The Oxford Paperback
Portuguese Dictionary

P9-CRG-912

The Oxford Paperback Portuguese Dictionary

PORTUGUESE–ENGLISH
Compiled by John Whitlam

ENGLISH–PORTUGUESE
Compiled by Lia Correia Raitt

Oxford   New York
OXFORD UNIVERSITY PRESS
1996

Oxford University Press, Walton Street, Oxford OX2 6DP

Oxford New York
Athens Auckland Bangkok Bombay
Calcutta Cape Town Dar es Salaam Delhi
Florence Hong Kong Istanbul Karachi
Kuala Lumpur Madras Madrid Melbourne
Mexico City Nairobi Paris Singapore
Taipei Tokyo Toronto
and associated companies in
Berlin Ibadan

Oxford is a trade mark of Oxford University Press

British Library Cataloguing in Publication Data
Data available

Library of Congress Cataloging in Publication Data
The Oxford paperback Portuguese dictionary: Portuguese–English,
English–Portuguese / Portuguese–English compiled by John Whitlam,
English–Portuguese compiled by Lia Correia Raitt.
p. cm.
1. Portuguese language—Dictionaries—English. 2. English language—
Dictionaries—Portuguese. I. Whitlam, John. II. Raitt, Lia Noêmia
Rodrigues Correia.
469.3'21—dc20 PC5333.093 1996 96–16941

ISBN 0–19–864528–7

10 9 8 7 6 5 4 3 2 1

Typeset by Pure Tech India Ltd.

Printed in Great Britain by
Mackays of Chatham

Contents • Índice

Preface

The Oxford Paperback Portuguese Dictionary has been written for speakers of both Portuguese and English and contains the most useful words and expressions in use today.

The dictionary provides a handy and comprehensive reference work for tourists, students, and business people who require quick and reliable answers to their translation needs.

Thanks are due to: Dr John Sykes, Prof. A. W. Raitt, Commander Virgílio Correia, Marcelo Affonso, Eng. Pedro Carvalho, Eng. Vasco Carvalho, Dr Iva Correia, Dr Ida Reis de Carvalho, Eng. J. Reis de Carvalho, Prof. A. Falcão, Bishop Manuel Falcão, Dr M. Luísa Falcão, Prof. J. Ferraz, Prof. M. de Lourdes Ferraz, Drs Ana and Jorge Fonseca, Mr Robert Howes, Irene Lakhani, Eng. Hugo Pires, Prof. M. Kaura Pires, Dr M. Alexandre Pires, Ambassador L. Pazos Alonso, Dr Teresa Pinto Pereira, Dr Isabel Tully, Carlos Wallenstein, Ligia Xavier, and Dr H. Martins and the members of his Mesa Lusófona at St Anthony's College, Oxford.

Prefácio

O *Oxford Paperback Portuguese Dictionary* foi escrito por pessoas de língua portuguesa e inglesa, e contém as palavras e expressões mais úteis em uso atualmente.

O dicionário constitui uma obra de referência prática e abrangente para turistas, estudantes e pessoas de negócios que necessitam de respostas rápidas e confiáveis para as suas traduções.

Agradecimentos a: Dr John Sykes, Prof. A. W. Raitt, Comandante Virgílio Correia, Marcelo Affonso, Eng. Pedro Carvalho, Eng. Vasco Carvalho, Dr Iva Correia, Dr Ida Reis de Carvalho, Eng. J. Reis de Carvalho, Prof. A. Falcão, Bispo Manuel Falcão, Dr M. Luísa Falcão, Prof. J. Ferraz, Prof. M. de Lourdes Ferraz, Drs Ana e Jorge Fonseca, Mr Robert Howes, Eng. Hugo Pires, Prof. M. Laura Pires, Dr M. Alexandre Pires, Embaixador L. Pazos Alonso, Dr Teresa Pinto Pereira, Dr Isabel Tully, Carlos Wallenstein, e Dr H. Martins e os membros de sua Mesa Lusófona do St Anthony's College, em Oxford.

Introduction

The swung dash (~) is used to replace a headword, or that part of a headword preceding the vertical bar (|).

In both English and Portuguese, only irregular plural forms are given. Plural forms of Portuguese nouns and adjectives ending in a single vowel are formed by adding an *s* (e.g. *livro*, *livros*). Those ending in *n*, *r*, *s* where the stress falls on the final syllable, and *z*, add *es* (e.g. *mulher*, *mulheres*, *falaz*, *falazes*). Nouns and adjectives ending in *m* change the final *m* to *ns* (e.g. *homem*, *homens*, *bom*, *bons*). Most of those ending in *ão* change their ending to *ões* (e.g. *estação*, *estações*).

Portuguese nouns and adjectives ending in an unstressed *o* form the feminine by changing the *o* to *a* (e.g. *belo*, *bela*). Those ending in *or* become *ora* (e.g. *trabalhador*, *trabalhadora*). All other masculine–feminine changes are shown at the main headword.

English and Portuguese pronunciation is given by means of the International Phonetic Alphabet. It is shown for all headwords, and for those derived words whose pronunciation is not easily deduced from that of a headword.

Portuguese verb tables will be found in the appendix.

Introdução

O sinal (~) é usado para substituir o verbete, ou parte deste precedendo a barra vertical (|).

Tanto em inglês como em português, somente as formas irregulares do plural são dadas. As formas regulares do plural dos substantivos ingleses recebem um *s* (ex. *teacher, teachers*), ou *es* quando terminarem em *ch, sh, s, ss, us, x* ou *z* (ex. *sash, sashes*). Os substantivos terminados em *y* e precedidos por uma consoante, mudam no plural para *ies* (ex. *baby, babies*).

O passado e o particípio passado dos verbos regulares ingleses são formados pelo acréscimo de *ed* à forma infinitiva (ex. *last, lasted*). Os verbos terminados em *e* recebem *d* (ex. *move, moved*). Aqueles terminados em *y* têm o *y* substituído por *ied* (*carry, carried*). As formas irregulares dos verbos aparecem no dicionário em ordem alfabética, remetidas à forma infinitiva, e também, na lista de verbos no apêndice.

As pronúncias inglesa e portuguesa são dadas em acordo com o Alfabeto Fonético Internacional. A pronúncia é dada para todos os verbetes, assim como para aquelas palavras derivadas cuja pronúncia não seja facilmente deduzida a partir do verbete.

Proprietary terms

This dictionary includes some words which are, or are asserted to be, proprietary names or trade marks. Their inclusion does not imply that they have acquired for legal purposes a non-proprietary or general significance, nor is any other judgement implied concerning their legal status. In cases where the editor has some evidence that a word is used as a proprietary name or trade mark this is indicated by the label *propr*, but no judgement concerning the legal status of such words is made or implied thereby.

Nomes comerciais

Este dicionário inclui algumas palavras que são, ou acredita-se ser, nomes comerciais ou marcas registradas. A sua inclusão no dicionário não implica que elas tenham adquirido para fins legais um significado geral ou não-comercial, assim como não afeta em nenhum dos conceitos implícitos o seu status legal.

Nos casos em que o editor tenha prova suficiente de que uma palavra seja usada como um nome comercial ou marca registrada, este emprego é indicado pela etiqueta *propr*. mas nenhuma apreciação relativa ao status legal de tais palavras é feita ou sugerida por esta indicação.

Portuguese Pronunciation

Vowels and Diphthongs

a, à, á, â	/ã/	chamam, ambos, antes	1) before *m* at the end of a word, or before *m* or *n* and another consonant, is nasalized
	/a/	aba, à, acolá, desânimo	2) in other positions is like *a* in English r*a*ther
ã	/ã/	irmã	is nasalized
e	/ẽ/	sem, venda	1) before *m* at the end of a word, or before *m* or *n* and another consonant, is nasalized
	/i/	arte	2) at the end of a word is like *y* in English happ*y*
	/e/	menas	3) in other positions is like *e* in English th*ey*
é	/ε/	artéria	is like *e* in English g*e*t
ê	/e/	fêmur	is like *e* in English th*ey*
i	/ĩ/	sim, vindo	1) before *m* at the end of a word, or before *m* or *n* and another consonant, is nasalized
	/i/	fila	2) in other positions is like *ee* in English s*ee*
o	/õ/	com, sombra, onda	1) before *m* at the end of a word, or before *m* or *n* and another consonant, is nasalized
	/u/	muito	2) at the end of a word, unstressed, is like *u* in English r*u*le

	/o/	comover	3) in other positions, unstressed, is like *o* in English p*o*le
	/o/	bo*b*o	4) stressed, is like *o* in English p*o*le or *o* in sh*o*p
	/ɔ/	l*o*ja	
ó	/ɔ/	*ó*pera	is like *o* in English sh*o*p
ô	/o/	t*ô*nica	is like *o* in English p*o*le
u, ú		g*u*erra, g*u*isado, q*u*e, q*u*ilo	1) is silent in *gue*, and *gui*, *que*, *qui*
	/u/	m*u*la, p*ú*rp*u*ra	2) in other positions is like *u* in English r*u*le
ü gü	/gw/	ung*ü*ento	in the combinations *güe* and *güi* is like *g* in English *g*ot, followed by English *w*
	/kw/	tranq*üi*lo	in the combinations *qüe* and *qüi* is like *qu* in English *qu*een
ãe	/ãj/	m*ãe*, p*ãe*s, alem*ãe*s	is like *y* in English b*y*, but nasalized
ai	/aj/	v*ai*, p*ai*, s*ai*, c*ai*ta	is like *y* in English b*y*
ao, au	/aw/	*ao*s, *au*todefesa	is like *ow* in English h*ow*
ão	/ãw/	n*ão*	is like *ow* in English h*ow*, but nasalized
ei	/ej/	l*ei*	is like *ey* in English th*ey*
eu	/ew/	d*eu*s, fl*eu*gma	both vowels pronounced separately
oẽ	/õj/	eleiç*õe*s	is like *oi* in English c*oi*n, but nasalized
oi	/oj/	n*oi*te	is like *oi* in English c*oi*n
ou	/o/	p*ou*co	is like *o* in English p*o*le

Consonants

b	/b/	*b*anho	is like *b* in English *b*all

c	/s/	*ci*nza, *ce*m	1) before *e* or *i* is like *s* in English *si*t
	/k/	*ca*sa	2) in other positions is like *c* in English *ca*t
ç	/s/	esta*ç*ão	is like *s* in English *si*t
ch	/ʃ/	*ch*á	is like *sh* in English *sh*out
d	/dʒ/	*di*zer, don*de*	1) before *i* or final unstressed *e* is like *j* in English *j*oin
	/d/	*d*ar	2) in other positions is like *d* in English *d*og
f	/f/	*f*alar	is like *f* in English *f*all
g	/ʒ/	a*ge*nte, *gi*ro	1) before *e* or *i* is like *s* in English vi*si*on
	/g/	*g*ato	2) in other positions is like *g* in English *g*et
h		*h*aver	is silent in Portuguese, but see *ch, lh, nh*
j	/ʒ/	*j*unta	is like *s* in English vi*si*on
k	/k/	*k*it	is like English *k* in *k*ey
l	/w/	fa*l*ta	1) between a vowel and a consonant, or following a vowel at the end of a word, is like *w* in English *w*ater
	/l/	*l*ata	2) in other positions is like *l* in English *l*ike
l	/λ/	ca*lh*ar	is like *lli* in English mi*lli*on
m		a*m*bas /ãbuʃ/	1) between a vowel and a consonant, or after a vowel at the end of a word, *m* nasalizes the preceding vowel
	co*m*	/kõ/	
	/m/	*m*ato, *m*ão	2) in other positions is like *m* in English *m*other
n		ci*n*za /'sĩza/	1) between a vowel and a consonant, *n* nasalizes the preceding vowel

	/n/	be*n*ig*n*o	2) in other positions is like *n* in English *n*ear
nh	/ɲ/	ba*nh*o	is like *ni* in English opi*ni*on
p	/p/	*p*az	is like *p* in English *p*oor
q	/k/	*q*ue, in*q*uieto	1) *qu* before *e* or *i* is like English *k*
	/kw/	*q*uase, *q*uórum	2) *qu* before *a* or *o*, or *qü* before *e* or *i*, is like *qu* in English *qu*een
r	/r/	apa*r*ato, go*r*do	1) between two vowels, or between a vowel and a consonant, is trilled
	/x/	*r*ato, ga*rr*a, mel*r*o, gen*r*o, Is*r*ael	2) at the beginning of a word, or in *rr*, or after *l*, *n*, or *s*, is like *ch* in Scottish lo*ch*
s	/ʃ/	depoi*s*	at the end of a word is like *sh* in English *sh*oot
	/z/	a*s*a, de*s*de, abi*s*mo, Israel	2) between two vowels, or before *b, d, g, l, m, n, r, v*, is like *z* inEnglish *z*ebra
	/s/	*s*uave	3) in other positions is like *s* in English *s*it
t	/tʃ/	*t*io, an*t*es	1) before *i* or final unstressed *e* is like *ch* in English *ch*eese
	/tʃi/	ki*t*	2) at the end of a word is like *chy* in English it*chy*
	/t/	a*t*ar	3) in other positions is like *t* in English *t*ap
v	/v/	lu*v*a	is like *v* in English *v*ain
w	/u/	*w*att	is shorter than English *w*
x	/z/	e*x*ato, e*x*emplo	1) in the prefix *ex* before a vowel, is pronounced like *z* in *z*ero

	/ʃ/	*x*ícara, bai*x*o, pei*x*e, frou*x*o	2) at the beginning of a word or after *ai*, *ei* or *ou*, is pronounced like *sh* in *sh*ow
	/s/	e*x*plodir,	3) is like *s* in English au*x*iliar*s*it
	/ks/	a*x*ila, fi*x*o	4) is like *x* in English e*x*it
			5) in the combination *xce*, *xci*, *x* is not pronounced in Portuguese e.g. e*x*celente, e*x*citar
z	/s/	fala*z*	1) at the end of a word, is like *s* in English *s*it
	/z/	di*z*er	2) in other positions, is like English *z*

Pronuncia Inglesa

Vogais e Ditongos

/iː/	s*ee*, t*ea*	como *i* em g*i*ro
/ɪ/	s*i*t, happ*y*	é um som mais breve do que *i* em l*i*
/e/	s*e*t	como *e* em t*é*pido
/æ/	h*a*t	é um som mais breve do que *a* em *a*mor
/aː/	*a*rm, c*a*lm	como *a* em c*a*rtaz
/ɒ/	g*o*t	como *o* em ex*ó*tico
/ɔː/	s*aw*, m*o*re	como *o* em c*o*rte
/ʊ/	p*u*t, l*oo*k	como *u* em m*u*rro
/uː/	t*oo*, d*ue*	como *u* em d*u*ro
/ʌ/	c*u*p, s*o*me	como *a* em p*a*no
/ɜː/	f*i*rm, f*u*r	como *e* em *e*nxerto
/ə/	*a*go, weath*er*	como *e* no português europeu part*e*
/eɪ/	p*a*ge, p*ai*n,	como *ei* em l*ei*te p*ay*
/əʊ/	h*o*me, r*oa*m	é um som mais longo do que *o* em c*o*ma
/aɪ/	f*i*ne, b*y*, g*uy*	como *ai* em s*ai*
/aɪə/	f*i*re, t*y*re	como *ai* em s*ai* seguido por /ə/
/aʊ/	n*ow*, sh*ou*t	como *au* em *au*la
/aʊə/	h*ou*r, fl*ow*er	como *au* em *au*la seguido por /ə/
/ɔɪ/	j*oi*n, b*oy*	como *oi* em d*ói*
/ɪə/	d*ea*r, h*e*re,	como *ia* em d*ia* b*ee*r
/eə/	h*ai*r, c*a*re,	como *e* em *e*téreo b*ea*r, th*e*re
/ʊə/	p*oo*r, d*u*ring	como *ua* em s*ua*

Consoantes

/p/	sna*p*	como *p* em *p*ato
/b/	*b*ath	como *b* em *b*ala
/t/	*t*ap	como *t* em *t*ela
/d/	*d*ip	como *d* em *d*ar
/k/	*c*at, *k*ite, stoma*ch*, pi*que*	como *c* em *c*asa
/ks/	e*x*ercise	como *x* em a*x*ila
/g/	*g*ot	como *g* em *g*ato
/tʃ/	*ch*in	como *t* em *t*io
/dʒ/	*J*une, *g*eneral, *j*u*dg*e	como *d* em *d*izer
/f/	*f*all	como *f* em *f*aca
/v/	*v*ine, o*f*	como *v* em *v*aca
/θ/	*th*in, mo*th*	não tem equivalente, soa como um *s* entre os dentes
/ð/	*th*is	não tem equivalente, soa com um *z* entre os dentes
/s/	*s*o, voi*c*e	como *s* em *s*uave
/z/	*z*oo, ro*s*e	como *z* em fa*z*er
/ʃ/	*sh*e, lun*ch*	como *ch* em *ch*egar
/ʒ/	mea*s*ure, vi*s*ion	como *j* em *j*amais
/h/	*h*ow	*h* aspirado
/m/	*m*an	como *m* em *m*ala
/n/	*n*one	como *n* em *n*ada
/ŋ/	si*ng*	como *n* em ci*n*to
/l/	*l*eg	como *l* em *l*uva
/r/	*r*ed, *wr*ite	como *r* em ca*r*a
/j/	*y*es, *y*oke	como *i* em *i*oga
/w/	*w*eather, s*w*itch	como *u* em ég*u*a

European Portuguese

Brazilian Portuguese, which is used in this dictionary, differs in a number of respects from that used in Portugal and the rest of the Portuguese-speaking world. These differences affect both spelling and pronunciation. Spelling variations appear on the Portuguese–English side. In so far as they affect pronunciation, the main variants are:

Brazilian Portuguese often omits the letters *b*, *c*, *m*, and *p*, which are retained by European Portuguese:

	Brazilian	**European**
b	su*b*til	su*b*til
c	a*c*ão	ac*c*ão
	ato	a*c*to
	elétrico	elé*c*trico
m	inde*m*nizar	inde*m*nizar
p	ba*p*tismo	ba*p*tismo
	exce*ç*ão	exce*p*ção

Letters *c* and *p* in such variant forms are usually silent, hence acto /'atu/, baptismo /ba'tiʒmu/. However, *c* is pronounced in the combination *ect*, hence eléctrico /i'lektriku/.

The combinations *gü* and *qü* become *gu* and *qu*:

	Brazilian	**European**
	un*gü*ento	un*gu*ento
	tran*qü*ilo	tran*qu*ilo

However, they are still pronounced /gw/ and /kw/ respectively.

The other main differences in pronunciation are:

d	/d/	*d*ar, *d*izer, bal*d*e, *d*onde	1) at the beginning of a word, or after *l*, or *n*, is like *d* in English *d*og

	/ð/	ci*d*ade, me*d*roso	2) in other positions is a sound between *d* in English *d*og and *th* in English *th*is
e	/ə/	art*e*	at the end of a word, is like *e* in English quarr*e*l
r	/rr/	*r*ato, ga*rr*a, mel*r*o, gen*r*o, Is*r*ael, guel*r*a, ten*r*o, is*r*aelense	at the beginning of a word, or in *rr*, or after *l, n,* or *s,* is strongly trilled
s	/ʃ/	depoi*s*, a*s*co, , ra*s*par co*s*tura	1) at the end of a word, or before *c, f, p, qu,* or *t,* is like English *sh*
	/ʒ/	de*s*de, I*s*lã, abi*s*mo, I*s*rael	2) before *b, d, g, l, m, n, r,* or *v* is like *s* in English vi*s*ion
t	/t/	a*t*ar, an*t*es, *t*io	is like *t* in English *t*ap
z	/ʃ/	fala*z*	at the end of a word, is like *sh* in English *sh*ake

Abbreviations • Abreviaturas

adjective	a	adjetivo
abbreviation	abbr/abr	abreviatura
something	aco	alguma coisa
adverb	adv	advérbio
somebody, someone	alg	algúem
article	art	artigo
American (English)	Amer	(inglês) americano
anatomy	anat	anatomia
architecture	arquit	arquitetura
astrology	astr/astrol	astrologia
motoring	auto	automobilismo
aviation	aviat	aviação
Brazilian Portuguese	B	português do Brasil
biology	biol	biologia
botany	bot	botânica
Brazilian Portuguese	Bras	português do Brasil
cinema	cine	cinema
colloquial	colloq	coloquial
commerce	comm/com	comércio
computing	comput	computação
conjunction	conj	conjunção
cookery	culin	cozinha
electricity	electr/eletr	eletricidade
feminine	f	feminina
familiar	fam	familiar
figurative	fig	figurativo
geography	geog	geografia
grammar	gramm/	gramática gram

infinitive	inf	infinitivo
interjection	int	interjeição
interrogative	interr	interrogativo
invariable	invar	invariável
legal, law	jur/jurid	jurídico
language	lang	linguagem
literal	lit	literal
masculine	m	masculino
mathematics	mat	matemática
mechanics	mech	mecânica
medicine	med	medicina
military	mil	militar
music	mus	música
noun	n	substantivo
nautical	naut	náutico
negative	neg	negativo
oneself	o.s.	se, si mesmo
European Portuguese	P	português de Portugal
pejorative	pej	pejorativo
philosophy	phil	filosofia
plural	pl	plural
politics	pol	política
European Portuguese	Port	português de Portugal
past participle	pp	particípio passado
prefix	pref	prefixo
preposition	prep	preposição
present	pres	presente
present participle	pres p	particípio presente
pronoun	pron	pronome
psychology	psych/psic	psicologia

past tense	pt	pretérito
relative	rel	relativo
religion	relig	religião
somebody	sb	alguém
singular	sing	singular
slang	sl	gíria
someone	s.o.	alguém
something	sth	alguma coisa
subjunctive	subj	subjuntivo
technology	techn/tecn	tecnologia
theatre	theat/teat	teatro
television	TV	televisão
university	univ	universidade
auxiliary verb	v aux	verbo auxiliar
intransitive verb	vi	verbo intransitivo
pronominal verb	vpr	verbo pronominal
transitive verb	vt	verbo transitivo
transitive & intransitive verb	vt/i	verbo transitivo e intransitivo

PORTUGUÊS-INGLÊS
PORTUGUESE-ENGLISH

A

a¹ /a/ *artigo* the □ *pron* (*mulher*) her; (*coisa*) it; (*você*) you

a² /a/ *prep* (*para*) to; (*em*) at; **às 3 horas** at 3 o'clock; **à noite** at night; **a lápis** in pencil; **a mão** by hand

à /a/ = **a² + a¹**

aba /'aba/ *f* (*de chapéu*) brim; (*de camisa*) tail; (*de mesa*) flap

abacate /aba'katʃi/ *m* avocado (pear)

abacaxi /abaka'ʃi/ *m* pineapple; (*fam: problema*) pain, headache

aba|de /a'badʒi/ *m* abbot; **~dia** *f* abbey

aba|fado /aba'fadu/ *a* (*tempo*) humid, close; (*quarto*) stuffy; **~far** *vt* (*asfixiar*) stifle; muffle <*som*>; smother <*fogo*>; suppress <*informação*>; cover up <*escândalo, assunto*>

abagunçar /abagũ'sar/ *vt* mess up

abaixar /aba'ʃar/ *vt* lower; turn down <*som, rádio*> □ *vi* **~-se** *vpr* bend down

abaixo /a'baʃu/ *adv* down; **~ de** below; **mais ~** further down; **~-assinado** *m* petition

abajur /aba'ʒur/ *m* (*quebra-luz*) lampshade; (*lâmpada*) (table) lamp

aba|lar /aba'lar/ *vt* shake; (*fig*) shock; **~lar-se** *vpr* be shocked, be shaken; **~lo** *m* shock

abanar /aba'nar/ *vt* shake, wave; wag <*rabo*>; (*com leque*) fan

abando|nar /abãdo'nar/ *vt* abandon; (*deixar*) leave; **~no** /o/ *m* abandonment; (*estado*) neglect

abarcar /abar'kar/ *vt* comprise, cover

abarro|tado /abaxo'tadu/ *a* crammed full; (*lotado*) crowded, packed; **~tar** *vt* cram full, stuff

abastado /abas'tadu/ *a* wealthy

abaste|cer /abaste'ser/ *vt* supply; fuel <*motor*>; fill up (with petrol) <*carro*>; refuel <*avião*>; **~cimento** *m* supply; (*de carro, avião*) refuelling

aba|ter /aba'ter/ *vt* knock down; cut down, fell <*árvore*>; shoot down <*avião, ave*>; slaughter <*gado*>; knock down, cut <*preço*>; **~ter alg** <*trabalho*> get s.o. down, wear s.o. out; <*má notícia*> sadden s.o.; <*doença*> lay s.o. low, knock the stuffing out of s.o.; **~tido** *a* dispirited, dejected; <*cara*> haggard, worn;

~timento *m* dejection; (*de preço*) reduction

abaulado /abaw'ladu/ *a* convex; <*estrada*> cambered

abcesso /ab'sɛsu/ *m* (*Port*) *veja* **abscesso**

abdi|cação /abidʒika'sãw/ *f* abdication; **~car** *vt/i* abdicate

abdômen /abi'dome/ *m* abdomen

abecedário /abese'dariu/ *m* alphabet, ABC

abeirar-se /abe'rarsi/ *vr* draw near

abe|lha /a'beʎa/ *f* bee; **~lhudo** *a* inquisitive, nosy

abençoar /abẽso'ar/ *vt* bless

aber|to /a'bɛrtu/ *pp de* **abrir** □ *a* open; <*céu*> clear; <*gás, torneira*> on; <*sinal*> green; **~tura** *f* opening; (*foto*) aperture; (*pol*) liberalization

abeto /a'betu/ *m* fir (tree)

abis|mado /abiz'madu/ *a* astonished; **~mo** *m* abyss

abjeto /abi'ʒɛtu/ *a* abject

abóbada /a'bɔbada/ *f* vault

abobalhado /aboba'ʎadu/ *a* silly

abóbora /a'bɔbora/ *f* pumpkin

abobrinha /abo'briɲa/ *f* courgette, (*Amer*) zucchini

abo|lição /aboli'sãw/ *f* abolition; **~lir** *vt* abolish

abomi|nação /abomina'sãw/ *f* abomination; **~nável** (*pl* **~náveis**) *a* abominable

abo|nar /abo'nar/ *vt* guarantee <*dívida*>; give a bonus to <*empregado*>; **~no** /o/ *m* guarantee; (*no salário*) bonus; (*subsídio*) allowance, benefit; (*reforço*) endorsement

abordar /abor'dar/ *vt* approach <*pessoa*>; broach, tackle <*assunto*>; (*naut*) board

aborre|cer /aboxe'ser/ *vt* (*irritar*) annoy; (*entediar*) bore; **~cer-se** *vpr* get annoyed; get bored; **~cido** *a* annoyed; bored; **~cimento** *m* annoyance; boredom

abor|tar /abor'tar/ *vi* miscarry, have a miscarriage □ *vt* abort; **~to** /o/ *m* abortion; (*natural*) miscarriage

aboto|adura /abotoa'dura/ *f* cufflink; **~ar** *vt* button (up) □ *vi* bud

abra|çar /abra'sar/ *vt* hug, embrace;

embrace <*causa*>; ~ço *m* hug, embrace

abrandar /abrã'dar/ *vt* ease <*dor*>; temper <*calor, frio*>; mollify, appease, placate <*povo*>; tone down, smooth over <*escândalo*> □ *vi* <*dor*> ease; <*calor, frio*> become less extreme; <*tempestade*> die down

abranger /abrã'ʒer/ *vt* cover; (*entender*) take in, grasp; ~ a extend to

abrasileirar /abrazile'rar/ *vt* Brazilianize

abre-|garrafas /abriga'xafas/ *m invar* (*Port*) bottle-opener; ~latas *m invar* (*Port*) can-opener

abreugrafia /abrewgra'fia/ *f* X-ray

abrevi|ar /abrevi'ar/ *vt* abbreviate <*palavra*>; abridge <*livro*>; ~atura *f* abbreviation

abridor /abri'dor/ *m* ~ **(de lata)** can-opener; ~ **de garrafa** bottle-opener

abri|gar /abri'gar/ *vt* shelter; house <*sem-teto*>; ~gar-se *vpr* (take) shelter; ~go *m* shelter

abril /a'briw/ *m* April

abrir /a'brir/ *vt* open; (*a chave*) unlock; turn on <*gás, torneira*>; make <*buraco, exceção*> □ *vi* open; <*céu, tempo*> clear (up); (*sinal*) turn green; ~-se *vpr* open; (*desabafar*) open up

abrupto /a'bruptu/ *a* abrupt

abrutalhado /abruta'ʎadu/ *a* <*sapato*> heavy; <*pessoa*> coarse

abscesso /abi'sεsu/ *m* abscess

absolu|tamente /abisoluta'mẽtʃi/ *adv* absolutely; (*não*) not at all; ~to *a* absolute; **em** ~**to** not at all, absolutely not

absol|ver /abisow'ver/ *vt* absolve; (*jurid*) acquit; ~vição *f* absolution; (*jurid*) acquittal

absor|ção /abisor'sãw/ *f* absorption; ~to *a* absorbed; ~vente *a* <*tecido*> absorbent; <*livro*> absorbing; ~ver *vt* absorb; ~ver-se *vpr* get absorbed

abs|têmio /abis'temiu/ *a* abstemious; (*de álcool*) teetotal □ *m* teetotaller; ~tenção *f* abstention; ~tencionista *a* abstaining □ *m/f* abstainer; ~ter-se *vpr* abstain; ~ter-se de refrain from; ~tinência *f* abstinence

abstra|ção /abistra'sãw/ *f* abstraction; (*mental*) distraction; ~ir *vt* separate; ~to *a* abstract

absurdo /abi'surdu/ *a* absurd □ *m* nonsense

abun|dância /abũ'dãsia/ *f* abundance; ~dante *a* abundant; ~dar *vi* abound

abu|sar /abu'zar/ *vi* go too far; ~sar de abuse; (*aproveitar-se*) take advantage of; ~so *m* abuse

abutre /a'butri/ *m* vulture

aca|bado /aka'badu/ *a* finished; (*exausto*) exhausted; (*velho*) decrepit; ~bamento *m* finish; ~bar *vt* finish □ *vi* finish, end; (*esgotar-se*) run out; ~bar-se *vpr* end, be over; (*esgotar-se*) run out; ~bar com put an end to, end; (*abolir, matar*) do away with; split up with <*namorado*>; wipe out <*adversário*>; ~bou de chegar he has just arrived; ~bar fazendo or por fazer end up doing

acabrunhado /akabru'ɲadu/ *a* dejected

aca|demia /akade'mia/ *f* academy; (*de ginástica etc*) gym; ~dêmico *a* & *m* academic

açafrão /asa'frãw/ *m* saffron

acalentar /akalẽ'tar/ *vt* lull to sleep <*bebê*>; cherish <*esperanças*>; have in mind <*planos*>

acalmar /akaw'mar/ *vt* calm (down) □ *vi* <*vento*> drop; <*mar*> grow calm; ~-se *vpr* calm down

acam|pamento /akãpa'mẽtu/ *m* camp; (*ato*) camping; ~par *vi* camp

aca|nhado /aka'ɲadu/ *a* shy; ~nhamento *m* shyness; ~nhar-se *vpr* be shy

ação /a'sãw/ *f* action; (*jurid*) lawsuit; (*com*) share

acariciar /akarisi'ar/ *vt* (*com a mão*) caress, stroke; (*adular*) make a fuss of; cherish <*esperanças*>

acarretar /akaxe'tar/ *vt* bring, cause

acasalar /akaza'lar/ *vt* mate; ~-se *vpr* mate

acaso /a'kazu/ *m* chance; **ao** ~ at random; **por** ~ by chance

aca|tamento /akata'mẽtu/ *m* respect, deference; ~tar *vt* respect, defer to <*pessoa, opinião*>; obey, abide by <*leis, ordens*>; take in <*criança*>

acc-, acç- (*Port*) *veja* ac-, aç-

acautelar-se /akawte'larsi/ *vpr* be cautious

acei|tação /asejta'sãw/ *f* acceptance; ~tar *vt* accept; ~tável (*pl* ~táveis) *a* acceptable

acele|ração /aselera'sãw/ *f* acceleration; ~rador *m* accelerator; ~rar *vi* accelerate □ *vt* speed up

acenar /ase'nar/ *vi* signal; (*saudando*) wave; ~ com promise, offer

acender /asẽ'der/ *vt* light <*cigarro, fogo, vela*>; switch on <*luz*>; heat up <*debate*>

aceno /a'senu/ *m* signal; (*de saudação*) wave

acen|to /a'sẽtu/ *m* accent; ~tuar *vt* accentuate; accent <*letra*>

acepção /asep'sãw/ *f* sense

acepipes /ase'pipʃ/ *m pl* (*Port*) cocktail snacks

acerca /a'serka/ ~ **de** *prep* about, concerning

acercar-se /aser'karsi/ *vpr* ~ **de** approach

acertar /aser'tar/ *vt* find <*(com o) caminho*>, *(a) casa*>; put right, set <*relógio*>; get right <*pergunta*>; guess (correctly) <*solução*>; hit <*alvo*>; make <*acordo, negócio*>; fix, arrange <*encontro*> □ *vi* *(ter razão)* be right; *(atingir o alvo)* hit the mark; ~ **com** find, happen upon; ~ **em** hit

acervo /a'servu/ *m* collection; *(jurid)* estate

aceso /a'sezu/ *pp de* **acender** □ *a* <*luz*> on; <*fogo*> alight

aces|sar /ase'sar/ *vt* access; ~**sível** *(pl* ~**síveis)** *a* accessible; affordable <*preço*>; ~**so** /ɛ/ *m* access; *(de raiva, tosse)* fit; *(de febre)* attack; ~**sório** *a* & *m* accessory

acetona /ase'tona/ *f (para unhas)* nail varnish remover

achado /a'ʃadu/ *m* find

achaque /a'ʃaki/ *m* ailment

achar /a'ʃar/ *vt* find; *(pensar)* think; ~**se** *vpr (estar)* be; *(considerar-se)* think that one is; **acho que sim/não** I think so/I don't think so

achatar /aʃa'tar/ *vt* flatten; cut <*salário*>

aciden|tado /asidẽ'tadu/ *a* rough <*terreno*>; bumpy <*estrada*>; eventful <*viagem, vida*>; injured <*pessoa*>; ~**tal** *(pl* ~**tais)** *a* accidental; ~**te** *m* accident

acidez /asi'des/ *f* acidity

ácido /'asidu/ *a* & *m* acid

acima /a'sima/ *adv* above; ~ **de** above; **mais** ~ higher up

acio|nar /asio'nar/ *vt* operate; *(jurid)* sue; ~**nista** *m/f* shareholder

acirrado /asi'xadu/ *a* stiff, tough

acla|mação /aklama'sãw/ *f* acclaim; *(de rei)* acclamation; ~**mar** *vt* acclaim

aclarar /akla'rar/ *vt* clarify, clear up □ *vi* clear up; ~**se** *vpr* become clear

aclimatar /aklima'tar/ *vt* acclimatize, *(Amer)* acclimate; ~**se** *vpr* get acclimatized, *(Amer)* get acclimated

aço /'asu/ *m* steel; ~ **inoxidável** stainless steel

acocorar-se /akoko'rarsi/ *vpr* squat (down)

acolá /ako'la/ *adv* over there

acolcho|ado /akowʃo'adu/ *m* quilt; ~**ar** *vt* quilt; upholster <*móveis*>

aco|lhedor /akoʎe'dor/ *a* welcoming; ~**lher** *vt* welcome <*hóspede*>; take in <*criança, refugiado*>; accept <*decisão, convite*>; respond to <*pedido*>; ~**lhida** *f,* ~**lhimento** *m* welcome; *(abrigo)* refuge

acomodar /akomo'dar/ *vt* accommodate; *(ordenar)* arrange; *(tornar có-*

modo) make comfortable; ~**se** *vpr* make o.s. comfortable

acompa|nhamento /akõpaɲa'mẽtu/ *m (mus)* accompaniment; *(prato)* side dish; *(comitiva)* escort; ~**nhante** *m/f* companion; *(mus)* accompanist; ~**nhar** *vt* accompany, go with; watch <*jogo, progresso*>; keep up with <*eventos, caso*>; keep up with, follow <*aula, conversa*>; share <*política, opinião*>; *(mus)* accompany; **a estrada** ~**nha o rio** the road runs alongside the river

aconche|gante /akõʃe'gãtʃi/ *a* cosy, *(Amer)* cozy; ~**gar** *vt (chegar a si)* cuddle; *(agasalhar)* wrap up; *(na cama)* tuck up; *(tornar cômodo)* make comfortable; ~**gar-se** *vpr* ensconce o.s.; ~**gar-se com** snuggle up to; ~**go** /e/ *m* cosiness, *(Amer)* coziness; *(abraço)* cuddle

acondicionar /akõdʒisio'nar/ *vt* condition; pack, package <*mercadoria*>

aconse|lhar /akõse'ʎar/ *vt* advise; ~**lhar-se** *vpr* consult; ~**lhar alg a** advise s.o. to; ~**lhar aco a alg** recommend sth to s.o.; ~**lhável** *(pl* ~**lháveis)** *a* advisable

aconte|cer /akõte'ser/ *vi* happen; ~**cimento** *m* event

acordar /akor'dar/ *vt/i* wake up

acorde /a'kɔrdʒi/ *m* chord

acordeão /akordʒi'ãw/ *m* accordion

acordo /a'kordu/ *m* agreement; **de** ~ **com** in agreement with <*pessoa*>; in accordance with <*lei etc*>; **estar de** ~ agree

Açores /a'soris/ *m pl* Azores

açoriano /asori'ano/ *a* & *m* Azorean

acorrentar /akoxẽ'tar/ *vt* chain (up)

acossar /ako'sar/ *vt* hound, badger

acos|tamento /akosta'mẽtu/ *m* hard shoulder, *(Amer)* berm; ~**tar-se** *vpr* lean back

acostu|mado /akostu'madu/ *a* usual, customary; **estar** ~**mado a** be used to; ~**mar** *vt* accustom; ~**mar-se a** get used to

acotovelar /akotove'lar/ *vt (empurrar)* jostle; *(para avisar)* nudge

açou|gue /a'sogi/ *m* butcher's (shop); ~**gueiro** *m* butcher

acovardar /akovar'dar/ *vt* cow, intimidate

acre /'akri/ *a* <*gosto*> bitter; <*aroma*> acrid, pungent; <*tom*> harsh

acredi|tar /akredʒi'tar/ *vt* believe; accredit <*representante*>; ~**tar em** believe <*pessoa, história*>; believe in <*Deus, fantasmas*>; *(ter confiança)* have faith in; ~**tável** *(pl* ~**táveis)** *a* believable

acre-doce /akri'dosi/ *a* sweet and sour

acrescentar /akrese'tar/ *vt* add
acres|cer /akre'ser/ *vt* (*juntar*) add; (*aumentar*) increase □ *vi* increase; **~cido de** with the addition of; **~ce que** add to that the fact that
acréscimo /a'kresimu/ *m* addition; (*aumento*) increase
acriançado /akriã'sadu/ *a* childish
acrílico /a'kriliku/ *a* acrylic
acroba|cia /akroba'sia/ *f* acrobatics; **~ta** *m/f* acrobat
act- (*Port*) *veja* **at-**
acuar /aku'ar/ *vt* corner
açúcar /a'sukar/ *m* sugar
açuca|rar /asuka'rar/ *vt* sweeten; sugar <*café, chá*>; **~reiro** *m* sugar bowl
açude /a'sudʒi/ *m* dam
acudir /aku'dʒir/ *vt/i* **~ (a)** come to the rescue (of)
acumular /akumu'lar/ *vt* accumulate; combine <*cargos*>
acupuntura /akupũ'tura/ *f* acupuncture
acu|sação /akuza'sãw/ *f* accusation; **~sar** *vt* accuse; (*jurid*) charge; (*revelar*) reveal, show up; acknowledge <*recebimento*>
acústi|ca /a'kustʃika/ *f* acoustics; **~co** *a* acoustic
adap|tação /adapta'sãw/ *f* adaptation; **~tado** *a* <*criança*> well-adjusted; **~tar** *vt* adapt; (*para encaixar*) tailor; **~tar-se** *vpr* adapt; **~tável** (*pl* **~táveis**) *a* adaptable
adega /a'dɛga/ *f* wine cellar
adentro /a'dẽtru/ *adv* inside; **selva ~** into the jungle
adepto /a'dɛptu/ *m* follower; (*Port: de equipa*) supporter
ade|quado /ade'kwadu/ *a* appropriate, suitable; **~quar** *vt* adapt, tailor
adereços /ade'resus/ *m pl* props
ade|rente /ade'rẽtʃi/ *m/f* follower; **~rir** *vi* (*colar*) stick; join <*a partido, causa*>; follow <*a moda*>; **~são** *f* adhesion; (*apoio*) support; **~sivo** *a* sticky, adhesive □ *m* sticker
ades|trado /ades'tradu/ *a* skilled; **~trador** *m* trainer; **~trar** *vt* train; break in <*cavalo*>
adeus /a'dews/ *int* goodbye □ *m* goodbye, farewell
adian|tado /adʒiã'tadu/ *a* advanced; <*relógio*> fast; **chegar ~tado** be early; **~tamento** *m* progress; (*pagamento*) advance; **~tar** *vt* advance <*dinheiro*>; put forward <*relógio*>; bring forward <*data, reunião*>; get ahead with <*trabalho*> □ *vi* <*relógio*> gain; (*ter efeito*) be of use; **~tar-se** *vpr* progress, get ahead; **não ~ta (fazer)** it's no use (doing); **~te** *adv* ahead

adia|r /adʒi'ar/ *vt* postpone; adjourn <*sessão*>; **~mento** *m* postponement, adjournment
adi|ção /adʒi'sãw/ *f* addition; **~cionar** *vt* add; **~do** *m* attaché
adivi|nhação /adʒiviɲa'sãw/ *f* guesswork; (*por adivinho*) fortune-telling; **~nhar** *vt* guess; tell <*futuro, sorte*>; read <*pensamento*>; **~nho** *m* fortune-teller
adjetivo /adʒe'tʃivu/ *m* adjective
adminis|tração /adʒiministra'sãw/ *f* administration; (*de empresas*) management; **~trador** *m* administrator; manager; **~trar** *vt* administer; manage <*empresa*>
admi|ração /adʒimira'sãw/ *f* admiration; (*assombro*) wonder(ment); **~rado** *a* admired; (*surpreso*) amazed, surprised; **~rador** *m* admirer □ *a* admiring; **~rar** *vt* admire; (*assombrar*) amaze; **~rar-se** *vpr* be amazed; **~rável** (*pl* **~ráveis**) *a* admirable; (*assombroso*) amazing
admis|são /adʒimi'sãw/ *f* admission; (*de escola*) intake; **~sível** (*pl* **~síveis**) *a* admissible
admitir /adʒimi'tʃir/ *vt* admit; (*permitir*) permit, allow; (*contratar*) take on
adoção /ado'sãw/ *f* adoption
ado|çar /ado'sar/ *vt* sweeten; **~cicado** *a* slightly sweet
adoecer /adoe'ser/ *vi* fall ill □ *vt* make ill
adoles|cência /adole'sẽsia/ *f* adolescence; **~cente** *a* & *m* adolescent
adopt- (*Port*) *veja* **adot-**
adorar /ado'rar/ *vt* (*amar*) adore; worship <*deus*>; (*fam: gostar de*) love
adorme|cer /adorme'ser/ *vi* fall asleep; <*perna*> go to sleep, go numb; **~cido** *a* sleeping; <*perna*> numb
ador|nar /ador'nar/ *vt* adorn; **~no** /o/ *m* adornment
ado|tar /ado'tar/ *vt* adopt; **~tivo** *a* adopted
adquirir /adʒiki'rir/ *vt* acquire
adu|bar /adu'bar/ *vt* fertilize; **~bo** *m* fertilizer
adu|lação /adula'sãw/ *f* flattery; (*do público*) adulation; **~lar** *vt* make a fuss of; (*com palavras*) flatter
adulterar /aduwte'rar/ *vt* adulterate; cook, doctor <*contas*> □ *vi* commit adultery
adúltero /a'duwteru/ *m* adulterer (*f* -ess) □ *a* adulterous
adul|tério /aduw'tɛriu/ *m* adultery; **~to** *a* & *m* adult
advento /adʒi'vẽtu/ *m* advent
advérbio /adʒi'vɛrbiu/ *m* adverb

adver|sário /adʒiver'sariu/ *m* opponent; (*inimigo*) adversary; **~sidade** *f* adversity; **~so** *a* adverse; (*adversário*) opposed

adver|tência /adʒiver'tẽsia/ *f* warning; **~tir** *vt* warn

advo|cacia /adʒivoka'sia/ *f* legal practice; **~gado** *m* lawyer; **~gar** *vt* advocate; (*jurid*) plead □ *vi* practise law

aéreo /a'ɛriu/ *a* air

aero|dinâmica /aerodʒi'namika/ *f* aerodynamics; **~dinâmico** *a* aerodynamic; **~dromo** *m* airfield; **~moça** /o/ *f* air hostess; **~nauta** *m* airman (*f*-woman); **~náutica** *f* (*força*) air force; (*ciência*) aeronautics; **~nave** *f* aircraft; **~porto** /o/ *m* airport

aeros|sol /aero'sɔw/ (*pl* **~sóis**) *m* aerosol

afabilidade /afabili'dadʒi/ *f* friendliness, kindness

afagar /afa'gar/ *vt* stroke

afamado /afa'madu/ *a* renowned, famed

afas|tado /afas'tadu/ *a* remote; <*parente*> distant; **~tado de** (far) away from; **~tamento** *m* removal; (*distância*) distance; (*de candidato*) rejection; **~tar** *vt* move away; (*tirar*) remove; ward off <*perigo, ameaça*>; put out of one's mind <*idéia*>; **~tar-se** *vpr* move away; (*distanciar-se*) distance o.s.; (*de cargo*) step down

afá|vel /a'favew/ (*pl* **~veis**) *a* friendly, genial

afazeres /afa'zeris/ *m pl* business; **~domésticos** (household) chores

afect- (*Port*) *veja* afet-

Afeganistão /afeganis'tãw/ *m* Afghanistan

afe|gão /afe'gãw/ *a & m* (*f* **~gã**) Afghan

afeição /afej'sãw/ *f* affection, fondness

afeiçoado /afejsu'adu/ *a* (*devoto*) devoted; (*amoroso*) fond

afeminado /afemi'nadu/ *a* effeminate

aferir /afe'rir/ *vt* check, inspect <*pesos, medidas*>; (*avaliar*) assess; (*cotejar*) compare

aferrar /afe'xar/ *vt* grasp; **~-se a** cling to

afe|tação /afeta'sãw/ *f* affectation; **~tado** *a* affected; **~tar** *vt* affect; **~tivo** *a* (*carinhoso*) affectionate; (*sentimental*) emotional; **~to** /ɛ/ *m* affection; **~tuoso** /o/ *a* affectionate

afi|ado /afi'adu/ *a* sharp; skilled <*pessoa*>; **~ar** *vt* sharpen

aficionado /afisio'nadu/ *m* enthusiast

afilhado /afi'ʎadu/ *m* godson (*f* -daughter)

afili|ação /afilia'sãw/ *f* affiliation; **~ada** *f* affiliate; **~ar** *vt* affiliate

afim /a'fĩ/ *a* related, similar

afinado /afi'nadu/ *a* in tune

afinal /afi'naw/ *adv* **~ (de contas)** (*por fim*) in the end; (*pensando bem*) after all

afinar /afi'nar/ *vt* tune □ *vi* taper

afinco /a'fĩku/ *m* perseverance, determination

afinidade /afini'dadʒi/ *f* affinity

afir|mação /afirma'sãw/ *f* assertion; **~mar** *vt* claim, assert; **~mativo** *a* affirmative

afivelar /afive'lar/ *vt* buckle

afixar /afik'sar/ *vt* stick, post

afli|ção /afli'sãw/ *f* (*física*) affliction; (*cuidado*) anxiety; **~gir** *vt* <*doença*> afflict; (*inquietar*) trouble; **~gir-se** *vpr* worry; **~to a** troubled, worried

afluente /aflu'ẽtʃi/ *m* tributary

afo|bação /afoba'sãw/ *f* fluster, flap; **~bado** *a* in a flap, flustered; **~bar** *vt* fluster; **~bar-se** *vpr* get flustered, get in a flap

afo|gado /afo'gadu/ *a* drowned; **morrer ~gado** drown; **~gador** *m* choke; **~gar** *vt/i* drown; (*auto*) flood; **~gar-se** *vpr* (*matar-se*) drown o.s.

afoito /a'fojtu/ *a* bold, daring

afora /a'fɔra/ *adv* **pelo mundo ~** throughout the world

afortunado /afortu'nadu/ *a* fortunate

afresco /a'fresku/ *m* fresco

África /'afrika/ *f* Africa; **~ do Sul** South Africa

africano /afri'kanu/ *a & m* African

afrodisíaco /afrodʒi'ziaku/ *a & m* aphrodisiac

afron|ta /a'frõta/ *f* affront, insult; **~tar** *vt* affront, insult

afrouxar /afro'ʃar/ *vt/i* loosen; (*de rapidez*) slow down; (*de disciplina*) relax

afta /'afta/ *f* (*mouth*) ulcer

afugentar /afuʒẽ'tar/ *vt* drive away; rout <*inimigo*>

afundar /afũ'dar/ *vt* sink; **~-se** *vpr* sink

agachar /aga'ʃar/ *vi* **~-se** *vpr* bend down

agarrar /aga'xar/ *vt* grab, snatch; **~-se** *vpr* **~-se a** cling to, hold on to

agasa|lhar /agaza'ʎar/ *vt* **~lhar-se** *vpr* wrap up (warmly); **~lho** *m* (*casaco*) coat; (*suéter*) sweater

agência /a'ʒẽsia/ *f* agency; **~ de correio** post office; **~ de viagens** travel agency

agenda /a'ʒẽda/ *f* diary

agente /a'ʒẽtʃi/ *m/f* agent

ágil /'aʒiw/ (*pl* **ágeis**) *a* <*pessoa*> agile; <*serviço*> quick, efficient

agili|dade /aʒili'dadʒi/ *f* agility; (*rapidez*) speed; **~zar** *vt* speed up, streamline

ágio /'aʒiu/ *m* premium

agiota /aʒi'ɔta/ *m/f* loan shark
agir /a'ʒir/ *vi* act
agi|tado /aʒi'tadu/ *a* agitated; *<mar>*
rough; ~**tar** *vt* wave *<braços>*; wag
<rabo>; shake *<garrafa>*; (*pertur-*
bar) agitate; ~**tar-se** *vpr* get agitated;
<mar> get rough
aglome|ração /aglomera'sãw/ *f* col-
lection; (*de pessoas*) crowd; ~**rar**
collect; ~**rar-se** *vpr* gather
agonia /ago'nia/ *f* anguish; (*da morte*)
death throes
agora /a'gɔra/ *adv* now; (*há pouco*)
just now; ~ **mesmo** right now; **de** ~
em diante from now on; **até** ~ so far,
up till now
agosto /a'gostu/ *m* August
agouro /a'goru/ *m* omen
agraciar /agrasi'ar/ *vt* decorate
agra|dar /agra'dar/ *vt* please; (*fazer*
agrados) be nice to, fuss over □ *vi* be
pleasing, please; (*cair no gosto*) go
down well; ~**dável** (*pl* ~**dáveis**) *a*
pleasant
agrade|cer /agrade'ser/ *vt* ~**cer aco**
a alg, ~**cer a alg por aco** thank s.o.
for sth □ *vi* say thank you; ~**cido** *a*
grateful; ~**cimento** *m* gratitude; *pl*
thanks
agrado /a'gradu/ *m* **fazer** ~**s a** be
nice to, make a fuss of
agrafa|r /agra'far/ *vt* (*Port*) staple;
~**dor** *m* stapler
agrário /a'grariu/ *a* land, agrarian
agra|vante /agra'vãtʃi/ *a* aggravating
□ *f* aggravating circumstance; ~**var**
vt aggravate, make worse; ~**var-se**
vpr get worse
agredir /agre'dʒir/ *vt* attack
agregado /agre'gadu/ *m* (*em casa*)
lodger
agres|são /agre'sãw/ *f* aggression;
(*ataque*) assault; ~**sivo** *a* aggressive;
~**sor** *m* aggressor
agreste /a'grestʃi/ *a* rural
agrião /agri'ãw/ *m* watercress
agrícola /a'grikola/ *a* agricultural
agricul|tor /agrikuw'tor/ *m* farmer;
~**tura** *f* agriculture, farming
agridoce /agri'dosi/ *a* bittersweet
agropecuá|ria /agropeku'aria/ *f*
farming; ~**rio** *a* agricultural
agru|pamento /agrupa'mẽtu/ *m*
grouping; ~**par** *vt* group; ~**par-se**
vpr group (together)
água /'agwa/ *f* water; **dar** ~ **na boca**
be mouthwatering; **ir por** ~ **abaixo**
go down the drain; ~ **benta** holy
water; ~ **doce** fresh water; ~
mineral mineral water; ~ **salgada**
salt water; ~ **sanitária** household
bleach
aguaceiro /agwa'seru/ *m* downpour

água-de|-coco /agwadʒi'koku/ *f* coco-
nut water; ~**-colônia** *f* eau de cologne
aguado /a'gwadu/ *a* watery
aguardar /agwar'dar/ *vt* wait for,
await □ *vi* wait
aguardente /agwar'dẽtʃi/ *f* spirit
aguarrás /agwa'xas/ *m* turpentine
água-viva /agwa'viva/ *f* jellyfish
agu|çado /agu'sadu/ *a* pointed; *<sen-*
tidos> acute; ~**çar** *vt* sharpen;
~**deza** *f* sharpness; (*mental*) per-
ceptiveness; ~**do** *a* sharp; *<som>*
shrill; (*fig*) acute
agüentar /agwẽ'tar/ *vt* stand, put up
with; hold *<peso>* □ *vi* <*pessoa>* hold
out; *<suporte>* hold
águia /'agia/ *f* eagle
agulha /a'guʎa/ *f* needle
ai /aj/ *m* sigh; (*de dor*) groan □ *int* ah!;
(*de dor*) ouch!
aí /a'i/ *adv* there; (*então*) then
aidético /aj'dɛtʃiku/ *a* suffering from
Aids □ *m* Aids sufferer
AIDS /'ajdʒis/ *f* Aids
ainda /a'ĩda/ *adv* still; **melhor** ~
even better; **não ...** ~ not ... yet; ~
assim even so; ~ **bem** just as well; ~
por cima moreover, in addition; ~
que even if
aipim /aj'pĩ/ *m* cassava
aipo /'ajpu/ *m* celery
ajeitar /aʒej'tar/ *vt* (*arrumar*) sort
out; (*arranjar*) arrange; (*ajustar*)
adjust; ~**-se** *vpr* adapt; (*dar certo*)
turn out right, sort o.s. out
ajoe|lhado /aʒoe'ʎadu/ *a* kneeling
(down); ~**lhar** *vi*, ~**lhar-se** *vpr*
kneel (down)
aju|da /a'ʒuda/ *f* help; ~**dante** *m/f*
helper; ~**dar** *vt* help
ajuizado /aʒui'zadu/ *a* sensible
ajus|tar /aʒus'tar/ *vt* adjust; settle
<disputa>; take in *<roupa>*; ~**tar-**
se *vpr* conform; ~**tável** (*pl*
~**táveis**) *a* adjustable; ~**te** *m* adjust-
ment; (*acordo*) settlement
ala /'ala/ *f* wing
ala|gação /alaga'sãw/ *f* flooding;
~**gadiço** *a* marshy □ *m* marsh;
~**gar** *vt* flood
alameda /ala'meda/ *f* avenue
álamo /'alamu/ *m* poplar (tree)
alarde /a'lardʒi/ *m* **fazer** ~ **de** flaunt;
make a big thing of *<notícia>*; ~**ar**
vt/i flaunt
alargar /alar'gar/ *vt* widen; (*fig*)
broaden; let out *<roupa>*
alarido /ala'ridu/ *m* outcry
alar|ma /a'larma/ *m* alarm; ~**mante**
a alarming; ~**mar** *vt* alarm; ~**me** *m*
alarm; ~**mista** *a* & *m* alarmist
alastrar /alas'trar/ *vt* scatter; (*disse-*
minar) spread □ *vi* spread

alavanca /ala'vãka/ *f* lever; ~ **de mudanças** gear lever

alban|ês /awba'nes/ *a & m* (*f* ~**esa**) Albanian

Albânia /aw'bania/ *f* Albania

albergue /aw'bɛrgi/ *m* hostel

álbum /'awbũ/ *m* album

alça /'awsa/ *f* handle; (*de roupa*) strap; (*de fusil*) sight

alcachofra /awka'ʃofra/ *f* artichoke

alçada /aw'sada/ *f* competence, power

álcali /'awkali/ *m* alkali

alcan|çar /awkã'sar/ *vt* reach; (*conseguir*) attain; (*compreender*) understand □ *vi* reach; ~**çável** (*pl* ~**çáveis**) *a* reachable; attainable; ~**ce** *m* reach; (*de tiro*) range; (*importância*) consequence; (*compreensão*) understanding

alcaparra /awka'paxa/ *f* caper

alcatra /aw'katra/ *f* rump steak

alcatrão /awka'trãw/ *m* tar

álcool /'awkɔw/ *m* alcohol

alcoó|latra /awko'ɔlatra/ *m/f* alcoholic; ~**lico** *a & m* alcoholic

alcunha /aw'kuɲa/ *f* nickname

aldeia /aw'deja/ *f* village

aleatório /alia'tɔriu/ *a* random, arbitrary

alecrim /ale'krĩ/ *m* rosemary

ale|gação /alega'sãw/ *f* allegation; ~**gar** *vt* allege

ale|goria /alego'ria/ *f* allegory; ~**górico** *a* allegorical

ale|grar /ale'grar/ *vt* cheer up; brighten up <*casa*>; ~**grar-se** *vpr* cheer up; ~**gre** /ɛ/ *a* cheerful; <*cores*> bright; ~**gria** *f* joy

alei|jado /ale'ʒadu/ *a* crippled □ *m* cripple; ~**jar** *vt* cripple

alei|tamento /alejta'mẽtu/ *m* breastfeeding; ~**tar** *vt* breast-feed

além /a'lẽj/ *adv* beyond; ~ **de** (*ao lado de lá de*) beyond; (*mais de*) over; (*ademais de*) apart from

Alemanha /ale'maɲa/ *f* Germany

alemão /ale'mãw/ (*pl* ~**mães**) *a & m* (*f* ~**mã**) German

alen|tador /alẽta'dor/ *a* encouraging; ~**tar** *vt* encourage; ~**tar-se** *vpr* cheer up; ~**to** *m* courage; (*fôlego*) breath

alergia /aler'ʒia/ *f* allergy

alérgico /a'lɛrʒiku/ *a* allergic (a to)

aler|ta /a'lɛrta/ *a & m* alert □ *adv* on the alert; ~**tar** *vt* alert

alfa|bético /awfa'bɛtʃiku/ *a* alphabetical; ~**betização** *f* literacy; ~**betizar** *vt* teach to read and write; ~**beto** *m* alphabet

alface /aw'fasi/ *f* lettuce

alfaiate /awfaj'atʃi/ *m* tailor

al|fândega /aw'fãdʒiga/ *f* customs; ~**fandegário** *a* customs □ *m* customs officer

alfine|tada /awfine'tada/ *f* prick; (*dor*) stabbing pain; (*fig*) dig; ~**te** /e/ *m* pin; ~**te de segurança** safety pin

alforreca /alfo'xeka/ *f* (*Port*) jellyfish

alga /'awga/ *f* seaweed

algarismo /awga'rizmu/ *m* numeral

algazarra /awga'zaxa/ *f* uproar, racket

alge|mar /awʒe'mar/ *vt* handcuff; ~**mas** /e/ *f pl* handcuffs

algibeira /alʒi'bejra/ *f* (*Port*) pocket

algo /'awgu/ *pron* something; (*numa pergunta*) anything □ *adv* somewhat

algodão /awgo'dãw/ *m* cotton; ~**(-doce)** candy floss, (*Amer*) cotton candy; ~ **(hidrófilo)** cotton wool, (*Amer*) absorbent cotton

alguém /aw'gẽj/ *pron* somebody, someone; (*numa pergunta*) anybody, anyone

al|gum /aw'gũ/ (*f* ~**guma**) *a* some; (*numa pergunta*) any; (*nenhum*) no, not one □ *pron pl* some; ~**guma coisa** something

algures /aw'guris/ *adv* somewhere

alheio /a'ʎeju/ *a* (*de outra pessoa*) someone else's; (*de outras pessoas*) other people's; ~ **a** foreign to; (*impróprio*) irrelevant to; (*desatento*) unaware of; ~ **de** removed from

alho /'aʎu/ *m* garlic; ~**-poró** *m* leek

ali /a'li/ *adv* (over) there

ali|ado /ali'adu/ *a* allied □ *m* ally; ~**ança** *f* alliance; (*anel*) wedding ring; ~**ar** *vt*, ~**ar-se** *vpr* ally

aliás /a'ljaʃ/ *adv* (*além disso*) what's more, furthermore; (*no entanto*) however; (*diga-se de passagem*) by the way, incidentally; (*senão*) otherwise

álibi /'alibi/ *m* alibi

alicate /ali'katʃi/ *m* pliers; ~ **de unhas** nail clippers

alicerce /ali'sɛrsi/ *m* foundation; (*fig*) basis

alie|nado /alie'nadu/ *a* alienated; (*demente*) insane; ~**nar** *vt* alienate; transfer <*bens*>; ~**nígena** *a & m/f* alien

alimen|tação /alimẽta'sãw/ *f* (*ato*) feeding; (*comida*) food; (*tecn*) supply; ~**tar** *a* food; <*hábitos*> eating □ *vt* feed; (*fig*) nurture; ~**tar-se de** live on; ~**tício** *a* gêneros ~**tícios** foodstuffs; ~**to** *m* food

ali|nhado /ali'ɲadu/ *a* aligned; <*pessoa*> smart, (*Amer*) sharp; ~**nhar** *vt* align

alíquota /a'likwota/ *f* (*de imposto*) bracket

alisar /ali'zar/ *vt* smooth (out); straighten <*cabelo*>

alistar /alis'tar/ *vt* recruit; ~-se *vpr* enlist

aliviar /alivi'ar/ *vt* relieve

alívio /a'liviu/ *m* relief

alma /'awma/ *f* soul

almanaque /awma'naki/ *m* yearbook

almejar /awme'ʒar/ *vt* long for

almirante /awmi'rātʃi/ *m* admiral

almo|çar /awmo'sar/ *vi* have lunch □ *vt* have lunch for; ~ço /o/ *m* lunch

almofada /awmo'fada/ *f* cushion; (*Port: de cama*) pillow

almôndega /aw'mõdʒiga/ *f* meatball

almoxarifado /awmoʃari'fadu/ *m* storeroom

alô /a'lo/ *int* hallo

alocar /alo'kar/ *vt* allocate

alo|jamento /aloʒa'mẽtu/ *m* accommodation, (*Amer*) accommodations, (*habitação*) housing; ~jar *vt* accommodate; house <*sem-teto*>; ~jar-se *vpr* stay

alongar /alõ'gar/ *vt* lengthen; extend, stretch out <*braço*>

alpendre /aw'pēdri/ *m* shed; (*pórtico*) porch

Alpes /'awpis/ *m pl* Alps

alpinis|mo /awpi'nizmu/ *m* mountaineering; ~ta *m/f* mountaineer

alqueire /aw'keri/ *m = 4.84 hectares,* (*in São Paulo = 2.42 hectares*)

alquimi|a /awki'mia/ *f* alchemy; ~sta *mf* alchemist

alta /'awta/ *f* rise; **dar** ~ **a** discharge; **ter** ~ be discharged

altar /aw'tar/ *m* altar

alterar /awte'rar/ *vt* alter; (*falsificar*) falsify; ~-se *vpr* change; (*zangar-se*) get angry

alter|nado /awter'nadu/ *a* alternate; ~nar *vt/i*, ~nar-se *vpr* alternate; ~nativa *f* alternative; ~nativo *a* alternative; <*corrente*> alternating

al|teza /aw'teza/ *f* highness; ~titude *f* altitude

alti|vez /awtʃi'ves/ *f* arrogance; ~vo *a* arrogant; (*elevado*) majestic

alto /'awtu/ *a* high; <*pessoa*> tall; <*barulho*> loud □ *adv* high; <*falar*> loud(ly); <*ler*> aloud □ *m* top; **os** ~**s e baixos** the ups and downs □ *int* halt!; ~**falante** *m* loudspeaker

altura /aw'tura/ *f* height; (*momento*) moment; **ser à** ~ **de** be up to

aluci|nação /alusina'sãw/ *f* hallucination; ~nante *a* mind-boggling, crazy

aludir /alu'dʒir/ *vi* allude (a to)

alu|gar /alu'gar/ *vt* rent <*casa*>; hire, rent <*carro*>; <*locador*> let, rent out, hire out; ~guel (*Port*), ~guer /ɛ/ *m* rent; (*ato*) renting

alumiar /alumi'ar/ *vt* light (up)

alumínio /alu'miniu/ *m* aluminium, (*Amer*) aluminum

aluno /a'lunu/ *m* pupil

alusão /alu'zãw/ *f* allusion (a to)

alvará /awva'ra/ *m* permit, licence

alve|jante /awve'ʒãtʃi/ *m* bleach; ~jar *vt* bleach; (*visar*) aim at

alvenaria /awvena'ria/ *f* masonry

alvo /'awvu/ *m* target

alvorada /awvo'rada/ *f* dawn

alvoro|çar /awvoro'sar/ *vt* stir up, agitate; (*entusiasmar*) excite; ~ço /o/ *m* (*tumulto*) uproar; (*entusiasmo*) excitement

amabilidade /amabili'dadʒi/ *f* kindness

amaci|ante /amasi'ãtʃi/ *m* (*de roupa*) (fabric) conditioner; ~ar *vt* soften; run in <*carro*>

amador /ama'dor/ *a & m* amateur; ~ismo *m* amateurism; ~ístico *a* amateurish

amadurecer /amadure'ser/ *vt/i* <*fruta*> ripen; (*fig*) mature

âmago /'amagu/ *m* heart, core; (*da questão*) crux

amaldiçoar /amawdʒiso'ar/ *vt* curse

amamentar /amamẽ'tar/ *vt* breast-feed

amanhã /ama'ɲã/ *m & adv* tomorrow; **depois de** ~ the day after tomorrow

amanhecer /amaɲe'ser/ *vi & m* dawn

amansar /amã'sar/ *vt* tame; (*fig*) placate <*pessoa*>

a|mante /a'mãtʃi/ *m/f* lover; ~mar *vt/i* love

amarelo /ama'rɛlu/ *a & m* yellow

amar|go /a'margu/ *a* bitter; ~gura *f* bitterness; ~gurar *vt* embitter; (*sofrer*) endure

amarrar /ama'xar/ *vt* tie (up); (*naut*) moor; ~ **a cara** frown, scowl

amarrotar /amaxo'tar/ *vt* crease

amassar /ama'sar/ *vt* crush, squash; screw up <*papel*>; crease <*roupa*>; dent <*carro*>; knead <*pão*>; mash <*batatas*>

amá|vel /a'mavew/ (*pl* ~veis) *a* kind

Ama|zonas /ama'zonas/ *m* Amazon; ~zônia *f* Amazonia

âmbar /'ãbar/ *m* amber

ambi|ção /ãbi'sãw/ *f* ambition; ~cionar *vt* aspire to; ~cioso /o/ *a* ambitious

ambien|tal /ãbiẽ'taw/ (*pl* ~tais) *a* environmental; ~tar *vt* set <*filme, livro*>; set up <*casa*>; ~tar-se *vpr* settle in; ~te *m* environment; (*atmosfera*) atmosphere

am|bigüidade /ãbigwi'dadʒi/ *f* ambiguity; ~bíguo *a* ambiguous

âmbito /'ãbitu/ *m* scope, range

ambos /'ãbus/ *a & pron* both

ambu|lância /ābu'lāsia/ *f* ambulance; **~lante** *a* (*que anda*) walking; <*músico*> wandering; <*venda*> mobile; **~latório** *m* out-patient clinic

amea|ça /ami'asa/ *f* threat; **~çador** *a* threatening; **~çar** *vt* threaten

ameba /a'mɛba/ *f* amoeba

amedrontar /amedrõ'tar/ *vt* scare; **~-se** *vpr* get scared

ameixa /a'mefa/ *f* plum; (*passa*) prune

amém /a'mēj/ *int* amen □ *m* agreement; **dizer ~ a** go along with

amêndoa /a'mēdoa/ *f* almond

amendoim /amēdo'ĩ/ *m* peanut

ame|nidade /ameni'dadʒi/ *f* pleasantness; *pl* pleasantries, small talk; **~nizar** *vt* ease; calm <*ânimos*>; settle <*disputa*>; tone down <*repreensão*>; **~no** /e/ *a* pleasant; mild <*clima*>

América /a'mɛrika/ *f* America; **~ do Norte/Sul** North/South America

america|nizar /amerikani'zar/ *vt* Americanize; **~no** *a & m* American

amestrar /ames'trar/ *vt* train

ametista /ame'tʃista/ *f* amethyst

amianto /ami'ātu/ *m* asbestos

ami|gar-se /ami'garsi/ *vpr* make friends; **~gável** (*pl* **~gáveis**) *a* amicable

amígdala /a'migdala/ *f* tonsil

amigdalite /amigda'litʃi/ *f* tonsillitis

amigo /a'migu/ *a* friendly □ *m* friend; **~ da onça** false friend

amistoso /amis'tozu/ *a & m* friendly

amiúde /ami'udʒi/ *adv* often

amizade /ami'zadʒi/ *f* friendship

amnésia /ami'nɛzia/ *f* amnesia

amnistia /amnis'tia/ *f* (*Port*) *veja* anistia

amo|lação /amola'sãw/ *f* annoyance; **~lante** *a* annoying; **~lar** *vt* annoy, bother; sharpen <*faca*>; **~lar-se** *vpr* get annoyed

amolecer /amole'ser/ *vt/i* soften

amol|gadura /amowga'dura/ *f* dent; **~gar** *vt* dent

amoníaco /amo'niaku/ *m* ammonia

amontoar /amõto'ar/ *vt* pile up; amass <*riquezas*>; **~-se** *vpr* pile up

amor /a'mor/ *m* love; **~ próprio** self-esteem

amora /a'mɔra/ *f* **~ preta**, (*Port*) **~ silvestre** blackberry

amordaçar /amorda'sar/ *vt* gag

amoroso /amo'rozu/ *adj* loving

amor-perfeito /amorper'fejtu/ *m* pansy

amorte|cedor /amortese'dor/ *m* shock absorber; **~cer** *vt* deaden; absorb <*impacto*>; break <*queda*> □ *vi* fade

amostra /a'mɔstra/ *f* sample

ampa|rar /āpa'rar/ *vt* support; (*fig*) protect; **~rar-se** *vpr* lean; **~ro** *m* (*apoio*) support; (*proteção*) protection; (*ajuda*) aid

ampère /ã'pɛri/ *m* amp(ere)

ampli|ação /āplia'sãw/ *f* (*de foto*) enlargement; (*de casa*) extension; **~ar** *vt* enlarge <*foto*>; extend <*casa*>; broaden <*conhecimentos*>

amplifi|cador /āplifika'dor/ *m* amplifier; **~car** *vt* amplify

amplo /'āplu/ *a* <*sala*> spacious; <*roupa*> full; <*sentido, conhecimento*> broad

ampola /ā'pola/ *f* ampoule

amputar /āpu'tar/ *vt* amputate

Amsterdã /amister'dā/, (*Port*) **Amsterdão** /amiʃter'dãw/ *f* Amsterdam

amu|ado /amu'adu/ *a* in a sulk, sulky; **~ar** *vi* sulk

amuleto /amu'leto/ *m* charm

amuo /a'muu/ *m* sulk

ana|crônico /ana'kroniku/ *a* anachronistic; **~cronismo** *m* anachronism

anais /a'najs/ *m pl* annals

analfabeto /anawfa'bɛtu/ *a & m* illiterate

analisar /anali'zar/ *vt* analyse

análise /a'nalizi/ *f* analysis

ana|lista /ana'lista/ *m/f* analyst; **~lítico** *a* analytical

analogia /analo'ʒia/ *f* analogy

análogo /a'nalogu/ *a* analogous

ananás /ana'naʃ/ *m invar* (*Port*) pineapple

anão /a'nãw/ *a & m* (*f* **anã**) dwarf

anarquia /anar'kia/ *f* anarchy; (*fig*) chaos

anárquico /a'narkiku/ *a* anarchic

anarquista /anar'kista/ *m/f* anarchist

ana|tomia /anato'mia/ *f* anatomy; **~tômico** *a* anatomical

anca /'āka/ *f* (*de pessoa*) hip; (*de animal*) rump

anchova /ā'ʃova/ *f* anchovy

ancinho /ā'siɲu/ *m* rake

âncora /'ākora/ *f* anchor

anco|radouro /ākora'doru/ *m* anchorage; **~rar** *vt/i* anchor

andaime /ā'dajmi/ *m* scaffolding

an|damento /āda'mẽtu/ *m* (*progresso*) progress; (*rumo*) course; **dar ~damento a** set in motion; **~dar** *m* (*jeito de andar*) gait, walk; (*de prédio*) floor; (*Port: apartamento*) flat, (*Amer*) apartment □ *vi* (*ir a pé*) walk; (*de trem, ônibus*) travel; (*a cavalo, de bicicleta*) ride; (*funcionar, progredir*) go; **ele anda deprimido** he's been depressed lately

Andes /'ãdʒis/ m pl Andes

andorinha /ãdo'riɲa/ f swallow

anedota /ane'dæta/ f anecdote

anel /a'nɛw/ (pl **anéis**) m ring; (no cabelo) curl; ~ **viário** ringroad

anelado /ane'ladu/ a curly

anemia /ane'mia/ f anaemia

anêmico /a'nemiku/ a anaemic

anes|tesia /aneste'zia/ f anaesthesia; (droga) anaesthetic; ~**tesiar** vt anaesthetize; ~**tésico** a & m anaesthetic; ~**tesista** m/f anaesthetist

ane|xar /anek'sar/ vt annex <terras>; (em carta) enclose; (juntar) attach; ~**xo** /ɛ/ a attached; (em carta) enclosed □ m annexe; (em carta) enclosure

anfíbio /ã'fibiu/ a amphibious □ m amphibian

anfiteatro /ãfitʃi'atru/ m amphitheatre; (no teatro) dress circle

anfi|trião /ãfitri'ãw/ m (f ~**triã**) host (f -ess)

angariar /ãgari'ar/ vt raise <fundos>; (em carta) canvass for <votos>; win <adeptos, simpatia>

angli|cano /ãgli'kanu/ a & m Anglican; ~**cismo** m Anglicism

anglo-saxônico /ãglusak'soniku/ a Anglo-Saxon

Angola /ã'gɔla/ f Angola

angolano /ãgo'lanu/ a & m Angolan

angra /'ãgra/ f inlet, cove

angular /ãgu'lar/ a angular

ângulo /'ãgulu/ m angle

angústia /ã'gustʃia/ f anguish, anxiety

angustiante /ãgustʃi'ãtʃi/ a distressing; <momento> anxious

ani|mado /ani'madu/ a (vivo) lively; (alegre) cheerful; (entusiasmado) enthusiastic; ~**mador** a encouraging □ m presenter; ~**mal** (pl ~**mais**) a & m animal; ~**mar** vt encourage; liven up <festa>; ~**mar-se** vpr cheer up; <festa> liven up

ânimo /'animu/ m courage, spirit; pl tempers

animosidade /animozi'dadʒi/ f animosity

aniquilar /aniki'lar/ vt destroy; (prostrar) shatter

anis /a'nis/ m aniseed

anistia /anis'tʃia/ f amnesty

aniver|sariante /aniversari'ãtʃi/ m/f birthday boy (f girl); ~**sário** m birthday; (de casamento etc) anniversary

anjo /'ãʒu/ m angel

ano /'anu/ m year; **fazer** ~**s** have a birthday; ~ **bissexto** leap year; ~ **letivo** academic year; ~**-bom** m New Year

anoite|cer /anojte'ser/ m nightfall □ vi ~**ceu** night fell

anomalia /anoma'lia/ f anomaly

anonimato /anoni'matu/ m anonymity

anônimo /a'nonimu/ a anonymous

anor|mal /anor'maw/ (pl ~**mais**) a abnormal

ano|tação /anota'sãw/ f note; ~**tar** vt note down, write down

ânsia /'ãsia/ f anxiety; (desejo) longing; ~**s de vômito** nausea

ansi|ar /ãsi'ar/ vi ~ **por** long for; ~**edade** f anxiety; (desejo) eagerness; ~**oso** /o/ a anxious

antártico /ã'tartʃiku/ a & m Antarctic

antebraço /ãtʃi'brasu/ m forearm

antece|dência /ãtese'dẽsia/ f com ~**dência** in advance; ~**dente** a preceding; ~**dentes** m pl record, past

antecessor /ãtese'sor/ m (f ~**a**) predecessor

anteci|pação /ãtʃisipa'sãw/ f anticipation; **com** ~**pação** in advance; ~**padamente** adv in advance; ~**pado** a advance; ~**par** vt anticipate, forestall; (adiantar) bring forward; ~**par-se** vpr be previous

antena /ã'tena/ f aerial, (Amer) antenna; (de inseto) feeler

anteontem /ãtʃi'õtẽ/ adv the day before yesterday

antepassado /ãtʃipa'sadu/ m ancestor

anterior /ãteri'or/ a previous; (dianteiro) front

antes /'ãtʃis/ adv before; (ao contrário) rather; ~ **de/que** before

ante-sala /ãtʃi'sala/ f ante-room

anti|biótico /ãtʃibi'ɔtʃiku/ a & m antibiotic; ~**caspa** a anti-dandruff; ~**concepcional** (pl ~**concepcionais**) a & m contraceptive; ~**congelante** m antifreeze; ~**corpo** m antibody

antídoto /ã'tʃidotu/ m antidote

antiético /ãtʃi'ɛtʃiku/ a unethical

antigamente /ãtʃiga'mẽtʃi/ adv formerly

anti|go /ã'tʃigu/ a old; (da antiguidade) ancient; <móveis etc> antique; (anterior) former; ~**guidade** f antiquity; (numa firma) seniority; pl (monumentos) antiquities; (móveis etc) antiques

anti-|higiênico /ãtʃiʒi'eniku/ a unhygienic; ~**histamínico** a & m antihistamine; ~**horário** a anticlockwise

antilhano /ãtʃi'ʎanu/ a & m West Indian

Antilhas /ã'tʃiʎas/ f pl West Indies

anti|patia /ãtʃipa'tʃia/ f dislike; ~**pático** a unpleasant, unfriendly

antiquado /ătʃi'kwadu/ *a* antiquated, out-dated

anti-|semitismo /ătʃisemi'tʃizmu/ *m* anti-Semitism; **~séptico** *a* & *m* antiseptic; **~social** (*pl* **~sociais**) *a* antisocial

antítese /ă'tʃitezi/ *f* antithesis

antologia /ătolo'ʒia/ *f* anthology

antônimo /ă'tonimu/ *m* antonym

antro /'ătru/ *m* cavern; (*de animal*) lair; (*de ladrões*) den

antro|pófago /ătro'pofagu/ *a* man-eating; **~pologia** *f* anthropology; **~pólogo** *m* anthropologist

anu|al /anu'aw/ (*pl* **~ais**) *a* annual, yearly

anu|lação /anula'sãw/ *f* cancellation; **~lar** *vt* cancel; annul <*casamento*>; (*compensar*) cancel out □ *m* ring finger

anunciar /anũsi'ar/ *vt* announce; advertise <*produto*>

anúncio /a'nũsiu/ *m* announcement; (*propaganda, classificado*) advert(isement); (*cartaz*) notice

ânus /'anus/ *m invar* anus

an|zol /ã'zɔw/ (*pl* **~zóis**) *m* fish-hook

aonde /a'õdʒi/ *adv* where

apadrinhar /apadri'ɲar/ *vt* be godfather to <*afilhado*>; be best man for <*noivo*>; (*proteger*) protect; (*patrocinar*) support

apa|gado /apa'gadu/ *a* <*fogo*> out; <*luz, TV*> off; (*indistinto*) faint <*pessoa*> dull; **~gar** *vt* put out <*cigarro, fogo*>; blow out <*vela*>; switch off <*luz, TV*>; rub out <*erro*>; clean <*quadro-negro*>; **~gar-se** *vpr* <*fogo, luz*> go out; <*lembrança*> fade; (*desmaiar*) pass out; (*fam: dormir*) nod off

apaixo|nado /apaʃo'nadu/ *a* in love (por with); **~nante** *a* captivating; **~nar-se** *vpr* fall in love (por with)

apalpar /apaw'par/ *vt* touch, feel; <*médico*> examine

apanhar /apa'ɲar/ *vt* catch; (*do chão*) pick up; pick <*flores, frutas*>; (*ir buscar*) pick up; (*alcançar*) catch up □ *vi* be beaten

aparafusar /aparafu'zar/ *vt* screw

apa|ra-lápis /apara'lapiʃ/ *m invar* (*Port*) pencil sharpener; **~rar** *vt* catch <*bola*>; parry <*golpe*>; trim <*cabelo*>; sharpen <*lápis*>

aparato /apa'ratu/ *m* pomp, ceremony

apare|cer /apare'ser/ *vi* appear; **~ça!** do drop in!; **~cimento** *m* appearance

apare|lhagem /apare'ʎaʒẽ/ *f* equipment; **~lhar** *vt* equip; **~lho** /e/ *m* apparatus; (*máquina*) machine; (*de chá*) set, service; (*fone*) phone

aparência /apa'rẽsia/ *f* appearance; **na ~** apparently

aparen|tado /aparẽ'tadu/ *a* related; **~tar** *vt* show; (*fingir*) feign; **~te** *a* apparent

apar|tamento /aparta'mẽtu/ *m* flat, (*Amer*) apartment; **~tar** *vt*, **~tar-se** *vpr* separate; **~te** *m* aside

apatia /apa'tʃia/ *f* apathy

apático /a'patʃiku/ *a* apathetic

apavo|rante /apavo'rătʃi/ *a* terrifying; **~rar** *vt* terrify; **~rar-se** *vpr* be terrified

apaziguar /apazi'gwar/ *vt* appease

apear-se /api'arsi/ *vpr* (*de cavalo*) dismount; (*de ônibus*) alight

ape|gar-se /ape'garsi/ *vpr* become attached (a to); **~go** /e/ *m* attachment

ape|lação /apela'sãw/ *f* appeal; (*fig*) exhibitionism; **~lar** *vi* appeal (**de** against); **~lar para** appeal to; (*fig*) resort to

apeli|dar /apeli'dar/ *vt* nickname; **~do** *m* nickname

apelo /a'pelu/ *m* appeal

apenas /a'penas/ *adv* only

apêndice /a'pẽdʒisi/ *m* appendix

apendicite /apẽdʒi'sitʃi/ *f* appendicitis

aperceber-se /aperse'bersi/ *vpr* **~(de)** notice, realize

aperfeiçoar /aperfejso'ar/ *vt* perfect

aperitivo /aperi'tʃivu/ *m* aperitif

aper|tado /aper'tadu/ *a* tight; (*sem dinheiro*) hard-up; **~tar** *vt* (*segurar*) hold tight; tighten <*cinto*>; press <*botão*>; squeeze <*esponja*>; take in <*vestido*>; fasten <*cinto de segurança*>; step up <*vigilância*>; cut down on <*despesas*>; break <*coração*>; (*fig*) pressurize <*pessoa*> □ *vi* <*sapato*> pinch; <*chuva, frio*> get worse; <*estrada*> narrow; **~tar-se** *vpr* (*gastar menos*) tighten one's belt; (*não ter dinheiro*) feel the pinch; **~tar a mão de alg** shake hands with s.o.; **~to** /e/ *m* pressure; (*de botão*) press; (*dificuldade*) tight spot, jam; **~to de mãos** handshake

apesar /ape'zar/ **~ de** *prep* in spite of

apeti|te /ape'tʃitʃi/ *m* appetite; **~toso** /o/ *a* appetizing

apetrechos /ape'treʃus/ *m pl* gear; (*de pesca*) tackle

apimentado /apimẽ'tadu/ *a* spicy, hot

apinhar /api'ɲar/ *vt* crowd, pack; **~se** *vpr* crowd

api|tar /api'tar/ *vi* whistle □ *vt* referee <*jogo*>; **~to** *m* whistle

aplanar /apla'nar/ *vt* level <*terreno*>; (*fig*) smooth <*caminho*>; smooth over <*problema*>

aplau|dir /aplaw'dʒir/ *vt* applaud; **~so(s)** *m* (*pl*) applause

apli|cação /aplika'sãw/ *f* application; (*de dinheiro*) investment; (*de lei*) enforcement; ~**car** *vt* apply; invest <*dinheiro*>; enforce <*lei*>; ~**car-se** *vpr* apply (**a** to); (*ao estudo etc*) apply o.s. (**a** to); ~**que** *m* hairpiece

apoderar-se /apode'rarsi/ *vpr* ~ **de** take possession of; <*raiva*> take hold of

apodrecer /apodre'ser/ *vt/i* rot

apoi|ar /apoj'ar/ *vt* lean; (*fig*) support; (*basear*) base; ~**ar-se** *vpr* ~**ar-se em** lean on; (*fig*) be based on, rest on; ~**o** *m* support

apólice /a'pɔlisi/ *f* policy; (*ação*) bond

apon|tador /apõta'dor/ *m* pencil sharpener; ~**tar** *vt* (*com o dedo*) point at, point to; point out <*erro, caso interessante*>; aim <*arma*>; name <*nomes*>; put forward <*razão*> □ *vi* <*sol, planta*> come up; (*com o dedo*) point (**para** to)

apoquentar /apokẽ'tar/ *vt* annoy

aporrinhar /apoxi'ɲar/ *vt* annoy

após /a'pɔs/ *adv* after; **loção ~-barba** after-shave (lotion)

aposen|tado /apozẽ'tadu/ *a* retired □ *m* pensioner; ~**tadoria** *f* retirement; (*pensão*) pension; ~**tar** *vt*, ~**tar-se** *vpr* retire; ~**to** *m* room

após-guerra /apɔz'gɛxa/ *m* post-war period

apos|ta /a'pɔsta/ *f* bet; ~**tar** *vt* bet (**em** on); (*fig*) have faith (**em** in)

apostila /apos'tʃila/ *f* revision aid, book of key facts

apóstolo /a'pɔstolu/ *m* apostle

apóstrofo /a'pɔstrofu/ *m* apostrophe

apre|ciação /apresia'sãw/ *f* appreciation; ~**ciar** *vt* appreciate; think highly of <*pessoa*>; ~**ciativo** *a* appreciative; ~**ciável** (*pl* ~**ciáveis**) *a* appreciable; ~**ço** /e/ *m* regard

apreen|der /apriẽ'der/ *vt* seize <*contrabando*>; apprehend <*criminoso*>; grasp <*sentido*>; ~**são** *f* apprehension; (*de contrabando*) seizure; ~**sivo** *a* apprehensive

apregoar /aprego'ar/ *vt* proclaim; cry <*mercadoria*>

apren|der /aprẽ'der/ *vt/i* learn; ~**diz** *m/f* (*de ofício*) apprentice; (*de direção*) learner; ~**dizado** *m*, ~**dizagem** *f* (*de ofício*) apprenticeship; (*de profissão*) training; (*escolar*) learning

apresen|tação /aprezẽta'sãw/ *f* presentation; (*teatral etc*) performance; (*de pessoas*) introduction; ~**tador** *m* presenter; ~**tar** *vt* present; introduce <*pessoa*>; ~**tar-se** *vpr* (*identificar-se*) introduce o.s.; <*ocasião, problema*> present o.s., arise; ~**tar-se a** report to <*polícia etc*>; go in for <*exame*>; stand for <*eleição*>; ~**tável** (*pl* ~**táveis**) *a* presentable

apres|sado /apre'sadu/ *a* hurried; ~**sar** *vt* hurry; ~**sar-se** *vpr* hurry (up)

aprimorar /aprimo'rar/ *vt* perfect, refine

aprofundar /aprofũ'dar/ *vt* deepen; study carefully <*questão*>; ~**se** *vpr* get deeper; ~**se em** go deeper into

aprontar /aprõ'tar/ *vt* get ready; pick <*briga*> □ *vi* act up; ~**se** *vpr* get ready

apropriado /apropri'adu/ *a* appropriate, suitable

apro|vação /aprova'sãw/ *f* approval; (*num exame*) pass; ~**var** *vt* approve of; approve <*lei*> □ *vi* make the grade; **ser ~vado** (*num exame*) pass

aprovei|tador /aprovejta'dor/ *m* opportunist; ~**tamento** *m* utilization; ~**tar** *vt* take advantage of; take <*ocasião*>; (*utilizar*) use □ *vi* make the most of it; (*Port: adiantar*) be of use; ~**tar-se** *vpr* take advantage (**de** of); ~**te!** (*divirta-se*) have a good time!

aproxi|mação /aprosima'sãw/ *f* (*chegada*) approach; (*estimativa*) approximation; ~**mado** *a* <*valor*> approximate; ~**mar** *vt* move nearer; (*aliar*) bring together; ~**mar-se** *vpr* approach, get nearer (**de** to)

ap|tidão /aptʃi'dãw/ *f* aptitude, suitability; ~**to** *a* suitable

apunhalar /apuɲa'lar/ *vt* stab

apu|rado /apu'radu/ *a* refined; ~**rar** *vt* (*aprimorar*) refine; (*descobrir*) ascertain; investigate <*caso*>; collect <*dinheiro*>; count <*votos*>; ~**rar-se** *vpr* (*com a roupa*) dress smartly; ~**ro** *m* refinement; (*no vestir*) elegance; (*dificuldade*) difficulty; *pl* trouble

aquarela /akwa'rɛla/ *f* watercolour

aquariano /akwari'anu/ *a* & *m* Aquarian

aquário /a'kwariu/ *m* aquarium; **Aquário** Aquarius

aquartelar /akwarte'lar/ *vt* billet

aquático /a'kwatʃiku/ *a* aquatic, water

aque|cedor /akese'dor/ *m* heater; ~**cer** *vt* heat □ *vi*, ~**cer-se** *vpr* heat up; ~**cimento** *m* heating

aqueduto /ake'dutu/ *m* aqueduct

aquele /a'keli/ *a* that; *pl* those □ *pron* that one; *pl* those; ~ **que** the one that

àquele = a² + aquele

aqui /a'ki/ *adv* here

aquilo /a'kilu/ *pron* that

àquilo = a² + aquilo

aquisi|ção /akizi'sãw/ *f* acquisition; ~**tivo** *a* **poder ~tivo** purchasing power

ar /ar/ *m* air; (*aspecto*) look, air; (*Port: no carro*) choke; **ao ~ livre** in the open air; **no** ~ (*fig*) up in the air; (*TV*) on air; ~ **condicionado** air conditioning

árabe /'arabi/ *a & m* Arab; (*ling*) Arabic

Arábia /a'rabia/ *f* Arabia; ~ **Saudita** Saudi Arabia

arado /a'radu/ *m* plough, (*Amer*) plow

aragem /a'raʒē/ *f* breeze

arame /a'rami/ *m* wire; ~ **farpado** barbed wire

aranha /a'raɲa/ *f* spider

arar /a'rar/ *vt* plough, (*Amer*) plow

arara /a'rara/ *f* parrot

arbi|trar /arbi'trar/ *vt/i* referee <*jogo*>; arbitrate <*disputa*>; ~**trário** *a* arbitrary

arbítrio /ar'bitriu/ *m* judgement; **livre** ~ free will

árbitro /'arbitru/ *m* arbiter <*da moda etc*>; (*jurid*) arbitrator; (*de futebol*) referee; (*de tênis*) umpire

arborizado /arbori'zadu/ *a* wooded, green; <*rua*> tree-lined

arbusto /ar'bustu/ *m* shrub

ar|ca /'arka/ *f* ~**ca de Noé** Noah's Ark; ~**cada** *f* (*galeria*) arcade; (*arco*) arch

arcaico /ar'kajku/ *a* archaic

arcar /ar'kar/ *vt* ~ **com** deal with

arcebispo /arse'bispu/ *m* archbishop

arco /'arku/ *m* (*arquit*) arch; (*arma, mus*) bow; (*eletr, mat*) arc; ~**da-velha** *m* **coisa do** ~**-da-velha** amazing thing; ~**-íris** *m invar* rainbow

ar|dente /ar'dētʃi/ *a* burning; (*fig*) ardent; ~**der** *vi* burn; <*olhos, ferida*> sting

ar|dil /ar'dʒiw/ (*pl* ~**dis**) *m* trick, ruse

ardor /ar'dor/ *m* heat; (*fig*) ardour; **com** ~ ardently

árduo /'arduu/ *a* strenuous, arduous

área /'aria/ *f* area; (**grande**) ~ penalty area; ~ (**de serviço**) yard

arear /ari'ar/ *vt* scour <*panela*>

areia /a'reja/ *f* sand

arejar /are'ʒar/ *vt* air □ *vi*, ~**-se** *vpr* get some air; (*descansar*) have a breather

are|na /a'rena/ *f* arena; ~**noso** /o/ *a* sandy

arenque /a'rēki/ *m* herring

argamassa /arga'masa/ *f* mortar

Argélia /ar'ʒɛlia/ *f* Algeria

argelino /arʒe'linu/ *a & m* Algerian

Argentina /arʒē'tʃina/ *f* Argentina

argentino /arʒē'tʃinu/ *a & m* Argentinian

argila /ar'ʒila/ *f* clay

argola /ar'gɔla/ *f* ring

argumen|tar /argumē'tar/ *vt/i* argue; ~**to** *m* argument; (*de filme etc*) subject-matter

ariano /ari'anu/ *a & m* (*do signo Aries*) Arian

árido /'aridu/ *a* arid; barren <*deserto*>; (*fig*) dull, dry

Aries /'aris/ *f* Aries

arisco /a'risku/ *a* timid

aristo|cracia /aristokra'sia/ *f* aristocracy; ~**crata** *m/f* aristocrat; ~**crático** *a* aristocratic

aritmética /aritʃ'mɛtʃika/ *f* arithmetic

arma /'arma/ *f* weapon; *pl* arms; ~ **de fogo** firearm

ar|mação /arma'sãw/ *f* frame; (*de óculos*) frames; (*naut*) rigging; ~**madilha** *f* trap; ~**madura** *f* suit of armour; (*armação*) framework; ~**mar** *vt* (*dar armas a*) arm; (*montar*) put up, assemble; set up <*máquina*>; set, lay <*armadilha*>; fit out <*navio*>; hatch <*plano, complô*>; cause <*briga*>; ~**mar-se** *vpr* arm o.s.

armarinho /arma'riɲu/ *m* haberdashery, (*Amer*) notions

armário /ar'mariu/ *m* cupboard; (*de roupa*) wardrobe

arma|zém /arma'zēj/ *m* warehouse; (*loja*) general store; (*depósito*) storeroom; ~**zenagem** *f*, ~**zenamento** *m* storage; ~**zenar** *vt* store

Armênia /ar'menia/ *f* Armenia

armênio /ar'meniu/ *a & m* Armenian

aro /'aru/ *m* (*de roda, óculos*) rim; (*de porta*) frame

aro|ma /a'roma/ *f* aroma; (*perfume*) fragrance; ~**mático** *a* aromatic; fragrant

ar|pão /ar'pãw/ *m* harpoon; ~**poar** *vt* harpoon

arquear /arki'ar/ *vt* arch; ~**-se** *vpr* bend, bow

arque|ologia /arkiolo'ʒia/ *f* archaeology; ~**ológico** *a* archaeological; ~**ólogo** *m* archaeologist

arquétipo /ar'kɛtʃipu/ *m* archetype

arquibancada /arkibã'kada/ *f* terraces, (*Amer*) bleachers

arquipélago /arki'pɛlagu/ *m* archipelago

arquite|tar /arkite'tar/ *vt* think up; ~**to** /ɛ/ *m* architect; ~**tônico** *a* architectural; ~**tura** *f* architecture

arqui|var /arki'var/ *vt* file <*papéis*>; shelve <*plano, processo*>; ~**vista** *m/ f* archivist; ~**vo** *m* file; (*conjunto*) files; (*móvel*) filing cabinet; *pl* (*do Estado etc*) archives

arran|cada /axã'kada/ *f* lurch; (*de atleta, fig*) spurt; ~**car** *vt* pull out <*cabelo etc*>; pull off <*botão etc*>; pull up <*erva daninha etc*>; take out <*dente*>; (*das mãos de alg*) wrench, snatch; extract <*confissão, dinheiro*> □ *vi* <*carro*> roar off; <*pessoa*> take off; (*dar solavanco*) lurch forward; ~**car-se** *vpr* take off; ~**co** *m* pull, tug; *veja* ~**cada**

arranha-céu /axaɲa'sɛw/ *m* skyscraper

arra|nhadura /axaɲa'dura/ *f* scratch; ~**nhão** *m* scratch; ~**nhar** *vt* scratch; have a smattering of <*língua*>

arran|jar /axã'ʒar/ *vt* arrange; (*achar*) get, find; (*resolver*) settle, sort out; ~**jar-se** *vpr* manage; ~**jo** *m* arrangement

arrasar /axa'zar/ *vt* devastate; raze, flatten <*casa, cidade*>; ~**-se** *vpr* be devastated

arrastar /axas'tar/ *vt* drag; <*corrente, avalancha*> sweep away; (*atrair*) draw □ *vi* trail; ~**-se** *vpr* crawl; <*tempo*> drag; <*processo*> drag out

arreba|tador /axebata'dor/ *a* entrancing; shocking <*notícia*>; ~**tar** *vt* (*enlevar*) entrance, send; (*chocar*) shock

arreben|tação /axebẽta'sãw/ *f* surf; ~**tar** *vi* <*bomba*> explode; <*corda*> snap, break; <*balão, pessoa*> burst; <*onda*> break; <*guerra, incêndio*> break out □ *vt* snap, break <*corda*>; burst <*balão*>; break down <*porta*>

arrebitar /axebi'tar/ *vt* turn up <*nariz*>; prick up <*orelhas*>

arreca|dação /axekada'sãw/ *f* (*dinheiro*) tax revenue; ~**dar** *vt* collect

arredar /axe'dar/ *vt* **não** ~ **pé** stand one's ground

arredio /axe'dʒiu/ *a* withdrawn

arredondar /axedõ'dar/ *vt* round up <*quantia*>; round off <*ângulo*>

arredores /axe'dɔris/ *m pl* surroundings; (*de cidade*) outskirts

arrefecer /axefe'ser/ *vt/i* cool

arregaçar /axega'sar/ *vt* roll up

arrega|lado /axega'ladu/ *a* <*olhos*> wide; ~**lar** *vt* ~**lar os olhos** be wide-eyed with amazement

arreganhar /axega'ɲar/ *vt* bare <*dentes*>; ~**-se** *vpr* grin

arrema|tar /axema'tar/ *vt* finish off; (*no tricô*) cast off; ~**te** *m* conclusion; (*na costura*) finishing off; (*no futebol*) finishing

arremes|sar /axeme'sar/ *vt* hurl; ~**so** /e/ *m* throw

arrepen|der-se /axepẽ'dersi/ *vpr* be sorry; <*pecador*> repent; ~**der-se de regret**; ~**dido** *a* sorry; <*pecador*> repentant; ~**dimento** *m* regret; (*de pecado, crime*) repentance

arrepi|ado /axepi'adu/ *a* <*cabelo*> standing on end; <*pele, pessoa*> covered in goose pimples; ~**ar** *vt* (*dar calafrios*) make shudder; make stand on end <*cabelo*>; **me** ~**a (a pele)** it

gives me goose pimples; ~**ar-se** *vpr* (*estremecer*) shudder; <*cabelo*> stand on end; (*na pele*) get goose pimples; ~**o** *m* shudder; **me dá** ~**os** it makes me shudder

arris|cado /axis'kadu/ *a* risky; ~**car** *vt* risk; ~**car-se** *vpr* take a risk, risk it; ~**car-se a fazer** risk doing

arro|char /axo'ʃar/ *vt* tighten up □ *vi* be tough; ~**cho** /o/ *m* squeeze

arro|gância /axo'gãsia/ *f* arrogance; ~**gante** *a* arrogant

arro|jado /axo'ʒadu/ *a* bold; ~**jar** *vt* throw

arrombar /axõ'bar/ *vt* break down <*porta*>; break into <*casa*>; crack <*cofre*>

arro|tar /axo'tar/ *vi* burp, belch; ~**to** /o/ *m* burp

arroz /a'xoz/ *m* rice; ~ **doce** rice pudding; ~**al** (*pl* ~**ais**) *m* rice field

arrua|ça /axu'asa/ *f* riot; ~**ceiro** *m* rioter

arruela /axu'ɛla/ *f* washer

arruinar /axui'nar/ *vt* ruin; ~**-se** *vpr* be ruined

arru|madeira /axuma'dera/ *f* (*de hotel*) chambermaid; ~**mar** *vt* tidy (up) <*casa*>; sort out <*papéis, vida*>; pack <*mala*>; (*achar*) find, get; make up <*desculpa*>; (*vestir*) dress up; ~**mar-se** *vpr* (*aprontar-se*) get ready; (*na vida*) sort o.s. out

arse|nal /arse'naw/ (*pl* ~**nais**) *m* arsenal

arsênio /ar'seniu/ *m* arsenic

arte /'artʃi/ *f* art; **fazer** ~ <*criança*> get up to mischief; ~**fato** *m* product, article

arteiro /ar'teru/ *a* mischievous

artéria /ar'tɛria/ *f* artery

artesa|nal /arteza'naw/ (*pl* ~**nais**) *a* craft; ~**nato** *m* craftwork

arte|são /arte'zãw/ (*pl* ~**s**) *m* (*f* ~**sã**) artisan, craftsman (*f* -woman)

ártico /'artʃiku/ *a* & *m* arctic

articu|lação /artʃikula'sãw/ *f* articulation; (*anat, tecn*) joint; ~**lar** *vt* articulate

arti|ficial /artʃifisi'aw/ (*pl* ~**ficiais**) *a* artificial; ~**fício** *m* trick

artigo /ar'tʃigu/ *m* article; (*com*) item

arti|lharia /artʃiʎa'ria/ *f* artillery; ~**lheiro** *m* (*mil*) gunner; (*no futebol*) striker

artimanha /artʃi'maɲa/ *f* trick; (*método*) clever way

ar|tista /ar'tʃista/ *m/f* artist; ~**tístico** *a* artistic

artrite /ar'tritʃi/ *f* arthritis

árvore /'arvori/ *f* tree

arvoredo /arvo'redu/ *m* grove

as /as/ *artigo & pron veja* **a**[1]

ás /as/ *m* ace

às = a² + as

asa /'aza/ f wing; (de xícara) handle; ~-delta f hang-glider

ascen|dência /asē'dēsia/ f ancestry; (superioridade) ascendancy; ~dente a rising; ~der vi rise; ascend <ao trono>; ~são f rise; (relig) Ascension; **em ~são** rising; (fig) up and coming; ~sor m lift, (Amer) elevator; ~sorista m/f lift operator

asco /'asku/ m revulsion, disgust; **dar ~** be revolting

asfalto /as'fawtu/ m asphalt

asfixiar /asfiksi'ar/ vt/i asphyxiate

Asia /'azia/ f Asia

asiático /azi'atʃiku/ a & m Asian

as|ma /'azma/ f asthma; ~mático a & m asthmatic

asneira /az'nera/ f stupidity; (uma) stupid thing

aspas /'aspas/ f pl inverted commas

aspargo /as'pargu/ m asparagus

aspecto /as'pɛktu/ m appearance, look; (de um problema) aspect

aspereza /aspe'reza/ f roughness; (do clima, de um som) harshness; (fig) rudeness

áspero /'asperu/ a rough; <clima, som> harsh; (fig) rude

aspi|ração /aspira'sãw/ f aspiration; (med) inhalation; ~rador m vacuum cleaner; ~rar vt inhale, breathe in <ar, fumaça>; suck up <líquido>; ~rar a aspire to

aspirina /aspi'rina/ f aspirin

asqueroso /aske'rozu/ a revolting, disgusting

assa|do /a'sadu/ a & m roast; ~dura f (na pele) sore patch

assalariado /asalari'adu/ a salaried □ m salaried worker

assal|tante /asaw'tãtʃi/ m robber; (na rua) mugger; (de casa) burglar; ~tar vt rob; burgle, (Amer) burglarize <casa>; ~to m (roubo) robbery; (a uma casa) burglary; (ataque) assault; (no boxe) round

assanhado /asa'ɲadu/ a worked up; <criança> excitable; (erótico) amorous

assar /a'sar/ vt roast

assassi|nar /asasi'nar/ vt murder; (pol) assassinate; ~nato m murder; (pol) assassination; ~no m murderer; (pol) assassin

asseado /asi'adu/ a well-groomed

as|sediar /asedʒi'ar/ vt besiege <cidade>; (fig) pester; ~sédio m siege; (fig) pestering

assegurar /asegu'rar/ vt (tornar seguro) secure; (afirmar) guarantee; ~ a alg aco/que assure s.o. of sth/

that; ~-se de/que make sure of/that

assembléia /asē'blɛja/ f (pol) assembly; (com) meeting

assemelhar /aseme'ʎar/ vt liken; ~-se vpr be alike; ~-se a resemble, be like

assen|tar /asē'tar/ vt (estabelecer) establish, define; settle <povo>; lay <tijolo> □ vi <pó> settle; ~tar-se vpr settle down; ~tar com go with; ~tar a <roupa> suit; ~to m seat; (fig) basis; **tomar ~to** take a seat; <pó> settle

assen|tir /asē'tʃir/ vi agree; ~timento m agreement

assessor /ase'sor/ m adviser; ~ar vt advise

assexuado /aseksu'adu/ a asexual

assiduidade /asidui'dadʒi/ f (à escola) regular attendance; (diligência) diligence

assíduo /a'siduu/ a (que freqüenta) regular; (diligente) assiduous

assim /a'sī/ adv like this, like that; (portanto) therefore; **e ~ por diante** and so on; ~ **como** as well as; ~ **que** as soon as

assimétrico /asi'mɛtriku/ a asymmetrical

assimilar /asimi'lar/ vt assimilate; ~-se vpr be assimilated

assinalar /asina'lar/ vt (marcar) mark; (distinguir) distinguish; (apontar) point out

assi|nante /asi'nãtʃi/ m/f subscriber; ~nar vt/i sign; ~natura f (nome) signature; (de revista) subscription

assis|tência /asis'tēsia/ f assistance; (presença) attendance; (público) audience; ~tente a assistant □ m/f assistant; ~tente social social worker; ~tir (a) vt/i (ver) watch; (presenciar) attend; assist <doente>

assoalho /aso'aʎu/ m floor

assoar /aso'ar/ vt ~ o nariz, (Port) ~-se blow one's nose

assobi|ar /asobi'ar/ vt/i whistle; ~o m whistle

associ|ação /asosia'sãw/ f association; ~ado a & m associate; ~ar vt associate (a with); ~ar-se vpr associate; (com) go into partnership (a with)

assolar /aso'lar/ vt devastate

assom|bração /asõbra'sãw/ f ghost; ~brar vt astonish, amaze; ~brar-se vpr be amazed; ~bro m amazement, astonishment; (coisa) marvel; ~broso /o/ a astonishing, amazing

assoprar /aso'prar/ vi blow □ vt blow; blow out <vela>

assovi- veja assobi-

assu|mido /asu'midu/ a (confesso) confirmed, self-confessed; ~mir vt assume, take on; accept, admit <*defeito*> □ *vi* take office

assunto /a'sũtu/ *m* subject; (*negócio*) matter

assus|tador /asusta'dor/ *a* frightening; ~**tar** *vt* frighten, scare; ~**tar-se** *vpr* get frightened, get scared

asterisco /aste'risku/ *m* asterisk

as|tral /as'traw/ (*pl* ~**trais**) *m* (*fam*) state of mind; ~**tro** *m* star; ~**trologia** *f* astrology; ~**trólogo** *m* astrologer; ~**tronauta** *m/f* astronaut; ~**tronave** *f* spaceship; ~**tronomia** *f* astronomy; ~**tronômico** *a* astronomical; ~**trônomo** *m* astronomer

as|túcia /as'tusia/ *f* cunning; ~**tuto** *a* cunning; <*comerciante*> astute

ata /'ata/ *f* minutes

ataca|dista /ataka'dʒista/ *m/f* wholesaler; ~**do m por** ~**do** wholesale

ata|cante /ata'kãtʃi/ *a* attacking □ *m/f* attacker; ~**car** *vt* attack; tackle <*problema*>

atadura /ata'dura/ *f* bandage

ata|lhar /ata'ʎar/ *vi* take a shortcut; ~**lho** *m* shortcut

ataque /a'taki/ *m* attack; (*de raiva, riso*) fit

atar /a'tar/ *vt* tie

atarantado /atarã'tadu/ *a* flustered, in a flap

atarefado /atare'fadu/ *a* busy

atarracado /ataxa'kadu/ *a* stocky

atarraxar /ataxa'ʃar/ *vt* screw

até /a'tɛ/ *prep* (up) to, as far as; (*tempo*) until □ *adv* even; ~ **logo** goodbye; ~ **que** until

atéia /a'tɛja/ *a* & *f veja* ateu

ateliê /ateli'e/ *m* studio

atemorizar /atemori'zar/ *vt* frighten

Atenas /a'tenas/ *f* Athens

aten|ção /atẽ'sãw/ *f* attention; *pl* (*bondade*) thoughtfulness; **com** ~**ção** attentively; ~**cioso** *a* thoughtful, considerate

aten|der /atẽ'der/ ~**der (a)** *vt/i* answer <*telefone, porta*>; answer to <*nome*>; serve <*freguês*>; see <*paciente, visitante*>; grant, meet <*pedido*>; heed <*conselho*>; ~**dimento** *m* service; (*de médico etc*) consultation

aten|tado /atẽ'tadu/ *m* murder attempt; (*pol*) assassination attempt; (*ataque*) attack (**contra** on); ~**tar** *vi* ~**tar contra** make an attempt on

atento /a'tẽtu/ *a* attentive; ~ **a** mindful of

aterrador /atexa'dor/ *a* terrifying

ater|ragem /ate'xaʒẽ/ *f* (*Port*) landing; ~**rar** *vi* (*Port*) land

aterris|sagem /atexi'saʒẽ/ *f* landing; ~**sar** *vi* land

ater-se /a'tersi/ *vpr* ~ **a** keep to, go by

ates|tado /ates'tadu/ *m* certificate; ~**tar** *vt* attest (to)

ateu /a'tew/ *a* & *m* (*f* **atéia**) atheist

atiçar /atʃi'sar/ *vt* poke <*fogo*>; stir up <*ódio, discórdia*>; arouse <*pessoa*>

atinar /atʃi'nar/ *vt* work out, guess; ~ **com** find; ~ **em** notice

atingir /atʃĩ'ʒir/ *vt* reach; hit <*alvo*>; (*conseguir*) attain; (*afetar*) affect

atirar /atʃi'rar/ *vt* throw □ *vi* shoot; ~ **em** fire at

atitude /atʃi'tudʒi/ *f* attitude; **tomar uma** ~ take action

ati|va /a'tʃiva/ *f* active service; ~**var** *vt* activate; ~**vidade** *f* activity; ~**vo** *a* active □ *m* (*com*) assets

Atlântico /at'lãtʃiku/ *m* Atlantic

atlas /'atlas/ *m* atlas

at|leta /at'lɛta/ *m/f* athlete; ~**lético** *a* athletic; ~**letismo** *m* athletics

atmosfera /atʃimos'fɛra/ *f* atmosphere

ato /'atu/ *m* act; (*ação*) action; **no** ~ on the spot

ato|lar /ato'lar/ *vt* bog down; ~**lar-se** *vpr* get bogged down; ~**leiro** *m* bog; (*fig*) fix, spot of trouble

atômico /a'tomiku/ *a* atomic

atomizador /atomiza'dor/ *m* atomizer spray

átomo /'atomu/ *m* atom

atônito /a'tonitu/ *a* astonished, stunned

ator /a'tor/ *m* actor

atordoar /atordo'ar/ *vt* <*golpe, notícia*> stun; <*som*> deafen; (*alucinar*) bewilder

atormentar /atormẽ'tar/ *vt* plague, torment

atração /atra'sãw/ *f* attraction

atracar /atra'kar/ *vt/i* (*naut*) moor; ~**se** *vpr* grapple; (*fam*) neck

atractivo (*Port*) *veja* **atrativo**

atraente /atra'ẽtʃi/ *a* attractive

atraiçoar /atrajso'ar/ *vt* betray

atrair /atra'ir/ *vt* attract

atrapalhar /atrapa'ʎar/ *vt/i* (*confundir*) confuse; (*estorvar*) hinder; (*perturbar*) disturb; ~**-se** *vpr* get mixed up

atrás /a'traʃ/ *adv* behind; (*no fundo*) at the back; ~ **de** behind; (*depois de, no encalço de*) after; **um mês** ~ **a** month ago; **ficar** ~ be left behind

atra|sado /atra'zadu/ *a* late; <*país, criança*> backward; <*relógio*> slow; <*pagamento*> overdue; <*idéias*> old-fashioned; ~**sar** *vt* delay; put back <*relógio*> □ *vi* be late; <*relógio*> lose; ~**sar-se** *vpr* be late; (*num trabalho*) get behind; (*no pagar*) get into arrears; ~**so** *m* delay; (*de país etc*) backwardness; *pl* (*com*) arrears; **com** ~**so** late

atrativo /atra'tʃivu/ *m* attraction

através /atra'vɛs/ ~ **de** *prep* through; *(de um lado ao outro)* across

atravessado /atrave'sadu/ *a* <*espinha*> stuck; **estar com alg ~ na garganta** be fed up with s.o.

atravessar /atrave'sar/ *vt* go through; cross <*rua, rio*>

atre|ver-se /atre'versi/ *vpr* dare; ~**ver-se a** dare to; ~**vido** *a* daring; *(insolente)* impudent; ~**vimento** *m* daring, boldness; *(insolência)* impudence

atribu|ir /atribu'ir/ *vt* attribute (**a** to); confer <*prêmio, poderes*> (**a** on); attach <*importância*> (**a** to); ~**to** *m* attribute

atrito /a'tritu/ *m* friction; *(desavença)* disagreement

atriz /a'tris/ *f* actress

atrocidade /atrosi'dadʒi/ *f* atrocity

atrope|lar /atrope'lar/ *vt* run over, knock down <*pedestre*>; *(empurrar)* jostle; mix up <*palavras*>; ~**lamento** *m* *(de pedestre)* running over; ~**lo** /e/ *m* scramble

atroz /a'tros/ *a* awful, terrible; heinous <*crime*>; cruel <*pessoa*>

atuação /atua'sãw/ *f (ação)* action; *(desempenho)* performance

atu|al /atu'aw/ *(pl* ~**ais)** *a* current, present; <*assunto, interesse*> topical; <*pessoa, carro*> up-to-date; ~**alidade** *f (presente)* present (time); *(de um livro)* topicality; *pl* current affairs; ~**alizado** *a* up-to-date; ~**alizar** *vt* update; ~**alizar-se** *vpr* bring o.s. up to date; ~**almente** *adv* at present, currently

atum /a'tũ/ *m* tuna

aturdir /atur'dʒir/ *vt veja* **atordoar**

audácia /aw'dasia/ *f* boldness; *(insolência)* audacity

audi|ção /awdʒi'sãw/ *f* hearing; *(concerto)* recital; ~**ência** *f* audience; *(jurid)* hearing

audiovisu|al /awdʒiovizu'aw/ *(pl* ~**ais)** *a* audiovisual

auditório /awdʒi'tɔriu/ *m* auditorium; **programa de ~** variety show

auge /'awʒi/ *m* peak, height

aula /'awla/ *f* class, lesson; **dar ~** teach

aumen|tar /awmẽ'tar/ *vt* increase; raise <*preço, salário*>; extend <*casa*>; *(com lente)* magnify; *(acrescentar)* add ~ *vi* increase; <*preço, salário*> go up; ~**to** *m* increase; *(de salário)* rise, *(Amer)* raise

au|sência /aw'zẽsia/ *f* absence; ~**sente** *a* absent □ *m/f* absentee

aus|pícios /aws'pisius/ *m pl* auspices; ~**picioso** /o/ *a* auspicious

auste|ridade /awsteri'dadʒi/ *f* austerity; ~**ro** /ɛ/ *a* austere

Austrália /aw'stralia/ *f* Australia

australiano /awstrali'anu/ *a* & *m* Australian

Austria /'awstria/ *f* Austria

austríaco /aws'triaku/ *a* & *m* Austrian

autarquia /awtar'kia/ *f* public authority

autêntico /aw'tẽtʃiku/ *a* authentic; genuine <*pessoa*>; true <*fato*>

autobio|grafia /awtobiogra'fia/ *f* autobiography; ~**gráfico** *a* autobiographical

autocarro /awto'kaxu/ *m* *(Port)* bus

autocrata /awto'krata/ *a* autocratic

autodefesa /awtode'feza/ *f* self-defence

autodidata /awtodʒi'data/ *a* & *m/f* self-taught (person)

autódromo /aw'tɔdromu/ *m* race track

auto-escola /awtois'kɔla/ *f* driving school

auto-estrada /awtois'trada/ *f* motorway, *(Amer)* expressway

autógrafo /aw'tɔgrafu/ *m* autograph

auto|mação /awtoma'sãw/ *f* automation; ~**mático** *a* automatic; ~**matizar** *vt* automate

auto|mobilismo /awtomobi'lizmu/ *m* motoring; *(esporte)* motor racing; ~**móvel** *(pl* ~**móveis)** *m* motor car, *(Amer)* automobile

au|tonomia /awtono'mia/ *f* autonomy; ~**tônomo** *a* autonomous; <*trabalhador*> selfemployed

autopeça /awto'pɛsa/ *f* car spare

autópsia /aw'tɔpsia/ *f* autopsy

autor /aw'tor/ *m (f* ~**a)** author; *(de crime)* perpetrator; *(jurid)* plaintiff

auto-retrato /awtoxe'tratu/ *m* self-portrait

autoria /awto'ria/ *f* authorship; *(de crime)* responsibility (**de** for)

autori|dade /awtori'dadʒi/ *f* authority; ~**zação** *f* authorization; ~**zar** *vt* authorize

autuar /awtu'ar/ *vt* sue

au|xiliar /awsili'ar/ *a* auxiliary □ *m/f* assistant □ *vt* assist; ~**xílio** *m* assistance, aid

aval /a'vaw/ *(pl* **avais**) *m* endorsement; *(com)* guarantee

avali|ação /avalia'sãw/ *f (de preço)* valuation; *(fig)* evaluation; ~**ar** *vt* value <*quadro etc*> (**em** at); assess <*danos, riscos*>; *(fig)* evaluate

avan|çar /avã'sar/ *vt* move forward □ *vi* move forward; *(mil, fig)* advance; ~**çar a** *(montar)* amount to; ~**ço** *m* advance

avar|eza /ava'reza/ *f* meanness; ~**ento** *a* mean

ava|ria /ava'ria/ f damage; (de máquina) breakdown; ~riado a damaged; <máquina> out of order; <carro> broken down; ~riar vt damage □ vi be damaged; <máquina> break down

ave /'avi/ f bird; ~ de rapina bird of prey

aveia /a'veja/ f oats

avelã /ave'lã/ f hazelnut

avenida /ave'nida/ f avenue

aven|tal /avẽ'taw/ (pl ~tais) m apron

aventu|ra /avẽ'tura/ f adventure; (amorosa) fling; ~rar vt venture; ~rar-se vpr venture (a to); ~reiro a adventurous □ m adventurer

averiguar /averi'gwar/ vt check (out)

avermelhado /averme'ʎadu/ a reddish

aver|são /aver'sãw/ f aversion; ~so a averse (a to)

aves|sas /a'vɛsas/ às ~sas the wrong way round; (de cabeça para baixo) upside down; ~so /e/ m ao ~so inside out

avestruz /aves'trus/ m ostrich

avi|ação /avia'sãw/ f aviation; ~ão m (aero)plane, (Amer) (air)plane; ~ão a jato jet

avi|dez /avi'des/ f (cobiça) greediness; ~do a greedy

avi|sar /avi'zar/ vt (informar) tell, let know; (advertir) warn; ~so m notice; (advertência) warning

avistar /avis'tar/ vt catch sight of

avo /'avu/ m um doze ~s one twelfth

avó /a'vɔ/ f grandmother; ~s m pl grandparents

avô /a'vo/ m grandfather

avoado /avo'adu/ a dizzy, scatterbrained

avulso /a'vuwsu/ a loose, odd

avultado /avuw'tadu/ a bulky

axila /ak'sila/ f armpit

azaléia /aza'lɛja/ f azalea

azar /a'zar/ m bad luck; ter ~ be unlucky; ~ado, ~ento a unlucky

aze|dar /aze'dar/ vt sour □ vi go sour; ~do /e/ a sour

azei|te /a'zejtʃi/ m oil; ~tona /o/ f olive

azevinho /aze'viɲu/ m holly

azia /a'zia/ f heartburn

azucrinar /azukri'nar/ vt annoy

azul /a'zuw/ (pl azuis) a blue

azulejo /azu'leʒu/ m (ceramic) tile

azul-marinho /azuwma'riɲu/ a invar navy blue

B

babá /ba'ba/ f nanny; ~ eletrônica baby alarm

ba|bado /ba'badu/ m frill; ~bador m

bib; ~bar vt/i, ~bar-se vpr drool (por over); <bebê> dribble; ~beiro (Port) m bib

baby-sitter /bejbi'siter/ (pl ~s) m/f babysitter

bacalhau /baka'ʎaw/ m cod

bacana /ba'kana/ (fam) a great

bacha|rel /baʃa'rɛw/ (pl ~réis) bachelor; ~relado m bachelor's degree; ~relar-se vpr graduate

bacia /ba'sia/ f basin; (da privada) bowl; (anat) pelvis

baço /'basu/ m spleen

bacon /'bejkõ/ m bacon

bactéria /bak'tɛria/ f bacterium; pl bacteria

bada|lado /bada'ladu/ a (fam) talked about; ~lar vt ring <sino> □ vi ring; (fam) go out and about; ~lativo (fam) a fun-loving, gadabout

badejo /ba'deʒu/ m sea bass

baderna /ba'dɛrna/ f (tumulto) commotion; (desordem) mess

badulaque /badu'laki/ m trinket

bafafá /bafa'fa/ (fam) m to-do, kerfuffle

ba|fo /'bafu/ m bad breath; ~fômetro m Breathalyser; ~forada f puff

bagaço /ba'gasu/ m pulp; (Port: aguardente) brandy

baga|geiro /baga'ʒeru/ m (de carro) roofrack; (Port: homem) porter; ~gem f luggage; (cultural etc) baggage

bagatela /baga'tɛla/ f trifle

Bagdá /bagi'da/ f Baghdad

bago /'bagu/ m berry; (de chumbo) pellet

bagulho /ba'guʎu/ m piece of junk; pl junk; ele é um ~ he's as ugly as sin

bagun|ça /ba'gũsa/ f mess; ~çar vt mess up; ~ceiro a messy □ m messer

baía /ba'ia/ f bay

baiano /ba'janu/ a & m Bahian

baila /'bajla/ f trazer/vir à ~ bring/come up

bai|lar /baj'lar/ vt/i dance; ~larino m ballet dancer; ~le m dance; (de gala) ball

bainha /ba'iɲa/ f (de vestido) hem; (de arma) sheath

baioneta /bajo'neta/ f bayonet

bairro /'bajxu/ m neighbourhood, area

baixa /'baʃa/ f drop, fall; (de guerra) casualty; (dispensa) discharge; ~mar f low tide

baixar /ba'ʃar/ vt lower; issue <ordem>; pass <lei> □ vi drop, fall; (fam: pintar) turn up

baixaria /baʃa'ria/ f sordidness; (uma) sordid thing

baixela /ba'ʃɛla/ f set of cutlery

baixeza /ba'ʃeza/ f baseness

baixo /'baʃu/ a low; <*pessoa*> short; <*som, voz*> quiet, soft; <*cabeça, olhos*> lowered; (*vil*) sordid □ adv low; <*falar*> softly, quietly □ m bass; **em ~** underneath; (*em casa*) downstairs; **em ~ de** under; **para ~** down; (*em casa*) downstairs; **por ~ de** under(neath)

baju|lador /baʒula'dor/ a obsequious □ m sycophant; **~lar** vt fawn on

bala /'bala/ f (*de revólver*) bullet; (*doce*) sweet

balada /ba'lada/ f ballad

balaio /ba'laju/ m linen basket

balan|ça /ba'lãsa/ f scales; **Balança** (*signo*) Libra; **~ça de pagamentos** balance of payments; **~çar** vt/i (*no ar*) swing; (*numa cadeira etc*) rock; <*carro, avião*> shake; <*navio*> roll; **~çar-se** vpr swing; **~cete** /e/ m trial balance; **~ço** m (*com*) balance sheet; (*brinquedo*) swing; (*movimento no ar*) swinging; (*de carro, avião*) shaking; (*de navio*) rolling; (*de cadeira*) rocking; **fazer um ~ço de** (*fig*) take stock of

balangandã /balãgã'dã/ m bauble

balão /ba'lãw/ m balloon; **soltar um ~-de-ensaio** (*fig*) put out feelers

balar /ba'lar/ vi bleat

balbu|ciar /bawbusi'ar/ vt/i babble; **~cio** m babble, babbling

balbúrdia /baw'burdʒia/ f hubbub

bal|cão /baw'kãw/ m (*em loja*) counter; (*de informações, bilhetes*) desk; (*de cozinha*) worktop, (*Amer*) counter; (*no teatro*) circle; **~conista** m/f shop assistant

balde /'bawdʒi/ m bucket

baldeação /bawdʒia'sãw/ f **fazer ~** change (trains)

baldio /baw'dʒiu/ a fallow; **terreno ~** (*piece of*) waste ground

balé /ba'lɛ/ m ballet

balear /bali'ar/ vt shoot

baleia /ba'leja/ f whale

balido /ba'lidu/ m bleat, bleating

balísti|ca /ba'listʃika/ f ballistics; **~co** a ballistic

bali|za /ba'liza/ f marker; (*luminosa*) beacon; **~zar** vt mark out

balneário /bawni'ariu/ m seaside resort

balofo /ba'lofu/ a fat, tubby

baloiço, balouço /ba'lojsu, ba'losu/ (*Port*) m (*de criança*) swing

balsa /'bawsa/ f (*de madeira etc*) raft; (*que vai e vem*) ferry

bálsamo /'bawsamu/ m balm

báltico /'bawtʃiku/ a & m Baltic

baluarte /balu'artʃi/ m bulwark

bambo /'bãbu/ a loose, slack; <*pernas*> limp; <*mesa*> wobbly

bambo|lê /bãbo'le/ m hula hoop; **~lear** vi <*pessoa*> sway, totter; <*coisa*> wobble

bambu /bã'bu/ m bamboo

ba|nal /ba'naw/ (*pl* **~nais**) a banal; **~nalidade** f banality

bana|na /ba'nana/ f banana □ (*fam*) m/f wimp; **~nada** f banana fudge; **~neira** f banana tree; **plantar ~neira** do a handstand

banca /'bãka/ f (*de trabalho*) bench; (*de jornais*) newsstand; **~ examinadora** examining board; **~da** f (*pol*) bench

bancar /bã'kar/ vt (*custear*) finance; (*fazer papel de*) play; (*fingir*) pretend

bancário /bã'kariu/ a bank □ m bank employee

bancarrota /bãka'xota/ f bankruptcy; **ir à ~** go bankrupt

banco /'bãku/ m (*com*) bank; (*no parque*) bench; (*na cozinha, num bar*) stool; (*de bicicleta*) saddle; (*de carro*) seat; **~ de areia** sandbank; **~ de dados** database

banda /'bãda/ f band; (*lado*) side; **de ~** sideways on; **nestas ~s** in these parts; **~ desenhada** (*Port*) cartoon

bandei|ra /bã'dera/ f flag; (*divisa*) banner; **dar ~ra** (*fam*) give o.s. away; **~rante** m/f pioneer □ f girl guide; **~rinha** m linesman'

bandeja /bã'deʒa/ f tray

bandido /bã'dʒidu/ m bandit

bando /'bãdu/ m (*de pessoas*) band; (*de pássaros*) flock

bandolim /bãdo'lĩ/ m mandolin

bangalô /bãga'lo/ m bungalow

Bangcoc /bã'koki/ f Bangkok

bangue-bangue /bãgi'bãgi/ (*fam*) m western

banguela /bã'gɛla/ a toothless

banha /'bana/ f lard; *pl* (*no corpo*) flab

banhar /ba'nar/ vt (*molhar*) bathe; (*lavar*) bath; **~-se** vpr bathe

banhei|ra /ba'nera/ f bath, (*Amer*) bathtub; **~ro** m bathroom; (*Port*) lifeguard

banhista /ba'nista/ m/f bather

banho /'banu/ m bath; (*no mar*) bathe, dip; **tomar ~** have a bath; (*no chuveiro*) have a shower; **tomar um ~ de loja/cultura** go on a shopping/cultural spree; **~ de espuma** bubble bath; **~ de sol** sunbathing; **~-maria** (*pl* **~s-maria**) m bain marie

ba|nimento /bani'mẽtu/ m banishment; **~nir** vt banish

banjo /'bãʒu/ m banjo

banqueiro /bã'keru/ m banker

banqueta /bã'keta/ f foot-stool

banque|te /bã'ketʃi/ m banquet; **~teiro** m caterer

banzé /bã'zɛ/ (*fam*) m commotion, uproar

bapt- (*Port*) *veja* **bat-**

baque /'baki/ *m* thud, crash; (*revés*) blow; **~ar** *vi* topple over □ *vt* hit hard, knock for six

bar /bar/ *m* bar

barafunda /bara'fũda/ *f* jumble; (*barulho*) racket

bara|lhada /bara'ʎada/ *f* jumble; **~lho** *m* pack of cards, (*Amer*) deck of cards

barão /ba'rãw/ *m* baron

barata /ba'rata/ *f* cockroach

bara|tear /barat∫i'ar/ *vt* cheapen; **~teiro** *a* cheap

baratinar /barat∫i'nar/ *vt* fluster; (*transtornar*) rattle, shake up

barato /ba'ratu/ *a* cheap □ *adv* cheaply □ (*fam*) *m* **um ~** great; **que ~!** that's brilliant!

barba /'barba/ *f* beard; *pl* (*de gato etc*) whiskers; **fazer a ~** shave; **~da** *f* walkover; (*cavalo*) favourite; **~do** *a* bearded

barbante /bar'bãt∫i/ *m* string

bar|baridade /barbari'dadʒi/ *f* barbarity; (*fam: muito dinheiro*) fortune; **~bárie** *f*, **~barismo** *m* barbarism

bárbaro /'barbaru/ *m* barbarian □ *a* barbaric; (*fam: forte, bom*) terrific

barbatana /barba'tana/ *f* fin

bar|beador /barbia'dor/ *m* shaver; **~bear** *vt* shave; **~bear-se** *vpr* shave; **~bearia** *f* barber's shop; **~beiragem** (*fam*) *f* bit of bad driving; **~beiro** *m* barber; (*fam: motorista*) bad driver

bar|ca /'barka/ *f* barge; (*balsa*) ferry; **~caça** *f* barge; **~co** *m* boat; **~co a motor** motorboat; **~co a remo/vela** rowing/sailing boat, (*Amer*) rowboat/ sailboat

barga|nha /bar'gaɲa/ *f* bargain; **~nhar** *vt/i* bargain

barítono /ba'ritonu/ *m* baritone

barômetro /ba'rometru/ *m* barometer

baronesa /baro'neza/ *f* baroness

barra /'baxa/ *f* bar; (*sinal gráfico*) slash, stroke; (*fam: situação*) situation; **segurar a ~** hold out; **forçar a ~** force the issue

barra|ca /ba'xaka/ *f* (*de acampar*) tent; (*na feira*) stall; (*casinha*) hut; (*guarda-sol*) sunshade; **~cão** *m* shed; **~co** *m* shack, shanty

barragem /ba'xaʒẽ/ *f* (*represa*) dam

barra-pesada /baxape'zada/ (*fam*) *a invar* <*bairro*> rough; <*pessoa*> shady; (*difícil*) tough

bar|rar /ba'xar/ *vt* bar; **~reira** *f* barrier; (*em corrida*) hurdle; (*em futebol*) wall

barrento /ba'xẽtu/ *a* muddy

barricada /baxi'kada/ *f* barricade

barri|ga /ba'xiga/ *f* stomach, (*Amer*) belly; **~ga da perna** calf; **~gudo** *a* pot-bellied

bar|ril /ba'xiw/ (*pl* **~ris**) *m* barrel

barro /'baxu/ *m* (*argila*) clay; (*lama*) mud

barroco /ba'xoku/ *a & m* baroque

barrote /ba'xɔt∫i/ *m* beam, joist

baru|lheira /baru'ʎera/ *f* racket, din; **~lhento** *a* noisy; **~lho** *m* noise

base /'bazi/ *f* base; (*fig: fundamento*) basis; **com ~ em** on the basis of; **na ~ de** based on; **~ado** *a* based; (*firme*) well-founded □ (*fam*) *m* joint; **~ar** *vt* base; **~ar-se em** be based on

básico /'baziku/ *a* basic

basquete /bas'kɛt∫i/ *m*, **basquetebol** /basketʃi'bɔw/ *m* basketball

bas|ta /'basta/ *m* **dar um ~ta em** call a halt to; **~tante** *a* (*muito*) quite a lot of; (*suficiente*) enough □ *adv* (*com adjetivo, advérbio*) quite; (*com verbo*) quite a lot; (*suficientemente*) enough

bastão /bas'tãw/ *m* stick; (*num revezamento, de comando*) baton

bastar /bas'tar/ *vi* be enough

bastidores /bast∫i'doris/ *m pl* (*no teatro*) wings; **nos ~** (*fig*) behind the scenes

bata /'bata/ *f* (*de mulher*) smock; (*de médico etc*) overall

bata|lha /ba'taʎa/ *f* battle; **~lhador** *a* plucky, feisty □ *m* fighter; **~lhão** *m* battalion; **~lhar** *vi* battle; (*esforçar-se*) fight hard □ *vt* fight hard to get

batata /ba'tata/ *f* potato; **~ doce** sweet potato; **~ frita** chips, (*Amer*) French fries; (*salgadinhos*) crisps, (*Amer*) potato chips

bate-boca /bat∫i'boka/ *m* row, argument

bate|deira /bate'dera/ *f* whisk; (*de manteiga*) churn; **~dor** *m* (*policial etc*) outrider; (*no criquete*) batsman; (*no beisebol*) batter; (*de caça*) beater; **~dor de carteiras** pickpocket

batelada /bate'lada/ *f* batch; **~s de** heaps of

batente /ba'tẽt∫i/ *m* (*de porta*) doorway; **para o/no ~** (*fam: ao trabalho*) to/at work

bate-papo /bat∫i'papu/ *m* chat.

bater /ba'ter/ *vt* beat; stamp <*pé*>; slam <*porta*>; strike <*horas*>; take <*foto*>; flap <*asas*>; (*datilografar*) type; (*lavar*) wash; (*usar muito*) wear a lot <*roupa*>; (*fam*) pinch <*carteira*> □ *vi* <*coração*> beat; <*porta*> slam; <*janela*> bang; <*horas*> strike; <*sino*> ring; (*à porta*) knock; (*com o carro*) crash; **~-se** *vpr* (*lutar*) fight; **~ à máquina** type; **~ à**

ou **na porta** knock at the door; ∼ **em** hit; harp on <*assunto*>; <*luz, sol*> shine on; ∼ **com o carro** crash one's car, have a crash; ∼ **com a cabeça** bang one's head; **ele batia os dentes de frio** his teeth were chattering with cold; **ele não bate bem** (*fam*) he's not all there

bate|ria /bate'ria/ *f* (*eletr*) battery; (*mus*) drums; ∼**ria de cozinha** kitchen utensils; ∼**rista** *m/f* drummer

bati|da /ba'tʃida/ *f* beat; (*à porta*) knock; (*no carro*) crash; (*policial*) raid; (*bebida*) cocktail of rum, sugar and fruit juice; ∼**do** *a* beaten; <*roupa*> well worn; <*assunto*> hackneyed □ *m* ∼**do de leite** (*Port*) milkshake

batina /ba'tʃina/ *f* cassock

ba|tismo /ba'tʃizmu/ *m* baptism; ∼**tizado** *m* christening; ∼**tizar** *vt* baptize; (*pôr nome*) christen

batom /ba'tõ/ *m* lipstick

batu|cada /batu'kada/ *f* samba percussion group; ∼**car** *vt/i* drum in a samba rhythm; ∼**que** *m* samba rhythm

batuta /ba'tuta/ *f* baton; **sob a** ∼ **de** under the direction of

baú /ba'u/ *m* trunk

baunilha /baw'niʎa/ *f* vanilla

bazar /ba'zar/ *m* bazaar; (*loja*) stationery and haberdashery shop

bê-a-bá /bea'ba/ *m* ABC

bea|titude /beatʃi'tudʒi/ *f* (*felicidade*) bliss; (*devoção*) piety, devoutness; ∼**to** *a* (*devoto*) pious, devout; (*feliz*) blissful

bêbado /'bebadu/ *a & m* drunk

bebê /be'be/ *m* baby; ∼ **de proveta** test-tube baby

bebe|deira /bebe'dera/ *f* (*estado*) drunkenness; (*ato*) drinking bout; ∼**dor** *m* drinker; ∼**douro** *m* drinking fountain

beber /be'ber/ *vt/i* drink

bebericar /beberi'kar/ *vt/i* sip

bebida /be'bida/ *f* drink

beca /'bɛka/ *f* gown

beça /'bɛsa/ *f* à ∼ (*fam*) (*com substantivo*) loads of; (*com adjetivo*) really; (*com verbo*) a lot

beco /'beku/ *m* alley; ∼ **sem saída** dead end

bedelho /be'deʎu/ *m* **meter o** ∼ (**em**) stick one's oar in(to)

bege /'bɛʒi/ *a invar* beige

bei|cinho /bej'siɲu/ *m* **fazer** ∼**cinho** pout; ∼**ço** *m* lip; ∼**çudo** *a* thicklipped

beija-flor /bejʒa'flor/ *m* hummingbird

bei|jar /be'ʒar/ *vt* kiss; ∼**jo** *m* kiss; ∼**joca** /ɔ/ *f* peck

bei|ra /'bera/ *f* edge; (*fig: do desastre etc*) verge, brink; **à** ∼**ra de** at the edge of; (*fig*) on the verge of; ∼**rada** *f* edge; ∼**ra-mar** *f* seaside; ∼**rar** *vt* (*ficar*) border (on); (*andar*) skirt; (*fig*) border on, verge on; **ele está** ∼**rando os 30 anos** he's nearing thirty

beisebol /bejsi'bɔw/ *m* baseball

belas-artes /bɛlaʃ'artʃiʃ/ *f pl* fine arts

beldade /bew'dadʒi/ *f*, **beleza** /be'leza/ *f* beauty

belga /'bɛwga/ *a & m* Belgian

Bélgica /'bɛwʒika/ *f* Belgium

beliche /be'liʃi/ *m* bunk

bélico /'bɛliku/ *a* war

belicoso /beli'kozu/ *a* warlike

belis|cão /belis'kãw/ *m* pinch; ∼**car** *vt* pinch; nibble <*comida*>

Belize /be'lizi/ *m* Belize

belo /'bɛlu/ *a* beautiful

beltrano /bew'tranu/ *m* such-and-such

bem /bej/ *adv* well; (*bastante*) quite; (*muito*) very □ *m* good; *pl* goods, property; **está** ∼ (it's) fine, OK; **fazer** ∼ **a** be good for; **tudo** ∼? (*fam*) how's things?; **se** ∼ **que** even though; ∼ **feito (por você)** (*fam*) it serves you right; **muito** ∼! well done!; **de** ∼ **com alg** on good terms with s.o.; ∼ **como** as well as

bem|-apessoado /bẽʒapeso'adu/ *a* nice-looking; ∼**-comportado** *a* wellbehaved; ∼**-disposto** *a* keen, willing; ∼**-estar** *m* well-being; ∼**-humorado** *a* good-humoured; ∼**-intencionado** *a* well-intentioned; ∼**-passado** *a* <*carne*> well-done; ∼**-sucedido** *a* successful; ∼**-vindo** *a* welcome; ∼**-visto** *a* well thought of

bênção /'bẽsãw/ (*pl* ∼**s**) *f* blessing

bendito /bẽ'dʒitu/ *a* blessed

benefi|cência /benefi'sẽsia/ *f* (*bondade*) goodness, kindness; (*caridade*) charity; ∼**cente** *a* <*associação*> charitable; <*concerto, feira*> charity; ∼**ciado** *m* beneficiary; ∼**ciar** *vt* benefit; ∼**ciar-se** *vpr* benefit (de from)

benefício /bene'fisiu/ *m* benefit; **em** ∼ **de** in aid of

benéfico /be'nɛfiku/ *a* beneficial (a to)

benevolência /benevo'lẽsia/ *f* benevolence

benévolo /be'nɛvolu/ *a* benevolent

benfeitor /bẽfej'tor/ *m* benefactor

bengala /bẽ'gala/ *f* walking stick; (*pão*) French stick

benigno /be'niginu/ *a* benign

ben|to /'bẽtu/ *a* blessed; <*água*> holy; ∼**zer** *vt* bless; ∼**zer-se** *vpr* cross o.s.

berço /'bersu/ *m* (*de embalar*) cradle; (*caminha*) cot; (*fig*) birthplace; **ter** ∼ be from a good family

berimbau /berĩ'baw/ *m Brazilian percussion instrument shaped like a bow*

berinjela /berĩ'ʒɛla/ *f* aubergine, (*Amer*) eggplant

Berlim /ber'lĩ/ *f* Berlin

berma /'bɛrma/ (*Port*) *f* hard shoulder, (*Amer*) berm

bermuda /ber'muda/ *f* Bermuda shorts

Berna /'bɛrna/ *f* Berne

ber|rante /be'xãtʃi/ *a* loud, flashy; ~**rar** *vi* <*pessoa*> shout; <*criança*> bawl; <*boi*> bellow; ~**reiro** *m* (*gritaria*) yelling, shouting; (*choro*) crying, bawling; ~**ro** /ɛ/ *m* yell, shout; (*de boi*) bellow; **aos** ~**ros** shouting

besouro /be'zoru/ *m* beetle

bes|ta /'besta/ *a* (*idiota*) stupid; (*cheio de si*) full of o.s.; (*pedante*) pretentious □ *f* (*pessoa*) dimwit, numbskull; **ficar** ~**ta** (*fam*) be taken aback; ~**teira** *f* stupidity; (*uma*) stupid thing; **falar** ~**teira** talk rubbish; ~**tial** (*pl* ~**tiais**) *a* bestial; ~**tificar** *vt* astound, dumbfound

besuntar /bezũ'tar/ *vt* coat; (*sujar*) smear

betão /be'tãw/ (*Port*) *m* concrete

beterraba /bete'xaba/ *f* beetroot

betoneira /beto'nera/ *f* cement mixer

bexiga /be'ʃiga/ *f* bladder

bezerro /be'zeru/ *m* calf

bibelô /bibe'lo/ *m* ornament

Bíblia /'biblia/ *f* Bible

bíblico /'bibliku/ *a* biblical

biblio|grafia /bibliogra'fia/ *f* bibliography; ~**teca** /ɛ/ *f* library; ~**tecário** *m* librarian □ *a* library

bica /'bika/ *f* tap; (*Port: cafezinho*) espresso; **suar em** ~**s** drip with sweat

bicama /bi'kama/ *f* truckle bed

bicar /bi'kar/ *vt* peck

bíceps /'bisɛps/ *m invar* biceps

bicha /'biʃa/ *f* (*Port: fila*) queue; (*Bras: fam*) queer, fairy

bicheiro /bi'ʃeru/ *m* organizer of illegal numbers game, racketeer

bicho /'biʃu/ *m* animal; (*inseto*) insect, (*Amer*) bug; **que** ~ **te mordeu?** what's got into you?; ~**-da-seda** (*pl* ~**s-da-seda**) *m* silkworm; ~**-de-sete-cabeças** (*fam*) *m* big deal, big thing; ~**-do-mato** (*pl* ~**s-do-mato**) *m* very shy person

bicicleta /bisi'klɛta/ *f* bicycle, bike

bico /'biku/ *m* (*de ave*) beak; (*de faca*) point; (*de sapato*) toe; (*de bule*) spout; (*de caneta*) nib; (*do seio*) nipple; (*de gás*) jet; (*fam*) (*emprego*) odd job, sideline; (*boca*) mouth

bidê /bi'de/ *m* bidet

bidimensio|nal /bidʒimẽsio'naw/ (*pl* ~**nais**) *a* two-dimensional

biela /bi'ɛla/ *f* connecting rod

Bielo-Rússia /bielo'xusia/ *f* Byelorussia

bielo-russo /bielo'xusu/ *a & m* Byelorussian

bie|nal /bie'naw/ (*pl* ~**nais**) *a* biennial □ *f* biennial art exhibition

bife /'bifi/ *m* steak

bifo|cal /bifo'kaw/ (*pl* ~**cais**) *a* bifocal

bifur|cação /bifurka'sãw/ *f* fork; ~**car-se** *vpr* fork

bigamia /biga'mia/ *f* bigamy

bígamo /'bigamu/ *a* bigamous □ *m* bigamist

bigo|de /bi'gɔdʒi/ *m* moustache; ~**dudo** *a* with a big moustache

bigorna /bi'gɔrna/ *f* anvil

bijuteria /biʒute'ria/ *f* costume jewellery

bilate|ral /bilate'raw/ (*pl* ~**rais**) *a* bilateral

bilhão /bi'ʎãw/ *m* thousand million, (*Amer*) billion

bilhar /bi'ʎar/ *m* pool, billiards

bilhe|te /bi'ʎetʃi/ *m* ticket; (*recado*) note; ~**te de ida e volta** return ticket, (*Amer*) round-trip ticket; **o** ~**te azul** (*fam*) the sack; ~**teria** *f*, (*Port*) ~**teira** *f* (*no cinema, teatro*) box office; (*na estação*) ticket office

bilíngüe /bi'lĩgwi/ *a* bilingual

bilionário /bilio'nariu/ *a & m* billionaire

bílis /'bilis/ *f* bile

binário /bi'nariu/ *a* binary

bingo /'bĩgu/ *m* bingo

binóculo /bi'nɔkulu/ *m* binoculars

biodegradá|vel /biodegra'davew/ (*pl* ~**veis**) *a* biodegradable

bio|grafia /biogra'fia/ *f* biography; ~**gráfico** *a* biographical

biógrafo /bi'ɔgrafu/ *m* biographer

bio|logia /biolo'ʒia/ *f* biology; ~**lógico** *a* biological

biólogo /bi'ɔlogu/ *m* biologist

biombo /bi'õbu/ *m* screen

biônico /bi'oniku/ *a* bionic; (*pol*) unelected

biópsia /bi'ɔpsia/ *f* biopsy

bioquími|ca /bio'kimika/ *f* biochemistry; ~**co** *a* biochemical □ *m* biochemist

biquíni /bi'kini/ *m* bikini

birma|nês /birma'nes/ *a & m* (*f* ~**nesa**) Burmese

Birmânia /bir'mania/ *f* Burma

birô /bi'ro/ *m* bureau

bir|ra /'bixa/ *f* wilfulness; **fazer** ~**ra** have a tantrum; ~**rento** *a* wilful

biruta /bi'ruta/ (*fam*) *a* crazy □ *f* windsock

bis /bis/ *int* encore!, more! □ *m invar* encore

bisa|vó /biza'vɔ/ f great-grandmother; ~**vós** m pl great-grandparents; ~**vô** m great-grandfather

bisbilho|tar /bizbiʎo'tar/ vt pry into □ vi pry; ~**teiro** a prying □ m busybody; ~**tice** f prying

bisca|te /bis'katʃi/ m odd job; ~**teiro** m odd-job man

biscoito /bis'kojtu/ m biscuit, (Amer) cookie

bisnaga /biz'naga/ f (pão) bridge roll; (tubo) tube

bisne|ta /biz'nɛta/ f great-granddaughter; ~**to** /ɛ/ m great-grandson; pl great-grandchildren

bis|pado /bis'padu/ m bishopric; ~**po** m bishop

bissexto /bi'sestu/ a occasional; ano ~ leap year

bissexu|al /biseksu'aw/ (pl ~**ais**) a & m/f bisexual

bisturi /bistu'ri/ m scalpel

bito|la /bi'tɔla/ f gauge; ~**lado** a narrow-minded

bizarro /bi'zaxu/ a bizarre

blablablá /blabla'bla/ (fam) m chit-chat

black /'blɛki/ m black market; ~**-tie** m evening dress

blas|femar /blasfe'mar/ vi blaspheme; ~**fêmia** f blasphemy; ~**femo** /e/ a blasphemous □ m blasphemer

blecaute /ble'kawtʃi/ m power cut

ble|far /ble'far/ vi bluff; ~**fe** /ɛ/ m bluff

blin|dado /blĩ'dadu/ a armoured; ~**dagem** f armour-plating

blitz /blits/ f invar police spot-check (on vehicles)

blo|co /'blɔku/ m block; (pol) bloc; (de papel) pad; (no carnaval) section; ~**quear** vt block; (mil) blockade; ~**queio** m blockage; (psic) mental block; (mil) blockade

blusa /'bluza/ f shirt; (de mulher) blouse; (de lã) sweater

boa /'boa/ f de bom; **numa** ~ (fam) well; (sem problemas) easily; **estar numa** ~ (fam) be doing fine; ~**gente** (fam) a invar nice; ~**-pinta** (pl ~**s-pintas**) (fam) a nice-looking; ~**-praça** (pl ~**s-praças**) (fam) a friendly, sociable

boate /bo'atʃi/ f nightclub

boato /bo'atu/ m rumour

boa|-nova /boa'nɔva/ (pl ~**s-novas**) f good news; ~**-vida** (pl ~**s-vidas**) m/f good-for-nothing, waster; ~**zinha** a sweet, kind

bo|bagem /bo'baʒẽ/ f silliness; (uma) silly thing; ~**beada** f slip-up; ~**bear** vi slip up; ~**beira** f veja **bobagem**

bobe /'bɔbi/ m curler, roller

bobina /bo'bina/ f reel; (eletr) coil

bobo /'bobu/ a silly □ m fool; (da corte) jester; ~**ca** /ɔ/ (fam) a stupid □ m/f twit

bo|ca /'boka/ f mouth; (no fogão) ring; ~**ca da noite** nightfall; ~**cado** m (na boca) mouthful; (pedaço) piece, bit; ~**cal** (pl ~**cais**) m mouthpiece

boce|jar /bose'ʒar/ vi yawn; ~**jo** /e/ m yawn

boche|cha /bo'ʃeʃa/ f cheek; ~**char** vi rinse one's mouth; ~**cho** /e/ m mouthwash; ~**chudo** a with puffy cheeks

bodas /'bodas/ f pl wedding anniversary; ~ **de prata/ouro** silver/golden wedding

bode /'bɔdʒi/ m (billy) goat; ~ **expiatório** scapegoat

bodega /bo'dɛga/ f (de bebidas) off-licence, (Amer) liquor store; (de secos e molhados) grocer's shop, corner shop

boêmio /bo'emiu/ a & m Bohemian

bofe|tada /bofe'tada/ f, **bofe|tão** /bofe'tãw/ m slap; ~**tear** vt slap

boi /boj/ m bullock, (Amer) steer

bói /bɔj/ m office boy

bóia /'bɔja/ f (de balizamento) buoy; (de cortiça, isopor etc) float; (câmara de borracha) rubber ring; (de braço) armband, water wing; (na caixa-d'água) ballcock; (fam: comida) grub; ~ **salva-vidas** lifebelt; ~**-fria** (pl ~**s-frias**) m/f itinerant farm labourer

boiar /bo'jar/ vt/i float; (fam) be lost

boico|tar /bojko'tar/ vt boycott; ~**te** /ɔ/ m boycott

boiler /'bojler/ (pl ~**s**) m boiler

boina /'bojna/ f beret

bo|jo /'boʒu/ m bulge; ~**judo** a (cheio) bulging; (arredondado) bulbous

bola /'bɔla/ f ball; **dar** ~ **para** (fam) give attention to <pessoa>; care about <coisa>; ~ **de gude** marble; ~ **de neve** snowball

bolacha /bo'laʃa/ f (biscoito) biscuit, (Amer) cookie; (descanso) beermat; (fam: tapa) slap

bo|lada /bo'lada/ f large sum of money; ~**lar** vt think up, devise

boléia /bo'lɛja/ f cab; (Port: carona) lift

boletim /bole'tʃĩ/ m bulletin; (escolar) report

bolha /'boʎa/ f bubble; (na pele) blister □ (fam) m/f pain

boliche /bo'liʃi/ m skittles

Bolívia /bo'livia/ f Bolivia

boliviano /bolivi'anu/ a & m Bolivian

bolo /'bolu/ m cake

bo|lor /bo'lor/ m mould, mildew; ~**lorento** a mouldy

bolota /bo'lɔta/ *f* (*glande*) acorn; (*bolinha*) little ball

bol|sa /'bowsa/ *f* bag; ~**sa (de estudo)** scholarship; ~**sa (de valores)** stock exchange; ~**sista** *m/f*, (*Port*) ~**seiro** *m* scholarship student; ~**so** /o/ *m* pocket

bom /bõ/ *a* (*f* **boa**) good; (*de saúde*) well; <*comida*> nice; **está** ~ that's fine

bomba¹ /'bõba/ *f* (*explosiva*) bomb; (*doce*) eclair; (*fig*) bombshell; **levar** ~ (*fam*) fail

bomba² /'bõba/ *f* (*de bombear*) pump

Bombaim /bõba'ĩ/ *f* Bombay

bombar|dear /bõbardʒi'ar/ *vt* bombard; (*do ar*) bomb; ~**deio** *m* bombardment; (*do ar*) bombing

bomba|-relógio /bõbaxe'lɔʒiu/ (*pl* ~**s-relógio**) *f* time bomb

bom|bear /bõbi'ar/ *vt* pump; ~**beiro** *m* fireman; (*encanador*) plumber

bombom /bõ'bõ/ *m* chocolate

bombordo /bõ'bɔrdu/ *m* port

bondade /bõ'dadʒi/ *f* goodness

bonde /'bõdʒi/ *m* tram; (*teleférico*) cable car

bondoso /bõ'dozu/ *a* good(-hearted)

boné /bo'nɛ/ *m* cap

bone|ca /bo'nɛka/ *f* doll; ~**co** /ɛ/ *m* dummy

bonificação /bonifika'sãw/ *f* bonus

bonito /bo'nitu/ *a* <*mulher*> pretty; <*homem*> handsome; <*tempo, casa etc*> lovely

bônus /'bonus/ *m invar* bonus

boqui|aberto /bokia'bɛrtu/ *a* openmouthed, flabbergasted; ~**nha** *f* snack

borboleta /borbo'leta/ *f* butterfly; (*roleta*) turnstile

borbotão /borbo'tãw/ *m* spurt

borbu|lha /bor'buʎa/ *f* bubble; ~**lhar** *vi* bubble

borda /'bɔrda/ *f* edge; ~**do** *a* edged; (*à linha*) embroidered □ *m* embroidery

bordão /bor'dãw/ *m* (*frase*) catchphrase

bordar /bor'dar/ *vt* (*à linha*) embroider

bor|del /bor'dɛw/ (*pl* ~**déis**) *m* brothel

bordo /'bordu/ *m* **a** ~ aboard

borra /'boxa/ *f* dregs; (*de café*) grounds

borra|cha /bo'xaʃa/ *f* rubber; ~**cheiro** *m* tyre fitter

bor|rão /bo'xãw/ *m* (*de tinta*) blot; (*rascunho*) rough draft; ~**rar** *vt* (*sujar*) blot; (*riscar*) cross out; (*pintar*) daub

borrasca /bo'xaska/ *f* squall

borri|far /boxi'far/ *vt* sprinkle; ~**fo** *m* sprinkling

bosque /'bɔski/ *m* wood

bosta /'bɔsta/ *f* (*de animal*) dung; (*chulo*) crap

bota /'bɔta/ *f* boot

botâni|ca /bo'tanika/ *f* botany; ~**co** *a* botanical □ *m* botanist

bo|tão /bo'tãw/ *m* button; (*de flor*) bud; **falar com os seus** ~**tões** say to o.s.

botar /bo'tar/ *vt* put; put on <*roupa*>; set <*mesa, despertador*>; lay <*ovo*>; find <*defeito*>

bote¹ /'bɔtʃi/ *m* (*barco*) dinghy; ~ **salva-vidas** lifeboat; (*de borracha*) liferaft

bote² /'bɔtʃi/ *m* (*de animal etc*) lunge

botequim /butʃi'kĩ/ *m* bar

botoeira /boto'era/ *f* buttonhole

boxe /'bɔksi/ *m* boxing; ~**ador** *m* boxer

brabo /'brabu/ *a* <*animal*> ferocious; <*calor, sol*> fierce; <*doença*> bad; <*prova, experiência*> tough; (*zangado*) angry

bra|çada /bra'sada/ *f* armful; (*em natação*) stroke; ~**çadeira** (*faixa*) armband; (*ferragem*) bracket; (*de atleta*) sweatband; ~**çal** (*pl* ~**çais**) *a* manual; ~**celete** /e/ *m* bracelet; ~**ço** *m* arm; ~**ço direito** (*fig*: *pessoa*) right-hand man

bra|dar /bra'dar/ *vt/i* shout; ~**do** *m* shout

braguilha /bra'giʎa/ *f* fly, flies

braile /'brajli/ *m* Braille

bra|mido /bra'midu/ *m* roar; ~**mir** *vi* roar

branco /'brãku/ *a* white □ *m* (*homem*) white man; (*espaço*) blank; **em** ~ <*cheque etc*> blank; **noite em** ~ sleepless night

bran|do /'brãdu/ *a* gentle; <*doença*> mild; (*indulgente*) lenient, soft; ~**dura** *f* gentleness; (*indulgência*) softness, leniency

brasa /'braza/ *f* **em** ~ red-hot; **mandar** ~ (*fam*) go to town

brasão /bra'zãw/ *m* coat of arms

braseiro /bra'zeru/ *m* brasier

Brasil /bra'ziw/ *m* Brazil

brasi|leiro /brazi'leru/ *a* & *m* Brazilian; ~**liense** *a* & *m/f* (*person*) from Brasília

bra|vata /bra'vata/ *f* bravado; ~**vio** *a* wild; <*mar*> rough; ~**vo** *a* (*corajoso*) brave; (*zangado*) angry; <*mar*> rough; ~**vura** *f* bravery

breca /'brɛka/ *f* **levado da** ~ very naughty

brecar /bre'kar/ *vt* stop <*carro*>; (*fig*) curb □ *vi* brake

brecha /'brɛʃa/ *f* gap; (*na lei*) loophole

bre|ga /'brɛga/ (*fam*) *a* tacky, naff; ~**guice** (*fam*) *f* tack, tackiness

brejo /'brɛʒu/ *m* marsh; **ir para o ~** (*fig*) go down the drain

brenha /'brɛɲa/ *f* thicket

breque /'brɛki/ *m* brake

breu /brew/ *m* tar, pitch

bre|ve /'brɛvi/ *a* short, brief; **em ~ve** soon, shortly; **~vidade** *f* shortness, brevity

briga /'briga/ *f* fight; (*bate-boca*) argument

briga|da /bri'gada/ *f* brigade; **~deiro** *m* brigadier; (*doce*) chocolate truffle

bri|gão /bri'gãw/ *a* (*f* **~gona**) belligerent; (*na fala*) argumentative □ *m* (*f* **~gona**) troublemaker; **~gar** *vi* fight; (*com palavras*) argue; <*cores*> clash

bri|lhante /bri'ʎãtʃi/ *a* (*reluzente*) shiny; (*fig*) brilliant; **~lhar** *vi* shine; **~lho** *m* (*de sapatos etc*) shine; (*dos olhos, de metais*) gleam; (*das estrelas*) brightness; (*de uma cor*) brilliance; (*fig: esplendor*) splendour

brin|cadeira /brĩka'dera/ *f* (*piada*) joke; (*brinquedo, jogo*) game; **de ~ cadeira** for fun; **~calhão** (*f* **~calhona**) *a* playful □ *m* joker; **~car** *vi* (*divertir-se*) play; (*gracejar*) joke

brinco /'brĩku/ *m* earring

brin|dar /brĩ'dar/ *vt* (*saudar*) toast, drink to; (*presentear*) give a gift to; **~dar alg com aco** afford s.o. sth; (*de presente*) give s.o. sth as a gift; **~de** *m* (*saudação*) toast; (*presente*) free gift

brinquedo /brĩ'kedu/ *m* toy

brio /'briu/ *m* self-esteem, character; **~so** /o/ *a* self-confident

brisa /'briza/ *f* breeze

britadeira /brita'dera/ *f* pneumatic drill

britânico /bri'taniku/ *a* British □ *m* Briton; **os ~s** the British

broca /'brɔka/ *f* drill

broche /'brɔʃi/ *m* brooch

brochura /bro'ʃura/ *f* **livro de ~** paperback

brócolis /'brɔkulis/ *m* *pl*, (*Port*) **brócolos** /'brɔkuluʃ/ *m* *pl* broccoli

bron|ca /'brõka/ *f* (*fam*) telling-off; **dar uma ~ca em alg** tell s.o. off; **~co** *a* coarse, rough

bronquite /brõ'kitʃi/ *f* bronchitis

bronze /'brõzi/ *m* bronze; **~ado** *a* tanned, brown □ *m* (sun)tan; **~ador** *a* tanning □ *m* suntan lotion; **~amento** *m* tanning; **~ar** *vt* tan; **~ar-se** *vpr* go brown, tan

bro|tar /bro'tar/ *vt* sprout <*folhas, flores*>; spout <*lágrimas, palavras*> □ *vi* (*planta*) sprout; <*lágrimas*> spout; <*idéias*> pop up; **~tinho** (*fam*) *m* youngster; **~to** /o/ *m* shoot; (*fam*) youngster

broxa /'brɔʃa/ *f* (large) paint brush □ (*fam*) *a* impotent

bruços /'brusus/ **de ~** face down

bru|ma /'bruma/ *f* mist; **~moso** /o/ *a* misty

brusco /'brusku/ *a* brusque, abrupt

bru|tal /bru'taw/ (*pl* **~tais**) *a* brutal; **~talidade** *f* brutality; **~to** *a* <*feições*> coarse; <*homem*> brutish; <*tom, comentário*> aggressive; <*petróleo*> crude; <*peso, lucro, salário*> gross □ *m* brute

bruxa /'bruʃa/ *f* witch; (*feia*) hag; **~ria** *f* witchcraft

Bruxelas /bru'ʃɛlas/ *f* Brussels

bruxo /'bruʃu/ *m* wizard

bruxulear /bruʃuli'ar/ *vi* flicker

bucha /'buʃa/ *f* (*tampão*) bung; (*para paredes*) rawlplug (R); **acertar na ~** (*fam*) hit the nail on the head

bucho /'buʃu/ *m* gut; **~ de boi** tripe

budis|mo /bu'dʒizmu/ *m* Buddhism; **~ta** *a* & *m/f* Buddhist

bueiro /bu'eru/ *m* storm drain

búfalo /'bufalu/ *m* buffalo

bu|fante /bu'fãtʃi/ *a* full, puffed; **~far** *vi* snort; (*reclamar*) grumble, moan

bufê /bu'fe/ *m* (*refeição*) buffet; (*serviço*) catering service; (*móvel*) sideboard

bugiganga /buʒi'gãga/ *f* knickknack

bujão /bu'ʒãw/ *m* **~ de gás** gas cylinder

bula /'bula/ *f* (*de remédio*) directions; (*do Papa*) bull

bulbo /'buwbu/ *m* bulb

bule /'buli/ *m* (*de chá*) teapot; (*de café etc*) pot

Bulgária /buw'garia/ *f* Bulgaria

búlgaro /'buwgaru/ *a* & *m* Bulgarian

bulhufas /bu'ʎufas/ (*fam*) *pron* nothing

bulício /bu'lisiu/ *m* bustle

bumbum /bũ'bũ/ (*fam*) *m* bottom, bum

bunda /'bũda/ *f* bottom

buquê /bu'ke/ *m* bouquet

buraco /bu'raku/ *m* hole; (*de agulha*) eye; (*jogo de cartas*) rummy; **~ da fechadura** keyhole

burburinho /burbu'riɲu/ *m* (*de vozes*) hubbub

bur|guês /bur'ges/ *a* & *m* (*f* **~guesa**) bourgeois; **~guesia** *f* bourgeoisie

burlar /bur'lar/ *vt* get round <*lei*>; get past <*defesas, vigilância*>

buro|cracia /burokra'sia/ *f* bureaucracy; **~crata** *m/f* bureaucrat; **~crático** *a* bureaucratic; **~cratizar** *vt* make bureaucratic

bur|rice /bu'xisi/ *f* stupidity; (*uma*) stupid thing; **~ro** *a* stupid; (*ignorante*) dim □ *m* (*animal*) donkey; (*pessoa*) halfwit, dunce; **~ro de carga** (*fig*) workhorse

bus|ca /'buska/ *f* search; **dar ~ca em**
search; **~ca-pé** *m* banger; **~car** *vt*
fetch; (*de carro*) pick up; **mandar**
~car send for

bússola /'busola/ *f* compass; (*fig*)
guide

busto /'bustu/ *m* bust

butique /bu'tʃiki/ *f* boutique

buzi|na /bu'zina/ *f* horn; **~nada** *f*
toot (of the horn); **~nar** *vi* sound
the horn, toot the horn

C

cá /ka/ *adv* here; **o lado de ~** this
side; **para ~** here; **de ~ para lá** back
and forth; **de lá para ~** since then; **~**
entre nós between you and me

ca|bal /ka'baw/ (*pl* **~bais**) *a* com-
plete, full; <*prova*> conclusive

cabana /ka'bana/ *f* hut; (*casinha no*
campo) cottage

cabeça /ka'besa/ *f* head; (*de lista*) top;
(*pessoa inteligente*) mind □ *m/f* (*chefe*)
ringleader; (*integrante mais inteli-*
gente) brains; **de ~** <*saber*> off the
top of one's head; <*calcular*> in one's
head; **de ~ para baixo** upside down;
deu-lhe na ~ de he took it into his
head to; **esquentar a ~** (*fam*) get
worked up; **fazer a ~ de alg** convince s.o.; **quebrar a ~** rack one's
brains; **subir à ~** go to s.o.'s head;
ter a ~ no lugar have one's head
screwed on; **~da** *f* (*no futebol*)
header; (*pancada*) head butt; **dar**
uma ~da no teto bang one's head on
the ceiling; **~-de-porco** (*pl* **~s-de-**
porco) *f* tenement; **~-de-vento** (*pl*
~s-de-vento) *m/f* scatterbrain,
airhead; **~lho** *m* heading

cabe|cear /kabesi'ar/ *vt* head <*bola*>;
~ceira *f* head; **~çudo** *a* pigheaded

cabe|dal /kabe'daw/ (*pl* **~dais**) *m*
wealth

cabelei|ra /kabe'lera/ *f* head of hair;
(*peruca*) wig; **~reiro** *m* hairdresser

cabe|lo /ka'belu/ *m* hair; **cortar o**
~lo have one's hair cut; **~ludo** *a*
hairy; (*difícil*) complicated; <*palavra,*
piada> dirty

caber /ka'ber/ *vi* fit; (*ter cabimento*) be
fitting; **~ a** <*mérito, parte*> be due to;
<*tarefa*> fall to; **cabe a você** it is
up to you to go; **~ em alg** <*roupa*> fit
s.o.

cabide /ka'bidʒi/ *m* (*peça de madeira,*
arame etc) hanger; (*móvel*) hat stand;
(*na parede*) coat rack

cabimento /kabi'mẽtu/ *m* **ter ~** be
fitting, be appropriate; **não ter ~** be
out of the question

cabine /ka'bini/ *f* cabin; (*de avião*)
cockpit; (*de loja*) changing room; **~**
telefônica phone box, (*Amer*) phone
booth

cabisbaixo /kabiz'baʃu/ *a* crestfallen

cabí|vel /ka'bivew/ (*pl* **~veis**) *a* ap-
propriate, fitting

cabo¹ /'kabu/ *m* (*militar*) corporal; **ao**
~ de after; **levar a ~** carry out; **~**
eleitoral campaign worker

cabo² /'kabu/ *m* (*fio*) cable; (*de panela*
etc) handle; **TV por ~** cable TV; **~ de**
extensão extension lead; **~ de força**
tug of war

caboclo /ka'boklu/ *a & m* mestizo

ca|bra /'kabra/ *f* goat; **~brito** *m* kid

ca|ça /'kasa/ *f* (*atividade*) hunting; (*ca-*
çada) hunt; (*animais*) game □ *m*
(*avião*) fighter; **à ~ça de** in pursuit
of; **~ça das bruxas** (*fig*) witch hunt;
~çador *m* hunter; **~ça-minas** *m in-*
var minesweeper; **~ça-níqueis** *m in-*
var slot machine; **~çar** *vt* hunt
<*animais, criminoso etc*>; (*procurar*)
hunt for □ *vi* hunt

cacareco /kaka'rɛku/ *m* piece of junk;
pl junk

cacare|jar /kakare'ʒar/ *vi* cluck; **~jo**
/e/ *m* clucking

caçarola /kasa'rɔla/ *f* saucepan

cacau /ka'kaw/ *m* cocoa

cace|tada /kase'tada/ *f* blow with a
club; (*fig*) annoyance; **~te** /e/ *m* club
□ (*fam*) *int* damn

cachaça /ka'ʃasa/ *f* white rum

cachê /ka'ʃe/ *m* fee

cache|col /kaʃe'kɔw/ (*pl* **~cóis**) *m*
scarf

cachimbo /ka'ʃĩbu/ *m* pipe

cacho /'kaʃu/ *m* (*de banana, uva*)
bunch; (*de cabelo*) lock; (*fam: caso*)
affair

cachoeira /kaʃo'era/ *f* waterfall

cachor|rinho /kaʃo'xinu/ *m* (*nado*)
doggy paddle; **~ro** /o/ *m* dog; (*Port*)
puppy; (*pessoa*) scoundrel; **~ro-**
quente (*pl* **~ros-quentes**) *m* hot dog

cacife /ka'sifi/ *m* (*fig*) pull

caci|que /ka'siki/ *m* (*índio*) chief; (*po-*
lítico) boss; **~quia** *f* leadership

caco /'kaku/ *m* shard; (*pessoa*) old
crock

cacto /'kaktu/ *m* cactus

caçula /ka'sula/ *m/f* youngest child □
a youngest

cada /'kada/ *a* each; **~ duas horas**
every two hours; **custam £5 ~ (um)**
they cost £5 each; **~ vez mais** more
and more; **~ vez mais fácil** easier
and easier; **ele fala ~ coisa** (*fam*)
he says the most amazing things

cadafalso /kada'fawsu/ *m* gallows

cadarço /ka'darsu/ *m* shoelace

cadas|trar /kadas'trar/ *vt* register;
~tro *m* register; (*ato*) registration;

(*policial, bancário*) records, files; (*imobiliário*) land register

ca|dáver /ka'daver/ *m* (dead) body, corpse; **~daverico** *a* cadaverous, corpse-like; <*exame*> post-mortem

cadê /ka'de/ (*fam*) *adv* where is/ are...?

cadeado /kadʒi'adu/ *m* padlock

cadeia /ka'deja/ *f* (*de eventos, lojas etc*) chain; (*prisão*) prison; (*rádio, TV*) network

cadeira /ka'dera/ *f* (*móvel*) chair; (*no teatro*) stall; (*de político*) seat; (*função de professor*) chair; (*matéria*) subject; *pl* (*anat*) hips; **~ de balanço** rocking chair; **~ de rodas** wheelchair; **~ elétrica** electric chair

ca|dência /ka'dẽsia/ *f* (*mus, da voz*) cadence; (*compasso*) rhythm; **~denciado** *a* rhythmic; <*passos*> measured

cader|neta /kader'neta/ *f* notebook; (*de professor*) register; (*de banco*) passbook; **~neta de poupança** savings account; **~no** /ɛ/ *m* exercise book; (*pequeno*) notebook; (*no jornal*) section

cadete /ka'detʃi/ *m* cadet

cadu|car /kadu'kar/ *vi* <*pessoa*> become senile; <*contrato*> lapse; **~co** *a* <*pessoa*> senile; <*contrato*> lapsed; **~quice** *f* senility

cafajeste /kafa'ʒestʃi/ *m* swine

ca|fé /ka'fɛ/ *m* coffee; (*botequim*) café; **~fé da manhã** breakfast; **tomar ~fé** have breakfast; **~fé-com-leite** *a invar* coffee-coloured, light brown □ *m* white coffee; **~feeiro** *a* coffee □ *m* coffee plant; **~feicultura** *f* coffee-growing; **~feína** *f* caffein(e)

cafetã /kafe'tã/ *m* caftan

cafetão /kafe'tãw/ *m* pimp

cafe|teira /kafe'tera/ *f* coffee pot; **~zal** (*pl* **~zais**) *m* coffee plantation; **~zinho** *m* small black coffee

cafo|na /ka'fona/ (*fam*) *a* naff, tacky; **~nice** *f* tackiness; (*coisa*) tacky thing

cágado /'kagadu/ *m* turtle

caiar /kaj'ar/ *vt* whitewash

cãibra /'kãjbra/ *f* cramp

caí|da /ka'ida/ *f* fall; *veja* **queda**; **~do** *a* <*árvore etc*> fallen; <*beiços etc*> drooping; (*deprimido*) dejected; (*apaixonado*) smitten

caimento /kaj'mẽtu/ *m* fall

caipi|ra /kaj'pira/ *a* <*pessoa*> countrified; <*festa, música*> country; <*sotaque*> rural □ *m/f* country person; (*depreciativo*) country bumpkin; **~rinha** *f* cachaça with limes, sugar and ice

cair /ka'ir/ *vi* fall; <*dente, cabelo*> fall out; <*botão etc*> fall off; <*comércio, trânsito etc*> fall off; <*tecido, cortina*>

hang; **~ bem/mal** <*roupa*> go well/ badly; <*ato, dito*> go down well, badly; **estou caindo de sono** I'm really sleepy

cais /kajs/ *m* quay; (*Port: na estação*) platform

caixa /'kaʃa/ *f* box; (*de loja etc*) cash-desk □ *m/f* cashier; **~ de correio** letter box; **~ de mudanças**, (*Port*) **~ de velocidades** gear box; **~ postal** post office box, PO Box; **~-d'água** (*pl* **~s-d'água**) *f* water tank; **~-forte** (*pl* **~s-fortes**) *f* vault

cai|xão /ka'ʃãw/ *m* coffin; **~xeiro** *m* (*em loja*) assistant; salesman; **~xilho** *m* frame; **~xote** /ɔ/ *m* crate

caju /ka'ʒu/ *m* cashew fruit; **~eiro** *m* cashew tree

cal /kaw/ *f* lime

calado /ka'ladu/ *a* quiet

calafrio /kala'friu/ *m* shudder, shiver

calami|dade /kalami'dadʒi/ *f* calamity; **~toso** /o/ *a* calamitous

calar /ka'lar/ *vi* be quiet □ *vt* keep quiet about <*segredo, sentimento*>; silence <*pessoa*>; **~-se** *vpr* go quiet

calça /'kawsa/ *f* trousers, (*Amer*) pants

calça|da /kaw'sada/ *f* pavement, (*Amer*) sidewalk; (*Port: rua*) roadway; **~dão** *m* pedestrian precinct; **~deira** *f* shoe-horn; **~do** *a* paved □ *m* shoe; *pl* footwear

calcanhar /kawka'ɲar/ *m* heel

calção /kaw'sãw/ *m* shorts; **~ de banho** swimming trunks

calcar /kaw'kar/ *vt* (*pisar*) trample; (*comprimir*) press; **~ aco em** (*fig*) base sth on, model sth on

calçar /kaw'sar/ *vt* put on <*sapatos, luvas*>; take <*número*>; pave <*rua*>; (*com calço*) wedge □ *vi* <*sapato*> fit; **~-se** *vpr* put one's shoes on

calcário /kaw'kariu/ *m* limestone □ *a* <*água*> hard

calças /'kawsas/ *f pl veja* **calça**

calcinha /kaw'siɲa/ *f* knickers, (*Amer*) panties

cálcio /'kawsiu/ *m* calcium

calço /'kawsu/ *m* wedge

calcu|ladora /kawkula'dora/ *f* calculator; **~lar** *vt/i* calculate; **~lista** *a* calculating □ *m/f* opportunist

cálculo /'kawkulu/ *m* calculation; (*diferencial*) calculus; (*med*) stone

cal|da /'kawda/ *f* syrup; *pl* hot springs; **~deira** *f* boiler; **~deirão** *m* cauldron; **~do** *m* (*sopa*) broth; (*suco*) juice; **~do de carne/galinha** beef/ chicken stock

calefação /kalefa'sãw/ *f* heating

caleidoscópio /kalejdos'kɔpiu/ *m* kaleidoscope

calejado /kale'ʒadu/ a <mãos> calloused; <pessoa> experienced

calendário /kalē'dariu/ m calendar

calha /'kaʎa/ f (no telhado) gutter; (sulco) gulley

calhamaço /kaʎa'masu/ m tome

calhambeque /kaʎã'bɛki/ (fam) m banger

calhar /ka'ʎar/ vi **calhou que** it so happened that; **calhou pegar em o mesmo trem** they happened to get the same train; ~ **de** happen to; **vir a** ~ come at the right time

cali|brado /kali'bradu/ a (bêbado) tipsy; ~**brar** vt calibrate; check (the pressure of) <pneu>; ~**bre** m calibre; **coisas desse** ~**bre** things of this order

cálice /'kalisi/ m (copo) liqueur glass; (na missa) chalice

caligrafia /kaligra'fia/ f (letra) handwriting; (arte) calligraphy

calista /ka'lista/ m/f chiropodist, (Amer) podiatrist

cal|ma /'kawma/ f calm; **com** ~**ma** calmly □ int calm down; ~**mante** m tranquilizer; ~**mo** a calm

calo /'kalu/ m (na mão) callus; (no pé) corn

calombo /ka'lõbu/ m bump

calor /ka'lor/ m heat; (agradável, fig) warmth; **estar com** ~ be hot

calo|rento /kalo'rētu/ a <pessoa> sensitive to heat; <lugar> hot; ~**ria** f calorie; ~**roso** /o/ a warm; <protesto> lively

calota /ka'lɔta/ f hubcap

calo|te /ka'lɔtʃi/ m bad debt; ~**teiro** m bad risk

calouro /ka'loru/ m (na faculdade) freshman; (em outros ramos) novice

ca|lúnia /ka'lunia/ f slander; ~**luniar** vt slander; ~**lunioso** /o/ a slanderous

cal|vície /kaw'visi/ f baldness; ~**vo** a bald

cama /'kama/ f bed; ~ **de casal/solteiro** double/single bed; ~**-beliche** (pl ~**s-beliches**) f bunk bed

camada /ka'mada/ f layer; (de tinta) coat

câmara /'kamara/ f chamber; (fotográfica) camera; **em** ~ **lenta** in slow motion; ~ **municipal** town council; (Port) town hall

camarada /kama'rada/ a friendly □ m/f comrade; ~**gem** f comradeship; (convivência agradável) camaraderie

câmara-de-ar /kamaradʒi'ar/ (pl **câmaras-de-ar**) f inner tube

camarão /kama'rãw/ m shrimp; (maior) prawn

cama|reira /kama'rera/ f chambermaid; ~**rim** m dressing room;

~**rote** /ɔ/ m (no teatro) box; (num navio) cabin

cambada /kã'bada/ f gang, horde

cambalacho /kãba'laʃu/ m scam

camba|lear /kãbali'ar/ vi stagger; ~**lhota** f somersault

cambi|al /kãbi'aw/ (pl ~**ais**) a exchange; ~**ante** m shade; ~**ar** vt change

câmbio /'kãbiu/ m exchange; (taxa) rate of exchange; ~ **oficial/paralelo** official/black market exchange rate

cambista /kã'bista/ m/f (de entradas) ticket-tout, (Amer) scalper; (de dinheiro) money changer

Camboja /kã'bɔʒa/ m Cambodia

cambojano /kãbo'ʒanu/ a & m Cambodian

camburão /kãbu'rãw/ m police van

camélia /ka'mɛlia/ f camelia

camelo /ka'melu/ m camel

camelô /kame'lo/ m street vendor

camião /kami'ãw/ (Port) m veja **caminhão**

caminhada /kami'ɲada/ f walk

caminhão /kami'ɲãw/ m lorry, (Amer) truck

cami|nhar /kami'ɲar/ vi walk; (fig) advance, progress; ~**nho** m way; (estrada) road; (trilho) path; **a** ~**nho** on the way; **a meio** ~**nho** halfway; ~**nho de ferro** (Port) railway, (Amer) railroad

caminho|neiro /kamiɲo'neru/ m lorry driver, (Amer) truck driver; ~**nete** /ɛ/ m van

camio|neta /kamio'neta/ f van; ~**nista** (Port) m/f veja **caminhoneiro**

cami|sa /ka'miza/ f shirt; ~**sa-de-força** (pl ~**sas-de-força**) f straitjacket; ~**sa-de-vênus** (pl ~**sas-de-vênus**) f condom; ~**seta** /e/ f T-shirt; (de baixo) vest; ~**sinha** (fam) f condom; ~**sola** /ɔ/ f nightdress; (Port) sweater

camomila /kamo'mila/ f camomile

campainha /kãpa'iɲa/ f bell; (da porta) doorbell

campanário /kãpa'nariu/ m belfry

campanha /kã'paɲa/ f campaign

campe|ão /kãpi'ãw/ m (f ~**ã**) champion; ~**onato** m championship

cam|pestre /kã'pɛstri/ a rural; ~**pina** f grassland

cam|ping /'kãpi/ m camping; (lugar) campsite; ~**pismo** (Port) m camping

campo /'kãpu/ m field; (interior) country; (de futebol) pitch; (de golfe) course; ~ **de concentração** concentration camp; ~**nês** m (f ~**nesa**) peasant

camu|flagem /kamu'flaʒē/ f camouflage; ~**flar** vt camouflage

camundongo /kamũ'dõgu/ m mouse

cana   29   capital

cana /'kana/ f cane; ~ **de açúcar** sugar cane

Canadá /kana'da/ m Canada

canadense /kana'dẽsi/ a & m Canadian

ca|nal /ka'naw/ (pl ~**nais**) m channel; (hidrovia) canal

canalha /ka'naʎa/ m/f scoundrel

canali|zação /kanaliza'sãw/ f piping; ~**zador** (Port) m plumber; ~**zar** vt channel < líquido, esforço, recursos>; canalize < rio>; pipe for water and drainage < cidade>

canário /ka'nariu/ m canary

canastrão /kanas'trãw/ m (f ~**trona**) ham actor (f actress)

canavi|al /kanavi'aw/ (pl ~**ais**) m cane field; ~**eiro** a sugar cane

canção /kã'sãw/ f song

cance|lamento /kãsela'mẽtu/ m cancellation; ~**lar** vt cancel; (riscar) cross out

câncer /'kãser/ m cancer; **Câncer** (signo) Cancer

cance|riano /kãseri'anu/ a & m Cancerian; ~**rígeno** a carcinogenic; ~**roso** /o/ a cancerous □ m person with cancer

cancro /'kãkru/ m (Port: câncer) cancer; (fig) canker

candango /kã'dãgu/ m person from Brasilia

cande|eiro /kãdʒi'eru/ m (oil-)lamp; ~**labro** m candelabra

candida|tar-se /kãdʒida'tarsi/ vpr (a vaga) apply (a for); (à presidência etc) stand, (Amer) run (a for); ~**to** m candidate (a for); (a vaga) applicant (a for); ~**tura** f candidature; (a vaga) application (a for)

cândido /'kãdʒidu/ a innocent

candomblé /kãdõ'blɛ/ m Afro-Brazilian cult; (reunião) candomble meeting

candura /kã'dura/ f innocence

cane|ca /ka'nɛka/ f mug; ~**co** /ɛ/ m tankard

canela¹ /ka'nɛla/ f (condimento) cinnamon

canela² /ka'nɛla/ f (da perna) shin; ~**da** f **dar uma ~da em alg** kick s.o. in the shins; **dar uma ~da em aco** hit one's shins on sth

cane|ta /ka'neta/ f pen; ~ **esferográfica** ball-point pen; ~**ta-tinteiro** (pl ~**tas-tinteiro**) f fountain pen

cangote /kã'gotʃi/ m nape of the neck

canguru /kãgu'ru/ m kangaroo

canhão /ka'ɲãw/ m (arma) cannon; (vale) canyon

canhoto /ka'ɲotu/ a left-handed □ m (talão) stub

cani|bal /kani'baw/ (pl ~**bais**) m/f cannibal; ~**balismo** m cannibalism

caniço /ka'nisu/ m reed; (pessoa) skinny person

canícula /ka'nikula/ f heat wave

ca|nil /ka'niw/ (pl ~**nis**) m kennel

canivete /kani'vɛtʃi/ m penknife

canja /'kãʒa/ f chicken soup; (fam) piece of cake

canjica /kã'ʒika/ f corn porridge

cano /'kanu/ m pipe; (de bota) top; (de arma de fogo) barrel

cano|a /ka'noa/ f canoe; ~**agem** f canoeing; ~**ista** m/f canoeist

canonizar /kanoni'zar/ vt canonize

can|saço /kã'sasu/ m tiredness; ~**sado** a tired; ~**sar** vt tire; (aborrecer) bore □ vi, ~**sar-se** vpr get tired; ~**sativo** a tiring; (aborrecido) boring; ~**seira** f tiredness; (lida) toil

can|tada /kã'tada/ f (fam) chat-up; ~**tar** vt/i sing; (fam) chat up

cântaro /'kãtaru/ m **chover a ~s** pour down, bucket down

cantarolar /kãtaro'lar/ vt/i hum

cantei|ra /kã'tera/ f quarry; ~**ro** m (de flores) flowerbed; (artífice) stonemason; ~**ro de obras** site office

cantiga /kã'tʃiga/ f ballad

can|til /kã'tʃiw/ (pl ~**tis**) m canteen; ~**tina** f canteen

canto¹ /'kãtu/ m (ângulo) corner

can|to² /'kãtu/ m (cantar) singing; ~**tor** m singer; ~**toria** f singing

canudo /ka'nudu/ m (de beber) straw; (tubo) tube; (fam: diploma) diploma

cão /kãw/ (pl **cães**) m dog

caolho /ka'oʎu/ a one-eyed

ca|os /kaws/ m chaos; ~**ótico** a chaotic

capa /'kapa/ f (de livro, revista) cover; (roupa sem mangas) cape; ~ **de chuva** raincoat

capacete /kapa'setʃi/ m helmet

capacho /ka'paʃu/ m doormat

capaci|dade /kapasi'dadʒi/ f capacity; (aptidão) ability; ~**tar** vt enable; (convencer) convince

capataz /kapa'tas/ m foreman

capaz /ka'pas/ a capable (**de** of); **ser ~ de** (poder) be able to; (ser provável) be likely to

cape|la /ka'pɛla/ f chapel; ~**lão** (pl ~**lães**) m chaplain

capen|ga /ka'pẽga/ a doddery; ~**gar** vi dodder

capeta /ka'peta/ m (diabo) devil; (criança) little devil

capilar /kapi'lar/ a hair

ca|pim /ka'pĩ/ m grass; ~**pinar** vt/i weed

capi|tal /kapi'taw/ (pl ~**tais**) a & m/f capital; (dinheiro) capitalism; ~**talismo** m capitalism; ~**talista** a & m/f capitalist; ~**talizar** vt (com) capitalize; (aproveitar) capitalize on

capi|tanear /kapitani'ar/ vt captain <*navio*>; (*fig*) lead; **~tania** f captaincy; **~tania do porto** port authority; **~tão** (*pl* **~tães**) m captain

capitulação /kapitula'sãw/ f capitulation, surrender

capítulo /ka'pitulu/ m chapter; (*de telenovela*) episode

capô /ka'po/ m bonnet, (*Amer*) hood

capoeira /kapo'era/ f Brazilian kick-boxing

capo|ta /ka'pɔta/ f roof; **~tar** vi overturn

capote /ka'pɔtʃi/ m overcoat

capri|char /kapri'ʃar/ vi excel o.s.; **~cho** m (*esmero*) care; (*desejo*) whim; (*teimosia*) contrariness; **~choso** /o/ a (*cheio de caprichos*) capricious; (*com esmero*) painstaking, meticulous

Capricórnio /kapri'kɔrniu/ m Capricorn

capricorniano /kaprikorni'anu/ a & m Capricorn

cápsula /'kapsula/ f capsule

cap|tar /kap'tar/ vt pick up <*emissão, sinais*>; tap <*água*>; catch, grasp <*sentido*>; win <*simpatia, admiração*>; **~tura** f capture; **~turar** vt capture

capuz /ka'pus/ m hood

caquético /ka'kɛtʃiku/ a broken-down, on one's last legs

caqui /ka'ki/ m persimmon

cáqui /'kaki/ a invar & m khaki

cara /'kara/ f face; (*aparência*) look; (*ousadia*) cheek □ (*fam*) m guy; **~ a ~** face to face; **de ~** straightaway; **dar de ~ com** run into; **está na ~** it's obvious; **fechar a ~** frown; **~ de pau** cheek; **~ de tacho** (*fam*) sheepish look

cara|col /kara'kɔw/ (*pl* **~cóis**) m snail

caracte|re /karak'tɛri/ m character; **~rística** f characteristic, feature; **~rístico** a characteristic; **~rizar** vt characterize; **~rizar-se** vpr be characterized

cara-de-pau /karadʒi'paw/ (*pl* **caras-de-pau**) a cheeky, brazen

caramba /ka'rãba/ int (*de espanto*) wow; (*de desagrado*) damn

caramelo /kara'mɛlu/ m caramel; (*bala*) toffee

caramujo /kara'muʒu/ m water snail

caranguejo /karã'geʒu/ m crab

caratê /kara'te/ m karate

caráter /ka'rater/ m character

caravana /kara'vana/ f caravan

car|boidrato /karboi'dratu/ m carbohydrate; **~bono** /o/ m carbon

carbu|rador /karbura'dor/ m carburettor, (*Amer*) carburator; **~rante** m fuel

carcaça /kar'kasa/ f carcass; (*de navio etc*) frame

cárcere /'karseri/ m jail

carcereiro /karse'reru/ m jailer, warder

carcomido /karko'midu/ a worm-eaten; <*rosto*> pock-marked

cardápio /kar'dapiu/ m menu

carde|al /kardʒi'aw/ (*pl* **~ais**) a cardinal

cardíaco /kar'dʒiaku/ a cardiac; **ataque ~** heart attack

cardio|lógico /kardʒio'lɔʒiku/ a heart; **~logista** m/f heart specialist, cardiologist

cardume /kar'dumi/ m shoal

careca /ka'rɛka/ a bald □ f bald patch

ca|recer /kare'ser/ **~recer de** vt lack; **~rência** f lack; (*social*) deprivation; (*afetiva*) lack of affection; **~rente** a lacking; (*socialmente*) deprived; (*afetivamente*) in need of affection

carestia /kares'tʃia/ f high cost; (*geral*) high cost of living; (*escassez*) shortage

careta /ka'reta/ f grimace □ a (*fam*) straight, square

car|ga /'karga/ f load; (*mercadorias*) cargo; (*elétrica*) charge; (*de cavalaria*) charge; (*de caneta*) refill; (*fig*) burden; **~ga horária** workload; **~go** m (*função*) post, job; **a ~go de** in the charge of; **~gueiro** m (*navio*) cargo ship, freighter

cariar /kari'ar/ vi decay

Caribe /ka'ribi/ m Caribbean

caricatu|ra /karika'tura/ f caricature; **~rar** vt caricature; **~rista** m/f caricaturist

carícia /ka'risia/ f (*com a mão*) stroke, caress; (*carinho*) affection

cari|dade /kari'dadʒi/ f charity; **obra de ~dade** charity; **~doso** /o/ a charitable

cárie /'kari/ f tooth decay

carim|bar /karĩ'bar/ vt stamp; postmark <*carta*>; **~bo** m stamp; (*do correio*) postmark

cari|nho /ka'riɲu/ m affection; (*um*) caress; **~nhoso** /o/ a affectionate

carioca /kari'ɔka/ a from Rio de Janeiro □ m/f person from Rio de Janeiro □ (*Port*) m weak coffee

caris|ma /ka'rizma/ m charisma; **~mático** a charismatic

carna|val /karna'vaw/ (*pl* **~vais**) m carnival; **~valesco** /e/ a carnival; <*roupa*> over the top, overdone □ m carnival organizer

car|ne /'karni/ f (*humana etc*) flesh; (*comida*) meat; **~neiro** m sheep; (*macho*) ram; (*como comida*) mutton; **~niça** f carrion; **~nificina** f slaughter; **~nívoro** *a* carnivorous □ *m* carnivore; **~nudo** *a* fleshy

caro /'karu/ *a* expensive; (*querido*) dear □ *adv* <*custar, cobrar*> a lot; <*comprar, vender*> at a high price; **pagar ~** pay a high price (for)

caroço /ka'rosu/ *m* (*de pêssego etc*) stone; (*de maçã*) core; (*em sopa, molho etc*) lump

carona /ka'rona/ *f* lift

carpete /kar'petʃi/ *m* fitted carpet

carpin|taria /karpīta'ria/ *f* carpentry; **~teiro** *m* carpenter

carran|ca /ka'xāka/ *f* scowl; **~cudo** *a* <*cara*> scowling; <*pessoa*> sullen

carrapato /kaxa'patu/ *m* (*animal*) tick; (*fig*) hanger-on

carrasco /ka'xasku/ *m* executioner; (*fig*) butcher

carre|gado /kaxe'gadu/ *a* <*céu*> dark, black; <*cor*> dark; <*ambiente*> tense; **~gador** *m* porter; **~gamento** *m* loading; (*carga*) load; **~gar** *vt* load <*navio, arma, máquina fotográfica*>; (*levar*) carry, charge <*bateria, pilha*>; **~gar em** overdo; pronounce strongly <*letra*>; (*Port*) press

carreira /ka'xera/ *f* career

carre|tel /kaxe'tɛw/ (*pl* **~téis**) *m* reel

car|ril /ka'xiw/ (*pl* **~ris**) (*Port*) *m* rail

carrinho /ka'xiɲu/ *m* (*para bagagem, compras*) trolley; (*de criança*) pram; **~ de mão** wheel-barrow

carro /'kaxu/ *m* car; (*de bois*) cart; **~ alegórico** float; **~ esporte** sports car; **~ fúnebre** hearse; **~ça** /ɔ/ *f* cart; **~ceria** *f* bodywork; **~chefe** (*pl* **~s-chefes**) *m* (*no carnaval*) main float; (*fig*) centrepiece; **~-forte** (*pl* **~s-fortes**) *m* security van

carros|sel /kaxo'sɛw/ (*pl* **~séis**) *m* merry-go-round

carruagem /kaxu'aʒē/ *f* carriage, coach

carta /'karta/ *f* letter; (*mapa*) chart; (*do baralho*) card; **~ branca** (*fig*) carte blanche; **~ de condução** (*Port*) driving licence, (*Amer*) driver's license; **~-bomba** (*pl* **~s-bomba**) *f* letter bomb; **~da** *f* (*fig*) move

cartão /kar'tãw/ *m* card; (*Port: papelão*) cardboard; **~ de crédito** credit card; **~ de visita** visiting card; **~-postal** (*pl* **cartões-postais**) *m* postcard

car|taz /kar'tas/ *m* poster, (*Amer*) bill; **em ~** showing, (*Amer*) playing; **~teira** *f* (*para dinheiro*) wallet; (*cartão*) card; (*mesa*) desk; **~teira de identidade** identity card; **~teira de motorista** driving licence, (*Amer*) driver's license; **~teiro** *m* postman

car|tel /kar'tɛw/ (*pl* **~téis**) *m* cartel

cárter /'karter/ *m* sump

carto|la /kar'tɔla/ *f* top hat □ *m* director; **~lina** *f* card; **~mante** *m*/*f* tarot reader, fortune-teller

cartório /kar'tɔriu/ *m* registry office

cartucho /kar'tuʃu/ *m* cartridge; (*de dinamite*) stick; (*de amendoim etc*) bag

car|tum /kar'tũ/ *m* cartoon; **~tunista** *m*/*f* cartoonist

caruncho /ka'rũʃu/ *m* woodcorm

carvalho /kar'vaʎu/ *m* oak

car|vão /kar'vãw/ *m* coal; (*de desenho*) charcoal; **~voeiro** *a* coal

casa /'kaza/ *f* house; (*comercial*) firm; (*de tabuleiro*) square; (*de botão*) hole; **em ~** at home; **para ~** home; **na ~ dos 30 anos** in one's thirties; **~ da moeda** mint; **~ de banho** (*Port*) bathroom; **~ de campo** country house; **~ de saúde** private hospital; **~ decimal** decimal place; **~ popular** council house

casaco /ka'zaku/ *m* (*sobretudo*) coat; (*paletó*) jacket; (*de lã*) pullover

ca|sal /ka'zaw/ (*pl* **~sais**) *m* couple; **~samento** *m* marriage; (*cerimônia*) wedding; **~sar** *vt* marry; (*fig*) combine □ *vi* get married; (*fig*) go together; **~sar-se** *vpr* get married; (*fig*) combine; **~sar-se com** marry

casarão /kaza'rãw/ *m* mansion

casca /'kaska/ *f* (*de árvore*) bark; (*de laranja, limão*) peel; (*de banana*) skin; (*de noz, ovo*) shell; (*de milho*) husk; (*de pão*) crust; (*de ferida*) scab

cascalho /kas'kaʎu/ *m* gravel

cascata /kas'kata/ *f* waterfall; (*fam*) fib

casca|vel /kaska'vɛw/ (*pl* **~véis**) *m* (*cobra*) rattlesnake □ *f* (*mulher*) shrew

casco /'kasku/ *m* (*de cavalo etc*) hoof; (*de navio*) hull; (*garrafa vazia*) empty

ca|sebre /ka'zɛbri/ *m* hovel, shack; **~seiro** *a* <*comida*> home-made; <*pessoa*> home-loving; <*vida*> home □ *m* housekeeper

caserna /ka'zɛrna/ *f* barracks

casmurro /kaz'muxu/ *a* sullen

caso /'kazu/ *m* case; (*amoroso*) affair; (*conto*) story □ *conj* in case; **em todo ou qualquer ~** in any case; **fazer ~ de** take notice of; **vir ao ~** be relevant; **~ contrário** otherwise

casório /ka'zɔriu/ (*fam*) *m* wedding

caspa /'kaspa/ *f* dandruff

casquinha /kas'kiɲa/ *f* (*de sorvete*) cone, cornet

cassar /ka'sar/ *vt* revoke, withdraw <*direitos, autorização*>; ban <*político*>

cassete /ka'sɛtʃi/ *m* cassette

cassetete /kase'tɛtʃi/ *m* truncheon, (*Amer*) nightstick

cassino /ka'sinu/ *m* casino; **~ de oficiais** officers' mess casta|nha /kas'taɲa/ f chestnut; ~nha de caju cashew nut; ~nha-do-pará (pl ~nhas-do-pará) f Brazil nut; ~nheiro m chestnut tree; ~nho a chestnut(-coloured); ~nholas /ɔ/ f pl castanets

castelhano /kaste'ʎanu/ a & m Castilian

castelo /kas'tɛlu/ m castle

casti|cal /kastʃi'saw/ (pl ~çais) m candlestick

cas|tidade /kastʃi'dadʒi/ f chastity; ~tigar vt punish; ~tigo m punishment; ~to a chaste

castor /kas'tor/ m beaver

castrar /kas'trar/ vt castrate

casu|al /kazu'aw/ (pl ~ais) a chance; (fortuito) fortuitous; ~alidade f chance

casulo /ka'zulu/ m (de larva) cocoon

cata /'kata/ f à ~ de in search of

cata|lão /kata'lãw/ (pl ~lães) a & m (f ~lã) Catalan

catalisador /kataliza'dor/ m catalyst; (de carro) catalytic convertor

catalogar /katalo'gar/ vt catalogue

catálogo /ka'talogu/ m catalogue; (de telefones) phone book

Catalunha /kata'luɲa/ f Catalonia

catapora /kata'pora/ f chicken pox

catar /ka'tar/ vt (procurar) search for; (recolher) gather; (do chão) pick up; sort <arroz, café>

catarata /kata'rata/ f waterfall; (no olho) cataract

catarro /ka'taxu/ m catarrh

catástrofe /ka'tastrofi/ f catastrophe

catastrófico /katas'trɔfiku/ a catastrophic

catecismo /kate'sizmu/ m catechism

cátedra /'katedra/ f chair

cate|dral /kate'draw/ (pl ~drais) f cathedral; ~drático m professor

cate|goria /katego'ria/ f category; (social) class; (qualidade) quality; ~górico a categorical; ~gorizar vt categorize

catinga /ka'tʃĩga/ f body odour, stink

cati|vante /katʃi'vãtʃi/ a captivating; ~var vt captivate; ~veiro m captivity; ~vo a & m captive

catolicismo /katoli'sizmu/ m Catholicism

católico /ka'tɔliku/ a & m Catholic

catorze /ka'torzi/ a & m fourteen

cau|da /'kawda/ f tail; ~dal (pl ~dais) m torrent

caule /'kawli/ m stem

cau|sa /'kawza/ f cause; (jurid) case; por ~sa de because of; ~sar vt cause

caute|la /kaw'tɛla/ f caution; (documento) ticket; ~loso /o/ a cautious, careful

cava /'kava/ f armhole

cava|do /ka'vadu/ a <vestido> low-cut; <olhos> deep-set; ~dor a hard-working ▫ m hard worker

cava|laria /kavala'ria/ f cavalry; ~lariça f stable; ~leiro m horseman; (na Idade Média) knight

cavalete /kava'letʃi/ m easel

caval|gadura /kavawga'dura/ f mount; ~gar vt/i ride; sit astride <muro, banco>; (saltar) jump

cavalhei|resco /kavaʎe'resku/ a gallant, gentlemanly; ~ro m gentleman ▫ a gallant, gentlemanly

cavalo /ka'valu/ m horse; a ~ on horseback; ~-vapor (pl ~s-vapor) horsepower

cavanhaque /kava'ɲaki/ m goatee

cavaquinho /kava'kiɲu/ m ukulele

cavar /ka'var/ vt dig; (fig) go all out for ▫ vi dig; (fig) go all out; ~ em (vasculhar) delve into; ~ a vida make a living

caveira /ka'vera/ f skull

caverna /ka'vɛrna/ f cavern

caviar /kavi'ar/ m caviar

cavidade /kavi'dadʒi/ f cavity

cavilha /ka'viʎa/ f peg

cavo /'kavu/ a hollow

cavoucar /kavo'kar/ vt excavate

caxemira /kaʃe'mira/ f cashmere

caxumba /ka'ʃũba/ f mumps

cear /si'ar/ vt have for supper ▫ vi have supper

cebo|la /se'bola/ f onion; ~linha f spring onion

ceder /se'der/ vt give up; (dar) give; (emprestar) lend ▫ vi (não resistir) give way; ~ a yield to

cedilha /se'dʒiʎa/ f cedilla

cedo /'sedu/ adv early; mais ~ ou mais tarde sooner or later

cedro /'sɛdru/ m cedar

cédula /'sedula/ f (de banco) note, (Amer) bill; (eleitoral) ballot paper

ce|gar /se'gar/ vt blind; blunt <faca>; ~go /ɛ/ a blind; <faca> blunt ▫ m blind man; às ~gas blindly

cegonha /se'goɲa/ f stork

cegueira /se'gera/ f blindness

ceia /'seja/ f supper

cei|fa /'sejfa/ f harvest; (massacre) slaughter; ~far vt reap; claim <vidas>; (matar) mow down

cela /'sɛla/ f cell

cele|bração /selebra'sãw/ f celebration; ~brar vt celebrate

célebre /'sɛlebri/ a celebrated

celebridade /selebri'dadʒi/ f celebrity

celeiro /se'leru/ m granary

célere /'sɛleri/ a swift, fast

celeste /se'lɛstʃi/ a celestial

celeuma /se'lewma/ f pandemonium

celibato /seli'batu/ *m* celibacy

celofane /selo'fani/ *m* cellophane

celta /'sɛwta/ *a* Celtic □ *m/f* Celt □ *m* (*língua*) Celtic

célula /'sɛlula/ *f* cell

celu|lar /selu'lar/ *a* cellular; **~lite** *f* cellulite; **~lose** /ɔ/ *f* cellulose

cem /sẽj/ *a* & *m* hundred

cemitério /semi'tɛriu/ *m* cemetery; (*fig*) graveyard

cena /'sena/ *f* scene; (*palco*) stage; **em ~** on stage

cenário /se'nariu/ *m* scenery; (*de crime etc*) scene

cênico /'seniku/ *a* stage

cenoura /se'nora/ *f* carrot

cen|so /'sẽsu/ *m* census; **~sor** *m* censor; **~sura** *f* (*de jornais etc*) censorship; (*órgão*) censor(s); (*condenação*) censure; **~surar** *vt* censor <*jornal, filme etc*>; (*condenar*) censure

centavo /sẽ'tavu/ *m* cent

centeio /sẽ'teju/ *m* rye

centelha /sẽ'teʎa/ *f* spark; (*fig: de gênio etc*) flash

cente|na /sẽ'tena/ *f* hundred; **uma ~na de** about a hundred; **às ~nas** in their hundreds; **~nário** *m* centenary

centésimo /sẽ'tɛzimu/ *a* hundredth

centí|grado /sẽ'tʃigradu/ *m* centigrade; **~litro** *m* centilitre; **~metro** *m* centimetre

cento /'sẽtu/ *a* & *m* hundred; **por ~** per cent

cen|tral /sẽ'traw/ (*pl* **~trais**) *a* central; **~tralizar** *vt* centralize; **~trar** *vt* centre; **~tro** *m* centre

cepti- (*Port*) *veja* **ceti-**

cera /'sera/ *f* wax; **fazer ~** waste time, faff about

cerâmi|ca /se'ramika/ *f* ceramics, pottery; **~co** *a* ceramic

cer|ca /'serka/ *f* fence; **~ca viva** hedge □ *adv* **~ca de** around, about; **~cado** *m* enclosure; (*para criança*) playpen; **~car** *vt* surround; (*com muro, cerca*) enclose; (*assediar*) besiege

cercear /sersi'ar/ *vt* (*fig*) curtail, restrict

cerco /'serku/ *m* (*mil*) siege; (*policial*) dragnet

cere|al /seri'aw/ (*pl* **~ais**) *m* cereal

cere|bral /sere'braw/ (*pl* **~brais**) *a* cerebral

cérebro /'sɛrebru/ *m* brain; (*inteligência*) intellect

cere|ja /se'reʒa/ *f* cherry; **~jeira** *f* cherry tree

cerimônia /seri'monia/ *f* ceremony; **sem ~** unceremoniously; **fazer ~** stand on ceremony

cerimoni|al /serimoni'aw/ (*pl* **~ais**) *a* & *m* ceremonial; **~oso** /o/ *a* ceremonious

cer|rado /se'xadu/ *a* <*barba, mata*> thick; <*punho, dentes*> clenched □ *m* scrubland; **~rar** *vt* close; **~rar-se** *vpr* close; <*noites, trevas*> close in

certeiro /ser'teru/ *a* well-aimed, accurate

certeza /ser'teza/ *f* certainty; **com ~** certainly; **ter ~** be sure (**de** of; **de que** that)

certidão /sertʃi'dãw/ *f* certificate; **~ de nascimento** birth certificate

certifi|cado /sertʃifi'kadu/ *m* certificate; **~car** *vt* certify; **~car-se de** make sure of

certo /'sɛrtu/ *a* (*correto*) right; (*seguro*) certain; (*algum*) a certain □ *adv* right; **dar ~** work

cerveja /ser'veʒa/ *f* beer; **~ria** *f* brewery; (*bar*) pub

cervo /'sɛrvu/ *m* deer

cer|zidura /serzi'dura/ *f* darning; **~zir** *vt* darn

cesariana /sezari'ana/ *f* Caesarian

césio /'sɛziu/ *m* caesium

cessar /se'sar/ *vt/i* cease

ces|ta /'sesta/ *f* basket; (*de comida*) hamper; **~to** /e/ *m* basket; **~to de lixo** wastepaper basket

ceticismo /setʃi'sizmu/ *m* scepticism

cético /'sɛtʃiku/ *a* sceptical □ *m* sceptic

cetim /se'tʃĩ/ *m* satin

céu /sɛw/ *m* sky; (*na religião*) heaven; **~ da boca** roof of the mouth

cevada /se'vada/ *f* barley

chá /ʃa/ *m* tea

chacal /ʃa'kaw/ (*pl* **~cais**) *m* jackal

chácara /'ʃakara/ *f* smallholding; (*casa*) country cottage

chaci|na /ʃa'sina/ *f* slaughter; **~nar** *vt* slaughter

chá-de-bar /ʃadʒi'bar/ (*pl* **~s-de-bar**) *m* bachelor party; **~-de-panela** (*pl* **~s-de-panela**) *m* hen night, (*Amer*) wedding shower

chafariz /ʃafa'ris/ *m* fountain

chaga /'ʃaga/ *f* sore

chaleira /ʃa'lera/ *f* kettle

chama /'ʃama/ *f* flame

cha|mada /ʃa'mada/ *f* call; (*dos presentes*) roll call; (*dos alunos*) register; **~mado** *m* call □ *a* (*depois do substantivo*) called; (*antes do substantivo*) so-called; **~mar** *vt* call; (*para sair etc*) ask, invite; attract <*atenção*> □ *vi* call; <*telefone*> ring; **~mar-se** *vpr* be called; **~mariz** *m* decoy; **~mativo** *a* showy, flashy

chamejar /ʃame'ʒar/ *vi* flare

chaminé /ʃami'nɛ/ *f* (*de casa, fábrica*) chimney; (*de navio, trem*) funnel

champanhe /ʃɐ̃'paɲi/ *m* champagne

champu /ʃɐ̃'pu/ (*Port*) *m* shampoo

chamuscar /ʃamuʃ'kar/ *vt* singe, scorch

chance /'ʃãsi/ *f* chance

chanceler /ʃãse'ler/ *m* chancellor

chanchada /ʃɐ̃'ʃada/ *f* (*peça*) second-rate play; (*filme*) B movie

chanta|gear /ʃãtaʒi'ar/ *vt* blackmail; ~**gem** *f* blackmail; ~**gista** *m/f* blackmailer

chão /ʃãw/ (*pl* ~s) *m* ground; (*dentro de casa etc*) floor

chapa /'ʃapa/ *f* sheet; (*foto*) plate; ~ **eleitoral** electoral list; ~ **de matrícula** (*Port*) number plate, (*Amer*) license plate □ (*fam*) *m* mate

chapéu /ʃa'pɛw/ *m* hat

charada /ʃa'rada/ *f* riddle

char|ge /ʃarʒi/ *f* (political) cartoon; ~**gista** *m/f* cartoonist

charla|tanismo /ʃarlata'nizmu/ *m* charlatanism; ~**tão** (*pl* ~**tães**) *m* (*f* ~**tona**) charlatan

char|me /'ʃarmi/ *m* charm; **fazer** ~**me** turn on the charm; ~**moso** /o/ *a* charming

charneca /ʃar'nɛka/ *f* moor

charuto /ʃa'rutu/ *m* cigar

chassi /ʃa'si/ *m* chassis

chata /'ʃata/ *f* (*barca*) barge

chate|ação /ʃatʃia'sãw/ *f* annoyance; ~**ar** *vt* annoy; ~**ar-se** *vpr* get annoyed

cha|tice /ʃa'tʃisi/ *f* nuisance; ~**to** *a* (*tedioso*) boring; (*irritante*) annoying; (*mal-educado*) rude; (*plano*) flat

chauvinis|mo /ʃovi'nizmu/ *m* chauvinism; ~**ta** *m/f* chauvinist □ *a* chauvinistic

cha|vão /ʃa'vãw/ *m* cliché; ~**ve** *f* key; (*ferramenta*) spanner; ~**ve de fenda** screwdriver; ~**ve inglesa** wrench; ~**veiro** *m* (*aro*) keyring; (*pessoa*) locksmith

chávena /'ʃavena/ *f* soup bowl; (*Port: xícara*) cup

checar /ʃe'kar/ *vt* check

che|fe /'ʃɛfi/ *m/f* (*patrão*) boss; (*gerente*) manager; (*dirigente*) leader; ~**fia** *f* leadership; (*de empresa*) management; (*sede*) headquarters; ~**fiar** *vt* lead; be in charge of <*trabalho*>

che|gada /ʃe'gada/ *f* arrival; ~**gado** *a* <*amigo, relação*> close; ~**gar** *vi* arrive; (*deslocar-se*) move up; (*ser suficiente*) be enough □ *vt* bring up <*prato, cadeira*>; ~**gar a fazer** go as far as to do as doing; **aonde você quer** ~**gar?** what are you driving at?; ~**gar lá** (*fig*) make it

cheia /'ʃeja/ *f* flood

cheio /'ʃeju/ *a* full; (*fam: farto*) fed up

chei|rar /ʃe'rar/ *vt/i* smell (**a** of); ~**roso** /o/ *a* scented

cheque /'ʃɛki/ *m* cheque, (*Amer*) check; ~ **de viagem** traveller's cheque; ~ **em branco** blank cheque

chi|ado /ʃi'adu/ *m* (*de pneus, freios*) screech; (*de porta*) squeak; (*de vapor, numa fita*) hiss; ~**ar** *vi* <*porta*> squeak; <*pneus, freios*> screech; <*vapor, fita*> hiss; <*fritura*> sizzle; (*fam: reclamar*) grumble, moan

chiclete /ʃi'klɛtʃi/ *m* chewing gum; ~ **de bola** bubble gum

chico|tada /ʃiko'tada/ *f* lash; ~**te** /ɔ/ *m* whip; ~**tear** *vt* whip

chi|frar /ʃi'frar/ (*fam*) *vt* cheat on <*marido, esposa*>; **two-time** <*namorado, namorada*>; ~**fre** *m* horn; ~**frudo** *a* horned; (*fam*) cuckolded □ *m* cuckold

Chile /'ʃili/ *m* Chile

chileno /ʃi'lenu/ *a* & *m* Chilean

chilique /ʃi'liki/ (*fam*) *m* funny turn

chil|rear /ʃiwxi'ar/ *vi* chirp, twitter; ~**reio** *m* chirping, twittering

chimarrão /ʃima'xãw/ *m* unsweetened maté tea

chimpanzé /ʃĩpã'zɛ/ *m* chimpanzee

China /'ʃina/ *f* China

chinelo /ʃi'nɛlu/ *m* slipper

chi|nês /ʃi'nes/ *a* & *m* (*f* ~**nesa**) Chinese

chinfrim /ʃĩ'frĩ/ *a* tatty, shoddy

chio /'ʃiu/ *m* squeak; (*de pneus*) screech; (*de vapor*) hiss

chique /'ʃiki/ *a* <*pessoa, aparência, roupa*> smart, (*Amer*) sharp; <*hotel, bairro, loja etc*> smart, up-market, posh

chiqueiro /ʃi'keru/ *m* pigsty

chis|pa /'ʃispa/ *f* flash; ~**pada** *f* dash; ~**par** *vi* (*soltar chispas*) flash; (*correr*) dash

choca|lhar /ʃoka'ʎar/ *vt/i* rattle; ~**lho** *m* rattle

cho|cante /ʃo'kãtʃi/ *a* shocking; (*fam*) incredible; ~**car** *vt/i* hatch <*ovos*>; (*ultrajar*) shock; ~**car-se** *vpr* <*carros etc*> crash; <*teorias etc*> clash

chocho /'ʃoʃu/ *a* dull, insipid

chocolate /ʃoko'latʃi/ *m* chocolate

chofer /ʃo'fɛr/ *m* chauffeur

chope /'ʃopi/ *m* draught lager

choque /'ʃɔki/ *m* shock; (*colisão*) collision; (*conflito*) clash

cho|radeira /ʃora'dera/ *f* fit of crying; ~**ramingar** *vi* whine; ~**ramingas** *m/f* *invar* whiner; ~**rão** *m* (*salgueiro*) weeping willow □ *a* (~**rona**) tearful; ~**rar** *vi* cry; ~**ro** /o/ *m* crying; ~**roso** /o/ *a* tearful

chouriço /ʃo'risu/ *m* black pudding; (*Port*) sausage

chover /ʃo'ver/ *vi* rain

chuchu /ʃu'ʃu/ *m* chayote

chucrute /ʃu'krutʃi/ *m* sauerkraut

chumaço /ʃu'masu/ *m* wad

chum|bado /ʃũ'badu/ (*fam*) *a* knocked out; **~bar** (*Port*) *vt* fill <*dente*>; fail <*aluno*> □ *vi* <*aluno*> fail; **~bo** *m* lead; (*Port: obturação*) filling

chu|par /ʃu'par/ *vt* suck; <*esponja*> suck up; **~peta** /e/ *f* dummy, (*Amer*) pacifier

churras|caria /ʃuxaska'ria/ *f* barbecue restaurant; **~co** *m* barbecue; **~queira** *f* barbecue; **~quinho** *m* kebab

chu|tar /ʃu'tar/ *vt/i* kick; (*fam: adivinhar*) guess; **~te** *m* kick; **~teira** *f* football boot

chu|va /'ʃuva/ *f* rain; **~va de pedra** hail; **~varada** *f* torrential rainstorm; **~veiro** *m* shower; **~viscar** *vi* drizzle; **~visco** *m* drizzle; **~voso** /o/ *a* rainy

cica|triz /sika'tris/ *f* scar; **~trizar** *vt* scar □ *vi* <*ferida*> heal

cic|lismo /si'klizmu/ *m* cycling; **~lista** *m/f* cyclist; **~lo** *m* cycle; **~lone** /o/ *m* cyclone; **~lovia** *f* cycle lane

cida|dania /sidada'nia/ *f* citizenship; **~dão** (*pl* **~dãos**) *m* (*f* **~dã**) citizen; **~de** *f* town; (*grande*) city; **~dela** /ɛ/ *f* citadel

ciência /si'ẽsia/ *f* science

cien|te /si'ẽtʃi/ *a* aware; **~tífico** *a* scientific; **~tista** *m/f* scientist

ci|fra /'sifra/ *f* figure; (*código*) cipher; **~frão** *m* dollar sign; **~frar** *vt* encode

cigano /si'ganu/ *a* & *m* gypsy

cigarra /si'gaxa/ *f* cicada; (*dispositivo*) buzzer

cigar|reira /siga'xera/ *f* cigarette case; **~ro** *m* cigarette

cilada /si'lada/ *f* trap; (*estratagema*) trick

cilindrada /silĩ'drada/ *f* (engine) capacity

cilíndrico /si'lĩdriku/ *a* cylindrical

cilindro /si'lĩdru/ *m* cylinder; (*rolo*) roller

cílio /'siliu/ *m* eyelash

cima /'sima/ *f* **em ~** on top; (*na casa*) upstairs; **em ~ de** on, on top of; **para ~** up; (*na casa*) upstairs; **por ~** over the top; **por ~ de** over; **de ~** from above; **ainda por ~** moreover

címbalo /'sĩbalu/ *m* cymbal

cimeira /si'mera/ *f* crest; (*Port: cúpula*) summit

cimen|tar /simẽ'tar/ *vt* cement; **~to** *m* cement

cinco /'sĩku/ *a* & *m* five

cine|asta /sini'asta/ *m/f* film-maker; **~ma** /e/ *m* cinema

Cingapura /sĩga'pura/ *f* Singapore

cínico /'siniku/ *a* cynical □ *m* cynic

cinismo /si'nizmu/ *m* cynicism

cinqüen|ta /sĩ'kwẽta/ *a* & *m* fifty; **~tão** *a* & *m* (*f* **~tona**) fifty-year-old

cinti|lante /sĩtʃi'lãtʃi/ *a* glittering; **~lar** *vi* glitter

cin|to /'sĩtu/ *m* belt; **~to de segurança** seatbelt; **~tura** *f* waist; **~turão** *m* belt

cin|za /'sĩza/ *f* ash □ *a invar* grey; **~zeiro** *m* ashtray

cin|zel /sĩ'zɛw/ (*pl* **~zéis**) *m* chisel; **~zelar** *vt* carve

cinzento /sĩ'zẽtu/ *a* grey

cipó /si'pɔ/ *m* vine, liana, **~poal** (*pl* **~poais**) *m* jungle

cipreste /si'prɛstʃi/ *m* cypress

cipriota /sipri'ɔta/ *a* & *m* Cypriot

ciranda /si'rãda/ *f* (*fig*) merry-go-round

cir|cense /sir'sẽsi/ *a* circus; **~co** *m* circus

circu|ito /sir'kuitu/ *m* circuit; **~lação** *f* circulation; **~lar** *a* & *f* circular □ *vt* circulate □ *vi* <*dinheiro, sangue*> circulate; <*carro*> drive; <*ônibus*> run; <*trânsito*> move; <*pessoa*> go round

círculo /'sirkulu/ *m* circle

circunci|dar /sirkũsi'dar/ *vt* circumcise; **~ção** *f* circumcision

circun|dar /sirkũ'dar/ *vt* surround; **~ferência** *f* circumference; **~flexo** /ɛks/ *a* & *m* circumflex; **~scrição** *f* district; **~scrição eleitoral** constituency; **~specto** /ɛ/ *a* circumspect; **~stância** *f* circumstance; **~stanciado** *a* detailed; **~stancial** (*pl* **~stanciais**) *a* circumstantial; **~stante** *m/f* bystander

cirrose /si'xɔzi/ *f* cirrhosis

cirur|gia /sirur'ʒia/ *f* surgery; **~gião** *m* (*f* **~giã**) surgeon

cirúrgico /si'rurʒiku/ *a* surgical

cisão /si'zãw/ *f* split, division

cisco /'sisku/ *m* speck

cisma¹ /'sizma/ *m* schism

cis|ma² /'sizma/ *f* (*mania*) fixation; (*devaneio*) imagining, daydream; (*prevenção*) irrational dislike; (*de criança*) whim; **~mar** *vt/i* be lost in thought; <*criança*> be insistent; **~mar em** brood over; **~mar de** *ou* **em fazer** insist on doing; **~mar que** insist on thinking that; **~mar com alg** take a dislike to s.o.

cisne /'sizni/ *m* swan

cistite /sis'tʃitʃi/ *f* cystitis

ci|tação /sita'sãw/ *f* quotation; (*jurid*) summons; **~tar** *vt* quote; (*jurid*) summon ciúme /si'umi/ *m* jealousy; ter ~s de be jealous of

ciu|meira /siu'mera/ *f* fit of jealousy; ~mento *a* jealous

cívico /'siviku/ *a* civic

ci|vil /si'viw/ (*pl* ~vis) *a* civil □ *m* civilian; ~vilidade *f* civility

civili|zação /siviliza'sãw/ *f* civilization; ~zado *a* civilized; ~zar *vt* civilize

civismo /si'vizmu/ *m* public spirit

cla|mar /kla'mar/ *vt/i* cry out, clamour (por for); ~mor *m* outcry; ~moroso /o/ *a* <*protesto*> loud, noisy; <*erro, injustiça*> blatant

clandestino /klãdes'tʃinu/ *a* clandestine

cla|ra /'klara/ *f* egg white; ~rabóia *f* skylight; ~rão *m* flash; ~rear *vt* brighten; clarify <*questão*> □ *vi* brighten up; (*fazer-se dia*) become light; ~reira *f* clearing; ~reza /e/ *f* clarity; ~ridade *f* brightness; (*do dia*) daylight

cla|rim /kla'rĩ/ *m* bugle; ~rinete /e/ *m* clarinet

clarividente /klariviˈdẽtʃi/ *m/f* clairvoyant

claro /'klaru/ *a* clear; <*luz*> bright; <*cor*> light □ *adv* clearly □ *int* of course; ~ que sim/não of course/of course not; às claras openly; noite em ~ sleepless night; já é dia ~ it's already daylight

classe /'klasi/ *f* class; ~ média middle class

clássico /'klasiku/ *a* classical; (*famoso, exemplar*) classic □ *m* classic

classifi|cação /klasifika'sãw/ *f* classification; (*numa competição esportiva*) placing, place; ~cado *a* classified; <*candidato*> successful; <*esportista, time*> qualified; ~car *vt* classify; (*considerar*) describe (de as); ~carse *vpr* <*candidato, esportista*> qualify; (*chamar-se*) describe o.s. (de as); ~catório *a* qualifying

classudo /kla'sudu/ (*fam*) *a* classy

claustro|fobia /klawstrofo'bia/ *f* claustrophobia; ~fóbico *a* claustrophobic

cláusula /'klawzula/ *f* clause

cla|ve /'klavi/ *f* clef; ~vícula *f* collar bone

cle|mência /kle'mẽsia/ *f* clemency; ~mente *a* <*pessoa*> lenient; <*tempo*> clement

cleptomaníaco /kleptoma'niaku/ *m* kleptomaniac

clérigo /'klɛrigu/ *m* cleric, clergyman

clero /'klɛru/ *m* clergy

clien|te /kliˈẽtʃi/ *m/f* (*de loja*) customer; (*de advogado, empresa*) client; ~tela /ɛ/ *f* (*de loja*) customers; (*de restaurante, empresa*) clientele

cli|ma /'klima/ *m* climate; ~mático *a* climatic

clímax /'klimaks/ *m invar* climax

clíni|ca /'klinika/ *f* clinic; ~ca geral general practice; ~co *a* clinical □ *m* ~co geral general practitioner, GP

clipe /'klipi/ *m* clip; (*para papéis*) paper clip

clone /'kloni/ *m* clone

cloro /'kloru/ *m* chlorine

close /'klozi/ *m* close-up

clube /'klubi/ *m* club

coação /koa'sãw/ *f* coercion

coadjuvante /koadʒu'vãtʃi/ *a* <*ator*> supporting □ *m/f* (*em peça, filme*) co-star; (*em crime*) accomplice

coador /koa'dor/ *m* strainer; (*de legumes*) colander; (*de café*) filter bag

coadunar /koadu'nar/ *vt* combine

coagir /koa'ʒir/ *vt* compel

coagular /koagu'lar/ *vt/i* clot; ~-se *vpr* clot

coágulo /ko'agulu/ *m* clot

coalhar /koa'ʎar/ *vt/i* curdle; ~-se *vpr* curdle

coalizão /koali'zãw/ *f* coalition

coar /ko'ar/ *vt* strain

coaxar /koa'ʃar/ *vi* croak □ *m* croaking

cobaia /ko'baja/ *f* guinea pig

cober|ta /ko'berta/ *f* (*de cama*) bedcover; (*de navio*) deck; ~to /ɛ/ *a* covered □ *pp de* cobrir; ~tor *m* blanket; ~tura *f* (*revestimento*) covering; (*reportagem*) coverage; (*seguro*) cover; (*apartamento*) penthouse

cobi|ça /ko'bisa/ *f* greed, covetousness; ~çar *vt* covet; ~çoso /o/ *a* covetous

cobra /'kɔbra/ *f* snake

co|brador /kobra'dor/ *m* (*no ônibus*) conductor; ~brança *f* (*de dívida*) collection; (*de preço*) charging; (*de atitudes*) asking for something in return (de for); ~brança de pênalti/falta penalty (kick)/free kick; ~brar *vt* collect <*dívida*>; ask for <*coisa prometida*>; take <*pênalti*>; ~brar aco a alg (*em dinheiro*) charge s.o. for sth; (*fig*) make s.o. pay for sth; ~brar uma falta (*no futebol*) take a free kick

cobre /'kɔbri/ *m* copper

cobrir /ko'brir/ *vt* cover; ~-se *vpr* <*pessoa*> cover o.s. up; <*coisa*> be covered

cocaína /koka'ina/ *f* cocaine

coçar /ko'sar/ *vt* scratch □ *vi* (*esfregar-se*) scratch; (*comichar*) itch; ~-se *vpr* scratch o.s.

cócegas /'kɔsegas/ *f pl* fazer ~ em tickle; sentir ~ be ticklish coceira /ko'sera/ *f* itch

cochi|char /koʃi'ʃar/ *vt/i* whisper; ∼cho *m* whisper

cochi|lada /koʃi'lada/ *f* doze; ∼lar *vi* doze; ∼lo *m* snooze

coco /'koku/ *m* coconut

cócoras /'kɔkoras/ *f pl* de ∼ squatting; ficar de ∼ squat

côdea /'kodʒia/ *f* crust

codificar /kodʒifi'kar/ *vt* encode <*mensagem*>; codify <*leis*>

código /'kɔdʒigu/ *m* code; ∼ de barras bar code

codinome /kodʒi'nomi/ *m* codename

coeficiente /koefisi'ẽtʃi/ *m* coefficient; (*fig: fator*) factor

coelho /ko'eʎu/ *m* rabbit

coentro /ko'ẽtru/ *m* coriander

coerção /koer'sãw/ *f* coercion

coe|rência /koe'rẽsia/ *f* (*lógica*) coherence; (*consequência*) consistency; ∼rente *a* (*lógico*) coherent; (*consequiente*) consistent

coexis|tência /koezis'tẽsia/ *f* coexistence; ∼tir *vi* coexist

cofre /'kɔfri/ *m* safe; (*de dinheiro público*) coffer

cogi|tação /koʒita'sãw/ *f* contemplation; fora de ∼tação out of the question; ∼tar *vt/i* contemplate

cogumelo /kogu'mɛlu/ *m* mushroom

coibir /koi'bir/ *vt* restrict; ∼-se de keep o.s. from

coice /'kojsi/ *m* kick

coinci|dência /koĩsi'dẽsia/ *f* coincidence; ∼dir *vi* coincide

coisa /'kojza/ *f* thing

coitado /koj'tadu/ *m* poor thing; ∼ do pai poor father

cola /'kɔla/ *f* glue; (*cópia*) crib

colabo|ração /kolabora'sãw/ *f* collaboration; (*de escritor etc*) contribution; ∼rador *m* collaborator; (*em jornal, livro*) contributor; ∼rar *vi* collaborate; (*em jornal, livro*) contribute (em to)

colagem /ko'laʒẽ/ *f* collage

colágeno /ko'laʒenu/ *m* collagen

colapso /ko'lapsu/ *m* collapse

colar¹ /ko'lar/ *m* necklace

colar² /ko'lar/ *vt* (*grudar*) stick; (*copiar*) crib □ *vi* stick; (*copiar*) crib; <*desculpa etc*> stand up, stick

colarinho /kola'riɲu/ *m* collar; (*de cerveja*) head

colate|ral /kolate'raw/ (*pl* ∼rais) *a* efeito ∼ral side effect

col|cha /'kowʃa/ *f* bedspread; ∼chão *m* mattress

colchete /kow'ʃetʃi/ *m* fastener; (*sinal de pontuação*) square bracket; ∼ de pressão press stud, popper

colchonete /kowʃo'nɛtʃi/ *m* (foldaway) mattress

coldre /'kɔwdri/ *m* holster

cole|ção /kole'sãw/ *f* collection; ∼cionador *m* collector; ∼cionar *vt* collect

colega /ko'lɛga/ *m/f* (*amigo*) friend; (*de trabalho*) colleague

colegi|al /koleʒi'aw/ (*pl* ∼ais) *a* school □ *m/f* schoolboy (*f* -girl)

colégio /ko'lɛʒiu/ *m* secondary school, (*Amer*) high school

coleira /ko'lera/ *f* collar

cólera /'kɔlera/ *f* (*doença*) cholera; (*raiva*) fury

colérico /ko'lɛriku/ *a* (*furioso*) furious □ *m* (*doente*) cholera victim

colesterol /koleste'rɔw/ *m* cholesterol

cole|ta /ko'lɛta/ *f* collection; ∼tânea *f* collection; ∼tar *vt* collect

colete /ko'letʃi/ *m* waistcoat, (*Amer*) vest; ∼ salva-vidas life-jacket, (*Amer*) life-preserver

coletivo /kole'tʃivu/ *a* collective; <*transporte*> public □ *m* bus

colheita /ko'ʎejta/ *f* harvest; (*produtos colhidos*) crop

colher¹ /ko'ʎɛr/ *f* spoon

colher² /ko'ʎer/ *vt* pick <*flores, frutos*>; gather <*informações*>

colherada /koʎe'rada/ *f* spoonful

colibri /koli'bri/ *m* hummingbird

cólica /'kɔlika/ *f* colic

colidir /koli'dʒir/ *vi* collide

coli|gação /koliga'sãw/ *f* (*pol*) coalition; ∼gado *m* (*pol*) coalition partner; ∼gar *vt* bring together; ∼gar-se *vpr* join forces; (*pol*) form a coalition

colina /ko'lina/ *f* hill

colírio /ko'liriu/ *m* eyewash

colisão /koli'zãw/ *f* collision

collant /ko'lã/ (*pl* ∼s) *m* body; (*de ginástica*) leotard

colmeia /kow'meja/ *f* beehive

colo /'kɔlu/ *f* (*regaço*) lap; (*pescoço*) neck

colo|cação /koloka'sãw/ *f* placing; (*emprego*) position; (*exposição de fatos*) statement; (*de aparelho, pneus, carpete etc*) fitting; ∼cado *a* placed; o primeiro ∼cado (*em ranking*) person in first place; ∼cador *m* fitter; ∼car *vt* put; fit <*aparelho, pneus, carpete etc*>; put forward, state <*opinião, idéias*>; (*empregar*) get a job for

Colômbia /ko'lõbia/ *f* Colombia

colombiano /kolõbi'anu/ *a & m* Colombian

cólon /'kɔlõ/ *m* colon

colônia¹ /ko'lonia/ *f* (*colonos*) colony

colônia² /ko'lonia/ *f* (*perfume*) cologne

coloni|al /koloni'aw/ (*pl* ∼ais) *a* colonial; ∼alismo *m* colonialism;

~**alista** *a & m/f* colonialist; ~**zar** *vt* colonize

colono /ko'lonu/ *m* settler, colonist; (*lavrador*) tenant farmer

coloqui|al /koloki'aw/ (*pl* ~**ais**) *a* colloquial

colóquio /ko'lɔkiu/ *m* (*conversa*) conversation; (*congresso*) conference

colo|rido /kolo'ridu/ *a* colourful □ *m* colouring; ~**rir** *vt* colour

colu|na /ko'luna/ *f* column; (*vertebral*) spine; ~**nável** (*pl* ~**náveis**) *a* famous □ *m/f* celebrity; ~**nista** *m/f* columnist

com /kõ/ *prep* with; **o comentário foi comigo** the comment was meant for me; **você está ~ a chave?** have you got the key?; ~ **seis anos de idade** at six years of age

coma /'koma/ *f* coma

comadre /ko'madri/ *f* (*madrinha*) godmother of one's child; (*mãe do afilhado*) mother of one's godchild; (*urinol*) bedpan

coman|dante /komã'dãtʃi/ *m* commander; ~**dar** *vt* lead; (*ordenar*) command; (*elevar-se acima de*) dominate; ~**do** *m* command; (*grupo*) commando group

comba|te /kõ'batʃi/ *m* combat; (*a drogas, doença etc*) fight (**a** against); ~**ter** *vt/i* fight; ~**ter-se** *vpr* fight

combi|nação /kõbina'sãw/ *f* combination; (*acordo*) arrangement; (*plano*) scheme; (*roupa*) petticoat; ~**nar** *vt* (*juntar*) combine; (*ajustar*) arrange □ *vi* go together, match; ~**nar com** go with, match; ~**nar de sair** arrange to go out; ~**nar-se** *vpr* (*juntar-se*) combine; (*harmonizar-se*) go together, match

comboio /kõ'boju/ *m* convoy; (*Port: trem*) train

combusti|vel /kõbus'tʃivew/ (*pl* ~**veis**) *m* fuel

come|çar /kome'sar/ *vt/i* start, begin; ~**ço** /e/ *m* beginning, start

comédia /ko'mɛdʒia/ *f* comedy

comediante /komedʒi'ãtʃi/ *m/f* comedian (*f* comedienne)

comemo|ração /komemora'sãw/ *f* (*celebração*) celebration; (*lembrança*) commemoration; ~**rar** *vt* (*festejar*) celebrate; (*lembrar*) commemorate; ~**rativo** *a* commemorative

comen|tar /komē'tar/ *vt* comment on; (*falar mal de*) make comments about; ~**tário** *m* comment; (*de texto, na TV etc*) commentary; **sem** ~**tários** no comment; ~**tarista** *m/f* commentator

comer /ko'mer/ *vt* eat; <*ferrugem etc*> eat away; take <*peça de xadrez*> □ *vi* eat; ~**-se** *vpr* (*de raiva etc*) be

consumed (**de** with); **dar de ~ a** feed

comerci|al /komersi'aw/ (*pl* ~**ais**) *a & m* commercial; ~**alizar** *vt* market; ~**ante** *m/f* trader; ~**ar** *vi* do business, trade; ~**ário** *m* shopworker

comércio /ko'mɛrsiu/ *m* (*atividade*) trade; (*loja etc*) business; (*lojas*) shops

comes /'komis/ *m pl* ~ **e bebes** (*fam*) food and drink; ~**tíveis** *m pl* foods, food; ~**tível** (*pl* ~**tíveis**) *a* edible

cometa /ko'meta/ *m* comet

cometer /kome'ter/ *vt* commit <*crime*>; make <*erro*>

comichão /komi'ʃãw/ *f* itch

comício /ko'misiu/ *m* rally

cômico /'komiku/ *a* (*de comédia*) comic; (*engraçado*) comical

comida /ko'mida/ *f* food; (*uma*) meal

comigo = **com + mim**

comi|lão /komi'lãw/ *a* (*f* ~**lona**) greedy □ *m* (*f* ~**lona**) glutton

cominho /ko'miɲu/ *m* cummin

comiserar-se /komize'rarsi/ *vpr* commiserate (**de** with)

comis|são /komi'sãw/ *f* commission; ~**sário** *m* commissioner; ~**sário de bordo** (*aéreo*) steward; (*de navio*) purser; ~**sionar** *vt* commission

comi|tê /komi'te/ *m* committee; ~**tiva** *f* group; (*de uma pessoa*) retinue

como /'komu/ *adv* (*na condição de*) as; (*da mesma forma que*) like; (*de que maneira*) how □ *conj* as; ~? (*pedindo repetição*) pardon?; ~ **se** as if; **assim** ~ as well as

cômoda /'komoda/ *f* chest of drawers, (*Amer*) bureau

como|didade /komodʒi'dadʒi/ *f* comfort; (*conveniência*) convenience; ~**dismo** *m* complacency; ~**dista** *a* complacent

cômodo /'komodu/ *a* comfortable; (*conveniente*) convenient □ *m* (*aposento*) room

como|vente /komo'vẽtʃi/ *a* moving; ~**ver** *vt* move □ *vi* be moving; ~**ver-se** *vpr* be moved

compacto /kõ'paktu/ *a* compact □ *m* single

compadecer-se /kõpade'sersi/ *vpr* feel pity (**de** for)

compadre /kõ'padri/ *m* (*padrinho*) godfather of one's child; (*pai do afilhado*) father of one's godchild

compaixão /kõpa'ʃãw/ *f* compassion

companhei|rismo /kõpaɲe'rizmu/ *m* companionship; ~**ro** *m* (*de viagem etc*) companion; (*amigo*) friend, mate

companhia /kõpa'ɲia/ *f* company; **fazer ~ a alg** keep s.o. company

compa|ração /kõpara'sãw/ *f* comparison; ~**rar** *vt* compare; ~**rativo**

a comparative; ~**rável** (*pl* ~**ráveis**)
a comparable
compare|cer /kõpare'ser/ *vi* appear;
~**cer a** attend; ~**cimento** *m* attendance
comparsa /kõ'parsa/ *m/f* (*ator*) bit
player; (*cúmplice*) sidekick
comparti|lhar /kõpartʃi'ʎar/ *vt/i*
share (**de** in); ~**mento** *m* compartment
compassado /kõpa'sadu/ *a* (*medido*)
measured; (*ritmado*) regular
compassivo /kõpa'sivu/ *a* compassionate
compasso /kõ'pasu/ *m* (*mus*) beat,
time; (*instrumento*) compass, pair of
compasses
compatí|vel /kõpa'tʃivew/ (*pl* ~**veis**)
a compatible
compatriota /kõpatri'ɔta/ *m/f* compatriot,   fellow   countryman   (*f*
-woman)
compelir /kõpe'lir/ *vt* compel
compene|tração /kõpenetra'sãw/ *f*
conviction;   ~**trar**   *vt*   convince;
~**trar-se** *vpr* convince o.s.
compen|sação /kõpẽsa'sãw/ *f* compensation; (*de cheques*) clearing;
~**sar** *vt* make up for <*defeitos, danos*>; offset <*peso, gastos*>; clear
<*cheques*> □ *vi* <*crime*> pay
compe|tência /kõpe'tẽsia/ *f* competence; ~**tente** *a* competent
compe|tição /kõpetʃi'sãw/ *f* competition; ~**tidor** *m* competitor; ~**tir**
vi compete; ~**tir a** be up to; ~**tividade** *f* competitiveness; ~**titivo** *a*
competitive
compla|cência /kõpla'sẽsia/ *f* complaisance; ~**cente** *a* obliging
complemen|tar /kõplemẽ'tar/ *vt*
complement   □   *a*   complementary;
~**to** *m* complement
comple|tar /kõple'tar/ *vt* complete;
top up <*copo, tanque etc*>; ~**tar 20
anos** turn 20; ~**to** /ɛ/ *a* complete;
(*cheio*) full up; **por** ~**to** completely;
escrever por ~**to** write out in full
comple|xado /kõplek'sadu/ *a* with a
complex; ~**xidade** *f* complexity; ~**xo**
/ɛ/ *a & m* complex
compli|cação /kõplika'sãw/ *f* complication; ~**cado** *a* complicated;
~**car** *vt* complicate; ~**car-se** *vpr* get
complicated
complô /kõ'plo/ *m* conspiracy, plot
com|ponente /kõpo'nẽtʃi/ *a & m*
component;   ~**por** *vt/i* compose;
~**por-se por** (*controlar-se*) compose
o.s.; ~**por-se de** be composed of
compor|tamento /kõporta'mẽtu/ *m*
behaviour;   ~**tar** *vt* hold;   bear   <*dor,
prejuízo*>;   ~**tar-se** *vpr* behave
composi|ção /kõpozi'sãw/ *f* composi-
tion;   (*acordo*) conciliation;   ~**tor** *m*
(*de música*) composer; (*gráfico*) compositor
compos|to /kõ'postu/ *pp de* **compor** □
a compound; <*pessoa*> level-headed □
m compound; ~**to de** made up of;
~**tura** *f* composure
compota /kõ'pɔta/ *f* fruit in syrup
com|pra /'kõpra/ *f* purchase; *pl*
shopping;   **fazer** ~**pras** go shopping;   ~**prador** *m* buyer;   ~**prar**
vt buy;   bribe <*oficial, juiz*>;   pick
<*briga*>
compreen|der /kõprië'der/ *vt* (*conter
em si*) contain; (*estender-se a*) cover,
take in; (*entender*) understand; ~**são**
f understanding; ~**sível** (*pl* ~**síveis**)
a understandable; ~**sivo** *a* understanding
compres|sa /kõ'prɛsa/ *f* compress;
~**são** *f* compression;   ~**sor** *m*
compressor; **rolo** ~**sor** steamroller
compri|do /kõ'pridu/ *a* long;
~**mento** *m* length
compri|mido /kõpri'midu/ *m* pill,
tablet □ *a* <*ar*> compressed; ~**mir**
vt (*apertar*) press; (*reduzir o volume
de*) compress
compromete|dor /kõpromete'dor/ *a*
compromising; ~**ter** *vt* (*envolver*) involve; (*prejudicar*) compromise; ~**ter
alg a fazer** commit s.o. to doing;
~**ter-se** *vpr* (*obrigar-se*) commit o.s.;
(*prejudicar-se*)   compromise   o.s.;
~**tido** *a* (*ocupado*) busy; (*noivo*)
spoken for
compromisso /kõpro'misu/ *m* commitment; (*encontro marcado*) appointment; **sem** ~ without obligation
compro|vação /kõprova'sãw/ *f* proof;
~**vante** *m* receipt; ~**var** *vt* prove
compul|são /kõpuw'sãw/ *f* compulsion;   ~**sivo** *a* compulsive;
~**sório** *a* compulsory
compu|tação /kõputa'sãw/ *f* computation; (*matéria, ramo*) computing;
~**tador** *m* computer; ~**tadorizar** *vt*
computerize; ~**tar** *vt* compute
comum /ko'mũ/ *a* common; ~ (*não especial*) ordinary; **fora do** ~ out of the
ordinary;   **em** ~ <*trabalho*> joint;
<*atuar*> jointly; **ter muito em** ~
have a lot in common
comungar /komũ'gar/ *vi* take communion
comunhão /komu'ɲãw/ *f* communion; (*relig*) (Holy) Communion
comuni|cação /komunika'sãw/ *f*
communication;   ~**cação social/visual** media studies/ graphic design;
~**cado** *m* notice; (*pol*) communiqué;
~**car** *vt* communicate; (*unir*) connect
□   *vi*,   ~**car-se** *vpr* communicate;
~**cativo** *a* communicative

comu|nidade /komuni'dadʒi/ f community; **~nismo** m communism; **~nista** a & m/f communist; **~ nitário** a (da comunidade) community; (para todos juntos) communal

côncavo /'kõkavu/ a concave

conce|ber /kõse'ber/ vt conceive; (imaginar) conceive of □ vi conceive; **~bível** (pl **~bíveis**) a conceivable

conceder /kõse'der/ vt grant; **~ em** accede to

concei|to /kõ'sejtu/ m concept; (opinião) opinion; (fama) reputation; **~tuado** a highly thought of; **~tuar** vt (imaginar) conceptualize; (avaliar) assess

concen|tração /kõsẽtra'sãw/ f concentration; (de jogadores) training camp; **~trar** vt concentrate; **~trar-se** vpr concentrate

concepção /kõsep'sãw/ f conception; (opinião) view

concernir /kõser'nir/ vt **~ a** concern

concerto /kõ'sertu/ m concert

conces|são /kõse'sãw/ f concession; **~sionária** f dealership; **~sionário** m dealer

concha /'kõʃa/ f (de molusco) shell; (colher) ladle

concili|ação /kõsilia'sãw/ f conciliation; **~ador** a conciliatory; **~ar** vt reconcile

concílio /kõ'siliu/ m council

conci|são /kõsi'zãw/ f conciseness; **~so** a concise

conclamar /kõkla'mar/ vt call <eleição, greve>; call upon <pessoa>

conclu|dente /kõklu'dẽtʃi/ a conclusive; **~ir** vt/i conclude; **~são** f conclusion; **~sivo** a concluding

concor|dância /kõkor'dãsia/ f agreement; **~dante** a consistent; **~dar** vi agree (em to) □ vt bring into line; **~data** f abrir **~data** go into liquidation

concórdia /kõ'kɔrdʒia/ f concord

concor|rência /kõko'xẽsia/ f competition (a for); **~rente** a competing; **~rer** vi compete (a for); **~rer para** contribute to; **~rido** a popular

concre|tizar /kõkretʃi'zar/ vt realize; **~tizar-se** vpr be realized; **~to** /ɛ/ a & m concrete

concurso /kõ'kursu/ m contest; (prova) competition

con|dado /kõ'dadu/ m county; **~de** m count

condeco|ração /kõdekora'sãw/ f decoration; **~rar** vt decorate

conde|nação /kõdena'sãw/ f condemnation; (jurid) conviction; **~nar** vt condemn; (jurid) convict

conden|sação /kõdẽsa'sãw/ f condensation; **~sar** vt condense; **~sar-se** vpr condense

condescen|dência /kõdesẽ'dẽsia/ f acquiescence; **~dente** a acquiescent; **~der** vi acquiesce; **~der a** comply with <pedido, desejo>; **~der a ir** condescend to go

condessa /kõ'desa/ f countess

condi|ção /kõdʒi'sãw/ f condition; (qualidade) capacity; **ter ~ção** ou **~ções para be able to; em boas ~ções** in good condition; **~cionado** a conditioned; **~cional** (pl **~cionais**) a conditional; **~cionamento** m conditioning

condimen|tar /kõdʒimẽ'tar/ vt season; **~to** m seasoning

condoer-se /kõdo'ersi/ vpr **~ de** feel sorry for

condolência /kõdo'lẽsia/ f sympathy; pl condolences

condomínio /kõdo'miniu/ m (taxa) service charge

condu|ção /kõdu'sãw/ f (de carro etc) driving; (transporte) transport; **~cente** a conducive (a to); **~ta** f conduct; **~to** m conduit; **~tor** m (de carro) driver; (eletr) conductor; **~zir** vt lead; drive <carro>; (eletr) conduct □ vi (de carro) drive; (levar) lead (a to)

cone /'koni/ m cone

conectar /konek'tar/ vt connect

cone|xão /konek'sãw/ f connection; **~xo** /ɛ/ a connected

confec|ção /kõfek'sãw/ f (roupa) off-the-peg outfit; (loja) clothes shop, boutique; (fábrica) clothes manufacturer; **~cionar** vt make

confederação /kõfedera'sãw/ f confederation

confei|tar /kõfej'tar/ vt ice; **~taria** f cake shop; **~teiro** m confectioner

confe|rência /kõfe'rẽsia/ f conference; (palestra) lecture; **~rencista** m/f speaker

conferir /kõfe'rir/ vt check (com against); (conceder) confer (a on) □ vi (controlar) check; (estar exato) tally

confes|sar /kõfe'sar/ vt/i confess; **~sar-se** vpr confess; **~sionário** m confessional; **~sor** m confessor

confete /kõ'fɛtʃi/ m confetti

confi|ança /kõfi'ãsa/ f (convicção) confidence; (fé) trust; **~ante** a confident (em of); **~ar** (dar) entrust; **~ar em** trust; **~ável** (pl **~áveis**) a reliable; **~dência** f confidence; **~dencial** (pl **~denciais**) a confidential; **~denciar** vt tell in confidence; **~dente** m/f confidant (f confidante)

configu|ração /kõfigura'sãw/ f configuration; **~rar** vt (representar) represent; (formar) shape; (comput) configure

con|finar /kõfi'nar/ *vi* ~**finar com** border on; ~**fins** *m pl* borders

confir|mação /kõfirma'sãw/ *f* confirmation; ~**mar** *vt* confirm; ~**mar-se** *vpr* be confirmed

confis|car /kõfis'kar/ *vt* confiscate; ~**co** *m* confiscation

confissão /kõfi'sãw/ *f* confession

confla|gração /kõflagra'sãw/ *f* conflagration; ~**grar** *vt* set alight; (*fig*) throw into turmoil

confli|tante /kõfli'tãtʃi/ *a* conflicting; ~**to** *m* conflict

confor|mação /kõforma'sãw/ *f* resignation; ~**mado** *a* resigned (**com** to); ~**mar** *vt* adapt (**a** to); ~**mar-se com** conform to <*regra, política*>; resign o.s. to, come to terms with <*destino, evento*>; ~**me** /ɔ/ *prep* according to □ *conj* depending on; ~**me** it depends; ~**midade** *f* conformity; ~**mismo** *m* conformism; ~**mista** *a* & *m/f* conformist

confor|tar /kõfor'tar/ *vt* comfort; ~**tável** (*pl* ~**táveis**) *a* comfortable; ~**to** /o/ *m* comfort

confraternizar /kõfraterni'zar/ *vi* fraternize

confron|tação /kõfrõta'sãw/ *f* confrontation; ~**tar** *vt* confront; (*comparar*) compare; ~**to** *m* confrontation; (*comparação*) comparison

con|fundir /kõfũ'dʒir/ *vt* confuse; ~**fundir-se** *vpr* get confused; ~**fusão** *f* confusion; (*desordem*) mess; (*tumulto*) commotion; ~**fuso** *a* (*confundido*) confused; (*que confunde*) confusing

conge|lador /kõʒela'dor/ *m* freezer; ~**lamento** *m* (*de preços etc*) freeze; ~**lar** *vt* freeze; ~**lar-se** *vpr* freeze

congênito /kõ'ʒenitu/ *a* congenital

congestão /kõʒes'tãw/ *f* congestion

congestio|nado /kõʒestʃio'nadu/ *a* <*rua, cidade*> congested; <*pessoa, rosto*> flushed; <*olhos*> bloodshot; ~**namento** *m* (*de trânsito*) traffic jam; ~**nar** *vt* congest; ~**nar-se** *vpr* <*rua*> get congested; <*rosto*> flush

conglomerado /kõglome'radu/ *m* conglomerate

congratular /kõgratu'lar/ *vt* congratulate (**por** on)

congre|gação /kõgrega'sãw/ *f* (*na igreja*) congregation; (*reunião*) gathering; ~**gar** *vt* bring together; ~**gar-se** *vpr* congregate

congresso /kõ'grɛsu/ *m* congress

conhaque /ko'ɲaki/ *m* brandy

conhe|cedor /koɲese'dor/ *a* knowing □ *m* connoisseur; ~**cer** *vt* know; (*ser apresentado a*) get to know; (*visitar*) go to, visit; ~**cido** *a* known; (*famoso*) well-known □ *m* acquaintance;

~**cimento** *m* knowledge; **tomar** ~**cimento de** learn of; **travar** ~**cimento com alg** make s.o.'s acquaintance, become acquainted with s.o.

cônico /'koniku/ *a* conical

coni|vência /koni'vẽsia/ *f* connivance; ~**vente** *a* conniving (**em** at)

conjetu|ra /kõʒe'tura/ *f* conjecture; ~**rar** *vt/i* conjecture

conju|gação /kõʒuga'sãw/ *f* (*ling*) conjugation; ~**gar** *vt* conjugate <*verbo*>

cônjuge /'kõʒuʒi/ *m/f* spouse

conjun|ção /kõʒũ'sãw/ *f* conjunction; ~**tivo** *a* & *m* subjunctive; ~**to** *a* joint □ *m* set; (*roupa*) outfit; (*musical*) group; **o** ~**to de** the body of; **em** ~**to** jointly; ~**tura** *f* state of affairs; (*econômica*) state of the economy

conosco = **com** + **nós**

cono|tação /konota'sãw/ *f* connotation; ~**tar** *vt* connote

conquanto /kõ'kwãtu/ *conj* although, even though

conquis|ta /kõ'kista/ *f* conquest; (*proeza*) achievement; ~**tador** *m* conqueror □ *a* conquering; ~**tar** *vt* conquer <*terra, país*>; win <*riqueza, independência*>; win over <*pessoa*>

consa|gração /kõsagra'sãw/ *f* (*de uma igreja*) consecration; (*dedicação*) dedication; ~**grado** *a* <*artista, expressão*> established; ~**grar** *vt* consecrate <*igreja*>; establish <*artista, estilo*>; (*dedicar*) dedicate (**a** to); ~**grar-se a** dedicate o.s. to

consci|ência /kõsi'ẽsia/ *f* (*moralidade*) conscience; (*sentidos*) consciousness; (*no trabalho*) conscientiousness; (*de um fato etc*) awareness; ~**encioso** /o/ *a* conscientious; ~**ente** *a* conscious; ~**entizar** *vt* make aware (**de** of); ~**entizar-se** *vpr* become aware (**de** of)

consecutivo /kõseku'tʃivu/ *a* consecutive

conse|guinte /kõse'gĩtʃi/ **a por** ~**guinte** consequently; ~**guir** *vt* get; ~**guir fazer** manage to do □ *vi* succeed

conse|lheiro /kõse'ʎeru/ *m* counsellor, adviser; ~**lho** /e/ *m* piece of advice; *pl* advice; (*órgão*) council

consen|so /kõ'sẽsu/ *m* consensus; ~**timento** *m* consent; ~**tir** *vt* allow □ *vi* consent (**em** to)

conse|qüência /kõse'kwẽsia/ *f* consequence; **por** ~**qüência** consequently; ~**qüente** *a* consequent; (*coerente*) consistent

conser|tar /kõser'tar/ *vt* repair; ~**to** /e/ *m* repair

conser|va /kõ'sɛrva/ f (*em vidro*) preserve; (*em lata*) tinned food; ~**vação** f preservation; ~**vador** *a* & *m* conservative; ~**vadorismo** *m* conservatism; ~**vante** *a* & *m* preservative; ~**var** *vt* preserve; (*manter, guardar*) keep; ~**var-se** *vpr* keep; ~**vatório** *m* conservatory

conside|ração /kõsidera'sãw/ f consideration; (*estima*) esteem; **levar em** ~**ração** take into consideration; ~**rar** *vt* consider; (*estimar*) think highly of □ *vi* consider; ~**rar-se** *vpr* consider o.s.; ~**rável** (*pl* ~**ráveis**) *a* considerable

consig|nação /kõsigna'sãw/ f consignment; ~**nar** *vt* consign

consigo = **com** + **si**

consis|tência /kõsis'tẽsia/ f consistency; ~**tente** *a* firm; ~**tir** *vi* consist (**em** in)

consoante /kõso'ãtʃi/ f consonant

conso|lação /kõsola'sãw/ f consolation; ~**lador** *a* consoling; ~**lar** *vt* console; ~**lar-se** *vpr* console o.s.

consolidar /kõsoli'dar/ *vt* consolidate; mend <*fratura*>

consolo /kõ'solu/ *m* consolation

consórcio /kõ'sɔrsiu/ *m* consortium

consorte /kõ'sɔrtʃi/ *m/f* consort

conspícuo /kõs'pikuu/ *a* conspicuous

conspi|ração /kõspira'sãw/ f conspiracy; ~**rador** *m* conspirator; ~**rar** *vi* conspire

cons|tância /kõs'tãsia/ f constancy; ~**tante** *a* & *f* constant; ~**tar** *vi* (*em lista etc*) appear; **não me** ~**ta** I am not aware; ~**ta que** it is said that; ~**tar de** consist of

consta|tação /kõstata'sãw/ f observation; ~**tar** *vt* note, notice; certify <*óbito*>

conste|lação /kõstela'sãw/ f constellation; ~**lado** *a* star-studded

conster|nação /kõsterna'sãw/ f consternation; ~**nar** *vt* dismay

consti|pação /kõstʃipa'sãw/ f (*Port: resfriado*) cold; ~**pado** *a* (*resfriado*) with a cold; (*no intestino*) constipated; ~**par-se** *vpr* (*Port: resfriar-se*) get a cold

constitu|cional /kõstʃitusio'naw/ (*pl* ~**cionais**) *a* constitutional; ~**ição** f constitution; ~**inte** *a* constituent □ f **Constituinte** Constituent Assembly; ~**ir** *vt* form <*governo, sociedade*>; (*representar*) constitute; (*nomear*) appoint

constran|gedor /kõstrãʒe'dor/ *a* embarrassing; ~**ger** *vt* embarrass; (*coagir*) constrain; ~**ger-se** *vpr* get embarrassed; ~**gimento** *m* (*embaraço*) embarrassment; (*coação*) constraint

constru|ção /kõstru'sãw/ f construction; (*terreno*) building site; ~**ir** *vt* build <*casa, prédio*>; (*fig*) construct; ~**tivo** *a* constructive; ~**tor** *m* builder; ~**tora** f building firm

cônsul /'kõsuw/ (*pl* ~**es**) *m* consul

consulado /kõsu'ladu/ *m* consulate

consul|ta /kõ'suwta/ f consultation; ~**tar** *vt* consult; ~**tor** *m* consultant; ~**toria** f consultancy; ~**tório** *m* (*médico*) surgery, (*Amer*) office

consu|mação /kõsuma'sãw/ f (*taxa*) minimum charge; ~**mado** *a* **fato** ~**mado** fait accompli; ~**mar** *vt* accomplish <*projeto*>; carry out <*crime, sacrifício*>; consummate <*casamento*>

consu|midor /kõsumi'dor/ *a* & *m* consumer; ~**mir** *vt* consume; take up <*tempo*>; ~**mismo** *m* consumerism; ~**mista** *a* & *m/f* consumerist; ~**mo** *m* consumption

conta /'kõta/ f (*a pagar*) bill; (*bancária*) account; (*contagem*) count; (*de vidro etc*) bead; *pl* (*com*) accounts; **em** ~ economical; **por** ~ **de** on account of; **por** ~ **própria** on one's own account; **ajustar** ~**s** settle up; **dar** ~ **de** (*fig*) be up to; **dar** ~ **do recado** (*fam*) deliver the goods; **dar-se** ~ **de** realize; **fazer de** ~ pretend; **ficar por** ~ **de** be left to; **levar** *ou* **ter em** ~ take into account; **prestar** ~**s de** account for; **tomar** ~ **de** take care of; ~ **bancária** bank account; ~ **corrente** current account

contabi|lidade /kõtabili'dadʒi/ f accountancy; (*contas*) accounts; (*seção*) accounts department; ~**lista** (*Port*) *m/f* accountant; ~**lizar** *vt* write up <*quantia*>; (*fig*) notch up

contact- (*Port*) *veja* **contat-**

conta|dor /kõta'dor/ *m* (*pessoa*) accountant; (*de luz etc*) meter; ~**gem** f counting; (*de pontos num jogo*) scoring; ~**gem regressiva** countdown

contagi|ante /kõtaʒi'ãtʃi/ *a* infectious; ~**ar** *vt* infect; ~**ar-se** *vpr* become infected

contágio /kõ'taʒiu/ *m* infection

contagioso /kõtaʒi'ozu/ *a* contagious

contami|nação /kõtamina'sãw/ f contamination; ~**nar** *vt* contaminate

contanto /kõ'tãtu/ *adv* ~ **que** provided that

contar /kõ'tar/ *vt/i* count; (*narrar*) tell; ~ **com** count on

conta|tar /kõta'tar/ *vt* contact; ~**to** *m* contact; **entrar em** ~**to com** get in touch with; **tomar** ~**to com** come into contact with

contem|plação /kõtẽpla'sãw/ f contemplation; ~**plar** *vt* (*considerar*) contemplate; *(dizer respeito a)* concern; **~plar alg com** treat s.o. to □ *vi* ponder; **~plativo** *a* contemplative

contemporâneo /kõtẽpo'raniu/ *a & m* contemporary

contenção /kõtẽ'sãw/ *f* containment

conten|cioso /kõtẽsi'ozu/ *a* contentious; **~da** *f* dispute

conten|tamento /kõtẽta'mẽtu/ *m* contentment; **~tar** *vt* satisfy; **~tar-se** *vpr* be content; **~te** *a (feliz)* happy; *(satisfeito)* content; **~to** *m* a **~to** satisfactorily

conter /kõ'ter/ *vt* contain; **~-se** *vpr* contain o.s.

conterrâneo /kõte'xaniu/ *m* fellow countryman *(f* -woman)

contestar /kõtes'tar/ *vt* question; *(jurid)* contest

conteúdo /kõte'udu/ *m (de recipiente)* contents; *(fig: de carta etc)* content

contexto /kõ'testu/ *m* context

contigo = com + ti

continência /kõtʃi'nẽsia/ *f (mil)* salute

continen|tal /kõtʃinẽ'taw/ *(pl* **~tais)** *a* continental; **~te** *m* continent

contin|gência /kõtʃĩ'ʒẽsia/ *f* contingency; **~gente** *a (eventual)* possible; *(incerto)* contingent □ *m* contingent

continu|ação /kõtʃinua'sãw/ *f* continuation; **~ar** *vt/i* continue; **eles ~am ricos** they are still rich; **~idade** *f* continuity

contínuo /kõ'tʃinuu/ *a* continuous □ *m* office junior

con|tista /kõ'tʃista/ *m/f* (short) story writer; **~to** *m* (short) story; **~to de fadas** fairy tale; **~to-do-vigário** *(pl* **~tos-do-vigário)** *m* confidence trick, swindle

contorcer /kõtor'ser/ *vt* twist; **~-se** *vpr (de dor)* writhe

contor|nar /kõtor'nar/ *vt* go round; *(fig)* get round *<obstáculo, problema>*; *(cercar)* surround; *(delinear)* outline; **~no** /o/ *m* outline; *(da paisagem)* contour

contra /'kõtra/ *prep* against

contra-|atacar /kõtrata'kar/ *vt* counterattack; **~-ataque** *m* counterattack

contrabaixo /kõtra'baʃu/ *m* double bass

contrabalançar /kõtrabalã'sar/ *vt* counterbalance

contraban|dear /kõtrabãdʒi'ar/ *vt* smuggle; **~dista** *m/f* smuggler; **~do** *m (ato)* smuggling; *(artigos)* contraband

contração /kõtra'sãw/ *f* contraction

contracenar /kõtrase'nar/ *vi* **~ com** play up to

contraceptivo /kõtrasep'tʃivu/ *a & m* contraceptive

contracheque /kõtra'ʃɛki/ *m* pay slip

contradi|ção /kõtradʒi'sãw/ *f* contradiction; **~tório** *a* contradictory; **~zer** *vt* contradict; **~zer-se** *vpr <pessoa>* contradict o.s.; *<idéias etc>* be contradictory

contragosto /kõtra'gostu/ *m* **a ~** reluctantly

contrair /kõtra'ir/ *vt* contract; pick up *<hábito, vício>*; **~-se** *vpr* contract

contramão /kõtra'mãw/ *f* opposite direction □ *a invar* one way

contramestre /kõtra'mestri/ *m* supervisor; *(em navio)* bosun

contra-ofensiva /kõtraofẽ'siva/ *f* counter-offensive

contrapartida /kõtrapar'tʃida/ *f (fig)* compensation; **em ~** on the other hand

contraproducente /kõtraprodu-'sẽtʃi/ *a* counter-productive

contrari|ar /kõtrari'ar/ *vt* go against, run counter to; *(aborrecer)* annoy; **~edade** *f* adversity; *(aborrecimento)* annoyance

contrário /kõ'trariu/ *a* opposite; *(desfavorável)* adverse; **~a** contrary to; *<pessoa>* opposed to □ *m* opposite; **pelo** *ou* **ao ~** on the contrary; **ao ~ de** contrary to; **em ~** to the contrary

contras|tante /kõtras'tãtʃi/ *a* contrasting; **~tar** *vt/i* contrast; **~te** *m* contrast

contra|tante /kõtra'tãtʃi/ *m/f* contractor; **~tar** *vt* employ, take on *<operários>*

contra|tempo /kõtra'tẽpu/ *m* hitch

contra|to /kõ'tratu/ *m* contract; **~tual** *(pl* **~tuais)** *a* contractual

contraven|ção /kõtravẽ'sãw/ *f* contravention; **~tor** *m* offender

contribu|ição /kõtribui'sãw/ *f* contribution; **~inte** *m/f* contributor; *(pagador de impostos)* taxpayer; **~ir** *vt* contribute □ *vi* contribute; *(pagar impostos)* pay tax

contrição /kõtri'sãw/ *f* contrition

contro|lar /kõtro'lar/ *vt* control; *(fiscalizar)* check; **~le** /o/, *(Port)* **~lo** /o/ *m* control; *(fiscalização)* check

contro|vérsia /kõtro'vɛrsia/ *f* controversy; **~verso** /ɛ/ *a* controversial

contudo /kõ'tudu/ *conj* nevertheless

contundir /kõtũ'dʒir/ *vt (dar hematoma em)* bruise; injure *<jogador>*; **~-se** *vpr* bruise o.s.; *<jogador>* get injured

conturbado /kõtur'badu/ *a* troubled

contu|são /kõtu'zãw/ *f* bruise; *(de jogador)* injury; **~so** *a* bruised; *<jogador>* injured

convales|cença /kõvale'sẽsa/ f convalescence; **~cer** vi convalesce
convenção /kõvẽ'sãw/ f convention
conven|cer /kõvẽ'ser/ vt convince; **~cido** a (convicto) convinced; (metido) conceited; **~cimento** m (convicção) conviction; (imodéstia) conceitedness
convencio|nal /kõvẽsio'naw/ (pl **~nais**) a conventional
conveni|ência /kõveni'ẽsia/ f convenience; **~ente** a convenient; (cabível) appropriate
convênio /kõ'veniu/ m agreement
convento /kõ'vẽtu/ m convent
convergir /kõver'ʒir/ vi converge
conver|sa /kõ'vɛrsa/ f conversation; a **~sa dele** the things he says; **~sa fiada** idle talk; **~sação** f conversation; **~sado** a <pessoa> talkative; <assunto> talked about; **~sador** a talkative
conversão /kõver'sãw/ f conversion
conversar /kõver'sar/ vi talk
conver|sível /kõver'sivew/ (pl **~síveis**) a & m convertible; **~ter** vt convert; **~ter-se** vpr be converted; **~tido** m convert
con|vés /kõ'vɛs/ (pl **~veses**) m deck
convexo /kõ'vɛksu/ a convex
convic|ção /kõvik'sãw/ f conviction; **~to** a convinced; (ferrenho) confirmed; <criminoso> convicted
convi|dado /kõvi'dadu/ m guest; **~dar** vt invite; **~dativo** a inviting
convincente /kõvĩ'sẽtʃi/ a convincing
convir /kõ'vir/ vi (ficar bem) be appropriate; (concordar) agree (em on); **~ a** suit, be convenient for; **convém notar que** one should note that
convite /kõ'vitʃi/ m invitation
convi|vência /kõvi'vẽsia/ f coexistence; (relação) close contact; **~ver** vi coexist; (ter relações) associate (com with)
convívio /kõ'viviu/ m association (com with)
convocar /kõvo'kar/ vt call <eleições, greve>; call upon <pessoa> (a to); (ao serviço militar) call up
convosco = com + vós
convul|são /kõvuw'sãw/ f (do corpo) convulsion; (da sociedade etc) upheaval; **~sionar** vt convulse <corpo>; (fig) churn up; **~sivo** a convulsive
cooper /'kuper/ m jogging; **fazer ~** go jogging
coope|ração /koopera'sãw/ f cooperation; **~rar** vi cooperate; **~rativa** f cooperative; **~rativo** a cooperative
coorde|nação /koordena'sãw/ f coordination; **~nada** f coordinate; **~nar** vt coordinate

copa /'kɔpa/ f (de árvore) top; (aposento) breakfast room; (torneio) cup; pl (naipe) hearts; **a Copa (do Mundo)** the World Cup; **~-cozinha** (pl **~s-cozinhas**) f kitchen-diner
cópia /'kɔpia/ f copy
copiar /kopi'ar/ vt copy
co-piloto /kopi'lotu/ m co-pilot
copioso /kopi'ozu/ a ample; <refeição> substantial
copo /'kɔpu/ m glass
coque /'kɔki/ m (penteado) bun
coqueiro /ko'keru/ m coconut palm
coqueluche /koke'luʃi/ f (doença) whooping cough; (mania) fad
coque|tel /koke'tɛw/ (pl **~téis**) m cocktail; (reunião) cocktail party
cor[1] /kɔr/ m **de ~** by heart
cor[2] /kor/ f colour; **TV a ~es** colour TV; **pessoa de ~** coloured person
coração /kora'sãw/ m heart
cora|gem /ko'raʒẽ/ f courage; **~joso** /o/ a courageous
co|ral[1] /ko'raw/ (pl **~rais**) m (animal) coral
co|ral[2] /ko'raw/ (pl **~rais**) m (de cantores) choir □ a choral
co|rante /ko'rãtʃi/ a & m colouring; **~rar** vt colour □ vi blush
cor|da /'kɔrda/ f rope; (mus) string; (para roupa lavada) clothes line; **dar ~da em** wind <relógio>; **~da bamba** tightrope; **~das vocais** vocal chords; **~dão** m cord; (de sapatos) lace; (policial) cordon
cordeiro /kor'deru/ m lamb
cor|del /kor'dɛw/ (pl **~déis**) (Port) m string; **literatura de ~del** trash
cor-de-rosa /kordʒi'rɔza/ a invar pink
cordi|al /kordʒi'aw/ (pl **~ais**) a & m cordial; **~alidade** f cordiality
cordilheira /kordʒi'ʎera/ f chain of mountains
coreano /kori'anu/ a & m Korean
Coréia /ko'rεja/ f Korea
core|ografia /koriogra'fia/ f choreography; **~ógrafo** m choreographer
coreto /ko'retu/ m bandstand
coriza /ko'riza/ f runny nose
corja /'kɔrʒa/ f pack; (de pessoas) rabble
córner /'kɔrner/ m corner
coro /'kɔru/ m chorus
coro|a /ko'roa/ f crown; (de flores etc) wreath □ (fam) m/f old man (f woman); **~ação** f coronation; **~ar** vt crown
coro|nel /koro'nɛw/ (pl **~néis**) m colonel
coronha /ko'roɲa/ f butt
corpete /kor'petʃi/ m bodice
corpo /'kɔrpu/ m body; (físico de mulher) figure; (físico de homem)

physique; ~ **de bombeiros** fire brigade; ~ **diplomático** diplomatic corps; ~ **docente** teaching staff, (*Amer*) faculty; ~**-a-**~ *m invar* pitched battle; ~**ral** (*pl* ~**rais**) *a* physical; <*pena*> corporal

corpu|lência /korpu'lẽsia/ *f* stoutness; ~**lento** *a* stout

correção /koxe'sãw/ *f* correction

corre-corre /kɔxi'kɔxi/ *m* (*debandada*) stampede; (*correria*) rush

correct- (*Port*) *veja* **corret-**

corre|diço /koxe'dʒisu/ *a* <*porta*> sliding; ~**dor** *m* (*atleta*) runner; (*passagem*) corridor

correia /ko'xeja/ *f* strap; (*peça de máquina*) belt; (*para cachorro*) lead, (*Amer*) leash

correio /ko'xeju/ *m* post, mail; (*repartição*) post office; **pôr no** ~ post, (*Amer*) mail; ~ **aéreo** air mail

correlação /koxela'sãw/ *f* correlation

correligionário /koxeliʒio'nariu/ *m* party colleague

corrente /ko'xẽtʃi/ *a* <*água*> running; <*mês, conta*> current; <*estilo*> fluid; (*usual*) common □ *f* (*de água, eletricidade*) current; (*cadeia*) chain; ~ **de ar** draught; ~**za** /e/ *f* current; (*de ar*) draught

cor|rer /ko'xer/ *vi* (*à pé*) run; (*de carro*) drive fast, speed; (*fazer rápido*) rush; <*água, sangue*> flow; <*tempo*> elapse; <*boato*> go round □ *vt* draw <*cortina*>; run <*risco*>; ~**reria** *f* rush

correspon|dência /koxespõ'dẽsia/ *f* correspondence; ~**dente** *a* corresponding □ *m/f* correspondent; (*equivalente*) equivalent; ~**der** *vi* ~**der a** correspond to; (*retribuir*) return; ~**der-se** *vpr* correspond (*com* with)

corre|tivo /koxe'tʃivu/ *a* corrective □ *m* punishment; ~**to** /ɛ/ *a* correct

corretor /koxe'tor/ *m* broker; ~ **de imóveis** estate agent, (*Amer*) realtor

corrida /ko'xida/ *f* (*prova*) race; (*ação de correr*) run; (*de taxi*) ride

corrigir /koxi'ʒir/ *vt* correct

corrimão /koxi'mãw/ (*pl* ~**s**) *m* handrail; (*de escada*) banister

corriqueiro /koxi'keru/ *a* ordinary, run-of-the-mill

corroborar /koxobo'rar/ *vt* corroborate

corroer /koxo'er/ *vt* corrode <*metal*>; (*fig*) erode; ~**-se** *vpr* corrode; (*fig*) erode

corromper /koxõ'per/ *vt* corrupt; ~**-se** *vpr* be corrupted

corro|são /koxo'zãw/ *f* (*de metal*) corrosion; (*fig*) erosion; ~**sivo** *a* corrosive

corrup|ção /koxup'sãw/ *f* corruption; ~**to** *a* corrupt

cor|tada /kor'tada/ *f* (*em tênis*) smash; (*em pessoa*) put-down; ~**tante** *a* cutting; ~**tar** *vt* cut; cut off <*luz, telefone, perna etc*>; cut down <*árvore*>; cut out <*efeito, vício*>; take away <*prazer*>; (*com o carro*) cut up; (*desprazar*) cut dead □ *vi* cut; ~**tar o cabelo** (*no cabeleireiro*) get one's hair cut; ~**te**[1] /ɔ/ *m* cut; (*gume*) blade; (*desenho*) cross-section; **sem** ~**te** <*faca*> blunt; ~**te de cabelo** haircut

cor|te[2] /'kortʃi/ *f* court; ~**tejar** *vt* court; ~**tejo** /e/ *m* (*séquito*) retinue; (*fúnebre*) cortège; ~**tês** *a* (*f* ~**tesa**) courteous, polite; ~**tesão** (*pl* ~**tesãos**) *m* courtier; ~**tesia** *f* courtesy

corti|ça /kor'tʃisa/ *f* cork; ~**ço** *m* (*casa popular*) slum tenement

cortina /kor'tʃina/ *f* curtain

cortisona /kortʃi'zona/ *f* cortisone

coruja /ko'ruʒa/ *f* owl □ *a* <*pai, mãe*> proud, doting

coruscar /korus'kar/ *vi* flash

corvo /'korvu/ *m* crow

cós /kɔs/ *m invar* waistband

coser /ko'zer/ *vt/i* sew

cosmético /koz'mɛtʃiku/ *a & m* cosmetic

cósmico /'kɔzmiku/ *a* cosmic

cosmo /'kɔzmu/ *m* cosmos; ~**nauta** *m/f* cosmonaut; ~**polita** *a* cosmopolitan □ *m/f* globetrotter

costa /'kɔsta/ *f* coast; *pl* (*dorso*) back; **Costa do Marfim** Ivory Coast; **Costa Rica** Costa Rica

costarriquenho /kostaxi'keɲu/ *a & m* Costa Rican

cos|teiro /kos'teru/ *a* coastal; ~**tela** /ɛ/ *f* rib; ~**teleta** /e/ *f* chop; *pl* (*suíças*) sideburns; ~**telinha** *f* (*de porco*) spare rib

costu|mar /kostu'mar/ *vt* ~**ma fazer** he usually does; ~**mava fazer** used to do; ~**me** *m* (*uso*) custom; (*traje*) costume; **de** ~**me** usually; **como de** ~**me** as usual; **ter o** ~**me de** have a habit of; ~**meiro** *a* customary

costu|ra /kos'tura/ *f* sewing; ~**rar** *vt/i* sew; ~**reira** *f* (*mulher*) dressmaker; (*caixa*) needlework box

co|ta /'kɔta/ *f* quota; ~**tação** *f* (*preço*) rate; (*apreço*) rating; ~**tado** *a* <*ação*> quoted; (*conceituado*) highly rated; ~**tar** *vt* rate; quote <*ações*>

cote|jar /kote'ʒar/ *vt* compare; ~**jo** /e/ *m* comparison

cotidiano /kotʃidʒi'anu/ *a* everyday □ *m* everyday life

cotonete /koto'nɛtʃi/ *m* cotton bud

cotove|lada /kotove'lada/ *f* (*para abrir caminho*) nudge; **~lo** /e/ *m* elbow

coura|ça /ko'rasa/ *f* (*armadura*) breastplate; (*de navio, animal*) armour; **~çado** (*Port*) *m* battleship

couro /'koru/ *m* leather; **~ cabeludo** scalp

couve /'kovi/ *f* spring greens; **~-de-bruxelas** (*pl* **~s-de-bruxelas**) *f* Brussels sprout; **~-flor** (*pl* **~s-flores**) *f* cauliflower

couvert /ku'vɛr/ (*pl* **~s**) *m* cover charge

cova /'kɔva/ *f* (*buraco*) pit; (*sepultura*) grave

covar|de /ko'vardʒi/ *m/f* coward □ *a* cowardly; **~dia** *f* cowardice

coveiro /ko'veru/ *m* gravedigger

covil /ko'viw/ (*pl* **~vis**) *m* den, lair

covinha /ko'viɲa/ *f* dimple

co|xa /'koʃa/ *f* thigh; **~xear** *vi* hobble

coxia /ko'ʃia/ *f* aisle

coxo /'koʃu/ *a* hobbling; **ser ~** hobble

co|zer /ko'zer/ *vt/i* cook; **~zido** *m* stew, casserole

cozi|nha /ko'ziɲa/ *f* (*aposento*) kitchen; (*comida, ação*) cooking; (*arte*) cookery; **~nhar** *vt/i* cook; **~nheiro** *m* cook

crachá /kra'ʃa/ *m* badge, (*Amer*) button

crânio /'kraniu/ *m* skull; (*pessoa*) genius

crápula /'krapula/ *m/f* scoundrel

craque /'kraki/ *m* (*de futebol*) soccer star; (*fam*) expert

crase /'krazi/ *f* contraction; **a com ~** a grave (à)

crasso /'krasu/ *a* crass

cratera /kra'tɛra/ *f* crater

cravar /kra'var/ *vt* drive in <*prego*>; dig <*unha*>; stick <*estaca*>; **~ com os olhos** stare at; **~-se** *vpr* stick

cravejar /krave'ʒar/ *vt* nail; (*com balas*) spray, riddle

cravo¹ /'kravu/ *m* (*flor*) carnation; (*condimento*) clove

cravo² /'kravu/ *m* (*na pele*) blackhead; (*prego*) nail

cravo³ /'kravu/ *m* (*instrumento*) harpsichord

creche /'krɛʃi/ *f* crèche

credenci|ais /kredēsi'ajs/ *f pl* credentials; **~ar** *vt* qualify

credi|ário /kredʒi'ariu/ *m* hire purchase agreement, credit plan; **~bilidade** *f* credibility; **~tar** *vt* credit

crédito /'krɛdʒitu/ *m* credit; **a ~** on credit

cre|do /'krɛdu/ *m* creed □ *int* heavens; **~dor** *m* creditor □ *a* <*saldo*> credit

crédulo /'krɛdulu/ *a* gullible

cre|mação /krema'sãw/ *f* cremation; **~mar** *vt* cremate; **~matório** *m* crematorium

cre|me /'krɛmi/ *a invar & m* cream; **~me Chantilly** whipped cream; **~me de leite** (sterilized) cream; **~moso** /o/ *a* creamy

cren|ça /'krēsa/ *f* belief; **~dice** *f* superstition; **~te** *m* believer; (*protestante*) Protestant □ *a* religious; (*protestante*) Protestant; **estar ~te que** believe that

crepe /'krɛpi/ *m* crepe

crepitar /krepi'tar/ *vi* crackle

crepom /kre'põ/ *m* crepe; **papel ~** tissue paper

crepúsculo /kre'puskulu/ *m* twilight

crer /krer/ *vt/i* believe (**em** in); **creio que** I think (that); **~-se** *vpr* believe o.s. to be

cres|cendo /kre'sēdu/ *m* crescendo; **~cente** *a* growing □ *m* crescent; **~cer** *vi* grow; <*bolo*> rise; **~cido** *a* grown; **~cimento** *m* growth

crespo /'krespu/ *a* <*cabelo*> frizzy; <*mar*> choppy

cretino /kre'tʃinu/ *m* cretin

cria /'kria/ *f* baby; *pl* young

criação /kria'sãw/ *f* creation; (*educação*) upbringing; (*de animais*) raising; (*gado*) livestock

criado /kri'adu/ *m* servant; **~-mudo** (*pl* **~s-mudos**) *m* bedside table

criador /kria'dor/ *m* creator; (*de animais*) farmer, breeder

crian|ça /kri'āsa/ *f* child □ *a* childish; **~çada** *f* kids; **~cice** *f* childishness; (*uma*) childish thing

criar /kri'ar/ *vt* (*fazer*) create; bring up <*filhos*>; rear <*animais*>; grow <*planta*>; pluck up <*coragem*>; **~-se** *vpr* be brought up, grow up

criati|vidade /kriatʃivi'dadʒi/ *f* creativity; **~vo** *a* creative

criatura /kria'tura/ *f* creature

crime /'krimi/ *m* crime

crimi|nal /krimi'naw/ (*pl* **~nais**) *a* criminal; **~nalidade** *f* crime; **~noso** *m* criminal

crina /'krina/ *f* mane

crioulo /kri'olu/ *a & m* creole; (*negro*) black

cripta /'kripta/ *f* crypt

crisálida /kri'zalida/ *f* chrysalis

crisântemo /kri'zãtemu/ *m* chrysanthemum

crise /'krizi/ *f* crisis

cris|ma /'krizma/ *f* confirmation; **~mar** *vt* confirm; **~mar-se** *vpr* get confirmed

crista /'krista/ *f* crest

cris|tal /kris'taw/ (*pl* **~tais**) *m* crystal; (*vidro*) glass; **~talino** *a* crystal-clear; **~talizar** *vt/i* crystallize

cris|tandade /kristã'dadʒi/ f Christendom; ~tão (pl ~tãos) a & m (f ~tã) Christian; ~tianismo m Christianity

Cristo /'kristu/ m Christ

cri|tério /kri'tɛriu/ m discretion; (norma) criterion; ~terioso a perceptive, discerning

crítica /'kritʃika/ f criticism; (análise) critique; (de filme, livro) review; (críticos) critics

criticar /kritʃi'kar/ vt criticize; review <filme, livro>

crítico /'kritʃiku/ a critical □ m critic

crivar /kri'var/ vt (furar) riddle

crí|vel /'krivew/ (pl ~veis) a credible

crivo /'krivu/ m sieve; (fig) scrutiny

crocante /kro'kãtʃi/ a crunchy

crochê /kro'ʃe/ m crochet

crocodilo /kroko'dʒilu/ m crocodile

cromo /'kromu/ m chrome

cromossomo /kromo'somu/ m chromosome

crôni|ca /'kronika/ f (histórica) chronicle; (no jornal) feature; (conto) short story; ~co a chronic

cronista /kro'nista/ m/f (de jornal) feature writer; (contista) short story writer; (historiador) chronicler

crono|grama /krono'grama/ m schedule; ~logia f chronology; ~lógico a chronological; ~metrar vt time

cronômetro /kro'nometru/ m stopwatch

croquete /kro'kɛtʃi/ m savoury meatball in breadcrumbs

croqui /kro'ki/ m sketch

crosta /'krosta/ f crust; (em ferida) scab

cru /kru/ a (f ~a) raw; <luz, tom, palavra> harsh; crude; <verdade> unvarnished, plain

cruci|al /krusi'aw/ (pl ~ais) a crucial

crucifi|cação /krusifika'sãw/ f crucifixion; ~car vt crucify; ~xo /ks/ m crucifix

cru|el /kru'ɛw/ (pl ~éis) a cruel; ~eldade f cruelty; ~ento a bloody

crupe /'krupi/ m croup

crustáceos /krus'tasius/ m pl shellfish

cruz /krus/ f cross

cruza|da /kru'zada/ f crusade; ~do¹ m (soldado) crusader

cru|zado² /kru'zadu/ m (moeda) cruzado; ~zador m cruiser; ~zamento m (de ruas) crossroads, junction, (Amer) intersection; (de raças) cross; ~zar vt cross □ vi <navio> cruise; ~zar com pass; ~zar-se vpr cross; <pessoas> pass each other;

~zeiro m (moeda) cruzeiro; (viagem) cruise; (cruz) cross

cu /ku/ m (chulo) arse, (Amer) ass

Cuba /'kuba/ f Cuba

cubano /ku'banu/ a & m Cuban

cúbico /'kubiku/ a cubic

cubículo /ku'bikulu/ m cubicle

cubis|mo /ku'bizmu/ m cubism; ~ta a & m/f cubist

cubo /'kubu/ m cube; (de roda) hub

cuca /'kuka/ (fam) f head

cuco /'kuku/ m cuckoo; (relógio) cuckoo clock

cu|-de-ferro /kudʒi'fɛxu/ (pl ~s-de-ferro) (fam) m swot

cueca /ku'ɛka/ f underpants; pl (Port: de mulher) knickers

cueiro /ku'eru/ m baby wrap

cuia /'kuia/ f gourd

cuidado /kui'dadu/ m care; com ~ carefully; ter ou tomar ~ be careful; ~so /o/ a careful

cuidar /kui'dar/ vi ~ de take care of; ~-se vpr look after o.s.

cujo /'kuʒu/ pron whose

culatra /ku'latra/ f breech; sair pela ~ (fig) backfire

culiná|ria /kuli'naria/ f cookery; ~rio a culinary

culmi|nância /kuwmi'nãsia/ f culmination; ~nante a culminating; ~nar vi culminate (em in)

cul|pa /'kuwpa/ f guilt; foi ~pa minha it was my fault; ter ~pa de be to blame for; ~pabilidade f guilt; ~pado a guilty □ m culprit; ~par vt blame (de for); (na justiça) find guilty (de of); ~par-se vpr take the blame (de for); ~pável (pl ~páveis) a culpable, guilty

culti|var /kuwtʃi'var/ vt cultivate; grow <plantas>; ~vo m cultivation; (de plantas) growing

cul|to /'kuwtu/ a cultured □ m cult; ~tura f culture; (de terra) cultivation; ~tural (pl ~turais) a cultural

cumbuca /kũ'buka/ f bowl

cume /'kumi/ m peak

cúmplice /'kũplisi/ m/f accomplice

cumplicidade /kũplisi'dadʒi/ f complicity

cumprimen|tar /kũprimẽ'tar/ vt/i (saudar) greet; (parabenizar) compliment; ~to m (saudação) greeting; (elogio) compliment; (de lei, ordem) compliance (de with); (de promessa, palavra) fulfilment

cumprir /kũ'prir/ vt keep <promessa, palavra>; comply with <lei, ordem>; do <dever>; carry out <obrigações>; serve <pena>; ~ com keep to □ vi cumpre-nos ir we should go; ~-se vpr be fulfilled

cúmulo /'kumulu/ *m* height; **é o ~!** that's the limit!

cunha /'kuɲa/ *f* wedge

cunha|da /ku'ɲada/ *f* sister-in-law; **~do** *m* brother-in-law

cunhar /'kuɲar/ *vt* coin <*palavra, expressão*>; mint <*moedas*>

cunho /'kuɲu/ *m* hallmark

cupim /ku'pĩ/ *m* termite

cupom /ku'põ/ *m* coupon

cúpula /'kupula/ *f* (*abóbada*) dome; (*de abajur*) shade; (*chefia*) leadership; (**reunião de**) ~ summit (meeting)

cura /'kura/ *f* cure □ *m* curate, priest

curandeiro /kurã'deru/ *m* (*religioso*) faith-healer; (*índio*) medicine man; (*charlatão*) quack

curar /ku'rar/ *vt* cure; dress <*ferida*>; **~-se** *vpr* be cured

curativo /kura'tʃivu/ *m* dressing

curá|vel /ku'ravew/ (*pl* ~**veis**) *a* curable

curin|ga /ku'rĩga/ *m* wild card; **~gão** *m* joker

curio|sidade /kuriozi'dadʒi/ *f* curiosity; **~so** /o/ *a* curious □ *m* (*espectador*) onlooker

cur|ral /ku'xaw/ (*pl* ~**rais**) *m* pen

currículo /ku'xikulu/ *m* curriculum; (*resumo*) curriculum vitae, CV

cur|sar /kur'sar/ *vt* attend <*escola, aula*>; study <*matéria*>; **~so** *m* course; **~sor** *m* cursor

curta|-metragem /kurtame'traʒẽ/ (*pl* ~**s-metragens**) *m* short (film)

cur|tição /kurtʃi'sãw/ (*fam*) *f* enjoyment; **~tir** *vt* (*fam*) enjoy; tan <*couro*>

curto /'kurtu/ *a* short; <*conhecimento, inteligência*> limited; **~-circuito** (*pl* ~**s-circuitos**) *m* short circuit

cur|va /'kurva/ *f* curve; (*de estrada, rio*) bend; **~va fechada** hairpin bend; **~var** *vt* bend; **~var-se** *vpr* bend; (*fig*) bow (**a** to); **~vo** *a* curved <*estrada*> winding

cus|parada /kuspa'rada/ *f* spit; **~pe** *m* spit, spittle; **~pir** *vt/i* spit

cus|ta /'kusta/ *f* **à ~ta de** at the expense of; **~tar** *vt* cost □ *vi* (*ser difícil*) be hard; **~tar a fazer** (*ter dificuldade*) find it hard to do; (*demorar*) take a long time to do; **~tear** *vt* finance, fund; **~teio** *m* funding; (*relação de despesas*) costing; **~to** *m* cost; **a ~to** with difficulty

custódia /kus'tɔdʒia/ *f* custody

cutelo /ku'telu/ *m* cleaver

cutícula /ku'tʃikula/ *f* cuticle

cútis /'kutʃis/ *f invar* complexion

cutucar /kutu'kar/ *vt* (*com o cotovelo,* *joelho*) nudge; (*com o dedo*) poke; (*com instrumento*) prod

czar /zar/ *m* tsar

D

da = **de** + **a**

dádiva /'dadʒiva/ *f* gift; (*donativo*) donation

dado /'dadu/ *m* (*de jogar*) die, dice; (*informação*) fact, piece of information; *pl* data

daí /da'i/ *adv* (*no espaço*) from there; (*no tempo*) then; ~ **por diante** from then on; **e ~?** (*fam*) so what?

dali /da'li/ *adv* from over there

dália /'dalia/ *f* dahlia

dal|tônico /daw'toniku/ *a* colourblind; **~tonismo** *m* colour-blindness

dama /'dama/ *f* lady; (*em jogos*) queen; *pl* (*jogo*) draughts, (*Amer*) checkers; **~ de honra** bridesmaid

da|nado /da'nadu/ *a* damned; (*zangado*) angry; (*travesso*) naughty; **~nar-se** *vpr* get angry; **~ne-se!** (*fam*) who cares?

dan|ça /'dãsa/ *f* dance; **~çar** *vt* dance □ *vi* dance; (*fam*) miss out; <*coisa*> go by the board; <*crimonoso*> get caught; **~çarino** *m* dancer; **~ceteria** *f* discotheque

da|nificar /danifi'kar/ *vt* damage; **~ninho** *a* undesirable; **~no** *m* (*pl*) damage; **~noso** /o/ *a* damaging

dantes /'dãtʃis/ *adv* formerly

daquela(s), daquele(s) = **de** + **aquela(s), aquele(s)**

daqui /da'ki/ *adv* from here; ~ **a 2 dias** in 2 days(' time); ~ **a pouco** in a minute; ~ **em diante** from now on

daquilo = **de** + **aquilo**

dar /dar/ *vt* give; have <*dormida, lida etc*>; do <*pulo, cambalhota etc*>; cause <*problemas*>; produce <*frutas, leite*>; deal <*cartas*>; (*lecionar*) teach □ *vi* (*ser possível*) be possible; (*ser suficiente*) be enough; ~ **com** come across; ~ **em** lead to; **ele dá para ator** he'd make a good actor; ~ **por** (*considerar como*) consider to be; (*reparar em*) notice; **~-se** *vpr* <*coisa*> happen; <*pessoa*> get on

dardo /'dardu/ *m* dart; (*no atletismo*) javelin

das = **de** + **as**

da|ta /'data/ *f* date; **de longa ~** long since; **~tar** *vt/i* date

dati|lografar /datʃilogra'far/ *vt/i* type; **~lografia** *f* typing; **~lógrafo** *m* typist

de /dʒi/ *prep* of; (*procedência*) from; ~ **carro** by car; **trabalho ~ repórter** I work as a reporter

debaixo /dʒiˈbaʃu/ *adv* below; ~ **de** under

debalde /dʒiˈbawdʒi/ *adv* in vain

debandada /debãˈdada/ *f* stampede

deba|te /deˈbatʃi/ *m* debate; ~**ter** *vt* debate; ~**ter-se** *vpr* grapple

debelar /debeˈlar/ *vt* overcome

dé|bil /ˈdɛbiw/ (*pl* ~**beis**) *a* feeble; ~**bil mental** retarded (person)

debili|dade /debiliˈdadʒi/ *f* debility; ~**tar** *vt* debilitate; ~**tar-se** *vpr* become debilitated

debitar /debiˈtar/ *vt* debit

débito /ˈdɛbitu/ *m* debit

debo|chado /deboˈʃadu/ *a* sardonic; ~**char** *vt* mock; ~**che** /ɔ/ *m* jibe

debruar /debruˈar/ *vt/i* edge

debruçar-se /debruˈsarsi/ *vpr* bend over; ~ **sobre** study

debrum /deˈbrũ/ *m* edging

debulhar /debuˈʎar/ *vt* thresh

debu|tante /debuˈtãtʃi/ *f* debutante; ~**tar** *vi* debut, make one's debut

década /ˈdɛkada/ *f* decade; **a ~ dos 60** the sixties

deca|dência /dekaˈdẽsia/ *f* decadence; ~**dente** *a* decadent

decair /dekaˈir/ *vi* decline; (*degringolar*) go downhill; <*planta*> wilt

decal|car /dekawˈkar/ *vt* trace; ~**que** *m* tracing

decapitar /dekapiˈtar/ *vt* decapitate

decatlo /deˈkatlu/ *m* decathlon

de|cência /deˈsẽsia/ *f* decency; ~**cente** *a* decent

decepar /deseˈpar/ *vt* cut off

decep|ção /desepˈsãw/ *f* disappointment; ~**cionar** *vt* disappoint; ~**cionar-se** *vpr* be disappointed

decerto /dʒiˈsɛrtu/ *adv* certainly

deci|dido /desiˈdʒidu/ *a* <*pessoa*> determined; ~**dir** *vt/i* decide; ~**dir-se** *vpr* make up one's mind; ~**dir-se por** decide on

decíduo /deˈsiduu/ *a* deciduous

decifrar /desiˈfrar/ *vt* decipher

deci|mal /desiˈmaw/ (*pl* ~**mais**) *a* & *m* decimal

décimo /ˈdɛsimu/ *a* & *m* tenth; ~ **primeiro** eleventh; ~ **segundo** twelfth; ~ **terceiro** thirteenth; ~ **quarto** fourteenth; ~ **quinto** fifteenth; ~ **sexto** sixteenth; ~ **sétimo** seventeenth; ~ **oitavo** eighteenth; ~ **nono** nineteenth

deci|são /desiˈzãw/ *f* decision; ~**sivo** *a* decisive

decla|ração /deklaraˈsãw/ *f* declaration; ~**rado** *a* <*inimigo*> sworn; <*crente*> avowed; <*ladrão*> self-confessed; ~**rar** *vt* declare

decli|nação /deklinaˈsãw/ *f* declension; ~**nar** *vt* ~**nar (de)** decline □ *vi* decline; <*sol*> go down; <*chão*> slope down

declínio /deˈkliniu/ *m* decline

declive /deˈklivi/ *m* (downward) slope, incline

decodificar /dekodʒifiˈkar/ *vt* decode

deco|lagem /dekoˈlaʒẽ/ *f* take-off; ~**lar** *vi* take off; (*fig*) get off the ground

decom|por /dekõˈpor/ *vt* break down; contort <*feições*>; ~**por-se** *vpr* break down; <*cadáver*> decompose; ~ **posição** *f* (*de cadáver*) decomposition

deco|ração /dekoraˈsãw/ *f* decoration; (*aprendizagem*) learning by heart; ~**rar** *vt* (*adornar*) decorate; (*aprender*) learn by heart, memorize; ~**rativo** *a* decorative; ~**reba** /ɛ/ (*fam*) *f* rote-learning; ~**ro** /o/ *m* decorum; ~**roso** /o/ *a* decorous

decor|rência /dekoˈxẽsia/ *f* consequence; ~**rente** *a* resulting (**de** from); ~**rer** *vi* <*tempo*> elapse; <*acontecimento*> pass off; (*resultar*) result (**de** from) □ *m* **no ~rer de** in the course of; **com o ~rer do tempo** in time, with the passing of time

deco|tado /dekoˈtadu/ *a* low-cut; ~**te** /ɔ/ *m* neckline

decrépito /deˈkrɛpitu/ *a* decrepit

decres|cente /dekreˈsẽtʃi/ *a* decreasing; ~**cer** *vi* decrease

decre|tar /dekreˈtar/ *vt* decree; declare <*estado de sítio*>; ~**to** /ɛ/ *m* decree; ~**to-lei** (*pl* ~**tos-leis**) *m* act

decurso /deˈkursu/ *m* course

de|dal /deˈdaw/ (*pl* ~**dais**) *m* thimble; ~**dão** *m* (*da mão*) thumb; (*do pé*) big toe

dedetizar /dedetʃiˈzar/ *vt* spray with insecticide

dedi|cação /dedʒikaˈsãw/ *f* dedication; ~**car** *vt* dedicate; devote <*tempo*>; ~**car-se** *vpr* dedicate o.s. (**a** to); ~**catória** *f* dedication

dedilhar /dedʒiˈʎar/ *vt* pluck

dedo /ˈdedu/ *m* finger; (*do pé*) toe; **cheio de ~s** all fingers and thumbs; (*sem graça*) awkward; ~**duro** (*pl* ~**s-duros**) *m* sneak; (*político, criminoso*) informer

dedução /deduˈsãw/ *f* deduction

dedurar /deduˈrar/ *vt* sneak on; (*à polícia*) inform on

dedu|tivo /deduˈtʃivu/ *a* deductive; ~**zir** *vt* (*descontar*) deduct; (*concluir*) deduce

defa|sado /defaˈzadu/ *a* out of step; ~**sagem** *f* gap, lag

defecar /defeˈkar/ *vi* defecate

defei|to /deˈfejtu/ *m* defect; **botar ~to em** find fault with; ~**tuoso** /o/ *a* defective

defen|der /defẽ'der/ *vt* defend; **~der-se** *vpr* (*virar-se*) fend for o.s.; (*contra-atacar*) defend o.s. (**de** against); **~siva** *f* **na ~siva** on the defensive; **~sor** *m* defender; (*advogado*) defence counsel

defe|rência /defe'rẽsia/ *f* deference; **~rente** *a* deferential

defesa /de'feza/ *f* defence □ *m* defender

defici|ência /defisi'ẽsia/ *f* deficiency; **~ente** *a* deficient; (*física ou mentalmente*) handicapped □ *m/f* handicapped person

déficit /'dɛfisitʃi/ (*pl* **~s**) *m* deficit

deficitário /defisitʃi'ariu/ *a* in deficit; <*empresa*> loss-making

definhar /defi'ɲar/ *vi* waste away; <*planta*> wither

defi|nição /defini'sãw/ *f* definition; **~nir** *vt* define; **~nir-se** *vpr* (*descrever-se*) define o.s.; (*decidir-se*) come to a decision; (*explicar-se*) make one's position clear; **~nitivo** *a* definitive; **~nível** (*pl* **~níveis**) *a* definable

defla|ção /defla'sãw/ *f* deflation; **~cionário** *a* deflationary

deflagrar /defla'grar/ *vt* set off □ *vi* break out

defor|mar /defor'mar/ *vt* misshape; deform <*corpo*>; distort <*imagem*>; **~midade** *f* deformity

defraudar /defraw'dar/ *vt* defraud (**de** of)

defron|tar /defrõ'tar/ *vt* **~tar com** face; **~te** *adv* opposite; **~te de** opposite

defumar /defu'mar/ *vt* smoke

defunto /de'fũtu/ *a & m* deceased

dege|lar /deʒe'lar/ *vt/i* thaw; **~lo** /e/ *m* thaw

degeneração /deʒenera'sãw/ *f* degeneration

degenerar /deʒene'rar/ *vi* degenerate (**em** into)

degolar /dego'lar/ *vt* cut the throat of

degra|dação /degrada'sãw/ *f* degradation; **~dante** *a* degrading; **~dar** *vt* degrade

degrau /de'graw/ *m* step

degringolar /degrĩgo'lar/ *vi* deteriorate, go downhill

degustar /degus'tar/ *vt* taste

dei|tada /dej'tada/ *f* lie-down; **~tado** *a* lying down; (*dormindo*) in bed; (*fam: preguiçoso*) idle; **~tar** *vt* lay down; (*na cama*) put to bed; (*pôr*) put; (*Port: jogar*) throw □ *vi*, **~tar-se** *vpr* lie down; (*ir para cama*) go to bed

dei|xa /'deʃa/ *f* cue; **~xar** *vt* leave; (*permitir*) let; **~xar de** (*parar*) stop; (*omitir*) fail; **não pôde ~xar de rir** he couldn't help laughing; **~xar alg**

nervoso make s.o. annoyed; **~xar cair** drop; **~xar a desejar** leave a lot to be desired; **~xa** (**para lá**) (*fam*) never mind, forget it

dela(s) = **de** + **ela(s)**

delatar /dela'tar/ *vt* report

délavé /dela've/ *a invar* faded

dele(s) = **de** + **ele(s)**

dele|gação /delega'sãw/ *f* delegation; **~gacia** *f* police station; **~gado** *m* delegate; **~gado de polícia** police chief; **~gar** *vt* delegate

delei|tar /delej'tar/ *vt* delight; **~tar-se** *vpr* delight (**com** in); **~te** *m* delight; **~toso** /o/ *a* delightful

delgado /dew'gadu/ *a* slender

delibe|ração /delibera'sãw/ *f* deliberation; **~rar** *vt/i* deliberate

delica|deza /delika'deza/ *f* delicacy; (*cortesia*) politeness; **~do** *a* delicate; (*cortês*) polite

delícia /de'lisia/ *f* delight; **ser uma ~** <*comida*> be delicious; <*sol etc*> be lovely

delici|ar /delisi'ar/ *vt* delight; **~ar-se** delight (**com** in); **~oso** /o/ *a* delightful, lovely; <*comida*> delicious

deline|ador /delinia'dor/ *m* eye-liner; **~ar** *vt* outline

delin|qüência /delĩ'kwẽsia/ *f* delinquency; **~qüente** *a & m* delinquent

deli|rante /deli'rãtʃi/ *a* rapturous; (*med*) delirious; **~rar** *vi* go into raptures; <*doente*> be delirious

delírio /de'liriu/ *m* (*febre*) delirium; (*excitação*) raptures

delito /de'litu/ *m* crime

delonga /de'lõga/ *f* delay

delta /'dɛwta/ *f* delta

dema|gogia /demago'ʒia/ *f* demagogy; **~gógico** *a* demagogic; **~gogo** /o/ *m* demagogue

demais /dʒi'majs/ *a & adv* (*muito*) very much; (*em demasia*) too much; **os ~** the rest, the others; **é ~!** (*fam*) it's great!

deman|da /de'mãda/ *f* demand; (*jurid*) action; **~dar** *vt* sue

demão /de'mãw/ *f* coat

demar|car /demar'kar/ *vt* demarcate; **~catório** *a* demarcation

demasia /dema'zia/ *f* excess; **em ~** too much (much, many)

de|mência /de'mẽsia/ *f* insanity; (*med*) dementia; **~mente** *a* insane; (*med*) demented

demissão /demi'sãw/ *f* sacking, dismissal; **pedir ~** resign

demitir /demi'tʃir/ *vt* sack, dismiss; **~-se** *vpr* resign

demo|cracia /demokra'sia/ *f* democracy; **~crata** *m/f* democrat; **~crático** *a* democratic; **~cratizar**

vt democratize; **~grafia** *f* demography; **~gráfico** *a* demographic
demo|lição /demoli'sãw/ *f* demolition; **~lir** *vt* demolish
demônio /de'moniu/ *m* demon
demons|tração /demõstra'sãw/ *f* demonstration; **~trar** *vt* demonstrate; **~trativo** *a* demonstrative
demo|ra /de'mɔra/ *f* delay; **~rado** *a* lengthy; **~rar** *vi* (*levar*) take; (*tardar a voltar, terminar etc*) be long; (*levar muito tempo*) take a long time □ *vt* delay
dendê /dẽ'de/ *m* (*óleo*) palm oil
denegrir /dene'grir/ *vt* denigrate
dengoso /dẽ'gozu/ *a* coy
dengue /'dẽgi/ *m* dengue
denomi|nação /denomina'sãw/ *f* denomination; **~nar** *vt* name
denotar /deno'tar/ *vt* denote
den|sidade /dẽsi'dadʒi/ *f* density; **~so** *a* dense
den|tado /dẽ'tadu/ *a* serrated; **~tadura** *f* (set of) teeth; (*postiça*) dentures, false teeth; **~tal** (*pl* **~tais**) *a* dental; **~tário** *a* dental; **~te** *m* tooth; (*de alho*) clove; **~te do siso** wisdom tooth; **~tição** *f* teething; (*dentadura*) teeth; **~tifrico** *m* toothpaste; **~tista** *m/f* dentist
dentre = de + entre
dentro /'dẽtru/ *adv* inside; **lá ~** in there; **por ~** on the inside; **~ de** inside; (*tempo*) within
dentu|ça /dẽ'tusa/ *f* buck teeth; **~ço** *a* with buck teeth
denúncia /de'nũsia/ *f* (*à polícia etc*) report; (*na imprensa etc*) disclosure
denunciar /denũsi'ar/ *vt* (*à polícia etc*) report; (*na imprensa etc*) denounce
deparar /depa'rar/ *vi* **~ com** come across
departamento /departa'mẽtu/ *m* department
depauperar /depawpe'rar/ *vt* impoverish
depenar /depe'nar/ *vt* pluck <*aves*>; (*roubar*) fleece
depen|dência /depẽ'dẽsia/ *f* dependence; *pl* premises; **~dente** *a* dependent (**de** on) □ *m/f* dependant; **~der** *vi* depend (**de** on)
depi|lação /depila'sãw/ *f* depilation; **~lar** *vt* depilate; **~latório** *m* depilatory cream
deplo|rar /deplo'rar/ *vt* deplore; **~rável** (*pl* **~ráveis**) *a* deplorable
de|poente /depo'ẽtʃi/ *m/f* witness; **~poimento** *m* (*à polícia*) statement; (*na justiça, fig*) testimony
depois /de'pojs/ *adv* after(wards); **~ de** after; **~ que** after
depor /de'por/ *vi* (*na polícia*) make a

statement; (*na justiça*) give evidence, testify □ *vt* lay down <*armas*>; depose <*rei, presidente*>
depor|tação /deporta'sãw/ *f* deportation; **~tar** *vt* deport
deposi|tante /depozi'tãtʃi/ *m/f* depositor; **~tar** *vt* deposit; cast <*voto*>; place <*confiança*>
depósito /de'pɔzitu/ *m* deposit; (*armazém*) warehouse
depra|vação /deprava'sãw/ *f* depravity; **~vado** *a* depraved; **~var** *vt* deprave
depre|ciação /depresia'sãw/ *f* (*perda de valor*) depreciation; (*menosprezo*) depreciation; **~ciar** *vt* (*desvalorizar*) devalue; (*menosprezar*) depreciate; **~ciar-se** *vpr* <*bens*> depreciate; <*pessoa*> deprecate o.s.; **~ciativo** *a* deprecatory
depre|dação /depreda'sãw/ *f* depredation; **~dar** *vt* wreck
depressa /dʒi'prɛsa/ *adv* fast, quickly
depres|são /depre'sãw/ *f* depression; **~sivo** *a* depressive
depri|mente /depri'mẽtʃi/ *a* depressing; **~mido** *a* depressed; **~mir** *vt* depress; **~mir-se** *vpr* get depressed
depurar /depu'rar/ *vt* purify
depu|tação /deputa'sãw/ *f* deputation; **~tado** *m* deputy, MP, (*Amer*) congressman (*f* -woman); **~tar** *vt* delegate
deque /'dɛki/ *m* (sun)deck
deri|va /de'riva/ *f* **à ~va** adrift; **andar à ~va** drift; **~vação** *f* derivation; **~var** *vt* derive; (*desviar*) divert □ *vi*, **~var-se** *vpr* derive, be derived (**de** from); <*navio*> drift
dermatolo|gia /dermatolo'ʒia/ *f* dermatology; **~gista** *m/f* dermatologist
derradeiro /dexa'deru/ *a* last, final
derra|mamento /dexama'mẽtu/ *m* spill, spillage; **~mamento de sangue** bloodshed; **~mar** *vt* spill; shed <*lágrimas*>; **~mar-se** *vpr* spill; **~me** *m* spill, spillage; **~me cerebral** stroke
derra|pagem /dexa'paʒẽ/ *f* skidding; (*uma*) skid; **~par** *vi* skid
derreter /dexe'ter/ *vt* melt; **~-se** *vpr* melt
derro|ta /de'xɔta/ *f* defeat; **~tar** *vt* defeat; **~tismo** *m* defeatism; **~tista** *a* & *m/f* defeatist
derrubar /dexu'bar/ *vt* knock down; bring down <*governo*>
desaba|far /dʒizaba'far/ *vi* speak one's mind; **~fo** *m* outburst
desa|bamento /dʒizaba'mẽtu/ *m* collapse; **~bar** *vi* collapse; <*chuva*> pour down

desabotoar /dʒiaboto'ar/ vt unbutton

desabri|gado /dʒizabri'gadu/ a homeless; ~**gar** vt make homeless

desabrochar /dʒizabro'ʃar/ vi blossom, bloom

desaca|tar /dʒizaka'tar/ vt defy; ~**to** m (de pessoa) disrespect; (da lei etc) disregard

desacerto /dʒiza'sertu/ m mistake

desacompanhado /dʒizakõpa-'ɲadu/ a unaccompanied

desaconse|lhar /dʒizakõse'ʎar/ vt advise against; ~**lhável** (pl ~**lháveis**) a inadvisable

desacor|dado /dʒizakor'dadu/ a unconscious; ~**do** /o/ m disagreement

desacostu|mado /dʒizakostu'madu/ a unaccustomed; ~**mar** vt ~**mar alg de** break s.o. of the habit of; ~**mar-se de** get out of the habit of

desacreditar /dʒizakredʒi'tar/ vt discredit

desafeto /dʒiza'fɛtu/ m disaffection

desafi|ador /dʒizafia'dor/ a <tarefa> challenging; <pessoa> defiant; ~**ar** vt challenge; (fazer face a) defy <perigo, morte>

desafi|nado /dʒizafi'nadu/ a out of tune; ~**nar** vi (cantando) sing out of tune; (tocando) play out of tune □ vt put out of tune

desafio /dʒiza'fiu/ m challenge

desafivelar /dʒizafive'lar/ vt unbuckle

desafo|gar /dʒizafo'gar/ vt vent; (desapertar) relieve; ~**gar-se** vpr give vent to one's feelings; ~**go** /o/ m (alívio) relief

desafo|rado /dʒizafo'radu/ a cheeky; ~**ro** /o/ m cheek; (um) liberty

desafortunado /dʒizafortu'nadu/ a unfortunate

desagra|dar /dʒizagra'dar/ vt displease; ~**dável** (pl ~**dáveis**) a unpleasant; ~**do** m displeasure

desagravo m redress, amends

desagregar /dʒizagre'gar/ vt split up; ~**-se** vpr split up

desaguar /dʒiza'gwar/ vt drain □ vi <rio> flow (em into)

desajeitado /dʒizaʒej'tadu/ a clumsy

desajuizado /dʒizaʒui'zadu/ a foolish

desajus|tado /dʒizaʒus'tadu/ a (psic) maladjusted; ~**te** m (psic) maladjustment

desalen|tar /dʒizalẽ'tar/ vt dishearten; ~**tar-se** vpr get disheartened; ~**to** m discouragement

desali|nhado /dʒizali'ɲadu/ a untidy; ~**nho** m untidiness

desalojar /dʒizalo'ʒar/ vt turn out <inquilino>; flush out <inimigo, ladrões>

desamarrar /dʒizama'xar/ vt untie □ vi cast off

desamarrotar /dʒizamaxo'tar/ vt smooth out

desamassar /dʒizama'sar/ vt smooth out

desambientado /dʒizãbiẽ'tadu/ a unsettled

desampa|rar /dʒizãpa'rar/ vt abandon; ~**ro** m abandonment

desandar /dʒizã'dar/ vi <molho> separate; ~ **a** start to

de|sanimar /dʒizani'mar/ vt discourage □ vi <pessoa> lose heart; <fato> be discouraging; ~**sânimo** m discouragement

desapaixonado /dʒizapaiʃo'nadu/ a dispassionate

desaparafusar /dʒizaparafu'zar/ vt unscrew

desapare|cer /dʒizapare'ser/ vi disappear; ~**cimento** m disappearance

desapego /dʒiza'pegu/ m detachment; (indiferença) indifference

desapercebido /dʒizaperse'bidu/ a unnoticed

desapertar /dʒizaper'tar/ vt loosen

desapon|tamento /dʒizapõta'mẽtu/ m disapointment; ~**tar** vt disappoint

desapropriar /dʒizapropri'ar/ vt expropriate

desapro|vação /dʒizaprova'sãw/ f disapproval; ~**var** vt disapprove of

desaproveitado /dʒizaprovej'tadu/ a wasted

desar|mamento /dʒizarma'mẽtu/ m disarmament; ~**mar** vt disarm; take down <barraca>

desarran|jar /dʒizaxã'ʒar/ vt mess up; upset <estômago>; ~**jo** m mess; (do estômago) upset

desarregaçar /dʒizaxega'sar/ vt roll down

desarru|mado /dʒizaxu'madu/ a untidy; ~**mar** vt untidy; unpack <mala>

desarticular /dʒizartʃiku'lar/ vt dislocate

desarvorado /dʒizarvo'radu/ a disoriented, at a loss

desassociar /dʒizasosi'ar/ vt disassociate; ~**-se** vpr disassociate o.s.

desas|trado /dʒizas'tradu/ a accident-prone; ~**tre** m disaster; ~**troso** /o/ a disastrous

desatar /dʒiza'tar/ vt untie; ~ **a chorar** dissolve in tears

desatarraxar /dʒizataxa'ʃar/ vt unscrew

desaten|cioso /dʒizatẽsi'ozu/ a inattentive; ~**to** a oblivious (a to)

desati|nar /dʒizatʃi'nar/ vt bewilder □ vi not think straight; ~**no** m mental aberration, bewilderment; (um) folly

desativar /dʒizatʃi'var/ *vt* deactivate; shut down <*fábrica*>
desatrelar /dʒizatre'lar/ *vt* unhitch
desatualizado /dʒizatuali'zadu/ *a* out-of-date
desavença /dʒiza'vẽsa/ *f* disagreement
desavergonhado /dʒizavergo'ɲadu/ *a* shameless
desbancar /dʒizbã'kar/ *vt* outdo
desbaratar /dʒizbara'tar/ *vt* (*desperdiçar*) waste
desbocado /dʒizbo'kadu/ *a* outspoken
desbotar /dʒizbo'tar/ *vt/i* fade
desbra|vador /dʒizbrava'dor/ *m* explorer; ~**var** *vt* explore
desbun|dante /dʒizbũ'dãtʃi/ (*fam*) *a* mind-blowing; ~**dar** (*fam*) *vt* blow the mind of □ *vi* flip, freak out; ~**de** (*fam*) *m* knockout
descabido /dʒiska'bidu/ *a* inappropriate
descalabro /dʒiska'labru/ *m* débâcle
descalço /dʒis'kawsu/ *a* barefoot
descambar /dʒiskã'bar/ *vi* deteriorate, degenerate
descan|sar /dʒiskã'sar/ *vt/i* rest; ~**so** *m* rest; (*de prato, copo*) mat
desca|rado /dʒiska'radu/ *a* blatant; ~**ramento** *m* cheek
descarga /dʒis'karga/ *f* (*eletr*) discharge; (*da privada*) flush; **dar** ~ flush (the toilet)
descarregar /dʒiskaxe'gar/ *vt* unload <*mercadorias*>; discharge <*poluentes*>; vent <*raiva*> □ *vi* <*bateria*> go flat; ~ **em cima de alg** take it out on s.o.
descarrilhar /dʒiskaxi'ʎar/ *vt/i* derail
descar|tar /dʒiskar'tar/ *vt* discard; ~**tável** (*pl* ~**táveis**) *a* disposable
descascar /dʒiskas'kar/ *vt* peel <*frutas, batatas*>; shell <*nozes*> □ *vi* <*pessoa, pele*> peel
descaso /dʒis'kazu/ *m* indifference
descen|dência /dʒesẽ'dẽsia/ *f* descent; ~**dente** *a* descended □ *m/f* descendant; ~**der** *vi* descend (de from)
descentralizar /dʒisẽtrali'zar/ *vt* decentralize
des|cer /de'ser/ *vi* go down; <*avião*> descend; (*do ônibus, trem*) get off; (*do carro*) get out □ *vt* go down <*escada, ladeira*>; ~**cida** *f* descent
desclassificar /dʒisklasifi'kar/ *vt* disqualify
desco|berta /dʒisko'bɛrta/ *f* discovery; ~**berto** /ɛ/ *a* uncovered; <*conta*> overdrawn; **a** ~**berto** overdrawn; ~**bridor** *m* discoverer; ~**brimento** *m* discovery; ~**brir** *vt* discover; (*expor*) uncover

descolar /dʒisko'lar/ *vt* unstick; (*fam*) (*dar*) give; (*arranjar*) get hold of, rustle up; (*Port*) <*avião*> take off
descom|por /dʒiskõ'por/ *vt* (*censurar*) scold; ~**-se** *vpr* <*pessoa*> lose one's composure; ~**postura** *f* (*estado*) loss of composure; (*censura*) talking-to
descomprometido /dʒiskõprome-'tʃidu/ *a* free
descomu|nal /dʒiskomu'naw/ (*pl* ~**nais**) *a* extraordinary; (*grande*) huge
desconcentrar /dʒiskõsẽ'trar/ *vt* distract
desconcer|tante /dʒiskõser'tãtʃi/ *a* disconcerting; ~**tar** *vt* disconcert
desconexo /dʒisko'nɛksu/ *a* incoherent
desconfi|ado /dʒiskõfi'adu/ *a* suspicious; ~**ança** *f* mistrust; ~**ar** *vi* suspect
desconfor|tável /dʒiskõfor'tavew/ (*pl* ~**táveis**) *a* uncomfortable; ~**to** /o/ *m* discomfort
descongelar /dʒiskõʒe'lar/ *vt* defrost <*geladeira*>; thaw <*comida*>
descongestio|nante /dʒiskõʒestʃio'nãtʃi/ *a & m* decongestant; ~**nar** *vt* decongest
desconhe|cer /dʒiskoɲe'ser/ *vt* not know; ~**cido** *a* unknown □ *m* stranger
desconsiderar /dʒiskõside'rar/ *vt* ignore
desconsolado /dʒiskõso'ladu/ *a* disconsolate
descontar /dʒiskõ'tar/ *vt* deduct; (*não levar em conta*) discount
desconten|tamento /dʒiskõtẽta-'mẽtu/ *m* discontent; ~**te** *a* discontent
desconto /dʒis'kõtu/ *m* discount; **dar um** ~ (*fig*) make allowances
descontra|ção /dʒiskõtra'sãw/ *f* informality; ~**ído** *a* informal, casual; ~**ir** *vt* relax; ~**ir-se** *vpr* relax
descontro|lar-se /dʒiskõtro'larsi/ *vpr* <*pessoa*> lose control; <*coisa*> go out of control; ~**le** /o/ *m* lack of control
desconversar /dʒiskõver'sar/ *vi* change the subject
descortesia /dʒiskorte'zia/ *f* rudeness
descostu|rar /dʒiskostu'rar/ *vt* unrip; ~**rar-se** *vpr* come undone
descrédito /dʒis'krɛdʒitu/ *m* discredit
descren|ça /dʒis'krẽsa/ *f* disbelief; ~**te** *a* sceptical, disbelieving
des|crever /dʒiskre'ver/ *vt* describe; ~**crição** *f* description; ~**critivo** *a* descriptive
descui|dado /dʒiskui'dadu/ *a* careless; ~**dar** *vt* neglect; ~**do** *m* carelessness; (*um*) oversight

descul|pa /dʒisˈkuwpa/ *f* excuse; **pe-dir ~pas** apologize; **~par** *vt* excuse; **~pe!** sorry!; **~par-se** *vpr* apologize; **~pável** (*pl* **~páveis**) *a* excusable

desde /ˈdezdʒi/ *prep* since; **~ que** since

des|dém /dezˈdẽj/ *m* disdain; **~denhar** *vt* disdain; **~nhoso** /o/ *a* disdainful

desdentado /dʒizdẽˈtadu/ *a* toothless

desdita /dʒizˈdʒita/ *f* unhappiness

desdizer /dʒizdʒiˈzer/ *vt* take back, withdraw □ *vi* take back what one said

desdo|bramento /dʒizdobraˈmẽtu/ *m* implication; **~brar** *vt* (*abrir*) unfold; break down <*dados, contas*>; **~brar-se** *vpr* unfold; (*empenhar-se*) go to a lot of trouble, bend over backwards

dese|jar /dezeˈʒar/ *vt* want; (*apaixonadamente*) desire; **~jar aco a alg** wish s.o. sth; **~jável** (*pl* **~jáveis**) *a* desirable; **~jo** /e/ *m* wish; (*forte*) desire; **~joso** /o/ *a* desirous

deselegante /dʒizeleˈgãtʃi/ *a* inelegant

desemaranhar /dʒizemaraˈɲar/ *vt* untangle

desembara|çado /dʒizĩbaraˈsadu/ *a* <*pessoa*> confident, nonchalant; **~çar-se** *vpr* rid o.s. (de of); **~ço** *m* confidence, ease

desembar|car /dʒizĩbarˈkar/ *vt/i* disembark; **~que** *m* disembarkation; (*seção do aeroporto*) arrivals

desembocar /dʒizĩboˈkar/ *vi* flow

desembol|sar /dʒizĩbowˈsar/ *vt* spend, pay out; **~so** /o/ *m* expenditure

desembrulhar /dʒizĩbruˈʎar/ *vt* unwrap

desembuchar /dʒizĩbuˈʃar/ (*fam*) *vi* (*desabafar*) get things off one's chest; (*falar logo*) spit it out

desempacotar /dʒizĩpakoˈtar/ *vt* unpack

desempatar /dʒizĩpaˈtar/ *vt* decide <*jogo*>

desempe|nhar /dʒizĩpeˈɲar/ *vt* perform; play <*papel*>; **~nho** *m* performance

desempre|gado /dʒizĩpreˈgadu/ *a* unemployed; **~go** /e/ *m* unemployment

desencadear /dʒizĩkadʒiˈar/ *vt* set off, trigger

desencaminhar /dʒizĩkamiˈɲar/ *vt* lead astray; embezzle <*dinheiro*>

desencantar /dʒizĩkãˈtar/ *vt* disenchant

desencon|trar-se /dʒizĩkõˈtrarsi/ *vpr* miss each other, fail to meet; **~tro** *m* failure to meet

desencorajar /dʒizĩkoraˈʒar/ *vt* discourage

desenferrujar /dʒizĩfexuˈʒar/ *vt* derust <*metal*>; stretch <*pernas*>; brush up <*língua*>

desenfreado /dʒizĩfriˈadu/ *a* unbridled

desenganar /dʒizĩgaˈnar/ *vt* disabuse; declare incurable <*doente*>

desengonçado /dʒizĩgõˈsadu/ *a* <*pessoa*> ungainly

desengre|nado /dʒizĩgreˈnadu/ *a* <*carro*> in neutral; **~nar** *vt* put in neutral <*carro*>; (*tec*) disengage

dese|nhar /dezeˈɲar/ *vt* draw; **~nhista** *m/f* drawer; (*industrial*) designer; **~nho** /e/ *m* drawing

desenlace /dʒizĩˈlasi/ *m* dénouement, outcome

desenredar /dʒizĩxeˈdar/ *vt* unravel

desenrolar /dʒizĩxoˈlar/ *vt* unroll <*rolo*>

desenten|der /dʒizĩtẽˈder/ *vt* misunderstand; **~der-se** *vpr* (*não se dar bem*) not get on; **~dimento** *m* misunderstanding

desenterrar /dʒizĩteˈxar/ *vt* dig up <*cadáver*>; unearth <*informação*>

desentortar /dʒizĩtorˈtar/ *vt* straighten out

desentupir /dʒizĩtuˈpir/ *vt* unblock

desenvol|to /dʒizĩˈvowtu/ *a* casual, nonchalant; **~tura** *f* casualness, nonchalance; **com ~tura** nonchalantly; **~ver** *vt* develop; **~ver-se** *vpr* develop; **~vimento** *m* development

desequi|librado *a* unbalanced; **~librar** *vt* unbalance; **~librar-se** *vpr* become unbalanced; **~líbrio** *m* imbalance

deser|ção /dezerˈsãw/ *f* desertion; **~tar** *vt/i* desert; **~to** /ɛ/ *a* deserted; **ilha ~ta** desert island □ *m* desert; **~tor** *m* deserter

desespe|rado /dʒizispeˈradu/ *a* desperate; **~rador** *a* hopeless; **~rar** *vt* (*desesperançar*) make despair □ *vi*, **~rar-se** *vpr* despair; **~ro** /e/ *m* despair

desestabilizar /dʒizistabiliˈzar/ *vt* destabilize

desestimular /dʒizistʃimuˈlar/ *vt* discourage

desfal|car /dʒisfawˈkar/ *vt* embezzle; **~que** *m* embezzlement

desfal|ecer /dʒisfaleˈser/ *vt* (*desmaiar*) faint; **~ecimento** *m* faint

desfavor /dʒisfaˈvor/ *m* disfavour

desfavo|rável /dʒisfavoˈravew/ (*pl* **~ráveis**) *a* unfavourable; **~recer** *vt* be unfavourable to; treat less favourably <*minorias etc*>

desfazer /dʒisfaˈzer/ *vt* undo; unpack <*mala*>; strip <*cama*>; break <*contrato*>; clear up <*mistério*>; **~se**

vpr come undone; <*casamento*> break up; <*sonhos*> crumble; **~-se em lágrimas** dissolve into tears

desfe|char /dʒisfe'ʃar/ *vt* throw <*murro, olhar*>; **~cho** /e/ *m* outcome, dénouement

desfeita /dʒis'fejta/ *f* slight, insult

desferir /dʒisfe'rir/ *vt* give <*pontapé*>; launch <*ataque*>; fire <*flecha*>

desfiar /dʒisfi'ar/ *vt* pick the meat off <*frango*>; **~-se** *vpr* <*tecido*> fray

desfigurar /dʒisfigu'rar/ *vt* disfigure; (*fig*) distort

desfi|ladeiro /dʒisfila'deru/ *m* pass; **~lar** *vi* parade; **~le** *m* parade; **~le de modas** fashion show

desflorestamento /dʒisfloresta-'mẽtu/ *m* deforestation

desforra /dʒis'fɔxa/ *f* revenge

desfraldar /dʒisfraw'dar/ *vt* unfurl

desfrutar /dʒisfru'tar/ *vt* enjoy

desgas|tante /dʒizgas'tãtʃi/ *a* wearing, stressful; **~tar** *vt* wear out; **~te** *m* (*de máquina etc*) wear and tear; (*de pessoa*) stress and strain

desgosto /dʒiz'gostu/ *m* sorrow

desgovernar-se /dʒizgover'narsi/ *vpr* go out of control

desgraça /dʒiz'grasa/ *f* misfortune; **~do** *a* wretched □ *m* wretch

desgravar /dʒizgra'var/ *vt* erase

desgrenhado /dʒizgre'ɲadu/ *a* unkempt

desgrudar /dʒizgru'dar/ *vt* unstick; **~-se** *vpr* <*pessoa*> tear o.s. away

desidra|tação /dʒizidrata'sãw/ *f* dehydration; **~tar** *vt* dehydrate

desig|nação /dʒizigna'sãw/ *f* designation; **~nar** *vt* designate

desi|gual /dʒizi'gwaw/ (*pl* **~guais**) *a* unequal; <*terreno*> uneven; **~gualdade** *f* inequality; (*de terreno*) unevenness

desilu|dir /dʒizilu'dʒir/ *vt* disillusion; **~são** *f* disillusionment

desinfe|tante /dʒizĩfe'tãtʃi/ *a & m* disinfectant; **~tar** *vt* disinfect

desinibido /dʒizini'bidu/ *a* uninhibited

desintegrar-se /dʒizĩte'grarsi/ *vpr* disintegrate

desinteres|sado /dʒizĩtere'sadu/ *a* uninterested; **~sante** *a* uninteresting; **~sar-se** *vpr* lose interest (**de** in); **~se** /e/ *m* disinterest

desis|tência /dezis'tẽsia/ *f* giving up; **~tir** *vt/i* **~tir (de)** give up

desle|al /dʒizle'aw/ (*pl* **~ais**) *a* disloyal; **~aldade** *f* disloyalty

deslei|xado /dʒizle'ʃadu/ *a* sloppy; (*no vestir*) scruffy; **~xo** *m* carelessness; (*no vestir*) scruffiness

desli|gado /dʒizli'gadu/ *a* <*luz, TV*> off; <*pessoa*> absent-minded; **~gar** *vt*

turn off <*luz, TV, motor*>; hang up, put down <*telefone*> □ *vi* (*ao telefonar*) hang up, put the phone down

deslindar /dʒizlĩ'dar/ *vt* clear up, solve

desli|zante /dʒizli'zãtʃi/ *a* slippery; <*inflação*> creeping; **~zar** *vi* slip; **~zar-se** *vpr* creep; **~ze** *m* slip; (*fig: erro*) slip-up

deslo|cado *a* <*membro*> dislocated; (*fig*) out of place; **~car** *vt* move; (*med*) dislocate; **~car-se** *vpr* move

deslum|brado /dʒizlũ'bradu/ *a* (*fig*) starry-eyed; **~bramento** *m* (*fig*) wonderment; **~brante** *a* dazzling; **~brar** *vt* dazzle; **~brar-se** *vpr* (*fig*) be dazzled

desmai|ado /dʒizmaj'adu/ *a* unconscious; **~ar** *vi* faint; **~o** *m* faint

desman|cha-prazeres /dʒizmã-ʃapra'zeris/ *m/f invar* spoilsport; **~char** *vt* break up; break off <*noivado*>; shatter <*sonhos*>; **~char-se** *vpr* break up; (*no ar, na água, em lágrimas*) dissolve

desmantelar /dʒizmãte'lar/ *vt* dismantle

desmarcar /dʒizmar'kar/ *vt* cancel <*encontro*>

desmascarar /dʒizmaske'rar/ *vt* unmask

desma|tamento /dʒizmata'mẽtu/ *m* deforestation; **~tar** *vt* clear (of forest)

desmedido /dʒizme'didu/ *a* excessive

desmemoriado /dʒizmemori'adu/ *a* forgetful

desmen|tido /dʒizmẽ'tʃidu/ *m* denial; **~tir** *vt* deny

desmiolado /dʒizmio'ladu/ *a* brainless

desmontar /dʒizmõ'tar/ *vt* dismantle

desmorali|zante /dʒizmorali'zãtʃi/ *a* demoralizing; **~zar** *vt* demoralize

desmoro|namento /dʒizmorona-'mẽtu/ *m* collapse; **~nar** *vt* destroy; **~nar-se** *vpr* collapse

desnatar /dʒizna'tar/ *vi* skim <*leite*>

desnecessário /dʒiznese'sariu/ *a* unnecessary

desní|vel /dʒiz'nivew/ (*pl* **~veis**) *m* difference in height

desnortear /dʒiznortʃi'ar/ *vt* disorientate, (*Amer*) disorient

desnutrição /dʒiznutri'sãw/ *f* malnutrition

desobe|decer /dʒizobede'ser/ *vt/i* **~decer (a)** disobey; **~diência** *f* disobedience; **~diente** *a* disobedient

desobrigar /dʒizobri'gar/ *vt* release (**de** from)

desobstruir /dʒizobistru'ir/ *vt* unblock; empty <*casa*>

desocupado /dʒizoku'padu/ *a* unoccupied

desodorante /dʒizodo'rātʃi/ *m*, (*Port*) **desodorizante** /dʒizoduri'zātʃi/ *m* deodorant

deso|lação /dezola'sãw/ *f* desolation; **~lado** *a* <*lugar*> desolate; <*pessoa*> desolated; **~lar** *vt* desolate

desones|tidade /dʒizonestʃi'dadʒi/ *f* dishonesty; **~to** /ɛ/ *a* dishonest

deson|ra /dʒi'zõxa/ *f* dishonour; **~rar** *vt* dishonour; **~roso** /o/ *a* dishonourable

desor|deiro /dʒizor'deru/ *a* troublemaking □ *m* troublemaker; **~dem** *f* disorder; **~denado** *a* disorganized; <*vida*> disordered; **~denar** *vt* disorganize

desorgani|zação /dʒizorganiza'sãw/ *f* disorganization; **~zar** *vt* disorganize; **~zar-se** *vpr* get disorganized

desorientar /dʒizoriẽ'tar/ *vt* disorientate, (*Amer*) disorient

desossar /dʒizo'sar/ *vt* bone

deso|va /dʒi'zɔva/ *f* roe; **~var** *vi* spawn

despa|chado /dʒispa'ʃadu/ *a* efficient; **~chante** *m/f* (*de mercadorias*) shipping agent; (*de documentos*) documentation agent; **~char** *vt* deal with; dispatch, forward <*mercadorias*>; **~cho** *m* dispatch

desparafusar /dʒisparafu'zar/ *vt* unscrew

despedaçar /dʒispeda'sar/ *vt* (*rasgar*) tear to pieces; (*quebrar*) smash; **~-se** *vpr* <*vidro, vaso*> smash; <*papel, tecido*> tear

despe|dida /dʒispe'dʒida/ *f* farewell; **~dida de solteiro** stag night, (*Amer*) bachelor party; **~dir** *vt* dismiss; sack <*empregado*>; **~dir-se** *vpr* say goodbye (**de** to)

despei|tado /dʒispej'tadu/ *a* spiteful; **~to** *m* spite; **a ~to de** despite, in spite of

despe|jar /dʒispe'ʒar/ *vt* pour out <*líquido*>; empty <*recipiente*>; evict <*inquilino*>; **~jo** /e/ *m* (*de inquilino*) eviction

despencar /dʒispẽ'kar/ *vi* plummet

despender /dʒispẽ'der/ *vt* spend <*dinheiro*>

despensa /dʒis'pẽsa/ *f* pantry, larder

despentear /dʒispẽtʃi'ar/ *vt* mess up <*cabelo*>; mess up the hair of <*pessoa*>

despercebido /dʒisperse'bidu/ *a* unnoticed

desper|diçar /dʒisperdʒi'sar/ *vt* waste; **~dício** *m* waste

desper|tador /dʒisperta'dor/ *m* alarm clock; **~tar** *vt* rouse <*pessoa*>;

(*fig*) arouse <*interesse, suspeitas etc*> □ *vi* awake

despesa /dʒis'peza/ *f* expense

des|pido /des'pidu/ *a* bare, stripped (**de** of); **~pir** *vt* strip (**de** of); strip off <*roupa*>; **~pir-se** *vpr* strip (off), get undressed

despo|jar /dʒispo'ʒar/ *vt* strip (**de** of); **~jar-se** *vpr* divest o.s. (**de** of); **~jo** /o/ *m* spoils, booty; **~jos mortais** mortal remains

despontar /dʒispõ'tar/ *vi* emerge

despor|tista /diʃpur'tiʃta/ (*Port*) *m/f* sportsman (*f* -woman); **~tivo** (*Port*) *a* sporting; **~to** /o/ (*Port*) *m* sport; **carro de ~to** sports car

déspota /'dɛspota/ *m/f* despot

despótico /des'pɔtʃiku/ *a* despotic

despovoar /dʒispovo'ar/ *vt* depopulate

desprender /dʒisprẽ'der/ *vt* detach; (*da parede*) take down; **~-se** *vpr* come off; (*fig*) detach o.s.

despreocupado /dʒisprioku'padu/ *a* unconcerned

despreparado /dʒisprepa'radu/ *a* unprepared

despretensioso /dʒispretẽsi'ozu/ *a* unpretentious

desprestigiar /dʒisprestʃiʒi'ar/ *vt* discredit

desprevenido /dʒispreve'nidu/ *a* off one's guard, unprepared; **apanhar ~** catch unawares

despre|zar /dʒispre'zar/ *vt* despise; (*ignorar*) ignore; **~zível** (*pl* **~zíveis**) *a* despicable; **~zo** /e/ *m* contempt

desproporção /dʒispropor'sãw/ *f* disproportion

desproporcio|nado /dʒisproporsio'nadu/ *a* disproportionate; **~nal** (*pl* **~nais**) *a* disproportional

despropositado /dʒispropozi'tadu/ *a* (*absurdo*) preposterous

desprovido /dʒispro'vidu/ *a* **~ de** without

desqualificar /dʒiskwalifi'kar/ *vt* disqualify

desqui|tar-se /dʒiski'tarsi/ *vpr* (legally) separate; **~te** *m* (legal) separation

desrespei|tar /dʒizxespej'tar/ *vt* not respect; (*ignorar*) disregard; **~to** *m* disrespect; **~toso** /o/ *a* disrespectful

dessa(s), **desse(s)** = **de** + **essa(s)**, **esse(s)**

desta = **de** + **esta**

desta|camento /dʒistaka'mẽtu/ *m* detachment; **~car** *vt* detach; (*ressaltar*) bring out, make stand out; **~carse** *vpr* (*desprender-se*) come off; <*corredor*> break away; (*sobressair*) stand out (**sobre** against); **~cável** (*pl*

~**cáveis**) *a* detachable; <*caderno*> pull-out

destam|pado /dʒistã'padu/ *a* (*panela*) uncovered; ~**par** *vt* remove the lid of

destapar /dʒista'par/ *vt* uncover

destaque /dʒis'taki/ *m* prominence; (*coisa, pessoa*) highlight; (*do notíciario*) headline

destas, deste = de + estas, este

destemido /dʒiste'midu/ *a* intrepid, courageous

desterrar /dʒiste'xar/ *vt* (*exilar*) exile

destes = de + estes

destilar /desti'lar/ *vt* distil; ~**ia** *f* distillery

desti|nado /destʃi'nadu/ *a* (*fadado*) destined; ~**nar** *vt* intend, mean (**para** for); ~**natário** *m* addressee; ~**no** *m* (*de viagem*) destination; (*sorte*) fate

destituir /destʃitu'ir/ *vt* remove

desto|ante /dʒisto'ãtʃi/ *a* <*sons*> discordant; <*cores*> clashing; ~**ar** *vi* ~**ar de** clash with

destrancar /dʒistrã'kar/ *vt* unlock

destreza /des'treza/ *f* skill

destrinchar /dʒistrĩ'ʃar/ *vt* (*expor*) dissect; (*resolver*) sort out

destro /'destru/ *a* skilful

destro|çar /dʒistro'sar/ *vt* wreck; ~**ços** *m pl* wreckage

destronar /dʒistro'nar/ *vt* depose

destroncar /dʒistrõ'kar/ *vt* rick

destru|ição /dʒistrui'sãw/ *f* destruction; ~**idor** *a* destructive □ *m* destroyer; ~**ir** *vt* destroy

desumano /dʒizu'manu/ *a* inhuman; (*cruel*) inhumane

desunião /dʒizuni'ãw/ *f* disunity

desu|sado /dʒizu'zadu/ *a* disused; ~**so** *m* disuse

desvairado /dʒizvaj'radu/ *a* delirious, raving

desvalori|zação /dʒizvaloriza'sãw/ *f* devaluation; ~**zar** *vt* devalue

desvanta|gem /dʒizvã'taʒẽ/ *f* disadvantage; ~**joso** /o/ *a* disadvantageous

desve|lar /dʒizve'lar/ *vt* unveil; uncover <*segredo*>; ~**lar-se** *vpr* go to a lot of trouble; ~**lo** /e/ *m* great care

desvencilhar /dʒizvẽsi'ʎar/ *vt* extricate, free

desvendar /dʒizvẽ'dar/ *vt* reveal <*segredo*>; solve <*mistério*>

desventura /dʒizvẽ'tura/ *f* misfortune; (*infelicidade*) unhappiness

desviar /dʒizvi'ar/ *vt* divert <*trânsito, rio, atenção, dinheiro*>; avert <*golpe, suspeitas, olhos*>; ~**se** *vpr* deviate; <*do tema*> digress

desvincular /dʒizvĩku'lar/ *vt* free

desvio /dʒiz'viu/ *m* diversion; (*do trânsito*) diversion, (*Amer*) detour; (*linha ferroviária*) siding

desvirtuar /dʒizvirtu'ar/ *vt* misrepresent <*verdade*>

deta|lhado /deta'ʎadu/ *a* detailed; ~**lhar** *vt* detail; ~**lhe** *m* detail

detec|tar /detek'tar/ *vt* detect; ~**tive** (*Port*) *m veja* **detetive**; ~**tor** *m* detector

de|tenção /detẽ'sãw/ *f* (*prisão*) detention; ~**tentor** *m* holder; ~**ter** *vt* (*ter*) hold; (*prender*) detain

detergente /deter'ʒẽtʃi/ *m* detergent

deterio|ração /deteriora'sãw/ *f* deterioration; ~**rar** *vt* damage; ~**rar-se** *vpr* deteriorate

determi|nação /determina'sãw/ *f* determination; ~**nado** *a* (*certo*) certain; (*resoluto*) determined; ~**nar** *vt* determine

detestar /detes'tar/ *vt* hate

detetive /dete'tʃivi/ *m* detective

detido /de'tʃidu/ *pp de* **deter** □ *a* thorough □ *m* detainee

detonar /deto'nar/ *vt* detonate; (*fam: criticar*) pull to pieces □ *vi* detonate

detrás /de'traʃ/ *adv* behind □ *prep* ~ **de** behind

detrito /de'tritu/ *m* detritus

deturpar /detur'par/ *vt* misrepresent, distort

deus /dews/ *m* (*f* **deusa**) god (*f* goddess); ~**-dará** *m* **ao** ~**-dará** at the mercy of chance

devagar /dʒiva'gar/ *adv* slowly

deva|near /devani'ar/ *vi* daydream; ~**neio** *m* daydream

devas|sar /deva'sar/ *vt* expose; ~**sidão** *f* debauchery; ~**so** *a* debauched

devastar /devas'tar/ *vt* devastate

de|vedor /deve'dor/ *a* debit □ *m* debtor; ~**ver** *vt* owe □ *vaux* ~**ve** fazer (*obrigação*) he has to do; ~**ve** chegar (*probabilidade*) he should arrive; ~**ve ser** (*suposição*) he must be; ~**ve ter ido** he must have gone; ~**v(er)ia fazer** he ought to do; ~**v(er)ia ter feito** he ought to have done; ~**vidamente** *adv* duly; ~**vido** *a* due (**a** to)

devoção /devo'sãw/ *f* devotion

de|volução /devolu'sãw/ *f* return; ~**volver** *vt* return

devorar /devo'rar/ *vt* devour

devo|tar /devo'tar/ *vt* devote; ~**tar-se** *vpr* devote o.s. (**a** to); ~**to** /ɔ/ *a* devout

dez /dɛs/ *a* & *m* ten

dezanove /dza'nɔv/ (*Port*) *a* & *m* nineteen

dezas|seis /dza'sejʃ/ (*Port*) *a* & *m* sixteen; ~**sete** /ɛ/ (*Port*) *a* & *m* seventeen

dezembro /de'zẽbru/ *m* December

deze|na /de'zena/ *f* ten; **uma ~ (de)** about ten; **~nove** /ɔ/ *a & m* nineteen
dezes|seis /dʒize'sejs/ *a & m* sixteen; **~sete** /ɛ/ *a & m* seventeen
dezoito /dʒi'zojtu/ *a & m* eighteen
dia /'dʒia/ *m* day; **de ~** by day; **(no) ~ 20 de julho** (on) July 20th; **~ de folga** day off; **~ útil** working day; **~-a-~ m** everyday life
dia|bete /dʒia'bɛtʃi/ *f* diabetes; **~bético** *a & m* diabetic
dia|bo /dʒi'abu/ *m* devil; **~bólico** *a* diabolical, devilish; **~brete** /e/ *m* little devil; **~brura** *f (de criança)* bit of mischief; *pl* mischief
diadema /dʒia'dema/ *m* tiara
diafragma /dʒia'fragima/ *m* diaphragm
dia|gnosticar /dʒiagnostʃi'kar/ *vt* diagnose; **~gnóstico** *m* diagnosis □ *a* diagnostic
diago|nal /dʒiago'naw/ *(pl ~nais)* *a & f* diagonal
diagra|ma /dʒia'grama/ *m* diagram; **~mação** *f* design; **~mador** *m* designer; **~mar** *vt* design *<livro, revista>*
dialect- *(Port)* veja **dialet-**
dia|lética /dʒia'lɛtʃika/ *f* dialectics; **~leto** /ɛ/ *m* dialect
dialogar /dʒialo'gar/ *vi* talk; *(pol)* hold talks
diálogo /dʒi'alogu/ *m* dialogue
diamante /dʒia'mãtʃi/ *m* diamond
diâmetro /dʒi'ametru/ *m* diameter
dian|te /dʒi'ãtʃi/ *adv* **de ... em ~te** from ... on(wards); **~te de** *(enfrentando)* faced with; *(perante)* before; **~teira** *f* lead; **~teiro** *a* front
diapasão /dʒiapa'zãw/ *m* tuning-fork
diapositivo /dʒiapozi'tʃivu/ *m* transparency
diá|ria /dʒi'aria/ *f* daily rate; **~rio** *a* daily
diarista /dʒia'rista/ *m/f* day labourer; *(faxineira)* daily (help)
diarréia /dʒia'xeja/ *f* diarrhoea
dica /'dʒika/ *f* tip, hint
dicção /dʒik'sãw/ *f* diction
dicionário /dʒisio'nariu/ *m* dictionary
didáti|ca /dʒi'datʃika/ *f* teaching methodology; **~co** *a* teaching; *<livro>* educational; *<estilo>* didactic
die|ta /dʒi'eta/ *f* diet; **de ~ta** on a diet; **~tista** *m/f* dietician
difa|mação /dʒifama'sãw/ *f* defamation; **~mar** *vt* defame; **~matório** *a* defamatory
diferen|ça /dʒife'rẽsa/ *f* difference; **~cial** *(pl ~ciais)* *a & f* differential; **~ciar** *vt* differentiate; **~ciar-se** *vpr* differ; **~te** *a* different

dife|rimento /dʒiferi'mẽtu/ *m* deferment; **~rir** *vt* defer □ *vi* differ
difí|cil /dʒi'fisiw/ *(pl ~ceis)* *a* difficult; *(improvável)* unlikely
dificilmente /dʒifisiw'mẽtʃi/ *adv* **~ poderá fazê-lo** he's unlikely to be able to do it
dificul|dade /dʒifikuw'dadʒi/ *f* difficulty; **~tar** *vt* make difficult
difteria /dʒifte'ria/ *f* diphtheria
difun|dir /dʒifũ'dʒir/ *vt* spread; *(pela rádio)* broadcast; diffuse *<luz, calor>*; **~dir-se** *vpr* spread
difu|são /dʒifu'zãw/ *f* diffusion; **~so** *a* diffuse
dige|rir /dʒiʒe'rir/ *vt* digest; **~rível** *(pl ~ríveis)* *a* digestible
diges|tão /dʒiʒes'tãw/ *f* digestion; **~tivo** *a* digestive
digi|tal /dʒiʒi'taw/ *(pl ~tais)* *a* digital; **impressão ~tal** fingerprint; **~tar** *vt* key
dígito /'dʒiʒitu/ *m* digit
digladiar /dʒigladʒi'ar/ *vi* do battle
dig|nar-se /dʒig'narsi/ *vpr* deign (de to); **~nidade** *f* dignity; **~nificar** *vt* dignify; **~no** *a* worthy (de of); *(decoroso)* dignified
dilace|rante /dʒilase'rãtʃi/ *a* *<dor>* excruciating; **~rar** *vt* tear to pieces
dilapidar /dʒilapi'dar/ *vt* squander
dilatar /dʒila'tar/ *vt* expand; *(med)* dilate; **~se** *vpr* expand; *(med)* dilate
dilema /dʒi'lema/ *m* dilemma
diletante /dʒile'tãtʃi/ *a & m/f* dilettante
dili|gência /dʒili'ʒẽsia/ *f* diligence; *(carruagem)* stagecoach; **~gente** *a* diligent, hard-working
diluir /dʒilu'ir/ *vt* dilute
dilúvio /dʒi'luviu/ *m* deluge
dimen|são /dʒimẽ'sãw/ *f* dimension; **~sionar** *vt* size up
diminu|ição /dʒiminui'sãw/ *f* reduction; **~ir** *vt* reduce □ *vi* lessen; *<carro, motorista>* slow down; **~tivo** *a & m* diminutive; **~to** *a* minute
Dinamarca /dʒina'marka/ *f* Denmark
dinamar|quês /dʒinamar'kes/ *(f ~quesa)* *a* Danish □ *m* Dane
dinâmi|ca /dʒi'namika/ *f* dynamics; **~co** *a* dynamic
dina|mismo /dʒina'mizmu/ *m* dynamism; **~mite** *f* dynamite
dínamo /'dʒinamu/ *m* dynamo
dinastia /dʒinas'tʃia/ *f* dynasty
dinda /'dʒĩda/ *(fam)* *f* godmother
dinheiro /dʒi'ɲeru/ *m* money
dinossauro /dʒino'sawru/ *m* dinosaur
diocese /dʒio'sɛzi/ *f* diocese
dióxido /dʒi'ɔksidu/ *m* dioxide; **~ de carbono** carbon dioxide
diplo|ma /dʒi'ploma/ *m* diploma; **~macia** *f* diplomacy; **~mar-se** *vpr*

take one's diploma; ~mata *m/f* diplomat □ *a* diplomatic; ~mático *a* diplomatic

direção /dʒire'sãw/ *f* (*sentido*) direction; (*de empresa*) management; (*condução de carro*) driving; (*manuseio do volante*) steering

direct- (*Port*) *veja* diret-

direi|ta /dʒi'rejta/ *f* right; ~tinho *adv* exactly right; ~tista *a* rightwing □ *m/f* rightwinger, rightist; ~to *a* right; (*ereto*) straight □ *adv* properly □ *m* right

dire|tas /dʒi'rɛtas/ *f pl* direct (presidential) elections; ~to *a* direct □ *adv* directly; ~tor *m* director; (*de escola*) headteacher; (*de jornal*) editor; ~tor-gerente managing director; ~toria *f* (*diretores*) board of directors; (*sala*) boardroom; ~tório *m* directory; ~triz *f* directive

diri|gente /dʒiri'ʒẽtʃi/ *a* leading □ *m/f* leader; ~gir *vt* direct; manage <*empresa*>; drive <*carro*>; ~gir-se *vpr* (*ir*) make one's way; ~gir-se a (*falar com*) address

dis|cagem /dʒis'kaʒẽ/ *f* dialling; ~car *vt/i* dial

discente /dʒi'sẽtʃi/ *a* corpo ~ student body

discer|nimento /dʒiserni'mẽtu/ *m* discernment; ~nir *vt* discern

discipli|na /dʒisi'plina/ *f* discipline; ~nador *a* disciplinary; ~nar *vt* discipline

discípulo /dʒi'sipulu/ *m* disciple

disc-jóquei /dʒisk'ʒɔkej/ *m* disc-jockey

disco /'dʒisku/ *m* disc; (*de música*) record; (*no atletismo*) discus □ (*fam*) *f* disco; ~ flexível/rígido floppy/hard disk; ~ laser CD, compact disc; ~ voador flying saucer

discor|dante /dʒiskor'dãtʃi/ *a* conflicting; ~dar *vi* disagree (de with)

discote|ca /dʒisko'tɛka/ *f* discotheque; ~cário *m* DJ

discre|pância /dʒiskre'pãsia/ *f* discrepancy; ~pante *a* inconsistent; ~par *vi* diverge (de from)

dis|creto /dʒis'krɛtu/ *a* discreet; ~crição *f* discretion

discrimi|nação /dʒiskrimina'sãw/ *f* discrimination; (*descrição*) description; ~nar *vt* discriminate; ~natório *a* discriminatory

discur|sar /dʒiskur'sar/ *vi* speak; ~so *m* speech

discussão /dʒisku'sãw/ *f* discussion; (*briga*) argument

discu|tir /dʒisku'tʃir/ *vt/i* discuss; (*brigar*) argue; ~tível (*pl* ~tíveis) *a* debatable

disenteria /dʒizẽte'ria/ *f* dysentery

disfar|çar /dʒisfar'sar/ *vt* disguise; ~çar-se *vpr* disguise o.s.; ~ce *m* disguise

dis|lético /dʒiz'lɛtʃiku/ *a* & *m* dyslexic; ~lexia *f* dyslexia; ~léxico *a* & *m* dyslexic

dispa|rada /dʒispa'rada/ *f* bolt; ~rado *adv* o melhor ~rado the best by a long way; ~rar *vt* fire <*arma*> □ *vi* (*com arma*) fire; <*preços, inflação*> shoot up; <*corredor*> surge ahead

disparate /dʒispa'ratʃi/ *m* piece of nonsense; *pl* nonsense

dis|pêndio /dʒis'pẽdʒiu/ *m* expenditure; ~pendioso /o/ *a* costly

dispen|sa /dʒis'pẽsa/ *f* exemption; ~sar *vt* (*distribuir*) dispense; (*isentar*) exempt (de from); (*prescindir de*) dispense with; ~sável (*pl* ~sáveis) *a* dispensable

dispersar /dʒisper'sar/ *vt* disperse; waste <*energias*> □ *vi*, ~-se *vpr* disperse

disperso /dʒis'pɛrsu/ *adj* scattered

dispo|nibilidade /dʒisponibili'dadʒi/ *f* availability; ~nível (*pl* ~níveis) *a* available

dis|por /dʒis'por/ *vt* arrange □ *vi* ~por de have at one's disposal; ~por-se *vpr* form up □ *m* ao seu ~por at your disposal; ~posição *f* (*vontade*) willingness; (*arranjo*) arrangement; (*de espírito*) frame of mind; (*de testamento etc*) provision; à ~posição de alg at s.o.'s disposal; ~positivo *m* device; ~posto *a* prepared, willing (a to)

dispu|ta /dʒis'puta/ *f* dispute; ~tar *vt* dispute; (*tentar ganhar*) compete for

disquete /dʒis'ketʃi/ *m* diskette, floppy (disk)

dissabores /dʒisa'boris/ *m pl* troubles

disseminar /dʒisemi'nar/ *vt* disseminate

dissertação /dʒiserta'sãw/ *f* dissertation, lecture

dissi|dência /dʒisi'dẽsia/ *f* dissidence; ~dente *a* & *m* dissident

dissídio /dʒi'sidʒiu/ *m* dispute

dissimular /dʒisimu'lar/ *vt* hide □ *vi* dissimulate

disso = de + isso

dissipar /dʒisi'par/ *vt* clear <*nevoeiro*>; dispel <*dúvidas, suspeitas, ilusões*>; dissipate <*fortuna*>; ~-se *vpr* <*nevoeiro*> clear; <*dúvidas etc*> be dispelled

dissolu|ção /dʒisolu'sãw/ *f* dissolution; ~to *a* dissolute

dissolver /dʒisow'ver/ *vt* dissolve; ~-se *vpr* dissolve

dissuadir /dʒisua'dʒir/ *vt* dissuade (de from)

distância /dʒis'tãsia/ *f* distance
distan|ciar /dʒistãsi'ar/ *vt* distance;
~**ciar-se** *vpr* distance o.s.; ~**te** *a* distant
disten|der /dʒistẽ'der/ *vt* stretch
<*pernas*>; relax <*músculo*>; ~**der-se** *vpr* relax; ~**são** *f* (*med*) pull;
~**são muscular** pulled muscle
distin|ção /dʒistʃĩ'sãw/ *f* distinction;
~**guir** *vt* distinguish (**de** from);
~**guir-se** *vpr* distinguish o.s.; ~**tivo** *a* distinctive □ *m* badge; ~**to** *a* distinct; <*senhor*> distinguished
disto = **de** + **isto**
distor|ção /dʒistor'sãw/ *f* distortion;
~**cer** *vt* distort
distra|ção /dʒistra'sãw/ *f* distraction;
~**ído** *a* absent-minded; ~**ir** *vt* distract; (*divertir*) amuse; ~**ir-se** *vpr* be distracted; (*divertir-se*) amuse o.s.
distribu|ição /dʒistribui'sãw/ *f* distribution; ~**idor** *m* distributor;
~**idora** *f* distributor, distribution company; ~**ir** *vt* distribute
distrito /dʒis'tritu/ *m* district
distúrbio /dʒis'turbiu/ *m* trouble
di|tado /dʒi'tadu/ *m* dictation; (*provérbio*) saying; ~**tador** *m* dictator;
~**tadura** *f* dictatorship; ~**tame** *m* dictate; ~**tar** *vt* dictate; ~**tatorial** (*pl* ~**tatoriais**) *a* dictatorial
dito /'dʒitu/ *a* ~ **e feito** no sooner said than done □ *m* remark
ditongo /dʒi'tõgu/ *m* diphthong
DIU /'dʒiu/ *m* IUD, coil
diurno /dʒi'urnu/ *a* day
divã /dʒi'vã/ *m* couch
divagar /dʒiva'gar/ *vi* digress
diver|gência /dʒiver'ʒẽsia/ *a* divergence; ~**gente** *a* divergent; ~**gir** *vi* diverge (**de** from); ~**são** *f* diversion; (*divertimento*) amusement; ~**sidade** *f* diversity; ~**sificar** *vt*/*i* diversify;
~**so** /ɛ/ *a* (*diferente*) diverse; *pl* (*vários*) several; ~**tido** *a* (*engraçado*) funny; (*que se curte*) enjoyable; ~**timento** *m* enjoyment, fun; (*um*) amusement; ~**tir** *vt* amuse; ~**tir-se** *vpr* enjoy o.s., have fun
dívida /'dʒivida/ *f* debt; ~ **externa** foreign debt
divi|dendo /dʒivi'dẽdu/ *m* dividend;
~**dido** *a* <*pessoa*> torn; ~**dir** *vt* divide; (*compartilhar*) share; ~**dir-se** *vpr* be divided
divindade /dʒivĩ'dadʒi/ *f* divinity
divino /dʒi'vinu/ *a* divine
divi|sa /dʒi'viza/ *f* (*lema*) motto; (*galão*) stripes; (*fronteira*) border; *pl* foreign currency; ~**são** *f* division;
~**sória** *f* partition; ~**sório** *a* dividing
divorci|ado /dʒivorsi'adu/ *a* divorced □ *m* divorcé (*f* divorcée); ~**ar** *vt*

divorce; ~**ar-se** *vpr* get divorced;
~**ar-se de** divorce
divórcio /dʒi'vɔrsiu/ *m* divorce
divul|gado /dʒivuw'gadu/ *a* widespread; ~**gar** *vt* spread; publish <*notícia*>; divulge <*segredo*>; ~**gar-se** *vpr* be spread
dizer /dʒi'zer/ *vt* say; ~ **a alg que** tell sb that; ~ **para alg fazer** tell s.o. to do □ *vi* ~ **com** go with; ~**-se** *vpr* claim to be □ *m* saying
dizimar /dʒizi'mar/ *vt* decimate
do = **de** +**o**
dó /dɔ/ *m* pity; **dar** ~ be pitiful; **ter** ~ **de** feel sorry for
do|ação /doa'sãw/ *f* donation; ~**ador** *m* donor; ~**ar** *vt* donate
do|bra /'dɔbra/ *f* fold; (*de calça*) turn-up, (*Amer*) cuff; ~**bradiça** *f* hinge;
~**bradiço** *a* pliable; ~**brado** *a* (*duplo*) double; ~**brar** *vt* (*duplicar*) double; (*fazer dobra em*) fold; (*curvar*) bend; go round <*esquina*>; ring <*sinos*>; (*Port*) dub <*filme*> □ *vi* double; <*sinos*> ring; ~**brar-se** *vpr* bend; ~**bro** *m* double
doca /'dɔka/ *f* dock
doce /'dosi/ *a* sweet; <*água*> fresh □ *m* sweet; ~ **de leite** fudge
docente /do'sẽtʃi/ *a* teaching; **corpo** ~ teaching staff, (*Amer*) faculty
dó|cil /'dɔsiw/ (*pl* ~**ceis**) *a* docile
documen|tação /dokumẽta'sãw/ *f* documentation; ~**tar** *vt* document;
~**tário** *a* & *m* documentary; ~**to** *m* document
doçura /do'sura/ *f* sweetness
dodói /do'dɔj/ (*fam*) *m* **ter** ~ have a pain □ *a* poorly, ill
doen|ça /do'ẽsa/ *f* illness; (*infecciosa, fig*) disease; ~**te** *a* ill; ~**tio** *a* <*criança, aspecto*> sickly; <*interesse, curiosidade*> morbid
doer /do'er/ *vi* hurt; <*cabeça, músculo*> ache
dog|ma /'dɔgima/ *m* dogma; ~**mático** *a* dogmatic
doido /'dojdu/ *a* crazy
dois /dojs/ *a* & *m* (*f* **duas**) two
dólar /'dɔlar/ *m* dollar
dolo|rido /dolo'ridu/ *a* sore; ~**roso** /o/ *a* painful
dom /dõ/ *m* gift
do|mador /doma'dor/ *m* tamer;
~**mar** *vt* tame
doméstica /do'mɛstʃika/ *f* housemaid
domesticar /domestʃi'kar/ *vt* domesticate
doméstico /do'mɛstʃiku/ *a* domestic
domi|ciliar /domisili'ar/ *a* home;
~**cílio** *m* home
domi|nação /domina'sãw/ *f* domination; ~**nador** *a* domineering;
~**nante** *a* dominant; ~**nar** *vt* dom-

inate; have a command of <*língua*>; ~**nar-se** *vpr* control o.s.

domin|go /do'mĩgu/ *m* Sunday; ~**gueiro** *a* Sunday

domini|cal /domini'kaw/ (*pl* ~**cais**) *a* Sunday; ~**cano** *a* & *m* Dominican

domínio /do'miniu/ *m* command

dona /'dona/ *f* owner; **Dona** (*com nome*) Miss; ~ **de casa** *f* housewife

donativo /dona'tʃivu/ *m* donation

donde /'dõdʒi/ *adv* from where; (*motivo*) from whence

dono /'donu/ *m* owner

donzela /dõ'zɛla/ *f* maiden

dopar /do'par/ *vt* drug

dor /dor/ *f* pain; (*menos aguda*) ache; ~ **de cabeça** headache

dor|mente /dor'mẽtʃi/ *a* numb □ *m* sleeper; ~**mida** *f* sleep; ~**minhoco** /o/ *m* sleepyhead; ~**mir** *vi* sleep; ~**mitar** *vi* doze; ~**mitório** *m* bedroom; (*comunitário*) dormitory

dorso /'dorsu/ *m* back; (*de livro*) spine

dos = **de** + **os**

do|sagem /do'zaʒẽ/ *f* dosage; ~**sar** *vt* moderate; ~**se** /ɔ/ *f* dose; (*de uísque etc*) shot, measure

dossiê /dosi'e/ *m* file

do|tação /dota'sãw/ *f* endowment; ~**tado** *a* gifted; ~**tado de** endowed with; ~**tar** *vt* endow (**de** with); ~**te** /ɔ/ *m* (*de noiva*) dowry; (*dom*) endowment

dou|rado /do'radu/ *a* (*de cor*) golden; (*revestido de ouro*) gilded, gilt □ *m* gilt; ~**rar** *vt* gild

dou|to /'dotu/ *a* learned; ~**tor** *m* doctor; ~**torado** *m* doctorate, PhD; ~**trina** *f* doctrine; ~**trinar** *vt* indoctrinate

doze /'dozi/ *a* & *m* twelve

dragão /dra'gãw/ *m* dragon

dragar /dra'gar/ *vt* dredge

drágea /'draʒia/ *f* lozenge

dra|ma /'drama/ *m* drama; ~**malhão** *m* melodrama; ~**mático** *a* dramatic; ~**matizar** *vt* dramatize; ~**maturgo** *m* dramatist, playwright

drapeado /drapi'adu/ *a* draped

drástico /'drastʃiku/ *a* drastic

dre|nagem /dre'naʒẽ/ *f* drainage; ~**nar** *vt* drain; ~**no** /ɛ/ *m* drain

driblar /dri'blar/ *vt* (*em futebol*) dribble round, beat; (*fig*) get round

drinque /'drĩki/ *m* drink

drive /'drajvi/ *m* disk drive

dro|ga /'drɔga/ *f* drug; (*fam*) (*coisa sem valor*) dead loss; (*coisa chata*) drag □ *int* damn; ~**gado** *a* on drugs □ *m* drug addict; ~**gar** *vt* drug; ~**gar-se** *vpr* take drugs; ~**garia** *f* dispensing chemist's, pharmacy

duas /'duas/ *veja* **dois**

dúbio /'dubiu/ *a* dubious

dub|lagem /du'blaʒẽ/ *f* dubbing; ~**lar** *vt* dub <*filme*>; mime <*música*>; ~**lê** *m* double

ducentésimo /dusẽ'tɛzimu/ *a* two-hundredth

ducha /'duʃa/ *f* shower

ducto /'duktu/ *m* duct

duelo /du'ɛlu/ *m* duel

duende /du'ẽdʒi/ *m* elf

dueto /du'etu/ *m* duet

duna /'duna/ *f* dune

duodécimo /duo'dɛsimu/ *a* twelfth

duodeno /duo'dɛnu/ *m* duodenum

dupla /'dupla/ *f* pair, duo; <*no tênis*> doubles

duplex /du'plɛks/ *a invar* two-floor □ *m invar* two-floor apartment, (*Amer*) duplex

dupli|car /dupli'kar/ *vt/i* double; ~**cidade** *f* duplicity; ~**cata** *f* duplicate

duplo /'duplu/ *a* double

duque /'duki/ duke; ~**sa** /e/ *f* duchess

du|ração /dura'sãw/ *f* duration; ~**radouro** *a* lasting; ~**rante** *prep* during; ~**rar** *vi* last; ~**rável** (*pl* ~**ráveis**) *a* durable

durex /du'rɛks/ *m invar* sellotape

du|reza /du'reza/ *f* hardness; ~**ro** *a* hard; (*fam: sem dinheiro*) hard up, broke

dúvida /'duvida/ *f* doubt; (*pergunta*) query

duvi|dar /duvi'dar/ *vt/i* doubt; ~**doso** /o/ *a* doubtful

duzentos /du'zẽtus/ *a* & *m* two hundred

dúzia /'duzia/ *f* dozen

E

e /i/ *conj* and

ébano /'ɛbanu/ *m* ebony

ébrio /'ɛbriu/ *a* drunk □ *m* drunkard

ebulição /ebuli'sãw/ *f* boiling

eclesiástico /eklezi'astʃiku/ *a* ecclesiastical

eclético /e'klɛtʃiku/ *a* eclectic

eclip|sar /eklip'sar/ *vt* eclipse; ~**se** *m* eclipse

eclodir /eklo'dʒir/ *vi* emerge; (*estourar*) break out; open

eco /'ɛku/ *m* echo; **ter** ~ have repercussions; ~**ar** *vt/i* echo

eco|logia /ekolo'ʒia/ *f* ecology; ~**lógico** *a* ecological; ~**logista** *m/f* ecologist

eco|nomia /ekono'mia/ *f* economy; (*ciência*) economics; *pl* (*dinheiro poupado*) savings; ~**nômico** *a* economic; (*rentável, barato*) economical; ~**nomista** *m/f* economist; ~**nomizar** *vt* save □ *vi* economize

écran /ɛ'krã/ (*Port*) *m* screen

eczema /ek'zema/ *m* eczema

edição /edʒi'sãw/ *f* edition; (*de filmes*) editing

edificante /edʒifi'kãtʃi/ *a* edifying

edifício /edʒi'fisiu/ *m* building

Edimburgo /edʒĩ'burgu/ *f* Edinburgh

edi|tal /edʒi'taw/ (*pl* ~**tais**) *m* announcement; ~**tar** *vt* publish; (*comput*) edit; ~**to** *m* edict; ~**tor** *m* publisher; ~**tora** *f* publishing company; ~**torial** (*pl* ~**toriais**) *a* publishing □ *m* editorial

edredom /edre'dõ/ *m*, (*Port*) **edredão** /edre'dãw/ *m* quilt

educa|ção /eduka'sãw/ *f* (*ensino*) education; (*polidez*) good manners; **é falta de** ~**ção** it's rude; ~**cional** (*pl* ~**cionais**) *a* education

edu|cado /edu'kadu/ *a* polite; ~**car** *vt* educate; ~**cativo** *a* educational

efeito /e'fejtu/ *m* effect; **fazer** ~ have an effect; **para todos os** ~**s** to all intents and purposes; ~ **colateral** side effect; ~ **estufa** greenhouse effect

efêmero /e'fêmeru/ *a* ephemeral

efeminado /efemi'nadu/ *a* effeminate

efervescente /eferve'stʃi/ *a* effervescent

efe|tivar /efetʃi'var/ *vt* bring into effect; (*contratar*) make a permanent member of staff; ~**tivo** *a* real, effective; <*cargo, empregado*> permanent; ~**tuar** *vt* carry out, effect

efi|cácia /efi'kasia/ *f* effectiveness; ~**caz** *a* effective

efici|ência /efisi'ẽsia/ *f* efficiency; ~**ente** *a* efficient

efígie /e'fiʒi/ *f* effigy

efusivo /efu'zivu/ *a* effusive

Egeu /e'ʒew/ *a & m* Aegean

égide /'ɛʒidʒi/ *f* aegis

egípcio /e'ʒipsiu/ *a & m* Egyptian

Egito /e'ʒitu/ *m* Egypt

ego /'ɛgu/ *m* ego; ~**cêntrico** *a* self-centred, egocentric; ~**ísmo** *m* selfishness; ~**ísta** *a* selfish □ *m/f* egoist □ *m* (*de rádio etc*) earplug

égua /'ɛgwa/ *f* mare

eis /ejs/ *adv* (*aqui está*) here is/are; (*isso é*) that is

eixo /'ejʃu/ *m* axle; (*mat, entre cidades*) axis; **pôr nos** ~**s** set straight

ela /'ɛla/ *pron* she; (*coisa*) it; (*com preposição*) her; (*coisa*) it

elaborar /elabo'rar/ *vt* (*fazer*) make, produce; (*desenvolver*) work out

elasticidade /elastʃisi'dadʒi/ *f* (*de coisa*) elasticity; (*de pessoa*) suppleness

elástico /e'lastʃiku/ *a* elastic □ *m* (*de borracha*) elastic band; (*de calcinha etc*) elastic

ele /'eli/ *pron* he; (*coisa*) it; (*com preposição*) him; (*coisa*) it

electr- (*Port*) *veja* **eletr-**

eléctrico /i'lɛktriku/ (*Port*) *m* tram, (*Amer*) streetcar □ *a veja* **elétrico**

elefante /ele'fãtʃi/ *m* elephant

ele|gância /ele'gãsia/ *f* elegance; ~**gante** *a* elegant

eleger /ele'ʒer/ *vt* elect; ~**-se** *vpr* get elected

elegia /ele'ʒia/ *f* elegy

elei|ção /elej'sãw/ *f* election; ~**to** *a* elected, elect; <*povo*> chosen; ~**tor** *m* voter; ~**torado** *m* electorate; ~**toral** (*pl* ~**torais**) *a* electoral

elemen|tar /elemẽ'tar/ *a* elementary; ~**to** *m* element

elenco /e'lẽku/ *m* (*de filme, peça*) cast

eletri|cidade /eletrisi'dadʒi/ *f* electricity; ~**cista** *m/f* electrician

elétrico /e'lɛtriku/ *a* electric

eletri|ficar /eletrifi'kar/ *vt* electrify; ~**zar** *vt* electrify

eletro /e'lɛtru/ *m* ECG; ~**cutar** *vt* electrocute; ~**do** /o/ *m* electrode; ~**domésticos** *m pl* electrical appliances

eletrôni|ca /ele'tronika/ *f* electronics; ~**co** *a* electronic

ele|vação /eleva'sãw/ *f* elevation; (*aumento*) rise; ~**vado** *a* high; <*sentimento, estilo*> elevated; ~**vador** *m* lift, (*Amer*) elevator; ~**var** *vt* raise; (*promover*) elevate; ~**var-se** *vpr* rise

elimi|nar /elimi'nar/ *vt* eliminate; ~**natória** *f* heat; ~**natório** *a* eliminatory

elipse /e'lipsi/ *f* ellipse

elíptico /e'liptʃiku/ *a* elliptical

eli|te /e'litʃi/ *f* elite; ~**tismo** *m* elitism; ~**tista** *a & m/f* elitist

elmo /'ɛwmu/ *m* helmet

elo /'ɛlu/ *m* link

elo|giar /eloʒi'ar/ *vt* praise; ~**giar alg por** compliment s.o. on; ~**gio** *m* (*louvor*) praise; (*um*) compliment; ~**gioso** /o/ *a* complimentary

elo|quência /elo'kwẽsia/ *f* eloquence; ~**qüente** *a* eloquent

eluci|dar /elusi'dar/ *vt* elucidate; ~**dativo** *a* elucidatory

em /j/ *prep* in; (*sobre*) on; **ela está no Eduardo** she's at Eduardo's (house); **de casa** ~ **casa** from house to house; **aumentar** ~ **10%** increase by 10%

emagre|cer /emagre'ser/ *vi* lose weight, get thinner □ *vt* make thinner; ~**cimento** *m* slimming

emanar /ema'nar/ *vi* emanate (**de** from)

emanci|pação /emãsipa'sãw/ *f* emancipation; ~**par** *vt* emancipate; ~**par-se** *vpr* become emancipated

emara|nhado /emara'ɲadu/ *a* tangled □ *m* tangle; ~**nhar** *vt* tangle; (*envolver*) entangle; ~**nhar-se** *vpr* get tangled up; (*envolver-se*) become entangled (**em in**)

embaçar /ība'sar/, (*Port*) **embaciar** /ībasi'ar/ *vt* steam up <*vidro*> □ *vi* <*vidro*> steam up; <*olhos*> grow misty

embainhar /ībaj'ɲar/ *vt* hem <*vestido, calça*>

embaixa|da /ība'ʃada/ *f* embassy; **~dor** *m* ambassador; **~triz** *f* ambassador; (*esposa*) ambassador's wife

embaixo /ī'baʃu/ *adv* underneath; (*em casa*) downstairs; **~ de** under

emba|lagem /ība'laʒē/ *f* packaging; **~lar**¹ *vt* pack

emba|lar² /ība'lar/ *vt* rock <*criança*>; **~lo** *m* (*fig*) excitement, thrill

embalsamar /ībawsa'mar/ *vt* embalm

embara|çar /ībara'sar/ *vt* embarrass; **~çar-se** *vpr* get embarrassed (**com** by); **~ço** *m* embarrassment; **~çoso** /o/ *a* embarrassing

embaralhar /ībara'ʎar/ *vt* muddle up; shuffle <*cartas*>; **~se** *vpr* get muddled up

embar|cação /ībarka'sāw/ *f* vessel; **~cadouro** *m* wharf; **~car** *vt/i* board, embark

embar|gado /ībar'gadu/ *a* <*voz*> faltering; **~go** *m* embargo

embarque /ī'barki/ *m* boarding; (*seção do aeroporto*) departures

embasba|cado /ībazba'kadu/ *a* openmouthed; **~car-se** *vpr* be left openmouthed

embate /ī'batʃi/ *m* (*de carros etc*) crash; (*fig*) clash

embebedar /ībebe'dar/ *vt* make drunk; **~se** *vpr* get drunk

embeber /ībe'ber/ *vt* soak; **~se de** soak up; **~se em** get absorbed in

embele|zador /ībeleza'dor/ *a* <*cirurgia*> cosmetic; **~zar** *vt* embellish; spruce up <*casa*>; **~zar-se** *vpr* make o.s. beautiful

embevecer /ībeve'ser/ *vt* captivate, engross; **~se** *vpr* get engrossed, be captivated

emblema /ē'blema/ *m* emblem

embocadura /īboka'dura/ *f* (*de instrumento*) mouthpiece; (*de freio*) bit; (*de rio*) mouth; (*de rua*) entrance

êmbolo /'ēbulu/ *m* piston

embolsar /ībow'sar/ *vt* pocket; (*reembolsar*) reimburse

embora /ī'bɔra/ *adv* away □ *conj* although

emborcar /ībor'kar/ *vi* overturn; <*barco*> capsize

emboscada /ībos'kada/ *f* ambush

embrai|agem /ēbraj'aʒē/ (*Port*) *f veja* **embreagem**; **~ar** (*Port*) *vi veja* **embrear**

embre|agem /ēbri'aʒē/ *f* clutch; **~ar** *vi* let in the clutch

embria|gar /ēbria'gar/ *vt* intoxicate; **~gar-se** *vpr* get drunk, become intoxicated; **~guez** /e/ *f* drunkenness; **~guez no volante** drunken driving

embri|ão /ēbri'āw/ *m* embryo; **~onário** *a* embryonic

embro|mação /ībroma'sāw/ *f* flannel; **~mar** *vt* flannel, string along; (*enganar*) con □ *vi* stall, drag one's feet

embru|lhada /ībru'ʎada/ *f* muddle; **~lhar** *vt* wrap up <*pacote*>; upset <*estômago*>; (*confundir*) muddle up; **~lhar-se** *vpr* <*pessoa*> get muddled up; **~lho** *m* parcel; (*fig*) mix-up

embur|rado /ību'xadu/ *a* sulky; **~rar** *vi* sulk

embuste /ī'bustʃi/ *m* hoax, put-up job

embu|tido /ību'tʃidu/ *a* built-in, fitted; **~tir** *vt* build in, fit

emen|da /e'mēda/ *f* correction, improvement; (*de lei*) amendment; **~dar** *vt* correct; amend <*lei*>; **~dar-se** *vpr* mend one's ways

ementa /i'mēta/ (*Port*) *f* menu

emer|gência /emer'ʒēsia/ *f* emergency; **~gente** *a* emergent; **~gir** *vi* surface

emi|gração /emigra'sāw/ *f* emigration; (*de aves etc*) migration; **~grado** *a* & *m* émigré; **~grante** *a* & *m/f* emigrant; **~grar** *vi* emigrate; <*aves, animais*> migrate

emi|nência /emi'nēsia/ *f* eminence; **~nente** *a* eminent

emis|são /emi'sāw/ *f* (*de ações etc*) issue; (*na rádio, TV*) transmission, broadcast; (*de som, gases*) emission; **~sário** *m* emissary; **~sor** *m* transmitter; **~sora** *f* (*de rádio*) radio station; (*de TV*) TV station

emitir /emi'tʃir/ *vt* issue <*ações, selos etc*>; emit <*sons*>; (*pela rádio, TV*) transmit, broadcast

emoção /emo'sāw/ *f* emotion; (*excitação*) excitement

emocio|nal /emosio'naw/ (*pl* **~nais**) *a* emotional; **~nante** *a* (*excitante*) exciting; (*comovente*) touching, emotional; **~nar** *vt* (*excitar*) excite; (*comover*) move, touch; **~nar-se** *vpr* get emotional

emoldurar /emowdu'rar/ *vt* frame

emotivo /emo'tʃivu/ *a* emotional

empacar /īpa'kar/ *vi* <*cavalo*> baulk; <*negociações etc*> grind to a halt; <*orador*> dry up

empacotar /īpako'tar/ *vt* pack up; (*pôr em pacotes*) packet

empa|da /ē'pada/ *f* pie; **~dão** *m* (large) pie

empalhar /īpa'ʎar/ *vt* stuff

empalidecer /īpalide'ser/ *vi* turn pale

empanar¹ /ēpa'nar/ vt tarnish, dull

empanar² /ēpa'nar/ vt cook in batter <carne etc>

empanturrar /ĩpãtu'xar/ vt stuff; ~se vpr stuff o.s. (de with)

empapar /ĩpa'par/ vt soak

empaltar /ēpa'tar/ vt draw <jogo> □ vi <times> draw; <corredores> tie; ~te m (em jogo) draw; (em corrida, votação) tie; (em xadrez, fig) stalemate

empatia /ēpa'tʃia/ f empathy

empecilho /ēpe'siʎu/ m hindrance

empenar /ēpe'nar/ vt/i warp

empe|nhar /ĩpe'nar/ vt (penhorar) pawn; (prometer) pledge; ~nhar-se vpr do one's utmost (em to); ~nho /e/ m (compromisso) pledge; (diligência) effort, commitment

emperrar /ĩpe'xar/ vt make stick □ vi stick

emperti|gado /ĩpertʃi'gadu/ a upright; ~gar-se vpr stand up straight

empilhar /ĩpi'ʎar/ vt pile up

empi|nado /ĩpi'nadu/ a erect; (íngreme) sheer, steep; <nariz> turned-up; (fig) stuck-up; ~nar vt stand upright; fly <pipa>; tip up <copo>

empírico /ē'piriku/ a empirical

emplacar /ĩpla'kar/ vt notch up <pontos, sucessos, anos>; license <carro>

emplastro /ĩ'plastru/ m surgical plaster; ~ de nicotina nicotine patch

empobre|cer /ĩpobre'ser/ vt impoverish; ~cimento m impoverishment

empoleirar /ĩpole'rar/ vt perch; ~-se vpr perch

empol|gação /ĩpowga'sãw/ f fascination; ~gante a fascinating; ~gar vt fascinate

empossar /ĩpo'sar/ vt swear in

empreen|dedor /ēpriēde'dor/ a enterprising □ m entrepreneur; ~der vt undertake; ~dimento m undertaking

empre|gada /ĩpre'gada/ f (doméstica) maid; ~gado m employee; ~gador m employer; ~gar vt employ; ~gar-se vpr get a job; ~gatício a vínculo ~gatício contract of employment; ~go /e/ m (trabalho) job; (uso) use; ~guismo m patronage

emprei|tada /ĩprej'tada/ f commission, contract; (empreendimento) venture; ~teira f contractor, firm of contractors; ~teiro m contractor

empre|sa /ĩ'preza/ f company; ~sariado m business community; ~sarial (pl ~sariais) a business; ~sário m businessman; (de cantor etc) manager

empres|tado /ĩpres'tadu/ a on loan; pedir ~tado (ask to) borrow; tomar ~tado borrow; ~tar vt lend

empréstimo /ĩ'prestʃimu/ m loan

empur|rão /ĩpu'xãw/ m push; ~rar vt push

emular /emu'lar/ vt emulate

enamorado /enamo'radu/ a (apaixonado) in love

encabeçar /ĩkabe'sar/ vt head

encabu|lado /ĩkabu'ladu/ a shy; ~lar vt embarrass; ~lar-se vpr be shy

encadear /ĩkade'ar/ vt chain ou link together

encader|nação /ĩkaderna'sãw/ f binding; ~nado a bound; (com capa dura) hardback; ~nar vt bind

encai|xar /ĩka'ʃar/ vt/i fit; ~xe m (cavidade) socket; (juntura) joint

encalço /ĩ'kawsu/ m pursuit; no ~ de in pursuit of

encalhar /ĩka'ʎar/ vi <barco> run aground; (fig) get bogged down; <mercadoria> not sell; (fam: ficar solteiro) be left on the shelf

encaminhar /ĩkami'nar/ vt (dirigir) steer, direct; (remeter) pass on; set in motion <processo>; ~-se vpr set out

encana|dor /ĩkana'dor/ m plumber; ~mento m plumbing

encan|tador /ĩkãta'dor/ a enchanting; ~tamento m enchantment; ~tar vt enchant; ~to m charm

encaraco|lado /ĩkarako'ladu/ a curly; ~lar vt curl; ~lar-se vpr curl up

encarar /ĩka'rar/ vt confront, face

encarcerar /ĩkarse'rar/ vt imprison

encardido /ĩkar'dʒidu/ a grimy

encarecidamente /ĩkaresida'mētʃi/ adv insistently

encargo /ĩ'kargu/ m task, responsibility

encar|nação /ĩkarna'sãw/ f (do espírito) incarnation; (de um personagem) embodiment; ~nar vt embody; play <papel>

encarre|gado /ĩkaxe'gadu/ a in charge (de of) □ m person in charge; (de operários) foreman; ~gado de negócios chargé d'affaires; ~gar vt ~gar alg de put s.o. in charge of; ~gar-se de undertake to

encarte /ĩ'kartʃi/ m insert

ence|nação /ĩsena'sãw/ f (de peça) production; (fingimento) playacting; ~nar vt put on □ vi put it on

ence|radeira /ĩsera'dera/ f floor polisher; ~rar vt wax

encer|rado /ĩse'xadu/ a <assunto> closed; ~ramento m close; ~rar vt close; ~rar-se vpr close

encharcar /ĩʃar'kar/ vt soak

en|chente /ē'ʃētʃi/ f flood; ~cher vt fill; (fam) annoy □ (fam) vi be annoying; ~cher-se vpr fill up; (fam: fartar-se) get fed up (de with)

enciclopédia /ẽsiklo'pɛdʒia/ *f* encyclopaedia

enco|berto /ĩko'bɛrtu/ *a* <*céu, tempo*> overcast; **~brir** *vt* cover up □ *vi* <*tempo*> become overcast

encolher /ĩko'ʎer/ *vt* shrug <*ombros*>; pull up <*pernas*>; shrink <*roupa*> □ *vi* <*roupa*> shrink; **~se** *vpr (de medo)* shrink; *(de frio)* huddle; *(espremer-se)* squeeze up

encomen|da /ĩko'mẽda/ *f* order; **de ou sob ~da** to order; **~dar** *vt* order (a from)

encon|trão /ĩkõ'trãw/ *m* bump; *(empurrão)* shove; **~trar** *vt (achar)* find; *(ver)* meet; **~trar com** meet; **~trar-se** *vpr (ver-se)* meet; *(estar)* be; **~tro** *m* meeting; *(mil)* encounter; **ir ao ~tro de** go to meet; *(fig)* meet; **ir de ~tro a** run into; *(fig)* go against

encorajar /ĩkora'ʒar/ *vt* encourage

encor|pado /ĩkor'padu/ *a* stocky; <*vinho*> full-bodied; **~par** *vt/i* fill out

encos|ta /ĩ'kɔsta/ *f* slope; **~tar** *vt (apoiar)* lean; park <*carro*>; leave on the latch <*porta*>; *(pôr de lado)* put aside □ *vi* <*carro*> pull in; **~tar-se** *vpr* lean; **~to** /o/ *m* back

encra|vado /ĩkra'vadu/ *a* <*unha, pêlo*> ingrowing; **~var** *vt* stick

encren|ca /ĩ'krẽka/ *f* fix, jam; *pl* trouble; **~car** *vt* get into trouble <*pessoa*>; complicate <*situação*> □ *vi* <*situação*> get complicated; <*carro*> break down; **~car-se** *vpr* <*pessoa*> get into trouble; **~queiro** *m* troublemaker

encres|pado /ĩkres'padu/ *a* <*mar*> choppy; **~par** *vt* frizz <*cabelo*>; **~par-se** *vpr* <*cabelo*> go frizzy; <*mar*> get choppy

encruzilhada /ĩkruzi'ʎada/ *f* cross-roads

encurralar /ĩkuxa'lar/ *vt* hem in, pen in

encurtar /ĩkur'tar/ *vt* shorten

endere|çar /ĩdere'sar/ *vt* address; **~ço** /e/ *m* address

endinheirado /ĩdʒiɲe'radu/ *a* well-off

endireitar /ĩdʒirej'tar/ *vt* straighten; **~se** *vpr* straighten up

endivi|dado /ĩdʒivi'dadu/ *a* in debt; **~dar** *vt* put into debt; **~dar-se** *vpr* get into debt

endoidecer /ĩdojde'ser/ *vi* get mad

endos|sar /ĩdo'sar/ *vt* endorse; **~so** /o/ *m* endorsement

endurecer /ĩdure'ser/ *vt/i* harden

ener|gético /ener'ʒetʃiku/ *a* energy; **~gia** *f* energy

enérgico /e'nɛrʒiku/ *a* vigorous; <*remédio, discurso*> powerful

enevoado /enevu'adu/ *a (com névoa)* misty; *(com nuvens)* cloudy

enfarte /ĩ'fartʃi/ *m* heart attack

ênfase /'ẽfazi/ *f* emphasis; **dar ~ a** emphasize

enfático /ẽ'fatʃiku/ *a* emphatic

enfatizar /ẽfatʃi'zar/ *vt* emphasize

enfei|tar /ĩfej'tar/ *vt* decorate; **~tar-se** *vpr* dress up; **~te** *m* decoration

enfeitiçar /ĩfejtʃi'sar/ *vt* bewitch

enfer|magem /ĩfer'maʒẽ/ *f* nursing; **~maria** *f* ward; **~meira** *f* nurse; **~meiro** *m* male nurse; **~midade** *f* illness; **~mo** *a* sick □ *m* patient

enferru|jado /ĩfexu'ʒadu/ *a* rusty; **~jar** *vt/i* rust

enfezado /ĩfe'zadu/ *a* bad- tempered

enfiar /ẽfi'ar/ *vt* put; slip on <*roupa*>; thread <*agulha*>; string <*pérolas*>

enfileirar /ĩfilej'rar/ *vt* line up; **~se** *vpr* line up

enfim /ẽ'fĩ/ *adv (finalmente)* finally; *(resumindo)* anyway

enfo|car /ĩfo'kar/ *vt* tackle; **~que** *m* approach

enfor|camento /ĩforka'mẽtu/ *m* hanging; **~car** *vt* hang; **~car-se** *vpr* hang o.s.

enfraquecer /ĩfrake'ser/ *vt/i* weaken

enfrentar /ĩfrẽ'tar/ *vt* face

enfumaçado /ĩfuma'sadu/ *a* smoky

enfurecer /ĩfure'ser/ *vt* infuriate; **~se** *vpr* get furious

enga|jamento /ĩgaʒa'mẽtu/ *m* commitment; **~jado** *a* committed; **~jar-se** *vpr* get involved (**em** in)

engalfinhar-se /ĩgawfi'ɲarsi/ *vpr* grapple

enga|nado /ĩga'nadu/ *a (errado)* mistaken; **~nar** *vt* deceive; cheat on <*marido, esposa*>; stave off <*fome*>; **~nar-se** *vpr* be mistaken; **~no** *m (erro)* mistake; *(desonestidade)* deception

engarra|famento /ĩgaxafa'mẽtu/ *m* traffic jam; **~far** *vt* bottle <*vinho etc*>; block <*trânsito*>

engas|gar /ĩgaz'gar/ *vt* choke □ *vi* choke; <*motor*> backfire; **~go** *m* choking

engastar /ĩgaʃ'tar/ *vt* set <*jóias*>

engatar /ĩga'tar/ *vt* hitch <*reboque etc*> (**a** to); engage <*marcha*>

engatinhar /ĩgatʃi'ɲar/ *vi* crawl; *(fig)* start out

engave|tamento /ĩgaveta'mẽtu/ *m* pile-up; **~tar** *vt* shelve

engelhar /ĩʒe'ʎar/ *vi (pele)* wrinkle

enge|nharia /ĩʒeɲa'ria/ *f* engineering; **~nheiro** *m* engineer; **~nho** /e/ *m (de pessoa)* ingenuity; *(de açúcar)* sugar mill; *(máquina)* device; **~nhoca** /ɔ/ *f* gadget; **~nhoso** *a* ingenious

engessar /ĩʒe'sar/ *vt* put in plaster
engodo /ĩ'godu/ *m* lure
engolir /ĩgo'lir/ *vt/i* swallow; ~ **em seco** gulp
engomar /ĩgo'mar/ *vt* press; (*com goma*) starch
engordar /ĩgor'dar/ *vt* make fat; fatten <*animais*> □ *vi* <*pessoa*> put on weight; <*comida*> be fattening
engraçado /ĩgra'sadu/ *a* funny
engradado /ĩgra'dadu/ *m* crate
engravidar /ĩgravi'dar/ *vt* make pregnant □ *vi* get pregnant
engraxar /ĩgra'ʃar/ *vt* polish
engre|nado /ĩgre'nadu/ *a* <*carro*> in gear; ~**nagem** *f* gear; (*fig*) mechanism; ~**nar** *vt* put into gear <*carro*>; strike up <*conversa*>; ~**nar-se** *vpr* mesh; (*fig*) <*pessoas*> get on
engrossar /ĩgro'sar/ *vt* thicken; raise <*voz*> □ *vi* thicken; <*pessoa*> turn nasty
enguia /ẽ'gia/ *f* eel
engui|çar /ẽgi'sar/ *vi* break down; ~**ço** *m* breakdown
enig|ma /e'nigima/ *m* enigma; ~**mático** *a* enigmatic
enjaular /ĩʒaw'lar/ *vt* cage
enjo|ar /ĩʒo'ar/ *vt* sicken □ *vi*, ~**ar-se** *vpr* get sick (**de** of); ~**ativo** *a* <*comida*> sickly; <*livro etc*> boring
enjôo /ĩ'ʒou/ *m* sickness
enlameado /ĩlami'adu/ *a* muddy
enlatado /ĩla'tadu/ *a* tinned, canned; ~**s** *m pl* tinned foods
enle|var /ẽle'var/ *vt* enthral; ~**vo** /e/ *m* rapture
enlouquecer /ĩloke'ser/ *vt* drive mad □ *vi* go mad
enluarado /ĩlua'radu/ *a* moonlit
enor|me /e'nɔrmi/ *a* enormous; ~**midade** *f* enormity
enquadrar /ĩkwa'drar/ *vt* fit □ *vi*, ~**se** *vpr* fit in
enquanto /ĩ'kwãtu/ *conj* while; ~ **isso** meanwhile; **por** ~ for the time being
enquête /ã'kɛtʃi/ *f* survey
enraivecer /ĩxajve'ser/ *vt* enrage
enredo /ẽ'redu/ *m* plot
enrijecer /ĩxiʒe'ser/ *vt* stiffen; ~**se** *vpr* stiffen
enrique|cer /ĩxike'ser/ *vt* (*dar dinheiro a*) make rich; (*fig*) enrich □ *vi* get rich; ~**cimento** *m* enrichment
enro|lado /ĩxo'ladu/ *a* complicated; ~**lar** *vt* (*envolver*) roll up; (*complicar*) complicate; (*enganar*) cheat; ~**lar-se** *vpr* (*envolver-se*) roll up; (*confundir-se*) get mixed up
enroscar /ĩxos'kar/ *vt* twist
enrouquecer /ĩxoke'ser/ *vi* go hoarse
enrugar /ĩxu'gar/ *vt* wrinkle <*pele, tecido*>; furrow <*testa*>

enrustido /ĩxus'tʃidu/ *a* repressed
ensaboar /ĩsabo'ar/ *vt* soap
ensai|ar /ĩsaj'ar/ *vt* (*provar*) try out; (*repetir*) rehearse; ~**o** *m* (*prova*) test; (*repetição*) rehearsal; (*escrito*) essay
ensangüentado /ĩsãgwẽ'tadu/ *a* bloody, bloodstained
enseada /ĩsi'ada/ *f* inlet
ensebado /ĩse'badu/ *a* greasy
ensimesmado /ĩsimez'madu/ *a* lost in thought
ensi|nar /ẽsi'nar/ *vt/i* teach (**aco a alg** s.o. sth); ~**nar alg a nadar** teach s.o. to swim; ~**no** *m* teaching; (*em geral*) education
ensolarado /ĩsola'radu/ *a* sunny
enso|pado /ĩso'padu/ *a* soaked □ *m* stew; ~**par** *vt* soak
ensurde|cedor /ĩsurdese'dor/ *a* deafening; ~**cer** *vt* deafen □ *vi* go deaf
entabular /ĩtabu'lar/ *vt* open, start
entalar /ĩta'lar/ *vt* wedge, jam; (*em apertos*) get; ~**se** *vpr* get wedged, get jammed; (*em apertos*) get caught up
entalhar /ĩta'ʎar/ *vt* carve
entanto /ĩ'tãtu/ *m* **no** ~ however
então /ĩ'tãw/ *adv* then; (*nesse caso*) so
entardecer /ĩtarde'ser/ *m* sunset
ente /'ẽtʃi/ *m* being
entea|da /ẽtʃi'ada/ *f* stepdaughter; ~**do** *m* stepson
entedi|ante /ĩtedʒi'ãtʃi/ *a* boring; ~**ar** *vt* bore; ~**ar-se** *vpr* get bored
enten|der /ĩtẽ'der/ *vt* understand; ~**der-se** *vpr* (*dar-se bem*) get on (**com** with); **dar a** ~**der** give to understand; ~**der de futebol** know about football; ~**dimento** *m* understanding
enternecedor /ĩternese'dor/ *a* touching
enter|rar /ĩte'xar/ *vt* bury; ~**ro** /e/ *m* burial; (*cerimônia*) funeral
entidade /ẽtʃi'dadʒi/ *f* entity; (*órgão*) body
entornar /ĩtor'nar/ *vt* tip over, spill
entorpe|cente /ĩtorpe'sẽtʃi/ *m* drug, narcotic; ~**cer** *vt* numb
entortar /ĩtor'tar/ *vt* make crooked
entrada /ẽ'trada/ *f* entry; (*onde se entra*) entrance; (*bilhete*) ticket; (*prato*) starter; (*pagamento*) deposit; *pl* (*no cabelo*) receding hairline; **dar** ~ **a** enter; ~ **proibida** no entry
entranhas /ĩ'traɲas/ *f pl* entrails
entrar /ẽ'trar/ *vi* go/come in; ~ **com** enter <*dados*>; put in <*dinheiro*>; ~ **em detalhes** go into details; ~ **em vigor** come into force
entravar /ẽtra'var/ *vt* hamper
entre /'ẽtri/ *prep* between; (*em meio a*) among
entreaberto /ẽtria'bɛrtu/ *a* half-open

entrecortar /ētrikor'tar/ *vt* intersperse; (*cruzar*) intersect

entre|ga /ī'trega/ *f* delivery; (*rendição*) surrender; **~ga a domicílio** home delivery; **~gar** *vt* hand over; deliver <*mercadorias, cartas*>; hand in <*caderno, trabalho escolar*>; **~gar-se** *vpr* give o.s. up (**a** to); **~gue** *pp de* **entregar**

entrelaçar /ētrela'sar/ *vt* intertwine; clasp <*mãos*>

entrelinhas /ētri'liɲas/ *f pl* **ler nas ~** read between the lines

entremear /ētrimi'ar/ *vt* intersperse

entreolhar-se /ētrio'ʎarsi/ *vpr* look at one another

entretanto /ētre'tãtu/ *conj* however

entre|tenimento /ētreteni'mētu/ *m* entertainment; **~ter** *vt* entertain

entrever /ētre'ver/ *vt* glimpse

entrevis|ta /ētre'vista/ *f* interview; **~tador** *m* interviewer; **~tar** *vt* interview

entristecer /ītriste'ser/ *vt* sadden □ *vi* be saddened (**com** by)

entroncamento /ītrõka'mētu/ *m* junction

entrosar /ītro'zar/ *vt/i* integrate

entu|lhar /ītu'ʎar/ *vt* cram (**de** with); **~lho** *m* rubble

entupir /ītu'pir/ *vt* block; **~pir-se** *vpr* get blocked; (*de comida*) stuff o.s. (**de** with)

enturmar-se /ītur'marsi/ *vpr* mix in, fit in

entusias|mar /ītuziaz'mar/ *vt* fill with enthusiasm; **~mar-se** *vpr* get enthusiastic (**com** about); **~mo** *m* enthusiasm; **~ta** *m/f* enthusiast □ *a* enthusiastic

entusiástico /ītuzi'astʃiku/ *a* enthusiastic

enumerar /enume'rar/ *vt* enumerate

envelope /ēve'lɔpi/ *m* envelope

envelhecer /īveʎe'ser/ *vt/i* age

envenenar /īvene'nar/ *vt* poison; (*fam*) soup up <*carro*>

envergadura /īverga'dura/ *f* wingspan; (*fig*) scale

envergo|nhado /īvergo'ɲadu/ *a* ashamed; (*constrangido*) embarrassed; **~nhar** *vt* disgrace; (*constranger*) embarrass; **~nhar-se** *vpr* be ashamed; (*acanhar-se*) get embarrassed

envernizar /īverni'zar/ *vt* varnish

en|viado /ēvi'adu/ *m* envoy; **~viar** *vt* send; **~vio** *m* (*ato*) sending; (*remessa*) consignment

envidraçar /īvidra'sar/ *vt* glaze

enviesado /īvie'zadu/ *a* (*não vertical*) slanting; (*torto*) crooked

envol|vente /īvow'vētʃi/ *a* compelling, gripping; **~ver** *vt* (*embrulhar*) wrap; (*enredar*) involve; **~ver-se** *vpr* (*enrolar-se*) wrap o.s.; (*enredar-se*) get involved; **~vimento** *m* involvement

enxada /ē'ʃada/ *f* hoe

enxaguar /ēʃa'gwar/ *vt* rinse

enxame /ē'ʃami/ *m* swarm

enxaqueca /ēʃa'keka/ *f* migraine

enxergar /īʃer'gar/ *vt/i* see

enxer|tar /īʃer'tar/ *vt* graft; **~to** /e/ *m* graft

enxotar /īʃo'tar/ *vt* drive away

enxofre /ē'ʃofri/ *m* sulphur

enxo|val /ēʃo'vaw/ (*pl* **~vais**) *m* (*de noiva*) trousseau; (*de bebê*) layette

enxugar /īʃu'gar/ *vt* dry; **~-se** *vpr* dry o.s.

enxurrada /īʃu'xada/ *f* torrent; (*fig*) flood

enxuto /ī'ʃutu/ *a* dry; <*corpo*> shapely

enzima /ē'zima/ *f* enzyme

epicentro /epi'sētru/ *m* epicentre

épico /'ɛpiku/ *a* epic

epidemia /epide'mia/ *f* epidemic

epi|lepsia /epilep'sia/ *f* epilepsy; **~léptico** *a &* *m* epileptic

epílogo /e'pilogu/ *m* epilogue

episódio /epi'zɔdʒiu/ *m* episode

epitáfio /epi'tafiu/ *m* epitaph

época /'ɛpoka/ *f* time; (*da história*) age, period; **fazer ~** make history; **móveis da ~** period furniture

epopéia /epo'pɛja/ *f* epic

equação /ekwa'sãw/ *f* equation

equador /ekwa'dor/ *m* equator; **o Equador** Ecuador

equatori|al /ekwatori'aw/ (*pl* **~ais**) *a* equatorial; **~ano** *a & m* Ecuadorian

equilibrar /ekili'brar/ *vt* balance; **~-se** *vpr* balance

equilíbrio /eki'libriu/ *m* balance

equipa /e'kipa/ (*Port*) *f* team

equi|pamento /ekipa'mētu/ *m* equipment; **~par** *vt* equip

equiparar /ekipa'rar/ *vt* equate (**com** with); **~-se** *vpr* compare (**a** with)

equipe /e'kipi/ *f* team

equitação /ekita'sãw/ *f* riding

equiva|lência /ekiva'lēsia/ *f* equivalence; **~lente** *a* equivalent; **~ler** *vi* be equivalent (**a** to)

equivo|cado /ekivo'kadu/ *a* mistaken; **~car-se** *vpr* make a mistake

equívoco /e'kivoku/ *a* equivocal □ *m* mistake

era /'ɛra/ *f* era

erário /e'rariu/ *m* exchequer

ereção /ere'sãw/ *f* erection

eremita /ere'mita/ *m/f* hermit

ereto /e'rɛtu/ *a* erect

erguer /er'ger/ *vt* raise; erect <*monumento etc*>; **~-se** *vpr* rise

eri|çado /eri'sadu/ *a* bristling; **~çar-se** *vpr* bristle

ermo /'ermu/ *a* deserted □ *m* wilderness

erosão /ero'zãw/ *f* erosion

erótico /e'rɔtʃiku/ *a* erotic

erotismo /ero'tʃizmu/ *m* eroticism

er|rado /e'xadu/ *a* wrong; **~rante** *a* wandering; **~rar** *vt* (*não fazer certo*) get wrong; miss <*alvo*> □ *vi* (*enganar-se*) be wrong; (*vaguear*) wander; **~ro** /e/ *m* mistake; **fazer um ~ro** make a mistake; **~rôneo** *a* erroneous

erudi|ção /erudʒi'sãw/ *f* learning; **~to** *a* learned; <*música*> classical □ *m* scholar

erupção /erup'sãw/ *f* (*vulcânica*) eruption; (*cutânea*) rash

erva /'ɛrva/ *f* herb; **~ daninha** weed; **~-doce** *f* aniseed

ervilha /er'viʎa/ *f* pea

esban|jador /izbaʒa'dor/ *a* extravagant □ *m* spendthrift; **~jar** *vt* squander; burst with <*saúde, imaginação, energia etc*>

esbar|rão /izba'xãw/ *m* bump; **~rar** *vi* **~rar com** *ou* **em** bump into <*pessoa*>; come up against <*problema*>

esbelto /iz'bɛwtu/ *a* svelte

esbo|çar /izbo'sar/ *vt* sketch <*desenho etc*>; outline <*plano etc*>; **~çar um sorriso** give a hint of a smile; **~ço** /o/ *m* (*desenho*) sketch; (*plano*) outline; (*de um sorriso*) hint

esbofetear /izbofetʃi'ar/ *vt* slap

esborrachar /izboxa'ʃar/ *vt* squash; **~-se** *vpr* crash

esbravejar /izbrave'ʒar/ *vi* rant, rail

esbura|cado /izbura'kadu/ *a* full of holes; **~car** *vt* make holes in

esbuga|lhado /izbuga'ʎadu/ *a* <*olhos*> bulging; **~lhar-se** *vpr* <*olhos*> pop out

escabroso /iska'brozu/ *a* (*fig*) difficult, tough

escada /is'kada/ *f* (*dentro de casa*) stairs; (*na rua*) steps; (*de mão*) ladder; **~ de incêndio** fire escape; **~ rolante** escalator; **~ria** *f* staircase

escafan|drista /iskafã'drista/ *m/f* diver; **~dro** *m* diving suit

escala /is'kala/ *f* scale; (*de navio*) port of call; (*de avião*) stopover; **fazer ~** stop over; **sem ~** <*vôo*> non-stop

esca|lada /iska'lada/ *f* (*fig*) escalation; **~lão** *m* echelon, level; **~lar** *vt* (*subir a*) scale; (*designar*) select

escaldar /iskaw'dar/ *vt* scald; blanch <*vegetais*>

escalfar /iskaw'far/ *vt* poach

escalonar /iskalo'nar/ *vt* schedule <*pagamento*>

escama /is'kama/ *f* scale

escanca|rado /iskãka'radu/ *a* wide open; **~rar** *vt* open wide

escandalizar /iskãdali'zar/ *vt* scandalize; **~-se** *vpr* be scandalized

escândalo /is'kãdalu/ *m* (*vexame*) scandal; (*tumulto*) fuss, uproar; **fazer um ~** make a scene

escandaloso /iskãda'lozu/ *a* (*chocante*) scandalous; (*espalhafatoso*) outrageous, loud

Escandinávia /iskãdʒi'navia/ *f* Scandinavia

escandinavo /iskãdʒi'navu/ *a* & *m* Scandinavian

escanga|lhado /iskãga'ʎadu/ *a* broken; **~lhar** *vt* break up; **~lhar-se** *vpr* fall to pieces; **~lhar-se de rir** split one's sides laughing

escaninho /iska'niɲu/ *m* pigeonhole

escanteio /iskã'teju/ *m* corner

esca|pada /iska'pada/ *f* (*fuga*) escape; (*aventura*) escapade; **~pamento** *m* exhaust; **~par** *vi* **~par a** *ou* **de** (*livrar-se*) escape from; (*evitar*) escape; **~pou-lhe a palavra** the word slipped out; **o copo ~pou-me das mãos** the glass slipped out of my hands; **o nome me ~pa** the name escapes me; **~par de boa** have a narrow escape; **~patória** *f* way out; (*desculpa*) pretext; **~pe** *m* escape; (*de carro etc*) exhaust; **~pulir** *vi* escape (de from)

escaramuça /iskara'musa/ *f* skirmish

escaravelho /iskara'vɛʎu/ *m* beetle

escarcéu /iskar'sɛw/ *m* uproar, fuss

escarlate /iskar'latʃi/ *a* scarlet

escarnecer /iskarne'ser/ *vt* mock

escárnio /is'karniu/ *m* derision

escarpado /iskar'padu/ *a* steep

escarrado /iska'xadu/ *m* **ele é o pai ~** he's the spitting image of his father

escarro /is'kaxu/ *m* phlegm

escas|sear /iskasi'ar/ *vi* run short; **~sez** *f* shortage; **~so** *a* (*raro*) scarce; (*ralo*) scant

esca|vadeira /iskava'dera/ *f* digger; **~var** *vt* excavate

esclare|cer /isklare'ser/ *vt* explain <*fatos*>; enlighten <*pessoa*>; **~cer-se** *vpr* <*fato*> be explained; <*pessoa*> find out; **~cimento** *m* (*de pessoas*) enlightenment; (*de fatos*) explanation

esclerosado /isklero'zadu/ *a* senile

escoar /isko'ar/ *vt/i* drain

esco|cês /isko'ses/ *a* (*f* **~cesa**) Scottish □ *m* (*f* **~cesa**) Scot

Escócia /is'kɔsia/ *f* Scotland

esco|la /is'kɔla/ *f* school; **~la de samba** samba school; **~lar** *a* school □ *m/f* schoolchild; **~laridade** *f* schooling

esco|lha /is'koʎa/ *f* choice; **~lher** *vt* choose

escol|ta /is'kɔwta/ *f* escort; **~tar** *vt* escort

escombros /is'kõbrus/ *m pl* debris

escon|de-esconde /iskõdʒis'kõdʒi/ *m* hide-and-seek; **~der** *vt* hide; **~der-se** *vpr* hide; **~derijo** *m* hiding place; *(de bandidos)* hideout; **~didas** *f pl* às **~didas** secretly

esco|ra /is'kɔra/ *f* prop; **~rar** *vt* prop up; **~rar-se** *vpr* <argumento etc> be based (**em** on)

escore /is'kɔri/ *m* score

escória /is'kɔria/ *f* scum, dross

escori|ação /iskoria'sãw/ *f* graze, abrasion; **~ar** *vt* graze

escorpião /iskorpi'ãw/ *m* scorpion; **Escorpião** Scorpio

escorredor /iskoxe'dor/ *m* drainer

escorrega /isko'xega/ *m* slide

escorre|gador /iskoxega'dor/ *m* slide; **~gão** *m* slip; **~gar** *vi* slip

escor|rer /isko'xer/ *vt* drain □ *vi* trickle; **~rido** *a* <cabelo> straight

escoteiro /isko'teru/ *m* boy scout

escotilha /isko'tʃiʎa/ *f* hatch

esco|va /is'kova/ *f* brush; **fazer ~va no cabelo** blow-dry one's hair; **~va de dentes** toothbrush; **~var** *vt* brush; **~vinha** *f* **cabelo à ~vinha** crew-cut

escra|chado /iskra'ʃadu/ *(fam) a* outspoken; **~char** *(fam) vt* tell off

escra|vatura /iskrava'tura/ *f* slavery; **~vidão** *f* slavery; **~vizar** *vt* enslave; **~vo** *m* slave

escre|vente /iskre'vẽtʃi/ *m/f* clerk; **~ver** *vt/i* write

escri|ta /is'krita/ *f* writing; **~to** *pp de* **escrever** □ *a* written; **por ~to** in writing; **~tor** *m* writer; **~tório** *m* office; *(numa casa)* study

escritu|ra /iskri'tura/ *f (a Bíblia)* scripture; *(contrato)* deed; **~ração** *f* bookkeeping; **~rar** *vt* keep, write up <contas>; draw up <documento>

escri|vaninha /iskriva'niɲa/ *f* bureau, writing desk; **~vão** *m (f ~vã)* registrar

escrúpulo /is'krupulu/ *m* scruple

escrupuloso /iskrupu'lozu/ *a* scrupulous

escrutínio /iskru'tʃiniu/ *m* ballot

escu|dar /isku'dar/ *vt* shield; **~deria** *f* team; **~do** *m* shield; *(moeda)* escudo

escula|chado /iskula'ʃadu/ *(fam) a* sloppy; **~char** *(fam) vt* mess up <coisa>; tell off <pessoa>; **~cho** *(fam) m (bagunça)* mess; *(bronca)* telling-off

escul|pir /iskuw'pir/ *vt* sculpt; **~tor** *m* sculptor; **~tura** *f* sculpture; **~tural** *(pl ~turais) a* statuesque

escuma /is'kuma/ *f* scum; **~deira** *f* skimmer

escuna /is'kuna/ *f* schooner

escu|ras /is'kuras/ *f pl* às **~ras** in the dark; **~recer** *vt* darken □ *vi* get dark; **~ridão** *f* darkness; **~ro** *a & m* dark

escuso /is'kuzu/ *a* shady

escu|ta /is'kuta/ *f* listening; **estar à ~ta** be listening; **~ta telefônica** phone tapping; **~tar** *vt (perceber)* hear; *(prestar atenção a)* listen to □ *vi (poder ouvir)* hear; *(prestar atenção)* listen

esdrúxulo /iz'druʃulu/ *a* weird

esfacelar /isfase'lar/ *vt* wreck

esfalfar /isfaw'far/ *vt* wear out; **~-se** *vpr* get worn out

esfaquear /isfaki'ar/ *vt* stab

esfarelar /isfare'lar/ *vt* crumble; **~-se** *vpr* crumble

esfarrapado /isfaxa'padu/ *a* ragged; <desculpa> lame

es|fera /is'fɛra/ *f* sphere; **~férico** *a* spherical

esferográfi|co /isfero'grafiku/ *a* **caneta ~ca** ball-point pen

esfiapar /isfia'par/ *vt* fray; **~-se** *vpr* fray

esfinge /is'fiʒi/ *f* sphinx

esfolar /isfo'lar/ *vt* skin; *(fig)* overcharge

esfomeado /isfomi'adu/ *a* starving, famished

esfor|çar-se /isfor'sarsi/ *vpr* make an effort; **~ço** /o/ *m* effort; **fazer ~ço** make an effort

esfre|gaço /isfre'gasu/ *m* smear; **~gar** *vt* rub; *(para limpar)* scrub

esfriar /isfri'ar/ *vt* cool □ *vi* cool (down); *(sentir frio)* get cold

esfumaçado /isfuma'sadu/ *a* smoky

esfuziante /isfuzi'ãtʃi/ *a* irrepressible, exuberant

esganar /izga'nar/ *vt* throttle

esganiçado /izgani'sadu/ *a* shrill

esgarçar /izgar'sar/ *vt/i* fray

esgo|tado /izgo'tadu/ *a* exhausted; <estoque, lotação> sold out; **~tamento** *m* exhaustion; **~tamento nervoso** nervous breakdown; **~tar** *vt* exhaust; *(gastar)* use up; **~tar-se** *vpr* <pessoa> become exhausted; <estoque, lotação> sell out; <recursos, provisões> run out; **~to** /o/ *m* drain; *(de detritos)* sewer

esgri|ma /iz'grima/ *f* fencing; **~mir** *vt* brandish □ *vi* fence; **~mista** *m/f* fencer

esgrouvinhado /izgrovi'ɲadu/ *a* tousled, dishevelled

esgueirar-se /izge'rarsi/ *vpr* slip, sneak

esguelha /iz'geʎa/ *f* **de ~** askew; <olhar> askance

esgui|char /izgi'ʃar/ *vt/i* spurt, squirt; **~cho** *m* jet, spurt

esguio /iz'gio/ *a* slender

eslavo /iz'lavu/ *a* Slavic □ *m* Slav

esmaecer /izmaj'ser/ *vi* fade

esma|gador /izmaga'dor/ *a* <*vitória, maioria*> overwhelming; <*provas*> incontrovertible; ~**gar** *vt* crush

esmalte /iz'mawtʃi/ *m* enamel; ~ **de unhas** nail varnish

esmeralda /izme'rawda/ *f* emerald

esme|rar-se /izme'rarsi/ *vpr* take great care (**em** over); ~**ro** /e/ *m* great care

esmigalhar /izmiga'ʎar/ *vt* crumble <*pão etc*>; shatter <*vidro, copo*>; ~**se** *vpr* <*pão etc*> crumble; <*vidro, copo*> shatter

esmiuçar /izmiu'sar/ *vt* examine in detail

esmo /'ezmu/ *m* **a** ~ <*escolher*> at random; <*andar*> aimlessly; <*falar*> nonsense

esmola /iz'mɔla/ *f* donation; *pl* charity

esmorecer /izmore'ser/ *vi* flag

esmurrar /izmu'xar/ *vt* punch

esno|bar /izno'bar/ *vt* snub □ *vi* be snobbish; ~**be** /iz'nɔbi/ *a* snobbish □ *m/f* snob; ~**bismo** *m* snobbishness

esotérico /ezo'tɛriku/ *a* esoteric

espa|çar /ispa'sar/ *vt* space out; make less frequent <*visitas, consultas etc*>; ~**cial** (*pl* ~**ciais**) *a* space; ~**ço** *m* space; (*cultural etc*) venue; ~**çoso** /o/ *a* spacious

espada /is'pada/ *f* sword; *pl* (*naipe*) spades; ~**chim** *m* swordsman

espádua /is'padua/ *f* shoulder blade

espaguete /ispa'gɛtʃi/ *m* spaghetti

espaire|cer /ispajre'ser/ *vt* amuse □ *vi* relax; (*dar uma volta*) go for a walk; ~**cimento** *m* recreation

espaldar /ispaw'dar/ *m* back

espalhafato /ispaʎa'fatu/ *m* (*barulho*) fuss, uproar; (*de roupa etc*) extravagance; ~**so** /o/ *a* (*barulhento*) noisy, rowdy; (*ostentoso*) extravagant

espalhar /ispa'ʎar/ *vt* scatter; spread <*notícia, terror etc*>; shed <*luz*>; ~**se** *vpr* spread; <*pessoas*> spread out

espa|nador /ispana'dor/ *m* feather duster; ~**nar** *vt* dust

espan|camento /ispãka'mẽtu/ *m* beating; ~**car** *vt* beat up

Espanha /is'paɲa/ *f* Spain

espa|nhol /ispa'ɲɔw/ (*pl* ~**nhóis**) *a* (*f* ~**nhola**) Spanish □ *m* (*f* ~**nhola**) Spaniard; (*língua*) Spanish; **os** ~**nhóis** the Spanish

espan|talho /ispã'taʎu/ *m* scarecrow; ~**tar** *vt* (*admirar*) amaze; (*assustar*) scare; (*afugentar*) drive away; ~**tar-se** *vpr* (*admirar-se*) be amazed; (*assustar-se*) get scared; ~**to** *m* (*susto*) fright; (*admiração*) amazement; ~**toso** /o/ *a* amazing

esparadrapo /ispara'drapu/ *m* sticking plaster

espargo /is'pargu/ (*Port*) *m* asparagus

esparramar /ispaxa'mar/ *vt* scatter; ~**se** *vpr* be scattered, spread

espartano /ispar'tanu/ *a* spartan

espartilho /ispar'tʃiʎu/ *m* corset

espas|mo /is'pazmu/ *m* spasm; ~**módico** *a* spasmodic

espatifar /ispatʃi'far/ *vt* smash; ~**se** *vpr* smash; <*carro, avião*> crash

especi|al /ispesi'aw/ (*pl* ~**ais**) *a* special; ~**alidade** *f* speciality; ~**alista** *m/f* specialist

especiali|zado /ispesiali'zadu/ *a* specialized; <*mão-de-obra*> skilled; ~**zar-se** *vpr* specialize (**em** in)

especiaria /ispesia'ria/ *f* spice

espécie /is'pɛsi/ *f* sort, kind; (*de animais*) species

especifi|cação /ispesifika'sãw/ *f* specification; ~**car** *vt* specify

específico /ispe'sifiku/ *a* specific

espécime /is'pesimi/ *m* specimen

espectador /ispekta'dor/ *m* (*de TV*) viewer; (*de jogo, espetáculo*) spectator; (*de acidente etc*) onlooker

espectro /is'pɛktru/ *m* (*fantasma*) spectre; (*de cores*) spectrum

especu|lação /ispekula'sãw/ *f* speculation; ~**lador** *m* speculator; ~**lar** *vi* speculate (**sobre** on); ~**lativo** *a* speculative

espe|lhar /ispe'ʎar/ *vt* mirror; ~**lhar-se** *vpr* be mirrored; ~**lho** /e/ *m* mirror; ~**lho retrovisor** rearview mirror

espelunca /ispe'lũka/ (*fam*) *f* dive

espera /is'pɛra/ *f* wait; **à** ~ **de** waiting for

esperan|ça /ispe'rãsa/ *f* hope; ~**çoso** /o/ *a* hopeful

esperar /ispe'rar/ *vt* (*aguardar*) wait for; (*desejar*) hope for; (*contar com*) expect □ *vi* wait (**por** for); **fazer alg** ~ keep s.o. waiting; **espero que ele venha** I hope (that) he comes; **espero que sim/não** I hope so/not

esperma /is'pɛrma/ *m* sperm

espernear /isper'niar/ *vi* kick; (*fig: reclamar*) kick up

esper|talhão /isperta'ʎãw/ *m* (*f* ~**talhona**) wise guy; ~**teza** /e/ *f* cleverness; (*uma*) clever move; ~**to** /e/ *a* clever

espes|so /is'pesu/ *a* thick; ~**sura** *f* thickness

espe|tacular /ispetaku'lar/ *a* spectacular; ~**táculo** *m* (*no teatro etc*) show; (*cena impressionante*) spectacle; ~**taculoso** /o/ *a* spectacular

espe|tar /ispe'tar/ *vt* (*cravar*) stick; (*furar*) skewer; ~**tar-se** *vpr* (*cravarse*) stick; (*ferir-se*) prick o.s.; ~**tinho**

m skewer; (*de carne etc*) kebab; ~**to** /e/ *m* spit

espevitado /ispevi'tadu/ *a* cheeky

espezinhar /ispezi'ɲar/ *vt* walk all over

espi|a /is'pia/ *m/f* spy; ~**ão** *m* (*f* ~**ã**) spy; ~**ada** *f* peep; ~**ar** *vt* (*observar*) spy on; (*aguardar*) watch for □ *vi* peer, peep

espicaçar /ispika'sar/ *vt* goad <*pessoa*>; excite <*imaginação, curiosidade*>

espichar /ispi'ʃar/ *vt* stretch □ *vi* shoot up; ~**se** stretch out

espiga /is'piga/ *f* (*de trigo etc*) ear; (*de milho*) cob

espina|fração /ispinafra'sãw/ (*fam*) *f* telling-off; ~**frar** (*fam*) *vt* tell off; ~**fre** *m* spinach

espingarda /ispĩ'garda/ *f* rifle, shotgun

espinha /is'piɲa/ *f* (*de peixe*) bone; (*na pele*) spot; ~ **dorsal** spine

espinho /is'piɲu/ *m* thorn; ~**so** /o/ *a* thorny; (*fig*) difficult, tough

espio|nagem /ispio'naʒẽ/ *f* espionage, spying; ~**nar** *vt* spy on □ *vi* spy

espi|ral /ispi'raw/ (*pl* ~**rais**) *a & f* spiral

espírita /is'pirita/ *a & m/f* spiritualist

espiritismo /ispiri'tʃizmu/ *m* spiritualism

espírito /is'piritu/ *m* spirit; (*graça*) wit

espiritu|al /ispiritu'aw/ (*pl* ~**ais**) *a* spiritual; ~**oso** /o/ *a* witty

espir|rar /ispi'xar/ *vt* spurt □ *vi* <*pessoa*> sneeze; <*lama, tinta etc*> spatter; <*fogo, lenha, fritura etc*> spit; ~**ro** *m* sneeze

esplêndido /is'plẽdʒidu/ *a* splendid

esplendor /isplẽ'dor/ *m* splendour

espoleta /ispo'leta/ *f* fuse

espoliar /ispoli'ar/ *vt* plunder, pillage

espólio /is'poliu/ *m* (*herdado*) estate; (*roubado*) spoils

espon|ja /is'põʒa/ *f* sponge; ~**joso** /o/ *a* spongy

espon|taneidade /ispõtanej'dadʒi/ *f* spontaneity; ~**tâneo** *a* spontaneous

espora /is'pora/ *f* spur

esporádico /ispo'radʒiku/ *a* sporadic

esporear /ispori'ar/ *vt* spur on

espor|te /is'portʃi/ *m* sport □ *a invar* <*roupa*> casual; **carro** ~**te** sports car; ~**tista** *m/f* sportsman (*f* -woman); ~**tiva** *f* sense of humour; ~**tivo** *a* sporting

espo|sa /is'poza/ *f* wife; ~**so** *m* husband

espregui|cadeira /ispregisa'dera/ *f* (*tipo cadeira*) deckchair; (*tipo cama*) sun lounger; ~**çar-se** *vpr* stretch

esprei|ta /is'prejta/ *f* **ficar à** ~**ta** lie in wait; ~**tar** *vt* stalk <*caça, vítima*>; spy on <*vizinhos, inimigos etc*>; look out for <*ocasião*> □ *vi* peep, spy

espre|medor /ispreme'dor/ *m* squeezer; ~**mer** *vt* squeeze; wring out <*roupa*>; squash <*pessoa*>; ~**mer-se** *vpr* squeeze up

espu|ma /is'puma/ *f* foam; ~**ma de borracha** foam rubber; ~**mante** *a* <*vinho*> sparkling; ~**mar** *vi* foam, froth

espúrio /is'puriu/ *a* spurious

esqua|dra /is'kwadra/ *f* squad; ~**dra de polícia** (*Port*) police station; ~**drão** *m* squadron; ~**dria** *f* doors and windows; ~**drinhar** *vt* explore; ~**dro** *m* set square

esqualidez /iskwali'des/ *f* squalor

esquálido /is'kwalidu/ *a* squalid

esquartejar /iskwarte'ʒar/ *vt* chop up

esque|cer /iske'ser/ *vt/i* forget; ~**cer-se de** forget; ~**cido** *a* forgotten; (*com memória fraca*) forgetful; ~**cimento** *m* oblivion; (*memória fraca*) forgetfulness

esque|lético /iske'lɛtʃiku/ *a* skinny, skeleton-like; ~**leto** /e/ *m* skeleton

esque|ma /is'kema/ *m* outline, draft; (*operação*) scheme; ~**ma de segurança** security operation; ~**mático** *a* schematic

esquentar /iskẽ'tar/ *vt* warm up □ *vi* warm up; <*roupa*> be warm; ~**se** *vpr* get annoyed; ~ **a cabeça** (*fam*) get worked up

esquer|da /is'kerda/ *f* left; **à** ~**da** (*posição*) on the left; (*direção*) to the left; ~**dista** *a* left-wing □ *m/f* left-winger; ~**do** /e/ *a* left

esqui /is'ki/ *m* ski; (*esporte*) skiing; ~ **aquático** water skiing; ~**ador** *m* skier; ~**ar** *vi* ski

esquilo /is'kilu/ *m* squirrel

esquina /is'kina/ *f* corner

esquisi|tice /iskizi'tʃisi/ *f* strangeness; (*uma*) strange thing; ~**to** *a* strange

esqui|var-se /iski'varsi/ *vpr* dodge out of the way; ~**var-se de** dodge; ~**vo** *a* elusive; <*pessoa*> aloof, antisocial

esquizo|frenia /iskizofre'nia/ *f* schizophrenia; ~**frênico** *a & m* schizophrenic

es|sa /'ɛsa/ *pron* that (one); ~**sa é boa** that's a good one; ~**sa não** come off it; **por** ~**sas e outras** for these and other reasons; ~**se** /e/ *a* that; *pl* those; (*fam: este*) this; *pl* these □ *pron* that one; *pl* those; (*fam: este*) this one; *pl* these

essência /e'sẽsia/ *f* essence

essenci|al /esẽsi'aw/ (pl ~ais) a essential; **o ~al** what is essential

estabele|cer /istabele'ser/ vt establish; **~cer-se** vpr establish o.s.; **~cimento** m establishment

estabili|dade /istabili'dadʒi/ f stability; **~zar** vt stabilize; **~zar-se** vpr stabilize

estábulo /is'tabulu/ m cowshed

estaca /is'taka/ f stake; (de barraca) peg; **voltar à ~ zero** go back to square one

estação /ista'sãw/ f (do ano) season; (ferroviária etc) station; **~ balneária** seaside resort

estacar /ista'kar/ vi stop short

estacio|namento /istasiona'mẽtu/ m (ação) parking; (lugar) car park, (Amer) parking lot; **~nar** vt/i park

estada /is'tada/ f, **estadia** /ista'dʒia/ f stay

estádio /is'tadʒiu/ m stadium

esta|dista /ista'dʒista/ m/f statesman (f -woman); **~do** m state; **~do civil** marital status; **~do de espírito** state of mind; **Estados Unidos da América** United States of America; **Estado-Maior** m Staff; **~dual** (pl ~duais) a state

esta|fa /is'tafa/ f exhaustion; **~fante** a exhausting; **~far** vt tire out; **~far-se** vpr get tired out

estagi|ar /istaʒi'ar/ vi do a traineeship; **~ário** m trainee

estágio /is'taʒiu/ m traineeship

estag|nado /istagi'nadu/ a stagnant; **~nar** vi stagnate

estalagem /ista'laʒẽ/ f inn

estalar /ista'lar/ vt (quebrar) crack; (fazer barulho com) click □ vi crack

estaleiro /ista'leru/ m shipyard

estalo /is'talu/ m crack; (de dedos, língua) click; **me deu um ~** it clicked (in my mind)

estam|pa /is'tãpa/ f print; **~pado** a <tecido> patterned □ m (desenho) pattern; (tecido) print; **~par** vt print

estampido /istã'pidu/ m bang

estancar /istã'kar/ vt staunch; **~-se** vpr dry up

estância /is'tãsia/ f **~ hidromineral** spa

estandarte /istã'dartʃi/ m banner

estanho /is'taɲu/ m tin

estanque /is'tãki/ a watertight

estante /is'tãtʃi/ f bookcase

estapafúrdio /istapa'furdʒiu/ a weird, odd

estar /is'tar/ vi be; (~ em casa) be in; **está chovendo**, (Port) **está a chover** it's raining; **~ com** have; **~ com calor/sono** be hot/sleepy; **~ para terminar** be about to finish; **ele não está para ninguém** he's not avail-

able to see anyone; **o trabalho está por terminar** the work is yet to be finished

estardalhaço /istarda'ʎasu/ m (barulho) fuss; (ostentação) extravagance

estarre|cedor /istaxese'dor/ a horrifying; **~cer** vt horrify; **~cer-se** vpr be horrified

esta|tal /ista'taw/ (pl ~tais) a state-owned □ f state company

estate|lado /istate'ladu/ a sprawling; **~lar** vt knock down; **~lar-se** vpr go sprawling

estático /is'tatʃiku/ a static

estatísti|ca /ista'tʃistʃika/ f statistics; **~co** a statistical

estati|zação /istatʃiza'sãw/ f nationalization; **~zar** vt nationalize

estátua /is'tatua/ f statue

estatueta /istatu'eta/ f statuette

estatura /ista'tura/ f stature

estatuto /ista'tutu/ m statute

está|vel /is'tavew/ (pl ~veis) a stable

este¹ /'estʃi/ m a invar & m east

este² /'estʃi/ a this; pl these □ pron this one; pl these; (mencionado por último) the latter

esteio /is'teju/ m prop; (fig) mainstay

esteira /is'tera/ f (tapete) mat; (rastro) wake

estelionato /istelio'natu/ m fraud

estender /istẽ'der/ vt (desdobrar) spread out; (alongar) stretch; (ampliar) extend; hold out <mão>; hang out <roupa>; roll out <massa>; draw out <conversa>; **~-se** vpr (deitar-se) stretch out; (ir longe) stretch, extend; **~-se sobre** dwell on

esteno|datilógrafo /istenodatʃi'lografu/ m shorthand typist; **~grafia** f shorthand

estepe /is'tɛpi/ m spare wheel

esterco /is'terku/ m dung

estéreo /is'teriu/ a invar stereo

estere|otipado /isteriotʃi'padu/ a stereotypical; **~ótipo** m stereotype

esté|ril /is'teriw/ (pl ~reis) a sterile

esterili|dade /isterili'dadʒi/ f sterility; **~zar** vt sterilize

esterli|no /ister'linu/ a **libra ~na** pound sterling

esteróide /iste'rɔjdʒi/ m steroid

estética /is'tɛtʃika/ f aesthetics

esteticista /istetʃi'sista/ m/f beautician

estético /is'tɛtʃiku/ a aesthetic

estetoscópio /istetos'kɔpiu/ m stethoscope

estiagem /istʃi'aʒẽ/ f dry spell

estibordo /istʃi'bordu/ m starboard

esti|cada /istʃi'kada/ f **dar uma ~cada** go on; **~car** vt stretch □ (fam) vi go on; **~car-se** vpr stretch out

estigma /isˈtʃigima/ m stigma;
~**tizar** vt brand (**de** as)
estilha|çar /istʃiʎaˈsar/ vt shatter;
~**çar-se** vpr shatter; ~**ço** m shard,
fragment
estilingue /istʃiˈligi/ m catapult
estilis|mo /istʃiˈlizmu/ m fashion
design; ~**ta** m/f fashion designer
esti|lístico /istʃiˈlistʃiku/ a stylistic;
~**lizar** vt stylize; ~**lo** m style; ~**lo
de vida** lifestyle
esti|ma /esˈtʃima/ f esteem; ~**mação**
f estimation; **cachorro de** ~**mação**
pet dog; ~**mado** a esteemed; **Estima-
do Senhor** Dear Sir; ~**mar** vt value
<*bens, jóias etc*> (**em** at); estimate
<*valor, preço etc*> (**em** at); think
highly of <*pessoa*>; ~**mativa** f estimate
estimu|lante /istʃimuˈlãtʃi/ a stimu-
lating □ m stimulant; ~**lar** vt stimulate; (*incentivar*) encourage
estímulo /isˈtʃimulu/ m stimulus; (*incentivo*) incentive
estio /isˈtʃiu/ m summer
estipu|lação /istʃipulaˈsãw/ f stipu-
lation; ~**lar** vt stipulate
estirar /istʃiˈrar/ vt stretch; ~**-se** vpr
stretch
estirpe /isˈtʃirpi/ f stock, line
estivador /istʃivaˈdor/ m docker
estocada /istoˈkada/ f thrust
estocar /istoˈkar/ vt stock □ vi stock
up
Estocolmo /istoˈkɔwmu/ f Stockholm
esto|far /istoˈfar/ vt upholster
<*móveis*>; ~**fo** /o/ m upholstery
estóico /isˈtɔjku/ a é m stoic
estojo /isˈtoʒu/ m case
estômago /isˈtomagu/ m stomach
Estônia /isˈtonia/ f Estonia
estonte|ante /istõtʃiˈãtʃi/ a stunning,
mind-boggling; ~**ar** vt stun
estopim /istoˈpĩ/ m fuse; (*fig*) flash-
point
estoque /isˈtɔki/ m stock
estore /isˈtɔri/ m blind
estória /isˈtɔria/ f story
estor|var /istorˈvar/ vt hinder; ob-
struct <*entrada, trânsito*>; ~**vo** /o/
m hindrance
estou|rado /istoˈradu/ a <*pessoa*>
explosive; ~**rar** vi <*bomba, escândalo, pessoa*> blow up; <*pneu*> burst;
<*guerra*> break out; <*moda, cantor
etc*> make it big; ~**ro** m (*de bomba,
moda etc*) explosion; (*de pessoa*) outburst; (*de pneu*) blowout; (*de guerra*)
outbreak
estrábico /isˈtrabiku/ a <*olhos*>
squinty; <*pessoa*> squint-eyed
estrabismo /istraˈbizmu/ m squint
estraçalhar /istrasaˈʎar/ vt tear to
pieces

estrada /isˈtrada/ f road; ~ **de ferro**
railway, (*Amer*) railroad; ~ **de
rodagem** highway; ~ **de terra** dirt
road
estrado /isˈtradu/ m podium; (*de
cama*) base
estraga-prazeres /istragapraˈzeris/
m/f invar spoilsport
estragão /istraˈgãw/ m tarragon
estra|gar /istraˈgar/ vt (*tornar desa-
gradável*) spoil; (*acabar com*) ruin □
vi (*quebrar*) break; (*apodrecer*) go off;
~**go** m damage; pl damage; (*da guerra, do tempo*) ravages
estrangeiro /istrãˈʒeru/ a foreign □
m foreigner; **do** ~ from abroad; **para
o/no** ~ abroad
estrangular /istrãguˈlar/ vt strangle
estra|nhar /istraˈɲar/ vt (*achar es-
tranho*) find strange; (*não se adaptar
a*) find it hard to get used to; (*não se
sentir à vontade com*) be shy with;
~**nhar que** find it strange that; **estou te** ~**nhando** that's not like you;
não é de se ~**nhar** it's not
surprising; ~**nheza** /e/ f (*esquisitice*)
strangeness; (*surpresa*) surprise;
~**nho** a strange □ m stranger
estratagema /istrataˈʒema/ m stratagem
estraté|gia /istraˈtɛʒia/ f strategy;
~**gico** a strategic
estrato /isˈtratu/ m (*camada*)
stratum; (*nuvem*) stratus; ~**sfera** f
stratosphere
estre|ante /istriˈãtʃi/ a new □ m/f
newcomer; ~**ar** vt première <*peça,
filme*>; embark on <*carreira*>; wear
for the first time <*roupa*> □ vi <*pessoa*> make one's début; <*filme, peça*>
open
estrebaria /istrebaˈria/ f stable
estréia /isˈtrɛja/ f (*de pessoa*) début;
(*de filme, peça*) première
estrei|tar /istrejˈtar/ vt narrow; take
in <*vestido*>; make closer <*relações,
laços*> □ vi narrow; ~**tar-se** vpr <*relações*> become closer; ~**to** a narrow;
<*relações, laços*> close; <*saia*>
straight □ m strait
estre|la /isˈtrela/ f star; ~**lado** a
<*céu*> starry; <*ovo*> fried; ~**lado
por** <*filme etc*> starring; ~**la-do-
mar** (pl ~**las-do-mar**) f starfish;
~**lar** vt fry <*ovo*>; star in <*filme,
peça*>; ~**lato** m stardom; ~**lismo** m
star quality
estreme|cer /istremeˈser/ vt shake;
strain <*relações, amizade*> □ vi shudder; <*relações, amizade*> become
strained; ~**cimento** m shudder; (*de
relações, amizade*) strain
estrepar-se /istreˈparsi/ (*fam*) vpr
come a cropper

estrépito /isˈtrɛpitu/ m noise; **com ~** noisily

estrepitoso /istrepiˈtozu/ a noisy; <*sucesso etc*> resounding

estres|sante /istreˈsãtʃi/ a stressful; **~sar** vt stress; **~se** /ɛ/ m stress

estria /isˈtria/ f streak; (*no corpo*) stretch mark

estribeira /istriˈbera/ f stirrup; **perder as ~s** lose control

estribilho /istriˈbiʎu/ m chorus

estribo /isˈtribu/ m stirrup

estridente /istriˈdẽtʃi/ a strident

estripulia /istripuˈlia/ f antic

estrito /isˈtritu/ a strict

estrofe /isˈtrɔfi/ f stanza, verse

estrogonofe /istrogoˈnɔfi/ m stroganoff

estrógeno /isˈtrɔʒenu/ m oestrogen

estron|do /isˈtrõdu/ m crash; **~doso** /o/ a loud; <*aplausos*> thunderous; <*sucesso, fracasso*> resounding

estropiar /istropiˈar/ vt cripple <*pessoa*>; mangle <*palavras*>

estrume /isˈtrumi/ m manure

estrutu|ra /istruˈtura/ f structure; **~ral** (pl **~rais**) a structural; **~rar** vt structure

estuário /istuˈariu/ m estuary

estudan|te /istuˈdãtʃi/ m/f student; **~til** (pl **~tis**) a student

estudar /istuˈdar/ vt/i study

estúdio /isˈtudʒiu/ m studio

estu|dioso /istudʒiˈozu/ a studious □ m scholar; **~do m** study

estufa /isˈtufa/ f (*para plantas*) greenhouse; (*de aquecimento*) stove; **~do m** stew

estupefato /istupeˈfatu/ a dumbfounded

estupendo /isteˈpẽdu/ a stupendous

estupidez /istupiˈdes/ f (*grosseria*) rudeness; (*uma*) rude thing; (*burrice*) stupidity; (*uma*) stupid thing

estúpido /isˈtupidu/ a (*grosso*) rude, coarse; (*burro*) stupid □ m lout

estupor /istuˈpor/ m stupor

estu|prador /istupraˈdor/ m rapist; **~prar** vt rape; **~pro m** rape

esturricar /istuxiˈkar/ vt parch

esvair-se /izvaˈirsi/ vpr fade; **~ em sangue** bleed to death

esvaziar /izvaziˈar/ vt empty; **~se** vpr empty

esverdeado /izverdʒiˈadu/ a greenish

esvoa|çante /izvoaˈsãtʃi/ a <*cabelo*> fly-away; **~çar** vi flutter

eta /ˈeta/ int what a

etapa /eˈtapa/ f stage; (*de corrida, turnê etc*) leg

etário /eˈtariu/ a age

éter /ˈɛter/ m ether

etéreo /eˈtɛriu/ a ethereal

eter|nidade /eterniˈdadʒi/ f eternity; **~no** /ɛ/ a eternal

éti|ca /ˈɛtʃika/ f ethics; **~co** a ethical

etimo|logia /etʃimoloˈʒia/ f etymology; **~lógico** a etymological

etíope /eˈtʃiopi/ a & m/f Ethiopian

Etiópia /etʃiˈɔpia/ f Ethiopia

etique|ta /etʃiˈketa/ f (*rótulo*) label; (*bons modos*) etiquette; **~tar** vt label

étnico /ˈɛtʃiniku/ a ethnic

eu /ew/ pron I □ m self; **mais alto do que ~** taller than me; **sou ~** it's me

EUA m pl USA

eucalipto /ewkaˈliptu/ m eucalyptus

eufemismo /ewfeˈmizmu/ m euphemism

euforia /ewfoˈria/ f euphoria

Europa /ewˈrɔpa/ f Europe

euro|peu /ewroˈpew/ a & m (f **~péia**) European

eutanásia /ewtaˈnazia/ f euthanasia

evacu|ação /evakuaˈsãw/ f evacuation; **~ar** vt evacuate

evadir /evaˈdʒir/ vt evade; **~-se** vpr escape (de from)

evan|gelho /evãˈʒeʎu/ m gospel; **~gélico** a evangelical

evaporar /evapoˈrar/ vt evaporate; **~-se** vpr evaporate

eva|são /evaˈzãw/ f escape; (*fiscal etc*) evasion; **~são escolar** truancy; **~siva** f excuse; **~sivo** a evasive

even|to /eˈvẽtu/ m event; **~tual** (pl **~tuais**) a possible; **~tualidade** f eventuality

evidência /eviˈdẽsia/ f evidence

eviden|ciar /evidẽsiˈar/ vt show up; **~ciar-se** vpr show up; **~te** a obvious, evident

evi|tar /eviˈtar/ vt avoid; **~tar de beber** avoid drinking; **~tável** (pl **~táveis**) a avoidable

evocar /evoˈkar/ vt call to mind, evoke <*passado etc*>; call up <*espíritos etc*>

evolu|ção /evoluˈsãw/ f evolution; **~ir** vi evolve

exacerbar /ezaserˈbar/ vt exacerbate

exage|rado /ezaʒeˈradu/ a over the top; **~rar** vt (*atribuir proporções irreais a*) exaggerate; (*fazer em excesso*) overdo □ vi (*ao falar*) exaggerate; (*exceder-se*) overdo it; **~ro** /e/ m exaggeration

exa|lação /ezalaˈsãw/ f fume; (*agradável*) scent; **~lar** vt give off <*perfume etc*>

exal|tação /ezawtaˈsãw/ f (*excitação*) agitation; (*engrandecimento*) exaltation; **~tar** vt (*excitar*) agitate; (*enfurecer*) infuriate; (*louvar*) exalt; **~tar-se** vpr (*excitar-se*) get agitated; (*enfurecer-se*) get furious

exa|me /eˈzami/ m examination; (*na escola*) exam(ination); **~me de**

sangue blood test; **~minar** *vt* examine

exaspe|ração /ezaspera'sãw/ *f* exasperation; **~rar** *vt* exasperate; **~rar-se** *vpr* get exasperated

exa|tidão /ezatʃi'dãw/ *f* exactness; **~to** *a* exact

exaurir /ezaw'rir/ *vt* exhaust; **~-se** *vpr* become exhausted

exaus|tivo /ezaws'tʃivu/ *a* <*estudo*> exhaustive; <*trabalho*> exhausting; **~to** *a* exhausted

exceção /ese'sãw/ *f* exception; **abrir ~** make an exception; **com ~ de** with the exception of

exce|dente /ese'dẽtʃi/ *a* & *m* excess, surplus; **~der** *vt* exceed; **~der-se** *vpr* overdo it

exce|lência /ese'lẽsia/ *f* excellence; (*tratamento*) excellency; **~lente** *a* excellent

excentricidade /esẽtrisi'dadʒi/ *f* eccentricity

excêntrico /e'sẽtriku/ *a* & *m* eccentric

excep|ção /iʃse'sãw/ (*Port*) *f veja* **exceção**; **~cional** (*pl* **~cionais**) *a* exceptional; (*deficiente*) handicapped

exces|sivo /ese'sivu/ *a* excessive; **~so** /ɛ/ *m* excess; **~so de bagagem** excess baggage; **~so de velocidade** speeding

exce|to /e'sɛtu/ *prep* except; **~tuar** *vt* except

exci|tação /esita'sãw/ *f* excitement; **~tante** *a* exciting; **~tar** *vt* excite; **~tar-se** *vpr* get excited

excla|mação /isklama'sãw/ *f* exclamation; **~mar** *vt/i* exclaim

exclu|ir /isklu'ir/ *vt* exclude; **~são** *f* exclusion; **com ~são de** with the exclusion of; **~sividade** *f* exclusive rights; **com ~sividade** exclusively; **~sivo** *a* exclusive; **~so** *a* excluded

excomungar /iskomũ'gar/ *vt* excommunicate

excremento /iskre'mẽtu/ *m* excrement

excur|são /iskur'sãw/ *f* excursion; (*a pé*) hike, walk; **~sionista** *m/f* day-tripper; (*a pé*) hiker, walker

execu|ção /ezeku'sãw/ *f* execution; **~tante** *m/f* performer; **~tar** *vt* carry out <*ordem, plano etc*>; perform <*papel, música*>; execute <*preso, criminoso etc*>; **~tivo** *a* & *m* executive

exem|plar /ezẽ'plar/ *a* exemplary □ *m* (*de espécie*) example; (*de livro, jornal etc*) copy; **~plificar** *vt* exemplify

exemplo /e'zẽplu/ *m* example; **a ~ de** following the example of; **por ~** for example; **dar o ~** set an example

exequí|vel /eze'kwivew/ (*pl* **~veis**) *a* feasible

exer|cer /ezer'ser/ *vt* exercise; exert <*pressão, influência*>; carry on <*profissão*>; **~cício** *m* exercise; (*mil*) drill; (*de profissão*) practice; (*financeiro*) financial year; **~citar** *vt* exercise; practise <*ofício*>; **~citar-se** *vpr* train

exército /e'zɛrsitu/ *m* army

exibição /ezibi'sãw/ *f* (*de filme, passaporte etc*) showing; (*de talento, força, ostentação*) show

exibicionis|mo /ezibisio'nizmu/ *m* exhibitionism; **~ta** *a* & *m/f* exhibitionist

exi|bido /ezi'bidu/ *a* <*pessoa*> pretentious □ *m* show-off; **~bir** *vt* show; (*ostentar*) show off; **~bir-se** *vpr* (*ostentar-se*) show off

exi|gência /ezi'ʒẽsia/ *f* demand; **~gente** *a* demanding; **~gir** *vt* demand

exíguo /e'zigwu/ *a* (*muito pequeno*) tiny; (*escasso*) minimal

exi|lado /ezi'lado/ *a* exiled □ *m* exile; **~lar** *vt* exile; **~lar-se** *vpr* go into exile

exílio /e'ziliu/ *m* exile

exímio /e'zimiu/ *a* distinguished

eximir /ezi'mir/ *vt* exempt (**de** from); **~-se de** get out of

exis|tência /ezis'tẽsia/ *f* existence; **~tencial** (*pl* **~tenciais**) *a* existential; **~tente** *a* existing; **~tir** *vi* exist

êxito /'ezitu/ *m* success; (*música, filme etc*) hit; **ter ~** succeed

êxodo /'ezodu/ *m* exodus

exonerar /ezone'rar/ *vt* (*de cargo*) dismiss, sack; **~-se** *vpr* resign

exorbitante /ezorbi'tãtʃi/ *a* exorbitant

exor|cismo /ezor'sizmu/ *m* exorcism; **~cista** *m/f* exorcist; **~cizar** *vt* exorcize

exótico /e'zɔtʃiku/ *a* exotic

expan|dir /ispã'dʒir/ *vt* spread; **~dir-se** *vpr* spread; <*pessoa*> open up; **~dir-se sobre** expand upon; **~são** *f* expansion; **~sivo** *a* expansive, open

expatri|ado /ispatri'ado/ *a* & *m* expatriate; **~ar-se** *vpr* leave one's country

expectativa /ispekta'tʃiva/ *f* expectation; **na ~ de** expecting; **estar na ~** wait to see what happens; **~ de vida** life expectancy

expedição /espedʒi'sãw/ *f* (*de encomendas, cartas*) dispatch; (*de passaporte, diploma etc*) issue; (*viagem*) expedition

expediente /ispedʒi'ẽtʃi/ *a* <*pessoa*> resourceful □ *m* (*horário*) working hours; (*meios*) expedient; **meio ~** part-time

expe|dir /ispe'dʒir/ vt dispatch <*encomendas, cartas*>; issue <*passaporte, diploma*>; ~**dito** a prompt, quick

expelir /ispe'lir/ vt expel

experi|ência /isperi'ēsia/ f experience; (*teste, tentativa*) experiment; ~**ente** a experienced

experimen|tação /isperimēta'sãw/ f experimentation; ~**tado** a experienced; ~**tar** vt (*provar*) try out; try on <*roupa*>; try <*comida*>; (*sentir, viver*) experience; ~**to** m experiment

expi|ar /espi'ar/ vt atone for; ~**atório** a bode ~**atório** scapegoat

expi|ração /espira'sãw/ f (*vencimento*) expiry; (*de ar*) exhalation; ~**rar** vt exhale □ vi (*morrer, vencer*) expire; (*expelir ar*) breath out, exhale

expli|cação /isplika'sãw/ f explanation; ~**car** vt explain; ~**car-se** vpr explain o.s.; ~**cável** (pl ~**cáveis**) a explainable

explicitar /isplisi'tar/ vt set out

explícito /is'plisitu/ a explicit

explodir /isplo'dʒir/ vt explode □ vi explode; <*ator etc*> make it big

explo|ração /isplora'sãw/ f (*uso, abuso*) exploitation; (*pesquisa*) exploration; ~**rar** vt (*tirar proveito de*) exploit; (*esquadrinhar*) explore

explo|são /isplo'zãw/ f explosion; ~**sivo** a & m explosive

expor /es'por/ vt (*sujeitar, arriscar*) expose (a to); display <*mercadorias*>; exhibit <*obras de arte*>; (*explicar*) expound; ~ **a vida** risk one's life; ~-**se** vpr expose o.s. (**a** to)

expor|tação /isporta'sãw/ f export; ~**tador** a exporting □ m exporter; ~**tadora** f export company; ~**tar** vt export

exposi|ção /ispozi'sãw/ f (*de arte etc*) exhibition; (*de mercadorias*) display; (*de filme fotográfico*) exposure; (*explicação*) exposition; ~**tor** m exhibitor

exposto /is'postu/ a exposed (**a** to); <*mercadoria, obra de arte*> on display

expres|são /ispre'sãw/ f expression; ~**sar** vt express; ~**sar-se** vpr express o.s.; ~**sivo** a expressive; <*número, quantia*> significant; ~**so** /ɛ/ a & m express

exprimir /ispri'mir/ vt express; ~-**se** vpr express o.s.

expropriar /ispropri'ar/ vt expropriate

expul|são /ispuw'sãw/ f expulsion; (*de jogador*) sending off; ~**sar** vt (*de escola, partido, país etc*) expel; (*de clube, bar, festa etc*) throw out; (*de jogo*) send off; ~**so** pp de **expulsar**

expur|gar /ispur'gar/ vt purge; expurgate <*livro*>; ~**go** m purge

êxtase /'estazi/ f ecstasy

extasiado /istazi'adu/ a ecstatic

exten|são /istē'sãw/ f extension; (*tamanho, alcance, duração*) extent; (*de terreno*) expanse; ~**sivo** a extensive; ~**so** a extensive; **por** ~**so** in full

extenu|ante /istenu'ātʃi/ a wearing, tiring; ~**ar** vt tire out; ~**ar-se** vpr tire o.s. out

exterior /isteri'or/ a outside, exterior; <*aparência*> outward; <*relações, comércio etc*> foreign □ m outside, exterior; (*de pessoa*) exterior; **o** ~ (*outros países*) abroad; **para o/no** ~ abroad

exter|minar /istermi'nar/ vt exterminate; ~**mínio** m extermination

exter|nar /ister'nar/ vt show; ~**na** /ɛ/ f location shot; ~**no** /ɛ/ a external; <*dívida etc*> foreign □ m day-pupil

extin|ção /istʃī'sãw/ f extinction; ~**guir** vt extinguish <*fogo*>; wipe out <*dívida, animal, povo*>; ~**guir-se** vpr <*fogo, luz*> go out; <*animal, planta*> become extinct; ~**to** a extinct; <*organização, pessoa*> defunct; ~**tor** m fire extinguisher

extirpar /istʃir'par/ vt remove <*tumor etc*>; uproot <*ervas daninhas*>; eradicate <*abusos*>

extor|quir /istor'kir/ vt extort; ~**são** f extortion

extra /'ɛstra/ a & m/f extra; **horas** ~**s** overtime

extração /istra'sãw/ f extraction; (*da loteria*) draw

extraconju|gal /estrakõʒu'gaw/ (pl ~**gais**) a extramarital

extracurricular /estrakuxiku'lar/ a extracurricular

extradi|ção /istradʒi'sãw/ f extradition; ~**tar** vt extradite

extrair /istra'ir/ vt extract; draw <*números da loteria*>

extrajudici|al /estraʒudʒisi'aw/ (pl ~**ais**) a out-of-court; ~**almente** adv out of court

extraordinário /istraordʒi'nariu/ a extraordinary

extrapolar /istrapo'lar/ vt (*exceder*) overstep; (*calcular*) extrapolate □ vi overstep the mark, go too far

extra-sensori|al /istrasēsori'aw/ (pl ~**ais**) a extra-sensory

extraterrestre /estrate'xestri/ a & m extraterrestrial

extrato /is'trato/ m extract; (*de conta*) statement

extrava|gância /istrava'gāsia/ f extravagance; ~**gante** a extravagant

extravasar /istrava'zar/ vt release, let out <*emoções, sentimentos*> □ vi overflow

extra|viado /istravi'adu/ a lost; ~**viar** vt lose, mislay <*papéis, car-**

ta>; lead astray <*pessoa*>; embezzle <*dinheiro*>; ~**viar-se** *vpr* go astray; <*carta*> get lost; ~**vio** *m* (*perda*) misplacement; (*de dinheiro*) embezzlement

extre|midade /estremi'dadʒi/ *f* end; (*do corpo*) extremity; ~**mismo** *m* extremism; ~**mista** *a* & *m/f* extremist; ~**mo** /e/ *a* & *m* extreme; **o Extremo Oriente** the Far East; ~**moso** /o/ *a* doting

extrovertido /istrover'tʃido/ *a* & *m* extrovert

exube|rância /ezube'rãsia/ *f* exuberance; ~**rante** *a* exuberant

exultar /ezuw'tar/ *vi* exult

exumar /ezu'mar/ *vt* exhume <*cadáver*>; dig up <*documentos etc*>

F

fã /fã/ *m/f* fan

fábrica /'fabrika/ *f* factory

fabri|cação /fabrika'sãw/ *f* manufacture; ~**cante** *m/f* manufacturer; ~**car** *vt* manufacture; (*inventar*) fabricate

fábula /'fabula/ *f* fable; (*fam: dinheirão*) fortune

fabuloso /fabu'lozu/ *a* fabulous

faca /'faka/ *f* knife; ~**da** *f* knife blow; **dar uma** ~**da em** (*fig*) get some money off

façanha /fa'saɲa/ *f* feat

facção /fak'sãw/ *f* faction

face /'fasi/ *f* face; (*do rosto*) cheek; ~**ta** /e/ *f* facet

fachada /fa'ʃada/ *f* façade

facho /'faʃu/ *m* beam

faci|al /fasi'aw/ (*pl* ~**ais**) *a* facial

fá|cil /'fasiw/ (*pl* ~**ceis**) *a* easy; <*pessoa*> easy-going

facili|dade /fasili'dadʒi/ *f* ease; (*talento*) facility; ~**tar** *vt* facilitate

fã-clube /fã'klubi/ *m* fan club

fac-símile /fak'simili/ *m* facsimile; (*fax*) fax

fact- (*Port*) *veja* **fat-**

facul|dade /fakuw'dadʒi/ *f* (*mental etc*) faculty; (*escola*) university, (*Amer*) college; **fazer** ~**dade** go to university; ~**tativo** *a* optional

fada /'fada/ *f* fairy; ~**do** *a* destined, doomed; ~**-madrinha** (*pl* ~**s-madrinhas**) *f* fairy godmother

fadiga /fa'dʒiga/ *f* fatigue

fa|dista /fa'dʒista/ *m/f* fado singer; ~**do** *m* fado

fagote /fa'gɔtʃi/ *m* bassoon

fagulha /fa'guʎa/ *f* spark

faia /'faja/ *f* beech

faisão /faj'zãw/ *m* pheasant

faísca /fa'iska/ *f* spark

fais|cante /fajs'kãtʃi/ *a* sparkling; ~**car** *vi* spark; (*cintilar*) sparkle

faixa /'faʃa/ *f* strip; (*cinto*) sash; (*em karatê, judô*) belt; (*da estrada*) lane; (*para pedestres*) zebra crossing, (*Amer*) crosswalk; (*atadura*) bandage; (*de disco*) track; ~ **etária** age group

fajuto /fa'ʒutu/ (*fam*) *a* fake

fala /'fala/ *f* speech

falácia /fa'lasia/ *f* fallacy

fa|lado /fa'ladu/ *a* <*língua*> spoken; <*caso, pessoa*> talked about; ~**lante** *a* talkative; ~**lar** *vt/i* speak; (*dizer*) say; ~**lar com** talk to; ~**lar de** *ou* **em** talk about; **por** ~**lar em** speaking of; **sem** ~**lar em** not to mention; ~**lou!** (*fam*) OK!; ~**latório** *m* (*boatos*) talk; (*som de vozes*) talking

falaz /fa'las/ *a* fallacious

falcão /faw'kãw/ *m* falcon

falcatrua /fawka'trua/ *f* swindle

fale|cer /fale'ser/ *vi* die, pass away; ~**cido** *a* & *m* deceased; ~**cimento** *m* death

falência /fa'lẽsia/ *f* bankruptcy; **ir à** ~ go bankrupt

falésia /fa'lezia/ *f* cliff

fa|lha /'faʎa/ *f* fault; (*omissão*) failure; ~**lhar** *vi* fail; ~**lho** *a* faulty

fálico /'faliku/ *a* phallic

fa|lido /fa'lidu/ *a* & *m* bankrupt; ~**lir** *vi* go bankrupt; ~**lível** (*pl* ~**líveis**) *a* fallible

falo /'falu/ *m* phallus

fal|sário /faw'sariu/ *m* forger; ~**sear** *vt* falsify; ~**sete** *m* falsetto; ~**sidade** *f* falseness; (*mentira*) falsehood

falsifi|cação /fawsifika'sãw/ *f* forgery; ~**cador** *m* forger; ~**car** *vt* falsify; forge <*documentos, notas*>

falso /'fawsu/ *a* false

fal|ta /'fawta/ *f* lack; (*em futebol*) foul; **em** ~**ta** at fault; **por** ~**ta de** for lack of; **sem** ~**ta** without fail; **fazer** ~**ta** be needed; **sentir a** ~**ta de** miss; ~ **tar** *vi* be missing; <*aluno*> be absent; ~**tam dois dias para** it's two days until; **me** ~**ta ... I** don't have ...; ~**tar a** miss <*aula etc*>; **break** <*palavra, promessa*>; ~**to** *a* short (**de** of)

fa|ma /'fama/ *f* reputation; (*celebridade*) fame; ~**migerado** *a* notorious

família /fa'milia/ *f* family

famili|ar /famili'ar/ *a* familiar; (*de família*) family; ~**aridade** *f* familiarity; ~**arizar** *vt* familiarize; ~**arizar-se** *vpr* familiarize o.s.

faminto /fa'mĩtu/ *a* starving

famoso /fa'mozu/ *a* famous

fanático /fa'natʃiku/ *a* fanatical □ *m* fanatic

fanatismo /fana'tʃizmu/ *m* fanaticism

fanfarrão /fãfaˈxãw/ *m* braggart

fanhoso /faˈɲozu/ *a* nasal; **ser ~** talk through one's nose

fanta|sia /fãtaˈzia/ *f* (*faculdade*) imagination; (*devaneio*) fantasy; (*roupa*) fancy dress; **~siar** *vt* dream up □ *vi* fantasize; **~siar-se** *vpr* dress up (**de** as); **~sioso** /o/ *a* fanciful; <*pessoa*> imaginative; **~sista** *a* imaginative

fantasma /fãˈtazma/ *m* ghost; **~górico** *a* ghostly

fantástico /fãˈtastʃiku/ *a* fantastic

fantoche /fãˈtɔʃi/ *m* puppet

faqueiro /faˈkeru/ *m* canteen of cutlery

fara|ó /faraˈɔ/ *m* pharaoh; **~ônico** *a* (*fig*) of epic proportions

farda /ˈfarda/ *f* uniform; **~do** *a* uniformed

fardo /ˈfardu/ *m* (*fig*) burden

fare|jador /fareʒaˈdor/ *a* **cão ~jador** sniffer dog; **~jar** *vt* sniff out □ *vi* sniff

farelo /faˈrɛlu/ *m* bran; (*de pão*) crumb; (*de madeira*) sawdust

farfalhar /farfaˈʎar/ *vi* rustle

farináceo /fariˈnasiu/ *a* starchy; **~s** *m pl* starchy foods

farin|ge /faˈrĩʒi/ *f* pharynx; **~gite** *f* pharyngitis

farinha /faˈriɲa/ *f* flour; **~ de rosca** breadcrumbs

far|macêutico /farmaˈsewtʃiku/ *a* pharmaceutical □ *m* (*pessoa*) pharmacist; **~mácia** *f* (*loja*) chemist's, (*Amer*) pharmacy; (*ciência*) pharmacy

faro /ˈfaru/ *f* sense of smell; (*fig*) nose

faroeste /faroˈɛstʃi/ *m* (*filme*) western; (*região*) wild west

faro|fa /faˈrɔfa/ *f* fried manioc flour; **~feiro** (*fam*) *m* day-tripper

fa|rol /faˈrow/ (*pl* **~róis**) *m* (*de carro*) headlight; (*de trânsito*) traffic light; (*à beira-mar*) lighthouse; **~rol alto** full beam; **~rol baixo** dipped beam; **~roleiro** *a* boastful □ *m* bighead; **~rolete** /e/ *m*, (*Port*) **~rolim** *m* side-light; (*traseiro*) tail-light

farpa /ˈfarpa/ *f* splinter; (*de metal, fig*) barb; **~do a arame~do** barbed wire

farra /ˈfaxa/ (*fam*) *f* partying; **cair na ~** go out and party

farrapo /faˈxapu/ *m* rag

far|rear /faxiˈar/ (*fam*) *vi* party; **~rista** (*fam*) *m/f* raver

far|sa /ˈfarsa/ *f* (*peça*) farce; (*fingimento*) pretence; **~sante** *m/f* (*brincalhão*) joker; (*pessoa sem seriedade*) unreliable character

far|tar /farˈtar/ *vt* satiate; **~tar-se** *vpr* (*saciar-se*) gorge o.s. (**de** with); (*cansar*) tire (**de** of); **~to a** (*abundante*) plentiful; (*cansado*) fed up (**de** with); **~tura** *f* abundance

fascículo /faˈsikulu/ *m* instalment

fasci|nação /fasinaˈsãw/ *f* fascination; **~nante** *a* fascinating; **~nar** *vt* fascinate

fascínio /faˈsiniu/ *m* fascination

fas|cismo /faˈsizmu/ *m* fascism; **~cista** *a* & *m/f* fascist

fase /ˈfazi/ *f* phase

fa|tal /faˈtaw/ (*pl* **~tais**) *a* fatal; **~talismo** *m* fatalism; **~talista** *a* fatalistic □ *m/f* fatalist; **~talmente** *adv* inevitably

fatia /faˈtʃia/ *f* slice

fatídico /faˈtʃidʒiku/ *a* fateful

fati|gante /fatʃiˈgãtʃi/ *a* tiring; **~gar** *vt* tire, fatigue

fato¹ /ˈfatu/ *m* fact; **de ~** as a matter of fact, in fact; **~ consumado** fait accompli

fato² /ˈfatu/ (*Port*) *m* suit

fator /faˈtor/ *m* factor

fátuo /ˈfatuu/ *a* fatuous

fatu|ra /faˈtura/ *f* invoice; **~ramento** *m* turnover; **~rar** *vt* invoice for <*encomenda*>; make <*dinheiro*>; (*fig: emplacar*) notch up □ *vi* (*fam*) rake it in

fauna /ˈfawna/ *f* fauna

fava /ˈfava/ *f* broad bean; **mandar alg às ~s** tell s.o. where to get off

favela /faˈvɛla/ *f* shanty town; **~do** *m* shanty-dweller

favo /ˈfavu/ *m* honeycomb

favor /faˈvor/ *m* favour; **a ~ de** in favour of; **por ~** please; **faça ~** please

favo|rável /favoˈravew/ (*pl* **~ráveis**) *a* favourable; **~recer** *vt* favour; **~ritismo** *m* favouritism; **~rito** *a* & *m* favourite

faxi|na /faˈʃina/ *f* clean-up; **~neiro** *m* cleaner

fazen|da /faˈzẽda/ *f* (*de café, gado etc*) farm; (*tecido*) fabric, material; (*pública*) treasury; **~deiro** *m* farmer

fazer /faˈzer/ *vt* do; (*produzir*) make; ask <*pergunta*>; **~-se** *vpr* (*tornar-se*) become; **~-se de** make o.s. out to be; **~ anos** have a birthday; **~ 20 anos** be twenty; **faz dois dias que ele está aqui** he's been here for two days; **faz dez anos que ele morreu** it's ten years since he died; **tanto faz** it doesn't matter

faz-tudo /fasˈtudu/ *m/f invar* jack of all trades

fé /fɛ/ *f* faith

fe|bre /ˈfɛbri/ *f* fever; **~bre amarela** yellow fever; **~bre do feno** hay fever; **~bril** (*pl* **~bris**) *a* feverish

fe|chado /feˈʃadu/ *a* closed; <*curva*> sharp; <*sinal*> red; <*torneira*> off; <*tempo*> overcast; <*cara*> stern; <*pessoa*> reserved; **~chadura** *f* lock; **~chamento** m closure; **~char** vt close, shut; turn off <*torneira*>; do up <*calça, casaco*>; close <*negócio*> □ vi close, shut; <*sinal*> go red; <*tempo*> cloud over; **~char à chave** lock; **~char a cara** frown; **~cho** /e/ m fastener; **~cho ecler** zip

fécula /ˈfɛkula/ f starch

fecun|dar /fekũˈdar/ vt fertilize; **~do** a fertile

feder /feˈder/ vi stink

fede|ração /federaˈsãw/ f federation; **~ral** (pl **~rais**) a federal; (fam) huge; **~rativo** a federal

fedor /feˈdor/ m stink, stench; **~ento** a stinking

feérico /feˈɛriku/ a magical

feições /fejˈsõjs/ f pl features

fei|jão /feˈʒãw/ m bean; (coletivo) beans; **~joada** f bean stew; **~joeiro** m bean plant

feio /ˈfeju/ a ugly; <*palavra, situação, tempo*> nasty; <*olhar*> dirty; **~so** /o/ a plain

fei|ra /ˈfera/ f market; (industrial) trade fair; **~rante** m/f market trader

feiti|caria /fejtʃiˈsera/ f magic; **~ceira** f witch; **~ceiro** m wizard □ a bewitching; **~ço** m spell

fei|tio /fejˈtʃiu/ m (de pessoa) make-up; **~to** pp de fazer □ m (ato) deed; (proeza) feat □ conj like; **bem ~to por ele** (it) serves him right; **~tura** f making

feiúra /fejˈura/ f ugliness

feixe /ˈfeʃi/ m bundle

fel /fɛw/ f gall; (fig) bitterness

felicidade /felisiˈdadʒi/ f happiness

felici|tações /felisitaˈsõjs/ f pl congratulations; **~tar** vt congratulate (por on)

felino /feˈlinu/ a feline

feliz /feˈlis/ a happy; **~ardo** a lucky; **~mente** adv fortunately

fel|pa /ˈfewpa/ f (de pano) nap; (penugem) down, fluff; **~pudo** a fluffy

feltro /ˈfewtru/ m felt

fêmea /ˈfemia/ a & f female

femi|nil /femiˈniw/ (pl **~nis**) a feminine; **~nilidade** f femininity; **~nino** a female; <*palavra*> feminine; **~nismo** m feminism; **~nista** a & m/f feminist

fêmur /ˈfemur/ m femur

fen|da /ˈfeda/ f crack; **~der** vt/i split, crack

feno /ˈfenu/ m hay

fenome|nal /fenomeˈnaw/ (pl **~nais**) a phenomenal

fenômeno /feˈnomenu/ m phenomenon

fera /ˈfɛra/ f wild beast; **ficar uma ~** get really angry; **ser ~ em** (fam) be brilliant at

féretro /ˈfɛretru/ m coffin

feriado /feriˈadu/ m public holiday

férias /ˈfɛrias/ f pl holiday(s), (Amer) vacation; **de ~** on holiday; **tirar ~** take a holiday

feri|da /feˈrida/ f injury; (com arma) wound; **~do** a injured; (mil) wounded □ m injured person; **os ~dos** the injured; (mil) the wounded; **~r** vt injure; (com arma) wound; (magoar) hurt

fermen|tar /fermẽˈtar/ vt/i ferment; **~to** m yeast; (fig) ferment; **~to em pó** baking powder

fe|rocidade /ferosiˈdadʒi/ f ferocity; **~roz** a ferocious

fer|rado /feˈxadu/ a **estou ~rado** (fam) I've had it; **~rado no sono** fast asleep; **~radura** f horseshoe; **~ragem** f ironwork; pl hardware; **~ramenta** f tool; (coletivo) tools; **~rão** m (de abelha) sting; **~rar** vt brand <*gado*>; shoe <*cavalo*>; **~rar-se** (fam) vpr come a cropper; **~reiro** m blacksmith; **~renho** a <*partidário etc*> staunch; <*vontade*> iron

férreo /ˈfɛxeu/ a iron

ferro /ˈfɛxu/ m iron; **~lho** /o/ m bolt; **~-velho** (pl **~s-velhos**) m (pessoa) scrap-metal dealer; (lugar) scrap-metal yard; **~via** f railway, (Amer) railroad; **~viário** a railway □ m railway worker

ferrugem /feˈxuʒẽ/ f rust

fér|til /ˈfɛrtʃiw/ (pl **~teis**) a fertile

fertili|dade /fertʃiliˈdadʒi/ f fertility; **~zante** m fertilizer; **~zar** vt fertilize

fer|vente /ferˈvẽtʃi/ a boiling; **~ver** vi boil; (de raiva) seethe; **~vilhar** vi bubble; **~vilhar de** swarm with; **~vor** m fervour; **~vura** f boiling

fes|ta /ˈfɛsta/ f party; (religiosa) festival; **~tejar** vt/i celebrate; (acolher) fete; **~tejo** /e/ m celebration; **~tim** m feast; **~tival** (pl **~tivais**) m festival; **~tividade** f festivity; **~tivo** a festive

feti|che /feˈtʃiʃi/ m fetish; **~chismo** m fetishism; **~chista** m/f fetishist □ a fetishistic

fétido /ˈfɛtʃidu/ a fetid

feto¹ /ˈfɛtu/ m (no útero) foetus

feto² /ˈfɛtu/ (Port) m (planta) fern

feu|dal /fewˈdaw/ (pl **~dais**) a feudal; **~dalismo** m feudalism

fevereiro /feveˈreru/ m February

fezes /ˈfɛzis/ f pl faeces

fiação /fiaˈsãw/ f (eletr) wiring; (fábrica) mill

fia|do /fiˈadu/ a <*conversa*> idle □ adv <*comprar*> on credit; **~dor** m guarantor

fiambre /fiˈãbri/ m cooked ham

fiança /fiˈãsa/ f surety; (*jurid*) bail

fiapo /fiˈapu/ m thread

fiar /fiˈar/ vt spin < lã etc>

fiasco /fiˈasku/ m fiasco

fibra /ˈfibra/ f fibre

ficar /fiˈkar/ vi (*tornar-se*) become; (*estar, ser*) be; (*manter-se*) stay; ~ fazendo keep (on) doing; ~ com keep; get < impressão, vontade>; ~ com medo get scared; ~ de fazer arrange to do; ~ para be left for; ~ bom turn out well; (*recuperar-se*) get better; ~ bem look good

fic|ção /fikˈsãw/ f fiction; ~ção científica science fiction; ~cionista m/f fiction writer

fi|cha /ˈfiʃa/ f (*de telefone*) token; (*de jogo*) chip; (*da caixa*) ticket; (*de fichário*) file card; (*na polícia*) record; (*Port: tomada*) plug; ~chário m, (Port) ~cheiro m file; (*móvel*) filing cabinet

fictício /fikˈtʃisiu/ a fictitious

fidalgo /fiˈdalgu/ m nobleman

fide|digno /fideˈdʒignu/ a trustworthy; ~lidade f fidelity

fiduciário /fidusiˈariu/ a fiduciary □ m trustee

fi|el /fiˈew/ (*pl* ~éis) a faithful □ m os ~éis (*na igreja*) the congregation

figa /ˈfiga/ f talisman

fígado /ˈfigadu/ f liver

fi|go /ˈfigu/ m fig; ~gueira f fig tree

figu|ra /fiˈgura/ f figure; (*carta de jogo*) face card; (*fam: pessoa*) character; **fazer (má)** ~ra make a (bad) impression; ~rado a figurative; ~rante m/f extra; ~rão m big shot; ~rar vi appear, figure; ~rativo a figurative; ~rinha f sticker; ~rino m fashion plate; (*de filme, peça*) costume design; (*fig*) model; **como manda o** ~rino as it should be

fila /ˈfila/ f line; (*de espera*) queue, (*Amer*) line; (*fileira*) row; **fazer** ~ queue up, (*Amer*) stand in line; ~ indiana single file

filamento /filaˈmẽtu/ m filament

filante /fiˈlãtʃi/ (*fam*) m/f sponger

filan|tropia /filãtroˈpia/ f philanthropy; ~trópico a philanthropic; ~tropo /o/ m philanthropist

filão /fiˈlãw/ m (*de ouro*) seam; (*fig*) money-spinner

filar /fiˈlar/ (*fam*) vt sponge, cadge

filar|mônica /filarˈmonika/ f philharmonic (orchestra); ~mônico a philharmonic

filate|lia /filateˈlia/ f philately; ~lista m/f philatelist

filé /fiˈlɛ/ m fillet

fileira /fiˈlera/ f row

filete /fiˈlɛtʃi/ m fillet

fi|lha /ˈfiʎa/ f daughter; ~lho m son; *pl* (*crianças*) children; ~lho da puta

(*chulo*) bastard, (*Amer*) son of a bitch; ~lho de criação foster child; ~lho único only child; ~lhote m (*de cão*) pup; (*de lobo etc*) cub; *pl* young

fili|ação /filiaˈsãw/ f affiliation; ~al (*pl* ~ais) a filial □ f branch

Filipinas /filiˈpinas/ f *pl* Philippines

filipino /filiˈpinu/ a & m Filipino

fil|madora /fiwmaˈdora/ f camcorder; ~magem f filming; ~mar vt/i film; ~me m film

fi|lologia /filoloˈʒia/ f philology; ~lólogo m philologist

filo|sofar /filozoˈfar/ vi philosophize; ~sofia f philosophy; ~sófico a philosophical

filósofo /fiˈlozofu/ m philosopher

fil|trar /fiwˈtrar/ vt filter; ~tro m filter

fim /fĩ/ m end; **a** ~ **de** (*para*) in order to; **estar a** ~ **de** fancy; **por** ~ finally; **sem** ~ endless; **ter** ~ come to an end; ~ **de semana** weekend

fi|nado /fiˈnadu/ a & m deceased, departed; ~nal (*pl* ~nais) a final □ m end □ f final; ~nalista m/f finalist; ~nalizar vt/i finish

finan|ças /fiˈnãsas/ f *pl* finances; ~ceiro a financial □ m financier; ~ciamento m financing; (*um*) loan; ~ciar vt finance; ~cista m/f financier

fincar /fiˈkar/ vt plant; ~ **o pé** (*fig*) dig one's heels in

findar /fiˈdar/ vt/i end

fineza /fiˈneza/ f finesse; (*favor*) kindness

fin|gido /fiˈʒidu/ a feigned; <*pessoa*> insincere; ~gimento m pretence; ~gir vt pretend; feign <*doença etc*> □ vi pretend; ~gir-se de pretend to be

finito /fiˈnitu/ a finite

finlan|dês /filãˈdes/ a (*f* ~desa) Finnish □ m (*f* ~desa) Finn; (*língua*) Finnish

Finlândia /fiˈlãdʒia/ f Finland

fi|ninho /fiˈniɲu/ adv **sair de** ~ninho slip away; ~no a (*não grosso*) thin; < *areia, pó etc*> fine; (*refinado*) refined; ~nório a crafty; ~nura f thinness; fineness

fio /ˈfiu/ m thread; (*elétrico*) wire; (*de sangue, água*) trickle; (*de luz, esperança*) glimmer; (*de navalha etc*) edge; **horas a** ~ hours on end

fir|ma /ˈfirma/ f firm; (*assinatura*) signature; ~mamento m firmament; ~mar vt fix; (*basear*) base □ vi settle; ~mar-se vpr be based (em on); ~me a firm; < *tempo*> settled □ adv firmly; ~meza f firmness

fis|cal /fisˈkaw/ (*pl* ~cais) m inspector; ~calização f inspection;

~**calizar** *vt* inspect; ~**co** *m* inland revenue, (*Amer*) internal revenue service

fis|gada /fiz'gada/ *f* stabbing pain; ~**gar** *vt* hook

físi|ca /'fizika/ *f* physics; ~**co** *a* physical □ *m* (*pessoa*) physicist; (*corpo*) physique

fisio|nomia /fizionɔ'mia/ *f* face; ~**nomista** *m/f* ser ~**nomista** have a good memory for faces; ~**terapeuta** *m/f* physiotherapist; ~**terapia** *f* physiotherapy

fissura /fi'sura/ *f* fissure; (*fam*) craving; ~**do** *a* ~**do em** (*fam*) mad about

fita /'fita/ *f* tape; (*fam: encenação*) playacting; **fazer** ~ (*fam*) put on an act; ~ **adesiva** (*Port*) adhesive tape; ~ **métrica** tape measure

fitar /fi'tar/ *vt* stare at

fivela /fi'vɛla/ *f* buckle

fi|xador /fiksa'dor/ *m* (*de cabelo*) setting lotion; (*de fotos*) fixative; ~**xar** *vt* fix; stick up <*cartaz*>; ~**xo** *a* fixed

flácido /'flasidu/ *a* flabby

flagelo /fla'ʒɛlu/ *m* scourge

fla|grante /fla'grãtʃi/ *a* flagrant; **apanhar em** ~**grante (delito)** catch in the act; ~**grar** *vt* catch

flame|jante /flame'ʒãtʃi/ *a* blazing; ~**jar** *vi* blaze

flamengo /fla'mẽgu/ *a* Flemish □ *m* Fleming; (*língua*) Flemish

flamingo /fla'mĩgu/ *m* flamingo

flâmula /'flamula/ *f* pennant

flanco /'flãku/ *m* flank

flanela /fla'nɛla/ *f* flannel

flanquear /flãki'ar/ *vt* flank

flash /flɛʃ/ *m invar* flash

flau|ta /'flawta/ *f* flute; ~**tista** *m/f* flautist

flecha /'flɛʃa/ *f* arrow

fler|tar /fler'tar/ *vi* flirt; ~**te** *m* flirtation

fleuma /'flewma/ *f* phlegm

fle|xão /flek'sãw/ *f* press-up, (*Amer*) push-up; (*ling*) inflection; ~**xibilidade** *f* flexibility; ~**xionar** *vt/i* flex <*perna, braço*>; (*ling*) inflect; ~**xível** (*pl* ~**xíveis**) *a* flexible

fliperama /flipe'rama/ *m* pinball machine

floco /'flɔku/ *m* flake

flor /flor/ *f* flower; **a fina** ~ the cream; **à** ~ **da pele** (*fig*) on edge

flo|ra /'flɔra/ *f* flora; ~**reado** *a* full of flowers; (*fig*) florid; ~**reio** *m* clever turn of phrase; ~**rescer** *vi* flower; ~**resta** /ɛ/ *f* forest; ~**restal** (*pl* ~**restais**) *a* forest; ~**rido** *a* in flower; (*fig*) florid; ~**rir** *vi* flower

flotilha /flo'tʃiʎa/ *f* flotilla

flu|ência /flu'ẽsia/ *f* fluency; ~**ente** *a* fluent

flui|dez /flui'des/ *f* fluidity; ~**do** *a* & *m* fluid

fluir /flu'ir/ *vi* flow

fluminense /flumi'nẽsi/ *a* & *m* (person) from Rio de Janeiro state

fluorescente /fluore'sẽtʃi/ *a* fluorescent

flutu|ação /flutua'sãw/ *f* fluctuation; ~**ante** *a* floating; ~**ar** *vi* float; <*bandeira*> flutter; (*hesitar*) waver

fluvi|al /fluvi'aw/ (*pl* ~**ais**) *a* river

fluxo /'fluksu/ *m* flow; ~**grama** *m* flowchart

fobia /fo'bia/ *f* phobia

foca /'fɔka/ *f* seal

focalizar /fokali'zar/ *vt* focus on

focinho /fo'siɲu/ *m* snout

foco /'fɔku/ *m* focus; (*fig*) centre

fofo /'fofu/ *a* soft; <*pessoa*> cuddly

fofo|ca /fo'fɔka/ *f* piece of gossip; *pl* gossip; ~**car** *vi* gossip; ~**queiro** *m* gossip □ *a* gossipy

fo|gão /fo'gãw/ *m* stove; (*de cozinhar*) cooker; ~**go** /o/ *m* fire; **tem** ~**go?** have you got a light?; **ser** ~**go** (*fam*) (*ser chato*) be a pain in the neck; (*ser incrível*) be amazing; ~**gos de artifício** fireworks; ~**goso** /o/ *a* fiery; ~**gueira** *f* bonfire; ~**guete** /e/ *m* rocket

foice /'fojsi/ *f* scythe

fol|clore /fow'klɔri/ *m* folklore; ~**clórico** *a* folk

fole /'fɔli/ *m* bellows

fôlego /'folegu/ *m* breath; (*fig*) stamina

fol|ga /'fowga/ *f* rest, break; (*fam: cara-de-pau*) cheek; ~**gado** *a* <*roupa*> full, loose; <*vida*> leisurely; (*fam: atrevido*) cheeky; ~**gar** *vt* loosen □ *vi* have time off

fo|lha /'foʎa/ *f* leaf; (*de papel*) sheet; **novo em** ~**lha** brand new; ~**lha de pagamento** payroll; ~**lhagem** *f* foliage; ~**lhear** *vt* leaf through; ~**lheto** /e/ *m* pamphlet; ~**lhinha** *f* tear-off calendar; ~**lhudo** *a* leafy

foli|a /fo'lia/ *f* revelry; ~**ão** *m* (*f* ~**ona**) reveller

folículo /fo'likulu/ *m* follicle

fome /'fomi/ *f* hunger; **estar com** ~ be hungry

fomentar /fomẽ'tar/ *vt* foment

fone /'foni/ *m* (*do telefone*) receiver; (*de rádio etc*) headphones

fonema /fo'nema/ *m* phoneme

fonéti|ca /fo'nɛtʃika/ *f* phonetics; ~**co** *a* phonetic

fonologia /fonolo'ʒia/ *f* phonology

fonte /'fõtʃi/ *f* (*de água*) spring; (*fig*) source

fora /'fɔra/ *adv* outside; (*não em casa*) out; (*viajando*) away □ *prep* except; **dar um** ~ drop a clanger; **dar um**

~ **em alg** cut s.o. dead; chuck <*namorado*>; **por** ~ on the outside; ~**-de-lei** *m/f invar* outlaw

foragido /fora'ʒidu/ *a* at large, on the run □ *m* fugitive

forasteiro /foras'teru/ *m* outsider

forca /'forka/ *f* gallows

for|ça /'forsa/ *f* (*vigor*) strength; (*violência*) force; (*elétrica*) power; **dar uma** ~**ça a alg** help s.o. out; **fazer** ~**ça** make an effort; ~**ças armadas** armed forces; ~**çar** *vt* force; ~**ça-tarefa** (*pl* ~**ças-tarefa**) *f* task force

fórceps /'fɔrseps/ *m invar* forceps

forçoso /for'sozu/ *a* forced

for|ja /'fɔrʒa/ *f* forge; ~**jar** *vt* forge

forma /'fɔrma/ *f* form; (*contorno*) shape; (*maneira*) way; **de qualquer** ~ anyway; **manter a** ~ keep fit

fôrma /'forma/ *f* mould; (*de cozinha*) baking tin

for|mação /forma'sãw/ *f* formation; (*educação*) education; (*profissionalizante*) training; ~**mado** *m* graduate; ~**mal** (*pl* ~**mais**) *a* formal; ~**malidade** *f* formality; ~**malizar** *vt* formalize; ~**mar** *vt* form; (*educar*) educate; ~**mar-se** *vpr* be formed; <*estudante*> graduate; ~**mato** *m* format; ~**matura** *f* graduation

formidá|vel /formi'davew/ (*pl* ~**veis**) *a* formidable; (*muito bom*) tremendous

formi|ga /for'miga/ *f* ant; ~**gamento** *m* pins and needles; ~**gar** *vi* swarm (**de** with); <*perna, mão etc*> tingle; ~**gueiro** *m* ants' nest

formosura /formo'zura/ *f* beauty

fórmula /'fɔrmula/ *f* formula

formu|lação /formula'sãw/ *f* formulation; ~**lar** *vt* formulate; ~**lário** *m* form

fornalha /for'naʎa/ *f* furnace

forne|cedor /fornese'dor/ *m* supplier; ~**cer** *vt* supply; ~**cer aco a alg** supply s.o. with sth; ~**cimento** *m* supply

forno /'fornu/ *m* oven; (*para louça etc*) kiln

foro /'foru/ *m* forum

forra /'fɔxa/ *f* **ir à** ~ get one's own back

for|ragem /fo'xaʒẽ/ *f* fodder; ~**rar** *vt* line <*roupa, caixa etc*>; cover <*sofá etc*>; carpet <*assoalho, sala etc*>; ~**ro** /o/ *m* (*de roupa, caixa etc*) lining; (*de sofá etc*) cover; (*carpete*) (fitted) carpet

forró /fo'xɔ/ *m* type of Brazilian dance

fortale|cer /fortale'ser/ *vt* strengthen; ~**cimento** *m* strengthening; ~**za** /e/ *f* fort-ress

for|te /'fɔrtʃi/ *a* strong; <*golpe*> hard; <*chuva*> heavy; <*físico*> muscular □ *adv* strongly; <*bater, chover*> hard □

m (*militar*) fort; (*habilidade*) strong point, forte; ~**tificação** *f* fortification; ~**tificar** *vt* fortify

fortu|ito /for'tuitu/ *a* chance; ~**na** *f* fortune

fosco /'fosku/ *a* dull; <*vidro*> frosted

fosfato /fos'fatu/ *m* phosphate

fósforo /'fɔsforu/ *m* match; (*elemento químico*) phosphor

fossa /'fɔsa/ *f* pit; **na** ~ (*fig*) miserable, depressed

fós|sil /'fɔsiw/ (*pl* ~**seis**) *m* fossil

fosso /'fosu/ *m* ditch; (*de castelo*) moat

foto /'fɔtu/ *f* photo; ~**cópia** *f* photocopy; ~**copiadora** *f* photocopier; ~**copiar** *vt* photocopy; ~**gênico** *a* photogenic; ~**grafar** *vt* photograph; ~**grafia** *f* photography; ~**gráfico** *a* photographic

fotógrafo /fo'tɔgrafu/ *m* photographer

foz /fɔs/ *f* mouth

fração /fra'sãw/ *f* fraction

fracas|sado /fraka'sadu/ *a* failed □ *m* failure; ~**sar** *vi* fail; ~**so** *m* failure

fracionar /frasio'nar/ *vt* break up

fraco /'fraku/ *a* weak; <*luz, som*> faint; <*medíocre*> poor □ *m* weakness, weak spot

fract- (*Port*) *veja* **frat-**

frade /'fradʒi/ *m* friar

fragata /fra'gata/ *f* frigate

frá|gil /'fraʒiw/ (*pl* ~**geis**) *a* fragile; <*pessoa*> frail

fragilidade /fraʒili'dadʒi/ *f* fragility; (*de pessoa*) frailty

fragmen|tar /fragmē'tar/ *vt* fragment; ~**tar-se** *vpr* fragment; ~**to** *m* fragment

fra|grância /fra'grãsia/ *f* fragrance; ~**grante** *a* fragrant

fralda /'frawda/ *f* nappy, (*Amer*) diaper

framboesa /frãbo'eza/ *f* raspberry

França /'frãsa/ *f* France

fran|cês /frã'ses/ *a* (*f* ~**cesa**) French □ *m* (*f* ~**cesa**) Frenchman (*f* -woman); (*língua*) French; **os** ~**ceses** the French

franco /'frãku/ *a* (*honesto*) frank; (*óbvio*) clear; (*gratuito*) free □ *m* franc; ~**-atirador** (*pl* ~**-atiradores**) *m* sniper; (*fig*) maverick

frangalho /frã'gaʎu/ *m* tatter

frango /'frãgu/ *m* chicken

franja /'frãʒa/ *f* fringe; (*do cabelo*) fringe, (*Amer*) bangs

fran|quear /frãki'ar/ *vt* frank <*carta*>; ~**queza** /e/ *f* frankness; ~**quia** *f* (*de cartas*) franking; (*jur*) franchise

fran|zino /frã'zinu/ *a* skinny; ~**zir** *vt* gather <*tecido*>; wrinkle <*testa*>

fraque /'fraki/ *m* morning suit

fraqueza /fra'keza/ *f* weakness; (*de luz, som*) faintness
frasco /'frasku/ *m* bottle
frase /'frazi/ *f* (*oração*) sentence; (*locução*) phrase; ~**ado** *m* phrasing
frasqueira /fras'kera/ *f* vanity case
frater|nal /frater'naw/ (*pl* ~**nais**) *a* fraternal; ~**nidade** *f* fraternity; ~**nizar** *vi* fraternize; ~**no** *a* fraternal
fratu|ra /fra'tura/ *f* fracture; ~**rar** *vt* fracture; ~**rar-se** *vpr* fracture
frau|dar /fraw'dar/ *vt* defraud; ~**de** *f* fraud; ~**dulento** *a* fraudulent
frear /fri'ar/ *vt/i* brake
freezer /'frizer/ *m* freezer
fre|guês /fre'ges/ *m* (*f* ~**guesa**) customer; ~**guesia** *f* (*de loja etc*) clientele; (*paróquia*) parish
frei /frej/ *m* brother
freio /'freju/ *m* brake; (*de cavalo*) bit
freira /'frera/ *f* nun
freixo /'freʃu/ *m* ash
fremir /fre'mir/ *vi* shake
frêmito /'fremitu/ *m* wave
frenesi /frene'zi/ *m* frenzy
frenético /fre'netʃiku/ *a* frantic
frente /'frētʃi/ *f* front; **em ~ a** *ou* **de** in front of; **para a ~** forward; **pela ~** ahead; **fazer ~ a** face
freqüência /fre'kwēsia/ *f* frequency; (*assiduidade*) attendance; **com muita ~** often
freqüen|tador /frekwēta'dor/ *m* regular visitor (**de** to); ~**tar** *vt* frequent; (*cursar*) attend; ~**te** *a* frequent
fres|cão /fres'kãw/ *m* air-conditioned coach; ~**co** /e/ *a* < *comida etc*> fresh; < *vento, água, quarto*> cool; (*fam*) (*afetado*) affected; (*exigente*) fussy; ~**cobol** *m* kind of racquetball; ~**cor** *m* freshness; ~**cura** *f* (*fam*) (*afetação*) affectation; (*ser exigente*) fussiness; (*coisa sem importância*) trifle
fresta /'frɛsta/ *f* slit
fre|tar /fre'tar/ *vt* charter < *avião*>; hire < *caminhão*>; ~**te** /ɛ/ *m* freight; (*aluguel de avião*) charter; (*de caminhão*) hire
frevo /'frevu/ *m* type of Brazilian dance
fria /'fria/ (*fam*) *f* difficult situation, spot; ~**gem** *f* chill
fric|ção /frik'sãw/ *f* friction; ~**cionar** *vt* rub
fri|eira /fri'era/ *f* chilblain; ~**eza** /e/ *f* coldness
frigideira /friʒi'dera/ *f* frying pan
frígido /'friʒidu/ *a* frigid
frigorífico /frigo'rifiku/ *m* cold store, refrigerator, fridge
frincha /'frĩʃa/ *f* chink
frio /'friu/ *a* & *m* cold; **estar com ~** be cold; ~**rento** *a* sensitive to the cold

frisar /fri'zar/ *vt* (*enfatizar*) stress; crimp < *cabelo*>
friso /'frizu/ *m* frieze
fri|tada /fri'tada/ *f* fry-up; ~**tar** *vt* fry; ~**tas** *f pl* chips, (*Amer*) French fries; ~**to a** fried; **está ~to** (*fam*) he's had it; ~**tura** *f* fried food
frivolidade /frivoli'dadʒi/ *f* frivolity; **frívolo** *a* frivolous
fronha /'froɲa/ *f* pillowcase
fronte /'frõtʃi/ *f* forehead, brow
frontei|ra /frõ'tera/ *f* border; ~**riço** *a* border
frota /'frɔta/ *f* fleet
frou|xidão /froʃi'dãw/ *f* looseness; (*moral*) laxity; ~**xo** *a* loose; < *regulamento*> lax; < *pessoa*> lackadaisical
fru|gal /fru'gaw/ (*pl* ~**gais**) *a* frugal; ~**galidade** *f* frugality
frus|tração /frustra'sãw/ *f* frustration; ~**trante** *a* frustrating; ~**trar** *vt* frustrate
fru|ta /'fruta/ *f* fruit; ~**ta-do-conde** (*pl* ~**tas-do-conde**) *f* sweetsop; ~**ta-pão** (*pl* ~**tas-pão**) *f* breadfruit; ~**teira** *f* fruitbowl; ~**tífero** *a* (*fig*) fruitful; ~**to** *m* fruit
fubá /fu'ba/ *m* maize flour
fu|çar /fu'sar/ *vi* nose around; ~**ças** (*fam*) *f pl* face, chops
fu|ga /'fuga/ *f* escape; ~**gaz** *a* fleeting; ~**gida** *f* escape; ~**gir** *vi* run away; (*soltar-se*) escape; ~**gir a** avoid; ~**gitivo** *a* & *m* fugitive
fulano /fu'lanu/ *m* whatever his name is
fuleiro /fu'leru/ *a* down-market, cheap and cheerful
fulgor /fuw'gor/ *m* brightness; (*fig*) splendour
fuligem /fu'liʒẽ/ *f* soot
fulmi|nante /fuwmi'nãtʃi/ *a* devastating; ~**nar** *vt* strike down; (*fig*) devastate; ~**nado por um raio** struck by lightning □ *vi* (*criticar*) rail
fu|maça /fu'masa/ *f* smoke; ~**maceira** *f* cloud of smoke; ~**mante**, (*Port*) ~**mador** *m* smoker; ~**mar** *vt/i* smoke; ~**mê** *a invar* smoked; ~**megar** *vi* smoke; ~**mo** *m* (*tabaco*) tobacco; (*Port*: *fumaça*) smoke; (*fumar*) smoking
função /fũ'sãw/ *f* function; **em ~ de** as a result of; **fazer as funções de** function as
funcho /'fũʃu/ *m* fennel
funcio|nal /fũsio'naw/ (*pl* ~**nais**) *a* functional; ~**nalismo** *m* civil service; ~**namento** *m* working; ~**nar** *vi* work; ~**nário** *m* employee; ~**nário público** civil servant
fun|dação /fũda'sãw/ *f* foundation; ~**dador** *m* founder □ *a* founding

fundamen|tal /fũdamẽ'taw/ (*pl* ~**tais**) *a* fundamental; ~**tar** *vt* (*basear*) base; (*justificar*) substantiate; ~**to** *m* foundation

fun|dar /fũ'dar/ *vt* (*criar*) found; (*basear*) base; ~**dar-se** *vpr* be based (**em** on); ~**dear** *vi* drop anchor, anchor; ~**dilho** *m* seat

fundir /fũ'dʒir/ *vt* melt <*ouro, ferro*>; cast <*sino, estátua*>; (*juntar*) merge; ~**-se** *vpr* <*ouro, ferro*> melt; (*juntarse*) merge

fundo /'fũdu/ *a* deep □ *m* (*parte de baixo*) bottom; (*parte de trás*) back; (*de quadro, foto*) background; (*de dinheiro*) fund; **no** ~ basically; ~**s** *m pl* (*da casa etc*) back; (*recursos*) funds

fúnebre /'funebri/ *a* funereal

funerário /fune'rariu/ *a* funeral

funesto /fu'nɛstu/ *a* fatal

fungar /fũ'gar/ *vt/i* sniff

fungo /'fũgu/ *m* fungus

fu|nil /fu'niw/ (*pl* ~**nis**) *m* funnel; ~**nilaria** *f* panel-beating; (*oficina*) bodyshop

furacão /fura'kãw/ *m* hurricane

furado /fu'radu/ *a* **papo** ~ (*fam*) hot air

furão /fu'rãw/ *m* (*animal*) ferret

furar /fu'rar/ *vt* pierce <*orelha etc*>; puncture <*pneu*>; make a hole in <*roupa etc*>; jump <*fila*>; break <*greve*> □ *vi* <*roupa etc*> go into a hole; <*pneu*> puncture; (*fam*) <*programa*> fall through

fur|gão /fur'gãw/ *m* van; ~**goneta** /e/ (*Port*) *f* van

fúria /'furia/ *f* fury

furioso /furi'ozu/ *a* furious

furo /'furu/ *m* hole; (*de pneu*) puncture; (*jornalístico*) scoop; (*fam: gafe*) blunder, faux pas; **dar um** ~ put one's foot in it

furor /fu'ror/ *m* furore

fur|ta-cor /furta'kor/ *a invar* iridescent; ~**tar** *vt* steal; ~**tivo** *a* furtive; ~**to** *m* theft

furúnculo /fu'rũkulu/ *m* boil

fusão /fu'zãw/ *f* fusion; (*de empresas*) merger

fusca /'fuska/ *f* VW beetle

fuselagem /fuze'laʒẽ/ *f* fuselage

fusí|vel /fu'zivew/ (*pl* ~**veis**) *m* fuse

fuso /'fuzu/ *m* spindle; ~ **horário** time zone

fustigar /fustʃi'gar/ *vt* lash; (*fig: com palavras*) lash out at

futebol /futʃi'bɔw/ *m* football; ~**ístico** *a* football

fú|til /'futʃiw/ (*pl* ~**teis**) *a* frivolous, inane

futilidade /futʃili'dadʒi/ *f* frivolity, inanity; (*uma*) frivolous thing

futu|rismo /futu'rizmu/ *m* futurism;

~**rista** *a* & *m* futurist; ~**rístico** *a* futuristic; ~**ro** *a* & *m* future

fu|zil /fu'ziw/ (*pl* ~**zis**) *m* rifle; ~**zilamento** *m* shooting; ~**zilar** *vt* shoot □ *vi* flash; ~**zileiro** *m* rifleman; ~**zileiro naval** marine

fuzuê /fuzu'e/ *m* commotion

G

gabar-se /ga'barsi/ *vpr* boast (**de** of)

gabarito /gaba'ritu/ *m* calibre

gabinete /gabi'netʃi/ *m* (*em casa*) study; (*escritório*) office; (*ministros*) cabinet

gado /'gadu/ *m* livestock; (*bovino*) cattle

gaélico /ga'ɛliku/ *a* & *m* Gaelic

gafanhoto /gafa'ɲotu/ *m* (*pequeno*) grasshopper; (*grande*) locust

gafe /'gafi/ *f* faux pas, gaffe

gafieira /gafi'era/ *f* dance; (*salão*) dance hall

gagá /ga'ga/ *a* (*fam*) senile

ga|go /'gagu/ *a* stuttering □ *m* stutterer; ~**gueira** *f* stutter; ~**guejar** *vi* stutter

gaiato /gaj'atu/ *a* funny

gaiola /gaj'ɔla/ *f* cage

gaita /'gajta/ *f* ~ **de foles** bagpipes

gaivota /gaj'vɔta/ *f* seagull

gajo /'gaʒu/ *m* (*Port*) guy, bloke

gala /'gala/ *f* **festa de** ~ gala; **roupa de** ~ formal dress

galã /ga'lã/ *m* leading man

galan|tear /galãtʃi'ar/ *vt* woo; ~**teio** *m* wooing; (*um*) courtesy

galão /ga'lãw/ *m* (*enfeite*) braid; (*mil*) stripe; (*medida*) gallon; (*Port: café*) white coffee

galáxia /ga'laksia/ *f* galaxy

galé /ga'lɛ/ *f* galley

galego /ga'legu/ *a* & *m* Galician

galera /ga'lɛra/ *f* (*fam*) crowd

galeria /gale'ria/ *f* gallery

Gales /'galis/ *m* **País de** ~ Wales

ga|lês /ga'les/ *a* (*f* ~**lesa**) Welsh □ *m* (*f* ~**lesa**) Welshman (*f* -woman); (*língua*) Welsh

galeto /ga'letu/ *m* spring chicken

galgar /gaw'gar/ *vt* (*transpor*) jump over; climb <*escada*>

galgo /'gawgu/ *m* greyhound

galheteiro /gaʎe'teru/ *m* cruet stand

galho /'gaʎu/ *m* branch; **quebrar um** ~ (*fam*) help out

galináceos /gali'nasius/ *m pl* poultry

gali|nha /ga'liɲa/ *f* chicken; ~**nheiro** *m* chicken coop

galo /'galu/ *m* cock; (*inchação*) bump

galocha /ga'lɔʃa/ *f* Wellington boot

galo|pante /galo'pãtʃi/ *a* galloping; ~**par** *vi* gallop; ~**pe** /ɔ/ *m* gallop

galpão /gaw'pãw/ *m* shed
galvanizar /gawvani'zar/ *vt* galvanize
gama /'gama/ *f* (*musical*) scale; (*fig*) range
gamado /ga'madu/ *a* besotted (**por** with)
gamão /ga'mãw/ *m* backgammon
gamar /ga'mar/ *vi* fall in love (**por** with)
gana /'gana/ *f* desire
ganância /ga'nãsia/ *f* greed
ganancioso /ganãsi'ozu/ *a* greedy
gancho /'gãʃu/ *m* hook
gangorra /gã'goxa/ *f* seesaw
gangrena /gã'grena/ *f* gangrene
gangue /'gãgi/ *m* gang
ga|nhador /gaɲa'dor/ *m* winner □ *a* winning; **~nhar** *vt* win <*corrida*, *prêmio*>; earn <*salário*>; get <*presente*>; gain <*vantagem, tempo, amigo*> □ *vi* win; **~nhar a vida** earn a living; **~nha-pão** *m* livelihood; **~nho** *m* gain; *pl* (*no jogo*) winnings □ *pp de* **ganhar**
ga|nido *m* squeal; (*de cachorro*) yelp; **~nir** *vi* squeal; <*cachorro*> yelp
ganso /'gãsu/ *m* goose
gara|gem /ga'raʒẽ/ *f* garage; **~gista** *m/f* garage attendant
garanhão /gara'ɲãw/ *m* stallion
garan|tia /garã'tʃia/ *f* guarantee; **~tir** *vt* guarantee
garatujar /garatu'ʒar/ *vt* scribble
gar|bo /'garbu/ *m* grace; **~boso** *a* graceful
garça /'garsa/ *f* heron
gar|çom /gar'sõ/ *m* waiter; **~çonete** /ɛ/ *f* waitress
gar|fada /gar'fada/ *f* forkful; **~fo** *m* fork
gargalhada /garga'ʎada/ *f* gale of laughter; **rir às ~s** roar with laughter
gargalo /gar'galu/ *m* bottleneck; **tomar no ~** drink out of the bottle
garganta /gar'gãta/ *f* throat
gargare|jar /gargare'ʒar/ *vi* gargle; **~jo** /e/ *m* gargle
gari /ga'ri/ *m/f* (*lixeiro*) dustman, (*Amer*) garbage collector; (*varredor de rua*) roadsweeper, (*Amer*) streetsweeper
garim|par /garĩ'par/ *vi* prospect; **~peiro** *m* prospector; **~po** *m* mine
garo|a /ga'roa/ *f* drizzle; **~ar** *vi* drizzle
garo|ta /ga'rota/ *f* girl; **~to** /o/ *m* boy; (*Port: café*) coffee with milk
garoupa /ga'ropa/ *f* grouper
garra /'gaxa/ *f* claw; (*fig*) drive, determination; *pl* (*poder*) clutches
garra|fa /ga'xafa/ *f* bottle; **~fada** *f* blow with a bottle; **~fão** *m* flagon

garrancho /ga'xãʃu/ *m* scrawl
garrido /ga'xidu/ *a* (*alegre*) lively
garupa /ga'rupa/ *f* (*de animal*) rump; (*de moto*) pillion seat
gás /gas/ *m* gas; *pl* (*intestinais*) wind, (*Amer*) gas; **~ lacrimogêneo** tear gas
gasóleo /ga'zɔliu/ *m* diesel oil
gasolina /gazo'lina/ *f* petrol
gaso|sa /ga'zɔza/ *f* fizzy lemonade, (*Amer*) soda; **~so** *a* gaseous; <*bebida*> fizzy
gáspea /'gaspia/ *f* upper
gas|tador /gasta'dor/ *a* & *m* spendthrift; **~tar** *vt* spend <*dinheiro*, *tempo*>; use up <*energia*>; wear out <*roupa, sapatos*>; **~to** *m* expense; *pl* spending, expenditure; **dar para o ~to** do
gastrenterite /gastrẽte'ritʃi/ *f* gastroenteritis
gástrico /'gastriku/ *a* gastric
gastrite /gas'tritʃi/ *f* gastritis
gastronomia /gastrono'mia/ *f* gastronomy
ga|ta /'gata/ *f* cat; (*fam*) sexy woman; **~tão** *m* (*fam*) hunk
gatilho /ga'tʃiʎu/ *m* trigger
ga|tinha /ga'tʃiɲa/ *f* (*fam*) sexy woman; **~to** *m* cat; (*fam*) hunk; **fazer alg de ~to-sapato** treat s.o. like a doormat
gatuno /ga'tunu/ *m* crook □ *a* crooked
gaúcho /ga'uʃu/ *a* & *m* (person) from Rio Grande do Sul
gaveta /ga'veta/ *f* drawer
gavião /gavi'ãw/ *m* hawk
gaze /'gazi/ *f* gauze
gazela /ga'zɛla/ *f* gazelle
gazeta /ga'zeta/ *f* gazette
geada /ʒi'ada/ *f* frost
ge|ladeira /ʒela'dera/ *f* fridge; **~lado** *a* frozen; (*muito frio*) freezing □ *m* (*Port*) ice cream; **~lar** *vt/i* freeze
gelati|na /ʒela'tʃina/ *f* (*sobremesa*) jelly; (*pó*) gelatine; **~noso** /o/ *a* gooey
geléia /ʒe'lɛja/ *f* jam
ge|leira /ʒe'lera/ *f* glacier; **~lo** /e/ *m* ice
gema /'ʒema/ *f* (*de ovo*) yolk; (*pedra*) gem; **carioca da ~** carioca born and bred; **~da** *f* egg yolk whisked with sugar
gêmeo /'ʒemiu/ *a* & *m* twin; **Gêmeos** (*signo*) Gemini
ge|mer /ʒe'mer/ *vi* moan, groan; **~mido** *m* moan, groan
gene /'ʒɛni/ *m* gene; **~alogia** *f* genealogy; **~alógico** *a* genealogical; **árvore ~alógica** family tree
Genebra /ʒe'nɛbra/ *f* Geneva
gene|ral /ʒene'raw/ (*pl* **~rais**) *m* general; **~ralidade** *f* generality; **~ralização** *f* generalization;

~ralizar *vt/i* generalize; ~ralizar-se *vpr* become generalized

genérico /ʒeˈnɛriku/ *a* generic

gênero /ˈʒeneru/ *m* type, kind; (*gramatical*) gender; (*literário*) genre; *pl* goods; ~s alimentícios foodstuffs; ela não faz o meu ~ she's not my type

gene|rosidade /ʒenerozi'dadʒi/ *f* generosity; ~roso /o/ *a* generous

genéti|ca /ʒeˈnɛtʃika/ *f* genetics; ~co *a* genetic

gengibre /ʒēˈʒibri/ *m* ginger

gengiva /ʒēˈʒiva/ *f* gum

geni|al /ʒeniˈaw/ (*pl* ~ais) *a* brilliant

gênio /ˈʒeniu/ *m* genius; (*temperamento*) temperament

genioso /ʒeniˈozu/ *a* temperamental

geni|tal /ʒeniˈtaw/ (*pl* ~tais) *a* genital

genitivo /ʒeniˈtʃivu/ *a & m* genitive

genocídio /ʒenoˈsidʒiu/ *m* genocide

genro /ˈʒēxu/ *m* son-in-law

gente /ˈʒētʃi/ *f* people; (*fam*) folks; a ~ (*sujeito*) we; (*objeto*) us □ *interj* (*fam*) gosh

gen|til /ʒēˈtʃiw/ (*pl* ~tis) *a* kind; ~tileza /e/ *f* kindness

genuíno /ʒenuˈinu/ *a* genuine

geo|grafia /ʒeograˈfia/ *f* geography; ~gráfico *a* geographical

geógrafo /ʒeˈɔgrafu/ *m* geographer

geo|logia /ʒeoloˈʒia/ *f* geology; ~lógico *a* geological

geólogo /ʒeˈɔlogu/ *m* geologist

geo|metria /ʒeomeˈtria/ *f* geometry; ~métrico *a* geometrical; ~político *a* geopolitical

Geórgia /ʒiˈɔrʒia/ *f* Georgia

georgiano /ʒiorʒiˈanu/ *a & m* Georgian

gera|ção /ʒeraˈsãw/ *f* generation; ~dor *m* generator

ge|ral /ʒeˈraw/ (*pl* ~rais) *a* general □ *f* (*limpeza*) spring-clean; em ~ral in general

gerânio /ʒeˈraniu/ *m* geranium

gerar /ʒeˈrar/ *vt* create; generate <*eletricidade*>

gerência /ʒeˈrēsia/ *f* management

gerenci|ador /ʒerēsiaˈdor/ *m* manager; ~al (*pl* ~ais) *a* management; ~ar *vt* manage

gerente /ʒeˈrētʃi/ *m* manager □ *a* managing

gergelim /ʒerʒeˈlĩ/ *m* sesame

geri|atria /ʒeriaˈtria/ *f* geriatrics; ~átrico *a* geriatric

geringonça /ʒerĩˈgõsa/ *f* contraption

gerir /ʒeˈrir/ *vt* manage

germânico /ʒerˈmaniku/ *a* Germanic

ger|me /ˈʒɛrmi/ *m* germ; ~me de trigo wheatgerm; ~minar *vi* germinate

gerúndio /ʒeˈrũdʒiu/ *m* gerund

gesso /ˈʒesu/ *m* plaster

ges|tação /ʒestaˈsãw/ *f* gestation; ~tante *f* pregnant woman

gestão /ʒesˈtãw/ *f* management

ges|ticular *vi* gesticulate; ~to /ˈʒestu/ *m* gesture

gibi /ʒiˈbi/ *m* (*fam*) comic

Gibraltar /ʒibrawˈtar/ *f* Gibraltar

gigan|te /ʒiˈgãtʃi/ *a & m* giant; ~tesco /e/ *a* gigantic

gilete /ʒiˈlɛtʃi/ *f* razor blade □ *a & m/f* (*fam*) bisexual

gim /ʒĩ/ *m* gin

ginásio /ʒiˈnaziu/ *m* (*escola*) secondary school; (*de ginástica*) gymnasium

ginasta /ʒiˈnasta/ *m/f* gymnast

ginásti|ca /ʒiˈnastʃika/ *f* gymnastics; (*aeróbica*) aerobics; ~co *a* gymnastic

ginecolo|gia /ʒinekoloˈʒia/ *f* gynaecology; ~gista *m/f* gynaecologist

gingar /ʒĩˈgar/ *vi* sway

gira-discos /ʒiraˈdiʃkuʃ/ *m invar* (*Port*) record player

girafa /ʒiˈrafa/ *f* giraffe

gi|rar /ʒiˈrar/ *vt/i* spin, revolve; ~rassol (*pl* ~rassóis) *m* sunflower; ~ratório *a* revolving

gíria /ˈʒiria/ *f* slang; (*uma ~*) slang expression

giro /ˈʒiru/ *m* spin, turn □ *a* (*Port fam*) great

giz /ʒis/ *m* chalk

gla|cê /glaˈse/ *m* icing; ~cial (*pl* ~ciais) *a* icy

glamour /glaˈmur/ *m* glamour; ~oso /o/ *a* glamorous

glândula /ˈglãdula/ *f* gland

glandular /glãduˈlar/ *a* glandular

glicerina /gliseˈrina/ *f* glycerine

glicose /gliˈkozi/ *f* glucose

glo|bal /gloˈbaw/ (*pl* ~bais) *a* (*mundial*) global; <*preço etc*> overall; ~bo /o/ *m* globe; ~bo ocular eyeball

glóbulo /ˈglɔbulu/ *m* globule; (*do sangue*) corpuscle

glória /ˈglɔria/ *f* glory

glori|ficar /glorifiˈkar/ *vt* glorify; ~oso /o/ *a* glorious

glossário /gloˈsariu/ *m* glossary

glu|tão /gluˈtãw/ *m* (*f* ~tona) glutton □ *a* (*f* ~tona) greedy

gnomo /giˈnomu/ *m* gnome

godê /goˈde/ *a* flared

goela /goˈɛla/ *f* gullet

gogó /goˈgɔ/ *m* (*fam*) Adam's apple

goia|ba /goiˈaba/ *f* guava; ~bada *f* guava jelly; ~beira *f* guava tree

gol /ˈgow/ (*pl* ~s) *m* goal

gola /ˈgɔla/ *f* collar

gole /ˈgɔli/ *m* mouthful

go|lear /goliˈar/ *vt* thrash; ~leiro *m* goalkeeper

golfe /ˈgowfi/ *m* golf

golfinho /gowˈfiɲu/ *m* dolphin

golfista /gow'fista/ *m/f* golfer
golo /'golu/ *m* (*Port*) goal
golpe /'gɔwpi/ *m* blow; (*manobra*) trick; ~ **(de estado)** coup (d'état); ~ **de mestre** masterstroke; ~ **de vento** gust of wind; ~ **de vista** glance; ~**ar** *vt* hit
goma /'goma/ *f* gum; (*para roupa*) starch
gomo /'gomu/ *m* segment
gôndola /'gõdola/ *f* rack
gongo /'gõgu/ *m* gong
gonorréia /gono'xeja/ *f* gonorrhea
gonzo /'gõzu/ *m* hinge
gorar /go'rar/ *vi* go wrong, fail
gor|do /'gordu/ *a* fat; ~**ducho** *a* plump
gordu|ra /gor'dura/ *f* fat; ~**rento** *a* greasy; ~**roso** /u/ *a* fatty; <*pele*> greasy, oily
gorgolejar /gorgole'ʒar/ *vi* gurgle
gorila /go'rila/ *m* gorilla
gor|jear /gorʒi'ar/ *vi* twitter; ~**jeio** *m* twittering
gorjeta /gor'ʒeta/ *f* tip
gorro /'goxu/ *m* hat
gos|ma /'gɔzma/ *f* slime; ~**mento** *a* slimy
gos|tar /gos'tar/ *vi* ~**tar de** like; ~**to** /o/ *m* taste; (*prazer*) pleasure; **para o meu** ~**to** for my taste; **ter** ~**to de** taste of; ~**toso** *a* nice; <*comida*> nice, tasty; (*fam*) <*pessoa*> gorgeous
go|ta /'gota/ *f* drop; (*que cai*) drip; (*doença*) gout; **foi a** ~**ta d'água** (*fig*) it was the last straw; ~**teira** *f* (*buraco*) leak; (*cano*) gutter; ~**tejar** *vi* drip; <*telhado*> leak □ *vt* drip
gótico /'gɔtʃiku/ *a* Gothic
gotícula /go'tʃicula/ *f* droplet
gover|nador /governa'dor/ *m* governor; ~**namental** (*pl* ~**namentais**) *a* government; ~**nanta** *f* housekeeper; ~**nante** *a* ruling □ *m/f* ruler; ~**nar** *vt* govern; ~**nista** *a* government □ *m/f* government supporter; ~**no** /e/ *m* government
go|zação /goza'sãw/ *f* joking; (*uma*) send-up; ~**zado** *a* funny; ~**zar** *vt* ~**zar (de)** enjoy; (*fam: zombar de*) make fun of □ *vi* (*ter orgasmo*) come; ~**zo** *m* (*prazer*) enjoyment; (*posse*) possession; (*orgasmo*) orgasm; **ser um** ~**zo** be funny
Grã-Bretanha /grãbre'taɲa/ *f* Great Britain
graça /'grasa/ *f* grace; (*piada*) joke; (*humor*) humour, funny side; (*jur*) pardon; **de** ~ for nothing; **sem** ~ (*enfadonho*) dull; (*não engraçado*) unfunny; (*envergonhado*) embarrassed; **ser uma** ~ be lovely; **ter** ~ be funny; **não tem** ~ **sair sozinho** it's no fun to go out alone; ~**s a** thanks to

grace|jar /grase'ʒar/ *vi* joke; ~**jo** /e/ *m* joke
graci|nha /gra'siɲa/ *f* **ser uma** ~**nha** be sweet; ~**oso** /o/ *a* gracious
grada|ção /grada'sãw/ *f* gradation; ~**tivo** *a* gradual
grade /'gradʒi/ *f* grille, grating; (*cerca*) railings; **atrás das** ~**s** behind bars; ~**ado** *a* <*janela*> barred
grado /'gradu/ *m* **de bom/mau** ~ willingly/unwillingly
gradu|ação /gradua'sãw/ *f* graduation; (*mil*) rank; (*variação*) gradation; ~**ado** *a* <*escala*> graduated; <*estudante*> graduate; <*militar*> high-ranking; (*eminente*) respected; ~**al** (*pl* ~**ais**) *a* gradual; ~**ar** *vt* graduate <*escala*>; (*ordenar*) grade; (*regular*) regulate; ~**ar-se** *vpr* <*estudante*> graduate
grafia /gra'fia/ *f* spelling
gráfi|ca /'grafika/ *f* (*arte*) graphics; (*oficina*) print shop; ~**co** *a* graphic □ *m* (*pessoa*) printer; (*diagrama*) graph; *pl* (*de computador*) graphics
grã-fino /grã'finu/ *a* posh, upper-class □ *m* posh person
grafite /gra'fitʃi/ *f* (*mineral*) graphite; (*de lápis*) lead; (*pichação*) piece of graffiti
gra|fologia /grafolo'ʒia/ *f* graphology; ~**fólogo** *m* graphologist
grama[1] /'grama/ *m* gramme
grama[2] /'grama/ *f* grass; ~**do** *m* lawn; (*campo de futebol*) field
gramática /gra'matʃika/ *f* grammar
gramati|cal /gramatʃi'kaw/ (*pl* ~**cais**) *a* grammatical
gram|peador /grãpia'dor/ *m* stapler; ~**pear** *vt* staple <*papéis etc*>; tap <*telefone*>; ~**po** *m* (*de cabelo*) hairclip; (*para papéis etc*) staple; (*ferramenta*) clamp
grana /'grana/ *f* (*fam*) cash
granada /gra'nada/ *f* (*projétil*) grenade; (*pedra*) garnet
gran|dalhão /grãda'ʎãw/ *a* (*f* ~**dalhona**) enormous; ~**dão** *a* (*f* ~**dona**) huge; ~**de** *a* big; (*fig*) <*escritor, amor etc*> great; ~**deza** /e/ *f* greatness; (*tamanho*) magnitude; ~**dioso** /o/ *a* grand
granel /gra'nɛw/ *m* **a** ~ in bulk
granito /gra'nitu/ *m* granite
granizo /gra'nizu/ *m* hail
gran|ja /'grãʒa/ *f* farm; ~**jear** *vt* win, gain
granulado /granu'ladu/ *a* granulated
grânulo /'granulu/ *m* granule
grão /grãw/ (*pl* ~**s**) *m* grain; (*de café*) bean; ~**-de-bico** (*pl* ~**s-de-bico**) *m* chickpea
grasnar /graz'nar/ *vi* <*pato*> quack; <*rã*> croak; <*corvo*> caw

grati|dão /grat∫i'dãw/ f gratitude; **~ficação** f (dinheiro a mais) gratuity; (recompensa) gratification; **~ficante** a gratifying; **~ficar** vt (dar dinheiro a) give a gratuity to; (recompensar) gratify

gratinado /grat∫i'nadu/ a & m gratin

grátis /'grat∫is/ adv free

grato /'gratu/ a grateful

gratuito /gra'tuitu/ a (de graça) free; (sem motivo) gratuitous

grau /graw/ m degree; **escola de 1°/2° ~** primary/secondary school

graúdo /gra'udu/ a big; (importante) important

gra|vação /grava'sãw/ f (de som) recording; (de desenhos etc) engraving; **~vador** m (pessoa) engraver; (máquina) tape recorder; **~vadora** f record company; **~var** vt record <música, disco>; (fixar na memória) memorize; (estampar) engrave

gravata /gra'vata/ f tie; (golpe) stranglehold; **~ borboleta** bowtie

grave /'gravi/ a serious; <voz, som> deep; <acento> grave

grávida /'gravida/ f pregnant

gravidade /gravi'dad3i/ f gravity

gravidez /gravi'des/ f pregnancy

gravura /gra'vura/ f engraving; (em livro) illustration

graxa /'gra∫a/ f (de sapatos) polish; (de lubrificar) grease

Grécia /'grɛsia/ f Greece

grego /'gregu/ a & m Greek

grei /grej/ f flock

gre|lha /'grɛʎa/ f grill; **~lhado** a grilled □ m grill; **~lhar** vt grill

grêmio /'gremiu/ m guild, association

grená /gre'na/ a & m dark red

gre|ta /'greta/ f crack; **~tar** vt/i crack

gre|ve /'grɛvi/ f strike; **entrar em ~ve** go on strike; **~ve de fome** hunger strike; **~vista** m/f striker

gri|fado /gri'fadu/ a in italics; **~far** vt italicize

griffe /'grifi/ f label, line

gri|lado /gri'ladu/ a (fam) hung-up; **~lar** (fam) vt bug; **~lar-se** vpr get hung-up (com about)

grilhão /gri'ʎãw/ m fetter

grilo /'grilu/ m (bicho) cricket; (fam) (preocupação) hang-up; (problema) hassle; (barulho) squeak

grinalda /gri'nawda/ f garland

gringo /'grĩgu/ (fam) a foreign □ m foreigner

gri|pado /gri'padu/ a **estar/ficar ~pado** have/get the flu; **~par-se** vpr get the flu; **~pe** f flu, influenza

grisalho /gri'zaʎu/ a grey

gri|tante /gri'tãt∫i/ a <erro> glaring, gross; <cor> loud, garish; **~tar** vt/i shout; (de medo) scream; **~taria** f

shouting; **~to** m shout; (de medo) scream; **aos ~tos** in a loud voice; **no ~to** (fam) by force

grogue /'grɔgi/ a groggy

grosa /'grɔza/ f gross

groselha /gro'zɛʎa/ f (vermelha) redcurrant; (espinhosa) gooseberry; **~ negra** blackcurrant

gros|seiro /gro'seru/ a rude; (tosco, malfeito) rough; **~seria** f rudeness; (uma) rude thing; **~so** /o/ a thick; <voz> deep; (fam) <pessoa, atitude> rude; **~sura** f thickness; (fam: grosseria) rudeness

grotesco /gro'tesku/ a grotesque

grua /'grua/ f crane

gru|dado /gru'dadu/ a stuck; (fig) very attached (em to); **~dar** vt/i stick; **~de** m glue; **~dento** a sticky

gru|nhido /gru'niɲdu/ m grunt; **~nhir** vi grunt

grupo /'grupu/ m group

gruta /'gruta/ f cave

guaraná /gwara'na/ m guarana

guarani /gwara'ni/ a & m/f Guarani

guarda /'gwarda/ f guard □ m/f guard; (policial) policeman (f -woman); **~ costeira** coastguard; **~chuva** m umbrella; **~costas** m invar bodyguard; **~dor** m parking attendant; **~florestal** (pl **~s-florestais**) m/f forest ranger; **~louça** m china cupboard; **~napo** m napkin, serviette; **~noturno** (pl **~s-noturnos**) m night watchman

guardar /gwar'dar/ vt (pôr no lugar) put away; (conservar) keep; (vigiar) guard; (não esquecer) remember; **~-se de** guard against

guarda|-redes /'gwarda-'xed∫/ m invar (Port) goalkeeper; **~roupa** m wardrobe; **~sol** (pl **~-sóis**) m sunshade

guardi|ão /gward3i'ãw/ (pl **~ães** ou **~ões**) m (f **~ã**) guardian

guarita /gwa'rita/ f sentry box

guar|necer /gwarne'ser/ vt (fortificar) garrison; (munir) equip; (enfeitar) garnish; **~nição** f (mil) garrison; (enfeite) garnish

Guatemala /gwate'mala/ f Guatemala

guatemalteco /gwatemal'tɛku/ a & m Guatemalan

gude /'gud3i/ m **bola de ~** marble

guelra /'gɛwxa/ f gill

guer|ra /'gɛxa/ f war; **~reiro** m warrior □ a warlike; **~rilha** f guerrilla war; **~rilheiro** a & m guerrilla

gueto /'getu/ m ghetto

guia /'gia/ m/f guide □ m guide(book) □ f delivery note

Guiana /gi'ana/ f Guyana

guianense /gia'nẽsi/ a & m/f Guyanan

guiar /gi'ar/ *vt* guide; drive <*veículo*> □ *vi* drive; ~**-se** *vpr* be guided

guichê /gi'ʃe/ *m* window

guidom /gi'dõ/, (*Port*) **guidão** /gi'dãw/ *m* handlebars

guilhotina /giʎo'tʃina/ *f* guillotine

guimba /'gĩba/ *f* butt

guinada /gi'nada/ *f* change of direction; **dar uma** ~ change direction

guinchar¹ /gĩ'ʃar/ *vi* squeal; <*freios*> screech

guinchar² /gĩ'ʃar/ *vt* tow <*carro*>; (*içar*) winch

guincho¹ /'gĩʃu/ *m* squeal; (*de freios*) screech

guincho² /'gĩʃu/ *m* (*máquina*) winch; (*veículo*) tow truck

guin|dar /gĩ'dar/ *vt* hoist; ~**daste** *m* crane

Guiné /gi'nɛ/ *f* Guinea

gui|sado /gi'zadu/ *m* stew; ~**sar** *vt* stew

guitar|ra /gi'taxa/ *f* (electric) guitar; ~**rista** *m/f* guitarist

guizo /'gizu/ *m* bell

gu|la /'gula/ *f* greed; ~**lodice** *f* greed; ~**loseima** *f* delicacy; ~**loso** /o/ *a* greedy

gume /'gumi/ *m* cutting edge

guri /gu'ri/ *m* boy; ~**a** *f* girl

guru /gu'ru/ *m* guru

gutu|ral /gutu'raw/ (*pl* ~**rais**) *a* guttural

H

há|bil /'abiw/ (*pl* ~**beis**) *a* clever, skilful

habili|dade /abili'dadʒi/ *f* skill; **ter** ~**dade com** be good with; ~**doso** /o/ *a* skilful; ~**tação** *f* qualification; ~**tar** *vt* qualify

habi|tação /abita'sãw/ *f* housing; (*casa*) dwelling; ~**tacional** (*pl* ~**tacionais**) *a* housing; ~**tante** *m/f* inhabitant; ~**tar** *vt* inhabit □ *vi* live; ~**tável** (*pl* ~**táveis**) *a* habitable

hábito /'abitu/ *m* habit

habitu|al /abitu'aw/ (*pl* ~**ais**) *a* habitual; ~**ar** *vt* accustom (a to); ~**ar-se** *vpr* get accustomed (a to)

hadoque /a'dɔki/ *m* haddock

Haia /'aja/ *f* the Hague

Haiti /aj'tʃi/ *m* Haiti

haitiano /ajtʃi'anu/ *a & m* Haitian

hálito /'alitu/ *m* breath

halitose /ali'tɔzi/ *f* halitosis

hall /xɔw/ (*pl* ~**s**) *m* hall; (*de hotel*) foyer

halte|re /aw'tɛri/ *m* dumbbell; ~**rofilismo** *m* weight lifting; ~**rofilista** *m/f* weight lifter

hambúrguer /ã'burger/ *m* hamburger

hangar /ã'gar/ *m* hangar

haras /'aras/ *m invar* stud farm

hardware /'xarduer/ *m* hardware

harmo|nia /armo'nia/ *f* harmony; ~**nioso** /o/ *a* harmonious; ~**nizar** *vt* harmonize; (*conciliar*) reconcile; ~**nizar-se** *vpr* (*combinar*) tone in; (*concordar*) coincide

har|pa /'arpa/ *f* harp; ~**pista** *m/f* harpist

haste /'astʃi/ *m* pole; (*de planta*) stem, stalk; ~**ar** *vt* hoist, raise

Havaí /ava'i/ *m* Hawaii

havaiano /avaj'anu/ *a & m* Hawaiian

haver /a'ver/ *m* credit; *pl* possessions □ *vt* (*auxiliar*) **havia sido** it had been; (*impessoal*) **há** there is/are; **ele trabalha aqui há anos** he's been working here for years; **ela morreu há vinte anos (atrás)** she died twenty years ago

haxixe /a'ʃiʃi/ *m* hashish

he|braico /e'brajku/ *a & m* Hebrew; ~**breu** *a & m* (*f* ~**bréia**) Hebrew

hectare /ek'tari/ *m* hectare

hediondo /edʒi'õdu/ *a* hideous

hein /ẽj/ *int* eh

hélice /'ɛlisi/ *f* propeller

helicóptero /eli'kɔpteru/ *m* helicopter

hélio /'ɛliu/ *m* helium

heliporto /eli'portu/ *m* heliport

hem /ẽj/ *int* eh

hematoma /ema'toma/ *m* bruise

hemisfério /emis'fɛriu/ *m* hemisphere; **Hemisfério Norte/Sul** Northern/Southern Hemisphere

hemo|filia /emofi'lia/ *f* haemophilia; ~**fílico** *a & m* haemophiliac; ~**globina** *f* haemoglobin; ~**grama** *m* blood count

hemor|ragia /emoxa'ʒia/ *f* haemorrhage; ~**róidas** *f pl* haemorrhoids

hené /e'ne/ *m* henna

hepatite /epa'tʃitʃi/ *f* hepatitis

hera /'ɛra/ *f* ivy

heráldi|ca /e'rawdʒika/ *f* heraldry; ~**co** *a* heraldic

herança /e'rãsa/ *f* inheritance; (*de um povo etc*) heritage

her|bicida /erbi'sida/ *m* weedkiller; ~**bívoro** *a* herbivorous □ *m* herbivore

her|dar /er'dar/ *vt* inherit; ~**deiro** *m* heir

hereditário /eredʒi'tariu/ *a* hereditary

here|ge /e'rɛʒi/ *m/f* heretic; ~**sia** *f* heresy

herético /e'rɛtʃiku/ *a* heretical

hermético /er'mɛtʃiku/ *a* airtight; (*fig*) obscure

hérnia /'ɛrnia/ *f* hernia

herói /e'rɔj/ *m* hero; ~**co** *a* heroic

hero|ína /ero'ina/ f (*mulher*) heroine; (*droga*) heroin; **~ismo** *m* heroism

herpes /'ɛrpis/ *m invar* herpes; **~zoster** *m* shingles

hesi|tação /ezita'sãw/ f hesitation; **~tante** *a* hesitant; **~tar** *vi* hesitate

hetero|doxo /etero'dɔksu/ *a* unorthodox; **~gêneo** *a* heterogeneous

heterossexu|al /eteroseksu'aw/ (*pl* **~ais**) *a & m* heterosexual

hexago|nal /eksago'naw/ (*pl* **~nais**) *a* hexagonal

hexágono /ek'sagonu/ *m* hexagon

hiato /i'atu/ *m* hiatus

hiber|nação /iberna'sãw/ f hibernation; **~nar** *vi* hibernate

híbrido /'ibridu/ *a & m* hybrid

hidrante /i'drãtʃi/ *m* fire hydrant

hidra|tante /idra'tãtʃi/ *a* moisturising □ *m* moisturizer; **~tar** *vt* moisturize *<pele>*; **~to** *m* **~to de carbono** carbohydrate

hidráuli|ca /i'drawlika/ f hydraulics; **~co** *a* hydraulic

hidrelétri|ca /idre'lɛtrika/ f hydroelectric power station; **~co** *a* hydroelectric

hidro|avião /idroavi'ãw/ *m* seaplane; **~carboneto** /e/ *m* hydrocarbon

hidrófilo /i'drɔfilu/ *a* absorbent; **algodão ~** cotton wool, (*Amer*) absorbent cotton

hidrofobia /idrofo'bia/ f rabies

hidro|gênio /idro'ʒeniu/ *m* hydrogen; **~massagem** f **banheira de ~massagem** jacuzzi; **~via** f waterway

hiena /i'ena/ f hyena

hierarquia /ierar'kia/ f hierarchy

hieróglifo /ie'rɔglifu/ *m* hieroglyphic

hífen /'ifẽ/ *m* hyphen

higi|ene /iʒi'eni/ f hygiene; **~ênico** *a* hygienic

hilari|ante /ilari'ãtʃi/ *a* hilarious; **~dade** f hilarity

Himalaia /ima'laja/ *m* Himalayas

hin|di /ĩ'dʒi/ *m* Hindi; **~du** *a & m/f* Hindu; **~duísmo** *m* Hinduism; **~duísta** *a & m/f* Hindu

hino /'inu/ *m* hymn; **~ nacional** national anthem

hipermercado /ipermer'kadu/ *m* hypermarket

hipersensí|vel /ipersẽ'sivew/ (*pl* **~veis**) *a* hypersensitive

hipertensão /ipertẽ'sãw/ f hypertension

hípico /'ipiku/ *a* horseriding

hipismo /i'pizmu/ *m* horseriding; (*corridas*) horseracing

hip|nose /ipi'nɔzi/ f hypnosis; **~nótico** *a* hypnotic; **~notismo** *m* hypnotism; **~notizador** *m* hypnotist; **~notizar** *vt* hypnotize

hipocondríaco /ipokõ'driaku/ *a & m* hypochondriac

hipocrisia /ipokri'zia/ f hypocrisy

hipócrita /i'pɔkrita/ *m/f* hypocrite □ *a* hypocritical

hipódromo /i'pɔdromu/ *m* race course, (*Amer*) race track

hipopótamo /ipo'pɔtamu/ *m* hippopotamus

hipote|ca /ipo'tɛka/ f mortgage; **~car** *vt* mortgage; **~cário** *a* mortgage

hipotermia /ipoter'mia/ f hypothermia

hipótese /i'pɔtezi/ f hypothesis; **na ~ de** in the event of; **na pior das ~s** at worst

hipotético /ipo'tɛtʃiku/ *a* hypothetical

hirto /'irtu/ *adj* rigid, stiff

hispânico /is'paniku/ *a* Hispanic

histamina /ista'mina/ f histamine

his|terectomia /isterekto'mia/ f hysterectomy; **~teria** f hysteria; **~térico** *a* hysterical; **~terismo** *m* hysteria

his|tória /is'tɔria/ f (*do passado*) history; (*conto*) story; *pl* (*amolação*) trouble; **~toriador** *m* historian; **~tórico** *a* historical; (*marcante*) historic □ *m* history

hoje /'oʒi/ *adv* today; **~ em dia** nowadays; **~ de manhã** this morning; **~ à noite** tonight

Holanda /o'lãda/ f Holland

holan|dês /olã'des/ *a* (f **~desa**) Dutch □ *m* (f **~desa**) Dutchman (f -woman); (*língua*) Dutch; **os ~deses** the Dutch

holding /'xɔwdʒĩ/ (*pl* **~s**) f holding company

holerite /ole'ritʃi/ *m* pay slip

holo|causto /olo'kawstu/ *m* holocaust; **~fote** /ɔ/ *m* spotlight; **~grama** *m* hologram

homem /'omẽ/ *m* man; **~ de negócios** businessman; **~-rã** (*pl* **homens-rã**) *m* frogman

homena|gear /omenaʒi'ar/ *vt* pay tribute to; **~gem** f tribute; **em ~gem a** in honour of

homeo|pata /omio'pata/ *m/f* homoeopath; **~patia** f homoeopathy; **~pático** *a* homoeopathic

homérico /o'mɛriku/ *a* (*estrondoso*) booming; (*extraordinário*) phenomenal

homi|cida /omi'sida/ *a* homicidal □ *m/f* murderer; **~cídio** *m* homicide; **~cídio involuntário** manslaughter

homo|geneizado /omoʒenej'zadu/ *a* *<leite>* homogenized; **~gêneo** *a* homogeneous

homologar /omolo'gar/ *vt* ratify

homólogo /o'mɔlogu/ *m* opposite number □ *a* equivalent

homônimo /o'monimu/ *m* (*xará*) namesake; (*vocábulo*) homonym

homossexu|al /omoseksu'aw/ (*pl* ~ais) *a* & *m* homosexual; ~alismo *m* homosexuality

Honduras /õ'duras/ *f* Honduras

hondurenho /õdu'reɲu/ *a* & *m* Honduran

hones|tidade /onestʃi'dadʒi/ *f* honesty; ~to /ɛ/ *a* honest

hono|rário /ono'rariu/ *a* honorary; ~rários *m pl* fees; ~rífico *a* honorific

hon|ra /'õxa/ *f* honour; ~radez *f* honesty, integrity; ~rado *a* honourable; ~rar *vt* honour; ~roso /o/ *a* honourable

hóquei /'ɔkej/ *m* (field) hockey; ~ sobre gelo ice hockey; ~ sobre patins roller hockey

hora /'ɔra/ *f* (*unidade de tempo*) hour; (*ocasião*) time; **que ~s são?** what's the time?; **a que ~s?** at what time?; **às três** ~**s** at three o'clock; **dizer as** ~**s** tell the time; **tem** ~**s?** do you have the time?; **de** ~ **em** ~ every hour; **em cima da** ~ at the last minute; **na** ~ (*naquele momento*) at the time; (*no ato*) on the spot; (*a tempo*) on time; **está na** ~ **de ir** it's time to go; **na** ~ **H** (*no momento certo*) at just the right moment; (*no momento crítico*) at the crucial moment; **meia** ~ half an hour; **toda** ~ all the time; **fazer** ~ kill time; **marcar** ~ make an appointment; **perder a** ~ lose track of time; **não tenho** ~ my time is my own; **não vejo a** ~ **de ir** I can't wait to go; ~**s extras** overtime; ~**s vagas** spare time

horário /o'rariu/ *a* hourly; **km** ~**s** km per hour □ *m* (*hora*) time; (*tabela*) timetable; (*de trabalho etc*) hours; ~ **nobre** prime time

horda /'ɔrda/ *f* horde

horista /o'rista/ *a* paid by the hour □ *m/f* worker paid by the hour

horizon|tal /orizõ'taw/ (*pl* ~tais) *a* & *f* horizontal; ~te *m* horizon

hor|monal /ormo'naw/ (*pl* ~monais) *a* hormonal; ~mônio *m* hormone

horóscopo /o'rɔskopu/ *m* horoscope

horrendo /o'xẽdu/ *a* horrid

horripi|lante /oxipi'lãtʃi/ *a* horrifying; ~lar *vt* horrify

horrí|vel /o'xivew/ (*pl* ~veis) *a* horrible, awful

horror /o'xor/ *m* horror (**a** of); (*coisa horrorosa*) horrible thing; **ser um** ~ be awful; **que** ~! how awful!

horro|rizar /oxori'zar/ *vt/i* horrify;

~rizar-se *vpr* be horrified; ~roso /o/ *a* horrible

horta /'ɔrta/ *f* vegetable plot; ~ comercial market garden, (*Amer*) truck farm; ~liça *f* vegetable

hortelã /orte'lã/ *f* mint; ~-pimenta peppermint

horti|cultor /ortʃikuw'tor/ *m* horticulturalist; ~cultura *f* horticulture; ~frutigranjeiros *m pl* fruit and vegetables; ~granjeiros *m pl* vegetables

horto /'ortu/ *m* market garden; (*viveiro*) nursery

hospe|dagem /ospe'daʒẽ/ *f* accommodation; ~dar *vt* put up; ~dar-se *vpr* stay

hóspede /'ɔspidʒi/ *m/f* guest

hospedei|ra /ospe'dera/ *f* landlady; ~ra de bordo (*Port*) stewardess; ~ro *m* landlord

hospício /os'pisiu/ *m* (*de loucos*) asylum

hospi|tal /ospi'taw/ (*pl* ~tais) *m* hospital; ~talar *a* hospital; ~taleiro *a* hospitable; ~talidade *f* hospitality; ~talizar *vt* hospitalize

hóstia /'ɔstʃia/ *f* Host, Communion wafer

hos|til /os'tʃiw/ (*pl* ~tis) *a* hostile; ~tilidade *f* hostility; ~tilizar *vt* antagonize

ho|tel /o'tɛw/ (*pl* ~téis) *m* hotel; ~teleiro *a* hotel □ *m* hotelier

huma|nidade /umani'dadʒi/ *f* humanity; ~nismo *m* humanism; ~nista *a* & *m/f* humanist; ~nitário *a* & *m* humanitarian; ~nizar *vt* humanize; ~no *a* human; (*compassivo*) humane; ~nos *m pl* humans

húmido /'umidu/ *adj* (*Port*) humid

humil|dade /umiw'dadʒi/ *f* humility; ~de *a* humble

humi|lhação /umiʎa'sãw/ *f* humiliation; ~lhante *a* humiliating; ~lhar *vt* humiliate

humor /u'mor/ *m* humour; (*disposição do espírito*) mood; **de bom/mau** ~ in a good/bad mood

humo|rismo /umo'rizmu/ *m* humour; ~rista *m/f* (*no palco*) comedian; (*escritor*) humorist; ~rístico *a* humorous

húngaro /'ũgaru/ *a* & *m* Hungarian

Hungria /ũ'gria/ *f* Hungary

hurra /'uxa/ *int* hurrah □ *m* cheer

I

ia|te /i'atʃi/ *m* yacht; ~tismo *m* yachting; ~tista *m/f* yachtsman (*f* -woman)

ibérico /i'bɛriku/ *a & m* Iberian

ibope /i'bɔpi/ *m* **dar ~** (*fam*) be popular

içar /i'sar/ *vt* hoist

iceberg /ajs'bɛrgi/ (*pl* ~**s**) *m* iceberg

ícone /'ikoni/ *m* icon

iconoclasta /ikono'klasta/ *m/f* iconoclast □ *a* iconoclastic

icterícia /ikte'risia/ *f* jaundice

ida /'ida/ *f* going; **na ~** on the way there; **~ e volta** return, (*Amer*) round trip

idade /i'dadʒi/ *f* age; **meia ~** middle age; **homem de meia ~** middle-aged man; **senhor de ~** elderly man; **Idade Média** Middle Ages

ide|al /ide'aw/ (*pl* ~**ais**) *a & m* ideal; **~alismo** *m* idealism; **~alista** *m/f* idealist □ *a* idealistic; **~alizar** *vt* (*criar*) devise; (*sublimar*) idealize; **~ar** *vt* devise; **~ário** *m* ideas

idéia /i'dɛja/ *f* idea; **mudar de ~** change one's mind

idem /'idẽ/ *adv* ditto

idêntico /i'dẽtʃiku/ *a* identical

identi|dade /idẽtʃi'dadʒi/ *f* identity; **~ficar** *vt* identify; **~ficar-se** *vpr* identify (**com** with)

ideo|logia /ideolo'ʒia/ *f* ideology; **~lógico** *a* ideological

idílico /i'dʒiliku/ *a* idyllic

idílio /i'dʒiliu/ *m* idyll

idio|ma /idʒi'oma/ *m* language; **~mático** *a* idiomatic

idio|ta /idʒi'ɔta/ *m/f* idiot □ *a* idiotic; **~tice** *f* stupidity; (*uma*) stupid thing

idola|trar /idola'trar/ *vt* idolize; **~tria** *f* idolatry

ídolo /'idulu/ *m* idol

idôneo /i'doniu/ *a* suitable

idoso /i'dozu/ *a* elderly

Iêmen /i'emẽ/ *m* Yemen

iemenita /ieme'nita/ *a & m/f* Yemeni

iene /i'ɛni/ *m* yen

iglu /i'glu/ *m* igloo

ignição /igni'sãw/ *f* ignition

ignomínia /igno'minia/ *f* ignominy

igno|rância /igno'rãsia/ *f* ignorance; **~rante** *a* ignorant; **~rar** (*desconsiderar*) ignore; (*desconhecer*) not know

igreja /i'greʒa/ *f* church

igu|al /i'gwaw/ (*pl* ~**ais**) *a* equal; (*em aparência*) identical; (*liso*) even □ *m/f* equal; **por ~al** equally; **~alar** *vt* equal; level <*terreno*>; **~alar(-se) a** be equal to; **~aldade** *f* equality; **~alitário** *a* egalitarian; **~almente** *adv* equally; (*como resposta*) the same to you; **~alzinho a** exactly the same (**a as**)

iguaria /igwa'ria/ *f* delicacy

iídiche /i'idiʃi/ *m* Yiddish

ile|gal /ile'gaw/ (*pl* ~**gais**) *a* illegal; **~galidade** *f* illegality

ilegítimo /ile'ʒitʃimu/ *a* illegitimate

ilegí|vel /ile'ʒivew/ (*pl* ~**veis**) *a* illegible

ileso /i'lɛzu/ *a* unhurt

iletrado /ile'tradu/ *adj & m* illiterate

ilha /'iʎa/ *f* island

ilharga /i'ʎarga/ *f* side

ilhéu /i'ʎɛw/ *m* (*f* **ilhoa**) islander

ilhós /i'ʎɔs/ *m invar* eyelet

ilhota /i'ʎɔta/ *f* small island

ilícito /i'lisitu/ *a* illicit

ilimitado /ilimi'tadu/ *a* unlimited

ilógico /i'lɔʒiku/ *a* illogical

iludir /ilu'dʒir/ *vt* delude; **~-se** *vpr* delude o.s.

ilumi|nação /ilumina'sãw/ *f* lighting; (*inspiração*) enlightenment; **~nar** *vt* light up, illuminate; (*inspirar*) enlighten

ilu|são /ilu'zãw/ *f* illusion; (*sonho*) delusion; **~sionista** *m/f* illusionist; **~sório** *a* illusory

ilus|tração /ilustra'sãw/ *f* illustration; (*erudição*) learning; **~trador** *m* illustrator; **~trar** *vt* illustrate; **~trativo** *a* illustrative; **~tre** *a* illustrious; **~tríssimo senhor** Dear Sir

ímã /'imã/ *m* magnet

imaculado /imaku'ladu/ *a* immaculate

imagem /i'maʒẽ/ *f* image; (*da TV*) picture

imagi|nação /imaʒina'sãw/ *f* imagination; **~nar** *vt* imagine; **~nário** *a* imaginary; **~nativo** *a* imaginative; **~nável** (*pl* ~**náveis**) *a* imaginable; **~noso** /o/ *a* imaginative

imatu|ridade /imaturi'dadʒi/ *f* immaturity; **~ro** *a* immature

imbatí|vel /ĩba'tʃivew/ (*pl* ~**veis**) *a* unbeatable

imbe|cil /ĩbe'siw/ (*pl* ~**cis**) *a* stupid □ *m/f* imbecile

imberbe /ĩ'bɛrbi/ *adj* (*sem barba*) beardless

imbricar /ĩbri'kar/ *vt* overlap; **~-se** *vpr* overlap

imedia|ções /imedʒia'sõjs/ *f pl* vicinity; **~tamente** *adv* immediately; **~to a** immediate

imemori|al /imemori'aw/ (*pl* ~**ais**) *a* immemorial

imen|sidão /imẽsi'dãw/ *f* vastness; **~so a** immense

imergir /imer'ʒir/ *vt* immerse

imi|gração /imigra'sãw/ *f* immigration; **~grante** *a & m/f* immigrant; **~grar** *vi* immigrate

imi|nência /imi'nẽsia/ *f* imminence; **~nente** *a* imminent

imiscuir-se /imisku'irsi/ *vpr* interfere

imi|tação /imita'sãw/ *f* imitation; **~tador** *m* imitator; **~tar** *vt* imitate

imobili|ária /imobili'aria/ *f* estate agent's, (*Amer*) realtor; **~ário** *a* property; **~dade** *f* immobility; **~zar** *vt* immobilize

imo|ral /imo'raw/ (*pl* **~rais**) *a* immoral; **~ralidade** *f* immorality

imor|tal /imor'taw/ (*pl* **~tais**) *a* immortal □ *m/f* member of the Brazilian Academy of Letters; **~talidade** *f* immortality; **~talizar** *vt* immortalize

imó|vel /i'mɔvew/ (*pl* **~veis**) *a* motionless, immobile □ *m* building, property; *pl* property, real estate

impaci|ência /ĩpasi'ẽsia/ *f* impatience; **~entar-se** *vpr* get impatient; **~ente** *a* impatient

impacto /ĩ'paktu/, (*Port*) **impacte** /ĩ'paktʃi/ *m* impact

impagá|vel /ĩpa'gavew/ (*pl* **~veis**) *a* priceless

ímpar /'ĩpar/ *a* unique; *<número>* odd

imparci|al /ĩparsi'aw/ (*pl* **~ais**) *a* impartial; **~alidade** *f* impartiality

impasse /ĩ'pasi/ *m* impasse

impassí|vel /ĩpa'sivew/ (*pl* **~veis**) *a* impassive

impecá|vel /ĩpe'kavew/ (*pl* **~veis**) *a* impeccable

impe|dido /ĩpe'dʒidu/ *a* *<rua>* blocked; (*Port: ocupado*) engaged, (*Amer*) busy; (*no futebol*) offside; **~dimento** *m* prevention; (*estorvo*) obstruction; (*no futebol*) offside position; **~dir** *vt* stop; (*estorvar*) hinder; block *<rua>*; **~dir alg de ir** *ou* **que alg vá** stop s.o. going

impelir /ĩpe'lir/ *vt* drive

impenetrá|vel /ĩpene'travew/ (*pl* **~veis**) *a* impenetrable

impensá|vel /ĩpẽ'savew/ (*pl* **~veis**) *a* unthinkable

impe|rador /ĩpera'dor/ *m* emperor; **~rar** *vi* reign, rule; **~rativo** *a* & *m* imperative; **~ratriz** *f* empress

imperceptí|vel /ĩpersep'tʃivew/ (*pl* **~veis**) *a* imperceptible

imperdí|vel /ĩper'dʒivew/ (*pl* **~veis**) *a* unmissable

imperdoá|vel /ĩperdo'avew/ (*pl* **~veis**) *a* unforgivable

imperfei|ção /ĩperfej'sãw/ *f* imperfection; **~to** *a* & *m* imperfect

imperi|al /ĩperi'aw/ (*pl* **~ais**) *a* imperial; **~alismo** *m* imperialism; **~alista** *a* & *m/f* imperialist

império /ĩ'pεriu/ *m* empire

imperioso /ĩperi'ozu/ *a* imperious; *<necessidade>* pressing

imperme|abilizar /ĩpermiabili'zar/ *vt* waterproof; **~ável** (*pl* **~áveis**) *a* waterproof; (*fig*) impervious (**a** to) □ *m* raincoat

imperti|nência /ĩpertʃi'nẽsia/ *f* impertinence; **~nente** *a* impertinent

impesso|al /ĩpeso'aw/ (*pl* **~ais**) *a* impersonal

ímpeto /'ĩpetu/ *m* (*vontade*) urge, impulse; (*de emoção*) surge; (*movimento*) start; (*na física*) impetus

impetuo|sidade /ĩpetuozi'dadʒi/ *f* impetuosity; **~so** /o/ *a* impetuous

impiedoso /ĩpie'dozu/ *a* merciless

impingir /ĩpĩ'ʒir/ *vt* foist (**a** on)

implacá|vel /ĩpla'kavew/ (*pl* **~veis**) *a* implacable

implan|tar /ĩplã'tar/ *vt* introduce; (*no corpo*) implant; **~te** *m* implant

implemen|tar /ĩplemẽ'tar/ *vt* implement; **~to** *m* implement

impli|cação /ĩplika'sãw/ *f* implication; **~cância** *f* (*ato*) harassment; (*antipatia*) grudge; **estar de ~cância com** have it in for; **~cante** *a* troublesome □ *m/f* troublemaker; **~car** *vt* (*comprometer*) implicate; **~car** (**em**) (*dar a entender*) imply; (*acarretar, exigir*) involve; **~car com** (*provocar*) pick on; (*antipatizar*) not get on with

implícito /ĩ'plisitu/ *a* implicit

implorar /ĩplo'rar/ *vt* plead for (**a** from)

imponente /ĩpo'nẽtʃi/ *a* imposing

impopular /ĩpopu'lar/ *a* unpopular

impor /ĩ'por/ *vt* impose (**a** on); command *<respeito>*; **~-se** *vpr* assert o.s.

impor|tação /ĩporta'sãw/ *f* import; **~tador** *m* importer; **~tadora** *f* import company; **~tados** *m pl* imported goods; **~tância** *f* importance; (*quantia*) amount; **ter ~tância** be important; **~tante** *a* important; **~tar** *vt* import *<mercadorias>* □ *vi* matter; **~tar em** (*montar a*) amount to; (*resultar em*) lead to; **~tar-se** (**com**) mind

importu|nar /ĩportu'nar/ *vt* bother; **~no** *a* annoying

imposição /ĩpozi'sãw/ *f* imposition

impossibili|dade /ĩposibili'dadʒi/ *f* impossibility; **~tar** *vt* make impossible; **~tar alg de ir**, **~tar a alg ir** prevent s.o. from going, make it impossible for s.o. to go

impossí|vel /ĩpo'sivew/ (*pl* **~veis**) *a* impossible

impos|to /ĩ'postu/ *m* tax; **~to de renda** income tax; **~to sobre o valor acrescentado** (*Port*) VAT; **~tor** *m* impostor; **~tura** *f* deception

impo|tência /ĩpo'tẽsia/ *f* impotence; **~tente** *a* impotent

impreci|são /ĩpresi'zãw/ *f* imprecision; **~so** *a* imprecise

impregnar /ĩpreg'nar/ *vt* impregnate

imprensa /ĩ'prẽsa/ *f* press; **~ marrom** gutter press

imprescindí|vel /ĩpresĩ'dʒivew/ (pl ~veis) a essential

impres|são /ĩpre'sãw/ f impression; (no prelo) printing; ~**são digital** fingerprint; ~**sionante** a (imponente) impressive; (comovente) striking; ~**sionar** vt (causar admiração) impress; (comover) make an impression on; ~**sionar-se** vpr be impressed (com by); ~**sionável** (pl ~sionáveis) a impressionable; ~**sionismo** m impressionism; ~**sionista** a & m/f impressionist; ~**so** a printed □ m printed sheet; pl printed matter; ~**sor** m printer; ~**sora** f printer

impresta|vel /ĩpres'tavew/ (pl ~veis) a useless

impre|visível /ĩprevi'zivew/ (pl ~visíveis) a unpredictable; ~**visto** a unforeseen □ m unforeseen circumstance

imprimir /ĩpri'mir/ vt print

impropério /ĩpro'pɛriu/ m term of abuse; pl abuse

impróprio /ĩ'prɔpriu/ a improper; (inadequado) unsuitable (para for)

imprová|vel /ĩpro'vavew/ (pl ~veis) a unlikely

improvi|sação /ĩproviza'sãw/ f improvisation; ~**sar** vt/i improvise; ~**so** m **de** ~**so** on the spur of the moment

impru|dência /ĩpru'dẽsia/ f recklessness; ~**dente** a reckless

impul|sionar /ĩpuwsio'nar/ vt drive; ~**sivo** a impulsive; ~**so** m impulse

impu|ne /ĩ'puni/ a unpunished; ~**nidade** f impunity

impu|reza /ĩpu'reza/ f impurity; ~**ro** a impure

imun|dície /imũ'dʒisi/ f filth; ~**do** a filthy

imu|ne /i'muni/ a immune (a to); ~**nidade** f immunity; ~**nizar** vt immunize

inabalá|vel /inaba'lavew/ (pl ~veis) a unshakeable

iná|bil /i'nabiw/ (pl ~bis) a (desafeitado) clumsy

inabitado /inabi'tadu/ a uninhabited

inacabado /inaka'badu/ a unfinished

inaceitá|vel /inasej'tavew/ (pl ~veis) a unacceptable

inacessí|vel /inase'sivew/ (pl ~veis) a inaccessible

inacreditá|vel /inakredʒi'tavew/ (pl ~veis) a unbelievable

inadequado /inade'kwadu/ a unsuitable

inadmissí|vel /inadʒimi'sivew/ (pl ~veis) a inadmissible

inadvertência /inadʒiver'tẽsia/ f oversight

inalar /ina'lar/ vt inhale

inalcançá|vel /inawkã'savew/ (pl ~veis) a unattainable

inalterá|vel /inawte'ravew/ (pl ~veis) a unchangeable

inanição /inani'sãw/ f starvation

inanimado /inani'madu/ a inanimate

inapto /i'naptu/ a (incapaz) unfit

inati|vidade /inatʃivi'dadʒi/ f inactivity; ~**vo** a inactive

inato /i'natu/ a innate

inaudito /inaw'dʒitu/ a unheard of

inaugu|ração /inawgura'sãw/ f inauguration; ~**ral** (pl ~rais) a inaugural; ~**rar** vt inaugurate

incabí|vel /ĩka'bivew/ (pl ~veis) a inappropriate

incalculá|vel /ĩkawku'lavew/ (pl ~veis) a incalculable

incandescente /ĩkãde'sẽtʃi/ a red-hot

incansá|vel /ĩkã'savew/ (pl ~veis) a tireless

incapaci|tado /ĩkapasi'tadu/ a <pessoa> disabled; ~**tar** vt incapacitate

incauto /ĩ'kawtu/ a reckless

incendi|ar /ĩsẽdʒi'ar/ vt set alight; ~**ar-se** vpr catch fire; ~**ário** a incendiary; (fig) <discurso> inflammatory □ m arsonist; (fig) agitator

incêndio /ĩ'sẽdʒiu/ m fire

incenso /ĩ'sẽsu/ m incense

incenti|var /ĩsẽtʃi'var/ vt encourage; ~**vo** m incentive

incer|teza /ĩser'teza/ f uncertainty; ~**to** /ɛ/ a uncertain

inces|to /ĩ'sɛstu/ m incest; ~**tuoso** /o/ a incestuous

in|chação /ĩʃa'sãw/ f swelling; ~**char** vt/i swell

inci|dência /ĩsi'dẽsia/ f incidence; ~**dente** m incident; ~**dir** vi ~**dir em** <luz> shine on; <imposto> be payable on

incinerar /ĩsine'rar/ vt incinerate

inci|são /ĩsi'zãw/ f incision; ~**sivo** a incisive

incitar /ĩsi'tar/ vt incite

incli|nação /ĩklina'sãw/ f (do chão) incline; (da cabeça) nod; (propensão) inclination; ~**nado** a <chão> sloping; <edifício> leaning; (propenso) inclined (a to); ~**nar** vt tilt; nod <cabeça> □ vi <chão> slope; <edifício> lean; (tender) incline (para towards); ~**nar-se** vpr lean

inclu|ir /ĩklu'ir/ vt include; ~**são** f inclusion; ~**sive** prep including □ adv inclusive; (até) even; ~**so** a included

incoe|rência /ĩkoe'rẽsia/ f (falta de nexo) incoherence; (inconseqüência) inconsistency; ~**rente** a (sem nexo) incoherent; (inconseqüente) inconsistent

incógni|ta /ĩ'kɔgnita/ *f* unknown; **~to** *adv* incognito
incolor /ĩko'lor/ *a* colourless
incólume /ĩ'kɔlumi/ *a* unscathed
incomodar /ĩkomo'dar/ *vt* bother □ *vi* be a nuisance; **~-se** *vpr* (*dar-se ao trabalho*) bother (**em** to); **~-se** (**com**) be bothered (by), mind
incômodo /ĩ'komodu/ *a* (*desagradável*) tiresome; (*sem conforto*) uncomfortable □ *m* nuisance
incompa|rável /ĩkõpa'ravew/ (*pl* **~ráveis**) *a* incomparable; **~tível** (*pl* **~tíveis**) *a* incompatible
incompe|tência /ĩkõpe'tẽsia/ *f* incompetence; **~tente** *a* incompetent
incompleto /ĩkõ'plɛtu/ *a* incomplete
incompreensí|vel /ĩkõpriẽ'sivew/ (*pl* **~veis**) *a* incomprehensible
inconcebí|vel /ĩkõse'bivew/ (*pl* **~veis**) *a* inconceivable
incondicio|nal /ĩkõdʒisio'naw/ (*pl* **~nais**) *a* unconditional; <*fã, partidário*> firm
inconformado /ĩkõfor'madu/ *a* unreconciled (**com** to)
inconfundí|vel /ĩkõfũ'dʒivew/ (*pl* **~veis**) *a* unmistakeable
inconsciente /ĩkõsi'ẽtʃi/ *a* & *m* unconscious
inconseqüente /ĩkõse'kwẽtʃi/ *a* inconsistent
incons|tância /ĩkõs'tãsia/ *f* changeability; **~tante** *a* changeable
inconstitucio|nal /ĩkõstʃitusio'naw/ (*pl* **~nais**) *a* unconstitutional
incontestá|vel /ĩkõtes'tavew/ (*pl* **~veis**) *a* indisputable
inconveniente /ĩkõveni'ẽtʃi/ *a* (*difícil*) inconvenient; (*desagradável*) annoying, tiresome; (*indecente*) unseemly □ *m* drawback
incorporar /ĩkorpo'rar/ *vt* incorporate
incorrer /ĩko'xer/ *vi* **~ em** <*multa etc*> incur
incorrigí|vel /ĩkoxi'ʒivew/ (*pl* **~veis**) *a* incorrigible
incrédulo /ĩ'krɛdulu/ *a* incredulous
incremen|tado /ĩkremẽ'tadu/ *a* (*fam*) stylish; **~tar** *vt* build up; (*fam*) jazz up; **~to** *m* development, growth
incriminar /ĩkrimi'nar/ *vt* incriminate
incrí|vel /ĩ'krivew/ (*pl* **~veis**) *a* incredible
incu|bação /ĩkuba'sãw/ *f* incubation; **~badora** *f* incubator; **~bar** *vt/i* incubate
inculto /ĩ'kuwtu/ *a* <*pessoa*> uneducated; <*terreno*> uncultivated
incum|bência /ĩkũ'bẽsia/ *f* task; **~bir** *vt* **~bir alg de aco/de ir** assign s.o. sth/to go □ *vi* **~bir a** be up to; **~bir-se de** take on
incurá|vel /ĩku'ravew/ (*pl* **~veis**) *a* incurable
incursão /ĩkur'sãw/ *f* incursion
incutir /ĩku'tʃir/ *vt* instil (**em** in)
indagar /ĩda'gar/ *vt* inquire (into)
inde|cência /ĩde'sẽsia/ *f* indecency; **~cente** *a* indecent
indecifrá|vel /ĩdesi'fravew/ (*pl* **~veis**) *a* indecipherable
indeciso /ĩde'sizu/ *a* undecided
indecoroso /ĩdeko'rozu/ *a* indecorous
indefi|nido /ĩdefi'nidu/ *a* indefinite; **~nível** (*pl* **~níveis**) *a* indefinable
indelé|vel /ĩde'lɛvew/ (*pl* **~veis**) *a* indelible
indelica|deza /ĩdelika'deza/ *f* impoliteness; (*uma*) impolite thing; **~do** *a* impolite
indeni|zação /ĩdeniza'sãw/ *f* compensation; **~zar** *vt* compensate
indepen|dência /ĩdepẽ'dẽsia/ *f* independence; **~dente** *a* independent
indescriti|vel /ĩdʒiskri'tʃivew/ (*pl* **~veis**) *a* indescribable
indesculpá|vel /ĩdʒiskuw'pavew/ (*pl* **~veis**) *a* inexcusable
indesejá|vel /ĩdeze'ʒavew/ (*pl* **~veis**) *a* undesirable
indestrutí|vel /ĩdʒistru'tʃivew/ (*pl* **~veis**) *a* indestructible
indeterminado /ĩdetermi'nadu/ *a* indeterminate
indevido /ĩde'vidu/ *a* undue
indexar /ĩdek'sar/ *vt* index; index-link <*salário, preços*>
Índia /'ĩdʒia/ *f* India
indiano /ĩdʒi'anu/ *a* & *m* Indian
indi|cação /ĩdʒika'sãw/ *f* indication; (*do caminho*) directions; (*nomeação*) nomination; (*recomendação*) recommendation; **~cador** *m* indicator; (*dedo*) index finger □ *a* indicative (**de** of); **~car** *vt* indicate; (*para cargo, prêmio*) nominate (**para** for); (*recomendar*) recommend; **~cativo** *a* & *m* indicative
índice /'ĩdʒisi/ *m* (*taxa*) rate; (*em livro etc*) index; **~ de audiência** ratings
indiciar /ĩdʒisi'ar/ *vt* charge
indício /ĩ'dʒisiu/ *m* sign, indication; (*de crime*) clue
indife|rença /ĩdʒife'rẽsa/ *f* indifference; **~rente** *a* indifferent
indígena /ĩ'dʒiʒena/ *a* indigenous, native □ *m/f* native
indiges|tão /ĩdʒiʒes'tãw/ *f* indigestion; **~to** *a* indigestible; (*fig*) heavygoing
indig|nação /ĩdʒigna'sãw/ *f* indignation; **~nado** *a* indignant; **~nar** *vt*

make indignant; ~**nar-se** *vpr* get indignant (**com** about)
indig|nidade /ĩdʒigni'dadʒi/ *f* indignity; ~**no** *a* <*pessoa*> unworthy; <*ato*> despicable
índio /'ĩdʒiu/ *a* & *m* Indian
indire|ta /ĩdʒi'rɛta/ *f* hint; ~**to** /ɛ/ *a* indirect
indis|creto /ĩdʒis'krɛtu/ *a* indiscreet; ~**crição** *f* indiscretion
indiscriminado /ĩdʒiskrimi'nadu/ *a* indiscriminate
indiscutí|vel /ĩdʒisku'tʃivew/ (*pl* ~**veis**) *a* unquestionable
indispensá|vel /ĩdʒispẽ'savew/ (*pl* ~**veis**) *a* indispensable
indisponí|vel /ĩdʒispo'nivew/ (*pl* ~**veis**) *a* unavailable
indis|por /ĩdʒis'por/ *vt* upset; ~**por alg contra** turn s.o. against; ~**por-se** *vpr* fall out (**com** with); ~**posição** *f* indisposition; ~**posto** *a* (*doente*) indisposed
indistinto /ĩdʒis'tʃĩtu/ *a* indistinct
individu|al /ĩdʒividu'aw/ (*pl* ~**ais**) *a* individual; ~**alidade** *f* individuality; ~**alismo** *m* individualism; ~**alista** *a* & *m/f* individualist
indivíduo /ĩdʒi'viduu/ *m* individual
indizí|vel /ĩdʒi'zivew/ (*pl* ~**veis**) *a* unspeakable
índole /'ĩdoli/ *f* nature
indo|lência /ĩdo'lẽsia/ *f* indolence; ~**lente** *a* indolent
indolor /ĩdo'lor/ *a* painless
Indonésia /ĩdo'nɛzia/ *f* Indonesia
indonésio /ĩdo'nɛziu/ *a* & *m* Indonesian
indubitá|vel /ĩdubi'tavew/ (*pl* ~**veis**) *a* undoubted
indul|gência /ĩduw'ʒẽsia/ *f* indulgence; ~**gente** *a* indulgent
indulto /ĩ'duwtu/ *m* pardon
indumentária /ĩdumẽ'taria/ *f* outfit
indústria /ĩ'dustria/ *f* industry
industri|al /ĩdustri'aw/ (*pl* ~**ais**) *a* industrial □ *m/f* industrialist; ~**alizado** *a* <*país*> industrialized; <*mercadoria*> manufactured; <*comida*> processed; ~**alizar** *vt* industrialize <*país, agricultura etc*>; process <*comida, lixo etc*>; ~**oso** /o/ *a* industrious
induzir /ĩdu'zir/ *vt* (*persuadir*) induce; (*inferir*) infer (**de** from); ~ **em erro** lead astray, mislead s.o.
inebriante /inebri'ãtʃi/ *a* intoxicating
inédito /i'nɛdʒitu/ *a* unheard-of, unprecedented; (*não publicado*) unpublished
ineficaz /inefi'kas/ *a* ineffective
inefici|ência /inefisi'ẽsia/ *f* inefficiency; ~**ente** *a* inefficient

inegá|vel /ine'gavew/ (*pl* ~**veis**) *a* undeniable
inépcia /i'nɛpsia/ *f* ineptitude
inepto /i'nɛptu/ *a* inept
inequívoco /ine'kivoku/ *a* unmistakeable
inércia /i'nɛrsia/ *f* inertia
inerente /ine'rẽtʃi/ *a* inherent (**a** in)
inerte /i'nɛrtʃi/ *a* inert
inesgotá|vel /inezgo'tavew/ (*pl* ~**veis**) *a* inexhaustible
inesperado /inespe'radu/ *a* unexpected
inesquecí|vel /ineske'sivew/ (*pl* ~**veis**) *a* unforgettable
inevitá|vel /inevi'tavew/ (*pl* ~**veis**) *a* inevitable
inexato /ine'zatu/ *a* inaccurate
inexis|tência /inezis'tẽsia/ *f* lack; ~**tente** *a* non-existent
inexperi|ência /inisperi'ẽsia/ *f* inexperience; ~**ente** *a* inexperienced
inexpressivo /inespre'sivu/ *a* expressionless
infalí|vel /ifa'livew/ (*pl* ~**veis**) *a* infallible
infame /ĩ'fami/ *a* despicable; (*péssimo*) dreadful
infâmia /ĩ'famia/ *f* disgrace
infância /ĩ'fãsia/ *f* childhood
infantaria /ĩfãta'ria/ *f* infantry
infan|til /ĩfã'tʃiw/ *a* <*roupa, livro*> children's; (*bobo*) childish; ~**tilidade** *f* childishness; (*uma*) childish thing
infarto /ĩ'fartu/ *m* heart attack
infec|ção /ĩfek'sãw/ *f* infection; ~**cionar** *vt* infect; ~**cioso** *a* infectious
infeliz /ĩfe'lis/ *a* (*não contente*) unhappy; (*inconveniente*) unfortunate; (*desgraçado*) wretched □ *m* (*desgraçado*) wretch; ~**mente** *adv* unfortunately
inferi|or /ĩferi'or/ *a* lower; (*em qualidade*) inferior (**a** to); ~**oridade** *f* inferiority
inferir /ĩfe'rir/ *vt* infer
infer|nal /ĩfer'naw/ (*pl* ~**nais**) *a* infernal; ~**nizar** *vt* ~**nizar a vida dele** make his life hell; ~**no** /ɛ/ *m* hell
infér|til /ĩ'fɛrtʃiw/ (*pl* ~**teis**) *a* infertile
infertilidade /ĩfertʃili'dadʒi/ *f* infertility
infestar /ĩfes'tar/ *vt* infest
infetar /ĩfe'tar/ *vt* infect
infidelidade /ĩfideli'dadʒi/ *f* infidelity
infi|el /ĩfi'ɛw/ (*pl* ~**éis**) *a* unfaithful
infiltrar /ĩfiw'trar/ *vt* infiltrate; ~**-se em** infiltrate
ínfimo /'ĩfimu/ *a* lowest; (*muito pequeno*) tiny
infindá|vel /ĩfĩ'davew/ (*pl* ~**veis**) *a* unending

infinidade /ĩfini'dadʒi/ f infinity; **uma ~ de** an infinite number of

infini|tesimal /ĩfinitezi'maw/ (pl **~tesimais**) a infinitesimal; **~tivo** a & m infinitive; **~to** a infinite □ m infinity

infla|ção /ĩfla'sãw/ f inflation; **~cionar** vt inflate; **~cionário** a inflationary; **~cionista** a & m/f inflationist

infla|mação /ĩflama'sãw/ f inflammation; **~mar** vt inflame; **~mar-se** vpr become inflamed; **~matório** a inflammatory; **~mável** (pl **~máveis**) a inflammable

in|flar /ĩ'flar/ vt inflate; **~flar-se** vpr inflate; **~flável** (pl **~fláveis**) a inflatable

infle|xibilidade /ĩfleksibili'dadʒi/ f inflexibility; **~xível** (pl **~xíveis**) a inflexible

infligir /ĩfli'ʒir/ vt inflict (**a** on)

influência /ĩflu'ẽsia/ f influence

influen|ciar /ĩflu'ẽsi'ar/ vt **~ciar** (**em**) influence; **~ciar-se** vpr be influenced; **~ciável** (pl **~ciáveis**) a open to influence; **~te** a influential

influir /ĩflu'ir/ vi **~ em** ou **sobre** influence

informação /ĩforma'sãw/ f information; (uma) a piece of information; (mil) intelligence; pl information

infor|mal /ĩfor'maw/ (pl **~mais**) a informal; **~malidade** f informality

infor|mar /ĩfor'mar/ vt inform; **~mar-se** vpr find out (**de** about); **~mática** f information technology; **~mativo** a informative; **~matizar** vt computerize; **~me** m (mil) piece of intelligence

infortúnio /ĩfor'tuniu/ m misfortune

infração /ĩfra'sãw/ f infringement

infra-estrutura /ĩfraistru'tura/ f infrastructure

infrator /ĩfra'tor/ m offender

infravermelho /ĩfraver'meʎu/ a infrared

infringir /ĩfrĩ'ʒir/ vt infringe

infrutífero /ĩfru'tʃiferu/ a fruitless

infundado /ĩfũ'dadu/ a unfounded

infundir /ĩfũ'dʒir/ vt (insuflar) infuse; (incutir) instil

infusão /ĩfu'zãw/ f infusion

ingenuidade /ĩʒenui'dadʒi/ f naivety

ingênuo /ĩ'ʒenuu/ a naive

Inglaterra /ĩgla'tɛxa/ f England

ingerir /ĩʒe'rir/ vt ingest; (engolir) swallow

in|glês /ĩ'gles/ a (f **~glesa**) English □ m (f **~glesa**) Englishman (f -woman); (língua) English; **os ~gleses** the English

ingra|tidão /ĩgratʃi'dãw/ f ingratitude; **~to** a ungrateful

ingrediente /ĩgredʒi'ẽtʃi/ m ingredient

íngreme /'ĩgrimi/ a steep

ingres|sar /ĩgre'sar/ vi **~sar em** join; **~so m** entry; (bilhete) ticket

inhame /i'ɲami/ m yam

ini|bição /inibi'sãw/ f inhibition; **~bir** vt inhibit

inici|ado /inisi'adu/ m initiate; **~al** (pl **~ais**) a & f initial; **~ar** vt (começar) begin; (em ciência, seita etc) initiate (**em** into) □ vi begin; **~ativa** f initiative

início /i'nisiu/ m beginning

inigualá|vel /inigwa'lavew/ (pl **~veis**) a unparalleled

inimaginá|vel /inimaʒi'navew/ (pl **~veis**) a unimaginable

inimi|go /ini'migu/ a & m enemy; **~zade** f enmity

ininterrupto /inĩte'xuptu/ a continuous

inje|ção /ĩʒe'sãw/ f injection; **~tado** a <olhos> bloodshot; **~tar** vt inject; **~tável** (pl **~táveis**) a <droga> intravenous

injúria /ĩ'ʒuria/ f insult

injuriar /ĩʒuri'ar/ vt insult

injus|tiça /ĩʒus'tʃisa/ f injustice; **~tiçado** a wronged; **~to** a unfair, unjust

ino|cência /ino'sẽsia/ f innocence; **~centar** vt clear (**de** of); **~cente** a innocent

inocular /inoku'lar/ vt inoculate

inócuo /i'nɔkuu/ a harmless

inodoro /ino'dɔru/ a odourless

inofensivo /inofe'sivu/ a harmless

inoportuno /inopor'tunu/ a inopportune

inorgânico /inor'ganiku/ a inorganic

inóspito /i'nɔspitu/ a inhospitable

ino|vação /inova'sãw/ f innovation; **~var** vt/i innovate

inoxidá|vel /inoksi'davew/ (pl **~veis**) a <aço> stainless

inquérito /ĩ'kɛritu/ m inquiry

inquie|tação /ĩkieta'sãw/ f concern; **~tador, ~tante** a worrying; **~tar** vt worry; **~tar-se** vpr worry; **~to** /ɛ/ a uneasy

inquili|nato /ĩkili'natu/ m tenancy; **~no** m tenant

inquirir /ĩki'rir/ vt cross-examine <testemunha>

Inquisição /ĩkizi'sãw/ f a **~ the Inquisition**

insaciá|vel /ĩsasi'avew/ (pl **~veis**) a insatiable

insalubre /ĩsa'lubri/ a unhealthy

insatis|fação /ĩsatʃisfa'sãw/ f dissatisfaction; **~fatório** a unsatisfactory; **~feito** a dissatisfied

ins|crever /ĩskre'ver/ *vt* (*registrar*) register; (*gravar*) inscribe; **~crever-se** *vpr* register; (*em escola etc*) enrol; **~crição** *f* (*registro*) registration; (*em clube, escola*) enrolment; (*em monumento etc*) inscription

insegu|rança /ĩsegu'rãsa/ *f* insecurity; **~ro** *a* insecure

insemi|nação /ĩsemina'sãw/ *f* insemination; **~nar** *vt* inseminate

insen|satez /ĩsẽsa'tes/ *f* folly; **~sato** *a* foolish; **~sibilidade** *f* insensitivity; **~sível** (*pl* **~síveis**) *a* insensitive

insepará|vel /ĩsepa'ravew/ (*pl* **~veis**) *a* inseparable

inserção /ĩser'sãw/ *f* insertion

inserir /ĩse'rir/ *vt* insert; enter <*dados*>

inse|ticida /ĩsetʃi'sida/ *m* insecticide; **~to** /ɛ/ *m* insect

insígnia /ĩ'signia/ *f* insignia

insignifi|cância /ĩsignifi'kãsia/ *f* insignificance; **~cante** *a* insignificant

insincero /ĩsĩ'sɛru/ *a* insincere

insinu|ante /ĩsinu'ãtʃi/ *a* suggestive; **~ar** *vt/i* insinuate

insípido /ĩ'sipidu/ *a* insipid

insis|tência /ĩsis'tẽsia/ *f* insistence; **~tente** *a* insistent; **~tir** *vt/i* insist (**em** on)

insolação /ĩsola'sãw/ *f* sunstroke

inso|lência /ĩso'lẽsia/ *f* insolence; **~lente** *a* insolent

insólito /ĩ'solitu/ *a* unusual

insolú|vel /ĩso'luvew/ (*pl* **~veis**) *a* insoluble

insone /ĩ'sɔni/ *a* <*noite*> sleepless; <*pessoa*> insomniac □ *m/f* insomniac

insônia /ĩ'sonia/ *f* insomnia

insosso /ĩ'sosu/ *a* bland; (*sem sabor*) tasteless; (*sem sal*) unsalted

inspe|ção /ĩspe'sãw/ *f* inspection; **~cionar** *vt* inspect; **~tor** *m* inspector

inspi|ração /ĩspira'sãw/ *f* inspiration; **~rar** *vt* inspire; **~rar-se** *vpr* take inspiration (**em** from)

instabilidade /ĩstabili'dadʒi/ *f* instability

insta|lação /ĩstala'sãw/ *f* installation; **~lar** *vt* install; **~lar-se** *vpr* install o.s.

instan|tâneo /ĩstã'taniu/ *a* instant; **~te** *m* instant

instaurar /ĩstaw'rar/ *vt* set up

instá|vel /ĩ'stavew/ (*pl* **~veis**) *a* unstable; <*tempo*> unsettled

insti|gação /ĩstʃiga'sãw/ *f* instigation; **~gante** *a* stimulating; **~gar** *vt* incite

instin|tivo /ĩstʃĩ'tʃivu/ *a* instinctive; **~to** *m* instinct

institu|cional /ĩstʃitusio'naw/ (*pl* **~cionais**) *a* institutional; **~ição** *f*

institution; **~ir** *vt* set up; set <*prazo*>; **~to** *m* institute

instru|ção /ĩstru'sãw/ *f* instruction; **~ir** *vt* instruct; train <*recrutas*>; (*informar*) advise (**sobre** of)

instrumen|tal /ĩstrumẽ'taw/ (*pl* **~tais**) *a* instrumental; **~tista** *m/f* instrumentalist; **~to** *m* instrument

instru|tivo /ĩstru'tʃivu/ *a* instructive; **~tor** *m* instructor

insubstituí|vel /ĩsubistʃitu'ivew/ (*pl* **~veis**) *a* irreplaceable

insucesso /ĩsu'sesu/ *m* failure

insufici|ência /ĩsufisi'ẽsia/ *f* insufficiency; (*dos órgãos*) failure; **~ente** *a* insufficient

insulina /ĩsu'lina/ *f* insulin

insul|tar /ĩsuw'tar/ *vt* insult; **~to** *m* insult

insuperá|vel /ĩsupe'ravew/ (*pl* **~veis**) *a* <*problema*> insurmountable; <*qualidade*> unsurpassed

insuportá|vel /ĩsupor'tavew/ (*pl* **~veis**) *a* unbearable

insur|gente /ĩsur'ʒẽtʃi/ *a* & *m/f* insurgent; **~gir-se** *vpr* rise up, revolt; **~reição** *f* insurrection

intato /ĩ'tatu/ *a* intact

íntegra /ĩ'tegra/ *f* full text; **na ~** in full

inte|gração /ĩtegra'sãw/ *f* integration; **~gral** (*pl* **~grais**) *a* whole; **arroz/pão ~gral** brown rice/bread; **~grante** *a* integral □ *m/f* member; **~grar** *vt* make up, form; **~grar-se em** become a part of; **~gridade** *f* integrity

íntegro /ĩ'tegru/ *a* honest

intei|ramente /ĩtera'mẽtʃi/ *adv* completely; **~rar** *vt* (*informar*) fill in, inform (**de** about); **~rar-se** *vpr* find out (**de** about); **~riço** *a* in one piece; **~ro** *a* whole

intelec|to /ĩte'lɛktu/ *m* intellect; **~tual** (*pl* **~tuais**) *a* & *m/f* intellectual

inteli|gência /ĩteli'ʒẽsia/ *f* intelligence; **~gente** *a* clever, intelligent; **~gível** (*pl* **~gíveis**) *a* intelligible

intem|périe /ĩtẽ'pɛri/ *f* bad weather; **~pestivo** *a* ill-timed

inten|ção /ĩtẽ'sãw/ *f* intention; **segundas ~ções** ulterior motives

intencio|nado /ĩtẽsio'nadu/ *a* **bem ~nado** well-meaning; **~nal** (*pl* **~nais**) *a* intentional; **~nar** *vt* intend

inten|sidade /ĩtẽsi'dadʒi/ *f* intensity; **~sificar** *vt* intensify; **~sificar-se** *vpr* intensify; **~sivo** *a* intensive; **~so** *a* intense

intento /ĩ'tẽtu/ *m* intention

intera|ção /ĩtera'sãw/ *f* interaction; **~gir** *vi* interact; **~tivo** *a* interactive

inter|calar /ĩterka'lar/ *vt* insert; **~câmbio** *m* exchange; **~ceptar** *vt* intercept

intercontinen|tal /ĩterkõtʃinẽ'taw/ (*pl* **~tais**) *a* intercontinental

interdepen|dência /ĩterdepẽ'dẽsia/ *f* interdependence; **~dente** *a* interdependent

interdi|ção /ĩterdʒi'sãw/ *f* closure; (*jurid*) injunction; **~tar** *vt* close <*rua etc*>; (*proibir*) ban

interes|sante /ĩtere'sãtʃi/ *a* interesting; **~sar** *vt* interest □ *vi* be relevant; **~sar-se** *vpr* be interested (**em** *ou* **por** in); **~se** /e/ *m* interest; (*próprio*) self-interest; **~seiro** *a* self-seeking

interestadu|al /ĩteristadu'aw/ (*pl* **~ais**) *a* interstate

interface /ĩter'fasi/ *f* interface

interfe|rência /ĩterfe'rẽsia/ *f* interference; **~rir** *vi* interfere

interfone /ĩter'foni/ *m* intercom

ínterim /'ĩteri/ *m* interim; **nesse ~** in the interim

interino /ĩte'rinu/ *a* temporary

interior /ĩteri'or/ *a* inner; (*dentro do país*) internal, domestic □ *m* inside; (*do país*) country, interior

inter|jeição /ĩterʒej'sãw/ *f* interjection; **~ligar** *vt* interconnect; **~locutor** *m* interlocutor; **~mediário** *a & m* intermediary

intermédio /ĩter'mɛdʒiu/ *m* **por ~ de** through

intermina|vel /ĩtermi'navew/ (*pl* **~veis**) *a* interminable

intermitente /ĩtermi'tẽtʃi/ *a* intermittent

internacio|nal /ĩternasio'naw/ (*pl* **~nais**) *a* international

inter|nar *vt* intern <*preso*>; admit to hospital <*doente*>; **~nato** *m* boarding school; **~no** *a* internal

interpelar /ĩterpe'lar/ *vt* question

interpor /ĩter'por/ *vt* interpose; **~-se** *vpr* intervene

interpre|tação /ĩterpreta'sãw/ *f* interpretation; **~tar** *vt* interpret; perform <*papel, música*>; **intérprete** *m/f* (*de línguas*) interpreter; (*de teatro etc*) performer

interro|gação /ĩtexoga'sãw/ *f* interrogation; **~gar** *vt* interrogate, question; **~gativo** *a* interrogative; **~gatório** *m* interrogation

inter|romper /ĩtexõ'per/ *vt* interrupt; **~rupção** *f* interruption; **~ruptor** *m* switch

interurbano /ĩterur'banu/ *a* long-distance □ *m* trunk call

intervalo /ĩter'valu/ *m* interval

inter|venção /ĩtervẽ'sãw/ *f* intervention; **~vir** *vi* intervene

intesti|nal /ĩtestʃi'naw/ (*pl* **~nais**) *a* intestinal; **~no** *m* intestine

inti|mação /ĩtʃima'sãw/ *f* (*da justiça*) summons; **~mar** *vt* order; (*à justiça*) summon

intimidade /ĩtʃimi'dadʒi/ *f* intimacy; (*entre amigos*) closeness; (*vida íntima*) private life; **ter ~ com** be close to

intimidar /ĩtʃimi'dar/ *vt* intimidate; **~-se** *vpr* be intimidated

íntimo /'ĩtʃimu/ *a* intimate; <*amigo*> close; <*vida*> private □ *m* close friend

intitular /ĩtʃitu'lar/ *vt* entitle

intocá|vel /ĩto'kavew/ (*pl* **~veis**) *a* untouchable

intole|rância /ĩtole'rãsia/ *f* intolerance; **~rante** *a* intolerant; **~rável** (*pl* **~ráveis**) *a* intolerable

intoxi|cação /ĩtoksika'sãw/ *f* poisoning; **~cação alimentar** food poisoning; **~car** *vt* poison

intragá|vel /ĩtra'gavew/ (*pl* **~veis**) *a* <*comida*> inedible; <*pessoa*> unbearable

intransigente /ĩtrãzi'ʒẽtʃi/ *a* uncompromising

intransi|tável /ĩtrãzi'tavew/ (*pl* **~táveis**) *a* impassable; **~tivo** *a* intransitive

intratá|vel /ĩtra'tavew/ (*pl* **~veis**) *a* <*pessoa*> difficult

intra-uterino /ĩtraute'rinu/ *a* dispositivo **~** intra-uterine device, IUD

intrépido /ĩ'trɛpidu/ *a* intrepid

intri|ga /ĩ'triga/ *f* intrigue; (*enredo*) plot; **~gante** *a* intriguing; **~gar** *vt* intrigue

intrincado /ĩtrĩ'kadu/ *a* intricate

intrínseco /ĩ'trĩsiku/ *a* intrinsic

introdu|ção /ĩtrodu'sãw/ *f* introduction; **~tório** *a* introductory; **~zir** *vt* introduce

introme|ter-se /ĩtrome'tersi/ *vpr* interfere; **~tido** *a* interfering □ *m* busybody

introspec|ção /ĩtrospek'sãw/ *f* introspection; **~tivo** *a* introspective

introvertido /ĩtrover'tʃidu/ *a* introverted □ *m* introvert

intruso /ĩ'truzu/ *a* intrusive □ *m* intruder

intu|ição /ĩtui'sãw/ *f* intuition; **~ir** *vt* intuit; **~itivo** *a* intuitive; **~to** *m* purpose

inumano /inu'manu/ *a* inhuman

inumerá|vel /inume'ravew/ (*pl* **~veis**) *a* innumerable

inúmero /i'numeru/ *a* countless

inun|dação /inũda'sãw/ *f* flood; **~dar** *vt/i* flood

inusitado /inuzi'tadu/ *a* unusual

inú|til /i'nutʃiw/ (*pl* **~teis**) *a* useless

inutilmente /inutʃiw'mẽtʃi/ *adv* in vain

inutilizar /inutʃili'zar/ *vt* render useless; damage <*aparelho*>; thwart <*esforços*>

invadir /ĩva'dʒir/ *vt* invade

invali|dar /ĩvali'dar/ *vt* invalidate; disable <*pessoa*>; **~dez** /e/ *f* disability

inválido /ĩ'validu/ *a* & *m* invalid

invariá|vel /ĩvari'avew/ (*pl* **~veis**) *a* invariable

inva|são /ĩva'zãw/ *f* invasion; **~sor** *m* invader □ *a* invading

inve|ja /ĩ'vɛʒa/ *f* envy; **~jar** *vt* envy; **~jável** (*pl* **~jáveis**) *a* enviable; **~joso** /o/ *a* envious

inven|ção /ĩvẽ'sãw/ *f* invention; **~tar** *vt* invent; **~tário** *m* inventory; **~tivo** *a* inventive; **~tor** *m* inventor

inver|nar /ĩver'nar/ *vi* winter, spend the winter; **~no** /ɛ/ *m* winter

inverossí|mil /ĩvero'simiw/ (*pl* **~meis**) *a* improbable

inver|são /ĩver'sãw/ *f* inversion; **~so** *a* inverse; <*ordem*> reverse □ *m* reverse; **~ter** *vt* reverse; (*colocar de cabeça para baixo*) invert

invertebrado /ĩverte'bradu/ *a* & *m* invertebrate

invés /ĩ'vɛs/ *m* **ao ~ de** instead of

investida /ĩves'tʃida/ *f* attack

investidura /ĩvestʃi'dura/ *f* investiture

investi|gação /ĩvestʃiga'sãw/ *f* investigation; **~gar** *vt* investigate

inves|timento /ĩvestʃi'mẽtu/ *m* investment; **~tir** *vt/i* invest; **~tir contra** attack

inveterado /ĩvete'radu/ *a* inveterate

inviá|vel /ĩvi'avew/ (*pl* **~veis**) *a* impracticable

invicto /ĩ'viktu/ *a* unbeaten

invisí|vel /ĩvi'zivew/ (*pl* **~veis**) *a* invisible

invocar /ĩvo'kar/ *vt* invoke; (*fam*) pester

invólucro /ĩ'vɔlukru/ *m* covering

involuntário /ĩvolũ'tariu/ *a* involuntary

invulnerá|vel /ĩvuwne'ravew/ (*pl* **~veis**) *a* invulnerable

iodo /i'odu/ *m* iodine

ioga /i'ɔga/ *f* yoga

iogurte /io'gurtʃi/ *m* yoghurt

ir /ir/ *vi* go; **~-se** *vpr* go away; **vou voltar** I will come back; **vou melhorando** I am (gradually) getting better

ira /'ira/ *f* wrath

Irã /i'rã/ *m* Iran

iraniano /irani'anu/ *a* & *m* Iranian

Irão /i'rãw/ *m* (*Port*) Iran

Iraque /i'raki/ *m* Iraq

iraquiano /iraki'anu/ *a* & *m* Iraqui

Irlanda /ir'lãda/ *f* Ireland

irlan|dês /irlã'des/ *a* (*f* **~desa**) Irish □ *m* (*f* **~desa**) Irishman (*f* -woman); (*língua*) Irish; **os ~deses** the Irish

irmã /ir'mã/ *f* sister

irmandade /irmã'dadʒi/ *f* (*associação*) brotherhood

irmão /ir'mãw/ (*pl* **~s**) *m* brother

ironia /iro'nia/ *f* irony

irônico /i'roniku/ *a* ironic

irracio|nal /ixasio'naw/ (*pl* **~nais**) *a* irrational

irradiar /ixadʒi'ar/ *vt* radiate; (*pelo rádio*) broadcast □ *vi* shine; **~-se** *vpr* spread, radiate

irre|al /ixe'aw/ (*pl* **~ais**) *a* unreal

irreconhecí|vel /ixekoɲe'sivew/ (*pl* **~veis**) *a* unrecognizable

irrecuperá|vel /ixekupe'ravew/ (*pl* **~veis**) *a* irretrievable

irrefletido /ixefle'tʃidu/ *a* rash

irregu|lar /ixegu'lar/ *a* irregular; (*inconstante*) erratic; **~laridade** *f* irregularity

irrelevante /ixele'vãtʃi/ *a* irrelevant

irreparáv|el /ixepa'ravew/ (*pl* **~veis**) *a* irreparable

irrepreensí|vel /ixepriẽ'sivew/ (*pl* **~veis**) *a* irreproachable

irrequieto /ixeki'etu/ *a* restless

irresistí|vel /ixezis'tʃivew/ (*pl* **~veis**) *a* irresistible

irresoluto /ixezo'lutu/ *a* <*questão*> unresolved; <*pessoa*> indecisive

irresponsá|vel /ixespõ'savew/ (*pl* **~veis**) *a* irresponsible

irreverente /ixeve'rẽtʃi/ *a* irreverent

irri|gação /ixiga'sãw/ *f* irrigation; **~gar** *vt* irrigate

irrisório /ixi'zɔriu/ *a* derisory

irri|tação /ixita'sãw/ *f* irritation; **~tadiço** *a* irritable; **~tante** *a* irritating; **~tar** *vt* irritate; **~tar-se** *vpr* get irritated

irromper /ixõ'per/ *vi* **~ em** burst into

isca /'iska/ *f* bait

isen|ção /izẽ'sãw/ *f* exemption; **~tar** *vt* exempt; **~to** *a* exempt

Islã /iz'lã/ *m* Islam

islâmico /iz'lamiku/ *a* Islamic

isla|mismo /izla'mizmu/ *m* Islam; **~mita** *a* & *m/f* Muslim

islan|dês /izlã'des/ *a* (*f* **~desa**) Icelandic □ *m* (*f* **~desa**) Icelander; (*língua*) Icelandic

Islândia /iz'lãdʒia/ *f* Iceland

iso|lamento /izola'mẽtu/ *m* isolation; (*eletr*) insulation; **~lante** *a* insulating; **~lar** *vt* isolate; (*eletr*) insulate □ *vi* (*contra azar*) touch wood, (*Amer*) knock on wood

isopor /izo'por/ *m* polystyrene

isqueiro /is'keru/ *m* lighter

Israel /izxa'ɛw/ m Israel
israe|lense /izraj'lẽsi/ a & m/f
Israeli; **~lita** a & m/f Israelite
isso /'isu/ pron that; **por ~** therefore
isto /'istu/ pron this; **~ é** that is
Itália /i'talia/ f Italy
italiano /itali'anu/ a & m Italian
itálico /i'taliku/ a & m italic
item /'itẽ/ m item
itine|rante /itʃine'rãtʃi/ a itinerant;
~rário m itinerary
Iugoslávia /iugoz'lavia/ f Yugoslavia
iugoslavo /iugoz'lavu/ a & m Yugoslavian

J

já /ʒa/ adv already; (agora) right away
□ conj on the other hand; **desde ~**
from now on; **~ não** no longer; **~
que** since; **~** in no time
jabuticaba /ʒabutʃi'kaba/ f jabuticaba
jaca /'ʒaka/ f jack fruit
jacaré /ʒaka'rɛ/ m alligator
jacinto /ʒa'sĩtu/ m hyacinth
jactância /ʒak'tãsia/ f boasting
jade /'ʒadʒi/ m jade
jaguar /ʒagu'ar/ m jaguar
jagunço /ʒa'gũsu/ m hired gunman
jamais /ʒa'majs/ adv never
Jamaica /ʒa'majka/ f Jamaica
jamaicano /ʒamaj'kanu/ a & m Jamaican
jamanta /ʒa'mãta/ f juggernaut
janeiro /ʒa'neru/ m January
janela /ʒa'nɛla/ f window
jangada /ʒã'gada/ f (fishing) raft
janta /'ʒãta/ f (fam) dinner
jantar /ʒã'tar/ m dinner □ vi have
dinner □ vt have for dinner
Japão /ʒa'pãw/ m Japan
japo|na /ʒa'pɔna/ f pea jacket □ m/f
(fam) Japanese; **~nês** a & m (f
~nesa) Japanese
jaqueira /ʒa'kera/ f jack-fruit tree
jaqueta /ʒa'keta/ f jacket
jarda /'ʒarda/ f yard
jar|dim /ʒar'dʒĩ/ m garden; **~dim-de-
infância** (pl **~dins-de-infância**) f
kindergarten
jardi|nagem /ʒardʒi'naʒẽ/ f gardening; **~nar** vi garden; **~neira** f (calça)
dungarees; (vestido) pinafore dress,
(Amer) jumper; (ônibus) open-sided
bus; (para flores) flower stand;
~neiro m gardener
jargão /ʒar'gãw/ m jargon
jar|ra /'ʒaxa/ f pot; **~ro** m jug
jasmim /ʒaz'mĩ/ m jasmine
jato /'ʒatu/ m jet
jaula /'ʒawla/ f cage

ja|zer /ʒa'zer/ vi lie; **~zida** f deposit;
~zigo m grave
jazz /dʒaz/ m jazz; **~ista** m/f jazz
artist; **~ístico** a jazzy
jeca /'ʒɛka/ m/f country bumpkin □ a
countrified; (cafona) tacky; **~-tatu**
m/f country bumpkin
jei|tão /ʒej'tãw/ m (fam) individual
style; **~tinho** m knack; **~to** m way;
(de pessoa) manner; (habilidade) skill;
de qualquer ~to anyway; **de ~to
nenhum** no way; **pelo ~to** by the
looks of things; **sem ~to** awkward;
dar um ~to to find a way; **dar um
~to em** (arrumar) tidy up; (consertar) fix; (torcer) twist <pé etc>; **ter
~to de** look like; **ter ou levar ~to
para** be good at; **tomar ~to** pull
one's socks up; **~toso** /o/ a skilful;
(de aparência) elegant
je|juar /ʒeʒu'ar/ vi fast; **~jum** m fast
Jeová /ʒio'va/ m **testemunha de ~**
Jehovah's witness
jérsei /'ʒersej/ m jersey
jesuíta /ʒezu'ita/ a & m/f Jesuit
Jesus /ʒe'zus/ m Jesus
jibóia /ʒi'bɔja/ f boa constrictor
jiboiar /ʒiboj'ar/ vi have a rest to let
one's dinner go down
jiló /ʒi'lɔ/ m okra
jipe /'ʒipi/ m jeep
jiu-jitsu /ʒiu'ʒitsu/ m jiu-jitsu
joa|lheiro /ʒoa'ʎeru/ m jeweller;
~lheria f jeweller's (shop)
joaninha /ʒoa'nĩa/ f ladybird,
(Amer) ladybug; (alfinete) safety pin
joão-ninguém /ʒoãwnĩ'gẽj/ (pl
joões-ninguém) m nobody
jocoso /ʒo'kozu/ a jocular
joe|lhada /ʒoe'ʎada/ f blow with the
knee; **~lheira** f kneepad; **~lho** /e/ m
knee; **de ~lhos** kneeling
jo|gada /ʒo'gada/ f move; **~gado** a
<pessoa> flat out; <papéis, roupa
etc> lying around; **~gador** m player;
(no cassino etc) gambler; **~gar** vt
play; (atirar) throw; (arriscar no jogo)
gamble □ vi play; (no cassino etc)
gamble; (balançar) toss; **~gar fora**
throw away; **~gatina** f gambling
jogging /'ʒogĩ/ m (cooper) jogging;
(roupa) track suit
jogo /'ʒogu/ m (partida) game; (ação
de jogar) play; (jogatina) gambling;
(conjunto) set; **em ~** at stake; **~ de
cintura** (fig) flexibility, room to
manoeuvre; **~ de luz** lighting
effects; **~ do bicho** illegal numbers
game; **Jogos Olímpicos** Olympic
Games; **~-da-velha** m noughts and
crosses
joguete /ʒo'getʃi/ m plaything
jóia /'ʒoja/ f jewel; (propina) entry fee
□ a (fam) great

joio /'ʒoju/ *m* chaff; **separar o ~ do trigo** separate the wheat from the chaff

jóquei /'ʒɔkej/ *m* (*pessoa*) jockey; (*lugar*) race course

Jordânia /ʒor'dania/ *f* Jordan

jordaniano /ʒordani'anu/ *a & m* Jordanian

jor|nada /ʒor'nada/ *f* (*viagem*) journey; **~nada de trabalho** working day; **~nal** (*pl* **~nais**) *m* newspaper; (*na TV*) news

jorna|leco /ʒorna'lɛku/ *m* rag, scandal sheet; **~leiro** *m* (*vendedor*) newsagent, (*Amer*) newsdealer; (*entregador*) paperboy; **~lismo** *m* journalism; **~lista** *m/f* journalist; **~lístico** *a* journalistic

jor|rar /ʒo'xar/ *vi* gush, spurt; **~ro** /'ʒoxu/ *m* spurt

jota /'ʒɔta/ *m* letter J

jovem /'ʒovẽ/ *a* young; (*criado por jovens*) youth □ *m/f* young man (*f* -woman); *pl* young people

jovi|al /ʒovi'aw/ (*pl* **~ais**) *a* jovial

juba /'ʒuba/ *f* mane

jubileu /ʒubi'lew/ *m* jubilee

júbilo /'ʒubilu/ *m* joy

ju|daico /ʒu'dajku/ *a* Jewish; **~daísmo** *m* Judaism; **~deu** *a* (*f* **~dia**) Jewish □ *m* (*f* **~dia**) Jew; **~diação** *f* ill-treatment; (*uma*) terrible thing; **~diar** *vi* **~diar de** ill-treat

judici|al /ʒudʒisi'aw/ (*pl* **~ais**) *a* judicial; **~ário** *a* judicial □ *m* judiciary; **~oso** /o/ *a* judicious

judô /ʒu'do/ *m* judo

judoca /ʒu'dɔka/ *m/f* judo player

jugo /'ʒugu/ *m* yoke

juiz /ʒu'is/ *m* (*f* **juíza**) judge; (*em jogos*) referee

juizado /ʒui'zadu/ *m* court

juízo /ʒu'izu/ *m* judgement; (*tino*) sense; (*tribunal*) court; **perder o ~** lose one's head; **ter ~** be sensible; **tomar** *ou* **criar ~** come to one's senses

jujuba /ʒu'ʒuba/ *f* (*bala*) fruit jelly

jul|gamento /ʒuwga'mẽtu/ *m* judgement; **~gar** *vt* judge; pass judgement on <*réu*>; (*imaginar*) think; **~gar-se** *vpr* consider o.s.

julho /'ʒuʎu/ *m* July

jumento /ʒu'mẽtu/ *m* donkey

junção /ʒũ'sãw/ *f* join; (*ação*) joining

junco /'ʒũku/ *m* reed

junho /'ʒuɲu/ *m* June

juni|no /ʒu'ninu/ *a* **festa ~na** St John's Day festival

júnior /'ʒunior/ *a & m* junior

jun|ta /'ʒũta/ *f* board; (*pol*) junta; **~tar** *vt* (*acrescentar*) add; (*uma coisa a outra*) join; (*uma coisa com outra*)

combine; save up <*dinheiro*>; gather up <*papéis, lixo etc*> □ *vi* gather together; **~tar-se** a join; **~to** *a* together □ *adv* together; **~to a** next to; **~to com** together with

ju|ra /'ʒura/ *f* vow; **~rado** *m* juror; **~ramentado** *a* accredited; **~ramento** *m* oath; **~rar** *vt/i* swear; **~ra?** (*fam*) really?

júri /'ʒuri/ *m* jury

jurídico /ʒu'ridʒiku/ *a* legal

juris|consulto /ʒuriskõ'suwtu/ *m* legal advisor; **~dição** *f* jurisdiction; **~prudência** *f* jurisprudence; **~ta** *m/f* jurist

juros /'ʒurus/ *m pl* interest

jus /ʒus/ *m* **fazer ~ a** live up to

jusante /ʒu'zãtʃi/ *f* **a ~** downstream

justamente /ʒusta'mẽtʃi/ *adv* exactly; (*com justiça*) fairly

justapor /ʒusta'por/ *vt* juxtapose

justi|ça /ʒus'tʃisa/ *f* (*perante a lei*) justice; (*para com outros*) fairness; (*tribunal*) court; **~ceiro** *a* fairminded □ *m* vigilante

justifi|cação /ʒustʃifika'sãw/ *f* justification; **~car** *vt* justify; **~cativa** *f* justification; **~cável** (*pl* **~cáveis**) *a* justifiable

justo /'ʒustu/ *a* fair; (*apertado*) tight □ *adv* just

juve|nil /ʒuve'niw/ (*pl* **~nis**) *a* youthful; (*para jovens*) for young people; <*time, torneio*> junior □ *m* junior championship

juventude /ʒuvẽ'tudʒi/ *f* youth

K

karaokê /karao'ke/ *m* karaoke

kart /'kartʃi/ (*pl* **~s**) *m* go-kart

ketchup /ke'tʃupi/ *m* ketchup

kit /'kitʃi/ (*pl* **~s**) *m* kit

kitchenette /kitʃe'netʃi/ *f* bedsitter

Kuwait /ku'wajtʃi/ *m* Kuwait

kuwaitiano /kuwajtʃi'anu/ *a & m* Kuwaiti

L

lá /la/ *adv* there; **até ~** <*ir*> there; <*esperar etc*> until then; **por ~** (*naquela direção*) that way; (*naquele lugar*) around there; **~ fora** outside; **sei ~** how should I know?

lã /lã/ *f* wool

labareda /laba'reda/ *f* flame

lábia /'labia/ *f* flannel; **ter ~** have the gift of the gab

lábio /'labio/ *m* lip

labirinto /labi'rĩtu/ *m* labyrinth

laboratório /labora'tɔriu/ *m* laboratory

laborioso /labori'ozu/ *a* hard-working

labu|ta /la'buta/ *f* drudgery; ~**tar** *vi* slog

laca /'laka/ *f* lacquer

laçada /la'sada/ *f* slipknot

lacaio /la'kaju/ *m* lackey

la|çar /la'sar/ *vt* lasso <*boi*>; ~**ço** *m* bow; (*de vaqueiro*) lasso; (*vínculo*) tie (de about)

lacônico /la'koniku/ *a* laconic

lacraia /la'kraja/ *f* centipede

la|crar /la'krar/ *vt* seal; ~**cre** *m* (*substância*) sealing wax; (*fechamento*) seal

lacri|mejar /lakrime'ʒar/ *vi* water; ~**mogêneo** *a* <*gás*> tear; <*filme*> tearjerking; ~**moso** /o/ *a* tearful

lácteo /'laktʃiu/ *a* milk; **Via Láctea** Milky Way

laticínio /laktʃi'siniu/ *m veja* **laticínio**

lacuna /la'kuna/ *f* gap

ladainha /lada'iɲa/ *f* litany

la|dear /ladʒi'ar/ *vt* flank; sidestep <*dificuldade*>; ~**deira** *f* slope

lado /'ladu/ *m* side; **o ~ de cá/lá** this/ that side; **ao ~ de** beside; **~ a ~** side by side; **para este ~** this way; **por outro ~** on the other hand

la|drão /la'drãw/ *m* (*f* ~**dra**) thief; (*tubo*) overflow pipe □ *a* thieving

ladrar /la'drar/ *vi* bark

ladri|lhar /ladri'ʎar/ *vt* tile; ~**lho** *m* tile

ladroagem /ladro'aʒẽ/ *f* stealing

lagar|ta /la'garta/ *f* caterpillar; (*numa roda*) caterpillar track; ~**tear** *vi* bask in the sun; ~**tixa** *f* gecko; ~**to** *m* lizard

lago /'lagu/ *m* lake

lagoa /la'goa/ *f* lagoon

lagos|ta /la'gosta/ *f* lobster; ~**tim** *m* crayfish, (*Amer*) crawfish

lágrima /'lagrima/ *f* tear

laia /'laja/ *f* kind

laico /'lajku/ *adj* <*pessoa*> lay; <*ensino*> secular

laivos /'lajvus/ *m pl* traces

laje /'laʒi/ *m* flagstone; ~**ar** *vt* pave

lajota /la'ʒota/ *f* small paving stone

lama /'lama/ *f* mud; ~**çal** (*pl* ~**çais**) *m* bog; ~**cento** *a* muddy

lamba|da /lã'bada/ *f* lambada; ~**teria** *f* lambada club

lam|ber /lã'ber/ *vt* lick; ~**bida** *f* lick

lambreta /lã'breta/ *f* moped

lambris /lã'bris/ *m pl* panelling

lambuzar /lãbu'zar/ *vt* smear; ~**-se** *vpr* get sticky

lamen|tar /lamẽ'tar/ *vt* (*lastimar*) lament; (*sentir*) be sorry; ~**tar-se de** lament; ~**tável** (*pl* ~**táveis**) *a* lamentable; ~**to** *m* lament

lâmina /'lamina/ *f* blade; (*de persiana*) slat

laminar /lami'nar/ *vt* laminate

lâmpada /'lãpada/ *f* light bulb; (*abajur*) lamp

lampe|jar /lãpe'ʒar/ *vi* flash; ~**jo** /e/ *m* flash

lampião /lãpi'ãw/ *m* lantern

lamúria /la'muria/ *f* moaning

lamuriar-se /lamuri'arsi/ *vpr* moan (de about)

lan|ça /'lãsa/ *f* spear; ~**çamento** *m* (*de navio, foguete, produto*) launch; (*de filme, disco*) release; (*novo produto*) new line; (*novo filme, disco*) release; (*novo livro*) new title; (*em livro comercial*) entry; ~**çar** *vt* (*atirar*) throw; launch <*navio, foguete, novo produto, livro*>; release <*filme, disco*>; (*em livro comercial*) enter; (*em leilão*) bid; ~**çar mão de** make use of; ~**ce** *m* (*num filme, jogo*) bit, moment; (*episódio*) episode; (*questão*) matter; (*jogada*) move; (*em leilão*) bid; (*de escada*) flight; (*de casas*) row

lancha /'lãʃa/ *f* launch

lan|char /lã'ʃar/ *vi* have a snack □ *vt* have a snack of; ~**che** *m* snack; ~**chonete** /ɛ/ *f* snack bar

lancinante /lãsi'nãtʃi/ *a* <*dor*> shooting; <*grito*> piercing

lânguido /'lãgidu/ *a* languid

lantejoula /lãte'ʒola/ *f* sequin

lanter|na /lã'terna/ *f* lantern; (*de bolso*) torch, (*Amer*) flashlight; ~**nagem** *f* panel-beating; (*oficina*) body-shop; ~**ninha** *m/f* usher (*f* usherette)

lanugem /la'nuʒẽ/ *f* down

lapela /la'pɛla/ *f* lapel

lapidar /lapi'dar/ *vt* cut <*pedra preciosa*>; (*fig*) polish

lápide /'lapidʒi/ *f* tombstone

lápis /'lapis/ *m invar* pencil

lapiseira /lapi'zera/ *f* propelling pencil; (*caixa*) pencil box

Lapônia /la'ponia/ *f* Lappland

lapso /'lapsu/ *m* lapse

la|quê /la'ke/ *m* lacquer; ~**quear** *vt* lacquer

lar /lar/ *m* home

laran|ja /la'rãʒa/ *f* orange □ *a invar* orange; ~**jada** *f* orangeade; ~**jeira** *f* orange tree

lareira /la'rera/ *f* hearth, fireplace

lar|gada /lar'gada/ *f* start; **dar a** ~**gada** start off; ~**gar** *vt* (*soltar*) let go of; give up <*estudos, emprego etc*>; ~**gar de fumar** give up smoking; ~**go** *a* wide; <*roupa*> loose □ *m* (*praça*) square; **ao** ~**go** (*no alto-mar*) out at sea; ~**gura** *f* width

larin|ge /la'rĩʒi/ *f* larynx; ~**gite** *f* laryngitis

larva /'larva/ *f* larva

lasanha /la'zaɲa/ f lasagna

las|ca /'laska/ f chip; **~car** vt/i chip; **de ~car** (fam) awful

lástima /'lastʃima/ f shame

lastro /'lastru/ m ballast

la|ta /'lata/ f (material) tin; (recipiente) tin, (Amer) can; **~ta de lixo** dustbin, (Amer) trash can; **~tão** m brass

late|jante /late'ʒãtʃi/ a throbbing; **~jar** vi throb

latente /la'tẽtʃi/ a latent

late|ral /late'raw/ (pl **~rais**) a side, lateral

laticínio /latʃi'siniu/ m dairy product

latido /la'tʃidu/ m bark

lati|fundiário /latʃifũdʒi'ariu/ a landowning □ m landowner; **~fúndio** m estate

latim /la'tʃĩ/ m Latin

latino /la'tʃinu/ a & m Latin; **~americano** a & m Latin American

latir /la'tʃir/ vi bark

latitude /latʃi'tudʒi/ f latitude

lauda /'lawda/ f side

laudo /'lawdu/ m report, findings

lava /'lava/ f lava

lava|bo /la'vabu/ m toilet; **~dora** f washing machine; **~gem** f washing; **~gem a seco** dry cleaning; **~gem cerebral** brainwashing

lavanda /la'vãda/ f lavender

lavanderia /lavãde'ria/ f laundry

lavar /la'var/ vt wash; **~ a seco** dry-clean; **~-se** vpr wash

lavatório /lava'tɔriu/ m (Port) wash-basin

lavoura /la'vora/ f (agricultura) farming; (terreno) field

lav|rador /lavra'dor/ m farmhand; **~rar** vt work; draw up <documento>

laxante /la'ʃãtʃi/ a & m laxative

lazer /la'zer/ m leisure

le|al /le'aw/ (pl **~ais**) a loyal; **~aldade** f loyalty

leão /le'ãw/ m lion; **Leão** (signo) Leo; **~-de-chácara** (pl **leões-de-chácara**) m bouncer

lebre /'lɛbri/ f hare

lecionar /lesio'nar/ vt/i teach

le|gação /lega'sãw/ f legation; **~gado** m (pessoa) legate; (herança) legacy

le|gal /le'gaw/ (pl **~gais**) a legal; (fam) good; <pessoa> nice; **tá ~gal** OK; **~galidade** f legality; **~galizar** vt legalize

legar /le'gar/ vt bequeath

legenda /le'ʒẽda/ f (de quadro) caption; (de filme) subtitle; (inscrição) inscription

legi|ão /leʒi'ãw/ f legion; **~onário** m (romano) legionary; (da legião estrangeira) legionnaire

legis|lação /leʒizla'sãw/ f legislation; **~lador** m legislator; **~lar** vi

legislate; ~lativo a legislative □ m

legislature; ~latura f legislature; **~ta** m/f legal expert

legiti|mar /leʒitʃi'mar/ vt legitimize; **~midade** f legitimacy

legítimo /le'ʒitʃimu/ a legitimate

legí|vel /le'ʒivew/ (pl **~veis**) a legible

légua /'lɛgwa/ f league

legume /le'gumi/ m vegetable

lei /lej/ f law

leigo /'lejgu/ a lay □ m layman

lei|lão /lej'lãw/ m auction; **~loar** vt auction; **~loeiro** m auctioneer

leitão /lej'tãw/ m sucking pig

lei|te /'lejtʃi/ m milk; **~te condensado/desnatado** condensed/skimmed milk; **~teira** f (jarro) milk jug; (panela) milk saucepan; **~teiro** m milkman □ a <vaca> dairy

leito /'lejtu/ m bed

leitor /lej'tor/ m reader

leitoso /lej'tozu/ a milky

leitura /lej'tura/ f (ação) reading; (material) reading matter

lema /'lema/ m motto

lem|brança /lẽ'brãsa/ f memory; (presente) souvenir; **~brar** vt/i remember; **~brar-se de** remember; **~brar aco a alg** remind s.o. of sth; **~brete** /e/ m reminder

leme /'lemi/ m rudder

len|ço /'lẽsu/ m (para o nariz) handkerchief; (para vestir) scarf; **~çol** /ɔ/ (pl **~çóis**) m sheet

len|da /'lẽda/ f legend; **~dário** a legendary

lenha /'leɲa/ f firewood; (uma) log; **~dor** m woodcutter

lente /'lẽtʃi/ f lens; **~ de contato** contact lens

lentidão /lẽtʃi'dãw/ f slowness

lentilha /lẽ'tʃiʎa/ f lentil

lento /'lẽtu/ a slow

leoa /le'oa/ f lioness

leopardo /leo'pardu/ m leopard

le|pra /'lɛpra/ f leprosy; **~proso** /o/ a leprous □ m leper

leque /'lɛki/ m fan; (fig) array

ler /ler/ vt/i read

ler|deza /ler'deza/ f sluggishness; **~do** /ɛ/ a sluggish

le|são /le'zãw/ f lesion, injury; **~sar** vt damage

lésbi|ca /'lɛzbika/ f lesbian; **~co** a lesbian

lesionar /lezio'nar/ vt injure

lesma /'lezma/ f slug

leste /'lestʃi/ m east

le|tal /le'taw/ (pl **~tais**) a lethal

le|tão /le'tãw/ a & m (f **~tã**) Latvian

letargia /letar'ʒia/ f lethargy

letivo /le'tʃivu/ a **ano ~** academic year

Letônia /le'tonia/ *f* Latvia

letra /'letra/ *f* letter; *(de música)* lyrics, words; *(caligrafia)* writing; **Letras** Modern Languages; **ao pé da ~** literally; **com todas as ~s** in no uncertain terms; **tirar de ~** take in one's stride; **~ de fôrma** block letter

letreiro /le'treru/ *m* sign

leucemia /lewse'mia/ *f* leukaemia

leva /ɛ/ *f* batch

levado /le'vadu/ *a* naughty

levan|tamento /levãta'mẽtu/ *m* *(enquete)* survey; *(rebelião)* uprising; **~tamento de pesos** weightlifting; **~tar** *vt* raise; lift *<peso>* □ *vi* get up; **~tar-se** *vpr* get up; *(revoltar-se)* rise up

levante /le'vãtʃi/ *m* east

levar /le'var/ *vt* take; lead *<vida>*; get *<tapa, susto etc>* □ *vi* lead (**a** to)

leve /'lɛvi/ *a* light; *(não grave)* slight; **de ~** lightly

levedura /leve'dura/ *f* yeast

leveza /le'veza/ *f* lightness

levi|andade /leviã'dadʒi/ *f* frivolity; **~ano** *a* frivolous

levitar /levi'tar/ *vi* levitate

lexi|cal /leksi'kaw/ *(pl ~cais) a* lexical

léxico /'lɛksiku/ *m* lexicon

lexicografia /leksikogra'fia/ *f* lexicography

lhe /ʎi/ *pron* (*a ele*) to him; (*a ela*) to her; (*a você*) to you; **~s** *pron* to them; (*a vocês*) to you

liba|nês /liba'nes/ *a & m* (*f* **~nesa**) Lebanese

Líbano /'libanu/ *m* Lebanon

libélula /li'bɛlula/ *f* dragonfly

libe|ração /libera'sãw/ *f* release; **~ral** (*pl* **~rais**) *a & m* liberal; **~ralismo** *m* liberalism; **~ralizar** *vt* liberalize; **~rar** *vt* release

liberdade /liber'dadʒi/ *f* freedom; **pôr em ~** set free; **~ condicional** probation

líbero /'liberu/ *m* sweeper

liber|tação /liberta'sãw/ *f* liberation; **~tar** *vt* free

Líbia /'libia/ *f* Libya

líbio /'libiu/ *a & m* Libyan

libi|dinoso /libidʒi'nozu/ *a* lecherous; **~do** *f* libido

li|bra /'libra/ *f* pound; **Libra** (*signo*) Libra; **~briano** *a & m* Libran

lição /li'sãw/ *f* lesson

licen|ça /li'sẽsa/ *f* leave; *(documento)* licence; **com ~ça** excuse me; **de ~ça** on leave; **sob ~ça** under licence; **~ciar** *vt* (*autorizar*) license; (*dar férias a*) give leave to; **~ciar-se** *vpr* (*tirar férias*) take leave; (*formar-se*) graduate; **~ciatura** *f* degree; **~cioso** /o/ *a* licentious

liceu /li'sew/ *m* (*Port*) secondary school, (*Amer*) high school

licor /li'kor/ *m* liqueur

lida /'lida/ *f* slog, grind; (*leitura*) read

lidar /li'dar/ *vt/i* **~ com** deal with

lide /'lidʒi/ *f* (*trabalho*) work

líder /'lider/ *m/f* leader

lide|rança /lide'rãsa/ *f* (*de partido etc*) leadership; (*em corrida, jogo etc*) lead; **~rar** *vt* lead

lido /'lidu/ *a* well-read

liga /'liga/ *f* (*aliança*) league; (*tira*) garter; (*presilha*) suspender; (*de metais*) alloy

li|gação /liga'sãw/ *f* connection; (*telefônica*) call; (*amorosa*) liaison; **~gada** *f* call, ring; **~gado** *a <luz, TV>* on; **~gado em** attached to *<pessoa>*; hooked on *<droga>*; **~gamento** *m* ligament; **~gar** *vt* join, connect; switch on *<luz, TV etc>*; start up *<carro>*; bind *<amigos>* □ *vi* ring up, call; **~gar para** (*telefonar*) ring, call; (*dar importância*) care about; (*dar atenção*) pay attention to; **~gar-se** *vpr* join

ligeiro /li'ʒeru/ *a* light; *<ferida, melhora>* slight; (*ágil*) nimble

lilás /li'las/ *m* lilac □ *a invar* mauve

lima¹ /'lima/ *f* (*ferramenta*) file

lima² /'lima/ *f* (*fruta*) sweet orange

limão /li'mãw/ *m* lime; (*amarelo*) lemon

limar /li'mar/ *vt* file

limeira /li'mera/ *f* sweet orange tree

limiar /limi'ar/ *m* threshold

limi|tação /limita'sãw/ *f* limitation; **~tar** *vt* limit; **~tar-se** *vpr* limit o.s.; **~tar(-se) com** border on; **~te** *m* limit; (*de terreno*) boundary; **passar dos ~tes** go too far; **~te de velocidade** speed limit

limo|eiro /limo'eru/ *m* lime tree; **~nada** *f* lemonade

lim|pador /lĩpa'dor/ *m* **~pador de pára-brisas** windscreen wiper; **~par** *vt* clean; wipe *<lágrimas, suor>*; (*fig*) clean up *<cidade, organização>*; **~peza** /e/ *f* (*ato*) cleaning; (*qualidade*) cleanness; (*fig*) clean-up; **~peza pública** sanitation; **~po** *a* clean; *<céu, consciência>* clear; *<lucro>* net, clear; (*fig*) pure; **passar a ~po** write up *<trabalho>*; (*fig*) sort out *<vida>*; **tirar a ~po** get to the bottom of *<caso>*

limusine /limu'zini/ *f* limousine

lince /'lĩsi/ *m* lynx

lindo /'lĩdu/ *a* beautiful

linear /lini'ar/ *a* linear

lingote /lĩ'gɔtʃi/ *m* ingot

língua /'lĩgwa/ *f* (*na boca*) tongue; (*idioma*) language; **~ materna** mother tongue

linguado /lĩ'gwadu/ *m* sole

lingua|gem /lĩ'gwaʒẽ/ *f* language; **~jar** *m* speech, dialect

lingüeta /lĩ'gweta/ *f* bolt

lingüiça /lĩ'gwisa/ *f* pork sausage

lin|güista /lĩ'gwiʃta/ *m/f* linguist; **~güística** *f* linguistics; **~güístico** *a* linguistic

linha /'liɲa/ *f* line; (*fio*) thread; **perder a ~** lose one's cool; **~ aérea** airline; **~ de fogo** firing line; **~ de montagem** assembly line; **~gem** *f* lineage

linho /'liɲu/ *m* linen; (*planta*) flax

linóleo /li'nɔliu/ *m* lino(leum)

lipoaspiração /lipoaspira'sãw/ *f* liposuction

liqui|dação /likida'sãw/ *f* liquidation; (*de loja*) clearance sale; (*de conta*) settlement; **~dar** *vt* liquidate; settle *<conta>*; pay off *<dívida>*; sell off, clear *<mercadorias>*

liqüidificador /likwidʒifika'dor/ *m* liquidizer

líqüido /'likidu/ *a* liquid; *<lucro, salário>* net □ *m* liquid

líri|ca /'lirika/ *f* (*mus*) lyrics; (*poesia*) lyric poetry; **~co** *a* lyrical; *<poesia>* lyric

lírio /'liriu/ *m* lily

Lisboa /liz'boa/ *f* Lisbon

lisboeta /lizbo'eta/ *a & m/f* (person) from Lisbon

liso /'lizu/ *a* smooth; (*sem desenho*) plain; *<cabelo>* straight; (*fam: duro*) broke

lison|ja /li'zõʒa/ *f* flattery; **~jear** *vt* flatter

lista /'lista/ *f* list; (*listra*) stripe; **~ telefônica** telephone directory

listra /'listra/ *f* stripe; **~do** *a* striped, stripey

lite|ral /lite'raw/ (*pl* **~rais**) *a* literal; **~rário** *a* literary; **~ratura** *f* literature

litígio /li'tʃiʒiu/ *m* dispute; (*jurid*) lawsuit

lito|ral /lito'raw/ (*pl* **~rais**) *m* coastline; **~râneo** *a* coastal

litro /'litru/ *m* litre

Lituânia /litu'ania/ *f* Lithuania

lituano /litu'anu/ *a & m* Lithuanian

living /'livĩ/ (*pl* **~s**) *m* living room

livrar /li'vrar/ *vt* free; (*salvar*) save; **~-se** *vpr* escape; **~-se de** get rid of

livraria /livra'ria/ *f* bookshop

livre /'livri/ *a* free; **~ de impostos** tax-free; **~-arbítrio** *m* free will

liv|reiro /li'vreru/ *m* bookseller; **~ro** *m* book; **~ro de consulta** reference book; **~ro de cozinha** cookery book; **~ro de texto** text book

li|xa /'liʃa/ *f* (*de unhas*) emery board; (*para madeira etc*) sandpaper; **~xar**

vt sand *<madeira>*; file *<unhas>*; **estou me ~xando** (*fam*) I couldn't care less

li|xeira /li'ʃera/ *f* dustbin, (*Amer*) garbage can; **~xeiro** *m* dustman, (*Amer*) garbage collector; **~xo** rubbish, (*Amer*) garbage; (*atômico*) waste

lobisomem /lobi'zomẽ/ *m* werewolf

lobo /'lobu/ *m* wolf; **~-marinho** (*pl* **~s-marinhos**) *m* sea lion

lóbulo /'lɔbulu/ *m* lobe

lo|cação /loka'sãw/ *f* (*de imóvel*) lease; (*de carro*) rental; **~cador** *m* (*de casa*) landlord; **~cadora** *f* rental company; (*de vídeos*) video shop

lo|cal /lo'kaw/ (*pl* **~cais**) *a* local □ *m* site; (*de um acidente etc*) scene; **~calidade** *f* locality; **~calização** *f* location; **~calizar** *vt* locate; **~calizar-se** *vpr* (*orientar-se*) get one's bearings

loção /lo'sãw/ *f* lotion; **~ apósbarba** aftershave lotion

locatário /loka'tariu/ *m* (*de imóvel*) tenant; (*de carro etc*) hirer

locomo|tiva /lokomo'tʃiva/ *f* locomotive; **~ver-se** *vpr* get around

locu|ção /loku'sãw/ *f* phrase; **~tor** *m* announcer

lodo /'lodu/ *m* mud; **~so** /o/ *a* muddy

logaritmo /loga'ritʃimu/ *m* logarithm

lógi|ca /'lɔʒika/ *f* logic; **~co** *a* logical

logo /'lɔgu/ *adv* (*em seguida*) straightaway; (*em breve*) soon; (*justamente*) just; **~ mais** later; **~ antes/depois** just before/straight after; **~ que** as soon as; **até ~** goodbye

logotipo /logo'tʃipu/ *m* logo

logradouro /logra'doru/ *m* public place

loiro /'lojru/ *a veja* **louro**

lo|ja /'lɔʒa/ *f* shop, (*Amer*) store; **~ja de departamentos** department store; **~ja maçônica** masonic lodge; **~jista** *m/f* shopkeeper

lom|bada /lõ'bada/ *f* (*de livro*) spine; (*na rua*) speed bump; **~binho** *m* tenderloin; **~bo** *m* back; (*carne*) loin

lona /'lona/ *f* canvas

Londres /'lõdris/ *f* London

londrino /lõ'drinu/ *a* London □ *m* Londoner

longa-metragem /lõgame'traʒẽ/ (*pl* **longas-metragens**) *m* feature film

longe /'lõʒi/ *adv* far, a long way; **de ~** from a distance; (*por muito*) by far; **~ disso** far from it

longevidade /lõʒevi'dadʒi/ *f* longevity

longínquo /lõ'ʒĩkwu/ *a* distant

longitude /lõʒi'tudʒi/ *f* longitude

longo /'lõgu/ *a* long □ *m* long dress; **ao ~ de** along; (*durante*) through, over

lontra /'lõtra/ *f* otter

lorde /'lɔrdʒi/ *m* lord

lorota /lo'rɔta/ (*fam*) *f* fib

losango /lo'zãgu/ *m* diamond

lo|tação /lota'sãw/ *f* capacity; (*ônibus*) bus; **~tação esgotada** full house; **~tado** *a* crowded; *< teatro, ônibus>* full; **~tar** *vt* fill □ *vi* fill up

lote /'lɔtʃi/ *m* (*quinhão*) portion; (*de terreno*) plot, (*Amer*) lot; (*em leilão*) lot; (*porção de coisas*) batch

loteria /lote'ria/ *f* lottery

louça /'losa/ *f* china; (*pratos etc*) crockery; **lavar a ~** wash up, (*Amer*) do the dishes

lou|co /'loku/ *a* mad, crazy □ *m* madman; **estou ~co para ir** (*fam*) I'm dying to go; **~cura** *f* madness; (*uma*) crazy thing

louro /'loru/ *a* blond □ *m* laurel; (*condimento*) bayleaf

lou|var /lo'var/ *vt* praise; **~vável** (*pl* **~váveis**) *a* praiseworthy; **~vor** /o/ *m* praise

lua /'lua/ *f* moon; **~-de-mel** *f* honeymoon

lu|ar /lu'ar/ *m* moonlight; **~arento** *a* moonlit

lubrifi|cação /lubrifika'sãw/ *f* lubrication; **~cante** *a* lubricating □ *m* lubricant; **~car** *vt* lubricate

lucidez /lusi'des/ *f* lucidity

lúcido /'lusidu/ *a* lucid

lu|crar /lu'krar/ *vt* profit (**com** by); **~cratividade** *f* profitability; **~crativo** *a* profitable, lucrative; **~cro** *m* profit

ludibriar /ludʒibri'ar/ *vt* cheat

lúdico /'ludʒiku/ *a* playful

lugar /lu'gar/ *m* place; (*espaço*) room; **em ~ de** in place of; **em primeiro ~** in the first place; **em algum ~** somewhere; **em todo ~** everywhere; **dar ~ a** give rise to; **ter ~** take place

lugarejo /luga'reʒu/ *m* village

lúgubre /'lugubri/ *a* gloomy, dismal

lula /'lula/ *f* squid

lume /'lumi/ *m* fire

luminária /lumi'naria/ *f* light, lamp; *pl* illuminations

luminoso /lumi'nozu/ *a* luminous; *< idéia>* brilliant

lunar /lu'nar/ *a* lunar □ *m* mole

lupa /'lupa/ *f* magnifying glass

lusco-fusco /lusku'fusku/ *m* twilight

lusitano /luzi'tanu/, **luso** /'luzu/ *a* & *m* Portuguese

lus|trar /lus'trar/ *vt* shine, polish; **~tre** *m* shine; (*fig*) lustre; (*luminária*) light, lamp; **~troso** /o/ *a* shiny

lu|ta /'luta/ *f* fight, struggle; **~ta livre** wrestling; **~tador** *m* fighter; (*de luta livre*) wrestler; **~tar** *vi* fight □ *vt* do *< judô etc>*

luto /'lutu/ *m* mourning

luva /'luva/ *f* glove

luxação /luʃa'sãw/ *f* dislocation

Luxemburgo /luʃẽ'burgu/ *m* Luxembourg

luxembur|guês /luʃẽbur'ges/ *a* (*f* **~guesa**) Luxemburg □ *m* (*f* **~guesa**) Luxemburger; (*língua*) Luxemburgish

luxo /'luʃu/ *m* luxury; **hotel de ~** luxury hotel; **cheio de ~** (*fam*) fussy

luxuoso /luʃu'ozu/ *a* luxurious

luxúria /lu'ʃuria/ *f* lust

luxuriante /luʃuri'ãtʃi/ *a* lush

luz /lus/ *f* light; **à ~ de** by the light of *< velas etc>*; in the light of *< fatos etc>*; **dar à ~** give birth to

luzidio /luzi'dʒio/ *a* shiny

luzir /lu'zir/ *vi* shine

M

maca /'maka/ *f* stretcher

maçã /ma'sã/ *f* apple

macabro /ma'kabru/ *a* macabre

maca|cão /maka'kãw/ *m* (*de trabalho*) overalls, (*Amer*) coveralls; (*tipo de calça*) dungarees; (*roupa inteiriça*) jumpsuit; (*para bebê*) romper suit; **~co** *m* monkey; (*aparelho*) jack

maçada /ma'sada/ *f* bore

maçaneta /masa'neta/ *f* doorknob

maçante /ma'sãtʃi/ *a* boring

macar|rão /maka'xãw/ *m* pasta; (*espaguete*) spaghetti; **~ronada** *f* pasta with tomato sauce and cheese

macarrônico /maka'xoniku/ *a* broken

macete /ma'setʃi/ *m* trick

machado /ma'ʃadu/ *m* axe

ma|chão /ma'ʃãw/ *a* tough □ *m* tough guy; **~chismo** *m* machismo; **~chista** *a* chauvinistic □ *m* male chauvinist; **~cho** *a* male; *< homem>* macho □ *m* male

machu|cado /maʃu'kadu/ *m* injury; (*na pele*) sore patch; **~car** *vt/i* hurt; **~car-se** *vpr* hurt o.s.

maciço /ma'sisu/ *a* solid; *< dose etc>* massive □ *m* massif

macieira /masi'era/ *f* apple tree

maciez /masi'es/ *f* softness

macilento /masi'lẽtu/ *a* haggard

macio /ma'siu/ *a* soft; *< carne>* tender

maço /'masu/ *m* (*de cigarros*) packet; (*de notas*) bundle

ma|çom /ma'sõ/ *m* freemason; **~çonaria** *f* freemasonry

maconha /ma'koɲa/ *f* marijuana

maçônico /ma'soniku/ *a* masonic

má-criação /makria'sãw/ *f* rudeness

macrobiótico /makrobi'ɔtʃiku/ *a* macrobiotic

macum|ba /ma'kũba/ f Afro-Brazil-ian cult; (*uma*) spell; **~beiro** m follower of macumba □ a macumba
madame /ma'dami/ f lady
Madeira /ma'dera/ f Madeira
madeira /ma'dera/ f wood □ m (*vinho*) Madeira; **~ de lei** hardwood
madeirense /made'rẽsi/ a & m Madeiran
madeixa /ma'deʃa/ f lock
madrasta /ma'drasta/ f stepmother
madrepérola /madre'pɛrola/ f mother of pearl
madressilva /madre'siwva/ f honeysuckle
Madri /ma'dri/ f Madrid
madrinha /ma'driɲa/ f (*de batismo*) godmother; (*de casamento*) bridesmaid
madru|gada /madru'gada/ f early morning; **~gador** m early riser; **~gar** vi get up early
maduro /ma'duru/ a <*fruta*> ripe; <*pessoa*> mature
mãe /mãj/ f mother; **~-de-santo** (*pl* **~s-de-santo**) f macumba priestess
maes|tria /majs'tria/ f expertise; **~tro** m conductor
máfia /'mafia/ f mafia
magazine /maga'zini/ m department store
magia /ma'ʒia/ f magic
mági|ca /'maʒika/ f magic; (*uma*) magic trick; **~co** a magic □ m magician
magis|tério /maʒis'tɛriu/ m teaching; (*professores*) teachers; **~trado** m magistrate
magnânimo /mag'nanimu/ a magnanimous
magnata /mag'nata/ m magnate
magnésio /mag'nɛziu/ m magnesium
mag|nético /mag'nɛtʃiku/ a magnetic; **~netismo** m magnetism; **~netizar** vt magnetize; (*fig*) mesmerize
mag|nificência /magnifi'sẽsia/ f magnificence; **~nífico** a magnificent
magnitude /magni'tudʒi/ f magnitude
mago /'magu/ m magician; **os reis ~s** the Three Wise Men
mágoa /'magoa/ f sorrow
magoar /mago'ar/ vt/i hurt; **~-se** vpr be hurt
ma|gricela /magri'sɛla/ a skinny; **~gro** a thin; <*leite*> skimmed; <*carne*> lean; (*fig*) meagre
maio /'maju/ m May
maiô /ma'jo/ m swimsuit
maionese /majo'nɛzi/ f mayonnaise
maior /ma'jɔr/ a bigger; <*escritor, amor etc*> greater; **o ~ carro** the biggest car; **o ~ escritor** the greatest writer; **~ de idade** of age

Maiorca /ma'jɔrka/ f Majorca
maio|ria /majo'ria/ f majority; **a ~ria dos brasileiros** most Brazilians; **~ridade** f majority, adulthood
mais /majs/ adv & pron more; **~ dois** two more; **dois dias a ~** two more days; **não trabalho ~** I don't work any more; **~ ou menos** more or less
maisena /maj'zɛna/ f cornflour, (*Amer*) cornstarch
maître /mɛtr/ m head waiter
maiúscula /ma'juskula/ f capital letter
majes|tade /maʒes'tadʒi/ f majesty; **~toso** a majestic
major /ma'ʒɔr/ m major
majoritário /maʒori'tariu/ a majority
mal /maw/ adv badly; (*quase não*) hardly □ conj hardly □ m evil; (*doença*) sickness; **não faz ~** never mind; **levar a ~** take offence at; **passar ~** be sick
mala /'mala/ f suitcase; (*do carro*) boot, (*Amer*) trunk; **~ aérea** air courier
malabaris|mo /malaba'rizmu/ m juggling act; **~ta** m/f juggler
malagradecido /malagrade'sidu/ a ungrateful
malagueta /mala'geta/ f chilli pepper
malaio /ma'laju/ a & m Malay
Malaísia /mala'izia/ f Malaysia
malaísio /mala'iziu/ a & m Malaysian
malan|dragem /malã'draʒẽ/ f hustling; (*uma*) clever trick; **~dro** a cunning □ m hustler
malária /ma'laria/ f malaria
mal-assombrado /malasõ'bradu/ a haunted
Malavi /mala'vi/ m Malawi
malcriado /mawkri'adu/ a rude
mal|dade /maw'dadʒi/ f wickedness; (*uma*) wicked thing; **por ~dade** out of spite; **~dição** f curse; **~dito** a cursed, damned; **~doso** /o/ a wicked
maleá|vel /mali'avew/ (*pl* **~veis**) a malleable
maledicência /maledi'sẽsia/ f malicious gossip
maléfico /ma'lɛfiku/ a evil; (*prejudicial*) harmful
mal-encarado /malĩka'radu/ a shady, dubious □ m shady character
mal-entendido /malĩtẽ'dʒidu/ m misunderstanding
mal-estar /malis'tar/ m (*doença*) ailment; (*constrangimento*) discomfort
maleta /ma'leta/ f overnight bag
malévolo /ma'lɛvolu/ a malevolent
malfei|to /maw'fejtu/ a badly done; <*roupa etc*> badly made; (*fig*) wrongful; **~tor** m wrongdoer; **~toria** f wrongdoing

ma|lha /'maʎa/ f (*ponto*) stitch; (*tricô*) in charge; ~**dão** a (f ~**dona**) bossy; knitting; (*tecido*) jersey; (*casaco*) jumper, (*Amer*) sweater; (*para ginástica*) leotard; (*de rede*) mesh; **fazer** ~**lha** knit; ~**lhado** a <*animal*> dappled; <*roque*> heavy; ~**lhar** vt beat; thresh <*trigo etc*> □ vi (*fam*) work out

mal-humorado /malumo'radu/ a in a bad mood, grumpy

malícia /ma'lisia/ f (*má índole*) malice; (*astúcia*) guile; (*humor*) innuendo

malicioso /malisi'ozu/ a (*mau*) malicious; (*astuto*) crafty; (*que põe malícia*) dirty-minded

maligno /ma'liginu/ a malignant

malmequer /mawme'ker/ m marigold

maloca /ma'lɔka/ f Indian village

malo|grar-se /malo'grarsi/ vpr go wrong, fail; ~**gro** /o/ m failure

mal-passado /mawpa'sadu/ a <*carne*> rare

Malta /'mawta/ f Malta

malte /'mawtʃi/ m malt

maltrapilho /mawtra'piʎu/ a scruffy

maltratar /mawtra'tar/ vt ill-treat, mistreat

malu|co /ma'luku/ a mad, crazy □ m madman; ~**quice** f madness; (*uma*) crazy thing

malvado /maw'vadu/ a wicked

malver|sação /mawversa'sãw/ f mismanagement; (*de fundos*) misappropriation; ~**sar** vt mismanage; misappropriate <*dinheiro*>

Malvinas /maw'vinas/ f pl Falklands

mamadeira /mama'dera/ f (baby's) bottle

mamãe /ma'mãj/ f mum

mamão /ma'mãw/ m papaya

ma|mar /ma'mar/ vi suckle; ~**mata** f (*fam*) fiddle

mamífero /ma'miferu/ m mammal

mamilo /ma'milu/ m nipple

mamoeiro /mamo'eru/ m papaya tree

manada /ma'nada/ f herd

mananci|al /manãsi'aw/ (pl ~**ais**) m spring; (*fig*) rich source

man|cada /mã'kada/ f blunder; ~**car** vi limp; ~**car-se** vpr (*fam*) take the hint, get the message

Mancha /'mãʃa/ f **o canal da** ~ the English Channel

man|cha /'mãʃa/ f stain; (*na pele*) mark; ~**char** vt stain

manchete /mã'ʃetʃi/ f headline

manco /'mãku/ a lame □ m cripple

mandachuva /mãda'ʃuva/ m (*fam*) bigwig; (*chefe*) boss

man|dado /mã'dadu/ m order; ~**dado de busca** search warrant; ~**dado de prisão** arrest warrant; ~**damento** m commandment; ~**dante** m/f person

dizer send word; ~**dar alg ir** tell s.o. to go; ~**dar ver** (*fam*) go to town; ~**dar em alg** order s.o. about; ~**dato** m mandate

mandíbula /mã'dʒibula/ f (lower) jaw

mandioca /mãdʒi'ɔka/ f manioc

maneira /ma'nera/ f way; pl (*boas*) manners; **desta** ~ in this way; **de qualquer** ~ anyway

mane|jar /mane'ʒar/ vt handle; operate <*máquina*>; ~**jável** (pl ~**jáveis**) a manageable; ~**jo** /e/ m handling

manequim /mane'kĩ/ m (*boneco*) dummy; (*medida*) size □ m/f mannequin, model

maneta /ma'neta/ a one-armed □ m/f person with one arm

manga¹ /'mãga/ f (*de roupa*) sleeve

manga² /'mãga/ f (*fruta*) mango

manganês /mãga'nes/ m manganese

mangue /'mãgi/ m mangrove swamp

mangueira¹ /mã'gera/ f (*tubo*) hose

mangueira² /mã'gera/ f (*árvore*) mango tree

manha /'maɲa/ f tantrum

manhã /ma'ɲã/ f morning; **de** ~ in the morning

manhoso /ma'ɲozu/ a wilful

mania /ma'nia/ f (*moda*) craze; (*doença*) mania

maníaco /ma'niaku/ a manic □ m maniac; ~**depressivo** a & m manic depressive

manicômio /mani'komiu/ m lunatic asylum

manicura /mani'kura/ f manicure; (*pessoa*) manicurist

manifes|tação /manifesta'sãw/ f manifestation; (*passeata*) demonstration; ~**tante** m/f demonstrator; ~**tar** vt manifest, demonstrate; ~**tar-se** vpr (*revelar-se*) manifest o.s.; (*exprimir-se*) express an opinion; ~**to** /ɛ/ a manifest, clear □ m manifesto

manipular /manipu'lar/ vt manipulate

manjedoura /mãʒe'dora/ f manger

manjericão /mãʒeri'kãw/ m basil

mano|bra /ma'nɔbra/ f manoeuvre; ~**brar** vt manoeuvre; ~**brista** m/f parking valet

mansão /mã'sãw/ f mansion

man|sidão /mãsi'dãw/ f gentleness; (*do mar*) calm; ~**sinho** adv **de** ~**sinho** (*devagar*) slowly; (*de leve*) gently; (*de fininho*) stealthily; ~**so** a gentle; <*mar*> calm; <*animal*> tame

manta /'mãta/ f blanket; (*casaco*) cloak

mantei|ga /mã'tejga/ f butter; ~**gueira** f butter dish

manter /mã'ter/ vt keep; ~**-se** vpr keep; (sustentar-se) keep o.s.

mantimentos /mãtʃi'mẽtus/ m pl provisions

manto /'mãtu/ m mantle

manu|al /manu'aw/ (pl ~**ais**) a & m manual; ~**fatura** f manufacture; (fábrica) factory; ~**faturar** vt manufacture

manuscrito /manus'kritu/ a hand-written □ m manuscript

manu|sear /manuzi'ar/ vt handle; ~**seio** m handling

manutenção /manutẽ'sãw/ f maintenance; (de prédio) upkeep

mão /mãw/ (pl ~**s**) f hand; (do trânsito) direction; (de tinta) coat; **abrir** ~ **de** give up; **agüentar a** ~ hang on; **dar a** ~ **a alg** hold s.o.'s hand; (cumprimentando) shake s.o.'s hand; **deixar alg na** ~ let s.o. down; **enfiar ou meter a** ~ **em** hit, slap; **lançar** ~ **de** make use of; **escrito à** ~ written by hand; **ter à** ~ have to hand; **de** ~**s dadas** hand in hand; **em segunda** ~ second-hand; **fora de** ~ out of the way; ~ **única** one way; ~**-de-obra** f labour

mapa /'mapa/ m map

maquete /ma'kɛtʃi/ f model

maqui|agem /maki'aʒẽ/ f make-up; ~**ar** vt make up; ~**ar-se** vpr put on make-up

maquiavélico /makia'vɛliku/ a Machiavellian

maqui|lagem, ~lar, (Port) ~**lhagem, ~lhar** veja **maqui|agem, ~ar**

máquina /'makina/ f machine; (ferroviária) engine; **escrever à** ~ type; ~ **de costura** sewing machine; ~ **de escrever** typewriter; ~ **de lavar (roupa)** washing machine; ~ **de lavar pratos** dishwasher; ~ **fotográfica** camera

maqui|nação /makina'sãw/ f machination; ~**nal** (pl ~**nais**) a mechanical; ~**nar** vt/i plot; ~**naria** f machinery; ~**nista** m/f (ferroviário) engine driver; (de navio) engineer

mar /mar/ m sea

maracu|já /maraku'ʒa/ m passion fruit; ~**jazeiro** m passion-fruit plant

marasmo /ma'razmu/ f stagnation

marato|na /mara'tona/ f marathon; ~**nista** m/f marathon runner

maravi|lha /mara'viʎa/ f marvel; **às mil ~lhas** wonderfully; ~**lhar** vt amaze; ~**lhar-se** vpr marvel (**de** at); ~**lhoso** /o/ a marvellous

mar|ca /'marka/ f (sinal) mark; (de carro, máquina) make; (de cigarro, sabão etc) brand; ~**ca registrada** regis-

tered trademark; ~**cação** f marking; (Port: discagem) dialling; ~**cador** m marker; (em livro) bookmark; (placar) scoreboard; (jogador) scorer; ~**cante** a outstanding; ~**capasso** m pacemaker; ~**car** vt mark; arrange <hora, encontro, jantar etc>; score <gol, ponto>; (Port: discar) dial; <relógio, termômetro> show; brand <gado>; (observar) keep a close eye on; (impressionar) leave one's mark on □ vi make one's mark; ~**car época** make history; ~**car hora** make an appointment; ~**car o compasso** beat time; ~**car os pontos** keep the score

marce|naria /marsena'ria/ f cabinet-making; (oficina) cabinet maker's workshop; ~**neiro** m cabinet maker

mar|cha /'marʃa/ f march; (de carro) gear; **pôr-se em** ~**cha** get going; ~**cha à ré,** (Port) ~**cha atrás** reverse; ~**char** vi march

marci|al /marsi'aw/ (pl ~**ais**) a martial; ~**ano** a & m Martian

marco¹ /'marku/ m (sinal) landmark

marco² /'marku/ m (moeda) mark

março /'marsu/ m March

maré /ma'rɛ/ f tide

mare|chal /mare'ʃaw/ (pl ~**chais**) m marshal

maresia /mare'zia/ f smell of the sea

marfim /mar'fĩ/ m ivory

margarida /marga'rida/ f daisy; (para impressora) daisywheel

margarina /marga'rina/ f margarine

mar|gem /'marʒẽ/ f (de rio) bank; (de lago) shore; (parte em branco, fig) margin; ~**ginal** (pl ~**ginais**) a marginal; (delinqüente) delinquent □ m/f delinquent □ f (rua) riverside road; ~**ginalidade** f delinquency; ~**ginalizar** vt marginalize

marido /ma'ridu/ m husband

marimbondo /marĩ'bõdu/ m hornet

marina /ma'rina/ f marina

mari|nha /ma'rina/ f navy; ~**nha mercante** merchant navy; ~**nheiro** m sailor; ~**nho** a marine

marionete /mario'nɛtʃi/ f puppet

mariposa /mari'poza/ f moth

mariscos /ma'riskus/ m seafood

mari|tal /mari'taw/ (pl ~**tais**) a marital

marítimo /ma'ritʃimu/ a sea; <cidade> seaside

marmanjo /mar'mãʒu/ m grown-up

marme|lada /marme'lada/ f (fam) fix; ~**lo** /ɛ/ m quince

marmita /mar'mita/ f (de soldado) mess tin; (de trabalhador) lunchbox

mármore /'marmori/ m marble

marmóreo /mar'mɔriu/ a marble

marquise /mar'kizi/ f awning

marreco /ma'xɛku/ m wild duck

Marrocos /ma'xɔkus/ *m* Morocco

marrom /ma'xõ/ *a* & *m* brown

marroquino /maxo'kinu/ *a* & *m* Moroccan

Marte /'martʃi/ *m* Mars

marte|lada /marte'lada/ *f* hammer blow; ~**lar** *vt/i* hammer; ~**lar em** (*fig*) go on and on about; ~**lo** /ɛ/ *m* hammer

mártir /'martʃir/ *m/f* martyr

mar|tírio /mar'tʃiriu/ *m* martyrdom; (*fig*) torture; ~**tirizar** *vt* martyr; (*fig*) torture

marujo /ma'ruʒu/ *m* sailor

mar|xismo /mark'sizmu/ *m* Marxism; ~**xista** *a* & *m/f* Marxist

mas /mas/ *conj* but

mascar /mas'kar/ *vt* chew

máscara /'maskara/ *f* mask; (*tratamento facial*) face-pack

mascarar /maska'rar/ *vt* mask

mascate /mas'katʃi/ *m* street vendor

mascavo /mas'kavu/ *a* **açúcar** ~ brown sugar

mascote /mas'kɔtʃi/ *f* mascot

masculino /masku'linu/ *a* male; (*para homens*) men's; <*palavra*> masculine □ *m* masculine

másculo /'maskulu/ *a* masculine

masmorra /maz'moxa/ *f* dungeon

masoquis|mo /mazo'kizmu/ *m* masochism; ~**ta** *m/f* masochist □ *a* masochistic

massa /'masa/ *f* mass; (*de pão*) dough; (*de torta, empada*) pastry; (*macarrão etc*) pasta; **cultura de** ~ mass culture; **em** ~ en masse; **as** ~**s** the masses

massa|crante /masa'krãtʃi/ *a* gruelling; ~**crar** *vt* massacre; (*fig: maçar*) wear out; ~**cre** *m* massacre

massa|gear /masaʒi'ar/ *vt* massage; ~**gem** *f* massage; ~**gista** *m/f* masseur (*f* masseuse)

mastigar /mastʃi'gar/ *vt* chew; (*ponderar*) chew over

mastro /'mastru/ *m* mast; (*de bandeira*) flagpole

mastur|bação /masturba'sãw/ *f* masturbation; ~**bar-se** *vpr* masturbate

mata /'mata/ *f* forest

mata-borrão /matabo'xãw/ *m* blotting paper

matadouro /mata'doru/ *m* slaughterhouse

mata|gal /mata'gaw/ (*pl* ~**gais**) *m* thicket

mata-moscas /mata'moskas/ *m invar* fly spray

ma|tança /ma'tãsa/ *f* slaughter; ~**tar** *vt* kill; satisfy <*fome*>; quench <*sede*>; guess <*charada*>; (*fazer nas coxas*) dash off; (*fam*) skive off <*aula, serviço*> □ *vi* kill

mata-ratos /mata'xatus/ *m invar* rat poison

mate[1] /'matʃi/ *m* (*chá*) maté

mate[2] /'matʃi/ *a invar* matt

matemáti|ca /mate'matʃika/ *f* mathematics; ~**co** *a* mathematical □ *m* mathematician

matéria /ma'tɛria/ *f* (*assunto, disciplina*) subject; (*no jornal*) article; (*substância*) matter; (*usada para fazer algo*) material; **em** ~ **de** in the way of

materi|al /materi'aw/ (*pl* ~**ais**) *a* materials □ *a* material; ~**alismo** *m* materialism; ~**alista** *a* materialistic □ *m/f* materialist; ~**alizar-se** *vpr* materialize

matéria-prima /matɛria'prima/ (*pl* **matérias-primas**) *f* raw material

mater|nal /mater'naw/ (*pl* ~**nais**) *a* maternal; ~**nidade** *f* maternity; (*clínica*) maternity hospital; ~**no** /ɛ/ *a* maternal; **língua** ~**na** mother tongue

mati|nal /matʃi'naw/ (*pl* ~**nais**) *a* morning; ~**nê** *f* matinée

matiz /ma'tʃis/ *m* shade; (*político*) colouring; (*pontinha: de ironia etc*) tinge

matizar /matʃi'zar/ *vt* tinge (**de** with)

mato /'matu/ *m* scrubland, bush

matraca /ma'traka/ *f* rattle; (*tagarela*) chatterbox

matreiro /ma'treru/ *a* cunning

matriar|ca /matri'arka/ *f* matriarch; ~**cal** (*pl* ~**cais**) *a* matriarchal

matrícula /ma'trikula/ *f* enrolment; (*taxa*) enrolment fee; (*Port: de carro*) number plate, (*Amer*) license plate

matricular /matriku'lar/ *vt* enrol; ~**se** *vpr* enrol

matri|monial /matrimoni'aw/ (*pl* ~**moniais**) *a* marriage; ~**mônio** *m* marriage

matriz /ma'tris/ *f* matrix; (*útero*) womb; (*sede*) head office

maturidade /maturi'dadʒi/ *f* maturity

matutino /matu'tʃinu/ *a* morning □ *m* morning paper

matuto /ma'tutu/ *a* countrified □ *m* country bumpkin

mau /maw/ *a* (*f* **má**) bad; ~**-caráter** *m invar* bad lot □ *a invar* no-good; ~**olhado** *m* evil eye

mausoléu /mawzo'lɛw/ *m* mausoleum

maus-tratos /maws'tratus/ *m pl* ill-treatment

maxilar /maksi'lar/ *m* jaw

máxima /'masima/ *f* maxim

maximizar /masimi'zar/ *vt* maximize; (*exagerar*) play up

máximo /'masimu/ *a* (*antes do substantivo*) utmost, greatest; (*depois do substantivo*) maximum □ *m* maximum; **o** ~ (*fam: o melhor*) really something; **ao** ~ to the maximum; **no** ~ at most

maxixe /maˈʃiʃi/ *m* gherkin

me /mi/ *pron* me; (*indireto*) (to) me; (*reflexivo*) myself

meada /miˈada/ *f* skein; **perder o fio da** ~ lose one's thread

meados /miˈadus/ *m pl* ~ **de maio** mid-May

meandro /miˈãdru/ *f* meander; *pl* (*fig*) twists and turns

mecâni|ca /meˈkanika/ *f* mechanics; ~**co** *a* mechanical □ *m* mechanic

meca|nismo /mekaˈnizmu/ *m* mechanism; ~**nizar** *vt* mechanize

mecenas /meˈsɛnas/ *m invar* patron

mecha /ˈmɛʃa/ *f* (*de vela*) wick; (*de bomba*) fuse; (*porção de cabelos*) lock; (*cabelo tingido*) highlight; ~**do** *a* highlighted

meda|lha /meˈdaʎa/ *f* medal; ~**lhão** *m* medallion; (*jóia*) locket

média /ˈmɛdʒia/ *f* average; (*café*) white coffee; **em** ~ on average

medi|ação /medʒiaˈsãw/ *f* mediation; ~**ador** *m* mediator; ~**ante** *prep* through, by; ~**ar** *vi* mediate

medica|ção /medʒikaˈsãw/ *f* medication; ~**mento** *m* medicine

medição /medʒiˈsãw/ *f* measurement

medicar /medʒiˈkar/ *vt* treat □ *vi* practise medicine; ~**-se** *vpr* dose o.s. up

medici|na /medʒiˈsina/ *f* medicine; ~**na legal** forensic medicine; ~**nal** (*pl* ~**nais**) *a* medicinal

médico /ˈmɛdʒiku/ *m* doctor □ *a* medical; ~**-legal** (*pl* ~**-legais**) *a* forensic; ~**-legista** (*pl* ~**s-legistas**) *m/f* forensic scientist

medi|da /meˈdʒida/ *f* measure; (*dimensão*) measurement; **à** ~**da que** as; **sob** ~**da** made to measure; **tirar as** ~**das de alg** take s.o.'s measurements; ~**dor** *m* meter

medie|val /medʒieˈvaw/ (*pl* ~**vais**) *a* medieval

médio /ˈmɛdʒiu/ *a* (*típico*) average; <*tamanho, prazo*> medium; <*classe, dedo*> middle

medíocre /meˈdʒiokri/ *a* mediocre

mediocridade /medʒiokriˈdadʒi/ *f* mediocrity

medir /meˈdʒir/ *vt* measure; weigh <*palavras*> □ *vi* measure; ~**-se** *vpr* measure o.s.; **quanto você mede?** how tall are you?

medi|tação /medʒitaˈsãw/ *f* meditation; ~**tar** *vi* meditate

mediterrâneo /medʒiteˈxaniu/ *a* Mediterranean □ *m* **o Mediterrâneo** the Mediterranean

médium /ˈmɛdʒiũ/ *m/f* medium

medo /ˈmedu/ *m* fear; **ter** ~ **de** be

afraid of; **com** ~ afraid; ~**nho** /o/ *a* frightful

medroso /meˈdrozu/ *a* fearful, timid

medula /meˈdula/ *f* marrow

megalomania /megalomaˈnia/ *f* megalomania

meia /ˈmeja/ *f* (*comprida*) stocking; (*curta*) sock; (*seis*) six; ~**-calça** (*pl* ~**s-calças**) *f* tights, (*Amer*) pantihose; ~**-idade** *f* middle age; ~**-noite** *f* midnight; ~**-volta** (*pl* ~**s-voltas**) *f* about-turn

mei|go /ˈmejgu/ *a* sweet; ~**guice** *f* sweetness

meio /ˈmeju/ *a* half □ *adv* rather □ *m* (*centro*) middle; (*ambiente*) environment; (*recurso*) means; ~ **litro** half a litre; **dois meses e** ~ two and a half months; **em** ~ **a** amid; **por** ~ **de** through; **o** ~ **ambiente** the environment; **os** ~**s de comunicação** the media; ~**-dia** *m* midday; ~**-fio** *m* kerb; ~**-termo** *m* (*acordo*) compromise

mel /mɛw/ *m* honey

mela|ço /meˈlasu/ *m* molasses; ~**do** *a* sticky □ *m* treacle

melancia /melãˈsia/ *f* watermelon

melan|colia /melãkoˈlia/ *f* melancholy; ~**cólico** *a* melancholy

melão /meˈlãw/ *m* melon

melar /meˈlar/ *vt* make sticky

melhor /meˈʎɔr/ *a* & *adv* better; **o** ~ the best

melho|ra /meˈʎɔra/ *f* improvement; ~**ras!** get well soon!; ~**ramento** *m* improvement; ~**rar** *vt* improve □ *vi* improve; <*doente*> get better

melin|drar /melĩˈdrar/ *vt* hurt; ~**drar-se** *vpr* be hurt; ~**droso** /o/ *a* delicate; <*pessoa*> sensitive

melodi|a /meloˈdʒia/ *f* melody; ~**oso** /o/ *a* melodious

melodra|ma /meloˈdrama/ *m* melodrama; ~**mático** *a* melodramatic

meloso /meˈlozu/ *a* sickly sweet

melro /ˈmɛwxu/ *m* blackbird

membrana /mẽˈbrana/ *f* membrane

membro /ˈmẽbru/ *m* member; (*braço, perna*) limb

memo|rando /memoˈrãdu/ *m* memo; ~**rável** (*pl* ~**ráveis**) *a* memorable

memória /meˈmɔria/ *f* memory; *pl* (*autobiografia*) memoirs

men|ção /mẽˈsãw/ *f* mention; **fazer** ~**ção de** mention; ~**cionar** *vt* mention

mendi|cância /mẽdʒiˈkãsia/ *f* begging; ~**gar** *vi* beg; ~**go** *m* beggar

menina /meˈnina/ *f* girl; **a** ~ **dos olhos de alg** the apple of s.o.'s eye

meningite /menĩˈʒitʃi/ *f* meningitis

meni|nice /meniˈnisi/ *f* (*idade*) childhood; ~**no** *m* boy

menopausa /meno'pawza/ f menopause

menor /me'nɔr/ a smaller ▫ m/f minor; **o/a** ~ the smallest; (*mínimo*) the slightest, the least

menos /'menos/ adv & pron less ▫ prep except; **dois dias a** ~ two days less; **a** ~ **que** unless; **ao** *ou* **pelo** ~ at least; **o** ~ **bonito** the least pretty; ~**prezar** vt look down upon; ~**prezo** /e/ m disdain

mensa|geiro /mẽsa'ʒeru/ m messenger; ~**gem** f message

men|sal /mẽ'saw/ (pl ~**sais**) a monthly; ~**salidade** f monthly payment; ~**salmente** adv monthly

menstru|ação /mẽstrua'sãw/ f menstruation; ~**ada** a **estar** ~**ada** be having one's period; ~**al** (pl ~**ais**) a menstrual; ~**ar** vi menstruate

menta /'mẽta/ f mint

men|tal /mẽ'taw/ (pl ~**tais**) a mental; ~**talidade** f mentality; ~**te** f mind

men|tir /mẽ'tʃir/ vi lie; ~**tira** f lie; ~**tiroso** /o/ a lying ▫ m liar

mentor /mẽ'tor/ m mentor

mercado /mer'kadu/ m market; ~**ria** f commodity; pl goods

mercan|te /mer'kãtʃi/ a merchant; ~**til** (pl ~**tis**) a mercantile; ~**tilismo** m commercialism

mercê /mer'se/ f **à** ~ **de** at the mercy of

merce|aria /mersia'ria/ f grocer's; ~**eiro** m grocer

mercenário /merse'nariu/ a & m mercenary

mercúrio /mer'kuriu/ m mercury; **Mercúrio** Mercury

merda /'mɛrda/ f (*chulo*) shit

mere|cedor /merese'dor/ a deserving; ~**cer** vt deserve ▫ vi be deserving; ~**cimento** m merit

merenda /me'rẽda/ f packed lunch; ~ **escolar** school dinner

mere|trício /mere'trisiu/ m prostitution; ~**triz** f prostitute

mergu|lhador /merguʎa'dor/ m diver; ~**lhar** vt dip (em into) ▫ vi (*na água*) dive; (*no trabalho*) bury o.s.; ~**lho** m dive; (*esporte*) diving; (*banho de mar*) dip

meridi|ano /meridʒi'anu/ m meridian; ~**onal** (pl ~**onais**) a southern

mérito /'mɛritu/ m merit

merluza /mer'luza/ f hake

mero /'mɛru/ a mere

mês /mes/ (pl **meses**) m month

mesa /'meza/ f table; (*de trabalho*) desk; ~ **de centro** coffee table; ~ **de jantar** dining table; ~ **telefônica** switchboard

mesada /me'zada/ f monthly allowance

mescla /'mɛskla/ f mixture, blend

mesmice /mez'misi/ f sameness

mesmo /'mezmu/ a same ▫ adv (*até*) even; (*justamente*) right; (*de verdade*) really; **você** ~ you yourself; **hoje** ~ this very day; ~ **assim** even so; ~ **que** even if; **dá no** ~ it comes to the same thing; **fiquei na mesma** I'm none the wiser

mesqui|nharia /meskiɲa'ria/ f meanness; (*uma*) mean thing; ~**nho** a mean

mesquita /mes'kita/ f mosque

Messias /me'sias/ m Messiah

mesti|çagem /mestʃi'saʒẽ/ f interbreeding; ~**ço** a <*pessoa*> of mixed race; <*animal*> crossbred ▫ m (*pessoa*) person of mixed race; (*animal*) mongrel

mes|trado /mes'tradu/ m master's degree; ~**tre** /ɛ/ m (f ~**tra**) master (f mistress); (*de escola*) teacher ▫ a main; <*chave*> master; ~**tre-de-obras** (pl ~**tres-de-obras**) m foreman; ~**tre-sala** (pl ~**tres-salas**) m master of ceremonies (*in carnival procession*); ~**tria** f expertise

meta /'mɛta/ f (*de corrida*) finishing post; (*gol, fig*) goal

meta|bólico /meta'bɔliku/ a metabolic; ~**bolismo** m metabolism

metade /me'tadʒi/ f half; **pela** ~ halfway

metafísi|ca /meta'fizika/ f metaphysics; ~**co** a metaphysical

metáfora /me'tafora/ f metaphor

metafórico /meta'fɔriku/ a metaphorical

me|tal /me'taw/ (pl ~**tais**) m metal; pl (*numa orquestra*) brass; ~**tálico** a metallic

meta|lurgia /metalur'ʒia/ f metallurgy; ~**lúrgica** f metal works; ~**lúrgico** a metallurgical ▫ m metalworker

metamorfose /metamor'fɔzi/ f metamorphosis

metano /me'tanu/ m methane

meteórico /mete'ɔriku/ a meteoric

meteoro /mete'ɔru/ m meteor; ~**logia** f meteorology; ~**lógico** a meteorological; ~**logista** m/f (*cientista*) meteorologist; (*na TV*) weather forecaster

meter /me'ter/ vt put; ~-**se** vpr (*envolver-se*) get (em into); (*intrometer-se*) meddle (em in); ~ **medo** be frightening

meticuloso /metʃiku'lozu/ a meticulous

metido /me'tʃidu/ a snobbish; **ele é** ~ **a perito** he thinks he's an expert

metódico /me'tɔdʒiku/ a methodical

metodista /meto'dʒista/ a & m/f Methodist

método /'mɛtodu/ *m* method

metra|lhadora /metra'ʎa'dora/ *f* machine gun; **~lhar** *vt* machine-gun

métri|co /'mɛtriku/ *a* metric; **fita ~ca** tape measure

metro¹ /'mɛtru/ *m* metre

metro² /'mɛtru/ *m* (*Port: metropolitano*) underground, (*Amer*) subway

metrô /me'tro/ *m* underground, (*Amer*) subway

metrópole /me'trɔpoli/ *f* metropolis

metropolitano /metropoli'tanu/ *a* metropolitan □ *m* (*Port*) underground, (*Amer*) subway

meu /mew/ *a* (*f* **minha**) my □ *pron* (*f* **minha**) mine; **um amigo ~** a friend of mine; **fico na minha** (*fam*) I keep myself to myself

mexer /me'ʃer/ *vt* move; (*com colher etc*) stir □ *vi* move; **~se** *vpr* move; (*apressar-se*) get a move on; **~ com** (*comover*) affect, get to; (*brincar com*) tease; (*trabalhar com*) work with; **~ em** touch

mexeri|ca /meʃe'rika/ *f* tangerine; **~car** *vi* gossip; **~co** *m* piece of gossip; *pl* gossip; **~queiro** *a* gossiping □ *m* gossip

mexicano /meʃi'kanu/ *a* & *m* Mexican

México /'mɛʃiku/ *m* Mexico

mexido /me'ʃidu/ *a* **ovos ~s** scrambled eggs

mexilhão /meʃi'ʎãw/ *m* mussel

mi|ado /mi'adu/ *m* miaow; **~ar** *vi* miaow

micróbio /mi'krɔbiu/ *m* microbe

micro|cosmo /mikro'kozmu/ *m* microcosm; **~empresa** /e/ *f* small business; **~empresário** *m* small businessman; **~filme** *m* microfilm; **~fone** *m* microphone; **~onda** *f* microwave; (**forno de**) **~s** *m* microwave (oven); **~ônibus** *m invar* minibus; **~processador** *m* microprocessor

microrganismo /mikrorga'nizmu/ *m* microorganism

microscó|pico /mikros'kɔpiku/ *a* microscopic; **~pio** *m* microscope

mídia /'midʒia/ *f* media

migalha /mi'gaʎa/ *f* crumb

mi|gração /migra'sãw/ *f* migration; **~grar** *vi* migrate; **~gratório** *a* migratory

mi|jar /mi'ʒar/ *vi* (*fam*) pee; **~jar-se** *vpr* wet o.s.; **~jo** *m* (*fam*) pee

mil /miw/ *a* & *m invar* thousand; **estar a ~** be on top form

mila|gre /mi'lagri/ *m* miracle; **~groso** /o/ *a* miraculous

milênio /mi'leniu/ *m* millennium

milésimo /mi'lɛzimu/ *a* thousandth

milha /'miʎa/ *f* mile

milhão /mi'ʎãw/ *m* million; **um ~ de dólares** a million dollars

milhar /mi'ʎar/ *m* thousand; **~es de vezes** thousands of times; **aos ~es** in their thousands

milho /'miʎo/ *m* maize, (*Amer*) corn

milico /mi'liku/ *m* (*fam*) military man; **os ~s** the military

mili|grama /mili'grama/ *m* milligram; **~litro** *m* millilitre; **~metro** /e/ *m* millimetre

milionário /milio'nariu/ *a* & *m* millionaire

mili|tante /mili'tãtʃi/ *a* & *m* militant; **~tar** *a* military □ *m* soldier

mim /mĩ/ *pron* me

mimar /mi'mar/ *vt* spoil

mímica /'mimika/ *f* mime; (*brincadeira*) charades

mi|na /'mina/ *f* mine; **~nar** *vt* mine; (*fig: prejudicar*) undermine

mindinho /mĩ'dʒiɲu/ *m* little finger, (*Amer*) pinkie

mineiro /mi'neru/ *a* mining; (*de MG*) from Minas Gerais □ *m* miner; (*de MG*) person from Minas Gerais

mine|ração /minera'sãw/ *f* mining; **~ral** (*pl* **~rais**) *a* & *m* mineral; **~rar** *vt/i* mine

minério /mi'neriu/ *m* ore

mingau /mĩ'gaw/ *m* porridge

mingua /'mĩgwa/ *f* lack

minguante /mĩ'gwãtʃi/ *a* **quarto ~** last quarter

minguar /mĩ'gwar/ *vi* dwindle

minha /'miɲa/ *a* & *pron veja* **meu**

minhoca /mi'ɲɔka/ *f* worm

miniatura /minia'tura/ *f* miniature

mini|malista /minima'lista/ *a* & *m/f* minimalist; **~mizar** *vt* minimize; (*subestimar*) play down

mínimo /'minimu/ *a* (*muito pequeno*) tiny; (*mais baixo*) minimum □ *m* minimum; **a mínima idéia** the slightest idea; **no ~** at least

minissaia /mini'saja/ *f* miniskirt

minis|terial /ministeri'aw/ (*pl* **~teriais**) *a* ministerial; **~tério** *m* ministry; **Ministério do Interior** Home Office, (*Amer*) Department of the Interior

minis|trar /minis'trar/ *vt* administer; **~tro** *m* minister; **primeiro ~tro** prime minister

Minorca /mi'nɔrka/ *f* Menorca

mino|ritário /minori'tariu/ *a* minority; **~ria** *f* minority

minúcia /mi'nusia/ *f* detail

minucioso /minusi'ozu/ *a* thorough

minúscu|la /mi'nuskula/ *f* small letter; **~lo** *a* < *letra*> small; (*muito pequeno*) minuscule

minuta /mi'nuta/ *f* (*rascunho*) rough draft

minuto /mi'nutu/ *m* minute
miolo /mi'olu/ *f* (*de fruta*) flesh; (*de pão*) crumb; *pl* brains
míope /'miopi/ *a* short-sighted
miopia /mio'pia/ *f* myopia
mira /'mira/ *f* sight; **ter em ~** have one's sights on
mirabolante /mirabo'lãtʃi/ *a* amazing; <*idéias, plano*> grandiose
mi|ragem /mi'raʒẽ/ *f* mirage; **~rante** *m* lookout; **~rar** *vt* look at; **~rar-se** *vpr* look at o.s.
mirim /mi'rĩ/ *a* little
miscelânea /mise'lania/ *f* miscellany
miscigenação /misiʒena'sãw/ *f* interbreeding
mise-en-plis /mizã'pli/ *m* shampoo and set
miserá|vel /mize'ravew/ (*pl* **~veis**) *a* miserable
miséria /mi'zɛria/ *f* misery; (*pobreza*) poverty; **uma ~** (*pouco dinheiro*) a pittance; **chorar ~** claim poverty
miseri|córdia /mizeri'kɔrdʒia/ *f* mercy; **~cordioso** *a* merciful
misógino /mi'zɔʒinu/ *m* misogynist □ *a* misogynistic
miss /'misi/ *f* beauty queen
missa /'misa/ *f* mass
missão /mi'sãw/ *f* mission
mís|sil /'misiw/ (*pl* **~seis**) *m* missile; **~sil de longo alcance** long-range missile
missionário /misio'nariu/ *m* missionary
missiva /mi'siva/ *f* missive
mis|tério /mis'tɛriu/ *m* mystery; **~terioso** /o/ *a* mysterious; **~ticismo** *m* mysticism
místico /'mistʃiku/ *m* mystic □ *a* mystical
misto /'mistu/ *a* mixed □ *m* mix; **~ quente** toasted ham and cheese sandwich
mistu|ra /mis'tura/ *f* mixture; **~rar** *vt* mix; (*confundir*) mix up; **~rar-se** *vpr* mix (**com** with)
mítico /'mitʃiku/ *a* mythical
mito /'mitu/ *m* myth; **~logia** *f* mythology; **~lógico** *a* mythological
miudezas /miu'dezas/ *f pl* odds and ends
miúdo /mi'udu/ *a* tiny, minute; <*chuva*> fine; <*despesas*> minor □ *m* (*criança*) child, little one; *pl* (*de galinha*) giblets; **trocar em ~s** go into detail
mixaria /miʃa'ria/ *f* (*fam*) (*soma irrisória*) pittance
mixórdia /mi'ʃɔrdʒia/ *f* muddle
mnemônico /ne'moniku/ *a* mnemonic
mobilar /mobi'lar/ *vt* (*Port*) furnish

mobília /mo'bilia/ *f* furniture
mobili|ar /mobili'ar/ *vt* furnish; **~ário** *m* furniture
mobili|dade /mobili'dadʒi/ *f* mobility; **~zar** *vt* mobilize
moça /'mosa/ *f* girl
moçambicano /mosãbi'kanu/ *a & m* Mozambican
Moçambique /mosã'biki/ *m* Mozambique
moção /mo'sãw/ *f* motion
mochila /mo'ʃila/ *f* rucksack
moço /'mosu/ *a* young □ *m* boy, lad
moda /'mɔda/ *f* fashion; **na ~** fashionable
modalidade /modali'dadʒi/ *f* (*esporte*) event
mode|lagem /mode'laʒẽ/ *f* modelling; **~lar** *vt* model (a on); **~lar-se** *vpr* model o.s. (**a** on) □ *a* model; **~lo** /e/ *m* model
mode|ração /modera'sãw/ *f* moderation; **~rado** *a* moderate; **~rar** *vt* moderate; reduce <*velocidade, despesas*>; **~rar-se** *vpr* restrain oneself
moder|nidade /moderni'dadʒi/ *f* modernity; **~nismo** *m* modernism; **~nista** *a & m/f* modernist; **~nizar** *vt* modernize; **~no** /ɛ/ *a* modern
modess /'mɔdʒis/ *m invar* sanitary towel
modéstia /mo'dɛstʃia/ *f* modesty
modesto /mo'dɛstu/ *a* modest
módico /'mɔdʒiku/ *a* modest
modifi|cação /modʒifika'sãw/ *f* modification; **~car** *vt* modify
mo|dismo /mo'dʒizmu/ *m* idiom; **~dista** *f* dressmaker
modo /'mɔdu/ *m* way; (*ling*) mood; *pl* (*maneiras*) manners
modular /modu'lar/ *vt* modulate □ *a* modular
módulo /'mɔdulu/ *m* module
moeda /mo'ɛda/ *f* (*peça de metal*) coin; (*dinheiro*) currency
mo|edor /moe'dor/ *m* **~edor de café** coffee-grinder; **~edor de carne** mincer; **~er** *vt* grind <*café, trigo*>; squeeze <*cana*>; mince <*carne*>; (*bater*) beat
mo|fado /mo'fadu/ *a* mouldy; **~far** *vi* moulder; **~fo** /o/ *m* mould
mogno /'mɔgnu/ *m* mahogany
moinho /mo'iɲu/ *m* mill; **~ de vento** windmill
moisés /moj'zɛs/ *m invar* carry-cot
moita /'mojta/ *f* bush
mola /'mɔla/ *f* spring
mol|dar /mow'dar/ *vt* mould; cast <*metal*>; **~de** /ɔ/ *m* mould; (*para costura etc*) pattern
moldu|ra /mow'dura/ *f* frame; **~rar** *vt* frame

mole /'mɔli/ a soft; <pessoa> listless; (fam) (fácil) easy □ adv easily; é ~? (fam) can you believe it?

molécula /mo'lɛkula/ f molecule

moleque /mo'lɛki/ m (menino) lad; (de rua) urchin; (homem) scoundrel

molestar /moles'tar/ vt bother

moléstia /mo'lɛstʃia/ f disease

moletom /mole'tõ/ m (tecido) knitted cotton; (blusa) sweatshirt

moleza /mo'leza/ f softness; (de pessoa) laziness; viver na ~ lead a cushy life; ser ~ be easy

mo|lhado /mo'ʎadu/ a wet; ~lhar vt wet; ~lhar-se vpr get wet

molho¹ /'mɔʎu/ m (de chaves) bunch; (de palha) sheaf

molho² /'mɔʎu/ m sauce; (para salada) dressing; deixar de ~ leave in soak <roupa>; ~ inglês Worcester sauce

molusco /mo'lusku/ m mollusc

momen|tâneo /momẽ'taniu/ a momentary; ~to m moment; (força) momentum

Mônaco /'monaku/ m Monaco

monar|ca /mo'narka/ m/f monarch; ~quia f monarchy; ~quista a & m/f monarchist

monástico /mo'nastʃiku/ a monastic

monção /mõ'sãw/ f monsoon

mone|tário /mone'tariu/ a monetary; ~tarismo m monetarism; ~tarista a & m/f monetarist

monge /'mõʒi/ m monk

monitor /moni'tor/ m monitor; ~ de vídeo VDU

monitorar /monito'rar/ vt monitor

mono|cromo /mono'krɔmu/ a monochrome; ~gamia f monogamy

monógamo /mo'nɔgamu/ a monogamous

monograma /mono'grama/ m monogram

monólogo /mo'nɔlogu/ m monologue

mononucleose /mononukli'ɔzi/ f glandular fever

mono|pólio /mono'pɔliu/ m monopoly; ~polizar vt monopolize

monossílabo /mono'silabu/ a monosyllabic □ m monosyllable

monotonia /monoto'nia/ f monotony

monótono /mo'nɔtonu/ a monotonous

monóxido /mo'nɔksidu/ m ~ de carbono carbon monoxide

mons|tro /'mõstru/ m monster; ~truosidade f monstrosity; ~truoso /o/ a monstrous

monta|dor /mõta'dor/ m (de cinema) editor; ~dora f assembly company; ~gem f assembly; (de filme) editing; (de peça teatral) production

monta|nha /mõ'taɲa/ f mountain; ~nha-russa (pl ~nhas-russas) f roller coaster; ~nhismo m mountaineering; ~nhoso /o/ a mountainous

mon|tante /mõ'tãtʃi/ m amount □ a rising; a ~tante upstream; ~tão m heap; ~tar vt ride <cavalo, bicicleta>; assemble <peças, máquina>; put up <barraca>; set up <empresa, escritório>; mount <guarda, diamante>; put on <espetáculo, peça>; edit <filme> □ vi ride; ~tar a <dívidas etc> amount to; ~tar em (subir em) mount; ~taria f mount; ~te m heap; um ~te de coisas (fam) loads of things; o Monte Branco Mont Blanc

Montevidéu /mõtʃivi'dɛw/ f Montevideo

montra /'mõtra/ f (Port) shop window

monumen|tal /monumẽ'taw/ (pl ~tais) a monumental; ~to m monument

mora|da /mo'rada/ f dwelling; (Port) address; ~dia f dwelling; ~dor m resident

mo|ral /mo'raw/ (pl ~rais) a moral □ f (ética) morals; (de uma história) moral □ m (ânimo) morale; (de pessoa) moral sense; ~ralidade f morality; ~ralista a moralistic □ m/f moralist; ~ralizar vi moralize

morango /mo'rãgu/ m strawberry

morar /mo'rar/ vi live

moratória /mora'tɔria/ f moratorium

mórbido /'mɔrbidu/ a morbid

morcego /mor'segu/ m bat

mor|daça /mor'dasa/ f gag; (para cão) muzzle; ~daz a scathing; ~der vt/i bite; ~dida f bite

mordo|mia /mordo'mia/ f (no emprego) perk; (de casa etc) comfort; ~mo /o/ m butler

more|na /mo'rena/ f brunette; ~no a dark; (bronzeado) brown □ m dark person

morfina /mor'fina/ f morphine

moribundo /mori'bũdu/ a dying

moringa /mo'rĩga/ f water jug

morma|cento /morma'sẽtu/ a sultry; ~ço m sultry weather

morno /'mornu/ a lukewarm

moro|sidade /morozi'dadʒi/ f slowness; ~so /o/ a slow

morrer /mo'xer/ vi die; <luz, dia, ardor, esperança etc> fade; <carro> stall

morro /'moxu/ m hill; (fig: favela) slum

mortadela /morta'dɛla/ f mortadella, salami

mor|tal /mor'taw/ (pl ~tais) a & m mortal; ~talha f shroud; ~talidade f mortality; ~tandade f slaughter; ~te /ɔ/ f death; ~tífero a deadly; ~tificar vt mortify; ~to /o/ a dead

mosaico /mo'zajku/ *m* mosaic

mosca /'moska/ *f* fly

Moscou /mos'ku/, (*Port*) **Moscovo** /moʃ'kovu/ *f* Moscow

mosquito /mos'kitu/ *m* mosquito

mostarda /mos'tarda/ *f* mustard

mosteiro /mos'teru/ *m* monastery

mos|tra /'mɔstra/ *f* display; **dar ~tras de** show signs of; **pôr à ~tra** show up; **~trador** *m* face, dial; **~trar** *vt* show; **~trar-se** *vpr* (*revelar-se*) show o.s. to be; (*exibir-se*) show off; **~truário** *m* display case

mo|tel /mo'tɛw/ (*pl* **~téis**) *m* motel

motim /mo'tʃĩ/ *m* riot; (*na marinha*) mutiny

moti|vação /motʃiva'sãw/ *f* motivation; **~var** *vt* (*incentivar*) motivate; (*provocar*) cause; **~vo** *m* (*razão*) reason; (*estímulo*) motive; (*na arte, música*) motif; **dar ~vo de** give cause for

moto /'mɔtu/ *f* motorbike; **~ca** /mo'tɔka/ *f* (*fam*) motorbike

motoci|cleta /motosi'klɛta/ *f* motorcycle; **~clismo** *m* motorcycling; **~clista** *m/f* motorcyclist

motoqueiro /moto'keru/ *m* (*fam*) biker

motor /mo'tor/ *m* (*de carro, avião etc*) engine; (*elétrico*) motor □ *a* (*f* **motriz**) *<força>* driving; (*anat*) motor; **~ de arranque** starter motor; **~ de popa** outboard motor

moto|rista /moto'rista/ *m/f* driver; **~rizado** *a* motorized; **~rizar** *vt* motorize

movedi|ço /move'dʒisu/ *a* unstable, moving; **areia ~ça** quicksand

mó|vel /'mɔvew/ (*pl* **~veis**) *a* *<peça, parte>* moving; *<tropas>* mobile; *<festa>* movable □ *m* piece of furniture; *pl* furniture

mo|ver /mo'ver/ *vt* move; (*impulsionar, fig*) drive; **~ver-se** *vpr* move; **~vido** *a* driven; **~vido a álcool** alcohol-powered

movimen|tação /movimẽta'sãw/ *f* bustle; **~tado** *a* *<rua, loja>* busy; *<música>* up-beat, lively; *<pessoa, sessão>* lively; **~tar** *vt* liven up; **~tar-se** *vpr* move; **~to** *m* movement; (*tecn*) motion; (*na rua etc*) activity

muam|ba /mu'ãba/ *f* contraband; **~beiro** *m* smuggler

muco /'muku/ *m* mucus

muçulmano /musuw'manu/ *a* & *m* Muslim

mu|da /'muda/ *f* (*planta*) seedling; **~da de roupa** change of clothes; **~dança** *f* change; (*de casa*) move; (*de carro*) transmission; **~dar** *vt/i* change; **~dar de assunto** change the subject; **~dar (de casa)** move (house); **~dar de cor** change colour;

~dar de idéia change one's mind; **~dar de lugar** change places; **~dar de roupa** change (clothes); **~dar-se** *vpr* move

mu|dez /mu'des/ *f* silence; **~do** *a* silent; (*deficiente*) dumb; *<telefone>* dead □ *m* mute

mu|gido /mu'ʒidu/ *m* moo; **~gir** *vi* moo

muito /'mũitu/ *a* a lot of; *pl* many □ *pron* a lot □ *adv* (*com adjetivo, advérbio*) very; (*com verbo*) a lot; **~ maior** much bigger; **~ tempo** a long time

mula /'mula/ *f* mule

mulato /mu'latu/ *a* & *m* mulatto

muleta /mu'leta/ *f* crutch

mulher /mu'ʎɛr/ *f* woman; (*esposa*) wife

mulherengo /muʎe'rẽgu/ *a* womanizing □ *m* womanizer, ladies' man

mul|ta /'muwta/ *f* fine; **~tar** *vt* fine

multicolor /muwtʃiko'lor/ *a* multicoloured

multidão /muwtʃi'dãw/ *f* crowd

multinacio|nal /muwtʃinasio'naw/ (*pl* **~nais**) *a* & *f* multinational

multipli|cação /muwtʃiplika-sãw/ *f* multiplication; **~car** *vt* multiply; **~car-se** *vpr* multiply; **~cidade** *f* multiplicity

múltiplo /'muwtʃiplu/ *a* & *m* multiple

multirraci|al /muwtʃixasi'aw/ (*pl* **~ais**) *a* multiracial

múmia /'mumia/ *f* mummy

mun|dano /mũ'danu/ *a* *<prazeres etc>* worldly; *<vida, mulher>* society; **~dial** (*pl* **~diais**) *a* world □ *m* world championship; **~do** *m* world; **todo (o) ~do** everybody

munição /muni'sãw/ *f* ammunition

muni|cipal /munisi'paw/ (*pl* **~cipais**) *a* municipal; **~cípio** *m* (*lugar*) borough, community; (*prédio*) town hall; (*autoridade*) local authority

munir /mu'nir/ *vt* provide (**de** with); **~-se** *vpr* equip o.s. (**de** with)

mu|ral /mu'raw/ (*pl* **~rais**) *a* & *m* mural; **~ralha** *f* wall

mur|char /mur'ʃar/ *vi* *<planta>* wither, wilt; *<salada>* go limp; *<beleza>* fade □ *vt* wither, wilt *<planta>*; **~cho** *a* *<planta>* wilting; *<pessoa>* broken

mur|murar /murmu'rar/ *vi* murmur; (*queixar-se*) mutter □ *vt* murmur; **~múrio** *m* murmur

muro /'muru/ *m* wall

murro /'muxu/ *m* punch

musa /'muza/ *f* muse

muscu|lação /muskula'sãw/ *f* weight-training; **~lar** *a* muscular; **~latura** *f* musculature

músculo /'muskulu/ *m* muscle

musculoso /musku'lozu/ a muscular
museu /mu'zew/ m museum
musgo /'muzgu/ m moss
música /'muzika/ f music; (*uma*)
song; ~ **de câmara** chamber music;
~ **de fundo** background music; ~
clássica ou **erudita** classical music
musi|cal /muzi'kaw/ (*pl* ~**cais**) a &
m musical; ~**car** vt set to music
músico /'muziku/ m musician □ a
musical
musse /'musi/ f mousse
mutilar /mutʃi'lar/ vt mutilate; maim
<*pessoa*>
mutirão /mutʃi'rãw/ m joint effort
mútuo /'mutuu/ a mutual
muxoxo /mu'ʃoʃu/ m **fazer** ~ tut

N

na = **em** + **a**
nabo /'nabu/ m turnip
nação /na'sãw/ f nation
nacio|nal /nasio'naw/ (*pl* ~**nais**) a
national; (*brasileiro*) home-produced;
~**nalidade** f nationality; ~**nalismo**
m nationalism; ~**nalista** a & m/f
nationalist; ~**nalizar** vt nationalize
naco /'naku/ m chunk
nada /'nada/ pron nothing □ adv not
at all; **de** ~ (*não há de quê*) don't
mention it; **que** ~!, ~ **disso!** no way!
na|dadeira /nada'dera/ f (*de peixe*)
fin; (*de mergulhador*) flipper;
~**dador** m swimmer; ~**dar** vi swim
nádegas /'nadegas/ f pl buttocks
nado /'nadu/ m ~ **borboleta** butterfly stroke; ~ **de costas** backstroke; ~
de peito breaststroke; **atravessar a**
~ swim across
náilon /'najlõ/ m nylon
naipe /'najpi/ m (*em jogo de cartas*) suit
namo|rada /namo'rada/ f girlfriend;
~**rado** m boyfriend; ~**rador** a
amorous □ m ladies' man; ~**rar** vt
(*ter relação com*) go out with; (*cobiçar*)
eye up □ vi <*casal*> (*ter relação*) go
out together; (*beijar-se etc*) kiss and
cuddle; <*homem*> have a girlfriend;
<*mulher*> have a boyfriend; ~**ro** /o/
m relationship
nanar /na'nar/ vi (*col*) sleep
nanico /na'niku/ a tiny
não /nãw/ adv not; (*resposta*) no □ m
no; ~**-alinhado** a non-aligned; ~**-**
conformista a & m/f non-conformist
naquela, naquele, naquilo = **em** +
aquela, aquele, aquilo
narci|sismo /narsi'zizmu/ m
narcissism; ~**sista** m/f narcissist □
a narcissistic; ~**so** m narcissus
narcótico /nar'kɔtʃiku/ a & m narcotic

nari|gudo /nari'gudu/ a with a big
nose; **ser** ~**gudo** have a big nose;
~**na** f nostril
nariz /na'ris/ m nose
nar|ração /naxa'sãw/ f narration;
~**rador** m narrator; ~**rar** vt nar-
rate; ~**rativa** f narrative; ~**rativo** a
narrative
nas = **em** + **as**
na|sal /na'zaw/ (*pl* ~**sais**) a nasal;
~**salizar** vt nasalize
nas|cença /na'sẽsa/ f birth; ~**cente** a
nascent □ f source; ~**cer** vi be born;
<*dente, espinha*> grow; <*planta*>
sprout; <*sol, lua*> rise; <*dia*> dawn;
(*fig*) <*empresa, projeto etc*> come into
being □ m o ~**cer do sol** sunrise;
~**cimento** m birth
nata /'nata/ f cream
natação /nata'sãw/ f swimming
Natal /na'taw/ m Christmas
na|tal /na'taw/ (*pl* ~**tais**) a <*país,*
terra> native
nata|lício /nata'lisiu/ a & m birth-
day; ~**lidade** f índice de ~**lidade**
birth rate; ~**lino** a Christmas
nati|vidade /natʃivi'dadʒi/ f nativity;
~**vo** a & m native
nato /'natu/ a born
natu|ral /natu'raw/ (*pl* ~**rais**) a nat-
ural; (*oriundo*) originating (de from)
□ m native (de of)
natura|lidade /naturali'dadʒi/ f
naturalness; **com** ~**lidade** matter-
of-factly; **de** ~**lidade carioca** born
in Rio de Janeiro; ~**lismo** m natural-
ism; ~**lista** a & m/f naturalist;
~**lizar** vt naturalize; ~**lizar-se** vpr
become naturalized
natureza /natu'reza/ f nature; ~
morta still life
naturis|mo /natu'rizmu/ m natur-
ism; ~**ta** m/f naturist
nau|fragar /nawfra'gar/ vi <*navio*>
be wrecked; <*tripulação*> be ship-
wrecked; (*fig*) <*plano, casamento*
etc> founder; ~**frágio** m shipwreck;
(*fig*) failure
náufrago /'nawfragu/ m castaway
náusea /'nawzia/ f nausea
nauseabundo /nawzia'bũdu/ a naus-
eating
náuti|ca /'nawtʃika/ f navigation;
~**co** a nautical
na|val /na'vaw/ (*pl* ~**vais**) a naval;
construção ~**val** shipbuilding
navalha /na'vaʎa/ f razor; ~**da** f cut
with a razor
nave /'navi/ f nave; ~ **espacial** spaceship
nave|gação /navega'sãw/ f naviga-
tion; (*tráfego*) shipping; ~**gador** m
navigator; ~**gante** m/f seafarer;
~**gar** vt navigate; sail <*mar*> □ vi

sail; (*traçar o rumo*) navigate; ~**gável** (*pl* ~**gáveis**) *a* navigable

navio /na'viu/ *m* ship; ~ **cargueiro** cargo ship; ~ **de guerra** warship; ~ **petroleiro** oil tanker

nazista /na'zista/, (*Port*) **nazi** /na'zi/ *a* & *m/f* Nazi

neblina /ne'blina/ *f* mist

nebulo|sa /nebu'lɔza/ *f* nebula; ~**sidade** *f* cloud; ~**so** /o/ *a* cloudy; (*fig*) obscure

neces|saire /nese'sɛr/ *m* toilet bag; ~**sário** *a* necessary; ~**sidade** *f* necessity; (*que se impõe*) need; (*pobreza*) need; ~**sitado** *a* needy □ *m* person in need; ~**sitar** *vt* require; (*tornar necessário*) necessitate; ~**sitar de** need

necro|lógio /nekro'lɔʒiu/ *m* obituary column; ~**tério** *m* mortuary, (*Amer*) morgue

néctar /'nɛktar/ *m* nectar

nectarina /nekta'rina/ *f* nectarine

nefasto /ne'fastu/ *a* fatal

ne|gação /nega'sãw/ *f* denial; (*ling*) negation; **ser uma** ~**gação em** be hopeless at; ~**gar** *vt* deny; ~**gar-se a** refuse to; ~**gativa** *f* refusal; (*ling*) negative; ~**gativo** *a* & *m* negative

negli|gência /negli'ʒẽsia/ *f* negligence; ~**genciar** *vt* neglect; ~**gente** *a* negligent

negoci|ação /negosia'sãw/ *f* negotiation; ~**ador** *m* negotiator; ~**ante** *m/f* dealer (**de** in); ~**ar** *vt/i* negotiate; ~**ar em** deal in; ~**ata** *f* shady deal; ~**ável** (*pl* ~**áveis**) *a* negotiable

negócio /ne'gɔsiu/ *m* deal; (*fam: coisa*) thing; *pl* business; **a** *ou* **de** ~**s** <*viajar*> on business

negocista /nego'sista/ *m* wheelerdealer □ *a* wheeler-dealing

ne|grito /ne'gritu/ *m* bold; ~**gro** /e/ *a* & *m* black; (*de raça*) Negro

nela, nele = **em** + **ela, ele**

nem /nẽj/ *adv* not even □ *conj* ~ ... ~ ... neither ... nor ...; ~ **sempre** not always; ~ **todos** not all; ~ **que** not even if; **que** ~ like; ~ **eu** nor do I

nenê /ne'ne/, **neném** /ne'nẽj/ *m* baby

nenhum /ne'ɲũ/ *a* (*f* **nenhuma**) no □ *pron* (*f* **nenhuma**) not one; ~ **dos dois** neither of them; ~ **erro** no mistakes; **erro** ~ no mistakes at all, not a single mistake; ~ **lugar** nowhere

nenúfar /ne'nufar/ *m* waterlily

neologismo /neolo'ʒizmu/ *m* neologism

néon /'nɛõ/ *m* neon

neozelan|dês /neozelã'des/ *a* (*f* ~**desa**) New Zealand □ *m* (*f* ~**desa**) New Zealander

Nepal /ne'paw/ *m* Nepal

nervo /'nervu/ *m* nerve; ~**sismo** *m* (*chateação*) annoyance; (*medo*) nerv-

ousness; ~**so** /o/ *a* <*sistema, doença*> nervous; (*chateado*) annoyed; (*medroso*) nervous; **deixar alg** ~**so** get on s.o.'s nerves

nessa(s), nesse(s) = **em** + **essa(s), esse(s)**

nesta(s), neste(s) = **em** + **esta(s), este(s)**

ne|ta /'nɛta/ *f* granddaughter; ~**to** /ɛ/ *m* grandson; *pl* grandchildren

neuro|logia /newrolo'ʒia/ *f* neurology; ~**lógico** *a* neurological; ~**logista** *m/f* neurologist

neu|rose /new'rɔzi/ *f* neurosis; ~**rótico** *a* neurotic

neutrali|dade /newtrali'dadʒi/ *f* neutrality; ~**zar** *vt* neutralize

neutrão /new'trãw/ *m* (*Port*) *veja* **nêutron**

neutro /'newtru/ *a* neutral

nêutron /'newtrõ/ *m* neutron

ne|vada /ne'vada/ *f* snowfall; ~**vado** *a* snow-covered; ~**var** *vi* snow; ~**vasca** *f* snowstorm; ~**ve** /ɛ/ *f* snow

névoa /'nɛvoa/ *f* haze

nevoeiro /nevo'eru/ *m* fog

nexo /'nɛksu/ *m* connection; **sem** ~ incoherent

Nicarágua /nika'ragwa/ *f* Nicaragua

nicaragüense /nikara'gwẽsi/ *a* & *m/f* Nicaraguan

nicho /'niʃu/ *m* niche

nicotina /niko'tʃina/ *f* nicotine

Níger /'niʒer/ *m* Niger

Nigéria /ni'ʒeria/ *f* Nigeria

nigeriano /niʒeri'anu/ *a* & *m* Nigerian

Nilo /'nilu/ *m* Nile

ninar /ni'nar/ *vt* lull to sleep

ninfa /'nĩfa/ *f* nymph

ninguém /nĩ'gẽj/ *pron* no-one, nobody

ninhada /ni'ɲada/ *f* brood

ninharia /niɲa'ria/ *f* trifle

ninho /'niɲu/ *m* nest

níquel /'nikew/ *m* nickel

nisei /ni'sej/ *a* & *m/f* Japanese Brazilian

nisso = **em** + **isso**

nisto = **em** + **isto**

nitidez /nitʃi'des/ *f* (*de imagem etc*) sharpness

nítido /'nitʃidu/ *a* <*imagem, foto*> sharp; <*diferença, melhora*> distinct, clear

nitrogênio /nitro'ʒeniu/ *m* nitrogen

ní|vel /'nivew/ (*pl* ~**veis**) *m* level; **a** ~**vel de** in terms of

nivelamento /nivela'mẽtu/ *m* levelling

nivelar /nive'lar/ *vt* level

no = **em** + **o**

nó /nɔ/ *m* knot; **dar um** ~ tie a knot; ~ **dos dedos** knuckle; **um** ~ **na garganta** a lump in one's throat

nobre /'nɔbri/ a noble; <*bairro*> exclusive □ m/f noble; ~**za** /e/ f nobility
noção /no'sãw/ f notion; pl (*rudimentos*) elements
nocaute /no'kawtʃi/ m knockout; **pôr alg ~** knock s.o. out; **~ar** vt knock out
nocivo /no'sivu/ a harmful
nódoa /'nodoa/ f (*Port*) stain
nogueira /no'gera/ f (*árvore*) walnut tree
noi|tada /noj'tada/ f night; **~te** f night; (*antes de dormir*) evening; **à ou de ~te** at night; (*antes de dormir*) in the evening; **hoje à ~te** tonight; **ontem à ~te** last night; **boa ~te** (*ao chegar*) good evening; (*ao despedir-se*) good night; **~te em branco** *ou* **claro** sleepless night
noi|vado /noj'vadu/ m engagement; **~va** f fiancée; (*no casamento*) bride; **~vo** m fiancé; (*no casamento*) bridegroom; **os ~vos** the engaged couple; (*no casamento*) the bride and groom; **ficar ~vo** get engaged
no|jento /no'ʒẽtu/ a disgusting; **~jo** /o/ m disgust
nômade /'nomadʒi/ m/f nomad □ a nomadic
nome /'nomi/ m name; **de ~** by name; **em ~ de** in the name of; **~ comercial** trade name; **~ de batismo** Christian name; **~ de guerra** professional name
nome|ação /nomia'sãw/ f appointment; **~ar** vt (*para cargo*) appoint; (*chamar pelo nome*) name
nomi|nal /nomi'naw/ (*pl* **~nais**) a nominal
nonagésimo /nona'ʒɛzimu/ a ninetieth
nono /'nonu/ a & m ninth
nora /'nɔra/ f daughter-in-law
nordes|te /nor'dɛstʃi/ m northeast; **~tino** a Northeastern □ m person from the Northeast (*of Brazil*)
nórdico /'nɔrdʒiku/ a Nordic
nor|ma /'nɔrma/ f norm; **~mal** (*pl* **~mais**) a normal
normali|dade /normali'dadʒi/ f normality; **~zar** vt bring back to normal; normalize <*relações diplomáticas*>; **~zar-se** vpr return to normal
noroeste /noro'ɛstʃi/ a & m northwest
norte /'nɔrtʃi/ a & m north; **~-africano** a & m North African; **~-americano** a & m North American; **~-coreano** a & m North Korean
nortista /nor'tʃista/ a Northern □ m/f Northerner
Noruega /noru'ɛga/ f Norway
norue|guês /norue'ges/ a & m (f **~guesa**) Norwegian

nos¹ = **em** + **os**
nos² /nus/ pron us; (*indireto*) (to) us; (*reflexivo*) ourselves
nós /nɔs/ pron we; (*depois de preposição*) us
nos|sa /'nɔsa/ int gosh; **~so** /ɔ/ a our □ pron ours
nos|talgia /nostaw'ʒia/ f nostalgia; **~tálgico** a nostalgic
nota /'nɔta/ f note; (*na escola etc*) mark; (*conta*) bill; **custar uma ~ (preta)** (*fam*) cost a bomb; **tomar ~** take note (**de** of); **~ fiscal** receipt
no|tação /nota'sãw/ f notation; **~tar** vt notice, note; **fazer ~tar** point out; **~tável** (*pl* **~táveis**) a & m/f notable
notícia /no'tʃisia/ f piece of news; pl news
notici|ar /notʃi'sjar/ vt report; **~ário** m (*na TV*) news; (*em jornal*) news section; **~arista** m/f (*na TV*) newsreader; (*em jornal*) news reporter; **~oso** /o/ a **agência ~osa** news agency
notifi|cação /notʃifika'sãw/ f notification; **~car** vt notify
notívago /no'tʃivagu/ a nocturnal □ m night person
notório /no'tɔriu/ a well-known
noturno /no'turnu/ a night; <*animal*> nocturnal
nova /'nɔva/ f piece of news; **~mente** adv again
novato /no'vatu/ m novice
nove /'nɔvi/ a & m nine; **~centos** a & m nine hundred
novela /no'vɛla/ f (*na TV*) soap opera; (*livro*) novella
novembro /no'vẽbru/ m November
noventa /no'vẽta/ a & m ninety
noviço /no'visu/ m novice
novidade /novi'dadʒi/ f novelty; (*notícia*) piece of news; pl (*notícias*) news
novilho /no'viʎu/ m calf
novo /'novu/ a new; (*jovem*) young; **de ~** again; **~ em folha** brand new
noz /nɔs/ f walnut; **~ moscada** nutmeg
nu /nu/ a (f **~a**) <*corpo, pessoa*> naked; <*braço, parede, quarto*> bare □ m nude; **~ em pêlo** stark naked; **a verdade ~a e crua** the plain truth
nuança /nu'ãsa/ f nuance
nu|blado /nu'bladu/ a cloudy; **~blar** vt cloud; **~blar-se** vpr cloud over
nuca /'nuka/ f nape of the neck
nuclear /nukli'ar/ a nuclear
núcleo /'nukliu/ m nucleus
nu|dez /nu'des/ f nakedness; (*na TV etc*) nudity; (*da parede etc*) bareness; **~dismo** m nudism; **~dista** m/f nudist
nulo /'nulu/ a void
num, numa(s) = **em** + **um, uma(s)**

nume|ral /nume'raw/ (*pl* ~**rais**) *a* & *m* numeral; ~**rar** *vt* number

numérico /nu'mɛriku/ *a* numerical

número /'numeru/ *m* number; (*de jornal, revista*) issue; (*de sapatos*) size; (*espetáculo*) act; **fazer** ~ make up the numbers

numeroso /nume'rozu/ *a* numerous

nunca /'nũka/ *adv* never; ~ **mais** never again

nuns = **em** + **uns**

nupci|al /nupsi'aw/ (*pl* ~**ais**) *a* bridal

núpcias /'nupsias/ *f pl* marriage

nu|trição /nutri'sãw/ *f* nutrition; ~**trir** *vt* nourish; (*fig*) harbour <*ódio, esperança*>; ~**tritivo** *a* nourishing; <*valor*> nutritional

nuvem /'nuvẽ/ *f* cloud

O

o /u/ *artigo* the □ *pron* (*homem*) him; (*coisa*) it; (*você*) you; ~ **que** (*a coisa que*) what; (*aquele que*) the one that; ~ **quê?** what?; **meu livro e** ~ **do João** my book and John's (one)

ó /ɔ/ *int* (*fam*) look

ô /o/ *int* oh

oásis /o'azis/ *m invar* oasis

oba /'oba/ *int* great

obcecar /obise'kar/ *vt* obsess

obe|decer /obede'ser/ *vt* ~**decer a** obey; ~**diência** *f* obedience; ~**diente** *a* obedient

obe|sidade /obezi'dadʒi/ *f* obesity; ~**so** /e/ *a* obese

óbito /'ɔbitu/ *m* death

obituário /obitu'ariu/ *m* obituary

obje|ção /obiʒe'sãw/ *f* objection; ~**tar** *vt/i* object (**a to**)

objeti|va /obiʒe'tʃiva/ *f* lens; ~**vidade** *f* objectivity; ~**vo** /ɔ/ *a* & *m* objective

objeto /obi'ʒetu/ *m* object

oblíquo /o'blikwu/ *a* oblique; <*olhar*> sidelong

obliterar /oblite'rar/ *vt* obliterate

oblongo /o'blõgu/ *a* oblong

obo|é /obo'ɛ/ *m* oboe; ~**ista** *m/f* oboist

obra /'ɔbra/ *f* work; **em** ~**s** being renovated; ~ **de arte** work of art; ~ **de caridade** charity; ~**prima** (*pl* ~**s-primas**) *f* masterpiece

obri|gação /obriga'sãw/ *f* obligation; (*título*) bond; ~**gado** *int* thank you; (*não querendo*) no thank you; ~**gar** *vt* force, oblige (**a to**); ~**gar-se** *vpr* undertake (**a to**); ~**gatório** *a* obligatory, compulsory

obsce|nidade /obiseni'dadʒi/ *f* obscenity; ~**no** /e/ *a* obscene

obscu|ridade /obiskuri'dadʒi/ *f* obscurity; ~**ro** *a* obscure

obséquio /obi'sekiu/ *m* favour

obsequioso /obiseki'ozu/ *a* obsequious

obser|vação /obiserva'sãw/ *f* observation; ~**vador** *a* observant □ *m* observer; ~**vância** *f* observance; ~**var** *vt* observe; ~**vatório** *m* observatory

obses|são /obise'sãw/ *f* obsession; ~**sivo** *a* obsessive

obsoleto /obiso'letu/ *a* obsolete

obstáculo /obis'takulu/ *m* obstacle

obstar /obis'tar/ *vt* stand in the way (**a of**)

obs|tetra /obis'tɛtra/ *m/f* obstetrician; ~**tetrícia** *f* obstetrics; ~**tétrico** *a* obstetric

obsti|nação /obistina'sãw/ *f* obstinacy; ~**nado** *a* obstinate; ~**nar-se** *vpr* insist (**em on**)

obstru|ção /obistru'sãw/ *f* obstruction; ~**ir** *vt* obstruct

ob|tenção /obitẽ'sãw/ *f* obtaining; ~**ter** *vt* obtain

obtu|ração /obitura'sãw/ *f* filling; ~**rador** *m* shutter; ~**rar** *vt* fill <*dente*>

obtuso /obi'tuzu/ *a* obtuse

óbvio /'ɔbviu/ *a* obvious

ocasi|ão /okazi'ãw/ *f* occasion; (*oportunidade*) opportunity; (*compra*) bargain; ~**onal** (*pl* ~**onais**) *a* chance; ~**onar** *vt* cause

Oceania /osia'nia/ *f* Oceania

oce|ânico /osi'aniku/ *a* ocean; ~**ano** *m* ocean

ociden|tal /osidẽ'taw/ (*pl* ~**tais**) *a* western □ *m/f* Westerner; ~**te** *m* West

ócio /'ɔsiu/ *m* (*lazer*) leisure; (*falta de trabalho*) idleness

ocioso /osi'ozu/ *a* idle □ *m* idler

oco /'oku/ *a* hollow; <*cabeça*> empty

ocor|rência /oko'xẽsia/ *f* occurrence; ~**rer** *vi* occur (**a to**)

ocu|lar /oku'lar/ *a* **testemunha** ~**lar** eye witness; ~**lista** *m/f* optician

óculos /'ɔkulus/ *m pl* glasses; ~ **de sol** sunglasses

ocul|tar /okuw'tar/ *vt* conceal; ~**to** *a* hidden; (*sobrenatural*) occult

ocu|pação /okupa'sãw/ *f* occupation; ~**pado** *a* (*pessoa*) busy; <*cadeira*> taken; <*telefone*> engaged, (*Amer*) busy; ~**par** *vt* occupy; take up <*tempo, espaço*>; hold <*cargo*>; ~**par-se** *vpr* keep busy; ~**par-se com** *ou* **de** be involved with <*política, literatura etc*>; take care of <*cliente, doente, problema*>; occupy one's time with <*leitura, palavras cruzadas etc*>

ode /'ɔdʒi/ *f* ode

odiar /o'dʒi'ar/ *vt* hate
ódio /'ɔdʒiu/ *m* hatred, hate; *(raiva)* anger
odioso /odʒi'ozu/ *a* hateful
odontologia /odõtolo'ʒia/ *f* dentistry
odor /o'dor/ *m* odour
oeste /o'ɛstʃi/ *a & m* west
ofe|gante /ofe'gãtʃi/ *a* panting; **~gar** *vi* pant
ofen|der /ofẽ'der/ *vt* offend; **~der-se** *vpr* take offence; **~sa** *f* insult; **~siva** *f* offensive; **~sivo** *a* offensive
ofere|cer /ofere'ser/ *vt* offer; **~cer-se** *vpr* **<***pessoa***>** offer o.s. (como as); **<***ocasião***>** arise; **~cer-se para ajudar** offer to help; **~cimento** *m* offer
oferenda /ofe'rẽda/ *f* offering
oferta /o'fɛrta/ *f* offer; **em ~** on offer; **a ~ e a demanda** supply and demand
ofici|al /ofisi'aw/ *(pl* **~ais)** *a* official □ *m* officer; **~alizar** *vt* make official; **~ar** *vi* officiate
oficina /ofi'sina/ *f* workshop; *(para carros)* garage, *(Amer)* shop
ofício /o'fisiu/ *m (profissão)* trade; *(na igreja)* service
oficioso /ofisi'ozu/ *a* unofficial
ofus|cante /ofus'kãtʃi/ *a* dazzling; **~car** *vt* dazzle **<***pessoa***>**; obscure **<***sol etc***>**; *(fig: eclipsar)* outshine
oi /oj/ *int (cumprimento)* hi; *(resposta)* yes?
oi|tavo /oi'tavu/ *a & m* eighth; **~tenta** *a & m* eighty; **~to** *a & m* eight; **~tocentos** *a & m* eight hundred
olá /o'la/ *int* hello
olaria /ola'ria/ *f* pottery
óleo /'ɔliu/ *m* oil
oleo|duto /oliu'dutu/ *m* oil pipeline; **~so** /o/ *a* oily
olfato /ow'fatu/ *m* sense of smell
olhada /o'ʎada/ *f* look; **dar uma ~** have a look
olhar /o'ʎar/ *vt* look at; *(assistir)* watch □ *vi* look □ *m* look; **~ para** look at; **~ por** look after; **e olhe lá** *(fam)* and that's pushing it
olheiras /o'ʎeras/ *f pl* dark rings under one's eyes
olho /'oʎu/ *m* eye; **a ~ nu** with the naked eye; **custar os ~s da cara** cost a fortune; **ficar de ~** keep an eye out; **ficar de ~ em** keep an eye on; **pôr alg no ~ da rua** throw s.o. out; **não pregar o ~** not sleep a wink; **~ gordo** *ou* **grande** envy; **~ mágico** peephole; **~ roxo** black eye
Olimpíada /olĩ'piada/ *f* Olympic Games
olímpico /o'lĩpiku/ *a* **<***jogos, vila***>** Olympic; *(fig)* blithe
oliveira /oli'vera/ *f* olive tree

olmo /'owmu/ *m* elm
om|breira /õ'brera/ *f (para roupa)* shoulder pad; **~bro** *m* shoulder; **dar de ~bros** shrug one's shoulders
omelete /ome'lɛtʃi/, *(Port)* **omeleta** /ome'leta/ *f* omelette
omis|são /omi'sãw/ *f* omission; **~so** *a* negligent, remiss
omitir /omi'tʃir/ *vt* omit
omni- *(Port) veja* oni-
omoplata /omo'plata/ *f* shoulder blade
onça¹ /'õsa/ *f (peso)* ounce
onça² /'õsa/ *f (animal)* jaguar
onda /'õda/ *f* wave; **pegar ~** *(fam)* surf
onde /'õdʒi/ *adv* where; **por ~?** which way?; **~ quer que** wherever
ondu|lação /õdula'sãw/ *f* undulation; *(do cabelo)* wave; **~lado** *a* wavy; **~lante** *a* undulating; **~lar** *vt* wave **<***cabelo***>** □ *vi* undulate
onerar /one'rar/ *vt* burden
ônibus /'onibus/ *m invar* bus; **~ espacial** space shuttle
onipotente /onipo'tẽtʃi/ *a* omnipotent
onírico /o'niriku/ *a* dreamlike
onisciente /onisi'ẽtʃi/ *a* omniscient
onomatopéia /onomato'pɛja/ *f* onomatopoeia
ontem /'õtẽ/ *adv* yesterday
onze /'õzi/ *a & m* eleven
opaco /o'paku/ *a* opaque
opala /o'pala/ *f* opal
opção /opi'sãw/ *f* option
ópera /'ɔpera/ *f* opera
ope|ração /opera'sãw/ *f* operation; *(bancária etc)* transaction; **~rador** *m* operator; **~rar** *vt* operate; operate on **<***doente***>**; work **<***milagre***>** □ *vi* operate; **~rar-se** *vpr (acontecer)* come about; *(fazer operação)* have an operation; **~rário** *a* working □ *m* worker
opereta /ope'reta/ *f* operetta
opinar /opi'nar/ *vt* think □ *vi* express one's opinion
opinião /opini'ãw/ *f* opinion; **na minha ~** in my opinion; **~ pública** public opinion
ópio /'ɔpiu/ *m* opium
opor /o'por/ *vt* put up **<***resistência, argumento***>**; *(pôr em contraste)* contrast (a with); **~-se a** *(não aprovar)* oppose; *(ser diferente)* contrast with
oportu|nidade /oportuni'dadʒi/ *f* opportunity; **~nista** *a & m/f* opportunist; **~no** *a* opportune
oposi|ção /opozi'sãw/ *f* opposition (a to); **~cionista** *a* opposition □ *m/f* opposition politician
oposto /o'postu/ *a & m* opposite

opres|são /opre'sãw/ *f* oppression; (*no peito*) tightness; **~sivo** *a* oppressive; **~sor** *m* oppressor

oprimir /opri'mir/ *vt* oppress; (*com trabalho*) weigh down □ *vi* be oppressive

optar /opi'tar/ *vi* opt (**por** for); **~ por** ir opt to go

óptica, óptico *veja* **ótica, ótico**

opu|lência /opu'lẽsia/ *f* opulence; **~lento** *a* opulent

ora /'ɔra/ *adv & conj* now □ *int* come; **~ essa!** come now!; **~ ..., ~ ...** first ..., then

oração /ora'sãw/ *f* (*prece*) prayer; (*discurso*) oration; (*frase*) clause

oráculo /o'rakulu/ *m* oracle

orador /ora'dor/ *m* orator

oral /o'raw/ (*pl* **orais**) *a & f* oral

orar /o'rar/ *vi* pray

órbita /'ɔrbita/ *f* orbit; (*do olho*) socket

orçamen|tário /orsamẽ'tariu/ *a* budgetary; **~to** *m* (*plano financeiro*) budget; (*previsão dos custos*) estimate

orçar /or'sar/ *vt* estimate (**em** at)

ordeiro /or'deru/ *a* orderly

ordem /'ɔrdẽ/ *f* order; **por ~ alfabética** in alphabetical order; **~ de pagamento** banker's draft; **~ do dia** agenda

orde|nação /ordena'sãw/ *f* ordering; (*de padre*) ordination; **~nado** *a* ordered □ *m* wages; **~nar** *vt* order; put in order <*papéis, livros etc*>; ordain <*padre*>

ordenhar /orde'ɲar/ *vt* milk

ordinário /ordʒi'nariu/ *a* (*normal*) ordinary; (*grosseiro*) vulgar; (*de má qualidade*) inferior; (*sem caráter*) rough

orégano /o'rɛganu/ *m* oregano

ore|lha /o'reʎa/ *f* ear; **~lhão** *m* phone booth; **~lhudo** *a* with big ears; **ser ~lhudo** have big ears

orfanato /orfa'natu/ *m* orphanage

ór|fão /'ɔrfãw/ (*pl* **~fãos**) *a & m* (*f* **~fã**) orphan

orgânico /or'ganiku/ *a* organic

orga|nismo /orga'nizmu/ *m* organism; (*do Estado etc*) institution; **~nista** *m/f* organist

organi|zação /organiza'sãw/ *f* organization; **~zador** *a* organizing □ *m* organizer; **~zar** *vt* organize

órgão /'ɔrgãw/ (*pl* **~s**) *m* organ; (*do Estado etc*) body

orgasmo /or'gazmu/ *m* orgasm

orgia /or'ʒia/ *f* orgy

orgu|lhar /orgu'ʎar/ *vt* make proud; **~lhar-se** *vpr* be proud (**de** of); **~lho** *m* pride; **~lhoso** /o/ *a* proud

orien|tação /oriẽta'sãw/ *f* orientation; (*direção*) direction; (*vocacional etc*) guidance; **~tador** *m* advisor; **~tal** (*pl* **~tais**) *a* eastern; (*da Ásia*) oriental; **~tar** *vt* direct; (*aconselhar*) advise; (*situar*) position; **~tar-se** *vpr* get one's bearings; **~tar-se por** be guided by; **~te** *m* east; **Oriente Médio** Middle East; **Extremo Oriente** Far East

orifício /ori'fisiu/ *m* opening; (*no corpo*) orifice

origem /o'riʒẽ/ *f* origin; **dar ~ a** give rise to; **ter ~** originate

origi|nal /oriʒi'naw/ (*pl* **~nais**) *a & m* original; **~nalidade** *f* originality; **~nar** *vt* give rise to; **~nar-se** *vpr* originate; **~nário** *a* <*planta, animal*> native (**de** to); <*pessoa*> originating (**de** from)

oriundo /o'rjũdu/ *a* originating (**de** from)

orla /'ɔrla/ *f* border; **~ marítima** seafront

ornamen|tação /ornamẽta'sãw/ *f* ornamentation; **~tal** (*pl* **~tais**) *a* ornamental; **~tar** *vt* decorate; **~to** *m* ornament

orques|tra /or'kɛstra/ *f* orchestra; **~tra sinfônica** symphony orchestra; **~tral** (*pl* **~trais**) *a* orchestral; **~trar** *vt* orchestrate

orquídea /or'kidʒia/ *f* orchid

ortodoxo /orto'dɔksu/ *a* orthodox

orto|grafia /ortogra'fia/ *f* spelling, orthography; **~gráfico** *a* orthographic

orto|pedia /ortope'dʒia/ *f* orthopaedics; **~pédico** *a* orthopaedic; **~pedista** *m/f* orthopaedic surgeon

orvalho /or'vaʎu/ *m* dew

os /us/ *artigo & pron veja* **o**

oscilar /osi'lar/ *vi* oscillate

ósseo /'ɔsiu/ *a* bone

os|so /'ɔsu/ *m* bone; **~sudo** *a* bony

ostensivo /ostẽ'sivu/ *a* ostensible

osten|tação /ostẽta'sãw/ *f* ostentation; **~tar** *vt* show off; **~toso** *a* showy, ostentatious

osteopata /ostʃio'pata/ *m/f* osteopath

ostra /'ɔstra/ *f* oyster

ostracismo /ostra'sizmu/ *m* ostracism

otário /o'tariu/ *m* (*fam*) fool

óti|ca /'ɔtʃika/ *f* (*ciência*) optics; (*loja*) optician's; (*ponto de vista*) viewpoint; **~co** *a* optical

otimis|mo /otʃi'mizmu/ *m* optimism; **~ta** *m/f* optimist □ *a* optimistic

ótimo /'ɔtʃimu/ *a* excellent

otorrino /oto'xinu/ *m* ear, nose and throat specialist

ou /o/ *conj* or; **~ ... ~ ...** either... or...; **~ seja** in other words

ouriço /o'risu/ *m* hedgehog; **~-do-mar** (*pl* **~s-do-mar**) *m* sea urchin

ouri|ves /o'rivis/ *m/f invar* jeweller; **~vesaria** *f* (*loja*) jeweller's

ouro /'oru/ *m* gold; *pl* (*naipe*) diamonds; **de ~** golden

ou|sadia /oza'dʒia/ *f* daring; (*uma*) daring step; **~sado** *a* daring; **~sar** *vt/i* dare

outdoor /'awtdor/ (*pl* **~s**) *m* billboard

outo|nal /oto'naw/ (*pl* **~nais**) *a* autumnal; **~no** /o/ *m* autumn, (*Amer*) fall

outorgar /otor'gar/ *vt* grant

ou|trem /o'trẽj/ *pron* (*outro*) someone else; (*outros*) others; **~tro** *a* other □ *pron* (*um*) another (one); *pl* others; **~tro copo** another glass; **~tra coisa** something else; **no ~tro dia** the other day; **no ~tro dia** the next day; **~tra vez** again; **~trora** *adv* once upon a time; **~trossim** *adv* equally

outubro /o'tubru/ *m* October

ou|vido /o'vidu/ *m* ear; **de ~vido** by ear; **dar ~vidos a** listen to; **~vinte** *m/f* listener; (*atentamente*) listen to □ *vi* hear; **~vir dizer que** hear that; **~vir falar de** hear of

ovação /ova'sãw/ *f* ovation

oval /o'vaw/ (*pl* **ovais**) *a* & *f* oval

ovário /o'variu/ *m* ovary

ovelha /o'veʎa/ *f* sheep

óvni /'ɔvni/ *m* UFO

ovo /'ovu/ *m* egg; **~ cozido/frito/ mexido/pochê** boiled/fried/ scrambled/poached egg

oxi|genar /oksiʒe'nar/ *vt* bleach <*cabelo*>; **~gênio** *m* oxygen

ozônio /o'zoniu/ *m* ozone

P

pá /pa/ *f* spade; (*de hélice*) blade; (*de moinho*) sail □ *m* (*Port: fam*) mate

pacato /pa'katu/ *a* quiet

paci|ência /pasi'ẽsia/ *f* patience; **~ente** *a* & *m/f* patient

pacificar /pasifi'kar/ *vt* pacify

pacífico /pa'sifiku/ *a* peaceful; **Oceano Pacífico** Pacific Ocean; **ponto ~** undisputed point

pacifis|mo /pasi'fizmu/ *m* pacifism; **~ta** *a* & *m/f* pacifist

paço /'pasu/ *m* palace

pacote /pa'kɔtʃi/ *m* (*de biscoitos etc*) packet; (*mandado pelo correio*) parcel; (*econômico, turístico, software*) package

pacto /'paktu/ *m* pact

padaria /pada'ria/ *f* baker's (shop), bakery

padecer /pade'ser/ *vt/i* suffer

padeiro /pa'deru/ *m* baker

padiola /padʒi'ɔla/ *f* stretcher

padrão /pa'drãw/ *m* standard; (*desenho*) pattern

padrasto /pa'drastu/ *m* stepfather

padre /'padri/ *m* priest

padrinho /pa'driɲu/ *m* (*de batismo*) godfather; (*de casamento*) best man

padroeiro /padro'eru/ *m* patron saint

padronizar /padroni'zar/ *vt* standardize

paetê /paj'te/ *m* sequin

paga /'paga/ *f* pay; **~mento** *m* payment

pa|gão /pa'gãw/ (*pl* **~gãos**) *a* & *m* (*f* **~gã**) pagan

pagar /pa'gar/ *vt* pay for <*compra, erro etc*>; pay <*dívida, conta, empregado etc*>; pay back <*empréstimo*>; repay <*gentileza etc*> □ *vi* pay; **eu pago para ver** I'll believe it when I see it

página /'paʒina/ *f* page

pago /'pagu/ *a* paid □ *pp de* **pagar**

pagode /pa'gɔdʒi/ *m* (*torre*) pagoda; (*fam*) singalong

pai /paj/ *m* father; *pl* (*pai e mãe*) parents; **~-de-santo** (*pl* **~s-de-santo**) *m* macumba priest

pai|nel /paj'nɛw/ (*pl* **~néis**) *m* panel; (*de carro*) dashboard

paio /'paju/ *m* pork sausage

pairar /paj'rar/ *vi* hover

país /pa'is/ *m* country; **País de Gales** Wales; **Países Baixos** Netherlands

paisa|gem /paj'zaʒẽ/ *f* landscape; **~gista** *m/f* landscape gardener

paisana /paj'zana/ *f* **à ~** <*policial*> in plain clothes; <*soldado*> in civilian clothes

paixão /paj'ʃãw/ *f* passion

pala /'pala/ *f* (*de boné*) peak; (*de automóvel*) sun visor

palácio /pa'lasiu/ *m* palace

paladar /pala'dar/ *m* palate, taste

palanque /pa'lãki/ *m* stand

palavra /pa'lavra/ *f* word; **pedir a ~** ask to speak; **ter ~** be reliable; **tomar a ~** start to speak; **sem ~** <*pessoa*> unreliable; **~ de ordem** watchword; **~s cruzadas** crossword

palavrão /pala'vrãw/ *m* swearword

palco /'pawku/ *m* stage

palestino /pales'tʃinu/ *a* & *m* Palestinian

palestra /pa'lɛstra/ *f* lecture

paleta /pa'leta/ *f* palette

paletó /pale'tɔ/ *m* jacket

palha /'paʎa/ *f* straw

palha|çada /paʎa'sada/ *f* joke; **~ço** *m* clown

paliativo /palia'tʃivu/ *a* & *m* palliative

palidez /pali'des/ *f* paleness

pálido /'palidu/ *a* pale

pali|tar /pali'tar/ *vt* pick □ *vi* pick one's teeth; **~teiro** *m* toothpick holder; **~to** *m* (*para dentes*) toothpick; (*de fósforo*) matchstick; (*pessoa magra*) beanpole

pal|ma /'pawma/ *f* palm; *pl* (*aplauso*) clapping; **bater ~mas** clap; **~meira** *f* palm tree; **~mito** *m* palm heart; **~mo** *m* span; **~mo a ~mo** inch by inch

palpá|vel /paw'pavew/ (*pl* **~veis**) *a* palpable

pálpebra /'pawpebra/ *f* eyelid

palpi|tação /pawpita'sãw/ *f* palpitation; **~tante** *a* (*fig*) thrilling; **~tar** *vi* <*coração*> flutter; <*pessoa*> tremble; (*dar palpite*) stick one's oar in; **~te** *m* (*pressentimento*) hunch; (*no jogo etc*) tip; **dar ~te** stick one's oar in

panacéia /pana'sɛja/ *f* panacea

Panamá /pana'ma/ *m* Panama

panamenho /pana'meɲu/ *a* & *m* Panamanian

pan-americano /panameri'kanu/ *a* Pan-American

pança /'pãsa/ *f* paunch

pancada /pã'kada/ *f* blow; **~ d'água** downpour; **~ria** *f* fight, punch-up

pâncreas /'pãkrias/ *m invar* pancreas

pançudo /pã'sudu/ *a* paunchy

panda /'pãda/ *f* panda

pandarecos /pãda'rɛkus/ *m pl* **aos** *ou* **em ~** battered

pandeiro /pã'deru/ *m* tambourine

pandemônio /pãde'moniu/ *m* pandemonium

pane /'pani/ *f* breakdown

panela /pa'nɛla/ *f* saucepan; **~ de pressão** pressure cooker

panfleto /pã'fletu/ *m* pamphlet

pânico /'paniku/ *m* panic; **em ~** in a panic; **entrar em ~** panic

panifica|ção /panifika'sãw/ *f* bakery; **~dora** *f* bakery

pano /'panu/ *m* cloth; **~ de fundo** backdrop; **~ de pó** duster; **~ de pratos** tea towel

pano|rama /pano'rama/ *m* panorama; **~râmico** *a* panoramic

panqueca /pã'kɛka/ *f* pancake

panta|nal /pãta'naw/ (*pl* **~nais**) *m* marshland

pântano /'pãtanu/ *m* marsh

pantanoso /pãta'nozu/ *a* marshy

pantera /pã'tɛra/ *f* panther

pão /pãw/ (*pl* **pães**) *m* bread; **~ de fôrma** sliced loaf; **~ integral** brown bread; **~-de-ló** *m* sponge cake; **~duro** (*pl* **pães-duros**) *a* (*fam*) a stingy, tight-fisted □ *m/f* skinflint; **~zinho** *m* bread roll

Papa /'papa/ *m* Pope

papa /'papa/ *f* (*de nenem*) food; (*arroz etc*) mush

papagaio /papa'gaju/ *m* parrot

papai /pa'paj/ *m* dad, daddy; **Papai Noël** Father Christmas

papar /pa'par/ *vt/i* (*fam*) eat

papari|car /papari'kar/ *vt* pamper; **~cos** *m pl* pampering

pa|pel /pa'pɛw/ (*pl* **~péis**) *m* (*de escrever etc*) paper; (*um*) piece of paper; (*numa peça, filme*) part; (*fig: função*) role; **de ~pel passado** officially; **~pel de alumínio** aluminium foil; **~pel higiênico** toilet paper; **~pelada** *f* paperwork; **~pelão** *m* cardboard; **~pelaria** *f* stationer's (shop); **~pelzinho** *m* scrap of paper

papo /'papu/ *f* (*fam: conversa*) talk; (*do rosto*) double chin; **bater um ~** (*fam*) have a chat; **~ furado** idle talk

papoula /pa'pola/ *f* poppy

páprica /'paprika/ *f* paprika

paque|ra /pa'kɛra/ *f* (*fam*) pick-up; **~rador** *a* flirtatious □ *m* flirt; **~rar** *vt* flirt with <*pessoa*>; eye up <*vestido, carro etc*> □ *vi* flirt

paquista|nês /pakista'nes/ *a* & *m* (*f* **~nesa**) Pakistani

Paquistão /pakis'tãw/ *m* Pakistan

par /par/ *a* even □ *m* pair; (*parceiro*) partner; **a ~ de** up to date with <*notícias etc*>; **sem ~** unequalled

para /'para/ *prep* for; (*a*) to; **~ que** so that; **~ quê?** what for?; **~ casa** home; **estar ~ sair** be about to leave; **era ~ eu ir** I was supposed to go

para|benizar /parabeni'zar/ *vt* congratulate (**por** on); **~béns** *m pl* congratulations

parábola /pa'rabola/ *f* (*conto*) parable; (*curva*) parabola

parabóli|co /para'bɔliku/ *a* **antena ~ca** satellite dish

pára|-brisa /para'briza/ *m* windscreen, (*Amer*) windshield; **~choque** *m* bumper

para|da /pa'rada/ *f* stop; (*interrupção*) stoppage; (*militar*) parade; (*fam: coisa difícil*) ordeal, challenge; **~da cardíaca** cardiac arrest; **~deiro** *m* whereabouts

paradisíaco /paradʒi'ziaku/ *a* idyllic

parado /pa'radu/ *a* <*trânsito, carro*> at a standstill, stopped; (*fig*) <*pessoa*> dull; **ficar ~** <*pessoa*> stand still; <*trânsito*> come to a standstill; (*fig: deixar de trabalhar*) stop work

parado|xal /paradok'saw/ (*pl* **~xais**) *a* paradoxical; **~xo** /ɔ/ *m* paradox

parafina /para'fina/ *f* paraffin

paráfrase /pa'rafrazi/ *f* paraphrase

parafrasear /parafrazi'ar/ *vt* paraphrase

parafuso /para'fuzu/ f screw; **entrar em ~** get into a state

para|gem /pa'raʒẽ/ f (*Port: parada*) stop; **nestas ~gens** in these parts

parágrafo /pa'ragrafu/ m paragraph

Paraguai /para'gwaj/ m Paraguay

paraguaio /para'gwaju/ a & m Paraguayan

paraíso /para'izu/ m paradise

pára-lama /para'lama/ m (*de carro*) wing; (*Amer*) fender; (*de bicicleta*) mudguard

parale|la /para'lɛla/ f parallel; *pl* (*aparelho*) parallel bars; **~lepípedo** m paving stone; **~lo** /ɛ/ a & m parallel

para|lisar /parali'zar/ vt paralyse; bring to a halt <*fábrica, produção*>; **~lisar-se** vpr become paralysed; <*fábrica, produção*> grind to a halt; **~lisia** f paralysis; **~lítico** a & m paralytic

paranói|a /para'nɔja/ f paranoia; **~co** a paranoid

parapeito /para'pejtu/ m (*muro*) parapet; (*da janela*) window-sill

pára-que|das /para'kɛdas/ m invar parachute; **~dista** m/f parachutist; (*militar*) paratrooper

parar /pa'rar/ vt/i stop; **~ de fumar** stop smoking; **ir ~** end up

pára-raios /para'xajus/ m invar lightning conductor

parasita /para'zita/ a & m/f parasite

parceiro /par'seru/ m partner

parce|la /par'sɛla/ f (*de terreno*) plot; (*prestação*) instalment; **~lar** vt spread <*pagamento*>

parceria /parse'ria/ f partnership

parci|al /parsi'aw/ (*pl* **~ais**) a partial; (*partidário*) biased; **~alidade** f bias

parco /'parku/ a frugal; <*recursos*> scant

par|dal /par'daw/ (*pl* **~dais**) m sparrow; **~do** a <*papel*> brown; <*pessoa*> mulatto

pare|cer /pare'ser/ vi (*ter aparência de*) seem; (*ter semelhança com*) be like; **~cer-se com** look like, resemble □ m opinion; **~cido** a similar (com to)

parede /pa'redʒi/ f wall

paren|te /pa'rẽtʃi/ m/f relative, relation; **~tesco** /e/ m relationship

parêntese /pa'rẽtʃizi/ f parenthesis; *pl* (*sinais*) brackets, parentheses

paridade /pari'dadʒi/ f parity

parir /pa'rir/ vt give birth to □ vi give birth

parlamen|tar /parlamẽ'tar/ a parliamentary □ m/f member of parliament; **~tarismo** m parliamentary system; **~to** m parliament

parmesão /parme'zãw/ a & m (**queijo**) ~ Parmesan (cheese)

paródia /pa'rɔdʒia/ f parody

parodiar /parodʒi'ar/ vt parody

paróquia /pa'rɔkia/ f parish

parque /'parki/ m park

parte /'partʃi/ f part; (*quinhão*) share; (*num litígio, contrato*) party; **a maior ~ de** most of; **à ~** (*de lado*) aside; (*separadamente*) separately; **um erro da sua ~** a mistake on your part; **em ~** in part; **em alguma ~** somewhere; **por toda ~** everywhere; **por ~ do pai** on one's father's side; **fazer ~ de** be part of; **tomar ~ em** take part in

parteira /par'tera/ f midwife

partici|pação /partʃisipa'sãw/ f participation; (*numa empresa, nos lucros*) share; **~pante** a participating □ m/f participant; **~par** vi take part (**de** ou **em** in)

particípio /partʃi'sipiu/ m participle

partícula /par'tʃikula/ f particle

particu|lar /partʃiku'lar/ a private; (*especial*) unusual □ m (*pessoa*) private individual; *pl* (*detalhes*) particulars; **em ~lar** (*especialmente*) in particular; (*a sós*) in private; **~laridade** f peculiarity

partida /par'tʃida/ f (*saída*) departure; (*de corrida*) start; (*de futebol, xadrez etc*) match; **dar ~ em** start up

par|tidário /partʃi'dariu/ a partisan □ m supporter; **~tido** a broken □ m (*político*) party; (*casamento, par*) match; **tirar ~tido de** benefit from; **tomar o ~tido de** side with; **~tilha** f division; **~tir** vi (*sair*) depart; <*corredor*> start □ vt break; **~tir-se** vpr break; **a ~tir de ...** from ... onwards; **~tir para** (*fam*) resort to; **~tir para outra** do something different, change direction; **~titura** f score

parto /'partu/ m birth

parvo /'parvu/ a (*Port*) stupid

Páscoa /'paskoa/ f Easter

pas|mar /paz'mar/ vt amaze; **~mar-se** vpr be amazed (**com** at); **~mo** a amazed □ m amazement

passa /'pasa/ f raisin

pas|sada /pa'sada/ f **dar uma ~sada em** call in at; **~sadeira** f (*mulher*) woman who irons; (*Port: faixa*) zebra crossing, (*Amer*) crosswalk; **~sado** a <*ano, mês, semana*> last; <*tempo, particípio etc*> past; <*fruta, comida*> off □ m past; **são duas horas ~sadas** it's gone two o'clock; **bem/mal ~sado** <*bife*> well done/rare

passa|geiro /pasa'ʒeru/ m passenger □ a passing; **~gem** f passage; (*bilhete*) ticket; **de ~gem** <*dizer etc*> in passing; **estar de ~gem** be passing through; ~**gem de ida e volta** return ticket, (*Amer*) round trip ticket

passaporte /pasa'pɔrtʃi/ *m* passport

passar /pa'sar/ *vt* pass; spend <*tempo*>; cross <*ponte, rio*>; (*a ferro*) iron <*roupa etc*>; (*aplicar*) put on <*creme, batom etc*> □ *vi* pass; <*dor, medo, chuva etc*> go; (*ser aceitável*) be passable □ *m* passing; ~**-se** *vpr* happen; **passou a beber muito** he started to drink a lot; **passei dos 30 anos** I'm over thirty; **não passa de um boato** it's nothing more than a rumour; ~ **por** go through; go along <*rua*>; (*ser considerado*) be taken for; **fazer-se** ~ **por** pass o.s. off as; ~ **por cima de** (*fig*) overlook; ~ **sem** go without

passarela /pasa'rɛla/ *f (sobre rua)* footbridge; (*para desfile de moda*) catwalk

pássaro /'pasaru/ *m* bird

passatempo /pasa'tẽpu/ *m* pastime

passe /'pasi/ *m* pass

pas|sear /pasi'ar/ *vi* go out and about; (*viajar*) travel around □ *vt* take for a walk; ~**seata** *f* protest march; ~**seio** *m* outing; (*volta a pé*) walk; (*volta de carro*) drive; **dar um** ~**seio** (*a pé*) go for a walk; (*de carro*) go for a drive

passio|nal /pasio'naw/ (*pl* ~**nais**) *a* **crime** ~**nal** crime of passion

passista /pa'sista/ *m/f* dancer

passí|vel /pa'sivew/ (*pl* ~**veis**) *a* ~**vel de** subject to

passi|vidade /pasivi'dadʒi/ *f* passivity; ~**vo** *a* passive □ *m* (*com*) liabilities; (*ling*) passive

passo /'pasu/ *m* step; (*velocidade*) pace; (*barulho*) footstep; ~ **a** ~ step by step; **a dois** ~**s** a stone's throw from; **dar um** ~ take a step

pasta /'pasta/ *f* (*matéria*) paste; (*bolsa*) briefcase; (*fichário*) folder; **ministro sem** ~ minister without portfolio; ~ **de dentes** toothpaste

pas|tagem /pas'taʒẽ/ *f* pasture; ~**tar** *vi* graze

pas|tel /pas'tɛw/ (*pl* ~**téis**) *m* (*para comer*) samosa; (*Port: doce*) pastry; (*para desenhar*) pastel; ~**telão** *m* (*comédia*) slapstick; ~**telaria** *f* (*loja*) samosa vendor, (*Port*) pastry shop; (*Port: pastéis*) pastries

pasteurizado /pastewri'zadu/ *a* pasteurized

pastilha /pas'tʃiʎa/ *f* pastille

pas|to /'pastu/ *m* (*erva*) fodder, feed; (*lugar*) pasture; ~**tor** *m* (*de gado*) shepherd; (*clérigo*) vicar; ~**tor alemão** (*cachorro*) Alsatian; ~**toral** (*pl* ~**torais**) *a* pastoral

pata /'pata/ *f* paw; ~**da** *f* kick

patamar /pata'mar/ *m* landing; (*fig*) level

patê /pa'te/ *m* pâté

patente /pa'tẽtʃi/ *a* obvious □ *f* (*mil*) rank; (*de invenção*) patent; ~**ar** *vt* patent <*produto, invenção*>

pater|nal /pater'naw/ (*pl* ~**nais**) *a* paternal; ~**nidade** *f* paternity; ~**no** /ɛ/ *a* paternal

pate|ta /pa'tɛta/ *a* daft, silly □ *m/f* fool; ~**tice** *f* stupidity; (*uma*) silly thing

patético /pa'tɛtʃiku/ *a* pathetic

patíbulo /pa'tʃibulu/ *m* gallows

pati|faria /patʃifa'ria/ *f* roguishness; (*uma*) dirty trick; ~**fe** *m* scoundrel

patim /pa'tʃĩ/ *m* skate; ~ **de rodas** roller skate

pati|nação /patʃina'sãw/ *f* skating; (*rinque*) skating rink; ~**nador** *m* skater; ~**nar** *vi* skate; <*carro*> skid; ~**nete** /ɛ/ *m* skateboard

pátio /'patʃiu/ *m* courtyard; (*de escola*) playground

pato /'patu/ *m* duck

pato|logia /patolo'ʒia/ *f* pathology; ~**lógico** *a* pathological; ~**logista** *m/f* pathologist

patrão /pa'trãw/ *m* boss

pátria /'patria/ *f* homeland

patriar|ca /patri'arka/ *m* patriarch; ~**cal** (*pl* ~**cais**) *a* patriarchal

patrimônio /patri'moniu/ *m* (*bens*) estate, property; (*fig: herança*) heritage

patri|ota /patri'ɔta/ *m/f* patriot; ~**ótico** *a* patriotic; ~**otismo** *m* patriotism

patroa /pa'troa/ *f* boss; (*fam: esposa*) missus, wife

patro|cinador /patrosina'dor/ *m* sponsor; ~**cinar** *vt* sponsor; ~**cínio** *m* sponsorship

patru|lha /pa'truʎa/ *f* patrol; ~**lhar** *vt/i* patrol

pau /paw/ *m* stick; (*fam: cruzeiro*) cruzeiro; (*chulo: pênis*) prick; *pl* (*naipe*) clubs; **a meio** ~ at half mast; **rachar** ~ (*fam: brigar*) row, fight like cat and dog; ~**lada** *f* blow with a stick

paulista /paw'lista/ *a & m/f* (person) from (the state of) São Paulo; ~**no** *a & m* (person) from (the city of) São Paulo

pausa /'pawza/ *f* pause; ~**do** *a* slow

pauta /'pawta/ *f* (*em papel*) lines; (*de música*) stave; (*fig: de discussão etc*) agenda; ~**do** *a* <*papel*> lined

pavão /pa'vãw/ *m* peacock

pavilhão /pavi'ʎãw/ *m* pavilion; (*no jardim*) summerhouse

pavimen|tar /pavimẽ'tar/ *vt* pave; ~**to** *m* floor; (*de rua etc*) surface

pavio /pa'viu/ *m* wick

pavor /pa'vor/ *m* terror; **ter** ~ **de** be terrified of; ~**oso** /o/ *a* dreadful

paz /pas/ *f* peace; **fazer as ~es** make up

pé /pɛ/ *m* foot; (*planta*) plant; (*de móvel*) leg; **a ~** on foot; **ao ~ da letra** literally; **estar de ~** <*festa etc*> be on; **ficar de ~** stand up; **em ~** standing (up); **em ~ de igualdade** on an equal footing

peão /pi'ãw/ *m* (*Port: pedestre*) pedestrian; (*no xadrez*) pawn

peça /'pɛsa/ *f* piece; (*de máquina, carro etc*) part; (*teatral*) play; **pregar uma ~ em** play a trick on; **~ de reposição** spare part; **~ de vestuário** item of clothing

pe|cado /pe'kadu/ *m* sin; **~cador** *m* sinner; **~caminoso** /o/ *a* sinful; **~car** *vi* (*contra a religião*) sin; (*fig*) fall down

pechin|cha /pe'ʃĩʃa/ *f* bargain; **~char** *vi* bargain, haggle

peçonhento /peso'ɲẽtu/ *a* **animais ~s** vermin

pecu|ária /peku'aria/ *f* livestock-farming; **~ário** *a* livestock; **~arista** *m/f* livestock farmer

peculi|ar /pekuli'ar/ *a* peculiar; **~aridade** *f* peculiarity

pecúlio /pe'kuliu/ *m* savings

pedaço /pe'dasu/ *m* piece; **aos ~s** in pieces; **cair aos ~s** fall to pieces

pedágio /pe'daʒiu/ *m* toll; (*cabine*) tollbooth

peda|gogia /pedago'ʒia/ *f* education; **~gógico** *a* educational; **~gogo** /o/ *m* educationalist

pe|dal /pe'daw/ (*pl* **~dais**) *m* pedal; **~dalar** *vt/i* pedal

pedante /pe'dãtʃi/ *a* pretentious □ *m/f* pseud

pé|-de-atleta /pɛdʒiat'lɛta/ *m* athlete's foot; **~-de-meia** (*pl* **~s-de-meia**) *m* nest egg; **~-de-pato** (*pl* **~s-de-pato**) *m* flipper

pederneira /peder'nera/ *f* flint

pedes|tal /pedes'taw/ (*pl* **~tais**) *m* pedestal

pedestre /pe'dɛstri/ *a* & *m/f* pedestrian

pé|-de-vento /pɛdʒi'vẽtu/ (*pl* **~s-de-vento**) *m* gust of wind

pedia|tra /pedʒi'atra/ *m/f* paediatrician; **~tria** *f* paediatrics

pedicuro /pedʒi'kuru/ *m* chiropodist, (*Amer*) podiatrist

pe|dido /pe'dʒidu/ *m* request; (*encomenda*) order; **a ~dido de** at the request of; **~dido de demissão** resignation; **~dido de desculpa** apology; **~dir** *vt* ask for; (*num restaurante etc*) order □ *vi* ask; (*num restaurante etc*) order; **~dir aco a alg** ask s.o. for sth; **~dir para alg ir** ask s.o. to go; **~dir desculpa**

apologize; **~dir em casamento** propose to

pedinte /pe'dʒĩtʃi/ *m/f* beggar

pedra /'pɛdra/ stone; **~ de gelo** ice cube; **chuva de ~** hail; **~ pomes** pumice stone

pedregoso /pedre'gozu/ *a* stony

pedreiro /pe'dreru/ *m* builder

pegada /pe'gada/ *f* footprint; (*de goleiro*) save

pegajoso /pega'ʒozu/ *a* sticky

pegar /pe'gar/ *vt* get; catch <*bola, doença, ladrão, ônibus*>; (*segurar*) get hold of; pick up <*emissora, hábito, mania*> □ *vi* (*aderir*) stick; <*doença*> be catching; <*moda*> catch on; <*carro, motor*> start; <*mentira, desculpa*> stick; **~-se** *vpr* come to blows; **~ bem/mal** go down well/badly; **~ fogo** catch fire; **pega essa rua** take that street; **~ em** grab; **~ no sono** get to sleep

pego /'pɛgu/ *pp de* **pegar**

pei|dar /pej'dar/ *vi* (*chulo*) fart; **~do** *m* (*chulo*) fart

pei|to /'pejtu/ *m* chest; (*seio*) breast; (*fig: coragem*) guts; **~toril** (*pl* **~toris**) *m* window-sill; **~tudo** *a* <*mulher*> busty; (*fig: corajoso*) gutsy

pei|xaria /pe'ʃaria/ *f* fishmonger's; **~xe** *m* fish; **Peixes** (*signo*) Pisces; **~xeiro** *m* fishmonger

pela = **por** + **a**

pelado /pe'ladu/ *a* (*nu*) naked, in the nude

pelan|ca /pe'lãka/ *f* roll of fat; *pl* flab; **~cudo** *a* flabby

pelar /pe'lar/ *vt* peel <*fruta, batata*>; skin <*animal*>; (*fam: tomar dinheiro de*) fleece

pelas = **por** + **as**

pele /'pɛli/ *f* skin; (*como roupa*) fur; **~teiro** *m* furrier; **~teria** *f* furrier's

pelica /pe'lika/ *f* **luvas de ~** kid gloves

pelicano /peli'kanu/ *m* pelican

película /pe'likula/ *f* skin

pelo = **por** + **o**

pêlo /'pelu/ *m* hair; (*de animal*) coat; **nu em ~** stark naked; **montar em ~** ride bareback

pelos = **por** + **os**

pelotão /pelo'tãw/ *m* platoon

pelúcia /pe'lusia/ *f* **bicho de ~** soft toy, fluffy animal

peludo /pe'ludu/ *a* hairy

pena¹ /'pena/ *f* (*de ave*) feather; (*de caneta*) nib

pena² /'pena/ *f* (*castigo*) penalty; (*de amor etc*) pang; **é uma ~ que** it's a pity that; **que ~!** what a pity!; **dar ~** be upsetting; **estar com** *ou* **ter ~ de** feel sorry for; **(não) vale a ~** it's (not) worth it; **vale a ~ tentar** it's worth trying; ~ **de morte** death penalty

penada /pe'nada/ *f* stroke of the pen

pe|nal /pe'naw/ (*pl* ~**nais**) *a* penal; ~**nalidade** *f* penalty; ~**nalizar** *vt* penalize

pênalti /'penawtʃi/ *m* penalty

penar /pe'nar/ *vi* suffer

pen|dente /pẽ'dẽtʃi/ *a* hanging; (*fig: causa*) pending; ~**der** *vi* hang; (*inclinar-se*) slope; (*tender*) be inclined (**a** to); ~**dor** *m* inclination

pêndulo /'pẽdulu/ *m* pendulum

pendu|rado /pẽdu'radu/ *a* hanging; (*fam: por fazer, pagar*) outstanding; ~**rar** *vt* hang (up); (*fam*) put on the slate <*compra*> □ *vi* (*fam*) pay later; ~**ricalho** *m* pendant

penedo /pe'nedu/ *m* rock

penei|ra /pe'nera/ *f* sieve; ~**rar** *vt* sieve, sift □ *vi* drizzle

pene|tra /pe'nɛtra/ *m/f* (*fam*) gatecrasher; ~**tração** *f* penetration; (*fig*) perspicacity; ~**trante** *a* <*som, olhar*> piercing; <*dor*> sharp; <*ferida*> deep; <*frio*> biting; <*análise, espírito*> incisive, perceptive; ~**trar** *vt* penetrate □ *vi* ~**trar em** enter <*casa*>; (*fig*) penetrate

penhasco /pe'ɲasku/ *m* cliff

penhoar /peɲo'ar/ *m* dressing gown

penhor /pe'ɲor/ *m* pledge; **casa de** ~**es** pawnshop

penicilina /penisi'lina/ *f* penicillin

penico /pe'niku/ *m* potty

península /pe'nĩsula/ *f* peninsula

pênis /'penis/ *m invar* penis

penitência /peni'tẽsia/ *f* (*arrependimento*) penitence; (*expiação*) penance

penitenciá|ria /penitẽsi'aria/ *f* prison; ~**rio** *a* prison □ *m* prisoner

penoso /pe'nozu/ *a* <*experiência, tarefa, assunto*> painful; <*trabalho, viagem*> hard, difficult

pensa|dor /pẽsa'dor/ *m* thinker; ~**mento** *m* thought

pensão /pẽ'sãw/ *f* (*renda*) pension; (*hotel*) guesthouse; ~ (**alimentícia**) (*paga por ex-marido*) alimony; ~ **completa** full board

pen|sar /pẽ'sar/ *vt/i* think (**em** of *ou* about); ~**sativo** *a* thoughtful, pensive

pên|sil /'pẽsiw/ (*pl* ~**seis**) *a* **ponte** ~**sil** suspension bridge

penso /'pẽsu/ *m* (*curativo*) dressing

pentágono /pẽ'tagonu/ *m* pentagon

pentatlo /pẽ'tatlu/ *m* pentathlon

pente /'pẽtʃi/ *m* comb; ~**adeira** *f* dressing table; ~**ado** *m* hairstyle, hairdo; ~**ar** *vt* comb; ~**ar-se** *vpr* do one's hair; (*com pente*) comb one's hair

Pentecostes /pẽte'kɔstʃis/ *m* Whitsun

pente-fino /pẽtʃi'finu/ *m* **passar a** ~ go over with a fine-tooth comb

pente|lhar /pẽte'ʎar/ *vt* (*fam*) bother; ~**lho** /e/ *m* pubic hair; (*fam: pessoa inconveniente*) pain (in the neck)

penugem /pe'nuʒẽ/ *f* down

penúltimo /pe'nuwtʃimu/ *a* last but one, penultimate

penumbra /pe'nũbra/ *f* half-light

penúria /pe'nuria/ *f* penury, extreme poverty

pepino /pe'pinu/ *m* cucumber

pepita /pe'pita/ *f* nugget

peque|nez /peke'nes/ *f* smallness; (*fig*) pettiness; ~**nininho** *a* tiny; ~**no** /e/ *a* small; (*mesquinho*) petty

Pequim /pe'kĩ/ *f* Peking, Beijing

pequinês /peki'nes/ *m* Pekinese

pêra /'pera/ *f* pear

perambular /perãbu'lar/ *vi* wander

perante /pe'rãtʃi/ *prep* before

percalço /per'kawsu/ *m* pitfall

perceber /perse'ber/ *vt* realize; (*Port: entender*) understand; (*psiqu*) perceive

percen|tagem /persẽ'taʒẽ/ *f* percentage; ~**tual** (*pl* ~**tuais**) *a & m* percentage

percep|ção /persep'sãw/ *f* perception; ~**tível** (*pl* ~**tíveis**) *a* perceptible

percevejo /perse'veʒu/ *m* (*bicho*) bedbug; (*tachinha*) drawing pin, (*Amer*) thumbtack

per|correr /perko'xer/ *vt* cross; cover <*distância*>; (*viajar por*) travel through; ~**curso** *m* journey

percus|são /perku'sãw/ *f* percussion; ~**sionista** *m/f* percussionist

percutir /perku'tʃir/ *vt* strike

perda /'perda/ *f* loss; ~ **de tempo** waste of time

perdão /per'dãw/ *f* pardon

perder /per'der/ *vt* lose; (*não chegar a ver, pegar*) miss <*ônibus, programa na TV etc*>; waste <*tempo*> □ *vi* lose; ~**-se** *vpr* get lost; ~**-se de alg** lose s.o.; ~ **aco de vista** lose sight of sth

perdiz /per'dʒis/ *f* partridge

perdoar /perdo'ar/ *vt* forgive (**aco a alg** s.o. for sth)

perdulário /perdu'lariu/ *a & m* spendthrift

perdurar /perdu'rar/ *vi* endure; <*coisa ruim*> persist

pere|cer /pere'ser/ *vi* perish; ~**cível** (*pl* ~**cíveis**) *a* perishable

peregri|nação /peregrina'sãw/ *f* peregrination; (*romaria*) pilgrimage; ~**nar** *vi* roam; (*por motivos religiosos*) go on a pilgrimage; ~**no** *m* pilgrim

pereira /pe'rera/ *f* pear tree

peremptório /perẽp'tɔriu/ *a* peremptory

perene /pe'reni/ *a* perennial

perereca /pere'rɛka/ *f* tree frog

perfazer /perfa'zer/ *vt* make up

perfeccionis|mo /perfeksio'nizmu/ *m* perfectionism; **~ta** *a* & *m/f* perfectionist

perfei|ção /perfej'sãw/ *f* perfection; **~to** *a* & *m* perfect

per|fil /per'fiw/ (*pl* **~fis**) *m* profile; **~filar** *vt* line up; **~filar-se** *vpr* line up

perfu|mado /perfu'madu/ *a* <*flor, ar*> fragrant; <*sabonete etc*> scented; <*pessoa*> with perfume on; **~mar** *vt* perfume; **~mar-se** *vpr* put perfume on; **~maria** *f* perfumery; (*fam*) trimmings, frills; **~me** *m* perfume

perfu|rador /perfura'dor/ *m* punch; **~rar** *vt* punch <*papel, bilhete*>; drill through <*chão*>; perforate <*úlcera, pulmão etc*>; **~ratriz** *f* drill

pergaminho /perga'miɲu/ *m* parchment

pergun|ta /per'gũta/ *f* question; **fazer uma ~ta** ask a question; **~tar** *vt/i* ask; **~tar aco a alg** ask s.o. sth; **~tar por** ask after

perícia /pe'risia/ *f* (*mestria*) expertise; (*inspeção*) investigation; (*peritos*) experts

perici|al /perisi'aw/ (*pl* **~ais**) *a* expert

pericli|tante /perikli'tãtʃi/ *a* precarious; **~tar** *vi* be at risk

peri|feria /perife'ria/ *f* periphery; (*da cidade*) outskirts; **~férico** *a* & *m* peripheral

perigo /pe'rigu/ *m* danger; **~so** /o/ *a* dangerous

perímetro /pe'rimetru/ *m* perimeter

periódico /peri'ɔdʒiku/ *a* periodic □ *m* periodical

período /pe'riodu/ *m* period; **trabalhar meio ~** work part-time

peripécias /peri'pɛsias/ *f pl* ups and downs, vicissitudes

periquito /peri'kitu/ *m* parakeet; (*de estimação*) budgerigar

periscópio /peris'kɔpiu/ *m* periscope

perito /pe'ritu/ *a* & *m* expert (**em at**)

per|jurar /perʒu'rar/ *vi* commit perjury; **~júrio** *m* perjury; **~juro** *m* perjurer

perma|necer /permane'ser/ *vi* remain; **~nência** *f* permanence; (*estadia*) stay; **~nente** *a* permanent □ *f* perm

permeá|vel /permi'avew/ (*pl* **~veis**) *a* permeable

permis|são /permi'sãw/ *f* permission; **~sível** (*pl* **~síveis**) *a* permissible; **~sivo** *a* permissive

permitir /permi'tʃir/ *vt* allow, permit; **~ a alg ir** allow s.o. to go

permutar /permu'tar/ *vt* exchange

perna /'pɛrna/ *f* leg

pernicioso /pernisi'ozu/ *a* pernicious

per|nil /per'niw/ (*pl* **~nis**) *m* leg

pernilongo /perni'lõgu/ *m* (large) mosquito

pernoi|tar /pernoj'tar/ *vi* spend the night; **~te** *m* overnight stay

pérola /'pɛrola/ *f* pearl

perpendicular /perpẽdʒiku'lar/ *a* perpendicular

perpetrar /perpe'trar/ *vt* perpetrate

perpetu|ar /perpetu'ar/ *vt* perpetuate; **~idade** *f* perpetuity

perpétu|o /per'pɛtuu/ *a* perpetual; **prisão ~a** life imprisonment

perple|xidade /perpleksi'dadʒi/ *f* puzzlement; **~xo** /ɛ/ *a* puzzled

persa /'pɛrsa/ *a* & *m/f* Persian

perse|guição /persegi'sãw/ *f* pursuit; (*de minorias etc*) persecution; **~guidor** *m* pursuer; (*de minorias etc*) persecutor; **~guir** *vt* pursue; persecute <*minoria, seita etc*>

perseve|rança /perseve'rãsa/ *f* perseverance; **~rante** *a* persevering; **~rar** *vi* persevere

persiana /persi'ana/ *f* blind

pérsico /'pɛrsiku/ *a* **Golfo Pérsico** Persian Gulf

persignar-se /persig'narsi/ *vt* cross o.s.

persis|tência /persis'tẽsia/ *f* persistence; **~tente** *a* persistent; **~tir** *vi* persist

perso|nagem /perso'naʒẽ/ *m/f* (*pessoa famosa*) personality; (*em livro, filme etc*) character; **~nalidade** *f* personality; **~nalizar** *vt* personalize; **~nificar** *vt* personify

perspectiva /perspek'tʃiva/ *f* (*na arte, ponto de vista*) perspective; (*possibilidade*) prospect

perspi|cácia /perspi'kasia/ *f* insight, perceptiveness; **~caz** *a* perceptive

persua|dir /persua'dʒir/ *vt* persuade (**alg a** s.o. to); **~são** *f* persuasion; **~sivo** *a* persuasive

perten|cente /pertẽ'sẽtʃi/ *a* belonging (**a** to); (*que tem a ver com*) pertaining (**a** to); **~cer** *vi* belong (**a** to); (*referir-se*) pertain (**a** to); **~ces** *m pl* belongings

perto /'pɛrtu/ *adv* near (**de** to); **aqui ~** near here, nearby; **de ~** closely; <*ver*> close up

pertur|bação /perturba'sãw/ *f* disturbance; (*do espírito*) anxiety; **~bado** *a* <*pessoa*> unsettled, troubled; **~bar** *vt* disturb; **~bar-se** *vpr* get upset, be perturbed

Peru /pe'ru/ *m* Peru

peru /pe'ru/ *m* turkey

perua /pe'rua/ *f* (*carro grande*) estate car, (*Amer*) station wagon; (*caminho-*

nete) van; (*para escolares etc*) minibus; (*fam: mulher*) brassy woman

peruano /peru'ano/ *a* & *m* Peruvian

peruca /pe'ruka/ *f* wig

perver|são /perver'sãw/ *f* perversion; **~so** *a* perverse; **~ter** *vt* pervert

pesadelo /peza'delu/ *m* nightmare

pesado /pe'zadu/ *a* heavy; <*estilo, livro*> heavy-going □ *adv* heavily

pêsames /'pezamis/ *m pl* condolences

pesar¹ /pe'zar/ *vt* weigh; (*fig: avaliar*) weigh up □ *vi* weigh; (*influir*) carry weight; **~ sobre** <*ameaça etc*> hang over; **~-se** *vpr* weigh o.s.

pesar² /pe'zar/ *m* sorrow; **~oso** /o/ *a* sorry, sorrowful

pes|ca /'pɛska/ *f* fishing; **ir à ~ca** go fishing; **~cador** *m* fisherman; **~car** *vt* catch; (*retirar da água*) fish out □ *vi* fish; (*fam*) (*entender*) understand; (*cochilar*) nod off; **~car de** (*fam*) know all about

pescoço /pes'kosu/ *m* neck

peseta /pe'zeta/ *f* peseta

peso /'pezu/ *m* weight; **de ~** (*fig*) <*pessoa*> influential; <*livro, argumento*> authoritative

pesqueiro /pes'keru/ *a* fishing

pesqui|sa /pes'kiza/ *f* research; (*uma*) study; *pl* research; **~sa de mercado** market research; **~sador** *m* researcher; **~sar** *vt/i* research

pêssego /'pesigu/ *m* peach

pessegueiro /pesi'geru/ *m* peach tree

pessimis|mo /pesi'mizmu/ *m* pessimism; **~ta** *a* pessimistic □ *m/f* pessimist

péssimo /'pɛsimu/ *a* terrible, awful

pesso|a /pe'soa/ *f* person; *pl* people; **em ~a** in person; **~al** (*pl* **~ais**) *a* personal □ *m* staff; (*fam*) folks

pesta|na /pes'tana/ *f* eyelash; **tirar uma ~na** (*fam*) have a nap; **~nejar** *vi* blink; **sem ~nejar** (*fig*) without batting an eyelid

pes|te /'pɛstʃi/ *f* (*doença*) plague; (*criança etc*) pest; **~ticida** *m* pesticide

pétala /'pɛtala/ *f* petal

peteca /pe'tɛka/ *f* kind of shuttlecock; (*jogo*) kind of badminton played with the hand

peteleco /pete'lɛku/ *m* flick

petição /petʃi'sãw/ *f* petition

petisco /pe'tʃisku/ *m* savoury, titbit

petrificar /petrifi'kar/ *vt* petrify; (*de surpresa*) stun; **~-se** *vpr* be petrified; (*de surpresa*) be stunned

petroleiro /petro'leru/ *a* oil □ *m* oil tanker

petróleo /pe'trɔliu/ *m* oil, petroleum; **~ bruto** crude oil

petrolífero /petro'liferu/ *a* oil-producing

petroquími|ca /petro'kimika/ *f* petrochemicals; **~co** *a* petrochemical

petu|lância /petu'lãsia/ *f* cheek; **~lante** *a* cheeky

peúga /pi'uga/ *f* (*Port*) sock

pevide /pe'vidʒi/ *f* (*Port*) pip

pia /'pia/ *f* (*do banheiro*) washbasin; (*da cozinha*) sink; **~ batismal** font

piada /pi'ada/ *f* joke

pia|nista /pia'nista/ *m/f* pianist; **~no** *m* piano; **~no de cauda** grand piano

piar /pi'ar/ *vi* <*pinto*> cheep; <*coruja*> hoot

picada /pi'kada/ *f* (*de agulha, alfinete etc*) prick; (*de abelha, vespa*) sting; (*de mosquito, cobra*) bite; (*de heroína*) shot; (*de avião*) nosedive; **o fim da ~** (*fig*) the limit

picadeiro /pika'deru/ *m* ring

picante /pi'kãtʃi/ *a* <*comida*> hot, spicy; <*piada*> risqué; <*filme, livro*> raunchy

pica-pau /pika'paw/ *m* woodpecker

picar /pi'kar/ *vt* (*com agulha, alfinete etc*) prick; <*abelha, vespa, urtiga*> sting; <*mosquito, cobra*> bite; <*pássaro*> peck; chop <*carne, alho etc*>; shred <*papel*> □ *vi* <*peixe*> bite; <*lã, cobertor*> prickle

picareta /pika'reta/ *f* pickaxe

pi|chação /piʃa'sãw/ *f* piece of graffiti; *pl* graffiti; **~char** *vt* spray with graffiti <*muro, prédio*>; spray <*grafite, desenho*>; **~che** *m* pitch

picles /'piklis/ *m pl* pickles

pico /'piku/ *m* peak; **20 anos e ~** (*Port*) just over 20

picolé /piko'lɛ/ *m* ice lolly

pico|tar /piko'tar/ *vt* perforate; **~te** /ɔ/ *m* perforations

pie|dade /pie'dadʒi/ *f* (*religiosidade*) piety; (*compaixão*) pity; **~doso** /o/ *a* merciful, compassionate

pie|gas /pi'ɛgas/ *a invar* <*filme, livro*> sentimental, schmaltzy; <*pessoa*> soppy; **~guice** *f* sentimentality

pifar /pi'far/ *vi* (*fam*) break down, go wrong

pigar|rear /pigaxi'ar/ *vi* clear one's throat; **~ro** *m* frog in the throat

pigmento /pig'mẽtu/ *m* pigment

pig|meu /pig'mew/ *a* & *m* (*f* **~méia**) pygmy

pijama /pi'ʒama/ *m* pyjamas

pilantra /pi'lãtra/ *m/f* (*fam*) crook

pilão /pi'lãw/ *m* (*na cozinha*) pestle; (*na construção*) ram

pilar /pi'lar/ *m* pillar

pilastra /pi'lastra/ *f* pillar

pileque /pi'lɛki/ *m* drinking session; **tomar um ~** get drunk

pilha /'piʎa/ *f* (*monte*) pile; (*elétrica*) battery

pilhar /pi'ʎar/ *vt* pillage

pilhéria /pi'ʎɛria/ *f* joke
pilotar /pilo'tar/ *vt* fly, pilot <*avião*>; drive <*carro*>
pilotis /pilo'tʃis/ *m pl* pillars
piloto /pi'lotu/ *m* pilot; (*de carro*) driver; (*de gás*) pilot light □ *a invar* pilot
pílula /'pilula/ *f* pill
pimen|ta /pi'mẽta/ *f* pepper; ~**ta de Caiena** cayenne pepper; ~**ta-do-reino** *f* black pepper; ~**ta-malague-ta** (*pl* ~**tas-malagueta**) *f* chilli pepper; ~**tão** *m* (bell) pepper; ~**teira** *f* pepper pot
pinacoteca /pinako'tɛka/ *f* art gallery
pin|ça /'pĩsa/ (*para tirar pêlos*) tweezers; (*para segurar*) tongs; (*de siri etc*) pincer; ~**çar** *vt* pluck <*sobrancelhas*>
pin|cel /pĩ'sɛw/ (*pl* ~**céis**) *m* brush; ~**celada** *f* brush stroke; ~**celar** *vt* paint
pin|ga /'pĩga/ *f* Brazilian rum; ~**gado** *a* <*café*> with a dash of milk; ~**gar** *vi* drip; (*começar a chover*) spit (with rain) □ *vt* drip; ~**gente** *m* pendant; ~**go** *m* drop; (*no i*) dot
pingue-pongue /pĩgi'põgi/ *m* table tennis
pingüim /pĩ'gwĩ/ *m* penguin
pi|nha /'piɲa/ *f* pine cone; ~**nheiro** *f* pine tree; ~**nho** *m* pine
pino /'pinu/ *m* pin; (*para trancar carro*) lock; **a** ~ upright; **bater** ~ <*carro*> knock
pin|ta /'pĩta/ *f* (*sinal*) mole; (*fam: aparência*) look; ~**tar** *vt* paint; dye <*cabelo*>; put make-up on <*rosto, olhos*> □ *vi* paint; (*fam*) <*pessoa*> show up; <*problema, oportunidade*> crop up; ~**tar-se** *vpr* put on make-up
pintarroxo /pĩta'xoʃu/ *m* robin
pinto /'pĩtu/ *m* chick
pin|tor /pĩ'tor/ *m* painter; ~**tura** *f* painting
pio[1] /'piu/ *m* (*de pinto*) cheep; (*de coruja*) hoot
pio[2] /'piu/ *a* pious
piolho /pi'oʎu/ *m* louse
pioneiro /pio'neru/ *m* pioneer □ *a* pioneering
pior /pi'ɔr/ *a & adv* worse; **o** ~ the worst
pio|ra /pi'ɔra/ *f* worsening; ~**rar** *vt* make worse, worsen □ *vi* get worse, worsen
pipa /'pipa/ *f* (*que voa*) kite; (*de vinho*) cask
pipilar /pipi'lar/ *vi* chirp
pipo|ca /pi'pɔka/ *f* popcorn; ~**car** *vi* spring up; ~**queiro** *m* popcorn seller
pique /'piki/ *m* (*disposição*) energy; **a** ~ vertically; **ir a** ~ <*navio*> sink

piquenique /piki'niki/ *m* picnic
pique|te /pi'ketʃi/ *m* picket; ~**teiro** *m* picket
pirado /pi'radu/ *a* (*fam*) crazy
pirâmide /pi'ramidʒi/ *f* pyramid
piranha /pi'raɲa/ *f* piranha; (*fam: mulher*) maneater
pirar /pi'rar/ (*fam*) *vi* flip out, go mad
pirata /pi'rata/ *a & m/f* pirate; ~**ria** *f* piracy
pires /'piris/ *m invar* saucer
pirilampo /piri'lãpu/ *m* glow-worm
Pirineus /piri'news/ *m pl* Pyrenees
pirra|ça /pi'xasa/ *f* spiteful act; **fazer** ~**ça** be spiteful; ~**cento** *a* spiteful
pirueta /piru'eta/ *f* pirouette
pirulito /piru'litu/ *m* lollipop
pi|sada /pi'zada/ *f* step; (*rastro*) footprint; ~**sar** *vt* tread on; tread <*uvas, palco*>; (*esmagar*) trample on □ *vi* step; ~**sar em** step on; (*entrar*) set foot in
pis|cadela /piska'dɛla/ *f* wink; ~**ca-pisca** *m* indicator; ~**car** *vi* (*com o olho*) wink; (*pestanejar*) blink; <*estrela, luz*> twinkle; <*motorista*> indicate □ *m* **num** ~**car de olhos** in a flash
piscicultura /pisikuw'tura/ *f* fish farming; (*lugar*) fish farm
piscina /pi'sina/ *f* swimming pool
piso /'pizu/ *m* floor
pisotear /pizotʃi'ar/ *vt* trample
pista /'pista/ *f* track; (*da estrada*) carriageway; (*para aviões*) runway; (*de circo*) ring; (*dica*) clue; ~ **de dança** dancefloor
pistache /pis'taʃi/ *m*, **pistacho** /pis-'taʃu/ *m* pistachio (nut)
pisto|la /pis'tɔla/ *f* pistol; (*para pintar*) spray gun; ~**lão** *m* influential contact; ~**leiro** *m* gunman
pitada /pi'tada/ *f* pinch
piteira /pi'tera/ *f* cigarette-holder
pitoresco /pito'resku/ *a* picturesque
pitu /pi'tu/ *m* crayfish
pivete /pi'vetʃi/ *m/f* child thief
pivô /pi'vo/ *m* pivot
pixaim /piʃa'ĩ/ *a* frizzy
pizza /'pitsa/ *f* pizza; ~**ria** *f* pizzeria
placa /'plaka/ *f* plate; (*de carro*) number plate, (*Amer*) license plate; (*comemorativa*) plaque; (*em computador*) board; ~ **de sinalização** roadsign
placar /pla'kar/ *m* scoreboard; (*escore*) scoreline
plácido /'plasidu/ *a* placid
plagi|ário /plaʒi'ariu/ *m* plagiarist; ~**ar** *vt* plagiarize
plágio /'plaʒiu/ *m* plagiarism
plaina /'plajna/ *f* plane
planador /plana'dor/ *m* glider
planalto /pla'nawtu/ *m* plateau
planar /pla'nar/ *vi* glide

planeamento, planear (*Port*) *veja*
planejamento, planejar

plane|jamento /planeʒaˈmẽtu/ *m*
planning; **~jamento familiar** family
planning; **~jar** *vt* plan

planeta /plaˈneta/ *m* planet

planície /plaˈnisi/ *f* plain

planificar /planifiˈkar/ *vt* (*progra-mar*) plan (out)

planilha /plaˈniʎa/ *f* spreadsheet

plano /ˈplanu/ *a* flat □ *m* plan; (*super-fície, nível*) plane; **primeiro ~** fore-ground

planta /ˈplãta/ *f* plant; (*do pé*) sole; (*de edifício*) ground plan; **~ção** *f* (*ato*) planting; (*terreno*) plantation; **~do** *a* **deixar alg ~do** (*fam*) keep s.o. wait-ing around

plantão /plãˈtãw/ *m* duty; (*noturno*) night duty; **estar de ~** be on duty

plantar /plãˈtar/ *vt* plant

plas|ma /ˈplazma/ *m* plasma; **~mar** *vt* mould, shape

plásti|ca /ˈplastʃika/ *f* face-lift; **~co** *a* & *m* plastic

plataforma /plataˈfɔrma/ *f* platform

plátano /ˈplatanu/ *m* plane tree

platéia /plaˈtɛja/ *f* audience; (*parte do teatro*) stalls, (*Amer*) orchestra

platina /plaˈtʃina/ *f* platinum; **~dos** *m pl* points

platônico /plaˈtoniku/ *a* platonic

plausí|vel /plawˈzivew/ (*pl* **~veis**) *a* plausible

ple|be /ˈplɛbi/ *f* common people; **~beu** *a* (*f* **~béia**) plebeian □ *m* (*f* **~béia**) commoner; **~biscito** *m* plebiscite

plei|tear /plejtʃiˈar/ *vt* contest; **~to** *m* (*litígio*) case; (*eleitoral*) contest

ple|namente /plenaˈmẽtʃi/ *adv* fully; **~nário** *a* plenary □ *m* plenary assembly; **~no** /e/ *a* full; **em ~no verão** in the middle of summer

plissado /pliˈsadu/ *a* pleated

pluma /ˈpluma/ *f* feather; **~gem** *f* plumage

plu|ral /pluˈraw/ (*pl* **~rais**) *a* & *m* plural

plutônio /pluˈtoniu/ *m* plutonium

pluvi|al /pluviˈaw/ (*pl* **~ais**) *a* rain

pneu /piˈnew/ *m* tyre; **~mático** *a* pneumatic □ *m* tyre

pneumonia /pineumoˈnia/ *f* pneumo-nia

pó /pɔ/ *f* powder; (*poeira*) dust; **leite em ~** powdered milk

pobre /ˈpɔbri/ *a* poor □ *m/f* poor man (*f* woman); **os ~s** the poor; **~za** /e/ *f* poverty

poça /ˈposa/ *f* pool; (*deixada pela chu-va*) puddle

poção /poˈsãw/ *f* potion

pocilga /poˈsiwga/ *f* pigsty

poço /ˈposu/ *f* (*de água, petróleo*) well; (*de mina, elevador*) shaft

podar /poˈdar/ *vt* prune

pó-de-arroz /pɔdʒiaˈxoz/ *m* (face) powder

poder /poˈder/ *m* power □ *v aux* can, be able; (*eventualidade*) may; **ele pode/podia/poderá vir** he can/could/might come; **ele pôde vir** he was able to come; **pode ser que** it may be that; **~ com** stand up to; **em ~ de alg** in sb's possession; **estar no ~** be in power

pode|rio /podeˈriu/ *m* might; **~roso** /o/ *a* powerful

pódio /ˈpɔdʒiu/ *m* podium

podre /ˈpodri/ *a* rotten; (*fam*) (*cansa-do*) exhausted; (*doente*) grotty; **~ de rico** filthy rich; **~s** *m pl* faults

poei|ra /poˈera/ *f* dust; **~rento** *a* dusty

poe|ma /poˈema/ *m* poem; **~sia** *f* (*arte*) poetry; (*poema*) poem; **~ta** *m* poet

poético /poˈɛtʃiku/ *a* poetic

poetisa /poeˈtʃiza/ *f* poetess

pois /pojs/ *conj* as, since; **~ é** that's right; **~ não** of course; **~ não?** can I help you?; **~ sim** certainly not

polaco /puˈlaku/ (*Port*) *a* Polish □ *m* Pole; (*língua*) Polish

polar /poˈlar/ *a* polar

polarizar /polariˈzar/ *vt* polarize; **~se** *vpr* polarize

pole|gada /poleˈgada/ *f* inch; **~gar** *m* thumb

poleiro /poˈleru/ *m* perch

polêmi|ca /poˈlemika/ *f* controversy, debate; **~co** *a* controversial

pólen /ˈpɔlẽ/ *m* pollen

polícia /poˈlisia/ *f* police □ *m/f* police-man (*f* -woman)

polici|al /poliˈsiaw/ (*pl* **~ais**) *a* <*carro, inquérito etc*> police; <*romance, filme*> detective □ *m/f* policeman (*f* -woman); **~amento** *m* policing; **~ar** *vt* police

poli|dez /poliˈdes/ *f* politeness; **~do** *a* polite

poli|gamia /poligaˈmia/ *f* polygamy; **~glota** *a* & *m/f* polyglot

Polinésia /poliˈnɛzia/ *f* Polynesia

polinésio /poliˈnɛziu/ *a* & *m* Polyne-sian

pólio /ˈpɔliu/ *f* polio

polir /poˈlir/ *vt* polish

polissílabo /poliˈsilabu/ *m* polysyl-lable

políti|ca /poˈlitʃika/ *f* politics; (*uma*) policy; **~co** *a* political □ *m* politician

pólo[1] /ˈpɔlu/ *m* pole

pólo[2] /ˈpɔlu/ *m* (*jogo*) polo; **~ aquá-tico** water polo

polo|nês /polo'nes/ *a* (*f* ~**nesa**) Polish □ *m* (*f* ~**nesa**) Pole; (*língua*) Polish

Polônia /po'lonia/ *f* Poland

polpa /'powpa/ *f* pulp

poltrona /pow'trona/ *f* armchair

polu|ente /polu'ētʃi/ *a & m* pollutant; ~**ição** *f* pollution; ~**ir** *vt* pollute

polvilhar /powvi'ʎar/ *vt* sprinkle

polvo /'powvu/ *m* octopus

pólvora /'pɔwvora/ *f* gunpowder

polvorosa /powvo'rɔza/ *f* uproar; **em ~** in uproar; <*pessoa*> in a flap

pomada /po'mada/ *f* ointment

pomar /po'mar/ *m* orchard

pom|ba /'põba/ *f* dove; ~**bo** *m* pigeon

pomo-de-Adão /pomudʃia'dãw/ *m* Adam's apple

pom|pa /'põpa/ *f* pomp; ~**poso** /o/ *a* pompous

ponche /'põʃi/ *m* punch

ponderar /põde'rar/ *vt/i* ponder

pônei /'ponej/ *m* pony

ponta /'põta/ *f* end; (*de faca, prego*) point; (*de nariz, dedo, língua*) tip; (*de sapato*) toe; (*Cin, Teat: papel curto*) walk-on part; (*no campo de futebol*) wing; (*jogador*) winger; **na ~ dos pés** on tip-toe; **uma ~ de** a touch of <*ironia etc*>; **agüentar as ~s** (*fam*) hold on; ~**-cabeça** /e/ *f de* ~**-cabeça** upside down

pontada /põ'tada/ *f* (*dor*) twinge

pontapé /põta'pɛ/ *m* kick; ~ **inicial** kick-off

pontaria /põta'ria/ *f* aim; **fazer ~** take aim

ponte /'põtʃi/ *f* bridge; ~ **aérea** shuttle; (*em tempo de guerra*) airlift; ~ **de safena** heart bypass; ~ **pênsil** suspension bridge

ponteiro /põ'teru/ *m* pointer; (*de relógio*) hand

pontiagudo /põtʃia'gudu/ *a* sharp

pontilhado /põtʃi'ʎadu/ *a* dotted

ponto /'põtu/ *m* point; (*de costura, tricô*) stitch; (*no final de uma frase*) full stop, (*Amer*) period; (*sinalzinho, no i*) dot; (*de ônibus*) stop; (*no teatro*) prompter; **a ~ de** on the point of; **ao ~** <*carne*> medium; **até certo ~** to a certain extent; **às duas em ~** at exactly two o'clock; **dormir no ~** (*fam*) miss the boat; **entregar os ~s** (*fam*) give up; **fazer ~** (*fam*) hang out; **dois ~s** colon; ~ **de exclamação/interrogação** exclamation/question mark; ~ **de táxi** taxi rank, (*Amer*) taxi stand; ~ **de vista** point of view; ~ **morto** neutral; ~**-e-vírgula** *m* semicolon

pontu|ação /põtua'sãw/ *f* punctuation; ~**al** (*pl* ~**ais**) *a* punctual; ~**alidade** *f* punctuality; ~**ar** *vt* punctuate

pontudo /põ'tudu/ *a* pointed

popa /'popa/ *f* stern

popu|lação /popula'sãw/ *f* population; ~**lacional** (*pl* ~**lacionais**) *a* population; ~**lar** *a* popular; ~**laridade** *f* popularity; ~**larizar** *vt* popularize; ~**larizar-se** *vpr* become popular

pôquer /'poker/ *m* poker

por /por/ *prep* for; (*através de*) through; (*indicando meio, agente*) by; (*motivo*) out of; ~ **ano/mês** *etc* per year/month/*etc*; ~ **cento** per cent; ~ **aqui** (*nesta área*) around here; (*nesta direção*) this way; ~ **dentro/fora** on the inside/outside; ~ **isso** for this reason; ~ **sorte** luckily; ~ **que** why; ~ **mais caro que seja** however expensive it may be; **está ~ acontecer/fazer** it is yet to happen/to be done

pôr /por/ *vt* put; put on <*roupa, chapéu, óculos*>; lay <*mesa, ovos*> □ *m* **o ~ do sol** sunset; ~**-se** *vpr* <*sol*> set; ~**-se a** start to; ~**-se a caminho** set off

porão /po'rãw/ *m* (*de prédio*) basement; (*de casa*) cellar; (*de navio*) hold

porca /'pɔrka/ *f* (*de parafuso*) nut; (*animal*) sow

porção /por'sãw/ *f* portion; **uma ~ de** (*muitos*) a lot of

porcaria /porka'ria/ *f* (*sujeira*) filth; (*coisa malfeita*) piece of trash; *pl* trash

porcelana /porse'lana/ *f* china

porcentagem /porsē'taʒē/ *f* percentage

porco /'porku/ *a* filthy □ *m* (*animal, fig*) pig; (*carne*) pork; ~**-espinho** (*pl* ~**s-espinhos**) *m* porcupine

porém /po'rēj/ *conj* however

pormenor /porme'nɔr/ *m* detail

por|nô /por'no/ *a* porn □ *m* porn film; ~**nografia** *f* pornography; ~**nográfico** *a* pornographic

poro /'pɔru/ *m* pore; ~**so** /o/ *a* porous

por|quanto /por'kwãtu/ *conj* since; ~**que** /por'ki/ *conj* because; (*Port: por quê?*) why; ~**quê** /por'ke/ *adv* (*Port*) why □ *m* reason why

porquinho|-da-índia /porkiɲuda'ĩdʒia/ (*pl* ~**s-da-índia**) *m* guinea pig

porrada /po'xada/ *f* (*fam*) beating

porre /'pɔxi/ *m* (*fam*) drinking session, booze-up; **de ~** drunk; **tomar um ~** get drunk

porta /'pɔrta/ *f* door

porta-aviões /pɔrtavi'õjs/ *m invar* aircraft carrier

portador /porta'dor/ *m* bearer

portagem /por'taʒē/ *f* (*Port*) toll

porta|chaves /pɔrta'ʃavis/ *m invar* key-holder *ou* key-ring; ~**-jóias** *m in-*

var jewellery box; ~**-lápis** *m invar* pencil holder; ~**-luvas** *m invar* glove compartment; ~**-malas** *m invar* boot, (*Amer*) trunk; ~**-níqueis** *m invar* purse

portanto /por'tãtu/ *conj* therefore

portão /por'tãw/ *m* gate

portar /por'tar/ *vt* carry; ~**-se** *vpr* behave

porta|-retrato /pɔrtaxe'tratu/ *m* photo frame; ~**-revistas** *m invar* magazine rack

portaria /porta'ria/ *f* (*entrada*) entrance; (*decreto*) decree

portá|til (*pl* ~**teis**) *a* portable

porta|-toalhas /pɔrtato'aʎas/ *m invar* towel rail; ~**-voz** *m/f* spokesman (*f* -woman)

porte /'pɔrtʃi/ *m* (*frete*) carriage; (*de cartas etc*) postage; (*de pessoa*) bearing; (*dimensão*) scale; **de grande/pequeno** ~ large-/small-scale

porteiro /por'teru/ *m* doorman; ~ **eletrônico** entryphone

porto /'portu/ *m* port; **o Porto** Oporto; ~ **de escala** port of call; **Porto Rico** *m* Puerto Rico; ~**-riquenho** /e/ *a & m* Puertorican

portuense /portu'ẽsi/ *a & m/f* (person) from Oporto

Portugal /portu'gaw/ *m* Portugal

portu|guês /portu'ges/ *a & m* (*f* ~**guesa**) Portuguese

portuário /portu'ariu/ *a* port □ *m* dock worker, docker

po|sar /po'zar/ *vi* pose; ~**se** /o/ *f* pose; (*de filme*) exposure

pós-datar /pɔzda'tar/ *vt* postdate

pós-escrito /pɔzis'kritu/ *m* postscript

pós-gradua|ção /pɔzgradua'sãw/ *f* postgraduation; ~**do** *a & m* postgraduate

pós-guerra /poz'gexa/ *m* post-war period; **a Europa do** ~ post-war Europe

posi|ção /pozi'sãw/ *f* position; ~**cionar** *vt* position; ~**tivo** *a & m* positive

posologia /pozolo'ʒia/ *f* dosage

pos|sante /po'sãtʃi/ *a* powerful; ~**se** /ɔ/ *f* (*de casa etc*) possession, ownership; (*do presidente etc*) swearing in; *pl* (*pertences*) possessions; **tomar** ~**se** take office; **tomar** ~**se de** take possession of

posses|são /pose'sãw/ *f* possession; ~**sivo** *a* possessive; ~**so** /ε/ *a* possessed; (*com raiva*) furious

possibili|dade /posibili'dadʒi/ *f* possibility; ~**tar** *vt* make possible

possí|vel /po'sivew/ (*pl* ~**veis**) *a* possible; **fazer todo o** ~**vel** do one's best

possuir /posu'ir/ *vt* possess; (*ser dono de*) own

posta /'pɔsta/ *f* (*de peixe*) steak

pos|tal /pos'taw/ (*pl* ~**tais**) *a* postal □ *m* postcard

postar /pos'tar/ *vt* place; ~**-se** *vpr* position o.s.

poste /'postʃi/ *m* post

pôster /'poster/ *m* poster

posteri|dade /posteri'dadʒi/ *f* posterity; ~**or** *a* (*no tempo*) subsequent, later; (*no espaço*) rear; ~**ormente** *adv* subsequently

postiço /pos'tʃisu/ *a* false

posto /'postu/ *m* post; ~ **de gasolina** petrol station, (*Amer*) gas station; ~ **de saúde** health centre □ *pp de* **pôr**; ~ **que** although

póstumo /'pɔstumu/ *a* posthumous

postura /pos'tura/ *f* posture

potá|vel /po'tavew/ (*pl* ~**veis**) *a* **água** ~**vel** drinking water

pote /'pɔtʃi/ *m* pot; (*de vidro*) jar

potência /po'tẽsia/ *f* power

poten|cial /potẽsi'aw/ (*pl* ~**ciais**) *a & m* potential; ~**te** *a* potent

potro /'potru/ *m* foal

pouco /'poku/ *a & pron* little; *pl* few □ *adv* not much □ *m* **um** ~ a little; ~ **a** ~ little by little; **aos** ~**s** gradually; **daqui a** ~ shortly; **por** ~ almost; ~ **tempo** a short time

pou|pança /po'pãsa/ *f* saving; (*conta*) savings account; ~**par** *vt* save; spare <*vida*>

pouquinho /po'kiɲu/ *m* **um** ~ (**de**) a little

pou|sada /po'zada/ *f* inn; ~**sar** *vi* land; ~**so** *m* landing

po|vão /po'vãw/ *m* common people; ~**vo** /o/ *m* people

povo|ação /povoa'sãw/ *f* settlement; ~**ar** *vt* populate

poxa /'poʃa/ *int* gosh

pra /pra/ *prep* (*fam*) *veja* **para**

praça /'prasa/ *f* (*largo*) square; (*mercado*) market □ *m* (*soldado*) private

prado /'pradu/ *m* meadow

pra-frente /pra'frẽtʃi/ *a invar* (*fam*) with it, modern

praga /'praga/ *f* curse; (*inseto, doença, pessoa*) pest

prag|mático /prag'matʃiku/ *a* pragmatic; ~**matismo** *m* pragmatism

praguejar /prage'ʒar/ *vt/i* curse

praia /'praja/ *f* beach

pran|cha /'prãʃa/ *f* plank; (*de surfe*) board; ~**cheta** /e/ *f* drawing board

pranto /'prãtu/ *m* weeping

pra|ta /'prata/ *f* silver; ~**taria** *f* (*coisas de prata*) silverware; ~**teado** *a* silver-plated; (*cor*) silver

prateleira /prate'lera/ *f* shelf

prática /'pratʃika/ *f* practice; **na** ~ in practice

prati|cante /pratʃi'kãtʃi/ *a* practising □ *m/f* apprentice; (*de esporte etc*) player; **~car** *vt* practise; (*cometer, executar*) carry out □ *vi* practise; **~cável** (*pl* **~cáveis**) *a* practicable

prático /'pratʃiku/ *a* practical

prato /'pratu/ *m* (*objeto*) plate; (*comida*) dish; (*parte de uma refeição*) course; (*do toca-discos*) turntable; *pl* (*instrumento*) cymbals; **~ fundo** dish; **~ principal** main course

praxe /'praʃi/ *f* normal practice; **de ~** usually

prazer /pra'zer/ *m* pleasure; **muito ~ (em conhecê-lo)** pleased to meet you; **~oso** /o/ *a* pleasurable

prazo /'prazu/ *m* term, time; **a ~ <compra etc>** on credit; **a curto/longo ~** in the short/long term; **último ~** deadline

preâmbulo /pri'ãbulu/ *m* preamble

precário /pre'kariu/ *a* precarious

precaução /prekaw'sãw/ *f* precaution

preca|ver-se /preka'versi/ *vpr* take precautions (**de** against); **~vido** *a* cautious

prece /'prɛsi/ *f* prayer

prece|dência /prese'dẽsia/ *f* precedence; **~dente** *a* preceding □ *m* precedent; **~der** *vt/i* precede

preceito /pre'sejtu/ *m* precept

precioso /presi'ozu/ *a* precious

precipício /presi'pisiu/ *m* precipice

precipi|tação /presipita'sãw/ *f* haste; (*chuva etc*) precipitation; **~tado** *a <fuga>* headlong; *<decisão, ato>* hasty, rash; **~tar** *vt* (*lançar*) throw; (*antecipar*) hasten; **~tar-se** *vpr* (*lançar-se*) throw o.s.; (*apressar-se*) rush; (*agir sem pensar*) act rashly

precisão /presi'zãw/ *f* precision, accuracy

precisamente /presiza'mẽtʃi/ *adv* precisely

preci|sar /presi'zar/ *vt* (*necessitar*) need; (*indicar com exatidão*) specify □ *vi* be necessary; **~sar de** need; **~so ir** I have to go; **~sa-se** wanted; **~so** *a* (*exato*) precise; (*necessário*) necessary

preço /'presu/ *m* price; **~ de custo** cost price; **~ fixo** set price

precoce /pre'kɔsi/ *a <fruto>* early; *<velhice, calvície etc>* premature; *<criança>* precocious

precon|cebido /prekõse'bidu/ *a* preconceived; **~ceito** *m* prejudice; **~ceituoso** *a* prejudiced

preconizar /prekoni'zar/ *vt* advocate

precursor /prekur'sor/ *m* forerunner

preda|dor /preda'dor/ *m* predator; **~tório** *a* predatory

predecessor /predese'sor/ *m* predecessor

predestinar /predestʃi'nar/ *vt* predestine

predeterminar /predetermi'nar/ *vt* predetermine

predição /predʒi'sãw/ *f* prediction

predile|ção /predʒile'sãw/ *f* preference; **~to** /ɛ/ *a* favourite

prédio /'predʒiu/ *m* building

predis|por /predʒis'por/ *vt* prepare (**para** for); (*tornar parcial*) prejudice (**contra** against); **~por-se** *vpr* prepare o.s.; **~posto** *a* predisposed; (*contra*) prejudiced

predizer /predʒi'zer/ *vt* predict, foretell

predomi|nância /predomi'nãsia/ *f* predominance; **~nante** *a* predominant; **~nar** *vi* predominate

predomínio /predo'miniu/ *m* predominance

preencher /prie'ʃer/ *vt* fill; fill in, (*Amer*) fill out *<formulário>*; meet *<requisitos>*

pré-escola /prɛis'kɔla/ *f* infant school, (*Amer*) preschool; **~-escolar** *a* pre-school; **~-estréia** *f* preview; **~-fabricado** *a* prefabricated

prefácio /pre'fasiu/ *m* preface

prefei|to /pre'fejtu/ *m* mayor; **~tura** *f* prefecture; (*prédio*) town hall

prefe|rência /prefe'rẽsia/ *f* preference; (*direito no trânsito*) right of way; **de ~** preferably; **~rencial** (*pl* **~renciais**) *a* preferential; *<rua>* main; **~rido** *a* favourite; **~rir** *vt* prefer (**a** to); **~rível** (*pl* **~ríveis**) *a* preferable

prefixo /pre'fiksu/ *m* prefix

prega /'prega/ *f* pleat

pregador[1] /prega'dor/ *m* (*de roupa*) peg

pre|gador[2] /prega'dor/ *m* (*quem prega*) preacher; **~gão** *m* (*de vendedor*) cry; **o ~gão** (*na bolsa de valores*) trading; (*em leilão*) bidding

pregar[1] /pre'gar/ *vt* fix; (*com prego*) nail; sew on *<botão>*; **não ~ olho** not sleep a wink; **~ uma peça em** play a trick on; **~ um susto em alg** give s.o. a fright

pregar[2] /pre'gar/ *vt/i* preach

prego /'prɛgu/ *m* nail

pregui|ça /pre'gisa/ *f* laziness; (*bicho*) sloth; **estou com ~ça de ir** I can't be bothered to go; **~çoso** *a* lazy

pré-histórico /prɛjs'tɔriku/ *a* prehistoric

preia-mar /preja'mar/ *f* high tide

prejudi|car /preʒudʒi'kar/ *vt* harm; damage *<saúde>*; **~car-se** *vpr* harm o.s.; **~cial** (*pl* **~ciais**) *a* harmful, damaging (**a** to)

prejuízo /preʒu'izu/ *m* damage; (*financeiro*) loss; **em ~ de** to the detriment of

prejulgar /preʒuw'gar/ *vt* prejudge

preliminar /prelimi'nar/ *a & m/f* preliminary

prelo /'prɛlu/ *m* printing press; **no ~** being printed

prelúdio /pre'ludʒiu/ *m* prelude

prematuro /prema'turu/ *a* premature

premeditar /premedʒi'tar/ *vt* premeditate

premente /pre'mẽtʃi/ *a* pressing

premi|ado /premi'adu/ *a* <*romance, atleta etc*> prize-winning; <*bilhete, número etc*> winning □ *m* prizewinner; **~ar** *vt* award a prize to <*romance, atleta etc*>; reward <*honestidade, mérito*>

prêmio /'premiu/ *m* prize; (*de seguro*) premium; **Grande Prêmio** (*de F1*) Grand Prix

premissa /pre'misa/ *f* premiss

premonição /premoni'sãw/ *f* premonition

pré-na|tal /prɛna'taw/ (*pl* **~tais**) *a* antenatal, (*Amer*) prenatal

prenda /'prẽda/ *f* (*Port*) present; **~s domésticas** household chores; **~do** *a* domesticated

pren|dedor /prẽde'dor/ *m* clip; **~dedor de roupa** clothes peg; **~der** *vt* (*pregar*) fix; (*capturar*) arrest; (*atar*) tie up <*cachorro*>; tie back <*cabelo*>; (*restringir*) restrict; (*ligar afetivamente*) bind; **~der (a atenção de) alg** grab s.o.('s attention)

prenhe /'prẽɲi/ *a* pregnant

prenome /pre'nomi/ *m* first name

pren|sa /'prẽsa/ *f* press; **~sar** *vt* press

preocu|pação /preokupa'sãw/ *f* concern; **~pante** *a* worrying; **~par** *vt* worry; **~par-se** *vpr* worry (**com** about)

prepa|ração /prepara'sãw/ *f* preparation; **~rado** *m* preparation; **~rar** *vt* prepare; **~rar-se** *vpr* prepare, get ready; **~rativos** *m pl* preparations; **~ro** *m* preparation; (*competência*) knowledge; **~ro físico** physical fitness

preponderar /prepõde'rar/ *vi* prevail (**sobre** over)

preposição /prepozi'sãw/ *f* preposition

prerrogativa /prexoga'tʃiva/ *f* prerogative

presa /'preza/ *f* (*de caça*) prey; (*de cobra*) fang; (*de elefante*) tusk; **~ de guerra** spoils of war

prescin|dir /presĩ'dʒir/ *vi* **~dir de** dispense with; **~dível** (*pl* **~díveis**) *a* dispensable

pres|crever /preskre'ver/ *vt* prescribe; **~crição** *f* prescription; (*norma*) rule

presen|ça /pre'zẽsa/ *f* presence; **~ça de espírito** presence of mind; **~ciar** *vt* (*estar presente a*) be present at; (*testemunhar*) witness; **~te** *a & m* present; **~tear** *vt* **~tear alg (com aco)** give s.o. (sth as) a present

presépio /pre'zɛpiu/ *m* crib

preser|vação /prezerva'sãw/ *f* preservation; **~var** *vt* preserve, protect; **~vativo** *m* (*em comida*) preservative; (*camisinha*) condom

presi|dência /prezi'dẽsia/ *f* presidency; (*de uma reunião*) chair; **~dencial** (*pl* **~denciais**) *a* presidential; **~dencialismo** *m* presidential system; **~dente** *m* (*f* **~denta**) president; (*de uma reunião*) chairperson

presidiário /prezidʒi'ariu/ *m* convict

presídio /pre'zidʒiu/ *m* prison

presidir /prezi'dʒir/ *vi* preside (**a** over)

presilha /pre'ziʎa/ *f* fastener; (*de cabelo*) slide

preso /'prezu/ *pp de* **prender** □ *m* prisoner; **ficar ~** get stuck; <*saia, corda etc*> get caught

pressa /'prɛsa/ *f* hurry; **às ~s** in a hurry, hurriedly; **estar com** *ou* **ter ~** be in a hurry

presságio /pre'saʒiu/ *m* omen

pressão /pre'sãw/ *f* pressure; **fazer ~ sobre** put pressure on; **~ arterial** blood pressure

pressen|timento /presẽtʃi'mẽtu/ *m* premonition, feeling; **~tir** *vt* sense

pressionar /presio'nar/ *vt* press <*botão*>; pressure <*pessoa*>

pressupor /presu'por/ *vt* <*pessoa*> presume; <*coisa*> presuppose

pressurizado /presuri'zadu/ *a* pressurized

pres|tação /presta'sãw/ *f* repayment, instalment; **~tar** *vt* render <*contas, serviço*> □ *vi* be of use; **não ~ta** he/it is no good; **~tar atenção** pay attention; **~tar juramento** take an oath; **~tativo** *a* helpful; **~tável** (*pl* **~táveis**) *a* serviceable

prestes /'prɛstʃis/ *a invar* **~ a** about to

prestidigita|ção /prestʃidʒiʒita'sãw/ *f* conjuring; **~dor** *m* conjurer

pres|tigiar /prestʃiʒi'ar/ *vt* give prestige to; **~tígio** *m* prestige; **~tigioso** /o/ *a* prestigious

préstimo /'prɛstʃimu/ *m* merit

presumir /prezu'mir/ *vt* presume

presun|ção /prezũ'sãw/ *f* presumption; **~çoso** /o/ *a* presumptuous

presunto /pre'zũtu/ *m* ham

pretendente /pretẽ'dẽtʃi/ m/f (candidato) candidate, applicant

preten|der /pretẽ'der/ vt intend; ~são f pretension; ~sioso /o/ a pretentious

preterir /prete'rir/ vt disregard

pretérito /pre'teritu/ m preterite

pretexto /pre'testu/ m pretext

preto /'pretu/ a & m black; ~-e-branco a invar black and white

prevalecer /prevale'ser/ vi prevail

prevenção /prevẽ'sãw/ f (impedimento) prevention; (parcialidade) bias

prevenir /preve'nir/ vt (evitar) prevent; (avisar) warn; ~-se vpr take precautions

preventivo /prevẽ'tʃivu/ a preventive

prever /pre'ver/ vt foresee, predict

previdência /previ'dẽsia/ f foresight; ~ social social security

prévio /'previu/ a prior

previ|são /previ'zãw/ f prediction, forecast; ~são do tempo weather forecast; ~sível (pl ~síveis) a predictable

pre|zado /pre'zadu/ a esteemed; **Prezado Senhor** Dear Sir; ~zar vt think highly of; ~zar-se vpr have self-respect

prima /'prima/ f cousin

primário /pri'mariu/ a primary; (fundamental) basic

primata /pri'mata/ m primate

primave|ra /prima'vera/ f spring; (flor) primrose; ~ril (pl ~ris) a spring

primazia /prima'zia/ f primacy

primei|ra /pri'mera/ f (marcha) first (gear); de ~ra first-rate; <carne> prime; ~ra-dama (pl ~ras-damas) f first lady; ~ranista m/f first-year (student); ~ro a & adv first; no dia ~ro de maio on the first of May; em ~ro lugar (para começar) in the first place; (numa corrida, competição) in first place; ~ro de tudo first of all; ~ros socorros first aid; ~ro-ministro (pl ~ros-ministros) m (f ~ra-ministra) prime-minister

primitivo /primi'tʃivu/ a primitive

primo /'primu/ m cousin □ a número ~ prime number; ~gênito a & m first-born

primor /pri'mor/ m perfection

primordi|al /primordʒi'aw/ (pl ~ais) a (primitivo) primordial; (fundamental) fundamental

primoroso /primo'rozu/ a exquisite

princesa /prĩ'seza/ f princess

princi|pado /prĩsipi'adu/ m principality; ~pal (pl ~pais) a main □ m principal

príncipe /'prĩsipi/ m prince

principiante /prĩsipi'ãtʃi/ m/f beginner

princípio /prĩ'sipiu/ m (início) beginning; (regra) principle; em ~ in principle; por ~ on principle

priori|dade /priori'dadʒi/ f priority; ~tário a priority

prisão /pri'zãw/ f (ato de prender) arrest; (cadeia) prison; (encarceramento) imprisonment; ~ perpétua life imprisonment; ~ de ventre constipation

prisioneiro /prizio'neru/ m prisoner

prisma /'prizma/ m prism

privação /priva'sãw/ f deprivation

privacidade /privasi'dadʒi/ f privacy

pri|vada /pri'vada/ f toilet; ~vado a private; ~vado de deprived of; ~var vt deprive (de of); ~var-se vpr deprive o.s. (de of)

privati|vo /priva'tʃivu/ a private; ~zar vt privatize

privi|legiado /privileʒi'adu/ a privileged; <tratamento> preferential; ~legiar vt favour; ~légio m privilege

pro (fam) = **para + o**

pró /prɔ/ adv for □ m os ~s e os contras the pros and cons

proa /'proa/ f bow, prow

probabilidade /probabili'dadʒi/ f probability

proble|ma /pro'blema/ m problem; ~mático a problematic

proce|dência /prose'dẽsia/ f origin; ~dente a logical; ~dente de coming from; ~der vi proceed; (comportar-se) behave; (na justiça) take legal action; ~der de come from; ~dimento m procedure; (comportamento) behaviour; (na justiça) proceedings

proces|sador /prosesa'dor/ m processor; ~sador de texto word processor; ~samento m processing; (na justiça) prosecution; ~samento de dados data processing; ~sar vt process; (por crime) prosecute; (por causa civil) sue; ~so /ɛ/ m process; (criminal) trial; (civil) lawsuit

procla|mação /proklama'sãw/ f proclamation; ~mar vt proclaim

procri|ação /prokria'sãw/ f procreation; ~ar vt/i procreate

procu|ra /pro'kura/ f search; (de produto) demand; à ~ra de in search of; ~ração f power of attorney; ~rado a sought after, in demand; ~rado pela polícia wanted by the police; ~rador m (mandatário) proxy; (advogado) public prosecutor; ~rar vt look for; (contatar) get in touch with; (ir visitar) lookup; ~rar saber try to find out

prodígio /pro'dʒiʒiu/ m wonder; (pessoa) prodigy

prodigioso /prodʒiʒi'ozu/ a prodigious

pródigo /'prɔdigu/ a lavish, extravagant

produ|ção /produ'sãw/ f production; ~**tividade** f productivity; ~**tivo** a productive; ~**to** m product; (renda) proceeds; ~**to nacional bruto** gross national product; ~**tos agrícolas** agricultural produce; ~**tor** m producer □ a **país** ~**tor de trigo** wheat-producing country; ~**zido** a (fam: arrumado) done up; ~**zir** vt produce

proeminente /proemi'nẽtʃi/ a prominent

proeza /pro'eza/ f achievement

profa|nar /profa'nar/ vt desecrate; ~**no** a profane

profecia /profe'sia/ f prophecy

proferir /profe'rir/ vt utter; give <discurso, palestra>; pass <sentença>

profes|sar /profe'sar/ vt profess; ~**so** /ɛ/ a professed; <político etc> seasoned; ~**sor** m teacher; ~**sor catedrático** professor

pro|feta /pro'fɛta/ m prophet; ~**fético** a prophetic; ~**fetizar** vt prophesy

profissão /profi'sãw/ f profession

profissio|nal /profisio'naw/ (pl ~**nais**) a & m/f professional; ~**nalismo** m professionalism; ~**nalizante** a vocational; ~**nalizar-se** vpr <esportista etc> turn professional

profun|didade /profũdʒi'dadʒi/ f depth; ~**do** a deep; <sentimento etc> profound

profusão /profu'zãw/ f profusion

prog|nosticar /prognostʃi'kar/ vt forecast; ~**nóstico** m forecast; (med) prognosis

progra|ma /pro'grama/ m programme; (de computador) program; (diversão) thing to do; ~**mação** f programming; ~**mador** m programmer; ~**mar** vt plan; program <computador etc>; ~**mável** (pl ~**máveis**) a programmable

progredir /progre'dʒir/ vi progress

progres|são /progre'sãw/ f progression; ~**sista** a & m/f progressive; ~**sivo** a progressive; ~**so** /ɛ/ m progress

proi|bição /proibi'sãw/ f ban (de on); ~**bido** a forbidden; ~**bir** vt forbid (alg de s.o. to); ban <livro, importações etc>; ~**bitivo** a prohibitive

proje|ção /proʒe'sãw/ f projection; ~**tar** vt plan <viagem, estrada etc>; design <casa, carro etc>; project <filme, luz>

projé|til /pro'ʒetʃiw/ (pl ~**teis**) m projectile

proje|tista /proʒe'tʃista/ m/f designer; ~**to** /ɛ/ m project; (de casa, carro) design; ~**to de lei** bill; ~**tor** m projector

prol /prɔw/ m em ~ **de** on behalf of

prole /'prɔli/ f offspring; ~**tariado** m proletariat; ~**tário** a & m proletarian

prolife|ração /prolifera'sãw/ f proliferation; ~**rar** vi proliferate

prolífico /pro'lifiku/ a prolific

prolixo /pro'liksu/ a verbose, long-winded

prólogo /'prɔlogu/ m prologue

prolon|gado /prolõ'gadu/ a prolonged; ~**gar** vt prolong; ~**gar-se** vpr go on

promessa /pro'mɛsa/ f promise

prome|tedor /promete'dor/ a promising; ~**ter** vt promise □ vi (dar esperança) show promise; ~**ter voltar** promise to return

promíscuo /pro'miskuu/ a promiscuous

promis|sor /promi'sor/ a promising; ~**sória** f promissory note

promoção /promo'sãw/ f promotion

promontório /promõ'tɔriu/ m promontory

promo|tor /promo'tor/ m promoter; (advogado) prosecutor; ~**ver** vt promote

promulgar /promuw'gar/ vt promulgate

prono|me /pro'nomi/ m pronoun; ~**minal** (pl ~**minais**) a pronominal

pron|tidão /prõtʃi'dãw/ f readiness; **com** ~**tidão** promptly; **estar de** ~**tidão** be at the ready; ~**tificar** vt ready; ~**tificar-se** vpr volunteer (**a** to; **para** for); ~**to** a ready; (rápido) prompt □ int that's that; ~**to-socorro** (pl ~**tos-socorros**) m casualty department; (Port: reboque) towtruck; ~**tuário** m (manual) manual, handbook; (médico) notes; (policial) record, file

pronúncia /pro'nũsia/ f pronunciation

pronunci|ado /pronũsi'adu/ a pronounced; ~**amento** m pronouncement; ~**ar** vt pronounce

propagar /propa'gar/ vt propagate <espécie>; spread <notícia, idéia, fé>; ~**se** vpr spread; <espécie> propagate

propen|são /propẽ'sãw/ f propensity; ~**so** a inclined (**a** to)

pro|piciar /propisi'ar/ vt provide; ~**pício** a propitious

propina /pro'pina/ f bribe; (Port: escolar) fee

propor /pro'por/ vt propose; ~**se** vpr set o.s. <objetivo>; ~**se a estudar** set out to study

proporção /propor'sãw/ *f* proportion

proporcio|nado /proporsio'nadu/ *a* proportionate (a to); **bem ~nado** well proportioned; **~nal** (*pl* **~nais**) *a* proportional; **~nar** *vt* provide

proposi|ção /propozi'sãw/ *f* proposition; **~tado** *a*, **~tal** (*pl* **~tais**) *a* intentional

propósito /pro'pɔzitu/ *m* intention; **a ~** by the way; **a ~ de** on the subject of; **chegar a ~** arrive at the right time; **de ~** on purpose

proposta /pro'pɔsta/ *f* proposal

propriamente /propria'mẽtʃi/ *adv* strictly; **a casa ~ dita** the house proper

proprie|dade /proprie'dadʒi/ *f* property; (*direito sobre bens*) ownership; **~tário** *m* owner; (*de casa alugada*) landlord

próprio /'prɔpriu/ *a* (*de si*) own; <*sentido*> literal; <*nome*> proper; **meu ~ carro** my own car; **um carro ~** a car of my own; **o ~ rei** the king himself; **~ a** peculiar to; **~ para** suited to

prorro|gação /proxoga'sãw/ *f* extension; (*de dívida*) deferment; (*em futebol etc*) extra time; **~gar** *vt* extend <*prazo*>; defer <*pagamento*>

pro|sa /'prɔza/ *f* prose; **~sador** *m* prose writer; **~saico** *a* prosaic

proscrever /proskre'ver/ *vt* proscribe

prospecto /pros'pɛktu/ *m* (*livro*) brochure; (*folheto*) leaflet

prospe|rar /prospe'rar/ *vi* prosper; **~ridade** *f* prosperity

próspero /'prɔsperu/ *a* prosperous

prosse|guimento /prosegi'mẽtu/ *m* continuation; **~guir** *vt* continue □ *vi* proceed, go on

prostitu|ição /prostʃitui'sãw/ *f* prostitution; **~ta** *f* prostitute

pros|tração /prostra'sãw/ *f* debility; **~trado** *a* prostrate; **~trar** *vt* prostrate; (*enfraquecer*) debilitate; **~trar-se** *vpr* prostrate o.s.

protago|nista /protago'nista/ *m/f* protagonist; **~nizar** *vt* be at the centre of <*acontecimento*>; feature in <*peça, filme*>

prote|ção /prote'sãw/ *f* protection; **~cionismo** *m* protectionism; **~cionista** *a & m/f* protectionist; **~ger** *vt* protect; **~gido** *m* protégé

proteína /prote'ina/ *f* protein

protelar /prote'lar/ *vt* put off

protes|tante /protes'tãtʃi/ *a & m/f* Protestant; **~tar** *vt/i* protest; **~to** /ɛ/ *m* protest

protetor /prote'tor/ *m* protector □ *a* protective

protocolo /proto'kɔlu/ *m* protocol; (*registro*) register

protótipo /pro'tɔtʃipu/ *m* prototype

protuberância /protube'rãsia/ *f* bulge

pro|va /'prɔva/ *f* (*que comprova*) proof; (*teste*) trial; (*exame*) exam; (*esportiva*) competition; (*de livro etc*) proof; *pl* (*na justiça*) evidence; **à ~va de bala** bulletproof; **pôr à ~va** put to the test; **~vado** *a* proven; **~var** *vt* try <*comida*>; try on <*roupa*>; try out <*carro, novo sistema etc*>; (*comprovar*) prove

provável /pro'vavew/ (*pl* **~veis**) *a* probable

proveito /pro'vejtu/ *m* profit, advantage; **tirar ~ de** (*beneficiar-se*) profit from; (*explorar*) take advantage of; **~so** /o/ *a* useful

proveni|ência /proveni'ẽsia/ *f* origin; **~ente** *a* originating (**de** from)

proventos /pro'vẽtus/ *m pl* proceeds

prover /pro'ver/ *vt* provide (**de** with)

provérbio /pro'vɛrbiu/ *m* proverb

proveta /pro'veta/ *f* test tube; **bebê de ~** test-tube baby

provi|dência /provi'dẽsia/ *f* (*medida*) measure, step; (*divina*) providence; **tomar ~dências** take steps, take action; **~denciar** *vt* (*prover*) get hold of, provide; (*resolver*) see to, take care of □ *vi* take action

província /pro'vĩsia/ *f* province; (*longe da cidade*) provinces

provinci|al /provĩsi'aw/ (*pl* **~ais**) *a* provincial; **~ano** *a & m* provincial

provir /pro'vir/ *vi* come (**de** from); (*resultar*) be due (**de** to)

provi|são /provi'zãw/ *f* provision; **~sório** *a* provisional

provo|cação /provoka'sãw/ *f* provocation; **~cador**, **~cante** *a* provocative; **~car** *vt* provoke; (*ocasionar*) cause

proximidade /prosimi'dadʒi/ *f* closeness; *pl* (*imediações*) vicinity

próximo /'prɔsimo/ *a* (*no tempo*) next; (*perto*) near, close (**de** to); <*parente*> close; <*futuro*> near □ *m* neighbour, fellow man

pru|dência /pru'dẽsia/ *f* prudence; **~dente** *a* prudent

prumo /'prumu/ *m* plumb line; **a ~** vertically

prurido /pru'ridu/ *m* itch

pseudônimo /pisew'donimu/ *m* pseudonym

psica|nálise /pisika'nalizi/ *f* psychoanalysis; **~nalista** *m/f* psychoanalyst

psi|cologia /pisikolo'ʒia/ *f* psychology; **~cológico** *a* psychological; **~cólogo** *m* psychologist

psico|pata /pisiko'pata/ *m/f* psychopath; **~se** /ɔ/ *f* psychosis; **~terapeuta** *m/f* psychotherapist; **~terapia** *f* psycho-therapy

psicótico /pisiˈkɔtʃiku/ a & m psychotic

psique /piˈsiki/ f psyche

psiqui|atra /pisikiˈatra/ m/f psychiatrist; **~atria** f psychiatry; **~átrico** a psychiatric

psíquico /piˈsikiku/ a psychological

pua /ˈpua/ f bit

puberdade /puberˈdadʒi/ f puberty

publi|cação /publikaˈsãw/ f publication; **~car** vt publish

publici|dade /publisiˈdadʒi/ f publicity; (reclame) advertising; **~tário** a publicity; (de reclame) advertising □ m advertising executive

público /ˈpubliku/ a public □ m public; (platéia) audience; **em ~** in public; **o grande ~** the general public

pudera /puˈdɛra/ int no wonder!

pudico /puˈdʒiku/ a prudish

pudim /puˈdʒĩ/ m pudding

pudor /puˈdor/ m modesty, shame

pue|ril /pueˈriw/ (pl **~ris**) a puerile

pugilis|mo /puʒiˈlizmu/ m boxing; **~ta** m boxer

pu|ído /puˈidu/ a worn through; **~ir** vt wear through

pujan|ça /puˈʒãsa/ f power; **~te** a powerful; (de saúde) robust

pular /puˈlar/ vt jump (over); (omitir) skip □ vi jump; **~ de contente** jump for joy; **~ carnaval** celebrate Carnival; **~ corda** skip

pulga /ˈpuwga/ f flea

pulmão /puwˈmãw/ m lung

pulo /ˈpulu/ m jump; **dar um ~ em** drop by; **dar ~s** jump up and down

pulôver /puˈlover/ m pullover

púlpito /ˈpuwpitu/ m pulpit

pul|sar /puwˈsar/ vi pulsate; **~seira** f bracelet; **~so** m (do braço) wrist; (batimento arterial) pulse

pulular /puluˈlar/ vi swarm (de with)

pulveri|zador /puwveriza'dor/ m spray; **~zar** vt spray <líquido>; (reduzir a pó, fig) pulverize

pun|gente /pũˈʒẽtʃi/ a consuming; **~gir** vt afflict

pu|nhado /puˈɲadu/ m handful; **~nhal** (pl **~nhais**) m dagger; **~nhalada** f stab wound; **~nho** m fist; (de camisa etc) cuff; (de espada) hilt

pu|nição /puniˈsãw/ f punishment; **~nir** vt punish; **~nitivo** a punitive

pupila /puˈpila/ f pupil

purê /puˈre/ m purée; **~ de batata** mashed potato

pureza /puˈreza/ f purity

pur|gante /purˈgãtʃi/ a & m purgative; **~gar** vt purge; **~gatório** m purgatory

purificar /purifiˈkar/ vt purify

puritano /puriˈtanu/ a & m puritan

puro /ˈpuru/ a pure; <aguardente> neat; **~ e simples** pure and simple; **~-sangue** (pl **~s-sangues**) a & m thoroughbred

púrpura /ˈpurpura/ a purple

purpurina /purpuˈrina/ f glitter

purulento /puruˈlẽtu/ a festering

pus /pus/ m pus

pusilânime /puziˈlanimi/ a faint-hearted

pústula /ˈpustula/ f pimple

puta /ˈputa/ f whore □ a invar (fam) **um ~ carro** one hell of a car; **filho da ~** (chulo) bastard; **~ que (o) pariu!** (chulo) fucking hell!

puto /ˈputu/ a (fam) furious

putrefazer /putrefaˈzer/ vi putrefy

puxa /ˈpuʃa/ int gosh

pu|xado /puˈʃadu/ a (fam) <exame> tough; <trabalho> hard; <aluguel, preço> steep; **~xador** m handle; **~xão** m pull, tug; **~xa-puxa** m toffee; **~xar** vt pull; strike up <conversa>; bring up <assunto>; **~xar de uma perna** limp; **~xar para** (parecer com) take after; **~xar por** (exigir muito de) push (hard); **~xa-saco** m (fam) creep

Q

QI /ke i/ m IQ

quadra /ˈkwadra/ f (de tênis etc) court; (quarteirão) block; **~do** a & m square

quadragésimo /kwadraˈʒezimu/ a fortieth

qua|dril /kwaˈdriw/ (pl **~dris**) m hip

quadrilha /kwaˈdriʎa/ f (bando) gang; (dança) square dance

quadrinho /kwaˈdriɲu/ m frame; **história em ~s** comic strip

quadro /ˈkwadru/ m picture; (pintado) painting; (tabela) table; (pessoal) staff; (equipe) team; (de uma peça) scene; **~-negro** (pl **~s-negros**) m blackboard

quadruplicar /kwadrupliˈkar/ vt/i quadruple

quádruplo /ˈkwadruplu/ a quadruple; **~s** m pl (crianças) quads

qual /kwaw/ (pl **quais**) pron which (one); **o/a ~** (coisa) that, which; (pessoa) that, who; **~ é o seu nome?** what's your name?; **seja ~ for a decisão** whatever the decision may be

qualidade /kwaliˈdadʒi/ f quality; **na ~ de** in one's capacity as, as

qualifi|cação /kwalifikaˈsãw/ f qualification; **~car** vt qualify; (descrever) describe (de as); **~car-se** vpr qualify

qualitativo /kwalita'tʃivu/ a qualitative

qualquer /kwaw'kɛr/ (pl **quaisquer**) a any; **um livro** ~ any old book; ~ **um** any one

quando /'kwãdu/ adv & conj when; ~ **quer que** whenever; ~ **de** at the time of; ~ **muito** at most

quantia /kwã'tʃia/ f amount

quanti|dade /kwãtʃi'dadʒi/ f quantity; **uma** ~**dade** de a lot of; **em** ~**dade** in large amounts; ~**ficar** vt quantify; ~**tativo** a quantitative

quanto /'kwãtu/ adv & pron how much; pl how many; ~ **tempo?** how long?; ~ **mais barato melhor** the cheaper the better; **tão alto** ~ **eu** as tall as me; ~ **ri!** how I laughed!; ~ **a** as for; ~ **antes** as soon as possible

quaren|ta /kwa'rẽta/ a & m forty; ~**tão** a & m (f ~**tona**) forty-year-old; ~**tena** /e/ f quarantine

quaresma /kwa'rezma/ f Lent

quarta /'kwarta/ f (dia) Wednesday; (marcha) fourth (gear); ~**-de-final** (pl ~**s-de-final**) f quarter final; ~**feira** (pl ~**s-feiras**) f Wednesday

quartanista /kwarta'nista/ m/f fourth-year (student)

quarteirão /kwarte'rãw/ m block

quar|tel /kwar'tɛw/ (pl ~**téis**) m barracks; ~**tel-general** (pl ~**téis-generais**) m headquarters

quarteto /kwar'tetu/ m quartet; ~ **de cordas** string quartet

quarto /'kwartu/ a fourth □ m (parte) quarter; (aposento) bedroom; (guarda) watch; **são três e/menos um** ~ (Port) it's quarter past/to three; ~ **de banho** (Port) bathroom; ~ **de hora** quarter of an hour; ~ **de hóspedes** guest room

quartzo /'kwartzu/ m quartz

quase /'kwazi/ adv almost, nearly; ~ **nada/nunca** hardly anything/ever

quatro /'kwatru/ a & m four; **de** ~ (no chão) on all fours; ~**centos** a & m four hundred

que /ki/ a which, what; ~ **dia é hoje?** what's the date today?; ~ **homem!** what a man!; ~ **triste!** how sad! □ pron what; ~ **é** ~ **é?** what is it? □ pron rel (coisa) which, that; (pessoa) who, that; (interrogativo) what; **o dia em** ~ ... the day when/that ... □ conj that; (porque) because; **espero** ~ **sim/não** I hope so/not

quê /ke/ pron what □ m **um** ~ something; **não tem de** ~ don't mention it

quebra /'kɛbra/ f break; (de empresa, banco) crash; (de força) cut; **de** ~ in addition; ~**-cabeça** m jigsaw (puzzle); (fig) puzzle; ~**diço** a breakable; ~**do** a broken; <carro> broken down;

~**dos** m pl small change; ~**galho** (fam) m stopgap; ~**mar** m breakwater; ~**molas** m invar speed bump; ~**nozes** m invar nutcrackers; ~**pau** (fam) m row; ~**quebra** m riot

quebrar /ke'brar/ vt break □ vi break; <carro etc> break down; <banco, empresa etc> crash, go bust; ~**-se** vpr break

queda /'kɛda/ f fall; **ter uma** ~ **por** have a soft spot for; ~**-de-braço** f arm wrestling

quei|jeira /ke'ʒera/ f cheese dish; ~**jo** m cheese; ~**jo prato** cheddar; ~**jo-de-minas** m Cheshire cheese

queima /'kejma/ f burning; ~**da** f forest fire; ~**do** a burnt; (bronzeado) tanned, brown; **cheiro de** ~**do** smell of burning

queimar /kej'mar/ vt burn; (bronzear) tan □ vi burn; <lâmpada> go; <fusível> blow; ~**-se** vpr burn o.s.; (bronzear-se) go brown

queima-roupa /kejma'xopa/ f à ~ point-blank

quei|xa /'keʃa/ f complaint; ~**xar-se** vpr complain (de about)

queixo /'keʃu/ m chin; **bater o** ~ shiver

queixoso /ke'ʃozu/ a plaintive □ m plaintiff

quem /kẽj/ pron who; (a pessoa que) anyone who, he who; **de** ~ **é este livro?** whose is this book?; ~ **quer que** whoever; **seja** ~ **for** whoever it is; ~ **falou isso fui eu** it was me who said that; ~ **me dera (que)** ... I wish ..., if only

Quênia /'kenia/ m Kenya

queniano /keni'anu/ a & m Kenyan

quen|tão /kẽ'tãw/ m mulled wine; ~**te** a hot; (com calor agradável) warm; ~**tura** f heat

quepe /'kɛpi/ m cap

quer /kɛr/ conj ~ ... ~ ... whether ... or ...

querer /ke'rer/ vt/i want; **quero ir** I want to go; **quero que você vá** I want you to go; **eu queria falar com o Sr X** I'd like to speak to Mr X; **vai** ~ **vir amanhã?** do you want to come tomorrow?; **vou** ~ **um cafezinho** I'd like a coffee; **se você quiser** if you want; **queira sentar** do sit down; ~ **dizer** mean; **quer dizer** (isto é) that is to say, I mean

querido /ke'ridu/ a dear □ m darling

quermesse /ker'mɛsi/ f fête, fair

querosene /kero'zeni/ m kerosene

questão /kes'tãw/ m question; (assunto) matter; **em** ~ in question; **fazer** ~ **de** really want to; **não faço** ~ **de ir** I don't mind not going

questio|nar /kestʃio'nar/ *vt/i* question; **~nário** *m* questionnaire; **~nável** (*pl* **~náveis**) *a* questionable
quiabo /ki'abu/ *m* okra
quibe /'kibi/ *m* savoury meatball
quicar /ki'kar/ *vt/i* bounce
quiche /'kiʃi/ *f* quiche
quie|to /ki'ɛtu/ *a* (*calado*) quiet; (*imóvel*) still; **~tude** *f* quiet
quilate /ki'latʃi/ *m* carat; (*fig*) calibre
quilha /'kiʎa/ *f* keel
quilo /'kilo/ *m* kilo; **~grama** *m* kilogram; **~metragem** *f* mileage; **~métrico** *a* mile-long
quilômetro /ki'lometru/ *m* kilometre
quimbanda /kĩ'bãda/ *m* Afro-Brazilian cult
qui|mera /ki'mɛra/ *f* fantasy; **~mérico** *a* fanciful
quími|ca /'kimika/ *f* chemistry; **~co** *a* chemical □ *m* chemist
quimioterapia /kimiotera'pia/ *f* chemotherapy
quimono /ki'mɔnu/ *m* kimono
quina /'kina/ *f* **de ~** edgeways
quindim /kĩ'dʒĩ/ *m* sweet made of coconut, sugar and egg yolks
quinhão /ki'ɲãw/ *m* share
quinhentos /ki'ɲɛtus/ *a* & *m* five hundred
quinina /ki'nina/ *f* quinine
qüinquagésimo /kwĩkwa'ʒɛzimu/ *a* fiftieth
quinquilharias /kĩkiʎa'rias/ *f pl* knick-knacks
quinta[1] /'kĩta/ *f* (*fazenda*) farm
quinta[2] /'kĩta/ *f* (*dia*) Thursday; **~-feira** (*pl* **~s-feiras**) *f* Thursday
quin|tal /kĩ'taw/ (*pl* **~tais**) *m* back yard
quinteiro /kĩ'tajru/ *m* (*Port*) farmer
quinteto /kĩ'tetu/ *m* quintet
quin|to /'kĩtu/ *a* & *m* fifth; **~tuplo** *a* fivefold; **~tuplos** *m pl* (*crianças*) quins
quinze /'kĩzi/ *a* & *m* fifteen; **às dez e ~** at quarter past ten; **são ~ para as dez** it's quarter to ten; **~na** /e/ *f* fortnight; **~nal** (*pl* **~nais**) *a* fortnightly; **~nalmente** *adv* fortnightly
quiosque /ki'ɔski/ *m* (*banca*) kiosk; (*no jardim*) gazebo
quiro|mância /kiro'mãsia/ *f* palmistry; **~mante** *m/f* palmist
quisto /'kistu/ *m* cyst
quitan|da /ki'tãda/ *f* grocer's (shop); **~deiro** *m* grocer
qui|tar /ki'tar/ *vt* pay off <*dívida*>; **~te** *a* **estar ~te** be quits
quociente /kwosi'ẽtʃi/ *m* quotient
quórum /'kwɔrũ/ *m* quorum

R

rã /xã/ *f* frog
rabanete /xaba'netʃi/ *m* radish
rabear /xabi'ar/ *vi* <*caminhão*> jackknife
rabino /xa'binu/ *m* rabbi
rabis|car /xabis'kar/ *vt* scribble □ *vi* (*escrever mal*) scribble; (*fazer desenhos*) doodle; **~co** *m* doodle
rabo /'xabu/ *m* (*de animal*) tail; **com o ~ do olho** out of the corner of one's eye; **~-de-cavalo** (*pl* **~s-de-cavalo**) *m* pony tail
rabugento /xabu'ʒẽtu/ *a* grumpy
raça /'xasa/ *f* (*de homens*) race; (*de animais*) breed
ração /xa'sãw/ *f* (*de comida*) ration; (*para animal*) food
racha /'xaʃa/ *f* crack; **~dura** *f* crack
rachar /xa'ʃar/ *vt* (*dividir*) split; (*abrir fendas em*) crack; chop <*lenha*>; split <*despesas*> □ *vi* (*dividir-se*) split; (*apresentar fendas*) crack; (*ao pagar*) split the cost
raci|al /xasi'aw/ (*pl* **~ais**) *a* racial
racio|cinar /xasiosi'nar/ *vi* reason; **~cínio** *m* reasoning; **~nal** (*pl* **~nais**) *a* rational; **~nalizar** *vt* rationalize
racio|namento /xasiona'mẽtu/ *m* rationing; **~nar** *vt* ration
racis|mo /xa'sizmu/ *m* racism; **~ta** *a* & *m/f* racist
radar /xa'dar/ *m* radar
radia|ção /xadʒia'sãw/ *f* radiation; **~dor** *m* radiator
radialista /xadʒia'lista/ *m/f* radio announcer
radiante /xadʒi'ãtʃi/ *a* (*de alegria*) overjoyed
radi|cal /xadʒi'kaw/ (*pl* **~cais**) *a* & *m* radical; **~car-se** *vpr* settle
rádio[1] /'xadʒiu/ *m* radio □ *f* radio station
rádio[2] /'xadʒiu/ *m* (*elemento*) radium
radioati|vidade /xadioatʃivi'dadʒi/ *f* radioactivity; **~vo** *a* radioactive
radiodifusão /xadʒiodʒifu'zãw/ *f* broadcasting
radiogra|far /xadʒiogra'far/ *vt* X-ray <*pulmões, osso etc*>; radio <*mensagem*>; **~fia** *f* X-ray
radiolo|gia /xadʒiolo'ʒia/ *f* radiology; **~gista** *m/f* radiologist
radio|novela /xadʒiono'vela/ *f* radio serial; **~patrulha** *f* patrol car; **~táxi** *m* radio taxi; **~terapia** *f* radiotherapy, ray treatment
raia /'xaja/ *f* (*em corrida*) lane; (*peixe*) ray

rainha /xa'iɲa/ f queen; **~-mãe** f queen mother

raio /'xaju/ m (de luz etc) ray; (de círculo) radius; (de roda) spoke; (relâmpago) bolt of lightning; **~ de ação** range

rai|va /'xajva/ f rage; (doença) rabies; **estar com ~va** be furious (de with); **ter ~va de alg** have it in for s.o.; **~voso** a furious; <cachorro> rabid

raiz /xa'iz/ f root; **~ quadrada/cúbica** square/cube root

rajada /xa'ʒada/ f (de vento) gust; (de tiros) burst

ra|lador /xala'dor/ m grater; **~lar** vt grate

ralé /xa'lɛ/ f rabble

ralhar /xa'ʎar/ vi scold

ralo[1] /'xalu/ m (ralador) grater; (de escoamento) drain

ralo[2] /'xalu/ a <cabelo> thinning; <sopa, tecido> thin; <vegetação> sparse; <café> weak

ra|mal /xa'maw/ (pl **~mais**) m (telefone) extension; (de ferrovia) branch line

ramalhete /xama'ʎetʃi/ m posy, bouquet

ramifi|cação /xamifika'sãw/ f branch; **~car-se** vi branch off

ramo /'xamu/ m branch; (profissional etc) field; (buquê) bunch; **Domingo de Ramos** Palm Sunday

rampa /'xãpa/ f ramp

rancor /xã'kor/ m resentment; **~oso** /o/ a resentful

rançoso /xã'sozu/ a rancid

ran|ger /xã'ʒer/ vt grind <dentes> □ vi creak; **~gido** m creak

ranhura /xa'ɲura/ f groove; (para moedas) slot

ranzinza /xã'zĩza/ a cantankerous

rapariga /xapa'riga/ f (Port) girl

rapaz /xa'pas/ m boy

rapé /xa'pɛ/ m snuff

rapidez /xapi'des/ f speed

rápido /'xapidu/ a fast □ adv <fazer> quickly; <andar> fast

rapina /xa'pina/ f **ave de ~** bird of prey

rapo|sa /xa'poza/ f vixen; **~so** m fox

rapsódia /xap'sodʒia/ f rhapsody

rap|tar /xap'tar/ vt abduct, kidnap <criança>; **~to** m abduction, kidnapping (de criança)

raquete /xa'kɛtʃi/ f, (Port) **raqueta** /xa'keta/ f racquet

raquítico /xa'kitʃiku/ a puny

ra|ramente /xara'mẽtʃi/ adv rarely; **~ridade** f rarity; **~ro** a rare □ adv rarely

rascunho /xas'kuɲu/ m rough version, draft

ras|gado /xaz'gadu/ a torn; (fig)

<elogios etc> effusive; **~gão** m tear; **~gar** vt tear; (em pedaços) tear up □ vi, **~gar-se** vpr tear; **~go** m tear; (fig) burst

raso /'xazu/ a <água> shallow; <sapato> flat; <colher etc> level

ras|pão /xas'pãw/ m graze; **atingir de ~pão** graze; **~par** vt shave <cabeça, pêlos>; plane <madeira>; (para limpar) scrape; (tocar de leve) graze; **~par em** scrape

ras|teiro /xas'teru/ a <planta> creeping; <animal> crawling; **~tejante** a crawling; <voz> slurred; **~tejar** vi crawl

rasto /'xastu/ m veja **rastro**

ras|trear /xastri'ar/ vt track <satélite etc>; scan <céu, corpo etc>; **~tro** m trail

ratear[1] /xatʃi'ar/ vi <motor> miss

ra|tear[2] /xatʃi'ar/ vt share; **~teio** m sharing

ratifi|cação /xatʃifika'sãw/ f ratification; **~car** vt ratify

rato /'xatu/ m rat; (camundongo) mouse; **~eira** f mousetrap

ravina /xa'vina/ f ravine

razão /xa'zãw/ f reason; (proporção) ratio □ m ledger; **à ~ de** at the rate of; **em ~ de** on account of; **ter ~** be right; **não ter ~** be wrong

razoá|vel /xazo'avew/ (pl **~veis**) a reasonable

ré[1] /xɛ/ f (na justiça) defendant

ré[2] /xɛ/ f (marcha) reverse; **dar ~** reverse

reabastecer /xeabaste'ser/ vt/i refuel

reabilitar /xeabili'tar/ vt rehabilitate

rea|ção /xea'sãw/ f reaction; **~ção em cadeia** chain reaction; **~cionário** a & m reactionary

readmitir /xeadʒimi'tʃir/ vt reinstate <funcionário>

reagir /xea'ʒir/ vi react; <doente> respond

reajus|tar /xeaʒus'tar/ vt readjust; **~te** m adjustment

re|al /xe'aw/ (pl **~ais**) a (verdadeiro) real; (da realeza) royal

realçar /xeaw'sar/ vt highlight; **~ce** m prominence

realejo /xea'leʒu/ m barrel organ

realeza /xea'leza/ f royalty

realidade /xeali'dadʒi/ f reality

realimentação /xealimẽta'sãw/ f feedback

realis|mo /xea'lizmu/ m realism; **~ta** a realistic □ m/f realist

reali|zado /xeali'zadu/ a <pessoa> fulfilled; **~zar** vt (fazer) carry out; (tornar real) realize <sonho, capital>; **~zar-se** vpr <sonho> come true; <pessoa> fulfil o.s.; <casamento, reunião etc> take place

realmente /xeaw'mẽtʃi/ *adv* really

reaparecer /xeapare'ser/ *vi* reappear

reativar /xeatʃi'var/ *vt* reactivate

reaver /xea'ver/ *vt* get back

reavivar /xeavi'var/ *vt* revive

rebaixar /xeba'ʃar/ *vt* lower <*preço*>; (*fig*) demean □ *vi* <*preços*> drop; ~-se *vpr* demean o.s.

rebanho /xe'baɲu/ *m* herd; (*fiéis*) flock

reba|te /xe'batʃi/ *m* alarm; ~ter *vt* return <*bola*>; refute <*acusação*>; (*à máquina*) retype

rebelar-se /xebe'larsi/ *vpr* rebel

rebel|de /xe'bɛwdʒi/ *a* rebellious □ *m/f* rebel; ~dia *f* rebelliousness

rebelião /xebeli'ãw/ *f* rebellion

reben|tar /xebẽ'tar/ *vt/i veja* **arrebentar**; ~to *m* (*de planta*) shoot; (*descendente*) offspring

rebite /xe'bitʃi/ *m* rivet

rebobinar /xebobi'nar/ *vt* rewind

rebo|cador /xeboka'dor/ *m* tug; ~car *vt* (*tirar*) tow; (*cobrir com reboco*) plaster; ~co /o/ *m* plaster

rebolar /xebo'lar/ *vi* swing one's hips

reboque /xe'bɔki/ *m* towing; (*veículo a* ~) trailer; (*com guindaste*) tow-truck; **a** ~ on tow

rebuçado /xebu'sadu/ *m* (*Port*) sweet, (*Amer*) candy

rebuliço /xebu'lisu/ *m* commotion

rebuscado /xebus'kadu/ *a* recherché

recado /xe'kadu/ *m* message

reca|ída /xeka'ida/ *f* relapse; ~ir *vi* relapse; <*acento, culpa*> fall

recal|cado /xekaw'kadu/ *a* repressed; ~car *vt* repress

recanto /xe'kãtu/ *m* nook, recess

recapitular /xekapitu'lar/ *vt* review □ *vi* recap

reca|tado /xeka'tadu/ *a* reserved, withdrawn; ~to *m* reserve

recear /xesi'ar/ *vt/i* fear (*por* for)

rece|ber /xese'ber/ *vt* receive; entertain <*convidados*> □ *vi* (~*ber salário*) get paid; (~*ber convidados*) entertain; ~bimento *m* receipt

receio /xe'seju/ *m* fear

recei|ta /xe'sejta/ *f* (*de cozinha*) recipe; (*médica*) prescription; (*dinheiro*) revenue; ~tar *vt* prescribe

recém-casados /xesẽjka'zadus/ *m pl* newly-weds; ~-chegado *m* newcomer; ~-nascido *a* newborn □ *m* newborn child, baby

recente /xe'sẽtʃi/ *a* recent; ~mente *adv* recently

receoso /xese'ozu/ *a* (*apreensivo*) afraid

recep|ção /xesep'sãw/ *f* reception; (*Port: de carta*) receipt; ~cionar *vt* receive; ~cionista *m/f* receptionist; ~táculo *m* receptacle; ~tivo *a* receptive; ~tor *m* receiver

reces|são /xese'sãw/ *f* recession; ~so /ɛ/ *m* recess

re|chear /xeʃi'ar/ *vt* stuff <*frango, assado*>; fill <*empada*>; ~cheio *m* (*para frango etc*) stuffing; (*de empada etc*) filling

rechonchudo /xeʃõ'ʃudu/ *a* plump

recibo /xe'sibu/ *m* receipt

reciclar /xesik'lar/ *vt* recycle

recife /xe'sifi/ *m* reef

recinto /xe'sĩtu/ *m* enclosure

recipiente /xesipi'ẽtʃi/ *m* container

reciprocar /xesipro'kar/ *vt* reciprocate

recíproco /xe'siproku/ *a* reciprocal; <*sentimento*> mutual

reci|tal /xesi'taw/ (*pl* ~tais) *m* recital; ~tar *vt* recite

recla|mação /xeklama'sãw/ *f* complaint; (*no seguro*) claim; ~mar *vt* claim □ *vi* complain (*de* about); (*no seguro*) claim; ~me *m*, (*Port*) ~mo *m* advertising

reclinar-se /xekli'narsi/ *vpr* recline

recluso /xe'kluzu/ *a* reclusive □ *m* recluse

recobrar /xeko'brar/ *vt* recover; ~-se *vpr* recover

recolher /xeko'ʎer/ *vt* collect; (*retirar*) withdraw; ~-se *vpr* retire

recomeçar /xekome'sar/ *vt/i* start again

recomen|dação /xekomẽda'sãw/ *f* recommendation; ~dar *vt* recommend; ~dável (*pl* ~dáveis) *a* advisable

recompen|sa /xekõ'pẽsa/ *f* reward; ~sar *vt* reward

reconcili|ação /xekõsilia'sãw/ *f* reconciliation; ~ar *vt* reconcile; ~ar-se *vpr* be reconciled

reconhe|cer /xekoɲe'ser/ *vt* recognize; (*admitir*) acknowledge; (*mil*) reconnoitre; identify <*corpo*>; ~cimento *m* recognition; (*gratidão*) gratitude; (*mil*) reconnaissance; (*de corpo*) identification; ~cível (*pl* ~cíveis) *a* recognizable

reconsiderar /xekõside'rar/ *vt/i* reconsider

reconstituinte /xekõstʃitu'ĩtʃi/ *m* tonic

reconstituir /xekõstʃitu'ir/ *vt* reform; reconstruct <*crime, cena*>

reconstruir /xekõstru'ir/ *vt* rebuild

recor|dação /xekorda'sãw/ *f* recollection; (*objeto*) memento; ~dar *vt* recollect; ~dar-se (**de**) recall

recor|de /xe'kɔrdʒi/ *a invar* & *m* record; ~dista *a* record-breaking □ *m/f* record-holder

recorrer /xeko'xer/ *vi* ~ **a** turn to <*médico, amigo*>; resort to <*violência, tática*>; ~ **de** appeal against

recor|tar /xekor'tar/ vt cut out; ~te /ɔ/ m cutting, (Amer) clipping

recostar /xekos'tar/ vt lean back; ~se vpr lean back

recreio /xe'kreju/ m recreation; (na escola) break

recriar /xekri'ar/ vt recreate

recriminação /xekrimina'sãw/ f recrimination

recrudescer /xekrude'ser/ vi intensify

recru|ta /xe'kruta/ m/f recruit; ~tamento m recruitment; ~tar vt recruit

recu|ar /xeku'ar/ vi move back; <tropas> retreat; (no tempo) go back; (ceder) back down; (não cumprir) back out (de of) □ vt move back; ~o m retreat; (fig: de intento) climbdown

recupe|ração /xekupera'sãw/ f recovery; ~rar vt recover; make up <atraso, tempo perdido>; ~rar-se vpr recover (de from)

recurso /xe'kursu/ m resort; (coisa útil) resource; (na justiça) appeal; pl resources

recu|sa /xe'kuza/ f refusal; ~sar vt refuse; turn down <convite, oferta>; ~sar-se vpr refuse (a to)

reda|ção /xeda'sãw/ f (de livro, contrato) draft; (pessoal) editorial staff; (seção) editorial department; (na escola) composition; ~tor m editor

rede /'xedʒi/ f net; (para deitar) hammock; (fig: sistema) network

rédea /'xedʒia/ f rein

redemoinho /xedemo'iɲu/ m veja rodamoinho

reden|ção /xedẽ'sãw/ f redemption; ~tor a redeeming □ m redeemer

redigir /xedʒi'ʒir/ vt draw up <contrato>; write <artigo>; edit <dicionário>

redimir /xedʒi'mir/ vt redeem

redobrar /xedo'brar/ vt redouble

redon|deza /xedõ'deza/ f roundness; pl vicinity; ~do a round

redor /xe'dɔr/ m ao ou em ~ de around

redução /xedu'sãw/ f reduction

redun|dante /xedũ'dãtʃi/ a redundant; ~dar vi. ~dar em develop into

redu|zido /xedu'zidu/ a limited; (pequeno) small; ~zir vt reduce; ~zir-se vpr (ficar reduzido) be reduced (a to); (resumir-se) come down (a to)

reeleger /xeele'ʒer/ vt re-elect; ~-se vpr be re-elected

reeleição /xeelej'sãw/ f re-election

reembol|sar /xeẽbow'sar/ vt reimburse <pessoa>; refund <dinheiro>; ~so /o/ m refund; ~so postal cash on delivery

reencarnação /xeẽkarna'sãw/ f reincarnation

reentrância /xeẽ'trãsia/ f recess

reescalonar /xeeskalo'nar/ vt reschedule

reescrever /xeeskre'ver/ vt rewrite

refastelar-se /xefaste'larsi/ vpr stretch out

refazer /xefa'zer/ vt redo; rebuild <vida>; ~-se vpr recover (de from)

refei|ção /xefej'sãw/ f meal; ~tório m dining hall

refém /xe'fẽj/ m hostage

referência /xefe'rẽsia/ f reference; com ~ a with reference to

referendum /xefe'rẽdũ/ m referendum

refe|rente /xefe'rẽtʃi/ a ~rente a regarding; ~rir vt report; ~rir-se vpr refer (a to)

refestelar-se /xefeste'larsi/ vpr (Port) veja refastelar-se

re|fil /xe'fiw/ (pl ~fis) m refill

refi|nado /xefi'nadu/ a refined; ~namento m refinement; ~nar vt refine; ~naria f refinery

refle|tido /xefle'tʃidu/ a <decisão> well-thought-out; <pessoa> thoughtful; ~tir vt/i reflect; ~tir-se vpr be reflected; ~xão /ks/ f reflection; ~xivo /ks/ a reflexive; ~xo /eks/ a <luz> reflected; <ação> reflex □ m (de luz etc) reflection; (físico) reflex; (no cabelo) streak

refluxo /xe'fluksu/ m ebb

refo|gado /xefo'gadu/ m lightly fried mixture of onions and garlic; ~gar vt fry lightly

refor|çar /xefor'sar/ vt reinforce; ~ço /o/ m reinforcement

refor|ma /xe'fɔrma/ f (da lei etc) reform; (na casa etc) renovation; (de militar) discharge; (pensão) pension; ~ma ministerial cabinet reshuffle; ~mado a reformed; (Port: aposentado) retired □ m (Port) pensioner; ~mar vt reform <lei, sistema etc>; renovate <casa, prédio>; (Port: aposentar) retire; ~mar-se vpr (Port: aposentar-se) retire; <criminoso> reform; ~matório m reform school; ~mista a & m/f reformist

refratário /xefra'tariu/ a <tigela etc> ovenproof, heatproof

refrear /xefri'ar/ vt rein in <cavalo>; (fig) curb, keep in check <paixões etc>; ~-se vpr restrain o.s.

refrega /xe'frega/ f clash, fight

refres|cante /xefres'kãtʃi/ a refreshing; ~car vt freshen, cool <ar>; refresh <pessoa, memória etc> □ vi get cooler; ~car-se vpr refresh o.s.; ~co /e/ m (bebida) soft drink; pl refreshments

refrige|rado /xefriʒe'radu/ *a* cooled; <*casa etc*> air-conditioned; (*na geladeira*) refrigerated; **~rador** *m* refrigerator; **~rante** *m* soft drink; **~rar** *vt* keep cool; (*na geladeira*) refrigerate

refugi|ado /xefuʒi'adu/ *m* refugee; **~ar-se** *vpr* take refuge

refúgio /xe'fuʒiu/ *m* refuge

refugo /xe'fugu/ *m* waste, refuse

refutar /xefu'tar/ *vt* refute

regaço /xe'gasu/ *m* lap

regador /xega'dor/ *m* watering can

regalia /xega'lia/ *f* privilege

regar /xe'gar/ *vt* water

regata /xe'gata/ *f* regatta

regatear /xegatʃi'ar/ *vi* bargain, haggle

re|gência /xe'ʒẽsia/ *f* (*de verbo etc*) government; **~gente** *m/f* (*de orquestra*) conductor; **~ger** *vt* govern □ *vi* rule

região /xeʒi'ãw/ *f* region; (*de cidade etc*) area

regi|me /xe'ʒimi/ *m* regime; (*dieta*) diet; **fazer ~me** diet; **~mento** *m* (*militar*) regiment; (*regulamento*) regulations

régio /'xɛʒiu/ *a* regal

regio|nal /xeʒio'naw/ (*pl* **~nais**) *a* regional

regis|trador /xeʒistra'dor/ *a* **caixa ~tradora** cash register; **~trar** *vt* register; (*anotar*) record; **~tro** *m* (*lista*) register; (*de um fato, em banco de dados*) record; (*ato de ~trar*) registration

rego /'xegu/ *m* (*de arado*) furrow; (*de roda*) rut; (*para escoamento*) ditch

regozi|jar /xegozi'ʒar/ *vt* delight; **~jar-se** *vpr* be delighted; **~jo** *m* delight

regra /'xɛgra/ *f* rule; *pl* (*menstruações*) periods; **em ~** as a rule

regres|sar /xegre'sar/ *vi* return; **~sivo** *a* regressive; **contagem ~siva** countdown; **~so** /ɛ/ *m* return

régua /'xɛgwa/ *f* ruler

regu|lagem /xegu'laʒẽ/ *f* (*de carro*) tuning; **~lamento** *m* regulations; **~lar** *a* regular; <*estatura, qualidade etc*> average □ *vt* regulate; tune <*carro, motor*>; set <*relógio*> □ *vi* work; **~lar-se por** go by, be guided by; **~laridade** *f* regularity; **~larizar** *vt* regularize

regurgitar /xegurʒi'tar/ *vt* bring up

rei /xej/ *m* king; **~nado** *m* reign

reincidir /xeĩsi'dʒir/ *vi* <*criminoso*> reoffend

reino /'xejnu/ *m* kingdom; (*fig: da fantasia etc*) realm; **Reino Unido** United Kingdom

reiterar /xejte'rar/ *vt* reiterate

reitor /xej'tor/ *m* chancellor, (*Amer*) president

reivindi|cação /xejvĩdʒika'sãw/ *f* demand; **~car** *vt* claim, demand

rejei|ção /xeʒej'sãw/ *f* rejection; **~tar** *vt* reject

rejuvenescer /xeʒuvene'ser/ *vt* rejuvenate □ *vi* be rejuvenated

relação /xela'sãw/ *f* relationship; (*relatório*) account; (*lista*) list; *pl* relations; **com** *ou* **em ~ a** in relation to, regarding

relacio|namento /xelasiona'mẽtu/ *m* relationship; **~nar** *vt* relate (**com** to); (*listar*) list; **~nar-se** *vpr* relate (**com** to)

relações-públicas /xelasõjs'publikas/ *m/f invar* public-relations person

relâmpago /xe'lãpagu/ *m* flash of lightning; *pl* lightning □ *a* lightning; **num ~** in a flash

relampejar /xelãpe'ʒar/ *vi* flash; **relampejou** there was a flash of lightning

relance /xe'lãsi/ *m* glance; **olhar de ~** glance (at)

rela|tar /xela'tar/ *vt* relate; **~tivo** *a* relative; **~to** *m* account; **~tório** *m* report

rela|xado /xela'ʃadu/ *a* relaxed; <*disciplina*> lax; <*pessoa*> lazy, complacent; **~xamento** *m* (*físico*) relaxation; (*de pessoa*) complacency; **~xante** *a* relaxing □ *m* tranquillizer; **~xar** *vt* relax □ *vi* (*descansar*) relax; (*tornar-se omisso*) get complacent; **~xar-se** *vpr* relax; **~xe** *m* relaxation

reles /'xɛlis/ *a invar* <*gente*> common; <*ação*> despicable

rele|vância /xele'vãsia/ *f* relevance; **~vante** *a* relevant; **~var** *vt* emphasize; **~vo** /e/ *m* relief; (*importância*) prominence

religi|ão /xeliʒi'ãw/ *f* religion; **~oso** /o/ *a* religious

relin|char /xelĩ'ʃar/ *vi* neigh; **~cho** *m* neighing

relíquia /xe'likia/ *f* relic

relógio /xe'lɔʒiu/ *m* clock; (*de pulso*) watch

relu|tância /xelu'tãsia/ *f* reluctance; **~tante** *a* reluctant; **~tar** *vi* be reluctant (**em** to)

reluzente /xelu'zẽtʃi/ *a* shining, gleaming

relva /'xɛwva/ *f* grass; **~do** *m* lawn

remador /xema'dor/ *m* rower

remanescente /xemane'sẽtʃi/ *a* remaining □ *m* remainder

remar /xe'mar/ *vt/i* row

rema|tar /xema'tar/ *vt* finish off; **~te** *m* finish; (*adorno*) finishing touch; (*de piada*) punch line

remediar /xemeˈdʒiˈar/ vt remedy

remédio /xeˈmɛdʒiu/ m (contra doença) medicine, drug; (a problema etc) remedy

remelento /xemeˈlẽtu/ a bleary

remen|dar /xemẽˈdar/ vt mend; (com pedaço de pano) patch; ~do m mend; (pedaço de pano) patch

remessa /xeˈmesa/ f (de mercadorias) shipment; (de dinheiro) remittance

reme|tente /xemeˈtẽtʃi/ m/f sender; ~ter vt send <mercadorias, dinheiro etc>; refer <leitor> (a to)

remexer /xemeˈʃer/ vt shuffle <papéis>; stir up <poeira, lama>; wave <braços> □ vi rummage; ~-se vpr move around

reminiscência /xeminiˈsẽsia/ f reminiscence

remir /xeˈmir/ vt redeem; ~-se vpr redeem o.s.

remissão /xemiˈsãw/ f (de pecados) redemption; (de doença, pena) remission; (num livro) cross-reference

remo /ˈxemu/ m oar; (esporte) rowing

remoção /xemoˈsãw/ f removal

remoinho /xemoˈiɲu/ m (Port) veja **rodamoinho**

remontar /xemõˈtar/ vi ~ a <coisa> date back to; <pessoa> think back to

remorso /xeˈmorsu/ m remorse

remo|to /xeˈmɔtu/ a remote; ~ver vt remove

remune|ração /xemuneraˈsãw/ f payment; ~rador a profitable; ~rar vt pay

rena /ˈxena/ f reindeer

re|nal /xeˈnaw/ (pl ~nais) a renal, kidney

Renascença /xenaˈsẽsa/ f Renaissance

renas|cer /xenaˈser/ vi be reborn; ~cimento m rebirth

renda[1] /ˈxẽda/ f (tecido) lace

ren|da[2] /ˈxẽda/ f income; (Port: aluguel) rent; ~der bring in, yield <lucro>; earn <juros>; fetch <preço>; bring <resultado> □ vi <investimento, trabalho, ação> pay off; <comida> go a long way; <produto comprado> give value for money; ~der-se vpr surrender; ~dição f surrender; ~dimento m (de renda) income; (de investimento, terreno) yield; (de motor etc) output; (de produto comprado) value for money; ~doso /o/ a profitable

rene|gado /xeneˈgadu/ a & m renegade; ~gar vt renounce

renhido /xeˈɲidu/ a hard-fought

Reno /ˈxenu/ m Rhine

reno|mado /xenoˈmadu/ a renowned; ~me /o/ m renown

reno|vação /xenovaˈsãw/ f renewal; ~var vt renew

renque /ˈxẽki/ m row

ren|tabilidade /xẽtabiliˈdadʒi/ f profitability; ~tável (pl ~táveis) a profitable

rente /ˈxẽtʃi/ adv ~ a close to □ a <cabelo> cropped

renúncia /xeˈnũsia/ f renunciation (a of); (a cargo) resignation (a from)

renunciar /xenũsiˈar/ vi <presidente etc> resign; ~ a give up; waive <direito>

reorganizar /xeorganiˈzar/ vt reorganize

repa|ração /xeparaˈsãw/ f reparation; (conserto) repair; ~rar vt (consertar) repair; make up for <ofensa, injustiça, erro>; make good <danos, prejuízo> □ vi ~rar (em) notice; ~ro m (conserto) repair

repar|tição /xepartʃiˈsãw/ f division; (seção do governo) department; ~tir vt divide up

repassar /xepaˈsar/ vt revise <matéria, lição>

repatriar /xepatriˈar/ vt repatriate

repe|lente /xepeˈlẽtʃi/ a & m repellent; ~lir vt repel; reject <idéia, proposta etc>

repensar /xepẽˈsar/ vt/i rethink

repen|te /xeˈpẽtʃi/ m de ~te suddenly; (fam: talvez) maybe; ~tino a sudden

reper|cussão /xeperkuˈsãw/ f repercussion; ~cutir vi <som> reverberate; (fig: ter efeito) have repercussions

repertório /xeperˈtɔriu/ m (músico etc) repertoire; (lista) list

repe|tição /xepetʃiˈsãw/ f repetition; ~tido a repeated; ~tidas vezes repeatedly; ~tir vt repeat □ vi (ao comer) have seconds; ~tir-se vpr <pessoa> repeat o.s.; <fato, acontecimento> recur; ~titivo a repetitive

repi|car /xepiˈkar/ vt/i ring; ~que m ring

replay /xeˈplej/ (pl ~s) m action replay

repleto /xeˈplɛtu/ a full up

réplica /ˈxɛplika/ f reply; (cópia) replica

replicar /xepliˈkar/ vt answer □ vi reply

repolho /xeˈpoʎu/ m cabbage

repor /xeˈpor/ vt (num lugar) put back; (substituir) replace

reportagem /xeporˈtaʒẽ/ f (uma) report; (ato) reporting

repórter /xeˈpɔrter/ m/f reporter

reposição /xepoziˈsãw/ f replacement

repou|sar /xepoˈsar/ vt/i rest; ~so m rest

repreen|der /xepriẽˈder/ vt rebuke, reprimand; ~são f rebuke, rep-

rimand; ~sível (pl ~síveis) a reprehensible
represa /xe'preza/ f dam
represália /xepre'zalia/ f reprisal
represen|tação /xeprezēta'sãw/ f representation; (espetáculo) performance; (ofício de ator) acting; ~tante m/f representative; ~tar vt represent; (no teatro) perform <peça>; play <papel, personagem> □ vi <ator> act; ~tativo a representative
repres|são /xepre'sãw/ f repression; ~sivo a repressive
repri|mido /xepri'midu/ a repressed; ~mir vt repress
reprise /xe'prizi/ f (na TV) repeat; (de filme) rerun
reprodu|ção /xeprodu'sãw/ f reproduction; ~zir vt reproduce; ~zir-se vpr (multiplicar-se) reproduce; (repetir-se) recur
repro|vação /xeprova'sãw/ f disapproval; (em exame) failure; ~var vt (rejeitar) disapprove of; (em exame) fail; ser ~vado <aluno> fail
rép|til /'xɛptʃiu/ (pl ~teis) m reptile
república /xe'publika/ f republic; (de estudantes) hall of residence
republicano /xepubli'kanu/ a & m republican
repudiar /xepudʒi'ar/ vt disown; repudiate <esposa>
repug|nância /xepug'nãsia/ f repugnance; ~nante a repugnant
repul|sa /xe'puwsa/ f repulsion; (recusa) rejection; ~sivo a repulsive
reputação /xeputa'sãw/ f reputation
requebrar /xeke'brar/ vt swing; ~-se vpr sway
requeijão /xeke'ʒãw/ m cheese spread, cottage cheese
reque|rer /xeke'rer/ vt (pedir) apply for; (exigir) require; ~rimento m application
requin|tado /xekĩ'tadu/ a refined; ~tar vt refine; ~te m refinement
requisi|ção /xekizi'sãw/ f requisition; ~tar vt requisition; ~to m requirement
rês /xes/ (pl reses) m head of cattle; pl cattle
rescindir /xesĩ'dʒir/ vt rescind
rés-do-chão /xɛzdu'ʃãw/ m invar (Port) ground floor, (Amer) first floor
rese|nha /xe'zeɲa/ f review; ~nhar vt review
reser|va /xe'zɛrva/ f reserve; (em hotel, avião etc, ressalva) reservation; ~var vt reserve; ~vatório m reservoir; ~vista m/f reservist
resfri|ado /xesfri'adu/ a estar ~ado have a cold □ m cold; ~ar vt cool □ vi get cold; (tornar-se morno) cool down; ~ar-se vpr catch a cold

resga|tar /xezga'tar/ vt (salvar) rescue; (remir) redeem; ~te m (salvamento) rescue; (pago por refém) ransom; (remissão) redemption
resguardar /xezgwar'dar/ vt protect; ~-se vpr protect o.s. (de from)
residência /xezi'dēsia/ f residence
residen|cial /xezidēsi'aw/ (pl ~ciais) a <bairro> residential; <telefone etc> home; ~te a a & m/f resident
residir /xezi'dʒir/ vi reside
resíduo /xe'ziduu/ m residue
resig|nação /xezigna'sãw/ f resignation; ~nado a resigned; ~nar-se vpr resign o.s. (com to)
resina /xe'zina/ f resin
resis|tência /xezis'tēsia/ f resistance; (de atleta, mental) endurance; (de material, objeto) toughness; ~tente a strong, tough; <tecido, roupa> hardwearing; <planta> hardy; ~tente a resistant to; ~tir vi (opor ~tência) resist; (agüentar) <pessoa> hold out; <objeto> hold; ~tir a (combater) resist; (agüentar) withstand; ~tir ao tempo stand the test of time
resmun|gar /xezmũ'gar/ vi grumble; ~go m grumbling
resolu|ção /xezolu'sãw/ f resolution; (firmeza) resolve; (de problema) solution; ~to a resolute; ~to a resolved to
resolver /xezow'ver/ vt (esclarecer) sort out; solve <problema, enigma>; (decidir) decide; ~-se vpr make up one's mind (a to)
respaldo /xes'pawdu/ m (de cadeira) back; (fig: apoio) backing
respectivo /xespek'tʃivu/ a respective
respei|tabilidade /xespejtabili'dadʒi/ f respectability; ~tador a respectful; ~tar vt respect; ~tável (pl ~táveis) a respectable; ~to m respect (por for); a ~to de about; a este ~to in this respect; com ~to a with regard to; dizer ~to a concern; ~toso /o/ a respectful
respin|gar /xespĩ'gar/ vt/i splash; ~go m splash
respi|ração /xespira'sãw/ f breathing; ~rador m respirator; ~rar vt/i breathe; ~ratório a respiratory; ~ro m breath; (descanso) break, breather
resplande|cente /xesplãde'sētʃi/ a resplendent; ~cer vi shine
resplendor /xesplē'dor/ m brilliance; (fig) glory
respon|dão /xespõ'dãw/ a (f ~dona) cheeky; ~der vt/i answer; (com insolência) answer back; ~der a answer; ~der por answer for, take responsibility for

responsabili|dade /xespõsabili-'dadʒi/ f responsibility; ~**zar** vt hold responsible (**por** for); ~**zar-se** vpr take responsibility (**por** for)

responsá|vel /xespõ'savew/ (pl ~**veis**) a responsible (**por** for)

resposta /xes'pɔsta/ f answer

resquício /xes'kisiu/ m vestige, remnant

ressabiado /xesabi'adu/ a wary, suspicious

ressaca /xe'saka/ f (depois de beber) hangover; (do mar) undertow

ressaltar /xesaw'tar/ vt emphasize □ vi stand out

ressalva /xe'sawva/ f reservation, proviso; (proteção) safeguard

ressarcir /xesar'sir/ vt refund

resse|cado /xese'kadu/ a <terra> parched; <pele> dry; ~**car** vt/i dry up

ressen|tido /xesē'tʃidu/ a resentful; ~**timento** m resentment; ~**tir-se** de (ofender-se) resent; (ser influenciado) show the effects of

ressequido /xese'kidu/ a veja **ressecado**

resso|ar /xeso'ar/ vi resound; ~**nância** f resonance; ~**nante** a resonant; ~**nar** vi (Port) snore

ressurgimento /xesurʒi'mētu/ m resurgence

ressurreição /xesuxej'sãw/ f resurrection

ressuscitar /xesusi'tar/ vt revive

restabele|cer /xestabele'ser/ vt restore; restore to health <doente>; ~**cer-se** vpr recover; ~**cimento** m restoration; (de doente) recovery

res|tante /xes'tãtʃi/ a remaining □ m remainder; ~**tar** vi remain; ~**ta-me dizer que** ... it remains for me to say that

restau|ração /xestawra'sãw/ f restoration; ~**rante** m restaurant; ~**rar** vt restore

restitu|ição /xestʃitui'sãw/ f return, restitution; ~**ir** vt (devolver) return; restore <forma, força etc>; reinstate <funcionário>

resto /'xɛstu/ m rest; pl (de comida) left-overs; (de cadáver) remains; **de** ~ besides

restrição /xestri'sãw/ f restriction

restringir /xestrĩ'ʒir/ vt restrict

restrito /xes'tritu/ a restricted

resul|tado /xezuw'tadu/ m result; ~**tante** a resulting (**de** from); ~**tar** vi result (**de** from; **em** in)

resu|mir /xezu'mir/ vt (abreviar) summarize; (conter em poucas palavras) sum up; ~**mir-se** vpr (ser expresso em poucas palavras) be summed up; ~**mir-se em** (ser

apenas) come down to; ~**mo** m summary; **em** ~**mo** briefly

resvalar /xezva'lar/ vi (sem querer) slip; (deslizar) slide

reta /'xɛta/ f (linha) straight line; (de pista etc) straight; ~ **final** home straight

retaguarda /xeta'gwarda/ f rearguard

retalho /xe'taʎu/ m scrap; **a** ~ (Port) retail

retaliação /xetalia'sãw/ f retaliation

retangular /xetãgu'lar/ a rectangular

retângulo /xe'tãgulu/ m rectangle

retar|dado /xetar'dadu/ a retarded □ m retard; ~**dar** vt delay; ~**datário** m latecomer

retenção /xetē'sãw/ f retention

reter /xe'ter/ vt keep <pessoa>; hold back <águas, riso, lágrimas>; (na memória) retain; ~**-se** vpr restrain o.s.

rete|sado /xete'zadu/ a taut; ~**sar** vt pull taut

reticência /xetʃi'sēsia/ f reticence

reti|dão /xetʃi'dãw/ f rectitude; ~**ficar** vt rectify

reti|rada /xetʃi'rada/ f (de tropas) retreat; (de dinheiro) withdrawal; ~**rado** a secluded; ~**rar** vt withdraw; (afastar) move away; ~**rar-se** vpr <tropas> retreat; (afastar-se) withdraw; (de uma atividade) retire; ~**ro** m retreat

reto /'xɛtu/ a <linha etc> straight; <pessoa> honest

retocar /xeto'kar/ vt touch up <desenho, maquiagem etc>; alter <texto>

reto|mada /xeto'mada/ f (continuação) resumption; (reconquista) retaking; ~**mar** vt (continuar com) resume; (conquistar de novo) retake

retoque /xe'tɔki/ m finishing touch

retorcer /xetor'ser/ vt twist; ~**-se** vpr writhe

retóri|ca /xe'tɔrika/ f rhetoric; ~**co** a rhetorical

retor|nar /xetor'nar/ vi return; ~**no** m return; (na estrada) turning place; **dar** ~**no** do a U-turn

retrair /xetra'ir/ vt retract, withdraw; ~**-se** vpr (recuar) withdraw; (encolher-se) retract

retrasa|do /xetra'zadu/ a **a semana** ~**da** the week before last

retratar[1] /xetra'tar/ vt (desdizer) retract

retra|tar[2] /xetra'tar/ vt (em quadro, livro) portray, depict; ~**to** m portrait; (foto) photo; (representação) portrayal; ~**to falado** identikit picture

retribuir /xetribu'ir/ vt return <favor, visita>; repay <gentileza>

retroativo /xetroa'tʃivu/ *a* retroactive; <*pagamento*> backdated

retro|ceder /xetrose'der/ *vi* retreat; (*desistir*) back down; ~**cesso** /ɛ/ *m* retreat; (*ao passado*) regression

retrógrado /xe'trɔgradu/ *a* retrograde

retrospec|tiva /xetrospek'tʃiva/ *f* retrospective; ~**tivo** *a* retrospective; ~**to** /ɛ/ *m* look back; **em** ~**to** in retrospect

retrovisor /xetrovi'zor/ *a* & *m* (**espelho**) ~ rear-view mirror

retrucar /xetru'kar/ *vt/i* retort

retum|bante /xetũ'bãtʃi/ *a* resounding; ~**bar** *vi* resound

réu /'xɛw/ *m* (*f* ré) defendant

reumatismo /xewma'tʃizmu/ *m* rheumatism

reu|nião /xeuni'ãw/ *f* meeting; (*descontraída*) get-together; (*de família*) reunion; ~**nião de cúpula** summit meeting; ~**nir** *vt* bring together <*pessoas*>; combine <*qualidades*>; ~**nir-se** *vpr* meet; <*amigos, familiares*> get together; ~**nir-se a** join

revanche /xe'vãʃi/ *f* revenge; (*jogo*) return match

reveillon /xeve'jõ/ (*pl* ~**s**) *m* New Year's Eve

reve|lação /xevela'sãw/ *f* revelation; (*de fotos*) developing; (*novo talento*) promising newcomer; ~**lar** *vt* reveal; develop <*filme, fotos*>; ~**lar-se** *vpr* (*vir a ser*) turn out to be

revelia /xeve'lia/ *f* à ~ by default; à ~ **de** without the knowledge of

reven|dedor /xevẽde'dor/ *m* dealer; ~**der** *vt* resell

rever /xe'ver/ *vt* (*ver de novo*) see again; (*revisar*) revise; (*examinar*) check

reve|rência /xeve'resia/ *f* reverence; (*movimento do busto*) bow; (*dobrando os joelhos*) curtsey; ~**rente** *a* reverent

reverso /xe'vɛrsu/ *m* reverse; **o** ~ **da medalha** the other side of the coin

revés /xe'vɛs/ (*pl* **reveses**) *m* setback

reves|timento /xevestʃi'mẽtu/ *m* covering; ~**tir** *vt* cover

reve|zamento /xeveza'mẽtu/ *m* alternation; ~**zar** *vt/i* alternate; ~**zar-se** *vpr* alternate

revi|dar /xevi'dar/ *vt* return <*golpe, insulto*>; refute <*crítica*>; (*retrucar*) retort □ *vi* hit back; ~**de** *m* response

revigorar /xevigo'rar/ *vt* strengthen □ *vi*, ~**-se** *vpr* regain one's strength

revi|rar /xevi'rar/ *vt* turn out <*bolsos, gavetas*>; turn over <*terra*>; turn inside out <*roupa*>; roll <*olhos*>; ~**rar-se** *vpr* toss and turn; ~**ravolta** /ɔ/ *f* (*na política etc*) about-face, about-turn; (*da situação*) turnabout, dramatic change

revi|são /xevi'zãw/ *f* (*de lições etc*) revision; (*de máquina, motor*) overhaul; (*de carro*) service; ~**são de provas** proofreading; ~**sar** *vt* revise <*provas, lições*>; service <*carro*>; ~**sor** *m* (*de bilhetes*) ticket inspector; ~**sor de provas** proofreader

revis|ta /xe'vista/ *f* (*para ler*) magazine; (*teatral*) revue; (*de tropas etc*) review; **passar** ~**ta a** a review; ~**tar** *vt* search

reviver /xevi'ver/ *vt* relive □ *vi* revive

revogar /xevo'gar/ *vt* revoke <*lei*>; cancel <*ordem*>

revol|ta /xe'vɔwta/ *f* (*rebelião*) revolt; (*indignação*) disgust; ~**tante** *a* disgusting; ~**tar** *vt* disgust; ~**tar-se** *vpr* (*rebelar-se*) revolt; (*indignar-se*) be disgusted; ~**to** /o/ *a* <*casa, gaveta*> upside down; <*cabelo*> dishevelled; <*mar*> rough; <*mundo, região*> troubled; <*anos*> turbulent

revolu|ção /xevolu'sãw/ *f* revolution; ~**cionar** *vt* revolutionize; ~**cionário** *a* & *m* revolutionary

revolver /xevow'ver/ *vt* turn over <*terra*>; roll <*olhos*>; go through <*gavetas, arquivos*>

revólver /xe'vɔwver/ *m* revolver

re|za /'xɛza/ *f* prayer; ~**zar** *vi* pray □ *vt* say <*missa, oração*>; (*dizer*) state

riacho /xi'aʃu/ *m* stream

ribalta /xi'bawta/ *f* footlights

ribanceira /xibã'sera/ *f* embankment

ribombar /xibõ'bar/ *vi* rumble

rico /'xiku/ *a* rich □ *m* rich man; **os** ~**s** the rich

ricochete /xiko'ʃetʃi/ *m* ricochet; ~**ar** *vi* ricochet

ricota /xi'kɔta/ *f* curd cheese, ricotta

ridicularizar /xidʒikulari'zar/ *vt* ridicule

ridículo /xi'dʒikulu/ *a* ridiculous

ri|fa /'xifa/ *f* raffle; ~**far** *vt* raffle

rifão /xi'fãw/ *m* saying

rifle /'xifli/ *m* rifle

rigidez /xiʒi'des/ *f* rigidity

rígido /'xiʒidu/ *a* rigid

rigor /xi'gor/ *m* severity; (*meticulosidade*) rigour; **vestido a** ~ evening dress; **de** ~ essential

rigoroso /xigo'rozu/ *a* strict; <*inverno, pena*> severe, harsh; <*lógica, estudo*> rigorous

rijo /'xiʒu/ *a* stiff; <*músculos*> firm

rim /xĩ/ *m* kidney; *pl* (*parte das costas*) small of the back

ri|ma /'xima/ *f* rhyme; ~**mar** *vt/i* rhyme

rí|mel /'ximew/ (*pl* ~**meis**) *m* mascara

ringue /'xĩgi/ *m* ring

rinoceronte /xinose'rõtʃi/ *m* rhinoceros

rinque /'xĩki/ *m* rink

rio /'xio/ *m* river

riqueza /xi'keza/ *f* wealth; (*qualidade*) richness; *pl* riches

rir /xir/ *vi* laugh (**de** at)

risada /xi'zada/ *f* laugh, laughter; **dar ~ laugh**

ris|ca /'xiska/ *f* stroke; (*listra*) stripe; (*do cabelo*) parting; **à ~ca** to the letter; **~car** *vt* (*apagar*) cross out <*erro*>; strike <*fósforo*>; scratch <*mesa, carro etc*>; write off <*amigo etc*>; **~co¹** *m* (*na parede etc*) scratch; (*no papel*) line; (*esboço*) sketch

risco² /'xisku/ *m* risk

riso /'xizu/ *m* laugh; **~nho** /o/ *a* smiling

ríspido /'xispidu/ *a* harsh

rítmico /'xitʃmiku/ *a* rhythmic

ritmo /'xitʃimu/ *m* rhythm

rito /'xitu/ *m* rite

ritu|al /xitu'aw/ (*pl* **~ais**) *a* & *m* ritual

ri|val /xi'vaw/ (*pl* **~vais**) *a* & *m/f* rival; **~validade** *f* rivalry; **~valizar** *vt* rival □ *vi* vie (**com** with)

rixa /'xiʃa/ *f* fight

robô /xo'bo/ *m* robot

robusto /xo'bustu/ *a* robust

roça /'xɔsa/ *f* (*campo*) country

rocambole /xokã'bɔli/ *m* roll

roçar /xo'sar/ *vt* graze; **~ em** brush against

ro|cha /'xɔʃa/ *f* rock; **~chedo** /e/ *m* cliff

roda /'xɔda/ *f* (*de carro etc*) wheel; (*de amigos etc*) circle; **~ dentada** cog; **~da** *f* round; **~do a saia ~da** full skirt; **~-gigante** (*pl* **~s-gigantes**) *f* big wheel, (*Amer*) ferris wheel; **~moinho** *m* (*de vento*) whirlwind; (*na água*) whirlpool; (*fig*) whirl, swirl; **~pé** *m* skirting board, (*Amer*) baseboard

rodar /xo'dar/ *vt* (*fazer girar*) spin; (*viajar por*) go round; do <*quilometragem*>; shoot <*filme*>; run <*programa*> □ *vi* (*girar*) spin; (*de carro*) drive round

rodear /xodʒi'ar/ *vt* (*circundar*) surround; (*andar ao redor de*) go round

rodeio /xo'deju/ *m* (*ao falar*) circumlocution; (*de gado*) round-up; **falar sem ~s** talk straight

rodela /xo'dɛla/ *f* (*de limão etc*) slice; (*peça de metal*) washer

rodízio /xo'dʒiziu/ *m* rota

rodo /'xodu/ *m* rake

rodopiar /xodopi'ar/ *vi* spin round

rodovi|a /xodo'via/ *f* highway; **~ária** *f* bus station; **~ário** *a* road; **polícia ~ária** traffic police

ro|edor /xoe'dor/ *m* rodent; **~er** *vt* gnaw; bite <*unhas*>; (*fig*) eat away

rogar /xo'gar/ *vi* request

rojão /xo'ʒãw/ *m* rocket

rol /xɔw/ (*pl* **róis**) *m* roll

rolar /xo'lar/ *vt* roll □ *vi* roll; (*fam*) (*acontecer*) happen

roldana /xow'dana/ *f* pulley

roleta /xo'leta/ *f* (*jogo*) roulette; (*borboleta*) turnstile

rolha /'xoʎa/ *f* cork

roliço /xo'lisu/ *a* <*objeto*> cylindrical; <*pessoa*> plump

rolo /'xolu/ *m* (*de filme, tecido etc*) roll; (*máquina, bobe*) roller; **~ compressor** steamroller; **~ de massa** rolling pin

Roma /'xoma/ *f* Rome

romã /xo'mã/ *f* pomegranate

roman|ce /xo'mãsi/ *m* (*livro*) novel; (*caso*) romance; **~cista** *m/f* novelist

romano /xo'manu/ *a* & *m* Roman

romântico /xo'mãtʃiku/ *a* romantic

romantismo /xomã'tʃizmu/ *m* (*amor*) romance; (*idealismo*) romanticism

romaria /xoma'ria/ *f* pilgrimage

rombo /'xõbu/ *m* hole

Romênia /xo'menia/ *f* Romania

romeno /xo'menu/ *a* & *m* Romanian

rom|per /xõ'per/ *vt* break; break off <*relações*> □ *vi* <*dia*> break; <*sol*> rise; **~per com** break up with; **~pimento** *m* break; (*de relações*) breaking off

ron|car /xõ'kar/ *vi* (*ao dormir*) snore; <*estômago*> rumble; **~co** *m* snoring; (*um*) snore; (*de motor*) roar

ron|da /'xõda/ *f* round, patrol; **~dar** *vt* (*patrulhar*) patrol; (*espreitar*) prowl around □ *vi* <*vigia etc*> patrol; <*animal, ladrão*> prowl around

ronronar /xõxo'nar/ *vi* purr

roque¹ /'xɔki/ *m* (*em xadrez*) rook

ro|que² /'xɔki/ *m* (*música*) rock; **~queiro** *m* rock musician

rosa /'xɔza/ *f* rose □ *a invar* pink; **~do** *a* rosy; <*vinho*> rosé

rosário /xo'zariu/ *m* rosary

rosbife /xoz'bifi/ *m* roast beef

rosca /'xoska/ *f* (*de parafuso*) thread; (*biscoito*) rusk; **farinha de ~** breadcrumbs

roseira /xo'zera/ *f* rosebush

roseta /xo'zeta/ *f* rosette

rosnar /xoz'nar/ *vi* <*cachorro*> growl; <*pessoa*> snarl

rosto /'xostu/ *m* face

rota /'xɔta/ *f* route

rota|ção /xota'sãw/ *f* rotation; **~tividade** *f* turnround; **~tivo** *a* rotating

rotei|rista /xote'rista/ *m/f* scriptwriter; **~ro** *m* (*de viagem*) itinerary;

(de filme, peça) script; *(de discussão etc)* outline

roti|na /xo't∫ina/ *f* routine; **~neiro** *a* routine

rótula /'xɔtula/ *f* kneecap

rotular /xotu'lar/ *vt* label (**de** as)

rótulo /'xɔtulu/ *m* label

rou|bar /xo'bar/ *vt* steal *<dinheiro, carro etc>*; rob *<pessoa, loja etc>* □ *vi* steal; *(em jogo)* cheat; **~bo** *m* theft, robbery

rouco /'xoku/ *a* hoarse; *<voz>* gravelly

rou|pa /'xopa/ *f* clothes; *(uma)* outfit; **~pa de baixo** underwear; **~pa de cama** bedclothes; **~pão** *m* dressing gown

rouquidão /xoki'dãw/ *f* hoarseness

rouxi|nol /xoʃi'nɔw/ *(pl* **~nóis**) *m* nightingale

roxo /'xoʃu/ *a* purple

rua /'xua/ *f* street

rubéola /xu'bɛola/ *f* German measles

rubi /xu'bi/ *m* ruby

rude /'xudʒi/ *a* rude

rudimentos /xudʒi'mẽtus/ *m pl* rudiments, basics

ruela /xu'ɛla/ *f* backstreet

rufar /xu'far/ *vi* *<tambor>* roll □ *m* roll

ruga /'xuga/ *f* *(na pele)* wrinkle; *(na roupa)* crease

ru|gido /xu'ʒidu/ *m* roar; **~gir** *vi* roar

ruibarbo /xui'barbu/ *m* rhubarb

ruído /xu'idu/ *m* noise

ruidoso /xui'dozu/ *a* noisy

ruim /xu'ĩ/ *a* bad

ruína /xu'ina/ *f* ruin

ruivo /'xuivu/ *a* *<cabelo>* red; *<pessoa>* red-haired □ *m* redhead

rulê /xu'le/ *a* **gola ~** roll-neck

rum /xũ/ *m* rum

ru|mar /xu'mar/ *vi* head (**para** for); **~mo** *m* course; **~mo a** heading for; **sem ~mo** *<vida>* aimless; *<andar>* aimlessly

rumor /xu'mor/ *m* *(da rua, de vozes)* hum; *(do trânsito)* rumble; *(boato)* rumour

ru|ral /xu'raw/ *(pl* **~rais**) *a* rural

rusga /'xuzga/ *f* quarrel, disagreement

rush /xaʃ/ *m* rush hour

Rússia /'xusia/ *f* Russia

russo /'xusu/ *a & m* Russian

rústico /'xustʃiku/ *a* rustic

S

Saará /saa'ra/ *m* Sahara

sábado /'sabadu/ *m* Saturday

sabão /sa'bãw/ *m* soap; **~ em pó** soap powder

sabatina /saba't∫ina/ *f* test

sabedoria /sabedo'ria/ *f* wisdom

saber /sa'ber/ *vt/i* know (**de** about); *(descobrir)* find out (**de** about) □ *m* knowledge; **eu sei cantar** I know how to sing, I can sing; **sei lá** I've no idea; **que eu saiba** as far as I know

sabiá /sabi'a/ *m* thrush

sabi|chão /sabi'ʃãw/ *a & m* (*f* **~chona**) know-it-all

sábio /'sabiu/ *a* wise □ *m* wise man

sabone|te /sabo'net∫i/ *m* bar of soap; **~teira** *f* soapdish

sabor /sa'bor/ *m* flavour; **ao ~ de** at the mercy of

sabo|rear /sabori'ar/ *vt* savour; **~roso** *a* tasty

sabo|tador /sabota'dor/ *m* saboteur; **~tagem** *f* sabotage; **~tar** *vt* sabotage

saca /'saka/ *f* sack

sacada /sa'kada/ *f* balcony

sa|cal /sa'kaw/ *(pl* **~cais**) *a* *(fam)* boring

saca|na /sa'kana/ *(fam)* *a* *(desonesto)* devious; *(lascivo)* dirty-minded, naughty □ *m/f* rogue; **~nagem** *(fam)* *f* *(esperteza)* trickery; *(sexo)* sex; *(uma)* dirty trick; **~near** *(fam)* *vt* *(enganar)* do the dirty on; *(amolar)* take the mickey out of

sacar /sa'kar/ *vt/i* withdraw *<dinheiro>*; draw *<arma>*; *(em tênis, vôlei etc)* serve; *(fam)* *(entender)* understand

saçaricar /sasari'kar/ *vi* play around

sacarina /saka'rina/ *f* saccharine

saca-rolhas /saka'xoʎas/ *m invar* corkscrew

sacer|dócio /saser'dɔsiu/ *m* priesthood; **~dote** /ɔ/ *m* priest; **~dotisa** *f* priestess

sachê /sa'ʃe/ *m* sachet

saciar /sasi'ar/ *vt* satisfy

saco /'saku/ *m* bag; **que ~!** *(fam)* what a pain!; **estar de ~ cheio (de)** *(fam)* be fed up (with), be sick (of); **encher o ~ de alg** *(fam)* get on s.o.'s nerves; **puxar o ~ de alg** *(fam)* suck up to s.o.; **~ de dormir** sleeping bag; **~la** /ɔ/ *f* bag; **~lão** *m* wholesale fruit and vegetable market; **~lejar** *vt* shake

sacramento /sakra'mẽtu/ *m* sacrament

sacri|ficar /sakrifi'kar/ *vt* sacrifice; have put down *<cachorro etc>*; **~fício** *m* sacrifice; **~légio** *m* sacrilege

sacrílego /sa'krilegu/ *a* sacrilegious

sacro /'sakru/ *a* *<música>* religious

sacrossanto /sakro'sãtu/ *a* sacrosanct

sacu|dida /saku'dʒida/ *f* shake; **~dir** *vt* shake

sádico /'sadʒiku/ *a* sadistic □ *m* sadist
sadio /sa'dʒiu/ *a* healthy
sadismo /sa'dʒizmu/ *m* sadism
safa|deza /safa'deza/ *f* (*desonestidade*) deviousness; (*libertinagem*) indecency; (*uma*) dirty trick; **~do** *a* (*desonesto*) devious; (*lascivo*) dirty-minded; (*esperto*) quick; <*criança*> naughty
safena /sa'fɛna/ *f* **ponte de ~** heart bypass; **~do** *m* bypass patient
safira /sa'fira/ *f* sapphire
safra /'safra/ *f* crop
sagitariano /saʒitari'anu/ *a* & *m* Sagittarian
Sagitário /saʒi'tariu/ *m* Sagittarius
sagrado /sa'gradu/ *a* sacred
saguão /sa'gwãw/ *m* (*de teatro, hotel*) foyer, (*Amer*) lobby; (*de estação, aeroporto*) concourse
saia /'saja/ *f* skirt; **~-calça** (*pl* **~s-calças**) *f* culottes
saída /sa'ida/ *f* (*partida*) departure; (*porta, fig*) way out; **de ~** at the outset; **estar de ~** be on one's way out
sair /sa'ir/ *vi* (*de dentro*) go/come out; (*partir*) leave; (*desprender-se*) come off; <*mancha*> come out; (*resultar*) turn out; **~-se** *vpr* fare; **~-se com** (*dizer*) come out with; **~ mais barato** to work out cheaper
sal /saw/ (*pl* **sais**) *m* salt; **~ de frutas** Epsom salts
sala /'sala/ *f* (*numa casa*) lounge; (*num lugar público*) hall; (*classe*) class; **fazer ~ a** entertain; **~ (de aula)** classroom; **~ de embarque** departure lounge; **~ de espera** waiting room; **~ de jantar** dining room; **~ de operação** operating theatre
sala|da /sa'lada/ *f* salad; (*fig*) jumble, mishmash; **~da de frutas** fruit salad; **~deira** *f* salad bowl
sala-e-quarto /sali'kwartu/ *m* two-room flat
sala|me /sa'lami/ *m* salami; **~minho** *m* pepperoni
salão /sa'lãw/ *m* hall; (*de cabeleireiro*) salon; (*de carros*) show; **~ de beleza** beauty salon
salari|al /salari'aw/ (*pl* **~ais**) *a* wage
salário /sa'lariu/ *m* salary
sal|dar /saw'dar/ *vt* settle; **~do** *m* balance
saleiro /sa'leru/ *m* salt cellar
sal|gadinhos /sawga'dʒiɲus/ *m pl* snacks; **~gado** *a* salty; <*preço*> exorbitant; **~gar** *vt* salt
salgueiro /saw'geru/ *m* willow; **~ chorão** weeping willow
saliência /sali'ẽsia/ *f* projection
salien|tar /saliẽ'tar/ *vt* (*deixar claro*) point out; (*acentuar*) highlight; **~tar-**

se *vpr* distinguish o.s.; **~te** *a* prominent
saliva /sa'liva/ *f* saliva
salmão /saw'mãw/ *m* salmon
salmo /'sawmu/ *m* psalm
salmonela /sawmo'nɛla/ *f* salmonella
salmoura /saw'mora/ *f* brine
salpicar /sawpi'kar/ *vt* sprinkle; (*sem querer*) spatter
salsa /'sawsa/ *f* parsley
salsicha /saw'siʃa/ *f* sausage
saltar /saw'tar/ *vt* (*pular*) jump; (*omitir*) skip □ *vi* jump; **~ à vista** be obvious; **~ do ônibus** get off the bus
saltear /sawtʃi'ar/ *vt* sauté <*batatas etc*>
saltitar /sawtʃi'tar/ *vi* hop
salto /'sawtu/ *m* (*pulo*) jump; (*de sapato*) heel; **~ com vara** pole vault; **~ em altura** high jump; **~ em distância** long jump; **~-mortal** (*pl* **~s-mortais**) *m* somersault
salu|bre /sa'lubri/ *a* healthy; **~tar** *a* salutary
salva[1] /'sawva/ *f* (*de canhões*) salvo; (*bandeja*) salver; **~ de palmas** round of applause
salva[2] /'sawva/ *f* (*erva*) sage
salva|ção /sawva'sãw/ *f* salvation; **~dor** *m* saviour
salvaguar|da /sawva'gwarda/ *f* safeguard; **~dar** *vt* safeguard
sal|vamento /sawva'mẽtu/ *m* rescue; (*de navio*) salvage; **~var** *vt* save; **~var-se** *vpr* escape; **~va-vidas** *m invar* (*bóia*) lifebelt □ *m/f* (*pessoa*) lifeguard □ *a* **barco ~va-vidas** lifeboat; **~vo** *a* safe □ *prep* save; **a ~vo** safe
samambaia /samã'baja/ *f* fern
sam|ba /'sãba/ *m* samba; **~ba-canção** (*pl* **~bas-canção**) *m* slow samba □ *a invar* **cueca ~ba-canção** boxer shorts; **~ba-enredo** (*pl* **~bas-enredo**) *m* samba story; **~bar** *vi* samba; **~bista** *m/f* (*dançarino*) samba dancer; (*compositor*) composer of sambas; **~bódromo** *m* Carnival parade ground
samovar /samo'var/ *m* tea urn
sanar /sa'nar/ *vt* cure
san|ção /sã'sãw/ *f* sanction; **~cionar** *vt* sanction
sandália /sã'dalia/ *f* sandal
sandes /'sãdiʃ/ *f invar* (*Port*) sandwich
sanduíche /sãdu'iʃi/ *m* sandwich
sane|amento /sania'mẽtu/ *m* (*esgotos*) sanitation; (*de finanças*) rehabilitation; **~ar** *vt* set straight <*finanças*>
sanfona /sã'fona/ *f* (*instrumento*) accordion; (*tricô*) ribbing; **~do** *a* <*porta*> folding; <*pulôver*> ribbed
san|grar /sã'grar/ *vt/i* bleed; **~grento** *a* bloody; <*carne*> rare;

~**gria** *f* bloodshed; *(de dinheiro)* extortion

sangue /'sãgi/ *m* blood; ~ **pisado** bruise; ~**-frio** *m* cool, coolness

sanguessuga /sãgi'suga/ *f* leech

sanguinário /sãgi'nariu/ *a* bloodthirsty

sanguíneo /sã'giniu/ *a* blood

sanidade /sani'dadʒi/ *f* sanity

sanitário /sani'tariu/ *a* sanitary; ~**s** *mpl* toilets

san|tidade /sãtʃi'dadʒi/ *f* sanctity; ~**tificar** *vt* sanctify; ~**to** *a* holy ○ *m* saint; **todo** ~**to dia** every single day; ~**tuário** *m* sanctuary

São /sãw/ *a* Saint

são /sãw/ *(pl* ~**s)** *a (f* **sã)** healthy; *(mentalmente)* sane; <*conselho*> sound

sapata /sa'pata/ *f* shoe; ~**ria** *f* shoe shop

sapate|ado /sapatʃi'adu/ *m* tap dancing; ~**ador** *m* tap dancer; ~**ar** *vi* tap one's feet; *(dançar)* tap-dance

sapa|teiro /sapa'teru/ *m* shoemaker; ~**tilha** *f* pump; ~**tilha de balé** ballet shoe; ~**to** *m* shoe

sapeca /sa'pɛka/ *a* saucy

sa|pinho /sa'piɲu/ *m* thrush; ~**po** *m* toad

saque¹ /'saki/ *m (do banco)* withdrawal; *(em tênis, vôlei etc)* serve

saque² /'saki/ *m (de loja etc)* looting; ~**ar** *vt* loot

saraiva /sa'rajva/ *f* hail; ~**da** *f* hailstorm; **uma** ~**da de** a hail of

sarampo /sa'rãpu/ *m* measles

sarar /sa'rar/ *vt* cure ○ *vi* get better; <*ferida*> heal

sar|casmo /sar'kazmu/ *m* sarcasm; ~**cástico** *a* sarcastic

sarda /'sarda/ *f* freckle

Sardenha /sar'deɲa/ *f* Sardinia

sardento /sar'dẽtu/ *a* freckled

sardinha /sar'dʒiɲa/ *f* sardine

sardônico /sar'doniku/ *a* sardonic

sargento /sar'ʒẽtu/ *m* sergeant

sarjeta /sar'ʒeta/ *f* gutter

Satanás /sata'nas/ *m* Satan

satânico /sa'taniku/ *a* satanic

satélite /sa'tɛlitʃi/ *a & m* satellite

sátira /'satʃira/ *f* satire

satírico /sa'tʃiriku/ *a* satirical

satirizar /satʃiri'zar/ *vt* satirize

satisfa|ção /satʃisfa'sãw/ *f* satisfaction; **dar** ~**ções** a answer to; ~**tório** *a* satisfactory; ~**zer** *vt* ~**zer (a)** satisfy ○ *vi* be satisfactory; ~**zer-se** *vpr* be satisfied

satisfeito /satʃis'fejtu/ *a* satisfied; *(contente)* content; *(de comida)* full

saturar /satu'rar/ *vt* saturate

Saturno /sa'turnu/ *m* Saturn

saudação /sawda'sãw/ *f* greeting

saudade /saw'dadʒi/ *f* longing; *(lembrança)* nostalgia; **estar com** ~**s de** miss; **matar** ~**s** catch up

saudar /saw'dar/ *vt* greet

saudá|vel /saw'davew/ *(pl* ~**veis)** *a* healthy

saúde /sa'udʒi/ *f* health ○ *int (ao beber)* cheers; *(ao espirrar)* bless you

saudo|sismo /sawdo'zizmu/ *m* nostalgia; ~**so** /o/ *a* longing; **estar** ~**so de** miss; **o nosso** ~**so amigo** our much-missed friend

sauna /'sawna/ *f* sauna

saxofo|ne /sakso'foni/ *m* saxophone; ~**nista** *m/f* saxophonist

sazo|nado /sazo'nadu/ *a* seasoned; ~**nal** *(pl* ~**nais)** *a* seasonal

se¹ /si/ *conj* if; **não sei** ~ ... I don't know if/whether

se² /si/ *pron (ele mesmo)* himself; *(ela mesma)* herself; *(você mesmo)* yourself; *(eles/elas)* themselves; *(vocês)* yourselves; *(um ao outro)* each other; **dorme-**~ **tarde no Brasil** people go to bed late in Brazil; **aqui** ~ **fala inglês** English is spoken here

sebo /'sebu/ *m (sujeira)* grease; *(livraria)* secondhand bookshop; ~**so** /o/ *a* greasy; <*pessoa*> slimy

seca /'seka/ *f* drought; ~**dor** *m* ~**dor de cabelo** hairdryer; ~**dora** *f* tumble dryer

seção /se'sãw/ *f* section; *(de loja)* department

secar /se'kar/ *vt/i* dry

sec|ção /sek'sãw/ *f veja* **seção**; ~**cionar** *vt* split up

seco /'seku/ *a* dry; <*resposta, tom*> curt; <*pessoa, caráter*> cold; <*barulho, pancada*> dull; **estar** ~ **por** I'm dying for

secretaria /sekreta'ria/ *f (de empresa)* general office; *(ministério)* department

secretá|ria /sekre'taria/ *f* secretary; ~**ria eletrônica** ansaphone; ~**rio** *m* secretary

secreto /se'krɛtu/ *a* secret

secular /seku'lar/ *a (não religioso)* secular; *(antigo)* age-old

século /'sɛkulu/ *m* century; *pl (muito tempo)* ages

secundário /sekũ'dariu/ *a* secondary

secura /se'kura/ *f* dryness; **estar com uma** ~ **de** be longing for/to

seda /'seda/ *f* silk

sedativo /seda'tʃivu/ *a & m* sedative

sede¹ /'sɛdʒi/ *f* headquarters; *(local do governo)* seat

sede² /'sedʒi/ *f* thirst *(de for)*; **estar com** ~ be thirsty

sedentário /sedẽ'tariu/ *a* sedentary

sedento /se'dẽtu/ *a* thirsty *(de for)*

sediar /sedʒi'ar/ *vt* host

sedimen|tar /sedʒimẽ'tar/ *vt* consolidate; ~**to** *m* sediment
sedoso /se'dozu/ *a* silky
sedu|ção /sedu'sãw/ *f* seduction; ~**tor** *a* seductive; ~**zir** *vt* seduce
segmento /seg'mẽtu/ *m* segment
segredo /se'gredu/ *m* secret; (*de cofre etc*) combination
segregar /segre'gar/ *vt* segregate
segui|da /se'gida/ *f* em ~**da** (*imediatamente*) straight away; (*depois*) next; ~**do** *a* followed (**de** by); **cinco horas ~das** five hours running; ~**dor** *m* follower; ~**mento** *m* continuation; **dar ~mento a** go on with
se|guinte /se'gĩtʃi/ *a* following; <*dia, semana etc*> next; ~**guir** *vt/i* follow; (*continuar*) continue; ~**guir-se** *vpr* follow; ~**guir em frente** (*ir embora*) go; (*indicação na rua*) go straight ahead
segun|da /se'gũda/ *f* (*dia*) Monday; (*marcha*) second; **de ~da** second-rate; ~**da-feira** (*pl* ~**das-feiras**) *f* Monday; ~**do** *a* & *m* second □ *adv* secondly □ *prep* according to □ *conj* according to what; ~**das intenções** ulterior motives; **de ~da mão** second-hand
segu|rança /segu'rãsa/ *f* security; (*estado de seguro*) safety; (*certeza*) assurance □ *m/f* security guard; ~**rar** *vt* hold; ~**rar-se** *vpr* (*controlar-se*) control o.s.; ~**rar-se em** hold on to; ~**ro** *a* secure; (*fora de perigo*) safe; (*com certeza*) sure □ *m* insurance; **estar no ~ro** <*bens*> be insured; **fazer ~ro de** insure; ~**ro-desemprego** *m* unemployment benefit
seio /'seju/ *m* breast, bosom; **no ~ de** within
seis /sejs/ *a* & *m* six; ~**centos** *a* & *m* six hundred
seita /'sejta/ *f* sect
seixo /'sejʃu/ *m* pebble
sela /'sɛla/ *f* saddle
selar¹ /se'lar/ *vt* saddle <*cavalo*>
selar² /se'lar/ *vt* seal; (*franquear*) stamp
sele|ção /sele'sãw/ *f* selection; (*time*) team; ~**cionar** *vt* select; ~**to** /ɛ/ *a* select
selim /se'lĩ/ *m* saddle
selo /'selu/ *m* seal; (*postal*) stamp; (*de discos*) label
selva /'sɛwva/ *f* jungle; ~**gem** *a* wild; ~**geria** *f* savagery
sem /sẽj/ *prep* without; ~ **eu saber** without me knowing; **ficar ~ dinheiro** run out of money
semáforo /se'maforu/ *m* (*na rua*) traffic lights; (*de ferrovia*) signal
sema|na /se'mana/ *f* week; ~**nal** (*pl*

~**nais**) *a* weekly; ~**nalmente** *adv* weekly; ~**nário** *m* weekly
semear /semi'ar/ *vt* sow
semelhan|ça /seme'ʎãsa/ *f* similarity; ~**te** *a* similar; (*tal*) such
sêmen /'semẽ/ *m* semen
semente /se'mẽtʃi/ *f* seed; (*em fruta*) pip
semestre /se'mɛstri/ *m* six months; (*da faculdade etc*) term, (*Amer*) semester
semi|círculo /semi'sirkulu/ *m* semicircle; ~**final** (*pl* ~**finais**) *f* semifinal
seminário /semi'nariu/ *m* (*aula*) seminar; (*colégio religioso*) seminary
sem-número /sẽ'numeru/ *m* **um ~ de** innumerable
sempre /'sẽpri/ *adv* always; **como ~** as usual; **para ~** for ever; ~ **que** whenever
sem|-terra /sẽ'tɛxa/ *m/f invar* landless labourer; ~**-teto** *a* homeless □ *m/f* homeless person; ~**-vergonha** *a invar* brazen □ *m/f invar* scoundrel
sena|do /se'nadu/ *m* senate; ~**dor** *m* senator
senão /si'nãw/ *conj* otherwise; (*mas antes*) but rather □ *m* snag
senda /'sẽda/ *f* path
senha /'seɲa/ *f* (*palavra*) password; (*número*) code; (*sinal*) signal
senhor /se'ɲor/ *m* gentleman; (*homem idoso*) older man; (*tratamento*) sir □ *a* (*f* ~**a**) mighty; **Senhor** (*com nome*) Mr; (*Deus*) Lord; **o ~** (*você*) you
senho|ra /se'ɲora/ *f* lady; (*mulher idosa*) older woman; (*tratamento*) madam; **Senhora** (*com nome*) Mrs; **a ~ra** (*você*) you; **nossa ~ra!** (*fam*) gosh; ~**ria** *f* **Vossa Senhoria** you; ~**rita** *f* young lady; (*tratamento*) miss; **Senhorita** (*com nome*) Miss
se|nil (*pl* ~**nis**) *a* senile; ~**nilidade** *f* senility
sensação /sẽsa'sãw/ *f* sensation
sensacio|nal /sẽsasio'naw/ (*pl* ~**nais**) *a* sensational; ~**nalismo** *m* sensationalism; ~**nalista** *a* sensationalist
sen|sato /sẽ'satu/ *a* sensible; ~**sibilidade** *f* sensitivity; ~**sível** (*pl* ~**síveis**) *a* sensitive; (*que se pode sentir*) noticeable; ~**so** *m* sense; ~**sual** (*pl* ~**suais**) *a* sensual
sen|tado /sẽ'tadu/ *a* sitting; ~**tar** *vt/i* sit; ~**tar-se** *vpr* sit down
sentença /sẽ'tẽsa/ *f* sentence
sentido /sẽ'tʃidu/ *m* sense; (*direção*) direction □ *a* hurt; **fazer** *ou* **ter ~** make sense
sentimen|tal /sẽtʃimẽ'taw/ (*pl* ~**tais**) *a* sentimental; **vida ~tal** love life; ~**to** *m* feeling

sentinela /sẽtʃi'nɛla/ f sentry

sentir /sẽ'tʃir/ vt feel; (notar) sense; smell <cheiro>; taste <gosto>; tell <diferença>; (ficar magoado por) be hurt by □ vi feel; ~-se vpr feel; **sinto muito** I'm very sorry

sepa|ração /separa'sãw/ f separation; ~**rado** a separate; <casal> separated; ~**rar** vt separate; ~**rar-se** vpr separate

séptico /'sɛptʃiku/ a septic

sepul|tar /sepuw'tar/ vt bury; ~**tura** f grave

seqüência /se'kwẽsia/ f sequence

sequer /se'kɛr/ adv nem ~ not even

seqües|trador /sekwestra'dor/ m kidnapper; (de avião) hijacker; ~**trar** vt kidnap <pessoa>; hijack <avião>; sequestrate <bens>; ~**tro** /ɛ/ m (de pessoa) kidnapping; (de avião) hijack; (de bens) sequestration

ser /ser/ vi be □ m being; é (como resposta) yes; **você gosta, não é?** you like it, don't you?; **ele foi morto** he was killed; **será que ele volta?** I wonder if he's coming back; **ou seja** in other words; **a não ~** except; **a não ~ que** unless; **não sou de fofocar** I'm not one to gossip

sereia /se'reja/ f mermaid

serenata /sere'nata/ f serenade

sereno /se'renu/ a serene; <tempo> fine

série /'sɛri/ f series; (na escola) grade; **fora de ~** (fam) incredible

seriedade /serie'dadʒi/ f seriousness

serin|ga /se'rĩga/ f syringe; ~**gueiro** m rubber tapper

sério /'sɛriu/ a serious; (responsável) responsible; ~? really?; **falar ~** be serious; **levar a ~** take seriously

sermão /ser'mãw/ m sermon

serpen|te /ser'pẽtʃi/ f serpent; ~**tear** vi wind; ~**tina** f streamer

serra¹ /'sɛxa/ f (montanhas) mountain range

serra² /'sɛxa/ f (de serrar) saw; ~**gem** f sawdust; ~**lheiro** m locksmith

serrano /se'xanu/ a mountain

serrar /se'xar/ vt saw

ser|tanejo /serta'neʒu/ a from the backwoods □ m backwoodsman; ~**tão** m backwoods

servente /ser'vẽtʃi/ m/f labourer

Sérvia /'sɛrvia/ f Serbia

servi|çal /servi'saw/ (pl ~**çais**) a helpful □ m/f servant; ~**ço** m service; (trabalho) work; (tarefa) job; **estar de ~ço** be on duty; ~**dor** m servant

ser|vil /ser'viw/ (pl ~**vis**) a servile

sérvio /'sɛrviu/ a & m Serbian

servir /ser'vir/ vt serve □ vi serve; (ser adequado) do; (ser útil) be of use; <roupa, sapato etc> fit; ~-**se**

vpr (ao comer etc) help o.s. (**de** to); ~-**se de** make use of; ~ **como** ou **de** serve as; **para que serve isso?** what is this (used) for?

sessão /se'sãw/ f session; (no cinema) showing, performance

sessenta /se'sẽta/ a & m sixty

seta /'sɛta/ f arrow; (de carro) indicator

sete /'sɛtʃi/ a & m seven; ~**centos** a & m seven hundred

setembro /se'tẽbru/ m September

setenta /se'tẽta/ a & m seventy

sétimo /'sɛtʃimu/ a seventh

setuagésimo /setua'ʒɛzimu/ a seventieth

setor /se'tor/ m sector

seu /sew/ a (f **sua**) (dele) his; (dela) her; (de coisa) its; (deles) their; (de você, de vocês) your □ pron (dele) his; (dela) hers; (deles) theirs; (de você, de vocês) yours; ~ **idiota!** you idiot!; **seu João** Mr John

seve|ridade /severi'dadʒi/ f severity; ~**ro** /ɛ/ a severe

sexagésimo /seksa'ʒɛzimu/ a sixtieth

sexo /'sɛksu/ m sex; **fazer ~** have sex

sex|ta /'sɛsta/ f Friday; ~**ta-feira** (pl ~**tas-feiras**) f Friday; **Sexta-feira Santa** Good Friday; ~**to** /e/ a & m sixth

sexu|al /seksu'aw/ (pl ~**ais**) a sexual; **vida** ~**al** sex life

sexy /'sɛksi/ a invar sexy

shopping /'ʃɔpĩ/ (pl ~**s**) m shopping centre, (Amer) mall

short /'ʃɔrtʃi/ m (pl ~**s**) shorts; **um ~** a pair of shorts

show /'ʃou/ (pl ~**s**) m show; (de música) concert

si /si/ pron (ele) himself; (ela) herself; (coisa) itself; (você) yourself; (eles) themselves; (vocês) yourselves; (qualquer pessoa) oneself; **em ~** in itself; **fora de ~** beside o.s.; **cheio de ~** full of o.s.; **voltar a ~** come round

sibilar /sibi'lar/ vi hiss

SIDA /'sida/ f (Port) AIDS

side|ral /side'raw/ (pl ~**rais**) a espaço ~**ral** outer space.

siderurgia /siderur'ʒia/ f iron and steel industry

siderúrgi|ca /side'rurʒika/ f steelworks; ~**co** a iron and steel □ m steelworker

sifão /si'fãw/ m syphon

sífilis /'sifilis/ f syphilis

sigilo /si'ʒilu/ m secrecy; ~**so** /o/ a secret

sigla /'sigla/ f acronym

signatário /signa'tariu/ m signatory

signifi|cação /signifika'sãw/ f significance; ~**cado** m meaning; ~**car** vt mean; ~**cativo** a significant

signo /'signu/ *m* sign
sílaba /'silaba/ *f* syllable
silenciar /silẽsi'ar/ *vt* silence
silêncio /si'lẽsiu/ *m* silence
silencioso /silẽsi'ozu/ *a* silent □ *m* silencer, (*Amer*) muffler
silhueta /siʎu'eta/ *f* silhouette
silício /si'lisiu/ *m* silicon
silicone /sili'koni/ *m* silicone
silo /'silu/ *m* silo
silvar /siw'var/ *vi* hiss
sil|vestre /siw'vɛstri/ *a* wild; **~vicultura** *f* forestry
sim /sĩ/ *adv* yes; **acho que ~** I think so
simbólico /sĩ'bɔliku/ *a* symbolic
simbo|lismo /sĩbo'lizmu/ *m* symbolism; **~lizar** *vt* symbolize
símbolo /'sĩbolu/ *m* symbol
si|metria /sime'tria/ *f* symmetry; **~métrico** *a* symmetrical
similar /simi'lar/ *a* similar
sim|patia /sĩpa'tʃia/ *f* (*qualidade*) pleasantness; (*afeto*) fondness (**por** for); (*compreensão, apoio*) sympathy; *pl* sympathies; **ter ~patia por** be fond of; **~pático** *a* nice
simpati|zante /sĩpatʃi'zãtʃi/ *a* sympathetic □ *m/f* sympathizer; **~zar** *vi* **~zar com** take a liking to <*pessoa*>; sympathize with <*idéias, partido etc*>
simples /'sĩplis/ *a invar* simple; (*único*) single □ *f* (*no tênis etc*) singles; **~mente** *adv* simply
simpli|cidade /sĩplisi'dadʒi/ *f* simplicity; **~ficar** *vt* simplify
simplório /sĩ'plɔriu/ *a* simple
simpósio /sĩ'pɔziu/ *m* symposium
simu|lação /simula'sãw/ *f* simulation; **~lar** *vt* simulate
simultâneo /simuw'taniu/ *a* simultaneous
sina /'sina/ *f* fate
sinagoga /sina'gɔga/ *f* synagogue
si|nal /si'naw/ (*pl* **~nais**) *m* sign; (*aviso, de rádio etc*) signal; (*de trânsito*) traffic light; (*no telefone*) tone; (*dinheiro*) deposit; (*na pele*) mole; **por ~nal** as a matter of fact; **~nal de pontuação** punctuation mark; **~naleira** *f* traffic lights; **~nalização** *f* (*na rua*) road signs; **~nalizar** *vt* signal; signpost <*rua, cidade*>
since|ridade /sĩseri'dadʒi/ *f* sincerity; **~ro** /ɛ/ *a* sincere
sincro|nia /sĩkro'nia/ *f* synchronization; **~nizar** *vt* synchronize
sindi|cal /sĩdʒi'kaw/ (*pl* **~cais**) *a* trade union; **~calismo** *m* trade unionism; **~calista** *m/f* trade unionist; **~calizar** *vt* unionize; **~cato** *m* trade union
síndico /'sĩdʒiku/ *m* house manager

síndrome /'sĩdromi/ *f* syndrome
sineta /si'neta/ *f* bell
sin|fonia /sĩfo'nia/ *f* symphony; **~fônica** *f* symphony orchestra
singe|leza /sĩʒe'leza/ *f* simplicity; **~lo** /ɛ/ *a* simple
singu|lar /sĩgu'lar/ *a* singular; (*estranho*) peculiar; **~larizar** *vt* single out
sinis|trado /sinis'tradu/ *a* damaged; **~tro** *a* sinister □ *m* accident
sino /'sinu/ *m* bell
sinônimo /si'nonimu/ *a* synonymous □ *m* synonym
sintaxe /sĩ'taksi/ *f* syntax
síntese /'sĩtezi/ *f* synthesis
sin|tético /sĩ'tɛtʃiku/ *a* (*artificial*) synthetic; (*resumido*) concise; **~tetizar** *vt* summarize
sinto|ma /sĩ'toma/ *m* symptom; **~mático** *a* symptomatic
sintoni|zador /sĩtoniza'dor/ *m* tuner; **~zar** *vt* tune <*rádio, TV*>; tune in to <*emissora*> □ *vi* be in tune (**com** with)
sinuca /si'nuka/ *f* snooker
sinuoso /sinu'ozu/ *a* winding
sinusite /sinu'zitʃi/ *f* sinusitis
sirene /si'rɛni/ *f* siren
siri /si'ri/ *m* crab
Síria /'siria/ *f* Syria
sírio /'siriu/ *a* & *m* Syrian
siso /'sizu/ *m* good sense
siste|ma /sis'tema/ *m* system; **~mático** *a* systematic
sisudo /si'zudu/ *a* serious
sítio /'sitʃiu/ *m* (*chácara*) farm; (*Port: local*) place; **estado de ~** state of siege
situ|ação /situa'sãw/ *f* situation; (*no governo*) party in power; **~ar** *vt* situate; **~ar-se** *vpr* be situated; <*pessoa*> position o.s.
smoking /iz'mokĩ/ (*pl* **~s**) *m* dinner jacket, (*Amer*) tuxedo
só /sɔ/ *a* alone; (*sentindo solidão*) lonely □ *adv* only; **um ~ voto** one single vote; **~ um carro** only one car; **a ~s** alone; **imagina ~** just imagine; **~ que** except (that)
soalho /so'aʎu/ *m* floor
soar /so'ar/ *vt/i* sound
sob /'sobi/ *prep* under
sobera|nia /sobera'nia/ *f* sovereignty; **~no** *a* & *m* sovereign
soberbo /so'berbu/ *a* <*pessoa*> haughty; (*magnífico*) splendid
sobra /'sobra/ *f* surplus; *pl* leftovers; **tempo de ~** (*muito*) plenty of time; **ficar de ~** be left over; **ter aco de ~** (*sobrando*) have sth left over
sobraçar /sobra'sar/ *vt* carry under one's arm
sobrado /so'bradu/ *m* (*casa*) house; (*andar*) upper floor

sobrancelha /sobrã'seʎa/ f eyebrow

so|brar /so'brar/ vi be left; **~bram-
me dois** I have two left

sobre /'sobri/ prep (em cima de) on;
(por cima de, acima de) over; (acerca
de) about

sobreaviso /sobria'vizu/ m **estar de
~** be on one's guard

sobrecapa /sobri'kapa/ f dust jacket

sobrecarregar /sobrikaxe'gar/ vt
overload

sobreloja /sobri'lɔʒa/ f mezzanine

sobremesa /sobri'meza/ f dessert

sobrenatu|ral /sobrinatu'raw/ (pl
~rais) a supernatural

sobrenome /sobri'nomi/ m surname

sobrepor /sobri'por/ vt superimpose

sobrepujar /sobripu'ʒar/ vt (em altura) tower over; (em valor, número
etc) surpass; overwhelm <adversá-
rio>; overcome <problemas>

sobrescritar /sobriskri'tar/ vt address

sobressair /sobrisa'ir/ vi stand out;
~-se vpr stand out

sobressalente /sobrisa'lẽtʃi/ a spare

sobressal|tar /sobrisaw'tar/ vt
startle; **~tar-se** vpr be startled;
~to m (movimento) start; (susto)
fright

sobretaxa /sobri'taʃa/ f surcharge

sobretudo /sobri'tudu/ adv above all
□ m overcoat

sobrevir /sobri'vir/ vi happen suddenly; (seguir) ensue; **~ a** follow

sobrevi|vência /sobrivi'vẽsia/ f sur-
vival; **~vente** a surviving □ m/f
survivor; **~ver** vt/i **~ver (a)** survive

sobrevoar /sobrivo'ar/ vt fly over

sobri|nha /so'briɲa/ f niece; **~nho** m
nephew

sóbrio /'sɔbriu/ a sober

socar /so'kar/ vt (esmurrar) punch;
(amassar) crush

soci|al /sosi'aw/ (pl **~ais**) a social;
camisa ~al dress shirt; **~alismo** m
socialism; **~alista** a & m/f socialist;
~alite /-a'lajtʃi/ m/f socialite; **~ável**
(pl **~áveis**) a sociable

sociedade /sosie'dadʒi/ f society;
(parceria) partnership; **~ anônima**
limited company

sócio /'sɔsiu/ m (de empresa) partner;
(de clube) member

socio-econômico /sosioeko'nomiku/
a socio-economic

soci|ologia /sosiolo'ʒia/ f sociology;
~ológico a sociological; **~ólogo** m
sociologist

soco /'soku/ m punch; **dar um ~ em**
punch

socor|rer /soko'xer/ vt help; **~ro** m
aid □ int help; **primeiros ~ros** first
aid

soda /'sɔda/ f (água) soda water; **~
cáustica** caustic soda

sódio /'sɔdʒiu/ m sodium

sofá /so'fa/ m sofa; **~-cama** (pl **~s-
camas**) m sofa-bed

sofisticado /sofistʃi'kadu/ a sophisticated

so|fredor /sofre'dor/ a martyred;
~frer vt suffer <dor, derrota, danos
etc>; have <acidente>; undergo
<operação, mudança etc> □ vi suffer;
~frer de suffer from <doença>; have
trouble with <coração etc>; **~frido** a
long-suffering; **~frimento** m
suffering; **~frível** (pl **~fríveis**) a
passable

soft /'sɔftʃi/ (pl **~s**) m software package; **~ware** m software; (um) software package

so|gra /'sɔgra/ f mother-in-law; **~gro**
/o/ m father-in-law; **~gros** /ɔ/ m pl in-
laws

soja /'sɔʒa/ f soya, (Amer) soy

sol /sɔw/ (pl **sóis**) m sun; **faz ~** it's
sunny

sola /'sɔla/ f sole; **~do** a <bolo> flat

solapar /sola'par/ vt undermine

solar[1] /so'lar/ a solar

solar[2] /so'lar/ vt sole <sapato> □ vi
<bolo> go flat

solavanco /sola'vãku/ m jolt; **dar ~s**
jolt

soldado /sow'dadu/ m soldier

sol|dadura /sowda'dura/ f weld;
~dar vt weld

soldo /'sowdu/ m pay

soleira /so'lera/ f doorstep

sole|ne /so'leni/ a solemn; **~nidade** f
(cerimônia) ceremony; (qualidade) so-
lemnity

soletrar /sole'trar/ vt spell

solici|tação /solisita'sãw/ f request
(de for); (por escrito) application (de
for); **~tante** m/f applicant; **~tar** vt
request; (por escrito) apply for

solícito /so'lisitu/ a helpful

solidão /soli'dãw/ f loneliness

soli|dariedade /solidarie'dadʒi/ f
solidarity; **~dário** a supportive
(com of)

soli|dez /soli'des/ f solidity; **~dificar**
vt solidify; **~dificar-se** vpr solidify

sólido /'sɔlidu/ a & m solid

solista /so'lista/ m/f soloist

solitá|ria /soli'taria/ f (verme) tape-
worm; (cela) solitary confinement;
~rio a solitary

solo[1] /'sɔlu/ m (terra) soil; (chão)
ground

solo[2] /'sɔlu/ m solo

soltar /sow'tar/ vt let go <prisio-
neiros, animal etc>; let loose <cães>;
(deixar de segurar) let go of; loosen
<gravata, corda etc>; let down

<cabelo>; let out <grito, suspiro etc>;
let off <foguetes>; tell <piada>; take
off <freio>; ~-se vpr <peça, parafu-
so> come loose; <pessoa> let o.s. go

soltei|ra /sow'tera/ f single woman;
~**rão** m bachelor; ~**ro** a single □ m
single man; ~**rona** f spinster

solto /'sowtu/ a (livre) free; <cães>
loose; <cabelo> down; <arroz> fluffy;
(frouxo) loose; (à vontade) relaxed;
(abandonado) abandoned; **correr** ~
run wild

solução /solu'sãw/ f solution

soluçar /solu'sar/ vi (ao chorar) sob;
(engasgar) hiccup

solucionar /solusio'nar/ vt solve

soluço /so'lusu/ m (ao chorar) sob;
(engasgo) hiccup; **estar com** ~**s** have
the hiccups

solú|vel /so'luvew/ (pl ~**veis**) a sol-
uble

solvente /sow'vẽtʃi/ a & m solvent

som /sõ/ m sound; (aparelho) stereo;
um ~ (fam) (música) a bit of music

so|ma /'soma/ f sum; ~**mar** vt add up
<números etc>; (ter como soma) add
up to

sombra /'sõbra/ f shadow; (área abri-
gada do sol) shade; **à** ~ **de** in the
shade of; **sem** ~ **de dúvida** without
a shadow of a doubt

sombre|ado /sõbri'adu/ a shady □ m
shading; ~**ar** vt shade

sombrinha /sõ'briɲa/ f parasol

sombrio /sõ'briu/ a gloomy

somente /so'mẽtʃi/ adv only

sonâmbulo /so'nãbulu/ m sleep-
walker

sonante /so'nãtʃi/ a **moeda** ~ hard
cash

sonata /so'nata/ f sonata

son|da /'sõda/ f probe; ~**dagem** f (no
mar) sounding; (de terreno) survey;
~**dagem de opinião** opinion poll;
~**dar** vt probe; sound <profundeza>;
(fig) sound out <pessoas, opiniões
etc>

soneca /so'nɛka/ f nap; **tirar uma** ~
have a nap

sone|gação /sonega'sãw/ f (de impos-
tos) tax evasion; ~**gador** m tax
dodger; ~**gar** vt withhold

soneto /so'netu/ m sonnet

so|nhador /soɲa'dor/ a dreamy □ m
dreamer; ~**nhar** vt/i dream (com
about); ~**nho** /'soɲu/ m dream; (doce)
doughnut

sono /'sonu/ m sleep; **estar com** ~ be
sleepy; **pegar no** ~ get to sleep;
~**lento** a sleepy

sono|plastia /sonoplas'tʃia/ f sound
effects; ~**ridade** f sound quality;
~**ro** /ɔ/ a sound; <voz> sonorous;
<consoante> voiced

sonso /'sõsu/ a devious

sopa /'sopa/ f soup

sopapo /so'papu/ m slap; **dar um** ~
em slap

sopé /so'pɛ/ m foot

sopeira /so'pera/ f soup tureen

soprano /so'pranu/ m/f soprano

so|prar /so'prar/ vt blow <folhas etc>;
blow up <balão>; blow out <vela> □
vi blow; ~**pro** m blow; (de vento) puff;
instrumento de ~**pro** wind instrument

soquete[1] /so'kɛtʃi/ f ankle sock

soquete[2] /so'ketʃi/ m socket

sordidez /sordʒi'des/ f sordidness;
(imundície) squalor

sórdido /'sɔrdʒidu/ a (reles) sordid;
(imundo) squalid

soro /'soru/ m (remédio) serum; (de
leite) whey

sorrateiro /soxa'teru/ a crafty

sor|ridente /soxi'dẽtʃi/ a smiling;
~**rir** vi smile; ~**riso** m smile

sorte /'sɔrtʃi/ f luck; (destino) fate;
pessoa de ~ lucky person; **por** ~
luckily; **ter ou dar** ~ be lucky; **tive a**
~ **de conhecê-lo** I was lucky enough
to meet him; **tirar a** ~ draw lots;
trazer ou dar ~ bring good luck

sor|tear /sortʃi'ar/ vt draw for
<prêmio>; select in a draw
<pessoa>; ~**teio** m draw

sorti|do /sor'tʃidu/ a assorted;
~**mento** m assortment

sorumbático /sorũ'batʃiku/ a
sombre, gloomy

sorver /sor'ver/ vt sip <bebida>

sósia /'sɔzia/ m/f double

soslaio /soz'laju/ m **de** ~ sideways;
<olhar> askance

sosse|gado /sose'gadu/ a <vida>
quiet; **ficar** ~**gado** <pessoa> rest
assured; ~**gar** vt reassure □ vi rest;
~**go** /e/ m peace

sótão /'sotãw/ (pl ~**s**) m attic, loft

sotaque /so'taki/ m accent

soterrar /sote'xar/ vt bury

soutien /suti'ã/ (pl ~**s**) m (Port) bra

sova|co /so'vaku/ m armpit; ~**queira**
f BO, body odour

soviético /sovi'ɛtʃiku/ a & m Soviet

sovi|na /so'vina/ a stingy, mean,
(Amer) cheap □ m/f cheapskate;
~**nice** f stinginess, meanness,
(Amer) cheapness

sozinho /so'ziɲu/ a (sem ninguém)
alone, on one's own; (por si próprio)
by o.s.; **falar** ~ talk to o.s.

spray /is'prej/ (pl ~**s**) m spray

squash /is'kwɛʃ/ m squash

stand /is'tãdʒi/ (pl ~**s**) m stand

status /is'tatus/ m status

stripper /is'triper/ (pl ~**s**) m/f stripper

strip-tease /istripi'tʃizi/ *m* striptease

sua /'sua/ *a & pron veja* **seu**

su|ado /su'adu/ *a <pessoa, roupa>* sweaty; (*fig*) hard-earned; ~**ar** *vt/i* sweat; ~**ar por/para** (*fig*) work hard for/to; ~**ar frio** come out in a cold sweat

sua|ve /su'avi/ *a <toque, subida>* gentle; *<gosto, cheiro, dor, inverno>* mild; *<música, voz>* soft; *<vinho>* smooth; *<trabalho>* light; *<presta-ções>* easy; ~**vidade** *f* gentleness; mildness; softness; smoothness; *veja* **suave**; ~**vizar** *vt* soften; soothe *<dor, pessoa>*

subalterno /subaw'tɛrnu/ *a & m* subordinate

subconsciente /subikõsi'ẽtʃi/ *a & m* subconscious

subdesenvolvido /subidʒizĩvow-'vidu/ *a* underdeveloped

súbdito /'subditu/ *m* (*Port*) *veja* **súdito**

subdividir /subidʒivi'dʒir/ *vt* sub-divide

subemprego /subĩ'pregu/ *m* menial job

subemprei|tar /subĩprej'tar/ *vt* sub-contract; ~**teiro** *m* subcontractor

subenten|der /subĩtẽ'der/ *vt* infer; ~**dido** *a* implied □ *m* insinuation

subestimar /subestʃi'mar/ *vt* under-estimate

su|bida /su'bida/ *f* (*ação*) ascent; (*ladeira*) incline; (*de preços etc, fig*) rise; ~**bir** *vi* go up; *<rio, águas>* rise □ *vt* go up, climb; ~**bir em** climb *<árvore>*; get up onto *<mesa>*; get on *<ônibus>*

súbito /'subitu/ *a* sudden; (**de**) ~ suddenly

subjacente /subiʒa'sẽtʃi/ *a* underly-ing

subjeti|vidade /subiʒetʃivi'dadʒi/ *f* subjectivity; ~**vo** *a* subjective

subjugar /subiʒu'gar/ *vt* subjugate

subjuntivo /subiʒũ'tʃivu/ *a & m* sub-junctive

sublevar-se /suble'varsi/ *vpr* rise up

sublime /su'blimi/ *a* sublime

subli|nhado /subli'ɲadu/ *m* under-lining; ~**nhar** *vt* underline

sublocar /sublo'kar/ *vt/i* sublet

submarino /subima'rinu/ *a* under-water □ *m* submarine

submer|gir /subimer'ʒir/ *vt* sub-merge; ~**gir-se** *vpr* submerge; ~**so** *a* submerged

submeter /subime'ter/ *vt* subject (**a** to); put down, subdue *<povo, rebeldes etc>*; submit *<projeto>*; ~**-se** *vpr* (*render-se*) submit; ~**-se a** (*sofrer*) under-go

submis|são /subimi'sãw/ *f* submis-sion; ~**so** *a* submissive

submundo /subi'mũdu/ *m* under-world

subnutrição /subinutri'sãw/ *f* mal-nutrition

subordi|nado /subordʒi'nadu/ *a & m* subordinate; ~**nar** *vt* subordinate (**a** to)

subor|nar /subor'nar/ *vt* bribe; ~**no** /o/ *m* bribe

subproduto /subipro'dutu/ *m* by-product

subs|crever /subiskre'ver/ *vt* sign *<carta etc>*; subscribe to *<opinião>*; subscribe *<dinheiro>* (**para** to); ~**crever-se** *vpr* sign one's name; ~**crição** *f* subscription; ~**crito** *pp de* ~**crever**

subseqüente /subise'kwẽtʃi/ *a* subse-quent

subserviente /subiservi'ẽtʃi/ *a* sub-servient

subsidiar /subisidʒi'ar/ *vt* subsidize

subsidiá|ria /subisidʒi'aria/ *f* sub-sidiary; ~**rio** *a* subsidiary

subsídio /subi'sidʒiu/ *m* subsidy

subsistência /subisis'tẽsia/ *f* subsis-tence

subsolo /subi'sɔlu/ *m* (*porão*) base-ment

substância /subis'tãsia/ *f* substance

substan|cial /subistãsi'aw/ (*pl* ~**ciais**) *a* substantial; ~**tivo** *m* noun

substitu|ição /subistʃitui'sãw/ *f* re-placement; substitution; ~**ir** *vt* (*pôr B no lugar de A*) replace (**A por B** A with B); (*usar B em vez de A*) substi-tute (**A por B** B for A); ~**to** *a & m* substitute

subterfúgio /subiter'fuʒiu/ *m* subter-fuge

subterrâneo /subite'xaniu/ *a* under-ground

sub|til /sub'til/ (*pl* ~**tis**) *a* (*Port*) *veja* **sutil**

subtra|ção /subitra'sãw/ *f* subtrac-tion; ~**ir** *vt* subtract *<números>*; (*roubar*) steal

suburbano /subur'banu/ *a* sub-urban

subúrbio /su'burbiu/ *m* suburbs

subven|ção /subivẽ'sãw/ *f* grant, subsidy; ~**cionar** *vt* subsidize

subver|são /subiver'sãw/ *f* subver-sion; ~**sivo** *a & m* subversive

suca|ta /su'kata/ *f* scrap metal; ~**tear** *vt* scrap

sucção /suk'sãw/ *f* suction

suce|der /suse'der/ *vi* (*acontecer*) hap-pen □ *vt* ~**der a** succeed *<rei etc>*; (*vir depois*) follow; ~**der-se** *vpr* fol-low on from one another; ~**dido** *a* **bem** ~**dido** successful

suces|são /suse'sãw/ *f* succession; **~sivo** *a* successive; **~so** /ε/ *m* success; *(música)* hit; **fazer** *ou* **ter ~so** be successful; **~sor** *m* successor

sucinto /su'sĩtu/ *a* succinct

suco /'suku/ *m* juice

suculento /suku'lẽtu/ *a* juicy

sucumbir /sukũ'bir/ *vi* succumb (a to)

sucur|sal /sukur'saw/ (*pl* **~sais**) *f* branch

Sudão /su'dãw/ *m* Sudan

sudário /su'dariu/ *m* shroud

sudeste /su'dεstʃi/ *a & m* southeast; **o Sudeste Asiático** Southeast Asia

súdito /'sudʒitu/ *m* subject

sudoeste /sudo'εstʃi/ *a & m* southwest

Suécia /su'εsia/ *f* Sweden

sueco /su'εku/ *a & m* Swedish

suéter /su'εter/ *m/f* sweater

sufici|ência /sufisi'ẽsia/ *f* sufficiency; **~ente** *a* enough, sufficient; **o ~ente** enough

sufixo /su'fiksu/ *m* suffix

suflê /su'fle/ *m* soufflé

sufo|cante /sufo'kãtʃi/ *a* stifling; **~car** *vt* (*asfixiar*) suffocate; *(fig)* stifle □ *vi* suffocate; **~co** /o/ *m* hassle; **estar num ~co** be having a tough time

sufrágio /su'fraʒiu/ *m* suffrage

sugar /su'gar/ *vt* suck

sugerir /suʒe'rir/ *vt* suggest

suges|tão /suʒes'tãw/ *f* suggestion; **dar uma ~tão** make a suggestion; **~tivo** *a* suggestive

Suíça /su'isa/ *f* Switzerland

suíças /su'isas/ *f pl* sideburns

sui|cida /sui'sida/ *a* suicidal □ *m/f* suicide (victim); **~cidar-se** *vpr* commit suicide; **~cídio** *m* suicide

suíço /su'isu/ *a & m* Swiss

suíno /su'inu/ *a & m* pig

suíte /su'itʃi/ *f* suite

su|jar /su'ʒar/ *vt* dirty; *(fig)* sully *<reputação etc>* □ *vi*, **~jar-se** *vpr* get dirty; **~jar-se com alg** queer one's pitch with s.o.; **~jeira** *f* dirt; *(uma)* dirty trick

sujei|tar /suʒej'tar/ *vt* subject (a to); **~tar-se** *vpr* subject o.s. (a to); **~to** *a* subject (a to) □ *m* *(de oração)* subject; *(pessoa)* person

su|jidade /suʒi'dadʒi/ *f* (*Port*) dirt; **~jo** *a* dirty

sul /suw/ *a invar & m* south; **~-africano** *a & m* South African; **~-americano** *a & m* South American; **~-coreano** *a & m* South Korean

sul|car /suw'kar/ *vt* furrow *<testa>*; **~co** *m* furrow

sulfúrico /suw'furiku/ *a* sulphuric

sulista /su'lista/ *a* southern □ *m/f* southerner

sultão /suw'tãw/ *m* sultan

sumário /su'mariu/ *a <justiça>* summary; *<roupa>* skimpy, brief

su|miço /su'misu/ *m* disappearance; **dar ~miço em** spirit away; **tomar chá de ~miço** disappear; **~mido** *a <cor, voz>* faint; **ele anda ~mido** he's disappeared; **~mir** *vi* disappear

sumo /'sumu/ *m* (*Port*) juice

sumptuoso /sũtu'ozu/ *a* (*Port*) *veja* **suntuoso**

sunga /'sũga/ *f* swimming trunks

suntuoso /sũtu'ozu/ *a* sumptuous

suor /su'or/ *m* sweat

superar /supe'rar/ *vt* overcome *<dificuldade etc>*; surpass *<expectativa, pessoa>*

superá|vel /supe'ravew/ (*pl* **~veis**) *a* surmountable; **~vit** (*pl* **~vits**) *m* surplus

superestimar /superestʃi'mar/ *vt* overestimate

superestrutura /superistru'tura/ *f* superstructure

superfici|al /superfisi'aw/ (*pl* **~ais**) *a* superficial

superfície /super'fisi/ *f* surface; *(medida)* area

supérfluo /su'perfluu/ *a* superfluous

superintendência /superĩtẽ'dẽsia/ *f* bureau

superi|or /superi'or/ *a* *(de cima)* upper; *<ensino>* higher; *<número, temperatura etc>* greater (a than); *(melhor)* superior (a to) □ *m* superior; **~oridade** *f* superiority

superlativo /superla'tʃivu/ *a & m* superlative

superlota|ção /superlota'sãw/ *f* overcrowding; **~do** *a* overcrowded

supermercado /supermer'kadu/ *m* supermarket

superpotência /superpo'tẽsia/ *f* superpower

superpovoado /superpovo'adu/ *a* overpopulated

supersecreto /superse'krεtu/ *a* top secret

supersensí|vel /superse'sivew/ (*pl* **~veis**) *a* oversensitive

supersônico /super'soniku/ *a* supersonic

supersti|ção /superstʃi'sãw/ *f* superstition; **~cioso** /o/ *a* superstitious

supervi|são /supervi'zãw/ *f* supervision; **~sionar** *vt* supervise; **~sor** *m* supervisor

supetão /supe'tãw/ *m* **de ~** all of a sudden

suplantar /suplã'tar/ *vt* supplant

suplemen|tar /suplemẽ'tar/ *a* supplementary □ *vt* supplement; **~to** *m* supplement

suplente /su'plẽtʃi/ *a* & *m/f* substitute

supletivo /suple'tʃivu/ *a* supplementary; **ensino ~** adult education

súplica /'suplika/ *f* plea; **tom de ~** pleading tone

suplicar /supli'kar/ *vt* plead for; (*em juízo*) petition for

suplício /su'plisiu/ *m* torture; (*fig: aflição*) torment

supor /su'por/ *vt* suppose

supor|tar /supor'tar/ *vt* (*sustentar*) support; (*tolerar*) stand, bear; **~tável** (*pl* **~táveis**) *a* bearable; **~te** /ɔ/ *m* support

suposição /supozi'sãw/ *f* supposition

supositório /supozi'tɔriu/ *m* suppository

supos|tamente /suposta'mẽtʃi/ *adv* supposedly; **~to** /o/ *a* supposed; **~to que** supposing that

supre|macia /suprema'sia/ *f* supremacy; **~mo** /e/ *a* supreme

supressão /supre'sãw/ *f* (*de lei, cargo, privilégio*) abolition; (*de jornal, informação, nomes*) suppression; (*de palavras, cláusula*) deletion

suprimento /supri'mẽtu/ *m* supply

suprimir /supri'mir/ *vt* abolish <*lei, cargo, privilégio*>; suppress <*jornal, informação, nomes*>; delete <*palavras, cláusula*>

suprir /su'prir/ *vt* provide for <*família, necessidades*>; make up for <*falta*>; make up <*quantia*>; supply <*o que falta*>; (*substituir*) take the place of; **~ alg de** provide s.o. with; **~ A por B** substitute B for A

supurar /supu'rar/ *vi* turn septic

sur|dez /sur'des/ *f* deafness; **~do** *a* deaf; <*consoante*> voiceless □ *m* deaf person; **os ~dos** the deaf; **~do-mudo** (*pl* **~dos-mudos**) *a* deaf and dumb □ *m* deaf-mute

sur|fe /'surfi/ *m* surfing; **~fista** *m/f* surfer

sur|gimento /surʒi'mẽtu/ *m* appearance; **~gir** *vi* arise; **~gir à mente** spring to mind

Suriname /suri'nami/ *m* Surinam

surpreen|dente /surpriẽ'dẽtʃi/ *a* surprising; **~der** *vt* surprise □ *vi* be surprising; **~der-se** *vpr* be surprised (**de at**)

surpre|sa /sur'preza/ *f* surprise; **de ~sa** by surprise; **~so** /e/ *a* surprised

sur|ra /'suxa/ *f* thrashing; **~rado** *a* <*roupa*> worn-out; **~rar** *vt* thrash <*pessoa*>; wear out <*roupa*>

surrealis|mo /suxea'lizmu/ *m* surrealism; **~ta** *a* & *m/f* surrealist

surtir /sur'tʃir/ *vt* produce; **~ efeito** be effective

surto /'surtu/ *m* outbreak

suscept- (*Port*) *veja* **suscet-**

susce|tibilidade /susetʃibili'dadʒi/ *f* (*de pessoa*) sensitivity; **~tível** (*pl* **~tíveis**) *a* <*pessoa*> touchy, sensitive; **~tível de** open to

suscitar /susi'tar/ *vt* cause; raise <*dúvida, suspeita*>

suspei|ta /sus'pejta/ *f* suspicion; **~tar** *vt/i* **~tar (de)** suspect; **~to** *a* suspicious; (*duvidoso*) suspect □ *m* suspect; **~toso** /o/ *a* suspicious

suspen|der /suspẽ'der/ *vt* suspend; **~são** *f* suspension; **~se** *m* suspense; **~so** *a* suspended; **~sórios** *m pl* braces, (*Amer*) suspenders

suspi|rar /suspi'rar/ *vi* sigh; **~rar por** long for; **~ro** *m* sigh; (*doce*) meringue

sussur|rar /susu'xar/ *vt/i* whisper; **~ro** *m* whisper

sustar /sus'tar/ *vt/i* stop

susten|táculo /sustẽ'takulu/ *m* mainstay; **~tar** *vt* support; (*afirmar*) maintain; **~to** *m* support; (*ganha-pão*) livelihood

susto /'sustu/ *m* fright

sutiã /sutʃi'ã/ *m* bra

su|til /su'tʃiw/ (*pl* **~tis**) *a* subtle; **~tileza** /e/ *f* subtlety

sutu|ra /su'tura/ *f* suture; **~rar** *vt* suture

T

tá /ta/ *int* (*fam*) OK; *veja* **estar**

taba|caria /tabaka'ria/ *f* tobacconist's; **~co** *m* tobacco

tabefe /ta'bɛfi/ *m* slap

tabe|la /ta'bɛla/ *f* table; **~lar** *vt* tabulate

tablado /ta'bladu/ *m* platform

tabu /ta'bu/ *a* & *m* taboo

tábua /'tabua/ *f* board; **~ de passar roupa** ironing board

tabuleiro /tabu'leru/ *m* (*de xadrez etc*) board

tabuleta /tabu'lɛta/ *f* (*letreiro*) sign

taça /'tasa/ *f* (*prêmio*) cup; (*de champanhe etc*) glass

ta|cada /ta'kada/ *f* shot; **de uma ~cada** in one go; **~car** *vt* hit <*bola*>; (*fam*) throw

tacha /'tasa/ *f* tack

tachar /ta'sar/ *vt* brand (**de as**)

tachinha /ta'siɲa/ *f* drawing pin, (*Amer*) thumbtack

tácito /'tasitu/ *a* tacit

taciturno /tasi'turnu/ *a* taciturn

taco /'taku/ *m* (*de golfe*) club; (*de bilhar*) cue; (*de hóquei*) stick

tact- (*Port*) *veja* **tat-**

tagare|la /taga'rɛla/ *a* chatty, talkative □ *m/f* chatterbox; **~lar** *vi* chatter

tailan|dês /tajlã'des/ *a & m* (*f* ~**desa**) Thai

Tailândia /taj'lãdʒia/ *f* Thailand

tailleur /ta'jɛr/ (*pl* ~ **s**) *m* suit

Taiti /taj'tʃi/ *m* Tahiti

tal /taw/ (*pl* **tais**) *a* such; **que** ~? what do you think?, (*Port*) how are you?; **que** ~ **uma cerveja?** how about a beer?; ~ **como** such as; ~ **qual** just like; **um** ~ **de João** someone called John; **e** ~ and so on

tala /'tala/ *f* splint

talão /ta'lãw/ *m* stub; ~ **de cheques** chequebook

talco /'tawku/ *m* talc

talen|to /ta'lẽtu/ *m* talent; ~**toso** /o/ *a* talented

talhar /ta'ʎar/ *vt* slice <*dedo, carne*>; carve <*pedra, imagem*>

talharim /taʎa'rĩ/ *m* tagliatelle

talher /ta'ʎɛr/ *m* set of cutlery; *pl* cutlery

talho /'taʎu/ *m* (*Port*) butcher's

talismã /taliz'mã/ *m* charm, talisman

talo /'talu/ *m* stalk

talvez /taw'ves/ *adv* perhaps; ~ **ele venha amanhã** he may come tomorrow

tamanco /ta'mãku/ *m* clog

tamanho /ta'maɲu/ *m* size □ *adj* such

tâmara /'tamara/ *f* date

tamarindo /tama'rĩdu/ *m* tamarind

também /tã'bẽj/ *adv* also; ~ **não** not ... either, neither

tam|bor /tã'bor/ *m* drum; ~**borilar** *vi* <*dedos*> drum; <*chuva*> patter; ~**borim** *m* tambourine

Tâmisa /'tamiza/ *m* Thames

tam|pa /'tãpa/ *f* lid; ~**pão** *m* (*vaginal*) tampon; ~**par** *vt* put the lid on <*recipiente*>; (*tapar*) cover; ~**pinha** *f* top□ *m/f* (*fam*) shorthouse

tampouco /tã'poku/ *adv* nor, neither

tanga /'tãga/ *f* G-string; (*avental*) loincloth

tangente /tã'ʒẽtʃi/ *f* tangent; **pela** ~ (*fig*) narrowly

tangerina /tãʒe'rina/ *f* tangerine

tango /'tãgu/ *m* tango

tanque /'tãki/ *m* tank; (*para lavar roupa*) sink

tanto /'tãtu/ *a & pron* so much; *pl* so many □ *adv* so much; ~ ... **como** ... both ... and ...; ~ **(...) quanto** as much (...) as; ~ **melhor** so much the better; ~ **tempo** so long; **vinte e** ~**s anos** twenty odd years; **nem** ~ not as much; **um** ~ **difícil** somewhat difficult; ~ **que** to the extent that

Tanzânia /tã'zania/ *f* Tanzania

tão /tãw/ *adv* so; ~ **grande quanto** as big as; ~**-somente** *adv* solely

tapa /'tapa/ *m ou f* slap; **dar um** ~ **em** slap

tapar /ta'par/ *vt* (*cobrir*) cover; block <*luz, vista*>; cork <*garrafa*>

tapeçaria /tapesa'ria/ *f* (*pano*) tapestry; (*loja*) carpet shop

tape|tar /tape'tar/ *vt* carpet; ~**te** /e/ *m* carpet

tapioca /tapi'ɔka/ *f* tapioca

tapume /ta'pumi/ *m* fence

taquicardia /takikar'dʒia/ *f* palpitations

taquigra|far /takigra'far/ *vt/i* write in shorthand; ~**fia** *f* shorthand

tara /'tara/ *f* fetish; ~**do** *a* sex-crazed □ *m* sex maniac; **ser** ~**do por** be crazy about

tar|dar /tar'dar/ *vi* (*atrasar*) be late; (*demorar muito*) be long □ *vt* delay; ~**dar a responder** take a long time to answer, be a long time answering; **o mais** ~**dar** at the latest; **sem mais** ~**dar** without further delay; ~**de** *adv* late □ *f* afternoon; **hoje à** ~**de** this afternoon; ~**de da noite** late at night; ~**dinha** *f* late afternoon; ~**dio** *a* late

tarefa /ta'rɛfa/ *f* task, job

tarifa /ta'rifa/ *f* tariff; ~ **de embarque** airport tax

tarimbado /tarĩ'badu/ *a* experienced

tarja /'tarʒa/ *f* strip

ta|rô /ta'ro/ *m* tarot; ~**rólogo** *m* tarot reader

tartamu|dear /tartamudʒi'ar/ *vi* stammer; ~**do** *a* stammering □ *m* stammerer

tártaro /'tartaru/ *m* tartar

tartaruga /tarta'ruga/ *f* (*bicho*) turtle; (*material*) tortoiseshell

tatear /tatʃi'ar/ *vt* feel □ *vi* feel one's way

táti|ca /'tatʃika/ *f* tactics; ~**co** *a* tactical

tá|til /'tatʃiw/ (*pl* ~**teis**) *a* tactile

tato /'tatu/ *m* (*sentido*) touch; (*diplomacia*) tact

tatu /ta'tu/ *m* armadillo

tatu|ador /tatua'dor/ *m* tattooist; ~**agem** *f* tattoo; ~**ar** *vt* tattoo

tauromaquia /tawroma'kia/ *f* bullfighting

taxa /'taʃa/ *f* (*a pagar*) charge; (*índice*) rate; ~ **de câmbio** exchange rate; ~ **de juros** interest rate; ~ **rodoviária** road tax

taxar /ta'ʃar/ *vt* tax

taxativo /taʃa'tʃivu/ *a* firm, categorical

táxi /'taksi/ *m* taxi

taxiar /taksi'ar/ *vi* taxi

taxímetro /tak'simetru/ *m* taxi meter

taxista /tak'sista/ *m/f* taxi driver

tchã /tʃã/ *m* (*fam*) special something

tchau /tʃaw/ *int* goodbye, bye

tcheco /'tʃɛku/ *a & m* Czech

Tchecoslováquia /tʃekoslo'vakia/ f Czechoslovakia

te /tʃi/ *pron* you; (*a ti*) to you

tear /tʃi'ar/ *m* loom

tea|tral /tʃia'traw/ (*pl* ~**trais**) *a* theatrical; <*grupo*> theatre; ~**tro** *m* theatre; ~**trólogo** *m* playwright

tece|lagem /tese'laʒẽ/ *f* (*trabalho*) weaving; (*fábrica*) textile factory; ~**lão** *m* (*f* ~**lã**) weaver

te|cer /te'ser/ *vt/i* weave; ~**cido** *m* cloth; (*no corpo*) tissue

te|cla /'tɛkla/ *f* key; ~**cladista** *m/f* (*músico*) keyboard player; (*de computador*) keyboard operator; ~**clado** *m* keyboard; ~**clar** *vt* key (in)

técni|ca /'tɛknika/ *f* technique; ~**co** *a* technical □ *m* specialist; (*de time*) manager; (*que mexe com máquinas*) technician

tecno|crata /tekno'krata/ *m/f* technocrat; ~**logia** *f* technology; ~**lógico** *a* technological

teco-teco /tɛku'tɛku/ *m* light aircraft

tecto /'tɛtu/ *m* (*Port*) *veja* **teto**

tédio /'tɛdʒiu/ *m* boredom

tedioso /tedʒi'ozu/ *a* boring, tedious

Teerã /tee'rã/ *f* Teheran

teia /'teja/ *f* web

tei|ma /'tejma/ *f* persistence; ~**mar** *vi* insist; ~**mar em ir** insist on going; ~**mosia** *f* stubbornness; ~**moso** /o/ *a* stubborn; <*ruído*> insistent

teixo /'tejʃu/ *m* yew

Tejo /'teʒu/ *m* Tagus

tela /'tɛla/ *f* (*de cinema, TV etc*) screen; (*tecido, pintura*) canvas

telecoman|dado /telekomã'dadu/ *a* remote-controlled; ~**do** *m* remote control

telecomunicação /telekomunika-'sãw/ *f* telecommunication

teleférico /tele'fɛriku/ *m* cable car

telefo|nar /telefo'nar/ *vi* telephone; ~**nar para alg** phone s.o.; ~**ne** /o/ *m* telephone; (*número*) phone number; ~**ne celular** cell phone; ~**ne sem fio** cordless phone; ~**nema** /e/ *m* phone call; ~**nia** *f* telephone technology

telefôni|co /tele'foniku/ *a* telephone; **cabine** ~**ca** phone box, (*Amer*) phone booth; **mesa** ~**ca** switchboard

telefonista /telefo'nista/ *m/f* (*da companhia telefônica*) operator; (*dentro de empresa etc*) telephonist

tele|grafar /telegra'far/ *vt/i* telegraph; ~**gráfico** *a* telegraphic

telégrafo /te'lɛgrafu/ *m* telegraph

tele|grama /tele'grama/ *m* telegram; ~**guiado** *a* remote- controlled

telejor|nal /teleʒor'naw/ (*pl* ~**nais**) *m* television news

tele|novela /teleno'vɛla/ *f* TV soap opera; ~**objetiva** *f* telephoto lens

tele|patia /telepa'tʃia/ *f* telepathy; ~**pático** *a* telepathic

telescó|pico /teles'kɔpiku/ *a* telescopic; ~**pio** *m* telescope

telespectador /telespekta'dor/ *m* television viewer □ *a* viewing

televi|são /televi'zãw/ *f* television; ~**são a cabo** cable television; ~**sionar** *vt* televise; ~**sivo** *a* television; ~**sor** *m* television set

telex /te'lɛks/ *m invar* telex

telha /'teʎa/ *f* tile; ~**do** *m* roof

te|ma /'tema/ *m* theme; ~**mático** *a* thematic

temer /te'mer/ *vt* fear □ *vi* be afraid; ~ **por** fear for

teme|rário /teme'rariu/ *a* reckless; ~**ridade** *f* recklessness; ~**roso** /o/ *a* fearful

te|mido /te'midu/ *a* feared; ~**mível** (*pl* ~**míveis**) *a* fearsome; ~**mor** *m* fear

tempão /tẽ'pãw/ *m* **um** ~ a long time

temperado /tẽpe'radu/ *a* <*clima*> temperate □ *pp de* **temperar**

temperamen|tal /tẽperamẽ'taw/ (*pl* ~**tais**) *a* temperamental; ~**to** *m* temperament

temperar /tẽpe'rar/ *vt* season <*comida*>; temper <*aço*>

temperatura /tẽpera'tura/ *f* temperature

tempero /tẽ'peru/ *m* seasoning

tempes|tade /tẽpes'tadʒi/ *f* storm; ~**tuoso** /o/ *a* stormy; (*fig*) tempestuous

templo /'tẽplu/ *m* temple

tempo /'tẽpu/ *m* (*período*) time; (*atmosférico*) weather; (*do verbo*) tense; (*de jogo*) half; **ao mesmo** ~ at the same time; **nesse meio** ~ in the meantime; **o** ~ **todo** all the time; **de todos os** ~**s** of all time; **quanto** ~ how long; **muito/pouco** ~ a long/ short time; ~ **integral** full time

têmpora /'tẽpora/ *f* temple

tempo|rada /tẽpo'rada/ *f* (*sazão*) season; (*tempo*) while; ~**ral** (*pl* ~**rais**) *a* temporal □ *m* storm; ~**rário** *a* temporary

te|nacidade /tenasi'dadʒi/ *f* tenacity; ~**naz** *a* tenacious □ *f* tongs

tenção /tẽ'sãw/ *f* intention

tencionar /tẽsio'nar/ *vt* intend

tenda /'tẽda/ *f* tent

tendão /tẽ'dãw/ *m* tendon; ~ **de Aquiles** Achilles tendon

tendência /tẽ'dẽsia/ *f* (*moda*) trend; (*propensão*) tendency

tendencioso /tẽdẽsi'ozu/ *a* tendentious

ten|der /tẽ'der/ *vi* tend (**para to-wards**); **~de a engordar** he tends to get fat; **o tempo ~de a ficar bom** the weather is improving

tenebroso /tene'brozu/ *a* dark; (*fig: terrível*) dreadful

tenente /te'nẽtʃi/ *m/f* lieutenant

tênis /'tenis/ *m invar* (*jogo*) tennis; (*sapato*) trainer; **um ~** (*par*) a pair of trainers; **~ de mesa** table tennis

tenista /te'nista/ *m/f* tennis player

tenor /te'nor/ *m* tenor

tenro /'tẽxu/ *a* tender

ten|são /tẽ'sãw/ *f* tension; **~são (arterial)** blood pressure; **~so** *a* tense

tentação /tẽta'sãw/ *f* temptation

tentáculo /tẽ'takulu/ *m* tentacle

ten|tador /tẽta'dor/ *a* tempting; **~tar** *vt* try; (*seduzir*) tempt □ *vi* try; **~tativa** *f* attempt; **~tativo** *a* tentative

tênue /'tenui/ *a* faint

teo|logia /teolo'ʒia/ *f* theology; **~lógico** *a* theological

teólogo /te'ɔlogu/ *m* theologian

teor /te'or/ *m* (*de gordura etc*) content; (*de carta, discurso*) drift

teo|rema /teo'rema/ *m* theorem; **~ria** *f* theory

teórico /te'ɔriku/ *a* theoretical

teorizar /teori'zar/ *vt* theorize

tépido /'tɛpidu/ *a* tepid

ter /ter/ *vt* have; **tenho vinte anos** I am twenty (years old); **~ medo/sede** be afraid/thirsty; **tenho que** *ou* **de ir** I have to go; **tem** (*há*) there is/are; **não tem de quê** don't mention it; **~ a ver com** have to do with

tera|peuta /tera'pewta/ *m/f* therapist; **~pêutico** *a* therapeutic; **~pia** *f* therapy

terça /'tersa/ *f* Tuesday; **~-feira** (*pl* **~s-feiras**) *f* Tuesday; **Terça-Feira Gorda** Shrove Tues-day

tercei|ra /ter'sera/ *f* (*marcha*) third; **~ranista** *m/f* third-year; **~ro** *a* third □ *m* third party

terço /'tersu/ *m* third

ter|çol (*pl* **~çóis**) *m* stye

tergal /ter'gaw/ *m* Terylene

térmi|co /'tɛrmiku/ *a* thermal; **garrafa ~ca** Thermos flask

termi|nal /termi'naw/ (*pl* **~nais**) *a* & *m* terminal; **~nal de vídeo** VDU; **~nante** *a* definite; **~nar** *vt* finish □ *vi* <*pessoa, coisa*> finish; <*coisa*> end; **~nar com alg** (*cortar relação*) break up with s.o.

ter|minologia /terminolo'ʒia/ *f* terminology; **~mo¹** /'termu/ *m* term; **pôr ~mo a** put an end to; **meio ~mo** compromise

termo² /'termu/ *m* (*Port*) Thermos flask

ter|mômetro /ter'mometru/ *m* thermometer; **~mostato** *m* thermostat

terno¹ /'ternu/ *m* suit

ter|no² /'ternu/ *a* tender; **~nura** *f* tenderness

terra /'tɛxa/ *f* land; (*solo, elétrico*) earth; (*chão*) ground; **a Terra** Earth; **por ~** on the ground; **~ natal** homeland

terraço /te'xasu/ *m* terrace

terra|cota /texa'kota/ *f* terracotta; **~moto** /texa'mɔtu/ *m* (*Port*) earthquake; **~plenagem** *f* earth moving

terreiro /te'xeru/ *m* meeting place for Afro-Brazilian cults

terremoto /texe'mɔtu/ *m* earthquake

terreno /te'xenu/ *a* earthly □ *m* ground; (*geog*) terrain; (*um*) piece of land; **~ baldio** piece of waste ground

térreo /'tɛxiu/ *a* ground-floor; **(andar) ~** ground floor, (*Amer*) first floor

terrestre /te'xɛstri/ *a* <*animal, batalha, forças*> land; (*da Terra*) of the Earth, the Earth's; <*alegrias etc*> earthly

terrificante /texifi'kãtʃi/ *a* terrifying

terrina /te'xina/ *f* tureen

territori|al /texitori'aw/ (*pl* **~ais**) *a* territorial

território /texi'tɔriu/ *m* territory

terrí|vel /te'xivew/ (*pl* **~veis**) *a* terrible

terror /te'xor/ *m* terror; **filme de ~** horror film

terroris|mo /texo'rizmu/ *m* terrorism; **~ta** *a* & *m/f* terrorist

tese /'tɛzi/ *f* theory; (*escrita*) thesis

teso /'tezu/ *a* (*apertado*) taut; (*rígido*) stiff

tesoura /te'zora/ *f* scissors; **uma ~** a pair of scissors

tesou|reiro /tezo'reru/ *m* treasurer; **~ro** *m* treasure; (*do Estado*) treasury

testa /'tɛsta/ *f* forehead; **~-de-ferro** (*pl* **~s-de-ferro**) *m* frontman

testamento /testa'mẽtu/ *m* will; (*na Bíblia*) testament

tes|tar /tes'tar/ *vt* test; **~te** /ɛ/ *m* test

testemu|nha /teste'muɲa/ *f* witness; **~nha ocular** eye witness; **~nhar** *vt* bear witness to □ *vi* testify; **~nho** *m* evidence, testimony

testículo /tes'tʃikulu/ *m* testicle

teta /'teta/ *f* teat

tétano /'tɛtanu/ *m* tetanus

teto /'tɛtu/ *m* ceiling; **~ solar** sun roof

tétrico /'tɛtriku/ *a* (*triste*) dismal; (*medonho*) horrible

teu /tew/ (*f* **tua**) *a* your □ *pron* yours

têx|til /'testʃiw/ (*pl* **~teis**) *m* textile

tex|to /'testu/ *m* text; **~tura** *f* texture

texugo /te'ʃugu/ *m* badger

tez /tes/ *f* complexion

ti /tʃi/ *pron* you

tia /'tʃia/ *f* aunt; **~-avó** (*pl* **~s-avós**) *f* great aunt

tiara /tʃi'ara/ *f* tiara

tíbia /'tʃibia/ *f* shinbone

ticar /tʃi'kar/ *vt* tick

tico /'tʃiku/ *m* **um ~ de** a little bit of

tiete /tʃi'ɛtʃi/ *m/f* fan

tifo /'tʃifu/ *m* typhoid

tigela /tʃi'ʒɛla/ *f* bowl; **de meia~** smalltime

tigre /'tʃigri/ *m* tiger; **~sa** /e/ *f* tigress

tijolo /tʃi'ʒolu/ *m* brick

til /tʃiw/ (*pl* **tis**) *m* tilde

tilintar /tʃili'tar/ *vi* jingle □ *m* jingling

timão /tʃi'mãw/ *m* tiller

timbre /'tʃibri/ *m* (*insígnia*) crest; (*em papel*) heading; (*de som*) tone; (*de vogal*) quality

time /'tʃimi/ *m* team

timidez /tʃimi'des/ *f* shyness

tímido /'tʃimidu/ *a* shy

tímpano /'tʃipanu/ *m* (*tambor*) kettledrum; (*no ouvido*) eardrum

tina /'tʃina/ *f* vat

tingir /tʃi'ʒir/ *vt* dye <*tecido, cabelo*>; (*fig*) tinge

ti|nido /tʃi'nidu/ *m* tinkling; **~nir** *vi* tinkle; <*ouvidos*> ring; (*tremer*) tremble; **estar ~nindo** (*fig*) be in peak condition

tino /'tʃinu/ *m* sense, judgement; **ter ~ para** have a flair for

tin|ta /'tʃita/ *f* (*para pintar*) paint; (*para escrever*) ink; (*para tingir*) dye; **~teiro** *m* inkwell

tintim /tʃi'tʃi/ *m* **contar ~ por ~** give a blow-by-blow account of

tin|to /'tʃitu/ *a* dyed; <*vinho*> red; **~tura** *f* dye; (*fig*) tinge; **~turaria** *f* dry cleaner's

tio /'tʃiu/ *m* uncle; *pl* (**~ e tia**) uncle and aunt; **~-avô** (*pl* **~s-avôs**) *m* great uncle

típico /'tʃipiku/ *a* typical

tipo /'tʃipu/ *m* type

tipóia /tʃi'pɔja/ *f* sling

tique /'tʃiki/ *m* (*sinal*) tick; (*do rosto etc*) twitch

tíquete /'tʃiketʃi/ *m* ticket

tiquinho /tʃi'kiɲu/ *m* **um ~ de** a tiny bit of

tira /'tʃira/ *f* strip □ *m/f* (*fam*) copper, (*Amer*) cop

tiracolo /tʃira'kɔlu/ *m* **a ~** <*bolsa*> over one's shoulder; <*pessoa*> in tow

tiragem /tʃi'raʒẽ/ *f* (*de jornal*) circulation

tira|-gosto /tʃira'gostu/ *m* snack; **~manchas** *m invar* stain remover

ti|rania /tʃira'nia/ *f* tyranny; **~rânico** *a* tyrannical; **~rano** *m* tyrant

tirar /tʃi'rar/ *vt* (*afastar*) take away; (*de dentro*) take out; take off <*roupa, sapato, tampa*>; take <*foto, cópia, férias*>; clear <*mesa*>; get <*nota, diploma, salário*>; get out <*mancha*>

tiritar /tʃiri'tar/ *vi* shiver

tiro /'tʃiru/ *m* shot; **~ ao alvo** shooting; **é ~ e queda** (*fam*) it can't fail; **~teio** *m* shoot-out

titânio /tʃi'taniu/ *m* titanium

títere /'tʃiteri/ *m* puppet

ti|tia /tʃi'tʃia/ *f* auntie; **~tio** *m* uncle

titiriti /tʃitʃi'tʃi/ *m* (*fam*) talk

titubear /tʃitubi'ar/ *vi* stagger, totter; (*fig: hesitar*) waver

titular /tʃitu'lar/ *m/f* title holder; (*de time*) captain □ *vt* title

título /'tʃitulu/ *m* title; (*obrigação*) bond; **a ~ de** on the basis of; **a ~ pessoal** on a personal basis

toa /'toa/ *f* **à ~** (*sem rumo*) aimlessly; (*ao acaso*) at random; (*sem motivo*) without reason; (*em vão*) for nothing; (*desocupado*) at a loose end; (*de repente*) out of the blue

toada /to'ada/ *f* melody

toalete /toa'lɛtʃi/ *m* toilet

toalha /to'aʎa/ *f* towel; **~ de mesa** tablecloth

tobogã /tobo'gã/ *m* (*rampa*) slide; (*trenó*) toboggan

toca /'tɔka/ *f* burrow

toca|-discos /tɔka'dʒiskus/ *m invar* record player; **~-fitas** *m invar* tape player

tocaia /to'kaja/ *f* ambush

tocante /to'kãtʃi/ *a* (*enternecedor*) moving

tocar /to'kar/ *vt* touch; play <*piano, música, disco etc*>; ring <*campainha*> □ *vi* touch; <*pianista, música, disco etc*> play; <*campainha, telefone, sino*> ring; **~-se** *vpr* touch; (*mancar-se*) take the hint; **~ a** (*dizer respeito*) concern; **~ em** touch; touch on <*assunto*>

tocha /'tɔʃa/ *f* torch

toco /'tɔku/ *m* (*de árvore*) stump; (*de cigarro*) butt

toda /'tɔda/ *f* **a ~** at full speed

todavia /toda'via/ *conj* however

todo /'todu/ *a* all; (*cada*) every; *pl* all; **~ o dinheiro** all the money; **~ dia, ~s os dias** every day; **~s os alunos** all the pupils; **o dia ~** all day; **em ~ lugar** everywhere; **~ mundo, ~s** everyone; **~s nós** all of us; **ao ~** in all; **~-poderoso** *a* almighty

tofe /'tɔfi/ *m* toffee

toga /'tɔga/ *f* gown; (*de romano*) toga

toicinho /toj'siɲu/ *m* bacon

toldo /'towdu/ *m* awning

tole|rância /tole'rãsia/ *f* tolerance; **~rante** *a* tolerant; **~rar** *vt* tolerate; **~rável** (*pl* **~ráveis**) *a* tolerable

to|lice /to'lisi/ *f* foolishness; (*uma*) foolish thing; **~lo** /o/ *a* foolish □ *m* fool

tom /tõ/ *m* tone

to|mada /to'mada/ *f* (*conquista*) capture; (*elétrica*) plughole; (*de filme*) shot; **~mar** *vt* take; (*beber*) drink; **~mar café** have breakfast

tomara /to'mara/ *int* I hope so; **~ que** let's hope that; **~-que-caia** *a invar* <*vestido*> strapless

tomate /to'matʃi/ *m* tomato

tom|bar /tõ'bar/ *vt* (*derrubar*) knock down; list <*edifício*> □ *vi* fall over; **~bo** *m* fall; **levar um ~bo** have a fall

tomilho /to'miʎu/ *m* thyme

tomo /'tomu/ *m* volume

tona /'tona/ *f* **trazer à ~** bring up; **vir à ~** emerge

tonalidade /tonali'dadʒi/ *f* (*de música*) key; (*de cor*) shade

to|nel /to'nɛw/ (*pl* **~néis**) *m* cask; **~nelada** *f* tonne

tôni|ca /'tonika/ *f* tonic; (*fig: assunto*) keynote; **~co** *a* & *m* tonic

tonificar /tonifi'kar/ *vt* tone up

ton|tear /tõtʃi'ar/ *vt* **~tear alg** make s.o.'s head spin; **~teira** *f* dizziness; **~to** *a* (*zonzo*) dizzy; (*bobo*) stupid; (*atrapalhado*) flustered; **~tura** *f* dizziness

to|pada /to'pada/ *f* trip; **dar uma ~pada em** stub one's toe on; **~par** *vt* agree to, accept; **~par com** bump into <*pessoa*>; come across <*coisa*>

topázio /to'paziu/ *m* topaz

topete /to'petʃi/ *m* quiff

tópico /'tɔpiku/ *a* topical □ *m* topic

topless /topi'lɛs/ *a invar* & *adv* topless

topo /'topu/ *m* top

topografia /topogra'fia/ *f* topography

topônimo /to'ponimu/ *m* place name

toque /'tɔki/ *m* touch; (*da campainha, do telefone*) ring; (*de instrumento*) playing; **dar um ~ em** (*fam*) have a word with

Tóquio /'tɔkiu/ *f* Tokyo

tora /'tɔra/ *f* log

toranja /to'rãʒa/ *f* grapefruit

tórax /'tɔraks/ *m invar* thorax

tor|ção /tor'sãw/ *f* (*do braço etc*) sprain; **~cedor** *m* supporter; **~cer** *vt* twist; (*machucar*) sprain; (*espremer*) wring <*roupa*>; (*centrifugar*) spin <*roupa*> □ *vi* (*gritar*) cheer (**por** for); (*desejar sucesso*) keep one's fingers crossed (**por** for; **para que** that); **~cer-se** *vpr* twist about;

~cicolo /ɔ/ *m* stiff neck; **~cida** *f* (*torção*) twist; (*torcedores*) supporters; (*gritaria*) cheering

tormen|ta /tor'mẽta/ *f* storm; **~to** *m* torment; **~toso** /o/ *a* stormy

tornado /tor'nadu/ *m* tornado

tornar /tor'nar/ *vt* make; **~-se** *vpr* become

torne|ado /torni'adu/ *a* **bem ~ado** shapely; **~ar** *vt* turn

torneio /tor'neju/ *m* tournament

torneira /tor'nera/ *f* tap, (*Amer*) faucet

torniquete /torni'ketʃi/ *m* (*para ferido*) tourniquet; (*Port: de entrada*) turnstile

torno /'tornu/ *m* lathe; (*de ceramista*) wheel; **em ~ de** around

tornozelo /torno'zelu/ *m* ankle

toró /to'rɔ/ *m* downpour

torpe /'torpi/ *a* dirty

torpe|dear /torpedʒi'ar/ *vt* torpedo; **~do** /e/ *m* torpedo

torpor /tor'por/ *m* torpor

torra|da /to'xada/ *f* piece of toast; *pl* toast; **~deira** *f* toaster

torrão /to'xãw/ *m* (*de terra*) turf; (*de açúcar*) lump

torrar /to'xar/ *vt* toast <*pão*>; roast <*café*>; blow <*dinheiro*>; sell off <*mercadorias*>

torre /'toxi/ *f* tower; (*em xadrez*) rook; **~ de controle** control tower; **~ão** *m* turret

torrefação /toxefa'sãw/ *f* (*ação*) roasting; (*fábrica*) coffee-roasting plant

torren|cial /toxẽsi'aw/ (*pl* **~ciais**) *a* torrential; **~te** *f* torrent

torresmo /to'xezmu/ *m* crackling

tórrido /'tɔxidu/ *a* torrid

torrone /to'xoni/ *m* nougat

torso /'torsu/ *m* torso

torta /'tɔrta/ *f* pie, tart

tor|to /'tortu/ *a* crooked; **a ~ e a direito** left, right and centre; **~tuoso** *a* winding

tortu|ra /tor'tura/ *f* torture; **~rador** *m* torturer; **~rar** *vt* torture

to|sa /'tɔza/ *f* (*de cachorro*) clipping; (*de ovelhas*) shearing; **~são** *m* fleece; **~sar** *vt* clip <*cachorro*>; shear <*ovelhas*>; crop <*cabelo*>

tosco /'tosku/ *a* rough, coarse

tosquiar /toski'ar/ *vt* shear <*ovelha*>

tos|se /'tɔsi/ *f* cough; **~se de cachorro** whooping cough; **~sir** *vi* cough

tostão /tos'tãw/ *m* penny

tostar /tos'tar/ *vt* brown <*carne*>; tan <*pele, pessoa*>; **~-se** *vpr* (*ao sol*) go brown

to|tal /to'taw/ (*pl* **~tais**) *a* & *m* total

totali|dade /totali'dadʒi/ *f* entirety; **~tário** *a* totalitarian; **~zar** *vt* total

touca /'toka/ f bonnet; (de freira) wimple; ~ **de banho** bathing cap; ~**dor** m dressing table

toupeira /to'pera/ f mole

tou|rada /to'rada/ f bullfight; ~**reiro** m bullfighter; ~**ro** m bull; **Touro** (signo) Taurus

tóxico /'tɔksiku/ a toxic □ m toxic substance

toxicômano /toksi'komanu/ m drug addict

toxina /tok'sina/ f toxin

traba|lhador /trabaʎa'dor/ a <pessoa> hard-working; <classe> working □ m worker; ~**lhar** vt work □ vi work; (numa peça, filme) act; ~**lheira** f big job; ~**lhista** a labour; ~**lho** m work; (um) job; (na escola) assignment; **dar-se o** ~**lho de** go to the trouble of; ~**lho de parto** labour; ~**lhos forçados** hard labour; ~**lhoso** a laborious

traça /'trasa/ f moth

tração /tra'sãw/ f traction

tra|çar /tra'sar/ vt draw; draw up <plano>; set out <ordens>; ~**ço** m stroke; (entre frases) dash; (vestígio) trace; (característica) trait; pl (do rosto) features

tractor /tra'tor/ m (Port) veja **trator**

tradi|ção /tradʒi'sãw/ f tradition; ~**cional** (pl ~**cionais**) a traditional

tradu|ção /tradu'sãw/ f translation; ~**tor** m translator; ~**zir** vt/i translate (de from; para into)

trafe|gar /trafe'gar/ vi run; ~**gável** (pl ~**gáveis**) a open to traffic

tráfego /'trafegu/ m traffic

trafi|cância /trafi'kãsia/ f trafficking; ~**cante** m/f trafficker; ~**car** vt/i traffic (com in)

tráfico /'trafiku/ m traffic

tra|gada /tra'gada/ f (de bebida) swallow; (de cigarro) drag; ~**gar** vt swallow; inhale <fumaça>

tragédia /tra'ʒɛdʒia/ f tragedy

trágico /'traʒiku/ a tragic

trago /'tragu/ m (de bebida) swallow; (de cigarro) drag; **de um** ~ in one go

trai|ção /traj'sãw/ f (ato) betrayal; (deslealdade) treachery; (da pátria) treason; ~**çoeiro** a treacherous; ~**dor** a treacherous □ m traitor

trailer /'trejler/ (pl ~**s**) m (de filme etc) trailer; (casa móvel) caravan, (Amer) trailer

traineira /traj'nera/ f trawler

training /'trejnĩ/ (pl ~**s**) m track suit

trair /tra'ir/ vt betray; be unfaithful to <marido, mulher>; ~**se** vpr give o.s. away

tra|jar /tra'ʒar/ vt wear; ~**jar-se** vpr dress (de in); ~**je** m outfit; ~**je a**

rigor evening dress; ~**je espacial** space suit

traje|to /tra'ʒɛtu/ m (percurso) journey; (caminho) route; ~**tória** f trajectory; (fig) course

tralha /'traʎa/ f (trastes) junk

tra|ma /'trama/ f plot; ~**mar** vt/i plot

trambi|que /trã'biki/ (fam) m con; ~**queiro** (fam) m con artist

tramitar /trami'tar/ vi be processed

trâmites /'tramitʃis/ m pl channels

tramóia /tra'mɔja/ f scheme

trampolim /trãpo'lĩ/ m (de ginástica) trampoline; (de piscina, fig) springboard

tranca /'trãka/ f bolt; (em carro) lock

trança /'trãsa/ f (de cabelo) plait

tran|cafiar /trãkafi'ar/ vt lock up; ~**car** vt lock; cancel <matrícula>

trançar /trã'sar/ vt plait <cabelo>; weave <palha etc>

tranco /'trãku/ m jolt; **aos** ~**s e barrancos** in fits and starts

tranqueira /trã'kera/ f junk

tranqüi|lidade /trãkwili'dadʒi/ f tranquillity; ~**lizador** a reassuring; ~**lizante** m tranquillizer □ a reassuring; ~**lizar** vt reassure; ~**lizar-se** vpr be reassured; ~**lo** a <bairro, sono> peaceful; <pessoa, voz, mar> calm; <consciência> clear; <sucesso, lucro> sure-fire □ adv with no trouble

transa /'trãza/ f (fam) (negócio) deal; (caso) affair; ~**ção** f transaction; ~**do** a (fam) <roupa, pessoa, casa> stylish; <relação> healthy

Transamazônica /trãzama'zonika/ f trans-Amazonian highway

transar /trã'zar/ (fam) vt set up; do <drogas> □ vi (negociar) deal; (fazer sexo) have sex

transatlântico /trãzat'lãtʃiku/ a transatlantic □ m liner

transbordar /trãzbor'dar/ vi overflow

transcen|dental /trãsẽdẽ'taw/ (pl ~**dentais**) a transcendental; ~**der** vt/i ~**der (a)** transcend

trans|crever /trãskre'ver/ vt transcribe; ~**crição** f transcription; ~**crito** a transcribed □ m transcript

transe /'trãzi/ m trance

transeunte /trãzi'ũtʃi/ m/f passer-by

transfe|rência /trãsfe'rẽsia/ f transfer; ~**ridor** m protractor; ~**rir** vt transfer; ~**rir-se** vpr transfer

transfor|mação /trãsforma'sãw/ f transformation; ~**mador** m transformer; ~**mar** vt transform; ~**mar-se** vpr be transformed

trânsfuga /'trãsfuga/ m/f deserter; (de um país) defector

transfusão /trãsfu'zãw/ f transfusion

trans|gredir /trãzgre'dʒir/ vt infringe; **~gressão** f infringement

transi|ção /trãzi'sãw/ f transition; **~cional** (pl **~cionais**) a transitional

transi|gente /trãzi'ʒẽtʃi/ a open to compromise; **~gir** vi compromise

transis|tor /trãzis'tor/ m transistor; **~torizado** a transistorized

transi|tar /trãzi'tar/ vi pass; **~tável** (pl **~táveis**) a passable; **~tivo** a transitive

trânsito /'trãzitu/ m traffic; **em ~** in transit

transitório /trãzi'tɔriu/ a transitory

translúcido /trãz'lusidu/ a translucent

transmis|são /trãzmi'sãw/ f transmission; **~sor** m transmitter

transmitir /trãzmi'tʃir/ vt transmit <programa, calor, doença>; convey <notícia, ordens>; transfer <herança, direito>; **~-se** vpr <doença> be transmitted

transpa|recer /trãspare'ser/ vi be visible; (fig) <emoção, verdade> come out; **~rência** f transparency; **~rente** a transparent

transpi|ração /trãspira'sãw/ f perspiration; **~rar** vt exude □ vi (suar) perspire; <notícia> trickle through; <verdade> come out

transplan|tar /trãsplã'tar/ vt transplant; **~te** m transplant

transpor /trãs'por/ vt cross <rio, fronteira>; get over <obstáculo, dificuldade>; transpose <letras, música>

transpor|tadora /trãsporta'dora/ f transport company; **~tar** vt transport; (em contas) carry forward; **~te** m transport; **~te coletivo** public transport

transposto /trãs'postu/ pp de transpor

transtor|nar /trãstor'nar/ vt mess up <papéis, casa>; disrupt <rotina, ambiente>; disturb, upset <pessoa>; **~nar-se** vpr <pessoa> be rattled; **~no** /o/ m (de casa, rotina) disruption; (de pessoa) disturbance; (contratempo) upset

transver|sal /trãzver'saw/ (pl **~sais**) a (**rua**) **~sal** cross street; **~so** /ɛ/ a transverse

transvi|ado /trãzvi'adu/ a wayward; **~ar** vt lead astray

trapa|ça /tra'pasa/ f swindle; **~cear** vi cheat; **~ceiro** a crooked □ m cheat

trapa|lhada /trapa'ʎada/ f bungle; **~lhão** a (f **~lhona**) bungling □ m (f **~lhona**) bungler

trapézio /tra'pɛziu/ m trapeze

trapezista /trape'zista/ m/f trapeze artist

trapo /'trapu/ m rag

traquéia /tra'kɛja/ f windpipe, trachea

traquejo /tra'keʒu/ m knack

traquinas /tra'kinas/ a invar mischievous

trás /tras/ adv **de ~** from behind; **a roda de ~** the back wheel; **de ~ para frente** back to front; **para ~** backwards; **deixar para ~** leave behind; **por ~ de** behind

traseiro /tra'zeru/ a rear, back □ m bottom

trasladar /trazla'dar/ vt transport

traspas|sado /traspa'sadu/ a <paletó> double-breasted; **~sar** vt pierce

traste /'trastʃi/ m (pessoa) pain; (coisa) piece of junk

tra|tado /tra'tadu/ m (pacto) treaty; (estudo) treatise; **~tamento** m treatment; (título) title; **~tar** vt treat; negotiate <preço, venda> □ vi (manter relações) have dealings (**com** with); (combinar) negotiate (**com** with); **~tar de** deal with; **~tar alg de** ou **por** address s.o. as; **~tar de voltar** (tentar) seek to return; (resolver) decide to return; **~tar-se de** be a matter of; **~tável** (pl **~táveis**) a <doença> treatable; <pessoa> accommodating; **~tos** m pl **maus ~tos** illtreatment

trator /tra'tor/ m tractor

trauma /'trawma/ m trauma; **~tizante** a traumatic; **~tizar** vt traumatize

tra|vão /tra'vãw/ m (Port) brake; **~var** vt lock <rodas, músculos>; stop <carro>; block <passagem>; strike up <amizade, conversa>; wage <luta, combate> □ vi (Port) brake

trave /'travi/ f beam, joist; (do gol) crossbar

traves|sa /tra'vesa/ f (trave) crossbar; (rua) side street; (prato) dish; (pente) slide; **~são** m dash; **~seiro** m pillow; **~sia** f crossing; **~so** /e/ a <criança> naughty; **~sura** f prank; pl mischief

travesti /traves'tʃi/ m transvestite; (artista) drag artist; **~do** a in drag

trazer /tra'zer/ vt bring; bear <nome, ferida>; wear <barba, chapéu, cabelo curto>

trecho /'treʃu/ m (de livro etc) passage; (de rua etc) stretch

treco /'trɛku/ (fam) m (coisa) thing; (ataque) turn

trégua /'trɛgwa/ f truce; (fig) respite

trei|nador /trejna'dor/ m trainer; **~namento** m training; **~nar** vt train <atleta, animal>; practise <língua etc> □ vi <atleta> train;

<pianista, principiante> practise;
~no *m* training; *(um)* training
session
trejeito /tre'ʒejtu/ *m* grimace
trela /'trɛla/ *f* lead, *(Amer)* leash
treliça /tre'lisa/ *f* trellis
trem /trẽj/ *m* train; **~ de aterrissagem** undercarriage; **~ de carga**
goods train, *(Amer)* freight train
trema /'trema/ *m* dieresis
treme|deira /treme'dera/ *f* shiver;
~licar *vi* tremble; **~luzir** *vi* glimmer, flicker
tremendo /tre'mẽdu/ *a* tremendous
tre|mer /tre'mer/ *vi* tremble; *<terra>*
shake; **~mor** *m* tremor; *(tremedeira)*
shiver; **~mular** *vi* *<bandeira>* flutter; *<luz, estrela>* glimmer, flicker
trêmulo /'tremulu/ *a* trembling;
<luz> flickering
trena /'trena/ *f* tape measure
trenó /tre'nɔ/ *m* sledge, *(Amer)* sled;
(puxado a cavalos etc) sleigh
tre|padeira /trepa'dera/ *f* climbing
plant; **~par** *vt* climb □ *vi* climb; *(chulo)* fuck
três /tres/ *a & m* three
tresloucado /trezlo'kadu/ *a* deranged
trevas /'trɛvas/ *f pl* darkness
trevo /'trevu/ *m* *(planta)* clover; *(rodoviário)* interchange
treze /'trezi/ *a & m* thirteen
trezentos /tre'zẽtus/ *a & m* three
hundred
triagem /tri'aʒẽ/ *f (escolha)* selection;
(separação) sorting; **fazer uma ~ de**
sort
tri|angular /triãgu'lar/ *a* triangular;
~ângulo *m* triangle
tri|bal /tri'baw/ *(pl ~bais)* *a* tribal;
~bo *f* tribe
tribu|na /tri'buna/ *f* rostrum; **~nal**
(pl ~nais) *m* court
tribu|tação /tributa'sãw/ *f* taxation;
~tar *vt* tax; **~tário** *a* tax □ *m*
tributary; **~to** *m* tribute
tri|cô /tri'ko/ *m* knitting; **artigos de
~cô** knitwear; **~cotar** *vt/i* knit
tridimensio|nal /tridʒimẽsio'naw/
(pl ~nais) *a* three- dimensional
trigêmeo /tri'ʒemiu/ *m* triplet
trigésimo /tri'ʒezimu/ *a* thirtieth
tri|go /'trigu/ *m* wheat; **~gueiro** *a*
dark
trilha /'triʎa/ *f* path; *(pista, de disco)*
track; **~ sonora** soundtrack
trilhão /tri'ʎãw/ *m* billion, *(Amer)*
trillion
trilho /'triʎu/ *m* track
trilogia /trilo'ʒia/ *f* trilogy
trimes|tral /trimes'traw/ *(pl ~-
trais)* *a* quarterly; **~tre** /ɛ/ *m* quarter; *(do ano letivo)* term
trincar /trĩ'kar/ *vt/i* crack

trincheira /trĩ'ʃera/ *f* trench
trinco /'trĩku/ *m* latch
trindade /trĩ'dadʒi/ *f* trinity
trinta /'trĩta/ *a & m* thirty
trio /'triu/ *m* trio; **~ elétrico** music
float
tripa /'tripa/ *f* gut
tripé /tri'pɛ/ *m* tripod
tripli|car /tripli'kar/ *vt/i*, **~car-se**
vpr treble; **~cata** *f* triplicate
triplo /'triplu/ *a & m* triple
tripu|lação /tripula'sãw/ *f* crew;
~lante *m/f* crew member; **~lar** *vt*
man
triste /'tristʃi/ *a* sad; **~za** /e/ *f* sad-
ness; **é uma ~za** *(fam)* it's pathetic
tritu|rador /tritura'dor/ *m (de papel)*
shredder; **~rador de lixo** waste dis-
posal unit; **~rar** *vt* shred *<legumes,
papel>*; grind up *<lixo>*
triun|fal /triũ'faw/ *(pl ~fais)* *a*
triumphal; **~fante** *a* triumphant;
~far *vi* triumph; **~fo** *m* triumph
trivi|al /trivi'aw/ *(pl ~ais)* *a* trivial;
~alidade *f* triviality; *pl* trivia
triz /tris/ *m* **por um ~** narrowly, by a
hair's breadth; **não foi atropelado
por um ~** he narrowly missed being
knocked down
tro|ca /'trɔka/ *f* exchange; **em ~ca de**
in exchange for; **~cadilho** *m* pun;
~cado *m* change; **~cador** *m*
conductor; **~car** *vt (dar e receber)* exchange *(por* for); change *<dinheiro,
lençóis, lâmpada, lugares etc>*; *(transpor)* change round; *(confundir)* mix
up; **~car-se** *vpr* change; **~car de
roupa/trem/lugar** change clothes/
trains/places; **~ca-troca** *m* swap;
~co /o/ *m* change; **a ~co de quê?**
what for?; **dar o ~co em alg** pay
s.o. back
troço /'trɔsu/ *(fam)* *m (coisa)* thing;
(ataque) turn; **me deu um ~** I had a
funny turn
troféu /tro'fɛw/ *m* trophy
trólebus /'trɔlebus/ *m invar* trolley
bus
trom|ba /'trõba/ *f (de elefante)* trunk;
(cara amarrada) long face; **~bada** *f*
crash; **~ba-d'água** *(pl ~bas-
d'água)* *f* downpour; **~badinha** *m*
bag snatcher; **~bar** *vi* **~bar com**
crash into *<poste, carro>*; bump into
<pessoa>
trombo|ne /trõ'bɔni/ *m* trombone;
~nista *m/f* trombonist
trompa /'trõpa/ *f* French horn; **~ de
Falópio** fallopian tube
trompe|te /trõ'pɛtʃi/ *m* trumpet;
~tista *m/f* trumpeter
tron|co /'trõku/ *m* trunk; **~cudo** *a*
stocky
trono /'tronu/ *m* throne

tropa /'trɔpa/ *f* troop; (*exército*) army; *pl* troops; ~ **de choque** riot police

trope|ção /trope'sãw/ *m* trip; (*erro*) slip-up; ~**çar** *vi* trip; (*errar*) slip up; ~**ço** /e/ *m* stumbling block

trôpego /'tropegu/ *a* unsteady

tropi|cal /tropi'kaw/ (*pl* ~**cais**) *a* tropical

trópico /'trɔpiku/ *m* tropic

tro|tar /tro'tar/ *vi* trot; ~**te** /ɔ/ *m* (*de cavalo*) trot; (*de estudantes*) practical joke; (*mentira*) hoax

trouxa /'troʃa/ *f* (*de roupa etc*) bundle □ *m/f* (*fam*) sucker □ *a* (*fam*) gullible

tro|vão /tro'vãw/ *m* clap of thunder; *pl* thunder; ~**vejar** *vi* thunder; ~**voada** *f* thunderstorm; ~**voar** *vi* thunder

trucidar /trusi'dar/ *vt* slaughter

trucu|lência /truku'lẽsia/ *f* barbarity; ~**lento** *a* (*cruel*) barbaric; (*brigão*) belligerent

trufa /'trufa/ *f* truffle

trunfo /'trũfu/ *m* trump; (*fig*) trump card

truque /'truki/ *m* trick

truta /'truta/ *f* trout

tu /tu/ *pron* you

tua /'tua/ *veja* **teu**

tuba /'tuba/ *f* tuba

tubarão /tuba'rãw/ *m* shark

tubá|rio /tu'bariu/ *a* **gravidez** ~**ria** ectopic pregnancy

tuberculose /tubercu'lɔzi/ *f* tuberculosis

tubo /'tubu/ *m* tube; (*no corpo*) duct

tubulação /tubula'sãw/ *f* ducting

tucano /tu'kanu/ *m* toucan

tudo /'tudu/ *pron* everything; ~ **bem?** (*cumprimento*) how are things?; ~ **de bom** all the best; **em** ~ **quanto é lugar** all over the place

tufão /tu'fãw/ *m* typhoon

tulipa /tu'lipa/ *f* tulip

tumba /'tũba/ *f* tomb

tumor /tu'mor/ *m* tumour; ~ **cerebral** brain tumour

túmulo /'tumulu/ *m* grave

tumul|to /tu'muwtu/ *m* commotion; (*motim*) riot; ~**tuado** *a* disorderly, rowdy; ~**tuar** *vt* disrupt □ *vi* cause a commotion; ~**tuoso** *a* tumultuous

tú|nel /'tunew/ (*pl* ~**neis**) *m* tunnel

túnica /'tunika/ *f* tunic

Tunísia /tu'nizia/ *f* Tunisia

tupiniquim /tupini'kĩ/ *a* Brazilian

turbante /tur'bãtʃi/ *m* turban

turbilhão /turbi'ʎãw/ *m* whirlwind

turbina /tur'bina/ *f* turbine

turbu|lência /turbu'lẽsia/ *f* turbulence; ~**lento** *a* turbulent

turco /'turku/ *a & m* Turkish

turfa /'turfa/ *f* peat

turfe /'turfe/ *m* horse-racing

turis|mo /tu'rizmu/ *m* tourism; **fazer** ~**mo** go sightseeing; ~**ta** *m/f* tourist

turístico /tu'ristʃiku/ *a* <*ponto, indústria*> tourist; <*viagem*> sightseeing

turma /'turma/ *f* group; (*na escola*) class

turnê /tur'ne/ *f* tour

turno /'turnu/ *m* (*de trabalho*) shift; (*de competição, eleição*) round

turquesa /tur'keza/ *m/f & a invar* turquoise

Turquia /tur'kia/ *f* Turkey

turra /'tuxa/ *f* **às** ~**s com** at loggerheads with

tur|var /tur'var/ *vt* cloud; ~**vo** *a* cloudy

tutano /tu'tanu/ *m* marrow

tutela /tu'tela/ *f* guardianship

tutor /tu'tor/ *m* guardian

tutu /tu'tu/ *m* (*vestido*) tutu; (*prato*) beans with bacon and manioc flour

TV /te've/ *f* TV

U

ubíquo /u'bikwu/ *a* ubiquitous

Ucrânia /u'krania/ *f* Ukraine

ucraniano /ukrani'anu/ *a & m* Ukrainian

ué /u'ɛ/ *int* hang on

ufa /'ufa/ *int* phew

ufanis|mo /ufa'nizmu/ *m* chauvinism; ~**ta** *a & m/f* chauvinist

Uganda /u'gãda/ *m* Uganda

ui /ui/ *int* (*de dor*) ouch; (*de nojo*) ugh; (*de espanto*) oh

uísque /u'iski/ *m* whisky

ui|var /ui'var/ *vi* howl; ~**vo** *m* howl

úlcera /'uwsera/ *f* ulcer

ulterior /uwteri'or/ *a* further

ulti|mamente /uwtʃima'mẽtʃi/ *adv* recently; ~**mar** *vt* finalize; ~**mato** *m* ultimatum

último /'uwtʃimu/ *a* last; <*moda, notícia etc*> latest; **em** ~ **caso** as a last resort; **nos** ~**s anos** in recent years; **por** ~ last

ultra|jante /uwtra'ʒãtʃi/ *a* offensive; ~**jar** *vt* offend; ~**je** *m* outrage

ultraleve /uwtra'levi/ *m* microlite

ultra|mar /uwtra'mar/ *m* overseas; ~**marino** *a* overseas

ultrapas|sado /uwtrapa'sadu/ *a* outdated; ~**sagem** *f* overtaking, (*Amer*) passing; ~**sar** *vt* (*de carro*) overtake, (*Amer*) pass; (*ser superior a*) surpass; (*exceder*) exceed; (*extrapolar*) go beyond □ *vi* overtake, (*Amer*) pass

ultra-sonografia /uwtrasonografi'a/ *f* ultrasound scan

ultravioleta /uwtravio'leta/ *a* ultraviolet

ulu|lante /ulu'lãtʃi/ *a* (*fig*) blatant; ~**lar** *vi* wail

um /ũ/ (*f* **uma**; *m pl* **uns**, *f pl* **umas**) *art* a, an; *pl* some □ *a & pron* one; ~ **ao outro** one another; **vieram umas 20 pessoas** about 20 people came

umbanda /ũ'bãda/ *m* Afro-Brazilian cult

umbigo /ũ'bigu/ *m* navel

umbili|cal /ũbili'kaw/ (*pl* ~**cais**) *a* umbilical

umedecer /umede'ser/ *vt* moisten; ~**se** *vpr* moisten

umidade /umi'dadʒi/ *f* moisture; (*de-sagradável*) damp; (*do ar*) humidity

úmido /'umidu/ *a* moist; <*parede, roupa etc*> damp; <*ar, clima*> humid

unânime /u'nanimi/ *a* unanimous

unanimidade /unanimi'dadʒi/ *f* unanimity

undécimo /ũ'dɛsimu/ *a* eleventh

ungüento /ũ'gwẽtu/ *m* ointment

unha /'uɲa/ *f* nail; (*de animal, utensílio*) claw

unhar /u'ɲar/ *vt* claw

união /uni'ãw/ *f* union; (*concórdia*) unity; (*ato de unir*) joining

unicamente /unika'mẽtʃi/ *adv* only

único /'uniku/ *a* only; (*ímpar*) unique

uni|dade /uni'dadʒi/ *f* unit; ~**do** *a* united; <*família*> close

unifi|cação /unifika'sãw/ *f* unification; ~**car** *vt* unify

unifor|me /uni'formi/ *a* uniform; <*superfície*> even □ *m* uniform; ~**midade** *f* uniformity; ~**mizado** *a* <*policial etc*> uniformed; (*padronizado*) standardized; ~**zar** *vt* (*padronizar*) standardize

unilate|ral /unilate'raw/ (*pl* ~**rais**) *a* unilateral

unir /u'nir/ *vt* unite <*povo, nações, família etc*>; (*ligar, casar*) join; (*combinar*) combine (**a** *ou* **com** with); ~**-se** *vpr* (*aliar-se*) unite (**a** with); (*juntar-se*) join together; (*combinar-se*) combine (**a** *ou* **com** with)

unissex /uni'sɛks/ *a invar* unisex

uníssono /u'nisonu/ *m* **em** ~ in unison

univer|sal /univer'saw/ (*pl* ~**sais**) *a* universal

universi|dade /universi'dadʒi/ *f* university; ~**tário** *a* university □ *m* university student

universo /uni'vɛrsu/ *m* universe

untar /ũ'tar/ *vt* grease <*fôrma*>; spread <*pão*>; smear <*corpo, rosto etc*>

upa /'upa/ *int* (*incentivando*) upsa-daisy; (*ao cair algo etc*) whoops

urânio /u'raniu/ *m* uranium

Urano /u'ranu/ *m* Uranus

urbanis|mo /urba'nizmu/ *m* town planning; ~**ta** *m/f* town planner

urbani|zado /urbani'zadu/ *a* built-up; ~**zar** *vt* urbanize

urbano /ur'banu/ *a* (*da cidade*) urban; (*refinado*) urbane

urdir /ur'dʒir/ *vt* weave; (*maquinar*) hatch

urdu /ur'du/ *m* Urdu

ur|gência /ur'ʒẽsia/ *f* urgency; ~**gente** *a* urgent; ~**gir** *vi* be urgent; <*tempo*> press; ~**ge irmos** we must go urgently

uri|na /u'rina/ *f* urine; ~**nar** *vt* pass □ *vi* urinate; ~**nol** (*pl* ~**nóis**) *m* (*penico*) chamber pot; (*em banheiro*) urinal

urna /'urna/ *f* (*para cinzas*) urn; (*para votos*) ballot box; *pl* (*fig*) polls

ur|rar /u'xar/ *vt/i* roar; ~**ro** *m* roar

urso /'ursu/ *m* bear; ~**-branco** (*pl* ~**s-brancos**) *m* polar bear

urti|cária /urtʃi'karia/ *f* nettle rash; ~**ga** *f* nettle

urubu /uru'bu/ *m* black vulture

Uruguai /uru'gwaj/ *m* Uruguay

uruguaio /uru'gwaju/ *a & m* Uruguayan

urze /'urzi/ *f* heather

usado /u'zadu/ *a* used; <*roupa*> worn; (*palavra*) common

usar /u'zar/ *vt* wear <*roupa, óculos, barba etc*>; ~ (**de**) (*utilizar*) use

usina /u'zina/ *f* plant; ~ **termonuclear** nuclear power station

uso /'uzu/ *m* use; (*de palavras, linguagem*) usage; (*praxe*) practice

usu|al /uzu'aw/ (*pl* ~**ais**) *a* common; ~**ário** *m* user; ~**fruir** *vt* enjoy <*coisas boas*>; have the use of <*prédio, jardim etc*>; ~**fruto** *m* use

usurário /uzu'rariu/ *a* money-grubbing □ *m* money-lender

usurpar /uzur'par/ *vt* usurp

uten|sílio /utẽ'siliu/ *m* utensil; ~**te** *m/f* (*Port*) user

útero /'uteru/ *m* uterus, womb

UTI /ute'i/ *f* intensive care unit

útil /'utʃiw/ (*pl* **úteis**) *a* useful; **dia** ~ workday

utili|dade /utʃili'dadʒi/ *f* usefulness; (*uma*) utility; ~**tário** *a* utilitarian; ~**zar** *vt* (*empregar*) use; (*tornar útil*) utilize; ~**zável** (*pl* ~**záveis**) *a* usable

utopia /uto'pia/ *f* Utopia

utópico /u'topiku/ *a* Utopian

uva /'uva/ *f* grape

úvula /'uvula/ *f* uvula

V

vaca /'vaka/ *f* cow

vaci|lante /vasi'lãtʃi/ *a* wavering; <*luz*> flickering; ~**lar** *vi* waver;

<*luz*> flicker; (*fam: bobear*) slip up

vaci|na /va'sina/ *f* vaccine; **~nação** *f* vaccination; **~nar** *vt* vaccinate

vácuo /'vakuu/ *m* vacuum

va|diar /vadʒi'ar/ *vi* (*viver ocioso*) laze around; (*fazer cera*) mess about; **~dio** *a* idle □ *m* idler

vaga /'vaga/ *f* (*posto*) vacancy; (*para estacionar*) parking place

vagabun|dear /vagabũdʒi'ar/ *vi* (*perambular*) roam; (*vadiar*) laze around; **~do** *a* <*pessoa, vida*> idle; <*produto, objeto*> shoddy □ *m* tramp; (*pessoa vadia*) bum

vaga-lume /vaga'lumi/ *m* glow-worm

va|gão /va'gãw/ *m* (*de passageiros*) carriage, (*Amer*) car; (*de carga*) wagon; **~gão-leito** (*pl* **~gões-leitos**) *m* sleeping car; **~gão-restaurante** (*pl* **~gões-restaurantes**) *m* dining car

vagar¹ /va'gar/ *vi* <*pessoa*> wander about; <*barco*> drift

vagar² /va'gar/ *vi* <*cargo, apartamento*> become vacant

vagaroso /vaga'rozu/ *a* slow

vagem /'vaʒẽ/ *f* green bean

vagi|na /va'ʒina/ *f* vagina; **~nal** (*pl* **~nais**) *a* vaginal

vago¹ /'vagu/ *a* (*indefinido*) vague

vago² /'vagu/ *a* (*desocupado*) vacant; <*tempo*> spare

vaguear /vagi'ar/ *vi* roam

vai|a /'vaja/ *f* boo; **~ar** *vi* boo

vai|dade /vaj'dadʒi/ *f* vanity; **~doso** *a* vain

vaivém /vaj'vẽj/ *m* comings and goings, toing and froing

vala /'vala/ *f* ditch; **~ comum** mass grave

vale¹ /'vali/ *m* (*de rio etc*) valley

vale² /'vali/ *m* (*ficha*) voucher; **~ postal** postal order

valen|tão /valẽ'tãw/ *a* (*f* **~tona**) tough □ *m* tough guy; **~te** *a* brave; **~tia** *f* bravery; (*uma*) feat

valer /va'ler/ *vt* be worth □ *vi* be valid; **~ aco a alg** earn s.o. sth; **~se de** avail o.s. of; **~ a pena** be worth it; **vale a pena tentar** it's worth trying; **mais vale desistir** it's better to give up; **vale tudo** anything goes; **fazer ~** enforce <*lei*>; stand up for <*direitos*>; **para ~** (*a sério*) for real; (*muito*) really

vale|-refeição /valirefej'sãw/ (*pl* **~s-refeição**) *m* luncheon voucher

valeta /va'leta/ *f* gutter

valete /va'letʃi/ *m* jack

valia /va'lia/ *f* value

validar /vali'dar/ *vt* validate

válido /'validu/ *a* valid

valioso /vali'ozu/ *a* valuable

valise /va'lizi/ *f* travelling bag

valor /va'lor/ *m* value; (*valentia*) valour; *pl* (*títulos*) securities; **no ~ de** to the value of; **sem ~** worthless; **objetos de ~** valuables; **~ nominal** face value

valori|zação /valoriza'sãw/ *f* (*apreciação*) valuing; (*aumento no valor*) increase in value; **~zado** *a* highly valued; **~zar** *vt* (*apreciar*) value; (*aumentar o valor de*) increase the value of; **~zar-se** *vt* <*coisa*> increase in value; <*pessoa*> value o.s.

val|sa /'vawsa/ *f* waltz; **~sar** *vi* waltz

válvula /'vawvula/ *f* valve

vampiro /vã'piru/ *m* vampire

vandalismo /vãda'lizmu/ *m* vandalism

vândalo /'vãdalu/ *m* vandal

vangloriar-se /vãglori'arsi/ *vpr* brag (de about)

vanguarda /vã'gwarda/ *f* vanguard; (*de arte*) avant-garde

vanta|gem /vã'taʒẽ/ *f* advantage; **contar ~gem** boast; **levar ~gem** have the advantage (a over); **tirar ~gem de** take advantage of; **~joso** /o/ *a* advantageous

vão /vãw/ (*pl* **~s**) *a* (*f* **vã**) vain □ *m* gap; **em ~** in vain

vapor /va'por/ *m* (*fumaça*) steam; (*gás*) vapour; (*barco*) steamer; **máquina a ~** steam engine; **a todo ~** at full blast

vaporizar /vapori'zar/ *vt* vaporize; (*com spray*) spray

vaqueiro /va'keru/ *m* cowboy

vaquinha /va'kina/ *f* collection, whip-round

vara /'vara/ *f* rod; **~ cívil** civil district; **~ mágica** *ou* **de condão** magic wand

va|ral /va'raw/ (*pl* **~rais**) *m* washing line

varanda /va'rãda/ *f* veranda

varão /va'rãw/ *m* male

varar /va'rar/ *vt* (*furar*) pierce; (*passar por*) sweep through

varejão /vare'ʒão/ *m* wholesale store

varejeira /vare'ʒera/ *f* bluebottle

vare|jista /vare'ʒista/ *a* retail □ *m/f* retailer; **~jo** /e/ *m* retail trade; **vender a ~jo** sell retail

vari|ação /varia'sãw/ *f* variation; **~ado** *a* varied; **~ante** *a* & *f* variant; **~ar** *vt/i* vary; **para ~ar** for a change; **~ável** (*pl* **~áveis**) *a* variable; <*tempo*> changeable

varicela /vari'sɛla/ *f* chickenpox

variedade /varie'dadʒi/ *f* variety

vários /'varius/ *a pl* several

varíola /va'riola/ *f* smallpox

variz /va'ris/ *f* varicose vein

varo|nil /varo'niw/ (*pl* ~**nis**) *a* manly

var|rer /va'xer/ *vt* sweep; (*fig*) sweep away; ~**rido** *a* **um doido** ~**rido** a raving lunatic

Varsóvia /var'sɔviɐ/ *f* Warsaw

vasculhar /vasku'ʎar/ *vt* search through

vasectomia /vazekto'miɐ/ *f* vasectomy

vaselina /vaze'linɐ/ *f* vaseline

vasilha /va'ziʎɐ/ *f* jug

vaso /'vazu/ *m* pot; (*para flores*) vase; ~ **sanguíneo** blood vessel

vassoura /va'sora/ *f* broom

vas|tidão /vastʃi'dãw/ *f* vastness; ~**to** *a* vast

vatapá /vata'pa/ *m* spicy North-Eastern dish

Vaticano /vatʃi'kɐnu/ *m* Vatican

vati|cinar /vatʃisi'nar/ *vt* prophesy; ~**cínio** *m* prophecy

va|zamento /vaza'mẽtu/ *m* leak; ~**zante** *f* ebb tide; ~**zão** *m* outflow; **dar** ~**zão a** (*fig*) give vent to; ~**zar** *vt/i* leak

vazio /va'ziu/ *a* empty □ *m* emptiness; (*um*) void

veado /vi'adu/ *m* deer

ve|dação /veda'sãw/ *f* (*de casa, janela*) insulation; (*em motor etc*) gasket; ~**dar** *vt* seal <*recipiente, abertura*>; stanch <*sangue*>; seal off <*saída, área*>; ~**dar aco (a alg)** prohibit sth (for s.o.)

vedete /ve'dɛte/ *f* star

vee|mência /vee'mẽsiɐ/ *f* vehemence; ~**mente** *a* vehement

vege|tação /veʒeta'sãw/ *f* vegetation; ~**tal** (*pl* ~**tais**) *a* & *m* vegetable; ~**tar** *vi* vegetate; ~**tariano** *a* & *m* vegetarian

veia /'veja/ *f* vein

veicular /veiku'lar/ *vt* convey; place <*anúncios*>

veículo /ve'ikulu/ *m* vehicle; (*de comunicação etc*) medium

vela¹ /'vɛla/ *f* (*de barco*) sail; (*esporte*) sailing

vela² /'vɛla/ *f* candle; (*em motor*) spark plug; **segurar a** ~ (*fam*) play gooseberry

velar¹ /ve'lar/ *vt* (*cobrir*) veil

velar² /ve'lar/ *vt* watch over □ *vi* keep vigil

veleidade /velej'dadʒi/ *f* whim

ve|leiro /ve'leru/ *m* sailing boat; ~**lejar** *vi* sail

velhaco /ve'ʎaku/ *a* crooked □ *m* crook

ve|lharia /veʎa'riɐ/ *f* old thing; ~**lhice** *f* old age; ~**lho** /ɛ/ *a* old □ *m* old man; ~**lhote** /ɔ/ *m* old man

velocidade /velosi'dadʒi/ *f* speed;

(*Port: marcha*) gear; **a toda** ~ at full speed; ~ **máxima** speed limit

velocímetro /velo'simetru/ *m* speedometer

velocista /velo'sista/ *m/f* sprinter

velório /ve'lɔriu/ *m* wake

veloz /ve'los/ *a* fast

veludo /ve'ludu/ *m* velvet; ~ **cotelê** corduroy

ven|cedor /vẽse'dor/ *a* winning □ *m* winner; ~**cer** *vt* win over <*adversário etc*>; win <*partida, corrida, batalha*> □ *vi* (*triunfar*) win; <*prestação, aluguel, dívida*> fall due; <*contrato, passaporte, prazo*> expire; <*apólice*> mature; ~**cido** *a* **dar-se por** ~**cido** give in; ~**cimento** *m* (*de dívida, aluguel*) due date; (*de contrato, prazo*) expiry date; (*de alimento, remédio etc*) best before date; (*salário*) payment; *pl* earnings

venda¹ /'vẽda/ *f* sale; (*loja*) general store; **à** ~ on sale; **pôr à** ~ put up for sale

ven|da² /'vẽda/ *f* blindfold; ~**dar** *vt* blindfold

venda|val /vẽda'vaw/ (*pl* ~**vais**) *m* gale, storm

ven|dável /vẽ'davew/ (*pl* ~**dáveis**) *a* saleable; ~**dedor** *m* (*de loja*) shop assistant; (*em geral*) seller; ~**der** *vt/i* sell; **estar** ~**dendo saúde** be bursting with health

vendeta /vẽ'deta/ *f* vendetta

veneno /ve'nenu/ *m* poison; (*de cobra etc, malignidade*) venom; ~**so** /o/ *a* poisonous; (*maldoso*) venomous

vene|ração /venera'sãw/ *f* reverence; (*de Deus etc*) worship; ~**rar** *vt* revere; worship <*Deus etc*>

vené|reo /ve'nɛriu/ *a* **doença** ~**rea** venereal disease

Veneza /ve'neza/ *f* Venice

veneziana /venezi'anɐ/ *f* shutter

Venezuela /venezu'ɛla/ *f* Venezuela

venezuelano /venezue'lanu/ *a* & *m* Venezuelan

venta /'vẽta/ *f* nostril

ven|tania /vẽta'niɐ/ *f* gale; ~**tar** *vi* be windy; ~**tarola** /ɔ/ *f* fan

venti|lação /vẽtʃila'sãw/ *f* ventilation; ~**lador** *m* fan; ~**lar** *vt* ventilate; air <*sala, roupa*>

ven|to /'vẽtu/ *m* wind; **de** ~**to em popa** smoothly; ~**toinha** *f* (*cata-vento*) weather vane; (*Port: ventilador*) fan; ~**tosa** /ɔ/ *f* sucker; ~**toso** /o/ *a* windy

ven|tre /'vẽtri/ *m* belly; ~**tríloquo** *m* ventriloquist

Vênus /'venus/ *f* Venus

ver /ver/ *vt* see; watch <*televisão*>; (*resolver*) see to □ *vi* see □ *m* **a meu** ~ in my view; ~**-se** *vpr* (*no espelho* *etc*) see o.s.; (*em estado, condição*) find o.s.; (*um ao outro*) see each other; **ter a ~ com** have to do with; **vai ~ que ela não sabe** (*fam*) I bet she doesn't know; **vê se você não volta tarde** see you don't get back late; **viu?** (*fam*) right?

veracidade /verasi'dadʒi/ *f* truthfulness

vera|near /verani'ar/ *vi* spend the summer; **~neio** *m* summer holiday, (*Amer*) summer vacation; **~nista** *m/f* holidaymaker, (*Amer*) vacationer

verão /ve'rãw/ *m* summer

veraz /ve'ras/ *a* truthful

verbas /'vɛrbas/ *f pl* funds

ver|bal /ver'baw/ (*pl* **~bais**) *a* verbal; **~bete** /e/ *m* entry; **~bo** *m* verb; **~borragia** *f* waffle; **~boso** /o/ *a* verbose

verda|de /ver'dadʒi/ *f* truth; **de ~de** <*coisa*> real; <*fazer*> really; **na ~de** actually; **para falar a ~de** to tell the truth; **~deiro** *a* <*declaração, pessoa*> truthful; (*real*) true

verde /'verdʒi/ *a & m* green; **jogar ~ para colher maduro** fish for information; **~abacate** *a invar* avocado; **~amarelo** *a* yellow and green; (*brasileiro*) Brazilian; (*nacionalista*) nationalistic; **~esmeralda** *a invar* emerald green; **~jar** *vi* turn green

verdu|ra /ver'dura/ *f* (*para comer*) greens; (*da natureza*) greenery; **~reiro** *m* greengrocer, (*Amer*) produce dealer

vereador /veria'dor/ *m* councillor

vereda /ve'reda/ *f* path

veredito /vere'dʒitu/ *m* verdict

vergar /ver'gar/ *vt/i* bend

vergo|nha /ver'goɲa/ *f* (*pudor*) shame; (*constrangimento*) embarrassment; (*timidez*) shyness; (*uma*) disgrace; **ter ~nha** be ashamed; be embarrassed; be shy; **cria** *ou* **tome ~nha na cara!** you should be ashamed of yourself!; **~nhoso** *a* shameful

verídico /ve'ridʒiku/ *a* true

verificar /verifi'kar/ *vt* check, verify <*fatos, dados etc*>; **~ que** ascertain that; **~ se** check that; **~-se** *vpr* <*previsão etc*> come true; <*acidente etc*> happen

verme /'vɛrmi/ *m* worm

verme|lhidão /vermeʎi'dãw/ *f* redness; **~lho** /e/ *a & m* red; **no ~lho** (*endividado*) in the red

vernáculo /ver'nakulu/ *a & m* vernacular

verniz /ver'nis/ *f* varnish; (*couro*) patent leather

veros|símil /vero'simiw/ (*pl*

~símeis) *a* plausible; **~similhança** *f* plausibility

verruga /ve'xuga/ *f* wart

ver|sado /ver'sadu/ *a* well-versed (**em** in); **~são** *f* version; **~sar** *vi* **~sar sobre** concern; **~sátil** (*pl* **~sáteis**) *a* versatile; **~satilidade** *f* versatility; **~sículo** *m* (*da Bíblia*) verse; **~so¹** /ɛ/ *m* verse

verso² /ɛ/ *m* (*de página*) reverse, other side; **vide ~** see over

vértebra /'vɛrtebra/ *f* vertebra

verte|brado /verte'bradu/ *a & m* vertebrate; **~bral** (*pl* **~brais**) *a* spinal

ver|tente /ver'tẽtʃi/ *f* slope; **~ter** *vt* (*derramar*) pour; shed <*lágrimas, sangue*>; (*traduzir*) render (**para into**)

verti|cal /vertʃi'kaw/ (*pl* **~cais**) *a & f* vertical; **~gem** *f* dizziness; **~ginoso** /o/ *a* dizzy

vesgo /'vezgu/ *a* cross-eyed

vesícula /ve'zikula/ *f* gall bladder

vespa /'vespa/ *f* wasp

véspera /'vɛspera/ *f* **a ~** the day before; **a ~ de** the eve of; **a ~ de Natal** Christmas Eve; **nas ~s de** on the eve of

vespertino /vesper'tʃinu/ *a* evening

ves|te /'vestʃi/ *f* robe; **~tiário** *m* (*para se trocar*) changing room; (*para guardar roupa*) cloakroom

vestibular /vestʃibu'lar/ *m* university entrance exam

vestíbulo /ves'tʃibulu/ *m* hall(way); (*do teatro*) foyer

vestido /ves'tʃidu/ *m* dress □ *a* dressed (**de** in)

vestígio /ves'tʃiʒiu/ *m* trace

ves|timenta /vestʃi'mẽta/ *f* (*de sacerdote*) vestments; **~tir** *vt* (*pôr*) put on; (*usar*) wear; (*pôr roupa em*) dress; (*dar roupa a*) clothe; **~tir-se** *vpr* dress; **~tir-se de branco/de padre** dress in white/as a priest; **~tuário** *m* clothing

vetar /ve'tar/ *vt* veto

veterano /vete'ranu/ *a & m* veteran

veterinário /veteri'nariu/ *a* veterinary □ *m* vet

veto /'vɛtu/ *m* veto

véu /vɛw/ *m* veil

vexa|me /ve'ʃami/ *m* disgrace; **dar um ~me** make a fool of o.s.; **~minoso** /o/ *a* disgraceful

vexar /ve'ʃar/ *vt* shame; **~-se** *vpr* be ashamed (**de** of)

vez /ves/ *f* (*ocasião*) time; (*turno*) turn; **às ~es** sometimes; **cada ~ mais** more and more; **de ~** for good; **desta ~** this time; **de ~ em quando** now and again, from time to time; **de uma ~** (*ao mesmo tempo*) at once; (*de um* *golpe*) in one go; **de uma ~ por todas** once and for all; **duas ~es** twice; **em ~ de** instead of; **fazer as ~es de** take the place of; **mais uma ~, outra ~** again; **muitas ~es** (*com muita freqüência*) often; (*repetidamente*) many times; **raras ~es** seldom; **repetidas ~es** repeatedly; **uma ~** once; **uma ~ que** since

via /'via/ *f* (*estrada*) road; (*rumo, meio*) way; (*exemplar*) copy; *pl* (*trâmites*) channels □ *prep* via; **em ~s de** on the point of; **por ~ aérea/marítima** by air/sea; **por ~ das dúvidas** just in case; **por ~ de regra** as a rule; **Via Láctea** Milky Way

viabili|dade /viabili'dadʒi/ *f* feasibility; **~zar** *vt* make feasible

viação /via'sãw/ *f* (*transporte*) road transport; (*estradas*) road network; (*companhia*) bus company

viaduto /via'dutu/ *m* viaduct; (*rodoviário*) flyover, (*Amer*) overpass

via|gem /vi'aʒẽ/ *f* (*uma*) trip, journey; (*em geral*) travelling; *pl* (*de uma pessoa*) travels; (*em geral*) travel; **boa ~gem!** have a good trip!; **~gem de negócios** business trip; **~jado** *a* well-travelled; **~jante** *a* travelling □ *m/f* traveller; **~jar** *vi* travel; **estar ~jando** (*fam*) (*com o pensamento longe*) be miles away

viário /vi'ariu/ *a* road; **anel ~** ring road

viatura /via'tura/ *f* vehicle

viá|vel /vi'avew/ (*pl* ~veis) *a* feasible

víbora /'vibora/ *f* viper

vi|bração /vibra'sãw/ *f* vibration; (*fig*) thrill; **~brante** *a* vibrant; **~brar** *vt* shake □ *vi* vibrate; (*fig*) be thrilled (**com** by)

vice /'visi/ *m/f* deputy

vice-cam|peão /visikãpi'ãw/ *m* (*f* ~peã) runner-up

vicejar /vise'ʒar/ *vi* flourish

vice-presiden|te /visiprezi'dẽtʃi/ *m* (*f* ~ta) vice-president

vice-rei /visi'xej/ *m* viceroy

vice-versa /visi'vɛrsa/ *adv* vice-versa

vici|ado /visi'adu/ *a* addicted (**em** to) □ *m* addict; **um ~ado em drogas** a drug addict; **~ar** *vt* (*falsificar*) tamper with; (*estragar*) ruin □ *vi* <*droga*> be addictive; **~ar-se** *vpr* get addicted (**em** to)

vício /'visiu/ *m* vice

vicioso /visi'ozu/ *a* **círculo ~** vicious circle

vicissitudes /visisi'tudʒis/ *f pl* ups and downs

viço /'visu/ *m* (*de plantas*) exuberance; (*de pessoa, pele*) freshness; **~so** /o/ *a* <*planta*> lush; <*pele, pessoa*> fresh

vida /'vida/ *f* life; **sem ~** lifeless; **dar ~ a** liven up

videira /vi'dera/ *f* vine

vidente /vi'dẽtʃi/ *m/f* clairvoyant

vídeo /'vidʒiu/ *m* video; (*tela*) screen

vídeo|cassete /vidʒiuka'sɛtʃi/ *m* (*fita*) video tape; (*aparelho*) video, (*Amer*) VCR; **~clipe** *m* video; **~clube** *m* video club; **~game** *m* videogame; **~teipe** *m* video tape

vidra|ça /vi'drasa/ *f* window pane; **~çaria** *f* (*fábrica*) glassworks; (*vidraças*) glazing; **~ceiro** *m* glazier

vi|drado /vi'dradu/ *a* glazed; **estar ~drado em** *ou* **por** (*fam*) love; **~drar** *vt* glaze □ *vi* (*fam*) fall in love (**em** *ou* **por** with); **~dro** *m* (*material*) glass; (*pote*) jar; (*janela*) window; **~dro fumê** tinted glass

viela /vi'ɛla/ *f* alley

Viena /vi'ɛna/ *f* Vienna

Vietnã /vietʃi'nã/ *m*, (*Port*) **Vietname** /viet'nam/ *m* Vietnam

vietnamita /vietna'mita/ *a & m/f* Vietnamese

viga /'viga/ *f* joist

vigarice /viga'risi/ *f* swindle

vigário /vi'gariu/ *m* vicar

vigarista /viga'rista/ *m/f* swindler, con artist

vi|gência /vi'ʒẽsia/ *f* (*qualidade*) force; (*tempo*) period in force; **~gente** *a* in force

vigésimo /vi'ʒɛzimu/ *a* twentieth

vigi|a /vi'ʒia/ *f* (*guarda*) watch; (*em navio*) porthole □ *m* night watchman; **~ar** *vt* (*observar*) watch; (*cuidar de*) watch over; (*como sentinela*) guard □ *vi* keep watch

vigi|lância /viʒi'lãsia/ *f* vigilance; **~lante** *a* vigilant

vigília /vi'ʒilia/ *f* vigil

vigor /vi'gor/ *m* vigour; **em ~** in force

vigo|rar /vigo'rar/ *vi* be in force; **~roso** *a* vigorous

vil /viw/ (*pl* vis) *a* base, despicable

vila /'vila/ *f* (*cidadezinha*) small town; (*casa elegante*) villa; (*conjunto de casas*) housing estate; **~ olímpica** Olympic village

vi|lania /vila'nia/ *f* villainy; **~lão** *m* (*f* ~lã) villain

vilarejo /vila'reʒu/ *m* village

vilipendiar /vilipẽdʒi'ar/ *vt* disparage

vime /'vimi/ *m* wicker

vina|gre /vi'nagri/ *m* vinegar; **~grete** /ɛ/ *m* vinaigrette

vin|car /vĩ'kar/ *vt* crease; line <*rosto*>; **~co** *m* crease; (*no rosto*) line

vincular /vĩku'lar/ *vt* bond, tie

vínculo /'vĩkulu/ *m* link, bond; **~ empregatício** contract of employment

vinda /'vĩda/ f coming; **dar as boas ~s** a welcome

vindicar /vĩdʒi'kar/ vt vindicate

vindima /vĩ'dʒima/ f vintage

vin|do /'vĩdu/ pp e pres de **vir**; **~douro** a coming

vin|gança /vĩ'gãsa/ f vengeance, revenge; **~gar** vt revenge □ vi <flores> thrive; <criança> survive; <plano, empreendimento> be successful; **~gar-se** vpr take one's revenge (**de** for; **em** on); **~gativo** a vindictive

vinha /'viɲa/ f vineyard

vinhedo /vi'ɲedu/ m vineyard

vinheta /vi'ɲeta/ f (na TV etc) sequence

vinho /'viɲu/ m wine □ a invar maroon; **~ do Porto** port

vinícola /vi'nikola/ a wine-growing

vinicul|tor /vinikuw'tor/ m wine grower; **~tura** f wine growing

vinil /vi'niw/ m vinyl

vinte /'vĩtʃi/ a & m twenty; **~na** /e/ f score

viola /vi'ɔla/ f viola

violação /viola'sãw/ f violation

violão /vio'lãw/ m guitar

violar /vio'lar/ vt violate

vio|lência /vio'lẽsia/ f violence; (uma) act of violence; **~lentar** vt rape <mulher>; **~lento** a violent

violeta /vio'leta/ f violet □ a invar violet

violi|nista /violi'nista/ m/f violinist; **~no m** violin

violonce|lista /violõse'lista/ m/f cellist; **~lo** /ɛ/ m cello

vir /vir/ vi come; **o ano que vem** next year; **venho lendo os jornais** I have been reading the papers; **vem cá** come here; (fam) listen; **isso não vem ao caso** that's irrelevant; **~ a ser** turn out to be; **~ com** give <argumento etc>

virabrequim /virabre'kĩ/ m crankshaft

viração /vira'sãw/ f breeze

vira-casaca /viraka'zaka/ m/f turncoat

vira|da /vi'rada/ f turn; **~do** a <roupa> inside out; (de cabeça para baixo) upside down; **~do para** facing

vira-lata /vira'lata/ m mongrel

virar /vi'rar/ vt turn; turn over <disco, barco etc>; turn inside out <roupa>; turn out <bolsos>; tip <balde, água etc> □ vi turn; <barco> turn over; (tornar-se) become; **~-se** vpr turn round; (na vida) get by, cope; **~-se para** turn to; **vira e mexe** every so often

viravolta /vira'vowta/ f about-turn

virgem /'virʒẽ/ a <fita> blank; <floresta, noiva etc> virgin □ f virgin; **Virgem** (signo) Virgo

virgindade /virʒĩ'dadʒi/ f virginity

vírgula /'virgula/ f comma; (decimal) point

vi|ril /vi'riw/ (pl **~ris**) a virile

virilha /vi'riʎa/ f groin

virilidade /virili'dadʒi/ f virility

virtu|al /virtu'aw/ (pl **~ais**) a virtual

virtude /vir'tudʒi/ f virtue

virtuo|sismo /virtuo'zizmu/ m virtuosity; **~so** /o/ a virtuous □ m virtuoso

virulento /viru'lẽtu/ a virulent

vírus /'virus/ m invar virus

visão /vi'zãw/ f vision; (aspecto, ponto de vista) view

visar /vi'zar/ vt aim at <caça, alvo>; **~ (a)** aim for <objetivo>; <medida, ação> be aimed at

vísceras /'viseras/ f pl innards

viscon|de /vis'kõdʒi/ m viscount; **~dessa** /e/ f viscountess

viscoso /vis'kozu/ a viscous

viseira /vi'zera/ f visor

visibilidade /vizibili'dadʒi/ f visibility

visionário /vizio'nariu/ a & m visionary

visi|ta /vi'zita/ f visit; (visitante) visitor; **fazer uma ~ta a alg** pay s.o. a visit; **~tante** a visiting □ m/f visitor; **~tar** vt visit

visí|vel /vi'zivew/ (pl **~veis**) a visible

vislum|brar /vizlũ'brar/ vt (entrever) glimpse; (imaginar) envisage; **~bre** m glimpse

visom /vi'zõ/ m mink

visor /vi'zor/ m viewfinder

vis|ta /'vista/ f sight; (dos olhos) eyesight; (panorama) view; **à ~ta** (visível) in view; (em dinheiro) in cash; **à primeira ~ta** at first sight; **pôr à ~ta** put on show; **de ~ta** <conhecer> by sight; **em ~ta de** in view of; **ter em ~ta** have in view; **dar na ~ta** attract attention; **fazer ~ta** look nice; **fazer ~ta grossa** turn a blind eye (**a** to); **perder de ~ta** lose sight of; **a perder de ~ta** as far as the eye can see; **uma ~ta de olhos** a quick look; **~to a** seen □ m visa; **pelo ~to** by the looks of things; **~to que** seeing that

visto|ria /visto'ria/ f inspection; **~riar** vt inspect

vistoso /vis'tozu/ a eye-catching

visu|al /vizu'aw/ (pl **~ais**) a visual □ m look; **~alizar** vt visualize

vi|tal /vi'taw/ (pl **~tais**) a vital; **~talício** a for life; **~talidade** f vitality

vita|mina /vita'mina/ *f* vitamin; (*bebida*) liquidized fruit drink; ~minado *a* with added vitamins; ~mínico *a* vitamin

vitela /vi'tɛla/ *f* (*carne*) veal

viticultura /vitʃikuw'tura/ *f* viticulture

vítima /'vitʃima/ *f* victim

viti|mar /vitʃi'mar/ *vt* (*matar*) claim the life of; ser ~mado por fall victim to

vitória /vi'tɔria/ *f* victory

vitorioso /vitori'ozu/ *a* victorious

vi|tral /vi'traw/ (*pl* ~trais) *m* stained glass window

vitrine /vi'trini/ *f* shop window

vitrola /vi'trɔla/ *f* jukebox

viú|va /vi'uva/ *f* widow; ~vo *a* widowed □ *m* widower

viva /'viva/ *f* cheer □ *int* hurray; ~ a rainha long live the queen

vivacidade /vivasi'dadʒi/ *f* vivacity

vivalma /vi'vawma/ *f* não há ~ lá fora there's not a soul outside

vivar /vi'var/ *vt/i* cheer

vivaz /vi'vas/ *a* lively, vivacious; <*planta*> hardy

viveiro /vi'veru/ *m* (*de plantas*) nursery; (*de peixes*) fishpond; (*de aves*) aviary; (*fig*) breeding ground

vivência /vi'vẽsia/ *f* experience

vívido /'vividu/ *a* vivid

viver /vi'ver/ *vt/i* live (**de** on) □ *m* life; ele vive reclamando he's always complaining

víveres /'viveris/ *m pl* provisions

vivissecção /vivisek'sãw/ *f* vivisection

vivo /'vivu/ *a* (*que vive*) living; (*animado*) lively; <*cor*> bright □ *m* os ~s the living; ao ~ live; estar ~ be alive; dinheiro ~ cash

vizi|nhança /vizi'ɲãsa/ *f* neighbourhood; ~nho *a* neighbouring □ *m* neighbour

vo|ador /voa'dor/ *a* flying; ~ar *vi* fly; (*explodir*) blow up; sair ~ando rush off

vocabulário /vokabu'lariu/ *m* vocabulary

vocábulo /vo'kabulu/ *m* word

voca|ção /voka'sãw/ *f* vocation; ~cional (*pl* ~cionais) *a* vocational; orientação ~cional careers guidance

vo|cal /vo'kaw/ (*pl* ~cais) *a* vocal

você /vo'se/ *pron* you; ~s *pron* you

vociferar /vosife'rar/ *vi* shout abuse

vodca /'vɔdʒka/ *f* vodka

voga /'vɔga/ *f* (*moda*) vogue

vo|gal /vo'gaw/ (*pl* ~gais) *f* vowel

volante /vo'lãtʃi/ *m* (*de carro*) steering wheel

volá|til /vo'latʃiw/ (*pl* ~teis) *a* volatile

vôlei /'volej/ *m*, voleibol /volej'bɔw/ *m* volleyball

volt /'vɔwtʃi/ (*pl* ~s) *m* volt

volta /'vɔwta/ *f* (*retorno*) return; (*da pista*) lap; (*resposta*) response; às ~s com tied up with; de ~ back; em ~ de around; na ~ on the way back; na ~ do correio by return of post; por ~ de around; dar a ~ ao mundo go round the world; dar a ~ por cima make a comeback; dar meia ~ turn round; dar uma ~ (*a pé*) go for a walk; (*de carro*) go for a drive; dar uma ~ em turn round; dar ~s spin round; ter ~ get a response; ~ e meia every so often; ~do *a* ~do para geared towards

voltagem /vow'taʒẽ/ *f* voltage

voltar /vow'tar/ *vi* go/come back, return □ *vt* rewind <*fita*>; ~se *vpr* turn round; ~se para/contra turn to/against; ~ a si come to; ~ a fazer do again; ~ atrás backtrack

volu|me /vo'lumi/ *m* volume; ~moso *a* sizeable; <*som*> loud

voluntário /volũ'tariu/ *a & m* volunteer

volúpia /vo'lupia/ *f* sensuality, lust

voluptuoso /voluptu'ozu/ *a* sensual; <*mulher*> voluptuous

volú|vel /vo'luvew/ (*pl* ~veis) *a* fickle

vomitar /vomi'tar/ *vt/i* vomit

vômito /'vomitu/ *m* vomit; *pl* vomiting

vontade /võ'tadʒi/ *f* will; à ~ (*bem*) at ease; (*quanto quiser*) as much as one likes; fique à ~ make yourself at home; tem comida à ~ there's plenty of food; estar com ~ de feel like; isso me dá ~ de chorar it makes me feel like crying; fazer a ~ de alg do what s.o. wants

vôo /'vou/ *m* flight; levantar ~ take off; ~ livre hang-gliding

voraz /vo'ras/ *a* voracious

vos /vus/ *pron* you; (*a vocês*) to you

vós /vɔs/ *pron* you

vosso /'vɔsu/ *a* your □ *pron* yours

vo|tação /vota'sãw/ *f* vote; ~tante *m/f* voter; ~tar *vt* vote on <*lei etc*>; (*dedicar*) devote; (*prometer*) vow □ *vi* vote (em for)

voto /'vɔtu/ *m* (*em votação*) vote; (*promessa*) vow; *pl* (*desejos*) wishes

vo|vó /vo'vɔ/ *f* grandma; ~vô *m* grandpa

voz /vɔs/ *f* voice; dar ~ de prisão a alg place s.o. under arrest

vozeirão /voze'rãw/ *m* loud voice

vozerio /voze'riu/ *m* shouting

vul|cânico /vuw'kaniku/ *a* volcanic; ~cão *m* volcano

vul|gar /vuw'gar/ *a* ordinary; (*baixo*) vulgar; **~garizar** *vt* popularize; (*tornar baixo*) vulgarize; **~go** *adv* commonly known as

vulne|rabilidade /vuwnerabili'dadʒi/ *f* vulnerability; **~rável** (*pl* **~ráveis**) *a* vulnerable

vul|to /'vuwtu/ *m* (*figura*) figure; (*tamanho*) bulk; (*importância*) importance; **de ~to** important; **~toso** /o/ *a* bulky; (*importante*) important

W

walkie-talkie /uɔki'tɔki/ (*pl* **~s**) *m* walkie-talkie

walkman /uɔk'mɛn/ *m invar* walkman

watt /u'ɔtʃi/ (*pl* **~s**) *m* watt

windsur|fe /uĩ'surfi/ *m* windsurfing; **~fista** *m/f* windsurfer

X

xadrez /ʃa'dres/ *m* (*jogo*) chess; (*desenho*) check; (*fam: prisão*) prison □ *a invar* check

xale /'ʃali/ *m* shawl

xampu /ʃã'pu/ *m* shampoo

xará /ʃa'ra/ *m/f* namesake

xarope /ʃa'rɔpi/ *m* syrup

xaxim /ʃa'ʃĩ/ *m* plant fibre

xenofobia /ʃenofo'bia/ *f* xenophobia

xenófobo /ʃe'nɔfobu/ *a* xenophobic □ *m* xenophobe

xepa /'ʃepa/ *f* scraps

xeque¹ /'ʃɛki/ *m* (*árabe*) sheikh

xeque² /'ʃɛki/ *m* (*no xadrez*) check; **~-mate** *m* checkmate

xere|ta /ʃe'reta/ (*fam*) *a* nosy □ *m/f* nosy parker; **~tar** (*fam*) *vi* nose around

xerez /ʃe'res/ *m* sherry

xerife /ʃe'rifi/ *m* sheriff

xerocar /ʃero'kar/ *vt* photocopy

xerox /ʃe'rɔks/ *m invar* photocopy

xexelento /ʃeʃe'lẽtu/ (*fam*) *a* scruffy □ *m* scruff

xícara /'ʃikara/ *f* cup

xiita /ʃi'ita/ *a* & *m/f* Shiite

xilofone /ʃilo'foni/ *m* xylophone

xingar /ʃĩ'gar/ *vt* swear at □ *vi* swear

xis /ʃis/ *m invar* letter X; **o ~ do problema** the crux of the problem

xixi /ʃi'ʃi/ (*fam*) *m* wee; **fazer ~** do a wee

xô /ʃo/ *int* shoo

xucro /'ʃukru/ *a* ignorant

Z

zagueiro /za'geru/ *m* fullback

Zaire /'zajri/ *m* Zaire

Zâmbia /'zãbia/ *f* Zambia

zan|gado /zã'gadu/ *a* cross, annoyed; **~gar** *vt* annoy; **~garse** *vpr* get cross, get annoyed (**com** with)

zanzar /zã'zar/ *vi* wander

zarpar /zar'par/ *vi* set off; (*de navio*) set sail

zebra /'zebra/ *f* zebra; (*pessoa*) fool; (*resultado*) upset

ze|lador /zela'dor/ *m* caretaker; (*Amer*) janitor; **~lar** *vt* **~lar (por)** take care of; **~lo** /e/ *m* zeal; **~lo por** devotion to; **~loso** /o/ *a* zealous

zero /'zɛru/ *m* zero; (*em escores*) nil; **~-quilômetro** *a invar* brand new

ziguezague /zigi'zagi/ *m* zigzag; **~ar** *vi* zigzag

Zimbábue /zĩ'babui/ *m* Zimbabwe

zinco /'zĩku/ *m* zinc

zíper /'ziper/ *m* zip, zipper

zodíaco /zo'dʒiaku/ *m* zodiac

zoeira /zo'era/ *f* din

zom|bador /zõba'dor/ *a* mocking; **~bar** *vi* **~bar (de)** mock; **~baria** *f* mockery

zona /'zona/ *f* (*área*) zone; (*de cidade*) district; (*desordem*) mess; (*tumulto*) commotion; (*bairro do meretrício*) red-light district

zonzo /'zõzu/ *a* dizzy

zôo /'zou/ *m* zoo

zoo|logia /zoolo'ʒia/ *f* zoology; **~lógico** *a* zoological

zoólogo /zo'ɔlogu/ *m* zoologist

zulu /zu'lu/ *a* & *m/f* Zulu

zum /zũ/ *m* zoom lens

zumbi /zũ'bi/ *m* zombie

zum|bido /zũ'bidu/ *m* buzz; (*no ouvido*) ringing; **~bir** *vi* buzz

zu|nido /zu'nidu/ *m* (*de vento, bala*) whistle; (*de inseto*) buzz; **~nir** *vi* <*vento, bala*> whistle; <*inseto*> buzz

zunzum /zũ'zũ/ *m* rumour

Zurique /zu'riki/ *f* Zurich

zurrar /zu'xar/ *vi* bray

ENGLISH-PORTUGUESE

INGLÊS-PORTUGUÊS

A

a /ə/; *emphatic* /eɪ/ (*before vowel* **an** /ən/; *emphatic* /æn/) *a* um. **two pounds a metre** duas libras o metro. **sixty miles an hour** sessenta milhas por hora, (P) à hora. **once a year** uma vez por ano

aback /ə'bæk/ *adv* **taken ~** desconcertado, (P) surpreendido

abandon /ə'bændən/ *vt* abandonar □ *n* abandono *m*. **~ed** *a* abandonado; (*behaviour*) livre, dissoluto. **~ment** *n* abandono *m*

abashed /ə'bæʃt/ *a* confuso, (P) atrapalhado

abate /ə'beɪt/ *vt/i* abater, abrandar, diminuir. **~ment** *n* abrandamento *m*, diminuição *f*

abattoir /'æbətwa:(r)/ *n* matadouro *m*

abbey /'æbɪ/ *n* abadia *f*, mosteiro *m*

abbreviat|e /ə'bri:vɪeɪt/ *vt* abreviar. **~ion** /-'eɪʃn/ *n* abreviação *f*; (*short form*) abreviatura *f*

abdicat|e /'æbdɪkeɪt/ *vt/i* abdicar. **~ion** /-'keɪʃn/ *n* abdicação *f*

abdom|en /'æbdəmən/ *n* abdômen *m*, (P) abdómen *m*. **~inal** /-'dɒmɪnl/ *a* abdominal

abduct /æb'dʌkt/ *vt* raptar. **~ion** /-ʃn/ *n* rapto *m*. **~or** *n* raptor, -a *mf*

aberration /æbə'reɪʃn/ *n* aberração *f*

abet /ə'bet/ *vt* (*pt* abetted) (*jur*) instigar; (*aid*) auxiliar

abeyance /ə'beɪəns/ *n* **in ~** (*matter*) em suspenso; (*custom*) em desuso

abhor /əb'hɔ:(r)/ *vt* (*pt* abhorred) abominar, ter horror a. **~rence** /-'hɒrəns/ *n* horror *m*. **~rent** /-'hɒrənt/ *a* abominável, execrável

abide /ə'baɪd/ *vt* (*pt* abided) suportar, tolerar. **~ by** (*promise*) manter; (*rules*) acatar

abiding /ə'baɪdɪŋ/ *a* eterno, perpétuo

ability /ə'bɪlətɪ/ *n* capacidade *f* (**to do** para *or* de fazer); (*cleverness*) habilidade *f*, esperteza *f*

abject /'æbdʒekt/ *a* abjeto, (P) abjecto

ablaze /ə'bleɪz/ *a* em chamas; (*fig*) aceso, (P) excitado

abl|e /'eɪbl/ *a* (**~er**, **~est**) capaz (**to** de). **be ~e to** (*have power, opportunity*) ser capaz de, poder; (*know how*

to) ser capaz de, saber. **~y** *adv* habilmente

ablutions /ə'blu:ʃnz/ *npl* ablução *f*, abluções *fpl*

abnormal /æb'nɔ:ml/ *a* anormal. **~ity** /-'mælətɪ/ *n* anormalidade *f*. **~ly** *adv* (*unusually*) excepcionalmente

aboard /ə'bɔ:d/ *adv* a bordo □ *prep* a bordo de

abode /ə'bəʊd/ *n* (*old use*) habitação *f*. **place of ~** domicílio *m*

aboli|sh /ə'bɒlɪʃ/ *vt* abolir, extinguir. **~tion** /æbə'lɪʃn/ *n* abolição *f*, extinção *f*

abominable /ə'bɒmɪnəbl/ *a* abominável, detestável

abominat|e /ə'bɒmɪneɪt/ *vt* abominar, detestar. **~ion** /-'neɪʃn/ *n* abominação *f*

abort /ə'bɔ:t/ *vt/i* (fazer) abortar. **~ive** *a* (*attempt etc*) abortado, malogrado

abortion /ə'bɔ:ʃn/ *n* aborto *m*. **have an ~** fazer um aborto, ter um aborto. **~ist** *n* abortad/or, -eira *mf*

abound /ə'baʊnd/ *vi* abundar (**in** em)

about /ə'baʊt/ *adv* (*approximately*) aproximadamente, cerca de; (*here and there*) aqui e ali; (*all round*) por todos os lados, em roda, em volta; (*in existence*) por aí □ *prep* acerca de, sobre; (*round*) em torno de; (*somewhere in*) em, por. **~-face**, **~-turn** *ns* reviravolta *f*. **~ here** por aqui. **be ~ to** estar prestes a. **he was ~ to eat** ia comer. **how** *or* **what ~ leaving?** e se nós fôssemos embora? **know/talk ~** saber/falar sobre

above /ə'bʌv/ *adv* acima, por cima □ *prep* sobre. **he's not ~ lying** ele não é de mentir. **~ all** sobretudo. **~-board** *a* franco, honesto □ *adv* com lisura. **~-mentioned** *a* acima, supracitado

abrasion /ə'breɪʒn/ *n* atrito *m*; (*injury*) escoriação *f*, esfoladura *f*

abrasive /ə'breɪsɪv/ *a* abrasivo; (*fig*) agressivo □ *n* abrasivo *m*

abreast /ə'brest/ *adv* lado a lado. **keep ~ of** manter-se a par de

abridge /ə'brɪdʒ/ *vt* abreviar. **~ment**

n abreviação *f*, abreviatura *f*, redução *f*; (*abridged text*) resumo *m*

abroad /əˈbrɔːd/ *adv* no estrangeiro; (*far and wide*) por todo o lado. **go ~** ir para o estrangeiro

abrupt /əˈbrʌpt/ *a* (*sudden, curt*) brusco; (*steep*) abrupto. **~ly** *adv* (*suddenly*) bruscamente; (*curtly*) com brusquidão. **~ness** *n* brusquidão *f*, (*steepness*) declive *m*

abscess /ˈæbsɪs/ *n* abscesso *m*, (P) abcesso *m*

abscond /əbˈskɒnd/ *vi* evadir-se, andar fugido

absen|t[1] /ˈæbsənt/ *a* ausente; (*look etc*) distraído. **~ce** *n* ausência *f*; (*lack*) falta *f*. **~t-minded** *a* distraído. **~t-mindedness** *n* distracção *f*, (P) distracção *f*

absent[2] /əbˈsent/ *v refl* **~ o.s.** ausentar-se

absentee /æbsənˈtiː/ *n* ausente *mf*, (P) absentista *mf*. **~ism** *n* absenteísmo *m*, (P) absentismo *m*

absolute /ˈæbsəluːt/ *a* absoluto; (*colloq: coward etc*) autêntico, (P) verdadeiro. **~ly** *adv* absolutamente

absolution /æbsəˈluːʃn/ *n* absolvição *f*

absolve /əbˈzɒlv/ *vt* (*from sin*) absolver (**from** de); (*from vow*) desligar (**from** de)

absor|b /əbˈsɔːb/ *vt* absorver. **~ption** *n* absorção *f*

absorbent /əbˈsɔːbənt/ *a* absorvente. **~ cotton** (*Amer*) algodão hidrófilo *m*

abst|ain /əbˈsteɪn/ *vi* abster-se (**from** de). **~ention** /-ˈstenʃn/ *n* abstenção *f*

abstemious /əbˈstiːmɪəs/ *a* abstêmio, (P) abstémio, sóbrio

abstinen|ce /ˈæbstɪməns/ *n* abstinência *f*. **~t** *a* abstinente

abstract[1] /ˈæbstrækt/ *a* abstrato, (P) abstracto

abstract[2] /əbˈstrækt/ *vt* (*take out*) extrair; (*separate*) abstrair. **~ed** *a* distraído. **~ion** /-ʃn/ *n* (*of mind*) distração *f*, (P) distracção *f*; (*idea*) abstração *f*, (P) abstracção *f*

absurd /əbˈsɜːd/ *a* absurdo. **~ity** *n* absurdo *m*

abundan|t /əˈbʌndənt/ *a* abundante. **~ce** *n* abundância *f*

abuse[1] /əˈbjuːz/ *vt* (*misuse*) abusar de; (*ill-treat*) maltratar; (*insult*) injuriar, insultar

abus|e[2] /əˈbjuːs/ *n* (*wrong use*) abuso *m* (**of** de); (*insults*) insultos *m* pl. **~ive** *a* injurioso, ofensivo

abysmal /əˈbɪzməl/ *a* abismal; (*colloq: bad*) abissal

abyss /əˈbɪs/ *n* abismo *m*

academic /ækəˈdemɪk/ *a* acadêmico, (P) académico, universitário; (*scholarly*) intelectual; (*pej*) acadêmico, (P) teórico □ *n* universitário

academy /əˈkædəmɪ/ *n* academia *f*

accede /əkˈsiːd/ *vi* **~ to** (*request*) aceder a; (*post*) assumir; (*throne*) ascender a, subir a

accelerat|e /əkˈseləreɪt/ *vt* acelerar □ *vi* acelerar-se; (*auto*) acelerar. **~ion** /-ˈreɪʃn/ *n* aceleração *f*

accelerator /əkˈseləreɪtə(r)/ *n* (*auto*) acelerador *m*

accent[1] /ˈæksənt/ *n* acento *m*; (*local pronunciation*) sotaque *m*

accent[2] /ækˈsent/ *vt* acentuar

accentuate /ækˈsentʃʊeɪt/ *vt* acentuar

accept /əkˈsept/ *vt* aceitar. **~able** *a* aceitável. **~ance** *n* aceitação *f*; (*approval*) aprovação *f*

access /ˈækses/ *n* acesso *m* (**to** a). **~ible** /əkˈsesəbl/ *a* acessível

accessory /əkˈsesərɪ/ *a* acessório □ *n* acessório *m*; (*jur: person*) cúmplice *m*

accident /ˈæksɪdənt/ *n* acidente *m*, desastre *m*; (*chance*) acaso *m*. **~al** /-ˈdentl/ *a* acidental, fortuito. **~ally** /-ˈdentəlɪ/ *adv* acidentalmente, por acaso

acclaim /əˈkleɪm/ *vt* aclamar □ *n* aplauso *m*, aclamações *fpl*

acclimatiz|e /əˈklaɪmətaɪz/ *vt/i* aclimatar(-se). **~ation** /-ˈzeɪʃn/ *n* aclimatação *f*

accommodat|e /əˈkɒmədeɪt/ *vt* acomodar; (*lodge*) alojar; (*adapt*) adaptar; (*supply*) fornecer; (*oblige*) fazer a vontade de. **~ing** *a* obsequioso, amigo de fazer vontades. **~ion** /-ˈdeɪʃn/ *n* acomodação *f*; (*rooms*) alojamento *m*, quarto *m*

accompan|y /əˈkʌmpənɪ/ *vt* acompanhar. **~iment** *n* acompanhamento *m*. **~ist** *n* (*mus*) acompanhad/or, (B) -eira *a*

accomplice /əˈkʌmplɪs/ *n* cúmplice *mf*

accomplish /əˈkʌmplɪʃ/ *vt* (*perform*) executar, realizar; (*achieve*) realizar, conseguir fazer. **~ed** *a* acabado. **~ment** *n* realização *f*; (*ability*) talento *m*, dote *m*

accord /əˈkɔːd/ *vi* concordar □ *vt* conceder □ *n* acordo *m*. **of one's own ~** por vontade própria, espontaneamente. **~ance** *n* **in ~ance with** em conformidade com, de acordo com

according /əˈkɔːdɪŋ/ *adv* **~ to** conforme. **~ly** *adv* (*therefore*) por conseguinte, por consequência; (*appropriately*) conformemente

accordion /əˈkɔːdɪən/ *n* acordeão *m*

accost /əˈkɒst/ *vt* abordar, abeirar-se de

account /əˈkaʊnt/ *n* (*comm*) conta *f*; (*description*) relato *m*; (*importance*)

importância *f* □ *vt* considerar. ~ **for**
dar contas de, explicar. **on** ~ **of** por
causa de. **on no** ~ em caso algum.
take into ~ ter *or* levar em conta.
~**able** /-əbl/ *a* responsável (**for** por).
~**ability** /-ə'bɪlətɪ/ *n* responsabilidade *f*

accountant /ə'kaʊntənt/ *n* conta-
dor(a) *m/f*, (P) contabilista *mf*

accrue /ə'kru:/ *vi* acumular-se. ~ **to**
reverter em favor de

accumulat|e /ə'kju:mjʊleɪt/ *vt/i* acu-
mular(-se). ~**ion** /-'leɪʃn/ *n* acumulação *f*, acréscimo *m*

accumulator /ə'kju:mjʊleɪtə(r)/ *n*
(*electr*) acumulador *m*

accura|te /'ækjərət/ *a* exato, (P) exac-
to, preciso. ~**cy** *n* exatidão *f*, (P)
exactidão *f*, precisão *f*. ~**tely** *adv*
com exatidão, (P) exactidão

accus|e /ə'kju:z/ *vt* acusar. **the** ~**ed** o
acusado. ~**ation** /ækju:'zeɪʃn/ *n*
acusação *f*

accustom /ə'kʌstəm/ *vt* acostumar,
habituar. ~**ed** *a* acostumado, habituado. **get** ~**ed to** acostumar-se a,
habituar-se a

ace /eɪs/ *n* ás *m*

ache /eɪk/ *n* dor *f* □ *vi* doer. **my leg** ~**s**
dói-me a perna, tenho dores na perna

achieve /ə'tʃi:v/ *vt* realizar, efetuar;
(*success*) alcançar. ~**ment** *n* realização *f*; (*feat*) feito *m*, façanha *f*,
sucesso *m*

acid /'æsɪd/ *a* ácido; (*wine*) azedo;
(*words*) áspero □ *n* ácido *m*. ~**ity**
/ə'sɪdətɪ/ *n* acidez *f*

acknowledge /ək'nɒlɪdʒ/ *vt* reconhecer. ~ (**receipt of**) acusar a recepção de. ~**ment** *n* reconhecimento *m*; (*letter etc*) acusação *f* de recebi-
mento, (P) aviso *m* de recepção

acne /'ækni/ *n* acne *f*

acorn /'eɪkɔːn/ *n* bolota *f*, glande *f*

acoustic /ə'ku:stɪk/ *a* acústico. ~**s**
npl acústica *f*

acquaint /ə'kweɪnt/ *vt* ~ **s.o. with**
sth pôr alg a par de alg coisa. **be**
~**ed with** (*person, fact*) conhecer.
~**ance** *n* (*knowledge, person*) conhecimento *m*; (*person*) conhecido *m*

acquiesce /ækwɪ'es/ *vi* consentir.
~**nce** /ækwɪ'esns/ *n* aquiescência *f*,
consentimento *m*

acqui|re /ə'kwaɪə(r)/ *vt* adquirir.
~**sition** /ækwɪ'zɪʃn/ *n* aquisição *f*

acquit /ə'kwɪt/ *vt* (*pt* **acquitted**)
absolver. ~ **o.s. well** sair-se bem.
~**tal** *n* absolvição *f*

acrid /'ækrɪd/ *a* acre

acrimon|ious /ækrɪ'məʊnɪəs/ *a*
acrimonioso. ~**y** /'ækrɪmənɪ/ *n* acrimónia *f*, (P) acrimónia *f*

acrobat /'ækrəbæt/ *n* acrobata *mf*.
~**ic** /-'bætɪk/ *a* acrobático. ~**ics**
/-'bætɪks/ *npl* acrobacia *f*

acronym /'ækrənɪm/ *n* sigla *f*

across /ə'krɒs/ *adv & prep* (*side to
side*) de lado a lado (de), de um lado
para o outro (de); (*on the other side*)
do outro lado (de); (*crosswise*) através
(de), de través. **go** *or* **walk** ~
atravessar. **swim** ~ atravessar a
nado

act /ækt/ *n* (*deed, theatr*) ato *m*, (P)
acto *m*; (*in variety show*) número *m*;
(*decree*) lei *f* □ *vi* agir, atuar, (P) actuar; (*theatr*) representar; (*function*)
funcionar; (*pretend*) fingir □ *vt* (*part,
role*) desempenhar. ~ **as** servir de.
~**ing** *a* interino □ *n* (*theatr*) desempenho *m*

action /'ækʃn/ *n* ação *f*, (P) acção *f*;
(*mil*) combate *m*. **out of** ~ fora de
combate; (*techn*) avariado. **take** ~
agir, atuar, (P) actuar

activ|e /'æktɪv/ *a* ativo, (P) activo; (*in-
terest*) vivo; (*volcano*) em atividade,
(P) actividade. ~**ity** /-'tɪvətɪ/ *n* atividade *f*, (P) actividade *f*

ac|tor /'æktə(r)/ *n* ator *m*, (P) actor *m*.
~**tress** *n* atriz *f*, (P) actriz *f*

actual /'æktʃʊəl/ *a* real, verdadeiro;
(*example*) concreto. **the** ~ **pen which**
a própria caneta que. ~**ity** /-'ælətɪ/ *n*
realidade *f*. ~**ly** *adv* (*in fact*) na realidade

acumen /ə'kju:men/ *n* agudeza *f*,
perspicácia *f*

acupunctur|e /'ækjʊpʌŋktʃə(r)/ *n*
acupuntura *f*, (P) acupunctura *f*.
~**ist** *n* acupunturador *m*, (P) acu-
puncturista *mf*

acute /ə'kju:t/ *a* agudo; (*mind*) perspicaz; (*emotion*) intenso, vivo; (*shortage*) grande. ~**ly** *adv* vivamente.

ad /æd/ *n* (*colloq*) anúncio *m*

AD *abbr* dC

adamant /'ædəmənt/ *a* inflexível

adapt /ə'dæpt/ *vt/i* adaptar(-se).
~**ation** /ædæp'teɪʃn/ *n* adaptação *f*.
~**or** (*electr*) *n* adaptador *m*

adaptab|le /ə'dæptəbl/ *a* adaptável.
~**ility** /-'bɪlətɪ/ *n* adaptabilidade *f*

add /æd/ *vt/i* acrescentar. ~ (**up**)
somar. ~ **up to** (*total*) elevar-se a

adder /'ædə(r)/ *n* víbora *f*

addict /'ædɪkt/ *n* viciado *m*. **drug** ~
(*B*) viciado em droga, viciado da droga, (P) toxicodependente *m*

addict|ed /ə'dɪktɪd/ *a* **be** ~**ed to**
(*drink, drugs; fig*) ter o vício de.
~**ion** /-ʃn/ *n* (*med*) dependência *f*,
(*fig*) vício *m*. ~**ive** *a* que produz dependência

addition /ə'dɪʃn/ *n* adição *f*. **in** ~
além disso. **in** ~ **to** além de. ~**al**
/-ʃənl/ *a* adicional, suplementar

address /ə'dres/ n endereço m; (speech) discurso m □ vt endereçar; (speak to) dirigir-se a
adenoids /'ædmɔıdz/ npl adenóides mpl
adept /'ædept/ a & n especialista (mf), perito (m) (at em)
adequa|te /'ædıkwət/ a adequado; (satisfactory) satisfatório. ~cy n adequação f; (of person) competência f. ~tely adv adequadamente
adhere /əd'hıə(r)/ vi aderir (to a)
adhesive /əd'hi:sıv/ a & n adesivo (m). ~ plaster esparadrapo m, (P) adesivo m
adjacent /ə'dʒeısnt/ a adjacente, contíguo (to a)
adjective /'ædʒektıv/ n adjetivo m, (P) adjectivo m
adjoin /ə'dʒɔın/ vt confinar com, ficar contíguo a
adjourn /ə'dʒɜ:n/ vt adiar □ vi suspender a sessão. ~ to (go) passar a, ir para
adjudicate /ə'dʒu:dıkeıt/ vt/i julgar; (award) adjudicar
adjust /ə'dʒʌst/ vt/i (alter) ajustar, regular; (arrange) arranjar. ~ (o.s.) to adaptar-se a. ~able a regulável. ~ment n (techn) regulação f, afinação f; (of person) adaptação f
ad lib /æd'lıb/ vi (pt ad libbed) (colloq) improvisar □ adv à vontade
administer /əd'mınıstə(r)/ vt administrar
administrat|e /əd'mınıstreıt/ vt administrar, gerir. ~ion /-'streıʃn/ n administração f. ~or n administrador m
administrative /əd'mınıstrətıv/ a administrativo
admirable /'ædmərəbl/ a admirável
admiral /'ædmərəl/ n almirante m
admir|e /əd'maıə(r)/ vt admirar. ~ation /-mı'reıʃn/ n admiração f. ~er /-'maıərə(r)/ n admirador m
admission /əd'mıʃn/ n admissão f; (to museum, theatre, etc) ingresso m, (P) entrada f; (confession) confissão f
admit /əd'mıt/ vt (pt admitted) (let in) admitir, permitir a entrada a; (acknowledge) reconhecer, admitir. ~ to confessar. ~tance n admissão f
admoni|sh /əd'mɒnıʃ/ vt admoestar. ~tion /-ə'nıʃn/ n admoestação f
adolescen|t /ædə'lesnt/ a & n adolescente (mf). ~ce n adolescência f
adopt /ə'dɒpt/ vt adotar, (P) adoptar. ~ed child filho adotivo, (P) adoptivo. ~ion /-ʃn/ n adoção f, (P) adopção f
ador|e /ə'dɔ:(r)/ vt adorar. ~able a adorável. ~ation /ædə'reıʃn/ n adoração f
adorn /ə'dɔ:n/ vt adornar, enfeitar

adrenalin /ə'drenəlm/ n adrenalina f
adrift /ə'drıft/ a & adv à deriva
adult /'ædʌlt/ a & n adulto (m). ~hood n idade f adulta, (P) maioridade f
adulterat|e /ə'dʌltəreıt/ vt adulterar. ~ion /'reıʃn/ n adulteração f
adulter|y /ə'dʌltərı/ n adultério m. ~er, ~ess ns adúlter/o, -a mf. ~ous a adúltero
advance /əd'va:ns/ vt/i avançar □ n avanço m; (payment) adiantamento m □ a (payment, booking) adiantado. in ~ com antecedência. ~d a avançado. ~ment n promoção f, ascensão f
advantage /əd'va:ntıdʒ/ n vantagem f. take ~ of aproveitar-se de, tirar partido de; (person) explorar. ~ous /ædvən'teıdʒəs/ a vantajoso
adventur|e /əd'ventʃə(r)/ n aventura f. ~er n aventureiro m, explorador m. ~ous a aventuroso
adverb /'ædvɜ:b/ n advérbio m
adversary /'ædvəsərı/ n adversário m, antagonista mf
advers|e /'ædvɜ:s/ a (contrary) adverso; (unfavourable) desfavorável. ~ity /əd'vɜ:sətı/ n adversidade f
advert /'ædvɜ:t/ n (colloq) anúncio m
advertise /'ædvətaız/ vt/i anunciar, fazer publicidade (de); (sell) pôr um anúncio (para). ~ for procurar; ~r /-ə(r)/ n anunciante mf
advertisement /əd'vɜ:tısmənt/ n anúncio m; (advertising) publicidade f
advice /əd'vaıs/ n conselho(s) mpl; (comm) aviso m
advis|e /əd'vaız/ vt aconselhar; (inform) avisar, informar. ~e against desaconselhar. ~able a aconselhável. ~er n conselheiro m; (in business) consultor m. ~ory a consultivo
advocate[1] /'ædvəkət/ n (jur) advogado m; (supporter) defensor(a) m/f
advocate[2] /'ædvəkeıt/ vt advogar, defender
aerial /'eərıəl/ a aéreo □ n antena f
aerobatics /eərə'bætıks/ npl acrobacia f aérea
aerobics /eə'rəubıks/ n ginástica f aeróbica
aerodynamic /eərəudar'næmık/ a aerodinâmico
aeroplane /'eərəpleın/ n avião m
aerosol /'eərəsɒl/ n aerossol m
aesthetic /i:s'θetık/ a estético.
affair /ə'feə(r)/ n (business) negócio m; (romance) ligação f, aventura f; (matter) assunto m. love ~ paixão f
affect /ə'fekt/ vt afetar, (P) afectar. ~ation /æfek'teıʃn/ n afetação f, (P)

afectação *f.* ~ed *a* afetado, (*P*) afectado, pretencioso

affection /ə'fekʃn/ *n* afeição *f*, afeto *m*, (*P*) afecto *m*

affectionate /ə'fekʃənət/ *a* afetuoso, (*P*) afectuoso, carinhoso

affiliat|e /ə'fɪlɪeɪt/ *vt* afiliar. ~ed company filial *f*. ~ion /-'eɪʃn/ *n* afiliação *f*

affirm /ə'fɜ:m/ *vt* afirmar. ~ation /æfə'meɪʃn/ *n* afirmação *f*

affirmative /ə'fɜ:mətɪv/ *a* afirmativo □ *n* afirmativa *f*

afflict /ə'flɪkt/ *vt* afligir. ~ion /-ʃn/ *n* aflição *f*

affluen|t /'æfluənt/ *a* rico, afluente. ~ce *n* riqueza *f*, afluência *f*

afford /ə'fɔ:d/ *vt* (*have money for*) permitir-se, ter meios (para). can you afford the time? você teria tempo? I can't afford a car eu não posso comprar um carro. we can't afford to lose não podemos perder

affront /ə'frʌnt/ *n* afronta *f* □ *vt* insultar

afield /ə'fi:ld/ *adv* far ~ longe

afloat /ə'fləʊt/ *adv* & *a* à tona, a flutuar; (*at sea*) no mar; (*business*) lançado, (*P*) sem dívidas

afraid /ə'freɪd/ *a* be ~ ter medo (of, to de; that que); (*be sorry*) lamentar, ter muita pena. I'm ~ (that) (*regret to say*) lamento *or* tenho muita pena de dizer que

afresh /ə'freʃ/ *adv* de novo

Africa /'æfrɪkə/ *n* áfrica *f*. ~n *a* & *n* africano (*m*)

after /ɑ:ftə(r)/ *adv* depois □ *prep* depois de □ *conj* depois que. ~ all afinal de contas. ~ doing, depois de fazer. be ~ (*seek*) querer, pretender. ~-effect *n* seqüela *f*, (*P*) sequela *f*, efeito *m* retardado; (*of drug*) efeito *m* secundário

aftermath /'ɑ:ftəmæθ/ *n* conseqüências *fpl*

afternoon /ɑ:ftə'nu:n/ *n* tarde *f*

aftershave /'ɑ:ftəʃeɪv/ *n* loção *f* após-barba, (*P*) loção *f* para a barba

afterthought /'ɑ:ftəθɔ:t/ *n* reflexão *f* posterior. as an ~ pensando melhor

afterwards /'ɑ:ftəwədz/ *adv* depois, mais tarde

again /ə'gen/ *adv* de novo, outra vez; (*on the other hand*) por outro lado. then ~ além disso

against /ə'genst/ *prep* contra

age /eɪdʒ/ *n* idade *f*; (*period*) época *f*, idade *f* □ *vt/i* (*pres p* ageing) envelhecer. ~s (*colloq: very long time*) há séculos *mpl*. of ~ (de) maior. ten years of ~ com/de dez anos. under ~ menor. ~-group *n* faixa etária *f*. ~less *a* sempre jovem

aged[1] /eɪdʒd/ *a* ~ six de seis anos de idade

aged[2] /'eɪdʒɪd/ *a* idoso, velho

agen|cy /'eɪdʒənsɪ/ *n* agência *f*; (*means*) intermédio *m*. ~t *n* agente *mf*

agenda /ə'dʒendə/ *n* ordem *f* do dia

aggravat|e /'ægrəveɪt/ *vt* agravar; (*colloq: annoy*) irritar. ~ion /-'veɪʃn/ *n* (*worsening*) agravamento *m*; (*exasperation*) irritação *f*; (*colloq: trouble*) aborrecimentos *mpl*

aggregate /'ægrɪgeɪt/ *vt/i* agregar (-se) □ *a* /'ægrɪgət/ total, global □ *n* (*total, mass, materials*) agregado *m*. in the ~ no todo

aggress|ive /ə'gresɪv/ *a* agressivo; (*weapons*) ofensivo. ~ion /-ʃn/ *n* agressão *f*. ~iveness *n* agressividade *f*. ~or *n* agressor *m*

aggrieved /ə'gri:vd/ *a* (*having a grievance*) lesado

agil|e /'ædʒaɪl/ *a* ágil. ~ity /ə'dʒɪlətɪ/ *n* agilidade *f*

agitat|e /'ædʒɪteɪt/ *vt* agitar. ~ion /-'teɪʃn/ *n* agitação *f*. ~or *n* agitador *m*

agnostic /æg'nɒstɪk/ *a* & *n* agnóstico (*m*)

ago /ə'gəʊ/ *adv* há. a month ~ há um mês. long ~ há muito tempo

agon|y /'ægənɪ/ *n* agonia *f*; (*mental*) angústia *f*. ~ize *vi* atormentar-se, torturar-se. ~izing *a* angustiante, (*P*) doloroso

agree /ə'gri:/ *vt/i* concordar; (*of figures*) acertar. ~ that reconhecer que. ~ to do concordar em *or* aceitar fazer. ~ to sth concordar com alguma coisa. seafood doesn't ~ with me não me dou bem com mariscos. ~d *a* (*time, place*) combinado. be ~d estar de acordo

agreeable /ə'gri:əbl/ *a* agradável. be ~ to estar de acordo com

agreement /ə'gri:mənt/ *n* acordo *m*; (*gramm*) concordância *f*; (*contract*) contrato *m*. in ~ de acordo

agricultur|e /'ægrɪkʌltʃə(r)/ *n* agricultura *f*. ~al /-'kʌltʃərəl/ *a* agrícola

aground /ə'graʊnd/ *adv* run ~ (*of ship*) encalhar

ahead /ə'hed/ *adv* à frente, adiante; (*in advance*) adiantado. ~ of sb diante de alguém, à frente de alguém. ~ of time antes da hora, adiantado. straight ~ sempre em frente

aid /eɪd/ *vt* ajudar □ *n* ajuda *f*. ~ and abet ser cúmplice de. in ~ of em auxílio de, a favor de

AIDS /eɪdz/ *n* (*med*) AIDS *f*, (*P*) sida *m*

ail /eɪl/ *vt* what ~s you? o que é que você tem? ~ing *a* doente. ~ment *n* doença *f*, achaque *m*

aim /eɪm/ vt (gun) apontar; (efforts) dirigir; (send) atirar (at para) □ vi visar □ n alvo m. ~ at visar. ~ to aspirar a, tencionar. **take** ~ fazer pontaria. ~**less** a, ~**lessly** adv sem objetivo, (P) objectivo

air /eə(r)/ n ar m □ vt arejar; (views) expor □ a (base etc) aéreo. **in the** ~ (rumour) espalhado; (plans) no ar. **on the** ~ (radio) no ar. ~**-conditioned** a com ar condicionado. ~**-conditioning** n condicionamento m do ar, (P) ar m condicionado. ~ **force** Força f Aérea. ~ **hostess** aeromoça f, (P) hospedeira f de bordo. ~ **raid** ataque m aéreo

airborne /'eəbɔ:n/ a (aviat: in flight) no ar; (diseases) levado pelo ar; (freight) por transporte aéreo

aircraft /'eəkrɑ:ft/ n (pl invar) avião m. ~**-carrier** n porta-aviões m

airfield /'eəfi:ld/ n campo m de aviação

airgun /'eəgʌn/ n espingarda f de pressão

airlift /'eəlɪft/ n ponte f aérea □ vt transportar em ponte aérea

airline /'eəlaɪn/ n linha f aérea

airlock /'eəlɒk/ n câmara f de vácuo; (in pipe) bolha f de ar

airmail /'eəmeɪl/ n correio m aéreo. **by** ~ por avião

airport /'eəpɔ:t/ n aeroporto m

airsick /'eəsɪk/ a enjoado. ~**ness** /-nɪs/ n enjôo m, (P) enjoo m

airstrip /'eəstrɪp/ n pista f de aterrissagem, (P) pista f de aterragem

airtight /'eətaɪt/ a hermético

airy /'eərɪ/ a (-ier, -iest) arejado; (manner) desenvolto

aisle /aɪl/ n (of church) nave f lateral; (gangway) coxia f

ajar /ə'dʒɑ:(r)/ adv & a entreaberto

alabaster /'æləbɑ:stə(r)/ n alabastro m

à la carte /ɑːlɑː'kɑːt/ adv & a à la carte, (P) à lista

alarm /ə'lɑːm/ n alarme m; (clock) campainha f □ vt alarmar. ~**-clock** n despertador m. ~**-bell** n campainha f de alarme. ~**ing** a alarmante. ~**ist** n alarmista mf

alas /ə'læs/ int ai! ai de mim!

albatross /'ælbətrɒs/ n albatroz m

album /'ælbəm/ n álbum m

alcohol /'ælkəhɒl/ n álcool m. ~**ic** /-'hɒlɪk/ a (person, drink) alcoólico □ n alcoólico m. ~**ism** n alcoolismo m

alcove /'ælkəʊv/ n recesso m, alcova f

ale /eɪl/ n cerveja f inglesa

alert /ə'lɜːt/ a (lively) vivo; (watchful) vigilante □ n alerta m □ vt alertar. **be on the** ~ estar alerta

algebra /'ældʒɪbrə/ n álgebra f. ~**ic** /-'breɪk/ a algébrico

Algeria /æl'dʒɪərɪə/ n Argélia f. ~**n** a & n argelino (m)

alias /'eɪlɪəs/ n (pl -ases) outro nome m, nome falso m, (P) pseudónimo m □ adv aliás

alibi /'ælɪbaɪ/ n (pl -is) álibi m, (P) alibi m

alien /'eɪlɪən/ n & a estrangeiro (m). ~ **to** (contrary) contrário a; (differing) alheio a, estranho a

alienat|e /'eɪlɪəneɪt/ vt alienar. ~**ion** /-'neɪʃn/ n alienação f

alight[1] /ə'laɪt/ vi descer; (bird) pousar

alight[2] /ə'laɪt/ a (on fire) em chamas; (lit up) aceso

align /ə'laɪn/ vt alinhar. ~**ment** n alinhamento m

alike /ə'laɪk/ a semelhante, parecido □ adv da mesma maneira. **look** or **be** ~ parecer-se

alimony /'ælɪmənɪ/ n pensão f alimentar, (P) de alimentos

alive /ə'laɪv/ a vivo. ~ **to** sensível a. ~ **with** fervilhando de, (P) a fervilhar de

alkali /'ælkəlaɪ/ n (pl -is) álcali m, (P) alcali m

all /ɔːl/ a & pron todo (f & pl -a, -os, -as) □ pron (everything) tudo □ adv completamente, de todo □ n tudo m. ~ **the better/less/more/worse** etc tanto melhor/menos/mais/pior etc. ~ **(the) men** todos os homens. ~ **of us** todos nós. ~ **but** quase, todos menos. ~ **in** (colloq: exhausted) estafado. ~**in** a tudo incluído. ~ **out** a fundo, (P) completamente. ~**-out** a (effort) máximo. ~ **over** (in one's body) todo; (finished) acabado; (in all parts of) por todo. ~ **right** bem; (as a response) está bem. ~ **round** em tudo; (for all) para todos. ~**-round** a geral. ~ **the same** apesar de tudo. **it's** ~ **the same to me** (para mim) tanto faz

allay /ə'leɪ/ vt acalmar

allegation /ælɪ'geɪʃn/ n alegação f

allege /ə'ledʒ/ vt alegar. ~**dly** /-ɪdlɪ/ adv segundo dizem, alegadamente

allegiance /ə'liːdʒəns/ n fidelidade f, lealdade f

allegor|y /'ælɪgərɪ/ n alegoria f. ~**ical** /-'gɒrɪkl/ a alegórico

allerg|y /'ælədʒɪ/ n alergia f. ~**ic** /ə'lɜːdʒɪk/ a alérgico

alleviate /ə'liːvɪeɪt/ vt aliviar

alley /'ælɪ/ n (pl -eys) (street) viela f; (for bowling) pista f

alliance /ə'laɪəns/ n aliança f

allied /'ælaɪd/ a aliado

alligator /'ælɪgeɪtə(r)/ n jacaré m

allocat|e /'æləkeɪt/ vt (share out) distribuir; (assign) destinar. ~**ion** /-'keɪʃn/ n atribuição f

allot /ə'lɒt/ vt (pt **allotted**) atribuir. **~ment** n atribuição f; (share) distribuição f; (land) horta f alugada

allow /ə'laʊ/ vt permitir; (grant) conceder, dar; (reckon on) contar com; (agree) admitir, reconhecer. **~ sb to** (+ inf) permitir a alg (+ inf or que + subj). **~ for** levar em conta

allowance /ə'laʊəns/ n (for employees) ajudas fpl de custo; (monthly, for wife, child) beneficio m; (tax) desconto m. **make ~s for** (person) levar em consideração, ser indulgente para com; (take into account) atender a, levar em consideração

alloy /ə'lɔɪ/ n liga f

allude /ə'luːd/ vi **~ to** aludir a

allure /ə'lʊə(r)/ vt seduzir, atrair

allusion /ə'luːʒn/ n alusão f

ally¹ /'ælaɪ/ n (pl -lies) aliado m

ally² /ə'laɪ/ vt aliar. **~ oneself with/ to** aliar-se com/a

almanac /'ɔːlmənæk/ n almanaque m

almighty /ɔːl'maɪtɪ/ a todo-poderoso; (colloq) grande, formidável

almond /'aːmənd/ n amêndoa f. **~ paste** maçapão m

almost /'ɔːlməʊst/ adv quase

alone /ə'ləʊn/ a & adv só. **leave ~** (abstain from interfering with) deixar em paz. **let ~** (without considering) sem or para não falar de

along /ə'lɒŋ/ prep ao longo de □ adv (onward) para diante. **all ~** durante todo o tempo. **~ with** com. **move ~, please** ande, por favor

alongside /əlɒŋ'saɪd/ adv (naut) atracado. **come ~** acostar □ prep ao lado de

aloof /ə'luːf/ adv à parte □ a distante. **~ness** n reserva f

aloud /ə'laʊd/ adv em voz alta

alphabet /'ælfəbet/ n alfabeto m. **~ical** /-'betɪkl/ a alfabético

alpine /'ælpaɪn/ a alpino, alpestre

Alps /ælps/ npl **the ~** os Alpes mpl

already /ɔːl'redɪ/ adv já

also /'ɔːlsəʊ/ adv também

altar /'ɔːltə(r)/ n altar m

alter /'ɔːltə(r)/ vt/i alterar(-se), modificar(-se). **~ation** /-'reɪʃn/ n alteração f; (to garment) modificação f

alternate¹ /ɔːl'tɜːnət/ a alternado. **~ly** adv alternadamente

alternate² /'ɔːltɜːneɪt/ vt/i alternar (-se). **~ing current** (elect) corrente f alterna. **~or** n (elect) alternador m

alternative /ɔːl'tɜːnətɪv/ a alternativo □ n alternativa f. **~ly** adv em alternativa. **or ~ly** ou então

although /ɔːl'ðəʊ/ conj embora, conquanto

altitude /'æltɪtjuːd/ n altitude f

altogether /ɔːltə'geðə(r)/ adv (completely) completamente; (in total) ao todo; (on the whole) de modo geral

aluminium /æljʊ'mɪnɪəm/ (Amer **aluminum** /ə'luːmɪnəm/) n alumínio m

always /'ɔːlweɪz/ adv sempre

am /æm/ see **be**

a.m. /eɪ'em/ adv da manhã

amalgamate /ə'mælgəmeɪt/ vt/i amalgamar(-se); (comm) fundir

amass /ə'mæs/ vt amontoar, juntar

amateur /'æmətə(r)/ n & a amador (m). **~ish** a (pej) de amador, (P) amadorístico

amaze /ə'meɪz/ vt assombrar, espantar. **~ed** a assombrado. **~ement** n assombro m. **~ingly** adv espantosamente

Amazon /'æməzən/ n **the ~** o Amazonas

ambassador /æm'bæsədə(r)/ n embaixador m

amber /'æmbə(r)/ n âmbar m; (traffic light) luz f amarela

ambiguous /æm'bɪgjʊəs/ a ambíguo. **~ity** /-'gjuːətɪ/ n ambigüidade f, (P) ambiguidade f

ambition /æm'bɪʃn/ n ambição f. **~ous** a ambicioso

ambivalent /æm'bɪvələnt/ a ambivalente. **~ce** n ambivalência f

amble /'æmbl/ vi caminhar sem pressa

ambulance /'æmbjʊləns/ n ambulância f

ambush /'æmbʊʃ/ n emboscada f □ vt fazer uma emboscada para, (P) fazer uma emboscada a

amenable /ə'miːnəbl/ a **~ to** (responsive) sensível a

amend /ə'mend/ vt emendar, corrigir. **~ment** n (to rule) emenda f. **~s** n **make ~s for** reparar, compensar

amenities /ə'miːnətɪz/ npl (pleasant features) atrativos mpl, (P) atractivos mpl; (facilities) confortos mpl, comodidades fpl

America /ə'merɪkə/ n América f. **~n** a & n americano (m). **~nism** /-nɪzəm/ n americanismo m. **~nize** vt americanizar

amiable /'eɪmɪəbl/ a amável

amicable /'æmɪkəbl/ a amigável, amigo

amid(st) /ə'mɪd(st)/ prep entre, no meio de

amiss /ə'mɪs/ a & adv mal. **sth ~** coisa que não está bem. **take sth ~** levar qq coisa a mal

ammonia /ə'məʊnɪə/ n amoníaco m

ammunition /æmjʊ'nɪʃn/ n munições fpl

amnesia /æm'niːzɪə/ n amnésia f

amnesty /'æmnəstɪ/ n anistia f, (P) amnistia f

amok /ə'mɒk/ adv run ~ enlouquecer; (crowd) correr desordenadamente

among(st) /ə'mʌŋ(st)/ prep entre, no meio de. ~ ourselves (aqui) entre nós

amoral /er'mɒrəl/ a amoral

amorous /'æmərəs/ a amoroso

amount /ə'maʊnt/ n quantidade f; (total) montante m; (sum of money) quantia f □ vi ~ to elevar-se a; (fig) equivaler a

amp /æmp/ n (colloq) ampère m

amphibi|an /æm'fɪbɪən/ n anfíbio m. ~ous a anfíbio

ampl|e /'æmpl/ a (-er, -est) (large, roomy) amplo; (enough) suficiente, bastante. ~y adv amplamente

amplif|y /'æmplɪfaɪ/ vt ampliar, amplificar. ~ier n amplificador m

amputat|e /'æmpjʊteɪt/ vt amputar. ~ion /-'teɪʃn/ n amputação f

amus|e /ə'mjuːz/ vt divertir. ~ement n divertimento m. ~ing a divertido

an /ən, æn/ see **a**

anachronism /ə'nækrənɪzəm/ n anacronismo m

anaem|ia /ə'niːmɪə/ n anemia f. ~ic a anêmico, (P) anémico

anaesthetic /ænɪs'θetɪk/ n anestético m, (P) anestésico m. give an ~ to anestesiar

anaesthetist /ə'niːsθətɪst/ n anestesista mf

anagram /'ænəgræm/ n anagrama m

analog(ue) /'ænəlɒg/ a análogo

analogy /ə'nælədʒɪ/ n analogia f

analys|e /'ænəlaɪz/ vt analisar. ~t /-ɪst/ n analista mf

analysis /ə'næləsɪs/ n (pl -yses) /-əsiːz/ análise f

analytic(al) /ænə'lɪtɪk(l)/ a analítico

anarch|y /'ænəkɪ/ n anarquia f. ~ist n anarquista mf

anatom|y /ə'nætəmɪ/ n anatomia f. ~ical /ænə'tɒmɪkl/ a anatômico, (P) anatómico

ancest|or /'ænsestə(r)/ n antepassado m. ~ral /-'sestrəl/ a ancestral (pl -ais)

ancestry /'ænsestrɪ/ n ascendência f, estirpe f

anchor /'æŋkə(r)/ n âncora f □ vt/i ancorar. ~age /-rɪdʒ/ n ancoradouro m

anchovy /'æntʃəvɪ/ n enchova f, (P) anchova f

ancient /'eɪnʃənt/ a antigo

ancillary /æn'sɪlərɪ/ a ancilar, (P) subordinado

and /ənd/; emphatic /ænd/ conj e. go ~ see vá ver. better ~ better/ less ~ less etc cada vez melhor/menos etc

anecdote /'ænɪkdəʊt/ n anedota f

angel /'eɪndʒl/ n anjo m. ~ic /æn'dʒelɪk/ a angélico, angelical

anger /'æŋgə(r)/ n cólera f, zanga f □ vt irritar

angle[1] /'æŋgl/ n ângulo m

angle[2] /'æŋgl/ vi (fish) pescar (à linha). ~ for (fig: compliments, information) andar à procura de. ~r /-ə(r)/ n pescador m

anglicism /'æŋglɪsɪzəm/ n anglicismo m

Anglo- /'æŋgləʊ/ pref anglo-

Anglo-Saxon /'æŋgləʊ'sæksn/ a & n anglo-saxão (m)

angr|y /'æŋgrɪ/ a (-ier, -iest) zangado. get ~y zangar-se (with com). ~ily adv furiosamente

anguish /'æŋgwɪʃ/ n angústia f

angular /'æŋgjʊlə(r)/ a angular; (features) anguloso

animal /'ænɪml/ a & n animal (m)

animate[1] /'ænɪmət/ a animado

animat|e[2] /'ænɪmeɪt/ vt animar. ~ion /-'meɪʃn/ n animação f. ~ed cartoon filme m de bonecos animados, (P) de desenhos animados

animosity /ænɪ'mɒsətɪ/ n animosidade f

aniseed /'ænɪsiːd/ n semente f de anis

ankle /'æŋkl/ n tornozelo m. ~ sock meia f soquete

annex /ə'neks/ vt anexar. ~ation /ænek'seɪʃn/ n anexação f

annexe /'æneks/ n anexo m

annihilate /ə'naɪəleɪt/ vt aniquilar

anniversary /ænɪ'vɜːsərɪ/ n aniversário m

announce /ə'naʊns/ vt anunciar. ~ment n anúncio m. ~r /-ə(r)/ n (radio, TV) locutor m

annoy /ə'nɔɪ/ vt irritar, aborrecer. ~ance n aborrecimento m. ~ed a aborrecido (with com). get ~ed aborrecer-se. ~ing a irritante

annual /'ænjʊəl/ a anual □ n (bot) planta f anual; (book) anuário m. ~ly adv anualmente

annuity /ə'njuːətɪ/ n anuidade f

annul /ə'nʌl/ vt (pt annulled) anular. ~ment n anulação f

anomal|y /ə'nɒməlɪ/ n anomalia f. ~ous a anômalo, (P) anómalo

anonym|ous /ə'nɒnɪməs/ a anônimo, (P) anónimo. ~ity /ænə'nɪmətɪ/ n anonimato m

anorak /'ænəræk/ n anoraque m, anorak m

another /ə'nʌðə(r)/ a & pron (um) outro. ~ ten minutes mais dez minutos. to one ~ um ao outro, uns aos outros

answer /'ɑːnsə(r)/ n resposta f; (solution) solução f □ vt responder a;

(*prayer*) atender a □ *vi* responder. ~ **the door** atender à porta. ~ **back** retrucar, (*P*) responder torto. ~ **for** responder por. ~**able** *a* responsável (for por; **to** perante). ~**ing machine** *n* secretária *f* eletrónica

ant /ænt/ *n* formiga *f*

antagonis|m /æn'tægənizəm/ *n* antagonismo *m*. ~**t** *n* antagonista *mf*. ~**tic** /-'nɪstɪk/ *a* antagónico, (*P*) antagónico, hostil

antagonize /æn'tægənaɪz/ *vt* antagonizar, hostilizar

Antarctic /æn'ta:ktɪk/ *n* Antártico, (*P*) Antárctico *m* □ *a* antártico, (*P*) antárctico

ante- /'æntɪ/ *pref* ante-

antecedent /æntɪ'si:dnt/ *a* & *n* antecedente (*m*)

antelope /'æntɪləʊp/ *n* antílope *m*

antenatal /æntɪ'neɪtl/ *a* pré-natal

antenna /æn'tenə/ *n* (*pl* -ae /-i:/) antena *f*

anthem /'ænθəm/ *n* cântico *m*. **national** ~ hino *m* nacional

anthology /æn'θɒlədʒɪ/ *n* antologia *f*

anthropolog|y /ænθrə'pɒlədʒɪ/ *n* antropologia *f*. ~**ist** *n* antropólogo *m*

anti- /æntɪ/ *pref* anti-. ~**-aircraft** /-eəkra:ft/ *a* antiaéreo

antibiotic /æntɪbar'ɒtɪk/ *n* antibiótico *m*

antibody /'æntɪbɒdɪ/ *n* anticorpo *m*

anticipat|e /æn'tɪsɪpeɪt/ *vt* (*foresee, expect*) prever; (*forestall*) anteciparse a. ~**ion** /-'peɪʃn/ *n* antecipação *f*; (*expectation*) expectativa *f*. **in** ~**ion of** na previsão *or* expectativa de

anticlimax /æntɪ'klaɪmæks/ *n* anticlímax *m*; (*let-down*) decepção *f*. **it was an** ~ não correspondeu à expectativa

anticlockwise /æntɪ'klɒkwaɪz/ *adv* & *a* no sentido contrário ao dos ponteiros dum relógio

antics /'æntɪks/ *npl* (*of clown*) palhaçadas *fpl*; (*behaviour*) comportamento *m* bizarro

anticyclone /ˌæntɪ'saɪkləʊn/ *n* anticiclone *m*

antidote /'æntɪdəʊt/ *n* antídoto *m*

antifreeze /'æntɪfri:z/ *n* anticongelante *m*

antihistamine /æntɪ'hɪstəmi:n/ *a* & *n* anti-histamínico (*m*)

antipathy /æn'tɪpəθɪ/ *n* antipatia *f*

antiquated /'æntɪkweɪtɪd/ *a* antiquado

antique /æn'ti:k/ *a* antigo □ *n* antiguidade *f*. ~ **dealer** antiquário *m*. ~ **shop** loja *f* de antiguidades, (*P*) antiquário *m*

antiquity /æn'tɪkwətɪ/ *n* antiguidade *f*

antiseptic /æntɪ'septɪk/ *a* & *n* antiséptico (*m*)

antisocial /æntɪ'səʊʃl/ *a* anti-social; (*unsociable*) insociável

antithesis /æn'tɪθəsɪs/ *n* (*pl* -eses) /-si:z/ antítese *f*.

antlers /'æntləz/ *npl* chifres *mpl*, esgalhos *mpl*

antonym /'æntənɪm/ *n* antônimo *m*, (*P*) antónimo *m*

anus /'eɪnəs/ *n* ânus *m*

anvil /'ænvɪl/ *n* bigorna *f*

anxiety /æŋ'zaɪətɪ/ *n* ansiedade *f*; (*eagerness*) ânsia *f*

anxious /'æŋkʃəs/ *a* (*worried, eager*) ansioso (**to** de, por). ~**ly** *adv* ansiosamente; (*eagerly*) impacientemente

any /'enɪ/ *a* & *pron* qualquer, quaisquer; (*in neg and interr sentences*) algum, alguns; (*in neg sentences*) nenhum, nenhuns; (*every*) todo. **at** ~ **moment** a qualquer momento. **at** ~ **rate** de qualquer modo, em todo o caso. **in** ~ **case** em todo o caso. **have you** ~ **money/friends?** você tem (algum) dinheiro/(alguns) amigos? **I don't have** ~ **time** não tenho nenhum tempo *or* tempo nenhum *or* tempo algum. **has she** ~? ela tem algum? **she doesn't have** ~ ela não tem nenhum □ *adv* (*at all*) de modo algum *or* nenhum; (*a little*) um pouco. ~ **the less/the worse** *etc* menos/pior *etc*

anybody /'enɪbɒdɪ/ *pron* qualquer pessoa; (*somebody*) alguém; (*after negative*) ninguém. **he didn't see** ~ ele não viu ninguém

anyhow /'enɪhaʊ/ *adv* (*no matter how*) de qualquer modo; (*badly*) de qualquer maneira, ao acaso; (*in any case*) em todo o caso. **you can try,** ~ em todo o caso, você pode tentar

anyone /'enɪwʌn/ *pron* = **anybody**

anything /'enɪθɪŋ/ *pron* (*something*) alguma coisa; (*no matter what*) qualquer coisa; (*after negative*) nada. **he didn't say** ~ não disse nada. **it is** ~ **but cheap** é tudo menos barato. ~ **you do** tudo o que você fizer

anyway /'enɪweɪ/ *adv* de qualquer modo; (*in any case*) em todo o caso

anywhere /'enɪweə(r)/ *adv* (*somewhere*) em qualquer parte; (*after negative*) em parte alguma/nenhuma. ~ **else** em qualquer outro lado. ~ **you go** onde quer que você vá. **he doesn't go** ~ ele não vai a lado nenhum

apart /ə'pa:t/ *adv* à parte; (*separated*) separado; (*into pieces*) aos bocados. ~ **from** à parte, além de. **ten metres** ~ a dez metros de distância entre si. **come** ~ desfazer-se. **keep** ~ manter separado. **take** ~ desmontar

apartment /ə'pa:tmənt/ n (*Amer*) apartamento m. **~s** aposentos mpl

apath|y /'æpəθɪ/ n apatia f. **~etic** /-'θetɪk/ a apático

ape /eɪp/ n macaco m □ vt macaquear

aperitif /ə'perətɪf/ n aperitivo m

aperture /'æpətʃə(r)/ n abertura f

apex /'eɪpeks/ n ápice m, cume m

apiece /ə'pi:s/ adv cada, por cabeça

apologetic /əpɒlə'dʒetɪk/ a (*tone etc*) apologético, de desculpas. **be ~** desculpar-se. **~ally** /-əlɪ/ adv desculpan-do-se

apologize /ə'pɒlədʒaɪz/ vi desculpar-se (**for** de, por; **to** junto de, perante), pedir desculpa (**for**, por; **to**, a)

apology /ə'pɒlədʒɪ/ n desculpa f; (*defence of belief*) apologia f

apostle /ə'pɒsl/ n apóstolo m

apostrophe /ə'pɒstrəfɪ/ n apóstrofe f

appal /ə'pɔ:l/ vt (pt **appalled**) estarrecer. **~ling** a estarrecedor

apparatus /æpə'reɪtəs/ n aparelho m

apparent /ə'pærənt/ a aparente. **~ly** adv aparentemente

apparition /æpə'rɪʃn/ n aparição f

appeal /ə'pi:l/ vi (*jur*) apelar (**to** para); (*attract*) atrair (**to** a); (*for funds*) angariar □ n apelo m; (*attractiveness*) atrativo m, (P) atractivo m; (*for funds*) angariação f. **~ to sb for sth** pedir uma coisa a alg. **~ing** a (*attractive*) atraente

appear /ə'pɪə(r)/ vi aparecer; (*seem*) parecer; (*in court, theatre*) apresentar-se. **~ance** n aparição f; (*aspect*) aparência f; (*in court*) comparecimento m, (P) comparência f

appease /ə'pi:z/ vt apaziguar

appendage /ə'pendɪdʒ/ n apêndice m

appendicitis /əpendɪ'saɪtɪs/ n apendicite f

appendix /ə'pendɪks/ n (pl **-ices** /-sì:z/) (*of book*) apêndice m; (pl **-ixes** /-ksɪz/) (*anat*) apêndice m

appetite /'æpɪtaɪt/ n apetite m

appetizer /'æpɪtaɪzə(r)/ n (*snack*) tira-gosto m; (*drink*) aperitivo m

appetizing /'æpɪtaɪzɪŋ/ a apetitoso

applau|d /ə'plɔ:d/ vt/i aplaudir. **~se** n aplauso(s) m(pl)

apple /'æpl/ n maçã f. **~ tree** macieira f

appliance /ə'plaɪəns/ n aparelho m, instrumento m, utensílio m. **household ~s** utensílios mpl domésticos

applicable /'æplɪkəbl/ a aplicável

applicant /'æplɪkənt/ n candidato m (**for** a)

application /æplɪ'keɪʃn/ n aplicação f; (*request*) pedido m; (*form*) formulário m; (*for job*) candidatura f

appl|y /ə'plaɪ/ vt aplicar □ vi **~y to** (*refer*) aplicar-se a; (*ask*) dirigir-se a.

~y for (*job, grant*) candidatar-se a. **~y o.s. to** aplicar-se a. **~ied** a aplicado

appoint /ə'pɔɪnt/ vt (*to post*) nomear; (*time, date*) marcar. **well-~ed** a bem equipado, bem provido. **~ment** n nomeação f; (*meeting*) entrevista f; (*with friends*) encontro m; (*with doctor etc*) consulta f, (P) marcação f; (*job*) posto m

apprais|e /ə'preɪz/ vt avaliar. **~al** n avaliação f

appreciable /ə'pri:ʃəbl/ a apreciável

appreciat|e /ə'pri:ʃɪeɪt/ vt (*value*) apreciar; (*understand*) compreender; (*be grateful for*) estar/ficar grato por □ vi encarecer. **~ion** /-'eɪʃn/ n apreciação f, (*rise in value*) encarecimento m; (*gratitude*) reconhecimento m. **~ive** /ə'pri:ʃɪətɪv/ a apreciador; (*grateful*) reconhecido

apprehen|d /æprɪ'hend/ vt (*seize, understand*) apreender; (*dread*) recear. **~sion** n apreensão f

apprehensive /æprɪ'hensɪv/ a apreensivo

apprentice /ə'prentɪs/ n aprendiz, -a mf □ vt pôr como aprendiz (**to** de). **~ship** n aprendizagem f

approach /ə'prəʊtʃ/ vt aproximar; (*with request or offer*) abordar □ vi aproximar-se □ n aproximação f. **~ to** (*problem*) abordagem f de; (*place*) acesso m a; (*person*) diligência junto de. **~able** a acessível

appropriate[1] /ə'prəʊprɪət/ a apropriado, próprio. **~ly** adv apropriadamente, a propósito

appropriate[2] /ə'prəʊprɪeɪt/ vt apropriar-se de

approval /ə'pru:vl/ n aprovação f. **on ~** (*comm*) sob condição, à aprovação

approv|e /ə'pru:v/ vt/i aprovar. **~e of** aprovar. **~ingly** adv com ar de aprovação

approximate[1] /ə'prɒksɪmət/ a aproximado. **~ly** adv aproximadamente

approximat|e[2] /ə'prɒksɪmeɪt/ vt/i aproximar(-se) de. **~ion** /-'meɪʃn/ n aproximação f

apricot /'eɪprɪkɒt/ n damasco m

April /'eɪprəl/ n Abril m. **~ Fool's Day** o primeiro de Abril, o dia das mentiras. **make an ~ fool of** pregar uma mentira em, (P) pregar uma mentira a

apron /'eɪprən/ n avental m

apt /æpt/ a apto; (*pupil*) dotado. **be ~ to** ser propenso a. **~ly** adv apropriadamente

aptitude /'æptɪtju:d/ n aptidão f, (P) aptitude f

aqualung /'ækwəlʌŋ/ n escafandro autônomo, (P) autónomo m

aquarium /ə'kweərɪəm/ n (pl -ums) aquário m

Aquarius /ə'kweərɪəs/ n (astr) Aquário m

aquatic /ə'kwætɪk/ a aquático; (sport) náutico, aquático

aqueduct /'ækwɪdʌkt/ n aqueduto m

Arab /'ærəb/ a & n árabe (mf). **~ic** a & n (lang) árabe (m), arábico (m). **a~ic numerals** algarismos mpl árabes or arábicos

Arabian /ə'reɪbɪən/ a árabe

arable /'ærəbl/ a arável

arbitrary /'a:bɪtrərɪ/ a arbitrário

arbitrat|e /'a:bɪtreɪt/ vi arbitrar. **~ion** /-'treɪʃn/ n arbitragem f. **~or** n árbitro m

arc /a:k/ n arco m. **~ lamp** lâmpada f de arco. **~ welding** soldadura f a arco

arcade /a:'keɪd/ n (shop) arcada f. **amusement ~** fliperama m

arch /a:tʃ/ n arco m; (vault) abóbada f □ vt/i arquear(-se)

arch- /a:tʃ/ pref arqui-.

archaeolog|y /a:kɪ'ɒlədʒɪ/ n arqueologia f. **~ical** /-ə'lɒdʒɪkl/ a arqueológico. **~ist** n arqueólogo m

archaic /a:'keɪk/ a arcaico

archbishop /a:tʃ'bɪʃəp/ n arcebispo m

arch-enemy /a:tʃ'enəmɪ/ n inimigo m número um

archer /'a:tʃə(r)/ n arqueiro m. **~y** n tiro m ao arco

archetype /'a:kɪtaɪp/ n arquétipo m

architect /'a:kɪtekt/ n arquiteto m, (P) arquitecto m

architectur|e /'a:kɪtektʃə(r)/ n arquitetura f, (P) arquitectura f. **~al** /-'tektʃərəl/ a arquitetônico, (P) arquitectónico

archiv|es /'a:kaɪvz/ npl arquivo m. **~ist** /-ɪvɪst/ n arquivista mf

archway /'a:tʃweɪ/ n arcada f

Arctic /'a:ktɪk/ n ártico m, (P) árctico m □ a ártico, (P) árctico. **~ weather** tempo m glacial

ardent /'a:dnt/ a ardente. **~ly** adv ardentemente

ardour /'a:də(r)/ n ardor m

arduous /'a:djʊəs/ a árduo

are /ə(r)/; emphatic /a:(r)/ see be

area /'eərɪə/ n área f

arena /ə'ri:nə/ n arena f

aren't /a:nt/ = are not

Argentin|a /a:dʒən'ti:nə/ n Argentina f. **~ian** /-'tɪnɪən/ a & n argentino (m)

argu|e /'a:gju:/ vi discutir; (reason) argumentar, arguir □ vt (debate) discutir. **~e that** alegar que. **~able** a alegável. **it's ~able that** pode-se sustentar que

argument /'a:gjʊmənt/ n (dispute) disputa f; (reasoning) argumento m. **~ative** /-'mentətɪv/ a que gosta de discutir, argumentativo

arid /'ærɪd/ a árido

Aries /'eəri:z/ n (astr) Áries m, Carneiro m

arise /ə'raɪz/ vi (pt arose, pp arisen) surgir. **~ from** resultar de

aristocracy /ærɪ'stɒkrəsɪ/ n aristocracia f

aristocrat /'ærɪstəkræt/ n aristocrata mf. **~ic** /-'krætɪk/ a aristocrático

arithmetic /ə'rɪθmətɪk/ n aritmética f

ark /a:k/ n Noah's **~** arca f de Noé

arm¹ /a:m/ n braço m. **~ in ~** de braço dado

arm² /a:m/ vt armar □ n (mil) arma f. **~ed robbery** assalto m à mão armada

armament /'a:məmənt/ n armamento m

armchair /'a:mtʃeə(r)/ n cadeira f de braços, poltrona f

armistice /'a:mɪstɪs/ n armistício m

armour /'a:mə(r)/ n armadura f; (on tanks etc) blindagem f. **~ed** a blindado

armoury /'a:mərɪ/ n arsenal m

armpit /'a:mpɪt/ n axila f, sovaco m

arms /a:mz/ npl armas fpl. **coat of ~** brasão m

army /'a:mɪ/ n exército m

aroma /ə'rəʊmə/ n aroma m. **~tic** /ærə'mætɪk/ a aromático

arose /ə'rəʊz/ see arise

around /ə'raʊnd/ adv em redor, em volta; (here and there) por aí □ prep em redor de, em torno de, em volta de; (approximately) aproximadamente. **~ here** por aqui

arouse /ə'raʊz/ vt despertar; (excite) excitar

arrange /ə'reɪndʒ/ vt arranjar; (time, date) combinar. **~ to do sth** combinar fazer alg coisa. **~ment** n arranjo m; (agreement) acordo m. **make ~ments (for)** (plans) tomar disposições (para); (preparations) fazer preparativos (para)

array /ə'reɪ/ vt revestir □ n **an ~ of** (display) um leque de, uma série de

arrears /ə'rɪəz/ npl dívidas fpl em atraso, atrasos mpl. **in ~** em atraso

arrest /ə'rest/ vt (by law) deter, prender; (process, movement) deter □ n captura f. **under ~** sob prisão

arrival /ə'raɪvl/ n chegada f. **new ~** recém-chegado m

arrive /ə'raɪv/ vi chegar

arrogan|t /'ærəgənt/ a arrogante. **~ce** n arrogância f. **~tly** adv com arrogância

arrow /'ærəʊ/ n flecha f, seta f

arsenal /'a:sənl/ n arsenal m

arsenic /'a:snɪk/ n arsênico m, (P) arsénico m

arson /'a:sn/ n fogo m posto. ~**ist** n incendiário m

art[1] /a:t/ n arte f. the ~s (univ) letras fpl. **fine** ~s belas-artes fpl. ~ **gallery** museu m (de arte); (private) galeria f de arte

artery /'a:tərɪ/ n artéria f

artful /'a:tfl/ a manhoso. ~**ness** n manha f

arthritis /a:'θraɪtɪs/ n artrite f

artichoke /'a:tɪtʃəʊk/ n alcachofra f. **Jerusalem** ~ topinambo m

article /'a:tɪkl/ n artigo m. ~**d** a (jur) em estágio, (P) a estagiar

articulate[1] /a:'tɪkjʊlət/ a que se exprime com clareza; (speech) bem articulado

articulat|e[2] /a:'tɪkjʊleɪt/ vt/i articular. ~**ed lorry** camião m articulado. ~**ion** /-'leɪʃn/ n articulação f

artifice /'a:tɪfɪs/ n artifício m

artificial /a:tɪ'fɪʃl/ a artificial

artillery /a:'tɪlərɪ/ n artilharia f

artisan /a:tɪ'zæn/ n artífice mf, artesão m, artesã f

artist /'a:tɪst/ n artista mf. ~**ic** /-'tɪstɪk/ a artístico. ~**ry** n arte f

artiste /a:'ti:st/ n artista mf

artless /'a:tlɪs/ a ingênuo, (P) ingênuo, simples

as /əz/; emphatic /æz/ adv & conj como; (while) enquanto; (when) quando. ~ **a gift** de presente. ~ **tall as** tão alto quanto, (P) tão alto como □ pron que. **I ate the same** ~ **he** comi o mesmo que ele. ~ **for,** ~ **to** quanto a. ~ **from** a partir de. ~ **if** como se. ~ **much** tanto, tantos. ~ **many** quanto, quantos. ~ **soon as** logo que. ~ **well** (also) também. ~ **well as** (in addition to) assim como

asbestos /æz'bestəs/ n asbesto m, amianto m

ascend /ə'send/ vt/i subir. ~ **the throne** ascender or subir ao trono

ascent /ə'sent/ n ascensão f; (slope) subida f, rampa f

ascertain /æsə'teɪn/ vt certificar-se de. ~ **that** certificar-se de que

ascribe /ə'skraɪb/ vt atribuir

ash[1] /æʃ/ n ~(-tree) freixo m

ash[2] /æʃ/ n cinza f. A~ **Wednesday** Quarta-feira f de Cinzas. ~**en** a pálido

ashamed /ə'ʃeɪmd/ a **be** ~ ter vergonha, ficar envergonhado (of de, por)

ashore /ə'ʃɔ:(r)/ adv em terra. **go** ~ desembarcar

ashtray /'æʃtreɪ/ n cinzeiro m

Asia /'eɪʃə/ n ásia f. ~**n** a & n asiático (m)

aside /ə'saɪd/ adv de lado, de parte □ n (theat) aparte m. ~ **from** (Amer) à parte

ask /a:sk/ vt/i pedir; (a question) perguntar; (invite) convidar. ~ **sb sth** pedir uma coisa a alguém. ~ **about** informar-se de. ~ **after sb** pedir notícias de alg, perguntar por alg. ~ **for** pedir. ~ **sb in** mandar entrar alg. ~ **sb to do sth** pedir alguém para fazer alguma coisa

askew /ə'skju:/ adv & a de través, de esguelha

asleep /ə'sli:p/ adv & a adormecido; (numb) dormente. **fall** ~ adormecer

asparagus /ə'spærəgəs/ n (plant) aspargo m, (P) espargo m; (culin) aspargos mpl, (P) espargo m

aspect /'æspekt/ n aspecto m; (direction) exposição f

aspersions /ə'spɜ:ʃnz/ npl **cast** ~ **on** caluniar

asphalt /'æsfælt/ n asfalto m □ vt asfaltar

asphyxiat|e /əs'fɪksɪeɪt/ vt/i asfixiar. ~**ion** /-'eɪʃn/ n asfixia f

aspir|e /əs'paɪə(r)/ vi ~**e to** aspirar a. ~**ation** /æspə'reɪʃn/ n aspiração f

aspirin /'æsprɪn/ n aspirina f

ass /æs/ n burro m. **make an** ~ **of o.s.** fazer papel de palhaço, (P) fazer figura de parvo

assail /ə'seɪl/ vt assaltar, agredir. ~**ant** n assaltante mf, agressor m

assassin /ə'sæsɪn/ n assassino m

assassinat|e /ə'sæsɪneɪt/ vt assassinar. ~**ion** /-'eɪʃn/ n assassinato m

assault /ə'sɔ:lt/ n assalto m □ vt assaltar, atacar

assemble /ə'sembl/ vt (people) reunir; (fit together) montar □ vi reunir-se

assembly /ə'semblɪ/ n assembléia f, (P) assembleia f. ~ **line** linha f de montagem

assent /ə'sent/ n assentimento m □ vi ~ **to** consentir em

assert /ə'sɜ:t/ vt afirmar; (one's rights) reivindicar. ~ **o.s.** impor-se. ~**ion** /-ʃn/ n asserção f. ~**ive** a dogmático, peremptório. ~**iveness** n assertividade f, (P) firmeza f

assess /ə'ses/ vt avaliar; (payment) estabelecer o montante de. ~**ment** n avaliação f. ~**or** n (valuer) avaliador m

asset /'æset/ n (advantage) vantagem f. ~**s** (comm) ativo m, (P) activo m (possessions) bens mpl

assiduous /ə'sɪdjʊəs/ a assíduo

assign /ə'saɪn/ vt atribuir, destinar

(*jur*) transmitir. ~ **sb to** designar alg para

assignation /æsɪg'neɪʃn/ *n* combinação *f* (de hora e local) de encontro

assignment /ə'saɪnmənt/ *n* tarefa *f*, missão *f*; (*jur*) transmissão *f*

assimilat|e /ə'sɪmɪleɪt/ *vt/i* assimilar(-se). ~**ion** /-'eɪʃn/ *n* assimilação *f*

assist /ə'sɪst/ *vt/i* ajudar. ~**ance** *n* ajuda *f*, assistência *f*

assistant /ə'sɪstənt/ *n* (*helper*) assistente *mf*, auxiliar *mf*; (*in shop*) ajudante *mf*, empregado *m* □ *a* adjunto

associat|e[1] /ə'səʊʃɪeɪt/ *vt* associar □ *vi* ~**e with** conviver com. ~**ion** /-'eɪʃn/ *n* associação *f*

associate[2] /ə'səʊʃɪət/ *a & n* associado (*m*)

assort|ed /ə'sɔ:tɪd/ *a* variados; (*foods*) sortidos. ~**ment** *n* sortimento *m*, (*P*) sortido *m*

assume /ə'sju:m/ *vt* assumir; (*presume*) supor, presumir

assumption /ə'sʌmpʃn/ *n* suposição *f*

assurance /ə'ʃʊərəns/ *n* certeza *f*, garantia *f*; (*insurance*) seguro *m*; (*self-confidence*) segurança *f*, confiança *f*

assure /ə'ʃʊə(r)/ *vt* assegurar. ~**d** *a* certo, garantido. **rest** ~**d that** ficar certo que

asterisk /'æstərɪsk/ *n* asterisco *m*

asthma /'æsmə/ *n* asma *f*. ~**tic** /-'mætɪk/ *a & n* asmático (*m*)

astonish /ə'stɒnɪʃ/ *vt* espantar. ~**ingly** *adv* espantosamente. ~**ment** *n* espanto *m*

astound /ə'staʊnd/ *vt* assombrar

astray /ə'streɪ/ *adv & a* **go** ~ perder-se, extraviar-se. **lead** ~ desencaminhar

astride /ə'straɪd/ *adv & prep* escarranchado (em)

astringent /ə'strɪndʒənt/ *a & n* adstringente (*m*)

strolog|y /ə'strɒlədʒɪ/ *n* astrologia *f*. ~**er** *n* astrólogo *m*

astronaut /'æstrənɔ:t/ *n* astronauta *mf*

astronom|y /ə'strɒnəmɪ/ *n* astronomia *f*. ~**er** *n* astrónomo *m*, (*P*) astrónomo *m*. ~**ical** /æstrə'nɒmɪkl/ *a* astronômico, (*P*) astronómico

astute /ə'stju:t/ *a* astuto, astucioso. ~**ness** *n* astúcia *f*

asylum /ə'saɪləm/ *n* asilo *m*

at /ət/; *emphatic* /æt/ *prep* a, em. ~ **home** em casa. ~ **night** à noite. ~ **once** imediatamente; (*simultaneously*) ao mesmo tempo. ~ **school** na escola. ~ **sea** no mar. ~ **the door** na porta. ~ **times** às vezes. **angry/ surprised** ~ zangado/surpreendido

com. **not** ~ **all** de nada. **no wind** ~ **all** nenhum vento

ate /et/ *see* **eat**

atheis|t /'eɪθɪɪst/ *n* ateu *m*. ~**m** /-zəm/ *n* ateísmo *m*

athlet|e /'æθli:t/ *n* atleta *mf*. ~**ic** /-'letɪk/ *a* atlético. ~**ics** /-'letɪks/ *n*(*pl*) atletismo *m*

Atlantic /ət'læntɪk/ *a* atlântico □ *n* ~ (**Ocean**) Atlântico *m*

atlas /'ætləs/ *n* atlas *m*

atmospher|e /'ætməsfɪə(r)/ *n* atmosfera *f*. ~**ic** /-'ferɪk/ *a* atmosférico

atom /'ætəm/ *n* átomo *m*. ~**ic** /ə'tɒmɪk/ *a* atômico, (*P*) atómico. ~(**ic**) **bomb** bomba *f* atômica, (*P*) atómica

atomize /'ætəmaɪz/ *vt* atomizar, vaporizar, pulverizar. ~**r** /-ə(r)/ *n* pulverizador *m*, vaporizador *m*

atone /ə'təʊn/ *vi* ~ **for** expiar. ~**ment** *n* expiação *f*

atrocious /ə'trəʊʃəs/ *a* atroz

atrocity /ə'trɒsətɪ/ *n* atrocidade *f*

atrophy /'ætrəfɪ/ *n* atrofia *f* □ *vt/i* atrofiar(-se)

attach /ə'tætʃ/ *vt/i* (*affix*) ligar(-se), prender(-se); (*join*) juntar(-se). ~**ed** *a* (*document*) junto, anexo. **be** ~**ed to** (*like*) estar apegado a. ~**ment** *n* ligação *f*; (*affection*) apego *m*; (*accessory*) acessório *m*

attaché /ə'tæʃeɪ/ *n* (*pol*) adido *m*. ~ **case** pasta *f*

attack /ə'tæk/ *n* ataque *m* □ *vt/i* atacar. ~**er** *n* atacante *mf*

attain /ə'teɪn/ *vt* atingir. ~**able** *a* atingível. ~**ment** *n* consecução *f*. ~**ments** *npl* conhecimentos *mpl*, talentos *mpl* adquiridos

attempt /ə'tempt/ *vt* tentar □ *n* tentativa *f*

attend /ə'tend/ *vt/i* atender (**to** a); (*escort*) acompanhar; (*look after*) tratar; (*meeting*) comparecer a; (*school*) freqüentar, (*P*) frequentar. ~**ance** *n* comparecimento *m*; (*times present*) freqüência *f*, (*P*) frequência *f*; (*people*) assistência *f*

attendant /ə'tendənt/ *a* concomitante, que acompanha □ *n* empregado *m*; (*servant*) servidor *m*

attention /ə'tenʃn/ *n* atenção *f*. ~**!** (*mil*) sentido! **pay** ~ prestar atenção (**to** a)

attentive /ə'tentɪv/ *a* atento; (*considerate*) atencioso

attest /ə'test/ *vt/i* ~ (**to**) atestar. ~ **a signature** reconhecer uma assinatura. ~**ation** /ætə'steɪʃn/ *n* atestação *f*, prova *f*

attic /'ætɪk/ *n* sótão *m*, águafurtada *f*

attitude /'ætɪtju:d/ *n* atitude *f*

attorney /ə'tɜːnɪ/ n (pl -eys) procurador m; (Amer) advogado m

attract /ə'trækt/ vt atrair. ~ion /-ʃn/ n atração f, (P) atracção f; (charm) atrativo m, (P) atractivo m

attractive /ə'træktɪv/ a atraente. ~ly adv atraentemente, agradavelmente

attribute¹ /ə'trɪbjuːt/ vt ~ to atribuir a

attribute² /'ætrɪbjuːt/ n atributo m

attrition /ə'trɪʃn/ n war of ~ guerra f de desgaste

aubergine /'əʊbəʒiːn/ n berinjela f

auburn /'ɔːbən/ a cor de acaju, castanho-avermelhado

auction /'ɔːkʃn/ n leilão m □ vt leiloar. ~eer /-ə'nɪə(r)/ n leiloeiro m, (P) pregoeiro m

audaci|ous /ɔː'deɪʃəs/ a audacioso, audaz. ~ty /-æsətɪ/ n audácia f

audible /'ɔːdəbl/ a audível

audience /'ɔːdɪəns/ n auditório m; (theat, radio; interview) audiência f

audiovisual /ɔːdɪəʊ'vɪʒʊəl/ a audiovisual

audit /'ɔːdɪt/ n auditoria f □ vt fazer uma auditoria

audition /ɔː'dɪʃn/ n audição f □ vt dar/fazer uma audição

auditor /'ɔːdɪtə(r)/ n perito-contador m, (P) perito-contabilista m

auditorium /ɔːdɪ'tɔːrɪəm/ n auditório m

augment /ɔːg'ment/ vt/i aumentar (-se)

augur /'ɔːgə(r)/ vi ~ well/ill ser de bom ou mau agouro

August /'ɔːgəst/ n Agosto m

aunt /aːnt/ n tia f

au pair /əʊ'peə(r)/ n au pair f

aura /'ɔːrə/ n aura f, emanação f

auspices /'ɔːspɪsɪz/ npl under the ~ of sob os auspícios or o patrocínio de

auspicious /ɔː'spɪʃəs/ a auspicioso

auster|e /ɔː'stɪə(r)/ a austero. ~ity /-erətɪ/ n austeridade f

Australia /ɒ'streɪlɪə/ n Austrália f. ~n a & n australiano (m)

Austria /'ɒstrɪə/ n áustria f. ~n a & n austríaco (m)

authentic /ɔː'θentɪk/ a autêntico. ~ity /-ən'tɪsətɪ/ n autenticidade f

authenticate /ɔː'θentɪkeɪt/ vt autenticar

author /'ɔːθə(r)/ n autor m, autora f. ~ship n (origin) autoria f

authoritarian /ɔːθɒrɪ'teərɪən/ a autoritário

authorit|y /ɔː'θɒrətɪ/ n autoridade f; (permission) autorização f. ~ative /-ɪtətɪv/ a (trusted) autorizado; (manner) autoritário

authoriz|e /'ɔːθəraɪz/ vt autorizar. ~ation /-'zeɪʃn/ n autorização f

autistic /ɔː'tɪstɪk/ a autista, autístico

autobiography /ɔːtə'baɪɒgrəfɪ/ n autobiografia f

autocrat /'ɔːtəkræt/ n autocrata mf. ~ic /-'krætɪk/ a autocrático

autograph /'ɔːtəgraːf/ n autógrafo m □ vt autografar

automat|e /'ɔːtəmeɪt/ vt automatizar. ~ion /ɔːtə'meɪʃn/ n automação f

automatic /ɔːtə'mætɪk/ a automático □ n (car) automático m. ~ally /-klɪ/ adv automaticamente

automobile /'ɔːtəməbiːl/ n (Amer) automóvel m

autonom|y /ɔː'tɒnəmɪ/ n autonomia f. ~ous a autônomo, (P) autónomo

autopsy /'ɔːtɒpsɪ/ n autópsia f

autumn /'ɔːtəm/ n outono m. ~al /-'tʌmnəl/ a outonal

auxiliary /ɔːg'zɪlɪərɪ/ a & n auxiliar (mf). ~ verb verbo m auxiliar

avail /ə'veɪl/ vt ~ o.s. of servir-se de □ vi (be of use) valer □ n of no ~ inútil. to no ~ sem resultado, em vão

availab|le /ə'veɪləbl/ a disponível. ~ility /-'bɪlətɪ/ n disponibilidade f

avalanche /'ævəlaːnʃ/ n avalanche f

avaric|e /'ævərɪs/ n avareza f. ~ious /-'rɪʃəs/ a avarento

avenge /ə'vendʒ/ vt vingar

avenue /'ævənjuː/ n avenida f; (fig line of approach) via f

average /'ævərɪdʒ/ n média f □ a médio □ vt tirar a média de; (produce do) fazer em média □ vi ~ out at dar de média, dar uma média de. on ~ em média

avers|e /ə'vɜːs/ a be ~e to ser avesso a. ~ion /-ʃn/ n aversão f, repug nância f

avert /ə'vɜːt/ vt (turn away) desviar (ward off) evitar

aviary /'eɪvɪərɪ/ n aviário m

aviation /eɪvɪ'eɪʃn/ n aviação f

avid /'ævɪd/ a ávido

avocado /ævə'kaːdəʊ/ n (pl -s) aba cate m

avoid /ə'vɔɪd/ vt evitar. ~able a que se pode evitar, evitável. ~ance n evitação f

await /ə'weɪt/ vt aguardar

awake /ə'weɪk/ vt/i (pt awoke, p awoken) acordar □ a be ~ estar acor dado

awaken /ə'weɪkən/ vt/i desperta ~ing n despertar m

award /ə'wɔːd/ vt atribuir, conferir (jur) adjudicar □ n recompensa j prêmio m, (P) prémio m; (scholarship bolsa f

aware /ə'weə(r)/ a ciente, cônscio. b ~ of estar consciente de or ter con sciência de. **become** ~ **of** tomar consciência de. **make sb** ~ **of** sensibilizar alg para. **~ness** n consciência f

away /əˈweɪ/ adv (at a distance) longe; (to a distance) para longe; (absent) fora; (persistently) sem parar; (entirely) completamente. **eight miles** ~ a oito milhas (de distância). **four days** ~ daí a quatro dias □ a & n ~ (**match**) jogo m fora de casa

awe /ɔː/ n assombro m, admiração f reverente, terror m respeitoso. **~some** a assombroso. **~struck** a assombrado, aterrado

awful /ˈɔːfl/ a terrível. **~ly** adv muito, terrivelmente

awhile /əˈwaɪl/ adv por algum tempo

awkward /ˈɔːkwəd/ a difícil; (clumsy, difficult to use) desajeitado, maljeitoso; (inconvenient) inconveniente; (embarrassing) embaraçoso; (embarrassed) embaraçado. **an** ~ **customer** (colloq) um preguês perigoso or intratável

awning /ˈɔːnɪŋ/ n toldo m

awoke, awoken /əˈwəʊk, əˈwəʊkən/ see **awake**

awry /əˈraɪ/ adv torto. **go** ~ dar errado. **be** ~ estar torto

axe /æks/ n machado m □ vt (pres p **axing**) (reduce) cortar; (dismiss) despedir

axiom /ˈæksɪəm/ n axioma m

axis /ˈæksɪs/ n (pl axes /-iːz/) eixo m

axle /ˈæksl/ n eixo (de roda) m

Azores /əˈzɔːz/ n Açores mpl

B

BA abbr see **Bachelor of Arts**

babble /ˈbæbl/ vi balbuciar; (baby) palrar; (stream) murmurar □ n balbucio m; (of baby) palrice f; (of stream) murmúrio m

baboon /bəˈbuːn/ n babuíno m

baby /ˈbeɪbɪ/ n bebê m, (P) bebé m. ~ **carriage** (Amer) carrinho m de bebê, (P) bebé. **~-sit** vi tomar conta de crianças. **~-sitter** n baby-sitter mf, babá f

babyish /ˈbeɪbɪʃ/ a infantil

bachelor /ˈbætʃələ(r)/ n solteiro m. **B~ of Arts/Science** Bacharel m em Letras/Ciências

back /bæk/ n (of person, hand, chair) costas fpl; (of animal) dorso m; (of car, train) parte f traseira; (of house, room) fundo m; (of coin) reverso m; (of page) verso m; (football) beque m; (zagueiro m, (P) defesa m □ a traseiro, posterior; (taxes) em atraso □ adv atrás, para trás; (returned) de volta □ vt (support) apoiar; (horse) apos-

tar em; (car) (fazer) recuar □ vi recuar. **at the** ~ **of beyond** em casa do diabo, no fim do mundo. **~-bencher** n (pol) deputado m sem pasta. ~ **down** desistir (from de). ~ **number** número m atrasado. ~ **out** (of an undertaking etc) fugir (ao combinado etc). ~ **up** (auto) fazer marcha à ré, (P) atrás; (comput) tirar um back-up de. **~-up** n apoio m; (comput) back-up m; (Amer: traffic-jam) engarrafamento m □ a de reserva; (comput) back-up

backache /ˈbækeɪk/ n dor f nas costas

backbiting /ˈbækbaɪtɪŋ/ n maledicência f

backbone /ˈbækbəʊn/ n espinha f dorsal

backdate /bækˈdeɪt/ vt antedatar

backer /ˈbækə(r)/ n (of horse) apostador m; (of cause) partidário m, apoiante mf; (comm) patrocinador m, financiador m

backfire /bækˈfaɪə(r)/ vi (auto) dar explosões no tubo de escape; (fig) sair o tiro pela culatra

background /ˈbækgraʊnd/ n (of picture) fundo m, segundo-plano m; (context) contexto m; (environment) meio m; (experience) formação f

backhand /ˈbækhænd/ n (tennis) esquerda f. **~ed** a com as costas da mão. **~ed compliment** cumprimento m ambíguo. **~er** /-ˈhændə(r)/ n (sl: bribe) suborno m, (P) luvas fpl (colloq)

backing /ˈbækɪŋ/ n apoio m; (comm) patrocínio m

backlash /ˈbæklæʃ/ n (fig) reação f violenta, repercussões fpl

backlog /ˈbæklɒg/ n acúmulo m (de trabalho etc)

backside /ˈbæksaɪd/ n (colloq: buttocks) traseiro m

backstage /bækˈsteɪdʒ/ a & adv por detrás dos bastidores

backstroke /ˈbækstrəʊk/ n nado m de costas

backtrack /ˈbæktræk/ vi (fig) voltar atrás

backward /ˈbækwəd/ a retrógrado; (retarded) atrasado; (step, look, etc) para trás

backwards /ˈbækwədz/ adv para trás; (walk) para trás; (fall) de costas, para trás; (in reverse order) de trás para diante, às avessas. **go** ~ **and forwards** ir e vir, andar para trás e para a frente. **know sth** ~ saber alg coisa de trás para a frente

backwater /ˈbækwɔːtə(r)/ n (pej: place) lugar m atrasado

bacon /ˈbeɪkən/ n toucinho m defumado; (in rashers) bacon m

bacteria /bæk'tɪərɪə/ *npl* bactérias *fpl*. ~l *a* bacteriano

bad /bæd/ *a* (**worse, worst**) mau; (*accident*) grave; (*food*) estragado; (*ill*) doente. **feel ~** sentir-se mal. **~ language** palavrões *mpl*. **~-mannered** *a* mal educado. **~-tempered** *a* mal humorado. **~ly** *adv* mal; (*seriously*) gravemente. **want ~ly** (*desire*) desejar imensamente, ter grande vontade de; (*need*) precisar muito de

badge /bædʒ/ *n* emblema *m*; (*policeman's*) crachá *m*, (*P*) distintivo *m*

badger /'bædʒə(r)/ *n* texugo *m* □ *vt* atormentar; (*pester*) importunar

badminton /'bædmɪntən/ *n* badminton *m*

baffle /'bæfl/ *vt* atrapalhar, desconcertar

bag /bæg/ *n* saco *m*; (*handbag*) bolsa *f*, carteira *f*. **~s** (*luggage*) malas *fpl* □ *vt* (*pt* **bagged**) ensacar; (*colloq: take*) embolsar

baggage /'bægɪdʒ/ *n* bagagem *f*

baggy /'bægɪ/ *a* (*clothes*) muito largo, bufante

bagpipes /'bægpaɪps/ *npl* gaita *f* de foles

Bahamas /bə'hɑːməz/ *npl* **the ~** as Bahamas *fpl*

bail¹ /beɪl/ *n* fiança *f* □ *vt* pôr em liberdade sob fiança. **be out on ~** estar solto sob fiança

bail² /beɪl/ *vt* ~ (**out**) (*naut*) esgotar, tirar água de

bailiff /'beɪlɪf/ *n* (*officer*) oficial *m* de diligências; (*of estate*) feitor *m*

bait /beɪt/ *n* isca *f* □ *vt* pôr isca; (*fig*) atormentar (com insultos), atazanar

bak|e /beɪk/ *vt/i* cozer (no forno); (*bread, cakes, etc*) assar; (*in the sun*) torrar. **~er** *n* padeiro *m*; (*of cakes*) doceiro *m*. **~ing** *n* cozedura *f*; (*batch*) fornada *f*. **~ing-powder** *n* fermento *m* em pó. **~ing tin** forma *f*

bakery /'beɪkərɪ/ *n* padaria *f*; (*cakes*) confeitaria *f*

balance /'bæləns/ *n* equilíbrio *m*; (*scales*) balança *f*; (*sum*) saldo *m*; (*comm*) balanço *m*. **~ of power** equilíbrio *m* político. **~ of trade** balança *f* comercial. **~-sheet** *n* balanço *m* □ *vt* equilibrar; (*weigh up*) pesar; (*budget*) equilibrar □ *vi* equilibrar-se. **~d** *a* equilibrado

balcony /'bælkənɪ/ *n* balcão *m*; (*in a house*) varanda *f*

bald /bɔːld/ *a* (**-er, -est**) calvo, careca; (*tyre*) careca. **~ing a** be **~ing** ficar calvo. **~ly** *adv* a nu e cru, (*P*) secamente. **~ness** *n* calvície *f*

bale¹ /beɪl/ *n* (*of straw*) fardo *m*; (*of cotton*) balote *m* □ *vt* enfardar

bale² /beɪl/ *vi* ~ **out** saltar em pára-quedas

balk /bɔːk/ *vt* frustrar, contrariar □ *vi* ~ **at** assustar-se com, recuar perante

ball¹ /bɔːl/ *n* bola *f*. **~-bearing** *n* rolamento *m* de esferas. **~-cock** *n* válvula *f* de depósito de água. **~-point** *n* esferográfica *f*

ball² /bɔːl/ *n* (*dance*) baile *m*

ballad /'bæləd/ *n* balada *f*

ballast /'bæləst/ *n* lastro *m*

ballerina /bælə'riːnə/ *n* bailarina *f*

ballet /'bæleɪ/ *n* balé *m*, (*P*) ballet *m*, bailado *m*

balloon /bə'luːn/ *n* balão *m*

ballot /'bælət/ *n* escrutínio *m*. ~ **(-paper)** *n* cédula *f* eleitoral, (*P*) boletim *m* de voto. **~-box** *n* urna *f* □ *vi* (*pt* **balloted**) (*pol*) votar □ *vt* (*members*) consultar por voto secreto

ballroom /'bɔːlruːm/ *n* salão *m* de baile

balm /bɑːm/ *n* bálsamo *m*. **~y** *a* balsâmico; (*mild*) suave

balustrade /bælə'streɪd/ *n* balaustrada *f*

bamboo /bæm'buː/ *n* bambu *m*

ban /bæn/ *vt* (*pt* **banned**) banir. ~ **from** proibir de □ *n* proibição *f*

banal /bə'nɑːl/ *a* banal. **~ity** /-ælətɪ/ *n* banalidade *f*

banana /bə'nɑːnə/ *n* banana *f*

band /bænd/ *n* (*for fastening*) cinta *f*, faixa *f*; (*strip*) tira *f*, banda *f*; (*mus: mil*) banda *f*; (*mus: dance, jazz*) conjunto *m*; (*group*) bando *m* □ *vi* ~ **together** juntar-se

bandage /'bændɪdʒ/ *n* atadura *f*, (*P*) ligadura *f* □ *vt* ligar

bandit /'bændɪt/ *n* bandido *m*

bandstand /'bændstænd/ *n* coreto *m*

bandwagon /'bændwægən/ *n* **climb on the ~** (*fig*) apanhar o trem

bandy /'bændɪ/ *vt* trocar. ~ **a story about** espalhar uma história

bandy-legged /'bændɪlegd/ *a* cambaio, de pernas tortas

bang /bæŋ/ *n* (*blow*) pancada *f*; (*loud noise*) estouro *m*, estrondo *m*; (*of gun*) detonação *f* □ *vt/i* (*hit, shut*) bater □ *vi* explodir □ *int* pum. ~ **in the middle** jogar no meio. **shut the door with a ~** bater (com) a porta

banger /'bæŋə(r)/ *n* (*firework*) bomba *f*; (*sl: sausage*) salsicha *f*. (**old**) ~ (*sl: car*) calhambeque *m* (*colloq*)

bangle /'bæŋgl/ *n* pulseira *f*, bracelete *m*

banish /'bænɪʃ/ *vt* banir, desterrar

banisters /'bænɪstəz/ *npl* corrimão *m*

banjo /'bændʒəʊ/ *pl* (**-os**) banjo *m*

bank¹ /bæŋk/ *n* (*of river*) margem *f*; (*of earth*) talude *m*; (*of sand*) banco *m*

□ *vt* amontoar □ *vi* (*aviat*) inclinar-se numa curva

bank² /bæŋk/ *n* (*comm*) banco *m* □ *vt* depositar no banco. **~ account** conta *f* bancária. **~ holiday** feriado *m* nacional. **~ on** contar com. **~ rate** taxa *f* bancária. **~ with** ter conta em

bank|er /'bæŋkə(r)/ *n* banqueiro *m*. **~ing** /-ŋ/ *n* operações *fpl* bancárias; (*career*) carreira *f* bancária, banca *f*

banknote /'bæŋknəʊt/ *n* nota *f* de banco

bankrupt /'bæŋkrʌpt/ *a* & *n* falido (*m*). **go ~** falir □ *vt* levar à falência. **~cy** *n* falência *f*, bancarrota *f*

banner /'bænə(r)/ *n* bandeira *f*, estandarte *m*

banns /bænz/ *npl* proclamas *mpl*, (*P*) banhos *mpl*

banquet /'bæŋkwɪt/ *n* banquete *m*

banter /'bæntə(r)/ *n* gracejo *m*, brincadeira *f* □ *vi* gracejar, brincar

baptism /'bæptɪzəm/ *n* batismo *m*, (*P*) baptismo *m*

Baptist /'bæptɪst/ *n* batista *mf*, (*P*) baptista *mf*

baptize /bæp'taɪz/ *vt* batizar, (*P*) baptizar

bar /ba:(r)/ *n* (*of chocolate*) tablette *f*, barra *f*; (*of metal, soap, sand etc*) barra *f*; (*of door, window*) tranca *f*; (*in pub*) bar *m*; (*counter*) balcão *m*, bar *m*; (*mus*) barra *f* de compasso; (*fig: obstacle*) barreira *f*, (*in lawcourt*) teia *f*. **the B~** a advocacia *f* □ *vt* (*pt* **barred**) (*obstruct*) barrar; (*prohibit*) proibir (**from** de); (*exclude*) excluir; (*door, window*) trancar □ *prep* salvo, exceto, (*P*) excepto **~ none** sem exceção, (*P*) excepção. **~ code** código *m* de barra. **behind ~s** na cadeia

Barbados /ba:'beɪdɒs/ *n* Barbados *mpl*

barbarian /ba:'beərɪən/ *n* bárbaro *m*

barbari|c /ba:'bærɪk/ *a* bárbaro. **~ty** /-ətɪ/ *n* barbaridade *f*

barbarous /'ba:bərəs/ *a* bárbaro

barbecue /'ba:bɪkju:/ *n* (*grill*) churrasqueira *f*; (*occasion, food*) churrasco *m* □ *vt* assar

barbed /ba:bd/ *a* **~ wire** arame *m* farpado

barber /'ba:bə(r)/ *n* barbeiro *m*

barbiturate /ba:'bɪtjʊərət/ *n* barbitúrico *m*

bare /beə(r)/ *a* (-**er**, -**est**) nu; (*room*) vazio; (*mere*) mero □ *vt* pôr à mostra, pôr a nu, descobrir

bareback /'beəbæk/ *adv* em pêlo

barefaced /'beəfeɪst/ *a* descarado

barefoot /'beə(r)fʊt/ *adv* descalço

barely /'beəlɪ/ *adv* apenas, mal

bargain /'ba:gɪn/ *n* (*deal*) negócio *m*;

(*good buy*) pechincha *f* □ *vi* negociar; (*haggle*) regatear. **~ for** esperar for

barge /ba:dʒ/ *n* barcaça *f* □ *vi* **~ in** interromper (despropositadamente); (*into room*) irromper

bark¹ /ba:k/ *n* (*of tree*) casca *f*

bark² /ba:k/ *n* (*of dog*) latido *m* □ *vi* latir. **his ~ is worse than his bite** cão que ladra não morde

barley /'ba:lɪ/ *n* cevada *f*. **~ sugar** *n* açúcar *m* de cevada. **~ water** *n* água *f* de cevada

barmaid /'ba:meɪd/ *n* empregada *f* de bar

barman /'ba:mən/ *n* (*pl* -**men**) barman *m*, empregado *m* de bar

barmy /'ba:mɪ/ *a* (*sl*) maluco

barn /ba:n/ *n* celeiro *m*

barometer /bə'rɒmɪtə(r)/ *n* barômetro *m*, (*P*) barómetro *m*

baron /'bærən/ *n* barão *m*. **~ess** *n* baronesa *f*

baroque /bə'rɒk/ *a* & *n* barroco (*m*)

barracks /'bærəks/ *n* quartel *m*, caserna *f*

barrage /'bæra:ʒ/ *n* barragem *f*; (*fig*) enxurrada *f*; (*mil*) fogo *m* de barragem

barrel /'bærəl/ *n* (*of oil, wine*) barril *m*; (*of gun*) cano *m*. **~-organ** *n* realejo *m*

barren /'bærən/ *a* estéril; (*soil*) árido, estéril

barricade /bærɪ'keɪd/ *n* barricada *f* □ *vt* barricar

barrier /'bærɪə(r)/ *n* barreira *f*; (*hindrance*) entrave *m*, barreira *f*

barring /'ba:rɪŋ/ *prep* salvo, exceto, (*P*) excepto

barrister /'bærɪstə(r)/ *n* advogado *m*

barrow /'bærəʊ/ *n* carrinho *m* de mão

barter /'ba:tə(r)/ *n* troca *f* □ *vt* trocar

base /beɪs/ *n* base *f* □ *vt* basear (**on** em) □ *a* baixo, ignóbil. **~less** *a* infundado

baseball /'beɪsbɔ:l/ *n* beisebol *m*

basement /'beɪsmənt/ *n* porão *m*, (*P*) cave *f*

bash /bæʃ/ *vt* bater com violência □ *n* pancada *f* forte. **have a ~ at** (*sl*) experimentar

bashful /'bæʃfl/ *a* tímido

basic /'beɪsɪk/ *a* básico, elementar, fundamental. **~ally** *adv* basicamente, no fundo

basil /'bæzl/ *n* mangericão *m*

basin /'beɪsn/ *n* bacia *f*; (*for food*) tigela *f*; (*naut*) ante-doca *f*; (*for washing*) pia *f*

basis /'beɪsɪs/ *n* (*pl* **bases** /-si:z/) base *f*

bask /ba:sk/ *vi* **~ in the sun** apanhar sol

basket /'ba:skɪt/ *n* cesto *m*

basketball /'ba:skɪtbɔ:l/ n basquete(-bol) m

Basque /ba:sk/ a & n basco (m)

bass[1] /bæs/ n (pl bass) (fish) perca f

bass[2] /beɪs/ a (mus) grave □ n (pl basses) (mus) baixo m

bassoon /bə'su:n/ n fagote m

bastard /'ba:stəd/ n (illegitimate child) bastardo m; (sl: pej) safado (sl) m; (colloq: not pej) cara (colloq) m

baste /beɪst/ vt (culin) regar (com molho)

bastion /'bæstɪən/ n bastião m, baluarte m

bat[1] /bæt/ n (cricket) pá f; (baseball) bastão m; (table tennis) rafuete f □ vt/i (pt batted) bater (em). without ~ting an eyelid sem pestanejar

bat[2] /bæt/ n (zool) morcego m

batch /bætʃ/ n (loaves) fornada f, (people) monte m; (goods) remessa f; (papers, letters etc) batelada f, monte m

bated /'beɪtɪd/ a with ~ breath com a respiração em suspenso, com a respiração suspensa

bath /ba:θ/ n (pl -s /ba:ðz/) banho m; (tub) banheira f. ~s (washing) banho m público; (swimming) piscina f □ vt dar banho a □ vi tomar banho

bathe /beɪð/ vt dar banho em; (wound) limpar □ vi tomar banho (de mar) □ n banho m (de mar). ~r /-ə(r)/ n banhista mf

bathing /'beɪðɪŋ/ n banho m de mar. ~-costume/-suit n traje m de banho, (P) fato m de banho

bathrobe /'ba:θrəub/ n (Amer) roupão m

bathroom /'ba:θru:m/ n banheiro m, (P) casa f de banho

baton /'bætən/ n (mus) batuta f; (policeman's) cassetete m; (mil) bastão m

battalion /bə'tælɪən/ n batalhão m

batter /'bætə(r)/ vt bater, espancar, maltratar □ n (culin: for cakes) massa f de bolos; (culin: for frying) massa f de empanar. ~ed a (car, pan) amassado; (child, wife) maltratado, espancado. ~ing n take a ~ing levar pancada or uma surra

battery /'bætərɪ/ n (mil, auto) bateria f; (electr) pilha f

battle /'bætl/ n batalha f, (fig) luta f □ vi combater, batalhar, lutar

battlefield /'bætlfi:ld/ n campo m de batalha

battlements /'bætlmənts/ npl ameias fpl

battleship /'bætlʃɪp/ n couraçado m

baulk /bɔ:lk/ vt/i = balk

bawdy /'bɔ:dɪ/ a (-ier, -iest) obsceno, indecente

bawl /bɔ:l/ vt/i berrar

bay[1] /beɪ/ n (bot) loureiro m

bay[2] /beɪ/ n (geog) baía f. ~ window janela f saliente

bay[3] /beɪ/ n (bark) latido m □ vi latir. at ~ (animal; fig) cercado, (P) em apuros. keep at ~ manter à distância

bayonet /'beɪənɪt/ n baioneta f

bazaar /bə'za:(r)/ n bazar m

BC abbr (before Christ) a C

be /bi:/ vi (pres am, are, is; pt was, were; pp been) (permanent quality/place) ser; (temporary place/state) estar; (become) ficar. ~ hot/right etc ter calor/razão etc. he's 30 (age) ele tem 30 anos. it's fine/cold etc (weather) faz bom tempo/frio etc. how are you? (health) como está? I'm a doctor — are you? eu sou médico — é mesmo? it's pretty, isn't it? é bonito, não é? he is to come (must) ele deve vir. how much is it? (cost) quanto é? ~ reading eating etc estar lendo/comendo etc. the money was found o dinheiro foi encontrado. have been to ter ido a, ter estado em

beach /bi:tʃ/ n praia f

beacon /'bi:kən/ n farol m; (marker) baliza f

bead /bi:d/ n conta f. ~ of sweat gota f de suor

beak /bi:k/ n bico m

beaker /'bi:kə(r)/ n copo m de plástico com bico; (in lab) proveta f

beam /bi:m/ n (of wood) trave f, viga f; (of light) raio m; (of torch) feixe m de luz □ vt/i (radiate) irradiar; (fig) sorrir radiante. ~ing a radiante

bean /bi:n/ n feijão m. broad ~ fava f. coffee ~s café m em grão. runner ~ feijão m verde

bear[1] /beə(r)/ n urso m

bear[2] /beə(r)/ vt/i (pt bore, pp borne) sustentar, suportar; (endure) agüentar, (P) aguentar, suportar; (child) dar à luz. ~ in mind ter em mente, lembrar. ~ left virar à esquerda. ~ on relacionar-se com, ter a ver com. ~ out confirmar. ~ up! coragem! ~able a tolerável, suportável. ~er n portador m

beard /bɪəd/ n barba f. ~ed a barbado, com barba

bearing /'beərɪŋ/ n (manner) porte m; (relevance) relação f; (naut) marcação f. get one's ~s orientar-se

beast /bi:st/ n (animal, person) besta f, animal m; (in fables) fera f. ~ of burden besta f de carga

beat /bi:t/ vt/i (pt beat, pp beaten) bater □ n (med) batimento m; (mus) compasso m, ritmo m; (of drum) toque m; (of policeman) ronda f, (P) giro m. ~ about the bush estar com rodeios. ~ a retreat bater em retirada. ~ it (*sl: go away*) pôr-se a andar. it ~s me (*colloq*) não consigo entender. ~ up espancar. ~er *n* (*culin*) batedeira *f*. ~ing *n* sova *f*

beautician /bjuːˈtɪʃn/ *n* esteticista *mf*

beautiful /ˈbjuːtɪfl/ *a* belo, lindo. ~ly *adv* lindamente

beautify /ˈbjuːtɪfaɪ/ *vt* embelezar

beauty /ˈbjuːtɪ/ *n* beleza *f*. ~ **parlour** instituto *m* de beleza. ~ **spot** sinal *m* no rosto, mosca *f*; (*place*) local *m* pitoresco

beaver /ˈbiːvə(r)/ *n* castor *m*

became /bɪˈkeɪm/ *see* **become**

because /bɪˈkɒz/ *conj* porque □ *adv* ~ **of** por causa de

beckon /ˈbekən/ *vt/i* ~ **(to)** fazer sinal (para)

become /bɪˈkʌm/ *vt/i* (*pt* **became**, *pp* **become**) tornar-se. **what has** ~ **of her?** que é feito dela?

becoming /bɪˈkʌmɪŋ/ *a* que fica bem, apropriado

bed /bed/ *n* cama *f*; (*layer*) camada *f*; (*of sea*) fundo *m*; (*of river*) leito *m*; (*of flowers*) canteiro *m* □ *vt/i* (*pt* **bedded**) ~ **down** ir deitar-se. ~ **in** plantar. ~ **and breakfast (b & b)** quarto *m* com café da manhã. ~**sit(ter)** *n* (*colloq*) misto *m* de quarto e sala. **go to** ~ ir para cama. **in** ~ na cama. ~**ding** *n* roupa *f* de cama

bedclothes /ˈbedkləʊðz/ *n* roupa *f* de cama

bedlam /ˈbedləm/ *n* confusão *f*, balbúrdia *f*

bedraggled /bɪˈdrægld/ *a* (*wet*) molhado; (*untidy*) desarrumado; (*dishevelled*) desgrenhado

bedridden /ˈbedrɪdn/ *a* preso ao leito, doente de cama

bedroom /ˈbedruːm/ *n* quarto *m* de dormir

bedside /ˈbedsaɪd/ *n* cabeceira *f*. ~ **manner** (*doctor's*) modos *mpl* que inspiram confiança

bedspread /ˈbedspred/ *n* colcha *f*

bedtime /ˈbedtaɪm/ *n* hora *f* de deitar, hora *f* de ir para a cama

bee /biː/ *n* abelha *f*. **make a** ~-**line for** ir direto a

beech /biːtʃ/ *n* faia *f*

beef /biːf/ *n* carne *f* de vaca

beefburger /ˈbiːfbɜːgə(r)/ *n* hambúrguer *m*

beehive /ˈbiːhaɪv/ *n* colméia *f*

been /biːn/ *see* **be**

beer /bɪə(r)/ *n* cerveja *f*

beet /biːt/ *n* beterraba *f*

beetle /ˈbiːtl/ *n* escaravelho *m*

beetroot /ˈbiːtruːt/ *n* (raiz de) beterraba *f*

before /bɪˈfɔː(r)/ *prep* (*time*) antes de; (*place*) em frente de □ *adv* antes; (*al-*

ready) já □ *conj* antes que. ~ **leaving** antes de partir. ~ **he leaves** antes que ele parta, antes de ele partir

beforehand /bɪˈfɔːhænd/ *adv* de antemão, antecipadamente

befriend /bɪˈfrend/ *vt* tornar-se amigo de; (*be helpful to*) auxiliar

beg /beg/ *vt/i* (*pt* **begged**) mendigar; (*entreat*) suplicar. ~ **sb's pardon** pedir desculpa a alg. ~ **the question** fazer uma petição de princípio. **it's going** ~**ging** está sobrando

began /bɪˈgæn/ *see* **begin**

beggar /ˈbegə(r)/ *n* mendigo *m*, pedinte *mf*; (*colloq: person*) cara (*colloq*) *m*

begin /bɪˈgɪn/ *vt/i* (*pt* **began**, *pp* **begun**, *pres p* **beginning**) começar, principiar. ~**ner** *n* principiante *mf*. ~**ning** *n* começo *m*, princípio *m*

begrudge /bɪˈgrʌdʒ/ *vt* ter inveja de; (*give*) dar de má vontade. ~ **doing** fazer de má vontade *or* a contragosto

beguile /bɪˈgaɪl/ *vt* enganar

begun /bɪˈgʌn/ *see* **begin**

behalf /bɪˈhɑːf/ *n* **on** ~ **of** em nome de; (*in the interest of*) em favor de

behave /bɪˈheɪv/ *vi* portar-se. ~ **(o.s.)** portar-se bem

behaviour /bɪˈheɪvjə(r)/ *n* conduta *f*, comportamento *m*

behead /bɪˈhed/ *vt* decapitar

behind /bɪˈhaɪnd/ *prep* atrás de □ *adv* atrás; (*late*) com atraso □ *n* (*colloq: buttocks*) traseiro (*colloq*) *m*. ~ **the times** antiquado, retrógrado. **leave** ~ deixar para trás

behold /bɪˈhəʊld/ *vt* (*pt* **beheld**) (*old use*) ver

beholden /bɪˈhəʊldən/ *a* em dívida (**to** para com)

beige /beɪʒ/ *a* & *n* bege (*m*), (*P*) beige (*m*)

being /ˈbiːɪŋ/ *n* ser *m*. **bring into** ~ criar. **come into** ~ nascer, originar-se

belated /bɪˈleɪtɪd/ *a* tardio, atrasado

belch /beltʃ/ *vi* arrotar □ *vt* ~ **out** (*smoke*) vomitar, lançar □ *n* arroto *m*

belfry /ˈbelfrɪ/ *n* campanário *m*

Belgi|um /ˈbeldʒəm/ *n* Bélgica *f*. ~**an** *a* & *n* belga (*mf*)

belief /bɪˈliːf/ *n* crença *f*; (*trust*) confiança *f*; (*opinion*) convicção *f*

believ|e /bɪˈliːv/ *vt/i* acreditar. ~**e in** acreditar em. ~**able** *a* crível. ~**er** /-ə(r)/ *n* crente *mf*

belittle /bɪˈlɪtl/ *vt* depreciar

bell /bel/ *n* sino *m*; (*small*) sineta *f*; (*on door, of phone*) campainha *f*; (*on cat, toy*) guizo *m*

belligerent /bɪˈlɪdʒərənt/ *a* & *n* beligerante (*mf*)

bellow /'beləʊ/ vt/i berrar, bramir. ~ out rugir

bellows /'beləʊz/ npl fole m

belly /'belɪ/ n barriga f, ventre m. ~-ache n dor f de barriga

bellyful /'belɪfʊl/ n have a ~ estar com a barriga cheia

belong /bɪ'lɒŋ/ vi ~ (to) pertencer (a); (club) ser sócio (de)

belongings /bɪ'lɒŋɪŋz/ npl pertences mpl. **personal** ~ objetos mpl de uso pessoal

beloved /bɪ'lʌvɪd/ a & n amado (m)

below /bɪ'ləʊ/ prep abaixo de, debaixo de □ adv abaixo, em baixo; (on page) abaixo

belt /belt/ n cinto m; (techn) correia f; (fig) zona f □ vt (sl: hit) zurzir □ vi (sl: rush) safar-se

bemused /bɪ'mjuːzd/ a estonteado, confuso; (thoughtful) pensativo

bench /bentʃ/ n banco m; (seat, working-table) bancada f. the ~ (jur) os magistrados (no tribunal)

bend /bend/ vt/i (pt & pp bent) curvar(-se); (arm, leg) dobrar; (road, river) fazer uma curva, virar □ n curva f. ~ over debruçar-se or inclinar-se sobre

beneath /bɪ'niːθ/ prep abaixo de, debaixo de; (fig) abaixo de □ adv debaixo, em baixo

benediction /benɪ'dɪkʃn/ n bênção f

benefactor /'benɪfæktə(r)/ n benfeitor m

beneficial /benɪ'fɪʃl/ a benéfico, proveitoso

benefit /'benɪfɪt/ n (advantage, performance) benefício m; (profit) proveito m; (allowance) subsídio m □ vt/i (pt benefited, pres p benefiting) (be useful to) beneficiar (by de); (do good to) beneficiar, fazer bem a; (receive benefit) lucrar, ganhar (by, from com)

beneficiary /benɪ'fɪʃərɪ/ n beneficiário m

benevolen|t /bɪ'nevələnt/ a benevolente. ~ce n benevolência f

benign /bɪ'naɪn/ a (incl med) benigno

bent /bent/ see **bend** □ n (for para) (skill) aptidão f, jeito m; (liking) queda f □ a curvado; (twisted) torcido; (sl: dishonest) desonesto. ~ on decidido a

bequeath /bɪ'kwiːð/ vt legar

bequest /bɪ'kwest/ n legado m

bereave|d /bɪ'riːvd/ a the ~d wife/ etc a esposa/etc do falecido. the ~d family a família enlutada. ~ment n luto m

bereft /bɪ'reft/ a ~ of privado de

beret /'bereɪ/ n boina f

Bermuda /bə'mjuːdə/ n Bermudas fpl

berry /'berɪ/ n baga f

berserk /bə'sɜːk/ a go ~ ficar louco de raiva, perder a cabeça

berth /bɜːθ/ n (in ship) beliche m; (in train) couchette f; (anchorage) ancoradouro m □ vi atracar. **give a wide** ~ **to** passar ao largo, (P) de largo

beside /bɪ'saɪd/ prep ao lado de, junto de. ~ o.s. fora de si. **be** ~ **the point** não ter nada a ver com o assunto, não vir ao caso

besides /bɪ'saɪdz/ prep além de; (except) fora, salvo □ adv além disso

besiege /bɪ'siːdʒ/ vt sitiar, cercar. ~ **with** assediar

best /best/ a & n (the) ~ (o/a) melhor (mf) □ adv melhor. ~ **man** padrinho m de casamento. **at (the)** ~ na melhor das hipóteses. **do one's** ~ fazer o (melhor) que se pode. **make the** ~ **of** tirar o melhor partido de. **the** ~ **part of** a maior parte de. **to the** ~ **of my knowledge** que eu saiba

bestow /bɪ'stəʊ/ vt conferir. ~ **praise** fazer or tecer elogios

best-seller /best'selə(r)/ n best-seller m

bet /bet/ n aposta f □ vt/i (pt bet or betted) apostar (on em)

betray /bɪ'treɪ/ vt trair. ~al n traição f

better /'betə(r)/ a & adv melhor □ vt melhorar □ n our ~s os nossos superiores mpl. **all the** ~ tanto melhor. ~ **off** (richer) mais rico. **he's** ~ **off at home** é melhor para ele ficar em casa. **I'd** ~ **go** é melhor irme embora. **the** ~ **part of it** a maior parte disso. **get** ~ melhorar. **get the** ~ **of sb** levar a melhor em relação a alg

betting-shop /'betɪŋʃɒp/ n agência f de apostas

between /bɪ'twiːn/ prep entre □ adv **in** ~ no meio, no intervalo. ~ **you and me** aqui entre nós

beverage /'bevərɪdʒ/ n bebida f

beware /bɪ'weə(r)/ vi acautelar-se (of com), tomar cuidado (of com)

bewilder /bɪ'wɪldə(r)/ vt desorientar. ~ment n desorientação f, confusão f

bewitch /bɪ'wɪtʃ/ vt encantar, cativar

beyond /bɪ'jɒnd/ prep além de; (doubt, reach) fora de □ adv além. **it's** ~ **me** isso ultrapassame. **he lives** ~ **his means** ele vive acima dos seus meios

bias /'baɪəs/ n parcialidade f; (pej: prejudice) preconceito m; (sewing) viés m □ vt (pt biased) influenciar. ~ed a parcial. ~ed **against** de prevenção contra, (P) de pé atrás contra

bib /bɪb/ n babeiro m, babette m

Bible /'baɪbl/ n Bíblia f

biblical /'bɪblɪkl/ a bíblico

bibliography /bɪblɪˈɒgrəfɪ/ n bibliografia f

bicarbonate /baɪˈkɑːbənət/ n ~ of soda bicarbonato m de soda

biceps /ˈbaɪseps/ n bíceps m

bicker /ˈbɪkə(r)/ vi questionar, discutir

bicycle /ˈbaɪsɪkl/ n bicicleta f □ vi andar de bicicleta

bid /bɪd/ n oferta f, lance m; (attempt) tentativa f □ vt/i (pt bid, pres p bidding) fazer uma oferta, lançar, oferecer como lance. ~der n licitante mf. the highest ~der quem dá or oferece mais

bide /baɪd/ vt ~ one's time esperar pelo bom momento

bidet /ˈbiːdeɪ/ n bidê m, (P) bidé m

biennial /baɪˈenɪəl/ a bienal

bifocals /baɪˈfəʊklz/ npl óculos mpl bifocais

big /bɪg/ a (bigger, biggest) grande; (sl: generous) generoso □ adv (colloq) em grande. ~-headed a pretensioso, convencido. ~ shot (sl) manda-chuva m. talk ~ gabar-se (colloq). think ~ (colloq) ter grandes planos

bigam|y /ˈbɪgəmɪ/ n bigamia f. ~ist n bígamo m. ~ous a bígamo

bigot /ˈbɪgət/ n fanático m, intolerante mf. ~ed a fanático, intolerante. ~ry n fanatismo m, intolerância f

bigwig /ˈbɪgwɪg/ n (colloq) mandachuva m

bike /baɪk/ n (colloq) bicicleta f

bikini /bɪˈkiːnɪ/ n (pl -is) biquíni m

bilberry /ˈbɪlbərɪ/ n arando m

bile /baɪl/ n bílis f

bilingual /baɪˈlɪŋgwəl/ a bilíngüe

bilious /ˈbɪlɪəs/ a bilioso

bill[1] /bɪl/ n (invoice) fatura f, (P) factura f; (in restaurant) conta f; (pol) projeto m, (P) projecto m de lei; (Amer: banknote) nota f de banco; (poster) cartaz m □ vt faturar, (P) facturar; (theatre) anunciar, pôr no programa. ~ of exchange letra f de câmbio. ~ sb for apresentar a alg a conta de

bill[2] /bɪl/ n (of bird) bico m

billiards /ˈbɪlɪədz/ n bilhar m

billion /ˈbɪlɪən/ n (10^9) mil milhões; (10^{12}) um milhão de milhões

bin /bɪn/ n (for storage) caixa f, lata f, (for rubbish) lata f do lixo, (P) caixote m

bind /baɪnd/ vt (pt bound) (tie) atar; (book) encadernar; (jur) obrigar; (cover the edge of) debruar □ n (sl: bore) chatice f (sl). be ~ing on ser obrigatório para

binding /ˈbaɪndɪŋ/ n encadernação f; (braid) debrum m

binge /bɪndʒ/ n (sl) go on a ~ cair na farra; (overeat) empanturrar-se

bingo /ˈbɪŋgəʊ/ n bingo m □ int acertei!

binoculars /bɪˈnɒkjʊləz/ npl binóculo m

biochemistry /baɪəʊˈkemɪstrɪ/ n bioquímica f

biodegradable /baɪəʊdɪˈgreɪdəbl/ a biodegradável

biograph|y /baɪˈɒgrəfɪ/ n biografia f. ~er n biógrafo m

biolog|y /baɪˈɒlədʒɪ/ n biologia f. ~ical /-əˈlɒdʒɪkl/ a biológico. ~ist n biólogo m

biopsy /ˈbaɪɒpsɪ/ n biópsia f

birch /bɜːtʃ/ n (tree) bétula f; (whip) vara f de vidoeiro

bird /bɜːd/ n ave f, pássaro m; (sl: girl) garota f (colloq). ~ sanctuary refúgio m ornitológico. ~-watcher n ornitófilo m

Biro /ˈbaɪərəʊ/ n (pl -os) (caneta) esferográfica f, Bic f

birth /bɜːθ/ n nascimento m. ~ certificate certidão f de nascimento. ~ control/rate controle m/índice m de natalidade. ~-place n lugar m de nascimento. give ~ to dar à luz

birthday /ˈbɜːθdeɪ/ n aniversário m, (P) dia m de anos. his ~ is on 9 July ele faz anos no dia 9 de julho

birthmark /ˈbɜːθmɑːk/ n sinal m

biscuit /ˈbɪskɪt/ n biscoito m, bolacha f

bisect /baɪˈsekt/ vt dividir ao meio

bishop /ˈbɪʃəp/ n bispo m

bit[1] /bɪt/ n (small piece, short time) pedaço m, bocado m; (of bridle) freio m; (of tool) broca f. a ~ um pouco

bit[2] /bɪt/ see bite

bitch /bɪtʃ/ n cadela f; (sl: woman) peste f (fig), cadela f (sl) □ vt/i (colloq: criticize) malhar, (P) cortar (em) (colloq); (colloq: grumble) resmungar. ~y a (colloq) maldoso

bite /baɪt/ vt/i (pt bit, pp bitten) morder; (insect) picar □ n mordida f; (sting) picada f. have a ~ (to eat) comer qualquer coisa

biting /ˈbaɪtɪŋ/ a cortante

bitter /ˈbɪtə(r)/ a amargo; (weather) glacial. ~ly adv amargamente. it's ~ly cold está um frio de rachar. ~ness n amargura f, (resentment) ressentimento m

bizarre /bɪˈzɑː(r)/ a bizarro

black /blæk/ a (-er, -est) negro, preto □ n negro m, preto m. a B~ (person) um preto, um negro □ vt enegrecer; (goods) boicotar. ~ and blue coberto de nódoas negras. ~ coffee café m (sem leite). ~ eye olho m negro. ~ ice gelo m negro sobre o asfalto. ~ market mercado m negro. ~ spot n (place) local m perigoso, ponto m negro

blackberry /'blækbərɪ/ n amora f silvestre

blackbird /'blækbɜ:d/ n melro m

blackboard /'blækbɔ:d/ n quadro m preto

blackcurrant /'blækkʌrənt/ n groselha f negra

blacken /'blækən/ vt/i escurecer. ~ sb's name difamar, denegrir

blackleg /'blækleg/ n fura-greves m

blacklist /'blæklɪst/ n lista f negra □ vt pôr na lista negra

blackmail /'blækmeɪl/ n chantagem f □ vt fazer chantagem. ~er n chantagista mf

blackout /'blækaʊt/ n (wartime) blecaute m; (med) desmaio m; (electr) falta f de corrente; (theatr) apagar m de luzes

blacksmith /'blæksmɪθ/ n ferreiro m

bladder /'blædə(r)/ n bexiga f

blade /bleɪd/ n lâmina f; (of oar, propeller) pá f; (of grass) ervinha f, folhinha f de erva

blame /bleɪm/ vt culpar □ n culpa f. be to ~ ser o culpado. ~less a irrepreensível; (innocent) inocente

bland /blænd/ a (-er, -est) (of manner) suave; (mild) brando; (insipid) insípido

blank /blæŋk/ a (space, cheque) em branco; (look) vago; (wall) nu □ n espaço m em branco; (cartridge) cartucho m sem bala

blanket /'blæŋkɪt/ n cobertor m; (fig) manto m □ vt (pt blanketed) cobrir com cobertor; (cover thickly) encobrir, recobrir. wet ~ desmancha-prazeres mf

blare /bleə(r)/ vt/i ressoar, atroar □ n clangor m; (of horn) buzinar m

blasé /'blɑ:zeɪ/ a blasé

blaspheme /blæs'fi:m/ vt/i blasfemar

blasphem|y /'blæsfəmɪ/ n blasfêmia f, (P) blasfêmia f. ~ous a blasfemo

blast /blɑ:st/ n (gust) rajada f; (sound) som m; (explosion) explosão f □ vt dinamitar. ~! droga! ~ed a maldito. ~-furnace n alto forno m. ~-off n (of missile) lançamento m, início m de combustão

blatant /'bleɪtnt/ a flagrante; (shameless) descarado

blaze /bleɪz/ n chamas fpl; (light) clarão m; (outburst) explosão f □ vi arder; (shine) resplandecer, brilhar. ~ a trail abrir o caminho, ser pioneiro

blazer /'bleɪzə(r)/ n blazer m

bleach /bli:tʃ/ n descolorante, descorante m; (household) água f sanitária □ vt/i branquear; (hair) oxigenar

bleak /bli:k/ a (-er, -est) (place) desolado; (chilly) frio; (fig) desanimador

bleary-eyed /'blɪərɪaɪd/ a com olhos injetados

bleat /bli:t/ n balido m □ vi balir

bleed /bli:d/ vt/i (pt bled) sangrar

bleep /bli:p/ n bip m. ~er n bip m

blemish /'blemɪʃ/ n defeito m; (on reputation) mancha f □ vt manchar

blend /blend/ vt/i misturar(-se); (go well together) combinar-se □ n mistura f. ~er n (culin) liquidificador m

bless /bles/ vt abençoar. ~ed with ter a felicidade de ter. ~ing n benção f; (thing one is glad of) felicidade f. it's a ~ing in disguise há males que vêm para bem

blessed /'blesɪd/ a bem-aventurado; (colloq: cursed) maldito

blew /blu:/ see blow

blight /blaɪt/ n doença f de plantas; (fig) influência f maligna □ vt arruinar, frustrar

blind /blaɪnd/ a cego □ vt cegar □ n (on window) persiana f; (deception) ardil m. ~ alley (incl fig) beco m sem saída. ~ man/woman cego m/cega f. be ~ to não ver. turn a ~ eye to fingir não ver, fechar os olhos a. ~ly adv às cegas. ~ness n cegueira f

blindfold /'blaɪndfəʊld/ a & adv de olhos vendados □ n venda f □ vt vendar os olhos a

blink /blɪŋk/ vi piscar

blinkers /'blɪŋkəz/ npl antolhos mpl

bliss /blɪs/ n felicidade f, beatitude f. ~ful a felicíssimo. ~fully adv maravilhosamente

blister /'blɪstə(r)/ n bolha f, empola f □ vi empolar

blizzard /'blɪzəd/ n tempestade f de neve, nevasca f

bloated /'bləʊtɪd/ a inchado

bloater /'bləʊtə(r)/ n arenque m salgado e defumado

blob /blɒb/ n pingo m grosso; (stain) mancha f

bloc /blɒk/ n bloco m

block /blɒk/ n bloco m; (buildings) quarteirão m; (in pipe) entupimento m. ~ (of flats) prédio m de andares □ vt bloquear, obstruir; (pipe) entupir. ~ letters maiúsculas fpl. ~age n obstrução f

blockade /blɒ'keɪd/ n bloqueio m □ vt bloquear

bloke /bləʊk/ n (colloq) sujeito m (colloq), cara m (colloq)

blond /blɒnd/ a & n louro (m)

blonde /blɒnd/ a & n loura (f)

blood /blʌd/ n sangue m □ a (bank, donor, transfusion, etc) de sangue; (poisoning) do sangue; (group, vessel) sangüíneo. ~-curdling a horrendo. ~ pressure tensão f arterial. ~ test exame *m* de sangue. ~**less** *a* (*fig*) pacífico

bloodhound /'blʌdhaʊnd/ *n* sabujo *m*

bloodshed /'blʌdʃed/ *n* derramamento *m* de sangue, carnificina *f*

bloodshot /'blʌdʃɒt/ *a* injetado *or* (*P*) injectado de sangue

bloodstream /'blʌdstri:m/ *n* sangue *m*, fluxo *m* sangüíneo

bloodthirsty /'blʌdθɜ:stɪ/ *a* sanguinário

bloody /'blʌdɪ/ *a* (-ier, -iest) ensangüentado; (*with much bloodshed*) sangrento; (*sl*) grande, maldito □ *adv* (*sl*) pra burro. ~-**minded** *a* (*colloq*) do contra (*colloq*), chato (*sl*)

bloom /blu:m/ *n* flor *f*; (*beauty*) frescura *f*, viço *m* □ *vi* florir; (*fig*) vicejar. **in** ~ em flor

blossom /'blɒsəm/ *n* flor *f*. **in** ~ em flor □ *vi* (*flower*) florir, desabrochar; (*develop, flourish*) florescer, desabrochar

blot /blɒt/ *n* mancha *f* □ *vt* (*pt* **blotted**) manchar; (*dry*) secar. ~ **out** apagar; (*hide*) tapar, toldar. ~**ter**, ~**ting-paper** *n* (papel) mata-borrão *m*

blotch /blɒtʃ/ *n* mancha *f*. ~**y** *a* manchado

blouse /blaʊz/ *n* blusa *f*; (*in uniform*) blusão *m*

blow¹ /bləʊ/ *vt/i* (*pt* **blew**, *pp* **blown**) soprar; (*fuse*) fundir-se, queimar; (*sl: squander*) esbanjar; (*trumpet etc*) tocar. ~ **a whistle** apitar. ~ **away** *or* **off** *vt* levar, soprar □ *vi* roar, ir pelos ares (fora). ~-**dry** *vt* (*hair*) fazer um brushing □ *n* brushing *m*. ~ **one's nose** assoar o nariz. ~ **out** (*candle*) apagar, soprar. ~-**out** *n* (*colloq: of tyre*) rebentar *m*; (*colloq: large meal*) comilança *f* (*colloq*). ~ **over** passar. ~ **up** *vt* (*explode*) explodir; (*tyre*) encher; (*photograph*) ampliar □ *vi* (*explode*) explodir

blow² /bləʊ/ *n* pancada *f*; (*slap*) bofetada *f*; (*punch*) murro *m*; (*fig*) golpe *m*

blowlamp /'bləʊlæmp/ *n* maçarico *m*

blown /bləʊn/ *see* **blow¹**

bludgeon /'blʌdʒən/ *n* moca *f* □ *vt* malhar em. ~ **to death** matar à pancada

blue /blu:/ *a* (-er, -est) azul; (*indecent*) indecente □ *n* azul *m*. **come out of the** ~ ser inesperado. ~**s** *n* (*mus*) blues. **have the** ~**s** estar deprimido (*colloq*)

bluebell /'blu:bel/ *n* jacinto *m* dos bosques

bluebottle /'blu:bɒtl/ *n* mosca *f* varejeira

blueprint /'blu:prɪnt/ *n* cópia *f* fotográfica de planta; (*fig*) projeto *m*, (*P*) projecto *m*

bluff /blʌf/ *vi* blefar, (*P*) fazer bluff □ *vt* enganar (fingindo), blefar □ *n* blefe *m*, (*P*) bluff *m*

blunder /'blʌndə(r)/ *vi* cometer um erro crasso; (*move*) avançar às cegas *or* tateando □ *n* erro *m* crasso, (*P*) bronca *f*

blunt /blʌnt/ *a* (-er, -est) embotado; (*person*) direto, (*P*) directo □ *vt* embotar. ~**ly** *adv* sem rodeios. ~**ness-** *n* franqueza *f* rude

blur /blɜ:(r)/ *n* mancha *f* □ *vt* (*pt* **blurred**) (*smear*) manchar; (*make indistinct*) toldar

blurb /blɜ:b/ *n* contracapa *f*, sinopse *f* de um livro

blurt /blɜ:t/ *vt* ~ **out** deixar escapar

blush /blʌʃ/ *vi* corar □ *n* rubor *m*, vermelhidão *f*

bluster /'blʌstə(r)/ *vi* (*wind*) soprar em rajadas; (*swagger*) andar com ar fanfarrão. ~**y** *a* borrascoso

boar /bɔ:(r)/ *n* varrão *m*. **wild** ~ javali *m*

board /bɔ:d/ *n* tábua *f*; (*for notices*) quadro *m*, (*P*) placard *m*; (*food*) pensão *f*; (*admin*) conselho *m* □ *vt/i* cobrir com tábuas; (*aircraft, ship, train*) embarcar (em); (*bus, train*) subir (em). **full** ~ pensão *f* completa. **half** ~ meia-pensão *f*. **on** ~ a bordo. ~ **up** entaipar. ~ **with** ser pensionista em casa de. ~**er** *n* pensionista *mf*; (*at school*) interno *m*. ~**ing-card** *n* cartão *m* de embarque. ~**ing-house** *n* pensão *f*. ~**ing-school** *n* internato *m*

boast /bəʊst/ *vi* gabar-se □ *vt* orgulhar-se de □ *n* gabarolice *f*. ~**er** *n* gabola *mf*. ~**ful** *a* vaidoso. ~**fully** *adv* com vaidade, gabando-se

boat /bəʊt/ *n* barco *m*. **in the same** ~ nas mesmas circunstâncias. ~**ing** *n* passear de barco

bob /bɒb/ *vt/i* (*pt* **bobbed**) (*curtsy*) inclinar-se; (*hair*) cortar pelos ombros, (*P*) cortar à Joãozinho. ~ (**up and down**) andar para cima e para baixo

bobbin /'bɒbɪn/ *n* bobina *f*; (*sewing-machine*) canela *f*, bobina *f*

bob-sleigh /'bɒbsleɪ/ *n* trenó *m*

bode /bəʊd/ *vi* ~ **well/ill** ser de bom/mau agouro

bodice /'bɒdɪs/ *n* corpete *m*

bodily /'bɒdɪlɪ/ *a* corporal, físico. □ *adv* (*in person*) fisicamente, em pessoa; (*lift*) em peso

body /'bɒdɪ/ *n* corpo *m*; (*organization*) organismo *m*. ~(**work**) *n* (*of car*) carroçaria *f*. **in a** ~ em massa. **the main** ~ **of** o grosso de. ~-**building** *n* body building *m*

bodyguard /'bɒdɪgɑːd/ n guarda-costas m; (escort) escolta f

bog /bɒg/ n pântano m □ vt get ~ged down atolar-se; (fig) ficar emperrado

boggle /'bɒgl/ vi the mind ~s não da para imaginar

bogus /'bəʊgəs/ a falso

boil¹ /bɔɪl/ n (med) furúnculo m

boil² /bɔɪl/ vt/i ferver. come to the ~ ferver. ~ down to resumir-se a. ~ over transbordar. ~ing hot fervendo. ~ing point ponto m de ebulição

boiler /'bɔɪlə(r)/ n caldeira f. ~ suit macacão m, (P) fato m de macaco

boisterous /'bɔɪstərəs/ a turbulento; (noisy and cheerful) animado

bold /bəʊld/ a (-er, -est) ousado; (of colours) vivo. ~ness n ousadia f

Bolivia /bə'lɪvɪə/ n Bolívia f. ~n a & n boliviano (m)

bollard /'bɒləd/ n (ship) abita f, (road) poste m

bolster /'bəʊlstə(r)/ n travesseiro m □ vt sustentar; ajudar. ~ one's spirits levantar o moral

bolt /bəʊlt/ n (on door etc) ferrolho m; (for nut) parafuso m; (lightning) relâmpago m □ vt aferrolhar; (food) engolir □ vi fugir, disparar. ~ upright reto como um fuso

bomb /bɒm/ n bomba f □ vt bombardear. ~er n (aircraft) bombardeiro m; (person) bombista mf

bombard /bɒm'bɑːd/ vt bombardear. ~ment n bombardeamento m

bombastic /bɒm'bæstɪk/ a bombástico

bombshell /'bɒmʃel/ n granada f, (fig) bomba f

bond /bɒnd/ n (agreement) compromisso m; (link) laço m, vínculo m; (comm) obrigação f. in ~ em depósito na alfândega

bondage /'bɒndɪdʒ/ n escravidão f, servidão f

bone /bəʊn/ n osso m; (of fish) espinha f □ vt desossar. ~-dry a completamente seco, ressecado. ~ idle preguiçoso

bonfire /'bɒnfaɪə(r)/ n fogueira f

bonnet /'bɒnɪt/ n chapéu m; (auto) capô m do motor, (P) capot m

bonus /'bəʊnəs/ n bônus m, (P) bónus m

bony /'bəʊnɪ/ a (-ier, -iest) ossudo; (meat, fish) cheio de ossos/de espinhas

boo /buː/ int fora □ vt/i vaiar □ n vaia f

boob /buːb/ n (sl: mistake) asneira f, disparate m □ vi (sl) fazer asneira(s)

booby /'buːbɪ/ n ~ prize prêmio m de consolação. ~ trap bomba f armadilhada

book /bʊk/ n livro m. ~s (comm) contas fpl, escrita f □ vt (enter) averbar, registrar; (comm) escriturar; (reserve) marcar, reservar. ~ of matches carteira f de fósforos. ~ of tickets (bus, tube) caderneta f de módulos. be fully ~ed ter a lotação esgotada. ~ing office bilheteria f, (P) bilheteira f

bookcase /'bʊkkeɪs/ n estante f

bookkeeper /'bʊkkiːpə(r)/ n guarda-livros m. ~ing n contabilidade f, escrituração f

booklet /'bʊklɪt/ n brochura f

bookmaker /'bʊkmeɪkə(r)/ n book (maker) m

bookmark /'bʊkmɑːk/ n marca f de livro, marcador m de página

bookseller /'bʊkselə(r)/ n livreiro m

bookshop /'bʊkʃɒp/ n livraria f

bookstall /'bʊkstɔːl/ n quiosque m

boom /buːm/ vi ribombar; (of trade) prosperar □ n (sound) ribombo m; (comm) boom m, prosperidade f

boon /buːn/ n benção f, vantagem f

boost /buːst/ vt desenvolver, promover; (morale) levantar; (price) aumentar □ n força f (colloq). ~er n (med) dose suplementar f; (vaccine) revacinação f, (P) reforço m

boot /buːt/ n bota f; (auto) portamala f □ vt ~ (up) (comput) to ~ (in addition) ainda por cima

booth /buːð/ n barraca f; (telephone, voting) cabine f

booty /'buːtɪ/ n saque m, pilhagem f

booze /buːz/ vi (colloq) embebedar-se (colloq), encharcar-se (colloq) □ n (colloq) pinga f (colloq)

border /'bɔːdə(r)/ n borda f, margem f; (frontier) fronteira f; (garden bed) canteiro m □ vi ~ on confinar com; (be almost the same as) atingir as raias de

borderline /'bɔːdəlaɪn/ n linha f divisória. ~ case caso m limite

bore¹ /bɔː(r)/ see bear²

bore² /bɔː(r)/ vt/i (techn) furar, perfurar □ n (of gun barrel) calibre m

bore³ /bɔː(r)/ vt aborrecer, entediar □ n maçante m; (thing) chatice f. be ~d aborrecer-se, maçar-se. ~dom n tédio m. boring a tedioso, maçante

born /bɔːn/ a nascido. be ~ nascer

borne /bɔːn/ see bear²

borough /'bʌrə/ n município m

borrow /'bɒrəʊ/ vt pedir emprestado (from a)

bosom /'bʊzəm/ n peito m; (woman's; fig: midst) seio m. ~ friend amigo m íntimo

boss /bɒs/ n (colloq) patrão m, patroa f, manda-chuva (colloq) m □ vt mandar. ~ sb about (colloq) mandar em alg

bossy /'bɒsɪ/ a mandão, autoritário

botan|y /'bɒtənɪ/ n botânica f. **~ical** /bə'tænɪkl/ a botânico. **~ist** /-ɪst/ n botânico m

botch /bɒtʃ/ vt atamancar; (spoil) estragar, escangalhar

both /bəʊθ/ a & pron ambos, os dois □ adv ~ ... and não só ... mas também, tanto ... como. **~ of us** nós dois. **~ the books** ambos os livros

bother /'bɒðə(r)/ vt/i incomodar(-se) □ n (inconvenience) incômodo m, (P) incómodo m, trabalho m; (effort) custo m, trabalho m; (worry) preocupação f. **don't ~** não se incomode. **I can't be ~ed** não posso me dar o trabalho

bottle /'bɒtl/ n garrafa f; (small) frasco m; (for baby) mamadeira f, (P) biberão m □ vt engarrafar. **~-opener** n sacarolhas m. **~ up** reprimir

bottleneck /'bɒtlnek/ n (obstruction) entrave m; (traffic-jam) engarrafamento m

bottom /'bɒtəm/ n fundo m; (of hill) sopé m; (buttocks) traseiro m □ a inferior; (last) último. **from top to ~** de alto a baixo. **~less** a sem fundo

bough /baʊ/ n ramo m

bought /bɔːt/ see buy

boulder /'bəʊldə(r)/ n pedregulho m

bounce /baʊns/ vi saltar; (of person) pular, dar pulos; (sl: of cheque) ser devolvido □ vt fazer saltar □ n (of ball) salto m, (P) ressalto m

bound¹ /baʊnd/ vi pular; (move by jumping) ir aos pulos □ n pulo m

bound² /baʊnd/ see bind □ a be ~ for ir com destino a, ir para. **be ~ to** (obliged) ser obrigado a; (certain) haver de. **she's ~ to like it** ela há de gostar disso

boundary /'baʊndrɪ/ n limite m

bound|s /baʊndz/ npl limites mpl. **out of ~s** interdito. **~ed by** limitado por. **~less** a sem limites

bouquet /bʊ'keɪ/ n ramo m de flores; (wine) aroma m

bout /baʊt/ n período m; (med) ataque m; (boxing) combate m

boutique /buː'tiːk/ n boutique f

bow¹ /bəʊ/ n (weapon, mus) arco m; (knot) laço m. **~-legged** a de pernas tortas. **~-tie** n gravata borboleta f, (P) laço m

bow² /baʊ/ n vênia f, (P) vénia f □ vt/i inclinar(-se), curvar-se

bow³ /baʊ/ n (naut) proa f

bowels /'baʊəlz/ npl intestinos mpl; (fig) entranhas fpl

bowl¹ /bəʊl/ n (basin) bacia f; (for food) tigela f; (of pipe) fornilho m

bowl² /bəʊl/ n (ball) boliche m, (P) bola f de madeira. **~s** npl boliche m,

(P) jogo m com bolas de madeira □ vt (cricket) lançar. **~ over** siderar, varar. **~ing** n boliche m, (P) bowling m. **~ing-alley** n pista f

bowler¹ /'bəʊlə(r)/ n (cricket) lançador m

bowler² /'bəʊlə(r)/ n ~ (hat) (chapéu de) coco m

box¹ /bɒks/ n caixa f; (theatr) camarote m □ vt pôr dentro duma caixa. **~ in** fechar. **~ office** n bilheteria f, (P) bilheteira f. **Boxing Day** feriado m no primeiro dia útil depois do Natal

box² /bɒks/ vt/i (sport) lutar boxe. **~ the ears of** esbofetear. **~er** n pugilista m, boxeur m. **~ing** n boxe m, pugilismo m

boy /bɔɪ/ n rapaz m. **~friend** n namorado m. **~hood** n infância f. **~ish** a de menino

boycott /'bɔɪkɒt/ vt boicotar □ n boicote m

bra /braː/ n soutien m

brace /breɪs/ n braçadeira f; (dental) aparelho m; (tool) berbequim m; (of birds) par m. **~s** npl (for trousers) suspensórios mpl □ vt apoiar, firmar. **~ o.s.** concentrar as energias, fazer força; (for blow) preparar-se

bracelet /'breɪslɪt/ n bracelete m, pulseira f

bracing /'breɪsɪŋ/ a tonificante, estimulante

bracken /'brækən/ n (bot) samambaia f, (P) feto m

bracket /'brækɪt/ n suporte m; (group) grupo m □ vt (pt bracketed) pôr entre parênteses; (put together) pôr em pé de igualdade, agrupar. **age/income ~** faixa f etária/ salarial. **round ~s** parênteses mpl. **square ~s** parênteses mpl, colchetes mpl

brag /bræg/ vi (pt bragged) gabar-se (about de)

braid /breɪd/ n galão m; (of hair) trança f

Braille /breɪl/ n braile m

brain /breɪn/ n cérebro m, miolos mpl (colloq); (fig) inteligência f. **~s** (culin) miolos mpl. **~-child** n invenção f. **~less** a estúpido

brainwash /'breɪnwɒʃ/ vt fazer uma lavagem cerebral

brainwave /'breɪnweɪv/ n idéia f, (P) ideia f genial

brainy /'breɪnɪ/ a (-ier, -iest) inteligente, esperto

braise /breɪz/ vt (culin) estufar

brake /breɪk/ n travão m □ vt/i travar. **~ light** farol m do freio

bran /bræn/ n (husks) farelo m

branch /braːntʃ/ n ramo m; (of road) ramificação f; (of railway line) ramal *m*; (*comm*) sucursal *f*; (*of bank*) balcão *m* □ *vi* ~ **(off)** bifurcar-se, ramificar-se

brand /brænd/ *n* marca *f* □ *vt* marcar. ~ **name** marca *f* de fábrica. ~**-new** *a* novo em folha. ~ **sb as** tachar alg de, (*P*) rotular alg de

brandish /'brændɪʃ/ *vt* brandir

brandy /'brændɪ/ *n* aguardente *f*, conhaque *m*

brass /brɑːs/ *n* latão *m*. **the** ~ (*mus*) os metais *mpl* □ *a* de cobre, de latão. **get down to** ~ **tacks** tratar das coisas sérias. **top** ~ (*sl*) os chefões (*colloq*)

brassière /'bræsɪə(r)/ *n* soutien *m*

brat /bræt/ *n* (*pej*) fedelho *m*

bravado /brə'vɑːdəʊ/ *n* bravata *f*

brave /breɪv/ *a* (**-er, -est**) bravo, valente □ *vt* arrostar. ~**ry** /-ərɪ/ *n* bravura *f*

brawl /brɔːl/ *n* briga *f*, rixa *f*, desordem *f* □ *vi* brigar

brawn /brɔːn/ *n* força *f* muscular, músculo *m*. ~**y** *a* musculoso

bray /breɪ/ *n* zurro *m* □ *vi* zurrar

brazen /'breɪzn/ *a* descarado

brazier /'breɪzɪə(r)/ *n* braseiro *m*

Brazil /brə'zɪl/ *n* Brasil *m*. ~**ian** *a* & *n* brasileiro (*m*). ~ **nut** castanha *f* do Pará

breach /briːtʃ/ *n* quebra *f*; (*gap*) brecha *f* □ *vt* abrir uma brecha em. ~ **of contract** quebra *f* de contrato. ~ **of the peace** perturbação *f* da ordem pública. ~ **of trust** abuso *m* de confiança

bread /bred/ *n* pão *m*. ~**-winner** *n* ganha-pão *m*

breadcrumbs /'bredkrʌmz/ *npl* migalhas *fpl*; (*culin*) farinha *f* de rosca

breadline /'bredlaɪn/ *n* **on the** ~ na miséria

breadth /bredθ/ *n* largura *f*; (*of mind, view*) abertura *f*

break /breɪk/ *vt* (*pt* **broke**, *pp* **broken**) partir, quebrar; (*vow, silence, etc*) quebrar; (*law*) transgredir; (*journey*) interromper; (*news*) dar; (*a record*) bater □ *vi* partir-se, quebrar-se; (*voice, weather*) mudar □ *n* quebra *f*, ruptura *f*; (*interval*) intervalo *m*; (*colloq: opportunity*) oportunidade *f*, chance *f*. ~ **one's arm/leg**quebrar o braço/a perna ~ **down** *vt* analisar □ *vi* (*of person*) ir-se abaixo; (*of machine*) avariar-se. ~ **in** forçar uma entrada. ~ **off** *vt* quebrar □ *vi* desligar-se. ~ **out** rebentar. ~ **up** *vt*/*i* terminar *vi* (*of schools*) entrar em férias. ~**able** *a* quebrável. ~**age** *n* quebra *f*

breakdown /'breɪkdaʊn/ *n* (*techni*) avaria *f*, pane *f*; (*med*) esgotamento *m* nervoso; (*of figures*) análise *f* □ *a*

(*auto*) de pronto-socorro. ~ **van** pronto-socorro *m*

breaker /'breɪkə(r)/ *n* vaga *f* de rebentação

breakfast /'brekfəst/ *n* café *m* da manhã

breakthrough /'breɪkθruː/ *n* descoberta *f* decisiva, avanço *m*

breakwater /'breɪkwɔːtə(r)/ *n* quebra-mar *m*

breast /brest/ *n* peito *m*. ~**-feed** *vt* (*pt* **-fed**) amamentar. ~**-stroke** *n* estilo *m* bruços

breath /breθ/ *n* respiração *f*. **bad** ~ mau hálito *m*. **out of** ~ sem fôlego. **under one's** ~ num murmúrio, baixo. ~**less** *a* ofegante

breathalyser /'breθəlaɪzə(r)/ *n* aparelho *m* para medir o nível de álcool no sangue, bafômetro *m* (*colloq*)

breath|e /briːð/ *vt*/*i* respirar. ~**e in** inspirar. ~ **out** expirar. ~**ing** *n* respiração *f*. ~**ing-space** *n* pausa *f*

breather /'briːðə(r)/ *n* pausa *f* de descanso, momento *m* para respirar

breathtaking /'breθteɪkɪŋ/ *a* assombroso, arrebatador

bred /bred/ *see* **breed**

breed /briːd/ *vt* (*pt* **bred**) criar □ *vi* reproduzir-se □ *n* raça *f*. ~**er** *n* criador *m*. ~**ing** *n* criação *f*; (*fig*) educação *f*

breez|e /briːz/ *n* brisa *f*. ~**y** *a* fresco

brevity /'brevɪtɪ/ *n* brevidade *f*

brew /bruː/ *vt* (*beer*) fabricar; (*tea*) fazer; (*fig*) armar, tramar □ *vi* fermentar; (*tea*) preparar; (*fig*) armar-se, preparar-se □ *n* decocção *f*; (*tea*) infusão *f*. ~**er** *n* cervejeiro *m*. ~**ery** *n* cervejaria *f*

bribe /braɪb/ *n* suborno *m*, (*P*) peita *f* □ *vt* subornar. ~**ry** /-ərɪ/ *n* suborno *m*, corrupção *f*

brick /brɪk/ *n* tijolo *m*

bricklayer /'brɪkleɪə(r)/ *n* pedreiro *m*

bridal /'braɪdl/ *a* nupcial

bride /braɪd/ *n* noiva *f*

bridegroom /'braɪdɡrʊm/ *n* noivo *m*

bridesmaid /'braɪdzmeɪd/ *n* dama *f* de honra, (*P*) noiva *f*

bridge[1] /brɪdʒ/ *n* ponte *f*; (*of nose*) cana *f* □ *vt* ~ **a gap** preencher uma lacuna

bridge[2] /brɪdʒ/ *n* (*cards*) bridge *m*

bridle /'braɪdl/ *n* cabeçada *f*, freio *m* □ *vt* refrear. ~**-path** *n* atalho *m*, carreiro *m*

brief[1] /briːf/ *a* (**-er, -est**) breve. ~**s** *npl* (*men's*) cueca *f*, (*P*) slip *m*; (*women's*) calcinhas *fpl*, (*P*) cuecas *fpl*. ~**ly** *adv* brevemente

brief[2] /briːf/ *n* (*jur*) sumário *m*; (*case*) causa *f*; (*instructions*) instruções *fpl* □ *vt* dar instruções a

briefcase /'bri:fkeɪs/ *n* pasta *f*

brigad|e /brɪ'geɪd/ *n* brigada *f*. **~ier** /-ə'dɪə(r)/ *n* brigadeiro *m*

bright /braɪt/ *a* (-er, -est) brilhante; (*of colour*) vivo; (*of light*) forte; (*room*) claro; (*cheerful*) alegre; (*clever*) inteligente. **~ness** *n* (*sheen*) brilho *m*; (*clarity*) claridade *f*; (*intelligence*) inteligência *f*

brighten /'braɪtn/ *vt* alegrar □ *vi* (*of weather*) clarear; (*of face*) animar-se, iluminar-se

brillian|t /'brɪljənt/ *a* brilhante. **~ce** *n* brilho *m*

brim /brɪm/ *n* borda *f*; (*of hat*) aba *f* □ *vi* (*pt* brimmed) **~ over** transbordar, cair por fora

brine /braɪn/ *n* salmoura *f*

bring /brɪŋ/ *vt* (*pt* brought) trazer. **~ about** causar. **~ back** trazer (de volta); (*call to mind*) relembrar. **~ down** trazer para baixo; (*bird, plane*) abater; (*prices*) baixar. **~ forward** adiantar, apresentar. **~ it off** ser bem sucedido (em alg coisa). **~ out** (*take out*) tirar; (*show*) revelar; (*book*) publicar. **~ round** *or* **to** reanimar, fazer voltar a si. **~ to bear** (*pressure etc*) exercer. **~ up** educar; (*med*) vomitar; (*question*) levantar

brink /brɪŋk/ *n* beira *f*, borda *f*

brisk /brɪsk/ *a* (-er, -est) (*pace, movement*) vivo, rápido; (*business, demand*) grande

bristl|e /'brɪsl/ *n* pêlo *m*. **~y** *a* eriçado

Britain /'brɪtən/ *n* Grã-Bretanha *f*

British /'brɪtɪʃ/ *a* britânico. **the ~** o povo *m* britânico, os britânicos *mpl*

brittle /'brɪtl/ *a* frágil

broach /brəʊtʃ/ *vt* abordar, entabular, encetar

broad /brɔːd/ *a* (-er, -est) largo; (*daylight*) pleno. **~ bean** fava *f*. **~-minded** *a* tolerante, liberal. **~ly** *adv* de modo geral

broadcast /'brɔːdkɑːst/ *vt/i* (*pt* broadcast) transmitir, fazer uma transmissão; (*person*) cantar, falar *etc* na rádio *or* na TV □ *n* emissão *f*. **~ing** *a* & *n* (de) rádiodifusão (*f*)

broaden /'brɔːdn/ *vt/i* alargar(-se)

broccoli /'brɒkəlɪ/ *n inv* brócolis *mpl*, (*P*) brócolos *mpl*

brochure /'brəʊʃə(r)/ *n* brochura *f*

broke /brəʊk/ *see* break □ *a* (*sl*) depenado (*sl*), liso (*sl*), (*P*) teso (*sl*)

broken /'brəʊkən/ *see* break □ *a* **~ English** inglês *m* estropeado. **~-hearted** *a* com o coração despedaçado

broker /'brəʊkə(r)/ *n* corretor *m*, broker *m*

bronchitis /brɒŋ'kaɪtɪs/ *n* bronquite *f*

bronze /brɒnz/ *n* bronze *m*

brooch /brəʊtʃ/ *n* broche *m*

brood /bru:d/ *n* ninhada *f* □ *vi* chocar; (*fig*) cismar. **~y** *a* (*hen*) choca; (*fig*) sorumbático, melancólico

brook /brʊk/ *n* regato *m*, ribeiro *m*

broom /bru:m/ *n* vassoura *f*; (*bot*) giesta *f*

broth /brɒθ/ *n* caldo *m*

brothel /'brɒθl/ *n* bordel *m*

brother /'brʌðə(r)/ *n* irmão *m*. **~-in-law** *n* (*pl* **~s-in-law**) cunhado *m*. **~hood** *n* irmandade *f*, fraternidade *f*. **~ly** *a* fraternal

brought /brɔːt/ *see* bring

brow /braʊ/ *n* (*forehead*) testa *f*; (*of hill*) cume *m*; (*eyebrow*) sobrancelha *f*

browbeat /'braʊbi:t/ *vt* (*pt* -beat, *pp* -beaten) intimidar

brown /braʊn/ *a* (-er, -est) castanho □ *n* castanho *m* □ *vt/i* acastanhar; (*in the sun*) bronzear, tostar; (*meat*) alourar

browse /braʊz/ *vi* (*through book*) folhear; (*of animal*) pastar; (*in a shop*) olhar sem comprar

bruise /bru:z/ *n* hematoma *m*, contusão *f* □ *vt* causar um hematoma. **~d** *a* coberto de hematomas, contuso; (*fruit*) machucado

brunette /bru:'net/ *n* morena *f*

brunt /brʌnt/ *n* **the ~ of** o maior peso de, o pior de

brush /brʌʃ/ *n* escova *f*; (*painter's*) pincel *m*; (*skirmish*) escaramuça *f*. **~ against** roçar. **~ aside** não fazer caso de. **~ off** (*colloq: reject*) mandar passear (*colloq*). **~ up (on)** aperfeiçoar

brusque /bru:sk/ *a* brusco

Brussels /'brʌslz/ *n* Bruxelas *f*. **~ sprouts** couve-de-Bruxelas *f*

brutal /'bru:tl/ *a* brutal. **~ity** /'tælətɪ/ *n* brutalidade *f*

brute /bru:t/ *n* & *a* (*animal, person*) bruto (*m*). **by ~ force** por força bruta

B Sc *abbr see* Bachelor of Science

bubb|le /'bʌbl/ *n* bolha *f*; (*of soap*) bola *f* de sabão □ *vi* borbulhar. **~le gum** *n* chiclete *m*, (*P*) pastilha *f* elástica. **~le over** transbordar. **~ly** *a* efervescente

buck[1] /bʌk/ *n* macho *m* □ *vi* dar galões, (*P*) corcovear. **~ up** *vt/i* (*sl*) animar(-se); (*sl: rush*) apressar-se, despachar-se

buck[2] /bʌk/ *n* (*Amer sl*) dólar *m*

buck[3] /bʌk/ *n* **pass the ~** (*sl*) fazer o jogo do empurra

bucket /'bʌkɪt/ *n* balde *m*

buckle /'bʌkl/ *n* fivela *f* □ *vt/i* afivelar(-se); (*bend*) torcer(-se), vergar. **~ down to** empenhar-se

bud /bʌd/ *n* botão *m*, rebento *m* □ *vi* (*pt* budded) rebentar. **in ~** em botão

Buddhis|t /'budɪst/ *a & n* budista (*mf*). ∼**m** /-zəm/ *n* budismo *m*

budding /'bʌdɪŋ/ *a* nascente, em botão, incipiente

budge /bʌdʒ/ *vt/i* mexer(-se)

budgerigar /'bʌdʒərɪga:(r)/ *n* periquito *m*

budget /'bʌdʒɪt/ *n* orçamento *m* □ *vi* (*pt* budgeted) ∼ **for** prever no orçamento *m*

buff /bʌf/ *n* (*colour*) côr *f* de camurça; (*colloq*) fanático *m*, entusiasta *mf* □ *vt* polir

buffalo /'bʌfələʊ/ *n* (*pl* -oes) búfalo *m*; (*Amer*) bisão *m*

buffer /'bʌfə(r)/ *n* pára-choque *m*

buffet[1] /'bʊfeɪ/ *n* (*meal, counter*) bufê *m*, (*P*) bufete *m*

buffet[2] /'bʌfɪt/ *vt* (*pt* buffeted) esbofetear; (*by wind, rain; fig*) fustigar

buffoon /bə'fu:n/ *n* palhaço *m*

bug /bʌg/ *n* (*insect*) bicho *m*; (*bed-bug*) percevejo *m*; (*sl: germ*) virus *m*; (*sl: device*) microfone *m* de escuta; (*sl: defect*) defeito *m* □ *vt* (*pt* bugged) grampear; (*Amer sl: annoy*) chatear (*sl*)

bugbear /'bʌgbeə(r)/ *n* papão *m*

buggy /'bʌgɪ/ *n* (*for baby*) carrinho *m*

bugle /'bju:gl/ *n* clarim *m*, corneta *f*

build /bɪld/ *vt/i* (*pt* built) construir, edificar □ *n* físico *m*, compleição *f*. ∼ **up** *vt/i* criar; (*increase*) aumentar; (*accumulate*) acumular(-se). ∼**-up** *n* acumulação *f*; (*fig*) publicidade *f*. ∼**er** *n* construtor *m*, empreiteiro *m*; (*workman*) operário *m*

building /'bɪldɪŋ/ *n* edifício *m*, prédio *m*. ∼ **site** canteiro *m* de obras. ∼ **society** sociedade *f* de investimentos imobiliários

built /bɪlt/ *see* build. ∼**-in** *a* incorporado. ∼**-in wardrobe** armário *m* embutido na parede. ∼**-up** *a* urbanizado

bulb /bʌlb/ *n* bolbo *m*; (*electr*) lâmpada *f*. ∼**ous** *a* bolboso

Bulgaria /bʌl'geərɪə/ *n* Bulgária *f*. ∼**n** *a & n* búlgaro (*m*)

bulg|e /bʌldʒ/ *n* bojo *m*, saliência *f* □ *vi* inchar; (*jut out*) fazer uma saliência. ∼**ing** *a* inchado; (*pocket etc*) cheio

bulk /bʌlk/ *n* quantidade *f*, volume *m*. **in** ∼ por grosso; (*loose*) a granel. **the** ∼ **of** a maior parte de. ∼**y** *a* volumoso

bull /bʊl/ *n* touro *m*. ∼**'s-eye** *n* (*of target*) centro *m* do alvo, mosca *f*

bulldog /'bʊldɒg/ *n* buldogue *m*

bulldoze /'bʊldəʊz/ *vt* terraplanar. ∼**r** /-ə(r)/ *n* bulldozer *m*

bullet /'bʊlɪt/ *n* bala *f*. ∼**-proof** *a* à prova de balas; (*vehicle*) blindado

bulletin /'bʊlətɪn/ *n* boletim *m*.

bullfight /'bʊlfaɪt/ *n* tourada *f*, corri-

da *f* de touros. ∼**er** *n* toureiro *m*. ∼**ing** *n* tauromaquia *f*

bullring /'bʊlrɪŋ/ *n* arena *f*, (*P*) praça *f* de touros

bully /'bʊlɪ/ *n* mandão *m*, pessoa *f* prepotente; (*schol*) terror *m*, o mau □ *vt* intimidar; (*treat badly*) atormentar; (*coerce*) forçar (**into** a)

bum[1] /bʌm/ *n* (*sl: buttocks*) traseiro *m*, bunda *f* (*sl*)

bum[2] /bʌm/ *n* (*Amer sl*) vagabundo *m*

bump /bʌmp/ *n* choque *m*, embate *m*; (*swelling*) inchaço *m*; (*on head*) galo *m* □ *vt/i* bater, chocar. ∼ **into** bater em, chocar com; (*meet*) esbarrar com, encontrar. ∼**y** *a* (*surface*) irregular; (*ride*) aos solavancos

bumper /'bʌmpə(r)/ *n* pára-choques *m inv* □ *a* excepcional

bun /bʌn/ *n* pãozinho *m* doce com passas; (*hair*) coque *m*

bunch /bʌntʃ/ *n* (*of flowers*) ramo *m*; (*of keys*) molho *m*; (*of people*) grupo *m*; (*of grapes*) cacho *m*

bundle /'bʌndl/ *n* molho *m* □ *vt* atar num molho; (*push*) despachar

bung /bʌŋ/ *n* batoque *m*, rolha *f* □ *vt* rolhar; (*sl: throw*) atirar, deitar. ∼ **up** entupir

bungalow /'bʌŋgələʊ/ *n* chalé *m*; (*outside Europe*) bungalô *m*, (*P*) bungalow *m*

bungle /'bʌŋgl/ *vt* fazer mal feito, estragar

bunion /'bʌnjən/ *n* (*med*) joanete *m*

bunk /bʌŋk/ *n* (*in train*) couchette *f*; (*in ship*) beliche *m*. ∼**-beds** *npl* beliches *mpl*

bunker /'bʌŋkə(r)/ *n* (*mil*) abrigo *m*, casamata *f*, bunker *m*; (*golf*) obstáculo *m* em cova de areia

buoy /bɔɪ/ *n* bóia *f* □ *vt* ∼ **up** animar

buoyan|t /'bɔɪənt/ *a* flutuante; (*fig*) alegre. ∼**cy** *n* (*fig*) alegria *f*, exuberância *f*

burden /'bɜːdn/ *n* fardo *m* □ *vt* collegar, sobrecarregar. ∼**some** *a* pesado

bureau /'bjʊərəʊ/ *n* (*pl* -eaux) /-əʊz/ (*desk*) secretária *f*; (*office*) seção *f*, (*P*) secção *f*

bureaucracy /bjʊə'rɒkrəsɪ/ *n* burocracia *f*

bureaucrat /'bjʊərəkræt/ *n* burocrata *mf*. ∼**ic** /-'krætɪk/ *a* burocrático

burger /'bɜːgə(r)/ *n* hambúrguer *m*

burglar /'bɜːglə(r)/ *n* ladrão *m*, assaltante *mf*. ∼ **alarm** *n* alarme *m* contra ladrões. ∼**ize** *vt* (*Amer*) assaltar. ∼**y** *n* assalto *m*

burgle /'bɜːgl/ *vt* assaltar

burial /'berɪəl/ *n* enterro *m*

burlesque /bɜː'lesk/ *n* paródia *f*

burly /'bɜːlɪ/ *a* (-ier, -iest) robusto e corpulento, forte

Burm|a /'bɜːmə/ n Birmânia f. ~ese /-'miːz/ a & n birmanês (m)

burn /bɜːn/ vt (pt burned or burnt) queimar □ vi queimar(-se), arder □ n queimadura f. ~ **down** reduzir a cinzas. ~**er** n (of stove) bico m de gás. ~**ing** a (thirst, desire) ardente; (topic) candente

burnish /'bɜːnɪʃ/ vt polir, brunir

burnt /bɜːnt/ see **burn**

burp /bɜːp/ n (colloq) arroto m □ vi (colloq) arrotar

burrow /'bʌrəʊ/ n toca f □ vi cavar, fazer uma toca

burst /bɜːst/ vt/i (pt burst) arrebentar □ n estouro m, rebentar m; (of anger, laughter) explosão f; (of firing) rajada f; (of energy) acesso m. ~ **into** (flames, room, etc) irromper em. ~ **into tears** desatar num choro, desfazer-se em lágrimas. ~ **out laughing** desatar a rir

bury /'berɪ/ vt sepultar, enterrar; (hide) esconder; (engross, thrust) mergulhar

bus /bʌs/ n (pl buses) ônibus m, (P) autocarro m. ~-**stop** n paragem f

bush /bʊʃ/ n arbusto m; (land) mato m. ~**y** a espesso

business /'bɪznɪs/ n (trade, shop, affair) negócio m; (task) função f; (occupation) ocupação f. **have no** ~ **to** não ter o direito de. **it's no** ~ **of yours** não é da sua conta. **mind your own** ~ cuide da sua vida. **that's my** ~ isso é meu problema. ~**like** a eficiente, sistemático. ~**man** n homem m de negócios, comerciante m

busker /'bʌskə(r)/ n músico m ambulante

bust[1] /bʌst/ n busto m

bust[2] /bʌst/ vt/i (pt busted or bust) (sl) = **burst**, **break** □ a falido. ~-**up** n (sl) discussão f, (P) bulha f. **go** ~ (sl) falir

bustl|e /'bʌsl/ vi andar numa azáfama; (hurry) apressar-se □ n azáfama f. ~**ing** a animado, movimentado

bus|y /'bɪzɪ/ a (-ier, -iest) ocupado; (street) movimentado; (day) atarefado □ vt ~**y o.s. with** ocupar-se com. ~**ily** adv ativamente, atarefadamente

busybody /'bɪzɪbɒdɪ/ n intrometido m, pessoa f abelhuda

but /bʌt/ conj mas □ prep exceto, (p) excepto, senão □ adv apenas, só. **all** ~ todos menos; (nearly) quase, por pouco não. ~ **for** sem, se não fosse. **last** ~ **one/two** penúltimo/antepenúltimo. **nobody** ~ ninguém a não ser

butcher /'bʊtʃə(r)/ n açougueiro m, (P) homem m do talho; (fig) carrasco

m □ vt chacinar. **the** ~'**s** açougue m, (P) talho m. ~**y** n chacina f

butler /'bʌtlə(r)/ n mordomo m

butt /bʌt/ n (of gun) coronha f; (of cigarette) ponta f; (target) alvo m de troça, de ridículo etc; (cask) barril m □ vt/i dar cabeçada em. ~ **in** interromper

butter /'bʌtə(r)/ n manteiga f □ vt pôr manteiga em. ~-**bean** n feijão m branco

buttercup /'bʌtəkʌp/ n botão-de-ouro m

butterfly /'bʌtəflaɪ/ n borboleta f

buttock /'bʌtək/ n nádega f

button /'bʌtn/ n botão m □ vt/i abotoar(-se)

buttonhole /'bʌtnhəʊl/ n casa f de botão; (in lapel) botoeira f □ vt (fig) obrigar a ouvir

buttress /'bʌtrɪs/ n contraforte m; (fig) esteio m □ vt sustentar

buxom /'bʌksəm/ a roliço, rechonchudo

buy /baɪ/ vt (pt bought) comprar (from a); (sl: believe) engolir (colloq) □ n compra f. ~**er** n comprador m

buzz /bʌz/ n zumbido m □ vi zumbir. ~ **off** (sl) pôr-se a andar. ~**er** n campainha f

by /baɪ/ prep (near) junto de, perto de; (along, past, means) por; (according to) conforme; (before) antes de. ~ **land/sea/air** por terra/mar/ar. ~ **bike/car** etc de bicicleta/carro etc. ~ **day/night** de dia/noite. ~ **the kilo** por quilo. ~ **now** a esta hora. ~ **accident/mistake** sem querer. ~ **oneself** sozinho □ adv (near) perto. ~ **and** ~ muito em breve. ~ **and large** no conjunto. ~-**election** n eleição f suplementar. ~-**law** n regulamento m. ~-**product** n derivado m

bye(-bye) /'baɪ(baɪ)/ int (colloq) adeus, adeusinho

bygone /'baɪgɒn/ a passado. **let** ~**s be** ~**s** o que passou, passou

bypass /'baɪpɑːs/ n (estrada) secundária f, desvio m; (med) by-pass m, ponte f de safena □ vt fazer um desvio; (fig) contornar

bystander /'baɪstændə(r)/ n circunstante mf, espectador m

byte /baɪt/ n

C

cab /kæb/ n táxi m; (of lorry, train) cabina f, cabine f

cabaret /'kæbəreɪ/ n variedades fpl, cabaré m

cabbage /'kæbɪdʒ/ n couve f, repolho m

cabin /'kæbɪn/ n cabana f; (in plane) cabina f; (in ship) camarote m

cabinet /'kæbmɪt/ n armário m. **C~** (pol) gabinete m

cable /'keɪbl/ n cabo m. **~-car** n funicular m, teleférico m. **~ railway** funicular m. **~ television** televisão f a cabo

cache /kæʃ/ n (esconderijo m de) tesouro m, armazém fpl, provisões f pl

cackle /'kækl/ n cacarejo m □ vi cacarejar

cactus /'kæktəs/ n (pl **~es** or **cacti** /-taɪ/) cacto m

caddie /'kædɪ/ n (golf) caddie m

caddy /'kædɪ/ n lata f para o chá

cadet /kə'det/ n cadete m

cadge /kædʒ/ vt/i filar, (P) cravar

Caesarean /sɪ'zeərɪən/ a **~ (section)** cesariana f

café /'kæfeɪ/ n café m

cafeteria /kæfɪ'tɪərɪə/ n cafeteria f, restaurante m self-service

caffeine /'kæfiːn/ n cafeína f

cage /keɪdʒ/ n gaiola f

cagey /'keɪdʒɪ/ a (colloq: secretive) misterioso, reservado

cajole /kə'dʒəʊl/ vt **~ sb into doing sth** convencer alguém (com lábia ou lisonjas) a fazer alg coisa

cake /keɪk/ n bolo m. **~d** a empastado. **his shoes were ~d with mud** tinha os sapatos cobertos de lama. **a piece of ~** (sl) canja f (sl)

calamity /kə'læmətɪ/ n calamidade f

calcium /'kælsɪəm/ n cálcio m

calculat|e /'kælkjʊleɪt/ vt/i calcular; (Amer: suppose) supor. **~ed** a (action) deliberado, calculado. **~ing** a calculista. **~ion** /-'leɪʃn/ n cálculo m. **~or** n calculador m, (P) maquina f de calcular

calendar /'kælɪmdə(r)/ n calendário m

calf[1] /kɑːf/ n (pl **calves**) (young cow or bull) vitelo m, bezerro m; (of other animals) cria f

calf[2] /kɑːf/ n (pl **calves**) (of leg) barriga f da perna

calibrat|e /'kælɪbreɪt/ vt calibrar. **~ion** /-breɪʃn/ n calibragem f

calibre /'kælɪbə(r)/ n calibre m

calico /'kælɪkəʊ/ n pano m de algodão; (printed) chita f, algodão m

call /kɔːl/ vt/i chamar; (summon) convocar; (phone) telefonar. **~ (in or round)** (visit) passar por casa de □ n chamada f; (bird's cry) canto m; (shout) brado m, grito m. **be ~ed** (named) chamar-se. **be on ~** estar de serviço. **~ back** (phone) tornar a telefonar; (visit) voltar. **~ for** (demand) pedir, requerer; (fetch) ir buscar. **~ off** cancelar. **~ on** (visit) visitar, fazer uma visita a. **~ out (to)** chamar. **~ up** (mil) mobilizar, recrutar; (phone) telefonar. **~-box** n

cabina f telefônica, (P) telefónica. **~er** n visitante f, visita f; (phone) chamador m, (P) pessoa f que faz a chamada. **~ing** n vocação f

callous /'kæləs/ a insensível. **~ly** adv sem piedade.

callow /'kæləʊ/ a (-er, -est) inexperiente, verde

calm /kɑːm/ a (-er, -est) calmo □ n calma f □ vt/i **~ (down)** acalmar (-se). **~ness** n calma f

calorie /'kælərɪ/ n caloria f

camber /'kæmbə(r)/ n (of road) abaulamento m

camcorder /'kæmkɔːdə(r)/ n câmera f de filmar

came /keɪm/ see **come**

camel /'kæml/ n camelo m

camera /'kæmərə/ n máquina f fotográfica; (cine, TV) câmera f. **~man** n (pl **-men**) operador m

camouflage /'kæməflɑːʒ/ n camuflagem f □ vt camuflar

camp[1] /kæmp/ n acampamento m □ vi acampar. **~-bed** n cama f de campanha. **~er** n campista mf; (car) auto-caravana f. **~ing** n campismo m

camp[2] /kæmp/ a afetado, efeminado

campaign /kæm'peɪn/ n campanha f □ vi fazer campanha

campsite /'kæmpsaɪt/ n área f de camping, (P) parque m de campismo

campus /'kæmpəs/ n (pl **-puses** /-pəsɪz/) campus m, (P) cidade f universitária

can[1] /kæn/ n vasilha f de lata; (for food) lata f (de conserva) □ vt (pt **canned**) enlatar. **~ned music** música f em fita para locais públicos. **~-opener** n abridor m de latas, (P) abrelatas m

can[2] /kæn/ v aux (be able to) poder, ser capaz de; (know how to) saber. **I ~not/~'t go** não posso ir

Canad|a /'kænədə/ n Canadá m. **~ian** /kə'neɪdɪən/ a & n canadense (mf), (P) canadiano (m)

canal /kə'næl/ n canal m

canary /kə'neərɪ/ n canário m. **C~ Islands** npl as (Ilhas) Canárias

cancel /'kænsl/ vt (pt **cancelled**) cancelar; (cross out) riscar; (stamps) inutilizar. **~ out** vi (fig) neutralizar-se mutuamente. **~lation** /-'leɪʃn/ n cancelamento m

cancer /'kænsə(r)/ n câncer m, cancro m. **C~** (astrol) Caranguejo m, Câncer m. **~ous** a canceroso

candid /'kændɪd/ a franco. **~ly** adv francamente

candida|te /'kændɪdeɪt/ n candidato m. **~cy** /-əsɪ/ n candidatura f

candle /'kændl/ n vela f; (in church) vela f, círio m. **~-light** n luz f de velas

candlestick /'kændlstɪk/ n castiçal m

candour /'kændə(r)/ n franqueza f, candura f

candy /'kændɪ/ n bala f, (P) açúcar cândi; (*Amer: sweet, sweets*) doce(s) m (*pl*). ~-**floss** n algodão-doce m

cane /keɪn/ n cana f; (*walking-stick*) bengala f; (*for baskets*) verga f; (*school: for punishment*) vergasta f □ vt vergastar

canine /'keɪnaɪn/ a & n canino (m)

canister /'kænɪstə(r)/ n lata f

cannabis /'kænəbɪs/ n cânhamo m, maconha f

cannibal /'kænɪbl/ n canibal mf. ~**ism** /-zəm/ n canibalismo m

cannon /'kænən/ n inv canhão m. ~**ball** n bala f de canhão

cannot /'kænət/ = **can not**

canny /'kænɪ/ a (-ier, -iest) astuto, manhoso

canoe /kə'nu:/ n canoa f □ vi andar de canoa. ~**ing** n (*sport*) canoagem f. ~**ist** n canoeiro m, (P) canoísta mf

canon /'kænən/ n cônego m, (P) cónego m; (*rule*) cânone m

canonize /'kænənaɪz/ vt canonizar

canopy /'kænəpɪ/ n dossel m; (*over doorway*) toldo m, marquise f; (*fig*) abóbada f

can't /ka:nt/ = **can not**

cantankerous /kæn'tæŋkərəs/ a irascível, intratável

canteen /kæn'ti:n/ n cantina f; (*flask*) cantil m; (*for cutlery*) estojo m

canter /'kæntə(r)/ n meio galope m, cânter m □ vi andar a meio galope

canton /'kæntɒn/ n cantão m

canvas /'kænvəs/ n lona f; (*for painting or tapestry*) tela f

canvass /'kænvəs/ vt/i angariar votos or fregueses

canyon /'kænjən/ n canhão m, (P) desfiladeiro m

cap /kæp/ n (*with peak*) boné m; (*without peak*) barrete m; (*of nurse*) touca f; (*of bottle, pen, tube, etc*) tampa f; (*mech*) tampa f, tampão m □ vt (*pt capped*) (*bottle, pen, tube, etc*) tapar, tampar; (*rates*) impor um limite a; (*outdo*) suplantar; (*sport*) seleccionar, (P) seleccionar. ~**ped with** encimado de, coroado de

capab|le /'keɪpəbl/ a (*person*) capaz (*of de*); (*things, situations*) suscetível, (P) susceptível (*of de*). ~**ility** /-'bɪlətɪ/ n capacidade f. ~**ly** adv capazmente

capacity /kə'pæsətɪ/ n capacidade f. **in one's** ~ **as** na (sua) qualidade de

cape¹ /keɪp/ n (*cloak*) capa f

cape² /keɪp/ n (*geog*) cabo m

caper¹ /'keɪpə(r)/ vi andar aos pinotes

caper² /'keɪpə(r)/ n (*culin*) alcaparra f

capillary /kə'pɪlərɪ/ n (*pl* -**ies**) vaso m capilar

capital /'kæpɪtl/ a capital □ n (*town*) capital f; (*money*) capital m. ~ (-**letter**) maiúscula f. ~ **punishment** pena f de morte

capitalis|t /'kæpɪtəlɪst/ a & n capitalista (*mf*). ~**m** /-zəm/ n capitalismo m

capitalize /'kæpɪtəlaɪz/ vi capitalizar; (*finance*) financiar; (*writing*) escrever com maiúscula. ~ **on** tirar partido de

capitulat|e /kə'pɪtʃuleɪt/ vi capitular. ~**ion** /'leɪʃn/ n capitulação f

capricious /kə'prɪʃəs/ a caprichoso

Capricorn /'kæprɪkɔ:n/ n (*astrol*) Capricórnio m

capsicum /'kæpsɪkəm/ n pimento m

capsize /kæp'saɪz/ vt/i virar(-se)

capsule /'kæpsju:l/ n cápsula f

captain /'kæptɪn/ n capitão m; (*navy*) capitão-de-mar-e-guerra m □ vt capitanear, comandar

caption /'kæpʃn/ n legenda f; (*heading*) título m

captivate /'kæptɪveɪt/ vt cativar

captiv|e /'kæptɪv/ a & n cativo (m), prisioneiro (m). ~**ity** /-'tɪvətɪ/ n cativeiro m

captor /'kæptə(r)/ n captor m

capture /'kæptʃə(r)/ vt capturar; (*attention*) prender □ n captura f

car /ka:(r)/ n carro m. ~ **ferry** barca f para carros. ~-**park** n (parque m de) estacionamento (m). ~ **phone** telefone m de carro. ~-**wash** n estação f de lavagem

carafe /kə'ræf/ n garrafa f para água ou vinho

caramel /'kærəmel/ n caramelo m.

carat /'kærət/ n quilate m

caravan /'kærəvæn/ n caravana f, reboque m

caraway /'kærəweɪ/ n ~ **seed** cariz f

carbohydrate /ka:bəʊ'haɪdreɪt/ n hidrato m de carbono

carbon /'ka:bən/ n carbono m. ~ **copy** cópia f em papel carbono, (P) químico. ~ **monoxide** óxido m de carbono. ~ **paper** papel m carbono, (P) químico

carburettor /ka:bjʊ'retə(r)/ n carburador m

carcass /'ka:kəs/ n carcaça f

card /ka:d/ n cartão m; (*postcard*) postal m; (*playing-card*) carta f. ~-**game(s)** n(pl) jogo(s) m(pl) de cartas. ~ **index** n fichário m, (P) ficheiro m

cardboard /'ka:dbɔ:d/ n cartão m, papelão m

cardiac /'ka:dɪæk/ a cardíaco

cardigan /'ka:dɪgən/ n casaco m de lã

cardinal /'ka:dml/ *a* cardeal, principal. ~ **number** numeral *m* cardinal □ *n* (*relig*) cardeal *m*
care /keə(r)/ *n* cuidado *m*; (*concern*) interesse *m* □ *vi* ~ **about** (*be interested*) estar interessado por; (*be worried*) estar preocupado com. ~ **for** (*like*) gostar de; (*look after*) tomar conta de. **take** ~ tomar cuidado. **take** ~ **of** cuidar de; (*deal with*) tratar de. **he couldn't** ~ **less** ele está pouco ligando, ele não dá a menor (*colloq*)
career /kə'rɪə(r)/ *n* carreira *f* □ *vi* ir a toda a velocidade, ir numa carreira
carefree /'keəfri:/ *a* despreocupado
careful /'keəfl/ *a* cuidadoso; (*cautious*) cauteloso. ~! cuidado! ~ly *adv* cuidadosamente; (*cautiously*) cautelosamente
careless /'keəlɪs/ *a* descuidado (**about** com). ~ly *adv* descuidadamente. ~ness *n* descuido *m*, negligência *f*
caress /kə'res/ *n* carícia *f* □ *vt* acariciar
caretaker /'keəteɪkə(r)/ *n* zelador *m* duma casa vizia; (*janitor*) zelador *m*, (*P*) porteiro *m*
cargo /'ka:gəʊ/ *n* (*pl* -oes) carregamento *m*, carga *f*
Caribbean /kærɪ'bi:ən/ *a* caraíba. **the** ~ as Caraíbas *fpl*
caricature /'kærɪkətjʊə(r)/ *n* caricatura *f* □ *vt* caricaturar
caring /'keərɪŋ/ *a* carinhoso, afetuoso, (*P*) afectuoso
carnage /'ka:nɪdʒ/ *n* carnificina *f*
carnation /ka:'neɪʃn/ *n* cravo *m*
carnival /'ka:nɪvl/ *n* carnaval *m*
carol /'kærəl/ *n* cântico *m* or canto *m* de Natal
carp[1] /ka:p/ *n inv* carpa *f*
carp[2] /ka:p/ *vi* ~ (**at**) criticar
carpent|er /'ka:pmtə(r)/ *n* carpinteiro *m*. ~ry *n* carpintaria *f*
carpet /'ka:pɪt/ *n* tapete *m* □ *vt* (*pt* **carpeted**) atapetar. **with fitted** ~**s** (estar) atapetado. **be on the** ~ (*colloq*) ser chamado à ordem. ~**sweeper** *n* limpador *m* de tapetes
carport /'ka:pɔ:t/ *n* abrigo *m*, (*P*) telheiro *m* para automóveis
carriage /'kærɪdʒ/ *n* carruagem *f*; (*of goods*) frete *m*, transporte *m*; (*cost, bearing*) porte *m*
carriageway /'kærɪdʒweɪ/ *n* faixa *f* de rodagem, pista *f*
carrier /'kærɪə(r)/ *n* transportador *m*; (*company*) transportadora *f*; (*med*) portador *m*. ~ (**bag**) saco *m* de plástico
carrot /'kærət/ *n* cenoura *f*
carry /'kærɪ/ *vt/i* levar; (*goods*) transportar; (*involve*) acarretar; (*have for*

sale) ter à venda. **be carried away** entusiasmar-se, deixar-se levar. ~**cot** *n* moisés *m*. ~ **off** levar à força; (*prize*) incluir. ~ **it off** sair-se bem (de). ~ **on** continuar; (*colloq: flirt*) flertar; (*colloq: behave*) portar-se (mal). ~ **out** executar; (*duty*) cumprir. ~ **through** levar a cabo
cart /ka:t/ *n* carroça *f*; carro *m* □ *vt* acarretar; (*collog*) carregar com
cartilage /'ka:tɪlɪdʒ/ *n* cartilagem *f*
carton /'ka:tn/ *n* embalagem *f* de cartão *or* de plástico; (*of yogurt*) embalagem *f*, pote *m*; (*of milk*) pacote *m*
cartoon /ka:'tu:n/ *n* desenho *m* humorístico, caricatura *f*; (*strip*) estória *f* em quadrinhos, (*P*) banda *f* desenhada; (*film*) desenhos *mpl* animados. ~**ist** *n* caricaturista *mf*; (*of strip, film*) desenhador *m*
cartridge /'ka:trɪdʒ/ *n* cartucho *m*
carv|e /ka:v/ *vt* esculpir, talhar; (*meat*) trinchar. ~**ing** *n* obra *f* de talha; (*on tree-trunk*) incisão *f*. ~**ing knife** faca *f* de trinchar, trinchante *m*
cascade /kæs'keɪd/ *n* cascata *f* □ *vi* cair em cascata
case[1] /keɪs/ *n* caso *m*; (*jur*) causa *f*, processo *m*; (*phil*) argumentos *mpl*. **in any** ~ em todo caso. **in** ~ (**of**) no caso (de). **in that** ~ nesse caso
case[2] /keɪs/ *n* caixa *f*; (*crate*) caixa *f*, caixote *m*; (*for camera, jewels, spectacles, etc*) estojo *m*; (*suitcase*) mala *f*; (*for cigarettes*) cigarreira *f*
cash /kæʃ/ *n* dinheiro *m*, numerário *m*, cash *m* □ *vt* (*obtain money for*) cobrar, receber; (*give money for*) pagar. **be short of** ~ ter pouco dinheiro. ~ **a cheque** (*receive/give*) cobrar/descontar um cheque. ~ **in** receber. ~ **in** (**on**) aproveitar-se de. **in** ~ em dinheiro. **pay** ~ pagar em dinheiro. ~ **desk** caixa *f*. ~ **dispenser** caixa *f* electrônica. ~-**flow** *n* cash-flow *m*. ~ **register** caixa *f* registradora, (*P*) registadora *f*
cashew /kæ'ʃu:/ *n* caju *m*
cashier /kæ'ʃɪə(r)/ *n* caixa *mf*
cashmere /kæʃ'mɪə(r)/ *n* caxemira *f*
casino /kə'si:nəʊ/ *n* (*pl* -os) casino *m*
cask /ka:sk/ *n* casco *m*, barril *m*
casket /'ka:skɪt/ *n* pequeno cofre *m*; (*Amer: coffin*) caixão *m*
casserole /'kæsərəʊl/ *n* caçarola *f*; (*stew*) estufado *m*
cassette /kə'set/ *n* cassette *f*. ~ **player** *n* gravador *m*. ~ **recorder** *n*
cast /ka:st/ *vt* (*pt* **cast**) lançar, arremessar; (*shed*) despojar-se de; (*vote*) dar; (*metal*) fundir; (*shadow*) projectar, (*P*) projectar □ *n* (*theatr*) elenco *m*; (*mould*) molde *m*; (*med*) aparelho

m de gesso. ~ **iron** *n* ferro *m* fundido. ~-**iron** *a* de ferro fundido; (*fig*) muito forte. ~-**offs** *npl* roupa *f* velha

castanets /kæstəˈnets/ *npl* castanholas *fpl*

castaway /ˈkɑ:stəweɪ/ *n* náufrago *m*

caste /kɑ:st/ *n* casta *f*

castigate /ˈkæstɪgeɪt/ *vt* castigar

castle /ˈkɑ:sl/ *n* castelo *m*; (*chess*) torre *f*

castor /ˈkɑ:stə(r)/ *n* roda *f* de pé de móvel. ~ **sugar** açúcar *m* em pó

castrat|e /kæˈstreɪt/ *vt* castrar. ~**ion** /-ʃn/ *n* castração *f*

casual /ˈkæʒʊəl/ *a* (*chance: meeting*) casual; (*careless, unmethodical*) descuidado; (*informal*) informal. ~ **clothes** roupa *f* prática *or* de lazer. ~ **work** trabalho *m* ocasional. ~**ly** *adv* casualmente; (*carelessly*) sem cuidado

casualty /ˈkæʒʊəltɪ/ *n* (*dead*) morto *m*; (*death*) morte *f*; (*injured*) ferido *m*; (*victim*) vítima *f*; (*mil*) baixa *f*

cat /kæt/ *n* gato *m*. ~'**s-eyes** *npl* (*P*) reflectores *mpl*

Catalonia /kætəˈləʊnɪə/ *n* Catalunha *f*

catalogue /ˈkætəlɒg/ *n* catálogo *m* □ *vt* catalogar

catalyst /ˈkætəlɪst/ *n* catalisador *m*

catapult /ˈkætəpʌlt/ *n* (*child's*) atiradeira *f*, (*P*) fisga *f* □ *vt* catapultar

cataract /ˈkætərækt/ *f* (*waterfall & med*) catarata *f*

catarrh /kəˈtɑ:(r)/ *n* catarro *m*

catastroph|e /kəˈtæstrəfɪ/ *n* catástrofe *f*. ~**ic** /kætəsˈtrɒfɪk/ *a* catastrófico

catch /kætʃ/ *vt* (*pt* **caught**) apanhar; (*grasp*) agarrar; (*hear*) perceber □ *vi* prender-se (**in** em); (*get stuck*) ficar preso □ *n* apanha *f*; (*of fish*) pesca *f*; (*trick*) ratoeira *f*; (*snag*) problema *m*; (*on door*) trinco *m*; (*fastener*) fecho *m*. ~ **fire** pegar fogo, (*P*) incendiar-se. ~ **on** (*colloq*) pegar, tornar-se popular. ~ **sb's eye** atrair a atenção de alg. ~ **sight of** avistar. ~ **up** (**with**) pôr-se a par (com); (*work*) pôr em dia. ~-**phrase** *n* clichê *m*

catching /ˈkætʃɪŋ/ *a* contagioso, infeccioso

catchment /ˈkætʃmənt/ *n* ~ **area** (*geog*) bacia *f* de captação; (*fig: of school, hospital*) área *f*

catchy /ˈkætʃɪ/ *a* (*tune*) que pega fácil

categorical /kætɪˈgɒrɪkl/ *a* categórico

category /ˈkætɪgərɪ/ *n* categoria *f*

cater /ˈkeɪtə(r)/ *vi* fornecer comida (para clubes, casamentos, etc). ~ **for** (*pander to*) satisfazer; (*consumers*) dirigir-se a. ~**er** *n* fornecedor *m*. ~**ing** *n* catering *m*

caterpillar /ˈkætəpɪlə(r)/ *n* lagarta *f*

cathedral /kəˈθi:drəl/ *n* catedral *f*

catholic /ˈkæθəlɪk/ *a* universal; (*eclectic*) eclético, (*P*) ecléctico. **C**~ *a* & *n* católico (*m*). **C**~**ism** /kəˈθɒlɪsɪzəm/ *n* catolicismo *m*

cattle /ˈkætl/ *npl* gado *m*

catty /ˈkætɪ/ *a* (dissimuladamente) maldoso, com perfídia

caught /kɔ:t/ *see* **catch**

cauldron /ˈkɔ:ldrən/ *n* caldeirão *m*

cauliflower /ˈkɒlɪflaʊə(r)/ *n* couve-flor *f*

cause /kɔ:z/ *n* causa *f* □ *vt* causar. ~ **sth to grow/move** *etc* fazer crescer/mexer *etc* alg coisa

causeway /ˈkɔ:zweɪ/ *n* estrada *f* elevada, caminho *m* elevado

caustic /ˈkɔ:stɪk/ *a* cáustico

cauti|on /ˈkɔ:ʃn/ *n* cautela *f*; (*warning*) aviso *m* □ *vt* avisar. ~**ous** /ˈkɔ:ʃəs/ *a* cauteloso. ~**ously** *adv* cautelosamente

cavalry /ˈkævəlrɪ/ *n* cavalaria *f*

cave /keɪv/ *n* caverna *f*, gruta *f* □ *vi* ~ **in** desabar, dar de si

caveman /ˈkeɪvmæn/ *n* (*pl* -**men**) troglodita *m*, homen *m* das cavernas; (*fig*) (tipo) primário *m*

cavern /ˈkævən/ *n* caverna *f*. ~**ous** *a* cavernoso

caviare /ˈkævɪɑ:(r)/ *n* caviar *m*

caving /ˈkeɪvɪŋ/ *n* espeleologia *f*

cavity /ˈkævətɪ/ *n* cavidade *f*

cavort /kəˈvɔ:t/ *vi* curvetear; (*person*) andar aos pinotes

CD /si:ˈdi:/ *see* **compact disc**

cease /si:s/ *vt*/*i* cessar. ~-**fire** *n* cessar-fogo *m*. ~**less** *a* incessante

cedar /ˈsi:də(r)/ *n* cedro *m*

cedilla /sɪˈdɪlə/ *n* cedilha *f*

ceiling /ˈsi:lɪŋ/ *n* (*lit & fig*) teto *m*, (*P*) tecto *m*

celebrat|e /ˈselɪbreɪt/ *vt*/*i* celebrar, festejar. ~**ion** /ˈbreɪʃn/ *n* celebração *f*, festejo *m*

celebrated /ˈselɪbreɪtɪd/ *a* célebre

celebrity /sɪˈlebrətɪ/ *n* celebridade *f*

celery /ˈselərɪ/ *n* aipo *m*

celiba|te /ˈselɪbət/ *a* celibatário. ~**cy** *n* celibato *m*

cell /sel/ *n* (*of prison, convent*) cela *f*; (*biol, pol, electr*) célula *f*

cellar /ˈselə(r)/ *n* porão *m*, cave *f*; (*for wine*) adega *f*, cave *f*

cell|o /ˈtʃeləʊ/ *n* (*pl* -**os**) violoncelo *m*. ~**ist** *n* violoncelista *mf*

Cellophane /ˈseləfeɪn/ *n* (*p*) celofane *m*

cellular /ˈseljʊlə(r)/ *a* celular

Celt /kelt/ *n* celta *mf*. ~**ic** *a* celta, céltico

cement /sɪˈment/ *n* cimento *m* □ *vt* cimentar. ~-**mixer** *n* betoneira *f*

cemetery /'semətrɪ/ n cemitério m

censor /'sensə(r)/ n censor m □ vt censurar. ~**ship** n censura f

censure /'senʃə(r)/ n censura f, crítica f □ vt censurar, criticar

census /'sensəs/ n recenseamento m, censo m

cent /sent/ n cêntimo m

centenary /sen'tiːnərɪ/ n centenário m

centigrade /'sentɪgreɪd/ a centígrado

centilitre /'sentɪliːtə(r)/ n centilitro m

centimetre /'sentɪmiːtə(r)/ n centímetro m

centipede /'sentɪpiːd/ n centopéia f, (P) centopeia f

central /'sentrəl/ a central. ~ **heating** aquecimento m central. ~**ize** vt centralizar. ~**ly** adv no centro

centre /'sentə(r)/ n centro m □ vt (pt **centred**) centrar □ vi ~ **on** concentrar-se em, fixar-se em

centrifugal /sen'trɪfjʊgl/ a centrífugo

century /'sentʃərɪ/ n século m

ceramic /sɪ'ræmɪk/ a (object) em cerâmica. ~**s** n cerâmica f

cereal /'sɪərɪəl/ n cereal m

cerebral /'serɪbrəl/ a cerebral

ceremonial /serɪ'məʊnɪəl/ a de cerimônia □ n cerimonial m

ceremon|y /'serɪmənɪ/ n cerimônia f, (P) cerimónia f. ~**ious** /-'məʊnɪəs/ a cerimonioso

certain /'sɜːtn/ a certo. be ~ ter a certeza. for ~ com certeza, ao certo. make ~ confirmar, verificar. ~**ly** adv com certeza, certamente. ~**ty** n certeza f

certificate /sə'tɪfɪkət/ n certificado m; (birth, marriage) certidão f; (health) atestado m

certif|y /'sɜːtɪfaɪ/ vt/i certificar. ~**ied** a (as insane) declarado

cervical /sɜː'vaɪkl/ a cervical; (of cervix) do útero

cesspit, cesspool /'sespɪt, 'sespuːl/ ns fossa f sanitária

chafe /tʃeɪf/ vt/i esfregar; (make/become sore) esfolar/ficar esfolado; (fig) irritar(-se)

chaff /tʃaːf/ vt brincar com □ n brincadeira f; (husk) casca f

chaffinch /'tʃæfɪntʃ/ n tentilhão m

chagrin /'ʃægrɪn/ n decepção f, desgosto m, aborrecimento m

chain /tʃeɪn/ n corrente f, cadeia f; (series) cadeia f □ vt acorrentar. ~ **reaction** reação f, (P) reacção f em cadeia. ~-**smoke** vi fumar cigarros um atrás do outro. ~ **store** loja f pertencente a uma cadeia

chair /tʃeə(r)/ n cadeira f; (position of chairman) presidência f, (univ) cátedra f □ vt presidir

chairman /'tʃeəmən/ n (pl -**men**) presidente mf

chalet /'ʃæleɪ/ n chalé m

chalk /tʃɔːk/ n greda f, cal f; (for writing) giz m □ vt traçar com giz

challeng|e /'tʃælɪndʒ/ n desafio m; (by sentry) interpelação f □ vt desafiar; (question truth of) contestar. ~**er** n (sport) pretendente mf (ao título). ~**ing** a estimulante, que constitui um desafio

chamber /'tʃeɪmbə(r)/ n (old use) aposento m. ~-**maid** n arrumadeira f. ~ **music** música f de câmara. **C**~ **of Commerce** Câmara f de Comércio

chamois /'ʃæmɪ/ n ~(-**leather**) camurça f

champagne /ʃæm'peɪn/ n champanhe m

champion /'tʃæmpɪən/ n campeão m, campeã f □ vt defender. ~**ship** n campeonato m

chance /tʃaːns/ n acaso m; (luck) sorte f; (opportunity) oportunidade f, chance f; (likelihood) hipótese f, probabilidade f; (risk) risco m □ a casual, fortuito □ vi calhar □ vt arriscar. **by** ~ por acaso

chancellor /'tʃaːnsələ(r)/ n chanceler m. **C**~ **of the Exchequer** Ministro m das Finanças

chancy /'tʃaːnsɪ/ a arriscado

chandelier /ʃændə'lɪə(r)/ n lustre m

change /tʃeɪndʒ/ vt mudar; (exchange) trocar (for por); (clothes, house, trains, etc) mudar de □ vi mudar; (clothes) mudar-se, mudar de roupa □ n mudança f; (money) troco m. a ~ **of clothes** uma muda de roupa. ~ **hands** (ownership) mudar de dono. ~ **into** (a butterfly etc) transformar-se em; (evening dress etc) pôr. ~ **one's mind** mudar de idéia. ~ **over** passar, mudar (to para). ~-**over** n mudança f. ~**able** a variável

channel /'tʃænl/ n canal m □ vt (pt **channelled**) canalizar. the **C**~ **Islands** as Ilhas do Canal da Mancha. the (**English**) **C**~ o Canal da Mancha

chant /tʃaːnt/ n cântico m; (of crowd etc) vt/i cantar, entoar

chao|s /'keɪɒs/ n caos m. ~**tic** /-'ɒtɪk/ a caótico

chap /tʃæp/ n (colloq) sujeito m, (B) cara m, (P) tipo m

chapel /'tʃæpl/ n capela f

chaperon /'ʃæpərəʊn/ n pau-de-cabeleira m, chaperon m □ vt servir de pau-de-cabeleira or de chaperon

chaplain /'tʃæplɪn/ n capelão m. ~**cy** n capelania f

chapter /'tʃæptə(r)/ n capítulo m

char /tʃaː(r)/ vt (pt **charred**) carbonizar

character /'kærəktə(r)/ *n* caráter *m*, (P) carácter *m*; (*in novel, play*) personagem *m*; (*reputation*) fama *f*; (*eccentric person*) excêntrico *m*; (*letter*) caractere *m*, (P) carácter *m*. ~**ize** *vt* caracterizar

characteristic /kærəktə'rɪstɪk/ *a* característico □ *n* característica *f*. ~**ally** *adv* tipicamente

charade /ʃə'ra:d/ *n* charada *f*

charcoal /'tʃa:kəʊl/ *n* carvão *m* de lenha

charge /tʃa:dʒ/ *n* preço *m*; (*electr, mil*) carga *f*; (*jur*) acusação *f*; (*task, custody*) cargo *m* □ *vt/i* (*price*) cobrar; (*enemy*) atacar; (*jur*) incriminar. be in ~ of ter a cargo. take ~ of encarregar-se de

chariot /'tʃærɪət/ *n* carro *m* de guerra *or* triunfal

charisma /kə'rɪzmə/ *n* carisma *m*. ~**tic** /kæriz'mætɪk/ *a* carismático

charit|y /'tʃærətɪ/ *n* caridade *f*; (*society*) instituição *f* de caridade. ~**able** *a* caridoso

charlatan /'ʃa:lətən/ *n* charlatão *m*

charm /tʃa:m/ *n* encanto *m*, charme *m*; (*spell*) feitiço *m*; (*talisman*) amuleto *m* □ *vt* encantar. ~**ing** *a* encantador

chart /tʃa:t/ *n* (*naut*) carta *f*; (*table*) mapa *m*, gráfico *m*, tabela *f* □ *vt* fazer o mapa de

charter /'tʃa:tə(r)/ *n* carta *f*. ~ (**flight**) (voo) charter *m* □ *vt* fretar. ~**ed accountant** *n* perito *m* contador, (P) perito *m* de contabilidade

charwoman /'tʃa:wʊmən/ *n* (*pl* -**women**) faxineira *f*, (P) mulher *f* a dias

chase /tʃeɪs/ *vt* perseguir □ *vi* (*colloq*) correr (**after** atrás de) □ *n* caça *f*, perseguição *f*. ~ **away** *or* **off** afugentar, expulsar

chasm /'kæzm/ *n* abismo *m*

chassis /'ʃæsɪ/ *n* chassi *m*

chaste /tʃeɪst/ *a* casto

chastise /tʃæs'taɪz/ *vt* castigar

chastity /'tʃæstətɪ/ *n* castidade *f*

chat /tʃæt/ *n* conversa *f* □ *vi* (*pt* **chatted**) conversar, cavaquear. **have a** ~ bater um papo, (P) dar dois dedos de conversa. ~**ty** *a* conversador

chatter /'tʃætə(r)/ *vi* tagarelar. **his teeth are** ~**ing** seus dentes estão tiritando □ *n* tagarelice *f*

chauffeur /'ʃəʊfə(r)/ *n* motorista *m*, chofer (particular) *m*, chauffeur *m*

chauvinis|t /'ʃəʊvɪnɪst/ *n* chauvinista *mf*. **male** ~**t** (*pej*) machista *m*. ~**m** /-zəm/ *n* chauvinismo *m*

cheap /tʃi:p/ *a* (-**er**, -**est**) barato; (*fare, rate*) reduzido. ~(**ly**) *adv* barato. ~**ness** *n* barateza *f*

cheapen /'tʃi:pən/ *vt* depreciar

cheat /tʃi:t/ *vt* enganar, trapacear □ *vi* (*at games*) roubar, (P) fazer batota; (*in exams*) copiar □ *n* intrujão *m*; (*at games*) trapaceiro *m*, (P) batoteiro *m*

check[1] /tʃek/ *vt/i* (*examine*) verificar; (*tickets*) revisar; (*restrain*) controlar, refrear □ *n* verificação *f*; (*tickets*) controle *m*; (*curb*) freio *m*; (*chess*) xeque *m*; (*Amer: bill*) conta *f*; (*Amer: cheque*) cheque *m*. ~ **in** assinar o registro; (*at airport*) fazer o check-in. ~-**in** *n* check-in *m*. ~ **out** pagar a conta. ~-**out** *n* caixa *f*. ~-**up** *n* exame *m* médico, check-up *m*

check[2] /tʃek/ *n* (*pattern*) xadrez *m*. ~**ed** *a* de xadrez

checkmate /'tʃekmeɪt/ *n* xeque-mate *m*

cheek /tʃi:k/ *n* face *f*; (*fig*) descaramento *m*. ~**y** *a* descarado

cheer /tʃɪə(r)/ *n* alegria *f*; (*shout*) viva *m* □ *vt/i* aclamar, aplaudir. ~**s!** à sua, (P) vossa (saúde)!; (*thank you*) obrigadinho. ~ (**up**) animar(-se). ~**ful** *a* bem disposto; alegre

cheerio /tʃɪərɪ'əʊ/ *int* (*colloq*) até logo, (P) adeusinho

cheese /tʃi:z/ *n* queijo *m*

cheetah /'tʃi:tə/ *n* chita *f*, lobo-tigre *m*

chef /ʃef/ *n* cozinheiro-chefe *m*

chemical /'kemɪkl/ *a* químico □ *n* produto *m* químico

chemist /'kemɪst/ *n* farmacêutico *m*; (*scientist*) químico *m*. ~**'s (shop)** *n* farmácia *f*. ~**ry** *n* química *f*

cheque /tʃek/ *n* cheque *m*. ~-**book** *n* talão *m* de cheques. ~-**card** *n* cartão *m* de banco

cherish /'tʃerɪʃ/ *vt* estimar, querer; (*hope*) acalentar

cherry /'tʃerɪ/ *n* cereja *f*. ~-**tree** *n* cerejeira *f*

chess /tʃes/ *n* jogo *m* de xadrez. ~-**board** *n* tabuleiro *m* de xadrez

chest /tʃest/ *n* peito *m*; (*for money, jewels*) cofre *m*. ~ **of drawers** cômoda *f*, (P) cómoda *f*

chestnut /'tʃesnʌt/ *n* castanha *f*. ~-**tree** *n* castanheiro *m*

chew /tʃu:/ *vt* mastigar. ~**ing-gum** *n* chiclete *m*, (P) pastilha *f* elástica

chic /ʃi:k/ *a* chique

chick /tʃɪk/ *n* pinto *m*

chicken /'tʃɪkɪn/ *n* galinha *f* □ *vi* ~ **out** (*sl*) acovardar-se. ~-**pox** *n* catapora *f*, (P) varicela *f*

chicory /'tʃɪkərɪ/ *n* (*for coffee*) chicória *f*; (*for salad*) endívia *f*

chief /tʃi:f/ *n* chefe *m* □ *a* principal. ~**ly** *adv* principalmente

chilblain /'tʃɪlbleɪn/ *n* frieira *f*

child /tʃaɪld/ *n* (*pl* **children** /'tʃɪldrən/) criança *f*; (*son*) filho *m*;

(*daughter*) filha *f*. ~**hood** *n* infância *f*, meninice *f*. ~**ish** *a* infantil; (*immature*) acriançado, pueril. ~**less** *a* sem filhos. ~**like** *a* infantil. ~-**minder** *n* babá *f* que cuida de crianças em sua propria casa

childbirth /'tʃaɪldbɜ:θ/ *n* parto *m*

Chile /'tʃɪlɪ/ *n* Chile *m*. ~**an** *a* & *n* chileno (*m*)

chill /tʃɪl/ *n* frio *m*; (*med*) resfriado *m*, (*P*) constipação *f* □ *vt/i* arrefecer; (*culin*) refrigerar. ~**y** *a* frio. be *or* feel ~**y** ter frio

chilli /'tʃɪlɪ/ *n* (*pl* -**ies**) malagueta *f*

chime /tʃaɪm/ *n* carrilhão *m*; (*sound*) música *m* de carrilhão □ *vt/i* tocar

chimney /'tʃɪmnɪ/ *n* (*pl* -**eys**) chaminé *f*. ~-**sweep** *n* limpador *m* de chaminés, (*P*) limpa-chaminés *m*

chimpanzee /tʃɪmpæn'zi:/ *n* chimpanzé *m*

chin /tʃɪn/ *n* queixo *m*

china /'tʃaɪnə/ *n* porcelana *f*; (*crockery*) louça *f*

Chin|a /'tʃaɪnə/ *n* China *f*. ~**ese** /-'ni:z/ *a* & *n* chinês (*m*)

chink[1] /tʃɪŋk/ *n* (*crack*) fenda *f*, fresta *f*

chink[2] /tʃɪŋk/ *n* tinir *m* □ *vt/i* (fazer) tinir

chip /tʃɪp/ *n* (*broken piece*) bocado *m*; (*culin*) batata *f* frita em palitos; (*gambling*) ficha *f*; (*electronic*) chip *m*, circuito *m* integrado □ *vt/i* (*pt* **chipped**) lascar(-se)

chipboard /'tʃɪpbɔ:d/ *n* compensado *m* (de madeira)

chiropodist /kɪ'rʊpədɪst/ *n* calista *mf*

chirp /tʃɜ:p/ *n* pipilar *m*; (*of cricket*) cricri *m* □ *vi* pipilar; (*cricket*) cantar, fazer cricri

chisel /'tʃɪzl/ *n* cinzel *m*, escopro *m* □ *vt* (*pt* **chiselled**) talhar

chivalr|y /'ʃɪvlrɪ/ *n* cavalheirismo *m*. ~**ous** *a* cavalheiresco

chive /tʃaɪv/ *n* cebolinho *m*

chlorine /'klɔ:ri:n/ *n* cloro *m*

chocolate /'tʃɒklɪt/ *n* chocolate *m*

choice /tʃɔɪs/ *n* escolha *f* □ *a* escolhido, seleto, (*P*) seleccionado

choir /'kwaɪə(r)/ *n* coro *m*

choirboy /'kwaɪəbɔɪ/ *n* menino *m* de coro, corista *m*, (*P*) coralista *m*

choke /tʃəʊk/ *vt/i* sufocar; (*on food*) engasgar(-se) □ *n* (*auto*) afogador *m*, (*P*) botão *m* do ar (*colloq*)

cholesterol /kə'lestərɒl/ *n* colesterol *m*

choose /tʃu:z/ *vt/i* (*pt* **chose**, *pp* **chosen**) escolher; (*prefer*) preferir. ~ **to do** decidir fazer

choosy /'tʃu:zɪ/ *a* (*colloq*) exigente, difícil de contentar

chop /tʃɒp/ *vt/i* (*pt* **chopped**) cortar □

n (*wood*) machadada *f*; (*culin*) costeleta *f*. ~ **down** abater. ~**per** *n* cutelo *m*; (*sl: helicopter*) helicóptero *m*

choppy /'tʃɒpɪ/ *a* (*sea*) picado

chopstick /'tʃɒpstɪk/ *n* fachi *m*, pauzinho *m*

choral /'kɔ:rəl/ *a* coral

chord /kɔ:d/ *n* (*mus*) acorde *m*

chore /tʃɔ:(r)/ *n* trabalho *m*; (*unpleasant task*) tarefa *f* maçante. **household** ~**s** afazeres *mpl* domésticos

choreograph|er /kɒrɪ'ɒgrəfə(r)/ *n* coreógrafo *m*. ~**y** *n* coreografia *f*

chortle /'tʃɔ:tl/ *n* risada *f* □ *vi* rir alto

chorus /'kɔ:rəs/ *n* coro *m*; (*of song*) refrão *m*, estribilho *m*

chose, chosen /tʃəʊz, 'tʃəʊzn/ *see* **choose**

Christ /kraɪst/ *n* Cristo *m*

christen /'krɪsn/ *vt* batizar, (*P*) baptizar. ~**ing** *n* batismo *m*, (*P*) baptismo *m*

Christian /'krɪstʃən/ *a* & *n* cristão (*m*). ~ **name** nome *m* de batismo, (*P*) baptismo. ~**ity** /-strˈænətɪ/ *n* cristandade *f*

Christmas /'krɪsməs/ *n* Natal *m* □ *a* do Natal. ~ **card** cartão *m* de Boas Festas. ~ **Day/Eve** dia *m*/véspera *f* de Natal. ~ **tree** árvore *f* de Natal

chrome /krəʊm/ *n* cromo *m*

chromosome /'krəʊməsəʊm/ *n* cromossoma *m*

chronic /'krɒnɪk/ *a* crônico, (*P*) crónico

chronicle /'krɒnɪkl/ *n* crônica *f*

chronological /krɒnə'lɒdʒɪkl/ *a* cronológico

chrysanthemum /krɪ'sænθəməm/ *n* crisântemo *m*

chubby /'tʃʌbɪ/ *a* (-**ier**, -**iest**) gorducho, rechonchudo

chuck /tʃʌk/ *vt* (*colloq*) deitar, atirar. ~ **out** (*person*) expulsar; (*thing*) jogar fora, (*P*) deitar fora

chuckle /'tʃʌkl/ *n* riso *m* abafado □ *vi* rir sozinho

chum /tʃʌm/ *n* (*colloq*) amigo *m* íntimo, camarada *mf*. ~**my** *a* amigável

chunk /tʃʌŋk/ *n* (grande) bocado *m*, naco *m*

church /tʃɜ:tʃ/ *n* igreja *f*

churchyard /'tʃɜ:tʃja:d/ *n* cemitério *m*

churlish /'tʃɜ:lɪʃ/ *a* grosseiro, indelicado

churn /tʃɜ:n/ *n* batedeira *f*; (*milk-can*) vasilha *f* de leite □ *vt* bater. ~ **out** produzir em série

chute /ʃu:t/ *n* calha *f*; (*for rubbish*) conduta *f* de lixo

chutney /'tʃʌtnɪ/ *n* (*pl* -**eys**) chutney *m*

cider /'saɪdə(r)/ *n* sidra *f*, (*P*) cidra *f*

cigar /sɪ'gɑ:(r)/ *n* charuto *m*

cigarette /ˌsɪgəˈret/ n cigarro m. ~-**case** n cigarreira f

cinder /ˈsɪndə(r)/ n brasa f. **burnt to a** ~ estorricado

cinema /ˈsɪnəmə/ n cinema m

cinnamon /ˈsɪnəmən/ n canela f

cipher /ˈsaɪfə(r)/ n cifra f

circle /ˈsɜːkl/ n círculo m; (theat) balcão m □ vt dar a volta a □ vi descrever círculos, voltear

circuit /ˈsɜːkɪt/ n circuito m

circuitous /sɜːˈkjuːrtəs/ a indireto, tortuoso

circular /ˈsɜːkjʊlə(r)/ a circular

circulat|e /ˈsɜːkjʊleɪt/ vt/i (fazer) circular. ~**ion** /-ˈleɪʃn/ n circulação f; (sales of newspaper) tiragem f

circumcis|e /ˈsɜːkəmsaɪz/ vt circuncidar. ~**ion** /-ˈsɪʒn/ n circuncisão f

circumference /səˈkʌmfərəns/ n circunferência f

circumflex /ˈsɜːkəmfleks/ n circunflexo m

circumstance /ˈsɜːkəmstəns/ n circunstância f. ~**s** (means) situação f económica, (P) econômica

circus /ˈsɜːkəs/ n circo m

cistern /ˈsɪstən/ n reservatório m; (of WC) autoclismo m

cit|e /saɪt/ vt citar. ~**ation** /-ˈteɪʃn/ n citação f

citizen /ˈsɪtɪzn/ n cidadão m, cidadã f; (of town) habitante mf. ~**ship** n cidadania f

citrus /ˈsɪtrəs/ n ~ **fruit** citrino m

city /ˈsɪtɪ/ n cidade f

civic /ˈsɪvɪk/ a cívico

civil /ˈsɪvl/ a civil; (rights) cívico; (polite) delicado. ~ **servant** funcionário m público. **C**~ **Service** Administração f Pública. ~ **war** guerra f civil. ~**ity** /-ˈvɪlətɪ/ n civilidade f, cortesia f

civilian /sɪˈvɪlɪən/ a & n civil (mf), paisano m

civiliz|e /ˈsɪvəlaɪz/ vt civilizar. ~**ation** /-ˈzeɪʃn/ n civilização f

claim /kleɪm/ vt reclamar; (assert) pretender □ vi (from insurance) reclamar □ n reivindicação f; (assertion) afirmação f; (right) direito m; (from insurance) reclamação f

clairvoyant /kleəˈvɔɪənt/ n vidente mf □ a clarividente

clam /klæm/ n molusco m

clamber /ˈklæmbə(r)/ vi trepar

clammy /ˈklæmɪ/ a (-ier, -iest) úmido, (P) húmido e pegajoso

clamour /ˈklæmə(r)/ n clamor m, vociferação f □ vi ~ **for** exigir aos gritos

clamp /klæmp/ n grampo m; (for car) bloqueador m □ vt prender com grampo; (a car) bloquear. ~ **down on**

apertar, suprimir; (colloq) cair em cima de (colloq)

clan /klæn/ n clã m

clandestine /klænˈdestɪn/ a clandestino

clang /klæŋ/ n tinir m

clap /klæp/ vt/i (pt **clapped**) aplaudir; (put) meter □ n aplauso m; (of thunder) ribombo m. ~ **one's hands** bater palmas

claptrap /ˈklæptræp/ n parlapatice f

claret /ˈklærət/ n clarete m

clarif|y /ˈklærɪfaɪ/ vt esclarecer. ~**ication** /-ɪˈkeɪʃn/ n esclarecimento m

clarinet /klærɪˈnet/ n clarinete m

clarity /ˈklærətɪ/ n claridade f

clash /klæʃ/ n choque m; (sound) estridor m; (fig) conflito m □ vt/i entrechocar(-se); (of colours) destoar

clasp /klɑːsp/ n (fastener) fecho m; (hold, grip) aperto m de mão □ vt apertar, serrar

class /klɑːs/ n classe f □ vt classificar

classic /ˈklæsɪk/ a & n clássico (m). ~**s** npl letras fpl clássicas, (P) estudos mpl clássicos. ~**al** a clássico

classif|y /-ˈklæsɪfaɪ/ vt classificar. ~**ication** /-ɪˈkeɪʃn/ n classificação f. ~**ied advertisement** (anúncio m) classificado (m)

classroom /ˈklɑːsruːm/ n sala f de aulas

clatter /ˈklætə(r)/ n estardalhaço m □ vi fazer barulho

clause /klɔːz/ n cláusula f; (gram) oração f

claustrophob|ia /klɔːstrəˈfəʊbɪə/ n claustrofobia f. ~**ic** a claustrofóbico

claw /klɔː/ n garra f; (of lobster) tenaz f, pinça f □ vt (seize) agarrar; (scratch) arranhar; (tear) rasgar

clay /kleɪ/ n argila f, barro m

clean /kliːn/ a (-er, -est) limpo □ adv completamente □ vt limpar □ vi ~ **up** fazer a limpeza. ~-**shaven** a de cara rapada. ~**er** n faxineira f, (P) mulher f da limpeza; (of clothes) empregado m da tinturaria. ~**ly** adv com limpeza, como deve ser

cleans|e /klenz/ vt limpar; (fig) purificar. ~**ing cream** creme m de limpeza

clear /klɪə(r)/ a (-er, -est) claro; (glass) transparente; (without obstacles) livre; (profit) líquido; (sky) limpo □ adv claramente □ vt (snow, one's name, etc) limpar; (the table) tirar; (jump) transpor; (debt) saldar; (jur) absolver; (through customs) despachar □ vi (fog) dissipar-se; (sky) limpar. ~ **of** (away from) afastado de. ~ **off** or **out** (sl) sair andando, zarpar. ~ **out** (clean) fazer a limpeza. ~ **up** (*tidy*) arrumar; (*mystery*) desvendar; (*of weather*) clarear, limpar. ~**ly** *adv* claramente

clearance /'klɪərəns/ *n* autorização *f*; (*for ship*) despacho *m*; (*space*) espaço *m* livre. ~ **sale** liquidação *f*, saldos *mpl*

clearing /'klɪərɪŋ/ *n* clareira *f*

clearway /'klɪəweɪ/ *n* rodovia *f* de estacionamento proibido

cleavage /'kli:vɪdʒ/ *n* divisão *f*; (*between breasts*) rego *m* (*of dress*) decote *m*

cleaver /'kli:və(r)/ *n* cutelo *m*

clef /klef/ *n* (*mus*) clave *f*

cleft /kleft/ *n* fenda *f*

clench /klentʃ/ *vt* (*teeth, fists*) cerrar; (*grasp*) agarrar

clergy /'klɜ:dʒɪ/ *n* clero *m*. ~**man** *n* (*pl* -**men**) clérigo *m*, sacerdote *m*

cleric /'klerɪk/ *n* clérigo *m*. ~**al** *a* (*relig*) clerical; (*of clerks*) de escritório

clerk /klɑ:k/ *n* auxiliar *m* de escritório

clever /'klevə(r)/ *a* (-**er**, -**est**) esperto, inteligente; (*skilful*) hábil, habilidoso. ~**ly** *adv* inteligentemente; (*skilfully*) habilmente, habilidosamente. ~**ness** *n* esperteza *f*, inteligência *f*

cliché /'kli:ʃeɪ/ *n* chavão *m*, lugar-comum *m*, clichê *m*

click /klɪk/ *n* estalido *m*, clique *m* □ *vi* dar um estalido

client /'klaɪənt/ *n* cliente *mf*

clientele /kli:ən'tel/ *n* clientela *f*

cliff /klɪf/ *n* penhasco *m*. ~**s** *npl* falésia *f*

climat|e /'klaɪmɪt/ *n* clima *m*. ~**ic** /'mætɪk/ *a* climático

climax /'klaɪmæks/ *n* clímax *m*, ponto *m* culminante

climb /klaɪm/ *vt* (*stairs*) subir; (*tree, wall*) subir em, trepar em; (*mountain*) escalar □ *vi* subir, trepar □ *n* subida *f*; (*mountain*) escalada *f*. ~ **down** descer; (*fig*) dar a mão à palmatória (*fig*). ~**er** *n* (*sport*) alpinista *mf*; (*plant*) trepadeira *f*

clinch /klɪntʃ/ *vt* (*deal*) fechar; (*argument*) resolver

cling /klɪŋ/ *vi* (*pt* **clung**) ~ (**to**) agarrar-se (a); (*stick*) colar-se (a)

clinic /'klɪnɪk/ *n* clínica *f*

clinical /'klɪnɪkl/ *a* clínico

clink /klɪŋk/ *n* tinido *m* □ *vt/i* (fazer) tilintar

clip[1] /klɪp/ *m* (*for paper*) clipe *m*; (*for hair*) grampo *m*, (*P*) gancho *m*; (*for tube*) braçadeira *f* □ *vt* (*pt* **clipped**) prender

clip[2] /klɪp/ *vt* (*pt* **clipped**) cortar; (*trim*) aparar □ *n* tosquia *f*; (*colloq: blow*) murro *m*. ~**ping** *n* recorte *m*

clique /kli:k/ *n* panelinha *f*, facção *f*, conventículo *m*

cloak /kləʊk/ *n* capa *f*, manto *m*

cloakroom /'kləʊkru:m/ *n* vestiário *m*; (*toilet*) toalete *m*, (*P*) lavabo *m*

clock /klɒk/ *n* relógio *m* □ *vi* ~**in/out** marcar o ponto (à entrada/à saída). ~ **up** (*colloq: miles etc*) fazer

clockwise /'klɒkwaɪz/ *a* & *adv* no sentido dos ponteiros do relógio

clockwork /'klɒkwɜ:k/ *n* mecanismo *m*. **go like** ~ ir às mil maravilhas

clog /klɒg/ *n* tamanco *m*, soco *m* □ *vt/i* (*pt* **clogged**) entupir(-se)

cloister /'klɒɪstə(r)/ *n* claustro *m*

close[1] /kləʊs/ *a* (-**er**, -**est**) próximo (**to** de); (*link, collaboration*) estreito; (*friend*) íntimo; (*weather*) abafado □ *adv* perto. ~ **at hand,** ~ **by** muito perto. ~ **together** (*crowded*) espremido. **have a** ~ **shave** (*fig*) escapar por um triz. ~**-up** *n* grande plano *m*. ~**ly** *adv* de perto. ~**ness** *n* proximidade *f*

close[2] /kləʊz/ *vt/i* fechar(-se); (*end*) terminar; (*of shop etc*) fechar □ *n* fim *m*. ~**d shop** organização *f* que só admite trabalhadores sindicalizados

closet /'klɒzɪt/ *n* (*Amer*) armário *m*

closure /'kləʊʒə(:)/ *n* encerramento *m*

clot /klɒt/ *n* coágulo *m* □ *vi* (*pt* **clotted**) coagular

cloth /klɒθ/ *n* pano *m*; (*tablecloth*) toalha *f* de mesa

cloth|e /kləʊð/ *vt* vestir. ~**ing** *n* vestuário *m*, roupa *f*

clothes /kləʊðz/ *npl* roupa *f*, vestuário *m*. ~**-line** *n* varal *m* para roupa

cloud /klaʊd/ *n* núvem *f* □ *vt/i* toldar(-se). ~**y** *a* nublado, toldado; (*liquid*) turvo

clout /klaʊt/ *n* cascudo *m*, (*P*) carolo *m*; (*colloq: power*) poder *m* efectivo □ *vt* (*colloq*) bater

clove /kləʊv/ *n* cravo *m*. ~ **of garlic** dente *m* de alho

clover /'kləʊvə(r)/ *n* trevo *m*

clown /klaʊn/ *n* palhaço *m* □ *vi* fazer palhaçadas

club /klʌb/ *n* clube *m*; (*weapon*) cacete *m*. ~**s** (*cards*) paus *mpl* □ *vt/i* (*pt* **clubbed**) dar bordoadas *or* cacetadas (em). ~ **together** (*share costs*) cotizar-se

cluck /klʌk/ *vi* cacarejar

clue /klu:/ *n* indício *m*, pista *f*; (*in crossword*) definição *f*. **not have a** ~ (*colloq*) não fazer a menor idéia

clump /klʌmp/ *n* maciço *m*, tufo *m*

clumsy /'klʌmzɪ/ *a* (-**ier**, -**iest**) desajeitado

clung /klʌŋ/ *see* **cling**

cluster /'klʌstə(r)/ n (pequeno) grupo m; (bot) cacho m □ vt/i agrupar(-se)

clutch /klʌtʃ/ vt agarrar (em), apertar □ vi agarrar-se (at a) □ n (auto) embreagem f, (P) embraiagem f. ~es npl garras fpl

clutter /'klʌtə(r)/ n barafunda f, desordem f □ vt atravancar

coach /kəʊtʃ/ n ônibus m, (P) camioneta f, (of train) carruagem f, (sport) treinador m □ vt (tutor) dar aulas a; (sport) treinar

coagulate /kəʊ'ægjʊleɪt/ vt/i coagular(-se)

coal /kəʊl/ n carvão m

coalfield /'kəʊlfiːld/ n região f carbonífera

coalition /kəʊə'lɪʃn/ n coligação f

coarse /kɔːs/ a (-er, -est) grosseiro

coast /kəʊst/ n costa f □ vi costear; (cycle) descer em roda-livre; (car) ir em ponto morto. ~al a costeiro

coastguard /'kəʊstgaːd/ n polícia f marítima

coastline /'kəʊstlaɪm/ n litoral m

coat /kəʊt/ n casaco m; (of animal) pêlo m; (of paint) camada f, demão f □ vt cobrir. ~ of arms brasão m. ~ing n camada f

coax /kəʊks/ vt levar com afagos ou lisonjas, convencer

cobble /'kɒbl/ n ~(-stone) n pedra f de calçada

cobweb /'kɒbweb/ n teia f de aranha

cocaine /kəʊ'keɪn/ n cocaína f

cock /kɒk/ n (male bird) macho m; (rooster) galo m □ vt (gun) engatilhar; (ears) fitar. ~-eyed a (sl: askew) de esguelha

cockerel /'kɒkərəl/ n frango m, galo m novo

cockle /'kɒkl/ n berbigão m

cockney /'kɒknɪ/ n (pl -eys) (person) londrino m; (dialect) dialeto m do leste de Londres

cockpit /'kɒkpɪt/ n cabine f

cockroach /'kɒkrəʊtʃ/ n barata f

cocktail /'kɒkteɪl/ n cocktail m, coquetel m. fruit ~ salada f de fruta

cocky /'kɒkɪ/ a (-ier, -iest) convencido (colloq)

cocoa /'kəʊkəʊ/ n cacau m

coconut /'kəʊkənʌt/ n coco m

cocoon /kə'kuːn/ n casulo m

cod /kɒd/ n (pl invar) bacalhau m. ~-liver oil óleo m de fígado de bacalhau

code /kəʊd/ n código m □ vt codificar

coeducational /kəʊedʒʊ'keɪʃənl/ a misto

coerc|e /kəʊ'ɜːs/ vt coagir. ~ion /-ʃn/ n coação f, (P) coacção f

coexist /kəʊɪg'zɪst/ vi coexistir. ~ence n coexistência f

coffee /'kɒfɪ/ n café m. ~ bar café m.

~-pot n cafeteira f. ~-table n mesa f baixa

coffin /'kɒfɪn/ n caixão m

cog /kɒg/ n dente m de roda. a ~ in the machine (fig) uma rodinha numa engrenagem

cogent /'kəʊdʒənt/ a convincente; (relevant) pertinente

cognac /'kɒnjæk/ n conhaque m

cohabit /kəʊ'hæbɪt/ vi coabitar

coherent /kə'hɪərənt/ a coerente

coil /kɔɪl/ vt/i enrolar(-se) □ n rolo m; (electr) bobina f, (one ring) espiral f, (contraceptive) dispositivo m intra-uterino, DIU

coin /kɔɪn/ n moeda f □ vt cunhar

coincide /kəʊm'saɪd/ vi coincidir

coinciden|ce /kəʊ'msɪdəns/ n coincidência f. ~tal /'dentl/ a que acontece por coincidência

colander /'kʌləndə(r)/ n peneira f, (P) coador m

cold /kəʊld/ a (-er, -est) frio □ n frio m; (med) resfriado m, constipação f. be or feel ~ estar com frio. it's ~ está frio. ~-blooded a (person) insensível; (deed) a sangue frio. ~ cream creme m para a pele. ~ness n frio m; (of feeling) frieza f

coleslaw /'kəʊlslɔː/ n salada f de repolho cru

colic /'kɒlɪk/ n cólica(s) f (pl)

collaborat|e /kə'læbəreɪt/ vi colaborar. ~ion /-'reɪʃn/ n colaboração f. ~or n colaborador m

collapse /kə'læps/ vi desabar; (med) ter um colapso □ n colapso m

collapsible /kə'læpsəbl/ a desmontável, dobrável

collar /'kɒlə(r)/ n gola f; (of shirt) colarinho m; (of dog) coleira f □ vt (colloq) pôr a mão a. ~-bone n clavícula f

colleague /'kɒliːg/ n colega mf

collect /kə'lekt/ vt (gather) juntar; (fetch) ir/vir buscar; (money, rent) cobrar; (as hobby) colecionar, (P) coleccionar □ vi juntar-se. call ~ (Amer) chamar a cobrar. ~ion /-ʃn/ n coleção f, (P) colecção f; (in church) coleta f, (P) colecta f; (of mail) tiragem f, coleta f, (P) abertura f. ~or n (as hobby) colecionador m, (P) coleccionador m

collective /kə'lektɪv/ a coletivo, (P) colectivo

college /'kɒlɪdʒ/ n colégio m

collide /kə'laɪd/ vi colidir

colliery /'kɒlɪərɪ/ n mina f de carvão

collision /kə'lɪʒn/ n colisão f, choque m; (fig) conflito m

colloquial /kə'ləʊkwɪəl/ a coloquial. ~ism n expressão f coloquial

collusion /kə'luːʒn/ n conluio m

colon /'kəʊlən/ n (gram) dois pontos mpl; (anat) cólon m

colonel /'kɜːnl/ n coronel m
colonize /'kɒlənaɪz/ vt colonizar
colon|y /'kɒlənɪ/ n colônia f, (P) colónia f. ~**ial** /kə'ləʊnɪəl/ a & n colonial (mf)
colossal /kə'lɒsl/ a colossal
colour /'kʌlə(r)/ n cor f □ a (photo, TV, etc) a cores; (film) colorido □ vt colorir, dar cor a □ vi (blush) corar. ~**blind** a daltónico, (P) daltónico. ~**ful** a colorido. ~**ing** n (of skin) cor f, (in food) corante m. ~**less** a descolorido
coloured /'kʌləd/ a (pencil, person) de cor □ n pessoa f de cor
column /'kɒləm/ n coluna f
columnist /'kɒləmnɪst/ n colunista mf
coma /'kəʊmə/ n coma m
comb /kəʊm/ n pente m □ vt pentear; (search) vasculhar. ~ **one's hair** pentear-se
combat /'kɒmbæt/ n combate m □ vt (pt **combated**) combater
combination /kɒmbɪ'neɪʃn/ n combinação f
combine /kəm'baɪn/ vt/i combinar (-se), juntar(-se), reunir(-se)
combustion /kəm'bʌstʃən/ n combustão f
come /kʌm/ vi (pt **came**, pp **come**) vir; (arrive) chegar; (occur) suceder. ~ **about** acontecer. ~ **across** encontrar, dar com. ~ **away** or **off** soltar-se. ~ **back** voltar. ~-**back** n regresso m; (retort) réplica f. ~ **by** obter. ~-**down** descer; (price) baixar. ~-**down** n humilhação f. ~ **from** vir de. ~ **in** entrar. ~ **into** (money) herdar. ~ **off** (succeed) ter êxito; (fare) sair-se. ~ **on!** vamos! ~ **out** sair. ~ **round** (after fainting) voltar a si; (be converted) deixar-se convencer. ~ **to** (amount to) montar a. ~ **up** subir; (seeds) despontar; (fig) surgir. ~ **up with** (idea) vir com, propor. ~-**uppance** n castigo m merecido
comedian /kə'miːdɪən/ n comediante mf
comedy /'kɒmədɪ/ n comédia f
comet /'kɒmɪt/ n cometa m
comfort /'kʌmfət/ n conforto m □ vt confortar, consolar. ~**able** a confortável
comic /'kɒmɪk/ a cómico, (P) cómico □ n cómico m, (P) cómico m; (periodical) estórias fpl em quadrinhos, (P) revista f de banda desenhada. ~ **strip** estória f em quadrinhos, (p) banda f desenhada. ~**al** a cómico, (P) cómico
coming /'kʌmɪŋ/ n vinda f □ a próximo. ~**s and goings** idas e vindas fpl
comma /'kɒmə/ n vírgula f
command /kə'mɑːnd/ n (mil) coman-

do m; (order) ordem f; (mastery) domínio m □ vt comandar; (respect) inspirar, impor. ~**er** n comandante m. ~**ing** a imponente
commandeer /kɒmən'dɪə(r)/ vt requisitar
commandment /kə'mɑːndmənt/ n mandamento m
commemorat|e /kə'meməreɪt/ vt comemorar. ~**ion** /-'reɪʃn/ n comemoração f. ~**ive** a comemorativo
commence /kə'mens/ vt/i começar. ~**ment** n começo m
commend /kə'mend/ vt louvar; (entrust) confiar. ~**able** a louvável. ~**ation** /kɒmen'deɪʃn/ n louvor m
comment /'kɒment/ n comentário m □ vi comentar. ~ **on** comentar, fazer comentários
commentary /'kɒməntrɪ/ n comentário m; (radio, TV) relato m
commentat|e /'kɒməntert/ vi fazer um relato. ~**or** n (radio, TV) comentarista mf, (P) comentador m
commerce /'kɒmɜːs/ n comércio m
commercial /kə'mɜːʃl/ a comercial □ n publicidade (comercial) f. ~**ize** vt comercializar
commiserat|e /kə'mɪzəreɪt/ vi ~ **with** compadecer-se de. ~**ion** /-'reɪʃn/ n comiseração f, pesar m
commission /kə'mɪʃn/ n comissão f; (order for work) encomenda f □ vt encomendar; (mil) nomear. ~ **to do** encarregar de fazer. **out of** ~ fora de serviço ativo, (P) activo. ~**er** n comissário m; (police) chefe m
commit /kə'mɪt/ vt (pt **committed**) cometer; (entrust) confiar. ~ **o.s.** comprometer-se, empenhar-se. ~ **suicide** suicidar-se. ~ **to memory** decorar. ~**ment** n compromisso m
committee /kə'mɪtɪ/ n comissão f, comitê m, (P) comité m
commodity /kə'mɒdətɪ/ n artigo m, mercadoria f
common /'kɒmən/ a (-er, -est) comum; (usual) usual, corrente; (pej: ill-bred) ordinário □ n prado m público, (P) baldio m. ~ **law** direito m consuetudinário. **C~ Market** Mercado m Comum. ~-**room** n sala f dos professores, ~ **sense** bom senso m, senso m comum. **House of C~s** Câmara f dos Comuns. **in** ~ em comum. ~**ly** adv mais comum
commoner /'kɒmənə(r)/ n plebeu m
commonplace /'kɒmənpleɪs/ a banal □ n lugar-comum m
commotion /kə'məʊʃn/ n agitação f, confusão f, barulheira f
communal /'kɒmjʊnl/ a (of a commune) comunal; (shared) comum

commune /'kɒmjuːn/ *n* comuna *f*

communicat|e /kə'mjuːnɪkeɪt/ *vt/i* comunicar. **~ion** /-'keɪʃn/ *n* comunicação *f*. **~ion cord** sinal *m* de alarme. **~ive** /-ətɪv/ *a* comunicativo

communion /kə'mjuːnɪən/ *n* comunhão *f*

communis|t /'kɒmjʊnɪst/ *n* comunista *mf* □ *a* comunista. **~m** /-zəm/ *n* comunismo *m*

community /kə'mjuːnətɪ/ *n* comunidade *f*. **~ centre** centro *m* comunitário

commute /kə'mjuːt/ *vi* viajar diariamente para o trabalho. **~r** /-ə(r)/ *n* pessoa *f* que viaja diariamente para o trabalho

compact[1] /kəm'pækt/ *a* compacto. **~ disc** /'kɒmpækt/ cd *m*

compact[2] /'kɒmpækt/ *n* estojo *m* de pó-de-arroz, (*P*) caixa *f*

companion /kəm'pænɪən/ *n* companheiro *m*. **~ship** *n* companhia *f*, convívio *m*

company /'kʌmpənɪ/ *n* companhia *f*; (*guests*) visitas *fpl*. **keep sb ~** fazer companhia a alg

comparable /'kɒmpərəbl/ *a* comparável

compar|e /kəm'peə(r)/ *vt/i* comparar(-se) (**to, with** com). **~ative** /'pærətɪv/ *a* comparativo; (*comfort etc*) relativo

comparison /kəm'pærɪsn/ *n* comparação *f*

compartment /kəm'paːtmənt/ *n* compartimento *m*

compass /'kʌmpəs/ *n* bússola *f*. **~es** compasso *m*

compassion /kəm'pæʃn/ *n* compaixão *f*. **~ate** *a* compassivo

compatib|le /kəm'pætəbl/ *a* compatível. **~ility** /-'bɪlətɪ/ *n* compatibilidade *f*

compel /kəm'pel/ *vt* (*pt* compelled) compelir, forçar. **~ling** *a* irresistível, convincente

compensat|e /'kɒmpənseɪt/ *vt/i* compensar. **~ion** /'seɪʃn/ *n* compensação *f*; (*financial*) indenização *f*, (*P*) indemnização *f*

compete /kəm'piːt/ *vi* competir. **~ with** rivalizar com

competen|t /'kɒmpɪtənt/ *a* competente. **~ce** *n* competência *f*

competition /kɒmpə'tɪʃn/ *n* competição *f*; (*comm*) concorrência *f*

competitive /kəm'petɪtɪv/ *a* (*sport, prices*) competitivo. **~ examination** concurso *m*

competitor /kəm'petɪtə(r)/ *n* competidor *m*, concorrente *mf*

compile /kəm'paɪl/ *vt* compilar, coligir. **~r** /-ə(r)/ *n* compilador *m*

complacen|t /kəm'pleɪsnt/ *a* satisfeito consigo mesmo, (*P*) complacente. **~cy** *n* (auto-)satisfação *f*, (*P*) complacência *f*

complain /kəm'pleɪn/ *vi* queixar-se (**about, of** de)

complaint /kəm'pleɪnt/ *n* queixa *f*; (*in shop*) reclamação *f*; (*med*) doença *f*, achaque *m*

complement /'kɒmplɪmənt/ *n* complemento *m* □ *vt* completar, complementar. **~ary** /-'mentrɪ/ *a* complementar

complet|e /kəm'pliːt/ *a* completo; (*finished*) acabado; (*downright*) perfeito □ *vt* completar; (*a form*) preencher. **~ely** *adv* completamente. **~ion** /-ʃn/ *n* conclusão *f*, feitura *f*, realização *f*

complex /'kɒmpleks/ *a* complexo □ *n* complexo *m*. **~ity** /kəm'pleksətɪ/ *n* complexidade *f*

complexion /kəm'plekʃn/ *n* cor *f* da tez; (*fig*) caráter *m*, (*P*) carácter *m*, aspecto *m*

compliance /kəm'plaɪəns/ *n* docilidade *f*; (*agreement*) conformidade *f*. **in ~ with** em conformidade com

complicat|e /'kɒmplɪkeɪt/ *vt* complicar. **~ed** *a* complicado. **~ion** /-'keɪʃn/ *n* complicação *f*

compliment /'kɒmplɪmənt/ *n* cumprimento *m* □ *vt* /'kɒmplɪment/ cumprimentar

complimentary /kɒmplɪ'mentrɪ/ *a* amável, elogioso. **~ copy** oferta *f*. **~ ticket** bilhete *m* grátis

comply /kəm'plaɪ/ *vi* **~ with** agir em conformidade com

component /kəm'pəʊnənt/ *n* componente *m*; (*of machine*) peça *f* □ *a* componente, constituinte

compose /kəm'pəʊz/ *vt* compor. **o.s.** acalmar-se, dominar-se. **~d** *a* calmo, senhor de si. **~r** /-ə(r)/ *n* compositor *m*

composition /kɒmpə'zɪʃn/ *n* composição *f*

compost /'kɒmpɒst/ *n* húmus *m*, adubo *m*

composure /kəm'pəʊʒə(r)/ *n* calma *f*, domínio *m* de si mesmo

compound /'kɒmpaʊnd/ *n* composto *m*; (*enclosure*) cercado *m*, recinto *m* □ *a* composto. **~ fracture** fratura *f*, (*P*) fractura *f* exposta

comprehen|d /kɒmprɪ'hend/ *vt* compreender. **~sion** *n* compreensão *f*

comprehensive /kɒmprɪ'hensɪv/ *a* compreensivo, vasto; (*insurance*) contra todos os riscos. **~ school** escola *f* de ensino secundário técnico e académico, (*P*) académico

compress /kəm'pres/ vt comprimir.
~ion /-ʃn/ n compressão f
comprise /kəm'praɪz/ vt compreender, abranger
compromise /'kɒmprəmaɪz/ n compromisso m □ vt comprometer □ vi chegar a um meio-termo
compulsion /kəm'pʌlʃn/ n (constraint) coação f; (psych) desejo m irresistível
compulsive /kəm'pʌlsɪv/ a (psych) compulsivo; (liar, smoker etc) inveterado
compulsory /kəm'pʌlsəri/ a obrigatório, compulsório
computer /kəm'pju:tə(r)/ n computador m. ~ science informática f. ~ize vt computerizar
comrade /'kɒmreɪd/ n camarada mf. ~ship n camaradagem f
con[1] /kɒn/ vt (pt conned) (sl) enganar □ n (sl) intrujice f, vigarice f, burla f. ~ man (sl) intrujão m, vigarista m, burlão m
con[2] /kɒn/ see pro
concave /'kɒnkeɪv/ a côncavo
conceal /kən'si:l/ vt ocultar, esconder.
~ment n encobrimento m
concede /kən'si:d/ vt conceder, admitir; (in a game etc) ceder
conceit /kən'si:t/ n presunção f. ~ed a presunçoso, presumido, cheio de si
conceivabl|e /kən'si:vəbl/ a concebível. ~y adv possivelmente
conceive /kən'si:v/ vt/i conceber
concentrat|e /'kɒnsntreɪt/ vt/i concentrar(-se). ~ion /-'treɪʃn/ n concentração f
concept /'kɒnsept/ n conceito m
conception /kən'sepʃn/ n concepção f
concern /kən'sɜ:n/ n (worry) preocupação f; (business) negócio m □ vt dizer respeito a, respeitar. ~ o.s. with, be ~ed with interessar-se por, ocupar-se de; (regard) dizer respeito a. it's no ~ of mine não me diz respeito. ~ing prep sobre, respeitante a
concerned /kən'sɜ:nd/ a inquieto, preocupado (about com)
concert /'kɒnsət/ n concerto m
concerted /kən'sɜ:tɪd/ a concertado
concession /kən'seʃn/ n concessão f
concise /kən'saɪs/ a conciso. ~ly adv concisamente
conclu|de /kən'klu:d/ vt concluir □ vi terminar. ~ding a final. ~sion n conclusão f
conclusive /kən'klu:sɪv/ a conclusivo. ~ly adv de forma conclusiva
concoct /kən'kɒkt/ vt preparar por mistura; (fig: invent) fabricar. ~ion /-ʃn/ n mistura f; (fig) invenção f, mentira f

concrete /'kɒnkri:t/ n concreto m, (P) cimento m □ a concreto □ vt concretar, (P) cimentar
concur /kən'kɜ:(r)/ vi (pt concurred) concordar; (of circumstances) concorrer
concussion /kən'kʌʃn/ n comoção f cerebral
condemn /kən'dem/ vt condenar.
~ation /kɒndem'neɪʃn/ n condenação f
condens|e /kən'dens/ vt/i condensar (-se). ~ation /kɒnden'seɪʃn/ n condensação f
condescend /kɒndɪ'send/ vi condescender; (lower o.s.) rebaixar-se
condition /kən'dɪʃn/ n condição f □ vt condicionar. on ~ that com a condição de que. ~al a condicional. ~er n (for hair) condicionador m, creme m rinse
condolences /kən'dəʊlənsɪz/ npl condolências fpl, pêsames mpl, sentimentos mpl
condom /'kɒndəm/ n preservativo m
condone /kən'dəʊn/ vt desculpar, fechar os olhos a
conducive /kən'dju:sɪv/ a be ~ to contribuir para, ser propício a
conduct[1] /kən'dʌkt/ vt conduzir, dirigir; (orchestra) reger
conduct[2] /'kɒndʌkt/ n conduta f
conductor /kən'dʌktə(r)/ n maestro m; (electr; of bus) condutor m
cone /kəʊn/ n cone m; (bot) pinha f; (for ice-cream) casquinha f, (P) cone m
confectioner /kən'fekʃnə(r)/ n confeiteiro m, (P) pasteleiro m. ~y n confeitaria f, (P) pastelaria f
confederation /kənfedə'reɪʃn/ n confederação f
confer /kən'fɜ:(r)/ (pt conferred) vt conferir, outorgar □ vi conferenciar
conference /'kɒnfərəns/ n conferência f. in ~ em reunião f
confess /kən'fes/ vt/i confessar; (relig) confessar(-se). ~ion /-ʃn/ n confissão f. ~ional n confissionário m. ~or n confessor m
confetti /kən'fetɪ/ n confetes mpl, (P) confetti mpl
confide /kən'faɪd/ vt confiar □ vi ~ in confiar em
confiden|t /'kɒnfɪdənt/ a confiante, confiado. ~ce n confiança f; (boldness) confiança f em si; (secret) confidência f. ~ce trick vigarice f. in ~ce em confidência
confidential /kɒnfɪ'denʃl/ a confidencial
confine /kən'faɪn/ vt fechar; (limit) limitar (to a). ~ment n detenção f; (med) parto m

confirm /kən'fɜːm/ vt confirmar.
~**ation** /kɒnfə'meɪʃn/ n confirmação
f. ~**ed** a (*bachelor*) inveterado

confiscat|e /'kɒnfɪskeɪt/ vt confiscar.
~**ion** /-'keɪʃn/ n confiscação f

conflict[1] /'kɒnflɪkt/ n conflito m

conflict[2] /kən'flɪkt/ vi estar em contradição. ~**ing** a contraditório

conform /kən'fɔːm/ vt/i conformar
(-se)

confound /kən'faʊnd/ vt confundir.
~**ed** a (*colloq*) maldito

confront /kən'frʌnt/ vt confrontar,
defrontar, enfrentar. ~ **with** confron-
tar-se com. ~**ation** /kɒnfrʌn'teɪʃn/ n
confrontação f

confus|e /kən'fjuːz/ vt confundir.
~**ed** a confuso. ~**ing** a que faz
confusão. ~**ion** /-ʒn/ n confusão f

congeal /kən'dʒiːl/ vt/i congelar, soli-
dificar

congenial /kən'dʒiːnɪəl/ a (*agreeable*)
simpático

congenital /kən'dʒenɪtl/ a congênito,
(P) congénito

congest|ed /kən'dʒestɪd/ a conges-
tionado. ~**ion** /-tʃn/ n (*traffic*) con-
gestionamento m; (*med*) congestão f

congratulat|e /kən'grætjuleɪt/ vt feli-
citar, dar os parabéns (**on** por).
~**ions** /-'leɪʃnz/ npl felicitações fpl,
parabéns mpl

congregat|e /'kɒngrɪgeɪt/ vi reunir-
se. ~**ion** /-'geɪʃn/ n (*in church*)
congregação f, fiéis mpl

congress /'kɒngres/ n congresso m.
C~ (*Amer*) Congresso m

conjecture /kən'dʒektʃə(r)/ n conjetura f, (P) conjectura f □ vt/i conjetu-
rar, (P) conjecturar

conjugal /'kɒndʒʊgl/ a conjugal

conjugat|e /'kɒndʒʊgeɪt/ vt conjugar.
~**ion** /-'geɪʃn/ n conjugação f

conjunction /kən'dʒʌŋkʃn/ n con-
junção f

conjur|e /'kʌndʒə(r)/ vi fazer truques
mágicos □ vt ~ **up** fazer aparecer.
~**or** n mágico m, prestidigitador m

connect /kə'nekt/ vt/i ligar(-se); (*of
train*) fazer ligação. ~**ed** a ligado. **be**
~**ed with** estar relacionado com

connection /kə'nekʃn/ n relação f;
(*rail; phone call*) ligação f; (*electr*)
contacto m

connoisseur /kɒnə'sɜː(r)/ n conhecedor m, apreciador m

connotation /kɒnə'teɪʃn/ n cono-
tação f

conquer /'kɒŋkə(r)/ vt vencer; (*country*) conquistar. ~**or** n conquistador
m

conquest /'kɒŋkwest/ n conquista f

conscience /'kɒnʃəns/ n consciência
f

conscientious /kɒnʃɪ'enʃəs/ a consciencioso

conscious /'kɒnʃəs/ a consciente.
~**ly** adv conscientemente. ~**ness** n
consciência f

conscript[1] /kən'skrɪpt/ vt recrutar.
~**ion** /-ʃn/ n serviço m militar obrigatório

conscript[2] /'kɒnskrɪpt/ n recruta m

consecrate /'kɒnsɪkreɪt/ vt consagrar

consecutive /kən'sekjʊtɪv/ a consecutivo, seguido

consensus /kən'sensəs/ n consenso m

consent /kən'sent/ vi consentir (**to**
em) □ n consentimento m

consequence /'kɒnsɪkwəns/ n con-
seqüência f, (P) consequência f

consequent /'kɒnsɪkwənt/ a resul-
tante (**on, upon** de). ~**ly** adv por con-
seqüência, (P) consequência, por
consequinte

conservation /kɒnsə'veɪʃn/ n conservação f

conservative /kən'sɜːvətɪv/ a conservador; (*estimate*) moderado. **C~** a & n
conservador (m)

conservatory /kən'sɜːvətrɪ/ n (*greenhouse*) estufa f; (*house extension*) jardim m de inverno

conserve /kən'sɜːv/ vt conservar

consider /kən'sɪdə(r)/ vt considerar;
(*allow for*) levar em consideração.
~**ation** /-'reɪʃn/ n consideração f.
~**ing** prep em vista de, tendo em
conta

considerabl|e /kən'sɪdərəbl/ a con-
siderável; (*much*) muito. ~**y** adv consideravelmente

considerate /kən'sɪdərət/ a atencioso, delicado

consign /kən'saɪn/ vt consignar.
~**ment** n consignação f

consist /kən'sɪst/ vi consistir (**of, in,
em**)

consisten|t /kən'sɪstənt/ a (*unchang-
ing*) constante; (*not contradictory*)
coerente. ~**t with** conforme com.
~**cy** n consistência f; (*fig*) coerência
f. ~**tly** adv regularmente

consol|e /kən'səʊl/ vt consolar.
~**ation** /kɒnsə'leɪʃn/ n consolação f.
~**ation prize** prêmio m de consolação

consolidat|e /kən'sɒlɪdeɪt/ vt/i conso-
lidar(-se). ~**ion** /-'deɪʃn/ n conso-
lidação f

consonant /'kɒnsənənt/ n consoante
f

consortium /kən'sɔːtɪəm/ n (*pl* -tia)
consórcio m

conspicuous /kən'spɪkjʊəs/ a conspi-
cuo, visível; (*striking*) notável. **make
o.s.** ~ fazer-se notar, chamar a atenção

conspira|cy /kən'spɪrəsɪ/ n conspiração f. ~**tor** n conspirador m

conspire /kən'spaɪə(r)/ vi conspirar

constable /'kʌnstəbl/ n polícia m

constant /'kɒnstənt/ a constante. ~**ly** adv constantemente

constellation /kɒnstə'leɪʃn/ n constelação f

consternation /kɒnstə'neɪʃn/ n consternação f

constipation /kɒnstɪ'peɪʃn/ n prisão f de ventre

constituency /kən'stɪtjʊənsɪ/ n (pl -cies) círculo m eleitoral

constituent /kən'stɪtjʊənt/ a & n constituinte (m)

constitut|e /'kɒnstɪtjuːt/ vt constituir. ~**ion** /-'tjuːʃn/ n constituição f. ~**ional** /-'tjuːʃənl/ a constitucional

constrain /kən'streɪn/ vt constranger

constraint /kən'streɪnt/ n constrangimento m

constrict /kən'strɪkt/ vt constringir, apertar. ~**ion** /-ʃn/ n constrição f

construct /kən'strʌkt/ vt construir. ~**ion** /-ʃn/ n construção f. under ~**ion** em construção

constructive /kən'strʌktɪv/ a construtivo

consul /'kɒnsl/ n cônsul m

consulate /'kɒnsjʊlət/ n consulado m

consult /kən'sʌlt/ vt consultar. ~**ation** /kɒnsl'teɪʃn/ n consulta f

consultant /kən'sʌltənt/ n consultor m; (med) especialista mf

consume /kən'sjuːm/ vt consumir. ~**r** /-ə(r)/ n consumidor m

consumption /kən'sʌmpʃn/ n consumo m

contact /'kɒntækt/ n contacto m; (person) relação f. ~ lenses fpl de contacto □ vt contactar

contagious /kən'teɪdʒəs/ a contagioso

contain /kən'teɪn/ vt conter. ~ o.s. conter-se. ~**er** n recipiente m; (for transport) contentor m

contaminat|e /kən'tæmɪneɪt/ vt contaminar. ~**ion** /-'neɪʃn/ n contaminação f

contemplat|e /'kɒntempleɪt/ vt contemplar; (intend) ter em vista; (consider) esperar, pensar em. ~**ion** /-'pleɪʃn/ n contemplação f

contemporary /kən'temprərɪ/ a & n contemporâneo (m)

contempt /kən'tempt/ n desprezo m. ~**ible** a desprezível. ~**uous** /-tʃʊəs/ a desdenhoso

contend /kən'tend/ vt afirmar, sustentar □ vi ~ with lutar contra. ~**er** n adversário m, contendor m

content[1] /kən'tent/ a satisfeito, contente □ vt contentar. ~**ed** a satisfeito,

contente. ~**ment** n contentamento m, satisfação f

content[2] /'kɒntent/ n conteúdo m. (table of) ~**s** índice m

contention /kən'tenʃn/ n disputa f, contenda f; (assertion) argumento m

contest[1] /'kɒntest/ n competição f; (struggle) luta f

contest[2] /kən'test/ vt contestar; (compete for) disputar. ~**ant** n concorrente mf

context /'kɒntekst/ n contexto m

continent /'kɒntɪmənt/ n continente m. the C~ a Europa (continental) f. ~**al** /-'nentl/ a continental; (of mainland Europe) europeu ~**al** breakfast café m da manhã europeu, (P) pequeno almoço m europeu. ~**al** quilt edredom m, (P) edredão m

contingen|t /kən'tɪndʒənt/ a & n contingente (m). ~**cy** n contingência f. ~**cy** plan plano m de emergência

continual /kən'tɪnjʊəl/ a contínuo. ~**ly** adv continuamente

continu|e /kən'tɪnjuː/ vt/i continuar. ~**ation** /-tɪnjʊ'eɪʃn/ n continuação f.

continuity /kɒntɪ'njuːətɪ/ n continuidade f

continuous /kən'tɪnjʊəs/ a contínuo. ~**ly** adv continuamente

contort /kən'tɔːt/ vt contorcer; (fig) distorcer. ~**ion** /-ʃn/ n contorção f

contour /'kɒntʊə(r)/ n contorno m

contraband /'kɒntrəbænd/ n contrabando m

contraception /kɒntrə'sepʃn/ n contracepção f

contraceptive /kɒntrə'septɪv/ a & n contraceptivo (m)

contract[1] /'kɒntrækt/ n contrato m

contract[2] /kən'trækt/ vt/i contrair (-se); (make a contract) contratar. ~**ion** /-ʃn/ n contração f, (P) contracção f

contractor /kən'træktə(r)/ n empreiteiro m; (firm) firma f empreiteira de serviços, (P) recrutadora f de mão de obra temporária

contradict /kɒntrə'dɪkt/ vt contradizer. ~**ion** /-ʃn/ n contradição f. ~**ory** a contraditório

contraflow /'kɒntrəfləʊ/ n fluxo m em sentido contrário

contrary[1] /'kɒntrərɪ/ a & n (opposite) contrário (m) □ adv ~ to contrariamente a. on the ~ ao ou pelo contrário

contrary[2] /kən'treərɪ/ a (perverse) do contra, embirrento

contrast[1] /'kɒntrɑːst/ n contraste m

contrast[2] /kən'trɑːst/ vt/i contrastar. ~**ing** a contrastante

contraven|e /kɒntrə'viːn/ vt infringir. ~**tion** /-'venʃn/ n contravenção f

contribut|e /kən'trɪbju:t/ *vt/i* contribuir (**to** para); (*to newspaper etc*) colaborar (**to** em). **~ion** /kɒntrɪ'bju:ʃn/ *n* contribuição *f*. **~or** /-'trɪbju:tə(r)/ *n* contribuinte *mf*; (*to newspaper*) colaborador *m*

contrivance /kən'traɪvəns/ *n* (*invention*) engenho *m*; (*device*) engenhoca *f*, (*trick*) maquinação *f*

contrive /kən'traɪv/ *vt* imaginar, inventar. **~ to do** conseguir fazer

control /kən'trəul/ *vt* (*pt* **controlled**) (*check, restrain*) controlar; (*firm etc*) dirigir □ *n* controle *m*; (*management*) direção *f*, (*P*) direcção *f*. **~s** (*of car, plane*) comandos *mpl*; (*knobs*) botões *mpl*. **be in ~ of** dirigir. **under ~** sob controle

controversial /kɒntrə'vɜ:ʃl/ *a* controverso, discutível

controversy /'kɒntrəvɜ:sɪ/ *n* controvérsia *f*

convalesce /kɒnvə'les/ *vi* convalescer. **~nce** *n* convalescença *f*. **~nt** /-nt/ *a & n* convalescente (*mf*). **~nt home** casa *f* de repouso

convene /kən'vi:n/ *vt* convocar □ *vi* reunir-se

convenience /kən'vi:nɪəns/ *n* conveniência *f*. **~s** (*appliances*) comodidades *fpl*; (*lavatory*) privada *f*, (*P*) casa *f* de banho. **at your ~** quando (e como) lhe convier. **~ foods** alimentos *mpl* semiprontos

convenient /kən'vi:nɪənt/ *a* conveniente. **be ~ for** convir a. **~ly** *adv* sem inconveniente; (*situated*) bem; (*arrive*) a propósito

convent /'kɒnvənt/ *n* convento *m*. **~ school** colégio *m* de freiras

convention /kən'venʃn/ *n* convenção *f*; (*custom*) uso *m*, costume *m*. **~al** *a* convencional

converge /kən'vɜ:dʒ/ *vi* convergir

conversant /kən'vɜ:snt/ *a* **be ~ with** conhecer; (*fact*) saber; (*machinery*) estar familiarizado com

conversation /kɒnvə'seɪʃn/ *n* conversa *f*. **~al** *a* de conversa, coloquial

converse[1] /kən'vɜ:s/ *vi* conversar

converse[2] /'kɒnvɜ:s/ *a & n* inverso (*m*). **~ly** /kən'vɜ:slɪ/ *adv* ao invés, inversamente

conver|t[1] /kən'vɜ:t/ *vt* converter; (*house*) transformar. **~sion** /-ʃn/ *n* conversão *f*; (*house*) transformação *f*. **~tible** *a* convertível, conversível □ *n* (*auto*) conversível *m*

convert[2] /'kɒnvɜ:t/ *n* convertido *m*, converso *m*

convex /'kɒnveks/ *a* convexo

convey /kən'veɪ/ *vt* transmitir; (*goods*) transportar; (*idea, feeling*) comunicar. **~ance** *n* transporte *m*.

~or belt tapete *m* rolante, correia *f* transportadora

convict[1] /kən'vɪkt/ *vt* declarar culpado. **~ion** /-ʃn/ *n* condenação *f*; (*opinion*) convicção *f*

convict[2] /'kɒnvɪkt/ *n* condenado *m*

convinc|e /kən'vɪns/ *vt* convencer. **~ing** *a* convincente

convoluted /kɒnvə'lu:tɪd/ *a* retorcido; (*fig*) complicado; (*bot*) convoluto

convoy /'kɒnvɔɪ/ *n* escolta *f*

convuls|e /kən'vʌls/ *vt* convulsionar; (*fig*) abalar. **be ~ed with laughter** torcer-se de riso. **~ion** /-ʃn/ *n* convulsão *f*

coo /ku:/ *vi* (*pt* **cooed**) arrulhar □ *n* arrulho *m*

cook /kʊk/ *vt/i* cozinhar □ *n* cozinheira *f*, cozinheiro *m*. **~ up** (*colloq*) cozinhar (*fig*), fabricar

cooker /'kʊkə(r)/ *n* fogão *m*

cookery /'kʊkərɪ/ *n* cozinha *f*. **~ book** livro *m* de culinária

cookie /'kʊkɪ/ *n* (*Amer*) biscoito *m*

cool /ku:l/ *a* (**-er, -est**) fresco; (*calm*) calmo; (*unfriendly*) frio □ *n* frescura *f*; (*sl: composure*) sangue-frio *m* □ *vt/i* arrefecer. **~-box** *n* geladeira *f* portátil. **in the ~** no fresco. **~ly** /'ku:llɪ/ *adv* calmamente; (*fig*) friamente. **~ness** *n* frescura *f*; (*fig*) frieza *f*

coop /ku:p/ *n* galinheiro *m* □ *vt* **~ up** engaislar, fechar

co-operat|e /kəʊ'ɒpəreɪt/ *vi* cooperar. **~ion** /-'reɪʃn/ *n* cooperação *f*

cooperative /kəʊ'ɒpərətɪv/ *a* cooperativo □ *n* cooperativa *f*

coordinat|e /kəʊ'ɔ:dɪneɪt/ *vt* coordenar. **~ion** /-'neɪʃn/ *n* coordenação *f*

cop /kɒp/ *n* (*sl*) porco *m* (*sl*), (*P*) xui *m* (*sl*)

cope /kəʊp/ *vi* aguentar-se, arranjar-se. **~ with** poder com, dar conta de

copious /'kəʊpɪəs/ *a* copioso

copper[1] /'kɒpə(r)/ *n* cobre *m* □ *a* de cobre

copper[2] /'kɒpə(r)/ *n* (*sl*) porco *m* (*sl*), (*P*) xui *m* (*sl*)

coppice /'kɒpɪs/, **copse** /kɒps/ *ns* mata *f* de corte

copulat|e /'kɒpjʊleɪt/ *vi* copular. **~ion** /-'leɪʃn/ *n* cópula *f*

copy /'kɒpɪ/ *n* cópia *f*; (*of book*) exemplar *m*; (*of newspaper*) número *m* □ *vt/i* copiar

copyright /'kɒpɪraɪt/ *n* direitos *mpl* autorais

coral /'kɒrəl/ *n* coral *m*

cord /kɔ:d/ *n* cordão *m*; (*electr*) fio *m*

cordial /'kɔ:dɪəl/ *a & n* cordial (*m*)

cordon /'kɔ:dn/ *n* cordão *m* □ *vt* **~ off** fechar (com um cordão de isolamento)

corduroy /'kɔ:dərɔɪ/ *n* veludo *m* cotelé

core /kɔː(r)/ n âmago m; (of apple, pear) coração m

cork /kɔːk/ n cortiça f; (for bottle) rolha f □ vt rolhar

corkscrew /'kɔːkskruː/ n sacarolhas m

corn[1] /kɔːn/ n trigo m; (Amer: maize) milho m; (seed) grão m. ~ **on the cob** espiga f de milho

corn[2] /kɔːn/ n (hard skin) calo m

corned /kɔːnd/ a ~ **beef** carne f de vaca enlatada

corner /'kɔːnə(r)/ n canto m; (of street) esquina f; (bend in road) curva f □ vt encurralar; (market) monopolizar □ vi dar uma curva, virar

cornet /'kɔːnɪt/ n (mus) cornetim m; (for ice-cream) casquinha f, (P) cone m

cornflakes /'kɔːnfleɪks/ npl cornflakes mpl, cereais mpl

cornflour /'kɔːnflaʊə(r)/ n fécula f de milho, maisena f

Corn|wall /'kɔːnwəl/ n Cornualha f. ~**ish** a da Cornualha

corny /'kɔːnɪ/ a (colloq) batido, (P) estafado

coronary /'kɒrənrɪ/ n ~ (**thrombosis**) infarto m, enfarte m

coronation /kɒrə'neɪʃn/ n coroação f

coroner /'kɒrənə(r)/ n magistrado m que investiga os casos de morte suspeita

corporal[1] /'kɔːpərəl/ n (mil) cabo m

corporal[2] /'kɔːpərəl/ a ~ **punishment** castigo m corporal

corporate /'kɔːpərət/ a coletivo, (P) colectivo; (body) corporativo

corporation /kɔːpə'reɪʃn/ n corporação f; (of town) municipalidade f

corps /kɔː(r)/ n (pl corps /kɔːz/) corpo m

corpse /kɔːps/ n cadáver m

corpuscle /'kɔːpʌsl/ n corpúsculo m

correct /kə'rekt/ a correto, (P) correcto. **the ~ time** a hora certa. **you are** ~ você tem razão □ vt corrigir. ~**ion** /-ʃn/ n correção f, (P) correcção f, emenda f

correlat|e /'kɒrəleɪt/ vt/i correlacionar(-se). ~**ion** /-'leɪʃn/ n correlação f

correspond /kɒrɪ'spɒnd/ vi corresponder (**to, with**, a); (write letters) corresponder-se (**with**, com). ~**ence** n correspondência f. ~**ent** n correspondente mf. ~**ing** a correspondente

corridor /'kɒrɪdɔː(r)/ n corredor m

corroborate /kə'rɒbəreɪt/ vt corroborar

corro|de /kə'rəʊd/ vt/i corroer(-se). ~**sion** n corrosão f

corrugated /'kɒrəgeɪtɪd/ a corrugado. ~ **cardboard** cartão m canelado. ~ **iron** chapa f ondulada

corrupt /kə'rʌpt/ a corrupto □ vt corromper. ~**ion** /-ʃn/ n corrupção f

corset /'kɔːsɪt/ n espartilho m; (elasticated) cinta f elástica

Corsica /'kɔːsɪkə/ n Córsega f

cosmetic /kɒz'metɪk/ n cosmético m □ a cosmético; (fig) superficial

cosmonaut /'kɒzmənɔːt/ n cosmonauta mf

cosmopolitan /kɒzmə'pɒlɪtən/ a & n cosmopolita (mf)

cosset /'kɒsɪt/ vt (pt cosseted) proteger

cost /kɒst/ vt (pt cost) custar; (pt costed) fixar o preço de □ n custo m. ~**s** (jur) custos mpl. **at all** ~**s** custe o que custar. **to one's** ~ à sua custa. ~ **of living** custo m de vida

costly /'kɒstlɪ/ a (-ier, -iest) a caro; (valuable) precioso

costume /'kɒstjuːm/ n traje m

cos|y /'kəʊzɪ/ a (-ier, -iest) confortável, íntimo □ n abafador m (do bule do chá). ~**iness** n conforto m

cot /kɒt/ n cama f de bêbê, berço m

cottage /'kɒtɪdʒ/ n pequena casa f de campo. ~ **cheese** requeijão m, ricota f. ~ **industry** artesanato m. ~ **pie** empada f de carne picada

cotton /'kɒtn/ n algodão m; (thread) fio m, linha f. ~ **wool** algodão m hidrófilo

couch /kaʊtʃ/ n divã m

couchette /kuː'ʃet/ n couchette f

cough /kɒf/ vi tossir □ n tosse f

could /kʊd, kəd/ pt of can[2]

couldn't /'kʊdnt/ = could not

council /'kaʊnsl/ n conselho m. ~ **house** casa f de bairro popular

councillor /'kaʊnsələ(r)/ n vereador m

counsel /'kaʊnsl/ n conselho m; (pl invar) (jur) advogado m. ~**lor** n conselheiro m

count[1] /kaʊnt/ vt/i contar □ n conta f. ~-**down** n (rocket) contagem f regressiva. ~ **on** contar com

count[2] /kaʊnt/ n (nobleman) conde m

counter[1] /'kaʊntə(r)/ n (in shop) balcão m; (in game) ficha f, (P) tento m

counter[2] /'kaʊntə(r)/ adv ~ **to** contrário a; (in the opposite direction) em sentido contrário a □ a oposto □ vt opor; (blow) aparar □ vi ripostar

counter- /'kaʊntə(r)/ pref contra-

counteract /kaʊntər'ækt/ vt neutralizar, frustrar

counter-attack /'kaʊntərətæk/ n contra-ataque m □ vt/i contra-atacar

counterbalance /'kaʊntəbæləns/ n contrapeso m □ vt contrabalançar

counterfeit /'kaʊntəfɪt/ a falsificado, falso □ n falsificação f □ vt falsificar

counterfoil /'kaʊntəfɔɪl/ n talão m, canhoto m

counterpart /'kaʊntəpɑːt/ n equivalente m; (person) homólogo m

counter-productive /'kaʊntəprə-dʌktɪv/ a contraproducente

countersign /'kaʊntəsam/ vt subscrever documento já assinado; (cheque) contrassinar

countess /'kaʊntɪs/ n condessa f

countless /'kaʊntlɪs/ a sem conta, incontável, inúmero

country /'kʌntrɪ/ n país m; (home-land) pátria f; (countryside) campo m

countryside /'kʌntrɪsaɪd/ n campo m

county /'kaʊntɪ/ n condado m

coup /kuː/ n ~ (d'état) golpe m (de estado)

couple /'kʌpl/ n par m, casal m □ vt/i unir(-se), ligar(-se); (techn) acoplar. a ~ of um par de

coupon /'kuːpɒn/ n cupão m

courage /'kʌrɪdʒ/ n coragem f. ~ous /kə'reɪdʒəs/ a corajoso

courgette /kʊə'ʒet/ n abobrinha f

courier /'kʊrɪə(r)/ n correio m; (for tourists) guia mf; (for parcels, mail) estafeta m

course /kɔːs/ n curso m; (series) série f; (culin) prato m; (for golf) campo m; (fig) caminho m. in due ~ na altura devida, oportunamente. in the ~ of durante. of ~ está claro, com certeza

court /kɔːt/ n (of monarch) corte f; (courtyard) pátio m; (tennis) court m, quadra f, (P) campo m; (jur) tribunal m □ vt cortejar; (danger) provocar. ~ martial (pl courts martial) conselho m de guerra

courteous /'kɜːtɪəs/ a cortês, delicado

courtesy /'kɜːtəsɪ/ n cortesia f

courtship /'kɔːtʃɪp/ n namoro m, corte f

courtyard /'kɔːtjɑːd/ n pátio m

cousin /'kʌzn/ n primo m. first/second ~ primo m em primeiro/segundo grau

cove /kəʊv/ n angra f, enseada f

covenant /'kʌvənənt/ n convenção f, convénio m; (jur) contrato m; (relig) aliança f

cover /'kʌvə(r)/ vt cobrir □ n cobertura f; (for bed) colcha f; (for book, furniture) capa f; (lid) tampa f; (shelter) abrigo m. ~ charge serviço m. ~ up tapar; (fig) encobrir. ~-up n (fig) encobrimento m. take ~ abrigar-se. under separate ~ em separado. ~ing n cobertura f. ~ing letter carta f (que acompanha um documento)

coverage /'kʌvərɪdʒ/ n (of events) reportagem f, cobertura f

covet /'kʌvɪt/ vt cobiçar

cow /kaʊ/ n vaca f

coward /'kaʊəd/ n covarde mf. ~ly a covarde

cowardice /'kaʊədɪs/ n covardia f

cowboy /'kaʊbɔɪ/ n cowboy m, vaqueiro m

cower /'kaʊə(r)/ vi encolher-se (de medo)

cowshed /'kaʊʃed/ n estábulo m

coy /kɔɪ/ a (-er, -est) (falsamente) tímido

crab /kræb/ n caranguejo m

crack /kræk/ n fenda f; (in glass) rachadura f; (noise) estalo m; (sl: joke) piada f; (drug) crack m □ a (colloq) de élite □ vt/i estalar; (nut) quebrar; (joke) contar; (problem) resolver; (voice) mudar. ~ down on (colloq) cair em cima de, arrochar. get ~ing (colloq) pôr mãos à obra

cracker /'krækə(r)/ n busca-pé m, bomba f de estalo; (culin) bolacha f de água e sal

crackers /'krækəz/ a (sl) desmiolado, maluco

crackle /'krækl/ vi crepitar □ n crepitação f

crackpot /'krækpɒt/ n (sl) desmiolado, maluco

cradle /'kreɪdl/ n berço m □ vt embalar

craft¹ /krɑːft/ n ofício m; (technique) arte f; (cunning) manha f, astúcia f

craft² /krɑːft/ n (invar) (boat) embarcação f

craftsman /'krɑːftsmən/ n (pl -men) artífice mf. ~ship n arte f

crafty /'krɑːftɪ/ a (-ier, -iest) manhoso, astucioso

crag /kræg/ n penhasco m. ~gy a escarpado, ingreme

cram /kræm/ vt (pt crammed) ~ (for an exam) decorar, (P) empinar. ~ into/with entulhar com

cramp /kræmp/ n cãimbra f □ vt restringir, tolher. ~ed a apertado

crane /kreɪn/ n grua f; (bird) grou m □ vt (neck) esticar

crank¹ /kræŋk/ n (techn) manivela f. ~shaft n (techn) cambota f

crank² /kræŋk/ n excêntrico m. ~y a excêntrico

crash /kræʃ/ n acidente m; (noise) estrondo m; (comm) falência f; (financial) colapso m, crash m □ vt/i (fall/strike) cair/bater com estrondo; (two cars) chocar, bater; (comm) abrir falência; (plane) cair □ a (course, programme) intensivo. ~-helmet n capacete m. ~-land vi fazer uma aterrissagem forçada

crate /kreɪt/ *n* engradado *m*

crater /'kreɪtə(r)/ *n* cratera *f*

crav|e /kreɪv/ *vt/i* ~**e** (for) ansiar por. ~**ing** *n* desejo *m* irresistível, ânsia *f*

crawl /krɔːl/ *vi* rastejar; (*of baby*) engatinhar, (*P*) andar de gatas; (*of car*) mover-se lentamente □ *n* rastejo *m*; (*swimming*) crawl *m*. **be** ~**ing with** fervilhar de, estar cheio de

crayfish /'kreɪfɪʃ/ *n* (*pl invar*) lagostim *m*

crayon /'kreɪən/ *n* crayon *m*, lápis *m* de pastel

craze /kreɪz/ *n* moda *f*, febre *f*

craz|y /'kreɪzɪ/ *a* (**-ier**, **-iest**) doido, louco (**about** por). ~**iness** *n* loucura *f*

creak /kriːk/ *n* rangido *m* □ *vi* ranger

cream /kriːm/ *n* (*milk fat; fig*) nata *f*, (*cosmetic; culin*) creme *m* □ *a* creme *invar* □ *vt* desnatar. ~ **cheese** queijo-creme *m*. ~**y** *a* cremoso

crease /kriːs/ *n* vinco *m* □ *vt/i* amar-rotar(-se)

creat|e /kriːˈeɪt/ *vt* criar. ~**ion** /-ʃn/ *n* criação *f*. ~**ive** *a* criador. ~**or** *n* criador *m*

creature /'kriːtʃə(r)/ *n* criatura *f*

crèche /kreɪʃ/ *n* creche *f*

credentials /krɪˈdenʃlz/ *npl* credenciais *fpl*; (*of competence etc*) referências *fpl*

credib|le /'kredəbl/ *a* crível, verosímil, (*P*) verossímil. ~**ility** /-'bɪlətɪ/ *n* credibilidade *f*

credit /'kredɪt/ *n* crédito *m*; (*honour*) honra *f*. ~**s** (*cinema*) créditos *mpl* □ *vt* (*pt* **credited**) acreditar em; (*comm*) creditar. ~ **card** cartão *m* de crédito. ~ **sb with** atribuir a alg. ~**or** *n* credor *m*

creditable /'kredɪtəbl/ *a* louvável, honroso

credulous /'kredjʊləs/ *a* crédulo

creed /kriːd/ *n* credo *m*

creek /kriːk/ *n* enseada *f* estreita. **be up the** ~ (*sl*) estar frito (*sl*)

creep /kriːp/ *vi* (*pt* **crept**) rastejar; (*move stealthily*) mover-se furtivamente □ *n* (*sl*) cara *m* nojento. **give sb the** ~**s** dar arrepios a alg. ~**er** *n* (planta *f*) trepadeira (*f*). ~**y** *a* arrepiante

cremat|e /krɪˈmeɪt/ *vt* cremar. ~**ion** /-ʃn/ *n* cremação *f*

crematorium /kreməˈtɔːrɪəm/ *n* (*pl* **-ia**) crematório *m*

crêpe /kreɪp/ *n* crepe *m*. ~ **paper** papel *m* crepom, (*P*) plissado

crept /krept/ *see* **creep**

crescent /'kresnt/ *n* crescente *m*; (*street*) rua *f* em semicírculo

cress /kres/ *n* agrião *m*

crest /krest/ *n* (*of bird, hill*) crista *f*; (*on coat of arms*) timbre *m*

Crete /kriːt/ *n* Creta *f*

crevasse /krɪˈvæs/ *n* fenda *f* (em geleira)

crevice /'krevɪs/ *n* racha *f*, fenda *f*

crew¹ /kruː/ *see* **crow**

crew² /kruː/ *n* tripulação *f*; (*gang*) bando *m*. ~**-cut** *n* corte *m* à escovinha. ~**-neck** *n* gola *f* redonda e um pouco subida

crib¹ /krɪb/ *n* berço *m*; (*Christmas*) presépio *m*

crib² /krɪb/ *vt/i* (*pt* **cribbed**) (*colloq*) colar (*sl*), (*P*) cabular (*sl*) □ *n* cópia *f*, plágio *m*; (*translation*) burro *m* (*sl*)

cricket¹ /'krɪkɪt/ *n* críquete *m*. ~**er** *n* jogador *m* de críquete

cricket² /'krɪkɪt/ *n* (*insect*) grilo *m*

crime /kraɪm/ *n* crime *m*; (*minor*) delito *m*; (*collectively*) criminalidade *f*

criminal /'krɪmɪnl/ *a* & *n* criminoso (*m*)

crimp /krɪmp/ *vt* preguear; (*hair*) frisar

crimson /'krɪmzn/ *a* & *n* carmesim (*m*)

cring|e /krɪndʒ/ *vi* encolher-se. ~**ing** *a* servil

crinkle /'krɪŋkl/ *vt/i* enrugar(-se) □ *n* vinco *m*, ruga *f*

cripple /'krɪpl/ *n* aleijado *m*, coxo *m* □ *vt* estropiar; (*fig*) paralisar

crisis /'kraɪsɪs/ *n* (*pl* **crises** /-siːz/) crise *f*

crisp /krɪsp/ *a* (**-er**, **est**) (*culin*) crocante; (*air*) fresco; (*manners, reply*) decidido. ~**s** *npl* batatas *fpl* fritas redondas

criterion /kraɪˈtɪərɪən/ *n* (*pl* **-ia**) critério *m*

critic /'krɪtɪk/ *n* crítico *m*. ~**al** *a* crítico. ~**ally** *adv* de forma crítica; (*ill*) gravemente

criticism /'krɪtɪsɪzəm/ *n* crítica *f*

criticize /'krɪtɪsaɪz/ *vt/i* criticar

croak /krəʊk/ *n* (*frog*) coaxar *m*; (*raven*) crocitar *m*, crocito *m* □ *vi* (*frog*) coaxar; (*raven*) crocitar

crochet /'krəʊʃeɪ/ *n* crochê *m* □ *vt* fazer em crochê

crockery /'krɒkərɪ/ *n* louça *f*

crocodile /'krɒkədaɪl/ *n* crocodilo *m*

crocus /'krəʊkəs/ *n* (*pl* **-uses** /-sɪz/) croco *m*

crony /'krəʊnɪ/ *n* camarada *mf*, amigão *m*, parceiro *m*

crook /krʊk/ *n* (*colloq: criminal*) vigarista *mf*; (*stick*) cajado *m*

crooked /'krʊkɪd/ *a* torcido; (*winding*) tortuoso; (*askew*) torto; (*colloq: dishonest*) desonesto. ~**ly** *adv* de través

crop /krɒp/ *n* colheita *f*, (*fig*) quantidade *f*; (*haircut*) corte *m* rente □ *vt* (*pt* cropped) cortar □ *vi* ~ **up** aparecer, surgir

croquet /'krəʊkeɪ/ *n* croquet *m*, croqué *m*

cross /krɒs/ *n* cruz *f* □ *vt/i* cruzar; (*cheque*) cruzar, (*P*) barrar; (*oppose*) contrariar; (*of paths*) cruzar-se □ *a* zangado. ~ **off** *or* **out** riscar. ~ **o.s.** benzer-se. ~ **sb's mind** passar pela cabeça *or* pelo espírito de alg, ocorrer a alg. **talk at** ~ **purposes** falar sem se entender. ~-**country** *a* & *adv* a corta-mato. ~-**examine** *vt* fazer o contra-interrogatório (de testemunhas). ~-**eyed** *a* vesgo, estrábico. ~-**fire** *n* fogo *m* cruzado. ~-**reference** *n* nota *f* remissiva. ~-**section** *n* corte *m* transversal; (*fig*) grupo *m or* sector *m* representativo. ~**ly** *adv* irritadamente

crossbar /'krɒsbɑ:(r)/ *n* barra *f* transversal *f*; (*of bicycle*) travessão *m*

crossing /'krɒsɪŋ/ *n* cruzamento *m*; (*by boat*) travessia *f*; (*on road*) passagem *f*

crossroads /'krɒsrəʊdz/ *n* encruzilhada *f*, cruzamento *m*

crossword /'krɒswɜːd/ *n* palavras *fpl* cruzadas

crotch /krɒtʃ/ *n* entrepernas *fpl*

crotchet /'krɒtʃɪt/ *n* (*mus*) semínima *f*

crouch /kraʊtʃ/ *vi* agachar-se

crow /krəʊ/ *n* corvo *m* □ *vi* (*cock*) (*pt* **crew**) cantar; (*fig*) rejubilar-se (**over** com). **as the** ~ **flies** em linha reta, (*P*) recta

crowbar /'krəʊbɑ:(r)/ *n* alavanca *f*, pé-de-cabra *m*

crowd /kraʊd/ *n* multidão *f* □ *vi* afluir □ *vt* encher. ~ **into** apinhar-se em. ~**ed** *a* cheio, apinhado

crown /kraʊn/ *n* coroa *f*; (*of hill*) topo *m*, cume *m* □ *vt* coroar; (*tooth*) pôr uma coroa em

crucial /'kru:ʃl/ *a* crucial

crucifix /'kru:sɪfɪks/ *n* crucifixo *m*

crucif|y /'kru:sɪfaɪ/ *vt* crucificar. ~**ixion** /-'fɪkʃn/ *n* crucificação *f*

crude /kru:d/ *a* (-**er**, -**est**) (*raw*) bruto; (*rough*, *vulgar*) grosseiro. ~ **oil** petróleo *m* bruto

cruel /krʊəl/ *a* (**crueller**, **cruellest**) cruel. ~**ty** *n* crueldade *f*

cruis|e /kru:z/ *n* cruzeiro *m* □ *vi* cruzar; (*of tourists*) fazer um cruzeiro; (*of car*) ir a velocidade de cruzeiro. ~**er** *n* cruzador *m*. ~**ing speed** velocidade *f* de cruzeiro

crumb /krʌm/ *n* migalha *f*, farelo *m*

crumble /'krʌmbl/ *vt/i* desfazer(-se); (*bread*) esmigalhar(-se); (*collapse*) desmoronar-se

crumple /'krʌmpl/ *vt/i* amarrotar (-se)

crunch /krʌntʃ/ *vt* trincar; (*under one's feet*) ranger

crusade /kru:'seɪd/ *n* cruzada *f*. ~**r** /-ə(r)/ *n* cruzado *m*; (*fig*) militante *mf*

crush /krʌʃ/ *vt* esmagar; (*clothes*, *papers*) amassar, amarrotar □ *n* aperto *m*. **a** ~ **on** (*sl*) uma paixonite, (*P*) paixoneta por.

crust /krʌst/ *n* côdea *f*, crosta *f*. ~**y** *a* crocante

crutch /krʌtʃ/ *n* muleta *f*; (*crotch*) entrepernas *fpl*

crux /krʌks/ *n* (*pl* **cruxes**) o ponto crucial

cry /kraɪ/ *n* grito *m* □ *vi* (*weep*) chorar; (*call out*) gritar. **a far** ~ **from** muito diferente de.

crying /'kraɪɪŋ/ *a* **a** ~ **shame** uma grande vergonha

crypt /krɪpt/ *n* cripta *f*

cryptic /'krɪptɪk/ *a* críptico, enigmático

crystal /'krɪstl/ *n* cristal *m*. ~**lize** *vt/i* cristalizar(-se)

cub /kʌb/ *n* cria *f*, filhote *m*. **C**~ (**Scout**) lobito *m*

Cuba /'kju:bə/ *n* Cuba *f*. ~**n** *a* & *n* cubano (*m*)

cubby-hole /'kʌbɪhəʊl/ *n* cochicho *m*; (*snug place*) cantinho *m*

cub|e /kju:b/ *n* cubo *m*. ~**ic** *a* cúbico

cubicle /'kju:bɪkl/ *n* cubículo *m*, compartimento *m*; (*at swimming-pool*) cabine *f*

cuckoo /'kʊku:/ *n* cuco *m*

cucumber /'kju:kʌmbə(r)/ *n* pepino *m*

cuddl|e /'kʌdl/ *vt/i* abraçar com carinho; (*nestle*) aninhar(-se) □ *n* abracinho *m*, festinha *f*. ~**y** *a* fofo, aconchegante

cudgel /'kʌdʒl/ *n* cacete *m*, moca *f* □ *vt* (*pt* **cudgelled**) dar cacetadas em

cue[1] /kju:/ *n* (*theat*) deixa *f*; (*hint*) sugestão *f*, sinal *m*

cue[2] /kju:/ *n* (*billiards*) taco *m*

cuff /kʌf/ *n* punho *m*; (*blow*) sopapo *m* □ *vt* dar um sopapo. ~-**link** *n* botão *m* de punho. **off the** ~ de improviso

cul-de-sac /'kʌldəsæk/ *n* (*pl* **culs-de-sac**) beco *m* sem saída

culinary /'kʌlɪnərɪ/ *a* culinário

cull /kʌl/ *vt* (*select*) escolher; (*kill*) abater seletivamente, (*P*) selectivamente □ *n* abate *m*

culminat|e /'kʌlmɪneɪt/ *vi* ~**e in** acabar em. ~**ion** /-'neɪʃn/ *n* auge *m*, ponto *m* culminante

culprit /'kʌlprɪt/ *n* culpado *m*

cult /kʌlt/ *n* culto *m*

cultivat|e /'kʌltɪveɪt/ *vt* cultivar. ~**ion** /-'veɪʃn/ *n* cultivo *m*, cultivação *f*

cultural /'kʌltʃərəl/ *a* cultural

culture /'kʌltʃə(r)/ *n* cultura *f*. ~**d** *a* culto

cumbersome /'kʌmbəsəm/ *a* (*unwieldy*) pesado, incômodo, (*P*) incómodo

cumulative /'kju:mjʊlətɪv/ *a* cumulativo

cunning /'kʌnɪŋ/ *a* astuto, manhoso □ *n* astúcia *f*, manha *f*

cup /kʌp/ *n* xícara *f*, (*P*) chávena *f*, (*prize*) taça *f*. **C~ Final** Final de Campeonato *f*

cupboard /'kʌbəd/ *n* armário *m*

cupful /'kʌpfʊl/ *n* xícara *f* cheia, (*P*) chávena *f* (cheia)

curable /'kjʊərəbl/ *a* curável

curator /kjʊə'reɪtə(r)/ *n* (*museum*) conservador *m*; (*jur*) curador *m*

curb/kɜ:b/ *n* freio *m* □ *vt* refrear; (*price increase etc*) sustar

curdle /'kɜ:dl/ *vt/i* coalhar

cure /kjʊə(r)/ *vt* curar □ *n* cura *f*

curfew /'kɜ:fju:/ *n* toque *m* de recolher

curio /'kjʊərɪəʊ/ *n* (*pl* -os) curiosidade *f*

curi|ous /'kjʊərɪəs/ *a* curioso. ~**osity** /-'ɒsətɪ/ *n* curiosidade *f*

curl /kɜ:l/ *vt/i* encaracolar(-se) □ *n* caracol *m*. ~ **up** enroscar(-se)

curler /'kɜ:lə(r)/ *n* rolo *m*

curly /'kɜ:lɪ/ *a* (-ier, -iest) encaracolado, crespo

currant /'kʌrənt/ *n* passa *f* de Corinto

currency /'kʌrənsɪ/ *n* moeda *f* corrente; (*general use*) circulação *f*. **foreign** ~ moeda *f* estrangeita

current /'kʌrənt/ *a* (*common*) corrente; (*event, price, etc*) atual, (*P*) actual □ *n* corrente *f*. ~ **account** conta *f* corrente. ~ **affairs** atualidades *fpl*, (*P*) actualidades *fpl*. ~**ly** *adv* atualmente, (*P*) actualmente

curriculum /kə'rɪkjʊləm/ *n* (*pl* -la) currículo *m*, programa *m* de estudos. ~ **vitae** *n* curriculum vitae *m*

curry[1] /'kʌrɪ/ *n* caril *m*

curry[2] /'kʌrɪ/ *vt* ~ **favour with** procurar agradar a

curse /kɜ:s/ *n* maldição *f*, praga *f*; (*bad language*) palavrão *m* □ *vt* amaldiçoar, praguejar contra □ *vi* praguejar; (*swear*) dizer palavrões

cursor /'kɜ:sə(r)/ *n* cursor *m*

cursory /'kɜ:sərɪ/ *a* apressado, superficial. **a** ~ **look** uma olhada superficial

curt /kɜ:t/ *a* brusco

curtail /kɜ:'teɪl/ *vt* abreviar; (*expenses etc*) reduzir

curtain /'kɜ:tn/ *n* cortina *f*; (*theat*) pano *m*

curtsy /'kɜ:tsɪ/ *n* reverência *f* □ *vi* fazer uma reverência

curve /kɜ:v/ *n* curva *f* □ *vt/i* curvar (-se); (*of road*) fazer uma curva

cushion /'kʊʃn/ *n* almofada *f* □ *vt* (*a blow*) amortecer; (*fig*) proteger

cushy /'kʊʃɪ/ *a* (-ier, -iest) (*colloq*) fácil, agradável. ~ **job** sinecura *f*, boca *f* (*fig*)

custard /'kʌstəd/ *n* creme *m*

custodian /kʌ'stəʊdɪən/ *n* guarda *m*

custody /'kʌstədɪ/ *n* (*safe keeping*) custódia *f*; (*jur*) detenção *f*; (*of child*) tutela *f*

custom /'kʌstəm/ *n* costume *m*; (*comm*) freguesia *f*, clientela *f*. ~**ary** *a* habitual

customer /'kʌstəmə(r)/ *n* freguês *m*, cliente *mf*

customs /'kʌstəmz/ *npl* alfândega *f* □ *a* alfandegário. ~ **clearance** desembaraço *m* alfandegário. ~ **officer** funcionário *m* da alfândega

cut /kʌt/ *vt/i* (*pt* cut, *pres p* cutting) cortar; (*prices etc*) reduzir □ *n* corte *m*, golpe *m*; (*of clothes, hair*) corte *m*; (*piece*) pedaço *m*; (*prices etc*) redução *f*, corte *m*; (*sl: share*) comissão *f*, (*P*) talhada *f* (*sl*). ~ **back** *or* **down** (*on*) reduzir. ~**-back** *n* corte *m*. ~ **in** intrometer-se; (*auto*) cortar. ~ **off** cortar; (*fig*) isolar. ~ **out** recortar; (*leave out*) suprimir. ~**-out** *n* figura *f* para recortar. ~**-price** *a* a preço(s) reduzido(s). ~ **short** encurtar, (*P*) atalhar

cute /kju:t/ *a* (-er, -est) (*colloq: clever*) esperto; (*attractive*) bonito, (*P*) giro (*colloq*)

cuticle /'kju:tɪkl/ *n* cutícula *f*

cutlery /'kʌtlərɪ/ *n* talheres *mpl*

cutlet /'kʌtlɪt/ *n* costeleta *f*

cutting /'kʌtɪŋ/ *a* cortante □ *n* (*from newspaper*) recorte *m*; (*plant*) estaca *f*. ~ **edge** gume *m*

CV *abbr see* **curriculum vitae**

cyanide /'saɪənaɪd/ *n* cianeto *m*

cycl|e /'saɪkl/ *n* ciclo *m*; (*bicycle*) bicicleta *f* □ *vi* andar de bicicleta. ~**ing** *n* ciclismo *m*. ~**ist** *n* ciclista *mf*

cyclone /'saɪkləʊn/ *n* ciclone *m*

cylind|er /'sɪlɪndə(r)/ *n* cilindro *m*. ~**rical** /-'lɪndrɪkl/ *a* cilíndrico

cymbals /'sɪmblz/ *npl* (*mus*) pratos *mpl*

cynic /'sɪnɪk/ *n* cínico *m*. ~**al** *a* cínico. ~**ism** /-sɪzəm/ *n* cinismo *m*

Cypr|us /'saɪprəs/ *n* Chipre *m*. ~**iot** /'sɪprɪət/ *a* & *n* cipriota (*mf*)

cyst /sɪst/ *n* quisto *m*

Czech /tʃek/ *a* & *n* tcheco (*m*), checo (*m*)

D

dab /dæb/ vt (pt **dabbed**) aplicar levemente □ **n** a ~ **of** uma aplicaçãozinha de. ~ **sth on** aplicar qq coisa em gestos leves

dabble /'dæbl/ vi ~ **in** interessar-se por, fazer um pouco de (como amador). ~**r** /-ə(r)/ n amador m

dad /dæd/ n (colloq) paizinho m. ~**dy** n (children's use) papai m, (P) papá m. ~**dy-long-legs** n pernilongo m

daffodil /'dæfədɪl/ n narciso m

daft /da:ft/ a (-er, -est) doido, maluco

dagger /'dægə(r)/ n punhal m. **at** ~**s drawn** prestes a lutar (**with** com)

daily /'deɪlɪ/ a diário, quotidiano □ adv diariamente, todos os dias □ n (newspaper) diário m; (colloq: charwoman) faxineira f, (P) mulher f a dias

dainty /'deɪntɪ/ a (-ier, -iest) delicado; (pretty, neat) gracioso

dairy /'deərɪ/ n leiteria f. ~ **products** laticínios mpl

daisy /'deɪzɪ/ n margarida f

dam /dæm/ n barragem f, represa f □ vt (pt **dammed**) represar

damag|e /'dæmɪdʒ/ n estrago(s) mpl. ~**es** (jur) perdas fpl e danos mpl □ vt estragar, danificar; (fig) prejudicar. ~**ing** a prejudicial

dame /deɪm/ n (old use) dama f, (Amer sl) mulher f

damn /dæm/ vt (relig) condenar aõ inferno; (swear at) amaldiçoar, maldizer; (fig: condemn) condenar □ int raios!, bolas! □ n **not care a** ~ (colloq) estar pouco ligando (colloq), (P) estar-se marimbando (colloq) □ a (colloq) do diabo, danado □ adv (colloq) muitíssimo. **I'll be** ~**ed if** que um raio me atinja se. ~**ation** /-'neɪʃn/ n danação f, condenação f. ~**ing** a comprometedor, condenatório

damp /dæmp/ n umidade f, (P) humidade f □ a (-er, -est) úmido, (P) húmido □ vt umedecer, (P) humedecer. ~**en** vt = **damp**. ~**ness** n umidade f, (P) humidade f

dance /da:ns/ vt/i dançar □ n dança f. ~ **hall** sala f de baile. ~**r** /-ə(r)/ n dançarino m; (professional) bailarino m

dandelion /'dændɪlaɪən/ n dente-de-leão m

dandruff /'dændrʌf/ n caspa f

Dane /deɪn/ n dinamarquês m

danger /'deɪndʒə(r)/ n perigo m. **be in** ~ **of** correr o risco de. ~**ous** a perigoso

dangle /'dæŋgl/ vi oscilar, pender □ vt

ter or trazer dependurado; (hold) balançar; (fig: hopes, etc) acenar com

Danish /'deɪnɪʃ/ a dinamarquês □ n (lang) dinamarquês m

dank /dæŋk/ a (-er, -est) frio e úmido, (P) húmido

dare /deə(r)/ vt ~ **to do** ousar fazer. ~ **sb to do** desafiar alg a fazer □ n desafio m. **I** ~ **say** creio

daredevil /'deədevl/ n louco m, temerário m

daring /'deərɪŋ/ a audacioso □ n audácia f

dark /da:k/ a (-er, -est) escuro, sombrio; (gloomy) sombrio; (of colour) escuro; (of skin) moreno □ n escuridão f, escuro m; (nightfall) anoitecer m, cair m da noite. ~ **horse** concorrente mf que é uma incógnita. ~-**room** n câmara f escura. **be in the** ~ **about** (fig) ignorar. ~**ness** n escuridão f

darken /'da:kən/ vt/i escurecer

darling /'da:lɪŋ/ a & n querido (m)

darn /da:n/ vt serzir, remendar

dart /da:t/ n dardo m, flecha f. ~**s** (game) jogo m de dardos □ vi lançar-se

dartboard /'da:tbɔ:d/ n alvo m

dash /dæʃ/ vi precipitar-se □ vt arremessar; (hopes) destruir □ n corrida f; (stroke) travessão m; (Morse) traço m. **a** ~ **of** um pouco de. ~ **off** partir a toda a velocidade; (letter) escrever às pressas

dashboard /'dæʃbɔ:d/ n painel m de instrumentos, quadro m de bordo

data /'deɪtə/ npl dados mpl. ~ **capture** aquisição f de informações, recolha f de dados. ~**base** n base f de dados. ~ **processing** processamento m or tratamento m de dados

date[1] /deɪt/ n data f; (colloq) encontro m marcado □ vt/i datar; (colloq) andar com. **out of** ~ desatualizado, (P) desactualizado. **to** ~ até a data. **up to** ~ (style) moderno; (information etc) em dia. ~**d** a antiquado

date[2] /deɪt/ n (fruit) tâmara f

daub /dɔ:b/ vt borrar, pintar toscamente

daughter /'dɔ:tə(r)/ n filha f. ~-**in-law** n (pl ~**s-in-law**) nora f

daunt /dɔ:nt/ vt assustar, intimidar, desencorajar

dawdle /'dɔ:dl/ vi perder tempo

dawn /dɔ:n/ n madrugada f □ vi madrugar, amanhecer. ~ **on** (fig) fazer-se luz no espírito de, começar a perceber

day /deɪ/ n dia m; (period) época f, tempo m. ~-**dream** n devaneio m □ vi devanear. **the** ~ **before** a véspera

daybreak /'deɪbreɪk/ n romper m do dia, aurora f, amanhecer m

daylight /'deɪlaɪt/ n luz f do dia. ~ **robbery** roubar descaradamente

daytime /'deɪtaɪm/ n dia m, dia m claro

daze /deɪz/ vt aturdir □ n **in a** ~ aturdido

dazzle /'dæzl/ vt deslumbrar; (with headlights) ofuscar

dead /ded/ a morto; (numb) dormente □ adv completamente, de todo □ n **in the** ~ **of the night** a horas mortas, na calada da noite. **the** ~ os mortos. **in the** ~ **centre** bem no meio. **stop** ~ estacar. ~ **beat** a (colloq) morto de cansaço. ~ **end** beco m sem saída. ~-**pan** a inexpressivo

deaden /'dedn/ vt (sound, blow) amortecer; (pain) aliviar

deadline /'dedlaɪn/ n prazo m final

deadlock /'dedlɒk/ n impasse m

deadly /'dedlɪ/ a (-ier, -iest) mortal; (weapon) mortífero

deaf /def/ a (-er, -est) surdo. **turn a** ~ **ear** fingir que não ouve. ~ **mute** surdo-mudo m. ~**ness** n surdez f

deafen /'defn/ vt ensurdecer. ~**ing** a ensurdecedor

deal /diːl/ vt (pt **dealt**) distribuir; (a blow, cards) dar □ vi negociar □ n negócio m; (cards) vez de dar f. **a great** ~ muito (of de). ~ **in** negociar em. ~ **with** (person) tratar (com); (affair) tratar de. ~**er** n comerciante m; (agent) concessionário m; representante m

dealings /'diːlɪŋz/ npl relações fpl; (comm) negócios mpl

dealt /delt/ see **deal**

dean /diːn/ n decano m

dear /dɪə(r)/ a (-er, -est) (cherished) caro, querido; (expensive) caro □ n amor m □ adv caro □ int **oh** ~! meu Deus! ~**ly** adv (very much) muito; (pay) caro

dearth /dɜːθ/ n escassez f

death /deθ/ n morte f. ~ **certificate** certidão f de óbito. ~ **penalty** pena f de morte. ~ **rate** taxa f de mortalidade. ~-**trap** n lugar m perigoso, ratoeira f. ~**ly** a de morte, mortal

debase /dɪ'beɪs/ vt degradar

debat|e /dɪ'beɪt/ n debate m □ vt debater. ~**able** a discutível

debauchery /dɪ'bɔːtʃərɪ/ n deboche m, devassidão f

debility /dɪ'bɪlətɪ/ n debilidade f

debit /'debɪt/ n débito m □ vt (pt **debited**) debitar

debris /'deɪbriː/ n destroços mpl

debt /det/ n dívida f. **in** ~ endividado. ~**or** n devedor m

debunk /dɪ'bʌŋk/ vt (colloq) desmitificar

début /'deɪbjuː/ n (of actor, play etc) estréia f

decade /'dekeɪd/ n década f

decaden|t /'dekədənt/ a decadente. ~**ce** n decadência f

decaffeinated /diː'kæfiːmeɪtɪd/ a sem cafeína

decanter /dɪ'kæntə(r)/ n garrafa f para vinho, de vidro ou cristal

decapitate /dɪ'kæpɪteɪt/ vt decapitar

decay /dɪ'keɪ/ vi apodrecer, estragar-se; (food; fig) deteriorar-se; (building) degradar-se □ n apodrecimento m; (of tooth) cárie f; (fig) declínio m, decadência f

deceased /dɪ'siːst/ a & n falecido (m), defunto (m)

deceit /dɪ'siːt/ n engano m. ~**ful** a enganador

deceive /dɪ'siːv/ vt enganar, iludir

December /dɪ'sembə(r)/ n dezembro m

decen|t /'diːsnt/ a decente; (colloq: good) (bastante) bom; (colloq: likeable) simpático. ~**cy** n decência f

decentralize /diː'sentrəlaɪz/ vt descentralizar

decept|ive /dɪ'septɪv/ a enganador, ilusório. ~**ion** /-ʃn/ n engano m

decibel /'desɪbel/ n decibel m

decide /dɪ'saɪd/ vt/i decidir. ~ **on** decidir-se por. ~ **to do** decidir fazer. ~**d** /-ɪd/ a decidido; (clear) definido, nítido. ~**dly** /-ɪdlɪ/ adv decididamente

decimal /'desɪml/ a decimal □ n (fração f, (P) fracção f) decimal m. ~ **point** vírgula f decimal

decipher /dɪ'saɪfə(r)/ vt decifrar

decision /dɪ'sɪʒn/ n decisão f

decisive /dɪ'saɪsɪv/ a decisivo; (manner) decidido. ~**ly** adv decisivamente

deck /dek/ n convés m; (of cards) baralho m. ~-**chair** n espreguiçadeira f

declar|e /dɪ'kleə(r)/ vt declarar. ~**ation** /deklə'reɪʃn/ n declaração f

decline /dɪ'klaɪn/ vt (refuse) declinar, recusar delicadamente; (gram) declinar □ vi (deteriorate) declinar; (fall) baixar □ n declínio m; (fall) abaixamento m

decode /diː'kəʊd/ vt descodificar

decompos|e /diːkəm'pəʊz/ vt/i decompor(-se). ~**ition** /-ɒmpə'zɪʃn/ n decomposição f

décor /'deɪkɔː(r)/ n decoração f

decorat|e /'dekəreɪt/ vt decorar, enfeitar; (paint) pintar; (paper) pôr papel em. ~**ion** /-'reɪʃn/ n decoração f; (medal etc) condecoração f. ~**ive** /-ətɪv/ a decorativo

decorum /dɪ'kɔːrəm/ n decoro m

decoy¹ /'diːkɔɪ/ n chamariz m, engodo m; (trap) armadilha f

decoy[2] /dɪ'kɔɪ/ vt atrair, apanhar

decrease[1] /di:'kri:s/ vt/i diminuir

decrease[2] /'di:kri:s/ n diminuição f

decree /dɪ'kri:/ n decreto m; (jur) decisão f judicial □ vt decretar

decrepit /dɪ'krepɪt/ a decrépito

dedicat|e /'dedɪkeɪt/ vt dedicar. ~ed a dedicado. ~ion /-'keɪʃn/ n dedicação f; (in book) dedicatória f

deduce /dɪ'dju:s/ vt deduzir

deduct /dɪ'dʌkt/ vt deduzir; (from pay) descontar

deduction /dɪ'dʌkʃn/ n dedução f; (from pay) desconto m

deed /di:d/ n ato m; (jur) contrato m

deem /di:m/ vt julgar, considerar

deep /di:p/ a (-er, -est) profundo □ adv profundamente. ~-freeze n congelador m □ vt congelar. take a ~ breath respirar fundo. ~ly adv profundamente

deepen /'di:pən/ vt/i aprofundar(-se); (mystery, night) adensar-se

deer /dɪə(r)/ n (pl invar) veado m

deface /dɪ'feɪs/ vt danificar, degradar

defamation /defə'meɪʃn/ n difamação f

default /dɪ'fɔ:lt/ vi faltar □ n by ~ à revelia. win by ~ (sport) ganhar por não comparecimento, (P) comparência □ a (comput) default m

defeat /dɪ'fi:t/ vt derrotar; (thwart) malograr □ n derrota f; (of plan, etc) malogro m

defect[1] /'di:fekt/ n defeito m. ~ive /dɪ'fektɪv/ a defeituoso

defect[2] /dɪ'fekt/ vi desertar. ~ion n defecção m. ~or n trânsfuga mf, dissidente mf; (political) asilado m político

defence /dɪ'fens/ n defesa f. ~less a indefeso

defend /dɪ'fend/ vt defender. ~ant n (jur) réu m, acusado m. ~er n advogado m de defesa, defensor m

defensive /dɪ'fensɪv/ a defensivo □ n on the ~ na defensiva f; (person, sport) na retranca f (colloq)

defer /dɪ'fɜ:(r)/ vt (pt deferred) adiar, diferir □ vi ~ to ceder, deferir

deferen|ce /'defərəns/ n deferência f. ~tial /-'renʃl/ a deferente

defian|ce /dɪ'faɪəns/ n desafio m. in ~ of sem respeito por. ~t a de desafio. ~tly adv com ar de desafio

deficien|t /dɪ'fɪʃnt/ a deficiente. be ~t in ter falta de. ~cy n deficiência f

deficit /'defɪsɪt/ n déficit m

define /dɪ'faɪn/ vt definir

definite /'defɪnɪt/ a definido; (clear) categórico, claro; (certain) certo. ~ly adv decididamente; (clearly) claramente

definition /defɪ'nɪʃn/ n definição f

definitive /dɪ'fɪnətɪv/ a definitivo

deflat|e /dɪ'fleɪt/ vt esvaziar; (person) desemproar, desinchar. ~ion /-ʃn/ n esvaziamento m; (econ) deflação f

deflect /dɪ'flekt/ vt/i desviar(-se)

deform /dɪ'fɔ:m/ vt deformar. ~ed a deformado, disforme. ~ity n deformidade f

defraud /dɪ'frɔ:d/ vt defraudar

defrost /di:'frɒst/ vt descongelar

deft /deft/ a (-er, -est) hábil

defunct /dɪ'fʌŋkt/ a (law etc) caduco, extinto

defuse /di:'fju:z/ vt (a bomb) desativar, (P) desactivar; (a situation) acalmar

defy /dɪ'faɪ/ vt desafiar; (attempts) resistir a; (the law) desobedecer a; (public opinion) opor-se a

degenerate /dɪ'dʒenəreɪt/ vi degenerar (into em)

degrad|e /dɪ'greɪd/ vt degradar. ~ation /degrə'deɪʃn/ n degradação f

degree /dɪ'gri:/ n grau m; (univ) diploma m. to a ~ ao mais alto grau, muito

dehydrate /di:'haɪdreɪt/ vt/i desidratar(-se)

de-ice /di:'aɪs/ vt descongelar, degelar; (windscreen) tirar o gelo de

deign /deɪn/ vt ~ to do dignar-se (a) fazer

deity /'di:ɪtɪ/ n divindade f

dejected /dɪ'dʒektɪd/ a abatido

delay /dɪ'leɪ/ vt atrasar; (postpone) retardar □ vi atrasar-se □ n atraso m, demora f

delegate[1] /'delɪgət/ n delegado m

delegat|e[2] /'delɪgeɪt/ vt delegar. ~ion /-'geɪʃn/ n delegação f

delet|e /dɪ'li:t/ vt riscar. ~ion /-ʃn/ n rasura f

deliberate[1] /dɪ'lɪbərət/ a deliberado; (steps etc) compassado. ~ly adv deliberadamente, de propósito

deliberat|e[2] /dɪ'lɪbəreɪt/ vt/i deliberar. ~ion /-'reɪʃn/ n deliberação f

delica|te /'delɪkət/ a delicado. ~cy n delicadeza f, (food) guloseima f, iguaria f, (P) acepipe m

delicatessen /delɪkə'tesn/ n (shop) mercearias fpl finas

delicious /dɪ'lɪʃəs/ a delicioso

delight /dɪ'laɪt/ n grande prazer m, delícia f; (thing) delícia f, encanto m □ vt deliciar □ vi ~ in deliciar-se com. ~ed a deliciado, encantado. ~ful a delicioso, encantador

delinquen|t /dɪ'lɪŋkwənt/ a & n delinquente mf, (P) delinquente mf. ~cy n delinquência f, (P) delinquência f

deliri|ous /dɪ'lɪrɪəs/ a delirante. be ~ous delirar. ~um /-əm/ n delírio m

deliver /dɪ'lɪvə(r)/ vt entregar;

(*letters*) distribuir; (*free*) libertar; (*med*) fazer o parto. ~**ance** *n* libertação *f*. ~**y** *n* entrega *f*; (*letters*) distribuição *f*; (*med*) parto *m*

delu|de /dɪˈluːd/ *vt* enganar. ~**de o.s.** ter ilusões. ~**sion** /-ʒn/ *n* ilusão *f*

deluge /ˈdeljuːdʒ/ *n* dilúvio *m* □ *vt* inundar

de luxe /dɪˈlʌks/ *a* de luxo

delve /delv/ *vi* ~ **into** pesquisar, rebuscar

demand /dɪˈmaːnd/ *vt* exigir; (*ask to be told*) perguntar □ *n* exigência *f*; (*comm*) procura *f*; (*claim*) reivindicação *f*. **in** ~ procurado. ~**ing** *a* exigente; (*work*) puxado, custoso

demean /dɪˈmiːn/ *vt* ~ **o.s.** rebaixar-se

demeanour /dɪˈmiːnə(r)/ *n* comportamento *m*, conduta *f*

demented /dɪˈmentɪd/ *a* louco, demente. **become** ~ enlouquecer

demo /ˈdeməʊ/ *n* (*pl* -**os**) (*colloq*) manifestação *f*, (*P*) manif *f*

democracy /dɪˈmɒkrəsɪ/ *n* democracia *f*

democrat /ˈdeməkræt/ *n* democrata *mf*. ~**ic** /ˈkrætɪk/ *a* democrático

demoli|sh /dɪˈmɒlɪʃ/ *vt* demolir. ~**tion** /deməˈlɪʃn/ *n* demolição *f*

demon /ˈdiːmən/ *n* demônio *m*

demonstrat|e /ˈdemənstreɪt/ *vt* demonstrar □ *vi* (*pol*) fazer uma manifestação, manifestar-se. ~**ion** /-ˈstreɪʃn/ *n* demonstração *f*; (*pol*) manifestação *f*. ~**or** *n* (*pol*) manifestante *mf*

demonstrative /dɪˈmɒnstrətɪv/ *a* demonstrativo

demoralize /dɪˈmɒrəlaɪz/ *vt* desmoralizar

demote /dɪˈməʊt/ *vt* fazer baixar de posto, rebaixar

demure /dɪˈmjʊə(r)/ *a* recatado, modesto

den /den/ *n* antro *m*, covil *m*; (*room*) cantinho *m*, recanto *m*

denial /dɪˈnaɪəl/ *n* negação *f*; (*refusal*) recusa *f*; (*statement*) desmentido *m*

denigrate /ˈdenɪgreɪt/ *vt* denegrir

denim /ˈdenɪm/ *n* brim *m*. ~**s** (*jeans*) blue-jeans *mpl*

Denmark /ˈdenmaːk/ *n* Dinamarca *f*

denomination /dɪnɒmɪˈneɪʃn/ *n* denominação *f*; (*relig*) confissão *f*, seita *f*; (*money*) valor *m*

denote /dɪˈnəʊt/ *vt* denotar

denounce /dɪˈnaʊns/ *vt* denunciar

dens|e /dens/ *a* (-**er**, -**est**) denso; (*colloq: person*) obtuso. ~**ely** *adv* (*packed etc*) muito. ~**ity** *n* densidade *f*

dent /dent/ *n* mossa *f*, depressão *f* □ *vt* dentear

dental /ˈdentl/ *a* dentário, dental

dentist /ˈdentɪst/ *n* dentista *mf*. ~**ry** *n* odontologia *f*

denture /ˈdentʃə(r)/ *n* dentadura *f* (postiça)

denunciation /dɪnʌnsɪˈeɪʃn/ *n* denúncia *f*

deny /dɪˈnaɪ/ *vt* negar; (*rumour*) desmentir; (*disown*) renegar; (*refuse*) recusar

deodorant /diːˈəʊdərənt/ *n* & *a* desodorante (*m*), (*P*) desodorizante (*m*)

depart /dɪˈpaːt/ *vi* partir. ~ **from** (*deviate*) afastar-se de, desviar-se de

department /dɪˈpaːtmənt/ *n* departamento *m*; (*in shop, office*) seção *f*, (*P*) secção *f*; (*government*) repartição *f*. ~ **store** loja *f* de departamentos, (*P*) grande armazém *m*

departure /dɪˈpaːtʃə(r)/ *n* partida *f*. **a** ~ **from** (*custom, diet etc*) uma mudança de. **a new** ~ uma nova orientação

depend /dɪˈpend/ *vi* ~ **on** depender de; (*trust*) contar com. ~**able** *a* de confiança. ~**ence** *n* dependência *f*. ~**ent (on)** *a* dependente (de)

dependant /dɪˈpendənt/ *n* dependente *mf*

depict /dɪˈpɪkt/ *vt* descrever; (*in pictures*) representar

deplete /dɪˈpliːt/ *vt* reduzir; (*use up*) esgotar

deplor|e /dɪˈplɔː(r)/ *vt* deplorar. ~**able** *a* deplorável

deport /dɪˈpɔːt/ *vt* deportar. ~**ation** /diːpɔːˈteɪʃn/ *n* deportação *f*

depose /dɪˈpəʊz/ *vt* depor

deposit /dɪˈpɒzɪt/ *vt* (*pt* **deposited**) depositar □ *n* depósito *m*. ~ **account** conta *f* de depósito a prazo. ~**or** *n* depositante *mf*

depot /ˈdepəʊ/ *n* (*mil*) depósito *m*; (*buses*) garagem *f*, (*Amer: station*) rodoviária *f*, estação *f* de trem, (*P*) de comboio

deprav|e /dɪˈpreɪv/ *vt* depravar. ~**ity** /-ˈprævətɪ/ *n* depravação *f*

depreciat|e /dɪˈpriːʃɪeɪt/ *vt/i* depreciar(-se). ~**ion** /ˈeɪʃn/ *n* depreciação *f*

depress /dɪˈpres/ *vt* deprimir; (*press down*) carregar em. ~**ion** /-ʃn/ *n* depressão *f*

deprivation /deprɪˈveɪʃn/ *n* privação *f*

deprive /dɪˈpraɪv/ *vt* ~ **of** privar de. ~**d** *a* privado; (*underprivileged*) deserdado (da sorte), destituído; (*child*) carente

depth /depθ/ *n* profundidade *f*. **be out of one's** ~ perder pé, (*P*) não ter pé; (*fig*) ficar desnorteado, estar perdido. **in the** ~(**s**) **of** no mais fundo de, nas profundezas de

deputation /depjʊ'teɪʃn/ n delegação f

deputy /'depjʊtɪ/ n (pl -ies) delegado m □ a adjunto. ~ **chairman** vice-presidente m

derail /dɪ'reɪl/ vt descarrilhar. **be** ~**ed** descarrilhar. ~**ment** n descarrilhamento m

deranged /dɪ'remdʒd/ a (mind) transtornado, louco

derelict /'derəlɪkt/ a abandonado

deri|de /dɪ'raɪd/ vt escarnecer de. ~**sion** /-'rɪʒn/ n escárnio m. ~**sive** a escarninho. ~**sory** a escarninho; (offer etc) irrisório

derivative /dɪ'rɪvətɪv/ a derivado; (work) pouco original □ n derivado m

deriv|e /dɪ'raɪv/ vt ~**e from** tirar de □ vi ~**e from** derivar de. ~**ation** /derɪ'veɪʃn/ n derivação f

derogatory /dɪ'rɒɡətrɪ/ a pejorativo; (remark) depreciativo

derv /dɜːv/ n gasóleo m

descend /dɪ'send/ vt/i descer, descender. **be** ~**ed from** descender de. ~**ant** n descendente mf

descent /dɪ'sent/ n descida f; (lineage) descendência f, origem f

descri|be /dɪs'kraɪb/ vt descrever. ~**ption** /-'krɪpʃn/ n descrição f; ~**ptive** /-'krɪptɪv/ a descritivo

desecrat|e /'desɪkreɪt/ vt profanar. ~**ion** /-'kreɪʃn/ n profanação f

desert[1] /'dezət/ a & n deserto (m). ~ **island** ilha f deserta

desert[2] /dɪ'zɜːt/ vt/i desertar. ~**ed** a abandonado. ~**er** n desertor m. ~**ion** /-ʃn/ n deserção f

deserv|e /dɪ'zɜːv/ vt merecer. ~**edly** /dɪ'zɜːvɪdlɪ/ adv merecidamente, a justo título. ~**ing** a (person) merecedor; (action) meritório

design /dɪ'zam/ n desenho m; (artistic) design m; (style of dress) modelo m; (pattern) padrão m, motivo m □ vt desenhar; (devise) conceber. ~**er** n desenhador m; (of dresses) costureiro m; (of machine) inventor m

designat|e /'dezɪgneɪt/ vt designar. ~**ion** /-'neɪʃn/ n designação f

desir|e /dɪ'zaɪə(r)/ n desejo m □ vt desejar. ~**able** a desejável, atraente

desk /desk/ n secretária f; (of pupil) carteira f; (in hotel) recepção f; (in bank) caixa f

desolat|e /'desələt/ a desolado. ~**ion** /-'leɪʃn/ n desolação f

despair /dɪ'speə(r)/ n desespero m □ vi desesperar (of de)

desperate /'despərət/ a desesperado; (criminal) capaz de tudo. **be** ~ **for** ter uma vontade doida de. ~**ly** adv desesperadamente

desperation /despə'reɪʃn/ n desespero m

despicable /dɪ'spɪkəbl/ a desprezível

despise /dɪ'spaɪz/ vt desprezar

despite /dɪ'spaɪt/ prep apesar de, a despeito de, mau grado

desponden|t /dɪ'spɒndənt/ a desanimado. ~**cy** n desânimo m

despot /'despɒt/ n déspota mf

dessert /dɪ'zɜːt/ n sobremesa f. ~**spoon** n colher f de sobremesa

destination /destɪ'neɪʃn/ n destino m, destinação f

destine /'destɪn/ vt destinar

destiny /'destɪnɪ/ n destino m

destitute /'destɪtjuːt/ a destituído, indigente

destr|oy /dɪ'strɔɪ/ vt destruir. ~**uction** /-'strʌkʃn/ n destruição f. ~**uctive** a destrutivo, destruidor

detach /dɪ'tætʃ/ vt separar, arrancar. ~**able** a separável; (lining etc) solto. ~**ed** a separado; (impartial) imparcial; (unemotional) desprendido. ~**ed house** casa f sem parede-meia com outra

detachment /dɪ'tætʃmənt/ n separação f; (indifference) desprendimento m; (mil) destacamento m; (impartiality) imparcialidade f

detail /'diːteɪl/ n pormenor m, detalhe m □ vt detalhar; (troops) destacar. ~**ed** a detalhado

detain /dɪ'tem/ vt reter; (in prison) deter. ~**ee** /diːteɪˈniː/ n detido m

detect /dɪ'tekt/ vt detectar. ~**ion** /-ʃn/ n detecção f. ~**or** n detector m

detective /dɪ'tektɪv/ n detective m. ~ **story** romance m policial

detention /dɪ'tenʃn/ n detenção f. **be given a** ~ (school) ficar de castigo na escola

deter /dɪ'tɜː(r)/ vt (pt **deterred**) dissuadir; (hinder) impedir

detergent /dɪ'tɜːdʒənt/ a & n detergente (m)

deteriorat|e /dɪ'tɪərɪəreɪt/ vi deteriorar(-se). ~**ion** /-'reɪʃn/ n deterioração f

determin|e /dɪ'tɜːmm/ vt determinar. ~**e to do** decidir fazer. ~**ation** /-'neɪʃn/ n determinação f. ~**ed** a determinado. ~**ed to do** decidido a fazer

deterrent /dɪ'terənt/ n dissuasivo m

detest /dɪ'test/ vt detestar. ~**able** a detestável

detonat|e /'detəneɪt/ vt/i detonar. ~**ion** /-'neɪʃn/ n detonação f. ~**or** n espoleta f, detonador m

detour /'diːtʊə(r)/ n desvio m

detract /dɪ'trækt/ vi ~ **from** depreciar, menosprezar

detriment /'detrɪmənt/ n detrimento m. ~**al** /-'mentl/ a prejudicial

devalu|e /diːˈvælju:/ vt desvalorizar. ~**ation** /-ˈeɪʃn/ n desvalorização f

devastat|e /ˈdevəsteɪt/ vi devastar; (fig: overwhelm) arrasar. ~**ing** a devastador; (criticism) de arrasar

develop /dɪˈveləp/ vt/i (pt developed) desenvolver(-se); (get) contrair; (build on) urbanizar; (film) revelar. ~ into tornar-se. ~**ing country** país m subdesenvolvido. ~**ment** n desenvolvimento m; (film) revelação f; (of land) urbanização f

deviat|e /ˈdiːvɪeɪt/ vi desviar-se. ~**ion** /-ˈeɪʃn/ n desvio m

device /dɪˈvaɪs/ n dispositivo m; (scheme) processo m. left to one's own ~s entregue a si mesmo

devil /ˈdevl/ n diabo m

devious /ˈdiːvɪəs/ a tortuoso; (fig: means) escuso; (fig: person) pouco franco

devise /dɪˈvaɪz/ vt imaginar, inventar

devoid /dɪˈvɔɪd/ a ~ of desprovido de, destituído de

devot|e /dɪˈvəʊt/ vt dedicar, devotar. ~**ed** a dedicado, devotado. ~**ion** /-ʃn/ n devoção f

devotee /devəˈtiː/ n ~ of adepto m de, entusiasta mf de

devour /dɪˈvaʊə(r)/ vt devorar

devout /dɪˈvaʊt/ a devota; (prayer) fervoroso

dew /djuː/ n orvalho m

dext|erity /dekˈsterətɪ/ n destreza f, jeito m. ~**rous** /ˈdekstrəs/ a destro, hábil

diabet|es /daɪəˈbiːtiːz/ n diabetes f. ~**ic** /-ˈbetɪk/ a & n diabético (m)

diabolical /daɪəˈbɒlɪkl/ a diabólico

diagnose /ˈdaɪəgnəʊz/ vt diagnosticar

diagnosis /daɪəgˈnəʊsɪs/ n (pl -oses /-siːz/) diagnóstico m

diagonal /daɪˈægənl/ a & n diagonal (f)

diagram /ˈdaɪəgræm/ n diagrama m, esquema m

dial /ˈdaɪəl/ n mostrador m □ vt (pt dialled) (number) marcar, discar. ~**ling code** código m de discagem. ~**ling tone** sinal m de discar

dialect /ˈdaɪəlekt/ n dialeto m, (P) dialecto m

dialogue /ˈdaɪəlɒg/ n diálogo m

diameter /daɪˈæmɪtə(r)/ n diâmetro m

diamond /ˈdaɪəmənd/ n diamante m, brilhante m; (shape) losango m. ~**s** (cards) ouros mpl

diaper /ˈdaɪəpə(r)/ n (Amer) fralda f

diaphragm /ˈdaɪəfræm/ n diafragma m

diarrhoea /daɪəˈrɪə/ n diarréia f, (P) diarreia f

diary /ˈdaɪərɪ/ n agenda f; (record) diário m

dice /daɪs/ n (pl invar) dado m

dictat|e /dɪkˈteɪt/ vt/i ditar. ~**ion** /-ʃn/ n ditado m

dictator /dɪkˈteɪtə(r)/ n ditador m. ~**ship** n ditadura f

diction /ˈdɪkʃn/ n dicção f

dictionary /ˈdɪkʃənrɪ/ n dicionário m

did /dɪd/ see **do**

diddle /ˈdɪdl/ vt (colloq) trapacear, enganar

didn't /ˈdɪdnt/ = **did not**

die /daɪ/ vi (pres p dying) morrer. be dying to estar doido para. ~ down diminuir, baixar. ~ out desaparecer, extinguir-se

diesel /ˈdiːzl/ n diesel m. ~ **engine** motor m diesel

diet /ˈdaɪət/ n dieta f □ vi fazer dieta, estar de dieta

differ /ˈdɪfə(r)/ vi diferir; (disagree) discordar

differen|t /ˈdɪfrənt/ a diferente. ~**ce** n diferença f; (disagreement) desacordo m. ~**ly** adv diferentemente

differentiate /dɪfəˈrenʃɪeɪt/ vt/i diferençar(-se), diferenciar(-se)

difficult /ˈdɪfɪkəlt/ a difícil. ~**y** n dificuldade f

diffiden|t /ˈdɪfɪdənt/ a acanhado, inseguro. ~**ce** n acanhamento m, insegurança f

diffuse[1] /dɪˈfjuːs/ a difuso

diffus|e[2] /dɪˈfjuːz/ vt difundir. ~**ion** /-ʒn/ n difusão f

dig /dɪg/ vt/i (pt dug, pres p digging) cavar; (thrust) espetar □ n (with elbow) cotovelada f; (with finger) cutucada f, (P) espetadela f; (remark) ferroada f; (archaeol) escavação f. ~**s** (colloq) quarto m alugado. ~ up desenterrar

digest /dɪˈdʒest/ vt/i digerir. ~**ible** a digerível, digestível. ~**ion** /-ʃn/ n digestão f

digestive /dɪˈdʒestɪv/ a digestivo

digit /ˈdɪdʒɪt/ n dígito m

digital /ˈdɪdʒɪtl/ a digital. ~ **clock** relógio m digital

dignif|y /ˈdɪgnɪfaɪ/ vt dignificar. ~**ied** a digno

dignitary /ˈdɪgnɪtərɪ/ n dignitário m

dignity /ˈdɪgnətɪ/ n dignidade f

digress /daɪˈgres/ vi digressar, divagar. ~ from desviar-se de. ~**ion** /-ʃn/ n digressão f

dike /daɪk/ n dique m

dilapidated /dɪˈlæpɪdeɪtɪd/ a (house) arruinado, degradado; (car) estragado

dilat|e /daɪˈleɪt/ vt/i dilatar(-se). ~**ion** /-ʃn/ n dilatação f

dilemma /dɪˈlemə/ n dilema m

diligen|t /ˈdɪlɪdʒənt/ a diligente, aplicado. ~**ce** n diligência f, aplicação f

dilute /dar'lju:t/ *vt* diluir □ *a* diluído

dim /dɪm/ *a* (**dimmer, dimmest**) (*weak*) fraco; (*dark*) sombrio; (*indistinct*) vago; (*colloq: stupid*) burro (*colloq*) □ *vt/i* (*pt* **dimmed**) (*light*) baixar. **~ly** *adv* (*shine*) fracamente; (*remember*) vagamente

dime /daɪm/ *n* (*Amer*) moeda *f* de dez centavos

dimension /dar'menʃn/ *n* dimensão *f*

diminish /dɪ'mɪnɪʃ/ *vt/i* diminuir

diminutive /dɪ'mɪnjʊtɪv/ *a* diminuto □ *n* diminutivo *m*

dimple /'dɪmpl/ *n* covinha *f*

din /dɪn/ *n* barulheira *f*, (*P*) chinfrim *m*

dine /daɪn/ *vi* jantar. **~r** /-ə(r)/ *n* (*person*) comensal *m*; (*rail*) vagão-restaurante *m*; (*Amer: restaurant*) lanchonete *f*

dinghy /'dɪŋgɪ/ *n* (*pl* **-ghies**) bote *m*; (*inflatable*) bote *m* de borracha, (*P*) barco *m* de borracha

dingy /'dɪndʒɪ/ *a* (**-ier, -iest**) com ar sujo, esquálido

dining-room /'daɪnɪŋru:m/ *n* sala *f* de jantar

dinner /'dɪnə(r)/ *n* jantar *m*; (*lunch*) almoço *m*. **~-jacket** *n* smoking *m*

dinosaur /'daɪnəsɔ:(r)/ *n* dinossauro *m*

dip /dɪp/ *vt/i* (*pt* **dipped**) mergulhar; (*lower*) baixar □ *n* mergulho *m*; (*bathe*) banho *m* rápido, mergulho *m*; (*slope*) descida *f*; (*culin*) molho *m*. **~ into** (*book*) folhear. **~ one's headlights** baixar para médios

diphtheria /dɪf'θɪərɪə/ *n* difteria *f*

diphthong /'dɪfθɒŋ/ *n* ditongo *m*

diploma /dɪ'pləʊmə/ *n* diploma *m*

diplomacy /dɪ'pləʊməsɪ/ *n* diplomacia *f*

diplomat /'dɪpləmæt/ *n* diplomata *mf*. **~ic** /-'mætɪk/ *a* diplomático

dire /daɪə(r)/ *a* (**-er, -est**) terrível; (*need, poverty*) extremo

direct /dɪ'rekt/ *a* direto, (*P*) directo □ *adv* diretamente, (*P*) directamente □ *vt* dirigir. **~ sb to** indicar a alg o caminho para

direction /dɪ'rekʃn/ *n* direção *f*, (*P*) direcção *f*, sentido *m*. **~s** instruções *fpl*. **~s for use** modo *m* de emprego

directly /dɪ'rektlɪ/ *adv* diretamente, (*P*) directamente; (*at once*) imediatamente, logo

director /dɪ'rektə(r)/ *n* diretor *m*, (*P*) director *m*

directory /dɪ'rektərɪ/ *n* (**telephone**) **~** lista *f* telefônica, (*P*) telefónica

dirt /dɜ:t/ *n* sujeira *f*. **~ cheap** (*colloq*) baratíssimo

dirty /'dɜ:tɪ/ *a* (**-ier, -iest**) sujo; (*word*) obsceno □ *vt/i* sujar(-se). **~ trick** golpe *m* baixo, (*P*) boa partida *f*

disability /dɪsə'bɪlətɪ/ *n* deficiência *f*

disable /dɪs'eɪbl/ *vt* incapacitar. **~d** *a* inválido, deficiente

disadvantage /dɪsəd'va:ntɪdʒ/ *n* desvantagem *f*

disagree /dɪsə'gri:/ *vi* discordar (**with** de). **~ with** (*food, climate*) não fazer bem. **~ment** *n* desacordo *m*; (*quarrel*) desintendimento *m*

disagreeable /dɪsə'gri:əbl/ *a* desagradável

disappear /dɪsə'pɪə(r)/ *vi* desaparecer. **~ance** *n* desaparecimento *m*

disappoint /dɪsə'pɔɪnt/ *vt* desapontar, decepcionar. **~ment** *n* desapontamento *m*, decepção *f*

disapprov|e /dɪsə'pru:v/ *vi* **~e (of)** desaprovar. **~al** *n* desaprovação *f*

disarm /dɪs'ɑ:m/ *vt/i* desarmar. **~ament** *n* desarmamento *m*

disast|er /dɪ'zɑ:stə(r)/ *n* desastre *m*. **~rous** *a* desastroso

disband /dɪs'bænd/ *vt/i* debandar; (*troops*) dispersar

disbelief /dɪsbɪ'li:f/ *n* incredulidade *f*

disc /dɪsk/ *n* disco *m*. **~ jockey** disc(o) jockey *m*

discard /dɪs'kɑ:d/ *vt* pôr de lado, descartar(-se) de; (*old clothes etc*) desfazer-se de

discern /dɪ'sɜ:n/ *vt* discernir. **~ible** *a* perceptível. **~ing** *a* perspicaz. **~ment** *n* discernimento *m*, perspicácia *f*

discharge[1] /dɪs'tʃɑ:dʒ/ *vt* descarregar; (*dismiss*) despedir, mandar embora; (*duty*) cumprir; (*liquid*) vazar, (*P*) deitar; (*patient*) dar alta a; (*prisoner*) absolver, pôr em liberdade; (*pus*) purgar, (*P*) deitar

discharge[2] /'dɪstʃɑ:dʒ/ *n* descarga *f*; (*dismissal*) despedimento *m*; (*of patient*) alta *f*; (*of prisoner*) absolvição *f*; (*med*) secreção *f*

disciple /dɪ'saɪpl/ *n* discípulo *m*

disciplin|e /'dɪsɪplɪn/ *n* disciplina *f* □ *vt* disciplinar; (*punish*) castigar. **~ary** *a* disciplinar

disclaim /dɪs'kleɪm/ *vt* (*jur*) repudiar; (*deny*) negar. **~er** *n* desmentido *m*

disclos|e /dɪs'kləʊz/ *vt* revelar. **~ure** /-ʒə(r)/ *n* revelação *f*

disco /'dɪskəʊ/ *n* (*pl* **-os**) (*colloq*) discoteca *f*

discolour /dɪs'kʌlə(r)/ *vt/i* descolorir(-se); (*in sunlight*) desbotar(-se)

discomfort /dɪs'kʌmfət/ *n* malestar *m*; (*lack of comfort*) desconforto *m*

disconcert /dɪskən'sɜ:t/ *vt* desconcertar. **~ing** *a* desconcertante

disconnect /dɪskə'nekt/ *vt* desligar

discontent /dɪskən'tent/ *n* descontentamento *m*. **~ed** *a* descontente

discontinue /dɪskən'tɪnju:/ *vt* descontinuar, suspender

discord /'dɪskɔ:d/ *n* discórdia *f*. ~ant /-'skɔ:dənt/ *a* discordante

discothèque /'dɪskətek/ *n* discoteca *f*

discount[1] /'dɪskaʊnt/ *n* desconto *m*

discount[2] /dɪs'kaʊnt/ *vt* descontar; (*disregard*) dar o desconto a

discourage /dɪs'kʌrɪdʒ/ *vt* desencorajar

discourte|ous /dɪs'kɜ:tɪəs/ *a* indelicado. ~sy /-sɪ/ *n* indelicadeza *f*

discover /dɪs'kʌvə(r)/ *vt* descobrir. ~y *n* descoberta *f*; (*of island etc*) descobrimento *m*

discredit /dɪs'kredɪt/ *vt* (*pt* discredited) desacreditar □ *n* descrédito *m*

discreet /dɪs'kri:t/ *a* discreto

discrepancy /dɪ'skrepənsɪ/ *n* discrepância *f*

discretion /dɪ'skreʃn/ *n* discrição *f*; (*prudence*) prudência *f*

discriminat|e /dɪs'krɪmɪneɪt/ *vt/i* discriminar. ~e against tomar partido contra, fazer discriminação contra. ~ing *a* discriminador; (*having good taste*) com discernimento *m*. ~ion /-'neɪʃn/ *n* discernimento *m*; (*bias*) discriminação *f*

discus /'dɪskəs/ *n* disco *m*

discuss /dɪ'skʌs/ *vt* discutir. ~ion /-ʃn/ *n* discussão *f*

disdain /dɪs'deɪn/ *n* desdém *m* □ *vt* desdenhar. ~ful *a* desdenhoso

disease /dɪ'zi:z/ *n* doença *f*. ~d *a* (*plant*) atacado por doença; (*person, animal*) doente

disembark /dɪsɪm'ba:k/ *vt/i* desembarcar

disembodied /dɪsɪm'bɒdɪd/ *a* desencarnado

disenchant /dɪsɪn'tʃa:nt/ *vt* desencantar. ~ment *n* desencantamento *m*

disengage /dɪsɪn'geɪdʒ/ *vt* desprender, soltar; (*mech*) desengatar

disentangle /dɪsɪn'tæŋgl/ *vt* desembaraçar, desenredar

disfavour /dɪs'feɪvə(r)/ *n* desfavor *m*, desgraça *f*

disfigure /dɪs'fɪgə(r)/ *vt* desfigurar

disgrace /dɪs'greɪs/ *n* vergonha *f*; (*disfavour*) desgraça *f* □ *vt* desonrar. ~ful *a* vergonhoso

disgruntled /dɪs'grʌntld/ *a* descontente

disguise /dɪs'gaɪz/ *vt* disfarçar □ *n* disfarce *m*. in ~ disfarçado

disgust /dɪs'gʌst/ *n* repugnância *f* □ *vt* repugnar. ~ing *a* repugnante

dish /dɪʃ/ *n* prato *m* □ *vt* ~ out (*colloq*) distribuir. ~ up servir. the ~es (*crockery*) a louça *f*

dishcloth /'dɪʃklɒθ/ *n* pano *m* de prato

dishearten /dɪs'ha:tn/ *vt* desencorajar, desalentar

dishevelled /dɪ'ʃevld/ *a* desgrenhado

dishonest /dɪs'ɒnɪst/ *a* desonesto. ~y *n* desonestidade *f*

dishonour /dɪs'ɒnə(r)/ *n* desonra *f* □ *vt* desonrar. ~able *a* desonroso

dishwasher /'dɪʃwɒʃə(r)/ *n* lavadora *f* de pratos, (P) máquina *f* de lavar louça

disillusion /dɪsɪ'lu:ʒn/ *vt* desiludir. ~ment *n* desilusão *f*

disinfect /dɪsɪn'fekt/ *vt* desinfetar, (P) desinfectar. ~ant *n* desinfetante *m*, (P) desinfectante *m*

disinherit /dɪsɪn'herɪt/ *vt* deserdar

disintegrate /dɪs'ɪntɪgreɪt/ *vt/i* desintegrar(-se)

disinterested /dɪs'ɪntrəstɪd/ *a* desinteressado

disjointed /dɪs'dʒɔɪntɪd/ *a* (*talk*) descosido, desconexo

disk /dɪsk/ *n* (*comput*) disco *m*; (*Amer*) = **disc**. ~ **drive** unidade *f* de disco

dislike /dɪs'laɪk/ *n* aversão *f*, antipatia *f* □ *vt* não gostar de, antipatizar com

dislocat|e /'dɪsləkeɪt/ *vt* (*limb*) deslocar. ~ion /-'keɪʃn/ *n* deslocação *f*

dislodge /dɪs'lɒdʒ/ *vt* desalojar

disloyal /dɪs'lɔɪəl/ *a* desleal. ~ty *n* deslealdade *f*

dismal /'dɪzməl/ *a* tristonho

dismantle /dɪs'mæntl/ *vt* desmantelar

dismay /dɪs'meɪ/ *n* consternação *f* □ *vt* consternar

dismiss /dɪs'mɪs/ *vt* despedir; (*from mind*) afastar, pôr de lado. ~al *n* despedimento *m*

dismount /dɪs'maʊnt/ *vi* desmontar

disobedien|t /dɪsə'bi:dɪənt/ *a* desobediente. ~ce *n* desobediência *f*

disobey /dɪsə'beɪ/ *vt/i* desobedecer (a)

disorder /dɪs'ɔ:də(r)/ *n* desordem *f*; (*med*) perturbações *fpl*, disfunção *f*. ~ly *a* desordenado; (*riotous*) desordeiro

disorganize /dɪs'ɔ:gənaɪz/ *vt* desorganizar

disorientate /dɪs'ɔ:rɪənteɪt/ *vt* desorientar

disown /dɪs'əʊn/ *vt* repudiar

disparaging /dɪ'spærɪdʒɪŋ/ *a* depreciativo

disparity /dɪ'spærətɪ/ *n* disparidade *f*

dispatch /dɪ'spætʃ/ *vt* despachar □ *n* despacho *m*

dispel /dɪs'pel/ *vt* (*pt* dispelled) dissipar

dispensary /dɪ'spensərɪ/ *n* dispensário *m*, farmácia *f*

dispense /dɪ'spens/ *vt* dispensar □ *vi*

~ **with** dispensar, passar sem. ~**r** /-ə(r)/ n (*container*) distribuidor m

dispers|e /dɪ'spɜːs/ vt/i dispersar (-se). ~**al** n dispersão f

dispirited /dɪ'spɪrɪtɪd/ a desanimado

displace /dɪ'spleɪs/ vt deslocar; (*take the place of*) substituir. ~**d person** deslocado m de guerra

display /dɪ'spleɪ/ vt exibir, mostrar; (*feeling*) manifestar, dar mostras de □ n exposição f; (*of computer*) apresentação f visual; (*comm*) objetos mpl expostos

displeas|e /dɪs'pliːz/ vt desagradar a. ~**ed with** descontente com. ~**ure** /'pleʒə(r)/ n desagrado m

disposable /dɪ'spəʊzəbl/ a descartável

dispos|e /dɪ'spəʊz/ vt dispor □ vi ~**e of** desfazer-se de. **well** ~**ed towards** bem disposto para com. ~**al** n (*of waste*) eliminação f. **at sb's** ~**al** à disposição de alg

disposition /dɪspə'zɪʃn/ n disposição f; (*character*) índole f

disproportionate /dɪsprə'pɔːʃənət/ a desproporcionado

disprove /dɪs'pruːv/ vt refutar

dispute /dɪ'spjuːt/ vt contestar; (*fight for, quarrel*) disputar □ n disputa f; (*industrial, pol*) conflito m. **in** ~ em questão

disqualif|y /dɪs'kwɒlɪfaɪ/ vt tornar inapto; (*sport*) desqualificar. ~**y from driving** apreender a carteira de motorista. ~**ication** /-ɪ'keɪʃn/ n desqualificação f

disregard /dɪsrɪ'gɑːd/ vt não fazer caso de □ n indiferença f (**for** por)

disrepair /dɪsrɪ'peə(r)/ n mau estado m, abandono m, degradação f

disreputable /dɪs'repjʊtəbl/ a pouco recomendável; (*in appearance*) com mau aspecto; (*in reputation*) vergonhoso, de má fama

disrepute /dɪsrɪ'pjuːt/ n descrédito m

disrespect /dɪsrɪ'spekt/ n falta f de respeito. ~**ful** a desrespeitoso, irreverente

disrupt /dɪs'rʌpt/ vt perturbar; (*plans*) transtornar; (*break up*) dividir. ~**ion** /-ʃn/ n perturbação f. ~**ive** a perturbador

dissatisf|ied /dɪ'sætɪsfaɪd/ a descontente. ~**action** /dɪsætɪs'fækʃn/ n descontentamento m

dissect /dɪ'sekt/ vt dissecar. ~**ion** /-ʃn/ n dissecação f

dissent /dɪ'sent/ vi dissentir, discordar □ n dissensão f, desacordo m

dissertation /dɪsə'teɪʃn/ n dissertação f

disservice /dɪs'sɜːvɪs/ n **do sb a** ~ prejudicar alg

dissident /'dɪsɪdənt/ a & n dissidente (mf)

dissimilar /dɪ'sɪmɪlə(r)/ a diferente

dissipate /'dɪsɪpeɪt/ vt dissipar; (*efforts, time*) desperdiçar. ~**d** a dissoluto

dissociate /dɪ'səʊʃɪeɪt/ vt dissociar, desassociar

dissolution /dɪsə'luːʃn/ n dissolução f

dissolve /dɪ'zɒlv/ vt/i dissolver(-se)

dissuade /dɪ'sweɪd/ vt dissuadir

distance /'dɪstəns/ n distância f. **from a** ~ de longe. **in the** ~ ao longe, à distância

distant /'dɪstənt/ a distante; (*relative*) afastado

distaste /dɪs'teɪst/ n aversão f. ~**ful** a desagradável

distemper /dɪ'stempə(r)/ n pintura f a têmpera; (*animal disease*) cinomose f □ vt pintar a têmpera

distend /dɪ'stend/ vt/i distender(-se)

distil /dɪ'stɪl/ vt (*pt* distilled) destilar. ~**lation** /'leɪʃn/ n destilação f

distillery /dɪ'stɪləri/ n destilaria f

distinct /dɪ'stɪŋkt/ a distinto; (*marked*) claro, nítido. ~**ion** /-ʃn/ n distinção f. ~**ive** a distintivo, característico. ~**ly** adv distintamente; (*markedly*) claramente

distinguish /dɪ'stɪŋgwɪʃ/ vt/i distinguir. ~**ed** a distinto

distort /dɪ'stɔːt/ vt distorcer; (*misrepresent*) deturpar. ~**ion** /-ʃn/ n distorção f; (*misrepresentation*) deturpação f

distract /dɪ'strækt/ vt distrair. ~**ed** a (*distraught*) desesperado, fora de si. ~**ing** a enlouquecedor. ~**ion** /-ʃn/ n distração f, (*P*) distracção f

distraught /dɪ'strɔːt/ a desesperado, fora de si

distress /dɪ'stres/ n (*physical*) dor f; (*anguish*) aflição f; (*poverty*) miséria f; (*danger*) perigo m □ vt afligir. ~**ing** a aflitivo, doloroso

distribut|e /dɪ'strɪbjuːt/ vt distribuir. ~**ion** /-'bjuːʃn/ n distribuição f. ~**or** n distribuidor m

district /'dɪstrɪkt/ n região f; (*of town*) zona f

distrust /dɪs'trʌst/ n desconfiança f □ vt desconfiar de

disturb /dɪ'stɜːb/ vt perturbar; (*move*) desarrumar; (*bother*) incomodar. ~**ance** n (*noise, disorder*) distúrbio m. ~**ed** a perturbado. ~**ing** a perturbador

disused /dɪs'juːzd/ a fora de uso, desusado, em desuso

ditch /dɪtʃ/ n fosso m □ vt (*sl: abandon*) abandonar, largar

dither /'dɪðə(r)/ vi hesitar

ditto /'dɪtəʊ/ *adv* idem

div|e /daɪv/ *vi* mergulhar; (*rush*) precipitar-se □ *n* mergulho *m*; (*of plane*) picada *f*; (*sl: place*) espelunca *f*. **~er** *n* mergulhador *m*. **~ing-board** *n* prancha *f* de saltos. **~ing-suit** *n* escafandro *m*

diverge /daɪ'vɜːdʒ/ *vi* divergir

divergent /daɪ'vɜːdʒənt/ *a* divergente

diverse /daɪ'vɜːs/ *a* diverso

diversify /daɪ'vɜːsɪfaɪ/ *vt* diversificar

diversity /daɪ'vɜːsətɪ/ *n* diversidade *f*

diver|t /daɪ'vɜːt/ *vt* desviar; (*entertain*) divertir. **~sion** /-ʃn/ *n* diversão *f*; (*traffic*) desvio *m*

divide /dɪ'vaɪd/ *vt/i* dividir(-se). **~ in two** (*branch, river, road*) bifurcar-se

dividend /'dɪvɪdend/ *n* dividendo *m*

divine /dɪ'vaɪn/ *a* divino

divinity /dɪ'vɪnətɪ/ *n* divindade *f*; (*theology*) teologia *f*

division /dɪ'vɪʒn/ *n* divisão *f*

divorce /dɪ'vɔːs/ *n* divórcio *m* □ *vt/i* divorciar(-se) de. **~d** *a* divorciado

divorcee /dɪvɔː'siː/ *n* divorciado *m*

divulge /daɪ'vʌldʒ/ *vt* divulgar

DIY *abbr see* do-it-yourself

dizz|y /'dɪzɪ/ *a* (**-ier, -iest**) tonto. **be** *or* **feel ~y** ter tonturas, sentir-se tonto. **~iness** *n* tontura *f*, vertigem *f*

do /duː/ *vt/i* (*3 sing pres* **does**, *pt* **did**, *pp* **done**) fazer; (*be suitable*) servir; (*be enough*) bastar (a); (*sl: swindle*) enganar, levar (*colloq*). **how ~ you ~?** como vai? **well done** muito bem!, (*P*) bravo!; (*culin*) bem passado. **done for** (*colloq*) liquidado (*colloq*), (*P*) anumado (*colloq*) □ *v aux* **~ you see?** vê?; **I ~ not smoke** não fumo. **don't you?, doesn't he?** *etc* não é? □ *n* (*pl* **dos** *or* **do's**) festa *f*. **~-it-yourself** *a* faça-você-mesmo. **~ away with** eliminar, suprimir. **~ in** (*sl*) matar, liquidar (*colloq*). **~ out** limpar. **~ up** (*fasten*) fechar; (*house*) renovar. **I could ~ with a cup of tea** apetecia-me uma xícara de chá. **it could ~ with a wash** precisa de uma lavagem

docile /'dəʊsaɪl/ *a* dócil

dock[1] /dɒk/ *n* doca *f* □ *vt* levar à doca □ *vi* entrar na doca. **~er** *n* estivador *m*

dock[2] /dɒk/ *n* (*jur*) banco *m* dos réus

dockyard /'dɒkjɑːd/ *n* estaleiro *m*

doctor /'dɒktə(r)/ *n* médico *m*, doutor *m*; (*univ*) doutor *m* □ *vt* (*cat*) capar; (*fig*) adulterar, falsificar

doctorate /'dɒktərət/ *n* doutorado *m*, (*P*) doutoramento *m*

doctrine /'dɒktrɪn/ *n* doutrina *f*

document /'dɒkjʊmənt/ *n* documento *m* □ *vt* documentar. **~ary** /-'mentrɪ/ *a* documental □ *n* documentário *m*

dodge /dɒdʒ/ *vt/i* esquivar(-se), furtar(-se) a □ *n* (*colloq*) truque *m*

dodgy /'dɒdʒɪ/ *a* (**-ier, -iest**) (*colloq*) delicado, difícil, embaraçoso

does /dʌz/ *see* do

doesn't /'dʌznt/ = does not

dog /dɒg/ *n* cão *m* □ *vt* (*pt* **dogged**) ir no encalço de, perseguir. **~-eared** *a* com os cantos dobrados

dogged /'dɒgɪd/ *a* obstinado, persistente

dogma /'dɒgmə/ *n* dogma *m*. **~tic** /-'mætɪk/ *a* dogmático

dogsbody /'dɒgzbɒdɪ/ *n* (*colloq*) pau-para-toda-obra *m* (*colloq*), factótum *m*

doldrums /'dɒldrəmz/ *npl* **be in the ~** estar com a neura; (*business*) estar parado

dole /dəʊl/ *vt* **~ out** distribuir □ *n* (*colloq*) auxílio *m* desemprego. **on the ~** (*colloq*) desempregado (titular de auxílio)

doleful /'dəʊlfl/ *a* tristonho, melancólico

doll /dɒl/ *n* boneca *f* □ *vt/i* **~ up** (*colloq*) embonecar(-se)

dollar /'dɒlə(r)/ *n* dólar *m*

dolphin /'dɒlfɪn/ *n* golfinho *m*

domain /dəʊ'meɪn/ *n* domínio *m*

dome /dəʊm/ *n* cúpula *f*; (*vault*) abóbada *f*

domestic /də'mestɪk/ *a* (*of home, animal, flights*) doméstico; (*trade*) interno; (*news*) nacional. **~ated** /-keɪtɪd/ *a* (*animal*) domesticado; (*person*) que gosta de trabalhos caseiros

dominant /'dɒmɪnənt/ *a* dominante

dominat|e /'dɒmɪneɪt/ *vt/i* dominar. **~ion** /-'neɪʃn/ *n* dominação *f*, domínio *m*

domineer /dɒmɪ'nɪə(r)/ *vi* **~ over** mandar (em), ser autocrático (para com). **~ing** *a* mandão, autocrático

dominion /də'mɪnjən/ *n* domínio *m*

domino /'dɒmɪnəʊ/ *n* (*pl* **-oes**) dominó *m*

donat|e /dəʊ'neɪt/ *vt* fazer doação de, doar, dar. **~ion** /-ʃn/ *n* donativo *m*

done /dʌn/ *see* do

donkey /'dɒŋkɪ/ *n* burro *m*

donor /'dəʊnə(r)/ *n* (*of blood*) doador *m*, (*P*) dador *m*

don't /dəʊnt/ = do not

doodle /'duːdl/ *vi* rabiscar

doom /duːm/ *n* ruína *f*; (*fate*) destino *m*. **be ~ed to** ser/estar condenado a. **~ed (to failure)** condenado ao fracasso

door /dɔː(r)/ *n* porta *f*

doorman /'dɔːmən/ *n* (*pl* **-men**) porteiro *m*

doormat /'dɔːmæt/ *n* capacho *m*

doorstep /'dɔːstep/ *n* degrau *m* da porta

doorway /'dɔːweɪ/ n vão m da porta, (P) entrada f

dope /dəʊp/ n (colloq) droga f; (sl: idiot) imbecil mf □ vt dopar, drogar

dormant /'dɔːmənt/ a dormente; (inactive) inativo, (P) inactivo; (latent) latente

dormitory /'dɔːmɪtrɪ/ n dormitório m; (Amer univ) residência f

dormouse /'dɔːmaʊs/ n (pl -mice) arganaz m

dos|e /dəʊs/ n dose f □ vt medicar. ~age n dosagem f; (on label) posologia f

doss /dɒs/ vi ~ (down) dormir sem conforto. ~-house n pensão f miserável, asilo m noturno, (P) nocturno. ~er n vagabundo m

dot /dɒt/ n ponto m. on the ~ no momento preciso □ vt be ~ted with estar semeado de. ~ted line linha f pontilhada

dote /dəʊt/ vi ~ on ser louco por, adorar

double /'dʌbl/ a duplo; (room, bed) de casal □ adv duas vezes mais □ n dobro m. ~s (tennis) dupla f, (P) pares mpl □ vt/i dobrar, duplicar; (fold) dobrar em dois. at the ~ a passo acelerado. ~-bass n contrabaixo m. ~ chin papada f. ~-cross vt enganar. ~-dealing n jogo m duplo. ~-decker n ônibus m, (P) autocarro m de dois andares. ~ Dutch algaraviada f, fala f incompreensível. ~ glazing (janela f de) vidro (m) duplo. doubly adv duplamente

doubt /daʊt/ n dúvida f □ vt duvidar de. ~ if or that duvidar que. ~ful a duvidoso; (hesitant) que tem dúvidas. ~less adv sem dúvida, indubitavelmente

dough /dəʊ/ n massa f

doughnut /'dəʊnʌt/ n sonho n, (P) bola f de Berlim

dove /dʌv/ n pomba f

dowdy /'daʊdɪ/ a (-ier, -iest) sem graça, sem gosto

down[1] /daʊn/ n (feathers, hair) penugem f

down[2] /daʊn/ adv (to lower place) abaixo, para baixo; (in lower place) em baixo. be ~ (level, price) descer; (sun) estar posto □ prep por (+n) (n+) abaixo. ~ the hill/street etc pelo monte/pela rua etc abaixo □ vt (colloq: knock down) jogar abaixo; (colloq: drink) esvaziar. come or go ~ descer. ~-and-out n marginal m. ~-hearted a desencorajado, desanimado. ~-to-earth a terra-a-terra invar. ~ under na Austrália. ~ with abaixo

downcast /'daʊnkɑːst/ a abatido, deprimido, desmoralizado

downfall /'daʊnfɔːl/ n queda f, ruína f

downhill /daʊn'hɪl/ adv go ~ descer; (fig) ir abaixo □ a /'daʊnhɪl/ a descer, descendente

downpour /'daʊnpɔː(r)/ n aguaceiro m forte, (P) chuvada f

downright /'daʊnraɪt/ a franco; (utter) autêntico, verdadeiro □ adv positivamente

downstairs /daʊn'steəz/ adv (at/to) em/para baixo, no/para o andar de baixo □ a /'daʊnsteəz/ (flat etc) de baixo, do andar de baixo

downstream /'daʊnstriːm/ adv rio abaixo

downtown /'daʊntaʊn/ a & adv (de, em, para) o centro da cidade. ~ Boston o centro de Boston

downtrodden /'daʊntrɒdn/ a espezinhado, oprimido

downward /'daʊnwəd/ a descendente. ~(s) adv para baixo

dowry /'daʊərɪ/ n dote m

doze /dəʊz/ vi dormitar. ~ off cochilar □ n soneca f, cochilo m

dozen /'dʌzn/ n dúzia f. ~s of (colloq) dezenas de, dúzias de

Dr abbr (Doctor) Dr

drab /dræb/ a insípido; (of colour) morto, apagado

draft[1] /drɑːft/ n rascunho m; (comm) ordem f de pagamento □ vt fazer o rascunho de; (draw up) redigir. the ~ (Amer: mil) recrutamento m

draft[2] /drɑːft/ n (Amer) = draught

drag /dræg/ vt/i (pt dragged) arrastar(-se); (river) dragar; (pull away) arrancar □ n (colloq: task) chatice f (sl); (colloq: person) estorvo m; (sl: clothes) travesti m

dragon /'drægən/ n dragão m

dragonfly /'drægənflaɪ/ n libélula f

drain /dreɪn/ vt drenar; (vegetables) escorrer; (glass, tank) esvaziar; (use up) esgotar □ vi ~ (off) escoar-se □ n cano m. ~s npl (sewers) esgotos mpl. ~age n drenagem f. ~(-pipe) cano m de esgoto. ~ing-board n escorredouro m

drama /'drɑːmə/ n arte f dramática, (play, event) drama m. ~tic /drə'mætɪk/ a dramático. ~tist /'dræmətɪst/ n dramaturgo m. ~tize /'dræmətaɪz/ vt dramatizar

drank /dræŋk/ see drink

drape /dreɪp/ vt ~ round/over dispor (tecido) em pregas à volta de or sobre. ~s npl (Amer) cortinas fpl

drastic /'dræstɪk/ a drástico, violento

draught /drɑːft/ n corrente f de ar; (naut) calado m. ~s (game) (jogo m das) damas fpl. ~ beer chope m, (P)

cerveja f à caneca, imperial f (colloq).
~y a com correntes de ar, ventoso

draughtsman /'drɑ:ftsmən/ n (pl -men) desenhista m, (P) desenhador m

draw /drɔ:/ vt (pt **drew**, pp **drawn**) puxar; (attract) atrair; (picture) desenhar; (in lottery) tirar à sorte; (line) traçar; (open curtains) abrir; (close curtains) fechar □ vi desenhar; (sport) empatar; (come) vir □ n (sport) empate m; (lottery) sorteio m. ~ **back** recuar. ~ **in** (of days) diminuir. ~ **near** aproximar-se. ~ **out** (money) levantar. ~ **up** deter-se, parar; (document) redigir; (chair) aproximar, chegar

drawback /'drɔ:bæk/ n inconveniente m, desvantagem f

drawer /drɔ:(r)/ n gaveta f

drawing /'drɔ:ɪŋ/ n desenho m. ~-**board** n prancheta f. ~-**pin** n percevejo m

drawl /drɔ:l/ n fala f arrastada

drawn /drɔ:n/ see **draw**

dread /dred/ n terror m □ vt temer

dreadful /'dredfl/ a medonho, terrível. ~**ly** adv terrivelmente

dream /dri:m/ n sonho m □ vt/i (pt **dreamed** or **dreamt**) sonhar (of com) □ a (ideal) dos seus sonhos. ~ **up** imaginar. ~**er** n sonhador m. ~**y** a sonhador; (music) romântico

dreary /'drɪərɪ/ a (-ier, -iest) tristonho; (boring) aborrecido

dredge /dredʒ/ n draga f □ vt/i dragar. ~**r** /-ə(r)/ n draga f; (for sugar) polvilhador m

dregs /dregz/ npl depósito m, sedimento m; (fig) escória f

drench /drentʃ/ vt encharcar

dress /dres/ n vestido m; (clothing) roupa f □ vt/i vestir(-se); (food) temperar; (wound) fazer curativo, (P) pensar, (P) tratar. ~ **rehearsal** ensaio m geral. ~ **up as** fantasiar-se de. **get** ~**ed** vestir-se

dresser /'dresə(r)/ n (furniture) guarda-louça m

dressing /'dresɪŋ/ n (sauce) tempero m; (bandage) curativo m, (P) penso m. ~-**gown** n roupão m. ~-**room** n (sport) vestiário m; (theat) camarim m. ~-**table** n toucador m

dressmak|er /'dresmeɪkə(r)/ n costureira f, modista f. ~**ing** n costura f

dressy /'dresɪ/ a (-ier, -iest) elegante, chique invar

drew /dru:/ see **draw**

dribble /'drɪbl/ vi pingar; (person) babar-se; (football) driblar

dried /draɪd/ a (fruit etc) seco

drier /'draɪə(r)/ n secador m

drift /drɪft/ vi ir à deriva; (pile up) amontoar-se □ n força f da corrente;

(pile) monte m; (of events) rumo m; (meaning) sentido m. ~**er** n pessoa f sem rumo

drill /drɪl/ n (tool) broca f; (training) exercício m, treino m; (routine procedure) exercícios mpl □ vt furar, perfurar; (train) treinar; (tooth) abrir □ vi treinar-se

drink /drɪŋk/ vt/i (pt **drank**, pp **drunk**) beber □ n bebida f. **a** ~ **of water** um copo de água. ~**able** a potável; (palatable) bebível. ~**er** n bebedor m. ~**ing water** água f potável

drip /drɪp/ vi (pt **dripped**) pingar □ n pingar m; (sl: person) banana mf (colloq). ~-**dry** vt deixar escorrer □ a que não precisa passar

dripping /'drɪpɪŋ/ n gordura f do assado

drive /draɪv/ vt (pt **drove**, pp **driven** /'drɪvn/) empurrar, impelir, levar; (car, animal) dirigir, conduzir, (P) guiar; (machine) acionar, (P) accionar □ vi dirigir, conduzir, (P) guiar □ n passeio m de carro; (private road) entrada f para veículos; (fig) energia f; (psych) drive m, compulsão f, impulso m; (campaign) campanha f. ~ **at** chegar a. ~ **away** (car) partir. ~ **in** (force in) enterrar. ~-**in** n (bank, cinema etc) banco m, cinema m etc em que se é atendido no carro, drive-in m. ~ **mad** (fazer) enlouquecer, pôr fora de si

drivel /'drɪvl/ n baboseira f, bobagem f

driver /'draɪvə(r)/ n condutor m; (of taxi, bus) chofer m, motorista mf

driving /'draɪvɪŋ/ n condução f. ~-**licence** n carteira f de motorista, (P) carta f de condução. ~-**school** auto-escola f, (P) escola f de condução. ~-**test** exame m de motorista, (P) de condução

drizzle /'drɪzl/ n chuvisco m □ vi chuviscar

drone /drəʊn/ n zumbido m; (male bee) zangão m □ vi zumbir; (fig) falar monotonamente

drool /dru:l/ vi babar(-se)

droop /dru:p/ vi pender, curvar-se

drop /drɒp/ n gota f; (fall) queda f; (distance) altura f de queda □ vt/i (pt **dropped**) (deixar) cair; (fall, lower) baixar. ~ (**off**) (person from car) deixar, largar. ~ **a line** escrever duas linhas (**to** a). ~ **in** passar por (**on em** casa de). ~ **off** (doze) adormecer. ~ **out** (withdraw) retirar-se; (of student) abandonar. ~-**out** n marginal mf, marginalizado m

droppings /'drɒpɪŋz/ npl excrementos mpl de animal; (of birds) cocô m (colloq), porcaria f (colloq)

dross /drɒs/ n escória f; (*refuse*) lixo m

drought /draʊt/ n seca f

drove /drəʊv/ see **drive**

drown /draʊn/ vt/i afogar(-se)

drowsy /'draʊzɪ/ a sonolento. **be or feel ~** ter vontade de dormir

drudge /drʌdʒ/ n mouro m de trabalho. **~ry** /-ərɪ/ n trabalho m penoso e monótono, estafa f

drug /drʌg/ n droga f; (*med*) medicamento m, remédio m □ vt (pt **drugged**) drogar. **~ addict** drogado m, tóxico-dependente m

drugstore /'drʌgstɔː(r)/ n (*Amer*) farmácia f que vende também sorvetes etc

drum /drʌm/ n (*mus*) tambor m; (*for oil*) barril m, tambor m. **~s** (*mus*) bateria f □ vi (pt **drummed**) tocar tambor; (*with one's fingers*) tamborilar □ vt **~ into sb** fazer entrar na cabeça de alg. **~ up** (*support*) conseguir obter; (*business*) criar. **~mer** n tambor m; (*in pop group etc*) baterista m, (P) bateria m

drunk /drʌŋk/ see **drink** □ a embriagado, bêbedo. **get ~** embebedar-se, embriagar-se □ n bêbedo m. **~ard** n alcoólico m, bêbedo m. **~en** a embriagado, bêbedo; (*habitually*) bêbedo

dry /draɪ/ a (**drier, driest**) seco; (*day*) sem chuva □ vt/i secar. **be or feel ~** ter sede. **~-clean** vt limpar a seco. **~-cleaner's** n (loja de) lavagem f a seco, lavanderia f. **~ up** (*dishes*) secar a louça f; (*of supplies*) esgotar-se. **~ness** n secura f

dual /'djuːəl/ a duplo. **~ carriageway** estrada f dividida por faixa central. **~-purpose** a com fim duplo

dub /dʌb/ vt (pt **dubbed**) (*film*) dobrar; (*nickname*) apelidar de

dubious /'djuːbɪəs/ a duvidoso; (*character, compliment*) dúbio. **feel ~ about** ter dúvidas quanto a

duchess /'dʌtʃɪs/ n duquesa f

duck /dʌk/ n pato m □ vi abaixar-se rapidamente □ vt (*head*) baixar; (*person*) batizar, pregar uma amona em. **~ling** n patinho m

duct /dʌkt/ n canal m, tubo m

dud /dʌd/ a (*sl: thing*) que não presta ou não funciona; (*sl: coin*) falso; (*sl: cheque*) sem fundos, (P) careca (*sl*)

due /djuː/ a devido; (*expected*) esperado □ adv **~ east/etc** exatamente, (P) exactamente a leste/etc □ n devido m. **~s** direitos mpl; (*of club*) cota f. **~ to** devido a, por causa de. **in ~ course** no tempo devido

duel /'djuːəl/ n duelo m

duet /djuː'et/ n dueto m

duffel /'dʌfl/ a **~ bag** saco m de lona. **~-coat** n casaco m de tecido de lã

dug /dʌg/ see **dig**

duke /djuːk/ n duque m

dull /dʌl/ a (**-er, -est**) (*boring*) enfadonho; (*colour*) morto; (*mirror*) embaçado; (*weather*) encoberto; (*sound*) surdo; (*stupid*) burro

duly /'djuːlɪ/ adv devidamente; (*in due time*) no tempo devido

dumb /dʌm/ a (**-er, -est**) mudo; (*colloq: stupid*) bronco, burro

dumbfound /dʌm'faʊnd/ vt pasmar

dummy /'dʌmɪ/ n imitação f, coisa f simulada; (*of tailor*) manequim m; (*of baby*) chupeta f

dump /dʌmp/ vt (*rubbish*) jogar fora; (*put down*) deixar cair; (*colloq: abandon*) largar □ n monte m de lixo; (*tip*) lixeira f; (*mil*) depósito m; (*colloq*) buraco m

dunce /dʌns/ n burro m. **~'s cap** orelhas fpl de burro

dune /djuːn/ n duna f

dung /dʌŋ/ n esterco m; (*manure*) estrume m

dungarees /dʌŋgə'riːz/ npl macacão m, (P) fato m de macaco

dungeon /'dʌndʒən/ n calabouço m, masmorra f

dupe /djuːp/ vt enganar □ n trouxa m

duplicate[1] /'djuːplɪkət/ n duplicado m □ a idêntico

duplicate[2] /'djuːplɪkeɪt/ vt duplicar, fazer em duplicado; (*on machine*) fotocopiar

duplicity /djuː'plɪsətɪ/ n duplicidade f

durable /'djʊərəbl/ a resistente; (*enduring*) duradouro, durável

duration /djʊ'reɪʃn/ n duração f

duress /djʊ'res/ n **under ~** sob coação f, (P) coacção f

during /'djʊərɪŋ/ prep durante

dusk /dʌsk/ n crepúsculo m, anoitecer m

dusky /'dʌskɪ/ a (**-ier, -iest**) escuro, sombrio

dust /dʌst/ n pó m, poeira f □ vt limpar o pó de; (*sprinkle*) polvilhar. **~-jacket** n sobrecapa f de livro

dustbin /'dʌstbɪn/ n lata f do lixo, (P) caixote m

duster /'dʌstə(r)/ n pano m do pó

dustman /'dʌstmən/ n (pl **-men**) lixeiro m, (P) homem m do lixo

dusty /'dʌstɪ/ a (**-ier, -iest**) poeirento, empoeirado

Dutch /dʌtʃ/ a holandês □ n (*lang*) holandês m. **~man** n holandês m. **~woman** n holandesa f. **go ~** pagar cada um a sua despesa

dutiful /'djuːtɪfl/ a cumpridor; (*showing respect*) respeitador

dut|y /'dju:tɪ/ *n* dever *m*; (*tax*) impostos *mpl*. **~ies** (*of official etc*) funções *fpl*. **off ~y** de folga. **on ~y** de serviço. **~y-free** *a* isento de impostos. **~y-free shop** free shop *m*

duvet /'dju:veɪ/ *n* edredom *m*, (*P*) edredão *m* de penas

dwarf /dwɔ:f/ *n* (*pl* **-fs**) anão *m*

dwell /dwel/ *vi* (*pt* **dwelt**) morar. **~ on** alongar-se sobre. **~er** *n* habitante. **~ing** *n* habitação *f*

dwindle /'dwɪndl/ *vi* diminuir, reduzir-se

dye /daɪ/ *vt* (*pres p* **dyeing**) tingir □ *n* tinta *f*

dying /'daɪɪŋ/ *see* **die**

dynamic /daɪ'næmɪk/ *a* dinâmico

dynamite /'daɪnəmaɪt/ *n* dinamite *f* □ *vt* dinamitar

dynamo /'daɪnəməʊ/ *n* (*pl* **-os**) dínamo *m*

dynasty /'dɪnəstɪ/ *n* dinastia *f*

dysentery /'dɪsəntrɪ/ *n* disenteria *f*

dyslex|ia /dɪs'leksɪə/ *n* dislexia *f*. **~ic** *a* disléxico

E

each /i:tʃ/ *a & pron* cada. **~ one** cada um. **~ other** um ao outro, uns aos outros. **they like ~ other** gostam um do outro/uns dos outros. **know/ love/etc ~ other** conhecer-se/amarse/etc

eager /'i:gə(r)/ *a* ansioso (**to** por), desejoso (**for** de); (*supporter*) entusiástico. **be ~ to** ter vontade de. **~ly** *adv* com impaciência, ansiosamente; (*keenly*) com entusiasmo. **~ness** *n* ansiedade *f*, desejo *m*; (*keenness*) entusiasmo *m*

eagle /'i:gl/ *n* águia *f*

ear /ɪə(r)/ *n* ouvido *m*; (*external part*) orelha *f*. **~-drum** *n* tímpano *m*. **~-ring** *n* brinco *m*

earache /'ɪəreɪk/ *n* dor *f* de ouvidos

earl /ɜ:l/ *n* conde *m*

early /'ɜ:lɪ/ (**-ier, -iest**) *adv* cedo □ *a* primeiro; (*hour*) matinal; (*fruit*) temporão; (*retirement*) antecipado. **have an ~ dinner** jantar cedo. **in ~ summer** no princípio do verão

earmark /'ɪəma:k/ *vt* destinar, reservar (**for** para)

earn /ɜ:n/ *vt* ganhar; (*deserve*) merecer

earnest /'ɜ:nɪst/ *a* sério. **in ~** a sério

earnings /'ɜ:nɪŋz/ *npl* salário *m*; (*profits*) ganhos *mpl*, lucros *mpl*

earshot /'ɪəʃɒt/ *n* **within ~** ao alcance da voz

earth /ɜ:θ/ *n* terra *f* □ *vt* (*electr*) ligar à terra. **why on ~?** por que diabo?, por

que cargas d'água? **~ly** *a* terrestre, terreno

earthenware /'ɜ:θənweə(r)/ *n* louça *f* de barro, faiança *f*

earthquake /'ɜ:θkweɪk/ *n* tremor *m* de terra, terremoto *m*

earthy /'ɜ:θɪ/ *a* terroso, térreo; (*coarse*) grosseiro

earwig /'ɪəwɪg/ *n* lacrainha *f*, (*P*) bicha-cadela *f*

ease /i:z/ *n* facilidade *f*; (*comfort*) bemestar *m* □ *vt/i* (*from pain, anxiety*) acalmar(-se); (*slow down*) afrouxar; (*slide*) deslizar. **at ~** à vontade; (*mil*) descansar. **ill at ~** pouco à vontade. **with ~** facilmente. **~ in/out** fazer entrar/sair com cuidado

easel /'i:zl/ *n* cavalete *m*

east /i:st/ *n* este *m*, leste *m*, pas-cente *m*, oriente *m*. **the E~** o Oriente □ *a* este, (de) leste, oriental □ *adv* a/para leste. **~ of** para o leste de **~erly** *a* oriental, leste, a/de leste **~ward** *a*, **~ward(s)** *adv* para leste

Easter /'i:stə(r)/ *n* Páscoa *f*. **~ egg** ovo *m* de Páscoa

eastern /'i:stən/ *a* oriental, leste

easy /'i:zɪ/ *a* (**-ier, -iest**) fácil; (*relaxed*) natural, descontraído. **take it ~** levar as coisas com calma. **~ chair** poltrona *f*. **~-going** *a* bonacheirão. **easily** *adv* facilmente

eat /i:t/ *vt/i* (*pt* **ate**, *pp* **eaten**) comer. **~ into** corroer. **~able** *a* comestível

eaves /i:vz/ *npl* beiral *m*

eavesdrop /'i:vzdrɒp/ *vi* (*pt* **-dropped**) escutar por detrás da porta

ebb /eb/ *n* vazante *f*, baixa-mar *m* □ *vi* vazar; (*fig*) declinar

EC /i:'si:/ *n* (*abbr of European Community*) CE *f*

eccentric /ɪk'sentrɪk/ *a & n* excêntrico (*m*). **~ity** /eksen'trɪsətɪ/ *n* excentricidade *f*

ecclesiastical /ɪkli:zɪ'æstɪkl/ *a* eclesiástico

echo /'ekəʊ/ *n* (*pl* **-oes**) eco *m* □ *vt/i* (*pt* **echoed**, *pres p* **echoing**) ecoar; (*fig*) repetir

eclipse /ɪ'klɪps/ *n* eclipse *m* □ *vt* eclipsar

ecolog|y /i:'kɒlədʒɪ/ *n* ecologia *f*. **~ical** /i:kə'lɒdʒɪkl/ *a* ecológico

economic /i:kə'nɒmɪk/ *a* econômico, (*P*) económico; (*profitable*) rentável. **~al** *a* econômico, (*P*) económico. **~s** *n* economia *f* política

economist /ɪ'kɒnəmɪst/ *n* economista *mf*

econom|y /ɪ'kɒnəmɪ/ *n* economia *f*. **~ize** *vt/i* economizar

ecstasy /'ekstəsɪ/ *n* êxtase *m*

ecstatic /ɪk'stætɪk/ *a* extático, extasiado

ecu /'eɪkju:/ *n* unidade *f* monetária européia

eczema /'eksɪmə/ *n* eczema *m*

edge /edʒ/ *n* borda *f*, beira *f*; (*of town*) periferia *f*, limite *m*; (*of knife*) fio *m* □ *vt* debruar □ *vi* (*move*) avançar pouco a pouco

edging /'edʒɪŋ/ *n* borda *f*, (*P*) bordadura *f*

edgy /'edʒɪ/ *a* irritadiço, nervoso

edible /'edɪbl/ *a* comestível

edict /'i:dɪkt/ *n* édito *m*

edifice /'edɪfɪs/ *n* edifício *m*

edit /'edɪt/ *vt* (*pt* edited) (*newspaper*) dirigir; (*text*) editar

edition /ɪ'dɪʃn/ *n* edição *f*

editor /'edɪtə(r)/ *n* (*of newspaper*) diretor *m*, (*P*) director *m*, editor *m* responsável; (*of text*) organizador *m* de texto. **the ~ (in chief)** redator-chefe *m*, (*P*) redactor-chefe *m*. **~ial** /edɪ'tɔ:rɪəl/ *a & n* editorial (*m*)

educat|e /'edʒʊkeɪt/ *vt* instruir; (*mind, public*) educar. **~ed** *a* instruído; educado. **~ion** /-'keɪʃn/ *n* educação *f*; (*schooling*) ensino *m*. **~ional** /'keɪʃənl/ *a* educativo, pedagógico

EEC /i:i:'si:/ *n* (*abbr of European Economic Community*) CEE *f*

eel /i:l/ *n* enguia *f*

eerie /'ɪərɪ/ *a* (**-ier, -iest**) arrepiante, misterioso

effect /ɪ'fekt/ *n* efeito *m* □ *vt* efetuar, (*P*) efectuar. **come into ~** entrar em vigor. **in ~** na realidade. **take ~** ter efeito

effective /ɪ'fektɪv/ *a* eficaz, eficiente; (*striking*) sensacional; (*actual*) efetivo, (*P*) efectivo. **~ly** *adv* (*efficiently*) eficazmente; (*strikingly*) de forma sensacional; (*actually*) efetivamente, (*P*) efectivamente. **~ness** *n* eficácia *f*

effeminate /ɪ'femɪnət/ *a* efeminado, afeminado

effervescent /efə'vesnt/ *a* efervescente

efficien|t /ɪ'fɪʃnt/ *a* eficiente, eficaz. **~cy** *n* eficiência *f*. **~tly** *adv* eficientemente

effigy /'efɪdʒɪ/ *n* efígie *f*

effort /'efət/ *n* esforço *m*. **~less** *a* fácil, sem esforço

effrontery /ɪ'frʌntərɪ/ *n* desfaçatez *f*

effusive /ɪ'fju:sɪv/ *a* efusivo, expansivo

e.g. /i:'dʒi:/ *abbr* por ex

egg[1] /eg/ *n* ovo *m*. **~-cup** *n* copinho *m* para ovo quente, oveiro *m*. **~-plant** *n* beringela *f*

egg[2] /eg/ *vt* **~ on** (*colloq*) incitar

eggshell /'egʃel/ *n* casca *f* de ovo

ego /'egəʊ/ *n* (*pl* -os) ego *m*, eu *m*. **~ism** *n* egoísmo *m*. **~ist** *n* egoísta *mf*. **~tism** *n* egotismo *m*. **~tist** *n* egotista *mf*

Egypt /'i:dʒɪpt/ *n* Egito *m*. **~ian** /ɪ'dʒɪpʃn/ *a & n* egípcio (*m*)

eh /eɪ/ *int* (*colloq*) hã?

eiderdown /'aɪdədaʊn/ *n* edredão *m*, edredom *m*

eight /eɪt/ *a & n* oito (*m*). **eighth** /eɪtθ/ *a & n* oitavo (*m*)

eighteen /eɪ'ti:n/ *a & n* dezoito (*m*). **~th** *a & n* décimo-oitavo (*m*)

eight|y /'eɪtɪ/ *a & n* oitenta (*m*). **~ieth** *a & n* octogésimo (*m*)

either /'aɪðə(r)/ *a & pron* um e outro; (*with negative*) nem um nem outro; (*each*) cada □ *adv* também não □ *conj* **~ ... or** ou ... ou; (*with negative*) nem ... nem

ejaculate /ɪ'dʒækjʊleɪt/ *vt/i* ejacular; (*exclaim*) exclamar

eject /ɪ'dʒekt/ *vt* expelir; (*expel*) expulsar, despejar

elaborate[1] /ɪ'læbərət/ *a* elaborado, rebuscado, minucioso

elaborate[2] /ɪ'læbəreɪt/ *vt* elaborar □ *vi* entrar em pormenores. **~ on** estender-se sobre

elapse /ɪ'læps/ *vi* decorrer

elastic /ɪ'læstɪk/ *a & n* elástico (*m*). **~ band** elástico *m*

elat|ed /ɪ'leɪtɪd/ *a* radiante, exultante. **~ion** *n* exultação *f*

elbow /'elbəʊ/ *n* cotovelo *m*

elder[1] /'eldə(r)/ *a* mais velho. **~s** *npl* pessoas *fpl* mais velhas

elder[2] /'eldə(r)/ *n* (*tree*) sabugueiro *m*

elderly /'eldəlɪ/ *a* idoso. **the ~** as pessoas de idade

eldest /'eldɪst/ *a & n* o mais velho (*m*)

elect /ɪ'lekt/ *vt* eleger □ *a* eleito. **~ion** /-kʃn/ *n* eleição *f*

electric /ɪ'lektrɪk/ *a* elétrico, (*P*) eléctrico. **~al** *a* elétrico, (*P*) eléctrico

electrician /ɪlek'trɪʃn/ *n* eletricista *m*, (*P*) electricista *m*

electricity /ɪlek'trɪsətɪ/ *n* eletricidade *f*, (*P*) electricidade *f*

electrify /ɪ'lektrɪfaɪ/ *vt* eletrificar, (*P*) electrificar; (*fig: excite*) eletrizar, (*P*) electrizar

electrocute /ɪ'lektrəkju:t/ *vt* eletrocutar, (*P*) electrocutar

electronic /ɪlek'trɒnɪk/ *a* eletrônico, (*P*) electrónico. **~s** *n* eletrônica *f*, (*P*) electrónica *f*

elegan|t /'elɪgənt/ *a* elegante. **~ce** *n* elegância *f*. **~tly** *adv* elegantemente, com elegância

element /'elɪmənt/ *n* elemento *m*; (*of heater etc*) resistência *f*. **~ary** /-'mentrɪ/ *a* elementar; (*school*) primário

elephant /'elɪfənt/ *n* elefante *m*

elevat|e /'elɪveɪt/ *vt* elevar. **~ion** /'veɪʃn/ *n* elevação *f*

elevator /'elɪveɪtə(r)/ *n* (*Amer: lift*) elevador *m*, ascensor *m*

eleven /ɪ'levn/ *a* & *n* onze (*m*). ~**th** *a* & *n* décimo primeiro (*m*). **at the** ~**th hour** à última hora

elf /elf/ *n* (*pl* **elves**) elfo *m*, duende *m*

elicit /ɪ'lɪsɪt/ *vt* extrair, obter

eligible /'elɪdʒəbl/ *a* (*for office*) idôneo, (*P*) idóneo (**for** para); (*desirable*) aceitável. **be** ~ **for** (*entitled to*) ter direito a

eliminat|e /ɪ'lɪmɪneɪt/ *vt* eliminar. ~**ion** /-'neɪʃn/ *n* eliminação *f*

élite /eɪ'liːt/ *n* elite *f*

ellip|se /ɪ'lɪps/ *n* elipse *f*. ~**tical** *a* elíptico

elm /elm/ *n* olmo *m*, ulmeiro *m*

elocution /elə'kjuːʃn/ *n* elocução *f*

elongate /'iːlɒŋgeɪt/ *vt* alongar

elope /ɪ'ləʊp/ *vi* fugir. ~**ment** *n* fuga *f* (de amantes), (*P*) (de amorosos)

eloquen|t /'eləkwənt/ *a* eloqüente, (*P*) eloquente. ~**ce** *n* eloqüência *f*, (*P*) eloquência *f*

else /els/ *adv* mais. **everybody** ~ todos os outros. **nobody** ~ mais ninguém. **nothing** ~ nada mais. **or** ~ ou então, senão. **somewhere** ~ noutro lado qualquer. ~**where** *adv* noutro lado

elude /ɪ'luːd/ *vt* escapar a; (*a question*) evadir

elusive /ɪ'luːsɪv/ *a* (*person*) esquivo, difícil de apanhar; (*answer*) evasivo

emaciated /ɪ'meɪʃɪeɪtɪd/ *a* emaciado, macilento

emancipat|e /ɪ'mænsɪpeɪt/ *vt* emancipar. ~**ion** /-'peɪʃn/ *n* emancipação *f*

embalm /ɪm'baːm/ *vt* embalsamar

embankment /ɪm'bæŋkmənt/ *n* (*of river*) dique *m*; (*of railway*) terrapleno *m*, talude *m*, (*P*) aterro *m*

embargo /ɪm'baːgəʊ/ *n* (*pl* -**oes**) embargo *m*

embark /ɪm'baːk/ *vt/i* embarcar. ~ **on** (*business etc*) embarcar em, meter-se em (*colloq*); (*journey*) começar

embarrass /ɪm'bærəs/ *vt* embaraçar, confundir. ~**ment** *n* embaraço *m*, atrapalhação *f*

embassy /'embəsɪ/ *n* embaixada *f*

embellish /ɪm'belɪʃ/ *vt* embelezar, enfeitar. ~**ment** *n* embelezamento *m*, enfeite *m*

embezzle /ɪm'bezl/ *vt* desviar (fundos). ~**ment** *n* desfalque *m*

embitter /ɪm'bɪtə(r)/ *vt* (*person*) amargurar; (*situation*) azedar

emblem /'embləm/ *n* emblema *m*

embod|y /ɪm'bɒdɪ/ *vt* encarnar; (*include*) incorporar, incluir. ~**iment** *n* personificação *f*

emboss /ɪm'bɒs/ *vt* (*metal*) gravar em relevo; (*paper*) gofrar

embrace /ɪm'breɪs/ *vt/i* abraçar(-se); (*offer, opportunity*) acolher □ *n* abraço *m*

embroider /ɪm'brɔɪdə(r)/ *vt* bordar. ~**y** *n* bordado *m*

embryo /'embrɪəʊ/ *n* (*pl* -**os**) embrião *m*. ~**nic** /-'ɒnɪk/ *a* embrionário

emerald /'emərəld/ *n* esmeralda *f*

emerge /ɪ'mɜːdʒ/ *vi* emergir, surgir

emergency /ɪ'mɜːdʒənsɪ/ *n* emergência *f*; (*urgent case*) urgência *f*. ~ **exit** saída *f* de emergência. **in an** ~ em caso de urgência

emigrant /'emɪgrənt/ *n* emigrante *mf*

emigrat|e /'emɪgreɪt/ *vi* emigrar. ~**ion** /-'greɪʃn/ *n* emigração *f*

eminen|t /'emɪnənt/ *a* eminente. ~**tly** *adv* eminentemente

emi|t /ɪ'mɪt/ *vt* (*pt* **emitted**) emitir. ~**ssion** /-ʃn/ *n* emissão *f*

emotion /ɪ'məʊʃn/ *n* emoção *f*. ~**al** *a* (*person, shock*) emotivo; (*speech, scene*) emocionante

emperor /'empərə(r)/ *n* imperador *m*

emphasis /'emfəsɪs/ *n* ênfase *f*. **lay** ~ **on** pôr em relevo

emphasize /'emfəsaɪz/ *vt* enfatizar, sublinhar; (*syllable, word*) acentuar

emphatic /ɪm'fætɪk/ *a* enfático; (*manner*) enérgico. ~**ally** *adv* enfaticamente

empire /'empaɪə(r)/ *n* império *m*

employ /ɪm'plɔɪ/ *vt* empregar. ~**ee** /emplɔɪ'iː/ *n* empregado *m*. ~**er** *n* patrão *m*. ~**ment** *n* emprego *m*. ~**ment agency** agência *f* de empregos

empower /ɪm'paʊə(r)/ *vt* autorizar (**to do** a fazer)

empress /'emprɪs/ *n* imperatriz *f*

empt|y /'emptɪ/ *a* vazio; (*promise*) falso □ *vt/i* esvaziar(-se). **on an** ~**y stomach** com o estômago vazio, em jejum. ~**ies** *npl* garrafas *fpl* vazias. ~**iness** *n* vazio *m*

emulate /'emjʊleɪt/ *vt* imitar, rivalizar com, emular com

emulsion /ɪ'mʌlʃn/ *n* emulsão *f*

enable /ɪ'neɪbl/ *vt* ~ **sb to do** permitir a alg fazer

enact /ɪ'nækt/ *vt* (*jur*) decretar; (*theat*) representar

enamel /ɪ'næml/ *n* esmalte *m* □ *vt* (*pt* **enamelled**) esmaltar

enamoured /ɪ'næməd/ *a* ~ **of** enamorado de, apaixonado por

encase /ɪn'keɪs/ *vt* encerrar (**in** em); (*cover*) revestir (**in** de)

enchant /ɪn'tʃaːnt/ *vt* encantar. ~**ing** *a* encantador. ~**ment** *n* encantamento *m*

encircle /ɪn'sɜːkl/ *vt* cercar, rodear

enclose /ɪn'kləʊz/ *vt* (*land*) cercar; (*with letter*) enviar incluso/junto. ~**d** *a* (*space*) fechado; (*with letter*) anexo, incluso, junto

enclosure /ɪnˈkləʊʒə(r)/ n cercado m, recinto m; (with letter) documento m anexo

encompass /ɪnˈkʌmpəs/ vt abranger

encore /ɒŋˈkɔː(r)/ int & n bis (m)

encounter /ɪnˈkaʊntə(r)/ vt encontrar, deparar com □ n encontro m

encourage /ɪnˈkʌrɪdʒ/ vt encorajar. ~ment n encorajamento m

encroach /ɪnˈkrəʊtʃ/ vi ~ on (land) invadir; (time) abusar de

encumb|er /ɪnˈkʌmbə(r)/ vt estorvar; (burden) sobrecarregar. ~rance n estorvo m, empecilho m; (burden) ônus m, (P) ónus m, encargo m

encyclopedia /ɪnˌsaɪkləˈpiːdɪə/ n enciclopédia f. ~ic a enciclopédico

end /end/ n fim m; (farthest part) extremo m, ponta f □ vt/i acabar, terminar. ~ up (arrive finally) ir parar (in a/em). ~ up doing acabar por fazer. in the ~ por fim. no ~ of (colloq) muito, enorme, imenso. on ~ (upright) em pé; (consecutive) a fio, de seguida

endanger /ɪnˈdeɪndʒə(r)/ vt pôr em perigo

endear|ing /ɪnˈdɪərɪŋ/ a cativante. ~ment n palavra f meiga; (act) carinho m

endeavour /ɪnˈdevə(r)/ n esforço m □ vi esforçar-se (to por)

ending /ˈendɪŋ/ n fim m; (of word) terminação f

endless /ˈendlɪs/ a interminável; (times) sem conta; (patience) infinito

endorse /ɪnˈdɔːs/ vt (document) endossar; (action) aprovar. ~ment n (auto) averbamento m

endow /ɪnˈdaʊ/ vt doar. ~ment n doação f

endur|e /ɪnˈdjʊə(r)/ vt suportar □ vi durar. ~able a suportável. ~ance n resistência f

enemy /ˈenəmɪ/ n & a inimigo (m)

energetic /enəˈdʒetɪk/ a enérgico

energy /ˈenədʒɪ/ n energia f

enforce /ɪnˈfɔːs/ vt aplicar

engage /ɪnˈɡeɪdʒ/ vt (staff) contratar; (mech) engrenar □ vi ~ in envolver-se em, lançar-se em. ~d a noivo; (busy) ocupado. ~ment n noivado m; (undertaking, appointment) compromisso m; (mil) combate m

engender /ɪnˈdʒendə(r)/ vt engendrar, produzir, causar

engine /ˈendʒɪn/ n motor m; (of train) locomotiva f

engineer /endʒɪˈnɪə(r)/ n engenheiro m □ vt engenhar. ~ing n engenharia f

England /ˈɪŋɡlənd/ n Inglaterra f

English /ˈɪŋɡlɪʃ/ a inglês □ n (lang) inglês m. the ~ os ingleses mpl.

~man n inglês m. ~-speaking a de lingua inglesa. ~woman n inglesa f

engrav|e /ɪnˈɡreɪv/ vt gravar. ~-ing n gravura f

engrossed /ɪnˈɡrəʊst/ a absorto (in em)

engulf /ɪnˈɡʌlf/ vt engolfar, tragar

enhance /ɪnˈhaːns/ vt aumentar; (heighten) realçar

enigma /ɪˈnɪɡmə/ n enigma m. ~tic /enɪɡˈmætɪk/ a enigmático

enjoy /ɪnˈdʒɔɪ/ vt gostar de; (benefit from) gozar de. ~ o.s. divertir-se. ~able a agradável. ~ment n prazer m

enlarge /ɪnˈlaːdʒ/ vt/i aumentar. ~ upon alargar-se sobre. ~ment n ampliação f

enlighten /ɪnˈlaɪtn/ vt esclarecer. ~ment n esclarecimento m, elucidação f

enlist /ɪnˈlɪst/ vt recrutar; (fig) aliciar, granjear □ vi alistar-se

enliven /ɪnˈlaɪvn/ vt animar

enmity /ˈenmətɪ/ n inimizade f

enormous /ɪˈnɔːməs/ a enorme

enough /ɪˈnʌf/ a, adv & n bastante (m), suficiente (m) □ int basta!, chega! have ~ of estar farto de

enquir|e /ɪnˈkwaɪə(r)/ vt/i perguntar, indagar. ~e about informar-se de, pedir informações sobre. ~y n pedido m de informações

enrage /ɪnˈreɪdʒ/ vt enfurecer, enraivecer

enrich /ɪnˈrɪtʃ/ vt enriquecer

enrol /ɪnˈrəʊl/ vt/i (pt enrolled) inscrever(-se); (schol) matricular(-se). ~ment n inscrição f; (schol) matrícula f

ensemble /ɒnˈsɒmbl/ n conjunto m

ensign /ˈensən/ n pavilhão m; (officer) guarda-marinha m

ensu|e /ɪnˈsjuː/ vi seguir-se. ~ing a decorrente

ensure /ɪnˈʃʊə(r)/ vt assegurar. ~ that assegurar-se de que

entail /ɪnˈteɪl/ vt acarretar

entangle /ɪnˈtæŋɡl/ vt emaranhar, enredar

enter /ˈentə(r)/ vt (room, club etc) entrar em; (register) registar; (data) entrar com □ vi entrar (into em). ~ for inscrever-se em

enterprise /ˈentəpraɪz/ n empresa f, empreendimento m; (fig) iniciativa f

enterprising /ˈentəpraɪzɪŋ/ a empreendedor

entertain /entəˈteɪn/ vt entreter; (guests) receber; (ideas) alimentar, nutrir. ~er n artista mf. ~ment n entretenimento m; (performance) espetáculo m, (P) espectáculo m

enthral /ɪn'θrɔːl/ vt (pt **enthralled**) fascinar

enthuse /ɪn'θjuːz/ vi ~ **over** entusiasmar-se por

enthusias|m /ɪn'θjuːzɪæzm/ n entusiasmo m. ~t n entusiasta mf. ~tic /-'æstɪk/ a entusiástico. ~tically /-'æstɪkəlɪ/ adv entusiasticamente

entice /ɪn'taɪs/ vt atrair. ~ **to do** induzir a fazer. ~ment n tentação f, engodo m

entire /ɪn'taɪə(r)/ a inteiro. ~ly adv inteiramente

entirety /ɪn'taɪərətɪ/ n **in its** ~ por inteiro, na (sua) totalidade

entitle /ɪn'taɪtl/ vt dar direito. ~d a (book) intitulado. **be** ~**d to sth** ter direito a alg coisa. ~ment n direito m

entity /'entətɪ/ n entidade f

entrance /'entrəns/ n entrada f (**to** para); (right to enter) admissão f

entrant /'entrənt/ n (sport) concorrente mf; (in exam) candidato m

entreat /ɪn'triːt/ vt rogar, suplicar. ~y n rogo m, súplica f

entrench /ɪn'trentʃ/ vt (mil) entrincheirar; (fig) fincar

entrust /ɪn'trʌst/ vt confiar

entry /'entrɪ/ n entrada f; (on list) item m; (in dictionary) verbete m. ~ **form** ficha f de inscrição, (P) boletim m de inscrição. **no** ~ entrada proibida

enumerate /ɪ'njuːməreɪt/ vt enumerar

envelop /ɪn'veləp/ vt (pt **enveloped**) envolver

envelope /'envələʊp/ n envelope m, sobrescrito m

enviable /'envɪəbl/ a invejável

envious /'envɪəs/ a invejoso. **be** ~ **of** ter inveja de. ~ly adv invejosamente, com inveja

environment /ɪn'vaɪərənmənt/ n meio m; (ecological) meio-ambiente m. ~al /-'mentl/ a do meio; (ecological) do ambiente

envisage /ɪn'vɪzɪdʒ/ vt encarar; (foresee) prever

envoy /'envɔɪ/ n enviado m

envy /'envɪ/ n inveja f □ vt invejar, ter inveja de

enzyme /'enzaɪm/ n enzima f

epic /'epɪk/ n epopéia f □ a épico

epidemic /epɪ'demɪk/ n epidemia f

epilep|sy /'epɪlepsɪ/ n epilepsia f. ~tic /'leptɪk/ a & n epiléptico (m)

episode /'epɪsəʊd/ n episódio m

epitaph /'epɪtɑːf/ n epitáfio m

epithet /'epɪθet/ n epíteto m

epitom|e /ɪ'pɪtəmɪ/ n (summary) epítome m; (embodiment) modelo m. ~ize vt (fig) representar, encarnar; (summarize) resumir

epoch /'iːpɒk/ n época f. ~**-making** a que marca uma época

equal /'iːkwəl/ a & n igual (m) □ vt (pt **equalled**) igualar, ser igual a. ~ **to** (task) à altura de. ~ity /iːˈkwɒlətɪ/ n igualdade f. ~ly adv igualmente; (similarly) de igual modo

equalize /'iːkwəlaɪz/ vt/i igualar; (sport) empatar

equanimity /ekwə'nɪmətɪ/ n equanimidade f, serenidade f

equate /ɪ'kweɪt/ vt equacionar (**with** com); (treat as equal) equiparar (**with** a)

equation /ɪ'kweɪʒn/ n equação f

equator /ɪ'kweɪtə(r)/ n equador m. ~ial /ekwə'tɔːrɪəl/ a equatorial

equilibrium /iːkwɪ'lɪbrɪəm/ n equilíbrio m

equip /ɪ'kwɪp/ vt (pt **equipped**) equipar (**with** com), munir (**with** de). ~ment n equipamento m

equitable /'ekwɪtəbl/ a eqüitativo, (P) equitativo

equity /'ekwətɪ/ n eqüidade f, (P) equidade f

equivalent /ɪ'kwɪvələnt/ a & n eqüivalente (m), (P) equivalente (m)

equivocal /ɪ'kwɪvəkl/ a equívoco

era /'ɪərə/ n era f, época f

eradicate /ɪ'rædɪkeɪt/ vt erradicar, suprimir

erase /ɪ'reɪz/ vt apagar. ~r /-ə(r)/ n borracha f (de apagar)

erect /ɪ'rekt/ a ereto, (P) erecto □ vt erigir. ~ion /-ʃn/ n ereção f, (P) erecção f; (building) construção f, edifício m

ero|de /ɪ'rəʊd/ vt corroer. ~sion /ɪ'rəʊʒn/ n erosão f

erotic /ɪ'rɒtɪk/ a erótico

err /ɜː(r)/ vi (pt **erred**) errar

errand /'erənd/ n recado m

erratic /ɪ'rætɪk/ a errático, irregular; (person) variável, imprevisível

erroneous /ɪ'rəʊnɪəs/ a errôneo, (P) erróneo, errado

error /'erə(r)/ n erro m

erudit|e /'eruːdaɪt/ a erudito. ~ion /-'dɪʃn/ n erudição f

erupt /ɪ'rʌpt/ vi (war, fire) irromper; (volcano) entrar em erupção. ~ion /-ʃn/ n erupção f

escalat|e /'eskəleɪt/ vt/i intensificar (-se); (of prices) subir em espiral. ~ion /'leɪʃn/ n escalada f

escalator /'eskəleɪtə(r)/ n escada f rolante

escapade /eskə'peɪd/ n peripécia f

escape /ɪ'skeɪp/ vi escapar-se □ vt escapar a □ n fuga f; (of prisoner) evasão f, fuga f. ~ **from sb** escapar de alguém. ~ **to** fugir para. **have a lucky** or **narrow** ~ escapar por um tris

escapism /ɪˈskeɪpɪzəm/ n escapismo m

escort[1] /ˈeskɔːt/ n escolta f; (of woman) cavalheiro m, acompanhante m

escort[2] /ɪˈskɔːt/ vt escoltar; (accompany) acompanhar

escudo /esˈkjuːdəʊ/ n (pl -os) escudo m

Eskimo /ˈeskɪməʊ/ n (pl -os) esquimó mf

especial /ɪˈspeʃl/ a especial. ~ly adv especialmente

espionage /ˈespɪənaːʒ/ n espionagem f

espouse /ɪˈspaʊz/ vt (a cause etc) abraçar

espresso /eˈspressəʊ/ n (pl -os) (coffee) expresso m

essay /ˈeseɪ/ n ensaio m; (schol) redação f, (P) redacção f

essence /ˈesns/ n essência f

essential /ɪˈsenʃl/ a essencial □ n the ~s o essencial m. ~ly adv essencialmente

establish /ɪˈstæblɪʃ/ vt estabelecer; (business, state) fundar; (prove) provar, apurar. ~ment n estabelecimento m; (institution) instituição f. the E~ment o Establishment m, a classe f dirigente

estate /ɪˈsteɪt/ n propriedade f; (possessions) bens mpl; (inheritance) herança f. ~ agent agente m imobiliário. (housing) ~ conjunto m habitacional. ~ car perua f

esteem /ɪˈstiːm/ vt estimar □ n estima f

estimate[1] /ˈestɪmət/ n cálculo m, avaliação f; (comm) orçamento m, estimativa f

estimat|e[2] /ˈestɪmeɪt/ vt calcular, estimar. ~ion /-ˈmeɪʃn/ n opinião f

estuary /ˈestʃʊərɪ/ n estuário m

etc abbr = et cetera /ɪtˈsetərə/ etc

etching /ˈetʃɪŋ/ n água-forte f

eternal /ɪˈtɜːnl/ a eterno

eternity /ɪˈtɜːnətɪ/ n eternidade f

ethic /ˈeθɪk/ n ética f. ~s ética f. ~al a ético

ethnic /ˈeθnɪk/ a étnico

etiquette /ˈetɪket/ n etiqueta f

etymology /etɪˈmɒlədʒɪ/ n etimologia f

eulogy /ˈjuːlədʒɪ/ n elogio m

euphemism /ˈjuːfəmɪzəm/ n eufemismo m

euphoria /juːˈfɔːrɪə/ n euforia f

Europe /ˈjʊərəp/ n Europa f. ~an /-ˈpɪən/ a & n europeu (m)

euthanasia /juːθəˈneɪzɪə/ n eutanásia f

evacuat|e /ɪˈvækjʊeɪt/ vt evacuar. ~ion /-ˈeɪʃn/ n evacuação f

evade /ɪˈveɪd/ vt evadir, esquivarse a

evaluate /ɪˈvæljʊeɪt/ vt avaliar

evangelical /iːvænˈdʒelɪkl/ a evangélico

evaporat|e /ɪˈvæpəreɪt/ vt/i evaporar(-se). ~ed milk leite m evaporado. ~ion /-ˈreɪʃn/ n evaporação f

evasion /ɪˈveɪʒn/ n evasão f

evasive /ɪˈveɪsɪv/ a evasivo

eve /iːv/ n véspera f

even /ˈiːvn/ a regular; (surface) liso, plano; (amounts) igual; (number) par □ vt/i ~ up igualar(-se), acertar □ adv mesmo. ~ better ainda melhor. get ~ with ajustar contas com. ~ly adv uniformemente; (amounts) em partes iguais

evening /ˈiːvnɪŋ/ n entardecer m, anoitecer m; (whole evening) serão m. ~ class aula f à noite (para adultos). ~ dress traje m de cerimónia, (P) trajo m de cerimónia or de rigor; (woman's) vestido m de noite

event /ɪˈvent/ n acontecimento m. in the ~ of no caso de. ~ful a movimentado, memorável

eventual /ɪˈventʃʊəl/ a final. ~ity /-ˈælətɪ/ n eventualidade f. ~ly adv por fim; (in future) eventualmente

ever /ˈevə(r)/ adv jamais; (at all times) sempre. do you ~ go? você já foi alguma vez?, vais alguma vez? the best I ~ saw o melhor que já vi. ~ since adv desde então □ prep desde □ conj desde que. ~ so (colloq) muitíssimo, tão. hardly ~ quase nunca

evergreen /ˈevəgriːn/ n sempre-verde f, planta f de folhas persistentes □ a persistente

everlasting /ˈevəlaːstɪŋ/ a eterno

every /ˈevrɪ/ a cada. ~ now and then de vez em quando, volta e meia. ~ one cada um. ~ other day dia sim dia não, de dois em dois dias. ~ three days de três em três dias

everybody /ˈevrɪbɒdɪ/ pron todo mundo, todos

everyday /ˈevrɪdeɪ/ a cotidiano, (P) quotidiano, diário; (common) do dia a dia, vulgar

everyone /ˈevrɪwʌn/ pron todo mundo, todos

everything /ˈevrɪθɪŋ/ pron tudo

everywhere /ˈevrɪweə(r)/ adv (position) em todo lugar, em toda parte; (direction) a todo lugar, a toda parte

evict /ɪˈvɪkt/ vt expulsar, despejar. ~ion /-ʃn/ n despejo m

evidence /ˈevɪdəns/ n evidência f; (proof) prova f; (testimony) testemunho m, depoimento m. ~ of sinal de. give ~ testemunhar. in ~ em evidência

evident /ˈevɪdənt/ a evidente. ~ly adv evidentemente

evil /'i:vl/ *a* mau □ *n* mal *m*
evo|ke /ɪ'vəuk/ *vt* evocar. ~**cative** /ɪ'vɒkətɪv/ *a* evocativo
evolution /i:və'lu:ʃn/ *n* evolução *f*
evolve /ɪ'vɒlv/ *vi* evolucionar, evoluir □ *vt* desenvolver, produzir
ex- /eks/ *pref* ex-
exacerbate /ɪg'zæsəbeɪt/ *vt* exacerbar
exact /ɪg'zækt/ *a* exato, (*P*) exacto □ *vt* exigir (**from** de). ~**ing** *a* exigente; (*task*) difícil. ~**ly** *adv* exatamente, (*P*) exactamente
exaggerat|e /ɪg'zædʒəreɪt/ *vt/i* exagerar. ~**ion** /-'reɪʃn/ *n* exagero *m*
exam /ɪg'zæm/ *n* (*colloq*) exame *m*
examination /ɪgzæmɪ'neɪʃn/ *n* exame *m*; (*jur*) interrogatório *m*
examine /ɪg'zæmɪn/ *vt* examinar; (*witness etc*) interrogar. ~**r** /-ə(r)/ *n* examinador *m*
example /ɪg'za:mpl/ *n* exemplo *m*. **for** ~ por exemplo. **make an** ~ **of** castigar para servir de exemplo
exasperat|e /ɪg'zæspəreɪt/ *vt* exasperar. ~**ion** /-'reɪʃn/ *n* exaspero *m*
excavat|e /'ekskəveɪt/ *vt* escavar; (*uncover*) desenterrar. ~**ion** /-'veɪʃn/ *n* escavação *f*
exceed /ɪk'si:d/ *vt* exceder; (*speed limit*) ultrapassar, exceder
excel /ɪk'sel/ *vi* (*pt* **excelled**) distinguir-se □ *vt* superar, ultrapassar
excellen|t /'eksələnt/ *a* excelente. ~**ce** *n* excelência *f*. ~**tly** *adv* excelentemente
except /ɪk'sept/ *prep* exceto, (*P*) excepto, fora □ *vt* excetuar, (*P*) exceptuar. ~ **for** a não ser, menos, salvo. ~**ing** *prep* à exceção de, (*P*) à excepção de. ~**ion** /-ʃn/ *n* exceção *f*, (*P*) excepção *f*. **take** ~**ion to** (*object to*) achar inaceitável; (*be offended by*) achar ofensivo
exceptional /ɪk'sepʃənl/ *a* excepcional. ~**ly** *adv* excepcionalmente
excerpt /'eksɜ:pt/ *n* trecho *m*, excerto *m*
excess[1] /ɪk'ses/ *n* excesso *m*
excess[2] /'ekses/ *a* excedente, em excesso. ~ **fare** excesso *m*, suplemento *m*. ~ **luggage** excesso *m* de peso
excessive /ɪk'sesɪv/ *a* excessivo. ~**ly** *adv* excessivamente
exchange /ɪks'tʃemdʒ/ *vt* trocar □ *n* troca *f*; (*of currency*) câmbio *m*. (**telephone**) ~ central *f* telefônica, (*P*) telefónica. ~ **rate** taxa *f* de câmbio
excise /'eksaɪz/ *n* imposto *m* (indireto, (*P*) indirecto)
excit|e /ɪk'saɪt/ *vt* excitar; (*rouse*) despertar; (*enthuse*) entusiasmar. ~**able** *a* excitável. ~**ed** *a* excitado. **get** ~**ed** excitar-se, entusiasmar-se. ~**ement** *n* excitação *f*. ~**ing** *a* excitante, emocionante

exclaim /ɪk'skleɪm/ *vi* exclamar
exclamation /eksklə'meɪʃn/ *n* exclamação *f*. ~ **mark** ponto *m* de exclamação
exclu|de /ɪk'sklu:d/ *vt* excluir. ~**ding** *prep* excluído. ~**sion** /ɪk'sklu:ʒn/ *n* exclusão *f*
exclusive /ɪk'sklu:sɪv/ *a* (*rights etc*) exclusivo; (*club etc*) seleto, (*P*) selecto; (*news item*) (em) exclusivo. ~ **of** sem incluir. ~**ly** *adv* exclusivamente
excruciating /ɪk'skru:ʃieɪtɪŋ/ *a* excruciante, atroz
excursion /ɪk'skɜ:ʃn/ *n* excursão *f*
excus|e[1] /ɪk'skju:z/ *vt* desculpar. ~**e me!** desculpe!, com licença! ~**e from** (*exempt*) dispensar de. ~**able** *a* desculpável
excuse[2] /ɪk'skju:s/ *n* desculpa *f*
ex-directory /eksdɪ'rektərɪ/ *a* que não vem no anuário, (*P*) na lista
execute /'eksɪkju:t/ *vt* executar
execution /eksɪ'kju:ʃn/ *n* execução *f*
executive /ɪg'zekjutɪv/ *a & n* executivo (*m*)
exemplary /ɪg'zemplərɪ/ *a* exemplar
exemplify /ɪg'zemplɪfaɪ/ *vt* exemplificar, ilustrar
exempt /ɪg'zempt/ *a* isento (**from** de) □ *vt* dispensar, eximir. ~**ion** /-ʃn/ *n* isenção *f*
exercise /'eksəsaɪz/ *n* exercício *m* □ *vt* (*powers, restraint etc*) exercer; (*dog*) levar para passear □ *vi* fazer exercício. ~ **book** caderno *m*
exert /ɪg'zɜ:t/ *vt* empregar, exercer. ~ **o.s.** esforçar-se, fazer um esforço. ~**ion** /-ʃn/ *n* esforço *m*
exhaust /ɪg'zɔ:st/ *vt* esgotar □ *n* (*auto*) (tubo de) escape *m*. ~**ed** *a* esgotado, exausto. ~**ion** /-stʃən/ *n* esgotamento *m*, exaustão *f*
exhaustive /ɪg'zɔ:stɪv/ *a* exaustivo, completo
exhibit /ɪg'zɪbɪt/ *vt* exibir, mostrar; (*thing, collection*) expor □ *n* objeto *m*, (*P*) objecto *m* exposto
exhibition /eksɪ'bɪʃn/ *n* exposição *f*; (*act of showing*) demonstração *f*
exhilarat|e /ɪg'zɪləreɪt/ *vt* regozijar; (*invigorate*) animar, estimular. ~**ion** /-'reɪʃn/ *n* animação *f*, alegria *f*
exhort /ɪg'zɔ:t/ *vt* exortar
exile /'eksaɪl/ *n* exílio *m*; (*person*) exilado *m* □ *vt* exilar, desterrar
exist /ɪg'zɪst/ *vi* existir. ~**ence** *n* existência *f*. **be in** ~**ence** existir
exit /'eksɪt/ *n* saída *f*
exonerate /ɪg'zɒnəreɪt/ *vt* exonerar
exorbitant /ɪg'zɔ:bɪtənt/ *a* exorbitante
exorcize /'eksɔ:saɪz/ *vt* esconjurar, exorcisar
exotic /ɪg'zɒtɪk/ *a* exótico

expan|d /ɪk'spænd/ *vt/i* expandir(-se); (*extend*) estender(-se), alargar(-se); (*gas, liquid, metal*) dilatar(-se). **~sion** /ɪk'spænʃn/ *n* expansão *f*; (*extension*) alargamento *m*; (*of gas etc*) dilatação *f*

expanse /ɪk'spæns/ *n* extensão *f*

expatriate /eks'pætrɪət/ *a & n* expatriado (*m*)

expect /ɪk'spekt/ *vt* esperar; (*suppose*) crer, supor; (*require*) contar com, esperar; (*baby*) esperar. **~ to do** contar fazer. **~ation** /ekspek'teɪʃn/ *n* expectativa *f*

expectan|t /ɪk'spektənt/ *a* **~t mother** gestante *f*. **~cy** *n* expectativa *f*

expedient /ɪk'spiːdɪənt/ *a* oportuno □ *n* expediente *m*

expedition /ekspr'dɪʃn/ *n* expedição *f*

expel /ɪk'spel/ *vt* (*pt* **expelled**) expulsar; (*gas, poison etc*) expelir

expend /ɪk'spend/ *vt* despender. **~able** *a* descartável

expenditure /ɪk'spendɪtʃə(r)/ *n* despesa *f*, gasto *m*

expense /ɪk'spens/ *n* despesa *f*; (*cost*) custo *m*. **at sb's** ~ à custa de alg. **at the** ~ **of** (*fig*) à custa de

expensive /ɪk'spensɪv/ *a* caro, dispendioso; (*tastes, habits*) de luxo

experience /ɪk'spɪərɪəns/ *n* experiência *f* □ *vt* experimentar; (*feel*) sentir. **~d** *a* experiente

experiment /ɪk'sperɪmənt/ *n* experiência *f* □ *vi* /ɪk'sperɪment/ fazer uma experiência. **~al** /-'mentl/ *a* experimental

expert /'eksp3ːt/ *a & n* perito (*m*). **~ly** *adv* com perícia, habilmente

expertise /eksp3ː'tiːz/ *n* perícia *f*, competência *f*

expir|e /ɪk'spaɪə(r)/ *vi* expirar. **~y** *n* fim *m* de prazo, expiração *f*

expl|ain /ɪk'splem/ / *vt* explicar. **~anation** /eksplə'neɪʃn/ *n* explicação *f*. **~anatory** /ɪk'splænətrɪ/ *a* explicativo

expletive /ɪk'spliːtɪv/ *n* imprecação *f*, praga *f*

explicit /ɪk'splɪsɪt/ *a* explícito

explo|de /ɪk'spləʊd/ *vt/i* (fazer) explodir. **~sion** /ɪk'spləʊʒn/ *n* explosão *f*. **~sive** *a & n* explosivo (*m*)

exploit[1] /'eksplɔɪt/ *n* façanha *f*

exploit[2] /ɪk'splɔɪt/ *vt* explorar. **~ation** /eksplɔɪ'teɪʃn/ *n* exploração *f*

exploratory /ɪk'splɒrətrɪ/ *a* exploratório; (*talks*) preliminar

explor|e /ɪk'splɔː(r)/ *vt* explorar; (*fig*) examinar. **~ation** /eksplə'reɪʃn/ *n* exploração *f*. **~er** *n* explorador *m*

exponent /ɪk'spəʊnənt/ *n* (*person*) expoente *mf*; (*math*) expoente *m*

export[1] /ɪk'spɔːt/ *vt* exportar. **~er** *n* exportador *m*

export[2] /'ekspɔːt/ *n* exportação *f*. **~s** *npl* exportações *fpl*

expos|e /ɪk'spəʊz/ *vt* expor; (*disclose*) revelar; (*unmask*) desmascarar. **~ure** /-ʒə(r)/ *n* exposição *f*; (*cold*) frio *m*

expound /ɪk'spaʊnd/ *vt* explanar, expor

express[1] /ɪk'spres/ *a* expresso, categórico □ *adv* (por) expresso □ *n* (*train*) rápido *m*, expresso *m*. **~ly** *adv* expressamente

express[2] /ɪk'spres/ *vt* exprimir. **~ion** /-ʃn/ *n* expressão *f*. **~ive** *a* expressivo

expulsion /ɪk'spʌlʃn/ *n* expulsão *f*

exquisite /'ekskwɪzɪt/ *a* requintado

extempore /ek'stempərɪ/ *a* improvisado □ *adv* de improviso, sem preparação prévia

exten|d /ɪk'stend/ *vt* (*stretch*) estender; (*enlarge*) aumentar, ampliar; (*prolong*) prolongar; (*grant*) oferecer □ *vi* (*stretch*) estender-se; (*in time*) prolongar-se. **~sion** /ɪk'stenʃn/ *n* (*incl phone*) extensão *f*; (*of deadline*) prorrogação *f*; (*building*) anexo *m*

extensive /ɪk'stensɪv/ *a* extenso; (*damage, study*) vasto. **~ly** *adv* muito

extent /ɪk'stent/ *n* extensão *f*; (*degree*) medida *f*. **to some** ~ até certo ponto, em certa medida. **to such an** ~ **that** a tal ponto que

exterior /ɪk'stɪərɪə(r)/ *a & n* exterior (*m*)

exterminat|e /ɪk'stɜːmmeɪt/ *vt* exterminar. **~ion** /'neɪʃn/ *n* exterminação *f*, extermínio *m*

external /ɪk'stɜːnl/ *a* externo. **~ly** *adv* exteriormente

extinct /ɪk'stɪŋkt/ *a* extinto. **~ion** /-ʃn/ *n* extinção *f*

extinguish /ɪk'stɪŋgwɪʃ/ *vt* extinguir, apagar. **~er** *n* extintor *m*

extol /ɪk'stəʊl/ *vt* (*pt* **extolled**) exaltar, elogiar, louvar

extort /ɪk'stɔːt/ *vt* extorquir (**from** a). **~ion** /-ʃn/ *n* extorsão *f*

extortionate /ɪk'stɔːʃənət/ *a* exorbitante

extra /'ekstrə/ *a* extra, adicional □ *adv* extra, excepcionalmente. **~ strong** extra-forte □ *n* extra *m*; (*cine, theat*) extra *mf*, figurante *mf*. **~ time** (*football*) prorrogação *f*

extra- /'ekstrə/ *pref* extra-

extract[1] /ɪk'strækt/ *vt* extrair; (*promise, tooth*) arrancar; (*fig*) obter. **~ion** /-ʃn/ *n* extração *f*, (*P*) extracção *f*; (*descent*) origem *f*

extract[2] /'ekstrækt/ *n* extrato *m*, (*P*) extracto *m*

extradit|e /'ekstrədaɪt/ *vt* extraditar. **~ion** /-'dɪʃn/ *n* extradição *f*

extramarital /ekstrə'mærɪtl/ a extraconjugal, extramatrimonial

extraordinary /ɪk'strɔːdnrɪ/ a extraordinário

extravagan|t /ɪk'strævəgənt/ a extravagante; (wasteful) esbanjador. ~ce n extravagância f; (wastefulness) esbanjamento m

extrem|e /ɪk'striːm/ a & n extremo (m). ~ely adv extremamente. ~ist n extremista mf

extremity /ɪk'stremətɪ/ n extremidade f

extricate /'ekstrɪkeɪt/ vt desembaraçar, livrar

extrovert /'ekstrəvɜːt/ n extrovertido m

exuberan|t /ɪg'zjuːbərənt/ a exuberante. ~ce n exuberância f

exude /ɪg'zjuːd/ vt (charm etc) destilar, ressumar, (P) transpirar

exult /ɪg'zʌlt/ vi exultar

eye /aɪ/ n olho m □ vt (pt eyed, pres p eyeing) olhar. **keep an ~ on** vigiar. **see ~ to ~** concordar inteiramente. ~-opener n revelação f. ~-shadow n sombra f

eyeball /'aɪbɔːl/ n globo m ocular

eyebrow /'aɪbraʊ/ n sobrancelha f

eyelash /'aɪlæʃ/ n pestana f

eyelid /'aɪlɪd/ n pálpebra f

eyesight /'aɪsaɪt/ n vista f

eyesore /'aɪsɔː(r)/ n monstruosidade f, horror m

eyewitness /'aɪwɪtnɪs/ n testemunha f ocular

F

fable /'feɪbl/ n fábula f

fabric /'fæbrɪk/ n tecido m; (structure) edifício m

fabricat|e /'fæbrɪkeɪt/ vt fabricar; (invent) urdir, inventar. ~ion /-'keɪʃn/ n fabrico m; (invention) invenção f

fabulous /'fæbjʊləs/ a fabuloso

façade /fə'saːd/ n fachada f

face /feɪs/ n face f, cara f, rosto m; (expression) face f; (grimace) careta f; (of clock) mostrador m □ vt (look towards) encarar; (confront) enfrentar □ vi (be opposite) estar de frente para. ~ **up to** enfrentar. ~ **to face** cara a cara, frente a frente. **in the ~ of** em vista de. **on the ~ of it** a julgar pelas aparências. **pull ~s** fazer caretas. ~-**cloth** n toalha f de rosto, (P) toalhete m de rosto. ~-**lift** n cirurgia f plástica do rosto. ~-**pack** n máscara de beleza f

faceless /'feɪslɪs/ a (fig) anônimo, (P) anónimo

facet /'fæsɪt/ n faceta f

facetious /fə'siːʃəs/ a faceto; (pej) engraçadinho (colloq pej)

facial /'feɪʃl/ a facial

facile /'fæsaɪl/ a fácil; (superficial) superficial

facilitate /fə'sɪlɪteɪt/ vt facilitar

facilit|y /fə'sɪlətɪ/ n facilidade f. ~ies (means) facilidades fpl; (installations) instalações fpl

facing /'feɪsɪŋ/ n revestimento m

facsimile /fæk'sɪməlɪ/ n fac-símile m

fact /fækt/ n fato m, (P) facto m. **in ~, as a matter of ~** na realidade

faction /'fækʃn/ n facção f

factor /'fæktə(r)/ n fator m, (P) factor m

factory /'fæktərɪ/ n fábrica f

factual /'fæktʃʊəl/ a concreto, real

faculty /'fækltɪ/ n faculdade f

fad /fæd/ n capricho m, mania f; (craze) moda f

fade /feɪd/ vt/i (colour) desbotar; (sound) diminuir; (disappear) apagar(-se)

fag /fæg/ n (colloq: chore) estafa f; (sl: cigarette) cigarro m. ~ged a estafado

fail /feɪl/ vt/i falhar; (in an examination) reprovar; (omit, neglect) deixar de; (comm) falir □ n **without ~** sem falta

failing /'feɪlɪŋ/ n deficiência f □ prep na falta de, à falta de

failure /'feɪljə(r)/ n fracasso m, (P) falhanço m; (of engine) falha f; (of electricity) falta f; (person) fracassado m.

faint /feɪnt/ a (-er, -est) (indistinct) apagado; (weak) fraco; (giddy) tonto □ vi desmaiar □ n desmaio m. ~-**hearted** a tímido. ~ly adv vagamente. ~ness n debilidade f; (indistinctness) apagado m

fair[1] /feə(r)/ n feira f. ~-**ground** n parque m de diversões, (P) largo m de feira

fair[2] /feə(r)/ a (-er, -est) (of hair) louro; (weather) bom; (moderate quality) razoável; (just) justo. ~ **play** jogo m limpo, fair-play m. ~ly adv razoavelmente. ~ness n justiça f

fairy /'feərɪ/ n fada f. ~ **story**, ~ **tale** conto m de fadas

faith /feɪθ/ n fé f; (religion) religião f; (loyalty) lealdade f. **in good ~** de boa fé, (P) à boa fé. ~-**healer** n curandeiro m

faithful /'feɪθfl/ a fiel. ~ly adv fielmente. **yours ~ly** atenciosamente. ~ness n fidelidade f

fake /feɪk/ n (thing) imitação f; (person) impostor m □ a falsificado □ vt falsificar; (pretend) simular, fingir

falcon /'fɔːlkən/ n falcão m

fall /fɔːl/ vi (pt fell, pp fallen) cair □ n quedas f; (Amer: autumn) outono m.

~s *npl* (*waterfall*) queda-d'água *f*. ~
back bater em retirada. ~ **back
on** recorrer a. ~ **behind** atrasar-se
(**with** em). ~ **down** *or* **off** cair. ~ **flat**
falhar, não resultar. ~ **flat on one's
face** estatelar-se. ~ **for** (*a trick*) cair
em, deixar-se levar por; (*colloq: a person*) apaixonar-se por, ficar caído por
(*colloq*). ~ **in** (*roof*) ruir; (*mil*) ali-
nhar-se, pôr-se em forma. ~ **out** brigar, (*P*) zangar-se (**with** com). ~-**out**
n poeira *f* radioativa, (*P*) radioactiva.
~ **through** (*of plans*) falhar

fallac|y /'fæləsɪ/ *n* falácia *f*, engano *m*.
~**ious** /fə'leɪʃəs/ *a* errôneo

fallen /'fɔːlən/ *see* **fall**

fallible /'fæləbl/ *a* falível

fallow /'fæləʊ/ *a* (*of ground*) de pou-
sio; (*uncultivated*) inculto

false /fɔːls/ *a* falso. ~ **teeth**. ~**ly** *adv*
falsamente. ~**ness** *n* falsidade *f*

falsehood /'fɔːlshʊd/ *n* falsidade *f*,
mentira *f*

falsify /'fɔːlsɪfaɪ/ *vt* (*pt* -**fied**) falsificar; (*a story*) deturpar

falter /'fɔːltə(r)/ *vi* vacilar; (*of the
voice*) hesitar

fame /feɪm/ *n* fama *f*. ~**d** *a* afamado

familiar /fə'mɪlɪə(r)/ *a* familiar; (*intimate*) íntimo. **be** ~ **with** estar familiarizado com

familiarity /fəmɪlɪ'ærɪtɪ/ *n* familiari-
dade *f*

familiarize /fə'mɪlɪəraɪz/ *vt* familia-
rizar (**with/to** com); (*make well
known*) tornar conhecido

family /'fæməlɪ/ *n* família *f*. ~ **doctor**
médico *m* da família. ~ **tree** árvore *f*
genealógica

famine /'fæmɪn/ *n* fome *f*

famished /'fæmɪʃt/ *a* esfomeado,
faminto. **be** ~ (*colloq*) estar morren-
do de fome, (*P*) estar a morrer de
fome

famous /'feɪməs/ *a* famoso

fan[1] /fæn/ *n* (*in the hand*) leque *m*;
(*mechanical*) ventilador *m*, (*P*)
ventoínha *f* □ *vt* (*pt* **fanned**) abanar;
(*a fire; fig*) atiçar □ *vi* ~ **out** abrir-se
em leque. ~ **belt** correia *f* da ventoí-
nhas

fan[2] /fæn/ *n* (*colloq*) fã *mf*. ~ **mail**
correio *m* de fãs

fanatic /fə'nætɪk/ *n* fanático *m*. ~**al** *a*
fanático. ~**ism** /-sɪzəm/ *n* fanatismo
m

fanciful /'fænsɪfl/ *a* fantasioso, fantasista

fancy /'fænsɪ/ *n* fantasia *f*; (*liking*)
gosto *m* □ *a* extravagante, fantástico;
(*of buttons etc*) de fantasia; (*of prices*)
exorbitante □ *vt* imaginar; (*colloq:
like*) gostar de; (*colloq: want*)
apetecer. **it took my** ~ gostei disso,

(*P*) deu-me no gosto. **a passing** ~ um
entusiasmo passageiro. ~ **dress** traje
m fantasia, (*P*) trajo *m* de fantasia

fanfare /'fænfeə(r)/ *n* fanfarra *f*

fang /fæŋ/ *n* presa *f*, dente *m* canino

fantastic /fæn'tæstɪk/ *a* fantástico

fantas|y /'fæntəsɪ/ *n* fantasia *f*. ~**ize**
vt fantasiar, imaginar

far /fɑː(r)/ *adv* longe; (*much, very*)
muito □ *a* distante, longínquo; (*end,
side*) outro. ~ **away**, ~ **off** ao longe.
as ~ **as** (*up to*) até. **as** ~ **as I know**
tanto quanto saiba. **the F~ East** o
Extremo-Oriente *m*. ~-**away** *a* distante, longínquo. ~-**fetched** *a* forçado; (*unconvincing*) pouco plausível.
~-**reaching** *a* de grande alcance

farc|e /fɑːs/ *n* farsa *f*. ~**ical** *a* de farsa;
ridículo

fare /feə(r)/ *n* preço *m* da passagem;
(*in taxi*) tarifa *f*, preço *m* da corrida;
(*passenger*) passageiro *m*; (*food*) comida *f* □ *vi* (*get on*) dar-se

farewell /feə'wel/ *int* & *n* adeus (*m*)

farm /fɑːm/ *n* quinta *f*, fazenda *f* □ *vt*
cultivar □ *vi* ser fazendeiro, (*P*)
lavrador. ~ **out** (*of work*) delegar a
tarefeiros. ~-**hand** *n* trabalhador *m*
rural. ~**er** *n* fazendeiro *m*, (*P*) lavrador *m*. ~**ing** *n* agricultura *f*, lavoura
f

farmhouse /'fɑːmhaʊs/ *n* casa *f* da
fazenda, (*P*) quinta

farmyard /'fɑːmjɑːd/ *n* quintal de fazenda *m*, (*P*) pátio *m* de quinta

farth|er /'fɑːðə(r)/ *adv* mais longe □ *a*
mais distante. ~**est** *adv* mais longe □
a o mais distante

fascinat|e /'fæsɪneɪt/ *vt* fascinar.
~**ion** /-'neɪʃn/ *n* fascínio *m*, fas-
cinação *f*

fascis|t /'fæʃɪst/ *n* fascista *mf*. ~**m**
/-zəm/ *n* fascismo *m*

fashion /'fæʃn/ *n* moda *f*; (*manner*)
maneira *f* □ *vt* amoldar, (*P*) moldar.
~**able** *a* na moda, (*P*) à moda.
~**ably** *adv* na moda, (*P*) à moda

fast[1] /fɑːst/ *a* (-**er**, -**est**) rápido; (*colour*)
fixo, que não desbota □ *adv* depressa;
(*firmly*) firmemente. **be** ~ (*of clock*)
adiantar-se, estar adiantado. ~
asleep profundamente adormecido,
ferrado no sono. ~ **food** *n* fast-food *f*

fast[2] /fɑːst/ *vi* jejuar □ *n* jejum *m*

fasten /'fɑːsn/ *vt/i* prender; (*door, window*) fechar(-se); (*seat-belt*) apertar.
~**er**, ~**ing** *ns* fecho *m*

fastidious /fə'stɪdɪəs/ *a* exigente

fat /fæt/ *n* gordura *f* □ *a* (**fatter, fat-
test**) gordo. ~**ness** *n* gordura *f*

fatal /'feɪtl/ *a* fatal. ~ **injuries** feri-
mentos *mpl* mortais. ~**ity** /fə'tælətɪ/
n fatalidade *f*. ~**ly** *adv* fatalmente,
mortalmente

fate /feɪt/ n (*destiny*) destino *m*; (*one's lot*) destino *m*, sorte *f*. ~**ful** a fatídico

fated /'feɪtɪd/ a predestinado; (*doomed*) condenado (**to**, a)

father /'fɑːðə(r)/ n pai *m* □ vt gerar. ~**-in-law** n (*pl* ~**s-in-law**) sogro *m*. ~**ly** a paternal

fathom /'fæðəm/ n braça *f* □ vt ~ (**out**) (*comprehend*) compreender

fatigue /fə'tiːɡ/ n fadiga *f* □ vt fatigar

fatten /'fætn/ vt/i engordar. ~**ing** a que engorda

fatty /'fætɪ/ a (**-ier, -iest**) gorduroso; (*tissue*) adiposo

fault /fɔːlt/ n defeito *m*, falha *f*; (*blame*) falta *f*, culpa *f*; (*geol*) falha *f*. **at** ~ culpado. **it's your** ~ é culpa sua. ~**less** a impecável. ~**y** a defeituoso

favour /'feɪvə(r)/ n favor *m* □ vt favorecer; (*prefer*) preferir. **do sb a** ~ fazer um favor a alg. ~**able** a favorável. ~**ably** adv favoravelmente

favourit|e /'feɪvərɪt/ a & n favorito (*m*). ~**ism** /-ɪzəm/ n favoritismo *m*

fawn[1] /fɔːn/ n cervo *m* novo □ a (*colour*) castanho claro

fawn[2] /fɔːn/ vi ~ **on** adular, bajular

fax /fæks/ n fax *m*, fac-símile *m* □ vt mandar um fax. ~ **machine** fax *m*

fear /fɪə(r)/ n medo *m*, receio *m*, temor *m*; (*likelihood*) perigo *m* □ vt recear, ter medo de. **for** ~ **of/that** com medo de/que. ~**ful** a (*terrible*) medonho; (*timid*) medroso, receoso. ~**less** a destemido, intrépido

feasib|le /'fiːzəbl/ a factível, praticável; (*likely*) plausível. ~**ility** /-'bɪlətɪ/ n possibilidade *f*, (*plausibility*) plausibilidade *f*

feast /fiːst/ n festim *m*; (*relig; fig*) festa *f* □ vt/i festejar; (*eat and drink*) banquetear-se. ~ **on** regalar-se com

feat /fiːt/ n feito *m*, façanha *f*

feather /'feðə(r)/ n pena *f*, pluma *f*

feature /'fiːtʃə(r)/ n feição *f*, traço *m*; (*quality*) característica *f*; (*film*) longa metragem *f*, (*article*) artigo *m* em destaque □ vt representar; (*film*) ter como protagonista a □ vi figurar

February /'febrʊərɪ/ n Fevereiro *m*

fed /fed/ see **feed** □ a **be** ~ **up** estar farto (*colloq*) (**with** de)

federa|l /'fedərəl/ a federal. ~**tion** /-'reɪʃn/ n federação *f*

fee /fiː/ n preço *m*. ~(**s**) (*of doctor, lawyer etc*) honorários *mpl*; (*member's subscription*) quota *f*; (*univ*) (*P*) propinas *fpl*. (**enrolment/registration**) matrícula *f* **school** ~**s** mensalidades *fpl* escolares, (*P*) mensalidades *fpl*

feeble /'fiːbl/ a (**-er, -est**) débil, fraco. ~**-minded** a débil mental, (*P*) deficiente

feed /fiːd/ vt (*pt* **fed**) alimentar, dar de

comer a; (*suckle*) alimentar; (*supply*) alimentar, abostecer □ vi alimentar-se □ n comida *f*, (*breast-feeding*) mamada *f*; (*mech*) alimentação *f*

feedback /'fiːdbæk/ n reação *f*, (*P*) reacção *f*; (*electr*) regeneração *f*

feel /fiːl/ vt (*pt* **felt**) sentir; (*touch*) apalpar, tatear □ vi (*tired, lonely etc*) sentir-se. ~ **hot/thirsty** ter calor/sede. ~ **as if** ter a impressão (de) que. ~ **like** ter vontade de

feeler /'fiːlə(r)/ n antena *f*

feeling /'fiːlɪŋ/ n sentimento *m*; (*physical*) sensação *f*

feet /fiːt/ see **foot**

feign /feɪn/ vt fingir

feline /'fiːlaɪn/ a felino

fell[1] /fel/ vt abater, derrubar

fell[2] /fel/ see **fall**

fellow /'feləʊ/ n companheiro *m*, camarada *m*; (*of society, college*) membro *m*; (*colloq*) cara *m*, (*P*) tipo *m* (*colloq*). ~**-traveller** n companheiro *m* de viagem. ~**-ship** n companheirismo *m*, camaradagem *f*, (*group*) associação *f*

felt[1] /felt/ n feltro *m*

felt[2] /felt/ see **feel**

female /'fiːmeɪl/ a (*animal etc*) fêmea *f*; (*voice, sex etc*) feminino □ n mulher *f*; (*animal*) fêmea *f*

feminin|e /'femənɪn/ a & n feminino (*m*). ~**ity** /-'nɪnətɪ/ n feminilidade *f*

feminist /'femɪnɪst/ n feminista *mf*

fenc|e /fens/ n tapume *m*, cerca *f* □ vt cercar □ vi esgrimir. ~**er** n esgrimista *mf*. ~**ing** n esgrima *f*, (*fences*) tapume *m*

fend /fend/ vi ~ **for o.s.** defender-se, virar-se (*colloq*), governar-se □ vt ~ **off** defender-se de

fender /'fendə(r)/ n guarda-fogo *m*; (*Amer: mudguard*) pára-lama *m*, guarda-lama *m*, (*P*) pára-choques *m*

fennel /'fenl/ n (*herb*) funcho *m*, erva-doce *f*

ferment[1] /fə'ment/ vt/i fermentar; (*excite*) excitar. ~**ation** /fɜːmen-'teɪʃn/ n fermentação *f*

ferment[2] /'fɜːment/ n fermento *m*; (*fig*) efervescência *f*

fern /fɜːn/ n feto *m*

feroc|ious /fə'rəʊʃəs/ a feroz. ~**ity** /-'rɒsətɪ/ n ferocidade *f*

ferret /'ferɪt/ n furão *m* □ vi (*pt* **ferreted**) caçar com furões □ vt ~ **out** desenterrar

ferry /'ferɪ/ n barco *m* de travessia, ferry(-boat) *m* □ vt transportar

fertil|e /'fɜːtaɪl/ a fértil, fecundo. ~**ity** /fə'tɪlətɪ/ n fertilidade *f*, fecundidade *f*. ~**ize** /-əlaɪz/ vt fertilizar, fecundar

fertilizer /'fɜːtəlaɪzə(r)/ n adubo *m*, fertilizante *m*

fervent /'fɜ:vənt/ a fervoroso
fervour /'fɜ:və(r)/ n fervor m, ardor m
fester /'festə(r)/ vt/i infectar; (fig) envenenar
festival /'festɪvl/ n festival m; (relig) festa f
festiv|e /'festɪv/ a festivo. ~e season periodo m das festas. ~ity /fes'tɪvətɪ/ n festividade f, regozijo m. ~ities festas fpl, festividades fpl
festoon /fe'stu:n/ vt engrinaldar
fetch /fetʃ/ vt (go for) ir buscar; (bring) trazer; (be sold for) vender-se por, render
fetching /'fetʃɪŋ/ a atraente
fête /feɪt/ n festa f or feira f de caridade ao ar livre □ vt festejar
fetish /'fetɪʃ/ n fetiche m, ídolo m; (obsession) mania f
fetter /'fetə(r)/ vt agrilhoar. ~s npl ferros mpl, grilhões mpl, grilhetas fpl
feud /fju:d/ n discórdia f, inimizade f. ~al a feudal
fever /'fi:və(r)/ n febre f. ~ish a febril
few /fju:/ a & n poucos (mpl). ~ books poucos livros. they are ~ são poucos. a ~ a & n alguns (mpl). a good ~, quite a ~ bastantes. ~er a & n menos (de). they were ~er eram menos numerosos. ~est a & n o menor número (de)
fiancé /fɪ'ɒnseɪ/ n noivo m. ~e n noiva f
fiasco /fɪ'æskəʊ/ n (pl -os) fiasco m
fib /fɪb/ n lorota f, cascata f, peta f, (P) mentira f □ vi (pt fibbed)
fibre /'faɪbə(r)/ n fibra f
fibreglass /'faɪbəɡlɑ:s/ n fibra f de vidro
fickle /'fɪkl/ a leviano, inconstante
fiction /'fɪkʃn/ n ficção f. (works of) ~ romances mpl, obras fpl de ficção. ~al a de ficção, fictício
fictitious /fɪk'tɪʃəs/ a fictício
fiddle /'fɪdl/ n (colloq) violino m; (sl: swindle) trapaça f □ vi (sl) trapacear (sl) □ vt (sl: falsify) falsificar, cozinhar (sl). ~ with (colloq) brincar com, mexer em, (P) estar a brincar com, estar a (re)mexer em. ~r /-ə(r)/ n (colloq) violinista m/f
fidelity /fɪ'delətɪ/ n fidelidade f
fidget /'fɪdʒɪt/ vi (pt fidgeted) estar irrequieto, remexer-se. ~ with mexer em. ~y a irrequieto; (impatient) impaciente
field /fi:ld/ n campo m □ vt/i (cricket) (estar pronto para) apanhar ou interceptar a bola. ~-day n grande dia m. ~-glasses npl binóculo m. F~ Marshal marechal-de-campo m
fieldwork /'fi:ldwɜ:k/ n trabalho m de campo; (mil) fortificação f de campanha

fiend /fi:nd/ n diabo m, demônio m, (P) demónio m. ~ish a diabólico
fierce /fɪəs/ a (-er, -est) feroz; (storm, attack) violento; (heat) intenso, abrasador. ~ness n ferocidade f; (of storm, attack) violência f; (of heat) intensidade f
fiery /'faɪərɪ/ a (-ier, -iest) ardente; (temper, speech) inflamado
fifteen /fɪf'ti:n/ a & n quinze (m). ~th a & n décimo quinto (m)
fifth /fɪfθ/ a & n quinto (m)
fift|y /'fɪftɪ/ a & n cinqüenta (m), (P) cinquenta (m). ~y-~y a meias. ~ieth a & n qüinquagésimo (m), (P) quinquagésimo (m)
fig /fɪɡ/ n figo m. ~-tree n figueira f
fight /faɪt/ vi (pt fought) lutar, combater □ vt lutar contra, combater □ n luta f; (quarrel, brawl) briga f. ~ over sth lutar por alg coisa. ~ shy of esquivar-se de, fugir de. ~er n lutador m; (mil) combatente mf; (plane) caça m. ~ing n combate m
figment /'fɪɡmənt/ n ~ of the imagination fruto m or produto m da imaginação
figurative /'fɪɡjərətɪv/ a figurado. ~ly adv em sentido figurado
figure /'fɪɡə(r)/ n (number) algarismo m; (diagram, body) figura f. ~s npl (arithmetic) contas fpl, aritmética f □ vt imaginar, supor □ vi (appear) figurar (in em). ~ of speech figura f de retórica. ~ out compreender. ~-head n figura f de proa; (pej: person) testa-de-ferro m, chefe m nominal
filament /'fɪləmənt/ n filamento m
fil|e¹ /faɪl/ n (tool) lixa f, lima f □ vt lixar, limar. ~ings npl limalha f
fil|e² /faɪl/ n fichário m, (P) dossier m; (box, drawer) fichário m, (P) ficheiro m; (comput) arquivo m (line) fila f □ vt arquivar □ vi ~e (past) desfilar, marchar em fila. ~e in/out entrar/sair em fila. (in) single ~e (em) fila indiana. ~ing cabinet fichário m, (P) ficheiro m
fill /fɪl/ vt/i encher(-se); (vacancy) preencher □ n eat one's ~ comer o que quiser. have one's ~ estar farto. ~ in (form) preencher. ~ out (get fat) engordar. ~ up encher até cima; (auto) encher o tanque
fillet /'fɪlɪt/ n (meat, fish) filé m, (P) filete m □ vt (pt filleted) (meat, fish) cortar em filés, (P) filetes
filling /'fɪlɪŋ/ n recheio m; (of tooth) obturação f, (P) chumbo m. ~ station posto m de gasolina
film /fɪlm/ n filme m □ vt/i filmar. ~ star estrela f or vedete f or (P) vedeta f de cinema, astro m
filter /'fɪltə(r)/ n filtro m □ vt/i filtrar

(-se). ~ **coffee** café *m* filtro. ~-**tip** *n* cigarro *m* com filtro

filth /fɪlθ/ *n* imundície *f*; (*fig*) obscenidade *f*. ~**y** *a* imundo; (*fig*) obsceno

fin /fɪn/ *n* barbatana *f*

final /'faɪnl/ *a* final; (*conclusive*) decisivo □ *n* (*sport*) final *f*. ~**s** *npl* (*exams*) finais *fpl*. ~**ist** *n* finalista *mf*. ~**ly** *adv* finalmente, por fim; (*once and for all*) definitivamente

finale /fɪ'nɑːlɪ/ *n* final *m*

finalize /'faɪnəlaɪz/ *vt* finalizar

financ|e /'faɪnæns/ *n* finança(s) *f* (*pl*) □ *a* financeiro □ *vt* financiar. ~**ier** /-'nænsɪə(r)/ *n* financeiro *m*

financial /faɪ'nænʃl/ *a* financeiro. ~**ly** *adv* financeiramente

find /faɪnd/ *vt* (*pt* found) (*sth lost*) achar, encontrar; (*think*) achar; (*discover*) descobrir; (*jur*) declarar □ *n* achado *m*. ~ **out** *vt* apurar, descobrir □ *vi* informar-se (**about** sobre)

fine[1] /faɪn/ *n* multa *f* □ *vt* multar

fine[2] /faɪn/ *a* (-er, -est) fino; (*splendid*) belo, lindo □ *adv* (muito) bem; (*small*) fino, fininho. ~ **arts** belas artes *fpl*. ~ **weather** bom tempo. ~**ly** *adv* lindamente; (*cut*) fininho, aos bocadinhos

finesse /fɪ'nes/ *n* finura *f*, sutileza *f*

finger /'fɪŋgə(r)/ *n* dedo *m* □ *vt* apalpar. ~-**mark** *n* dedada *f*. ~-**nail** *n* unha *f*

fingerprint /'fɪŋgəprɪnt/ *n* impressão *f* digital

fingertip /'fɪŋgətɪp/ *n* ponta *f* do dedo

finicky /'fɪnɪkɪ/ *a* meticuloso, miudinho

finish /'fɪnɪʃ/ *vt/i* acabar, terminar □ *n* fim *m*; (*of race*) chegada *f*; (*on wood, clothes*) acabamento *m*. ~ **doing** acabar de fazer. ~ **up doing** acabar por fazer. ~ **up in** ir parar a, acabar em

finite /'faɪnaɪt/ *a* finito

Fin|land /'fɪnlənd/ *n* Finlândia *f*. ~**n** *n* finlandês *m*. ~**nish** *a* & *n* (*lang*) finlandês (*m*)

fir /fɜː(r)/ *n* abeto *m*

fire /'faɪə(r)/ *n* fogo *m*; (*conflagration*) incêndio *m*; (*heater*) aquecedor *m* □ *vt* (*bullet, gun, etc*) disparar; (*dismiss*) despedir; (*fig: stimulate*) inflamar □ *vi* atirar, fazer fogo (**at** sobre). **on** ~ em chamas. **set** ~ **to** pôr fogo em. ~-**alarm** *n* alarme *m* de incêndio. ~-**brigade** bombeiros *mpl*. ~-**engine** *n* carro *m* de bombeiro, (*P*) da bomba. ~-**escape** *n* saída *f* de incêndio. ~-**extinguisher** *n* extintor *m* de incêndio. ~ **station** quartel *m* dos bombeiros

firearm /'faɪərɑːm/ *n* arma *f* de fogo

fireman /'faɪəmən/ *n* (*pl* -men) bombeiro *m*

fireplace /'faɪəpleɪs/ *n* chaminé *f*, lareira *f*

firewood /'faɪəwʊd/ *n* lenha *f*

firework /'faɪəwɜːk/ *n* fogo *m* de artifício

firing-squad /'faɪərɪŋskwɒd/ *n* pelotão *m* de execução

firm[1] /fɜːm/ *n* firma *f* comercial

firm[2] /fɜːm/ *a* (-er, -est) firme; (*belief*) firme, inabalável. ~**ly** *adv* firmemente. ~**ness** *n* firmeza *f*

first /fɜːst/ *a* & *n* primeiro (*m*); (*auto*) primeira (*f*) □ *adv* primeiro, em primeiro lugar. **at** ~ a princípio, no início. ~ **of all** antes de mais nada. **for the** ~ **time** pela primeira vez. ~ **aid** primeiros socorros *mpl*. ~-**class** *a* de primeira classe. ~ **name** nome de batismo *m*, (*P*) baptismo *m*. ~-**rate** *a* excelente. ~**ly** *adv* primeiramente, em primeiro lugar

fiscal /'fɪskl/ *a* fiscal

fish /fɪʃ/ *n* (*pl usually invar*) peixe *m* □ *vt/i* pescar. ~ **out** (*colloq*) tirar. ~**ing** *n* pesca *f*. **go** ~**ing** ir pescar, (*P*) ir à pesca. ~**ing-rod** *n* vara *f* de pescar. ~**y** *a* de peixe; (*fig: dubious*) suspeito

fisherman /'fɪʃəmən/ *n* (*pl* -men) pescador *m*

fishmonger /'fɪʃmʌŋgə(r)/ *n* dono *m*/ empregado *m* de peixaria. ~'**s** (**shop**) peixaria *f*

fission /'fɪʃn/ *n* fissão *f*, cisão *f*

fist /fɪst/ *n* punho *m*, mão *f* fechada, (*P*) punho *m*

fit[1] /fɪt/ *n* acesso *m*, ataque *m*; (*of generosity*) rasgo *m*

fit[2] /fɪt/ *a* (fitter, fittest) de boa saúde, em forma; (*proper*) próprio; (*good enough*) em condições; (*able*) capaz □ *vt/i* (*pt* fitted) (*clothes*) assentar, ficar bem (a); (*into space*) (*match*) ajustar (-se) (a); (*install*) instalar □ *n* **be a good** ~ assentar bem. **be a tight** ~ estar justo. ~ **out** equipar. ~**ted carpet** carpete *m*, (*P*) alcatifa *f*. ~**ness** *n* saúde *f*, (*P*) condição *f* física

fitful /'fɪtfl/ *a* intermitente

fitment /'fɪtmənt/ *n* móvel *m* de parede

fitting /'fɪtɪŋ/ *a* apropriado □ *n* (*clothes*) prova *f*. ~**s** (*fixtures*) instalações *fpl*; (*fitments*) mobiliário *m*. ~ **room** cabine *f*

five /faɪv/ *a* & *n* cinco (*m*)

fix /fɪks/ *vt* fixar; (*mend, prepare*) arranjar □ *n* **in a** ~ em apuros, (*P*) numa alhada. ~ **sb up with sth** conseguir alg coisa para alguém. ~**ed** *a* fixo

fixation /fɪk'seɪʃn/ *n* fixação *f*; (*obsession*) obsessão *f*

fixture /'fɪkstʃə(r)/ *n* equipamento *m*,

instalação *f*; (*sport*) (data *f* marcada para) competição *f*

fizz /fɪz/ *vi* efervescer, borbulhar □ *n* efervescência *f*. ~y *a* gasoso

fizzle /'fɪzl/ *vi* ~ **out** (*plan etc*) acabar em nada *or* (*P*) em águas de bacalhau (*colloq*)

flab /flæb/ *n* (*colloq*) gordura *f*, banha *f* (*colloq*). ~**by** *a* flácido

flabbergasted /'flæbəgɑːstɪd/ *a* (*colloq*) espantado, pasmado (*colloq*)

flag[1] /flæg/ *n* bandeira *f* □ *vt* (*pt* **flagged**) fazer sinal. ~ **down** fazer sinal para parar. ~**-pole** *n* mastro *m* (de bandeira)

flag[2] /flæg/ *vi* (*pt* **flagged**) (*droop*) cair, pender, tombar; (*of person*) esmorecer

flagrant /'fleɪɡrənt/ *a* flagrante

flagstone /'flæɡstəʊn/ *n* laje *f*

flair /fleə(r)/ *n* jeito *m*, habilidade *f*

flak|e /fleɪk/ *n* floco *m*; (*paint*) lasca *f* □ *vi* descamar-se, lascar-se. ~**y** *a* (*paint*) descamado, lascado

flamboyant /flæm'bɔɪənt/ *a* flamejante; (*showy*) flamante, vistoso; (*of manner*) extravagante

flame /fleɪm/ *n* chama *f*, labareda *f* □ *vi* flamejar. **burst into** ~**s** incendiar-se

flamingo /flə'mɪŋɡəʊ/ *n* (*pl* **-os**) flamingo *m*

flammable /'flæməbl/ *a* inflamável

flan /flæn/ *n* torta *f*, (*P*) tarte *f*

flank /flæŋk/ *n* flanco *m* □ *vt* flanquear

flannel /'flænl/ *n* flanela *f*; (*for face*) toalha *f*, (*P*) toalhete *m* de rosto

flap /flæp/ *vi* (*pt* **flapped**) bater □ *vt* ~ **its wings** bater as asas □ *n* (*of table, pocket*) aba *f*; (*sl: panic*) pânico *m*

flare /fleə(r)/ *vi* ~ **up** irromper em chamas; (*of war*) rebentar; (*fig: of person*) enfurecer-se □ *n* chamejar *m*; (*dazzling light*) clarão *m*; (*signal*) foguete *m* de sinalização. ~**d** *a* (*skirt*) évasé

flash /flæʃ/ *vi* brilhar subitamente; (*on and off*) piscar; (*auto*) fazer sinal com o pisca-pisca □ *vt* fazer brilhar; (*send*) lançar, dardejar; (*flaunt*) fazer alarde de, ostentar □ *n* clarão *m*, lampejo *m*; (*photo*) flash *m*. ~ **past** passar como uma bala, (*P*) passar como um bólide

flashback /'flæʃbæk/ *n* cena *f* retrospectiva, flashback *m*

flashlight /'flæʃlaɪt/ *n* lanterna *f* elétrica, (*P*) eléctrica

flashy /'flæʃɪ/ *a* espalhafatoso, que dá na vista

flask /flɑːsk/ *n* frasco *m*; (*vacuum flask*) garrafa *f* térmica, (*P*) garrafa *f* termos

flat /flæt/ *a* (**flatter, flattest**) plano, chato; (*tyre*) arriado, vazio; (*battery*) fraco; (*refusal*) categórico; (*fare, rate*) fixo; (*monotonous*) monótono; (*mus*) bemol; (*out of tune*) desafinado □ *n* apartamento *m*; (*colloq: tyre*) furo *m* no preu; (*mus*) bemol *m*. ~ **out** (*drive*); (*work*) a dar tudo por tudo. ~**ly** *adv* categoricamente

flatter /'flætə(r)/ *vt* lisonjear, adular. ~**er** *n* lisonjeiro *m*, adulador *m*. ~**ing** *a* lisonjeiro, adulador. ~**y** *n* lisonja *f*

flatulence /'flætjʊləns/ *n* flatulência *f*

flaunt /flɔːnt/ *vt/i* pavonear(-se), ostentar

flavour /'fleɪvə(r)/ *n* sabor *m* (**of** a) □ *vt* dar sabor a, temperar. ~**ing** *n* aroma *m* sintético; (*seasoning*) tempero *m*

flaw /flɔː/ *n* falha *f*, imperfeição *f*. ~**ed** *a* imperfeito. ~**less** *a* perfeito

flea /fliː/ *n* pulga *f*

fled /fled/ *see* **flee**

fledged /fledʒd/ *a* **fully-**~ (*fig*) treinado, experiente

flee /fliː/ *vi* (*pt* **fled**) fugir □ *vt* fugir de

fleece /fliːs/ *n* lã *f* de carneiro, velo *m* □ *vt* (*fig*) esfolar, roubar

fleet /fliːt/ *n* (*of warships*) esquadra *f*; (*of merchant ships, vehicles*) frota *f*

fleeting /'fliːtɪŋ/ *a* curto, fugaz

Flemish /'flemɪʃ/ *a* & *n* (*lang*) flamengo (*m*)

flesh /fleʃ/ *n* carne *f*; (*of fruit*) polpa *f*. ~**y** *a* carnudo

flew /fluː/ *see* **fly**[2]

flex[1] /fleks/ *vt* flexionar

flex[2] /fleks/ *n* (*electr*) fio *f* flexível

flexib|le /'fleksəbl/ *a* flexível. ~**ility** /-'bɪlətɪ/ *n* flexibilidade *f*

flexitime /'fleksɪtaɪm/ *n* horário *m* flexível

flick /flɪk/ *n* (*light blow*) safanão *m*; (*with fingertip*) piparote *m* □ *vt* dar um safanão em; (*with fingertip*) dar um piparote a. ~**-knife** *n* navalha *f* de ponta e mola. ~ **through** folhear

flicker /'flɪkə(r)/ *vi* vacilar, oscilar, tremular □ *n* oscilação *f*, tremular *m*; (*light*) luz *f* oscilante

flier /'flaɪə(r)/ *n* = **flyer**

flies /flaɪz/ *npl* (*of trousers*) braguilha *f*

flight[1] /flaɪt/ *n* (*flying*) voo *m*. ~ **of stairs** lance *m*, (*P*) lanço *m* de escada. ~**-deck** *n* cabine *f*, (*P*) cabina *f*

flight[2] /flaɪt/ *n* (*fleeing*) fuga *f*. **put to** ~ pôr em fuga. **take** ~ pôr-se em fuga

flimsy /'flɪmzɪ/ *a* (**-ier, -iest**) (*material*) fino; (*object*) frágil; (*excuse etc*) fraco, esfarrapado

flinch /flɪntʃ/ *vi* (*wince*) retrair-se; (*draw back*) recuar; (*hesitate*) hesitar

fling /flɪŋ/ *vt/i* (*pt* **flung**) atirar(-se), arremessar(-se); (*rush*) precipitar-se

flint /flɪnt/ *n* sílex *m*; (*for lighter*) pedra *f*

flip /flɪp/ *vt* (*pt* **flipped**) fazer girar com o dedo e o polegar □ *n* pancadinha *f*. ~ **through** folhear

flippant /'flɪpənt/ *a* irreverente, petulante

flipper /'flɪpə(r)/ *n* (*of seal*) nadadeira *f*; (*of swimmer*) pé-de-pato *m*

flirt /flɜːt/ *vt* namoriscar, flertar, (P) flartar □ *n* namorador *m*, namoradeira *f*. ~**ation** /-'teɪʃn/ *n* namorico *m*, flerte *m*, (P) flirt *m*. ~**atious** *a* namorador *m*, namoradeira *f*

flit /flɪt/ *vi* (*pt* **flitted**) esvoaçar

float /fləʊt/ *vt/i* (*fazer*) flutuar; (*company*) lançar □ *n* bóia *f*; (*low cart*) carro *m* de alegórico

flock /flɒk/ *n* (*of sheep; congregation*) rebanho *m*; (*of birds*) bando *m*; (*crowd*) multidão *f* □ *vi* afluir, juntar-se

flog /flɒg/ *vt* (*pt* **flogged**) açoitar; (*sl: sell*) vender

flood /flʌd/ *n* inundação *f*, cheia *f*; (*of tears*) dilúvio *m* □ *vt* inundar, alagar □ *vi* estar inundado; (*river*) transbordar; (*fig: people*) afluir

floodlight /'flʌdlaɪt/ *n* projetor *m*, (P) projector *m*, holofote *m* □ *vt* (*pt* **floodlit**) iluminar

floor /flɔː(r)/ *n* chão *m*, soalho *m*; (*for dancing*) pista *f*; (*storey*) andar *m* □ *vt* assoalhar; (*baffle*) desconcertar, embatucar

flop /flɒp/ *vi* (*pt* **flopped**) (*drop*) (deixar-se) cair; (*move helplessly*) debater-se; (*sl: fail*) ser um fiasco □ *n* (*sl*) fiasco *m*. ~**py** *a* mole, tombado. ~**py** (**disk**) disquete *m*

floral /'flɔːrəl/ *a* floral

florid /'flɒrɪd/ *a* florido

florist /'flɒrɪst/ *n* florista *mf*

flounce /flaʊns/ *n* babado *m*, debrum *m*

flounder /'flaʊndə(r)/ *vi* esbracejar, debater-se; (*fig*) meter os pés pelas mãos

flour /'flaʊə(r)/ *n* farinha *f*. ~**y** *a* farinhento

flourish /'flʌrɪʃ/ *vi* florescer, prosperar □ *vt* brandir □ *n* floreado *m*; (*movement*) gesto *m* elegante. ~**ing** *a* próspero

flout /flaʊt/ *vt* escarnecer (de)

flow /fləʊ/ *vi* correr, fluir; (*traffic*) mover-se; (*hang loosely*) flutuar; (*gush*) jorrar □ *n* corrente *f*, (*of tide; fig*) enchente *f*. ~ **into** (*of river*) desaguar em. ~ **chart** organograma *m*, (P) organigrama *m*

flower /'flaʊə(r)/ *n* flor *f* □ *vi* florir, florescer. ~**-bed** *n* canteiro *m*. ~**ed** *a* de flores, (P) florido, às flores. ~**y** *a* florido

flown /fləʊn/ *see* **fly**[2]

flu /fluː/ *n* (*colloq*) gripe *f*

fluctuate /'flʌktʃueɪt/ *vi* flutuar, oscilar. ~**ion** /-'eɪʃn/ *n* flutuação *f*, oscilação *f*

flue /fluː/ *n* cano *m* de chaminé

fluen|t /'fluːənt/ *a* fluente. **be** ~**t** (**in a language**) falar correntemente (uma língua). ~**cy** *n* fluência *f*. ~**tly** *adv* fluentemente

fluff /flʌf/ *n* cotão *m*; (*down*) penugem *f* □ *vt* (*colloq: bungle*) estender-se em (*sl*), executar mal. ~**y** *a* penugento, fofo

fluid /'fluːɪd/ *a* & *n* fluido (*m*)

fluke /fluːk/ *n* bambúrrio (*colloq*) *m*, golpe *m* de sorte

flung /flʌŋ/ *see* **fling**

flunk /flʌŋk/ *vt/i* (*Amer colloq*) levar pau (*colloq*), (P) chumbar (*colloq*)

fluorescent /fluə'resnt/ *a* fluorescente

fluoride /'fluəraɪd/ *n* flúor *m*, fluor *m*

flurry /'flʌrɪ/ *n* rajada *f*, rabanada *f*, lufada *f*; (*fig*) atrapalhação *f*, agitação *f*

flush[1] /flʌʃ/ *vi* corar, ruborizar-se □ *vt* lavar com água, (P) lavar a jorros de água □ *n* rubor *m*, vermelhidão *f*; (*fig*) excitação *f*; (*of water*) jorro *m* □ *a* ~ **with** ao nível de, rente a. ~ **the toilet** dar descarga

flush[2] /flʌʃ/ *vt* ~ **out** desalojar

fluster /'flʌstə(r)/ *vt* atarantar, perturbar, enervar

flute /fluːt/ *n* flauta *f*

flutter /'flʌtə(r)/ *vi* esvoaçar; (*wings*) bater; (*heart*) palpitar □ *vt* bater. ~ **one's eyelashes** pestanejar □ *n* (*of wings*) batimento *m*; (*fig*) agitação *f*

flux /flʌks/ *n* **in a state of** ~ em mudança *f* contínua

fly[1] /flaɪ/ *n* mosca *f*

fly[2] /flaɪ/ *vi* (*pt* **flew**, *pp* **flown**) voar; (*passengers*) ir de/viajar de avião; (*rush*) correr □ *vt* pilotar; (*passengers, goods*) transportar por avião; (*flag*) hastear, (P) arvorar □ *n* (*of trousers*) braguilha *f*

flyer /'flaɪə(r)/ *n* aviador *m*; (*Amer: circular*) prospecto *m*

flying /'flaɪɪŋ/ *a* voador. **with** ~ **colours** com grande êxito, esplendidamente. ~ **saucer** disco *m* voador. ~ **start** bom arranque *m*. ~ **visit** visita *f* de médico

flyleaf /'flaɪliːf/ *n* (*pl* -**leaves**) guarda *f*, folha *f* em branco

flyover /'flaɪəʊvə(r)/ *n* viaduto *m*

foal /fəʊl/ *n* potro *m*

foam /fəʊm/ *n* espuma *f* □ *vi* espumar. **~ (rubber)** *n* espuma *f* de borracha

fob /fɒb/ *vt* (*pt* **fobbed**) **~ off** iludir, entreter com artifícios. **~ off on** impingir a

focus /'fəʊkəs/ *n* (*pl* **-cuses** *or* **-ci** /-saɪ/) foco *m* □ *vt/i* (*pt* **focused**) focar; (*fig*) concentrar(-se). **in ~** focado, em foco. **out of ~** desfocado

fodder /'fɒdə(r)/ *n* forragem *f*

foetus /'fiːtəs/ *n* (*pl* **-tuses**) feto *m*

fog /fɒg/ *n* nevoeiro *m* □ *vt/i* (*pt* **fogged**) enevoar(-se). **~-horn** *n* sereia *f* de nevoeiro. **~gy** *a* enevoado, brumoso. **it is ~gy** está nevoento

foible /'fɔɪbl/ *n* fraqueza *f*, ponto *m* fraco

foil[1] /fɔɪl/ *n* papel *m* de alumínio; (*fig*) contraste *m*

foil[2] /fɔɪl/ *vt* frustrar

foist /fɔɪst/ *vt* impingir (**on** a)

fold /fəʊld/ *vt/i* dobrar(-se); (*arms*) cruzar; (*colloq: fail*) falir □ *n* dobra *f*. **~er** *n* pasta *f*; (*leaflet*) prospecto *m* (desdobrável). **~ing** *a* dobrável, dobradiço

foliage /'fəʊlɪdʒ/ *n* folhagem *f*

folk /fəʊk/ *n* povo *m*. **~s** (*family, people*) gente *f* (*colloq*) □ *a* folclórico, popular. **~lore** *n* folclore *m*

follow /'fɒləʊ/ *vt/i* seguir. **it ~s that** quer dizer que. **~ suit** (*cards*) servir o naipe jogado; (*fig*) seguir o exemplo, fazer o mesmo. **~ up** (*letter etc*) dar seguimento a. **~er** *n* partidário *m*, seguidor *m*. **~ing** *n* partidários *mpl* □ *a* seguinte □ *prep* em seguimento a

folly /'fɒlɪ/ *n* loucura *f*

fond /fɒnd/ *a* (**-er -est**) carinhoso; (*hope*) caro. **be ~ of** gostar de, ser amigo de. **~ness** *n* (*for people*) afeição *f*; (*for thing*) gosto *m*

fondle /'fɒndl/ *vt* acariciar

font /fɒnt/ *n* pia *f* batismal, (*P*) baptismal

food /fuːd/ *n* alimentação *f*, comida *f*; (*nutrient*) alimento *m* □ *a* alimentar. **~ poisoning** envenenamento *m* alimentar

fool /fuːl/ *n* idiota *mf*, parvo *m* □ *vt* enganar □ *vi* **~ around** andar sem fazer nada

foolhardy /'fuːlhaːdɪ/ *a* imprudente, atrevido

foolish /'fuːlɪʃ/ *a* idiota, parvo. **~ly** *adv* parvamente. **~ness** *n* idiotice *f*, parvoíce *f*

foolproof /'fuːlpruːf/ *a* infalível

foot /fʊt/ *n* (*pl* **feet**) (*of person, bed, stairs*) pé *m*; (*of animal*) pata *f*; (*measure*) pé *m* (= 30,48 cm) □ *vt* **~ the bill** pagar a conta. **on ~** a pé. **on** *or* **to one's feet** de pé. **put one's ~**

in it fazer uma gafe. **to be under sb's feet** atrapalhar alg. **~-bridge** *n* passarela *f*

football /'fʊtbɔːl/ *n* bola *f* de futebol; (*game*) futebol *m*. **~ pools** loteria *f* esportiva, (*P*) totobola *m*. **~er** *n* futebolista *mf*, jogador *m* de futebol

foothills /'fʊthɪlz/ *npl* contrafortes *mpl*

foothold /'fʊthəʊld/ *n* ponto *m* de apoio

footing /'fʊtɪŋ/ *n*: **firm ~** stor. **on an equal ~** em pé de igualdade

footlights /'fʊtlaɪts/ *npl* ribalta *f*

footnote /'fʊtnəʊt/ *n* nota *f* de rodapé

footpath /'fʊtpaːθ/ *n* (*pavement*) calçada *f*, (*P*) passeio *m*; (*in open country*) atalho *m*, caminho *m*

footprint /'fʊtprɪnt/ *n* pegada *f*

footstep /'fʊtstep/ *n* passo *m*

footwear /'fʊtweə(r)/ *n* calçado *m*

for /fə(r)/; *emphatic* /fɔː(r)/ *prep* para; (*in favour of; in place of*) por; (*during*) durante □ *conj* porque, visto que. **a liking ~** gosto por. **he has been away ~ two years** há dois anos que ele está fora. **~ ever** para sempre

forage /'fɒrɪdʒ/ *vi* forragear; (*rummage*) remexer à procura (de) □ *n* forragem *f*

forbade /fə'bæd/ *see* **forbid**

forbear /fɔː'beə(r)/ *vt/i* (*pt* **forbore**, *pp* **forborne**) abster-se (**from** de). **~ance** *n* paciência *f*, tolerância *f*

forbid /fə'bɪd/ *vt* (*pt* **forbade**, *pp* **forbidden**) proibir. **you are ~den to smoke** você está proibido de fumar, (*P*) estás proibido de fumar. **~ding** *a* severo, intimidante

force /fɔːs/ *n* força *f* □ *vt* forçar. **~ into** fazer entrar à força. **~ on** impor a. **come into ~** entrar em vigor. **the ~s** as Forças Armadas. **~d** *a* forçado. **~ful** *a* enérgico

force-feed /'fɔːsfiːd/ *vt* (*pt* **-fed**) alimentar à força

forceps /'fɔːseps/ *n* (*pl invar*) fórceps *m*

forcibl|e /'fɔːsəbl/ *a* convincente; (*done by force*) à força. **~y** *adv* à força

ford /fɔːd/ *n* vau *m* □ *vt* passar a vau, vadear

fore /fɔː(r)/ *a* dianteiro □ *n* **to the ~** em evidência

forearm /'fɔːraːm/ *n* antebraço *m*

foreboding /fɔː'bəʊdɪŋ/ *n* pressentimento *m*

forecast /'fɔːkaːst/ *vt* (*pt* **forecast**) prever □ *n* previsão *f*. **weather ~** boletim *m* meteorológico, previsão *f* do tempo

forecourt /'fɔːkɔːt/ *n* pátio *m* de entrada; (*of garage*) área *f* das bombas de gasolina

forefinger /'fɔ:fɪŋəg(r)/ n (dedo) indicador m

forefront /'fɔ:frʌnt/ n vanguarda f

foregone /'fɔ:gɒn/ a ~ **conclusion** resultado m previsto

foreground /'fɔ:graʊnd/ n primeiro plano m

forehead /'fɒrɪd/ n testa f

foreign /'fɒrən/ a estrangeiro; (trade) externo; (travel) ao/no estrangeiro. F~ Office Ministério m dos Negócios Estrangeiros. ~er n estrangeiro m.

foreman /'fɔ:mən/ n (pl **foremen**) contramestre m; (of jury) primeiro jurado m

foremost /'fɔ:məʊst/ a principal, primeiro □ adv **first and** ~ antes de mais nada, em primeiro lugar

forename /'fɔ:neɪm/ n

forensic /fə'rensɪk/ a forense. ~ **medicine** medicina f legal

forerunner /'fɔ:rʌnə(r)/ n precursor m

foresee /fɔ:'si:/ vt (pt **-saw**, pp **-seen**) prever. ~**able** a previsível

foreshadow /fɔ:'ʃædəʊ/ vt prefigurar, pressagiar

foresight /'fɔ:saɪt/ n previsão f, previdência f

forest /'fɒrɪst/ n floresta f

forestall /fɔ:'stɔ:l/ vt (do first) antecipar-se a; (prevent) prevenir; (anticipate) antecipar

forestry /'fɒrɪstrɪ/ n silvicultura f

foretell /fɔ:'tel/ vt (pt **foretold**) predizer, profetizar

forever /fə'revə(r)/ adv (endlessly) constantemente

foreword /'fɔ:wɜ:d/ n prefácio m

forfeit /'fɔ:fɪt/ n penalidade f, preço m; (in game) prenda f □ vt perder

forgave /fə'geɪv/ see **forgive**

forge[1] /fɔ:dʒ/ vi ~ **ahead** tomar a dianteira, avançar

forge[2] /fɔ:dʒ/ n forja f □ vt (metal, friendship) forjar; (counterfeit) falsificar, forjar. ~**r** /-ə(r)/ n falsificador m, forjador m. ~**ry** /-ərɪ/ n falsificação f

forget /fə'get/ vt/i (pt **forgot**, pp **forgotten**) esquecer. ~ **o.s.** portar-se com menos dignidade, esquecer-se de quem é. ~-**me-not** n miosótis m. ~**ful** a esquecido. ~**fulness** n esquecimento m

forgive /fə'gɪv/ vt (pt **forgave**, pp **forgiven**) perdoar (sb for sth alg coisa a alg). ~**ness** n perdão m

forgo /fɔ:'gəʊ/ vt (pt **forwent**, pp **forgone**) renunciar a

fork /fɔ:k/ n garfo m; (for digging etc) forquilha f; (in road) bifurcação f □ vi bifurcar. ~ **out** (sl) desembolsar. ~-**lift truck** empilhadeira f. ~**ed** a bifurcado; (lightning) em zigzag

forlorn /fə'lɔ:n/ a abandonado, desolado

form /fɔ:m/ n forma f; (document) impresso m, formulário m; (schol) classe f □ vt/i formar(-se)

formal /'fɔ:ml/ a formal; (dress) de cerimônia, (P) cerimónia. ~**ity** /-'mælətɪ/ n formalidade f. ~**ly** adv formalmente

format /'fɔ:mæt/ n formato m □ vt (pl **formatted**) (disk) formatar

formation /fɔ:'meɪʃn/ n formação f

former /'fɔ:mə(r)/ a antigo; (first of two) primeiro. **the** ~ aquele. ~**ly** adv antigamente

formidable /'fɔ:mɪdəbl/ a formidável, tremendo

formula /'fɔ:mjʊlə/ n (pl **-ae** /-i:/ or **-as**) fórmula f

formulate /'fɔ:mjʊleɪt/ vt formular

forsake /fə'seɪk/ vt (pt **forsook**, pp **forsaken**) abandonar

fort /fɔ:t/ n (mil) forte m

forth /fɔ:θ/ adv adiante, para a frente. **and so** ~ e assim por diante, etcetera. **go back and** ~ andar de trás para diante.

forthcoming /fɔ:θ'kʌmɪŋ/ a que está para vir, próximo; (communicative) comunicativo, receptivo; (book) no prelo

forthright /'fɔ:θraɪt/ a franco, direto, (P) directo

fortif|**y** /'fɔ:tɪfaɪ/ vt fortificar. ~**ication** /-ɪ'keɪʃn/ n fortificação f

fortitude /'fɔ:tɪtju:d/ n fortitude f, fortaleza f

fortnight /'fɔ:tnaɪt/ n quinze dias mpl, (P) quinzena f. ~**ly** a quinzenal □ adv de quinze em quinze dias

fortress /'fɔ:trɪs/ n fortaleza f

fortuitous /fɔ:'tju:ɪtəs/ a fortuito, acidental

fortunate /'fɔ:tʃənət/ a feliz, afortunado. **be** ~ ter sorte. ~**ly** adv felizmente

fortune /'fɔ:tʃən/ n sorte f; (wealth) fortuna f. **have the good** ~ **to** ter a sorte de. ~-**teller** n cartomante mf

fort|**y** /'fɔ:tɪ/ a & n quarenta (m). ~**ieth** a &n quadragésimo (m)

forum /'fɔ:rəm/ n fórum m, foro m

forward /'fɔ:wəd/ a (in front) dianteiro; (towards the front) para a frente; (advanced) adiantado; (pert) atrevido □ n (sport) atacante m, (P) avançado m □ adv ~(**s**) para a frente, para diante □ vt (letter) remeter; (goods) expedir; (fig: help) favorecer. **come** ~ apresentar-se. **go** ~ avançar. ~**ness** n adiantamento m; (pertness) atrevimento m

fossil /'fɒsl/ a & n fóssil (m)

foster /'fɒstə(r)/ vt fomentar; (child)

criar. **~-child** *n* filho *m* adotivo, (*P*) adoptivo. **~-mother** *n* mãe *f* adotiva, (*P*) adoptiva

fought /fɔ:t/ *see* **fight**

foul /faʊl/ *a* (**-er, -est**) infecto; (*language*) obsceno; (*weather*) mau □ *n* (*football*) falta *f* □ *vt* sujar, emporcalhar. **~-mouthed** *a* de linguagem obscena. **~ play** jogo *m* desleal; (*crime*) crime *m*

found[1] /faʊnd/ *see* **find**

found[2] /faʊnd/ *vt* fundar. **~ation** /-'deɪʃn/ *n* fundação *f*; (*basis*) fundamento *m*. **~ations** *npl* (*of building*) alicerces *mpl*

founder[1] /'faʊndə(r)/ *n* fundador *m*

founder[2] /'faʊndə(r)/ *vi* afundar-se

foundry /'faʊndrɪ/ *n* fundição *f*

fountain /'faʊntɪn/ *n* fonte *f*. **~-pen** *n* caneta-tinteiro *f*, (*P*) caneta *f* de tinta permanente

four /fɔ:(r)/ *a & n* quatro (*m*). **~fold** *a* quádruplo □ *adv* quadruplamente. **~th** *a & n* quarto (*m*)

foursome /'fɔ:səm/ *n* grupo *m* de quatro pessoas

fourteen /fɔ:'ti:n/ *a & n* catorze (*m*). **~th** *a & n* décimo quarto (*m*)

fowl /faʊl/ *n* ave *f* de capoeira

fox /fɒks/ *n* raposa *f* □ *vt* (*colloq*) mistificar, enganar. **be ~ed** ficar perplexo

foyer /'fɔɪeɪ/ *n* foyer *m*

fraction /'frækʃn/ *n* fração *f*, (*P*) fracção *f*; (*small bit*) bocadinho *m*, partícula *f*

fracture /'fræktʃə(r)/ *n* fratura *f*, (*P*) fractura *f* □ *vt/i* fraturar(-se), (*P*) fracturar(-se)

fragile /'frædʒaɪl/ *a* frágil

fragment /'frægmənt/ *n* fragmento *m*. **~ary** /'frægməntrɪ/ *a* fragmentário

fragran|t /'freɪɡrənt/ *a* fragrante, perfumado. **~ce** *n* fragrância *f*, perfume *m*

frail /freɪl/ *a* (**-er, -est**) frágil

frame /freɪm/ *n* (*techn; of spectacles*) armação *f*; (*of picture*) moldura *f*; (*of window*) caixilho *m*; (*body*) corpo *m*, (*P*) estrutura *f* □ *vt* colocar a armação em; (*picture*) emoldurar; (*fig*) formular; (*sl*) incriminar falsamente, tramar. **~ of mind** estado *m* de espírito

framework /'freɪmwɜ:k/ *n* estrutura *f*; (*context*) quadro *m*, esquema *m*

France /frɑ:ns/ *n* França *f*

franchise /'fræntʃaɪz/ *n* (*pol*) direito *m* de voto; (*comm*) concessão *f*, franchise *f*

frank[1] /fræŋk/ *a* franco. **~ly** *adv* francamente. **~ness** *n* franqueza *f*

frank[2] /fræŋk/ *vt* franquear

frantic /'fræntɪk/ *a* frenético

fraternal /frə'tɜ:nl/ *a* fraternal

fraternize /'frætənaɪz/ *vi* confraternizar

fraud /frɔ:d/ *n* fraude *f*; (*person*) impostor *m*. **~ulent** /'frɔ:djʊlənt/ *a* fraudulento

fraught /frɔ:t/ *a* **~ with** cheio de

fray[1] /freɪ/ *n* rixa *f*

fray[2] /freɪ/ *vt/i* desfiar(-se), puir, esgarçar(-se)

freak /fri:k/ *n* aberração *f*, anomalia *f* □ *a* anormal. **~ of nature** aborto *m* da natureza. **~ish** *a* anormal

freckle /'frekl/ *n* sarda *f*. **~d** *a* sardento

free /fri:/ *a* (**freer, freest**) livre; (*gratis*) grátis; (*lavish*) liberal □ *vt* (*pt* **freed**) libertar (**from** de); (*rid*) livrar (**of** de). **~ of charge** grátis, de graça. **a ~ hand** carta *f* branca. **~lance** *a* independente, free-lance. **~-range** *a* (*egg*) de galinha criada em galinheiro. **~ly** *adv* livremente

freedom /'fri:dəm/ *n* liberdade *f*

freez|e /fri:z/ *vt/i* (*pt* **froze**, *pp* **frozen**) gelar; (*culin; finance*) congelar (-se) □ *n* gelo *m*; (*culin; finance*) congelamento *m*. **~er** *n* congelador *m*. **~ing** *a* gélido, glacial. **below ~ing** abaixo de zero

freight /freɪt/ *n* frete *m*

French /frentʃ/ *a* francês □ *n* (*lang*) francês *m*. **the ~** os franceses. **~man** *n* francês *m*. **~-speaking** *a* francófono. **~ window** porta *f* envidraçada. **~woman** *n* francesa *f*

frenz|y /'frenzɪ/ *n* frenesi *m*. **~ied** *a* frenético

frequen|t[1] /'fri:kwənt/ *a* freqüente, (*P*) frequente. **~cy** *n* freqüência *f*, (*P*) frequência *f*. **~tly** *adv* freqüentemente, (*P*) frequentemente

frequent[2] /frɪ'kwent/ *vt* freqüentar, (*P*) frequentar

fresh /freʃ/ *a* (**-er, -est**) fresco; (*different, additional*) novo; (*colloq: cheeky*) descarado, atrevido. **~ly** *adv* recentemente. **~ness** *n* frescura *f*

freshen /'freʃn/ *vt/i* refrescar. **~ up** refrescar-se

fret /fret/ *vt/i* (*pt* **fretted**) ralar(-se). **~ful** *a* rabugento

friar /'fraɪə(r)/ *n* frade *m*; (*before name*) frei *m*

friction /'frɪkʃn/ *n* fricção *f*

Friday /'fraɪdɪ/ *n* sexta-feira *f*. **Good ~** sexta-feira *f* santa

fridge /frɪdʒ/ *n* (*colloq*) geladeira *f*, (*P*) frigorífico *m*

fried /fraɪd/ *see* **fry** □ *a* frito

friend /frend/ *n* amigo *m*. **~ship** *n* amizade *f*

friendl|y /'frendlɪ/ *a* (**-ier, -iest**)

amigável, amigo, simpático. ~**iness** n
simpatia f, gentileza f
frieze /friːz/ n friso m
frigate /ˈfrɪɡət/ n fragata f
fright /fraɪt/ n medo m, susto m. give
sb a ~ pregar um susto em alguém.
~**ful** a medonho, assustador
frighten /ˈfraɪtn/ vt assustar. ~ off
afugentar. ~**ed** a assustado. be ~**ed**
(**of**) ter medo (de)
frigid /ˈfrɪdʒɪd/ a frígido. ~**ity**
/-ˈdʒɪdətɪ/ n frigidez f, frieza f; (psych)
frigidez f
frill /frɪl/ n babado m, (P) folho m
fringe /frɪndʒ/ n franja f, (of area)
borda f; (of society) margem f. ~ **be-
nefits** (work) regalias fpl extras. ~
theatre teatro m alternativo, teatro
m de vanguarda
frisk /frɪsk/ vi pular, brincar □ vt revistar
fritter[1] /ˈfrɪtə(r)/ n bolinho m frito,
(P) frito m
fritter[2] /ˈfrɪtə(r)/ vt ~ **away** desperdiçar
frivol|ous /ˈfrɪvələs/ a frívolo. ~**ity**
/-ˈvɒlətɪ/ n frivolidade f
fro /frəʊ/ see **to and fro**
frock /frɒk/ n vestido m
frog /frɒɡ/ n rã f
frogman /ˈfrɒɡmən/ n (pl -men)
homem-rã m
frolic /ˈfrɒlɪk/ vi (pt frolicked) brincar, fazer travessuras □ n brincadeira
f, travessura f
from /frɒm/; emphatic /frɒm/ prep de;
(with time, prices etc) de, a partir de;
(according to) por, a julgar por
front /frʌnt/ n (meteo, mil, pol; of car,
train) frente f, (of shirt) peitilho m; (of
building; fig) fachada f; (promenade)
calçada f à beiramar □ a da frente;
(first) primeiro. in ~ (of) em frente
(de). ~ **door** porta f da rua. ~**-wheel
drive** tracção f, (P) tracção f dianteira.
~**age** n frontaria f. ~**al** a frontal
frontier /ˈfrʌntɪə(r)/ n fronteira f
frost /frɒst/ n gelo m, temperatura f
abaixo de zero; (on ground, plants etc)
geada f □ vt/i cobrir(-se) de geada. ~**-
bite** n queimadura f de frio. ~**-bitten**
a queimado pelo frio. ~**ed** a (glass)
fosco. ~**y** a glacial
froth /frɒθ/ n espuma f □ vi espumar,
fazer espuma. ~**y** a espumoso
frown /fraʊn/ vi franzir as sobrancelhas □ n franzir m de sobrancelhas. ~
on desaprovar
froze, frozen /frəʊz, ˈfrəʊzn/ see
freeze
frugal /ˈfruːɡl/ a poupado; (meal)
frugal. ~**ly** adv frugalmente
fruit /fruːt/ n fruto m; (collectively)
fruta f. ~ **machine** caça-níqueis ms/

pl. ~ **salad** salada f de frutas. ~**y** a
que tem gosto or cheiro de fruta
fruit|ful /ˈfruːtfl/ a frutífero, pro-
dutivo. ~**less** a infrutífero
fruition /fruːˈɪʃn/ n come to ~ realizar-se
frustrat|e /frʌˈstreɪt/ vt frustrar.
~**ion** /-ʃn/ n frustração f
fry /fraɪ/ vt/i (pt fried) fritar. ~**ing-
pan** n frigideira f
fudge /fʌdʒ/ n (culin) doce m de leite,
(P) doce m acaramelado □ vt/i ~ (**the
issue**) lançar a confusão
fuel /ˈfjuːəl/ n combustível m; (for
car) carburante m □ vt (pt fuelled)
abastecer de combustível; (fig) atear
fugitive /ˈfjuːdʒətɪv/ a & n fugitivo
(m)
fulfil /fʊlˈfɪl/ vt (pt fulfilled) cumprir,
realizar; (condition) satisfazer. ~ **o.s.**
realizar-se. ~**ling** a satisfatório.
~**ment** n realização f; (of condition)
satisfação f
full /fʊl/ a (-er, -est) cheio; (meal)
completo; (price) total, por inteiro;
(skirt) rodado □ adv in ~
integralmente. at ~ **speed** a toda
velocidade. to the ~ ao máximo. be
~ **up** (colloq: after eating) estar cheio
(colloq). ~ **moon** lua f cheia. ~**-scale**
a em grande. ~**-size** a em tamanho
natural. ~ **stop** ponto m final. ~**-
time** a & adv a tempo integral, full-
time. ~**y** adv completamente
fulsome /ˈfʊlsəm/ a excessivo
fumble /ˈfʌmbl/ vi tatear, (P) tactear;
(in the dark) andar tateando. ~ **with**
estar atrapalhado com, andar às voltas com
fume /fjuːm/ vi defumar, (P) deitar
fumo, fumegar; (with anger) ferver.
~**s** npl gases mpl
fumigate /ˈfjuːmɪɡeɪt/ vt fumigar
fun /fʌn/ n divertimento m. for ~ de
brincadeira. **make** ~ **of** zombar de,
fazer troça de. ~**-fair** n parque m de
diversões, (P) feira f de diversões, (P)
feira f popular
function /ˈfʌŋkʃn/ n função f □ vi
funcionar. ~**al** a funcional
fund /fʌnd/ n fundos mpl □ vt financiar
fundamental /fʌndəˈmentl/ a fundamental
funeral /ˈfjuːnərəl/ n enterro m, funeral m □ a fúnebre
fungus /ˈfʌŋɡəs/ n (pl -gi /-ɡaɪ/) fungo
m
funnel /ˈfʌnl/ n funil m; (of ship)
chaminé f
funn|y /ˈfʌnɪ/ a (-ier, -iest) engraçado,
divertido; (odd) esquisito. ~**ily** adv
comicamente; (oddly) estranhamente.
~**ily enough** por incrível que pareça

fur /fɜ:(r)/ n pêlo m; (for clothing) pele f; (in kettle) depósito m, crosta f. ~ coat casaco m de pele

furious /'fjʊərɪəs/ a furioso. ~ly adv furiosamente

furnace /'fɜ:nɪs/ n fornalha f

furnish /'fɜ:nɪʃ/ vt mobiliar, (P) mobilar; (supply) prover (with de). ~ings npl mobiliário m e equipamento m

furniture /'fɜ:nɪtʃə(r)/ n mobília f

furrow /'fʌrəʊ/ n sulco m; (wrinkle) ruga f □ vt sulcar; (wrinkle) enrugar

furry /'fɜ:rɪ/ a (-ier, -iest) peludo; (toy) de pelúcia

furth|er /'fɜ:ðə(r)/ a mais distante; (additional) adicional, suplementar □ adv mais longe; (more) mais □ vt promover. ~er education ensino m supletivo, cursos mpl livres, (P) educação f superior. ~est a o mais distante □ adv mais longe

furthermore /fɜ:ðə'mɔ:(r)/ adv além disso

furtive /'fɜ:tɪv/ a furtivo

fury /'fjʊərɪ/ n fúria f, furor m

fuse¹ /fju:z/ vt/i fundir(-se); (fig) amalgamar □ n fusível m. the lights ~d os fusíveis queimaram

fuse² /fju:z/ n (of bomb) espoleta f

fuselage /'fju:zəla:ʒ/ n fuselagem f

fusion /'fju:ʒn/ n fusão f

fuss /fʌs/ n história(s) f(pl), escarcéu m □ vi preocupar-se com ninharias. make a ~ of ligar demasiado para, criar caso com, fazer um espalhafato com. ~y a exigente, complicado

futile /'fju:taɪl/ a fútil

future /'fju:tʃə(r)/ a & n futuro (m). in ~ no futuro, de agora em diante

futuristic /fju:tʃə'rɪstɪk/ a futurista, futurístico

fuzz /fʌz/ n penugem f; (hair) cabelo m frisado

fuzzy /'fʌzɪ/ a (hair) frisado; (photo) pouco nítido, desfocado

G

gab /gæb/ n (colloq) have the gift of the ~ ter o dom da palavra

gabble /'gæbl/ vt/i tagarelar, falar, ou muito depressa □ n tagarelice f, algaravia f

gable /'geɪbl/ n empena f, oitão m

gad /gæd/ vi (pt gadded) ~ about (colloq) badalar

gadget /'gædʒɪt/ n pequeno utensílio m; (fitting) dispositivo m; (device) engenhoca f (colloq)

Gaelic /'geɪlɪk/ n galês m

gaffe /gæf/ n gafe f

gag /gæg/ n mordaça f; (joke) gag m, piada f □ vt (pt gagged) amordaçar

gaiety /'geɪətɪ/ n alegria f

gaily /'geɪlɪ/ adv alegremente

gain /geɪn/ vt ganhar □ vi (of clock) adiantar-se. ~ weight aumentar de peso. ~ on (get closer to) aproximar-se de □ n ganho m; (increase) aumento m. ~ful a lucrativo, proveitoso

gait /geɪt/ n (modo de) andar m

gala /'ga:lə/ n gala m; (sport) festival m

galaxy /'gæləksɪ/ n galáxia f

gale /geɪl/ n vento m forte

gall /gɔ:l/ n bílis f; (fig) fel m; (sl: impudence) descaramento m, desplante m, (P) lata f (sl). ~-bladder n vesícula f biliar. ~-stone n cálculo m biliar

gallant /'gælənt/ a galhardo, valente; (chivalrous) galante, cortês. ~ry n galhardia f, valentia f; (chivalry) galanteria f, cortesia f

gallery /'gælərɪ/ n galeria f

galley /'gælɪ/ n (pl -eys) galera f; (ship's kitchen) cozinha f

gallivant /gælɪ'vænt/ vi (colloq) vadiar, (P) andar na paródia

gallon /'gælən/ n galão m (= 4,546 litros; Amer = 3.785 litros)

gallop /'gæləp/ n galope m □ vi (pt galloped) galopar

gallows /'gæləʊz/ npl forca f

galore /gə'lɔ:(r)/ adv a beça, em abundância

galvanize /'gælvənaɪz/ vt galvanizar

gambit /'gæmbɪt/ n gambito m

gambl|e /'gæmbl/ vt/i jogar □ n jogo (de azar) m; (fig) risco m. ~e on apostar em. ~er n jogador m. ~ing n jogo m (de azar)

game /geɪm/ n jogo m; (football) desafio m; (animals) caça f □ a bravo. ~ for pronto para

gamekeeper /'geɪmki:pə(r)/ n guarda-florestal m

gammon /'gæmən/ n presunto m defumado

gamut /'gæmət/ n gama f

gang /gæŋ/ n bando m, gang m; (of workmen) turma f, (P) grupo m □ vi ~ up ligar-se (on contra)

gangling /'gæŋglɪŋ/ a desengonçado

gangrene /'gæŋgri:n/ n gangrena f

gangster /'gæŋstə(r)/ n gângster m, bandido m

gangway /'gæŋweɪ/ n passagem f; (aisle) coxia f; (on ship) portaló m; (from ship to shore) passadiço m

gaol /dʒeɪl/ n & vt = jail

gap /gæp/ n abertura f, brecha f; (in time) intervalo m; (deficiency) lacuna f

gap|e /geɪp/ vi ficar boquiaberto or embasbacado. ~ing a escancarado

garage /'gæra:ʒ/ n garagem f; (service station) posto m de gasolina, (P) estação *f* de serviço □ *vt* pôr na garagem

garbage /'ga:bɪdʒ/ *n* lixo *m*. ~ **can** (*Amer*) lata *f* do lixo, (*P*) caixote *m* do lixo

garble /'ga:bl/ *vt* deturpar

garden /'ga:dn/ *n* jardim *m* □ *vi* jardinar. ~**er** *n* jardineiro *m*. ~**ing** *n* jardinagem *f*

gargle /'ga:gl/ *vi* gargarejar □ *n* gargarejo *m*

gargoyle /'ga:gɔɪl/ *n* gárgula *f*

garish /'geərɪʃ/ *a* berrante, espalhafatoso

garland /'ga:lənd/ *n* grinalda *f*

garlic /'ga:lɪk/ *n* alho *m*

garment /'ga:mənt/ *n* peça *f* de vestuário, roupa *f*

garnish /'ga:nɪʃ/ *vt* enfeitar, guarnecer □ *n* guarnição *f*

garrison /'gærɪsn/ *n* guarnição *f* □ *vt* guarnecer

garrulous /'gærələs/ *a* tagarela

garter /'ga:tə(r)/ *n* liga *f*. ~**-belt** *n* (*Amer*) cinta *f* de ligas

gas /gæs/ *n* (*pl* gases) gás *m*; (*med*) anestésico *m*; (*Amer colloq: petrol*) gasolina *f* □ *vt* (*pt* gassed) asfixiar; (*mil*) gasear □ *vi* (*colloq*) fazer conversa fiada. ~ **fire** aquecedor *m* a gás. ~ **mask** máscara *f* anti-gás. ~ **meter** medidor *m* do gás

gash /gæʃ/ *n* corte *m*, lanho *m* □ *vt* cortar

gasket /'gæskɪt/ *n* junta *f*

gasoline /'gæsəli:n/ *n* (*Amer*) gasolina *f*

gasp /ga:sp/ *vi* arfar, arquejar; (*fig: with rage, surprise*) ficar sem ar □ *n* arquejo *m*

gassy /'gæsɪ/ *a* gasoso; (*full of gas*) cheio de gás

gastric /'gæstrɪk/ *a* gástrico

gastronomy /gæ'strɒnəmɪ/ *n* gastronomia *f*

gate /geɪt/ *n* portão *m*; (*of wood*) cancela *f*; (*barrier*) barreira *f*; (*airport*) porta *f*

gateau /'gætəʊ/ *n* (*pl* ~x /-təʊz/) bolo *m* grande com creme

gatecrash /'geɪtkræʃ/ *vt/i* entrar (numa festa) sem convite

gateway /'geɪtweɪ/ *n* (porta de) entrada *f*

gather /'gæðə(r)/ *vt* reunir, juntar; (*pick up, collect*) apanhar; (*amass, pile up*) acumular, juntar; (*conclude*) deduzir; (*cloth*) franzir □ *vi* reunir-se; (*pile up*) acumular-se. ~ **speed** ganhar velocidade. ~**ing** *n* reunião *f*

gaudy /'gɔ:dɪ/ *a* (-ier, -iest) (*bright*) berrante; (*showy*) espalhafatoso

gauge /geɪdʒ/ *n* medida *f* padrão; (*device*) indicador *m*; (*railway*) bitola *f* □ *vt* medir, avaliar

gaunt /gɔ:nt/ *a* emagrecido, macilento; (*grim*) lúgubre, desolado

gauntlet /'gɔ:ntlɪt/ *n* **run the ~ of** (*fig*) expor-se a. **throw down the ~** lançar um desafio, (*P*) atirar a luva

gauze /gɔ:z/ *n* gaze *f*

gave /geɪv/ *see* give

gawky /'gɔ:kɪ/ *a* (-ier, -iest) desajeitado

gay /geɪ/ *a* (-er, -est) alegre; (*colloq: homosexual*) homosexual, gay

gaze /geɪz/ *vi* ~ (**at**) olhar fixamente (para) □ *n* contemplação *f*

gazelle /gə'zel/ *n* gazela *f*

GB *abbr of* Great Britain

gear /gɪə(r)/ *n* equipamento *m*; (*techn*) engrenagem *f*; (*auto*) velocidade *f* □ *vt* equipar; (*adapt*) adaptar. **in ~** engrenado. **out of ~** em ponto morto. ~**-lever** *n* alavanca *f* de mudanças

gearbox /'gɪəbɒks/ *n* caixa *f* de mudança, caixa *f* de transmissão, (*P*) caixa *f* de velocidades

geese /gi:s/ *see* goose

gel /dʒel/ *n* geléia *f*, (*P*) geleia *f*

gelatine /'dʒeləti:n/ *n* gelatina *f*

gelignite /'dʒelɪgnaɪt/ *n* gelignite *f*

gem /dʒem/ *n* gema *f*, pedra *f* preciosa

Gemini /'dʒemɪnaɪ/ *n* (*astr*) Gêmeos *mpl*, (*P*) Gémeos *mpl*

gender /'dʒendə(r)/ *n* gênero *m*, (*P*) género *m*

gene /dʒi:n/ *n* gene *m*

genealogy /dʒi:nɪ'ælədʒɪ/ *n* genealogia *f*

general /'dʒenrəl/ *a* geral □ *n* general *m*. ~ **election** eleições *fpl* legislativas. ~ **practitioner** *n* clínico-geral *m*, (*P*) médico *m* de família. **in ~** em geral. ~**ly** *adv* geralmente

generaliz|e /'dʒenrəlaɪz/ *vt/i* generalizar. ~**ation** /-'zeɪʃn/ *n* generalização *f*

generate /'dʒenəreɪt/ *vt* gerar, produzir

generation /dʒenə'reɪʃn/ *n* geração *f*

generator /'dʒenəreɪtə(r)/ *n* gerador *m*

gener|ous /'dʒenərəs/ *a* generoso; (*plentiful*) abundante. ~**osity** /-'rɒsətɪ/ *n* generosidade *f*

genetic /dʒɪ'netɪk/ *a* genético. ~**s** *n* genética *f*

genial /'dʒi:nɪəl/ *a* agradável

genital /'dʒenɪtl/ *a* genital. ~**s** *npl* órgãos *mpl* genitais

genius /'dʒi:nɪəs/ *n* (*pl* -uses) gênio *m*, (*P*) génio *m*

genocide /'dʒenəsaɪd/ *n* genocídio *m*

gent /dʒent/ *n* **the G~s** (*colloq*) banheiros *mpl* de homens, (*P*) lavabos *mpl* para homens

genteel /dʒen'tiːl/ a elegante, fino, refinado

gentl|e /'dʒentl/ a (~er, ~est) brando, suave. ~eness n brandura f, suavidade f. ~y adv brandamente, suavemente

gentleman /'dʒentlmən/ n (pl -men) senhor m; (well-bred) cavalheiro m

genuine /'dʒenjʊm/ a genuíno, verdadeiro; (belief) sincero

geograph|y /dʒɪ'ɒgrəfɪ/ n geografia f. ~er n geógrafo m. ~ical /dʒɪə'græfɪkl/ a geográfico

geolog|y /dʒɪ'ɒlədʒɪ/ n geologia f. ~ical /dʒɪə'lɒdʒɪkl/ a geológico. ~ist n geólogo m

geometr|y /dʒɪ'ɒmətrɪ/ n geometria f. ~ic(al) /dʒɪə'metrɪk(l)/ a geométrico

geranium /dʒə'reɪnɪəm/ n gerânio m

geriatric /dʒerɪ'ætrɪk/ a geriátrico

germ /dʒɜːm/ n germe m, micróbio m

German /'dʒɜːmən/ a & n alemão (m), alemã (f); (lang) alemão (m). ~ measles rubéola f. ~ic /dʒə'mænɪk/ a germânico. ~y n Alemanha f

germinate /'dʒɜːmɪneɪt/ vi germinar

gestation /dʒe'steɪʃn/ n gestação f

gesticulate /dʒe'stɪkjʊleɪt/ vi gesticular

gesture /'dʒestʃə(r)/ n gesto m

get /get/ vt (pt got, pres p getting) (have) ter; (receive) receber; (catch) apanhar; (earn, win) ganhar; (fetch) ir buscar; (find) achar; (colloq: understand) entender. ~ sb to do sth fazer com que alguém faça alg coisa □ vi ir, chegar; (become) ficar. ~ married/ready casar-se/aprontar-se. ~ about andar dum lado para o outro. ~ across atravessar. ~ along or by (manage) ir indo. ~ along or on with entender-se com. ~ at (reach) chegar a; (attack) atacar; (imply) insinuar. ~ away ir-se embora; (escape) fugir. ~ back vi voltar □ vt recuperar. ~ by (pass) passar, escapar; (manage) aguentar-se. ~ down descer. ~ in entrar. ~ off vi descer; (leave) partir; (jur) ser absolvido □ vt (remove) tirar. ~ on (succeed) fazer progressos, ir; (be on good terms) dar-se bem. ~ out sair. ~ out of (fig) fugir de. ~ over (illness) restabelecer-se de. ~ round (person) convencer; (rule) contornar. ~ up vi levantar-se □ vt (mount) montar. ~-up n (colloq) apresentação f

getaway /'getəweɪ/ n fuga f

geyser /'giːzə(r)/ n aquecedor m; (geol) gêiser m, (P) géiser m

Ghana /'gɑːnə/ n Gana m

ghastly /'gɑːstlɪ/ a (-ier, -iest) horrível; (pale) lívido

gherkin /'gɜːkɪn/ n pepino m pequeno para conservas, cornichão m

ghetto /'getəʊ/ n (pl -os) gueto m, ghetto m

ghost /gəʊst/ n fantasma m, espectro m. ~ly a fantasmagórico, espectral

giant /'dʒaɪənt/ a & n gigante (m)

gibberish /'dʒɪbərɪʃ/ n algaravia f, linguagem f incompreensível

gibe /dʒaɪb/ n zombaria f □ vi ~ (at) zombar (de)

giblets /'dʒɪblɪts/ npl miúdos mpl, miudezas fpl

giddy /'gɪdɪ/ a (-ier, -iest) estonteante, vertiginoso. be or feel ~ ter tonturas or vertigens

gift /gɪft/ n presente m, dádiva f; (ability) dom m, dote m. ~-wrap vt (pt -wrapped) fazer um embrulho de presente

gifted /'gɪftɪd/ a dotado

gig /gɪg/ n (colloq) show m, sessão f de jazz etc

gigantic /dʒaɪ'gæntɪk/ a gigantesco

giggle /'gɪgl/ vi dar risadinhas nervosas □ n risinho f m nervoso

gild /gɪld/ vt dourar

gills /gɪlz/ npl guelras fpl

gilt /gɪlt/ a & n dourado (m). ~-edged a de toda a confiança

gimmick /'gɪmɪk/ n truque m, artifício m

gin /dʒɪn/ n gin m, genebra f

ginger /'dʒɪndʒə(r)/ n gengibre m □ a louro-avermelhado, ruivo. ~ ale, ~ beer cerveja f de gengibre, (P) ginger ale m

gingerbread /'dʒɪndʒəbred/ n pão m de gengibre

gingerly /'dʒɪndʒəlɪ/ adv cautelosamente

gipsy /'dʒɪpsɪ/ n = gypsy

giraffe /dʒɪ'rɑːf/ n girafa f

girder /'gɜːdə(r)/ n trave f, viga f

girdle /'gɜːdl/ n cinto m; (corset) cinta f □ vt rodear

girl /gɜːl/ n (child) menina f; (young woman) moça f, (P) rapariga f. ~-friend n amiga f; (of boy) namorada f. ~hood n (of child) meninice f; (youth) juventude f

giro /'dʒaɪrəʊ/ n sistema m de transferência de crédito entre bancos; (cheque) cheque m pago pelo governo a desempregados ou doentes

girth /gɜːθ/ n circunferência f, perímetro m

gist /dʒɪst/ n essencial m

give /gɪv/ vt/i (pt gave, pp given) dar; (bend, yield) ceder. ~ away dar; (secret) revelar, trair. ~ back devolver. ~ in dar-se por vencido, render-se. ~ off emitir. ~ out vt anunciar □ vi esgotar-se. ~ up vt/i desistir (de), renunciar (a). ~ **o.s. up** entregar-se. ~ **way** ceder; (*traffic*) dar prioridade; (*collapse*) dar de si

given /'gɪvn/ *see* **give** □ *a* dado. ~ **name** nome *m* de batismo, (*P*) baptismo

glacier /'glæsɪə(r)/ *n* glaciar *m*, geleira *f*

glad /glæd/ *a* contente. ~**ly** *adv* com (todo o) prazer

gladden /'glædn/ *vt* alegrar

glam|our /'glæmə(r)/ *n* fascinação *f*, encanto *m*. ~**orize** *vt* tornar fascinante. ~**orous** *a* fascinante, sedutor

glance /gla:ns/ *n* relance *m*, olhar *m* □ *vi* ~ **at** dar uma olhada a. **at first** ~ à primeira vista

gland /glænd/ *n* glândula *f*

glar|e /gleə(r)/ *vi* brilhar intensamente, faiscar □ *n* luz *f* crua; (*fig*) olhar *m* feroz. ~**e at** olhar ferozmente para. ~**ing** *a* brilhante; (*obvious*) flagrante

glass /gla:s/ *n* vidro *m*; (*vessel, its contents*) copo *m*; (*mirror*) espelho *m*. ~**es** óculos *mpl*. ~**y** *a* vítreo

glaze /gleɪz/ *vt* (*door etc*) envidraçar; (*pottery*) vidrar □ *n* vidrado *m*

gleam /gli:m/ *n* raio *m* de luz frouxa; (*fig*) vislumbre *m* □ *vi* luzir, brilhar

glean /gli:n/ *vt* catar

glee /gli:/ *n* alegria *f*. ~**ful** *a* cheio de alegria

glib /glɪb/ *a* que tem a palavra fácil, verboso. ~**ly** *adv* fluentemente, sem hesitação. ~**ness** *n* verbosidade *f*

glide /glaɪd/ *vi* deslizar; (*bird, plane*) planar. ~**r** /-ə(r)/ *n* planador *m*

glimmer /'glɪmə(r)/ *n* luz *f* trêmula □ *vi* tremular

glimpse /glɪmps/ *n* vislumbre *m*. **catch a** ~ **of** entrever, ver de relance

glint /glɪnt/ *n* brilho *m*, reflexo *m* □ *vi* brilhar, cintilar

glisten /'glɪsn/ *vi* reluzir

glitter /'glɪtə(r)/ *vi* luzir, resplandecer □ *n* esplendor *m*, cintilação *f*

gloat /gləʊt/ *vi* ~ **over** ter um prazer maligno em, exultar com

global /'gləʊbl/ *a* global

globe /gləʊb/ *n* globo *m*

gloom /glu:m/ *n* obscuridade *f*; (*fig*) tristeza *f*. ~**y** *a* sombrio; (*sad*) triste; (*pessimistic*) pessimista

glorif|y /'glɔːrɪfaɪ/ *vt* glorificar. **a** ~**ied waitress/***etc* pouco mais que uma garçonete/*etc*

glorious /'glɔːrɪəs/ *a* glorioso

glory /'glɔːrɪ/ *n* glória *f*; (*beauty*) esplendor *m* □ *vi* ~ **in** orgulhar-se de

gloss /glɒs/ *n* brilho *m* □ *a* brilhante □ *vt* ~ **over** minimizar, encobrir. ~**y** *a* brilhante

glossary /'glɒsərɪ/ *n* (*pl* -**ries**) glossário *m*

glove /glʌv/ *n* luva *f*. ~ **compartment** porta-luvas *m*. ~**d** *a* enluvado

glow /gləʊ/ *vi* arder; (*person*) resplandecer; (*eyes*) brilhar □ *n* brasa *f*. ~**ing** *a* (*fig*) entusiástico

glucose /'glu:kəʊs/ *n* glucose *f*

glue /glu:/ *n* cola *f* □ *vt* (*pres p* **gluing**) colar

glum /glʌm/ *a* (**glummer, glummest**) sorumbático; (*dejected*) abatido

glut /glʌt/ *n* superabundância *f*

glutton /'glʌtn/ *n* glutão *m*. ~**ous** *a* glutão. ~**y** *n* gula *f*

gnarled /na:ld/ *a* nodoso

gnash /næʃ/ *vt* ~ **one's teeth** ranger os dentes

gnat /næt/ *n* mosquito *m*

gnaw /nɔː/ *vt/i* roer

gnome /nəʊm/ *n* gnomo *m*

go /gəʊ/ *vi* (*pt* **went**, *pp* **gone**) ir; (*leave*) ir, ir-se; (*mech*) andar, funcionar; (*become*) ficar; (*be sold*) vender-se; (*vanish*) ir-se, desaparecer □ *n* (*pl* **goes**) (*energy*) dinamismo *m*; (*try*) tentativa *f*; (*success*) sucesso *m*; (*turn*) vez *f*. ~ **riding** ir andar *or* montar a cavalo. ~ **shopping** ir às compras. **be** ~**ing to do** ir fazer. ~ **ahead** ir para diante. ~ **away** ir-se embora. ~ **back** voltar atrás (**on** com). ~ **bad** estragar-se. ~ **by** (*pass*) passar. ~ **down** descer; (*sun*) pôr-se; (*ship*) afundar-se. ~ **for** ir buscar; (*like*) gostar de; (*sl: attack*) atirar-se a, ir-se a (*colloq*). ~ **in** entrar. ~ **in for** (*exam*) apresentar-se a. ~ **off** ir-se; (*explode*) rebentar; (*sound*) soar; (*decay*) estragar-se. ~ **on** continuar; (*happen*) acontecer. ~ **out** sair; (*light*) apagar-se. ~ **over** *or* **through** verificar, examinar. ~ **round** (**be** *enough*) chegar. ~ **under** ir abaixo. ~ **up** subir. ~ **without** passar sem. **on the** ~ em grande atividade, (*P*) actividade. ~**-ahead** *n* luz *f* verde □ *a* dinâmico, empreendedor. ~**-between** *n* intermediário *m*. ~**-kart** *n* kart *m*. ~**-slow** *n* operação *f* tartaruga, (*P*) greve *f* de zelo

goad /gəʊd/ *vt* aguilhoar, espicaçar

goal /gəʊl/ *n* meta *f*; (*area*) baliza *f*; (*score*) gol *m*, (*P*) golo *m*. ~**-post** *n* trave *f*

goalkeeper /'gəʊlkiːpə(r)/ *n* goleiro *m*, (*P*) guarda-redes *m*

goat /gəʊt/ *n* cabra *f*

gobble /'gɒbl/ *vt* comer com sofreguidão, devorar

goblet /'gɒblɪt/ *n* taça *f*, cálice *m*

goblin /'gɒblɪn/ *n* duende *m*

God /gɒd/ *n* Deus *m*. ~**-forsaken** *a* miserável, abandonado

god /gɒd/ *n* deus *m*. **~-daughter** *n*
afilhada *f*. **~dess** *n* deusa *f*. **~father**
n padrinho *m*. **~ly** *a* devoto.
~mother *n* madrinha *f*. **~son** *n* afilhado *m*

godsend /'gɒdsend/ *n* achado *m*,
dádiva *f* do céu

goggles /'gɒglz/ *npl* óculos *mpl* de
proteção, (*P*) protecção

going /'gəʊŋ/ *n* **it is slow/hard ~** é
demorado/difícil □ *a* (*price, rate*) corrente, atual, (*P*) actual. **~s-on** *npl*
acontecimentos *mpl* estranhos

gold /gəʊld/ *n* ouro *m* □ *a* de/em ouro.
~-mine *n* mina *f* de ouro

golden /'gəʊldən/ *a* de ouro; (*like
gold*) dourado; (*opportunity*) único.
~ wedding bodas *fpl* de ouro

goldfish /'gəʊldfɪʃ/ *n* peixe *m* doura-
do/vermelho

goldsmith /'gəʊldsmɪθ/ *n* ourives *m
inv*

golf /gɒlf/ *n* golfe *m*. **~ club** clube *m*
de golfe, associação *f* de golfe; (*stick*)
taco *m*. **~-course** *n* campo *m* de golfe.
~er *n* jogador *m* de golfe

gone /gɒn/ *see* **go** □ *a* ido, passado. **~
six o'clock** depois das seis

gong /gɒŋ/ *n* gongo *m*

good /gʊd/ *a* (**better, best**) bom □ *n*
bem *m*. **as ~ as** praticamente. **for ~**
para sempre. **it is no ~** não adianta.
it is no ~ shouting/*etc* não adianta
gritar/*etc*. **~ afternoon** *int* boa(s)
tarde(s). **~ evening/night** *int* boa(s)
noite(s). **G~ Friday** Sexta-feira
f Santa. **~-looking** *a* bonito. **~
morning** *int* bom dia. **~ name** bom
nome *m*

goodbye /gʊd'baɪ/ *int & n* adeus (*m*)

goodness /'gʊdnɪs/ *n* bondade *f*. **my
~ness!** meu Deus!

goods /gʊdz/ *npl* (*comm*) mercadorias
fpl. **~ train** trem *m* de carga, (*P*)
comboio *m* de mercadorias

goodwill /gʊd'wɪl/ *n* boa vontade *f*

goose /guːs/ *n* (*pl* **geese**) ganso *m*. **~-
flesh, ~-pimples** *ns* pele *f* de galinha

gooseberry /'gʊzbərɪ/ *n* (*fruit*) groselha *f*; (*bush*) groselheira *f*

gore¹ /gɔː(r)/ *n* sangue *m* coagulado

gore² /gɔː(r)/ *vt* perfurar

gorge /gɔːdʒ/ *n* desfiladeiro *m*, garganta *f* □ *vt* **~ o.s.** empanturrar-se

gorgeous /'gɔːdʒəs/ *a* magnífico, maravilhoso

gorilla /gə'rɪlə/ *n* gorila *m*

gormless /'gɔːmlɪs/ *a* (*sl*) estúpido

gorse /gɔːs/ *n* giesta *f*, tojo *m*, urze *f*

gory /'gɔːrɪ/ *a* (**-ier, -iest**) sangrento

gosh /gɒʃ/ *int* puxa!, (*P*) caramba!

gospel /'gɒspl/ *n* evangelho *m*

gossip /'gɒsɪp/ *n* bisbilhotice *f*, fofoca
f; (*person*) bisbilhoteiro *m*, fofoqueiro

m □ *vi* (*pt* **gossiped**) bisbilhotar. **~y**
a bisbilhoteiro, fofoqueiro

got /gɒt/ *see* **get**. **have ~** ter. **have ~
to do** ter de *or* que fazer

Gothic /'gɒθɪk/ *a* gótico

gouge /gaʊdʒ/ *vt* **~ out** arrancar

gourmet /'gʊəmeɪ/ *n* gastrônomo *m*,
(*P*) gastrónomo *m*, gourmet *m*

gout /gaʊt/ *n* gota *f*

govern /'gʌvn/ *vt/i* governar. **~ess** *n*
preceptora *f*. **~or** *n* governador *m*; (*of
school, hospital etc*) diretor *m*, (*P*)
director *m*

government /'gʌvənmənt/ *n* governo
m. **~al** /-'mentl/ *a* governamental

gown /gaʊn/ *n* vestido *m*; (*of judge,
teacher*) toga *f*

GP *abbr see* **general practitioner**

grab /græb/ *vt* (*pt* **grabbed**) agarrar,
apanhar

grace /greɪs/ *n* graça *f* □ *vt* honrar;
(*adorn*) ornar. **say ~** dar graças.
~ful *a* gracioso

gracious /'greɪʃəs/ *a* gracioso; (*kind*)
amável, afável

grade /greɪd/ *n* categoria *f*; (*of goods*)
classe *f*, qualidade *f*; (*on scale*) grau
m; (*school mark*) nota *f* □ *vt* classificar

gradient /'greɪdɪənt/ *n* gradiente *m*,
declive *m*

gradual /'grædʒʊəl/ *a* gradual,
progressivo. **~ly** *adv* gradualmente

graduate¹ /'grædʒʊət/ *n* diplomado
m, graduado *m*, licenciado *m*

graduat|e² /'grædʒʊeɪt/ *vt/i* formar
(-se). **~ion** /-'eɪʃn/ *n* colação *f* de
grau, (*P*) formatura *f*

graffiti /grə'fiːtiː/ *npl* graffiti *mpl*

graft /grɑːft/ *n* (*med, bot*) enxerto *m*;
(*work*) batalha *f* □ *vt* enxertar; (*work*)
batalhar

grain /greɪn/ *n* grão *m*; (*collectively*)
cereais *mpl*; (*in wood*) veio *m*.
against the ~ (*fig*) contra a maneira
de ser

gram /græm/ *n* grama *m*

grammar /'græmə(r)/ *n* gramática *f*.
~atical /grə'mætɪkl/ *a* gramatical

grand /grænd/ *a* (**-er, -est**) grandioso,
magnífico; (*duke, master*) grão. **~
piano** piano *m* de cauda.

grand|child /'græntʃaɪld/ *n* (*pl*
-children) neto *m*. **~daughter** *n*
neta *f*. **~father** *n* avô *m*. **~mother**
n avó *f*. **~parents** *npl* avós *mpl*.
~son *n* neto *m*

grandeur /'grændʒə(r)/ *n* grandeza *f*

grandiose /'grændɪəʊs/ *a* grandioso

grandstand /'grændstænd/ *n* tribuna
f principal

granite /'grænɪt/ *n* granito *m*

grant /grɑːnt/ *vt* conceder; (*a request*)
ceder a; (*admit*) admitir (**that** que) □
n subsídio *m*; (*univ*) bolsa *f*. **take for**

~**ed** ter como coisa garantida, contar com

grape /greɪp/ n uva f

grapefruit /'greɪpfruːt/ n inv grape-fruit m, toronja f

graph /grɑːf/ n gráfico m

graphic /'græfɪk/ a gráfico; (fig) vívido. ~**s** npl (comput) gráficos mpl

grapple /'græpl/ vi ~ **with** estar engalfinhado com; (fig) estar às voltas com

grasp /grɑːsp/ vt agarrar; (understand) compreender □ n domínio m; (reach) alcance m; (fig: understanding) compreensão f

grasping /'grɑːspɪŋ/ a ganancioso

grass /grɑːs/ n erva f; (lawn) grama f, (P) relva f; (pasture) pastagem f; (sl: informer) delator m □ vt cobrir com grama; (sl: betray) delatar. ~ **roots** (pol) bases fpl. ~**y** a coberto de erva

grasshopper /'grɑːshɒpə(r)/ n gafanhoto m

grate[1] /greɪt/ n (fireplace) lareira f; (frame) grelha f

grate[2] /greɪt/ vt ralar □ vi ranger. ~ **one's teeth** ranger os dentes. ~**r** /-ə(r)/ n ralador m

grateful /'greɪtfl/ a grato, agradecido. ~**ly** adv com reconhecimento, com gratidão

gratify /'grætɪfaɪ/ vt (pt -fied) contentar, satisfazer. ~**ing** a gratificante

grating /'greɪtɪŋ/ n grade f

gratis /'greɪtɪs/ a & adv grátis (invar), de graça

gratitude /'grætɪtjuːd/ n gratidão f, reconhecimento m

gratuitous /grə'tjuːɪtəs/ a gratuito; (uncalled-for) sem motivo

gratuity /grə'tjuːətɪ/ n gratificação f, gorjeta f

grave[1] /greɪv/ n cova f, sepultura f, túmulo m

grave[2] /greɪv/ a (-er, -est) grave, sério. ~**ly** adv gravemente

grave[3] /grɑːv/ a ~ **accent** acento m grave

gravel /'grævl/ n cascalho m miúdo, saibro m

gravestone /'greɪvstəʊn/ n lápide f, campa f

graveyard /'greɪvjɑːd/ n cemitério m

gravity /'grævətɪ/ n gravidade f

gravy /'greɪvɪ/ n molho m (de carne)

graze[1] /greɪz/ vt/i pastar

graze[2] /greɪz/ vt roçar; (scrape) esfolar □ n esfoladura f, (P) esfoladela f

greas|e /griːs/ n gordura f □ vt engordurar; (culin) untar; (mech) lubrificar. ~**e-proof paper** papel m vegetal. ~**y** a gorduroso

great /greɪt/ a (-er, -est) grande; (colloq: splendid) esplêndido. **G**~ **Brit-**ain Grã-Bretanha f. ~-**grandfather** n bisavô m. ~-**grandmother** f bisavó f. ~**ly** adv grandemente, muito. ~**ness** n grandeza f

Great Britain /greɪt'brɪtən/ n Grã-Bretanha f

Greece /griːs/ n Grécia f

greed /griːd/ n cobiça f, ganância f; (for food) gula f. ~**y** a cobiçoso, ganancioso; (for food) guloso

Greek /griːk/ a & n grego (m)

green /griːn/ a (-er, -est) verde □ n verde m; (grass) gramado m, (P) relvado m. ~**s** hortaliças fpl. ~ **belt** zona f verde, paisagem f protegida. ~ **light** luz f verde. ~**ery** n verdura f

greengrocer /'griːnɡrəʊsə(r)/ n quitandeiro m, (P) vendedor m de hortaliças

greenhouse /'griːnhaʊs/ n estufa f. ~ **effect** efeito estufa

Greenland /'griːnlənd/ n Groenlândia f

greet /griːt/ vt acolher. ~**ing** n saudação f; (welcome) acolhimento m. ~**ings** npl cumprimentos mpl; (Christmas etc) votos mpl, desejos mpl

gregarious /grɪ'ɡeərɪəs/ a gregário; (person) sociável

grenade /grɪ'neɪd/ n granada f

grew /gruː/ see **grow**

grey /greɪ/ a (-er, -est) cinzento; (of hair) grisalho □ n cinzento m

greyhound /'greɪhaʊnd/ n galgo m

grid /grɪd/ n (grating) gradeamento m, grade f; (electr) rede f

grief /griːf/ n dor f. **come to** ~ acabar mal

grievance /'griːvns/ n razão f de queixa

grieve /griːv/ vt sofrer, afligir □ vi sofrer. ~ **for** chorar por

grill /grɪl/ n grelha f; (food) grelhado m; (place) grill m □ vt grelhar; (question) submeter a interrogatório cerrado, apertar com perguntas □ vi grelhar

grille /grɪl/ n grade f; (of car) grelha f

grim /grɪm/ a (grimmer, grimmest) sinistro; (without mercy) implacável

grimace /grɪ'meɪs/ n careta f □ vi fazer careta(s)

grim|e /graɪm/ n sujeira f. ~**y** a encardido, sujo

grin /grɪn/ vi (pt grinned) sorrir abertamente, dar um sorriso largo □ n sorriso m aberto

grind /graɪnd/ vt (pt ground) triturar; (coffee) moer; (sharpen) amolar, afiar. ~ **one's teeth** ranger os dentes. ~ **to a halt** parar freando lentamente

grip /grɪp/ vt (pt gripped) agarrar;

(*interest*) prender □ *n* (*of hands*) aperto *m*; (*control*) controle *m*, domínio *m*. **come to ~s with** arcar com. **~ping** *a* apaixonante

grisly /'grɪzlɪ/ *a* (-ier, -iest) macabro, horrível

gristle /'grɪsl/ *n* cartilagem *f*

grit /grɪt/ *n* areia *f*, grão *m* de areia; (*fig: pluck*) coragem *f*, fortaleza *f* □ *vt* (*pt* gritted) (*road*) jogar areia em; (*teeth*) cerrar

groan /grəʊn/ *vi* gemer □ *n* gemido *m*

grocer /'grəʊsə(r)/ *n* dono/a *m/f* de mercearia. **~ies** *npl* artigos *mpl* de mercearia. **~y** *n* (*shop*) mercearia *f*

groggy /'grɒgɪ/ *a* (-ier, -iest) grogue, fraco das pernas

groin /grɔɪn/ *n* virilha *f*

groom /gru:m/ *n* noivo *m*; (*for horses*) moço *m* de estrebaria □ *vt* (*horse*) tratar de; (*fig*) preparar

groove /gru:v/ *n* ranhura *f*; (*for door, window*) calha *f*; (*in record*) estria *f*; (*fig*) rotina *f*

grope /grəʊp/ *vi* tatear. **~ for** procurar às cegas

gross /grəʊs/ *a* (-er, -est) (*vulgar*) grosseiro; (*flagrant*) flagrante; (*of error*) crasso; (*of weight, figure etc*) bruto □ *n* (*pl invar*) grosa *f*. **~ly** *adv* grosseiramente; (*very*) extremamente

grotesque /grəʊ'tesk/ *a* grotesco

grotty /'grɒtɪ/ *a* (*sl*) sórdido

grouch /graʊtʃ/ *vi* (*colloq*) ralhar. **~y** *a* (*colloq*) rabugento

ground¹ /graʊnd/ *n* chão *m*, solo *m*; (*area*) terreno *m*; (*reason*) razão *f*, motivo *m*. **~s** jardins *mpl*; (*of coffee*) borra(s) *f* (*pl*) □ *vt/i* (*naut*) encalhar; (*plane*) reter em terra. **~ floor** térreo *m*, (*P*) rés-do-chão *m*. **~less** *a* infundado, sem fundamento

ground² /graʊnd/ *see* **grind**

grounding /'graʊndɪŋ/ *n* bases *fpl*, conhecimentos *mpl* básicos

groundsheet /'graʊndʃi:t/ *n* impermeável *m* para o chão

groundwork /'graʊndwɜ:k/ *n* trabalhos *mpl* de base or preliminares

group /gru:p/ *n* grupo *m* □ *vt/i* agrupar(-se)

grouse¹ /graʊs/ *n* (*pl invar*) galo *m* silvestre

grouse² /graʊs/ *vi* (*colloq: grumble*) resmungar; (*colloq: complain*) queixar-se

grovel /'grɒvl/ *vi* (*pt* grovelled) humilhar-se; (*fig*) rebaixar-se

grow /grəʊ/ *vi* (*pt* grew, *pp* grown) crescer; (*become*) tornar-se □ *vt* cultivar. **~ old** envelhecer. **~ up** crescer, tornar-se adulto. **~er** *n* cultivador *m*, produtor *m*. **~ing** *a* crescente

growl /graʊl/ *vi* rosnar □ *n* rosnadela *f*

grown /grəʊn/ *see* **grow** □ *a* **~ man** homem feito. **~-up** *a* adulto □ (*increase*) aumento *m*; (*med*) tumor *m*

grub /grʌb/ *n* larva *f*; (*sl: food*) papança *f* (*collog*) (*B*) bóia (*sl*) *f*, (*P*) alimento *m*

grubby /'grʌbɪ/ *a* (-ier, -iest) sujo, porco

grudge /grʌdʒ/ *vt* dar/reconhecer de má vontade □ *n* má vontade *f*. **~ doing** fazer de má vontade. **~ sb sth** dar alg a alguém má vontade. **have a ~ against** ter ressentimento contra. **grudgingly** *adv* relutantemente

gruelling /'gru:əlɪŋ/ *a* estafante, extenuante

gruesome /'gru:səm/ *a* macabro

gruff /grʌf/ *a* (-er, -est) carrancudo, rude

grumble /'grʌmbl/ *vi* resmungar (at contra, por)

grumpy /'grʌmpɪ/ *a* (-ier, -iest) malhumorado, rabugento

grunt /grʌnt/ *vi* grunhir □ *n* grunhido *m*

guarantee /gærən'ti:/ *n* garantia *f* □ *vt* garantir

guard /gɑ:d/ *vt* guardar, proteger □ *vi* **~ against** precaver-se contra □ *n* guarda *f*; (*person*) guarda *m*; (*on train*) condutor *m*. **~ian** *n* guardião *m*, defensor *m*; (*of orphan*) tutor *m*

guarded /'gɑ:dɪd/ *a* cauteloso, circunspeto, (*P*) circunspecto

guerrilla /gə'rɪlə/ *n* guerrilheiro *m*, (*P*) guerrilha *m*. **~ warfare** guerrilha *f*, guerra *f* de guerrilhas

guess /ges/ *vt/i* adivinhar; (*suppose*) supor □ *n* suposição *f*, conjetura *f*, (*P*) conjectura *f*

guesswork /'gesw3:k/ *n* suposição *f*, conjetura(s) *f* (*pl*), (*P*) conjectura(s) *f* (*pl*)

guest /gest/ *n* convidado *m*; (*in hotel*) hóspede *mf*. **~-house** *n* pensão *f*

guffaw /gə'fɔ:/ *n* gargalhada *f* □ *vi* rir à(s) gargalhada(s)

guidance /'gaɪdns/ *n* orientação *f*, direção *f*, (*P*) direcção *f*

guide /gaɪd/ *n* guia *mf* □ *vt* guiar. **~d missile** míssil *m* guiado; (*remote-control*) míssil *m* teleguiado. **~-dog** *n* cão *m* de cego, cão-guia *m*. **~-lines** *npl* diretrizes *fpl*, (*P*) directrizes *fpl*

Guide /gaɪd/ *n* Guia *f*

guidebook /'gaɪdbʊk/ *n* guia *m* (turístico)

guild /gɪld/ *n* corporação *f*

guile /gaɪl/ *n* astúcia *f*, manha *f*

guilt /gɪlt/ *n* culpa *f*. **~y** *a* culpado

guinea-pig /'gɪnɪpɪg/ n cobaia f, por-quinho-da-India m

guitar /gɪ'ta:(r)/ n guitarra f, violão m, (P) viola f. ~ist n guitarrista mf, tocador m de violão, (P) de viola

gulf /gʌlf/ n golfo m; (hollow) abismo m

gull /gʌl/ n gaivota f

gullible /'gʌləbl/ a crédulo

gully /'gʌlɪ/ n barranco m; (drain) sarjeta f

gulp /gʌlp/ vt engolir, devorar □ vi engolir em seco □ n trago m

gum[1] /gʌm/ n (anat) gengiva f

gum[2] /gʌm/ n goma f; (chewing-gum) chiclete m, goma f elástica, (P) pastilha f □ vt (pt gummed) colar

gumboot /'gʌmbu:t/ n bota f de borracha

gumption /'gʌmpʃn/ n (colloq) iniciativa f e bom senso m, cabeça f, juizo m

gun /gʌn/ n (pistol) pistola f; (rifle) espingarda f; (cannon) canhão m □ vt (pt gunned) a tiro

gunfire /'gʌnfaɪə(r)/ n tiroteio m

gunman /'gʌnmən/ n (pl -men) bandido m armado

gunpowder /'gʌnpaʊdə(r)/ n pólvora f

gunshot /'gʌnʃɒt/ n tiro m

gurgle /'gɜ:gl/ n gorgolejo m □ vi gorgolejar

gush /gʌʃ/ vi jorrar □ n jorro m. ~ing a efusivo, derretido

gust /gʌst/ n (of wind) rajada f; (of smoke) nuvem f. ~y a ventoso

gusto /'gʌstəʊ/ n gosto m, entusiasmo m

gut /gʌt/ n tripa f. ~s (belly) barriga f; (colloq: courage) coragem f □ vt (pt gutted) estripar; (fish) limpar; (fire) destruir o interior de

gutter /'gʌtə(r)/ n calha f, canaleta f; (in street) sarjeta f, valeta f

guy /gaɪ/ n (sl: man) cara m, (P) tipo m (colloq)

guzzle /'gʌzl/ vt/i comer/beber com sofreguidão, encher-se (de)

gym /dʒɪm/ n (colloq: gymnasium) ginásio m; (colloq: gymnastics) ginástica f. ~-slip n uniforme m escolar

gym|nasium /dʒɪm'neɪzɪəm/ n ginásio m. ~nast /'dʒɪmnæst/ n ginasta mf. ~nastics /-'næstɪks/ npl ginástica f

gynaecolog|y /gaɪnɪ'kɒlədʒɪ/ n ginecologia f. ~ist n ginecologista mf

gypsy /'dʒɪpsɪ/ n cigano m

gyrate /dʒaɪ'reɪt/ vi girar

H

haberdashery /'hæbədæʃərɪ/ n armarinho m, (P) retrosaria f

habit /'hæbɪt/ n hábito m, costume m; (costume) hábito m. be in/get into the ~ of ter/apanhar o hábito de

habit|able /'hæbɪtəbl/ a habitável. ~ation /-'teɪʃn/ n habitação f

habitat /'hæbɪtæt/ n habitat m

habitual /hə'bɪtʃʊəl/ a habitual, costumeiro; (smoker, liar) inveterado. ~ly adv habitualmente

hack[1] /hæk/ n (horse) cavalo m de aluguel; (writer) escrevinhador (pej) m

hack[2] /hæk/ vt cortar, despedaçar. ~ to pieces cortar em pedaços

hackneyed /'hæknɪd/ a banal, batido

had /hæd/ see have

haddock /'hædək/ n invar hadoque m, eglefim m. smoked ~ hadoque m fumado

haemorrhage /'hemərɪdʒ/ n hemorragia f

haemorrhoids /'hemərɔɪdz/ npl hemorróidas fpl

haggard /'hægəd/ a desfigurado, com o rosto desfeito, magro e macilento

haggle /'hægl/ vi ~ (over) regatear

hail[1] /heɪl/ vt saudar; (taxi) fazer sinal para, chamar □ vi ~ from vir de

hail[2] /heɪl/ n granizo m, (P) saraiva f, (P) chuva de pedra f □ vi chover granizo, (P) saraivar

hailstone /'heɪlstəʊn/ n pedra f de granizo

hair /heə(r)/ n (on head) cabelo(s) m(pl); (on body) pêlos mpl; (single strand) cabelo m; (of animal) pêlo m. ~-do n (colloq) penteado m. ~-dryer n secador m de cabelo. ~-raising a horripilante, de pôr os cabelos em pé. ~-style n estilo m de penteado

hairbrush /'heəbrʌʃ/ n escova f para o cabelo

haircut /'heəkʌt/ n corte m de cabelo

hairdresser /'heədresə(r)/ n cabeleireiro m, cabeleireira f

hairpin /'heəpɪn/ n grampo m, (P) gancho m para o cabelo. ~ bend curva f techada, quase em W

hairy /'heərɪ/ a (-ier, -iest) peludo, cabeludo; (sl: terrifying) de pôr os cabelos em pé, horripilante

hake /heɪk/ n (pl invar) abrótea f

half /ha:f/ n (pl halves /ha:vz/) metade f, meio m □ a meio □ adv ao meio. ~ a dozen meia dúzia. ~ an hour meia hora. ~-caste n mestiço m. ~-hearted a sem grande entusiasmo. ~-**term** n férias fpl no meio do trimestre. ~-**time** n meiotempo m. ~-**way** a & adv a meio caminho. ~-**wit** n idiota mf. **go halves** dividir as despesas

halibut /'hælɪbət/ n (pl invar) halibute m

hall /hɔːl/ n sala f; (entrance) vestíbulo m, entrada f; (mansion) solar m. ~ **of residence** residência f de estudantes

hallmark /'hɔːlmɑːk/ n (on gold etc) marca f do contraste; (fig) cunho m, selo m

hallo /hə'ləʊ/ int & n (greeting, surprise) olá; (on phone) está

hallow /'hæləʊ/ vt consagrar, santificar

Halloween /hæləʊ'iːn/ n véspera f do Dia de Todos os Santos

hallucination /həluːsɪ'neɪʃn/ n alucinação f

halo /'heɪləʊ/ n (pl -oes) halo m, auréola f

halt /hɔːlt/ n parada f, (P) paragem f □ vt deter, fazer parar □ vi fazer alto, parar

halve /hɑːv/ vt dividir ao meio; (time etc) reduzir à metade

ham /hæm/ n presunto m

hamburger /'hæmbɜːgə(r)/ n hambúrguer m, (P) hamburgo m

hamlet /'hæmlɪt/ n aldeola f, lugarejo m

hammer /'hæmə(r)/ n martelo m □ vt/i martelar; (fig) bater com força

hammock /'hæmək/ n rede f (de dormir)

hamper[1] /'hæmpə(r)/ n cesto m, (P) cabaz m

hamper[2] /'hæmpə(r)/ vt dificultar, atrapalhar

hamster /'hæmstə(r)/ n hamster m

hand /hænd/ n mão f; (of clock) ponteiro m; (writing) letra f; (worker) trabalhador m; (cards) mão f; (measure) palmo m. (helping) ~ ajuda f, mão f □ vt dar, entregar. **at** ~ à mão. ~-**baggage** n bagagem f de mão. ~ **in** or over entregar. ~ **out** distribuir. ~-**out** n impresso m, folheto m; (money) esmola f, donativo m. **on the one** ~ ... **on the other** ~ por um lado ... por outro. **out of** ~ incontrolável. **to** ~ à mão

handbag /'hændbæg/ n carteira f, bolsa de mão f, mala de mão f

handbook /'hændbʊk/ n manual m

handbrake /'hændbreɪk/ n freio m de mão, (P) travão m de mão

handcuffs /'hændkʌfs/ npl algemas fpl

handful /'hændfʊl/ n mão-cheia f, punhado m; (a few) punhado m; (diffi-

cult task) mão-de-obra f. **she's a** ~ (colloq) ela é danada

handicap /'hændɪkæp/ n (in competition) handicap m; (disadvantage) desvantagem f □ vt (pt **handicapped**) prejudicar. ~**ped** a deficiente. **mentally** ~**ped** deficiente mental

handicraft /'hændɪkrɑːft/ n artesanato m, trabalho m manual

handiwork /'hændɪwɜːk/ n obra f, trabalho m

handkerchief /'hæŋkətʃɪf/ n lenço m

handle /'hændl/ n (of door etc) maçaneta f, puxador m; (of cup etc) asa f; (of implement) cabo m; (of pan etc) alça f, (P) pega f □ vt (touch) manusear, tocar; (operate with hands) manejar; (deal in) negociar em; (deal with) tratar de; (person) lidar com. **fly off the** ~ (colloq) perder as estribeiras

handlebar /'hændlbɑː(r)/ n guidão m, (P) guiador m

handmade /'hændmeɪd/ a feito à mão

handshake /'hændʃeɪk/ n aperto m de mão

handsome /'hænsəm/ a bonito; (fig) generoso

handwriting /'hændraɪtɪŋ/ n letra f, caligrafia f

handy /'hændɪ/ a (-ier, -iest) a (convenient, useful) útil, prático; (person) jeitoso; (near) à mão

handyman /'hændɪmæn/ n (pl -men) faz-tudo m

hang /hæŋ/ vt (pt **hung**) pendurar, suspender; (head) baixar; (pt **hanged**) (criminal) enforcar □ vi estar dependurado, pender; (criminal) ser enforcado. **get the** ~ **of** (colloq) pegar o jeito de, (P) apanhar. ~ **about** andar por aí. ~ **back** hesitar. ~-**gliding** n asa f delta. ~ **on** (wait) aguardar. ~ **on to** (hold tightly) agarrar-se a. ~ **out** (sl: live) morar. ~ **up** (phone) desligar. ~-**up** n (sl) complexo m

hangar /'hæŋə(r)/ n hangar m

hanger /'hæŋə(r)/ n (for clothes) cabide m. ~-**on** n parasita mf

hangover /'hæŋəʊvə(r)/ n (from drinking) ressaca f

hanker /'hæŋkə(r)/ vi ~ **after** ansiar por, suspirar por

haphazard /hæp'hæzəd/ a ~ **ly** adv ao acaso, à sorte

happen /'hæpən/ vi acontecer, suceder. **he** ~**s to be out** por acaso ele não está. ~-**ing** n acontecimento m

happy|**y** /'hæpɪ/ a (-ier, -iest) feliz. **be** ~**y with** estar contente com. ~**y-go-lucky** a despreocupado. ~**ily** adv com satisfação; (fortunately) felizmente. **she smiled** ~**ily** ela sorriu feliz. ~**iness** n felicidade f

harass /'hærəs/ vt amofinar, atormentar, perseguir. ~**ment** n amofinação f, perseguição f. **sexual** ~**ment** assédio m sexual

harbour /'ha:bə(r)/ n porto m; (shelter) abrigo m □ vt abrigar, dar asilo a; (fig: in the mind) ocultar, obrigar

hard /ha:d/ a (-er, -est) duro; (difficult) difícil □ adv muito, intensamente; (look) fixamente; (pull) com força; (think) a fundo, a sério. ~**back** n livro m encadernado ~**boiled egg** ovo m cozido. ~ **by** muito perto. ~ **disk** disco m rígido. ~**headed** a realista, prático. ~ **of hearing** meio surdo. ~ **shoulder** acostamento m, (P) berma f alcatroada. ~ **up** (colloq) sem dinheiro, teso (sl), liso (sl). ~ **water** água f dura

hardboard /'ha:dbɔ:d/ n madeira f compensada, madeira f prensada, (P) tabopan m

harden /'ha:dn/ vt/i endurecer. ~**ed** a (callous) calejado; (robust) enrijado

hardly /'ha:dlı/ adv mal, dificilmente, a custo. ~ **ever** quase nunca

hardship /'ha:dʃıp/ n provação f, adversidade f; (suffering) sofrimento m; (financial) privação f

hardware /'ha:dweə(r)/ n ferragens fpl; (comput) hardware m

hardy /'ha:dı/ a (-ier, -iest) resistente

hare /heə(r)/ n lebre f

hark /ha:k/ vi ~ **back to** voltar a, recordar

harm /ha:m/ n mal m □ vt prejudicar, fazer mal a. ~**ful** a prejudicial, nocivo. ~**less** a inofensivo. **out of** ~'s **way** a salvo. **there's no** ~ **in** não há mal em

harmonica /ha:'mɒnıkə/ n gaita f de boca, (P) beiços

harmon|y /'ha:mənı/ n harmonia f. ~**ious** /-'məʊnıəs/ a harmonioso. ~**ize** vt/i harmonizar(-se)

harness /'ha:nıs/ n arreios mpl □ vt arrear; (fig: use) aproveitar, utilizar

harp /ha:p/ n harpa f □ vi ~ **on (about)** repisar. ~**ist** n harpista mf

harpoon /ha:'pu:n/ n arpão m

harpsichord /'ha:psıkɔ:d/ n cravo m

harrowing /'hærəʊıŋ/ a dilacerante, lancinante

harsh /ha:ʃ/ a (-er, -est) duro, severo; (texture, voice) áspero; (light) cru; (colour) gritante; (climate) rigoroso. ~**ly** adv duramente. ~**ness** n dureza f

harvest /'ha:vıst/ n colheita f, ceifa f □ vt colher, ceifar

has /hæz/ see **have**

hash /hæʃ/ n picadinho m, carne f cozida; (fig: jumble) bagunça f. **make a** ~ **of** fazer uma bagunça

hashish /'hæʃıʃ/ n haxixe m

hassle /'hæsl/ n (colloq: quarrel) discussão f; (colloq: struggle) dificuldade f □ vt (colloq) aborrecer

haste /heıst/ n pressa f. **make** ~ apressar-se

hasten /'heısn/ vt/i apressar(-se)

hast|y /'heıstı/ a (-ier, -iest) apressado; (too quick) precipitado. ~**ily** adv às pressas, precipitadamente

hat /hæt/ n chapéu m

hatch[1] /hætʃ/ n (for food) postigo m; (naut) escotilha f

hatch[2] /hætʃ/ vt/i chocar; (a plot etc) tramar, urdir

hatchback /'hætʃbæk/ n carro m de três ou cinco portas

hatchet /'hætʃıt/ n machadinha f

hate /heıt/ n ódio m □ vt odiar, detestar. ~**ful** a odioso, detestável

hatred /'heıtrıd/ n ódio m

haughty /'hɔ:tı/ a (-ier, -iest) altivo, soberbo, arrogante

haul /hɔ:l/ vt arrastar, puxar; (goods) transportar em camião □ n (booty) presa f; (fish caught) apanha f; (distance) percurso m. ~**age** n transporte m de cargas. ~**ier** n (firm) transportadora f rodoviária; (person) fretador m

haunt /hɔ:nt/ vt rondar, freqüentar, (P) frequentar; (ghost) assombrar; (thought) obcecar □ n lugar m favorito. ~**ed house** casa f mal-assombrada

have /hæv/ vt (3 sing pres **has**, pt **had**) ter; (bath etc) tomar; (meal) fazer; (walk) dar □ v aux ter. ~ **done** ter feito. ~ **it out (with)** pôr a coisa em pratos limpos, pedir uma explicação (para). ~ **sth done** mandar fazer alg coisa

haven /'heıvn/ n porto m; (refuge) refúgio m

haversack /'hævəsæk/ n mochila f

havoc /'hævək/ n estragos mpl. **play** ~ **with** causar estragos em

hawk[1] /hɔ:k/ n falcão m

hawk[2] /hɔ:k/ vt vender de porta em porta. ~**er** n vendedor m ambulante

hawthorn /'hɔ:θɔ:n/ n pirilteiro m, estrepeiro m

hay /heı/ n feno m. ~ **fever** febre f do feno

haystack /'heıstæk/ n palheiro m, (P) meda f de feno

haywire /'heıwaıə(r)/ a **go** ~ (colloq) ficar transtornado

hazard /'hæzəd/ n risco m □ vt arriscar. ~ **warning lights** pisca-alerta m. ~**ous** a arriscado

haze /heɪz/ n bruma f, neblina f, cerração f

hazel /'heɪzl/ n aveleira f. ~-nut n avelã f

hazy /'heɪzɪ/ a (-ier, -iest) brumoso, encoberto; (*fig: vague*) vago

he /hi:/ pron ele □ n macho m

head /hed/ n cabeça f; (*chief*) chefe m; (*of beer*) espuma f □ a principal □ vt encabeçar, estar à frente de □ vi ~ **for** dirigir-se para. ~-**dress** n toucador m. ~ **first** de cabeça. ~-**on** a frontal □ adv de frente. ~s **or tails?** cara ou coroa? ~ **waiter** chefe de garçons m, (P) dos criados. ~**er** n (*football*) cabeçada f

headache /'hedeɪk/ n dor f de cabeça

heading /'hedɪŋ/ n cabeçalho m, título m; (*subject category*) rubrica f

headlamp /'hedlæmp/ n farol m

headland /'hedlənd/ n promontório m

headlight /'hedlaɪt/ n farol m

headline /'hedlaɪn/ n título m, cabeçalho m

headlong /'hedlɒŋ/ a de cabeça; (*rash*) precipitado □ adv de cabeça; (*rashly*) precipitadamente

head|master /hed'ma:stə(r)/ n director m, (P) director m. ~**mistress** n directora f, (P) directora f

headphone /'hedfəʊn/ n fone m de cabeça, (P) auscultador m

headquarters /hed'kwɔ:təz/ npl sede f; (*mil*) quartel m general

headrest /'hedrest/ n apoio m para a cabeça

headroom /'hedru:m/ n (*auto*) espaço m para a cabeça; (*bridge*) limite m de altura, altura f máxima

headstrong /'hedstrɒŋ/ a teimoso

headway /'hedweɪ/ n progresso m. **make** ~ fazer progressos

heady /'hedɪ/ a (-ier, -iest) empolgante

heal /hi:l/ vt/i curar(-se), sarar; (*wound*) cicatrizar

health /helθ/ n saúde f. ~ **centre** posto m de saúde. ~ **foods** alimentos mpl naturais. ~**y** a saudável, sadio

heap /hi:p/ n monte m, pilha f □ vt amontoar, empilhar. ~**s of money** (*colloq*) dinheiro aos montes (*colloq*)

hear /hɪə(r)/ vt/i (pt **heard** /hɜ:d/) ouvir. ~, **hear!** apoiado! ~ **from** ter notícias de. ~ **of** or **about** ouvir falar de. **I won't** ~ **of it** nem quero ouvir falar nisso. ~**ing** n ouvido m, audição f; (*jur*) audiência f. ~**ing-aid** n aparelho m de audição

hearsay /'hɪəseɪ/ n boato m. **it's only** ~ é só por ouvir dizer

hearse /hɜ:s/ n carro m funerário

heart /ha:t/ n coração m. ~**s** (*cards*) copas fpl. **at** ~ no fundo. **by** ~ de cor. ~ **attack** ataque m de coração. ~-**beat** n pulsação f, batida f. ~-**breaking** a de cortar o coração. ~-**broken** a com o coração partido, desfeito. ~-**to-heart** a com o coração nas mãos. **lose** ~ perder a coragem, desanimar

heartburn /'ha:tbɜ:n/ n azia f

hearten /'ha:tn/ vt animar, encorajar

heartfelt /'ha:tfelt/ a sincero, sentido

hearth /ha:θ/ n lareira f

heartless /'ha:tlɪs/ a insensível, desalmado, cruel

heart|y /'ha:tɪ/ a (-ier, -iest) caloroso; (*meal*) abundante. ~**ily** adv calorosamente; (*eat, laugh*) com vontade

heat /hi:t/ n calor m; (*fig*) ardor m; (*contest*) eliminatória f □ vt/i aquecer. ~**stroke** n insolação f. ~**wave** n onda f de calor. ~**er** n aquecedor m. ~**ing** n aquecimento m

heated /'hi:tɪd/ a (*fig*) acalorado, aceso

heathen /'hi:ðn/ n pagão m, pagã f

heather /'heðə(r)/ n urze f

heave /hi:v/ vt/i (*lift*) içar; (a sigh) soltar; (*retch*) ter náuseas; (*colloq: throw*) atirar

heaven /'hevn/ n céu m. ~**ly** a celestial; (*colloq*) divino

heav|y /'hevɪ/ a (-ier, -iest) pesado; (*blow, rain*) forte; (*cold, drinker*) grande; (*traffic*) intenso. ~**ily** adv pesadamente; (*drink, smoke etc*) inveterado

heavyweight /'hevɪweɪt/ n (*boxing*) peso-pesado m

Hebrew /'hi:bru:/ a hebreu, hebraico □ n (*lang*) hebreu m

heckle /'hekl/ vt interromper, interpelar

hectic /'hektɪk/ a muito agitado, febril

hedge /hedʒ/ n sebe f □ vt cercar □ vi (*in answering*) usar de evasivas. ~ **one's bets** (*fig*) resguardar-se

hedgehog /'hedʒhɒg/ n ouriço-cacheiro m

heed /hi:d/ vt prestar atenção a, escutar □ n **pay** ~ **to** prestar atenção a, dar ouvidos a. ~**less** a ~**less of** indiferente a, sem prestar atenção a

heel /hi:l/ n calcanhar m; (*of shoe*) salto m; (*sl*) canalha m

hefty /'heftɪ/ a (-ier, -iest) robusto e corpulento

height /haɪt/ n altura f; (*of mountain, plane*) altitude f; (*fig*) auge m, cúmulo m

heighten /'haɪtn/ vt/i aumentar, elevar(-se)

heir /eə(r)/ n herdeiro m. ~**ess** n herdeira f

heirloom /'eəluːm/ *n* peça *f* de família, (*P*) relíquia *f* de família
held /held/ *see* **hold**[1]
helicopter /'helɪkɒptə(r)/ *n* helicóptero *m*
hell /hel/ *n* inferno *m*. **for the ~ of it** só por gozo. **~-bent** *a* decidido a todo o custo (**on** a). **~ish** *a* infernal
hello /hə'ləʊ/ *int* & *n* = **hallo**
helm /helm/ *n* leme *m*
helmet /'helmɪt/ *n* capacete *m*
help /help/ *vt/i* ajudar □ *n* ajuda *f*. **home ~** empregada *f*, faxineira *f*, (*P*) mulher *f* a dias. **~ o.s.** to servir-se de. **he cannot ~ laughing** ele não pode conter o riso. **it can't be ~ed** não há remédio. **~er** *n* ajudante *mf*. **~ful** *a* útil; (*serviceable*) de grande ajuda. **~less** *a* impotente
helping /'helpɪŋ/ *n* porção *f*, dose *f*
hem /hem/ *n* bainha *f* □ *vt* (*pt* **hemmed**) fazer a bainha. **~ in** cercar, encurralar
hemisphere /'hemɪsfɪə(r)/ *n* hemisfério *m*
hemp /hemp/ *n* cânhamo *m*
hen /hen/ *n* galinha *f*
hence /hens/ *adv* (*from now*) a partir desta altura; (*for this reason*) daí, por isso. **a week ~** daqui a uma semana. **~forth** *adv* de agora em diante, doravante
henpecked /'henpekt/ *a* mandado, (*P*) dominado pela mulher
her /hɜː(r)/ *pron* a (a ela); (*after prep*) ela. (**to**) **~** lhe. **I know ~** conheço-a □ *a* seu(s), sua(s); dela
herald /'herəld/ *vt* anunciar
heraldry /'herəldrɪ/ *n* heráldica *f*
herb /hɜːb/ *n* erva *f* culinária *or* medicinal
herd /hɜːd/ *n* manada *f*; (*of pigs*) vara *f* □ *vi* **~ together** juntar-se em rebanho
here /hɪə(r)/ *adv* aqui □ *int* tome; aqui está. **to/from ~** para aqui/daqui
hereafter /hɪər'aːftə(r)/ *adv* de/para o futuro, daqui em diante □ *n* **the ~** a vida de além-túmulo, (*P*) a vida futura
hereby /hɪə'baɪ/ *adv* (*jur*) pelo presente ato ou decreto, etc, (*P*) pelo presente acto ou decreto, etc
hereditary /hɪ'redɪtrɪ/ *a* hereditário
heredity /hɪ'redətɪ/ *n* hereditariedade *f*
here|sy /'herəsɪ/ *n* heresia *f*. **~tic** *n* herege *mf*. **~tical** /hɪ'retɪkl/ *a* herético
heritage /'herɪtɪdʒ/ *n* herança *f*, patrimônio *m*, (*P*) património *m*
hermit /'hɜːmɪt/ *n* eremita *m*
hernia /'hɜːnɪə/ *n* hérnia *f*
hero /'hɪərəʊ/ *n* (*pl* **-oes**) herói *m*
heroic /hɪ'rəʊɪk/ *a* heróico

heroin /'herəʊɪn/ *n* heroína *f*
heroine /'herəʊɪn/ *n* heroína *f*
heroism /'herəʊɪzəm/ *n* heroísmo *m*
heron /'herən/ *n* garça *f*
herring /'herɪŋ/ *n* arenque *m*
hers /hɜːz/ *poss pron* o(s) seu(s), a(s) sua(s), o(s) dela, a(s) dela. **it is ~** é (o) dela *or* o seu
herself /hɜː'self/ *pron* ela mesma; (*reflexive*) se. **by ~** sozinha. **for ~** para si mesma. **to ~** a/para si mesma. **Mary ~ said so** foi a própria Maria que o disse
hesitant /'hezɪtənt/ *a* hesitante
hesitat|e /'hezɪteɪt/ *vt* hesitar. **~ion** /-'teɪʃn/ *n* hesitação *f*
heterosexual /hetərəʊ'seksjʊəl/ *a* & *n* heterossexual (*mf*)
hexagon /'heksəgən/ *n* hexágono *m*. **~al** /-'ægənl/ *a* hexagonal
hey /heɪ/ *int* eh, olá
heyday /'heɪdeɪ/ *n* auge *m*, apogeu *m*
hi /haɪ/ *int* olá, viva
hibernat|e /'haɪbəneɪt/ *vi* hibernar. **~ion** /-'neɪʃn/ *n* hibernação *f*
hiccup /'hɪkʌp/ *n* soluço *m* □ *vi* soluçar, estar com soluços
hide[1] /haɪd/ *vt/i* (*pt* **hid**, *pp* **hidden**) esconder(-se) (**from** de). **~-and-seek** *n* (*game*) esconde-esconde *m*. **~-out** *n* (*colloq*) esconderijo *m*
hide[2] /haɪd/ *n* pele *f*, couro *m*
hideous /'hɪdɪəs/ *a* horrendo, medonho
hiding /'haɪdɪŋ/ *n* (*colloq: thrashing*) sova *f*, surra *f*. **go into ~** esconder-se. **~-place** *n* esconderijo *m*
hierarchy /'haɪəraːkɪ/ *n* hierarquia *f*
hi-fi /haɪ'faɪ/ *a* & *n* (de) alta fidelidade (*f*)
high /haɪ/ *a* (**-er**, **-est**) alto; (*price, number*) elevado; (*voice, pitch*) agudo □ *n* alta *f* □ *adv* alto. **two metres ~** com dois metros de altura. **~ chair** cadeira *f* alta para crianças. **~-handed** *a* autoritário, prepotente. **~ jump** salto *m* em altura. **~-rise building** edifício *m* alto, (*P*) torre *f*. **~ school** escola *f* secundária. **in the ~ season** em plena estação. **~-speed** *a* ultra-rápido. **~-spirited** *a* animado, vivo. **~ spot** (*sl*) ponto *m* culminante. **~ street** rua *f* principal. **~ tide** maré *f* alta. **~er education** ensino *m* superior
highbrow /'haɪbraʊ/ *a* & *n* (*colloq*) intelectual (*m*)
highlight /'haɪlaɪt/ *n* (*fig*) ponto *m* alto □ *vt* salientar, pôr em relevo, realçar
highly /'haɪlɪ/ *adv* altamente, extremamente. **~-strung** *a* muito sensível, nervoso, tenso. **speak ~ of** falar bem de

Highness /'haɪnɪs/ n Alteza f

highway /'haɪweɪ/ n estrada f, rodovia f. **H∼ Code** Código m Nacional de Trânsito

hijack /'haɪdʒæk/ vt seqüestrar, (P) sequestrar □ n seqüestro m, (P) sequestro m. **∼er** n (of plane) pirata m (do ar)

hike /haɪk/ n caminhada no campo f □ vi fazer uma caminhada. **∼r** /-ə(r)/ n excursionista mf, caminhante mf

hilarious /hɪ'leərɪəs/ a divertido, desopilante

hill /hɪl/ n colina f, monte m; (slope) ladeira f, subida f. **∼y** a acidentado

hillside /'hɪlsaɪd/ n encosta f, vertente f

hilt /hɪlt/ n punho m. **to the ∼** completamente, inteiramente

him /hɪm/ pron o (a ele); (after prep) ele. **(to) ∼** lhe. **I know ∼** conheço-o

himself /hɪm'self/ pron ele mesmo; (reflexive) se. **by ∼** sozinho. **for ∼** para si mesmo. **to ∼** a/para si mesmo. **Peter ∼ saw it** foi o próprio Pedro que o viu

hind /haɪnd/ a traseiro, posterior

hind|er /'hɪndə(r)/ vt empatar, estorvar; (prevent) impedir. **∼rance** n estorvo m

hindsight /'haɪndsaɪt/ n **with ∼** em retrospecto

Hindu /hɪn'du:/ n & a hindu (mf). **∼ism** /-ɪzəm/ n hinduísmo m

hinge /hɪndʒ/ n dobradiça f □ vi **∼ on** depender de

hint /hɪnt/ n insinuação f, indireta f, (P) indirecta f; (advice) sugestão f, dica f (colloq) □ vt dar a entender, insinuar □ vi **∼ at** fazer alusão a

hip /hɪp/ n quadril m

hippie /'hɪpɪ/ n hippie mf

hippopotamus /hɪpə'pɒtəməs/ n (pl -muses) hipopótamo m

hire /'haɪə(r)/ vt alugar; (person) contratar □ n aluguel m, (P) aluguer m. **∼-purchase** n compra f a prestações, (P) crediário m

hirsute /'hɜ:sju:t/ a hirsuto

his /hɪz/ a seu(s), sua(s), dele □ poss pron o(s) seu(s), a(s) sua(s), o(s) dele, a(s) dele. **it is ∼** é (o) dele or o seu

Hispanic /hɪs'pænɪk/ a hispânico

hiss /hɪs/ n silvo m; (for disapproval) assobio m, vaia f □ vt/i sibilar; (for disapproval) assobiar, vaiar

historian /hɪ'stɔ:rɪən/ n historiador m

histor|y /'hɪstərɪ/ n história f. **∼ic(al)** /hɪ'stɒrɪk(l)/ a histórico

hit /hɪt/ vt (pt **hit**, pres p **hitting**) atingir, bater em; (knock against, collide with) chocar com, ir de encontro a; (strike a target) acertar em; (find)

descobrir; (affect) atingir □ vi **∼ on** dar com □ n pancada f; (fig: success) sucesso m. **∼ it off** dar-se bem (with com). **∼-and-run** a (driver) que foge depois do desastre. **∼-or-miss** a ao acaso

hitch /hɪtʃ/ vt atar, prender; (to a hook) enganchar □ n sacão m; (snag) problema m. **∼ a lift**, **∼-hike** viajar de carona, (P) boleia. **∼-hiker** n o que viaja de carona, boleia. **∼ up** puxar para cima

hive /haɪv/ n colméia f □ vt **∼ off** separar e tornar independente

hoard /hɔ:d/ vt juntar, açambarcar □ n provisão f; (of valuables) tesouro m

hoarding /'hɔ:dɪŋ/ n tapume m, outdoor m

hoarse /hɔ:s/ a (-er, -est) rouco. **∼ness** n rouquidão f

hoax /həʊks/ n (malicious) logro m, embuste m; (humorous) trote m □ vt (malicious) engancar; lograr; passar um trote, pregar uma peça

hob /hɒb/ n placa f de aquecimento (do fogão)

hobble /'hɒbl/ vi coxear □ vt pear

hobby /'hɒbɪ/ n passatempo m favorito. **∼-horse** n (fig) tópico m favorito

hock /hɒk/ n vinho m branco do Reno

hockey /'hɒkɪ/ n hóquei m

hoe /həʊ/ n enxada f □ vt trabalhar com enxada

hog /hɒg/ n porco m; (greedy person) glutão m □ vt (pt **hogged**) (colloq) açambarcar

hoist /hɔɪst/ vt içar □ n guindaste m, (P) monta-cargas m

hold¹ /həʊld/ vt (pt **held**) segurar; (contain) levar; (possess) ter, possuir; (occupy) ocupar; (keep, maintain) conservar, manter; (affirm) manter □ vi (of rope etc) agüentar(-se), (P) aguentar(-se) □ n (influence) domínio m. **get ∼ of** pôr as mãos em; (fig) apanhar. **∼ back** reter. **∼ on** (colloq) esperar. **∼ on to** guardar; (cling to) agarrar-se a. **∼ one's breath** suster a respiração. **∼ one's tongue** calar-se. **∼ the line** não desligar. **∼ out** resistir. **∼ up** (support) sustentar; (delay) demorar; (rob) assaltar. **∼-up** n atraso m; (auto) engarrafamento m; (robbery) assalto m. **∼ with** agüentar, (P) aguentar. **∼er** n detentor m; (of post, title etc) titular mf; (for object) suporte m

hold² /həʊld/ n (of ship, plane) porão m

holdall /'həʊldɔ:l/ n saco m de viagem

holding /'həʊldɪŋ/ n (land) propriedade f; (comm) ações fpl, (P) acções fpl, valores mpl, holding m

hole /həʊl/ n buraco m □ vt abrir buraco(s) em, esburacar

holiday /'hɒlədeɪ/ n férias fpl; (day off; public) feriado m □ vi passar férias. ~-maker n pessoa f em férias; (in summer) veranista mf, (P) veraneante mf

holiness /'həʊlmɪs/ n santidade f

Holland /'hɒlənd/ n Holanda f

hollow /'hɒləʊ/ a oco, vazio; (fig) falso; (cheeks) fundo; (sound) surdo □ n (in the ground) cavidade f; (in the hand) cova f

holly /'hɒlɪ/ n azevinho m

holster /'həʊlstə(r)/ n coldre m

holy /'həʊlɪ/ a (-ier, -iest) santo, sagrado; (water) benta. H~ Ghost, H~ Spirit Espírito m Santo

homage /'hɒmɪdʒ/ n homenagem f. pay ~ to prestar homenagem a

home /həʊm/ n casa f, lar m; (institution) lar m, asilo m; (country) país m natal □ a caseiro, doméstico; (of family) de família; (pol) nacional, interno; (football match) em casa □ adv (at) ~ em casa. come/go ~ vir/ir para casa. make oneself at ~ não fazer cerimónia, (P) cerimónia. ~-made a caseiro. H~ Office Ministério m do Interior. ~ town cidade f or terra f natal. ~ truth dura verdade f, verdade(s) f (pl) amarga(s). ~less a sem casa, desabrigado

homeland /'həʊmlænd/ n pátria f

homely /'həʊmlɪ/ a (-ier, -iest) (simple) simples; (Amer: ugly) sem graça

homesick /'həʊmsɪk/ a be ~ ter saudades

homeward /'həʊmwəd/ a (journey) de regresso

homework /'həʊmwɜːk/ n trabalho m de casa, dever m de casa

homicide /'hɒmɪsaɪd/ n homicídio m; (person) homicida mf

homoeopath|y /həʊmɪ'ɒpəθɪ/ n homeopatia f. ~ic a homeopático

homosexual /hɒmə'sekʃʊəl/ a & n homossexual (mf)

honest /'ɒnɪst/ a honesto; (frank) franco. ~ly adv honestamente; (frankly) francamente. ~y n honestidade f

honey /'hʌnɪ/ n mel m; (colloq: darling) querido m, querida f, meu bem m

honeycomb /'hʌnɪkəʊm/ n favo m de mel

honeymoon /'hʌnɪmuːn/ n lua de mel f

honorary /'ɒnərərɪ/ a honorário

honour /'ɒnə(r)/ n honra f □ vt honrar. ~able a honrado, honroso

hood /hʊd/ n capuz m; (car roof) capota f, (P) tejadilho m; (Amer: bonnet)

capô m, (P) capot m

hoodwink /'hʊdwɪŋk/ vt enganar

hoof /huːf/ n (pl -fs) casco m

hook /hʊk/ n gancho m; (on garment) colchete m; (for fishing) anzol m □ vt enganchar; (fish) apanhar, pescar. off the ~ livre de dificuldades; (phone) desligado

hooked /hʊkt/ a be ~ on (sl) ter o vício de, estar viciado em

hookey /'hʊkɪ/ n play ~ (Amer sl) fazer gazeta

hooligan /'huːlɪgən/ n desordeiro m

hoop /huːp/ n arco m; (of cask) cinta f

hooray /huː'reɪ/ int & n = **hurrah**

hoot /huːt/ n (of owl) pio m de mocho; (of horn) buzinada f; (jeer) apupo m □ vi (of owl) piar; (of horn) buzinar; (jeer) apupar. ~er n buzina f; (of factory) sereia f

Hoover /'huːvə(r)/ n aspirador de pó m, (P) aspirador m □ vt passar o aspirador

hop[1] /hɒp/ vi (pt hopped) saltar num pé só, (P) ao pé coxinho □ n salto m. ~ in (colloq) subir, saltar (colloq). ~ it (sl) pôr-se a andar (colloq). ~ out (colloq) descer, saltar (colloq)

hop[2] /hɒp/ n (plant) lúpulo m. ~s espigas fpl de lúpulo

hope /həʊp/ n esperança f □ vt/i esperar. ~ for esperar (ter). ~ful a esperançoso; (promising) promissor. be ~ful (that) ter esperança (que), confiar (em que). ~fully adv esperançosamente; (it is hoped that) é de esperar que. ~less a desesperado, sem esperança; (incompetent) incapaz

horde /hɔːd/ n horda f

horizon /hə'raɪzn/ n horizonte m

horizontal /hɒrɪ'zɒntl/ a horizontal

hormone /'hɔːməʊn/ n hormônio m, (P) hormona f

horn /hɔːn/ n chifre m, corno m; (of car) buzina f; (mus) trompa f. ~y a caloso, calejado

hornet /'hɔːnɪt/ n vespão m

horoscope /'hɒrəskəʊp/ n horóscopo m, (P) horoscópio m

horrible /'hɒrəbl/ a horrível, horroroso

horrid /'hɒrɪd/ a horrível, horripilante

horrific /hə'rɪfɪk/ a horrífico

horr|or /'hɒrə(r)/ n horror m □ a (film etc) de terror. ~ify vt horrorizar, horripilar

horse /hɔːs/ n cavalo m. ~-chestnut n castanha f da Índia. ~-racing n corrida f de cavalos, hipismo m. ~-radish n rábano m

horseback /'hɔːsbæk/ n on ~ a cavalo

horseplay /'hɔːspleɪ/ n brincadeira f grosseira, abrutalhada f

horsepower /'hɔːspauə(r)/ n cavalo-vapor m

horseshoe /'hɔːsʃuː/ n ferradura f

horticultur|e /'hɔːtɪkʌltʃə(r)/ n horticultura f. ~al /-'kʌltʃərəl/ a hortícola

hose /həuz/ n ~(-pipe) mangueira f □ vt regar com a mangueira

hospice /'hɒspɪs/ n hospício m; (for travellers) hospedaria f

hospit|able /hə'spɪtəbl/ a hospitaleiro. ~ality /-'tælətɪ/ n hospitalidade f

hospital /'hɒspɪtl/ n hospital m

host¹ /həust/ n anfitrião m, dono m da casa. ~ess n anfitriã f, dona f da casa

host² /həust/ n a ~ of uma multidão de, um grande número de

host³ /həust/ n (relig) hóstia f

hostage /'hɒstɪdʒ/ n refém m

hostel /'hɒstl/ n residência f de estudantes etc

hostil|e /'hɒstaɪl/ a hostil. ~ity /hɒ'stɪlətɪ/ n hostilidade f

hot /hɒt/ a (hotter, hottest) quente; (culin) picante. **be** or **feel** ~ estar com or ter calor. **it is** ~ está or faz calor □ vt/i (pt hotted) ~ up (colloq) aquecer. ~ **dog** cachorro-quente m. ~ **line** linha direta f, (P) directa esp entre chefes de estado. ~-**water bottle** saco m de água quente

hotbed /'hɒtbed/ n (fig) foco m

hotchpotch /'hɒtʃpɒtʃ/ n misturada f, (P) salgalhada f

hotel /həu'tel/ n hotel m. ~**ier** /-ɪə(r)/ n hoteleiro m

hound /haund/ n cão m de caça e de corrida, sabujo m □ vt acossar, perseguir

hour /'auə(r)/ n hora f. ~**ly** adv de hora em hora □ a de hora em hora. ~**ly pay** retribuição f horária. **paid** ~**ly** pago por hora

house¹ /haus/ n (pl ~s /'hauzɪz/) n casa f; (pol) câmara f. **on the** ~ por conta da casa. ~-**warming** n inauguração f da casa

house² /hauz/ vt alojar; (store) arrecadar, guardar

houseboat /'hausbəut/ n casa f flutuante

household /'haushəuld/ n família f, agregado m familiar. ~**er** n ocupante mf; (owner) proprietário m

housekeep|er /'hauskiːpə(r)/ n governanta f. ~**ing** n (work) tarefas fpl domésticas

housewife /'hauswaɪf/ n (pl -wives) dona f de casa

housework /'hauswɜːk/ n tarefas fpl domésticas

housing /'hauzɪŋ/ n alojamento m. ~ **estate** zona f residencial

hovel /'hɒvl/ n casebre m, tugúrio m

hover /'hɒvə(r)/ vi pairar; (linger) deixar-se ficar, demorar-se

hovercraft /'hɒvəkraːft/ n invar aerobarco m, hovercraft m

how /hau/ adv como. ~ **long/old is...?** que comprimento/idade tem...? ~ **far?** a que distância? ~ **many?** quantos? ~ **much?** quanto? ~ **often?** com que freqüência, (P) frequência? ~ **pretty it is** como é lindo. ~ **about a walk?** e se fôssemos dar uma volta? ~ **are you?** como vai? ~ **do you do?** muito prazer! **and** ~! oh se é!

however /hau'evə(r)/ adv de qualquer maneira; (though) contudo, no entanto, todavia. ~ **small it may be** por menor que seja

howl /haul/ n uivo m □ vi uivar

HP abbr see **hire-purchase**

hp abbr see **horsepower**

hub /hʌb/ n cubo m da roda; (fig) centro m. ~-**cap** n calota f, (P) tampão m da roda

hubbub /'hʌbʌb/ n chinfrim m

huddle /'hʌdl/ vt/i apinhar(-se). ~ **together** aconchegar-se

hue¹ /hjuː/ n matiz f, tom m

hue² /hjuː/ n ~ **and cry** clamor m, alarido m

huff /hʌf/ n **in a** ~ com raiva, zangado

hug /hʌɡ/ vt (pt hugged) abraçar, apertar nos braços; (keep close to) chegar-se a □ n abraço m

huge /hjuːdʒ/ a enorme

hulk /hʌlk/ n casco (esp de navio desmantelado) m. ~**ing** a (colloq) desajeitadão (colloq)

hull /hʌl/ n (of ship) casco m

hullo /hə'ləu/ int & n = **hallo**

hum /hʌm/ vt/i (pt hummed) cantar com a boca fechada; (of insect, engine) zumbir □ n zumbido m

human /'hjuːmən/ a humano □ n ~ (**being**) ser m humano

humane /hjuː'meɪn/ a humano, compassivo

humanitarian /hjuːmænɪ'teərɪən/ a humanitário

humanity /hjuː'mænətɪ/ n humanidade f

humbl|e /'hʌmbl/ a (-er, -est) humilde □ vt humilhar. ~**y** adv humildemente

humdrum /'hʌmdrʌm/ a monótono, rotineiro

humid /'hjuːmɪd/ a úmido, (P) húmido. ~**ity** /-'mɪdətɪ/ n umidade f, (P) humidade f

humiliat|e /hjuː'mɪlɪeɪt/ vt humilhar. ~**ion** /-'eɪʃn/ n humilhação f

humility /hju:'mɪlətɪ/ n humildade f

humorist /'hju:mərɪst/ n humorista mf

hum|our /'hju:mə(r)/ n humor m □ vt fazer a vontade de. **~orous** a humorístico; (person) divertido, espirituoso

hump /hʌmp/ n corcova f; (of the back) corcunda f □ vt corcovar, arquear. **the ~** (sl) a neura (colloq)

hunch[1] /hʌntʃ/ vt curvar. **~ed up** curvado

hunch[2] /hʌntʃ/ n (colloq) palpite m

hunchback /'hʌntʃbæk/ n corcunda mf

hundred /'hʌndrəd/ a cem □ n centena f, cento m. **~s of** centenas de. **~fold** a centuplo □ adv cem vezes mais. **~th** a & n centésimo (m)

hundredweight /'hʌndrədweɪt/ n quintal m (= 50,8 kg; Amer 45,36 kg)

hung /hʌŋ/ see **hang**

Hungar|y /'hʌŋgərɪ/ n Hungria f. **~ian** /-'geərɪən/ a & n húngaro (m)

hunger /'hʌŋgə(r)/ n fome f □ vi **~ for** ter fome de; (fig) desejar vivamente, ansiar por

hungr|y /'hʌŋgrɪ/ a (ier, -iest) esfomeado, faminto. **be ~y** ter fome, estar com fome. **~ily** adv avidamente

hunk /hʌŋk/ n grande naco m

hunt /hʌnt/ vt/i caçar □ n caça f. **~ for** andar à caça de, andar à procura de. **~er** n caçador m. **~ing** n caça f, caçada f

hurdle /'hɜːdl/ n obstáculo m

hurl /hɜːl/ vt arremessar, lançar com força

hurrah, hurray /hʊ'rɑː, hʊ'reɪ/ int & n hurra (m), viva (m)

hurricane /'hʌrɪkən/ n furacão m

hurried /'hʌrɪd/ a apressado. **~ly** adv apressadamente, às pressas

hurry /'hʌrɪ/ vt/i apressar(-se), despachar(-se) □ n pressa f. **be in a ~** estar com or ter pressa. **do sth in a ~** fazer alg coisa às pressas. **~up!** ande logo

hurt /hɜːt/ vt (pt hurt) fazer mal a; (injure, offend) magoar, ferir □ vi doer □ a magoado, ferido □ n mal m; (feelings) mágoa f. **~ful** a prejudicial; (remark etc) que magoa

hurtle /'hɜːtl/ vi despenhar-se; (move rapidly) precipitar-se □ vt arremessar

husband /'hʌzbənd/ n marido m, esposo m

hush /hʌʃ/ vt (fazer) calar. **~!** silencio! □ vi calar-se □ n silêncio m. **~hush** a (colloq) muito em segredo. **~ up** abafar, encobrir

husk /hʌsk/ n casca f

husky /'hʌskɪ/ a (-ier, -iest) (hoarse) rouco, enrouquecido; (burly) corpulento □ n cão m esquimó

hustle /'hʌsl/ vt empurrar, dar encon-trões a □ n empurrão m. **~ and bustle** grande movimento m

hut /hʌt/ n cabana f, barraca f de madeira

hutch /hʌtʃ/ n coelheira f

hyacinth /'haɪəsmθ/ n jacinto m

hybrid /'haɪbrɪd/ a & n híbrido (m)

hydrant /'haɪdrənt/ n hidrante m

hydraulic /har'drɔːlɪk/ a hidráulico

hydroelectric /ˌhaɪdrəʊɪ'lektrɪk/ a hidrelétrico, (P) hidroeléctrico

hydrofoil /'haɪdrəʊfɔɪl/ n

hydrogen /'haɪdrədʒən/ n hidrogénio m, (P) hidrogénio m

hyena /har'i:nə/ n hiena f

hygiene /'haɪdʒiːn/ n higiene f

hygienic /har'dʒiːnɪk/ a higiênico, (P) higiénico

hymn /hɪm/ n hino m, cântico m

hyper- /'haɪpə(r)/ pref hiper-

hypermarket /'haɪpəmɑːkɪt/ n hipermercado m

hyphen /'haɪfn/ n hífen m, traço-de-união m. **~ate** vt unir com hífen

hypno|sis /hɪp'nəʊsɪs/ n hipnose f. **~tic** /-'nɒtɪk/ a hipnótico

hypnot|ize /'hɪpnətaɪz/ vt hipnotizar. **~ism** /-ɪzəm/ n hipnotismo m

hypochondriac /haɪpə'kɒndriæk/ n hipocondríaco m

hypocrisy /hɪ'pɒkrəsɪ/ n hipocrisia f

hypocrit|e /'hɪpəkrɪt/ n hipócrita mf. **~ical** /-'krɪtɪkl/ a hipócrita

hypodermic /haɪpə'dɜːmɪk/ a hipodérmico □ n seringa f

hypothe|sis /har'pɒθəsɪs/ n (pl -theses /-siːz/) hipótese f. **~tical** /-ə'θetɪkl/ a hipotético

hyster|ia /hɪ'stɪərɪə/ n histeria f. **~ical** /hɪ'sterɪkl/ a histérico

I

I /aɪ/ pron eu

Iberian /aɪ'bɪərɪən/ a ibérico □ n íbero m

ice /aɪs/ n gelo m □ vt/i gelar; (cake) cobrir com glacê □ vi **~ up** gelar. **~box** n (Amer) geladeira f, (P) frigorífico m. **~(-cream)** n sorvete m, (P) gelado m. **~cube** n cubo m or pedra f de gelo. **~ hockey** hóquei m sobre o gelo. **~ lolly** picolé m. **~pack** n saco m de gelo. **~rink** n rinque m de patinação, (P) patinagem f no gelo. **~ skating** n patinação f, (P) patinagem f no gelo

iceberg /'aɪsbɜːg/ n iceberg m; (fig) pedaço m de gelo

Iceland /'aɪslənd/ n Islândia f. **~er** n islandês m. **~ic** /-'lændɪk/ a & n islandês (m)

icicle /'aɪsɪkl/ n pingente m de gelo

icing /'aɪsɪŋ/ n (*culin*) cobertura f de açúcar, glacê m

icy /'aɪsɪ/ a (**-ier, -iest**) gelado, gélido, glacial; (*road*) com gelo

idea /aɪ'dɪə/ n idéia f, (P) ideia f

ideal /aɪ'dɪəl/ a & n ideal (m). ~ize vt idealizar. ~ly adv idealmente

idealis|t /aɪ'dɪəlɪst/ n idealista mf. ~m /-zəm/ n idealismo m. ~tic /-'lɪstɪk/ a idealista

identical /aɪ'dentɪkl/ a idêntico

identif|y /aɪ'dentɪfaɪ/ vt identificar □ vi ~y with identificar-se com. ~ication /-ɪ'keɪʃn/ n identificação f, (*papers*) documentos mpl de identificação

identity /aɪ'dentətɪ/ n identidade f. ~ card carteira f de identidade

ideolog|y /aɪdɪ'ɒlədʒɪ/ n ideologia f. ~ical a /-ɪə'lɒdʒɪkl/ a ideológico

idiom /'ɪdɪəm/ n idioma m; (*phrase*) expressão f idiomática. ~atic /-'mætɪk/ a idiomático

idiosyncrasy /ɪdɪə'sɪŋkrəsɪ/ n idiossincrasia f, peculiaridade f

idiot /'ɪdɪət/ n idiota mf. ~ic /-'ɒtɪk/ a idiota

idl|e /'aɪdl/ a (**-er, -est**) (*not active; lazy*) ocioso; (*unemployed*) sem trabalho; (*of machines*) parado; (*fig: useless*) inútil □ vt/i (*of engine*) estar em ponto morto, P estar no ralenti. ~eness n ociosidade f. ~y adv ociosamente

idol /'aɪdl/ n ídolo m. ~ize vt idolatrar

idyllic /ɪ'dɪlɪk/ a idílico

i.e. abbr isto é, quer dizer

if /ɪf/ conj se

igloo /'ɪɡluː/ n iglu m

ignite /ɪɡ'naɪt/ vt/i inflamar(-se), acender; (*catch fire*) pegar fogo; (*set fire to*) atear fogo a, (P) deitar fogo a

ignition /ɪɡ'nɪʃn/ n (*auto*) ignição f. ~ (key) chave f de ignição

ignoran|t /'ɪɡnərənt/ a ignorante. ~ce n ignorância f. be ~t of ignorar

ignore /ɪɡ'nɔː(r)/ vt não fazer caso de, passar por cima de; (*person in the street etc*) fingir não ver

ill /ɪl/ a (*sick*) doente; (*bad*) mau □ adv mal □ n mal m. ~-advised a pouco aconselhável. ~ at ease pouco à vontade. ~-bred a mal educado. ~-fated a malfadado. ~-treat vt maltratar. ~ will má vontade f, animosidade f

illegal /ɪ'liːɡl/ a ilegal

illegible /ɪ'ledʒəbl/ a ilegível

illegitima|te /ɪlɪ'dʒɪtɪmət/ a ilegítimo. ~cy n ilegitimidade f

illitera|te /ɪ'lɪtərət/ a analfabeto; (*uneducated*) iletrado. ~cy n analfabetismo m

illness /'ɪlnɪs/ n doença f

illogical /ɪ'lɒdʒɪkl/ a ilógico

illuminat|e /ɪ'luːmɪneɪt/ vt iluminar; (*explain*) esclarecer. ~ion /-'neɪʃn/ n iluminação f. ~ions npl luminárias fpl

illusion /ɪ'luːʒn/ n ilusão f

illusory /ɪ'luːsərɪ/ a ilusório

illustrat|e /'ɪləstreɪt/ vt ilustrar. ~ion /-'streɪʃn/ n ilustração f. ~ive /-ətɪv/ a ilustrativo

illustrious /ɪ'lʌstrɪəs/ a ilustre

image /'ɪmɪdʒ/ n imagem f. (public) ~ imagem f pública

imaginary /ɪ'mædʒɪnərɪ/ a imaginário

imaginat|ion /ɪmædʒɪ'neɪʃn/ n imaginação f. ~ive /ɪ'mædʒɪnətɪv/ a imaginativo

imagin|e /ɪ'mædʒɪn/ vt imaginar. ~able a imaginável

imbalance /ɪm'bæləns/ n desequilíbrio m

imbecile /'ɪmbəsiːl/ a & n imbecil (mf)

imbue /ɪm'bjuː/ vt imbuir, impregnar

imitat|e /'ɪmɪteɪt/ vt imitar. ~ion /-'teɪʃn/ n imitação f

immaculate /ɪ'mækjʊlət/ a imaculado; (*impeccable*) impecável

immaterial /ɪmə'tɪərɪəl/ a (*of no importance*) irrelevante. that's ~ to me para mim tanto faz

immature /ɪmə'tjʊə(r)/ a imaturo

immediate /ɪ'miːdɪət/ a imediato. ~ly adv imediatamente □ conj logo que, assim que

immens|e /ɪ'mens/ a imenso. ~ely /-slɪ/ adv imensamente. ~ity n imensidade f

immers|e /ɪ'mɜːs/ vt mergulhar, imergir. be ~ed in (*fig*) estar imerso em. ~ion /-ʃn/ n imersão f. ~ion heater aquecedor m de água elétrico, (P) eléctrico

immigr|ate /'ɪmɪɡreɪt/ vi imigrar. ~ant n & a imigrante (mf), imigrado (m). ~ation /-'ɡreɪʃn/ n imigração f

imminen|t /'ɪmɪnənt/ a iminente. ~ce n iminência f

immobil|e /ɪ'məʊbaɪl/ a imóvel. ~ize /-əlaɪz/ vt imobilizar

immoderate /ɪ'mɒdərət/ a imoderado, descomedido

immoral /ɪ'mɒrəl/ a imoral. ~ity /ɪmə'rælətɪ/ n imoralidade f

immortal /ɪ'mɔːtl/ a imortal. ~ity /-'tælətɪ/ n imortalidade f. ~ize vt imortalizar

immun|e /ɪ'mjuːn/ a imune, imunizado (from, to contra). ~ity n imunidade f

imp /ɪmp/ n diabrete m

impact /'ɪmpækt/ n impacto m

impair /ɪm'peə(r)/ *vt* deteriorar; (*damage*) prejudicar

impale /ɪm'peɪl/ *vt* empalar

impart /ɪm'pa:t/ *vt* comunicar, transmitir (**to** a)

impartial /ɪm'pa:ʃl/ *a* imparcial. **~ity** /-ʃɪ'rælətɪ/ *n* imparcialidade *f*

impassable /ɪm'pa:səbl/ *a* (*road, river*) impraticável, intransitável; (*barrier etc*) intransponível

impasse /'æmpɑ:s/ *n* impasse *m*

impatien|t /ɪm'peɪʃənt/ *a* impaciente. **~ce** *n* impaciência *f*. **~tly** *adv* impacientemente

impeach /ɪm'pi:tʃ/ *vt* incriminar, acusar

impeccable /ɪm'pekəbl/ *a* impecável

impede /ɪm'pi:d/ *vt* impedir, estorvar

impediment /ɪm'pedɪmənt/ *n* impedimento *m*, obstáculo *m*. (**speech**) **~** defeito *m* (na fala)

impel /ɪm'pel/ *vt* (*pt* **impelled**) impelir, forçar (**to do** a fazer)

impending /ɪm'pendɪŋ/ *a* iminente

impenetrable /ɪm'penɪtrəbl/ *a* impenetrável

imperative /ɪm'perətɪv/ *a* imperativo; (*need etc*) imperioso □ *n* imperativo *m*

imperceptible /ɪmpə'septəbl/ *a* imperceptível

imperfect /ɪm'pɜ:fɪkt/ *a* imperfeito. **~ion** /-ə'fekʃn/ *n* imperfeição *f*

imperial /ɪm'pɪərɪəl/ *a* imperial; (*of measures*) legal (*na GB*). **~ism** /-lɪzəm/ *n* imperialismo *m*

imperious /ɪm'pɪərɪəs/ *a* imperioso

impersonal /ɪm'pɜ:sənl/ *a* impessoal

impersonat|e /ɪm'pɜ:səneɪt/ *vt* fazer-se passar por; (*theat*) fazer *or* representar (o papel) de. **~ion** /'neɪʃn/ *n* imitação *f*

impertinen|t /ɪm'pɜ:tɪnənt/ *a* impertinente. **~ce** *n* impertinência *f*. **~tly** *adv* com impertinência

impervious /ɪm'pɜ:vɪəs/ *a* **~ to** (*water*) impermeável a; (*fig*) insensível a

impetuous /ɪm'petʃʊəs/ *a* impetuoso

impetus /'ɪmpɪtəs/ *n* ímpeto *m*

impinge /ɪm'pɪndʒ/ *vi* **~ on** afetar, P afectar; (*encroach*) infringir

impish /'ɪmpɪʃ/ *a* travesso, malicioso

implacable /ɪm'plækəbl/ *a* implacável

implant /ɪm'plɑ:nt/ *vt* implantar

implement[1] /'ɪmplɪmənt/ *n* instrumento *m*, utensílio *m*

implement[2] /'ɪmplɪment/ *vt* implementar, executar

implicat|e /'ɪmplɪkeɪt/ *vt* implicar. **~ion** /-'keɪʃn/ *n* implicação *f*

implicit /ɪm'plɪsɪt/ *a* implícito; (*unquestioning*) absoluto, incondicional

implore /ɪm'plɔ:(r)/ *vt* implorar, suplicar, rogar

imply /ɪm'plaɪ/ *vt* implicar; (*hint*) sugerir, dar a entender, insinuar

impolite /ɪmpə'laɪt/ *a* indelicado, incorreto, (*P*) incorrecto

import[1] /ɪm'pɔ:t/ *vt* importar. **~ation** /-'teɪʃn/ *n* importação *f*. **~er** *n* importador *m*

import[2] /'ɪmpɔ:t/ *n* importação *f*; (*meaning*) significado *m*; (*importance*) importância *f*

importan|t /ɪm'pɔ:tnt/ *a* importante. **~ce** *n* importância *f*

impos|e /ɪm'pəʊz/ *vt* impôr; (*inflict*) infligir □ *vi* **~e on** abusar de. **~ition** /-ə'zɪʃn/ *n* imposição *f*; (*unfair burden*) abuso *m*

imposing /ɪm'pəʊzɪŋ/ *a* imponente

impossib|le /ɪm'pɒsəbl/ *a* impossível. **~ility** /-'bɪlətɪ/ *n* impossibilidade *f*

impostor /ɪm'pɒstə(r)/ *n* impostor *m*

impoten|t /'ɪmpətənt/ *a* impotente. **~ce** *n* impotência *f*

impound /ɪm'paʊnd/ *vt* apreender, confiscar

impoverish /ɪm'pɒvərɪʃ/ *vt* empobrecer

impracticable /ɪm'præktɪkəbl/ *a* impraticável

impractical /ɪm'præktɪkl/ *a* pouco prático

imprecise /ɪmprɪ'saɪs/ *a* impreciso

impregnable /ɪm'pregnəbl/ *a* inexpugnável; (*fig*) inabalável, irrefutável

impregnate /'ɪmpregneɪt/ *vt* impregnar (**with** de)

impresario /ɪmprɪ'sa:rɪəʊ/ *n* (*pl* **-os**) empresário *m*

impress /ɪm'pres/ *vt* impressionar, causar impressão a; (*imprint*) imprimir. **~ on** s.o. inculcar algo em alguém

impression /ɪm'preʃn/ *n* impressão *f*. **~able** *a* impressionável. **~ist** *n* impressionista *mf*

impressive /ɪm'presɪv/ *a* impressionante, imponente

imprint[1] /'ɪmprɪnt/ *n* impressão *f*, marca *f*

imprint[2] /ɪm'prɪnt/ *vt* imprimir

imprison /ɪm'prɪzn/ *vt* prender, aprisionar. **~ment** *n* aprisionamento *m*, prisão *f*

improbab|le /ɪm'prɒbəbl/ *a* improvável. **~ility** /-'bɪlətɪ/ *n* improbabilidade *f*

impromptu /ɪm'prɒmptju:/ *a* & *adv* de improviso □ *n* impromptu *m*

improper /ɪm'prɒpə(r)/ *a* impróprio; (*indecent*) indecente, pouco decente; (*wrong*) incorreto, (*P*) incorrecto

improve /ɪm'pru:v/ *vt/i* melhorar. **~ on** aperfeiçoar. **~ment** *n* melhoria *f*, (*in house etc*) melhoramento *m*; (*in health*) melhoras *fpl*

improvis|e /'mprəvaɪz/ *vt/i* improvisar. ~**ation** /-'zeɪʃn/ *n* improvisação *f*

imprudent /ɪm'pru:dnt/ *a* imprudente

impuden|t /'ɪmpjʊdənt/ *a* descarado, insolente. ~**ce** *n* descaramento *m*, insolência *f*

impulse /'ɪmpʌls/ *n* impulso *m*

impulsive /ɪm'pʌlsɪv/ *a* impulsivo

impur|e /ɪm'pjʊə(r)/ *a* impuro. ~**ity** *n* impureza *f*

in /ɪn/ *prep* em, dentro de □ *adv* dentro; (*at home*) em casa; (*in fashion*) na moda. ~ **Lisbon/English** em Lisboa/inglês. ~ **winter** no inverno. ~ **an hour** (*at end of, within*) numa hora. ~ **the rain** na chuva. ~ **doing** ao fazer. ~ **the evening** à tardinha. **the best** ~ o melhor em. **we are** ~ **for** vamos ter. ~**-laws** *npl* (*colloq*) sogros *mpl*. ~**-patient** *n* doente em internado. **the** ~**s and outs** meandros *mpl*

inability /ɪnə'bɪlətɪ/ *n* incapacidade *f* (**to do** para fazer)

inaccessible /ɪnæk'sesəbl/ *a* inacessível

inaccura|te /ɪn'ækjərət/ *a* inexato, (*P*) inexacto. ~**cy** *n* inexatidão *f*, (*P*) inexactidão *f*, falta *f* de rigor

inaction /ɪn'ækʃn/ *n* inação *f*, (*P*) inacção *f*

inactiv|e /ɪn'æktɪv/ *a* inativo, (*P*) inactivo. ~**ity** /-'tɪvətɪ/ *n* inação *f*, (*P*) inacção *f*

inadequa|te /ɪn'ædɪkwət/ *a* inadequado, impróprio; (*insufficient*) insuficiente. ~**cy** *n* inadequação *f*, (*insufficiency*) insuficiência *f*

inadmissible /ɪnəd'mɪsəbl/ *a* inadmissível

inadvertently /ɪnəd'vɜ:təntlɪ/ *adv* inadvertidamente; (*unintentionally*) sem querer, sem ser por mal

inadvisable /ɪnəd'vaɪzəbl/ *a* desaconselhável, não aconselhável

inane /ɪ'neɪn/ *a* tolo, oco

inanimate /ɪn'ænɪmət/ *a* inanimado

inappropriate /ɪnə'prəʊprɪət/ *a* impróprio, inadequado

inarticulate /ɪnɑ:'tɪkjʊlət/ *a* inarticulado; (*of person*) incapaz de se exprimir claramente

inattentive /ɪnə'tentɪv/ *a* desatento

inaugural /ɪ'nɔ:gjʊrəl/ *a* inaugural

inaugurat|e /ɪ'nɔ:gjʊreɪt/ *vt* inaugurar. ~**ion** /-'reɪʃn/ *n* inauguração *f*

inauspicious /ɪnɔ:'spɪʃəs/ *a* pouco auspicioso

inborn /ɪn'bɔ:n/ *a* inato

inbred /ɪn'bred/ *a* inato, congênito, (*P*) congénito

incalculable /ɪn'kælkjʊləbl/ *a* incalculável

incapable /ɪn'keɪpəbl/ *a* incapaz

incapacit|y /ɪnkə'pæsətɪ/ *n* incapacidade *f*. ~**ate** *vt* incapacitar

incarnat|e /ɪn'kɑ:neɪt/ *a* encarnado. **the devil** ~**e** o diabo em pessoa. ~**ion** /-'neɪʃn/ *n* encarnação *f*

incendiary /ɪn'sendɪərɪ/ *a* incendiário □ *n* bomba *f* incendiária

incense[1] /'ɪnsens/ *n* incenso *m*

incense[2] /ɪn'sens/ *vt* exasperar, enfurecer

incentive /ɪn'sentɪv/ *n* incentivo, estímulo

incessant /ɪn'sesənt/ *a* incessante. ~**ly** *adv* incessantemente, sem cessar

incest /'ɪnsest/ *n* incesto *m*. ~**uous** /ɪn'sestjʊəs/ *a* incestuoso

inch /ɪntʃ/ *n* polegada *f* (= *2.54 cm*) □ *vt/i* avançar palmo a palmo *or* pouco a pouco. **within an** ~ **of** a um passo de

incidence /'ɪnsɪdəns/ *n* incidência *f*; (*rate*) percentagem *f*

incident /'ɪnsɪdənt/ *n* incidente *m*

incidental /ɪnsɪ'dentl/ *a* incidental, acessório; (*casual*) acidental; (*expenses*) eventuais; (*music*) de cena, incidental. ~**ly** *adv* incidentalmente; (*by the way*) a propósito

incinerat|e /ɪn'sɪnəreɪt/ *vt* incinerar. ~**or** *n* incinerador *m*

incision /ɪn'sɪʒn/ *n* incisão *f*

incisive /ɪn'saɪsɪv/ *a* incisivo

incite /ɪn'saɪt/ *vt* incitar, instigar. ~**ment** *n* incitamento *m*

inclination /ɪnklɪ'neɪʃn/ *n* inclinação *f*, tendência *f*

incline[1] /ɪn'klaɪn/ *vt/i* inclinar(-se). **be** ~**d to** inclinar-se para; (*have tendency*) ter tendência para

incline[2] /'ɪnklaɪn/ *n* inclinação *f*, declive *m*

inclu|de /ɪn'klu:d/ *vt* incluir; (*in letter*) enviar junto *or* em anexo. ~**ding** *prep* inclusive. ~**sion** *n* inclusão *f*

inclusive /ɪn'klu:sɪv/ *a* & *adv* inclusive. **be** ~ **of** incluir

incognito /ɪnkɒg'ni:təʊ/ *a* & *adv* incógnito

incoherent /ɪnkə'hɪərənt/ *a* incoerente

income /'ɪnkʌm/ *n* rendimento *m*. ~ **tax** imposto sobre a renda, (*P*) sobre o rendimento

incoming /'ɪnkʌmɪŋ/ *a* (*tide*) enchente; (*tenant etc*) novo

incomparable /ɪn'kɒmpərəbl/ *a* incomparável

incompatible /ɪnkəm'pætəbl/ *a* incompatível

incompeten|t /ɪn'kɒmpɪtənt/ *a* incompetente. ~**ce** *n* incompetência *f*

incomplete /mkəm'pli:t/ a incompleteto

incomprehensible /mkɒmprɪ'hensəbl/ a incompreensível

inconceivable /mkən'si:vəbl/ a inconcebível

inconclusive /mkən'klu:sɪv/ a inconcludente

incongruous /m'kɒŋgruəs/ a incongruente; (*absurd*) absurdo

inconsequential /mkɒnsɪ'kwenʃl/ a sem importância

inconsiderate /mkən'sɪdərət/ a impensado, inconsiderado; (*lacking in regard*) pouco atencioso, sem consideração (pelos sentimentos *etc* de outrem)

inconsisten|t /mkən'sɪstənt/ a incoerente; (*at variance*) contraditório. ~t with incompatível com. ~cy n incoerência f. ~cies npl contradições fpl

inconspicuous /mkən'spɪkjuəs/ a que não dá nas vistas, que não chama a atenção

incontinen|t /m'kɒntɪmənt/ a incontinente. ~ce n incontinência f

inconvenien|t /mkən'vi:nɪənt/ a inconveniente, incômodo. ~ce n inconveniência f; (*drawback*) inconveniente m □ vt incomodar

incorporate /m'kɔ:pəreɪt/ vt incorporar; (*include*) incluir

incorrect /mkə'rekt/ a incorreto, (P) incorrecto

incorrigible /m'kɒrɪdʒəbl/ a incorrigível

increas|e¹ /m'kri:s/ vt/i aumentar. ~ing a crescente. ~ingly adv cada vez mais

increase² /'mkri:s/ n aumento m. on the ~ aumentando, crescendo

incredible /m'kredəbl/ a incrível

incredulous /m'kredjuləs/ a incrédulo

increment /'mkrəmənt/ n incremento m, aumento m

incriminat|e /m'krɪmmeɪt/ vt incriminar. ~ing a comprometedor

incubat|e /'mkjubeɪt/ vt incubar. ~ion /-'beɪʃn/ n incubação f. ~or n incubadora f

inculcate /'mkʌlkeɪt/ vt inculcar

incumbent /m'kʌmbənt/ n (*pol, relig*) titular mf □ a be ~ on incumbir a, caber a

incur /m'kɜ:r/ vt (*pt incurred*) (*displeasure, expense etc*) incorrer em; (*debts*) contrair

incurable /m'kjuərəbl/ a incurável, que não tem cura

indebted /m'detɪd/ a ~ to s.o. em dívida (para) com alg (for por)

indecen|t /m'di:snt/ a indecente. ~t assault atentado m contra o pudor. ~cy n indecência f

indecision /mdɪ'sɪʒn/ n indecisão f

indecisive /mdɪ'saɪsɪv/ a inconcludente, não decisivo; (*hesitating*) indeciso

indeed /m'di:d/ adv realmente, deveras, mesmo; (*in fact*) de fato, (P) facto. very much ~ muitíssimo

indefinite /m'defmət/ a indefinido; (*time*) indeterminado. ~ly adv indefinidamente

indelible /m'deləbl/ a indelével

indemnify /m'demnɪfaɪ/ vt indenizar, (P) indemnizar (for de); (*safeguard*) garantir (against contra)

indemnity /m'demnətɪ/ n (*legal exemption*) isenção f; (*compensation*) indenização f, (P) indemnização f; (*safeguard*) garantia f

indent /m'dent/ vt (*notch*) recortar; (*typ*) entrar. ~ation /-'teɪʃn/ n recorte m; (*typ*) entrada f

independen|t /mdɪ'pendənt/ a independente. ~ce n independência f. ~tly adv independentemente

indescribable /mdɪ'skraɪbəbl/ a indescritível

indestructible /mdɪ'strʌktəbl/ a indestrutível

indeterminate /mdɪ'tɜ:mmət/ a indeterminado

index /'mdeks/ n (pl **indexes**) n (*in book*) índice m; (*in library*) catálogo m □ vt indexar. ~ **card** ficha f (de fichário). ~ **finger** index m, (dedo) indicador m. ~-**linked** a ligado ao índice de inflação

India /'mdɪə/ n índia f. ~n a & n (*of India*) indiano (m); (*American*) índio (m)

indicat|e /'mdɪkeɪt/ vt indicar. ~ion /-'keɪʃn/ n indicação f. ~or n indicador m; (*auto*) pisca-pisca m; (*board*) quadro m

indicative /m'dɪkətɪv/ a & n indicativo (m)

indict /m'daɪt/ vt acusar. ~ment n acusação f

indifferen|t /m'dɪfrənt/ a indiferente; (*not good*) medíocre. ~ce n indiferença f

indigenous /m'dɪdʒməs/ a indígena, natural, nativo (to de)

indigest|ion /mdɪ'dʒestʃən/ n indigestão f. ~ible /-təbl/ a indigesto

indign|ant /m'dɪgnənt/ a indignado. ~ation /-'neɪʃn/ n indignação f

indirect /mdɪ'rekt/ a indireto, (P) indirecto. ~ly adv indiretamente, (P) indirectamente

indiscr|eet /mdɪ'skri:t/ a indiscreto; (*not wary*) imprudente. ~etion

/-'eʃn/ n indiscrição f; (action, remark etc) deslize m

indiscriminate /mdɪ'skrɪmmət/ a que tem falta de discernimento; (random) indiscriminado. **~ly** adv sem discernimento; (at random) indiscriminadamente, ao acaso

indispensable /mdɪ'spensəbl/ a indispensável

indispos|ed /mdɪ'spəʊzd/ a indisposto. **~ition** /-ə'zɪʃn/ n indisposição f

indisputable /mdɪ'spju:təbl/ a indisputável, incontestável

indistinct /mdɪ'stɪŋkt/ a indistinto

indistinguishable /mdɪ'stɪŋgwɪʃəbl/ a indistinguível, imperceptível; (identical) indiferenciável

individual /mdɪ'vɪdʒʊəl/ a individual □ n indivíduo m. **~ity** /-'ælətɪ/ n individualidade f. **~ly** adv individualmente

indivisible /mdɪ'vɪzəbl/ a indivisível

indoctrinat|e /m'dɒktrɪneɪt/ vt (en)doutrinar. **~ion** /-'neɪʃn/ n (en)doutrinação f

indolen|t /'mdələnt/ a indolente. **~ce** n indolência f

indoor /'mdɔ:(r)/ a (de) interior, interno; (under cover) coberto; (games) de salão. **~s** /m'dɔ:z/ adv dentro de casa, no interior

induce /m'dju:s/ vt induzir, levar; (cause) causar, provocar. **~ment** n incentivo m, encorajamento m

indulge /m'dʌldʒ/ vt satisfazer; (spoil) fazer a(s) vontade(s) de □ vi **~ in** entregar-se a

indulgen|t /m'dʌldʒənt/ a indulgente. **~ce** n (leniency) indulgência f; (desire) satisfação f

industrial /m'dʌstrɪəl/ a industrial; (unrest etc) trabalhista; (action) reivindicativo. **~ estate** zona f industrial. **~ist** n industrial m. **~ized** a industrializado

industrious /m'dʌstrɪəs/ a trabalhador, aplicado

industry /'mdəstrɪ/ n indústria f; (zeal) aplicação f, diligência f, zelo m

inebriated /ɪ'ni:brɪeɪtɪd/ a embriagado, ébrio

inedible /ɪ'nedɪbl/ a não comestível

ineffective /ɪnɪ'fektɪv/ a ineficaz; (person) ineficiente, incapaz

ineffectual /ɪnɪ'fektʃʊəl/ a ineficaz, improfícuo

inefficien|t /ɪnɪ'fɪʃnt/ a ineficiente. **~cy** n ineficiência f

ineligible /ɪn'elɪdʒəbl/ a inelegível; (undesirable) indesejável. **be ~ for** não ter direito a

inept /ɪ'nept/ a inepto

inequality /ɪnɪ'kwɒlətɪ/ n desigualdade f

inert /ɪ'nɜ:t/ a inerte. **~ia** /-ʃə/ n inércia f

inevitable /m'evɪtəbl/ a inevitável, fatal

inexcusable /mɪk'skju:zəbl/ a indesculpável, imperdoável

inexhaustible /mɪg'zɔ:stəbl/ a inesgotável, inexaurível

inexorable /m'eksərəbl/ a inexorável

inexpensive /mɪk'spensɪv/ a barato, em conta

inexperience /mɪk'spɪərɪəns/ n inexperiência f, falta de experiência f. **~d** a inexperiente

inexplicable /m'eksplɪkəbl/ a inexplicável

inextricable /m'ekstrɪkəbl/ a inextricável

infallib|le /m'fæləbl/ a infalível. **~ility** /-'bɪlətɪ/ n infalibilidade f

infam|ous /'mfəməs/ a infame. **~y** n infâmia f

infan|t /'mfənt/ n bebê m, (P) bebé m; (child) criança f. **~cy** n infância f; (babyhood) primeira infância f

infantile /'mfəntaɪl/ a infantil

infantry /'mfəntrɪ/ n infantaria f

infatuat|ed /m'fætʃʊeɪtɪd/ a **~ed with** cego or perdido por. **~ion** /-'eɪʃn/ n cegueira f, paixão f

infect /m'fekt/ vt infectar. **~ s.o. with** contagiar or contaminar alg com. **~ion** /-ʃn/ n infecção f, contágio m. **~ious** /-ʃəs/ a infeccioso, contagioso

infer /m'fɜ:(r)/ vt (pt inferred) inferir, deduzir. **~ence** /'mfərəns/ n inferência f

inferior /m'fɪərɪə(r)/ a inferior; (work etc) de qualidade inferior □ n inferior mf; (in rank) subalterno m. **~ity** /-'ɒrətɪ/ n inferioridade f

infernal /m'fɜ:nl/ a infernal

infertil|e /m'fɜ:taɪl/ a infértil, estéril. **~ity** /-ə'tɪlətɪ/ n infertilidade f, esterilidade f

infest /m'fest/ vt infestar (**with** de). **~ation** n infestação f

infidelity /mfɪ'delətɪ/ n infidelidade f

infiltrat|e /'mfɪltreɪt/ vt/i infiltrar (-se). **~ion** /-'treɪʃn/ n infiltração f

infinite /'mfɪnət/ a & n infinito (m). **~ly** adv infinitamente

infinitesimal /mfɪnɪ'tesɪml/ a infinitesimal, infinitésimo

infinitive /m'fɪnətɪv/ n infinitivo m

infinity /m'fɪnətɪ/ n infinidade f, infinito m

infirm /m'fɜ:m/ a débil, fraco. **~ity** n (illness) enfermidade f; (weakness) fraqueza f

inflam|e /m'fleɪm/ vt inflamar. **~mable** /-æməbl/ a inflamável. **~mation** /-ə'meɪʃn/ n inflamação f

inflate /ɪnˈfleɪt/ vt (balloon etc) encher de ar; (prices) causar inflação de

inflation /ɪnˈfleɪʃn/ n inflação f. ~ary a inflacionário

inflection /ɪnˈflekʃn/ n inflexão f; (gram) flexão f, desinência f

inflexible /ɪnˈfleksəbl/ a inflexível

inflict /ɪnˈflɪkt/ vt infligir, impor (on a)

influence /ˈɪnfluəns/ n influência f □ vt influenciar, influir sobre

influential /ɪnfluˈenʃl/ a influente

influenza /ɪnfluˈenzə/ n gripe f

influx /ˈɪnflʌks/ n afluência f, influxo m

inform /ɪnˈfɔːm/ vt informar. ~ against or on denunciar. **keep** ~**ed** manter ao corrente or a par. ~**ant** n informante mf. ~**er** n delator m, denunciante mf

informal /ɪnˈfɔːml/ a informal; (simple) simples, sem cerimónia, (P) cerimônia; (unofficial) oficioso; (colloquial) familiar; (dress) de passeio, à vontade; (dinner, gathering) íntimo. ~**ity** /-ˈmælətɪ/ n informalidade f; (simplicity) simplicidade f; (intimacy) intimidade f. ~**ly** adv informalmente, sem cerimónia, (P) cerimônia, à vontade

information /ɪnfəˈmeɪʃn/ n informação f; (facts, data) informações fpl. ~ **technology** tecnologia f da informação

informative /ɪnˈfɔːmətɪv/ a informativo

infra-red /ɪnfrəˈred/ a infravermelho

infrequent /ɪnˈfriːkwənt/ a pouco freqüente, (P) frequente. ~**ly** adv raramente

infringe /ɪnˈfrɪndʒ/ vt infringir. ~ **on** transgredir; (rights) violar. ~**ment** n infração f, (P) infracção f; (rights) violação f

infuriat|e /ɪnˈfjʊərɪeɪt/ vt enfurecer, enraivecer. ~**ing** a enfurecedor, de enfurecer, de dar raiva

infus|e /ɪnˈfjuːz/ vt infundir, incutir; (herbs, tea) pôr de infusão. ~**ion** /-ʒn/ n infusão f

ingen|ious /ɪnˈdʒiːnɪəs/ a engenhoso, bem pensado. ~**uity** /-ˈrnjuːətɪ/ n engenho m, habilidade f, imaginação f

ingenuous /ɪnˈdʒenjʊəs/ a cândido, ingênuo, (P) ingénuo

ingot /ˈɪŋgət/ n barra f, lingote m

ingrained /ɪnˈgreɪnd/ a arraigado, enraizado; (dirt) entranhado

ingratiate /ɪnˈgreɪʃɪeɪt/ vt ~ o.s. with insinuar-se junto de, cair nas or ganhar as boas graças de

ingratitude /ɪnˈgrætɪtjuːd/ n ingratidão f

ingredient /ɪnˈgriːdɪənt/ n ingrediente m

inhabit /ɪnˈhæbɪt/ vt habitar. ~**able** a habitável. ~**ant** n habitante mf

inhale /ɪnˈheɪl/ vt inalar, aspirar. ~**r** /-ə(r)/ n inalador m

inherent /ɪnˈhɪərənt/ a inerente. ~**ly** adv inerentemente, em si

inherit /ɪnˈherɪt/ vt herdar (from de). ~**ance** n herança f

inhibit /ɪnˈhɪbɪt/ vt inibir; (prevent) impedir. **be** ~**ed** ser (um) inibido. ~**ion** /-ˈbɪʃn/ n inibição f

inhospitable /ɪnˈhɒspɪtəbl/ a inóspito; (of person) inospitaleiro, pouco/nada hospitaleiro

inhuman /ɪnˈhjuːmən/ a desumano. ~**ity** /-ˈmænətɪ/ n desumanidade f

inhumane /ɪnhjuːˈmeɪm/ a inumano, cruel

inimitable /ɪˈnɪmɪtəbl/ a inimitável

iniquitous /ɪˈnɪkwɪtəs/ a iníquo

initial /ɪˈnɪʃl/ a & n inicial (f) □ vt (pt initialled) assinar com as iniciais, rubricar. ~**ly** adv inicialmente

initiat|e /ɪˈnɪʃɪeɪt/ vt iniciar (into em); (scheme) lançar. ~**ion** /-ˈeɪʃn/ n iniciação f; (start) início m

initiative /ɪˈnɪʃətɪv/ n iniciativa f

inject /ɪnˈdʒekt/ vt injetar, (P) injectar; (fig) insuflar. ~**ion** /-ʃn/ n injeção f, (P) injecção f

injure /ˈɪndʒə(r)/ vt (harm) fazer mal a, prejudicar, lesar; (hurt) ferir

injury /ˈɪndʒərɪ/ n ferimento m, lesão f; (wrong) mal m

injustice /ɪnˈdʒʌstɪs/ n injustiça f

ink /ɪŋk/ n tinta f. ~-**well** n tinteiro m. ~**y** a sujo de tinta

inkling /ˈɪŋklɪŋ/ n idéia f, (P) ideia f, suspeita f

inlaid /ɪnˈleɪd/ see **inlay**[1]

inland /ˈɪnlənd/ a interior □ adv /ɪnˈlænd/ no interior, para o interior. **the I**~ **Revenue** o Fisco, a Receita Federal

inlay[1] /ɪnˈleɪ/ vt (pt inlaid) embutir, incrustar

inlay[2] /ˈɪnleɪ/ n incrustação f, obturação f

inlet /ˈɪnlet/ n braço m de mar, enseada f; (techn) admissão f

inmate /ˈɪnmeɪt/ n residente mf; (in hospital) internado m; (in prison) presidiário m

inn /ɪn/ n estalagem f

innards /ˈɪnədz/ npl (colloq) tripas (colloq) fpl

innate /ɪˈneɪt/ a inato

inner /ˈɪnə(r)/ a interior, interno; (fig) íntimo. ~ **city** centro m da cidade. ~**most** a mais profundo, mais íntimo. ~ **tube** n câmara f de ar

innings /'mɪŋz/ *n* (*cricket*) vez *f* de bater; (*pol*) período *m* no poder

innocen|t /'ɪnəsnt/ *a* & *n* inocente (*mf*). ~**ce** *n* inocência *f*

innocuous /ɪ'nɒkjʊəs/ *a* inócuo, inofensivo

innovat|e /'ɪnəveɪt/ *vi* inovar. ~**ion** /-'veɪʃn/ *n* inovação *f*. ~**or** *n* inovador *m*

innuendo /mju:'endəʊ/ *n* (*pl* -oes) insinuação *f*, indireta *f*, (*P*) indirecta *f*

innumerable /ɪ'nju:mərəbl/ *a* inumerável

inoculat|e /ɪ'nɒkjʊleɪt/ *vt* inocular. ~**ion** /-'leɪʃn/ *n* inoculação *f*, vacina *f*

inoffensive /mə'fensɪv/ *a* inofensivo

inoperative /ɪn'ɒpərətɪv/ *a* inoperante, ineficaz

inopportune /ɪn'ɒpətju:n/ *a* inoportuno

inordinate /ɪ'nɔ:dmət/ *a* excessivo, desmedido. ~**ly** *adv* excessivamente, desmedidamente

input /'ɪnpʊt/ *n* (*data*) dados *mpl*; (*electr: power*) energia *f*; (*computer process*) entrada *f*, dados *mpl*

inquest /'ɪnkwest/ *n* inquérito *m*

inquir|e /ɪn'kwaɪə(r)/ *vi* informar-se □ *vt* perguntar, indagar, inquirir. ~**e about** procurar informações sobre, indagar. ~**e into** inquirir, indagar. ~**ing** *a* (*look*) interrogativo; (*mind*) inquisitivo. ~**y** *n* (*question*) pergunta *f*; (*jur*) inquérito *m*; (*investigation*) investigação *f*

inquisition /mkwɪ'zɪʃn/ *n* inquisição *f*

inquisitive /ɪn'kwɪzətɪv/ *a* curioso, inquisitivo; (*prying*) intrometido, bisbilhoteiro

insan|e /ɪn'sem/ *a* louco, doido. ~**ity** /ɪn'sænətɪ/ *n* loucura *f*, demência *f*

insanitary /ɪn'sænɪtrɪ/ *a* insalubre, anti-higiênico, (*P*) anti-higiénico

insatiable /ɪn'seɪʃəbl/ *a* insaciável

inscri|be /ɪn'skraɪb/ *vt* inscrever; (*book*) dedicar. ~**ption** /-ɪpʃn/ *n* inscrição *f*; (*in book*) dedicatória *f*

inscrutable /ɪn'skru:təbl/ *a* impenetrável, misterioso

insect /'ɪnsekt/ *n* inseto *m*, (*P*) insecto *m*

insecur|e /ɪnsɪ'kjʊə(r)/ *a* (*not firm*) inseguro, mal seguro; (*unsafe; psych*) inseguro. ~**ity** *n* insegurança *f*, falta *f* de segurança

insensible /ɪn'sensəbl/ *a* insensível; (*unconscious*) inconsciente

insensitive /ɪn'sensətɪv/ *a* insensível

inseparable /ɪn'seprəbl/ *a* inseparável

insert[1] /ɪn'sɜ:t/ *vt* inserir; (*key*) meter, colocar; (*add*) pôr, inserir. ~**ion** /-ʃn/ *n* inserção *f*

insert[2] /'ɪnsɜ:t/ *n* coisa *f* inserida

inside /ɪn'saɪd/ *n* interior *m*. ~**s** (*colloq*) tripas *fpl* (*colloq*) □ *a* interior, interno □ *adv* no interior, dentro, por dentro □ *prep* dentro de; (*of time*) em menos de. ~ **out** de dentro para fora, do avesso; (*thoroughly*) por dentro e por fora, a fundo

insidious /ɪn'sɪdɪəs/ *a* insidioso

insight /'ɪnsaɪt/ *n* penetração *f*, perspicácia *f*; (*glimpse*) vislumbre *m*

insignificant /ɪnsɪg'nɪfɪkənt/ *a* insignificante

insincer|e /ɪnsɪn'sɪə(r)/ *a* insincero. ~**ity** /-'serətɪ/ *n* insinceridade *f*, falta *f* de sinceridade

insinuat|e /ɪn'smjʊeɪt/ *vt* insinuar. ~**ion** /-'eɪʃn/ *n* (*act*) insinuação *f*; (*hint*) indireta *f*, (*P*) indirecta *f*, insinuação *f*

insipid /ɪn'sɪpɪd/ *a* insípido, sem sabor

insist /ɪn'sɪst/ *vt/i* ~ (on/that) insistir (em/em que)

insisten|t /ɪn'sɪstənt/ *a* insistente. ~**ce** *n* insistência *f*. ~**tly** *adv* insistentemente

insolen|t /'ɪnsələnt/ *a* insolente. ~**ce** *n* insolência *f*

insoluble /ɪn'sɒljʊbl/ *a* insolúvel

insolvent /ɪn'sɒlvənt/ *a* insolvente

insomnia /ɪn'sɒmnɪə/ *n* insônia *f*, (*P*) insónia *f*

inspect /ɪn'spekt/ *vt* inspecionar, (*P*) inspeccionar, examinar; (*tickets*) fiscalizar; (*passport*) controlar; (*troops*) passar revista a. ~**ion** /-ʃn/ *n* inspeção *f*, (*P*) inspecção *f*, exame *m*; (*ticket*) fiscalização *f*; (*troops*) revista *f*. ~**or** *n* inspetor *m*, (*P*) inspector *m*; (*on train*) fiscal *m*

inspir|e /ɪn'spaɪə(r)/ *vt* inspirar. ~**ation** /-ə'reɪʃn/ *n* inspiração *f*

instability /ɪnstə'bɪlətɪ/ *n* instabilidade *f*

install /ɪn'stɔ:l/ *vt* instalar; (*heater etc*) montar, instalar. ~**ation** /-ə'leɪʃn/ *n* instalação *f*

instalment /ɪn'stɔ:lmənt/ *n* prestação *f*; (*of serial*) episódio *m*

instance /'ɪnstəns/ *n* exemplo *m*, caso *m*. **for** ~ por exemplo. **in the first** ~ em primeiro lugar

instant /'ɪnstənt/ *a* imediato; (*food*) instantâneo □ *n* instante *m*. ~**ly** *adv* imediatamente, logo

instantaneous /ɪnstən'temɪəs/ *a* instantâneo

instead /ɪn'sted/ *adv* em vez disso, em lugar disso. ~ **of** em vez de, em lugar de

instigat|e /'ɪnstɪgeɪt/ *vt* instigar, incitar. ~**ion** /-'geɪʃn/ *n* instigação *f*. ~**or** *n* instigador *m*

instil /ɪn'stɪl/ vt (pt instilled) instilar, insuflar

instinct /'ɪnstɪŋkt/ n instinto m. ~ive /ɪn'stɪŋktɪv/ a instintivo

institut|e /'ɪnstɪtjuːt/ n instituto m □ vt instituir; (legal proceedings) intentar; (inquiry) ordenar. ~ion /-'tjuːʃn/ n instituição f; (school) estabelecimento m de ensino; (hospital) estabelecimento m hospitalar

instruct /ɪn'strʌkt/ vt instruir; (order) mandar, ordenar; (a solicitor etc) dar instruções a. ~ s.o. in sth ensinar alg coisa a alguém. ~ion /-ʃn/ n instrução f. ~ions /-ʃnz/ npl instruções fpl, modo m de emprego; (orders) ordens fpl. ~ive a instrutivo. ~or n instrutor m

instrument /'ɪnstrʊmənt/ n instrumento m. ~ panel painel m de instrumentos

instrumental /ɪnstrʊ'mentl/ a instrumental. be ~ in ter um papel decisivo em. ~ist n instrumentalista mf

insubordinat|e /ɪnsə'bɔːdɪmət/ a insubordinado. ~ion /-'neɪʃn/ n insubordinação f

insufferable /ɪn'sʌfrəbl/ a intolerável, insuportável

insufficient /ɪnsə'fɪʃnt/ a insuficiente

insular /'ɪnsjʊlə(r)/ a insular; (fig: narrow-minded) bitolado, limitado, (P) tacanho

insulat|e /'ɪnsjʊleɪt/ vt isolar. ~ing tape fita f isolante. ~ion /-'leɪʃn/ n isolamento m

insulin /'ɪnsjʊlɪn/ n insulina f

insult[1] /ɪn'sʌlt/ vt insular, injuriar. ~ing a insultante, injurioso

insult[2] /'ɪnsʌlt/ n insulto m, injúria f

insur|e /ɪn'ʃʊə(r)/ vt segurar, pôr no seguro; (Amer) = ensure. ~ance n seguro m. ~ance policy apólice f de seguro

insurmountable /ɪnsə'maʊntəbl/ a insuperável

intact /ɪn'tækt/ a intato, (P) intacto

intake /'ɪnteɪk/ n admissão f; (techn) admissão f, entrada f; (of food) ingestão f

intangible /ɪn'tændʒəbl/ a intangível

integral /'ɪntɪɡrəl/ a integral. be an ~ part of ser parte integrante de

integrat|e /'ɪntɪɡreɪt/ vt/i integrar (-se). ~ed circuit circuito m integrado. ~ion /'ɡreɪʃn/ n integração f

integrity /ɪn'teɡrəti/ n integridade f

intellect /'ɪntəlekt/ n intelecto m, inteligência f. ~ual /-'lektʃʊəl/ a & n intelectual (mf)

intelligen|t /ɪn'telɪdʒənt/ a inteligente. ~ce n inteligência f; (mil) informações fpl. ~tly adv inteligentemente

intelligible /ɪn'telɪdʒəbl/ a inteligível

intend /ɪn'tend/ vt tencionar; (destine) reservar, destinar. ~ed a intencional, propositado

intens|e /ɪn'tens/ a intenso; (person) emotivo. ~ely adv intensamente; (very) extremamente. ~ity n intensidade f

intensif|y /ɪn'tensɪfaɪ/ vt intensificar. ~ication /-ɪ'keɪʃn/ n intensificação f

intensive /ɪn'tensɪv/ a intensivo. ~ care tratamento m intensivo

intent /ɪn'tent/ n intento m, desígnio m, propósito m □ a atento, concentrado. ~ on absorto em; (intending to) decidido a. ~ly adv atentamente

intention /ɪn'tenʃn/ n intenção f. ~al a intencional. ~ally adv de propósito

inter /ɪn'tɜː(r)/ vt (pt interred) enterrar

inter- /'ɪntə(r)/ pref inter-

interact /ɪntə'rækt/ vi agir uns sobre os outros. ~ion /-ʃn/ n interação f, (P) interacção f

intercede /ɪntə'siːd/ vi interceder

intercept /ɪntə'sept/ vt interceptar

interchange[1] /ɪntə'tʃeɪndʒ/ vt permutar, trocar. ~able a permutável

interchange[2] /'ɪntətʃeɪndʒ/ n permuta f, intercâmbio m; (road junction) trevo m de trânsito, (P) nó m

intercom /'ɪntəkɒm/ n interfone m, (P) intercomunicador m

interconnected /ɪntəkə'nektɪd/ a (facts, events etc) ligado, relacionado

intercourse /'ɪntəkɔːs/ n (sexual) relações fpl sexuais

interest /'ɪntrəst/ n interesse m; (legal share) título m; (in finance) juro(s) m(pl). rate of ~ taxa f de juros □ vt interessar. ~ed a interessado. be ~ed in interessar-se por. ~ing a interessante

interface /'ɪntəfeɪs/ n interface f

interfer|e /ɪntə'fɪə(r)/ vi interferir, intrometer-se (in em); (meddle, hinder) interferir (with com); (tamper) mexer indevidamente (with em). ~ence n interferência f

interim /'ɪntərɪm/ n in the ~ nesse/neste ínterim m, (P) interim m □ a interino, provisório

interior /ɪn'tɪərɪə(r)/ a & n interior (m)

interjection /ɪntə'dʒekʃn/ n interjeição f

interlock /ɪntə'lɒk/ vt/i entrelaçar; (pieces of puzzle etc) encaixar(-se); (mech: wheels) engrenar, engatar

interloper /'ɪntələʊpə(r)/ n intruso m

intermarr|iage /ɪntəˈmærɪdʒ/ n casamento m entre membros de diferentes famílias, raças etc; (*between near relations*) casamento m consangüíneo, (P) consanguíneo. **~y** vi ligar-se por casamento

intermediary /ɪntəˈmiːdɪərɪ/ a & n intermediário (m)

intermediate /ɪntəˈmiːdɪət/ a intermédio, intermediário

interminable /ɪnˈtɜːmɪnəbl/ a interminável, infindável

intermission /ɪntəˈmɪʃn/ n intervalo m

intermittent /ɪntəˈmɪtnt/ a intermitente. **~ly** adv intermitentemente

intern /ɪnˈtɜːn/ vt internar. **~ee** /-ˈniː/ n internado m. **~ment** n internamento m

internal /ɪnˈtɜːnl/ a interno, interior. **~ly** adv internamente, interiormente

international /ɪntəˈnæʃnəl/ a & n internacional (m/f)

interpolate /ɪnˈtɜːpəleɪt/ vt interpolar

interpret /ɪnˈtɜːprɪt/ vt/i interpretar. **~ation** /-ˈteɪʃn/ n interpretação f. **~er** n intérprete m/f

interrelated /ɪntərɪˈleɪtɪd/ a inter-relacionado, correlacionado

interrogat|e /ɪnˈterəgeɪt/ vt interrogar. **~ion** /-ˈgeɪʃn/ n interrogação f; (*of police etc*) interrogatório m

interrogative /ɪntəˈrɒgətɪv/ a interrogativo □ n (*pronoun*) pronome m interrogativo

interrupt /ɪntəˈrʌpt/ vt interromper. **~ion** /-ʃn/ n interrupção f

intersect /ɪntəˈsekt/ vt/i intersectar (-se); (*roads*) cruzar-se. **~ion** /-ʃn/ n intersecção f; (*crossroads*) cruzamento m

intersperse /ɪntəˈspɜːs/ vt entremear, intercalar; (*scatter*) espalhar

interval /ˈɪntəvl/ n intervalo m. at **~s** a intervalos

interven|e /ɪntəˈviːn/ vi (*interfere*) intervir; (*of time*) passar-se, decorrer; (*occur*) sobrevir, intervir. **~tion** /-ˈvenʃn/ n intervenção f

interview /ˈɪntəvjuː/ n entrevista f □ vt entrevistar. **~ee** n entrevistado m. **~er** n entrevistador m

intestin|e /ɪnˈtestɪn/ n intestino m. **~al** a intestinal

intima|te[1] /ˈɪntɪmət/ a íntimo; (*detailed*) profundo. **~cy** n intimidade f. **~tely** adv intimamente

intimate[2] /ˈɪntɪmeɪt/ vt (*announce*) dar a conhecer, fazer saber; (*imply*) dar a entender

intimidat|e /ɪnˈtɪmɪdeɪt/ vt intimidar. **~ion** /-ˈdeɪʃn/ n intimidação f

into /ˈɪntə/; *emphatic* /ˈɪntʊ/ prep para dentro de. **divide ~ three** dividir em tres. **~ pieces** aos bocados. **translate ~** traduzir para

intolerable /ɪnˈtɒlərəbl/ a intolerável, insuportável

intoleran|t /ɪnˈtɒlərənt/ a intolerante. **~ce** n intolerância f

intonation /ɪntəˈneɪʃn/ n entonação f, entoação f, inflexão f

intoxicat|ed /ɪnˈtɒksɪkeɪtɪd/ a embriagado, etilizado. **~ion** /ˈkeɪʃn/ n embriaguez f

intra- /ˈɪntrə/ *pref* intra-

intractable /ɪnˈtræktəbl/ a intratável, difícil

intransigent /ɪnˈtrænsɪdʒənt/ a intransigente

intransitive /ɪnˈtrænsətɪv/ a (*verb*) intransitivo

intravenous /ɪntrəˈviːnəs/ a intravenoso

intrepid /ɪnˈtrepɪd/ a intrépido, arrojado

intrica|te /ˈɪntrɪkət/ a intrincado, complexo. **~cy** n complexidade f

intrigu|e /ɪnˈtriːg/ vt/i intrigar □ n intriga f. **~ing** a intrigante, curioso

intrinsic /ɪnˈtrɪnsɪk/ a intrínseco. **~ally** /-klɪ/ adv intrinsecamente

introduce /ɪntrəˈdjuːs/ vt (*programme, question*) apresentar; (*bring in, insert*) introduzir; (*initiate*) iniciar. **~ sb to sb** (*person*) apresentar alg a alguém

introduct|ion /ɪntrəˈdʌkʃn/ n introdução f; (*of/to person*) apresentação f. **~ory** /-tərɪ/ a introdutório, de introdução; (*letter, words*) de apresentação

introspective /ɪntrəˈspektɪv/ a introspectivo

introvert /ˈɪntrəvɜːt/ n & a introvertido (m)

intru|de /ɪnˈtruːd/ vi intrometer-se, ser a mais. **~der** n intruso m. **~sion** n intrusão f. **~sive** a intruso

intuit|ion /ɪntjuːˈɪʃn/ n intuição f. **~ive** /ɪnˈtjuːɪtɪv/ a intuitivo

inundate /ˈɪnʌndeɪt/ vt inundar (with de)

invade /ɪnˈveɪd/ vt invadir. **~r** /-ə(r)/ n invasor m

invalid[1] /ˈɪnvəlɪd/ n inválido m

invalid[2] /ɪnˈvælɪd/ a inválido. **~ate** vt invalidar

invaluable /ɪnˈvæljʊəbl/ a inestimável

invariabl|e /ɪnˈveərɪəbl/ a invariável. **~y** adv invariavelmente

invasion /ɪnˈveɪʒn/ n invasão f

invective /ɪnˈvektɪv/ n invectiva f

invent /m'vent/ *vt* inventar. ~**ion** *n* invenção *f*. ~**ive** *a* inventivo. ~**or** *n* inventor *m*

inventory /'mvəntrı/ *n* inventário *m*

inverse /m'vɜ:s/ *a & n* inverso (*m*). ~**ly** *adv* inversamente

inver|t /m'vɜ:t/ *vt* inverter. ~**ted commas** aspas *fpl*. ~**sion** *n* inversão *f*

invest /m'vest/ *vt* investir; (*time, effort*) dedicar □ *vi* fazer um investimento. ~ **in** (*colloq: buy*) gastar dinheiro em. ~**ment** *n* investimento *m*. ~**or** *n* investidor *m*, financiador *m*

investigat|e /m'vestıgeıt/ *vt* investigar. ~**ion** /-'geıʃn/ *n* investigação *f*. **under** ~**ion** em estudo. ~**or** *n* investigador *m*

inveterate /m'vetərət/ *a* inveterado

invidious /m'vıdıəs/ *a* antipático, odioso

invigorate /m'vıgəreıt/ *vt* revigorar; (*encourage*) estimular

invincible /m'vmsəbl/ *a* invencível

invisible /m'vızəbl/ *a* invisível

invit|e /m'vaıt/ *vt* convidar; (*bring on*) pedir, provocar. ~**ation** /mvı'teıʃn/ *n* convite *m*. ~**ing** *a* (*tempting*) tentador; (*pleasant*) acolhedor, convidativo

invoice /'mvɔıs/ *n* fatura *f*, (*P*) factura *f* □ *vt* faturar, (*P*) facturar

invoke /m'vəʊk/ *vt* invocar

involuntary /m'vɒləntrı/ *a* involuntário

involve /m'vɒlv/ *vt* implicar, envolver. ~**d** *a* (*complex*) complicado; (*at stake*) em jogo; (*emotionally*) envolvido. ~**d in** implicado em. ~**ment** *n* envolvimento *m*, participação *f*

invulnerable /m'vʌlnərəbl/ *a* invulnerável

inward /'mwəd/ *a* interior; (*thought etc*) íntimo. ~(**s**) *adv* para dentro, para o interior. ~**ly** *adv* interiormente, intimamente

iodine /'aıədi:n/ *n* iodo *m*; (*antiseptic*) tintura *f* de iodo

IOU /aıəʊ'ju:/ *n abbr* vale *m*

IQ /aı'kju:/ *abbr* (*intelligence quotient*) Q I *m*

Iran /ı'ra:n/ *n* Irã *m*. ~**ian** /ı'remıən/ *a & n* iraniano (*m*)

Iraq /ı'ra:k/ *n* Iraque *m*. ~**i** *a & n* iraquiano (*m*)

irascible /ı'ræsəbl/ *a* irascível

irate /aı'reıt/ *a* irado, enraivecido

Ireland /'aıələnd/ *n* Irlanda *f*

iris /'aıərıs/ *n* (*anat, bot*) íris *f*

Irish /'aıərıʃ/ *a & n* (*language*) irlandês (*m*). ~**man** *n* irlandês *m*. ~**woman** *n* irlandesa *f*

irk /ɜ:k/ *vt* aborrecer, ncomodar. ~**some** *a* aborrecido

iron /'aıən/ *n* ferro *m*; (*appliance*) ferro *m* de engomar □ *a* de ferro □ *vt* passar a ferro. ~ **out** fazer desaparecer; (*fig*) aplanar, resolver. ~**ing** *n* do the ~**ing** passar a roupa. ~**ing-board** *n* tábua *f* de passar roupa, (*P*) tábua *f* de engomar

ironic(al) /aı'rɒnık(l)/ *a* irônico, (*P*) irónico

ironmonger /'aıənmʌngə(r)/ *n* ferreiro *m*, (*P*) ferrageiro *m*. ~'**s** *n* (*shop*) loja *f* de ferragens

irony /'aıərənı/ *n* ironia *f*

irrational /ı'ræʃənl/ *a* irracional; (*person*) ilógico, que não raciocina

irreconcilable /ırekən'saıləbl/ *a* irreconciliável

irrefutable /ırı'fju:təbl/ *a* irrefutável

irregular /ı'regjʊlə(r)/ *a* irregular. ~**ity** /-'lærətı/ *n* irregularidade *f*

irrelevant /ı'reləvənt/ *a* irrelevante, que não é pertinente

irreparable /ı'repərəbl/ *a* irreparável, irremediável

irreplaceable /ırı'pleısəbl/ *a* insubstituível

irresistible /ırı'zıstəbl/ *a* irresistível

irresolute /ı'rezəlu:t/ *a* irresoluto

irrespective /ırı'spektıv/ *a* ~ **of** sem levar em conta, independente de

irresponsible /ırı'spɒnsəbl/ *a* irresponsável

irretrievable /ırı'tri:vəbl/ *a* irreparável

irreverent /ı'revərənt/ *a* irreverente

irreversible /ırı'vɜ:səbl/ *a* irreversível; (*decision*) irrevogável

irrigat|e /'ırıgeıt/ *vt* irrigar. ~**ion** /-'geıʃn/ *n* irrigação *f*

irritable /'ırıtəbl/ *a* irritável, irascível

irritat|e /'ırıteıt/ *vt* irritar. ~**ion** /-'teıʃn/ *n* irritação *f*

is /ız/ *see* **be**

Islam /'ızla:m/ *n* Islã *m*. ~**ic** /ız'læmık/ *a* islâmico

island /'aılənd/ *n* ilha *f*. **traffic** ~ abrigo *m* de pedestres, (*P*) placa *f* de refugio

isolat|e /'aısəleıt/ *vt* isolar. ~**ion** /-'leıʃn/ *n* isolamento *m*

Israel /'ızreıl/ *n* Israel *m*. ~**i** /ız'reılı/ *a & n* israelense (*mf*), (*P*) israelita (*mf*)

issue /'ıʃu:/ *n* questão *f*; (*outcome*) resultado *m*; (*of magazine etc*) número *m*; (*of stamps, money etc*) emissão *f* □ *vt* distribuir, dar; (*stamps, money etc*) emitir; (*orders*) dar □ *vi* ~ **from** sair de. **at** ~ em questão. **take** ~ **with** entrar em discussão com, discutir com

it /ɪt/ *pron* (*subject*) ele, ela; (*object*) o, a; (*non-specific*) isto, isso, aquilo. **~ is cold** está *or* faz frio. **~ is the 6th of May** hoje é seis de maio. **that's ~ é** isso. **take ~** leva isso. **who is ~?** quem é?

italic /ɪ'tælɪk/ *a* itálico. **~s** *npl* itálico *m*

Ital|y /'ɪtəlɪ/ *n* Itália *f*. **~ian** /ɪ'tælɪən/ *a & n* (*person, lang*) italiano (*m*)

itch /ɪtʃ/ coceira *f*, (*P*) comichão *f*; (*fig: desire*) desejo *m* ardente □ *vi* coçar, sentir comichão, comichar. **my arm ~es** estou com coceira no braço. **I am ~ing to** estou morto por (*colloq*). **~y** *a* que dá coceira

item /'aɪtəm/ *n* item *m*, artigo *m*; (*on programme*) número *m*; (*on agenda*) ponto *m*. **~ news** — notícia *f*. **~ize** /-aɪz/ *vt* discriminar, especificar

itinerant /aɪ'tɪnərənt/ *a* itinerante; (*musician, actor*) ambulante

itinerary /aɪ'tɪnərərɪ/ *n* itinerário *m*

its /ɪts/ *a* seu, sua, seus, suas

it's /ɪts/ = it is, it has

itself /ɪt'self/ *pron* ele mesmo, ele próprio, ela mesma, ela própria; (*reflexive*) se; (*after prep*) si mesmo, si próprio, si mesma, si própria. **by ~** sozinho, por si

ivory /'aɪvərɪ/ *n* marfim *m*

ivy /'aɪvɪ/ *n* hera *f*

J

jab /dʒæb/ *vt* (*pt jabbed*) espetar □ *n* espetadela *f*; (*colloq: injection*) picada *f*

jabber /'dʒæbə(r)/ *vi* tagarelar; (*indistinctly*) falar confusamente □ *n* tagarelice *f*, (*indistinct speech*) algaravia *f*, (*indistinct voices*) algaraviada *f*

jack /dʒæk/ *n* (*techn*) macaco *m*; (*cards*) valete *m* □ *vt* **~ up** levantar com macaco. **the Union J~** a bandeira *f* inglesa

jackal /'dʒækl/ *n* chacal *m*

jackdaw /'dʒækdɔː/ *n* gralha *f*

jacket /'dʒækɪt/ *n* casaco (curto) *m*; (*of book*) sobrecapa *f*; (*of potato*) casca *f*

jack-knife /'dʒæknaɪf/ *vi* (*lorry*) perder o controle

jackpot /'dʒækpɒt/ *n* sorte *f* grande. **hit the ~** ganhar a sorte grande

Jacuzzi /dʒə'kuːzi:/ *n* (*P*) jacuzzi *m*, banheira *f* de hidromassagem

jade /dʒeɪd/ *n* (*stone*) jade *m*

jaded /'dʒeɪdɪd/ *a* (*tired*) estafado; (*bored*) enfastiado

jagged /'dʒægɪd/ *a* recortado, denteado; (*sharp*) pontiagudo

jail /dʒeɪl/ *n* prisão *f* □ *vt* prender,

colocar na cadeia. **~er** *n* carcereiro *m*

jam¹ /dʒæm/ *n* geléia *f*, compota *f*

jam² /dʒæm/ *vt/i* (*pt jammed*) (*wedge*) entalar; (*become wedged*) entalar-se; (*crowd*) apinhar(-se); (*mech*) bloquear; (*radio*) provocar interferências em □ *n* (*crush*) aperto *m*; (*traffic*) engarrafamento *m*; (*colloq: difficulty*) apuro *m*, aperto *m*. **~ one's brakes on** (*colloq*) pôr o pé no freio, (*P*) no travão subitamente, apertar o freio subitamente. **~-packed** *a* (*colloq*) abarrotado (**with** de)

Jamaica /dʒə'meɪkə/ *n* Jamaica *f*

jangle /'dʒæŋgl/ *n* som *m* estridente □ *vi* retinir

janitor /'dʒænɪtə(r)/ *n* porteiro *m*; (*caretaker*) zelador *m*

January /'dʒænjʊərɪ/ *n* Janeiro *m*

Japan /dʒə'pæn/ *n* Japão *m*. **~ese** /dʒæpə'niːz/ *a & n* japonês (*m*)

jar¹ /dʒaː(r)/ *n* pote *m*. **jam-~** *n* frasco *m* de geléia

jar² /dʒaː(r)/ *vt/i* (*pt jarred*) ressoar, bater ruidosamente (**against** contra); (*of colours*) destoar; (*disagree*) discorder (**with** de) □ *n* (*shock*) choque *m*. **~ring** *a* dissonante

jargon /'dʒaːgən/ *n* jargão *m*, gíria *f* profissional

jaundice /'dʒɔːndɪs/ *n* icterícia *f*. **~d** *a* (*fig*) invejoso, despeitado

jaunt /dʒɔːnt/ *n* (*trip*) passeata *f*

jaunty /'dʒɔːntɪ/ *a* (**-ier, -iest**) (*cheerful*) alegre, jovial; (*sprightly*) desenvolto

javelin /'dʒævlɪn/ *n* dardo *m*

jaw /dʒɔː/ *n* maxilar *m*, mandíbula *f*

jay /dʒeɪ/ *n* gaio *m*. **~-walker** *n* pedestre *m* imprudente, (*P*) peão *m* indisciplinado

jazz /dʒæz/ *n* jazz *m* □ *vt* **~ up** animar. **~y** *a* (*colloq*) espalhafatoso

jealous /'dʒeləs/ *a* ciumento; (*envious*) invejoso. **~y** *n* ciúme *m*; (*envy*) inveja *f*

jeans /dʒiːnz/ *npl* (blue-)jeans *mpl*, calça *f* de zuarte, (*P*) calças *fpl* de ganga

jeep /dʒiːp/ *n* jipe *m*

jeer /dʒɪə(r)/ *vt/i* **~ at** (*laugh*) fazer troça de; (*scorn*) escarnecer de; (*boo*) vaiar □ *n* (*mockery*) troça *f*; (*booing*) vaia *f*

jell /dʒel/ *vi* tomar consistência, gelatinizar-se

jelly /'dʒelɪ/ *n* gelatina *f*.

jellyfish /'dʒelɪfɪʃ/ *n* água-viva *f*

jeopard|y /'dʒepədɪ/ *n* perigo *m*. **~ize** *vt* comprometer, pôr em perigo

jerk /dʒɜːk/ *n* solavanco *m*, (*P*) sacão *m*; (*sl: fool*) idiota *mf* □ *vt/i* sacudir; (*move*) mover-se aos solavancos, (*P*) mover(-se) aos sacões. ~y *a* sacudido

jersey /'dʒɜːzɪ/ *n* (*pl* -eys) camisola *f*, pulôver *m*, suéter *m*; (*fabric*) jérsei *m*

jest /dʒest/ *n* gracejo *m*, graça *f* □ *vi* gracejar, brincar

Jesus /'dʒiːzəs/ *n* Jesus *m*

jet¹ /dʒet/ *n* azeviche *m*. ~-**black** *a* negro de azeviche

jet² /dʒet/ *n* jato *m*, (*P*) jacto *m*; (*plane*) (avião *m*) jato *m*, (*P*) jacto *m*. ~ **lag** cansaço *m* provocado pela diferença de fuso horário. ~-**propelled** *a* de propulsão a jato, (*P*) jacto

jettison /'dʒetɪsn/ *vt* alijar; (*discard*) desfazer-se de; (*fig*) abandonar

jetty /'dʒetɪ/ *n* (*breakwater*) quebramar *m*; (*landing-stage*) desembarcadouro *m*, cais *m*

Jew /dʒuː/ *n* judeu *m*

jewel /'dʒuːəl/ *n* jóia *f*. ~**ler** *n* joalheiro *m*. ~**ler's** (**shop**) joalheria *f*. ~**lery** *n* jóias *fpl*

Jewish /'dʒuːɪʃ/ *a* judeu

jib /dʒɪb/ *vi* (*pt* **jibbed**) recusar-se a avançar; (*of a horse*) empacar. ~ **at** (*fig*) opor-se a, ter relutância em □ *n* (*sail*) bujarrona *f*

jig /dʒɪg/ *n* jiga *f*

jiggle /'dʒɪgl/ *vt* (*rock*) balançar; (*jerk*) sacolejar

jigsaw /'dʒɪgsɔː/ *n* ~(-**puzzle**) puzzle *m*, quebra-cabeça *m*, (*P*) quebracabeças *m*

jilt /dʒɪlt/ *vt* deixar, abandonar, dar um fora em (*colloq*), (*P*) mandar passear (*colloq*)

jingle /'dʒɪŋgl/ *vt/i* tilintar, tinir □ *n* tilintar *m*, tinido *m*; (*advertising etc*) música *f* de anúncio

jinx /dʒɪŋks/ *n* (*colloq*) pessoa *f or* coisa *f* azarenta; (*fig: spell*) azar *m*

jitter|s /'dʒɪtəz/ *npl* **the** ~**s** (*colloq*) nervos *mpl*. ~**y** /-ərɪ/ *a* **be** ~**y** (*colloq*) estar nervoso, ter os nervos a flor da pele (*colloq*)

job /dʒɒb/ *n* trabalho *m*; (*post*) emprego *m*. **have a** ~ **doing** ter dificuldade em fazer. **it is a good** ~ **that** felizmente que. ~**less** *a* desempregado

jobcentre /'dʒɒbsentə(r)/ *n* posto *m* de desemprego

jockey /'dʒɒkɪ/ *n* (*pl* -eys) jóquei *m*

jocular /'dʒɒkjʊlə(r)/ *a* jocoso, galhofeiro, brincalhão

jog /dʒɒg/ *vt* (*pt* **jogged**) dar um leve empurrão em, tocar em; (*memory*) refrescar □ *vi* (*sport*) fazer jogging. ~**ging** *n* jogging *m*

join /dʒɔɪn/ *vt* juntar, unir; (*become member*) fazer-se sócio de, entrar para. ~ **sb** juntar-se a alg □ *vi* (*of roads*) juntar-se, entroncar-se; (*of rivers*) confluir □ *n* junção *f*, junta *f*.

~ **in** *vt/i* participar (em). ~ **up** alistar-se

joiner /'dʒɔɪnə(r)/ *n* marceneiro *m*

joint /dʒɔɪnt/ *a* comum, conjunto; (*effort*) conjunto □ *n* junta *f*, junção *f*; (*anat*) articulação *f*; (*culin*) quarto *m*; (*roast meat*) carne *f* assada; (*sl: place*) espelunca *f*. ~ **author** co-autor *m*. ~**ly** *adv* conjuntamente

joist /dʒɔɪst/ *n* trave *f*, barrote *m*

jok|e /dʒəʊk/ *n* piada *f*, gracejo *m* □ *vi* gracejar. ~**er** *n* brincalhão *m*; (*cards*) curinga *f* de baralho, (*P*) diabo *m*. ~**ingly** *adv* brincadeira

joll|y /'dʒɒlɪ/ *a* (-ier, -iest) alegre, bem disposto □ *adv* (*colloq*) muito. ~**ity** *n* festança *f*, pândega *f*

jolt /dʒəʊlt/ *vt* sacudir, sacolejar □ *vi* ir aos solavancos □ *n* solavanco *m*; (*shock*) choque *m*, sobressalto *m*

jostle /'dʒɒsl/ *vt* dar um encontrão *or* encontrões em, empurrar □ *vi* empurrar, acotovelar-se

jot /dʒɒt/ *n* (**not a**) ~ nada □ *vt* (*pt* **jotted**) ~ (**down**) apontar, tomar nota de. ~**ter** *n* (*pad*) bloco *m* de notas

journal /'dʒɜːnl/ *n* diário *m*; (*newspaper*) jornal *m*; (*periodical*) periódico *m*, revista *f*. ~**ism** *n* jornalismo *m*. ~**ist** *n* jornalista *mf*

journey /'dʒɜːnɪ/ *n* (*pl* -eys) viagem *f*; (*distance*) trajeto *m*, (*P*) trajecto *m* □ *vi* viajar

jovial /'dʒəʊvɪəl/ *a* jovial

joy /dʒɔɪ/ *n* alegria *f*. ~-**ride** *n* passeio *m* em carro roubado. ~**ful**, ~**ous** *adjs* alegre

jubil|ant /'dʒuːbɪlənt/ *a* cheio de alegria, jubiloso. ~**ation** /-leɪʃn/ *n* júbilo *m*, regozijo *m*

jubilee /'dʒuːbɪliː/ *n* jubileu *m*

Judaism /'dʒuːdenzəm/ *n* judaísmo *m*

judder /'dʒʌdə(r)/ *vi* trepidar, vibrar □ *n* trepidação *f*, vibração *f*

judge /dʒʌdʒ/ *n* juiz *m* □ *vt* julgar. ~**ment** *n* (*judging*) julgamento *m*, juízo *m*; (*opinion*) juízo *m*; (*decision*) julgamento *m*

judic|iary /dʒuː'dɪʃərɪ/ *n* magistratura *f*; (*system*) judiciário *m*. ~**ial** *a* judiciário

judicious /dʒuː'dɪʃəs/ *a* judicioso

judo /'dʒuːdəʊ/ *n* judô *m*, (*P*) judo *m*

jug /dʒʌg/ *n* (*tall*) jarro *m*; (*round*) botija *f*; **milk-** ~ *n* leiteira *f*

juggernaut /'dʒʌgənɔːt/ *n* (*lorry*) jainanta *f*, (*P*) camião *m* TIR

juggle /'dʒʌgl/ *vt/i* fazer malabarismos (**with** com). ~**r** /-ə(r)/ *n* malabarista *mf*

juic|e /dʒuːs/ *n* suco *m*, (*P*) sumo *m*. ~**y** *a* suculento; (*colloq: story etc*) picante

juke-box /'dʒu:kbɒks/ *n* juke-box *m*, (*P*) máquina *f* de música

July /dʒu:'laɪ/ *n* julho *m*

jumble /'dʒʌmbl/ *vt* misturar □ *n* mistura *f*. ~ **sale** venda *f* de caridade de objetos usados

jumbo /'dʒʌmbəʊ/ *a* ~ **jet** (avião) jumbo *m*

jump /dʒʌmp/ *vt/i* saltar; (*start*) sobressaltar(-se); (*of prices etc*) subir repentinamente □ *n* salto *m*; (*start*) sobressalto *m*; (*of prices*) alta *f*. ~ **at** aceitar imediatamente. ~ **the gun** agir prematuramente. ~ **the queue** furar a fila. ~ **to conclusions** tirar conclusões apressadas

jumper /'dʒʌmpə(r)/ *n* pulôver *m*, suéter *m*, (*P*) camisada *f* de lã

jumpy /'dʒʌmpɪ/ *a* nervoso

junction /'dʒʌŋkʃn/ *n* junção *f*; (*of roads etc*) entroncamento *m*

June /dʒu:n/ *n* junho *m*

jungle /'dʒʌŋgl/ *n* selva *f*, floresta *f*

junior /'dʒu:nɪə(r)/ *a* júnior; (*in age*) mais novo (**to** que); (*in rank*) subalterno; (*school*) primária □ *n* o mais novo *m*; (*sport*) júnior *mf*. ~ **to** (*in rank*) abaixo de

junk /dʒʌŋk/ *n* ferro-velho *m*, velharias *fpl*; (*rubbish*) lixo *m*. ~ **food** comida *f* sem valor nutritivo. ~ **mail** material *m* impresso, enviado por correio, sem ter sido solicitado. ~ **shop** loja *f* de ferro-velho, bricabraque *m*

junkie /'dʒʌŋkɪ/ *n* (*sl*) drogado *m*

jurisdiction /dʒʊərɪs'dɪkʃn/ *n* jurisdição *f*

juror /'dʒʊərə(r)/ *n* jurado *m*

jury /'dʒʊərɪ/ *n* júri *m*

just /dʒʌst/ *a* justo □ *adv* justamente, exatamente, (*P*) exactamente; (*only*) só. **he has** ~ **left** ele acabou de sair. ~ **listen!** escuta só! ~ **as** assim como; (*with time*) assim que. ~ **as tall as** exatamente, (*P*) exactamente tão alto quanto. ~ **as well that** ainda bem que. ~ **before** um momento antes (de). ~**ly** *adv* com justiça, justamente

justice /'dʒʌstɪs/ *n* justiça *f*. **J~ of the Peace** juiz *m* de paz

justifiabl|e /'dʒʌstɪfaɪəbl/ *a* justificável. ~**y** *adv* com razão, justificadamente

justif|y /'dʒʌstɪfaɪ/ *vt* justificar. ~**ication** /-ɪ'keɪʃn/ *n* justificação *f*

jut /dʒʌt/ *vi* (*pt* jutted) ~ **out** fazer saliência, sobressair

juvenile /'dʒu:vənaɪl/ *a* (*youthful*) juvenil; (*childish*) pueril; (*delinquent*) jovem; (*court*) de menores □ *n* jovem *mf*

juxtapose /dʒʌkstə'pəʊz/ *vt* justapor

K

kaleidoscope /kə'laɪdəskəʊp/ *n* caleidoscópio *m*

kangaroo /kæŋgə'ru:/ *n* canguru *m*

karate /kə'ra:tɪ/ *n* klaratê *m*

kebab /kə'bæb/ *n* churrasquinho *m*, espetinho *m*

keel /ki:l/ *n* quilha *f* □ *vi* ~ **over** virar-se

keen /ki:n/ *a* (**-er, -est**) (*sharp*) agudo; (*eager*) entusiástico; (*of appetite*) devorador; (*of intelligence*) vivo; (*of wind*) cortante. ~**ly** *adv* vivamente; (*eagerly*) com entusiasmo. ~**ness** *n* vivacidade *f*; (*enthusiasm*) entusiasmo *m*

keep /ki:p/ (*pt* kept) *vt* guardar; (*family*) sustentar; (*animals*) ter, criar; (*celebrate*) festejar; (*conceal*) esconder; (*delay*) demorar; (*prevent*) impedir (**from** de); (*promise*) cumprir; (*shop*) ter □ *vi* manter-se, conservar-se; (*remain*) ficar. ~ (**on**) continuar (**doing** fazendo) □ *n* sustento *m*; (*of castle*) torre *f* de menagem. ~ **back** *vt* (*withhold*) reter □ *vi* manter-se afastado. ~ **in/out** impedir de entrar/de sair. ~ **up** conservar. ~ **up** (**with**) acompanhar. ~**er** *n* guarda *mf*

keeping /'ki:pɪŋ/ *n* guarda *f*, cuidado *m*. **in** ~ **with** em harmonia com, (*P*) de harmonia com

keepsake /'ki:pseɪk/ *n* (*thing*) lembrança *f*, recordação *f*

keg /keg/ *n* barril *m* pequeno

kennel /'kenl/ *n* casota *f* (de cão). ~**s** *npl* canil *m*

kept /kept/ *see* **keep**

kerb /kɜ:b/ *n* meio fio *m*, (*P*) borda *f* do passeio

kernel /'kɜ:nl/ *n* (*of nut*) miolo *m*

kerosene /'kerəsi:n/ *n* (*paraffin*) querosene *m*, (*P*) petróleo *m*; (*aviation fuel*) gasolina *f*

ketchup /'ketʃəp/ *n* molho *m* de tomate, ketchup *m*

kettle /'ketl/ *n* chaleira *f*

key /ki:/ *n* chave *f*; (*of piano etc*) tecla *f*; (*mus*) clave *f* □ *a* chave. ~**-ring** *n* chaveiro *m*, porta-chaves *m invar* □ *vt* ~ **in** digitar, bater. ~**ed up** tenso

keyboard /'ki:bɔ:d/ *n* teclado *m*

keyhole /'ki:həʊl/ *n* buraco *m* da fechadura

khaki /'ka:kɪ/ *a & n* cáqui (*invar m*), (*P*) caqui (*invar m*)

kick /kɪk/ *vt/i* dar um pontapé *or* pontapés (**a, em**); (*ball*) chutar (**em**); (*of horse*) dar um coice *or* coices, escoicear □ *n* pontapé *m*; (*of gun, horse*) coice *m*; (*colloq: thrill*) excitação *f*, prazer *m*. **~-off** *n* chute *m* inicial, kick-off *m*. **~ out** (*colloq*) pôr na rua. **~ up** (*colloq: fuss, racket*) fazer

kid /kɪd/ *n* (*goat*) cabrito *m*; (*sl: child*) garoto *m*; (*leather*) pelica *f* □ *vt/i* (*pt* **kidded**) (*colloq*) brincar (com)

kidnap /'kɪdnæp/ *vt* (*pt* **kidnapped**) raptar. **~ping** *n* rapto *m*

kidney /'kɪdnɪ/ *n* rim *m*

kill /kɪl/ *vt* matar; (*fig: put an end to*) acabar com □ *n* matança *f*. **~er** *n* assassino *m*. **~ing** *n* matança *f*, massacre *m*; (*of game*) caçada *f* □ *a* (*colloq: funny*) de morrer de rir; (*colloq: exhausting*) de morte

killjoy /'kɪldʒɔɪ/ *n* desmancha-prazeres *mf*

kiln /kɪln/ *n* forno *m*

kilo /'kiːləʊ/ *n* (*pl* **-os**) quilo *m*

kilogram /'kɪləgræm/ *n* quilograma *m*

kilometre /'kɪləmiːtə(r)/ *n* quilómetro *m*, (*P*) quilómetro *m*

kilowatt /'kɪləwɒt/ *n* quilowatt *m*, (*P*) quilovate *m*

kilt /kɪlt/ *n* kilt *m*, saiote *m* escocês

kin /km/ *n* família *f*, parentes *mpl*. next of **~** os parentes mais próximos

kind[1] /kamd/ *n* espécie *f*, gênero *m*, (*P*) género *m*, natureza *f*. in **~** em gêneros, (*P*) géneros; (*fig: in the same form*) na mesma moeda. **~ of** (*colloq: somewhat*) de certo modo, um pouco

kind[2] /kamd/ *a* (**-er, -est**) (*good*) bom; (*friendly*) gentil, amável. **~-hearted** *a* bom, bondoso. **~ness** *n* bondade *f*

kindergarten /'kmdəgɑːtn/ *n* jardim de infância *m*, (*P*) infantil

kindle /'kɪndl/ *vt/i* acender(-se), atear(-se)

kindly /'kamdlɪ/ *a* (**-ier, -iest**) benévolo, bondoso □ *adv* bondosamente, gentilmente, com simpatia. **~ wait** tenha a bondade de esperar

kindred /'kɪndrɪd/ *a* aparentado; (*fig: connected*) afim. **~ spirit** espírito *m* congênere, alma *f* gêmea

kinetic /kɪ'netɪk/ *a* cinético

king /kɪŋ/ *n* rei *m*. **~-size(d)** *a* de tamanho grande

kingdom /'kɪŋdəm/ *n* reino *m*

kingfisher /'kɪŋfɪʃə(r)/ *n* pica-peixe *m*, martim-pescador *m*

kink /kɪŋk/ *n* (*in rope*) volta *f*, nó *m*; (*fig*) perversão *f*. **~y** *a* (*colloq*) excêntrico, pervertido; (*of hair*) encarapinhado

kiosk /'kiːɒsk/ *n* quiosque *m*. **telephone ~** cabine telefônica, (*P*) telefônica

kip /kɪp/ *n* (*sl*) sono *m* □ *vi* (*pt* **kipped**) (*sl*) dormir

kipper /'kɪpə(r)/ *n* arenque *m* defumado

kiss /kɪs/ *n* beijo *m* □ *vt/i* beijar(-se)

kit /kɪt/ *n* equipamento *m*; (*set of tools*) ferramenta *f*; (*for assembly*) kit *m* □ *vt* (*pt* **kitted**) **~ out** equipar

kitbag /'kɪtbæg/ *n* mochila *f* (de soldado etc); saco *m* de viagem

kitchen /'kɪtʃɪn/ *n* cozinha *f*. **~ garden** horta *f*. **~ sink** pia *f*, (*P*) lavalouças *m*

kite /kaɪt/ *n* (*toy*) pipa *f*, (*P*) papagaio *m* de papel

kith /kɪθ/ *n* **~ and kin** parentes e amigos *mpl*

kitten /'kɪtn/ *n* gatinho *m*

kitty /'kɪtɪ/ *n* (*fund*) fundo *m* comum, vaquinha *f*; (*cards*) bolo *m*

knack /næk/ *n* jeito *m*

knapsack /'næpsæk/ *n* mochila *f*

knead /niːd/ *vt* amassar

knee /niː/ *n* joelho *m*

kneecap /'niːkæp/ *n* rótula *f*

kneel /niːl/ *vi* (*pt* **knelt**) **~ (down)** ajoelhar(-se)

knelt /nelt/ *see* **kneel**

knew /njuː/ *see* **know**

knickers /'nɪkəz/ *npl* calcinhas (de senhora) *fpl*

knife /naɪf/ *n* (*pl* **knives**) faca *f* □ *vt* esfaquear, apunhalar

knight /naɪt/ *n* cavaleiro *m*; (*chess*) cavalo *m*. **~hood** *n* grau *m* de cavaleiro

knit /nɪt/ *vt* (*pt* **knitted** *or* **knit**) tricotar □ *vi* tricotar, fazer tricô; (*fig: unite*) unir-se; (*of bones*) soldar-se. **~ one's brow** franzir as sobrancelhas. **~ting** *n* malha *f*, tricô *m*

knitwear /'nɪtweə(r)/ *n* roupa *f* de malha, malhas *fpl*

knob /nɒb/ *n* (*of door*) maçaneta *f*; (*of drawer*) puxador *m*; (*of radio, TV etc*) botão *m*; (*of butter*) noz *f*. **~bly** *a* nodoso

knock /nɒk/ *vt/i* bater (em); (*sl: criticize*) desancar (em). **~ about** *vt* tratar mal □ *vi* (*wander*) andar a esmo. **~ down** (*chair, pedestrian*) deitar no chão, derrubar; (*demolish*) jogar abaixo; (*colloq: reduce*) baixar, reduzir; (*at auction*) adjudicar (**to** a). **~ down** *a* (*price*) muito baixo. **~-kneed** *a* de pernas de tesoura. **~ off** *vt* (*colloq: complete quickly*) despachar; (*sl: steal*) roubar □ *vi* (*colloq*) parar de trabalhar, fechar a loja (*colloq*). **~ out** pôr fora de combate, eliminar; (*stun*) assombrar. **~-out** *n* (*boxing*) nocaute *m*, KO *m*. **~ over** entornar. **~ up** (*meal etc*) arranjar às pressas. **~er** *n* aldrava *f*

knot /nɒt/ *n* nó *m* □ *vt* (*pt* **knotted**) atar com nó, dar nó *or* nós em

knotty /'nɒtɪ/ *a* (**-ier, -iest**) nodoso, cheio de nós; (*difficult*) complicado, espinhoso

know /nəʊ/ *vt/i* (*pt* **knew,** *pp* **known**)
saber (**that** que); (*person, place*) conhecer □ *n* **in the ~** (*colloq*) por
dentro. **~ about** (*cars etc*) saber sobre, saber de. **~-all** *n* sabe-tudo *m*
(*colloq*). **~-how** *n* know-how *m*, conhecimentos *mpl* técnicos, culturais
etc. **~ of** ter conhecimento de, ter
ouvido falar de. **~ingly** *adv* com ar
conhecedor; (*consciously*) conscientemente

knowledge /'nɒlɪdʒ/ *n* conhecimento
m; (*learning*) saber *m*. **~able** *a* conhecedor, entendido, versado

known /nəʊn/ *see* **know** □ *a* conhecido

knuckle /'nʌkl/ *n* nó *m* dos dedos □ *vi*
~ under ceder, submeter-se

Koran /kə'raːn/ *n* Alcorão *m*, Corão *m*

Korea /kə'rɪə/ *n* Coréia *f*

kosher /'kəʊʃə(r)/ *a* aprovado pela lei
judaica; (*colloq*) como deve ser

kowtow /kaʊ'taʊ/ *vi* prosternar-se
(**to** diante de); (*act obsequiously*) bajular

L

lab /læb/ *n* (*colloq*) laboratório *m*

label /'leɪbl/ *n* (*on bottle etc*) rótulo *m*;
(*on clothes, luggage*) etiqueta *f* □ *vt* (*pt*
labelled) rotular; etiquetar, pôr etiqueta em

laboratory /lə'bɒrətrɪ/ *n* laboratório
m

laborious /lə'bɔːrɪəs/ *a* laborioso, tra-
balhoso

labour /'leɪbə(r)/ *n* trabalho *m*, labuta
f; (*workers*) mão-de-obra *f* □ *vi* trabalhar; (*try hard*) esforçar-se □ *vt* alongar-se sobre, insistir em. **in ~** em
trabalho de parto. **~ed** *a* (*writing*)
laborioso, sem espontaneidade;
(*breathing, movement*) difícil. **~-
saving** *a* que poupa trabalho

Labour /'leɪbə(r)/ *n* (*party*) Partido *m*
Trabalhista, os trabalhistas □ *a* trabalhista

labourer /'leɪbərə(r)/ *n* trabalhador
m; (*on farm*) trabalhador *m* rural

labyrinth /'læbərɪnθ/ *n* labirinto *m*

lace /leɪs/ *n* renda *f*; (*of shoe*) cordão *m*
de sapato, (*P*) atacador *m* □ *vt* atar;
(*drink*) juntar um pouco (de aguardente, rum etc)

lacerate /'læsəreɪt/ *vt* lacerar, rasgar

lack /læk/ *n* falta *f* □ *vt* faltar (a), não
ter. **be ~ing** faltar. **be ~ing in** care-
cer de

lackadaisical /lækə'deɪzɪkl/ *a* lânguido, apático, desinteressado

laconic /lə'kɒnɪk/ *a* lacônico, (*P*) lacónico

lacquer /'lækə(r)/ *n* laca *f*

lad /læd/ *n* rapaz *m*, moço *m*

ladder /'lædə(r)/ *n* escada de mão *f*,
(*P*) escadote *m*; (*in stocking*) fio *m* cor-
rido, (*P*) malha *f* caída □ *vi* deixar
correr um fio, (*P*) cair uma malha □
vt fazer malhas em

laden /'leɪdn/ *a* carregado (**with** de)

ladle /'leɪdl/ *n* concha (de sopa) *f*

lady /'leɪdɪ/ *n* senhora *f*; (*title*) Lady *f*.
~-in-waiting *n* dama *f* de compa-
nhia, (*P*) dama *f* de honor. **young ~**
jovem *f*. **~-like** *a* senhoril, elegante.
Ladies *n* (*toilets*) toalete *m* das Senhoras

ladybird /'leɪdɪbɜːd/ *n* joaninha *f*

lag¹ /læg/ *vi* (*pt* **lagged**) atrasar-se,
ficar para trás □ *n* atraso *m*

lag² /læg/ *vt* (*pt* **lagged**) (*pipes etc*)
revestir com isolante térmico

lager /'laːgə(r)/ *n* cerveja *f* leve e
clara, "loura" *f* (*sl*)

lagoon /lə'guːn/ *n* lagoa *f*

laid /leɪd/ *see* **lay²**

lain /leɪn/ *see* **lie²**

lair /leə(r)/ *n* toca *f*, covil *m*

laity /'leɪtɪ/ *n* leigos *mpl*

lake /leɪk/ *n* lago *m*

lamb /læm/ *n* cordeiro *m*, carneiro *m*;
(*meat*) carneiro *m*

lambswool /'læmzwʊl/ *n* lã *f*

lame /leɪm/ *a* (**-er, -est**) coxo; (*fig:
unconvincing*) fraco. **~ness** *n*
claudicação *f*, coxeadura *f*

lament /lə'ment/ *n* lamento *m*,
lamentação *f* □ *vt/i* lamentar(-se)
(de). **~able** *a* lamentável

laminated /'læmɪn.tɪd/ *a* laminado

lamp /læmp/ *n* lâmpada *f*

lamppost /'læmppəʊst/ *n* poste *m* (do
candeeiro) (de iluminação pública)

lampshade /'læmpʃeɪd/ *n* abajur *m*,
quebra-luz *m*

lance /laːns/ *n* lança *f* □ *vt* lancetar

lancet /'laːnsɪt/ *n* bisturi *m*, (*P*) lance-
ta *f*

land /lænd/ *n* terra *f*; (*country*) país *m*;
(*plot*) terreno *m*; (*property*) terras *fpl*
□ *a* de terra, terrestre; (*policy etc*)
agrário □ *vt/i* desembarcar; (*aviat*)
aterrissar, (*P*) aterrar; (*fall*) ir parar
(**on** em); (*colloq: obtain*) arranjar; (*a
blow*) aplicar, mandar. **~-locked** *a* ro-
deado de terra

landing /'lændɪŋ/ *n* desembarque *m*;
(*aviat*) aterrissagem *f*, (*P*) aterragem
f; (*top of stairs*) patamar *m*. **~-stage** *n*
cais *m* flutuante

land|lady /'lændleɪdɪ/ *n* (*of rented
house*) senhoria *f*, proprietária *f*;
(*who lets rooms*) dona *f* da casa; (*of
boarding-house*) dona *f* da pensão; (*of
inn etc*) proprietária *f*, estalajadeira *f*.
~lord *n* (*of rented house*) senhorio

m, proprietário *m*; (*of inn etc*) proprietário *m*, estalajadeiro *m*

landmark /'lændma:k/ *n* (*conspicuous feature*) ponto *m* de referência; (*fig*) marco *m*

landscape /'lændskeip/ *n* paisagem *f* □ *vt* projectar, (*P*) projectar paisagisticamente

landslide /'lændslaid/ *n* desabamento *m or* desmoronamento *m* de terras; (*fig: pol*) vitoria *f* esmagadora

lane /lem/ *n* senda *f*, caminho *m*; (*in country*) estrada *f* pequena; (*in town*) viela *f*, ruela *f*; (*of road*) faixa *f*, pista *f*; (*of traffic*) fila *f*; (*aviat*) corredor *m*; (*naut*) rota *f*

language /'læŋgwidʒ/ *n* língua *f*; (*speech, style*) linguagem *f*. **bad** ~ linguagem *f* grosseira. ~ **lab** laboratório *m* de línguas

languid /'læŋgwid/ *a* lânguido

languish /'læŋgwiʃ/ *vi* elanguescer

lank /læŋk/ *a* (*of hair*) escorrido, liso

lanky /'læŋki/ *a* (-ier, -iest) desengonçado, escanifrado

lantern /'læntən/ *n* lanterna *f*

lap[1] /læp/ *n* colo *m*; (*sport*) volta *f* completa. ~-**dog** *n* cãozinho *m* de estimação

lap[2] /læp/ *vt* ~ **up** beber lambendo □ *vi* marulhar

lapel /lə'pel/ *n* lapela *f*

lapse /læps/ *vi* decair, degenerar-se; (*expire*) caducar □ *n* lapso *m*; (*jur*) prescrição *f*. ~ **into** (*thought*) mergulhar em; (*bad habit*) adquirir

larceny /'la:sənı/ *n* furto *m*

lard /la:d/ *n* banha de porco *f*

larder /'la:də(r)/ *n* despensa *f*

large /la:dʒ/ *a* (-er, -est) grande. **at** ~ à solta, em liberdade. **by and** ~ em geral. ~**ly** *adv* largamente, em grande parte. ~**ness** *n* grandeza *f*

lark[1] /la:k/ *n* (*bird*) cotovia *f*

lark[2] /la:k/ *n* (*colloq*) pândega *f*, brincadeira *f* □ *vi* ~ **about** (*colloq*) fazer travessuras, brincar

larva /'la:və/ *n* (*pl* -**vae** /-vi:/) larva *f*

laryngitis /lærm'dʒaitis/ *n* laringite *f*

larynx /'lærmks/ *n* laringe *f*

lascivious /lə'sivıəs/ *a* lascivo, sensual

laser /'leizə(r)/ *n* laser *m*. ~ **printer** impressora *f* a laser

lash /læʃ/ *vt* chicotear, açoitar; (*rain*) fustigar □ *n* chicote *m*; (*stroke*) chicotada *f*; (*eyelash*) pestana *f*, cílio *m*. ~ **out** atacar, atirar-se a; (*colloq: spend*) esbanjar dinheiro em algo

lashings /'læʃmz/ *npl* ~ **of** (*sl*) montes de (*colloq*)

lasso /læ'su:/ *n* (*pl* -**os**) laço *m* □ *vt* laçar

last[1] /la:st/ *a* último □ *adv* no fim, em

último lugar; (*most recently*) a última vez □ *n* último *m*. **at** (**long**) ~ por fim, finalmente. ~-**minute** *a* de última hora. ~ **night** ontem à noite, a noite passada. **the** ~ **straw** a gota d'água. **to the** ~ até o fim. ~**ly** *adv* finalmente, em último lugar

last[2] /la:st/ *vt/i* durar, continuar. ~**ing** *a* duradouro, durável

latch /lætʃ/ *n* trinco *m*

late /leit/ *a* (-er, -est) atrasado; (*recent*) recente; (*former*) antigo, ex-, anterior; (*hour, fruit etc*) tardio; (*deceased*) falecido □ *adv* tarde. **in** ~ **July** no fim de julho. **of** ~ ultimamente. **at the** ~st o mais tardar. ~**ness** *n* atraso *m*

lately /'leitli/ *adv* nos últimos tempos, ultimamente

latent /'leitnt/ *a* latente

lateral /'lætərəl/ *a* lateral

lathe /leið/ *n* torno *m*

lather /'la:ðə(r)/ *n* espuma *f* de sabão □ *vt* ensaboar □ *vi* fazer espuma

Latin /'lætm/ *n* (*lang*) latim *m* □ *a* latino. ~ **America** *n* América *f* Latina. ~ **American** *a* & *n* latino-americano (*m*)

latitude /'lætitju:d/ *n* latitude *f*

latter /'lætə(r)/ *a* último, mais recente □ *n* **the** ~ este, esta. ~**ly** *adv* recentemente

lattice /'lætis/ *n* treliça *f*, (*P*) gradeamento *m* de ripas

laudable /'lɔ:dəbl/ *a* louvável

laugh /la:f/ *vi* rir (**at** de). ~ **off** disfarçar com uma piada □ *n* riso *m*. ~**able** *a* irrisório, ridículo. ~**ing-stock** *n* objeto *m*, (*P*) objecto *m* de troça

laughter /'la:ftə(r)/ *n* riso *m*, risada *f*

launch[1] /lɔ:ntʃ/ *vt* lançar □ *n* lançamento *m*. ~ **into** lançar-se or meter-se em. ~**ing pad** plataforma *f* de lançamento

launch[2] /lɔ:ntʃ/ *n* (*boat*) lancha *f*

launder /'lɔ:ndə(r)/ *vt* lavar e passar

launderette /lɔ:n'dret/ *n* lavanderia *f* automática

laundry /'lɔ:ndrı/ *n* lavanderia *f*; (*clothes*) roupa *f*. **do the** ~ lavar a roupa

laurel /'lɒrəl/ *n* loureiro *m*, louro *m*

lava /'la:və/ *n* lava *f*

lavatory /'lɒvətrı/ *n* privada *f*, (*P*) retrete *f*; (*room*) toalete *m*, (*P*) lavabo *m*

lavender /'lævəndə(r)/ *n* alfazema *f*, lavanda *f*

lavish /'lævıʃ/ *a* pródigo; (*plentiful*) copioso, generoso; (*lush*) suntuoso □ *vt* ser pródigoem, encher de. ~**ly** *adv* prodigamente; copiosamente; suntuosamente

law /lɔ:/ *n* lei *f*; (*profession, study*) direito *m*. ~-**abiding** *a* cumpridor da lei, respeitador da lei. ~ **and order** ordem *f* pública. ~**-breaker** *n* transgressor *m* da lei. ~**ful** *a* legal, legítimo. ~**fully** *adv* legalmente. ~**less** *a* sem lei; (*act*) ilegal; (*person*) rebelde

lawcourt /'lɔ:kɔ:t/ *n* tribunal *m*

lawn /lɔ:n/ *n* gramado *m*, (*P*) relvado *m*. ~**-mower** *n* cortador *m* de grama, (*P*) máquina *f* de cortar a relva

lawsuit /'lɔ:su:t/ *n* processo *m*, ação *f*, (*P*) acção *f* judicial

lawyer /'lɔ:jə(r)/ *n* advogado *m*

lax /læks/ *a* negligente; (*discipline*) frouxo; (*morals*) relaxado. ~**ity** *n* negligência *f*; (*of discipline*) frouxidão *f*; (*of morals*) relaxamento *m*

laxative /'læksətɪv/ *n* laxante *m*, laxativo *m*

lay[1] /leɪ/ *a* leigo. ~ **opinion** opinião *f* de um leigo

lay[2] /leɪ/ *vt* (*pt* **laid**) pôr, colocar; (*trap*) preparar, pôr; (*eggs, table, siege*) pôr; (*plan*) fazer □ *vi* pôr (ovos). ~ **aside** pôr de lado. ~ **down** pousar; (*condition, law, rule*) impôr; (*arms*) depor; (*one's life*) oferecer; (*policy*) ditar. ~ **hold of** agarrar(-se a). ~ **off** *vt* (*worker*) suspender do trabalho □ *vi* (*collog*) parar, desistir. ~**-off** *n* suspensão *f* temporária. ~ **on** (*gas, water etc*) instalar, ligar; (*entertainment etc*) organizar, providenciar; (*food*) servir. ~ **out** (*design*) traçar, planejar; (*spread out*) estender, espalhar; (*money*) gastar. ~ **up** *vt* (*store*) juntar; (*ship, car*) pôr fora de serviço

lay[3] /leɪ/ *see* **lie**

layabout /'leɪəbaʊt/ *n* (*sl*) vadio *m*

lay-by /'leɪbaɪ/ *n* acostamento *m*, (*P*) berma *f*

layer /'leɪə(r)/ *n* camada *f*

layman /'leɪmən/ *n* (*pl* **-men**) leigo *m*

layout /'leɪaʊt/ *n* disposição *f*; (*typ*) composição *f*

laze /leɪz/ *vi* descansar, vadiar

laz|y /'leɪzɪ/ *a* (**-ier, -iest**) preguiçoso. ~**iness** *n* preguiça *f*, ~**y-bones** *n* (*collog*) vadio *m*, vagabundo *m*

lead[1] /li:d/ *vt/i* (*pt* **led**) conduzir, guiar, levar; (*team etc*) chefiar, liderar; (*life*) levar; (*choir, band etc*) dirigir □ *n* (*distance*) avanço *m*; (*first place*) dianteira *f*; (*clue*) indício *m*, pista *f*; (*leash*) coleira *f*; (*electr*) cabo *m*; (*theatr*) papel *m* principal; (*example*) exemplo *m*. **in the** ~ na frente. ~ **away** levar. ~ **on** (*fig*) encorajar. ~ **the way** ir na frente. ~ **up to** conduzir a

lead[2] /led/ *n* chumbo *m*; (*of pencil*) grafite *f*. ~**en** *a* de chumbo; (*of colour*) plúmbeo

leader /'li:də(r)/ *n* chefe *m*, líder *m*; (*of country, club, union etc*) dirigente *mf*; (*pol*) líder; (*of orchestra*) regente *mf*, maestro *m*; (*in newspaper*) editorial *m*. ~**-ship** *n* direção *f*, (*P*) direcção *f*, liderança *f*

leading /'li:dɪŋ/ *a* principal. ~ **article** artigo *m* de fundo, editorial *m*

leaf /li:f/ *n* (*pl* **leaves**) folha *f*; (*flap of table*) aba *f* □ *vi* ~ **through** folhear. ~**y** *a* frondoso

leaflet /'li:flɪt/ *n* prospecto *m*, folheto *m* informativo

league /li:g/ *n* liga *f*; (*sport*) campeonato *m* da Liga. **in** ~ **with** de coligação com, em conluio com

leak /li:k/ *n* (*escape*) fuga *f*; (*hole*) buraco *m* □ *vt/i* (*roof, container*) pingar; (*eletr gas*) ter um escapamento, (*P*) ter uma fuga; (*naut*) fazer água. ~ **(out)** (*fig: divulge*) divulgar; (*fig: become known*) transpirar, divulgar-se. ~**age** *n* vazamento *m*. ~**y** *a* que tem um vazamento

lean[1] /li:n/ *a* (**-er, -est**) magro. ~**ness** *n* magreza *f*

lean[2] /li:n/ *vt/i* (*pt* **leaned** *or* **leant** /lent/) encostar(-se), apoiar-se (**on** em); (*be slanting*) inclinar(-se). ~ **back/forward** *or* **over** inclinar-se para trás/para a frente. ~ **on** (*collog*) pressionar. ~ **to** *n* alpendre *m*

leaning /'li:nɪŋ/ *a* inclinado □ *n* inclinação *f*

leap /li:p/ *vt* (*pt* **leaped** *or* **leapt**/lept/) galgar, saltar por cima de □ *vi* saltar □ *n* salto *m*, pulo *m*. ~**-frog** *n* eixo-badeixo *m*, (*P*) jogo *m* do eixo. ~ **year** ano *m* bissexto

learn /lɜ:n/ *vt/i* (*pt* **learned** *or* **learnt**) aprender; (*be told*) vir a saber, ouvir dizer. ~**er** *n* principiante *mf*, aprendiz *m*

learn|ed /'lɜ:nɪd/ *a* erudito. ~**ing** *n* saber *m*, erudição *f*

lease /li:s/ *n* arrendamento *m*, aluguel *m*, (*P*) aluguer *m* □ *vt* arrendar, (*P*) alugar

leash /li:ʃ/ *n* coleira *f*

least /li:st/ *a* o menor □ *n* o mínimo *m*, o menos *m* □ *adv* o menos. **at** ~ pelo menos. **not in the** ~ de maneira alguma

leather /'leðə(r)/ *n* couro *m*, cabedal *m*

leave /li:v/ *vt/i* (*pt* **left**) deixar; (*depart from*) sair/partir (de), ir-se (de) □ *n* licença *f*, permissão *f*. **be left (over)** restar, sobrar. ~ **alone** deixar em paz, não tocar. ~ **out** omitir. ~ **of absence** licença *f*. **on** ~ (*mil*) de licença. **take one's** ~ despedir-se (**of** de)

leavings /'li:vɪŋz/ *npl* restos *mpl*

Leban|on /'lebənən/ *n* Líbano *m*. **~ese** /'ni:z/ *a & n* libanês (*m*)

lecherous /'letʃərəs/ *a* lascivo

lectern /'lektən/ *n* estante *f* (de coro de igreja)

lecture /'lektʃə(r)/ *n* conferência *f*; (*univ*) aula *f* teórica; (*fig*) sermão *m* □ *vi* dar uma conferência; (*univ*) dar aula(s) □ *vt* pregar um sermão a alg (*colloq*). **~r** /-ə(r)/ *n* conferente *mf*, conferencista *mf*; (*univ*) professor *m*

led /led/ *see* **lead**[1]

ledge /ledʒ/ *n* rebordo *m*, saliência *f*; (*of window*) peitoril *m*

ledger /'ledʒə(r)/ *n* livro-mestre *m*, razão *m*

leech /li:tʃ/ *n* sanguessuga *f*

leek /li:k/ *n* alho-poró *m*, (*P*) alho-porro *m*

leer /lɪə(r)/ *vi* **~ (at)** olhar de modo malicioso *or* manhoso (para) □ *n* olhar *m* malicioso *or* manhoso

leeway /'li:weɪ/ *n* (*naut*) deriva *f*; (*fig*) liberdade *f* de ação, (*P*) acção, margem *f* (*colloq*)

left[1] /left/ *see* **leave**. **~ luggage** (*office*) depósito *m* de bagagens. **~-overs** *npl* restos *mpl*, sobras *fpl*

left[2] /left/ *a* esquerdo; (*pol*) de esquerda □ *n* esquerda *f* □ *adv* à/para à esquerda. **~-hand** *a* da esquerda; (*position*) à esquerda. **~-handed** *a* canhoto. **~-wing** *a* (*pol*) de esquerda

leg /leg/ *n* perna *f*; (*of table*) pé *m*, perna *f*; (*of journey*) etapa *f*. **pull sb's ~** brincar *or* mexer com alg. **stretch one's ~s** esticar as pernas. **~-room** *n* espaço *m* para as pernas

legacy /'legəsɪ/ *n* legado *m*

legal /'li:gl/ *a* legal; (*affairs etc*) jurídico. **~ adviser** advogado *m*. **~ity** /li:'gæləti/ *n* legalidade *f*. **~ly** *adv* legalmente

legalize /'li:gəlaɪz/ *vt* legalizar

legend /'ledʒənd/ *n* lenda *f*. **~ary** /'ledʒəndrɪ/ *a* lendário

leggings /'legɪŋz/ *npl* perneiras *fpl*; (*women's*) legging *m*

legib|le /'ledʒəbl/ *a* legível. **~ility** /-'bɪlətɪ/ *n* legibilidade *f*

legion /'li:dʒən/ *n* legião *f*

legislat|e /'ledʒɪsleɪt/ *vi* legislar. **~ion** /-'leɪʃn/ *n* legislação *f*

legislat|ive /'ledʒɪslətɪv/ *a* legislativo. **~ure** /-eɪtʃə(r)/ *n* corpo *m* legislativo

legitima|te /lɪ'dʒɪtɪmət/ *a* legítimo. **~cy** *n* legitimidade *f*

leisure /'leʒə(r)/ *n* lazer *m*, tempo livre *m*. **at one's ~** ao bel prazer, (*P*) a seu belo prazer. **~ centre** centro *m* de lazer. **~ly** *a* pausado, compassado □ *adv* sem pressa, devagar

lemon /'lemən/ *n* limão *m*

lemonade /lemə'neɪd/ *n* limonada *f*

lend /lend/ *vt* (*pt* **lent**) emprestar; (*contribute*) dar. **~ a hand to** (*help*) ajudar. **~ itself to** prestar-se a. **~er** *n* pessoa *f* que empresta. **~ing** *n* empréstimo *m*

length /leŋθ/ *n* comprimento *m*; (*in time*) período *m*; (*of cloth*) corte *m*. **at ~** extensamente; (*at last*) por fim, finalmente. **~y** *a* longo, demorado

lengthen /'leŋθən/ *vt/i* alongar(-se)

lengthways /'leŋθweɪz/ *adv* ao comprido, em comprimento, longitudinalmente

lenien|t /'li:nɪənt/ *a* indulgente, clemente. **~cy** *n* indulgência *f*, clemência *f*

lens /lenz/ *n* (*of spectacles*) lente *f*; (*photo*) objetiva *f*, (*P*) objectiva *f*

lent /lent/ *see* **lend**

Lent /lent/ *n* Quaresma *f*

lentil /'lentl/ *n* lentilha *f*

Leo /'li:əʊ/ *n* (*astr*) Leão *m*

leopard /'lepəd/ *n* leopardo *m*

leotard /'li:əʊta:d/ *n* collant(s) *m* (*pl*), (*P*) maillot *m* de ginástica ou dança

leper /'lepə(r)/ *n* leproso *m*

leprosy /'leprəsɪ/ *n* lepra *f*

lesbian /'lezbɪən/ *a* lésbico □ *n* lésbica *f*

less /les/ *a* (*in number*) menor (**than** que); (*in quantity*) menos (**than** que) □ *n, adv & prep* menos. **~ and ~** cada vez menos

lessen /'lesn/ *vt/i* diminuir

lesser /'lesə(r)/ *a* menor. **to a ~ degree** em menor grau

lesson /'lesn/ *n* lição *f*

let /let/ *vt* (*pt* **let**, *pres p* **letting**) deixar, permitir; (*lease*) alugar, arrendar □ *v aux* **~'s go** vamos. **~ him do it** que o faça ele. **~ me know** diga-me, avise-me □ *n* aluguel *m*, (*P*) aluguer *m*. **~ alone** deixar em paz; (*not to mention*) sem falar em, para não falar em. **~ down** baixar; (*deflate*) esvaziar; (*disappoint*) desapontar; (*fail to help*) deixar na mão. **~-down** *n* desapontamento *m*. **~ go** *vt/i* soltar. **~ in** deixar entrar. **~ o.s. in for** (*task, trouble*) meter-se em. **~ off** (*gun*) disparar; (*firework*) soltar, (*P*) deitar; (*excuse*) desculpar. **~ on** (*colloq*) *vt* revelar (**that** que) □ *vi* descoser-se (*colloq*), (*P*) descair-se (*colloq*). **~ out** deixar sair. **~ through** deixar passar. **~ up** (*colloq*) abrandar, diminuir. **~-up** *n* (*colloq*) pausa *f*, trégua *f*

lethal /'li:θl/ *a* fatal, mortal

letharg|y /'leθədʒɪ/ *n* letargia *f*, apatia *f*. **~ic** /lɪ'θa:dʒɪk/ *a* letárgico, apático

letter /'letə(r)/ *n* (*symbol*) letra *f*; (*message*) carta *f*. **~-bomb** *n* carta-bomba *f*. **~-box** *n* caixa *f* do correio. **~ing** *n* letras *fpl*

lettuce /'letɪs/ *n* alface *f*

leukaemia /lu:'ki:mɪə/ *n* leucemia *f*

level /'levl/ *a* plano; (*on surface*) horizontal; (*in height*) no mesmo nível (**with** que); (*spoonful etc*) raso □ *n* nível *m* □ *vt* (*pt* **levelled**) nivelar; (*gun, missile*) apontar; (*accusation*) dirigir. **on the** ~ (*colloq*) franco, sincero. ~ **crossing** passagem *f* de nível. ~-**headed** *a* equilibrado, sensato

lever /'li:və(r)/ *n* alavanca *f* □ *vt* ~ **up** levantar com alavanca

leverage /'li:vərɪdʒ/ *n* influência *f*

levity /'levətɪ/ *n* frivolidade *f*, leviandade *f*

levy /'levɪ/ *vt* (*tax*) cobrar □ *n* imposto *m*

lewd /lu:d/ *a* (-er, -est) libidinoso, obsceno

liabilit|y /laɪə'bɪlətɪ/ *n* responsabilidade *f*; (*colloq: handicap*) desvantagem *f*. ~**ies** dívidas *fpl*

liable /'laɪəbl/ *a* ~ **to do** suscetível, (*P*) susceptível de fazer; ~ **to** (*illness etc*) suscetível, (*P*) susceptível a; (*fine*) sujeito a. ~ **for** responsável por

liaise /lɪ'eɪz/ *vi* (*colloq*) servir de intermediário (**between** entre), fazer a ligação (**with** com)

liaison /lɪ'eɪzn/ *n* ligação *f*

liar /'laɪə(r)/ *n* mentiroso *m*

libel /'laɪbl/ *n* difamação *f* □ *vt* (*pt* **libelled**) difamar

liberal /'lɪbərəl/ *a* liberal. ~**ly** *adv* liberalmente

Liberal /'lɪbərəl/ *a* & *n* liberal (*mf*)

liberat|e /'lɪbəreɪt/ *vt* libertar. ~**ion** /-'reɪʃn/ *n* libertação *f*; (*of women*) emancipação *f*

libert|y /'lɪbətɪ/ *n* liberdade *f*. **at** ~**y to** livre de. **take** ~**ies** tomar liberdades

libido /lɪ'bi:dəʊ/ *n* (*pl* -os) libido *m*

Libra /'li:brə/ *n* (*astr*) Balança *f*, Libra *f*

librar|y /'laɪbrərɪ/ *n* biblioteca *f*. ~**ian** /-'breərɪən/ *n* bibliotecário *m*

Libya /'lɪbɪə/ *n* Líbia *f*. ~**n** *a* & *n* líbio (*m*)

lice /laɪs/ *n see* **louse**

licence /'laɪsns/ *n* licença *f*; d (*for TV*) taxa *f*; (*for driving*) carteira *f*, (*P*) carta *f*; (*behaviour*) libertinagem *f*

license /'laɪsns/ *vt* dar licença para, autorizar □ *n* (*Amer*) = **licence**. ~ **plate** placa *f* do carro, (*P*) placa *f* de matrícula

licentious /lar'senʃəs/ *a* licencioso

lichen /'laɪkən/ *n* líquen *m*

lick /lɪk/ *vt* lamber; (*sl: defeat*) bater (*colloq*), dar uma surra em (*colloq*) □ *n* lambidela *f*. **a** ~ **of paint** uma mão de pintura

lid /lɪd/ *n* tampa *f*

lido /'li:dəʊ/ *n* (*pl* ~os) piscina *f* pública ao ar livre

lie[1] /laɪ/ *n* mentira *f* □ *vi* (*pt* **lied**, *pres p* **lying**) mentir. **give the** ~ **to** desmentir

lie[2] /laɪ/ *vi* (*pt* **lay**, *pp* **lain**, *pres p* **lying**) estar deitado; (*remain*) ficar; (*be situated*) estar, encontrar-se; (*in grave, on ground*) jazer. ~ **down** descansar. ~ **in**, **have a** ~-**in** dormir até tarde. ~ **low** (*colloq: hide*) andar escondido

lieu /lu:/ *n* **in** ~ **of** em vez de

lieutenant /lef'tenənt/ *n* (*army*) tenente *m*; (*navy*) 1º tenente *m*

life /laɪf/ *n* (*pl* **lives**) vida *f*. ~ **cycle** ciclo *m* vital. ~ **expectancy** probabilidade *f* de vida. ~-**guard** *n* salva-vidas *m*. ~ **insurance** seguro *m* de vida. ~-**jacket** *n* colete *m* salva-vidas. ~-**size(d)** *a* (de) tamanho natural *invar*

lifebelt /'laɪfbelt/ *n* cinto *m* salva-vidas, (*P*) cinto *m* de salvação

lifeboat /'laɪfbəʊt/ *n* barco *m* salva-vidas

lifebuoy /'laɪfbɔɪ/ *n* bóia *f* salva-vidas, (*P*) bóia *f* de salvação

lifeless /'laɪflɪs/ *a* sem vida

lifelike /'laɪflaɪk/ *a* natural, real; (*of portrait*) muito parecido

lifelong /'laɪflɒŋ/ *a* de toda a vida, perpétuo

lifestyle /'laɪfstaɪl/ *n* estilo *m* de vida

lifetime /'laɪftaɪm/ *n* vida *f*. **the chance of a** ~ uma oportunidade única

lift /lɪft/ *vt/i* levantar(-se), erguer(-se); (*colloq: steal*) roubar, surripiar (*colloq*); (*of fog*) levantar, dispersar-se □ *n* ascensor *m*, elevador *m*. **give a** ~ **to** dar carona, (*P*) boleia a (*colloq*). ~-**off** *n* decolagem *f*, (*P*) descolagem *f*

ligament /'lɪgəmənt/ *n* ligamento *m*

light[1] /laɪt/ *n* luz *f*; (*lamp*) lâmpada *f*; (*on vehicle*) farol *m*; (*spark*) lume *m* □ *a* claro □ *vt* (*pt* **lit** *or* **lighted**) (*ignite*) acender; (*illuminate*) iluminar. **bring to** ~ trazer à luz, revelar. **come to** ~ vir à luz. ~ **up** iluminar(-se), acender(-se). ~-**year** *n* ano-luz *m*

light[2] /laɪt/ *a* & *adv* (-er, -est) leve. ~-**headed** *a* (*dizzy*) estonteado, tonto; (*frivolous*) leviano. ~-**hearted** *a* alegre, despreocupado. ~**ly** *adv* de leve, levemente, ligeiramente. ~**ness** *n* leveza *f*

lighten[1] /'laɪtn/ *vt/i* iluminar(-se); (*make brighter*) clarear

lighten[2] /'laɪtn/ *vt/i* (*load etc*) aligeirar(-se), tornar mais leve

lighter /'laɪtə(r)/ *n* isqueiro *m*

lighthouse /'laɪthaʊs/ *n* farol *m*

lighting /'laɪtɪŋ/ n iluminação f
lightning /'laɪtnɪŋ/ n relâmpago m; (*thunderbolt*) raio m □ a muito rápido. **like** ~ como um relâmpago
lightweight /'laɪtweɪt/ a leve
like[1] /laɪk/ a semelhante (a), parecido (com) □ *prep* como □ *conj* (*colloq*) como □ n igual m, coisa f parecida. ~**-minded** a da mesma opinião. **the** ~**s of you** gente como você(s).
like[2] /laɪk/ vt gostar (de). ~**s** npl gostos mpl. **I would** ~ gostaria (de), queria. **if you** ~ se quiser. **would you** ~? gostaria?, queria? ~**able** a simpático
like|**ly** /'laɪklɪ/ a (-ier, -iest) provável □ *adv* provavelmente. **he is** ~**ly to come** é provável que ele venha. **not** ~**ly!** (*colloq*) nem morto, nem por sonhos. ~**lihood** n probabilidade f
liken /'laɪkn/ vt comparar (**to** com)
likeness /'laɪknɪs/ n semelhança f
likewise /'laɪkwaɪz/ adv também; (*in the same way*) da mesma maneira
liking /'laɪkɪŋ/ n gosto m, inclinação f; (*for person*) afeição f. **take a** ~ **to** (*thing*) tomar gosto por; (*person*) simpatizar com
lilac /'laɪlək/ n lilás m □ a lilás *invar*
lily /'lɪlɪ/ n lírio m, lis m. ~ **of the valley** lírio m do vale
limb /lɪm/ n membro m
limber /'lɪmbə(r)/ vi ~ **up** fazer exercícios para desenferrujar (*colloq*)
lime[1] /laɪm/ n cal f
lime[2] /laɪm/ n (*fruit*) limão m
lime[3] /laɪm/ n ~(-**tree**) tília f
limelight /'laɪmlaɪt/ n **be in the** ~ estar em evidência
limerick /'lɪmərɪk/ n poema m humorístico (*de cinco versos*)
limit /'lɪmɪt/ n limite m □ vt limitar. ~**ation** /-'teɪʃn/ n limitação f. ~**ed company** sociedade f anônima, (P) anónima de responsabilidade limitada
limousine /'lɪməzi:n/ n limusine f
limp[1] /lɪmp/ vi mancar, coxear □ n **have a** ~ coxear
limp[2] /lɪmp/ a (-er, -est) mole, frouxo
line[1] /laɪn/ n linha f; (*string*) fio m; (*rope*) corda f; (*row*) fila f; (*of poem*) verso m; (*wrinkle*) ruga f, (*of business*) ramo m; (*of goods*) linha f; (*Amer: queue*) fila f, (P) bicha f □ vt marcar com linhas; (*streets etc*) ladear, enfileirar-se ao longo de. ~**d paper** papel m pautado. **in** ~ **with** de acordo com. ~ **up** alinhar(-se), enfileirar(-se); (*in queue*) pôr(-se) em fila, (P) bicha. ~-**up** n (*players*) formação f
line[2] /laɪn/ vt (*garment*) forrar (**with** de)
lineage /'lɪnɪdʒ/ n linhagem f
linear /'lɪnɪə(r)/ a linear

linen /'lɪnɪn/ n (*sheets etc*) roupa f (branca) de cama; (*material*) linho m
liner /'laɪnə(r)/ n navio m de linha regular, (P) paquete m
linesman /'laɪnzmən/ n (*football, tennis*) juiz m de linha
linger /'lɪŋgə(r)/ vi demorar-se, deixar-se ficar; (*of smells etc*) persistir
lingerie /'lænʒərɪ/ n roupa f de baixo (de senhora), lingerie f
linguist /'lɪŋgwɪst/ n lingüista mf, (P) linguista mf
linguistic /lɪŋ'gwɪstɪk/ a lingüístico, (P) linguístico. ~**s** n lingüística f, (P) linguística f
lining /'laɪnɪŋ/ n forro m
link /lɪŋk/ n laço m; (*of chain; fig*) elo m □ vt unir, ligar; (*relate*) ligar; (*arm*) enfiar. ~ **up** (*of roads*) juntar-se (**with** a). ~**age** n ligação f
lino, linoleum /'laɪnəʊ, lɪ'nəʊlɪəm/ n linóleo m
lint /lɪnt/ n (*med*) curativo m de fibra de algodão; (*fluff*) cotão m
lion /'laɪən/ n leão m. ~**ess** n leoa f
lip /lɪp/ n lábio m, beiço m; (*edge*) borda f; (*of jug etc*) bico m. ~-**read** vt/i entender pelos movimentos dos lábios. **pay** ~- **service to** fingir pena, admiração etc
lipstick /'lɪpstɪk/ n batom m, (P) bâton m
liquefy /'lɪkwɪfaɪ/ vt/i liquefazer(-se)
liqueur /lɪ'kjʊə(r)/ n licor m
liquid /'lɪkwɪd/ n & a líquido (m). ~**ize** vt liqüidificar, (P) liquidificar. ~**izer** n liqüidificador m, (P) liquidificador m
liquidat|**e** /'lɪkwɪdeɪt/ vt liquidar. ~**ion** /-'deɪʃn/ n liquidação f
liquor /'lɪkə(r)/ n bebida f alcoólica
liquorice /'lɪkərɪs/ n alcaçuz m
Lisbon /'lɪzbən/ n Lisboa f
lisp /lɪsp/ n ceceio m □ vi cecear
list[1] /lɪst/ n lista f □ vt fazer uma lista de; (*enter*) pôr na lista
list[2] /lɪst/ vi (*of ship*) adernar □ n adernamento m
listen /'lɪsn/ vi escutar, prestar atenção. ~ **to,** ~ **in (to)** escutar, pôr-se à escuta. ~**er** n ouvinte mf
listless /'lɪstlɪs/ a sem energia, apático
lit /lɪt/ *see* **light**[1]
literal /'lɪtərəl/ a literal. ~**ly** adv literalmente
litera|**te** /'lɪtərət/ a alfabetizado. ~**cy** n alfabetização f, instrução f
literature /'lɪtrətʃə(r)/ n literatura f; (*colloq: leaflets etc*) folhetos mpl
lithe /laɪð/ a ágil, flexível
litigation /lɪtɪ'geɪʃn/ n litígio m
litre /'li:tə(r)/ n litro m
litter /'lɪtə(r)/ n lixo m; (*animals*) ninhada f □ vt cobrir de lixo. ~**ed**

with coberto de. **~-bin** n lata f, (P) caixote m do lixo

little /'lɪtl/ a pequeno; (not much) pouco □ n pouco m □ adv pouco, mal, nem. **a ~ um** pouco (de). **he ~ knows** ele mal/nem sabe. **~ by ~** pouco a pouco

liturgy /'lɪtədʒɪ/ n liturgia f

live[1] /laɪv/ a vivo; (wire) eletrizado; (broadcast) em direto, (P) directo, ao vivo

live[2] /lɪv/ vt/i viver; (reside) habitar, morar, viver. **~ down** fazer esquecer. **~ it up** cair na farra. **~ on** viver de; (continue) continuar a viver. **~ up to** mostrar-se à altura de; (fulfil) cumprir

livelihood /'laɪvlɪhʊd/ n modo m de vida

livel|y /'laɪvlɪ/ a (-ier, -iest) vivo, animado. **~iness** n vivacidade f, animação f

liven /'laɪvn/ vt/i **~ up** animar(-se)

liver /'lɪvə(r)/ n fígado m

livery /'lɪvərɪ/ n libré f

livestock /'laɪvstɒk/ n gado m

livid /'lɪvɪd/ a lívido; (colloq: furious) furioso

living /'lɪvɪŋ/ a vivo □ n vida f; (livelihood) modo de vida m, sustento m. **earn** or **make a ~** ganhar a vida. **standard of ~** nível m de vida. **~-room** n sala f de estar

lizard /'lɪzəd/ n lagarto m

llama /'la:mə/ n lama m

load /ləʊd/ n carga f; (of lorry, ship) carga f, carregamento m; (weight, strain) peso m. **~s of** (colloq) montes de (colloq) □ vt carregar. **~ed** a (dice) viciado; (sl: rich) cheio da nota

loaf[1] /ləʊf/ n (pl **loaves**) pão m

loaf[2] /ləʊf/ vi vadiar. **~er** n preguiçoso m, vagabundo m

loan /ləʊn/ n empréstimo m □ vt emprestar. **on ~** emprestado

loath /ləʊθ/ a sem vontade de, pouco disposto a, relutante em

loath|e /ləʊð/ vt detestar. **~ing** n repugnância f, aversão f. **~some** a repugnante

lobby /'lɒbɪ/ n entrada f, vestíbulo m; (pol) lobby m, grupo m de pressão □ vt fazer pressão sobre

lobe /ləʊb/ n lóbulo m

lobster /'lɒbstə(r)/ n lagosta f

local /'ləʊkl/ a local; (shops etc) do bairro □ n pessoa f do lugar; (colloq: pub) taberna f do bairro, do bairro. **government** administração f municipal. **~ly** adv localmente; (nearby) na vizinhança

locale /ləʊ'ka:l/ n local m

locality /ləʊ'kælətɪ/ n localidade f; (position) lugar m

localized /'ləʊkəlaɪzd/ a localizado

locat|e /ləʊ'keɪt/ vt localizar; (situate) situar. **~ion** /-ʃn/ n localização f. **on ~ion** (cinema) em external, (P) no exterior

lock[1] /lɒk/ n (hair) mecha f de cabelo

lock[2] /lɒk/ n (on door etc) fecho m, fechadura f; (on canal) comporta f □ vt/i fechar à chave; (auto: wheels) imobilizar(-se). **~ in** fechar à chave, encerrar. **~ out** fechar a porta para, deixar na rua. **~-out** n lockout m. **~ up** fechar a casa. **under ~ and key** a sete chaves

locker /'lɒkə(r)/ n compartimento m com chave

locket /'lɒkɪt/ n medalhão m

locksmith /'lɒksmɪθ/ n serralheiro m, chaveiro m

locomotion /ləʊkə'məʊʃn/ n locomoção f

locomotive /'ləʊkəməʊtɪv/ n locomotiva f

locum /'ləʊkəm/ n (med) substituto m

locust /'ləʊkəst/ n gafanhoto m

lodge /lɒdʒ/ n casa f do guarda numa propriedade; (of porter) portaria f □ vt alojar; (money) depositar. **~ a complaint** apresentar uma queixa □ vi estar alojado (**with** em casa de); (become fixed) alojar-se. **~r** /-ə(r)/ n hóspede mf

lodgings /'lɒdʒɪŋz/ n quarto m mobiliado; (flat) apartamento m

loft /lɒft/ n sótão m

lofty /'lɒftɪ/ a (-ier, -iest) elevado; (haughty) altivo

log /lɒg/ n tronco m, toro m. **~(-book)** n (naut) diário m de bordo; (aviat) diario m de vôo. **sleep like a ~** dormir como uma pedra □ vt (pt **logged**) (naut/aviat) lançar no diário de bordo. **~ off** acabar de usar. **~ on** começar a usar

loggerheads /'lɒgəhedz/ npl **at ~** às turras (**with** com)

logic /'lɒdʒɪk/ a lógico. **~al** a lógico. **~ally** adv logicamente

logistics /lə'dʒɪstɪks/ n logística f

logo /'ləʊgəʊ/ n (pl **-os**) (colloq) emblema m, logotipo m, (P) logótipo m

loin /lɔɪn/ n (culin) lombo m, alcatra f

loiter /'lɔɪtə(r)/ vi andar vagarosamente; (stand about) rondar

loll /lɒl/ vi refestelar-se

loll|ipop /'lɒlɪpɒp/ n pirulito m, (P) chupa-chupa m. **~y** n (colloq) pirulito m, (P) chupa-chupa m; (sl: money) grana f

London /'lʌndən/ n Londres

lone /ləʊn/ a solitário. **~r** /-ə(r)/ n solitário m. **~some** a solitário

lonely /'ləʊnlɪ/ a (-ier, -iest) solitário; (person) só, solitário

long[1] /lɒŋ/ *a* (-er, -est) longo, comprido □ *adv* muito tempo, longamente. **how ~ is...?** (*in size*) qual é o comprimento de...? **how ~?** (*in time*) quanto tempo? **he will not be ~** ele não vai demorar. **a ~ time** muito tempo. **a ~ way** longe. **as** *or* **so ~ as** contanto que, desde que. **~ ago** há muito tempo. **before ~** (*future*) daqui a pouco, dentro em pouco; (*past*) pouco (tempo) depois. **in the ~ run** no fim de contas. **~ before** muito (tempo) antes. **~-distance** *a* (*flight*) de longa distância; (*phone call*) interurbano. **~ face** cara *f* triste. **~ jump** salto *m* em distância. **~-playing record** LP *m*. **~-range** *a* de longo alcance; (*forecast*) a longo prazo. **~-sighted** *a* que emxerga mal a distância. **~-standing** *a* de longa data. **~-suffering** *a* com paciência exemplar/de santo. **~-term** *a* a longo prazo. **~ wave** ondas *fpl* longas. **~-winded** *a* prolixo. **so ~!** (*colloq*) até logo!

long[2] /lɒŋ/ *vi* **~ for** ansiar por, ter grande desejo de. **~ to** desejar. **~ing** *n* desejo *m* ardente

longevity /lɒn'dʒevətɪ/ *n* longevidade *f*, vida *f* longa

longhand /'lɒŋhænd/ *n* escrita *f* à mão

longitude /'lɒndʒɪtjuːd/ *n* longitude *f*

loo /luː/ *n* (*colloq*) banheiro *m*, (*P*) casa *f* de banho

look /lʊk/ *vt/i* olhar; (*seem*) parecer □ *n* olhar *m*; (*appearance*) ar *m*, aspecto *m*. (**good**) **~s** beleza *f*. **~ after** tomar conta de, olhar por. **~ at** olhar para. **~ down on** desprezar. **~ for** procurar. **~ forward to** aguardar com impaciência. **~ in on** visitar. **~ into** examinar, investigar. **~ like** parecer-se com, ter ar de. **~ on** (*as spectator*) ver, assistir; (*regard as*) considerar. **~ out** ter cautela. **~ out for** procurar; (*watch*) estar à espreita de. **~-out** *n* (*mil*) posto *m* de observação; (*watcher*) vigia *m*. **~ round** olhar em redor. **~ up** (*word*) procurar; (*visit*) ir ver. **~ up to** respeitar

loom[1] /luːm/ *n* tear *m*

loom[2] /luːm/ *vi* surgir indistintamente; (*fig*) ameaçar

loony /'luːnɪ/ *n & a* (*sl*) maluco (*m*), doido (*m*)

loop /luːp/ *n* laçada *f*; (*curve*) volta *f*, arco *m*; (*aviat*) loop *m* □ *vt* dar uma laçada

loophole /'luːphəʊl/ *n* (*in rule*) saída *f*, furo *m*

loose /luːs/ *a* (-er, -est) (*knot etc*) frouxo; (*page etc*) solto; (*clothes*) folgado; (*not packed*) a granel; (*inexact*) vago; (*morals*) dissoluto, imoral. **at a ~ end** sem saber o que fazer, sem

ocupação definida. **break ~** soltar-se. **~ly** *adv* sem apertar; (*roughly*) vagamente

loosen /'luːsn/ *vt* (*slacken*) soltar, desapertar; (*untie*) desfazer, desatar

loot /luːt/ *n* saque *m* □ *vt* pilhar, saquear. **~er** *n* assaltante *mf*. **~ing** *n* pilhagem *f*, saque *m*

lop /lɒp/ *vt* (*pt* lopped) **~ off** cortar, podar

lop-sided /lɒp'saɪdɪd/ *a* torto, inclinado para um lado

lord /lɔːd/ *n* senhor *m*; (*title*) lord *m*. **the L~** o Senhor. **the L~'s Prayer** o Pai-Nosso. (**good**) **L~!** meu Deus! **~ly** *a* magnífico, nobre; (*haughty*) altivo, arrogante

lorry /'lɒrɪ/ *n* camião *m*, caminhão *m*

lose /luːz/ *vt/i* (*pt* lost) perder. **get lost** perder-se. **get lost** (*sl*) vai passear! (*colloq*). **~r** /-ə(r)/ *n* perdedor *m*

loss /lɒs/ *n* perda *f*. **be at a ~** estar perplexo. **at a ~ for words** sem saber o que dizer

lost /lɒst/ *see* lose □ *a* perdido. **~ property** objetos *mpl*, (*P*) objectos *mpl* perdidos (e achados)

lot[1] /lɒt/ *n* sorte *f*; (*at auction, land*) lote *m*. **draw ~s** tirar à sorte

lot[2] /lɒt/ *n* **the ~** tudo; (*people*) todos *mpl*. **a ~ (of)**, **~s (of)** (*colloq*) uma porção (de) (*colloq*). **quite a ~ (of)** (*colloq*) uma boa porção (de) (*colloq*)

lotion /'ləʊʃn/ *n* loção *f*

lottery /'lɒtərɪ/ *n* loteria *f*, (*P*) lotaria *f*

loud /laʊd/ *a* (-er, -est) alto, barulhento, ruidoso; (*of colours*) berrante □ *adv* alto. **~-hailer** *n* megafone *m*. **out ~** em voz alta. **~ly** *adv* alto

loudspeaker /laʊd'spiːkə(r)/ *n* alto-falante *m*

lounge /laʊndʒ/ *vi* recostar-se preguiçosamente □ *n* sala *f*, salão *m*

louse /laʊs/ *n* (*pl* lice) piolho *m*

lousy /'laʊzɪ/ *a* (-ier, -iest) piolhento; (*sl: very bad*) péssimo

lout /laʊt/ *n* pessoa *f* grosseira, arruaceiro *m*

lovable /'lʌvəbl/ *a* amoroso, adorável

love /lʌv/ *n* amor *m*; (*tennis*) zero *m*, nada *m* □ *vt* amar, estar apaixonado por; (*like greatly*) gostar muito de. **in ~** apaixonado (**with** por). **~ affair** aventura *f* amorosa. **she sends you her ~** ela lhe manda lembranças

lovely /'lʌvlɪ/ *a* (-ier, -iest) lindo; (*colloq: delightful*) encantador, delicioso

lover /'lʌvə(r)/ *n* namorado *m*, apaixonado *m*; (*illicit*) amante *m*; (*devotee*) admirador *m*, apreciador *m*

lovesick /'lʌvsɪk/ *a* perdido de amor

loving /'lʌvɪŋ/ *a* amoroso, terno, extremoso

low /ləʊ/ a (-er, -est) baixo □ adv baixo
□ n baixa f; (low pressure) área de
baixa pressão f. ~-cut a decotado.
~-down a baixo, reles □ n (colloq) a
verdade autêntica, (P) a verdade nua
e crua. ~-fat a de baixo teor de
gordura. ~-key a (fig) moderado,
discreto

lower /'ləʊə(r)/ a & adv see low □ vt
baixar. ~ o.s. (re)baixar-se (to a)

lowlands /'ləʊləndz/ npl planície(s) f
(pl)

lowly /'ləʊlɪ/ a (-ier, -iest) humilde,
modesto

loyal /'lɔɪəl/ a leal. ~ly adv leal-
mente. ~ty n lealdade f

lozenge /'lɒzɪndʒ/ n (shape) losango
m; (tablet) pastilha f

LP abbr see long-playing record

lubric|ate /'lu:brɪkeɪt/ vt lubrificar.
~ant n lubrificante m. ~ation
/-'keɪ/ n lubrificação f

lucid /'lu:sɪd/ a lúcido. ~ity /lu:-
'sɪdətɪ/ n lucidez f

luck /lʌk/ n sorte f. bad ~ pouca
sorte f. for ~ para dar sorte. good
~!

luck|y /'lʌkɪ/ a (-ier, -iest) sortudo,
com sorte; (event etc) feliz; (number
etc) que dá sorte. ~ily adv felizmente

lucrative /'lu:krətɪv/ a lucrativo, rentável

ludicrous /'lu:dɪkrəs/ a ridículo, absurdo

lug /lʌg/ vt (pt lugged) arrstar

luggage /'lʌgɪdʒ/ n bagagem f. ~-
rack n porta-bagagem m. ~-van n
furgão m

lukewarm /'lu:kwɔ:m/ a morno; (fig)
sem entusiasmo, indiferente

lull /lʌl/ vt (send to sleep) embalar;
(suspicions) acalmar □ n calmarica f,
(P) acalmia f

lullaby /'lʌləbaɪ/ n canção f de embalar

lumbago /lʌm'beɪgəʊ/ n lumbago m

lumber /'lʌmbə(r)/ n trastes mpl
velhos; (wood) madeira f cortada □
vt ~ sb with

luminous /'lu:mɪnəs/ a luminoso

lump /lʌmp/ n bocado m; (swelling)
caroço m; (in the throat) nó m; (in
liquid) grumo m; (of sugar) torrão m
□ vt ~ together amontoar, juntar
indiscriminadamente. ~ sum quantia f total; (payment) pagamento m
de uma vez. ~y a grumoso, encaroça-
do

lunacy /'lu:nəsɪ/ n loucura f

lunar /'lu:nə(r)/ a lunar

lunatic /'lu:nətɪk/ n lunático m. ~
asylum manicômio m, (P) manicômio m

lunch /lʌntʃ/ n almoço m □ vi
almoçar. ~-time n hora f do almoço

luncheon /'lʌntʃən/ n (formal)
almoço m. ~ meat carne f enlatada,
(P) 'merenda' f. ~ voucher senha f de
almoço

lung /lʌŋ/ n pulmão m

lunge /lʌndʒ/ n mergulho m,
movimento m súbito para a frente;
(thrust) arremetida f □ vi mergulhar,
arremessar-se (at para cima de,
contra)

lurch¹ /lɜ:tʃ/ n leave sb in the ~
deixar alg em apuros

lurch² /lɜ:tʃ/ vi ir aos ziguezagues,
dar guinadas; (stagger) cambalear

lure /lʊə(r)/ vt atrair, tentar □ n chamariz m, engodo m. the ~ of the sea
a atração, (P) atracção do mar

lurid /'lʊərɪd/ a berrante; (fig: sensa-
tional) sensacional; (fig: shocking)
horrífico

lurk /lɜ:k/ vi esconder-se à espreita;
(prowl) rondar; (be latent) estar latente

luscious /'lʌʃəs/ a apetitoso; (voluptuous) desejável

lush /lʌʃ/ a viçoso, luxuriante

Lusitanian /lusɪ'temɪən/ a & n lusitano (m)

lust /lʌst/ n luxúria f, sensualidade f;
(fig) cobiça f, desejo m ardente □ vi ~
after cobiçar, desejar ardentemente.
~ful a sensual

lustre /'lʌstə(r)/ n lustre m; (fig)
prestígio m

lusty /'lʌstɪ/ a (-ier, -iest) robusto,
vigoroso

lute /lu:t/ n alaúde m

Luxemburg /'lʌksəmbɜ:g/ n Luxemburgo m

luxuriant /lʌg'ʒʊərɪənt/ a luxuriante

luxurious /lʌg'ʒʊərɪəs/ a luxuoso

luxury /'lʌkʃərɪ/ n luxo m □ a de luxo

lying /'laɪŋ/ see lie¹, lie²

lynch /lɪntʃ/ vt linchar

lynx /lɪŋks/ n lince m

lyre /'laɪə(r)/ n lira f

lyric /'lɪrɪk/ a lírico. ~s npl (mus)
letra f. ~al a lírico

M

MA abbr see Master of Arts

mac /mæk/ n (colloq) impermeável m,
gabardine f

macabre /mə'ka:brə/ a macabro

macaroni /mækə'rəʊnɪ/ n macarrão
m

macaroon /mækə'ru:n/ n bolinho m
seco de amêndoa ralada

mace¹ /meɪs/ n (staff) maça f

mace² /meɪs/ n (spice) macis m

machination /mækɪ'neɪʃn/ n maquinação f

machine /mə'ʃiːn/ n máquina f □ vt fazer à máquina; (sewing) coser à máquina. ~-gun n metralhadora f. ~-readable a em linguagem de máquina. ~ tool máquina-ferramenta f

machinery /mə'ʃiːnərɪ/ n maquinaria f; (working parts; fig) mecanismo m

machinist /mə'ʃiːnɪst/ n maquinista m

macho /'mætʃəʊ/ a machista

mackerel /'mækrəl/ n (pl invar) cavala f

mackintosh /'mækɪntɒʃ/ n impermeável m, gabardine f

mad /mæd/ a (madder, maddest) doido, louco; (dog) raivoso; (colloq: angry) furioso (colloq). be ~ about ser doido por. like ~ como (um) doido. ~ly adv loucamente; (frantically) enlouquecidamente. ~ness n loucura f

Madagascar /mædə'gæskə(r)/ n Madagáscar m

madam /'mædəm/ n senhora f. no, ~ não senhora

madden /'mædn/ vt endoidecer, enlouquecer. it's ~ing é de enlouquecer

made /meɪd/ see make. ~ to measure feito sob medida

Madeira /mə'dɪərə/ n Madeira f; (wine) Madeira m

madman /'mædmən/ n (pl -men) doido m

madrigal /'mædrɪgl/ n madrigal m

Mafia /'mæfɪə/ n Máfia f

magazine /mægə'ziːn/ n revista f, magazine m; (of gun) carregador m

magenta /mə'dʒentə/ a & n magenta (m), carmin (m)

maggot /'mægət/ n larva f. ~y a bichento

Magi /'meɪdʒaɪ/ npl the ~ os Reis mpl Magos

magic /'mædʒɪk/ n magia f □ a mágico. ~al a mágico

magician /mə'dʒɪʃn/ n (conjuror) prestidigitador m; (wizard) feiticeiro m

magistrate /'mædʒɪstreɪt/ n magistrado m

magnanim|ous /mæg'nænɪməs/ a magnânimo. ~ity /-ə'nɪmətɪ/ n magnanimidade f

magnate /'mægneɪt/ n magnata m

magnet /'mægnɪt/ n ímã m, (P) íman m. ~ic /-'netɪk/ a magnético. ~ism /-ɪzəm/ n magnetismo m. ~ize vt magnetizar

magnificen|t /mæg'nɪfɪsnt/ a magnífico. ~ce n magnificência f

magnif|y /'mægnɪfaɪ/ vt aumentar; (sound) ampliar, amplificar. ~ication /-ɪ'keɪʃn/ n aumento m, ampliação f. ~ying glass lupa f

magnitude /'mægnɪtjuːd/ n magnitude f

magpie /'mægpaɪ/ n pega f

mahogany /mə'hɒgənɪ/ n mogno m

maid /meɪd/ n criada f, empregada f. old ~ solteirona f

maiden /'meɪdn/ n (old use) donzela f □ a (aunt) solteira; (speech, voyage) inaugural. ~ name nome m de solteira

mail[1] /meɪl/ n correio m; (letters) correio m, correspondência f □ a postal □ vt postar, pôr no correio; (send by mail) mandar pelo correio. ~-bag n mala f postal. ~-box n (Amer) caixa f do correio. ~ing-list n lista f de endereços. ~ order n encomenda f por correspondência, (P) por correio

mail[2] /meɪl/ n (armour) cota f de malha

mailman /'meɪlmæn/ n (pl -men) (Amer) carteiro m

maim /meɪm/ vt mutilar, aleijar

main[1] /meɪn/ a principal □ in the ~ em geral, essencialmente. ~ road estrada f principal. ~ly adv principalmente, sobretudo

main[2] /meɪn/ n (water/gas) ~ cano m de água/gás. the ~s (electr) a rede f elétrica

mainland /'meɪnlənd/ n continente m

mainstay /'meɪnsteɪ/ n (fig) esteio m

mainstream /'meɪnstriːm/ n tendência f dominante, linha f principal

maintain /meɪn'teɪn/ vt manter, sustentar; (rights) defender, manter

maintenance /'meɪntənəns/ n (care, continuation) manutenção f; (allowance) pensão f

maisonette /meɪzə'net/ n dúplex m

maize /meɪz/ n milho m

majestic /mə'dʒestɪk/ a majestoso. ~ally adv majestosamente

majesty /'mædʒəstɪ/ n majestade f

major /'meɪdʒə(r)/ a maior; (very important) de vulto □ n major m □ vi ~ in (Amer: univ) especializar-se em. ~ road estrada f principal

Majorca /mə'dʒɔːkə/ n Maiorca f

majority /mə'dʒɒrətɪ/ n maioria f; (age) maioridade f □ a majoritário, (P) maioritário. the ~ of people a maioria or a maior parte das pessoas

make /meɪk/ vt/i (pt made) fazer; (decision) tomar; (destination) chegar a; (cause to) fazer (+ inf) or (com) que (+ subj). you ~ me angry você me aborrece □ n (brand) marca f. on the ~ (sl) oportunista. be made of ser feito de. ~ o.s. at home estar à vontade/

como em sua casa. ~ it chegar; (*succeed*) triunfar. I ~ it two o'clock são duas pelo meu relógio. ~ as if to fazer *ou* fingir que. ~ believe fingir. ~-believe *a* fingido □ *n* fantasia *f*. ~ do with arranjar-se com, contentar-se com. ~ for dirigir-se para; (*contribute to*) ajudar a. ~ good *vi* triunfar □ *vt* compensar; (*repair*) reparar. ~ off fugir (with com). ~ out avistar, distinguir; (*understand*) entender; (*claim*) pretender; (*a cheque*) passar, emitir. ~ over ceder, transferir. ~ up *vt* fazer, compor; (*story*) inventar; (*deficit*) suprir □ *vi* fazer as pazes. ~ up (one's face) maquilar-se, (*P*) maquilhar-se. ~-up *n* maquilagem *f*, (*P*) maquilhagem *f*; (*of object*) composição *f*; (*psych*) maneira *f* de ser, natureza *f*. ~ up for compensar. ~ up one's mind decidir-se

maker /'meɪkə(r)/ *n* fabricante *mf*
makeshift /'meɪkʃɪft/ *n* solução *f* temporária □ *a* provisório
making /'meɪkɪŋ/ *n* be the ~ of fazer, ser a causa do sucesso de. in the ~ em formação. he has the ~s of ele tem as qualidades essenciais de
maladjusted /mælə'dʒʌstɪd/ *a* desajustado, inadaptado
maladministration /mælədmɪnɪ'streɪʃn/ *n* mau governo *m*, má gestão *f*
malaise /mæ'leɪz/ *n* mal-estar *m*
malaria /mə'leərɪə/ *n* malária *f*
Malay /mə'leɪ/ *a* & *n* malaio (*m*). ~sia /-ʒə/ *n* Malásia *f*
male /meɪl/ *a* (*voice, sex*) masculino; (*biol, techn*) macho □ *n* (*human*) homem *m*, indivíduo *m* do sexo masculino; (*arrival*) macho *m*
malevolen|t /mə'levələnt/ *a* malévolo. ~ce *n* malevolência *f*, má vontade *f*
malform|ation /mælfɔ:'meɪʃn/ *n* malformação *f*, deformidade *f*. ~ed *a* deformado
malfunction /mæl'fʌŋkʃn/ *n* mau funcionamento *m* □ *vi* funcionar mal
malice /'mælɪs/ *n* maldade *f*, malícia *f*. bear sb ~ guardar rancor a alg
malicious /mə'lɪʃəs/ *a* maldoso, malicioso. ~ly *adv* maldosamente, maliciosamente
malign /mə'laɪn/ *vt* caluniar, difamar
malignan|t /mə'lɪgnənt/ *a* (*tumour*) maligno; (*malevolent*) malévolo. ~cy *n* malignidade *f*; malevolência *f*
malinger /mə'lɪŋgə(r)/ *vi* fingir-se doente. ~er *n* pessoa *f* que se finge doente
mallet /'mælɪt/ *n* maço *m*
malnutrition /mælnju:'trɪʃn/ *n* desnutrição *f*, subalimentação *f*

malpractice /mæl'præktɪs/ *n* abuso *m*; (*incompetence*) incompetência *f* profissional, negligência *f*
malt /mɔ:lt/ *n* malte *m*
Malt|a /'mɔ:ltə/ *n* Malta *f*. ~ese /-'ti:z/ *a* & *n* maltês (*m*)
maltreat /mæl'tri:t/ *vt* maltratar. ~ment *n* mau(s) trato(s) *m* (*pl*)
mammal /'mæml/ *n* mamífero *m*
mammoth /'mæməθ/ *n* mamute *m* □ *a* gigantesco, colossal
man /mæn/ *n* (*pl* men) homem *m*; (*in sports team*) jogador *m*; (*chess*) peça *f* □ *vt* (*pt* manned) prover de pessoal; (*mil*) guarnecer; (*naut*) guarnecer, equipar, tripular; (*be on duty at*) estar de serviço em. ~ in the street o homem da rua. ~-hour *n* hora *f* de trabalho per capita, homem-hora *f*. ~-hunt *n* caça *f* ao homem. ~-made *a* artificial. ~ to man de homem para homem
manage /'mænɪdʒ/ *vt* (*household*) governar; (*tool*) manejar; (*boat, affair, crowd*) manobrar; (*shop*) dirigir, gerir. I could ~ another drink (*colloq*) até que tomaria mais um drinque (*colloq*) □ *vi* arranjar-se. ~ to do conseguir fazer. ~able *a* manejável; (*easily controlled*) controlável. ~ment *n* gerência *f*, direção *f*, (*P*) direcção *f*. managing director diretor *m*, (*P*) director *m* geral
manager /'mænɪdʒə(r)/ *n* diretor *m*, (*P*) director *m*; (*of bank, shop*) gerente *m*; (*of actor*) empresário *m*; (*sport*) treinador *m*. ~ess *f* /-'res/ *n* diretora *f*, (*P*) directora *f*; gerente *f*. ~ial /-'dʒɪərɪəl/ *a* diretivo, (*P*) directivo, administrativo. ~ial staff gestores *mpl*
mandarin /'mændərɪn/ *n* mandarim *m*. ~ (orange) mandarina *f*, tangerina *f*
mandate /'mændeɪt/ *n* mandato *m*
mandatory /'mændətrɪ/ *a* obrigatório
mane /meɪn/ *n* crina *f*; (*of lion*) juba *f*
mangle[1] /'mæŋgl/ *n* calandra *f* □ *vt* espremer (com a calandra)
mangle[2] /'mæŋgl/ *vt* (*mutilate*) mutilar, estropiar
mango /'mæŋgəʊ/ *n* (*pl* -oes) manga *f*
manhandle /'mænhændl/ *vt* mover à força de braço; (*treat roughly*) tratar com brutalidade
manhole /'mænhəʊl/ *n* poço *m* de inspeção, (*P*) inspecção *f*
manhood /'mænhʊd/ *n* idade adulta *f*; (*quality*) virilidade *f*
mania /'meɪnɪə/ *n* mania *f*. ~c /-ræk/ *n* maníaco *m*
manicur|e /'mænɪkjʊə(r)/ *n* manicure *f* □ *vt* fazer. ~ist *n* manicure *m*

manifest /'mænɪfest/ *a* manifes to □ *vt* manifestar. **~ation** /-'steɪʃn/ *n* manifestação *f*

manifesto /mænɪ'festəʊ/ *n* (*pl* **-os**) manifesto *m*

manipulat|e /mə'nɪpjʊleɪt/ *vt* manipular. **~ion** /'leɪʃn/ *n* manipulação *f*

mankind /mæn'kaɪnd/ *n* humanidade *f*, gênero *m*, (*P*) género *m* humano

manly /'mænlɪ/ *a* viril, másculo

manner /'mænə(r)/ *n* maneira *f*, modo *m*; (*attitude*) modo(s) *m* (*pl*); (*kind*) espécie *f*. **~s** maneiras *fpl*. **bad ~s** má-criação *f*, falta *f* de educação. **good ~s** (boa) educação *f*. **~ed** *a* afetado.

mannerism /'mænərɪzəm/ *n* maneirismo *m*

manoeuvre /mə'nu:və(r)/ *n* manobra *f* □ *vt/i* manobrar

manor /'mænə(r)/ *n* solar *m*

manpower /'mænpaʊə(r)/ *n* mão-de-obra *f*

mansion /'mænʃn/ *n* mansão *f*

manslaughter /'mænslɔ:tə(r)/ *n* homicídio *m* involuntário

mantelpiece /'mæntlpi:s/ *n* (*shelf*) consolo *m* da lareira, (*P*) prateleira *f* da chaminé

manual /'mænjʊəl/ *a* manual □ *n* manual *m*

manufacture /mænjʊ'fæktʃə(r)/ *vt* fabricar □ *n* fabrico *m*, fabricação *f*. **~r** /-ə(r)/ *n* fabricante *mf*

manure /mə'njʊə(r)/ *n* estrume *m*

manuscript /'mænjʊskrɪpt/ *n* manuscrito *m*

many /'menɪ/ *a* (**more, most**) muitos □ *n* muitos; (*many people*) muita gente *f*. **a great ~** muitíssimos. **~ a man/tear/etc** muitos homens/muitas lágrimas/*etc.* **you may take as ~ as you want** você pode levar quantos quiser. **~ of us/them/you** muitos de nós/deles/de vocês. **how ~?** quantos? **one too ~** um a mais

map /mæp/ *n* mapa *m* □ *vt* (*pt* **mapped**) fazer mapa de. **~ out** planear em pormenor; (*route*) traçar

maple /'meɪpl/ *n* bordo *m*

mar /ma:(r)/ *vt* (*pt* **marred**) estragar; (*beauty*) desfigurar

marathon /'mærəθən/ *n* maratona *f*

marble /'ma:bl/ *n* mármore *m*; (*for game*) bola *f* de gude, (*P*) berlinde *m*

March /ma:tʃ/ *n* março *m*

march /ma:tʃ/ *vi* marchar □ *vt* **~ off** fazer marchar, conduzir à força. **he was ~ed off to prison** fizeram-no marchar para a prisão □ *n* marcha *f*. **~-past** *n* desfile *m* em revista militar

mare /meə(r)/ *n* égua *f*

margarine /ma:dʒə'ri:n/ *n* margarina *f*

margin /'ma:dʒɪn/ *n* margem *f*. **~al** *a* marginal. **~al seat** (*pol*) lugar *m* ganho com pequena maioria. **~ally** *adv* por uma pequena margem, muito pouco

marigold /'mærɪgəʊld/ *n* cravo-de-defunto *m*, (*P*) malmequer *m*

marijuana /mærɪ'wa:nə/ *n* maconha *f*

marina /mə'ri:nə/ *n* marina *f*

marinade /mærɪ'neɪd/ *n* vinha d'alho, escalabeche *m* □ *vt* pôr na vinha d'alho

marine /mə'ri:n/ *a* marinho; (*of ship, trade etc*) marítimo □ *n* (*shipping*) marinha *f*; (*sailor*) fuzileiro *m* naval

marionette /mærɪə'net/ *n* fantoche *m*, marionete *f*

marital /'mærɪtl/ *a* marital, conjugal, matrimonial. **~ status** estado *m* civil

maritime /'mærɪtaɪm/ *a* marítimo

mark¹ /ma:k/ *n* (*currency*) marco *m*

mark² /ma:k/ *n* marca *f*; (*trace*) marca *f*, sinal *m*; (*stain*) mancha *f*; (*schol*) nota *f*; (*target*) alvo *m* □ *vt* marcar; (*exam etc*) marcar, classificar. **~ out** marcar. **~ out for** escolher para, designar para. **~ time** marcar passo. **make one's ~** ganhar nome. **~er** *n* marcador *m*. **~ing** *n* marcas *fpl*, marcação *f*

marked /ma:kt/ *a* marcado. **~ly** /-ɪdlɪ/ *adv* manifestamente, visivelmente

market /'ma:kɪt/ *n* mercado *m* □ *vt* vender; (*launch*) comercializar, lançar. **~ garden** horta *f* de legumes para venda. **~-place** *n* mercado *m*. **~ research** pesquisa *f* de mercado. **on the ~** à venda. **~ing** *n* marketing *m*

marksman /'ma:ksmən/ *n* (*pl* **-men**) atirador *m* especial

marmalade /'ma:məleɪd/ *n* compota *f* de laranja

maroon /mə'ru:n/ *a* & *n* bordô (*m*), (*P*) bordeaux (*m*)

marooned /mə'ru:nd/ *a* abandonado em ilha, costa deserta etc; (*fig: stranded*) encalhado (*fig*)

marquee /ma:'ki:/ *n* barraca *f ou* tenda *f* grande, (*Amer: awning*) toldo *m*

marriage /'mærɪdʒ/ *n* casamento *m*, matrimônio *m*, (*P*) matrimónio *m*. **~ certificate** certidão *f* de casamento. **~able** *a* casadouro

marrow /'mærəʊ/ *n* (*of bone*) tutano *m*, medula *f*; (*vegetable*) abóbora *f*. **chilled to the ~** gelado até os ossos

marr|y /'mærɪ/ *vt* casar(-se) com; (*give or unite in marriage*) casar □ *vi* casar-se. **~ied** *a* casado; (*life*) de casado, conjugal. **get ~ied** casar-se

Mars /ma:z/ *n* Marte *m*

marsh /ma:ʃ/ *n* pântano *m.* ~**y** *a* pantanoso

marshal /'ma:ʃl/ *n* (*mil*) marechal *m*; (*steward*) mestre *m* de cerimônias, (*P*) cerimónias □ *vt* (*pt* **marshalled**) dispor em ordem, ordenar; (*usher*) conduzir, escoltar

marshmallow /ma:ʃ'mæləʊ/ *n* marshmallow *m*

martial /'ma:ʃl/ *a* marcial. ~ **law** lei *f* marcial

martyr /'ma:tə(r)/ *n* mártir *mf* □ *vt* martirizar. ~**dom** *n* martírio *m*

marvel /'ma:vl/ *n* maravilha *f*, prodígio *m* □ *vi* (*pt* **marvelled**) (*feel wonder*) maravilhar-se (**at** com); (*be astonished*) pasmar (**at** com)

marvellous /'ma:vələs/ *a* maravilhoso

Marxis|**t** /'ma:ksɪst/ *a* & *n* marxista (*mf*). ~**m** /-zəm/ *n* marxismo *m*

marzipan /'ma:zɪpæn/ *n* maçapão *m*

mascara /mæ'ska:rə/ *n* rímel *m*

mascot /'mæskət/ *n* mascote *f*

masculin|**e** /'mæskjʊlɪn/ *a* masculino □ *n* masculino *m.* ~**ity** /' lmətɪ/ *n* masculinidade *f*

mash /mæʃ/ *n* (*pulp*) papa *f* □ *vt* esmagar. ~**ed potatoes** purê *m* de batata(s)

mask /ma:sk/ *n* máscara *f* □ *vt* mascarar

masochis|**t** /'mæsəkɪst/ *n* masoquista *mf.* ~**m** /-zəm/ *n* masoquismo *m*

mason /'meɪsn/ *n* maçom *m*; (*building*) pedreiro *m.* ~**ry** *n* maçonaria *f*; (*building*) alvenaria *f*

Mason /'meɪsn/ *n* Maçônico *m*, (*P*) Maçónico *m.* ~**ic** /mə'sɒnɪk/ *a* Maçônico, (*P*) Maçónico

masquerade /mæ:skə'reɪd/ *n* mascarada *f* □ *vi* ~ **as** mascarar-se de, disfarçar-se de

mass[1] /mæs/ *n* (*relig*) missa *f*

mass[2] /mæs/ *n* massa *f*; (*heap*) montão *m* □ *vt/i* aglomerar(-se), reunir(-se) em massa. ~-**produce** *vt* produzir em série. **the** ~**es** as massas, a grande massa

massacre /'mæsəkə(r)/ *n* massacre *m* □ *vt* massacrar

massage /'mæsa:ʒ/ *n* massagem *f* □ *vt* massagear, fazer massagens em, (*P*) dar massagens a

masseu|**r** /mæ'sɜ:(r)/ *n* massagista *m.* ~**se** /mæ'sɜ:z/ *n* massagista *f*

massive /'mæsɪv/ *a* (*heavy*) maciço; (*huge*) enorme

mast /ma:st/ *n* mastro *m*; (*for radio etc*) antena *f*

master /'ma:stə(r)/ *n* (*in school*) professor *m*, mestre *m*; (*expert*) mestre *m*; (*boss*) patrão *m*; (*owner*) dono *m.* **M**~ (*boy*) menino *m* □ *vt* dominar. ~-**key**

n chave-mestra *f.* ~-**mind** *n* (*of scheme etc*) cérebro *m* □ *vt* planejar, dirigir. **M**~ **of Arts**/*etc* Licenciado *m* em Letras/*etc.* ~-**stroke** *n* golpe *m* de mestre. ~**y** *n* domínio *m* (**over** sobre); (*knowledge*) conhecimento *m*; (*skill*) perícia *f*

masterly /'ma:stəlɪ/ *a* magistral

masterpiece /'ma:stəpi:s/ *n* obra-prima *f*

masturbat|**e** /'mæstəbeɪt/ *vi* masturbar-se. ~**ion** /'beɪʃn/ *n* masturbação *f*

mat /mæt/ *n* tapete *m* pequeno; (*at door*) capacho *m.* (**table-**)~ *n* (*of cloth*) paninho *m* de mesa; (*for hot dishes*) descanso *m* para pratos

match[1] /mætʃ/ *n* fósforo *m*

match[2] /mætʃ/ *n* (*contest*) competição *f*, torneio *m*; (*game*) partida *f*; (*equal*) par *m*, parceiro *m*, igual *mf*; (*fig: marriage*) casamento *m*; (*marriage partner*) partido *m* □ *vt/i* (*set against*) contrapôr (**against** a); (*equal*) igualar; (*go with*) condizer; (*be alike*) ir com, emparceirar com. **her shoes** ~**ed her bag** os sapatos dela combinavam com a bolsa. ~**ing** *a* condizente, a condizer

matchbox /'mætʃbɒks/ *n* caixa *f* de fósforos

mat|**e**[1] /meɪt/ *n* companheiro *m*, camarada *mf*; (*of birds, animals*) macho *m*, fêmea *f*; (*assistant*) ajudante *mf* □ *vt/i* acasalar(-se) (**with** com). ~**ing season** *n* época *f* de cio

mate[2] /meɪt/ *n* (*chess*) mate *m*, xeque-mate *m*

material /mə'tɪərɪəl/ *n* material *m*; (*fabric*) tecido *m*; (*equipment*) apetrechos *mpl* □ *a* material; (*significant*) importante

materialis|**m** /mə'tɪərɪəlɪzəm/ *n* materialismo *m.* ~**tic** /'lɪstɪk/ *a* materialista

materialize /mə'tɪərɪəlaɪz/ *vi* realizar-se, concretizar-se; (*appear*) aparecer

maternal /mə'tɜ:nəl/ *a* maternal

maternity /mə'tɜ:nətɪ/ *n* maternidade *f* □ *a* (*clothes*) de grávida. ~ **hospital** maternidade *f.* ~ **leave** licença *f* de maternidade

mathematic|**s** /mæθə'mætɪks/ *n* matemática *f.* ~**al** *a* matemático. ~**ian** /-ə'tɪʃn/ *n* matemático *m*

maths /mæθs/ *n* (*colloq*) matemática *f*

matinée /'mætɪneɪ/ *n* matinê *f*, (*P*) matinée *f*

matrimon|**y** /'mætrɪmənɪ/ *n* matrimônio *m*, (*P*) matrimónio *m.* ~**ial** /'məʊnɪəl/ *a* matrimonial, conjugal

matrix /'meɪtrɪks/ *n* (*pl* **matrices** /-si:z/) matriz *f*

matron /'meɪtrən/ *n* matrona *f*; (*in school*) inspetora *f*; (*former use: senior nursing officer*) enfermeira-chefe *f*. ~**ly** *a* respeitável, muito digno

matt /mæt/ *a* fosco, sem brilho

matted /'mætɪd/ *a* emaranhado

matter /'mætə(r)/ *n* (*substance*) matéria *f*; (*affair*) assunto *m*, caso *m*, questão *f*; (*pus*) pus *m* □ *vi* importar. **as a ~ of fact** na verdade. **it does not ~** não importa. ~**-of-fact** *a* prosaico, terra-a-terra. **no ~ what happens** não importa o que acontecer. **what is the ~?** o que é que há? **what is the ~ with you?** o que é que você tem?

mattress /'mætrɪs/ *n* colchão *m*

matur|e /mə'tjʊə(r)/ *a* maduro, amadurecido □ *vt/i* amadurecer; (*comm*) vencer-se. ~**ity** *n* madureza *f*, maturidade *f*; (*comm*) vencimento *m*

maul /mɔːl/ *vt* maltratar, atacar

Mauritius /mə'rɪʃəs/ *n* Ilha *f* Maurícia

mausoleum /mɔːsə'lɪəm/ *n* mausoléu *m*

mauve /məʊv/ *a & n* lilás (*m*)

maxim /'mæksɪm/ *n* máxima *f*

maxim|um /'mæksɪməm/ *a & n* (*pl* -ima) máximo (*m*). ~**ize** *vt* aumentar ao máximo, maximizar

may /meɪ/ *v aux* (*pt* might) poder. **he ~/might come** talvez venha/viesse. **you might have** podia ter. **you ~ leave** pode ir. ~ **I smoke?** posso fumar?, dá licença que eu fume? ~ **he be happy** que ele seja feliz. **I ~ or might as well go** talvez seja or fosse melhor eu ir

May /meɪ/ *n* maio *n*. ~ **Day** o primeiro de maio

maybe /'meɪbi:/ *adv* talvez

mayhem /'meɪhem/ *n* (*disorder*) distúrbios *mpl* violentos; (*havoc*) estragos *mpl*

mayonnaise /meɪə'neɪz/ *n* maionese *f*

mayor /meə(r)/ *n* prefeito *m*. ~**ess** *n* prefeita *f*; (*mayor's wife*) mulher *f* do prefeito

maze /meɪz/ *n* labirinto *m*

me /mi:/ *pron* me; (*after prep*) mim. **with ~** comigo. **he knows ~** ele me conhece. **it's ~** sou eu

meadow /'medəʊ/ *n* prado *m*, campina *f*

meagre /'mi:gə(r)/ *a* (*thin*) magro; (*scanty*) escasso

meal[1] /mi:l/ *n* refeição *f*

meal[2] /mi:l/ *n* (*grain*) farinha *f* grossa

mean[1] /mi:n/ *a* (-er, -est) mesquinho; (*unkind*) mau. ~**ness** *n* mesquinhez *f*

mean[2] /mi:n/ *a* médio □ *n* média *f*. **Greenwich ~ time** tempo *m* médio de Greenwich

mean[3] /mi:n/ *vt* (*pt* meant) (*intend*) tencionar *or* ter (a) intenção (**to de**); (*signify*) querer dizer, significar; (*entail*) dar em resultado, resultar provavelmente em; (*refer to*) referir-se a. **be meant for** destinar-se a. **I didn't ~ it** desculpe, foi sem querer. **he ~s what he says** ele está falando sério

meander /mɪ'ændə(r)/ *vi* serpentear; (*wander*) perambular

meaning /'mi:nɪŋ/ *n* sentido *m*, significado *m*. ~**ful** *a* significativo. ~**less** *a* sem sentido

means /mi:nz/ *n* meio(s) *m*(*pl*) □ *npl* meios *mpl* pecuniários, recursos *mpl*. **by all ~** com certeza. **by ~ of** por meio de, através de. **by no ~** de modo nenhum

meant /ment/ *see* **mean**[3]

mean|time /'mi:ntaɪm/ *adv* (**in the**) ~**time** entretanto. ~**while** /-waɪl/ *adv* entretanto

measles /'mi:zlz/ *n* sarampo *m*. **German ~** rubéola *f*

measly /'mi:zlɪ/ *a* (*sl*) miserável, ínfimo

measurable /'meʒərəbl/ *a* mensurável

measure /'meʒə(r)/ *n* medida *f* □ *vt/i* medir. **made to ~** feito sob medida. ~ **up to** mostrar-se à altura de. ~**d** *a* medido, calculado. ~**ment** *n* medida *f*

meat /mi:t/ *n* carne *f*. ~**y** *a* carnudo; (*fig: substantial*) substancial

mechanic /mɪ'kænɪk/ *n* mecânico *m*

mechanic|al /mɪ'kænɪkl/ *a* mecânico. ~**s** *n* mecânica *f*; *npl* mecanismo *m*

mechan|ism /'mekənɪzəm/ *n* mecanismo *m*. ~**ize** *vt* mecanizar

medal /'medl/ *n* medalha *f*. ~**list** *n* condecorado *m*. **be a gold ~list** ser medalha de ouro

medallion /mɪ'dælɪən/ *n* medalhão *m*

meddle /'medl/ *vi* (*interfere*) imiscuir-se, intrometer-se (**in em**); (*tinker*) mexer (**with em**). ~**some** *a* intrometido, abelhudo

media /'mi:dɪə/ *see* **medium** □ *npl* **the ~** a média, os meios de comunicação social *or* de massa

mediat|e /'mi:dɪeɪt/ *vi* servir de intermediário, mediar. ~**ion** /-'eɪʃn/ *n* mediação *f*. ~**or** *n* mediador *m*, intermediário *m*

medical /'medɪkl/ *a* médico □ *n* (*colloq: examination*) exame *m* médico

medicat|ed /'medɪkeɪtɪd/ *a* medicinal. ~**ion** /-'keɪʃn/ *n* medicamentação *f*

medicinal /mɪ'dɪsɪnl/ *a* medicinal

medicine /'medsn/ *n* medicina *f*; (*substance*) remédio *m*, medicamento *m*

medieval /medɪ'i:vl/ *a* medieval

mediocr|e /mi:dɪ'əʊkə(r)/ *a* medíocre. ~**ity** /-'ɒkrətɪ/ *n* mediocridade *f*

meditat|e /'medɪteɪt/ *vt/i* meditar. ~**ion** /-'teɪʃn/ *n* meditação *f*

Mediterranean /medɪtə'reɪnɪən/ *a* mediterrâneo □ *n* the ~ o Mediterrâneo

medium /'miːdɪəm/ *n* (*pl* media) meio *m*; (*pl* mediums) (*person*) médium *mf* □ *a* médio. ~ **wave** (*radio*) onda *f* média. **the happy** ~ o meio-termo

medley /'medlɪ/ *n* (*pl* -eys) miscelânea *f*

meek /miːk/ *a* (-er, -est) manso, submisso, sofrido

meet /miːt/ *vt* (*pt* met) encontrar; (*intentionally*) encontrar-se com, ir ter com; (*at station etc*) ir esperar, ir buscar; (*make the acquaintance of*) conhecer; (*conform with*) ir ao encontro de, satisfazer; (*opponent, obligation etc*) fazer face a; (*bill, expenses*) pagar □ *vi* encontrar-se; (*get acquainted*) familiarizar-se; (*in session*) reunir-se. ~ **with** encontrar; (*accident, misfortune*) sofrer, ter

meeting /'miːtɪŋ/ *n* reunião *f*, encontro *m*; (*between two people*) encontro *m*. ~-**place** *n* ponto *m* de encontro

megalomania /megələʊ'meɪnɪə/ *n* megalomania *f*, mania *f* de grandezas

megaphone /'megəfəʊn/ *n* megafone *m*, porta-voz *m*

melancholy /'melənkɒlɪ/ *n* melancolia *f* □ *a* melancólico

mellow /'meləʊ/ *a* (-er, -est) (*fruit, person*) amadurecido, maduro; (*sound, colour*) quente, suave □ *vt/i* amadurecer; (*soften*) suavizar

melodious /mɪ'ləʊdɪəs/ *a* melodioso

melodrama /'melədrɑːmə/ *n* melodrama *m*. ~**tic** /-ə'mætɪk/ *a* melodramático

melod|y /'melədɪ/ *n* melodia *f*. ~**ic** /mɪ'lɒdɪk/ *a* melódico

melon /'melən/ *n* melão *m*

melt /melt/ *vt/i* (*metals*) fundir(-se); (*butter, snow etc*) derreter (-se); (*fade away*) desvanecer (-se). ~**ing-pot** *n* cadinho *m*

member /'membə(r)/ *n* membro *m*; (*of club etc*) sócio *m*. **M**~ **of Parliament** deputado *m*. ~**ship** *n* qualidade *f* de sócio; (*members*) número *m* de sócios; (*fee*) cota *f*. ~**ship card** carteira *f*, (*P*) cartão *m* de sócio

membrane /'membreɪn/ *n* membrana *f*

memento /mɪ'mentəʊ/ *n* (*pl* -oes) lembrança *f*, recordação *f*

memo /'meməʊ/ *n* (*pl* -os) (*colloq*) nota *f*, apontamento *m*, lembrete *m*

memoir /'memwɑː(r)/ *n* (*record, essay*) memória *f*, memorial *m*; ~**s** *npl* (*autobiography*) memórias *fpl*

memorable /'memərəbl/ *a* memorável

memorandum /memə'rændəm/ *n* (*pl* -**da** *or* -**dums**) nota *f*, lembrete *m*; (*diplomatic*) memorando *m*

memorial /mɪ'mɔːrɪəl/ *n* monumento *m* comemorativo □ *a* comemorativo

memorize /'meməraɪz/ *vt* decorar, memorizar, aprender de cor

memory /'memərɪ/ *n* memória *f*. **from** ~ de memória, de cor. **in** ~ **of** em memória de

men /men/ *see* **man**

menac|e /'menəs/ *n* ameaça *f*; (*nuisance*) praga *f*, chaga *f* □ *vt* ameaçar. ~**ingly** *adv* ameaçadoramente, de modo ameaçador

menagerie /mɪ'nædʒərɪ/ *n* coleção *f*, (*P*) colecção *f* de animais ferozes em jaulas

mend /mend/ *vt* consertar, reparar; (*darn*) remendar □ *n* conserto *m*; (*darn*) remendo *m*. ~ **one's ways** corrigir-se, emendar-se. **on the** ~ melhorando

menial /'miːnɪəl/ *a* humilde

meningitis /menɪn'dʒaɪtɪs/ *n* meningite *f*

menopause /'menəpɔːz/ *n* menopausa *f*

menstruation /menstrʊ'eɪʃn/ *n* menstruação *f*

mental /'mentl/ *a* mental; (*hospital*) de doentes mentais, psiquiátrico

mentality /men'tælətɪ/ *n* mentalidade *f*

mention /'menʃn/ *vt* mencionar □ *n* menção *f*. **don't** ~ **it!** não tem de quê, de nada

menu /'menjuː/ *n* (*pl* -us) menu *m*, (*P*) ementa *f*

mercenary /'mɜːsɪnərɪ/ *a* & *n* mercenário (*m*)

merchandise /'mɜːtʃəndaɪz/ *n* mercadorias *fpl* □ *vt/i* negociar

merchant /'mɜːtʃənt/ *n* mercador *m* □ *a* (*ship, navy*) mercante. ~ **bank** banco *m* comercial

merciful /'mɜːsɪfl/ *a* misericordioso

merciless /'mɜːsɪlɪs/ *a* impiedoso, sem dó

mercury /'mɜːkjʊrɪ/ *n* mercúrio *m*

mercy /'mɜːsɪ/ *n* piedade *f*, misericórdia *f*. **at the** ~ **of** à mercê de

mere /mɪə(r)/ *a* mero, simples. ~**ly** *adv* meramente, simplesmente, apenas

merge /mɜːdʒ/ *vt/i* fundir(-se), amalgamar(-se); (*comm: companies*) fundir(-se). ~**r** /-ə(r)/ *n* fusão *f*

meringue /mə'ræŋ/ *n* merengue *m*, suspiro *m*

merit /'merɪt/ *n* mérito *m* □ *vt* (*pt* **merited**) merecer

mermaid /'mɜːmeɪd/ n sereia f

merriment /'merɪmənt/ n divertimento m, alegria f, folguedo m

merry /'merɪ/ a (-ier, -iest) alegre, divertido. **~ Christmas** Feliz Natal. **~-go-round** n carrossel m. **~-making** n festa f, divertimento m. **merrily** adv alegremente

mesh /meʃ/ n malha f. **~es** npl (network; fig) malhas fpl.

mesmerize /'mezməraɪz/ vt hipnotizar

mess /mes/ n (disorder) desordem f, trapalhada f; (trouble) embrulhada f, trapalhada f; (dirt) porcaria f; (mil: place) cantina f; (mil: food) rancho m □ vt ~ up (make untidy) desarrumar; (make dirty) sujar; (confuse) atrapalhar, estragar □ vi ~ about perder tempo; (behave foolishly) fazer asneiras. ~ about with (tinker with) entreter-se com, andar às voltas com. **make a ~ of** estragar

message /'mesɪdʒ/ n mensagem f; (informal) recado m

messenger /'mesmdʒə(r)/ n mensageiro m

Messiah /mɪ'saɪə/ n Messias m

messy /'mesɪ/ a (-ier, -iest) desarrumado, bagunçado; (dirty) sujo, porco

met /met/ see **meet**

metabolism /mɪ'tæbəlɪzm/ n metabolismo m

metal /'metl/ n metal m □ a de metal. **~lic** /mɪ'tælɪk/ a metálico; (paint, colour) metalizado

metamorphosis /metəˈmɔːfəsɪs/ n (pl -phoses /-siːz/) metamorfose f

metaphor /'metəfə(r)/ n metáfora f. **~ical** /'fɒrɪkl/ a metafórico

meteor /'miːtɪə(r)/ n meteoro m

meteorolog|y /miːtɪə'rɒlədʒɪ/ n meteorologia f. **~ical** /-ə'lɒdʒɪkl/ a meteorológico

meter[1] /'miːtə(r)/ n contador m

meter[2] /'miːtə(r)/ n (Amer) = **metre**

method /'meθəd/ n método m

methodical /mɪ'θɒdɪkl/ a metódico

Methodist /'meθədɪst/ n metodista mf

methylated /'meθɪleɪtɪd/ a ~ spirit álcool m metílico

meticulous /mɪ'tɪkjʊləs/ a meticuloso

metre /'miːtə(r)/ n metro m

metric /'metrɪk/ a métrico. **~ation** /-'keɪʃn/ n conversão f para o sistema métrico

metropol|is /mə'trɒpəlɪs/ n metrópole f. **~itan** /metrə'pɒlɪtən/ a metropolitano

mettle /'metl/ n têmpera f, caráter m, (P) carácter m; (spirit) brio m

mew /mjuː/ n miado m □ vi miar

Mexic|o /'meksɪkəʊ/ n México m. **~an** a & n mexicano (m)

miaow /miː'aʊ/ n & vi = **mew**

mice /maɪs/ see **mouse**

mickey /'mɪkɪ/ n **take the ~ out of** (sl) fazer troça de, gozar (colloq)

micro- /'maɪkrəʊ/ pref micro-

microbe /'maɪkrəʊb/ n micróbio m

microchip /'maɪkrəʊtʃɪp/ n microchip m

microcomputer /'maɪkrəʊkəmpjuː-tə(r)/ n microcomputador m

microfilm /'maɪkrəʊfɪlm/ n microfilme m

microlight /'maɪkrəʊlaɪt/ n (aviat) ultraleve m

microphone /'maɪkrəfəʊn/ n microfone m

microprocessor /maɪkrəʊ'prəʊse-sə(r)/ n microprocessador m

microscop|e /'maɪkrəskəʊp/ n microscópio m. **~ic** /'skɒpɪk/ a microscópico

microwave /'maɪkrəʊweɪv/ n microonda f. **~ oven** forno m de microondas

mid /mɪd/ a meio. **in ~-air** no ar, em pleno vôo. **in ~-March** em meados de março

midday /mɪd'deɪ/ n meio-dia m

middle /'mɪdl/ a médio, meio; (quality) médio, mediano □ n meio m. **in the ~ of** no meio de. **~-aged** a de meia idade. **M~ Ages** Idade f Média. **~ class** classe f média. **~-class** a burguês. **M~ East** Médio Oriente m. **~ name** segundo nome m

middleman /'mɪdlmæn/ n (pl -men) intermediário m

midge /mɪdʒ/ n mosquito m

midget /'mɪdʒɪt/ n anão m □ a minúsculo

Midlands /'mɪdləndz/ npl região f do centro da Inglaterra

midnight /'mɪdnaɪt/ n meia-noite f

midriff /'mɪdrɪf/ n diafragma m; (abdomen) ventre m

midst /mɪdst/ n **in the ~ of** no meio de

midsummer /mɪd'sʌmə(r)/ n pleno verão m; (solstice) solstício m do verão

midway /mɪd'weɪ/ adv a meio caminho

midwife /'mɪdwaɪf/ n (pl -wives) parteira f

might[1] /maɪt/ n potência f; (strength) força f. **~y** a poderoso; (fig: great) imenso □ adv (colloq) muito

might[2] /maɪt/ see **may**

migraine /'miːgreɪn/ n enxaqueca f

migrant /'maɪgrənt/ a migratório □ n (person) migrante mf, emigrante mf

migrat|e /maɪ'greɪt/ vi migrar. **~ion** /-ʃn/ n migração f

mike /maɪk/ n (colloq) microfone m

mild /maɪld/ *a* (-er, -est) brando, manso; (*illness, taste*) leve; (*climate*) temperado; (*weather*) ameno. ~ly *adv* brandamente, mansamente. **to put it ~ly** para não dizer coisa pior. ~ness *n* brandura *f*

mildew /'mɪldju:/ *n* bolor *m*, mofo *m*; (*in plants*) míldio *m*

mile /maɪl/ *n* milha *f* (= 1.6 km). ~s **too big**/*etc* (*colloq*) grande demais. ~age *n* (*loosely*) quilometragem *f*

milestone /'maɪlstəʊn/ *n* marco *m* miliário; (*fig*) data *f or* acontecimento *m* importante

militant /'mɪlɪtənt/ *a* & *n* militante (*mf*)

military /'mɪlɪtrɪ/ *a* militar

militate /'mɪlɪteɪt/ *vi* militar. ~ **against** militar contra

milk /mɪlk/ *n* leite *m* □ *a* (*product*) lácteo □ *vt* ordenhar; (*fig: exploit*) explorar. ~-**shake** *n* milk-shake *m*, leite *m* batido. ~y *a* (*like milk*) leitoso; (*tea etc*) com muito leite. **M**~ **Way** Via *f* Láctea

milkman /'mɪlkmən/ *n* (*pl* -men) leiteiro *m*

mill /mɪl/ *n* moinho *m*; (*factory*) fábrica *f* □ *vt* moer □ *vi* ~ **around** aglomerar-se; (*crowd*) apinhar-se, (P) agitar-se. ~**er** *n* moleiro *m*. **pepper-**~ *n* moedor *m* de pimenta

millennium /mɪ'lenɪəm/ *n* (*pl* -iums *or* -ia) milênio *m*, (P) milénio *m*

millet /'mɪlɪt/ *n* painço *m*, milhete *m*

milli- /'mɪlɪ/ *pref* mili-

milligram /'mɪlɪgræm/ *n* miligrama *m*

millilitre /'mɪlɪli:tə(r)/ *n* mililitro *m*

millimetre /'mɪlɪmi:tə(r)/ *n* milímetro *m*

million /'mɪlɪən/ *n* milhão *m*. **a** ~ **pounds** um milhão de libras. ~**aire** /-'neə(r)/ *n* milionário *m*

millstone /'mɪlstəʊn/ *n* mó *f*. **a** ~ **round one's neck** um peso nos ombros

mime /maɪm/ *n* mímica *f*; (*actor*) mímico *m* □ *vt/i* exprimir por mímica, mimar

mimic /'mɪmɪk/ *vt* (*pt* **mimicked**) imitar □ *n* imitador *m*, parodiante *mf*. ~**ry** *n* imitação *f*.

mince /mɪns/ *vt* picar □ *n* carne *f* moída, (P) carne *f* picada. ~-**pie** *n* pastel *m* recheado com massa de passas, amêndoas, especiarias etc. ~**r** *n* máquina *f* de moer

mincemeat /'mɪnsmi:t/ *n* massa *f* de passas, amêndoas, especiarias etc usada para recheio. **make** ~ **of** (*colloq*) arrasar, aniquilar

mind *n* espírito *m*, mente *f*; (*intellect*) intelecto *m*; (*sanity*) razão *f* □ *vt* (*look*

after) tomar conta de, tratar de; (*heed*) prestar atenção a; (*object to*) importar-se com, incomodar-se com. **do you** ~ **if I smoke?** você se incomoda que eu fume? **do you** ~ **helping me?** quer fazer o favor de me ajudar? **never** ~ não se importe, não tem importância. **to be out of one's** ~ estar fora de si. **have a good** ~ **to** estar disposto a. **make up one's** ~ decidir-se. **presence of** ~ presença *f* de espírito. **to my** ~ a meu ver. ~**ful of** atento a, consciente de. ~**less** *a* insensato

minder /'maɪndə(r)/ *n* pessoa *f* que toma conta *mf*; (*bodyguard*) guarda-costa *mf*, (P) guarda-costas *mf*

mine[1] /maɪn/ *poss pron* o(s) meu(s), a(s) minha(s). **it is** ~ é (o) meu *or* (a) minha

min|e[2] /maɪn/ *n* mina *f* □ *vt* escavar, explorar; (*extract*) extrair; (*mil*) minar. ~**er** *n* mineiro *m*. ~**ing** *n* exploração *f* mineira □ *a* mineiro

minefield /'maɪnfi:ld/ *n* campo *m* minado

mineral /'mɪnərəl/ *n* mineral *m*; (*soft drink*) bebida *f* gasosa. ~ **water** água *f* mineral

minesweeper /'maɪnswi:pə(r)/ *n* caça-minas *m*

mingle /'mɪŋgl/ *vt/i* misturar(-se) (**with** com)

mingy /'mɪndʒɪ/ *a* (-ier, -iest) (*colloq*) sovina, unha(s)-de-fome (*colloq*)

mini- /'mɪnɪ/ *pref* mini-

miniature /'mɪnɪtʃə(r)/ *n* miniatura *f* □ *a* miniatural

minibus /'mɪnɪbʌs/ *n* (*public*) micro-ônibus *m*, (P) autocarro *m* pequeno

minim /'mɪnɪm/ *n* (*mus*) mínima *f*

minim|um /'mɪnɪməm/ *a* & *n* (*pl* -ma) mínimo (*m*). ~**al** *a* mínimo. ~**ize** *vt* minimizar, dar pouca importância a

miniskirt /'mɪnɪskɜ:t/ *n* minissaia *f*

minist|er /'mɪnɪstə(r)/ *n* ministro *m*; (*relig*) pastor *m*. ~**erial** /-'stɪərɪəl/ *a* ministerial. ~**ry** *n* ministério *m*

mink /mɪŋk/ *n* (*fur*) marta *f*, visão *m*

minor /'maɪnə(r)/ *a* & *n* menor (*mf*)

minority /maɪ'nɒrətɪ/ *n* minoria *f* □ *a* minoritário

mint[1] /mɪnt/ *n* **the M**~ a Casa da Moeda. **a** ~ uma fortuna □ *vt* cunhar. **in** ~ **condition** em perfeito estado, como novo, impecável

mint[2] /mɪnt/ *n* (*plant*) hortelã *f*; (*sweet*) pastilha *f* de hortelã

minus /'maɪnəs/ *prep* menos; (*colloq: without*) sem □ *n* menos *m*

minute[1] /'mɪnɪt/ *n* minuto *m*. ~**s** (*of meeting*) ata *f*, (P) acta *f*

minute² /maɪˈnjuːt/ a diminuto, minúsculo; (*detailed*) minucioso

mirac|le /ˈmɪrəkl/ n milagre m. **~ulous** /mɪˈrækjʊləs/ a milagroso, miraculoso

mirage /ˈmɪrɑːʒ/ n miragem f

mire /maɪə(r)/ n lodo m, lama f

mirror /ˈmɪrə(r)/ n espelho m; (*in car*) retrovisor m □ vt refletir, (*P*) reflectir, espelhar

mirth /mɜːθ/ n alegria f, hilaridade f

misadventure /mɪsədˈventʃə(r)/ n desgraça f. **death by ~** morte f acidental

misanthropist /mɪˈsænθrəpɪst/ n misantropo m

misapprehension /mɪsæprɪˈhenʃn/ n mal-entendido m

misbehav|e /mɪsbɪˈheɪv/ vi portar-se mal, proceder mal. **~iour** /-ˈheɪvɪə(r)/ n mau comportamento m, má conduta f

miscalculat|e /mɪsˈkælkjʊleɪt/ vi calcular mal, enganar-se. **~ion** /-ˈleɪʃn/ n erro m de cálculo

miscarr|y /mɪsˈkærɪ/ vi abortar, ter um aborto; (*fail*) falhar, malograr-se. **~iage** /-ɪdʒ/ n aborto m. **~iage of justice** erro m judiciário

miscellaneous /mɪsəˈleɪnɪəs/ a variado, diverso

mischief /ˈmɪstʃɪf/ n (*of children*) diabrura f, travessura f; (*harm*) mal m, dano m. **get into ~** fazer disparates. **make ~** criar or semear discórdias

mischievous /ˈmɪstʃɪvəs/ a endiabrado, travesso

misconception /mɪskənˈsepʃn/ n idéia f errada, falso conceito m

misconduct /mɪsˈkɒndʌkt/ n conduta f imprópria

misconstrue /mɪskənˈstruː/ vt interpretar mal

misdeed /mɪsˈdiːd/ n má ação f, (*P*) acção f, (*crime*) crime m

misdemeanour /mɪsdɪˈmiːnə(r)/ n delito m

miser /ˈmaɪzə(r)/ n avarento m, sovina mf. **~ly** a avarento, sovina

miserable /ˈmɪzrəbl/ a infeliz; (*wretched, mean*) desgraçado, miserável

misery /ˈmɪzərɪ/ n infelicidade f

misfire /mɪsˈfaɪə(r)/ vi (*plan, gun, engine*) falhar

misfit /ˈmɪsfɪt/ n inadaptado m

misfortune /mɪsˈfɔːtʃən/ n desgraça f, infelicidade f, pouca sorte f

misgiving(s) /mɪsˈgɪvɪŋ(z)/ n(pl) dúvida(s) f(pl), receio(s) m(pl)

misguided /mɪsˈgaɪdɪd/ a (*mistaken*) desencaminhado; (*misled*) mal aconselhado, enganado

mishap /ˈmɪshæp/ n contratempo m, desastre m

misinform /mɪsɪnˈfɔːm/ vt informar mal

misinterpret /mɪsɪnˈtɜːprɪt/ vt interpretar mal

misjudge /mɪsˈdʒʌdʒ/ vt julgar mal

mislay /mɪsˈleɪ/ vt (*pt mislaid*) perder, extraviar

mislead /mɪsˈliːd/ vt (*pt misled*) induzir em erro, enganar. **~ing** a enganador

mismanage /mɪsˈmænɪdʒ/ vt dirigir mal. **~ment** n má gestão f, desgoverno m

misnomer /mɪsˈnəʊmə(r)/ n termo m impróprio

misogynist /mɪˈsɒdʒɪnɪst/ n misógino m

misprint /ˈmɪsprɪnt/ n erro m tipográfico

mispronounce /mɪsprəˈnaʊns/ vt pronunciar mal

misquote /mɪsˈkwəʊt/ vt citar incorretamente

misread /mɪsˈriːd/ vt (*pt misread* /-ˈred/) ler or interpretar mal

misrepresent /mɪsreprɪˈzent/ vt deturpar, desvirtuar

miss /mɪs/ vt/i (*chance, bus etc*) perder; (*target*) errar, falhar; (*notice the loss of*) dar pela falta de; (*regret the absence of*) sentir a falta de, ter saudades de. **he ~es her/Portugal**/*etc* ele sente a falta or tem saudades dela/de Portugal/*etc* □ n falha f. **it was a near ~** foi or escapou por um triz. **~ out** omitir. **~ the point** não compreender

Miss /mɪs/ n (*pl* **Misses**) Senhorita f, (*P*) Senhora f

misshapen /mɪsˈʃeɪpn/ a disforme

missile /ˈmɪsaɪl/ n míssil m; (*object thrown*) projétil m, (*P*) projéctil m

missing /ˈmɪsɪŋ/ a que falta; (*lost*) perdido; (*person*) desaparecido. **a book with a page ~** um livro com uma página a menos

mission /ˈmɪʃn/ n missão f

missionary /ˈmɪʃənrɪ/ n missionário m

misspell /mɪsˈspel/ vt (*pt misspelt or misspelled*) escrever mal

mist /mɪst/ n neblina f, névoa f, bruma f; (*fig*) névoa f □ vt/i enevoar(-se); (*window*) embaçar(-se)

mistake /mɪˈsteɪk/ n engano m, erro m □ vt (*pt mistook, pp mistaken*) compreender mal; (*choose wrongly*) enganar-se em. **~ for** confundir com, tomar por. **~n** /-ən/ a errado. **be ~n** enganar-se. **~nly** /-ənlɪ/ adv por engano

mistletoe /ˈmɪsltəʊ/ n visco m

mistreat /mɪsˈtriːt/ vt maltratar. **~ment** n mau trato m

mistress /'mɪstrɪs/ *n* senhora *f*, dona *f*; (*teacher*) professora *f*; (*lover*) amante *f*

mistrust /mɪs'trʌst/ *vt* desconfiar de, duvidar de □ *n* desconfiança *f*

misty /'mɪstɪ/ *a* (**-ier, -iest**) enevoado, brumoso; (*window*) embaçado; (*indistinct*) indistinto

misunderstand /mɪsʌndə'stænd/ *vt* (*pt* **-stood**) compreender mal. ~**ing** *n* mal-entendido *m*

misuse[1] /mɪs'juːz/ *vt* empregar mal; (*power etc*) abusar de

misuse[2] /mɪs'juːs/ *n* mau uso *m*; (*abuse*) abuso *m*; (*of funds*) desvio *m*

mitigat|e /'mɪtɪgeɪt/ *vt* atenuar, mitigar. ~**ing circumstances** circunstâncias *fpl* atenuantes

mitten /'mɪtn/ *n* luva *f* com uma única divisão entre o polegar e os dedos

mix /mɪks/ *vt/i* misturar(-se) □ *n* mistura *f*. ~ **up** misturar bem; (*fig: confuse*) confundir. ~**-up** *n* trapalhada *f*, confusão *f*. ~ **with** associar-se com. ~**er** *n* (*culin*) batedeira *f*

mixed /mɪkst/ *a* (*school etc*) misto; (*assorted*) sortido. **be** ~ **up** (*colloq*) estar confuso

mixture /'mɪkstʃə(r)/ *n* mistura *f*. **cough** ~ xarope *m* para a tosse

moan /məʊn/ *n* gemido *m* □ *vi* gemer; (*complain*) queixar-se, lastimar-se (**about** de). ~**er** *n* pessoa *f* lamurienta

moat /məʊt/ *n* fosso *m*

mob /mɒb/ *n* multidão *f*; (*tumultuous*) turba *f*; (*sl: gang*) bando *m* □ *vt* (*pt* **mobbed**) cercar, assediar

mobil|e /'məʊbaɪl/ *a* móvel. ~**e home** caravana *f*, trailer *m*. ~**ity** /-'bɪlətɪ/ *n* mobilidade *f*

mobiliz|e /'məʊbɪlaɪz/ *vt/i* mobilizar. ~**ation** /-'zeɪʃn/ *n* mobilização *f*

moccasin /'mɒkəsɪn/ *n* mocassim *m*

mock /mɒk/ *vt/i* zombar de, gozar □ *a* falso. ~**-up** *n* modelo *m*, maqueta *f*

mockery /'mɒkərɪ/ *n* troça *f*, gozação *f*. **a** ~ **of** uma gozação de

mode /məʊd/ *n* modo *m*; (*fashion*) moda *f*

model /'mɒdl/ *n* modelo *m* □ *a* modelo; (*exemplary*) exemplar; (*toy*) em miniatura □ *vt* (*pt* **modelled**) modelar; (*clothes*) apresentar □ *vi* ser or trabalhar como modelo

modem /'məʊdem/ *n* modem *m*

moderate[1] /'mɒdərət/ *a & n* moderado (*m*). ~**ly** *adv* moderadamente. ~**ly good** sofrível

moderat|e[2] /'mɒdəreɪt/ *vt/i* moderar (-se). ~**ion** /-'reɪʃn/ *n* moderação *f*. **in** ~**ion** com moderação

modern /'mɒdn/ *a* moderno. ~ **languages** línguas *fpl* vivas. ~**ize** *vt* modernizar

modest /'mɒdɪst/ *a* modesto. ~**y** *n* modéstia *f*. ~**ly** *adv* modestamente

modicum /'mɒdɪkəm/ *n* **a** ~ **of** um pouco de

modif|y /'mɒdɪfaɪ/ *vt* modificar. ~**ication** /-ɪ'keɪʃn/ *n* modificação *f*

modulat|e /'mɒdjʊleɪt/ *vt/i* modular. ~**ion** /-'leɪʃn/ *n* modulação *f*

module /'mɒdjuːl/ *n* módulo *m*

mohair /'məʊheə(r)/ *n* mohair *m*

moist /mɔɪst/ *a* (**-er, -est**) úmido, (*P*) húmido. ~**ure** /'mɔɪstʃə(r)/ *n* umidade *f*, (*P*) humidade *f*. ~**urizer** /-tʃəraɪzə(r)/ *n* creme *m* hidratante

moisten /'mɔɪsn/ *vt/i* umedecer, (*P*) humedecer

molasses /mə'læsɪz/ *n* melaço *m*

mole[1] /məʊl/ *n* (*on skin*) sinal na pele *m*

mole[2] /məʊl/ *n* (*animal*) toupeira *f*

molecule /'mɒlɪkjuːl/ *n* molécula *f*

molest /mə'lest/ *vt* meter-se com, molestar

mollusc /'mɒləsk/ *n* molusco *m*

mollycoddle /'mɒlɪkɒdl/ *vt* mimar

molten /'məʊltən/ *a* fundido

moment /'məʊmənt/ *n* momento *m*

momentar|y /'məʊməntrɪ/ *a* momentâneo. ~**ily** /'məʊməntrəlɪ/ *adv* momentâneamente

momentous /mə'mentəs/ *a* grave, importante

momentum /mə'mentəm/ *n* ímpeto *m*, velocidade *f* adquirida

Monaco /'mɒnəkəʊ/ *n* Mônaco *m*

monarch /'mɒnək/ *n* monarca *mf*. ~**y** *n* monarquia *f*

monast|ery /'mɒnəstrɪ/ *n* mosteiro *m*, convento *m*. ~**ic** /mə'næstɪk/ *a* monástico

Monday /'mʌndɪ/ *n* segunda-feira *f*

monetary /'mʌnɪtrɪ/ *a* monetário

money /'mʌnɪ/ *n* dinheiro *m*. ~**-box** *n* cofre *m*. ~**-lender** *n* agiota *mf*. ~ **order** vale *m* postal

mongrel /'mʌŋgrəl/ *n* (cão) vira-lata *m*, (*P*) rafeiro *m*

monitor /'mɒnɪtə(r)/ *n* chefe *m* de turma; (*techn*) monitor *m* □ *vt* controlar; (*a broadcast*) monitorar (a transmissão)

monk /mʌŋk/ *n* monge *m*, frade *m*

monkey /'mʌŋkɪ/ *n* (*pl* **-eys**) macaco *m*. ~**-nut** *n* amendoim *m*. ~**-wrench** *n* chave *f* inglesa

mono /'mɒnəʊ/ *n* (*pl* **-os**) gravação *f* mono □ *a* mono *invar*

monocle /'mɒnəkl/ *n* monóculo *m*

monogram /'mɒnəgræm/ *n* monograma *m*

monologue /'mɒnəlɒg/ *n* monólogo *m*

monopol|y /mə'nɒpəlɪ/ *n* monopólio *m*. ~**ize** *vt* monopolizar

monosyllab|le /'mɒnəsɪləbl/ *n*

monossílabo m. ~**ic** /-'læbɪk/ a monossilábico

monotone /'mɒnətəʊn/ n tom m uniforme

monoton|ous /mə'nɒtənəs/ a monótono. ~**y** n monotonia f

monsoon /mɒn'su:n/ n monção f

monst|er /'mɒnstə(r)/ n monstro m. ~**rous** a monstruoso

monstrosity /mɒn'strɒsətɪ/ n monstruosidade f

month /mʌnθ/ n mês m

monthly /'mʌnθlɪ/ a mensal □ adv mensalmente □ n (periodical) revista f mensal

monument /'mɒnjʊmənt/ n monumento m. ~**al** /-'mentl/ a monumental

moo /mu:/ n mugido m □ vi mugir

mood /mu:d/ n humor m, disposição f. **in a good/bad** ~ de bom/mau humor. ~**y** a de humor instável; (sullen) carrancudo

moon /mu:n/ n lua f

moon|light /'mu:nlaɪt/ n luar m. ~**lit** a iluminado pela lua, enluarado

moonlighting /'mu:nlaɪtɪŋ/ n (colloq) segundo emprego m, esp à noite

moor[1] /mʊə(r)/ n charneca f

moor[2] /mʊə(r)/ vt amarrar, atracar. ~**ings** npl amarras fpl; (place) amarradouro m, fundeadouro m

moose /mu:s/ n (pl invar) alce m

moot /mu:t/ a discutível □ vt levantar

mop /mɒp/ n esfregão m □ vt (pt mopped) ~ (**up**) limpar. ~ **of hair** trunfa f

mope /məʊp/ vi estar or andar abatido e triste

moped /'məʊped/ n (bicicleta) motorizada f

moral /'mɒrəl/ a moral □ n moral f. ~**s** moral f, bons costumes mpl. ~**ize** vi moralizar. ~**ly** adv moralmente

morale /mə'ra:l/ n moral m

morality /mə'rælətɪ/ n moralidade f

morass /mə'ræs/ n pântano m

morbid /'mɔ:bɪd/ a mórbido

more /mɔ:(r)/ a & adv mais (**than** (do) que) □ n mais m. (**some**) ~ **tea/pens/**etc mais chá/canetas/etc. **there is no** ~ **bread** não há mais pão. ~ **or less** mais ou menos

moreover /mɔ:'rəʊvə(r)/ adv além disso, de mais a mais

morgue /mɔ:g/ n morgue f, necrotério m

moribund /'mɒrɪbʌnd/ a moribundo, agonizante

morning /'mɔ:nɪŋ/ n manhã f. **in the** ~ de manhã

Morocc|o /mə'rɒkəʊ/ n Marrocos m. ~**an** a & n marroquino (m)

moron /'mɔ:rɒn/ n idiota mf

morose /mə'rəʊs/ a taciturno e insociável, carrancudo

morphine /'mɔ:fi:n/ n morfina f

Morse /mɔ:s/ n ~ (**code**) (alfabeto) Morse m

morsel /'mɔ:sl/ n bocado m (esp de comida)

mortal /'mɔ:tl/ a & n mortal (mf). ~**ity** /mɔ:'tælətɪ/ n mortalidade f

mortar /'mɔ:tə(r)/ n argamassa f; (bowl) almofariz m; (mil) morteiro m

mortgage /'mɔ:gɪdʒ/ n hipoteca f □ vt hipotecar

mortify /'mɔ:tɪfaɪ/ vt mortificar

mortuary /'mɔ:tʃərɪ/ n casa f mortuária

mosaic /məʊ'zeɪɪk/ n mosaico m

Moscow /'mɒskəʊ/ n Moscou m, (P) Moscovo m

mosque /mɒsk/ n mesquita f

mosquito /mə'ski:təʊ/ n (pl -oes) mosquito m

moss /mɒs/ n musgo m. ~**y** a musgoso

most /məʊst/ a o mais, o maior; (majority) a maioria de, a maior parte de □ n mais m; (majority) a maioria, a maior parte, o máximo □ adv o mais; (very) muito. **at** ~ no máximo. **for the** ~ **part** na maior parte, na grande maioria. **make the** ~ **of** aproveitar ao máximo, tirar o melhor partido de. ~**ly** adv sobretudo

motel /məʊ'tel/ n motel m

moth /mɒθ/ n mariposa f, (P) borboleta f nocturna. (**clothes-**)~ n traça f. ~-**ball** n bola f de naftalina. ~-**eaten** a roído por traças

mother /'mʌðə(r)/ n mãe f □ vt tratar como a um filho. ~**hood** n maternidade f. ~-**in-law** n (pl ~**s-in-law**) sogra f. ~-**of-pearl** n madrepérola f. **M**~'**s Day** o Dia das Mães. ~-**to-be** n futura mãe f. ~**ly** a maternal

motif /məʊ'ti:f/ n tema m

motion /'məʊʃn/ n movimento m; (proposal) moção f □ vt/i ~ (**to**) **sb to** fazer sinal a alg para. ~**less** a imóvel

motivat|e /'məʊtɪveɪt/ vt motivar. ~**ion** /-'veɪʃn/ n motivação f

motive /'məʊtɪv/ n motivo m

motor /'məʊtə(r)/ n motor m; (car) automóvel m □ a (anat) motor; (boat) a motor □ vi ir de automóvel. ~ **bike** (colloq) moto f (colloq). ~ **car** carro m. ~ **cycle** motocicleta f. ~ **cyclist** motociclista mf. ~ **vehicle** veículo m automóvel. ~**ing** n automobilismo m. ~**ized** a motorizado

motorist /'məʊtərɪst/ n motorista mf, automobilista mf

motorway /'məʊtəweɪ/ n autoestrada f

mottled /'mɒtld/ *a* sarapintado, pintalgado

motto /'mɒtəʊ/ *n* (*pl* **-oes**) divisa *f*, lema *m*

mould[1] /məʊld/ *n* (*container*) forma *f*, molde *m*; (*culin*) forma *f* □ *vt* moldar. **~ing** *n* (*archit*) moldura *f*

mould[2] /məʊld/ *n* (*fungi*) bolor *m*, mofo *m*. **~y** *a* bolorento

moult /məʊlt/ *vi* estar na muda

mound /maʊnd/ *n* monte *m* de terra *or* de pedras; (*small hill*) montículo *m*

mount /maʊnt/ *vt/i* montar □ *n* (*support*) suporte *m*; (*for gem etc*) engaste *m*. **~ up** aumentar, subir

mountain /'maʊntɪn/ *n* montanha *f*. **~ bike** mountain bike *f*. **~ous** *a* montanhoso

mountaineer /maʊntɪ'nɪə(r)/ *n* alpinista *mf*. **~ing** *n* alpinismo *m*

mourn /mɔːn/ *vt/i* **~ (for)** chorar (a morte de). **~ (over)** sofrer (por). **~er** *n* pessoa *f* que acompanha o enterro. **~ing** *n* luto *m*. **in ~ing** de luto

mournful /'mɔːnfl/ *a* triste; (*sorrowful*) pesaroso

mouse /maʊs/ *n* (*pl* **mice**) camundongo *m*

mousetrap /'maʊstræp/ *n* ratoeira *f*

mousse /muːs/ *n* mousse *f*

moustache /mə'stɑːʃ/ *n* bigode *m*

mouth[1] /maʊθ/ *n* boca *f*. **~-organ** gaita *f* de boca, (*P*) beiços

mouth[2] /maʊð/ *vt/i* declamar; (*silently*) articular sem som

mouthful /'maʊθfʊl/ *n* bocado *m*

mouthpiece /'maʊθpiːs/ *n* (*mus*) bocal *m*, boquilha *f*; (*fig: person*) portavoz *mf*

mouthwash /'maʊθwɒʃ/ *n* líquido *m* para bochecho

movable /'muːvəbl/ *a* móvel

move /muːv/ *vt/i* mover(-se), mexer (-se), deslocar(-se); (*emotionally*) comover; (*incite*) convencer, levar a; (*act*) agir; (*propose*) propor; (*depart*) ir, partir; (*go forward*) avançar. **~ (out)** mudar-se, sair □ *n* movimento *m*; (*in game*) jogada *f*; (*player's turn*) vez *f*; (*house change*) mudança *f*. **~ back** recuar. **~ forward** avançar. **~ in** mudar-se para. **~ on!** circulem! **~ over, please** chegue-se para lá, por favor. **on the ~** em marcha

movement /'muːvmənt/ *n* movimento *m*

movie /'muːvɪ/ *n* (*Amer*) filme *m*. **the ~s** o cinema

moving /'muːvɪŋ/ *a* (*touching*) comovente; (*movable*) móvil; (*in motion*) em movimento

mow /məʊ/ *vt* (*pp* **mowed** *or* **mown**) ceifar; (*lawn*) cortar a grama, (*P*) relva. **~ down** ceifar. **~er** *n* (*for lawn*) máquina *f* de cortar a grama, (*P*) relva

MP *abbr see* **Member of Parliament**

Mr /'mɪstə(r)/ *n* (*pl* **Messrs**) Senhor *m*. **~ Smith** o Sr Smith

Mrs /'mɪsɪz/ *n* Senhora *f*. **~ Smith** a Sra Smith. **Mr and ~ Smith** o Sr Smith e a mulher

Ms /mɪz/ *n* Senhora D *f*

much /mʌtʃ/ (**more, most**) *a*, *adv* & *n* muito (*m*). **very ~** muito, muitíssimo. **you may have as ~ as you need** você pode levar o que precisar. **~ of it** muito *or* grande parte dele. **so ~ the better/worse** tanto melhor/pior. **how ~?** quanto? **not ~** não muito. **too ~** demasiado, demais. **he's not ~ of a gardener** não é lá grande jardineiro

muck /mʌk/ *n* estrume *m*; (*colloq: dirt*) porcaria *f* □ *vi* **~ about** (*sl*) entreter-se, perder tempo. **~ in** (*sl*) ajudar, dar uma mão □ *vt* **~ up** (*sl*) estragar. **~y** *a* sujo

mucus /'mjuːkəs/ *n* muco *m*

mud /mʌd/ *n* lama *f*. **~dy** *a* lamacento, enlameado

muddle /'mʌdl/ *vt* baralhar, atrapalhar, confundir □ *vi* **~ through** sair-se bem, desenrascar-se (*sl*) □ *n* desordem *f*; (*mix-up*) confusão *f*, trapalhada *f*

mudguard /'mʌdgɑːd/ *n* para-lama *m*

muff /mʌf/ *n* (*for hands*) regalo *m*

muffle /'mʌfl/ *vt* abafar. **~ (up)** agasalhar(-se). **~d sounds** sons *mpl* abafados. **~r** /-ə(r)/ *n* cachecol *m*

mug /mʌg/ *n* caneca *f*; (*sl: face*) cara *f*; (*sl: fool*) trouxa *mf* (*colloq*) □ *vt* (*pt* **mugged**) assaltar, agredir. **~ger** *n* assaltante *mf*. **~ging** *n* assalto *m*

muggy /'mʌgɪ/ *a* abafado

mule /mjuːl/ *n* mulo *m*; (*female*) mula *f*

mull /mʌl/ *vt* **~ over** ruminar; (*fig*) matutar em

multi- /'mʌltɪ/ *pref* mult(i)-

multicoloured /'mʌltɪkʌləd/ *a* multicolor

multinational /mʌltɪ'næʃnəl/ *a* & *n* multinacional (*f*)

multiple /'mʌltɪpl/ *a* & *n* múltiplo (*m*)

multipl|y /'mʌltɪplaɪ/ *vt/i* multiplicar(-se). **~ication** /-ɪ'keɪʃn/ *n* multiplicação *f*

multi-storey /mʌltɪ'stɔːrɪ/ *a* (*car park*) em vários níveis

multitude /'mʌltɪtjuːd/ *n* multidão *f*

mum[1] /mʌm/ *a* **keep ~** (*colloq*) ficar calado

mum[2] /mʌm/ (*B*) mamãe *f* (*colloq*) *n* (*colloq*) (*P*) mamã

mumble /'mʌmbl/ *vt/i* resmungar, resmonear

mummy[1] /'mʌmɪ/ n (body) múmia f

mummy[2] /'mʌmɪ/ n (esp child's lang) mamã (B) mamãe f (colloq) mãezinha f (colloq), (P)

mumps /mʌmps/ n parotidite f, papeira f

munch /mʌntʃ/ vt mastigar

mundane /mʌn'dem/ a banal; (worldly) mundano

municipal /mju:'nɪsɪpl/ a municipal. ~ity /-'pælətɪ/ n municipalidade f

munitions /mju:'nɪʃnz/ npl munições fpl

mural /'mjʊərəl/ a & n mural (m)

murder /'mɜ:də(r)/ n assassínio m, assassinato m □ vt assassinar. ~er n assassino m, assassina f. ~ous a assassino, sanguinário; (of weapon) mortífero

murky /'mɜ:kɪ/ a (-ier, -iest) escuro, sombrio

murmur /'mɜ:mə(r)/ n murmúrio m □ vt/i murmurar

muscle /'mʌsl/ n músculo m □ vi ~ in (colloq) impor-se, intrometer-se

muscular /'mʌskjʊlə(r)/ a muscular; (brawny) musculoso

muse /mju:z/ vi meditar, cismar

museum /mju:'zɪəm/ n museu m

mush /mʌʃ/ n papa f de farinha de milho. ~y a mole; (sentimental) piegas inv

mushroom /'mʌʃrʊm/ n cogumelo m □ vi pulular, multiplicar-se com rapidez

music /'mju:zɪk/ n música f. ~al a musical □ n (show) comédia f musical, musical m. ~al box n caixa f de música. ~-stand n estante f de música

musician /mju:'zɪʃn/ n músico m

musk /mʌsk/ n almíscar m

Muslim /'mʊzlɪm/ a & n muçulmano (m)

muslin /'mʌzlɪn/ n musselina f

mussel /'mʌsl/ n mexilhão m

must /mʌst/ v aux dever. you ~ go é necessário que você parta. he ~ be old ele deve ser velho. I ~ have done it eu devo tê-lo feito □ n be a ~ (colloq) ser imprescindível

mustard /'mʌstəd/ n mostarda f

muster /'mʌstə(r)/ vt/i juntar(-se), reunir(-se). **pass** ~ ser aceitável

musty /'mʌstɪ/ a (-ier, -iest) mofado, bolorento

mutation /mju:'teɪʃn/ n mutação f

mute /mju:t/ a & n mudo (m)

muted /'mju:tɪd/ a (sound) em surdina; (colour) suave

mutilat|e /'mju:tɪleɪt/ vt mutilar. ~ion /-'leɪʃn/ n mutilação f

mutin|y /'mju:tɪnɪ/ n motim f □ vi amotinar-se. ~ous a amotinado

mutter /'mʌtə(r)/ vt/i resmungar

mutton /'mʌtn/ n (carne de) carneiro m

mutual /'mju:tʃʊəl/ a mútuo; (colloq: common) comum. ~ly adv mutuamente

muzzle /'mʌzl/ n focinho m; (device) focinheira f; (of gun) boca f □ vt amordaçar; (dog) pôr focinheira em

my /maɪ/ a meu(s), minha(s)

myself /maɪ'self/ pron eu mesmo, eu próprio; (reflexive) me; (after prep) mim (próprio, mesmo). **by** ~ sozinho

mysterious /mɪ'stɪərɪəs/ a misterioso

mystery /'mɪstərɪ/ n mistério m

mystic /'mɪstɪk/ a & n místico (m). ~al a místico. ~ism /-sɪzəm/ n misticismo m

mystify /'mɪstɪfaɪ/ vt deixar perplexo

mystique /mɪ'sti:k/ n mística f

myth /mɪθ/ n mito m. ~ical a mítico

mytholog|y /mɪ'θɒlədʒɪ/ n mitologia f. ~ical /mɪθə'lɒdʒɪkl/ a mitológico

N

nab /næb/ vt (pt nabbed) (sl) apanhar em flagrante, apanhar com a boca na botija (colloq), pilhar

nag /næg/ vt/i (pt nagged) implicar (com), criticar constantemente; (pester) apoquentar

nagging /'nægɪŋ/ a implicante; (pain) constante, contínuo

nail /neɪl/ n prego m; (of finger, toe) unha f □ vt pregar. ~-brush n escova f de unhas. ~-file n lixa f de unhas. ~ polish esmalte m, (P) verniz m para as unhas. **hit the** ~ **on the head** acertar em cheio. **on the** ~ sem demora

naïve /naɪ'i:v/ a ingênuo, (P) ingénuo

naked /'neɪkɪd/ a nu. **to the** ~ **eye** a olho nu, à vista desarmada ~ness f nudez f

name /neɪm/ n nome m; (fig) reputação f, fama f □ vt (mention; appoint) nomear; (give a name to) chamar, dar o nome de; (a date) marcar. **be** ~**d after** ter o nome de. ~less a sem nome, anônimo, (P) anónimo

namely /'neɪmlɪ/ adv a saber

namesake /'neɪmseɪk/ n homônimo m (P) homónimo m

nanny /'nænɪ/ n ama f, babá f

nap[1] /næp/ n soneca f □ vi (pt napped) dormitar, tirar um cochilo. **catch** ~**ping** apanhar desprevenido

nap[2] /næp/ n (of material) felpa f

nape /neɪp/ n nuca f

napkin /'næpkɪn/ n guardanapo m; (for baby) fralda f

nappy /'næpɪ/ *n* fralda *f.* ~**-rash** *n* assadura *f*

narcotic /nɑːˈkɒtɪk/ *a* & *n* narcótico (*m*)

narrat|e /nəˈreɪt/ *vt* narrar. ~**ion** /-ʃn/ *n* narrativa *f.* ~**or** *n* narrador *m*

narrative /'nærətɪv/ *n* narrativa *f* □ *a* narrativo

narrow /'nærəʊ/ *a* (-er, -est) estreito; (*fig*) restrito □ *vt/i* estreitar(-se); (*limit*) limitar(-se). ~**ly** *adv* (*only just*) por pouco; (*closely, carefully*) de perto, com cuidado. ~**-minded** *a* bitolado, de visão limitada. ~**ness** *n* estreiteza *f*

nasal /'neɪzl/ *a* nasal

nast|y /'nɑːstɪ/ *a* (-ier, -iest) (*malicious, of weather*) mau; (*unpleasant*) desagradável, intragável; (*rude*) grosseiro. ~**ily** *adv* maldosamente; (*unpleasantly*) desagradavelmente. ~**iness** *f* (*malice*) maldade *f*; (*rudeness*) grosseria *f*

nation /'neɪʃn/ *n* nação *f.* ~**-wide** *a* em todo o país, em escala *or* a nível nacional

national /'næʃnəl/ *a* nacional □ *n* natural *mf.* ~ **anthem** hino *m* nacional. ~**ism** *n* nacionalismo *m.* ~**ize** *vt* nacionalizar. ~**ly** *adv* em escala nacional

nationality /næʃəˈnælətɪ/ *n* nacionalidade *f*

native /'neɪtɪv/ *n* natural *mf*, nativo *m* □ *a* nativo; (*country*) natal; (*inborn*) inato. **be a** ~ **of** ser natural de. ~ **language** língua *f* materna. ~ **speaker of Portuguese** pessoa *f* de língua portuguesa, falante *m* nativo de Português

Nativity /nəˈtɪvətɪ/ *n* **the** ~ a Natividade *f*

natter /'nætə(r)/ *vi* fazer conversa fiada, falar à toa, tagarelar

natural /'nætʃrəl/ *a* natural. ~ **history** história *f* natural. ~**ist** *n* naturalista *mf.* ~**ly** *adv* naturalmente; (*by nature*) por natureza

naturaliz|e /'nætʃrəlaɪz/ *vt/i* naturalizar(-se); (*animal, plant*) aclimatar(-se). ~**ation** /-ˈzeɪʃn/ *n* naturalização *f*

nature /'neɪtʃə(r)/ *n* natureza *f*; (*kind*) gênero *m*, (*P*) género *m*; (*of person*) índole *f*

naughty /'nɔːtɪ/ *a* (-ier, -iest) (*child*) levado; (*indecent*) picante

nause|a /'nɔːsɪə/ *n* náusea *f.* ~**ate** /'nɔːsɪeɪt/ *vt* nausear. ~**ating,** ~**ous** *a* nauseabundo, repugnante

nautical /'nɔːtɪkl/ *a* náutico. ~ **mile** milha *f* marítima

naval /'neɪvl/ *a* naval; (*officer*) de marinha

nave /neɪv/ *n* nave *f*

navel /'neɪvl/ *n* umbigo *m*

navigable /'nævɪɡəbl/ *a* navegável

navigat|e /'nævɪɡeɪt/ *vt* (*sea etc*) navegar; (*ship*) pilotar □ *vi* navegar. ~**ion** /-'ɡeɪʃn/ *n* navegação *f.* ~**or** *n* navegador *m*

navy /'neɪvɪ/ *n* marinha *f* de guerra. ~ (**blue**) azul-marinho *m invar*

near /nɪə(r)/ *adv* perto, quaze □ *prep* perto de □ *a* próximo □ *vt* aproximar-se de, chegar-se a. **draw** ~ aproximar(-se) (**to de**). ~ **by** *adv* perto, próximo. **N**~ **East** Oriente *m* Próximo. ~ **to** perto de. ~**ness** *n* proximidade *f*

nearby /'nɪəbaɪ/ *a* & *adv* próximo, perto

nearly /'nɪəlɪ/ *adv* quase, por pouco. **not** ~ **as pretty**/*etc* **as** longe de ser tão bonita/*etc* como

neat /niːt/ *a* (-er, -est) (bem) cuidado; (*room*) bem arrumado; (*spirits*) puro, sem gelo. ~**ly** *adv* (*with care*) com cuidado; (*cleverly*) habilmente. ~**ness** *n* aspecto *m* cuidado

nebulous /'nebjʊləs/ *a* nebuloso; (*vague*) vago, confuso

necessar|y /'nesəsərɪ/ *a* necessário. ~**ily** *adv* necessariamente

necessitate /nɪˈsesɪteɪt/ *vt* exigir, obrigar a, tornar necessário

necessity /nɪˈsesətɪ/ *n* necessidade *f*; (*thing*) coisa *f* indispensável, artigo *m* de primeira necessidade

neck /nek/ *n* pescoço *m*; (*of dress*) gola *f.* ~ **and neck** emparelhados

necklace /'neklɪs/ *n* colar *m*

neckline /'neklaɪn/ *n* decote *m*

nectarine /'nektərɪn/ *n* pêssego *m*

née /neɪ/ *a* em solteira. **Ann Jones** ~ **Drewe** Ann Jones cujo nome de solteira era Drewe

need /niːd/ *n* necessidade *f* □ *vt* precisar de, necessitar de. **you** ~ **not come** não temde *or* não precisa vir. ~**less** *a* inútil, desnecessário. ~**lessly** *adv* inutilmente, sem necessidade

needle /'niːdl/ *a* agulha *f* □ *vt* (*colloq: provoke*) provocar

needlework /'niːdlwɜːk/ *n* costura *f*; (*embroidery*) bordado *m*

needy /'niːdɪ/ *a* (-ier, -iest) necessitado, carenciado

negation /nɪˈɡeɪʃn/ *n* negação *f*

negative /'neɡətɪv/ *a* negativo □ *n* negativa *f*, negação *f*; (*photo*) negativo *m.* **in the** ~ (*answer*) na negativa; (*gram*) na forma negativa. ~**ly** *adv* negativamente

neglect /nɪˈɡlekt/ *vt* descuidar; (*opportunity*) desprezar; (*family*) não cuidar de, abandonar; (*duty*) não cumprir □ *n* falta *f* de cuidado(s), descuido *m.* (**state of**) ~ abandono

m. ~ **to** (*omit to*) esquecer-se de. ~**ful**
a negligente
negligen|t /'neglɪdʒənt/ *a* negligente.
~**ce** *n* negligência *f*, desleixo *m*
negligible /'neglɪdʒəbl/ *a* insignificante, ínfimo
negotiable /nɪ'gəʊʃəbl/ *a* negociável
negotia|te /nɪ'gəʊʃɪeɪt/ *vt/i* negociar;
(*obstacle*) transpor; (*difficulty*) vencer.
~**ion** /-sɪ'eɪʃn/ *n* negociação *f.* ~**or** *n*
negociador *m*
Negro /'ni:grəʊ/ *a* & *n* (*pl* ~**oes**) negro (*m*), preto (*m*)
neigh /neɪ/ *n* relincho *m* □ *vi* relin-
char
neighbour /'neɪbə(r)/ *n* vizinho *m.*
~**hood** *n* vizinhança *f.* ~**ing** *a*
vizinho. ~**ly** *a* de boa vizinhança
neither /'naɪðə(r)/ *a* & *pron* nenhu-
m(a) (de dois *ou* duas), nem um nem
outro, nem uma nem outra □ *adv* tampouco, também não □ *conj* nem. ~
big nor small nem grande nem
pequeno. ~ **am I** nem eu
neon /'ni:ɒn/ *n* néon *m* □ *a* (*lamp etc*)
de néon
nephew /'nevju:/ *n* sobrinho *m*
nerve /nɜ:v/ *n* nervo *m*; (*fig: courage*)
coragem *f*; (*colloq: impudence*) descaramento *m*, (*P*) lata *f* (*colloq*). **get on
sb's nerves** irritar, dar nos nervos de
alg. ~**-racking** *a* de arrasar os nervos, enervante
nervous /'nɜ:vəs/ *a* nervoso. **be** *or*
feel ~ (*afraid*) ter receio/um certo
medo. ~ **breakdown** esgotamento *m*
nervoso. ~**ly** *adv* nervosamente.
~**ness** *n* nervosismo *m*; (*fear*) receio
m
nest /nest/ *n* ninho *m* □ *vi* aninhar-se,
fazer *or* ter ninho. ~**-egg** *n* pé-de-
meia *m*
nestle /'nesl/ *vi* aninhar-se
net¹ /net/ *n* rede *f* □ *vt* (*pt* **netted**)
apanhar na rede. ~**ting** *n* rede *f.*
wire ~**ting** rede *f* de arame
net² /net/ *a* (*weight etc*) líquido
Netherlands /'neðələndz/ *npl* the ~
os Países Baixos
nettle /'netl/ *n* urtiga *f*
network /'netwɜ:k/ *n* rede *f*, cadeia *f*
neuro|sis /njʊə'rəʊsɪs/ *n* (*pl* -**oses**
/-si:z/) neurose *f.* ~**tic** /-'rɒtɪk/ *a* & *n*
neurótico (*m*)
neuter /'nju:tə(r)/ *a* & *n* neutro (*m*) □
vt castrar, capar
neutral /'nju:trəl/ *a* neutro. ~ (**gear**)
ponto *m* morto. ~**ity** /-'trælətɪ/ *n* neu-
tralidade *f*
never /'nevə(r)/ *adv* nunca; (*colloq:
not*) não. he ~ **refuses** ele nunca
recusa. **I** ~ **saw him** (*colloq*) nunca
o vi. ~ **mind** não faz mal, deixe para
lá. ~**-ending** *a* interminável

nevertheless /nevəðə'les/ *adv* & *conj*
contudo, no entanto
new /nju:/ *a* (**-er**, **-est**) novo. ~**-born** *a*
recém-nascido. ~ **moon** lua *f* nova. ~
year ano *m* novo. N~ **Year's Day** dia
m de Ano Novo. N~ **Year's Eve**
véspera *f* de Ano Novo. N~ **Zealand**
Nova Zelândia *f.* N~ **Zealander** neo-
zelandês *m.* ~**ness** *n* novidade *f*
newcomer /'nju:kʌmə(r)/ *n* recém-
chegado *m*, (*P*) recém-vindo *m*
newfangled /nju:'fæŋgld/ *a* (*pej*)
moderno
newly /'nju:lɪ/ *adv* há pouco,
recentemente. ~**-weds** *npl* recém-
casados *mpl*
news /nju:z/ *n* notícia(s) *f*(*pl*); (*radio*)
noticiário *m*, notícias *fpl.* (*TV*) tele-
jornal *m.* ~**-caster**, ~**-reader** *n* locutor *m.* ~**-flash** *n* notícia *f* de última
hora
newsagent /'nju:zeɪdʒənt/ *n* jorna-
leiro *m*
newsletter /'nju:zletə(r)/ *n* boletim *m*
informativo
newspaper /'nju:zpeɪpə(r)/ *n* jornal *m*
newsreel /'nju:zri:l/ *n* atualidades
fpl, (*P*) actualidades *fpl*
newt /nju:t/ *n* tritão *m*
next /nekst/ *a* próximo; (*adjoining*)
pegado, ao lado, contíguo; (*following*)
seguinte □ *adv* a seguir □ *n* seguinte
mf. ~**-door** *a* do lado. ~ **of kin** parente *m* mais próximo. ~ **to** ao lado
de. ~ **to nothing** quase nada
nib /nɪb/ *n* bico *m*, (*P*) aparo *m*
nibble /'nɪbl/ *vt* mordiscar, dar denta-
dinhas em
nice /naɪs/ *a* (**-er**, **-est**) agradável,
bom; (*kind*) simpático, gentil; (*pretty*)
bonito; (*respectable*) bem educado,
correto, (*P*) correcto; (*subtle*) fino,
subtil. ~**ly** *adv* agradavelmente;
(*well*) bem
nicety /'naɪsətɪ/ *n* sutileza *f*, (*P*) subtileza *f*
niche /nɪtʃ/ *n* nicho *m*; (*fig*) bom lugar *m*
nick /nɪk/ *n* corte *m*, chanfradura *f*;
(*sl: prison*) cadeia *f* □ *vt* dar um corte
em; (*sl: steal*) roubar, limpar (*colloq*);
(*sl: arrest*) apanhar, pôr a mão em
(*colloq*). **in good** ~ (*colloq*) em boa
forma, em bom estado. **in the** ~ **of
time** mesmo a tempo
nickel /'nɪkl/ *n* níquel *m*; (*Amer*) moeda *f* de cinco cêntimos
nickname /'nɪknem/ *n* apelido *m*, (*P*)
alcunha *f*; (*short form*) diminutivo *m*
□ *vt* apelidar de
nicotine /'nɪkəti:n/ *n* nicotina *f*
niece /ni:s/ *n* sobrinha *f*
Nigeria /naɪ'dʒɪərɪə/ *n* Nigéria *f.* ~**n**
a & *n* nigeriano (*m*)

niggardly /'nɪgədlɪ/ a miserável

night /naɪt/ n noite f □ a de noite, noturno, (P) nocturno. **at ~** à/de noite. **by ~** de noite. **~-cap** n (drink) bebida f na hora de deitar. **~-club** n boate f, (P) boîte f. **~-dress, ~-gown** ns camisola f de dormir, (P) camisa f de noite. **~-life** n vida f noturna, (P) nocturna. **~-school** n escola f noturna, (P) nocturna. **~-time** n noite f. **~-watchman** n guarda-noturno m, (P) guarda-nocturno m

nightfall /'naɪtfɔːl/ n anoitecer m

nightingale /'naɪtɪŋgeɪl/ n rouxinol m

nightly /'naɪtlɪ/ a noturno, (P) nocturno □ adv de noite, à noite, todas as noites

nightmare /'naɪtmeə(r)/ n pesadelo m

nil /nɪl/ n nada m; (sport) zero m □ a nulo

nimble /'nɪmbl/ a (-er, -est) ágil, ligeiro

nin|e /naɪn/ a & n nove (m). **~th** a & n nono (m)

nineteen /naɪn'tiːn/ a & n dezenove (m), (P) dezanove (m). **~th** a & n décimo nono (m)

ninet|y /'naɪntɪ/ a & n noventa (m). **~ieth** a & n nonagésimo (m)

nip /nɪp/ vt/i (pt nipped) apertar, beliscar; (colloq: rush) ir correndo, ir num pulo (colloq) □ n aperto m, beliscão m; (drink) gole m, trago m. **a ~ in the air** um frio cortante. **~ in the bud** cortar pela raiz

nipple /'nɪpl/ n mamilo m

nippy /'nɪpɪ/ a (-ier, -iest) (colloq: quick) rápido; (colloq: chilly) cortante

nitrogen /'naɪtrədʒən/ n azoto m, nitrogênio m, (P) nitrogénio m

nitwit /'nɪtwɪt/ n (colloq) imbecil m

no /nəʊ/ a nenhum □ adv não □ n (pl noes) não m. **~ entry** entrada f proibida. **~ money/time/** etc nenhum dinheiro/tempo/etc. **~ man's land** terra f de ninguém. **~ one** = nobody. **~ smoking** é proibido fumar. **~ way!** (colloq) de modo nenhum!

nob|le /'nəʊbl/ a (-er, -est) nobre. **~ility** /-'bɪlətɪ/ n nobreza f

nobleman /'nəʊblmən/ n (pl -men) nobre m, fidalgo m

nobody /'nəʊbɒdɪ/ pron ninguém □ n nulidade f. **he knows ~** ele não conhece ninguém. **~ is there** não tem ninguém lá

nocturnal /nɒk'tɜːnl/ a noturno, (P) nocturno

nod /nɒd/ vt/i (pt nodded) **~ (one's head)** acenar (com) a cabeça; **~ (off)** cabecear □ n aceno m com a cabeça

(para dizer que sim or para cumprimentar)

noise /nɔɪz/ n ruído m, barulho m. **~less** a silencioso

nois|y /'nɔɪzɪ/ a (-ier, -iest) ruidoso, barulhento. **~ily** adv ruidosamente

nomad /'nəʊmæd/ n nômade mf, (P) nómade mf. **~ic** /'mædɪk/ a nômade, (P) nómade

nominal /'nɒmɪnl/ a nominal; (fee, sum) simbólico

nominat|e /'nɒmɪneɪt/ vt (appoint) nomear; (put forward) propor. **~ion** /-'neɪʃn/ n nomeação f

non- /nɒn/ pref não, sem, in-, a-, anti-, des-. **~-skid** a antiderrapante. **~-stick** a não-aderente

nonchalant /'nɒnʃələnt/ a indiferente, desinteressado

non-commissioned /nɒnkə'mɪʃnd/ a **~ officer** sargento m, cabo m

non-committal /nɒnkə'mɪtl/ a evasivo

nondescript /'nɒndɪskrɪpt/ a insignificante, medíocre, indefinível

none /nʌn/ pron (person) nenhum, ninguém; (thing) nenhum, nada. **~ of us** nenhum de nós. **I have ~** não tenho nenhum. **~ of that!** nada disso! □ adv **~ too** não muito. **he is ~ the happier** nem por isso ele é mais feliz. **~ the less** contudo, no entanto, apesar disso

nonentity /nɒ'nentətɪ/ n nulidade f, zero m à esquerda, João Ninguém m

non-existent /nɒnɪg'zɪstənt/ a inexistente

nonplussed /nɒn'plʌst/ a perplexo, pasmado

nonsens|e /'nɒnsns/ n absurdo m, disparate m. **~ical** /-'sensɪkl/ a absurdo, disparatado

non-smoker /nɒn'sməʊkə(r)/ n não-fumante m, (P) não-fumador m

non-stop /nɒn'stɒp/ a ininterrupto, contínuo; (train) direto, (P) directo; (flight) sem escala □ adv sem parar

noodles /'nuːdlz/ npl talharim m, (P) macarronete m

nook /nʊk/ n (re)canto m

noon /nuːn/ n meio-dia m

noose /nuːs/ n laço m corrediço

nor /nɔː(r)/ conj & adv nem, também não. **~ do I** nem eu

norm /nɔːm/ n norma f

normal /'nɔːml/ a & n normal (m). **above/below ~** acima/abaixo do normal. **~ity** /nɔː'mælətɪ/ n normalidade f. **~ly** adv normalmente

north /nɔːθ/ n norte m □ a norte, do norte; (of country, people etc) setentrional □ adv a, ao/para o norte. **N~ America** América f do Norte. **N~ American** a & n norte-americano

(m). ~-east n nordeste m. ~erly
/'nɔːðəlɪ/ a do norte. ~ward a ao
norte. ~ward(s) adv para o norte.
~-west n noroeste m

northern /'nɔːðən/ a do norte

Norw|ay /'nɔːweɪ/ n Noruega f.
~egian /nɔːˈwiːdʒən/ a & n norue-
guês (m)

nose /nəʊz/ n nariz m; (of animal)
focinho m □ vi ~ about farejar. **pay
through the** ~ pagar um preço exorbitante

nosebleed /'nəʊzbliːd/ n hemorragia f
nasal or pelo nariz

nosedive /'nəʊzdaɪv/ n vôo m picado

nostalg|ia /nɒˈstældʒə/ n nostalgia f.
~ic a nostálgico

nostril /'nɒstrəl/ n narina f; (of horse)
venta f (usually pl)

nosy /'nəʊzɪ/ a (-ier, -iest) (colloq) bisbilhoteiro

not /nɒt/ adv não. ~ **at all** nada, de
modo nenhum; (reply to thanks) de
nada. **he is ~ at all bored** ele não
está nem um pouco entediado. ~
yet ainda não. **I suppose ~** creio
que não

notable /'nəʊtəbl/ a notável □ n no-
tabilidade f

notably /'nəʊtəblɪ/ adv notavelmente;
(particularly) especialmente

notch /nɒtʃ/ n corte m em V □ vt marcar com cortes. ~ **up** (score etc) marcar

note /nəʊt/ n nota f; (banknote) nota
(de banco) f; (short letter) bilhete m □
vt notar

notebook /'nəʊtbʊk/ n livrinho m de
notas, (P) bloco-notas m

noted /'nəʊtɪd/ a conhecido, famoso

notepaper /'nəʊtpeɪpə(r)/ n papel m
de carta

noteworthy /'nəʊtwɜːðɪ/ a notável

nothing /'nʌθɪŋ/ n nada m; (person)
nulidade f, zero m □ adv nada, de
modo algum or nenhum, de maneira
alguma or nenhuma. **he eats ~** ele
não come nada. ~ **big**/etc nada (de)
grande/etc. ~ **else** nada mais. ~
much pouca coisa. **for** ~ (free) de
graça; (in vain) em vão

notice /'nəʊtɪs/ n anúncio m, notícia f;
(in street, on wall) letreiro m; (warning) aviso m; (attention) atenção f.
(advance) ~ pré-aviso m □ vt notar,
reparar. **at short** ~ num prazo curto.
a week's ~ o prazo de uma semana.
~-**board** n quadro m para afixar
anúncios etc. **hand in one's** ~ pedir
demissão. **take** ~ reparar (of em).
take no ~ não fazer caso (of de)

noticeabl|e /'nəʊtɪsəbl/ a visível. ~y
adv visivelmente

notif|y /'nəʊtɪfaɪ/ vt participar, noti-

ficar. ~**ication** /-ɪˈkeɪʃn/ n participação f, notificação f

notion /'nəʊʃn/ n noção f

notor|ious /nəʊˈtɔːrɪəs/ a notório.
~**iety** /-əˈraɪətɪ/ n fama f

notwithstanding /nɒtwɪθˈstændɪŋ/
prep apesar de, não obstante □ adv
mesmo assim, ainda assim □ conj embora, conquanto, apesar de que

nougat /'nuːgaː/ n nugá m, torrone m

nought /nɔːt/ n zero m

noun /naʊn/ n substantivo m, nome m

nourish /'nʌrɪʃ/ vt alimentar, nutrir.
~**ing** a alimentício, nutritivo.
~**ment** n alimento m, sustento m

novel /'nɒvl/ n romance m □ a novo,
original. ~**ist** n romancista mf. ~**ty**
n novidade f

November /nəʊˈvembə(r)/ n novembro m

novice /'nɒvɪs/ n (beginner) noviço m,
novato m; (relig) noviço m

now /naʊ/ adv agora □ conj ~ **(that)**
agora que. **by** ~ a estas horas, por
esta altura. **from** ~ **on** de agora em
diante. ~ **and again,** ~ **and then** de
vez em quando. **right** ~ já

nowadays /'naʊədeɪz/ adv hoje em
dia, presentemente, atualmente, (P)
actualmente

nowhere /'nəʊweə(r)/ adv (position)
em lugar nenhum, em lado nenhum;
(direction) a lado nenhum, a parte alguma or nenhuma

nozzle /'nɒzl/ n bico m, bocal m; (of
hose) agulheta f

nuance /'njuːaːns/ n nuance f, matiz
m

nuclear /'njuːklɪə(r)/ a nuclear

nucleus /'njuːklɪəs/ n (pl -lei /-laɪ/)
núcleo m

nud|e /njuːd/ a & n nu (m). **in the** ~e
nu. ~**ity** n nudez f

nudge /nʌdʒ/ vt tocar com o cotovelo,
cutucar □ n ligeira cotovelada f, cutucada f

nudis|t /'njuːdɪst/ n nudista mf. ~**m**
/-zəm/ n nudismo m

nuisance /'njuːsns/ n aborrecimento
m, chatice f (sl); (person) chato m (sl)

null /nʌl/ a nulo. ~ **and void** (jur)
írrito e nulo. ~**ify** vt anular, invalidar

numb /nʌm/ a entorpecido, dormente
□ vt entorpecer, adormecer

number /'nʌmbə(r)/ n número m;
(numeral) algarismo m □ vt numerar;
(amount to) ser em número de; (count)
contar, incluir. ~-**plate** n chapa (do
carro) f

numeral /'njuːmərəl/ n número m,
algarismo m

numerate /'njuːmərət/ a que tem conhecimentos básicos de matemática

numerical /nju:'merɪkl/ a numérico
numerous /'nju:mərəs/ a numeroso
nun /nʌn/ n freira f, religiosa f
nurs|e /nɜ:s/ n enfermeira f, enfermeiro m; (nanny) ama(-seca) f, babá f □ vt cuidar de, tratar de; (hopes etc) alimentar, acalentar. ~ing n enfermagem f. ~ing home clínica f de repouso
nursery /'nɜ:sərɪ/ n quarto m de crianças; (for plants) viveiro m. (day) ~ creche f. ~ rhyme poema m or canção f infantil. ~ school jardim m de infância
nurture /'nɜ:tʃə(r)/ vt educar
nut /nʌt/ n (bot) noz f; (techn) porca f de parafuso
nutcrackers /'nʌtkrækəz/ npl quebra-nozes m invar
nutmeg /'nʌtmeg/ n noz-moscada f
nutrient /'nju:trɪənt/ n substância f nutritiva, nutriente m
nutrit|ion /nju:'trɪʃn/ n nutrição f. ~ious a nutritivo
nutshell /'nʌtʃel/ n casca f de noz. in a ~ em poucas palavras
nuzzle /'nʌzl/ vt esfregar com o focinho
nylon /'naɪlɒn/ n nylon m. ~s meias fpl de nylon

O

oaf /əʊf/ n (pl oafs) imbecil m, idiota m
oak /əʊk/ n carvalho m
OAP abbr see old-age pensioner
oar /ɔ:(r)/ n remo m
oasis /əʊ'eɪsɪs/ n (pl oases /-si:z/) oásis m
oath /əʊθ/ n juramento m; (swearword) praga f
oatmeal /'əʊtmi:l/ n farinha f de aveia; (porridge) papa f de aveia
oats /əʊts/ npl aveia f
obedien|t /ə'bi:dɪənt/ a obediente. ~ce n obediência f. ~tly adv obedientemente
obes|e /əʊ'bi:s/ a obeso. ~ity n obesidade f
obey /ə'beɪ/ vt/i obedecer (a)
obituary /ə'bɪtʃʊərɪ/ n necrológio m, (P) necrologia f
object[1] /'ɒbdʒɪkt/ n objeto m, (P) objecto m; (aim) objetivo m, (P) objectivo m; (gram) complemento m
object[2] /əb'dʒekt/ vt/i objetar, (P) objectar (que). ~ to opor-se a, discordar de. ~ion /-ʃn/ n objeção f, (P) objecção f
objectionable /əb'dʒekʃnəbl/ a censurável; (unpleasant) desagradável
objectiv|e /əb'dʒektɪv/ a objetivo, (P) objectivo. ~ity /-'tɪvətɪ/ n objetividade f, (P) objectividade f
obligation /ɒblɪ'geɪʃn/ n obrigação f. be under an ~ to sb dever favores a alg
obligatory /ə'blɪgətrɪ/ a obrigatório
oblig|e /ə'blaɪdʒ/ vt obrigar; (do a favour) fazer um favor a, obsequiar. ~ed a obrigado (to a). ~ed to sb em dívida (para) com alg. ~ing a prestável, amável. ~ingly adv amavelmente
oblique /ə'bli:k/ a oblíquo
obliterat|e /ə'blɪtəreɪt/ vt obliterar. ~ion /-'reɪʃn/ n obliteração f
oblivion /ə'blɪvɪən/ n esquecimento m
oblivious /ə'blɪvɪəs/ a esquecido, sem consciência (of/to de)
oblong /'ɒblɒŋ/ a oblongo □ n retângulo m, (P) rectângulo m
obnoxious /əb'nɒkʃəs/ a ofensivo, detestável
oboe /'əʊbəʊ/ n oboé m
obscen|e /əb'si:n/ a obsceno. ~ity /-'enətɪ/ n obscenidade f
obscur|e /əb'skjʊə(r)/ a obscuro □ vt obscurecer; (conceal) encobrir. ~ity n obscuridade f
obsequious /əb'si:kwɪəs/ a demasiado obsequioso, subserviente
observan|t /əb'zɜ:vənt/ a observador. ~ce n observância f, cumprimento m
observatory /əb'zɜ:vətrɪ/ n observatório m
observ|e /əb'zɜ:v/ vt observar. ~ation /ɒbzə'veɪʃn/ n observação f. keep under ~ation vigiar. ~er n observador m
obsess /əb'ses/ vt obcecar. ~ion /-ʃn/ n obsessão f. ~ive a obsessivo
obsolete /'ɒbsəli:t/ a obsoleto, antiguado
obstacle /'ɒbstəkl/ n obstáculo m
obstetric|s /əb'stetrɪks/ n obstetrícia f. ~ian /ɒbstɪ'trɪʃn/ n obstetra mf
obstina|te /'ɒbstmət/ a obstinado. ~cy n obstinação f
obstruct /əb'strʌkt/ vt obstruir, bloquear; (hinder) estorvar, obstruir. ~ion /-ʃn/ n obstrução f; (thing) obstáculo m
obtain /əb'tem/ vt obter □ vi prevalecer, estar em vigor. ~able a que se pode obter
obtrusive /əb'tru:sɪv/ a importuno; (thing) demasiadamente em evidência, que dá muito na vista (colloq)
obvious /'ɒbvɪəs/ a óbvio, evidente. ~ly adv obviamente
occasion /ə'keɪʒn/ n ocasião f; (event) acontecimento m □ vt ocasionar. on ~ de vez em quando, ocasionalmente
occasional /ə'keɪʒənl/ a ocasional.

~ly *adv* de vez em quando, ocasionalmente

occult /ɒˈkʌlt/ *a* oculto

occupation /ɒkjʊˈpeɪʃn/ *n* ocupação *f*. ~al *a* profissional; (*therapy*) ocupacional

occup|y /ˈɒkjʊpaɪ/ *vt* ocupar. ~ant, ~ier *ns* ocupante *mf*

occur /əˈkɜː(r)/ *vi* (*pt* occurred) ocorrer, acontecer, dar-se; (*arise*) apresentar-se, aparecer. ~ **to sb** ocorrer a alg

occurrence /əˈkʌrəns/ *n* acontecimento *m*, ocorrência *f*

ocean /ˈəʊʃn/ *n* oceano *m*

o'clock /əˈklɒk/ *adv* it is one ~ é uma hora. **it is six** ~ são seis horas

octagon /ˈɒktəgən/ *n* octógono *m*. ~al /-ˈtægənl/ *a* octogonal

octave /ˈɒktɪv/ *n* oitava *f*

October /ɒkˈtəʊbə(r)/ *n* outubro *m*

octopus /ˈɒktəpəs/ *n* (*pl* -puses) polvo *m*

odd /ɒd/ *a* (-er, -est) estranho, singular; (*number*) ímpar; (*left over*) de sobra; (*not of set*) desemparelhado; (*occasional*) ocasional. ~ **jobs** (*paid*) biscates *mpl*; (*in garden etc*) trabalhos *mpl* diversos. **twenty** ~ vinte e tantos. ~ity *n* singularidade *f*; (*thing*) curiosidade *f*. ~ly *adv* de modo estranho

oddment /ˈɒdmənt/ *n* resto *m*, artigo *m* avulso

odds /ɒdz/ *npl* probabilidades *fpl*; (*in betting*) ganhos *mpl* líquidos. **at** ~ em desacordo; (*quarrelling*) de mal, brigado. **it makes no** ~ não faz diferença. ~ **and ends** artigos *mpl* avulsos, coisas *fpl* pequenas

odious /ˈəʊdɪəs/ *a* odioso

odour /ˈəʊdə(r)/ *n* odor *m*. ~less *a* inodoro

of /əv/; *emphatic* /ɒv/ *prep* de. **a friend** ~ **mine** um amigo meu. **the fifth** ~ **June** (no dia) cinco de junho. **take six** ~ **them** leve seis deles

off /ɒf/ *adv* embora, fora; (*switched off*) apagado, desligado; (*taken off*) tirado, desligado; (*cancelled*) cancelado; (*food*) estragado □ *prep* (fora) de; (*distant from*) a alguma distância de. **be** ~ (*depart*) ir-se embora, partir. **be well** ~ ser abastado. **be better/ worse** ~ estar em melhor/pior situação. **a day** ~ um dia de folga. **20%** ~ redução de 20%. **on the** ~ **chance that** no caso de. ~ **colour** indisposto, adoentado. ~-**licence** *n* loja *f* de bebidas alcoólicas. ~-**load** *vt* descarregar. ~-**putting** *a* desconcertante. ~-**stage** *adv* fora de cena. ~-**white** *a* branco-sujo

offal /ˈɒfl/ *n* miudezas *fpl*, fressura *f*

offence /əˈfens/ *n* (*feeling*) ofensa *f*;

(*crime*) delito *m*, transgressão *f*. **give** ~ **to** ofender. **take** ~ ofender-se (at com)

offend /əˈfend/ *vt* ofender. **be** ~ed ofender-se (at com). ~er *n* delinqüente *mf*, (P) delinquente *mf*

offensive /əˈfensɪv/ *a* ofensivo; (*disgusting*) repugnante □ *n* ofensiva *f*

offer /ˈɒfə(r)/ *vt* (*pt* offered) oferecer □ *n* oferta *f*. **on** ~ em promoção. ~ing *n* oferenda *f*

offhand /ɒfˈhænd/ *a* espontâneo; (*curt*) seco □ *adv* de improviso, sem pensar

office /ˈɒfɪs/ *n* escritório *m*; (*post*) cargo *m*; (*branch*) filial *f*. ~ **hours** horas *fpl* de expediente. **in** ~ no poder. **take** ~ assumir o cargo

officer /ˈɒfɪsə(r)/ *n* oficial *m*; (*policeman*) agente *m*

official /əˈfɪʃl/ *a* oficial □ *n* funcionário *m*. ~ly *adv* oficialmente

officiate /əˈfɪʃɪeɪt/ *vi* (*relig*) oficiar. ~ **as** presidir, exercer as funções de

officious /əˈfɪʃəs/ *a* intrometido

offing /ˈɒfɪŋ/ *n* in the ~ (*fig*) em perspectiva

offset /ˈɒfset/ *vt* (*pt* -set, *pres p* -setting) compensar, contrabalançar

offshoot /ˈɒfʃuːt/ *n* rebento *m*; (*fig*) efeito *m* secundário

offshore /ˈɒfʃɔː(r)/ *a* ao largo da costa

offside /ɒfˈsaɪd/ *a & adv* offside, em impedimento, (P) fora de jogo

offspring /ˈɒfsprɪŋ/ *n* (*pl* invar) descendência *f*, prole *f*

often /ˈɒfn/ *adv* muitas vezes, freqüentemente, (P) frequentemente. **every so** ~ de vez em quando. **how** ~? quantas vezes?

oh /əʊ/ *int* oh, ah

oil /ɔɪl/ *n* óleo *m*; (*petroleum*) petróleo *m* □ *vt* lubrificar. ~-**painting** *n* pintura *f* a óleo. ~ **rig** plataforma *f* de poço de petróleo. ~ **well** poço *m* de petróleo. ~y *a* oleoso; (*food*) gorduroso

oilfield /ˈɔɪlfiːld/ *n* campo *m* petrolífero

oilskins /ˈɔɪlskɪnz/ *npl* roupa *f* de oleado

ointment /ˈɔɪntmənt/ *n* pomada *f*

OK /əʊˈkeɪ/ *a & adv* (*colloq*) (está) bem, (está) certo, (está) legal

old /əʊld/ *a* (-er, -est) velho; (*person*) velho, idoso; (*former*) antigo. **how** ~ **is he?** que idade tem ele? **he is eight years** ~ ele tem oito anos (de idade). **of** ~ (d)antes, antigamente. ~ **age** velhice *f*. ~-**age pensioner** reformado *m*, aposentado *m*, pessoa *f* de terceira idade. ~ **boy** antigo aluno *m*. ~-**fashioned** *a* fora de moda. ~ **girl** antiga aluna *f*. ~ **maid** solteirona *f*

~ **man** homem *m* idoso, velho *m*. ~ **-time** *a* antigo. ~ **woman** mulher *f* idosa, velha *f*

olive /'ɒlɪv/ *n* azeitona *f* □ *a* de azeitona. ~ **oil** azeite *m*

Olympic /ə'lɪmpɪk/ *a* olímpico. ~**s** *npl* Olimpíadas *fpl*. ~ **Games** Jogos *mpl* Olímpicos

omelette /'ɒmlɪt/ *n* omelete *f*

omen /'əʊmən/ *n* agouro *m*, presságio *m*

ominous /'ɒmməs/ *a* agourento; (*fig: threatening*) ameaçador

omi|t /ə'mɪt/ *vt* (*pt* omitted) omitir. ~**ssion** /-ʃn/ *n* omissão *f*

on /ɒn/ *prep* sobre, em cima de, de, em □ *adv* para a diante, para a frente; (*switched on*) aceso, ligado; (*tap*) aberto; (*machine*) em funcionamento; (*put on*) posto; (*happening*) em curso. ~ **arrival** na chegada, ao chegar. ~ **foot** *etc* a pé *etc*. ~ **doing** ao fazer. ~ **time** na hora, dentro do horário. ~ **Tuesday** na terça-feira. ~ **Tuesdays** às terças-feiras. **walk**/*etc* ~ continuar a andar/*etc*. **be** ~ **at** (*film, TV*) estar levando *or* passando. ~ **and off** de vez em quando. ~ **and** ~ **sem** parar

once /wʌns/ *adv* uma vez; (*formerly*) noutro(s) tempo(s) □ *conj* uma vez que, desde que. **all at** ~ de repente; (*simultaneously*) todos ao mesmo tempo. **just this** ~ só esta vez. ~ **(and) for all** duma vez para sempre. ~ **upon a time** era uma vez. ~**-over** *n* (*colloq*) vista *f* de olhos

oncoming /'ɒnkʌmɪŋ/ *a* que se aproxima, próximo. **the** ~ **traffic** o trânsito que vem do sentido oposto, (*P*) no sentido contrário

one /wʌn/ *a* um(a); (*sole*) único □ *n* um(a) *mf* □ *pron* um(a) *mf*; (*impersonal*) se. ~ **by** ~ um a um. **a big/red**/*etc* ~ um grande/vermelho/*etc*. **this/that** ~ este/esse. ~ **another** um ao outro, uns aos outros. ~**-sided** *a* parcial. ~**-way** *a* (*street*) mão única; (*ticket*) simples

oneself /wʌn'self/ *pron* si, si mesmo/próprio; (*reflexive*) se. **by** ~ sozinho

onion /'ʌnɪən/ *n* cebola *f*

onlooker /'ɒnlʊkə(r)/ *n* espectador *m*, circunstante *mf*

only /'əʊnlɪ/ *a* único □ *adv* apenas, só, somente □ *conj* só que. **an** ~ **child** um filho único. **he** ~ **has six** ele só tem seis. **not** ~ ... **but also** não só ... mas também. ~ **too** muito, mais que

onset /'ɒnset/ *n* começo *m*; (*attack*) ataque *m*

onslaught /'ɒnslɔːt/ *n* ataque *m* violento, assalto *m*

onward(s) /'ɒnwəd(z)/ *adv* para a frente/diante

ooze /uːz/ *vt/i* escorrer, verter

opal /'əʊpl/ *n* opala *f*

opaque /əʊ'peɪk/ *a* opaco, tosco

open /'əʊpən/ *a* aberto; (*view*) aberto, amplo; (*free to all*) aberto ao público; (*attempt*) franco □ *vt/i* abrir(-se); (*of shop, play*) abrir. **in the** ~ **air** ao ar livre. **keep** ~ **house** receber muito, abrir a porta para todos. ~ **on to** dar para. ~ **out** *or* **up** abrir(-se). ~**-heart** *a* (*of surgery*) de coração aberto. ~**-minded** *a* imparcial. ~**-plan** *a* sem divisórias. ~ **secret** segredo *m* de polichinelo. ~ **sea** mar *m* alto. ~**ness** *n* abertura *f*; (*frankness*) franqueza *f*

opener /'əʊpənə(r)/ *n* (*tins*) abridor *m* de latas; (*bottles*) saca-rolhas *m invar*

opening /'əʊpənɪŋ/ *n* abertura *f*; (*beginning*) começo *m*; (*opportunity*) oportunidade *f*; (*job*) vaga *f*

openly /'əʊpənlɪ/ *adv* abertamente

opera /'ɒprə/ *n* ópera *f*. ~**-glasses** *npl* binóculo (de teatro) *m*, (*P*) binóculos *mpl*. ~**tic** /ɒpə'rætɪk/ *a* de ópera

operat|e /'ɒpəreɪt/ *vt/i* operar; (*techn*) (pôr a) funcionar. ~**e on** (*med*) operar. ~**ing-theatre** *n* (*med*) anfiteatro *m*, sala *f* de operações. ~**ion** /-'reɪʃn/ *n* operação *f*. **in** ~**ion** em vigor; (*techn*) em funcionamento. ~**ional** /'reɪʃənl/ *a* operacional. ~**or** *n* operador *m*; (*telephonist*) telefonista *mf*

operative /'ɒpərətɪv/ *a* (*surgical*) operatório; (*law etc*) em vigor

opinion /ə'pɪnɪən/ *n* opinião *f*, parecer *m*. **in my** ~ **a meu ver.** ~ **poll** *n* sondagem (de opinião) *f*. ~**ated** /-eɪtɪd/ *a* dogmático

opium /'əʊpɪəm/ *n* ópio *m*

Oporto /ə'pɔːtəʊ/ *n* Porto *m*

opponent /ə'pəʊnənt/ *n* adversário *m*, antagonista *mf*, oponente *mf*

opportune /'ɒpətjuːn/ *a* oportuno

opportunity /ɒpə'tjuːnətɪ/ *n* oportunidade *f*

oppos|e /ə'pəʊz/ *vt* opor-se a. ~**ed to** oposto a. ~**ing** *a* oposto

opposite /'ɒpəzɪt/ *a & n* oposto (*m*), contrário (*m*) □ *adv* em frente □ *prep* ~ **(to)** em frente de

opposition /ɒpə'zɪʃn/ *n* oposição *f*

oppress /ə'pres/ *vt* oprimir. ~**ion** /-ʃn/ *n* opressão *f*. ~**ive** *a* opressivo. ~**or** *n* opressor *m*

opt /ɒpt/ *vi* ~ **for** optar por. ~ **out** recusar-se a participar (**of** de). ~ **to do** escolher fazer

optical /'ɒptɪkl/ *a* óptico. ~ **illusion** ilusão *f* óptica

optician /ɒp'tɪʃn/ *n* oculista *mf*

optimis|t /'ɒptɪmɪst/ *n* otimista *mf*, (P) optimista *mf*. ~**m** /-zəm/ *n* otimismo *m*, (P) optimismo *m*. ~**tic** /-'mɪstɪk/ *a* otimista, (P) optimista. ~**tically** /-'mɪstɪklɪ/ *adv* com otimismo, (P) optimismo

optimum /'ɒptɪməm/ *a & n* (*pl* -**ima**) ótimo (*m*), (P) óptimo (*m*)

option /'ɒpʃn/ *n* escolha *f*, opção *f*. **have no ~ (but)** não ter outro remédio (senão)

optional /'ɒpʃənl/ *a* opcional, facultativo

opulen|t /'ɒpjʊlənt/ *a* opulento. ~**ce** *n* opulência *f*

or /ɔː(r)/ *conj* ou; (*with negative*) nem. ~ **else** senão

oracle /'ɒrəkl/ *n* oráculo *m*

oral /'ɔːrəl/ *a* oral

orange /'ɒrɪndʒ/ *n* laranja *f*; (*colour*) laranja *m*, cor *f* de laranja □ *a* de laranja; (*colour*) alaranjado, cor de laranja

orator /'ɒrətə(r)/ *n* orador *m*. ~**y** *n* oratória *f*

orbit /'ɔːbɪt/ *n* órbita *f* □ *vt* (*pt* **orbited**) gravitar em torno de

orchard /'ɔːtʃəd/ *n* pomar *m*

orchestra /'ɔːkɪstrə/ *n* orquestra *f*. ~**l** /'kestrəl/ *a* orquestral

orchestrate /'ɔːkɪstreɪt/ *vt* orquestrar

orchid /'ɔːkɪd/ *n* orquídea *f*

ordain /ɔː'deɪn/ *vt* decretar; (*relig*) ordenar

ordeal /ɔː'diːl/ *n* prova *f*, provação *f*

order /'ɔːdə(r)/ *n* ordem *f*, (*comm*) encomenda *f*, pedido *m* □ *vt* ordenar; (*goods etc*) encomendar. **in ~ that** para que. **in ~ to** para

orderly /'ɔːdəlɪ/ *a* ordenado, em ordem; (*not unruly*) ordeiro □ *n* (*mil*) ordenança *f*; (*med*) servente *m* de hospital

ordinary /'ɔːdɪnrɪ/ *a* normal, ordinário, vulgar. **out of the ~** fora do comum

ordination /ɔːdɪ'neɪʃn/ *n* (*relig*) ordenação *f*

ore /ɔː(r)/ *n* minério *m*

organ /'ɔːgən/ *n* órgão *m*. ~**ist** *n* organista *mf*

organic /ɔː'gænɪk/ *a* orgânico

organism /'ɔːgənɪzəm/ *n* organismo *m*

organiz|e /'ɔːgənaɪz/ *vt* organizar. ~**ation** /-'zeɪʃn/ *n* organização *f*. ~**er** *n* organizador *m*

orgasm /'ɔːgæzəm/ *n* orgasmo *m*

orgy /'ɔːdʒɪ/ *n* orgia *f*

Orient /'ɔːrɪənt/ *n* **the ~** o Oriente *m*. ~**al** /-'entl/ *a & n* oriental (*mf*)

orientat|e /'ɔːrɪənteɪt/ *vt* orientar. ~**ion** /-'teɪʃn/ *n* orientação *f*

orifice /'ɒrɪfɪs/ *n* orifício *m*

origin /'ɒrɪdʒɪn/ *n* origem *f*

original /ə'rɪdʒənl/ *a* original; (*not copied*) original. ~**ity** /-'nælətɪ/ *n* originalidade *f*. ~**ly** *adv* originalmente; (*in the beginning*) originariamente

originat|e /ə'rɪdʒəneɪt/ *vt/i* originar (-se). ~**e from** provir de. ~**or** *n* iniciador *m*, criador *m*, autor *m*

ornament /'ɔːnəmənt/ *n* ornamento *m*; (*object*) peça *f* decorativa. ~**al** /-'mentl/ *a* ornamental. ~**ation** /-en'teɪʃn/ *n* ornamentação *f*

ornate /ɔː'neɪt/ *a* florido, floreado

ornitholog|y /ɔːnɪ'θɒlədʒɪ/ *n* ornitologia *f*. ~**ist** *n* ornitólogo *m*

orphan /'ɔːfn/ *n* órfã(o) *f*(*m*) □ *vt* deixar órfão. ~**age** *n* orfanato *m*

orthodox /'ɔːθədɒks/ *a* ortodoxo

orthopaedic /ɔːθə'piːdɪk/ *a* ortopédico

oscillate /'ɒsɪleɪt/ *vi* oscilar, vacilar

ostensibl|e /ɒs'tensəbl/ *a* aparente, pretenso. ~**y** *adv* aparentemente, pretensamente

ostentati|on /ɒsten'teɪʃn/ *n* ostentação *f*. ~**ous** /-'teɪʃəs/ *a* ostentoso, ostensivo

osteopath /'ɒstɪəpæθ/ *n* osteopata *mf*

ostracize /'ɒstrəsaɪz/ *vt* pôr de lado, marginalizar

ostrich /'ɒstrɪtʃ/ *n* avestruz *mf*

other /'ʌðə(r)/ *a*, *n & pron* outro (*m*) □ *adv* ~ **than** diferente de, senão. (**some**) ~**s** outros. **the ~ day** no outro dia. **the ~ one** o outro

otherwise /'ʌðəwaɪz/ *adv* de outro modo □ *conj* senão, caso contrário

otter /'ɒtə(r)/ *n* lontra *f*

ouch /aʊtʃ/ *int* ai!, ui!

ought /ɔːt/ *v aux* (*pt* **ought**) dever. **you ~ to stay** você devia ficar. **he ~ to succeed** ele deve vencer. **I ~ to have done it** eu devia tê-lo feito

ounce /aʊns/ *n* onça *f* (= *28,35g*)

our /'aʊə(r)/ *a* nosso(s), nossa(s)

ours /'aʊəz/ *poss pron* o(s) nosso(s), a(s) nossa(s)

ourselves /aʊə'selvz/ *pron* nós mesmos/próprios; (*reflexive*) nos. **by ~** sozinhos

oust /aʊst/ *vt* expulsar, obrigar a sair

out /aʊt/ *adv* fora; (*of light, fire*) apagado; (*in blossom*) aberto, desabrochado; (*of tide*) baixo. **be ~** não estar em casa, estar fora (de casa); (*wrong*) enganar-se. **be ~ to** estar resolvido a. **run**/*etc* **~** sair correndo/*etc*. ~**-and-~** a completo, rematado. ~ **of** fora de; (*without*) sem. ~ **of pity**/*etc* por pena/*etc*. **made ~ of** feito *de or* em. **take ~ of** tirar de. **5 ~ of 6** 5 (de) entre 6. ~ **of date** fora de moda; (*not valid*) fora do prazo. ~ **of doors** ao ar livre. ~ **of one's mind** doido. ~ **of**

order quebrado. **~ of place** deslocado. **~ of the way** afastado. **~-patient** n doente mf de consulta externa

outboard /'autbɔ:d/ a ~ **motor** motor m de popa

outbreak /'autbreɪk/ n (of flu etc) surto m, epidemia f, (of war) deflagração f

outburst /'autbɜ:st/ n explosão f

outcast /'autka:st/ n pária m

outcome /'autkʌm/ n resultado m

outcry /'autkraɪ/ n clamor m; (protest) protesto m

outdated /aut'deɪtɪd/ a fora da moda, ultrapassado

outdo /aut'du:/ vt (pt -did, pp -done) ultrapassar, superar

outdoor /'autdɔ:(r)/ a ao ar livre. **~s** /-'dɔ:z/ adv fora de casa, ao ar livre

outer /'autə(r)/ a exterior. **~ space** espaço (cósmico) m

outfit /'autfɪt/ n equipamento m; (clothes) roupa f

outgoing /'autgəʊɪŋ/ a que vai sair; (of minister etc) demissionário; (fig) sociável. **~s** npl despesas fpl

outgrow /aut'grəʊ/ vt (pt -grew, pp -grown) crescer mais do que; (clothes) já não caber em

outhouse /'authaʊs/ n anexo m, dependência f

outing /'autɪŋ/ n saída f, passeio m

outlandish /aut'lændɪʃ/ a exótico, estranho

outlaw /'autlɔ:/ n fora-da-lei mf, bandido m □ vt banir, proscrever

outlay /'autleɪ/ n despesa(s) f(pl)

outlet /'autlet/ n saída f, escoadouro m; (for goods) mercado m, saída f; (for feelings) escape m, vazão m; (electr) tomada f

outline /'autlaɪn/ n contorno m; (summary) plano m geral, esquema m, esboço m □ vt contornar; (summarize) descrever em linhas gerais

outlive /aut'lɪv/ vt sobreviver a

outlook /'autlʊk/ n (view) vista f; (mental attitude) visão f; (future prospects) perspectiva(s) f(pl)

outlying /'autlaɪɪŋ/ a afastado, remoto

outnumber /aut'nʌmbə(r)/ vt ultrapassar em número

outpost /'autpəʊst/ n posto m avançado

output /'autpʊt/ n rendimento m; (of computer) saída f, output m

outrage /'autreɪdʒ/ n atrocidade f, crime m; (scandal) escândalo m □ vt ultrajar

outrageous /aut'reɪdʒəs/ a (shocking) escandaloso; (very cruel) atroz

outright /'autraɪt/ adv completamente; (at once) imediatamente;

(frankly) abertamente □ a completo; (refusal) claro

outset /'autset/ n início m, começo m, princípio m

outside¹ /aut'saɪd/ n exterior m □ adv (lá) (por) fora □ prep (para) fora de, além de; (in front of) diante de. **at the ~** no máximo

outside² /'autsaɪd/ a exterior

outsider /aut'saɪdə(r)/ n estranho m; (in race) cavalo m com poucas probabilidades, azarão m

outsize /'autsaɪz/ a tamanho extra invar

outskirts /'autskɜ:ts/ npl arredores mpl, subúrbios mpl

outspoken /aut'spəʊkn/ a franco

outstanding /aut'stændɪŋ/ a saliente, proeminente; (debt) por saldar; (very good) notável, destacado

outstretched /aut'stretʃt/ a (arm) estendido, esticado

outstrip /aut'strɪp/ vt (pt -stripped) ultrapassar, passar à frente de

outward /'autwəd/ a para o exterior; (sign etc) exterior; (journey) de ida. **~ly** adv exteriormente. **~s** adv para o exterior

outwit /aut'wɪt/ vt (pt -witted) ser mais esperto que, enganar

oval /'əʊvl/ n & a oval (m)

ovary /'əʊvərɪ/ n ovário m

ovation /əʊ'veɪʃn/ n ovação f

oven /'ʌvn/ n forno m

over /'əʊvə(r)/ prep sobre, acima de, por cima de; (across) de para o/do outro lado de; (during) durante, em; (more than) mais de □ adv por cima; (too) demais, demasiadamente; (ended) acabado. **the film is ~** o filme já acabou. **jump/etc ~** saltar/etc por cima. **he has some ~** ele tem uns de sobra. **all ~ the country** em/por todo o país. **all ~ the table** por toda a mesa. **~ and above** (besides, in addition to) (para) além de. **~ and ~** repetidas vezes. **~ there** ali, lá, acolá

over- /'əʊvə(r)/ pref sobre-, super-; (excessively) demais, demasiado

overall¹ /'əʊvərɔ:l/ n bata f. **~s** macacão m, (P) fato-macaco m

overall² /'əʊvərɔ:l/ a global; (length etc) total □ adv globalmente

overawe /əʊvər'ɔ:/ vt intimidar

overbalance /əʊvə'bæləns/ vt/i (fazer) perder o equilíbrio

overbearing /əʊvə'beərɪŋ/ a autoritário, despótico; (arrogant) arrogante

overboard /'əʊvəbɔ:d/ adv (pela) borda fora

overcast /əʊvə'ka:st/ a encoberto, nublado

overcharge /əʊvə'tʃa:dʒ/ vt ~ **sb (for)** cobrar demais a alg (por) overcoat /'əʊvəkəʊt/ n casacão m; (for men) sobretudo m

overcome /əʊvə'kʌm/ vt (pt -came, pp -come) superar, vencer. ~ by sucumbindo a, dominado or vencido por

overcrowded /əʊvə'kraʊdɪd/ a apinhado, superlotado; (country) superpovoado

overdo /əʊvə'du:/ vt (pt -did, pp -done) exagerar, levar longe demais. ~ne (culin) cozinhado demais

overdose /'əʊvədəʊs/ n dose f excessiva

overdraft /'əʊvədra:ft/ n saldo m negativo

overdraw /əʊvə'drɔ:/ vt (pt -drew, pp -drawn) sacar a descoberto

overdue /əʊvə'dju:/ a em atraso, atrasado; (belated) tardio

overestimate /əʊvər'estɪmeɪt/ vt sobreestimar, atribuir valor excessivo a

overexpose /əʊvərɪk'spəʊz/ vt expor demais

overflow[1] /əʊvə'fləʊ/ vt/i extravasar, transbordar (with de)

overflow[2] /'əʊvəfləʊ/ n (outlet) descarga f; (excess) excesso m

overgrown /əʊvə'grəʊn/ a que cresceu demais; (garden etc) invadido pela vegetação

overhang /əʊvə'hæŋ/ vt (pt -hung) estar sobranceiro a, pairar sobre □ vi projetar-se, (P) projectar-se para fora □ n saliência f

overhaul[1] /əʊvə'hɔ:l/ vt fazer uma revisão em

overhaul[2] /'əʊvəhɔ:l/ n revisão f

overhead[1] /əʊvə'hed/ adv em or por cima, ao or no alto

overhead[2] /'əʊvəhed/ a aéreo. ~s npl despesas fpl gerais

overhear /əʊvə'hɪə(r)/ vt (pt -heard) (eavesdrop) ouvir sem conhecimento do falante; (hear by chance) ouvir por acaso

overjoyed /əʊvə'dʒɔɪd/ a radiante, felicíssimo

overlap /əʊvə'læp/ vt/i (pt -lapped) sobrepor(-se) parcialmente; (fig) coincidir

overleaf /əʊvə'li:f/ adv no verso

overload /əʊvə'ləʊd/ vt sobrecarregar

overlook /əʊvə'lʊk/ vt deixar passar; (of window) dar para; (of building) dominar

overnight /əʊvə'naɪt/ adv durante a noite; (fig) dum dia para o outro □ a (train) da noite; (stay, journey, etc) noite, noturno; (fig) súbito

overpass /əʊvə'pa:s/ n passagem f superior

overpay /əʊvə'peɪ/ vt (pt -paid) pagar em excesso

overpower /əʊvə'paʊə(r)/ vt dominar, subjugar; (fig) esmagar. ~ing a esmagador; (heat) sufocante, insuportável

overpriced /əʊvə'praɪst/ a muito caro

overrate /əʊvə'reɪt/ vt sobreestimar, exagerar o valor de

override /əʊvə'raɪd/ vt (pt -rode, pp -ridden) prevalecer sobre, passar por cima de. ~ing a primordial, preponderante; (importance) maior

overripe /'əʊvəraɪp/ a demasiado maduro

overrule /əʊvə'ru:l/ vt anular, rejeitar; (claim) indeferir

overrun /əʊvə'rʌn/ vt (pt -ran, pp -run, pres p -running) invadir; (a limit) exceder, ultrapassar

overseas /əʊvə'si:z/ a ultramarino; (abroad) estrangeiro □ adv no ultramar, no estrangeiro

oversee /əʊvə'si:/ vt (pt -saw pp -seen) supervisionar. ~r /'əʊvəsɪə(r)/ n capataz m

overshadow /əʊvə'ʃædəʊ/ vt (fig) eclipsar, ofuscar

oversight /'əʊvəsaɪt/ n lapso m

oversleep /əʊvə'sli:p/ vi (pt -slept) acordar tarde, dormir demais

overt /'əʊvɜ:t/ a manifesto, claro, patente

overtake /əʊvə'teɪk/ vt/i (pt -took, pp -taken) ultrapassar

overthrow /əʊvə'θrəʊ/ vt (pt -threw, pp -thrown) derrubar □ n /'əʊvəθrəʊ/ (pol) derrubada f

overtime /'əʊvətaɪm/ n horas fpl extras

overtones /'əʊvətəʊnz/ npl (fig) tom m, implicação f

overture /'əʊvətjʊə(r)/ n (mus) abertura f; (fig) proposta f, abordagem f

overturn /əʊvə'tɜ:n/ vt/i virar(-se); (car, plane) capotar, virar-se

overweight /əʊvə'weɪt/ a be ~ ter excesso de peso

overwhelm /əʊvə'welm/ vt oprimir; (defeat) esmagar; (amaze) assoberbar. ~ing a esmagador; (urge) irresistível

overwork /əʊvə'wɜ:k/ vt/i sobrecarregar(-se) com trabalho □ n excesso m de trabalho

overwrought /əʊvə'rɔ:t/ a muito agitado, superexcitado

ow|e /əʊ/ vt dever. ~ing a devido. ~ing to devido a

owl /aʊl/ n coruja f

own[1] /əʊn/ a próprio. a house/etc of one's ~ uma casa/etc própria. get one's ~ back (colloq) ir à forra, (P) desforrar-se. hold one's ~ agüentar-se, (P) aguentar-se. on one's ~ sozinho

own[2] /əʊn/ *vt* possuir. ~ **up (to)** (*colloq*) confessar. ~**er** *n* proprietário *m*, dono *m*. ~**ership** *n* posse *f*, propriedade *f*

ox /ɒks/ *n* (*pl* **oxen**) boi *m*

oxygen /'ɒksɪdʒən/ *n* oxigênio *m*, (P) oxigénio *m*

oyster /'ɔɪstə(r)/ *n* ostra *f*

ozone /'əʊzəʊn/ *n* ozônio *m*, (P) ozono *m*. ~ **layer** camada *f* de ozônio, (P) ozono *m*

P

pace /peɪs/ *n* passo *m*; (*fig*) ritmo *m* □ *vt* percorrer passo a passo □ *vi* ~ **up and down** andar de um lado para o outro. **keep** ~ **with** acompanhar, manter-se a par de

pacemaker /'peɪsmeɪkə(r)/ *n* (*med*) marcapasso *m*, (P) pacemaker *m*

Pacific /pə'sɪfɪk/ *a* pacífico □ *n* ~ (**Ocean**) (Oceano) Pacífico *m*

pacifist /'pæsɪfɪst/ *n* pacifista *mf*

pacify /'pæsɪfaɪ/ *vt* pacificar, apaziguar

pack /pæk/ *n* pacote *m*; (*mil*) mochila *f*; (*of hounds*) matilha *f*; (*of lies*) porção *f*; (*of cards*) baralho *m* □ *vt* empacotar; (*suitcase*) fazer; (*box, room*) encher; (*press down*) atulhar, encher até não caber mais □ *vi* fazer as malas. ~ **into** (*cram*) apinhar em, comprimir em. **send** ~**ing** pôr a andar, mandar passear. ~**ed** *a* apinhado. ~**ed lunch** merenda *f*

package /'pækɪdʒ/ *n* pacote *m*, embrulho *m* □ *vt* embalar. ~ **deal** pacote *m* de propostas. ~ **holiday** pacote *m* turístico, (P) viagem *f* organizada

packet /'pækɪt/ *n* pacote *m*; (*of cigarettes*) maço *m*

pact /pækt/ *n* pacto *m*

pad /pæd/ *n* (*in clothing*) chumaço *m*; (*for writing*) bloco *m* de papel/de notas; (*for ink*) almofada (de carimbo) *f*. (**launching**) ~ rampa *f* de lançamento □ *vt* (*pt* **padded**) enchumaçar, acolchoar; (*fig: essay etc*) encher linguiça. ~**ding** *n* chumaço *m*; (*fig*) linguiça *f*

paddle[1] /'pædl/ *n* remo *m* de canoa. ~-**steamer** *n* vapor *m* movido a rodas

paddl|e[2] /'pædl/ *vi* chapinhar, molhar os pés. ~**ing pool** piscina *f* de plástico para crianças

paddock /'pædək/ *n* cercado *m*; (*at racecourse*) paddock *m*

padlock /'pædlɒk/ *n* cadeado *m* □ *vt* fechar com cadeado

paediatrician /piːdɪə'trɪʃn/ *n* pediatra *mf*

pagan /'peɪgən/ *a* & *n* pagão (*m*), pagã (*f*)

page[1] /peɪdʒ/ *n* (*of book etc*) página *f*

page[2] /peɪdʒ/ *vt* mandar chamar

pageant /'pædʒənt/ *n* espetáculo *m*, (P) espectáculo *m* (histórico); (*procession*) cortejo *m*. ~**ry** *n* pompa *f*

pagoda /pə'gəʊdə/ *n* pagode *m*

paid /peɪd/ *see* **pay** □ *a* **put** ~ **to** (*colloq: end*) pôr fim a

pail /peɪl/ *n* balde *m*

pain /peɪn/ *n* dor *f*. ~**s** esforços *mpl* □ *vt* magoar. **be in** ~ sofrer, ter dores. ~-**killer** *n* analgésico *m*. **take** ~**s to** esforçar-se por. ~**ful** *a* doloroso; (*grievous, laborious*) penoso. ~**less** *a* sem dor, indolor

painstaking /'peɪnzteɪkɪŋ/ *a* cuidadoso, esmerado, meticuloso

paint /peɪnt/ *n* tinta *f*. ~**s** (*in box*) tintas *fpl* □ *vt/i* pintar. ~**er** *n* pintor *m*. ~**ing** *n* pintura *f*

paintbrush /'peɪntbrʌʃ/ *n* pincel *m*

pair /peə(r)/ *n* par *m*. **a** ~ **of scissors** uma tesoura. **a** ~ **of trousers** um par de calças. **in** ~**s** aos pares □ *vi* ~ **off** formar pares

Pakistan /paːkɪ'staːn/ *n* Paquistão *m*. ~**i** *a* & *n* paquistanês (*m*)

pal /pæl/ *n* (*colloq*) colega *mf*, amigo *m*

palace /'pælɪs/ *n* palácio *m*

palat|e /'pælət/ *n* palato *m*. ~**able** *a* saboroso, gostoso; (*fig*) agradável

palatial /pə'leɪʃl/ *a* suntuoso, (P) sumptuoso

pale /peɪl/ *a* (-er, -est) pálido; (*colour*) claro □ *vi* empalidecer. ~**ness** *n* palidez *f*

Palestin|e /'pælɪstam/ *n* Palestina *f*. ~**ian** /-'stɪnɪən/ *a* & *n* palestino (*m*)

palette /'pælɪt/ *n* paleta *f*. ~-**knife** *n* espátula *f*

pall /pɔːl/ *vi* tornar-se enfadonho, perder o interesse (**on** para)

pallid /'pælɪd/ *a* pálido

palm /paːm/ *n* (*of hand*) palma *f*; (*tree*) palmeira *f* □ *vt* ~ **off** impingir (**on** a). **P**~ **Sunday** Domingo *m* de Ramos

palpable /'pælpəbl/ *a* palpável

palpitat|e /'pælpɪteɪt/ *vi* palpitar. ~**ion** /-'teɪʃn/ *n* palpitação *f*

paltry /'pɔːltrɪ/ *a* (-ier, -iest) irrisório

pamper /'pæmpə(r)/ *vt* mimar, paparicar

pamphlet /'pæmflɪt/ *n* panfleto *m*, folheto *m*

pan /pæn/ *n* panela *f*; (*for frying*) frigideira *f* □ *vt* (*pt* **panned**) (*colloq*) criticar severamente

panacea /pænə'sɪə/ *n* panacéia *f*

panache /pæ'næʃ/ *n* brio *m*, estilo *m*, panache *m*

pancake /'pænkeɪk/ *n* crepe *m*, panqueca *f*

pancreas /'pæŋkrɪəs/ n pâncreas m

panda /'pændə/ n panda m

pandemonium /pændɪ'məʊnɪəm/ n pandemônio m, (P) pandemónio m, caos m

pander /'pændə(r)/ vi ~ to prestar-se a servir, ir ao encontro de, fazer concessões a

pane /peɪn/ n vidraça f

panel /'pænl/ n painel m; (jury) júri m; (speakers) convidados mpl. (instrument) ~ painel m de instrumentos, (P) de bordo. ~led a apainelado. ~ling n apainelamento m. ~list n convidado m

pang /pæŋ/ n pontada f, dor f aguda e súbita. ~s (of hunger) ataques mpl de fome. ~s of conscience remorsos mpl

panic /'pænɪk/ n pânico m ▢ vt/i (pt panicked) desorientar(-se), (fazer) entrar em pânico. ~-stricken a tomado de pânico

panoram|a /pænə'rɑːmə/ n panorama m. ~ic /-'ræmɪk/ a panorâmico

pansy /'pænzɪ/ n amor-perfeito m

pant /pænt/ vi ofegar, arquejar

panther /'pænθə(r)/ n pantera f

panties /'pæntɪz/ npl (colloq) calcinhas fpl

pantomime /'pæntəmaɪm/ n pantomima f

pantry /'pæntrɪ/ n despensa f

pants /pænts/ npl (colloq: underwear) cuecas fpl; (colloq: trousers) calças fpl

papal /'peɪpl/ a papal

paper /'peɪpə(r)/ n papel m; (newspaper) jornal m; (exam) prova f escrita; (essay) comunicação f. ~s npl (for identification) documentos mpl ▢ vt forrar com papel. on ~ por escrito. ~-clip n clipe m

paperback /'peɪpəbæk/ a & n ~ (book) livro m de capa mole

paperweight /'peɪpəweɪt/ n pesa-papéis m invar, (P) pisa-papéis m invar

paperwork /'peɪpəwɜːk/ n trabalho m de secretária; (pej) papelada f

paprika /'pæprɪkə/ n páprica f, pimentão m doce

par /pɑː(r)/ n be below ~ estar abaixo do padrão desejado. on a ~ with em igualdade com

parable /'pærəbl/ n parábola f

parachut|e /'pærəʃuːt/ n pára-quedas m invar ▢ vi descer de pára-quedas. ~ist n pára-quedista f

parade /pə'reɪd/ n (mil) parada f militar; (procession) procissão f ▢ vi desfilar ▢ vt alardear, exibir

paradise /'pærədaɪs/ n paraíso m

paradox /'pærədɒks/ n paradoxo m. ~ical /-'dɒksɪkl/ a paradoxal

paraffin /'pærəfɪn/ n querosene m, (P) petróleo m

paragon /'pærəgən/ n modelo m de perfeição

paragraph /'pærəgrɑːf/ n parágrafo m

parallel /'pærəlel/ a & n paralelo (m) ▢ vt (pt parelleled) comparar(-se) a

paralyse /'pærəlaɪz/ vt paralisar

paraly|sis /pə'ræləsɪs/ n paralisia f. ~tic /-'lɪtɪk/ a & n paralítico (m)

parameter /pə'ræmɪtə(r)/ n parâmetro m

paramount /'pærəmaʊnt/ a supremo, primordial

parapet /'pærəpɪt/ n parapeito m

paraphernalia /pærəfə'neɪlɪə/ n equipamento m, tralha f (colloq)

paraphrase /'pærəfreɪz/ n paráfrase f ▢ vt parafrasear

paraplegic /pærə'pliːdʒɪk/ n paraplégico m

parasite /'pærəsaɪt/ n parasita mf

parasol /'pærəsɒl/ n sombrinha f, (on table) pára-sol m, guarda-sol m

parcel /'pɑːsl/ n embrulho m; (for post) encomenda f

parch /pɑːtʃ/ vt ressecar. be ~ed estar com muita sede

parchment /'pɑːtʃmənt/ n pergaminho m

pardon /'pɑːdn/ n perdão m; (jur) perdão m, indulto m ▢ vt (pt pardoned) perdoar. I beg your ~ perdão, desculpe. (I beg your) ~? como?

pare /peə(r)/ vt aparar, cortar; (peel) descascar

parent /'peərənt/ n pai m, mãe f. ~s npl pais mpl. ~al /pə'rentl/ a dos pais, paterno, materno

parenthesis /pə'renθəsɪs/ n (pl -theses) /-siːz/ parêntese m, parêntesis m

Paris /'pærɪs/ n Paris m

parish /'pærɪʃ/ n paróquia f; (municipal) freguesia f. ~ioner /pə'rɪʃənə(r)/ n paroquiano m

parity /'pærətɪ/ n paridade f

park /pɑːk/ n parque m ▢ vt estacionar. ~ing n estacionamento m. no ~ing estacionamento proibido. ~ing-meter n parquímetro m

parliament /'pɑːləmənt/ n parlamento m, assembléia f. ~ary /-'mentrɪ/ a parlamentar

parochial /pə'rəʊkɪəl/ a paroquial; (fig) provinciano, tacanho

parody /'pærədɪ/ n paródia f ▢ vt parodiar

parole /pə'rəʊl/ n on ~ em liberdade condicional ▢ vt pôr em liberdade condicional

parquet /'pɑːkeɪ/ n parquê m, parquete m

parrot /'pærət/ *n* papagaio *m*

parry /'pærɪ/ *vt* (a)parar □ *n* parada *f*

parsimonious /pɑ:sɪ'məʊnɪəs/ *a* parco; (*mean*) avarento

parsley /'pɑ:slɪ/ *n* salsa *f*

parsnip /'pɑ:snɪp/ *n* cherovia *f*, pastinaga *f*

parson /'pɑ:sn/ *n* pároco *m*, pastor *m*

part /pɑ:t/ *n* parte *f*; (*of serial*) episódio *m*; (*of machine*) peça *f*; (*theatre*) papel *m*; (*side in dispute*) partido *m* □ *a* parcial □ *adv* em parte □ *vt/i* separar (-se) (**from** de). **in ~** em parte. **on the ~ of** da parte de. **~-exchange** *n* troca *f* parcial. **~ of speech** categoria *f* gramatical. **~-time** *a* & *adv* a tempo parcial, parttime. **take ~ in** tomar parte em. **these ~s** estas partes

partial /'pɑ:ʃl/ *a* (*incomplete, biased*) parcial. **be ~ to** gostar de. **~ity** /-ɪ'ælətɪ/ *n* parcialidade *f*, (*liking*) predileção *f*, (*P*) predilecção *f* (**for** por). **~ly** *adv* parcialmente

particip|ate /pɑ:'tɪsɪpeɪt/ *vi* participar (**in** em). **~ant** *n* /-ənt/ participante *mf*. **~ation** /-'peɪʃn/ *n* participação *f*

participle /'pɑ:tɪsɪpl/ *n* particípio *m*

particle /'pɑ:tɪkl/ *n* partícula *f*, (*of dust*) grão *m*; (*fig*) mínimo *m*

particular /pə'tɪkjʊlə(r)/ *a* especial, particular; (*fussy*) exigente; (*careful*) escrupuloso. **~s** *npl* pormenores *mpl*. **in ~** em especial, particularmente. **~ly** *adv* particularmente

parting /'pɑ:tɪŋ/ *n* separação *f*; (*in hair*) risca *f* □ *a* de despedida

partisan /pɑ:tɪ'zæn/ *n* partidário *m*; (*mil*) guerrilheiro *m*

partition /pɑ:'tɪʃn/ *n* (*of room*) tabique *m*, divisória *f*; (*pol: division*) partilha *f*, divisão *f* □ *vt* dividir, repartir. **~ off** dividir por meio de tabique

partly /'pɑ:tlɪ/ *adv* em parte

partner /'pɑ:tnə(r)/ *n* sócio *m*; (*cards, sport*) parceiro *m*; (*dancing*) par *m*. **~ship** *n* associação *f*, (*comm*) sociedade *f*

partridge /'pɑ:trɪdʒ/ *n* perdiz *f*

party /'pɑ:tɪ/ *n* festa *f*, reunião *f*; (*group*) grupo *m*; (*pol*) partido *m*; (*jur*) parte *f*. **~ line** (*telephone*) linha *f* coletiva, (*P*) colectiva

pass /pɑ:s/ *vt/i* (*pt* **passed**) passar; (*overtake*) ultrapassar; (*exam*) passar; (*approve*) passar; (*law*) aprovar. **~ (by)** passar por □ *n* (*permit, sport*) passe *m*; (*geog*) desfiladeiro *m*, garganta *f*; (*in exam*) aprovação *f*. **make a ~ at** (*colloq*) atirar-se para (*colloq*). **~ away** falecer. **~ out** *or* **round** distribuir. **~ out** (*colloq: faint*) perder os sentidos, desmaiar. **~ over** (*disre-*

gard, overlook) passar por cima de. **~ up** (*colloq: forgo*) deixar perder

passable /'pɑ:səbl/ *a* passável; (*road*) transitável

passage /'pæsɪdʒ/ *n* passagem *f*; (*voyage*) travessia *f*; (*corridor*) corredor *m*, passagem *f*

passenger /'pæsɪndʒə(r)/ *n* passageiro *m*

passer-by /pɑ:sə'baɪ/ *n* (*pl* **passers-by**) transeunte *mf*

passion /'pæʃn/ *n* paixão *f*. **~ate** *a* apaixonado, exaltado

passive /'pæsɪv/ *a* passivo. **~ness** *n* passividade *f*

Passover /'pɑ:səʊvə(r)/ *n* Páscoa *f* dos judeus

passport /'pɑ:spɔ:t/ *n* passaporte *m*

password /'pɑ:swɜ:d/ *n* senha *f*

past /pɑ:st/ *a* passado; (*former*) antigo □ *n* passado □ *prep* para além de; (*in time*) mais de; (*in front of*) diante de □ *adv* em frente. **be ~ it** já não ser capaz. **it's five ~ eleven** são onze e cinco. **these ~ months** estes últimos meses

pasta /'pæstə/ *n* prato *m* de massa(s)

paste /peɪst/ *n* cola *f*; (*culin*) massa(s) *f(pl)*; (*dough*) massa *f*, (*jewellery*) strass *m* □ *vt* colar

pastel /'pæstl/ *n* pastel *m* □ *a* pastel *invar*

pasteurize /'pæstʃəraɪz/ *vt* pasteurizar

pastille /'pæstɪl/ *n* pastilha *f*

pastime /'pɑ:staɪm/ *n* passatempo *m*

pastoral /'pɑ:stərəl/ *a* & *n* pastoral (*f*)

pastry /'peɪstrɪ/ *n* massa *f* (de pastelaria); (*tart*) pastel *m*

pasture /'pɑ:stʃə(r)/ *n* pastagem *f*

pasty¹ /'pæstɪ/ *n* empadinha *f*

pasty² /'peɪstɪ/ *a* pastoso

pat /pæt/ *vt* (*pt* **patted**) (*hit gently*) dar pancadinhas em; (*caress*) fazer festinhas a □ *n* pancadinha *f*; (*caress*) festinha *f* □ *adv* a propósito; (*readily*) prontamente □ *a* preparado, pronto

patch /pætʃ/ *n* remendo *m*; (*over eye*) tapa-ôlho *m*; (*spot*) mancha *f*; (*small area*) pedaço *m*; (*of vegetables*) canteiro *m*, (*P*) leira *f* □ *vt* **~ up** remendar. **~ up a quarrel** fazer as pazes. **bad ~** mau bocado *m*. **not be a ~ on** não chegar aos pés de. **~-work** *n* obra *f* de retalhos. **~y** *a* desigual

pâté /'pæteɪ/ *n* patê *m*

patent /'peɪtnt/ *a* & *n* patente (*f*) □ *vt* patentear. **~ leather** verniz *m*, polimento *m*. **~ly** *adv* claramente

paternal /pə'tɜ:nl/ *a* paternal; (*relative*) paterno

paternity /pə'tɜ:nətɪ/ *n* paternidade *f*

path /pɑːθ/ n (pl -s /pɑːðz/) caminho m, trilha f; (in park) aléia f; (of rocket) trajetória f, (P) trajectória f

pathetic /pəˈθetɪk/ a patético; (colloq: contemptible) desgraçado (colloq)

patholog|y /pəˈθɒlədʒɪ/ n patologia f. ~ist n patologista mf

pathos /ˈpeɪθɒs/ n patos m, patético m

patience /ˈpeɪʃns/ n paciência f

patient /ˈpeɪʃnt/ a paciente □ n doente mf, paciente mf. ~ly adv pacientemente

patio /ˈpætɪəʊ/ n (pl -os) pátio m

patriot /ˈpætrɪət/ n patriota mf. ~ic /-ˈɒtɪk/ a patriótico. ~ism /-ɪzəm/ n patriotismo m

patrol /pəˈtrəʊl/ n patrulha f □ vt/i patrulhar. ~ car carro m de patrulha

patron /ˈpeɪtrən/ n (of the arts etc) patrocinador m, protetor m, (P) protector m; (of charity) benfeitor m; (customer) freguês m, cliente mf. ~ saint padroeiro m, patrono m

patron|age /ˈpætrənɪdʒ/ n freguesia f, clientela f; (support) patrocínio m. ~ize vt ser cliente de; (support) patrocinar; (condescend) tratar com ares de superioridade

patter[1] /ˈpætə(r)/ n (of rain) tamborilar m, rufo m. ~ of steps som m leve de passos miúdos, corridinha f leve

patter[2] /ˈpætə(r)/ n (of class, profession) gíria f, jargão m; (chatter) conversa f fiada

pattern /ˈpætn/ n padrão m; (for sewing) molde m; (example) modelo m

paunch /pɔːntʃ/ n pança f

pause /pɔːz/ n pausa f □ vi pausar, fazer (uma) pausa

pav|e /peɪv/ vt pavimentar. ~e the way preparar o caminho (for para). ~ing-stone n paralelepípedo m, laje f

pavement /ˈpeɪvmənt/ n passeio m

pavilion /pəˈvɪlɪən/ n pavilhão m

paw /pɔː/ n pata f □ vt dar patadas em; (horse) escarvar; (colloq: person) pôr as patas em cima de

pawn[1] /pɔːn/ n (chess) peão m; (fig) joguete m

pawn[2] /pɔːn/ vt empenhar. ~-shop casa f de penhores, prego m (colloq)

pawnbroker /ˈpɔːnbrəʊkə(r)/ n penhorista mf, dono m de casa de penhores, agiota mf

pay /peɪ/ vt/i (pt paid) pagar; (interest) render; (visit, compliment) fazer □ n pagamento m; (wages) vencimento m, ordenado m, salário m. in the ~ of em pagamento de. ~ attention prestar atenção. ~ back restituir. ~ for pagar. ~ homage prestar homenagem. ~ in depositar. ~-slip n contracheque m, (P) folha f de pagamento

payable /ˈpeɪəbl/ a pagável

payment /ˈpeɪmənt/ n pagamento m; (fig: reward) recompensa f

payroll /ˈpeɪrəʊl/ n folha f de pagamentos. be on the ~ fazer parte da folha de pagamento de uma firma

pea /piː/ n ervilha f

peace /piːs/ n paz f. disturb the ~ perturbar a ordem pública. ~able a pacífico

peaceful /ˈpiːsfl/ a pacífico; (calm) calmo, sereno

peacemaker /ˈpiːsmeɪkə(r)/ n mediador m, pacificador m

peach /piːtʃ/ n pêssego m

peacock /ˈpiːkɒk/ n pavão m

peak /piːk/ n pico m, cume m, cimo m; (of cap) pala f; (maximum) máximo m. ~ hours horas fpl de ponta; (electr) horas fpl de carga máxima. ~ed cap boné m de pala

peaky /ˈpiːkɪ/ a com ar doentio

peal /piːl/ n (of bells) repique m; (of laughter) gargalhada f, risada f

peanut /ˈpiːnʌt/ n amendoim m. ~s (sl: small sum) uma bagatela f

pear /peə(r)/ n pera f

pearl /pɜːl/ n pérola f. ~y a nacarado

peasant /ˈpeznt/ n camponês m, aldeão m

peat /piːt/ n turfa f

pebble /ˈpebl/ n seixo m, calhau m

peck /pek/ vt/i bicar; (attack) dar bicadas (em) □ n bicada f; (colloq: kiss) beijo m seco. ~ing order hierarquia f, ordem f de importância

peckish /ˈpekɪʃ/ a be ~ (colloq) ter vontade de comer

peculiar /pɪˈkjuːlɪə(r)/ a bizarro, singular; (special) peculiar (to a), característico (to de). ~ity /-ˈærətɪ/ n singularidade f, (feature) peculiaridade f

pedal /ˈpedl/ n pedal m □ vi (pt pedalled) pedalar

pedantic /pɪˈdæntɪk/ a pedante

peddle /ˈpedl/ vt vender de porta em porta; (drugs) fazer tráfico de

pedestal /ˈpedɪstl/ n pedestal m

pedestrian /pɪˈdestrɪən/ n pedestre mf, (P) peão m □ a pedestre; (fig) prosaico. ~ crossing faixa f para pedestres, (P) passadeira f

pedigree /ˈpedɪɡriː/ n estirpe f, linhagem f; (of animal) raça f □ a de raça

pedlar /ˈpedlə(r)/ n vendedor m ambulante

peek /piːk/ vi espreitar □ n espreitadela f

peel /piːl/ n casca f □ vt descascar □ vi (skin) pelar; (paint) escamar-se, descascar; (wallpaper) descolar-se. ~ings npl cascas fpl

peep /piːp/ vi espreitar □ n espreitadela *f*. ~-**hole** *n* vigia *f*; (*in door*) olho *m* mágico

peer[1] /pɪə(r)/ *vi* ~ **at/into** (*searchingly*) perscrutar; (*with difficulty*) esforçar-se por ver

peer[2] /pɪə(r)/ *n* (*equal, noble*) par *m*. ~**age** *n* pariato *m*

peeved /piːvd/ *a* (*sl*) irritado, chateado (*sl*)

peevish /ˈpiːvɪʃ/ *a* irritável

peg /peg/ *n* cavilha *f*; (*for washing*) pregador *m* de roupa, (*P*) mola *f*; (*for coats etc*) cabide *m*; (*for tent*) □ *vt* (*pt* **pegged**) prender com estacas. **off the** ~ prêt-à-porter

pejorative /prɪˈdʒɒrətɪv/ *a* pejorativo

pelican /ˈpelɪkən/ *n* pelicano *m*. ~ **crossing** passagem *f* com sinais manobrados pelos pedestres

pellet /ˈpelɪt/ *n* bolinha *f*; (*for gun*) grão *m* de chumbo

pelt[1] /pelt/ *n* pele *f*

pelt[2] /pelt/ *vt* bombardear (**with** com) □ *vi* chover a cántaros; (*run fast*) correr em disparada

pelvis /ˈpelvɪs/ *n* (*anat*) pélvis *m*, bacia *f*

pen[1] /pen/ *n* (*enclosure*) cercado *m*. **play-**~ *n* cercado *m*, (*P*) pargue *m* □ *vt* (*pt* **penned**) encurralar

pen[2] /pen/ *n* caneta *f* □ *vt* (*pt* **penned**) escrever. ~-**friend** *n* correspondente *mf*. ~-**name** *n* pseudônimo *m*, (*P*) pseudónimo *m*

penal /ˈpiːnl/ *a* penal. ~**ize** *vt* impôr uma penalidadea; (*sport*) penalizar

penalty /ˈpenltɪ/ *n* pena *f*; (*fine*) multa *f*, (*sport*) penalidade *f*. ~ **kick** pênalti *m*, (*P*) grande penalidade *f*

penance /ˈpenəns/ *n* penitência *f*

pence /pens/ *see* penny

pencil /ˈpensl/ *n* lápis *m* □ *vt* (*pt* **pencilled**) escrever *or* desenhar a lápis. ~-**sharpener** *n* apontador *m*, (*P*) apara-lápis *m invar*

pendant /ˈpendənt/ *n* berloque *m*

pending /ˈpendɪŋ/ *a* pendente □ *prep* (*during*) durante; (*until*) até

pendulum /ˈpendjʊləm/ *n* pêndulo *m*

penetrat|e /ˈpenɪtreɪt/ *vt/i* penetrar (em). ~**ing** *a* penetrante. ~**ion** /-ˈtreɪʃn/ *n* penetração *f*

penguin /ˈpeŋgwɪn/ *n* pingüim *m*, (*P*) pinguim *m*

penicillin /penɪˈsɪlɪn/ *n* penicilina *f*

peninsula /pəˈnɪnsjʊlə/ *n* península *f*

penis /ˈpiːnɪs/ *n* pênis *m*, (*P*) pénis *m*

peniten|t /ˈpenɪtənt/ *a* & *n* penitente (*mf*). ~**ce** *n* /-əns/ contrição *f*, penitência *f*

penitentiary /penɪˈtenʃərɪ/ *n* (*Amer*) penitenciária *f*, cadeia *f*

penknife /ˈpennaɪf/ *n* (*pl* -**knives**) canivete *m*

penniless /ˈpenɪlɪs/ *a* sem vintém, sem um tostão

penny /ˈpenɪ/ *n* (*pl* **pennies** *or* **pence**) pêni *m*, (*P*) péni *m*; (*fig*) centavo *m*, vintém *m*

pension /ˈpenʃn/ *n* pensão *f*; (*in retirement*) aposentadoria *f*, (*P*) reforma *f* □ *vt* ~ **off** reformar, aposentar. ~**er** *n* (**old-age**) ~**er** reformado *m*

pensive /ˈpensɪv/ *a* pensativo

Pentecost /ˈpentɪkɒst/ *n* Pentecostes *m*

penthouse /ˈpenthaʊs/ *n* cobertura *f*, (*P*) apartamento de luxo (no último andar)

pent-up /ˈpentʌp/ *a* reprimido

penultimate /penˈʌltɪmət/ *a* penúltimo

people /ˈpiːpl/ *npl* pessoas *fpl* □ *n* gente *f*, povo *m* □ *vt* povoar. **the Portuguese** ~ os portugueses *mpl*. ~ **say** dizem, diz-se

pep /pep/ *n* vigor *m* □ *vt* ~ **up** animar. ~ **talk** discurso *m* de encorajamento

pepper /ˈpepə(r)/ *n* pimenta *f*; (*vegetable*) pimentão *m*, (*P*) pimento *m* □ *vt* apimentar. ~**y** *a* apimentado, picante

peppermint /ˈpepəmɪnt/ *n* hortelã-pimenta *f*; (*sweet*) bala *f*, (*P*) pastilha *f* de hortelã-pimenta

per /pɜː(r)/ *prep* por. ~ **annum** por ano. ~ **cent** por cento. ~ **kilo**/*etc* o quilo/*etc*

perceive /pəˈsiːv/ *vt* perceber; (*notice*) aperceber-se de

percentage /pəˈsentɪdʒ/ *n* percentagem *f*

perceptible /pəˈseptəbl/ *a* perceptível

percept|ion /pəˈsepʃn/ *n* percepção *f*. ~**ive** /-tɪv/ *a* perceptivo, penetrante, perspicaz

perch[1] /pɜːtʃ/ *n* poleiro *m* □ *vi* empoleirar-se, pousar

perch[2] /pɜːtʃ/ *n* (*fish*) perca *f*

percolat|e /ˈpɜːkəleɪt/ *vt/i* filtrar(-se), passar. ~**or** *n* máquina *f* de café com filtro, cafeteira *f*

percussion /pəˈkʌʃn/ *n* percussão *f*

peremptory /pəˈremptərɪ/ *a* peremptório, decisivo

perennial /pəˈrenɪəl/ *a* perene; (*plant*) perene

perfect[1] /ˈpɜːfɪkt/ *a* perfeito. ~**ly** *adv* perfeitamente

perfect[2] /pəˈfekt/ *vt* aperfeiçoar. ~**ion** /-ʃn/ *n* perfeição *f*. ~**ionist** *n* perfeccionista *mf*

perforat|e /ˈpɜːfəreɪt/ *vt* perfurar. ~**ion** /ˈreɪʃn/ *n* perfuração *f*; (*line of holes*) pontilhado *m*, picotado *m*

perform /pəˈfɔːm/ *vt* (*a task; mus*) executar; (*a function; theat*) desempenhar □ *vi* representar; (*function*) funcionar. ~**ance** *n* (*of task; mus*) execução f; (of function; theat) desempenho m; (of car) performance f, comportamento m, rendimento m; (colloq: fuss) drama m, cena f. ~er n artista mf

perfume /'pɜːfjuːm/ n perfume m

perfunctory /pəˈfʌŋktərɪ/ a superficial, negligente

perhaps /pəˈhæps/ adv talvez

peril /'perəl/ n perigo m. ~ous a perigoso

perimeter /pəˈrɪmɪtə(r)/ n perímetro m

period /'pɪərɪəd/ n período m, época f; (era) época f; (lesson) hora f de aula, período m letivo, (P) lectivo; (med) período m; (full stop) ponto (final) m □ a (of novel) de costumes; (of furniture) de estilo. ~ic /-'ɒdɪk/ a periódico. ~ical /-'ɒdɪkl/ n periódico m. ~ically /-'ɒdɪklɪ/ adv periodicamente

peripher|y /pəˈrɪfərɪ/ n periferia f. ~al a periférico; (fig) marginal, à margem

perish /'perɪʃ/ vi morrer, perecer; (rot) estragar-se, deteriorar-se. ~able a (of goods) deteriorável

perjur|e /'pɜːdʒə(r)/ vpr ~e o.s. jurar falso, perjurar. ~y n perjúrio m

perk[1] /pɜːk/ vt/i ~ up (colloq) arrebitar(-se). ~y a (colloq) vivo, animado

perk[2] /pɜːk/ n (colloq) regalia f, extra m

perm /pɜːm/ n permanente f □ vt have one's hair ~ed fazer uma permanente

permanen|t /'pɜːmənənt/ a permanente. ~ce n permanência f. ~tly adv permanentemente, a título permanente

permeable /'pɜːmɪəbl/ a permeável

permeate /'pɜːmɪeɪt/ vt/i permear, penetrar

permissible /pəˈmɪsəbl/ a permissível, admissível

permission /pəˈmɪʃn/ n permissão f, licença f

permissive /pəˈmɪsɪv/ a permissivo. ~ society sociedade f permissiva. ~ness n permissividade f

permit[1] /pəˈmɪt/ vt (pt permitted) permitir, consentir (sb to a alguém que)

permit[2] /'pɜːmɪt/ n licença f, (pass) passe m

permutation /pɜːmjuːˈteɪʃn/ n permutação f

pernicious /pəˈnɪʃəs/ a pernicioso, prejudicial

perpendicular /pɜːpənˈdɪkjʊlə(r)/ a & n perpendicular (f)

perpetrat|e /'pɜːpɪtreɪt/ vt perpetrar. ~or n autor m

perpetual /pəˈpetʃʊəl/ a perpétuo

perpetuate /pəˈpetʃʊeɪt/ vt perpetuar

perplex /pəˈpleks/ vt deixar perplexo. ~ed a perplexo. ~ing a confuso. ~ity n perplexidade f

persecut|e /'pɜːsɪkjuːt/ vt perseguir. ~ion n /-'kjuːʃn/ n perseguição f

persever|e /pɜːsɪˈvɪə(r)/ vi perseverar. ~ance n perseverança f

Persian /'pɜːʃn/ a & n (lang) persa (m)

persist /pəˈsɪst/ vi persistir (in doing em fazer). ~ence n persistência f. ~ent a persistente; (obstinate) teimoso; (continual) contínuo, constante. ~ently adv persistentemente

person /'pɜːsn/ n pessoa f. in ~ em pessoa

personal /'pɜːsənl/ a pessoal; (secretary) particular. ~ stereo estereo m pessoal. ~ly adv pessoalmente

personality /pɜːsəˈnælətɪ/ n personalidade f; (on TV) vedete f

personify /pəˈsɒnɪfaɪ/ vt personificar

personnel /pɜːsəˈnel/ n pessoal m

perspective /pəˈspektɪv/ n perspectiva f

perspir|e /pəˈspaɪə(r)/ vi transpirar. ~ation /-əˈreɪʃn/ n transpiração f

persua|de /pəˈsweɪd/ vt persuadir (to a). ~sion /-'sweɪʒn/ n persuasão f, (belief) crença f, convicção f. ~sive /-'sweɪsɪv/ a persuasivo

pert /pɜːt/ a (saucy) atrevido, descarado; (lively) vivo

pertain /pəˈteɪn/ vi ~ to pertencer a; (be relevant) ser pertinente a, (P) ser próprio de

pertinent /'pɜːtɪnənt/ a pertinente

perturb /pəˈtɜːb/ vt perturbar, transtornar

Peru /pəˈruː/ n Peru m. ~vian a & n peruano (m), (P) peruviano (m)

peruse /pəˈruːz/ vt ler com atenção

perva|de /pəˈveɪd/ vt espalhar-se por, invadir. ~sive a penetrante

pervers|e /pəˈvɜːs/ a que insiste no erro; (wicked) perverso; (wayward) caprichoso. ~ity n obstinação f, (wickedness) perversidade f, (waywardness) capricho m, birra f

perver|t[1] /pəˈvɜːt/ vt perverter. ~sion n perversão f

pervert[2] /'pɜːvɜːt/ n pervertido m

peseta /pəˈseɪtə/ n peseta f

pessimis|t /'pesɪmɪst/ n pessimista mf. ~m /-zəm/ n pessimismo m. ~tic /-'mɪstɪk/ a pessimista

pest /pest/ n inseto m, (P) insecto m nocivo; (animal) animal m daninho; (person) peste f

pester /'pestə(r)/ vt incomodar (colloq)

pesticide /'pestɪsaɪd/ n pesticida m

pet /pet/ n animal m de estimação; (*favourite*) preferido m, querido m □ a (*rabbit etc*) de estimação □ vt (*pt petted*) acariciar. ~ **name** nome m usado em família

petal /'petl/ n pétala f

peter /'pi:tə(r)/ vi ~ **out** extinguir-se, acabar pouco a pouco, morrer (*fig*)

petition /pɪ'tɪʃn/ n petição f □ vt requerer

petrify /'petrɪfaɪ/ vt petrificar

petrol /'petrəl/ n gasolina f. ~ **pump** bomba f de gasolina. ~ **station** posto m de gasolina. ~ **tank** tanque m de gasolina

petroleum /pɪ'trəʊliəm/ n petróleo m

petticoat /'petɪkəʊt/ n combinação f, anágua f

petty /'petɪ/ a (-ier, -iest) pequeno, insignificante; (*mean*) mesquinho. ~ **cash** fundo m para pequenas despesas, caixa f pequena

petulan|t /'petjʊlənt/ a irritável. ~**ce** n irritabilidade f

pew /pju:/ n banco (de igreja) m

pewter /'pju:tə(r)/ n estanho m

phallic /'fælɪk/ a fálico

phantom /'fæntəm/ n fantasma m

pharmaceutical /ˌfa:mə'sju:tɪkl/ a farmacêutico

pharmac|y /'fa:məsɪ/ n farmácia f. ~**ist** n farmacêutico m

phase /feɪz/ n fase f □ vt ~ **in/out** introduzir/retirar progressivamente

PhD abbr of **Doctor of Philosophy** n doutorado m

pheasant /'feznt/ n faisão m

phenomen|on /fɪ'nɒmɪnən/ n (pl -ena) fenómeno m, (P) fenómeno m. ~**al** a fenomenal

philanthrop|ist /fɪ'lænθrəpɪst/ n filantropo m. ~**ic** /-ən'θrɒpɪk/ a filantrópico

Philippines /'fɪlɪpi:nz/ npl the ~ as Filipinas fpl

philistine /'fɪlɪstaɪn/ n filisteu m

philosoph|y /fɪ'lɒsəfɪ/ n filosofia f. ~**er** n filósofo m. ~**ical** /-ə'sɒfɪkl/ a filosófico

phlegm /flem/ n (*med*) catarro m, fleuma f

phobia /'fəʊbɪə/ n fobia f

phone /fəʊn/ n (*colloq*) telefone m □ vt/i (*colloq*) telefonar (para). **on the** ~ no telefone. ~ **back** voltar a telefonar, ligar de volta. ~ **book** lista f telefónica, (P) telefónica. ~ **box** cabine f telefónica, (P) telefónica. ~ **call** chamada f, telefonema m. ~**-in** n programa m de rádio ou tv com participação dos ouvintes

phonecard /'fəʊnka:d/ n cartão m para uso em telefone público

phonetic /fə'netɪk/ a fonetico. ~**s** n fonética f

phoney /'fəʊnɪ/ a (-ier, -iest) (*sl*) falso, fingido □ n (*sl: person*) fingido m; (*sl: thing*) falso m, (P) falsificação f

phosphate /'fɒsfeɪt/ n fosfato m

phosphorus /'fɒsfərəs/ n fósforo m

photo /'fəʊtəʊ/ n (pl -os) (*colloq*) retrato m, foto f

photocop|y /'fəʊtəʊkɒpɪ/ n fotocópia f □ vt fotocopiar. ~**ier** n fotocopiadora f

photogenic /fəʊtəʊ'dʒenɪk/ a fotogênico, (P) fotogénico

photograph /'fəʊtəgra:f/ n fotografia f □ vt fotografar. ~**er** /fə'tɒgrəfə(r)/ n fotógrafo m. ~**ic** /-'græfɪk/ a fotográfico. ~**y** /fə'tɒgrəfɪ/ n fotografia f

phrase /freɪz/ n expressão f, frase f; (*gram*) locução f, frase f elíptica □ vt exprimir. ~**-book** n livro m de expressões idiomáticas

physical /'fɪzɪkl/ a físico

physician /fɪ'zɪʃn/ n médico m

physicist /'fɪzɪsɪst/ n físico m

physics /'fɪzɪks/ n física f

physiology /fɪzɪ'ɒlədʒɪ/ n fisiologia f

physiotherap|y /fɪzɪəʊ'θerəpɪ/ n fisioterapia f. ~**ist** n fisioterapeuta mf

physique /fɪ'zi:k/ n físico m

pian|o /pɪ'ænəʊ/ n (pl -os) piano m. ~**ist** /'pɪənɪst/ n pianista mf

pick[1] /pɪk/ n (*tool*) picareta f

pick[2] /pɪk/ vt escolher; (*flowers, fruit etc*) colher; (*lock*) forçar; (*teeth*) palitar □ n escolha f; (*best*) o/a melhor. ~ **a quarrel with** puxar uma briga com. ~ **holes in an argument** descobrir os pontos fracos dum argumento. ~ **sb's pocket** bater a carteira de alg. ~ **off** tirar, arrancar. ~ **on** implicar com. ~ **out** escolher; (*identify*) identificar, reconhecer. ~ **up** vt apanhar; (*speed*) ganhar. **take one's** ~ escolher livremente

pickaxe /'pɪkæks/ n picareta f

picket /'pɪkɪt/ n piquete m; (*single striker*) grevista mf de piquete □ vt (*pt picketed*) colocar um piquete em □ vi fazer piquete

pickings /'pɪkɪŋz/ npl restos mpl

pickle /'pɪkl/ n vinagre m. ~**s** picles mpl, (P) pickles mpl □ vt conservar em vinagre. **in a** ~ (*colloq*) numa encrenca (*colloq*)

pickpocket /'pɪkpɒkɪt/ n batedor m de carteiras, (P) carteirista m

picnic /'pɪknɪk/ n piquenique m □ vi (*pt picnicked*) piquenicar, (P) fazer um piquenique

pictorial /pɪk'tɔ:rɪəl/ a ilustrado

picture /'pɪktʃə(r)/ n imagem f; (*illustration*) estampa f, ilustração f; (*painting*) quadro m, pintura f;

(*photo*) fotografia *f*, retrato *m*; (*drawing*) desenho *m*; (*fig*) descrição *f*, quadro *m* □ *vt* imaginar; (*describe*) pintar, descrever. **the ∼s** o cinema

picturesque /pɪktʃəˈresk/ *a* pitoresco

pidgin /ˈpɪdʒɪn/ *a* **∼ English** inglês *m* estropiado

pie /paɪ/ *n* torta *f*, (P) tarte *f*; (*of meat*) empada *f*

piece /piːs/ *n* pedaço *m*, bocado *m*; (*of machine, in game*) peça *f*; (*of currency*) moeda *f* □ *vt* **∼ together** juntar, montar. **a ∼ of advice/furniture/** *etc* um conselho/um móvel/*etc*. **∼-work** *n* trabalho *m* por, (P) a peça *or* por, (P) a tarefa. **take to ∼s** desmontar

piecemeal /ˈpiːsmiːl/ *a* aos poucos, pouco a pouco

pier /pɪə(r)/ *n* molhe *m*

pierc|e /pɪəs/ *vt* furar, penetrar. **∼ing** *a* penetrante; (*of scream, pain*) lancinante

piety /ˈpaɪətɪ/ *n* piedade *f*, devoção *f*

pig /pɪg/ *n* porco *m*. **∼-headed** *a* cabeçudo, teimoso

pigeon /ˈpɪdʒɪn/ *n* pombo *m*. **∼-hole** *n* escaninho *m*

piggy /ˈpɪgɪ/ *a* como um porco. **∼-back** *adv* nas costas. **∼ bank** cofre *m* de criança

pigment /ˈpɪgmənt/ *n* pigmento *m*. **∼ation** /-ˈteɪʃn/ *n* pigmentação *f*

pigsty /ˈpɪgstaɪ/ *n* pocilga *f*, chiqueiro *m*

pigtail /ˈpɪgteɪl/ *n* trança *f*

pike /paɪk/ *n* (*pl invar*) (*fish*) lúcio *m*

pilchard /ˈpɪltʃəd/ *n* peixe *m* pequeno da família do arenque, sardinha *f* européia

pile /paɪl/ *n* pilha *f*; (*of carpet*) pêlo *m* □ *vt/i* amontoar(-se), empilhar(-se) (**into** em). **a ∼ of** (*colloq*) um monte de (*colloq*). **∼ up** acumular(-se). **∼-up** *n* choque *m* em cadeia

piles /paɪlz/ *npl* hemorróidas *fpl*

pilfer /ˈpɪlfə(r)/ *vt* furtar. **∼age** *n* furto *m* (de coisas pequenas *or* em pequenas quantidades)

pilgrim /ˈpɪlgrɪm/ *n* peregrino *m*, romeiro *m*. **∼age** *n* peregrinação *f*, romaria *f*

pill /pɪl/ *n* pílula *f*, comprimido *m*

pillage /ˈpɪlɪdʒ/ *n* pilhagem *f*, saque *m* □ *vt* pilhar, saquear

pillar /ˈpɪlə(r)/ *n* pilar *m*. **∼-box** *n* marco *m* do correio

pillion /ˈpɪlɪən/ *n* assento *m* traseiro de motorizada. **ride ∼** ir no assento de trás

pillow /ˈpɪləʊ/ *n* travesseiro *m*

pillowcase /ˈpɪləʊkeɪs/ *n* fronha *f*

pilot /ˈpaɪlət/ *n* piloto *m* □ *vt* (*pt piloted*) pilotar. **∼-light** *n* piloto *m*;

(*electr*) lâmpada *f* testemunho; (*gas*) piloto *m*

pimento /pɪˈmentəʊ/ *n* (*pl* -os) pimentão *m* vermelho

pimple /ˈpɪmpl/ *n* borbulha *f*, espinha *f*

pin /pɪn/ *n* alfinete *m*; (*techn*) cavilha *f* □ *vt* (*pt pinned*) pregar *or* prender com alfinete(s); (*hold down*) prender, segurar. **have ∼s and needles** estar com cãibra. **∼ sb down** (*fig*) obrigar alg a definir-se, apertar alg (*fig*). **∼-point** *vt* localizar com precisão. **∼-stripe** *a* de listras finas. **∼ up** pregar. **∼-up** *n* (*colloq*) pin-up *f*

pinafore /ˈpɪnəfɔː(r)/ *n* avental *m*. **∼ dress** veste *f*

pincers /ˈpɪnsəz/ *npl* (*tool*) torquês *f*, (P) alicate *m*; (*med*) pinça *f*; (*zool*) pinça(s) *f*(*pl*), tenaz(es) *f* (*pl*)

pinch /pɪntʃ/ *vt* apertar; (*sl: steal*) surripiar (*colloq*) □ *n* aperto *m*; (*tweak*) beliscão *m*; (*small amount*) pitada *f*. **at a ∼** em caso de necessidade

pine[1] /paɪn/ *n* (*tree*) pinheiro *m*; (*wood*) pinho *m*

pine[2] /paɪn/ *vi* **∼ away** definhar, consumir-se. **∼ for** suspirar por

pineapple /ˈpaɪnæpl/ *n* abacaxi *m*, (P) ananás *m*

ping-pong /ˈpɪŋpɒŋ/ *n* pingue-pongue *m*

pink /pɪŋk/ *a & n* rosa (*m*)

pinnacle /ˈpɪnəkl/ *n* pináculo *m*

pint /paɪnt/ *n* quartilho *m* (= *0,57l*; *Amer* = *0,47l*)

pioneer /paɪəˈnɪə(r)/ *n* pioneiro *m* □ *vt* ser o pioneiro em, preparar o caminho para

pious /ˈpaɪəs/ *a* piedoso, devoto

pip /pɪp/ *n* (*seed*) pevide *f*

pipe /paɪp/ *n* cano *m*, tubo *m*; (*of smoker*) cachimbo *m* □ *vt* encanar, canalizer **∼ down** calar a boca

pipeline /ˈpaɪplaɪn/ *n* (*for oil*) oleoduto *m*; (*for gas*) gaseoduto *m*, (P) gasoduto *m*. **in the ∼** (*fig*) encaminhado

piping /ˈpaɪpɪŋ/ *n* tubagem *f*. **∼ hot** muito quente

piquant /ˈpiːkənt/ *a* picante

pira|te /ˈpaɪərət/ *n* pirata *m*. **∼cy** *n* pirataria *f*

Pisces /ˈpaɪsiːz/ *n* (*astr*) Peixe *m*, (P) Pisces *m*

pistol /ˈpɪstl/ *n* pistola *f*

piston /ˈpɪstən/ *n* êmbolo *m*, pistão *m*

pit /pɪt/ *n* (*hole*) cova *f*, fosso *m*; (*mine*) poço *m*; (*quarry*) pedreira *f* □ *vt* (*pt pitted*) picar, esburacar; (*fig*) opor. **∼ o.s. against** (*struggle*) medir-se com

pitch[1] /pɪtʃ/ *n* breu *m*. **∼-black** *a* escuro como breu

pitch² /pɪtʃ/ vt (*throw*) lançar; (*tent*) armar □ vi cair □ n (*slope*) declive m; (*of sound*) som m; (*of voice*) altura f; (*sport*) campo m

pitchfork /'pɪtʃfɔ:k/ n forcado m

pitfall /'pɪtfɔ:l/ n (*fig*) cilada f, perigo m inesperado

pith /pɪθ/ n (*of orange*) parte f branca da casca, mesocarpo m; (*fig: essential part*) cerne m, âmago m

pithy /'pɪθɪ/ a (-ier, -iest) preciso, conciso

piti|ful /'pɪtɪfl/ a lastimoso; (*contemptible*) miserável. ~**less** a impiedoso

pittance /'pɪtns/ n salário m miserável, miséria f

pity /'pɪtɪ/ n dó m, pena f, piedade f □ vt compadecer-se de. **it's a** ~ é uma pena. **take** ~ **on** ter pena de. **what a** ~**!** que pena!

pivot /'pɪvət/ n eixo m □ vt (*pt pivoted*) girar em torno de

placard /'plæka:d/ n (*poster*) cartaz m

placate /plə'keɪt/ vt apaziguar, aplacar

place /pleɪs/ n lugar m, sítio m; (*house*) casa f; (*seat, rank etc*) lugar m □ vt colocar, pôr. ~ **an order** fazer uma encomenda. **at/to my** ~ em a or na minha casa. ~**-mat** n pano m de mesa individual, (P) napperon m à americana

placid /'plæsɪd/ a plácido

plagiar|ize /'pleɪdʒəraɪz/ vt plagiar. ~**ism** n plágio m

plague /pleɪg/ n peste f; (*of insects*) praga f □ vt atormentar, atazanar

plaice /pleɪs/ n (*pl invar*) solha f

plain /pleɪn/ a (-er, -est) claro; (*candid*) franco; (*simple*) simples; (*not pretty*) sem beleza; (*not patterned*) liso □ adv com franqueza □ n planície f. **in** ~ **clothes** à paisana. ~**ly** adv claramente; (*candidly*) francamente

plaintiff /'pleɪntɪf/ n queixoso m

plaintive /'pleɪntɪv/ a queixoso

plait /plæt/ vt entrançar □ n trança f

plan /plæn/ n plano m, projeto m, (P) projecto m; (*of a house, city etc*) plano m, planta f □ vt (*pt planned*) planear, planejar □ vi fazer planos. ~ **to do** ter a intenção de fazer

plane¹ /pleɪn/ n (*level*) plano m; (*aeroplane*) avião m □ a plano

plane² /pleɪn/ n (*tool*) plaina f □ vt aplainar

planet /'plænɪt/ n planeta m

plank /plæŋk/ n prancha f

planning /'plænɪŋ/ n planeamento m, planejamento m. ~ **permission** permissão f para construir

plant /pla:nt/ n planta f; (*techn*) aparelhagem f; (*factory*) fábrica f □ vt

plantar. ~ **a bomb** colocar uma bomba. ~**ation** /-'teɪʃn/ n plantação f

plaque /pla:k/ n placa f; (*on teeth*) tártaro m, pedra f

plaster /'pla:stə(r)/ n reboco m; (*adhesive*) esparadrapo m, band-aid m □ vt rebocar; (*cover*) cobrir (**with** com, de). **in** ~ engessado. ~ **of Paris** gesso m. ~**er** n rebocador m, caiador m

plastic /'plæstɪk/ a plástico □ n plástica f. ~ **surgery** cirurgia f plástica

plate /pleɪt/ n prato m; (*in book*) gravura f □ vt revestir de metal

plateau /'plætəʊ/ n (*pl -eaux* /-əʊz/) planalto m, platô m

platform /'plætfɔ:m/ n estrado m; (*for speaking*) tribuna f; (*rail*) plataforma f, cais m; (*fig*) programa m de partido político. ~ **ticket** bilhete m de gare

platinum /'plætɪnəm/ n platina f

platitude /'plætɪtjuːd/ n banalidade f, lugar-comum m

platonic /plə'tɒnɪk/ a platônico, (P) platónico

plausible /'plɔ:zəbl/ a plausível; (*person*) convincente

play /pleɪ/ vt/i (*for amusement*) brincar; (*instrument*) tocar; (*cards, game*) jogar; (*opponent*) jogar contra; (*match*) disputar □ n jogo m; (*theatre*) peça f; (*movement*) folga f, margem f. ~ **down** minimizar. ~ **on** (*take advantage of*) aproveitar-se de. ~ **safe** jogar pelo seguro. ~ **up** (*colloq*) dar problemas (a). ~**-group** n jardim m de infância, (P) jardim m infantil. ~**-pen** n cercado m para crianças

playboy /'pleɪbɔɪ/ n play-boy m

player /'pleɪə(r)/ n jogador m; (*theat*) artista mf; (*mus*) artista mf, executante mf, instrumentista mf

playful /'pleɪfl/ a brincalhão m

playground /'pleɪgraʊnd/ n pátio m de recreio

playing /'pleɪɪŋ/ n atuação f, (P) actuação f. ~**-card** n carta f de jogar. ~**-field** n campo m de jogos

playwright /'pleɪraɪt/ n dramaturgo m

plc abbr (*of public limited company*) SARL

plea /pli:/ n súplica f; (*reason*) pretexto m, desculpa f; (*jur*) alegação f da defesa

plead /pli:d/ vt/i pleitear; (*as excuse*) alegar. ~ **guilty** confessar-se culpado. ~ **with** implorar a

pleasant /'pleznt/ a agradável

pleas|e /pli:z/ vt/i agradar (a), dar prazer (a) □ adv por favor, (P) se faz favor. **they** ~**e themselves, they do as they** ~**e** eles fazem como bem entendem. ~**ed** *a* contente, satisfeito (with com). ~**ing** *a* agradável

pleasur|e /'pleʒə(r)/ *n* prazer *m*. ~**able** *a* agradável

pleat /pli:t/ *n* prega *f* □ *vt* preguear

pledge /pledʒ/ *n* penhor *m*, garantia *f*; (*fig*) promessa *f* □ *vt* prometer; (*pawn*) empenhar

plentiful /'plentɪfl/ *a* abundante

plenty /'plentɪ/ *n* abundância *f*, fartura *f*. ~ (of) muito (de); (*enough*) bastante (de)

pliable /'plaɪəbl/ *a* flexível

pliers /'plaɪəz/ *npl* alicate *m*

plight /plaɪt/ *n* triste situação *f*

plimsoll /'plɪmsəl/ *n* alpargata *f*, tênis *m*, (*P*) ténis *m*

plinth /plɪnθ/ *n* plinto *m*

plod /plɒd/ *vi* (*pt* **plodded**) caminhar lentamente; (*work*) trabalhar, marrar (*sl*). ~**der** *n* trabalhador *m* lento mas perseverante. ~**ding** *a* lento

plonk /plɒŋk/ *n* (*sl*) vinho *m* ordinário, (*P*) carrascão *m*

plot /plɒt/ *n* complô *m*, conspiração *f*; (*of novel etc*) trama *f*; (*of land*) lote *m* □ *vt/i* (*pt* **plotted**) conspirar; (*mark out*) traçar

plough /plaʊ/ *n* arado *m* □ *vt/i* arar. ~ **back** reinvestir. ~ **into** colidir. ~ **through** abrir caminho por

ploy /plɔɪ/ *n* (*colloq*) estratagema *m*

pluck /plʌk/ *vt* apanhar; (*bird*) depenar; (*eyebrows*) depilar; (*mus*) tanger □ *n* coragem *f*. ~ **up courage** ganhar coragem. ~**y** *a* corajoso

plug /plʌg/ *n* tampão *m*; (*electr*) tomada *f*, (*P*) ficha *f* □ *vt* (*pt* **plugged**) tapar com tampão; (*colloq: publicize*) fazer grande propaganda de □ *vi* ~ **away** (*colloq*) trabalhar com afinco. ~ **in** (*electr*) ligar. ~**hole** *n* buraco *m* do cano

plum /plʌm/ *n* ameixa *f*

plumb /plʌm/ *adv* exatamente, (*P*) exactamente, mesmo □ *vt* sondar. ~**line** *n* fio *m* de prumo

plumb|er /'plʌmə(r)/ *n* bombeiro *m*, encanador *m*, (*P*) canalizador *m*. ~**ing** *n* encanamento *m*, (*P*) canalização *f*

plummet /'plʌmɪt/ *vi* (*pt* **plummeted**) despencar

plump /plʌmp/ *a* (-er, -est) rechonchudo, roliço □ *vi* ~ **for** optar por. ~**ness** *n* gordura *f*

plunder /'plʌndə(r)/ *vt* pilhar, saquear □ *n* pilhagem *f*, saque *m*; (*goods*) despojo *m*

plunge /plʌndʒ/ *vt/i* mergulhar, atirar(-se), afundar(-se) □ *n* mergulho *m*. **take the** ~ (*fig*) decidir-se, dar o salto (*fig*)

plunger /'plʌndʒə(r)/ *n* (*of pump*)

êmbolo *m*, pistão *m*; (*for sink etc*) desentupidor *m*

pluperfect /plu:'pɜ:fɪkt/ *n* mais-que-perfeito *m*

plural /'plʊərəl/ *a* plural; (*noun*) no plural □ *n* plural *m*

plus /plʌs/ *prep* mais □ *a* positivo □ *n* sinal +; (*fig*) qualidade *f* positiva

plush /plʌʃ/ *n* pelúcia *f* □ *a* de pelúcia; (*colloq*) de luxo

ply /plaɪ/ *vt* (*tool*) manejar; (*trade*) exercer □ *vi* (*ship*, *bus*) fazer carreira entre dois lugares. ~ **sb with drink** encher alguém de bebidas

plywood /'plaɪwʊd/ *n* madeira *f* compensada

p.m. /pi:'em/ *adv* da tarde, da noite

pneumatic /nju:'mætɪk/ *a* pneumático. ~ **drill** broca *f* pneumática

pneumonia /nju:'məʊnɪə/ *n* pneumonia *f*

PO *abbr see* **Post Office**

poach /pəʊtʃ/ *vt/i* (*steal*) caçar/pescar em propriedade alheia; (*culin*) fazer pochê, (*P*) escalfar. ~**ed eggs** ovos *mpl* pochês, (*P*) ovos *mpl* escalfados

pocket /'pɒkɪt/ *n* bolso *m*, algibeira *f* □ *a* de algibeira □ *vt* meter no bolso. ~-**book** *n* (*notebook*) livro *m* de apontamentos; (*Amer: handbag*) carteira *f*. ~-**money** *n* (*monthly*) mesada *f*; (*weekly*) semanada *f*, dinheiro *m* para pequenas despesas

pod /pɒd/ *n* vagem *f*

poem /'pəʊɪm/ *n* poema *m*

poet /'pəʊɪt/ *n* poeta *m*, poetisa *f*. ~**ic** /-'etɪk/ *a* poético

poetry /'pəʊɪtrɪ/ *n* poesia *f*

poignant /'pɔɪnjənt/ *a* pungente, doloroso

point /pɔɪnt/ *n* ponto *m*; (*tip*) ponta *f*; (*decimal point*) vírgula *f*; (*meaning*) sentido *m*, razão *m*; (*electr*) tomada *f*. ~**s** (*rail*) agulhas *fpl* □ *vt/i* (*aim*) apontar (**at** para); (*show*) apontar, indicar (**at/to** para). **on the** ~ **of** prestes a, quase a. ~-**blank** *a* & *adv* à queima-roupa; (*fig*) categórico. ~ **of view** ponto *m* de vista. ~ **out** apontar, fazer ver. **that is a good** ~ (*remark*) é uma boa observação. **to the** ~ a propósito. **what is the** ~? de que adianta?

pointed /'pɔɪntɪd/ *a* ponteagudo; (*of remark*) intencional, contundente

pointer /'pɔɪntə(r)/ *n* ponteiro *m*; (*colloq: hint*) sugestão *f*

pointless /'pɔɪntlɪs/ *a* inútil, sem sentido

poise /pɔɪz/ *n* equilíbrio *m*; (*carriage*) porte *m*; (*fig: self-possession*) presença *f*, segurança *f*. ~**d** *a* equilibrado; (*person*) seguro de si

poison /'pɔɪzn/ n veneno m, peçonha f □ vt envenenar. **blood-~ing** n envenenamento m do sangue. **food-~ing** n intoxicação f alimentar. **~ous** a venenoso

poke /pəʊk/ vt/i espetar; (with elbow) acotovelar; (fire) atiçar □ n espetadela f; (with elbow) cotovelada f. ~ **about** esgaravatar, remexer, procurar. ~ **out** (head) enfiar. ~ **fun at** fazer troça/pouco de. ~ **out** (head) enfiar

poker[1] /'pəʊkə(r)/ n atiçador m

poker[2] /'pəʊkə(r)/ n (cards) pôquer m, (P) póquer m

poky /'pəʊki/ a (-ier, -iest) acanhado, apertado

Poland /'pəʊlənd/ n Polônia f, (P) Polónia f

polar /'pəʊlə(r)/ a polar. ~ **bear** urso m branco

polarize /'pəʊləraɪz/ vt polarizar

pole[1] /pəʊl/ n vara f; (for flag) mastro m; (post) poste m

pole[2] /pəʊl/ n (geog) pólo m

Pole /pəʊl/ n polaco m

polemic /pə'lemɪk/ n polêmica f, (P) polémica f

police /pə'li:s/ n polícia f □ vt policiar. ~ **state** estado m policial. ~ **station** distrito m, delegacia f, (P) esquadra f de polícia

police|man /pə'li:smən/ n (pl -men) policial m, (P) polícia m, guarda m, agente m de polícia. **~-woman** (pl -women) n polícia f feminina, (P) mulher-polícia f

policy[1] /'pɒlɪsɪ/ n (plan of action) política f

policy[2] /'pɒlɪsɪ/ n (insurance) apólice f de seguro

polio /'pəʊlɪəʊ/ n polio f

polish /'pɒlɪʃ/ vt polir, dar lustro em; (shoes) engraxar; (floor) encerar □ n (for shoes) graxa f; (for floor) cera f; (for nails) esmalte m, (P) verniz m; (shine) polimento m; (fig) requinte m. ~ **off** acabar (rapidamente). ~ **up** (language) aperfeiçoar. **~ed** a requintado, elegante

Polish /'pəʊlɪʃ/ a & n polonês (m), (P) polaco (m)

polite /pə'laɪt/ a polido, educado, delicado. **~ly** adv delicadamente. **~ness** n delicadeza f, cortesia f

political /pə'lɪtɪkl/ a político

politician /pɒlɪ'tɪʃn/ n político m

politics /'pɒlətɪks/ n política f

polka /'pɒlkə/ n polca f. ~ **dots** bolas fpl

poll /pəʊl/ n votação f; (survey) sondagem f, pesquisa f □ vt (votes) obter. **go to the ~s** votar, ir às urnas. **~ing-booth** n cabine f de voto

pollen /'pɒlən/ n pólen m

pollut|e /pə'lu:t/ vt poluir. **~ion** /-ʃn/ n poluição f

polo /'pəʊləʊ/ n pólo m. ~ **neck** gola f rolê

polyester /pɒlɪ'estə/ n poliéster m

polytechnic /pɒlɪ'teknɪk/ n politécnica f

polythene /'pɒlɪθi:n/ n politeno m. ~ **bag** n saco m de plástico

pomegranate /'pɒmɪgrænɪt/ n romã f

pomp /pɒmp/ n pompa f

pompon /'pɒmpɒn/ n pompom m

pomp|ous /'pɒmpəs/ a pomposo. **~osity** /-'pɒsətɪ/ n imponência f

pond /pɒnd/ n lagoa f, lago m; (artificial) tanque m, lago m

ponder /'pɒndə(r)/ vt/i ponderar, meditar (over sobre)

pong /pɒŋ/ n (sl) pivete m □ vi (sl) cheirar mal, tresandar

pony /'pəʊnɪ/ n pônei m, (P) pónei m. **~-tail** n rabo m de cavalo. **~-trekking** n passeio m de pônei, (P) pónei

poodle /'pu:dl/ n cão m de água, caniche m

pool[1] /pu:l/ n (puddle) charco m, poça f; (for swimming) piscina f

pool[2] /pu:l/ n (fund) fundo m comum; (econ, comm) pool m; (game) forma f de bilhar. **~s** loteca f, (P) totobola m □ vt pôr num fundo comum

poor /pʊə(r)/ a (-er, -est) pobre; (not good) medíocre. **~ly** adv mal □ a doente

pop[1] /pɒp/ n estalido m, ruído m seco □ vt/i (pt popped) dar um estalido, estalar; (of cork) saltar. ~ **in/out/off** entrar/sair/ir-se embora. ~ **up** aparecer de repente, saltar

pop[2] /pɒp/ n música f pop □ a pop invar

popcorn /'pɒpkɔ:n/ n pipoca f

pope /pəʊp/ n papa m

poplar /'pɒplə(r)/ n choupo m, álamo m

poppy /'pɒpɪ/ n papoula f

popular /'pɒpjʊlə(r)/ a popular; (in fashion) em voga, na moda. **be ~ with** ser popular entre. **~ity** /-'lærətɪ/ n popularidade f. **~ize** vt popularizar, vulgarizar

populat|e /'pɒpjʊleɪt/ vt povoar. **~ion** /-'leɪʃn/ n população f

populous /'pɒpjʊləs/ a populoso

porcelain /'pɔ:slɪn/ n porcelana f

porch /pɔ:tʃ/ n alpendre m; (Amer) varanda f

porcupine /'pɔ:kjʊpaɪn/ n porco-espinho m

pore[1] /pɔ:(r)/ n poro m

pore[2] /pɔ:(r)/ vi ~ **over** examinar, estudar

pork /pɔ:k/ n carne f de porco

pornograph|y /pɔːˈnɒɡrəfɪ/ n pornografia f. **~ic** /-əˈɡræfɪk/ a pornográfico

porous /ˈpɔːrəs/ a poroso

porpoise /ˈpɔːpəs/ n toninha f, (P) golfinho m

porridge /ˈpɒrɪdʒ/ n (papa f de) flocos mpl de aveia

port[1] /pɔːt/ n (harbour) porto m

port[2] /pɔːt/ n (wine) (vinho do) Porto m

portable /ˈpɔːtəbl/ a portátil

porter[1] /ˈpɔːtə(r)/ n (carrier) carregador m

porter[2] /ˈpɔːtə(r)/ n (doorkeeper) porteiro m

portfolio /pɔːtˈfəʊlɪəʊ/ n (pl -os) (case, post) pasta f; (securities) carteira f de investimentos

porthole /ˈpɔːθəʊl/ n vigia f

portion /ˈpɔːʃn/ n (share, helping) porção f; (part) parte f

portly /ˈpɔːtlɪ/ a (-ier, -iest) corpulento e digno

portrait /ˈpɔːtrɪt/ n retrato m

portray /pɔːˈtreɪ/ vt retratar, pintar; (fig) descrever. **~al** n retrato m

Portug|al /ˈpɔːtjʊɡl/ n Portugal m. **~uese** /-ˈɡiːz/ a & n invar português (m)

pose /pəʊz/ vt/i (fazer) posar; (question) fazer □ n pose f, postura f. **~ as** fazer-se passar por

poser /ˈpəʊzə(r)/ n quebra-cabeças m

posh /pɒʃ/ a (sl) chique invar

position /pəˈzɪʃn/ n posição f; (job) lugar m, colocação f; (state) situação f □ vt colocar

positive /ˈpɒzətɪv/ a positivo; (definite) categórico, definitivo; (colloq: downright) autêntico. **she's ~ that** ela tem certeza que. **~ly** adv positivamente; (absolutely) completamente

possess /pəˈzes/ vt possuir. **~ion** /-ʃn/ n posse f; (thing possessed) possessão f. **~or** n possuidor m

possessive /pəˈzesɪv/ a possessivo

possib|le /ˈpɒsəbl/ a possível. **~ility** /-ˈbɪlətɪ/ n possibilidade f

possibly /ˈpɒsəblɪ/ adv possivelmente, talvez. **if I ~ can** se me fôr possível. **I cannot ~ leave** estou impossibilitado de partir

post[1] /pəʊst/ n (pole) poste m □ vt (notice) afixar, pregar

post[2] /pəʊst/ n (station, job) posto m □ vt colocar; (appoint) colocar

post[3] /pəʊst/ n (mail) correio m □ a postal □ vt mandar pelo correio. **keep ~ed** manter informado. **~code** n código m postal. **P~ Office** agência f dos correios, (P) estação f dos correios; (corporation) Departamento m dos Correios e Telégrafos, (P) Cor-

reios, Telégrafos e Telefones mpl (CTT)

post- /pəʊst/ pref pós-

postage /ˈpəʊstɪdʒ/ n porte m

postal /ˈpəʊstl/ a postal. **~ order** vale m postal

postcard /ˈpəʊstkaːd/ n cartão-postal m, (P) (bilhete) postal m

poster /ˈpəʊstə(r)/ n cartaz m

posterity /pɒˈsterətɪ/ n posteridade f

postgraduate /pəʊstˈɡrædʒʊet/ n pós-graduado m

posthumous /ˈpɒstjʊməs/ a póstumo. **~ly** adv a título póstumo

postman /ˈpəʊstmən/ n (pl -men) carteiro m

postmark /ˈpəʊstmaːk/ n carimbo m do correio

post-mortem /pəʊstˈmɔːtəm/ n autópsia f

postpone /pəˈspəʊn/ vt adiar. **~ment** n adiamento m

postscript /ˈpəʊsskrɪpt/ n post scriptum m

postulate /ˈpɒstjʊleɪt/ vt postular

posture /ˈpɒstʃə(r)/ n postura f, posição f □ vi posar

post-war /ˈpəʊstwɔː(r)/ a de após-guerra

posy /ˈpəʊzɪ/ n raminho m de flores

pot /pɒt/ n pote m; (for cooking) panela f; (for plants) vaso m; (sl: marijuana) maconha f □ vt (pt potted) **~ (up)** plantar em vaso. **go to ~** (sl: business) arruinar, degringolar (colloq); (sl: person) estar arruinado or liquidado. **~-belly** n pança f, barriga f. **take ~ luck** aceitar o que houver. **take a ~-shot** dar um tiro de perto (at em); (at random) dar um tiro a esmo (at em)

potato /pəˈteɪtəʊ/ n (pl -oes) batata f

poten|t /ˈpəʊtnt/ a potente, poderoso; (drink) forte. **~cy** n potência f

potential /pəˈtenʃl/ a & n potencial (m). **~ly** adv potencialmente

pothol|e /ˈpɒthəʊl/ n caverna f, caldeirão m; (in road) buraco m. **~ing** n espeleologia f

potion /ˈpəʊʃn/ n poção f

potted /ˈpɒtɪd/ a (of plant) de vaso; (preserved) de conserva

potter[1] /ˈpɒtə(r)/ n oleiro m, ceramista mf. **~y** n olaria f, cerâmica f

potter[2] /ˈpɒtə(r)/ vi entreter-se com isto ou aquilo

potty[1] /ˈpɒtɪ/ a (-ier, -iest) (sl) doido, pirado (sl), (P) chanfrado (colloq)

potty[2] /ˈpɒtɪ/ n (-ties) (colloq) penico m de criança

pouch /paʊtʃ/ n bolsa f; (for tobacco) tabaqueira f

poultice /ˈpəʊltɪs/ n cataplasma f

poultry /'pəʊltrɪ/ *n* aves *fpl* domésticas

pounce /paʊns/ *vi* atirar-se (**on** sobre, para cima de) □ *n* salto *m*

pound[1] /paʊnd/ *n* (*weight*) libra *f* (= 453 g); (*money*) libra *f*

pound[2] /paʊnd/ *n* (*for dogs*) canil municipal *m*; (*for cars*) parque de viaturas rebocadas *m*

pound[3] /paʊnd/ *vt/i* (*crush*) esmagar, pisar; (*of heart*) bater com força; (*bombard*) bombardear; (*on piano etc*) martelar

pour /pɔː(r)/ *vt* deitar □ *vi* correr; (*rain*) chover torrencialmente. ~ **in/out** (*of people*) afluir/sair em massa. ~ **off** *or* **out** esvaziar, vazar. ~**ing rain** chuva *f* torrencial

pout /paʊt/ *vt/i* ~ (**one's lips**) (*sulk*) fazer beicinho; (*in annoyance*) ficar de trombas □ *n* beicinho *m*

poverty /'pɒvətɪ/ *n* pobreza *f*, miséria *f*. ~-**stricken** *a* pobre

powder /'paʊdə(r)/ *n* pó *m*; (*for face*) pó-de-arroz *m* □ *vt* polvilhar; (*face*) empoar. ~**ed** *a* em pó. ~-**room** *n* toalete *m*, toucador *m*. ~**y** *a* como pó

power /'paʊə(r)/ *n* poder *m*; (*maths, mech*) potência *f*; (*energy*) energia *f*; (*electr*) corrente *f*. ~ **cut** corte *m* de energia, blecaute *m*. ~ **station** central *f* elétrica, (*P*) eléctrica. ~**ed by** movido a; (*jet etc*) de propulsão. ~**ful** *a* poderoso; (*mech*) potente. ~**less** *a* impotente

practicable /'præktɪkəbl/ *a* viável

practical /'præktɪkl/ *a* prático. ~ **joke** brincadeira *f* de mau gosto

practically /'præktɪklɪ/ *adv* praticamente

practice /'præktɪs/ *n* prática *f*; (*of law etc*) exercício *m*; (*sport*) treino *m*; (*clients*) clientela *f*. **in** ~ (*in fact*) na prática; (*well-trained*) em forma. **out of** ~ destreinado, sem prática. **put into** ~ pôr em prática

practis|e /'præktɪs/ *vt/i* (*skill, sport*) praticar, exercitar-se em; (*profession*) exercer; (*put into practice*) pôr em prática. ~**ed** *a* experimentado, experiente. ~**ing** *a* (*Catholic etc*) praticante

practitioner /præk'tɪʃənə(r)/ *n* praticante *mf*. **general** ~ médico *m* de clínica geral *or* de família

pragmatic /præg'mætɪk/ *a* pragmático

prairie /'preərɪ/ *n* pradaria *f*

praise /preɪz/ *vt* louvar, elogiar □ *n* elogio(s) *m(pl)*, louvor(es) *m(pl)*

praiseworthy /'preɪzwɜːðɪ/ *a* louvável, digno de louvor

pram /præm/ *n* carrinho *m* de bebê, (*P*) bebé

prance /pra:ns/ *vi* (*of horse*) curvetear, empinar-se; (*of person*) pavonear-se

prank /præŋk/ *n* brincadeira *f* de mau gosto

prattle /'prætl/ *vi* tagarelar

prawn /prɔːn/ *n* camarão *m* grande, (*P*) gamba *f*

pray /preɪ/ *vi* rezar, orar

prayer /preə(r)/ *n* oração *f*. **the Lord's P~** o Padre-Nosso. ~-**book** *n* missal *m*

pre- /priː/ *pref* pré-

preach /priːtʃ/ *vt/i* pregar (**at, to** a). ~**er** *n* pregador *m*

preamble /priː'æmbl/ *n* preâmbulo *m*

prearrange /priːə'reɪndʒ/ *vt* combinar *or* arranjar de antemão

precarious /prɪ'keərɪəs/ *a* precário; (*of position*) instável, inseguro

precaution /prɪ'kɔːʃn/ *n* precaução *f*. ~**ary** *a* de precaução

preced|e /prɪ'siːd/ *vt* preceder. ~**ing** *a* precedente

precedent /'presɪdənt/ *n* precedente *m*

precinct /'priːsɪŋkt/ *n* precinto *m*; (*Amer: district*) circunscrição *f*. (**pedestrian**) ~ área *f* de pedestres, (*P*) zona *f* para peões

precious /'preʃəs/ *a* precioso

precipice /'presɪpɪs/ *n* precipício *m*

precipitat|e /prɪ'sɪpɪteɪt/ *vt* precipitar □ *a* /-ɪtət/ precipitado. ~**ion** /-'teɪʃn/ *n* precipitação *f*

precis|e /prɪ'saɪs/ *a* preciso; (*careful*) meticuloso. ~**ely** *adv* precisamente. ~**ion** /-'sɪʒn/ *n* precisão *f*

preclude /prɪ'kluːd/ *vt* evitar, excluir, impedir

precocious /prɪ'kəʊʃəs/ *a* precoce

preconc|eived /priːkən'siːvd/ *a* preconcebido. ~**eption** /priːkən'sepʃn/ *n* idéia *f* preconcebida

precursor /priː'kɜːsə(r)/ *n* precursor *m*

predator /'predətə(r)/ *n* animal *m* de rapina, predador *m*. ~**y** *a* predatório

predecessor /'priːdɪsesə(r)/ *n* predecessor *m*

predicament /prɪ'dɪkəmənt/ *n* situação *f* difícil

predict /prɪ'dɪkt/ *vt* predizer, prognosticar. ~**able** *a* previsível. ~**ion** /-ʃn/ *n* predição *f*, prognóstico *m*

predominant /prɪ'dɒmɪnənt/ *a* predominante, preponderante. ~**ly** *adv* predominantemente, preponderantemente

predominate /prɪ'dɒmɪneɪt/ *vi* predominar

pre-eminent /priː'emɪnənt/ *a* preeminente, superior

pre-empt /priː'empt/ *vt* adquirir por

preempção. **~ive** a antecipado; (mil)
preventivo

preen /priːn/ vt alisar. **~ o.s.** enfeitar-
se

prefab /'priːfæb/ n (colloq) casa f pré-
fabricada. **~ricated** /-'fæbrɪkeɪtɪd/ a
pré-fabricado

preface /'prefɪs/ n prefácio m

prefect /'priːfekt/ n aluno m autoriza-
do a disciplinar outros; (official) prefeito m

prefer /prɪ'fɜː(r)/ vt (pt **preferred**)
preferir. **~able** /'prefrəbl/ a preferível

preferen|ce /'prefrəns/ n preferência
f. **~tial** /-ə'renʃl/ a preferencial, pri-
vilegiada

prefix /'priːfɪks/ n (pl **-ixes**) prefixo m

pregnan|t /'pregnənt/ a (woman)
grávida; (animal) prenhe. **~cy** n
gravidez f

prehistoric /priːhɪ'stɒrɪk/ a pré-
histórico

prejudice /'predʒʊdɪs/ n preconceito
m, idéia f preconcebida, prejuízo m;
(harm) prejuízo m □ vt influenciar.
~d a com preconceitos

preliminar|y /prɪ'lɪmɪnərɪ/ a pre-
liminar. **~ies** npl preliminares mpl,
preâmbulos mpl

prelude /'prelju:d/ n prelúdio m

premarital /priː'mærɪtl/ a antes do
casamento, pré-marital

premature /'premətjʊə(r)/ a prematuro

premeditated /priː'medɪteɪtɪd/ a pre-
meditado

premier /'premɪə(r)/ a primeiro □ n
(pol) primeiro-ministro m

premises /'premɪsɪz/ npl local m,
edifício m. **on the ~** neste estabelecimento, no local

premium /'priːmɪəm/ n prêmio m, (P)
prémio m. **at a ~** a peso de ouro

premonition /priːmə'nɪʃn/ n pressentimento m

preoccup|ation /priːɒkjʊ'peɪʃn/ n
preocupação f. **~ied** /-'ɒkjʊpaɪd/ a
preocupado

preparation /prepə'reɪʃn/ n preparação f. **~s** preparativos mpl

preparatory /prɪ'pærətrɪ/ a pre-
paratório. **~ school** escola f primária
particular

prepare /prɪ'peə(r)/ vt/i preparar(-se)
(for para). **~d** to pronto a, preparado
para

preposition /prepə'zɪʃn/ n preposição f

preposterous /prɪ'pɒstərəs/ a absurdo, disparatado, ridículo

prerequisite /priː'rekwɪzɪt/ n condição f prévia

prerogative /prɪ'rɒgətɪv/ n prerrogativa f

Presbyterian /prezbɪ'tɪərɪən/ a & n
presbiteriano (m)

prescri|be /prɪ'skraɪb/ vt prescrever;
(med) receitar, prescrever. **~ption**
/-ɪpʃn/ n prescrição f; (med) receita f

presence /'prezns/ n presença f. **~ of
mind** presença f de espírito

present[1] /'preznt/ a & n presente
(mf). **at ~** no momento, presentemente

present[2] /'preznt/ n (gift) presente m

present[3] /prɪ'zent/ vt apresentar;
(film etc) dar. **~ sb with** oferecer a
alg. **~able** a apresentável. **~ation**
/prezn'teɪʃn/ n apresentação f. **~er** n
apresentador n

presently /'prezntlɪ/ adv dentro em
pouco, daqui a pouco; (Amer: now)
neste momento

preservative /prɪ'zɜːvətɪv/ n preservativo m

preserv|e /prɪ'zɜːv/ vt preservar;
(maintain; culin) conservar □ n reserva f; (fig) área f, terreno m; (jam)
compota f. **~ation** /prezə'veɪʃn/ n
conservação f

preside /prɪ'zaɪd/ vi presidir (over a)

presiden|t /'prezɪdənt/ n presidente
mf. **~cy** n presidência f. **~tial**
/-'denʃl/ a presidencial

press /pres/ vt/i carregar (on em);
(squeeze) espremer; (urge) pressionar;
(iron) passar a ferro □ n imprensa f;
(mech) prensa f; (for wine) lagar m.
be ~ed for estar apertado com falta
de. **~ on (with)** continuar (com),
prosseguir (com). **~ conference** entrevista f coletiva. **~-stud** n mola f,
botão m de pressão

pressing /'presɪŋ/ a premente, ur-
gente

pressure /'preʃə(r)/ n pressão f □ vt
fazer pressão sobre. **~-cooker** n panela f de pressão. **~ group** grupo m
de pressão

pressurize /'preʃəraɪz/ vt pressionar,
fazer pressão sobre

prestige /pre'stiːʒ/ n prestígio m

prestigious /pre'stɪdʒəs/ a prestigio-
so

presumably /prɪ'zjuːməblɪ/ adv provavelmente

presum|e /prɪ'zjuːm/ vt presumir. **~e
to** tomar a liberdade de, atrever-se a.
~ption /-ʌmpʃn/ n presunção f

presumptuous /prɪ'zʌmptʃʊəs/ a
presunçoso

pretence /prɪ'tens/ n fingimento m;
(claim) pretensão f; (pretext) desculpa
f, pretexto m

pretend /prɪ'tend/ vt/i fingir (to do
fazer). **~ to** (lay claim to) ter pretensões a, ser pretendente a; (profess to
have) pretender ter

pretentious /prɪˈtenʃəs/ a pretencioso

pretext /ˈpriːtekst/ n pretexto m

pretty /ˈprɪtɪ/ a (-ier, -iest) bonito, lindo □ adv bastante

prevail /prɪˈveɪl/ vi prevalecer. ~ on sb to convencer alguéma. ~ing a dominante

prevalen|t /ˈprevələnt/ a geral, dominante. ~ce n frequência f

prevent /prɪˈvent/ vt impedir (from doing de fazer). ~able a que se pode evitar, evitável. ~ion /-ʃn/ n prevenção f. ~ive a preventivo

preview /ˈpriːvjuː/ n pré-estréia f, (P) ante-estréia f

previous /ˈpriːvɪəs/ a precedente, anterior. ~ to antes de. ~ly adv antes, anteriormente

pre-war /priːˈwɔː(r)/ a do pré-guerra, (P) de antes da guerra

prey /preɪ/ n presa f □ vi ~ on dar caça a; (worry) preocupar, atormentar. **bird of** ~ ave f de rapina, predador m

price /praɪs/ n preço m □ vt marcar o preço de. ~less a inestimável; (colloq: amusing) impagável

prick /prɪk/ vt picar, furar □ n picada f. ~ **up one's ears** arrebitar a(s) orelha(s)

prickl|e /ˈprɪkl/ n pico m, espinho m; (sensation) picada f. ~y a espinhoso, que pica; (person) irritável

pride /praɪd/ n orgulho m □ vpr ~ o.s. on orgulhar-se de

priest /priːst/ n padre m, sacerdote m. ~hood n sacerdócio m; (clergy) clero m

prim /prɪm/ a (primmer, primmest) formal, cheio de nove-horas; (prudish) pudico

primary /ˈpraɪmərɪ/ a primário; (chief, first) primeiro. ~ **school** escola f primária

prime[1] /praɪm/ a primeiro, principal; (first-rate) de primeira qualidade. P~ **Minister** Primeiro-Ministro m. ~ **number** número m primo

prime[2] /praɪm/ vt aprontar, aprestar; (with facts) preparar; (surface) preparar, aparelhar. ~r /-ə(r)/ n (paint) aparelho m

primeval /praɪˈmiːvl/ a primitivo

primitive /ˈprɪmɪtɪv/ a primitivo

primrose /ˈprɪmrəʊz/ n primavera f, prímula f

prince /prɪns/ n príncipe m

princess /prɪnˈses/ n princesa f

principal /ˈprɪnsəpl/ a principal □ n (schol) diretor m, (P) director m. ~ly adv principalmente

principle /ˈprɪnsəpl/ n princípio m. **in/on** ~ em/por princípio

print /prɪnt/ vt imprimir; (write) escrever em letra de imprensa □ n marca f, impressão f; (letters) letra f de imprensa; (photo) prova (fotográfica) f; (engraving) gravura f. **out of** ~ esgotado. ~-**out** n cópia f impressa. ~**ed matter** impressos mpl

print|er /ˈprɪntə(r)/ n tipógrafo m; (comput) impressora f. ~**ing** n impressão f, tipografia f

prior[1] /ˈpraɪə(r)/ a anterior, precedente. ~ **to** antes de

priority /praɪˈɒrətɪ/ n prioridade f

prise /praɪz/ vt forçar (com alavanca). ~ **open** arrombar

prison /ˈprɪzn/ n prisão f. ~**er** n prisioneiro m

pristine /ˈprɪstiːn/ a primitivo; (condition) perfeito, como novo

privacy /ˈprɪvəsɪ/ n privacidade f, intimidade f; (solitude) isolamento m

private /ˈpraɪvət/ a privado; (confidential) confidencial; (lesson, life, house etc) particular; (ceremony) íntimo □ n soldado m raso. **in** ~ em particular; (of ceremony) na intimidade. ~**ly** adv particularmente; (inwardly) no fundo, interiormente

privet /ˈprɪvɪt/ n (bot) alfena f, ligustro m

privilege /ˈprɪvəlɪdʒ/ n privilégio m. ~**d** a privilegiado. **be** ~**d to** ter o privilégio de

prize /praɪz/ n prêmio m, (P) prémio m □ a premiado; (fool etc) perfeito □ vt ter em grande apreço, apreciar muito. ~-**giving** n distribuição f de prêmios, (P) prémios. ~-**winner** n premiado m, vencedor m

pro[1] /prəʊ/ n the ~s and cons os prós e os contras

pro- /prəʊ/ pref (acting for) pro-; (favouring) pró-

probab|le /ˈprɒbəbl/ a provável. ~**ility** /-ˈbɪlətɪ/ n probabilidade f. ~**ly** adv provavelmente

probation /prəˈbeɪʃn/ n (testing) estágio m, tirocínio m; (jur) liberdade f condicional. ~**ary** a probatório

probe /prəʊb/ n (med) sonda f, (fig: investigation) inquérito m □ vt/i ~ (into) sondar, investigar

problem /ˈprɒbləm/ n problema m □ a difícil. ~**atic** /-ˈmætɪk/ a problemático

procedure /prəˈsiːdʒə(r)/ n procedimento m, processo m, norma f

proceed /prəˈsiːd/ vi prosseguir, ir para diante, avançar. ~ **to do** passar a fazer. ~ **with** sth continuar or avançar com alguma coisa. ~**ing** n procedimento m

proceedings /prəˈsiːdɪŋz/ npl (jur) processo m; (report) ata f, (P) acta f

proceeds /'prəʊsi:dz/ npl produto m, luco m, proventos mpl

process /'prəʊses/ n processo m □ vt tratar; (photo) revelar. **in ~** em curso. **in the ~ of doing** sendo feito

procession /prə'seʃn/ n procissão f, cortejo m

procl|aim /prə'kleɪm/ vt proclamar. **~amation** /prɒklə'meɪʃn/ n proclamação f

procure /prə'kjʊə(r)/ vt obter

prod /prɒd/ vt/i (pt prodded) (push) empurrar; (poke) espetar; (fig: urge) incitar □ n espetadela f; (fig) incitamento m

prodigal /'prɒdɪgl/ a pródigo

prodigious /prə'dɪdʒəs/ a prodigioso

prodigy /'prɒdɪdʒɪ/ n prodígio m

produc|e¹ /prə'dju:s/ vt/i produzir; (bring out) tirar, extrair; (show) apresentar, mostrar; (cause) causar, provocar; (theat) pôr em cena. **~er** n produtor m. **~tion** /-'dʌkʃn/ n produção f; (theat) encenação f

produce² /'prɒdju:s/ n produtos (agrícolas) mpl

product /'prɒdʌkt/ n produto m

productiv|e /prə'dʌktɪv/ a produtivo. **~ity** /prɒdʌk'tɪvətɪ/ n produtividade f

profan|e /prə'feɪn/ a profano; (blasphemous) blasfemo. **~ity** /-'fænətɪ/ n profanidade f

profess /prə'fes/ vt professar. **~ to do** alegar fazer

profession /prə'feʃn/ n profissão f. **~al** a profissional; (well done) de profissional; (person) que exerce uma profissão liberal □ n profissional mf

professor /prə'fesə(r)/ n professor (universitário) m

proficien|t /prə'fɪʃnt/ a proficiente, competente. **~cy** n proficiência f, competência f

profile /'prəʊfaɪl/ n perfil m

profit /'prɒfɪt/ n proveito m; (money) lucro m □ vi (pt profited) **~ by** aproveitar-se de; **~ from** tirar proveito de. **~able** a proveitoso; (of business) lucrativo, rentável

profound /prə'faʊnd/ a profundo. **~ly** adv profundamente

profus|e /prə'fju:s/ a profuso. **~ely** adv profusamente, em abundância. **~ion** /-ʒn/ n profusão f

program /'prəʊgræm/ n (computer) **~ programa** m □ vt (pt programmed) programar. **~mer** n programador m

programme /'prəʊgræm/ n programa m

progress¹ /'prəʊgres/ n progresso m. **in ~** em curso, em andamento

progress² /prə'gres/ vi progredir. **~ion** /-ʃn/ n progressão f

progressive /prə'gresɪv/ a progressivo; (reforming) progressista. **~ly** adv progressivamente

prohibit /prə'hɪbɪt/ vt proibir (sb from doing alg de fazer)

project¹ /prə'dʒekt/ vt projetar, (P) projectar □ vi ressaltar, sobressair. **~ion** /-ʃn/ n projeção f, (P) projecção f; (protruding) saliência f, ressalto m

project² /'prɒdʒekt/ n projeto m, (P) projecto m

projectile /prə'dʒektaɪl/ n projétil m, (P) projéctil m

projector /prə'dʒektə(r)/ n projetor m, (P) projector m

proletari|at /prəʊlɪ'teərɪət/ n proletariado m. **~an** a & n proletário (m)

proliferat|e /prə'lɪfəreɪt/ vi proliferar. **~ion** /-'reɪʃn/ n proliferação f

prolific /prə'lɪfɪk/ a prolífico

prologue /'prəʊlɒg/ n prólogo m

prolong /prə'lɒŋ/ vt prolongar

promenade /prɒmə'na:d/ n passeio m □ vt/i passear

prominen|t /'prɒmɪnənt/ a (projecting; important) proeminente; (conspicuous) bem à vista, conspícuo. **~ce** n proeminência f. **~tly** adv bem à vista

promiscu|ous /prə'mɪskjʊəs/ a promíscuo, de costumes livres. **~ity** /prɒmɪs'kju:ətɪ/ n promiscuidade f, liberdade f de costumes

promis|e /'prɒmɪs/ n promessa f □ vt/i prometer. **~ing** a prometedor, promissor

promot|e /prə'məʊt/ vt promover. **~ion** /-'məʊʃn/ n promoção f

prompt /prɒmpt/ a pronto, rápido, imediato; (punctual) pontual □ adv em ponto □ vt levar; (theat) soprar, servir de ponto para. **~er** n ponto m. **~ly** adv prontamente; pontualmente. **~ness** n prontidão f

prone /prəʊn/ a deitado (de bruços). **~ to** propenso a

prong /prɒŋ/ n (of fork) dente m

pronoun /'prəʊnaʊn/ n pronome m

pron|ounce /prə'naʊns/ vt pronunciar; (declare) declarar. **~ounced** a pronunciado. **~ouncement** n declaração f. **~unciation** /-ʌnsɪ'eɪʃn/ n pronúncia f

proof /pru:f/ n prova f; (of liquor) teor m alcóolico, graduação f □ a **~ against** à prova de

prop¹ /prɒp/ n suporte m; (lit & fig) apoio m, esteio m □ vt (pt propped) sustentar, suportar, apoiar. **~ against** apoiar contra

prop^2 /prɒp/ n (colloq: theat) acessório m, (P) adereço m

propaganda /ˌprɒpə'gændə/ n propaganda f

propagat|e /'prɒpəgeɪt/ vt/i propagar(-se). ~**ion** /-'geɪʃn/ n propagação f

propel /prə'pel/ vt (pt **propelled**) propulsionar, impelir

propeller /prə'pelə(r)/ n hélice f

proper /'prɒpə(r)/ a correto, (P) correcto; (seemly) conveniente; (real) propriamente dito; (colloq: thorough) belo. ~ **noun** substantivo m próprio. ~**ly** adv corretamente, (P) correctamente, (rightly) com razão, acertadamente; (accurately) propriamente

property /'prɒpətɪ/ n (house) imóvel m; (land, quality) propriedade f; (possessions) bens mpl

prophecy /'prɒfəsɪ/ n profecia f

prophesy /'prɒfɪsaɪ/ vt/i profetizar. ~ that predizer que

prophet /'prɒfɪt/ n profeta m. ~**ic** /prə'fetɪk/ a profético

proportion /prə'pɔ:ʃn/ n proporção f. ~**al**, ~**ate** adjs proporcional

proposal /prə'pəʊzl/ n proposta f; (of marriage) pedido m de casamento

propos|e /prə'pəʊz/ vt propor □ vi pedir em casamento. ~**e to do** propor-se fazer. ~**ition** /prɒpə'zɪʃn/ n proposição f; (colloq: matter) caso m, questão f

propound /prə'paʊnd/ vt propor

proprietor /prə'praɪətə(r)/ n proprietário m

propriety /prə'praɪətɪ/ n propriedade f, correção f, (P) correcção f

propulsion /prə'pʌlʃn/ n propulsão f

prosaic /prə'zeɪk/ a prosaico

prose /prəʊz/ n prosa f

prosecut|e /'prɒsɪkju:t/ vt (jur) processar. ~**ion** /-'kju:ʃn/ n (jur) acusação f

prospect^1 /'prɒspekt/ n perspectiva f

prospect^2 /prə'spekt/ vt/i pesquisar, prospectar

prospective /prə'spektɪv/ a futuro; (possible) provável

prosper /'prɒspə(r)/ vi prosperar

prosper|ous /'prɒspərəs/ a próspero. ~**ity** /-'sperətɪ/ n prosperidade f

prostitut|e /'prɒstɪtju:t/ n prostituta f. ~**ion** /-'tju:ʃn/ n prostituição f

prostrate /'prɒstreɪt/ a prostrado

protect /prə'tekt/ vt proteger. ~**ion** /-ʃn/ n proteção f, (P) protecção f. ~**ive** a protetor, (P) protector. ~**or** n protetor m, (P) protector m

protégé /'prɒtɪʒeɪ/ n protegido m. ~**e** n protegida f

protein /'prəʊti:n/ n proteína f

protest^1 /'prəʊtest/ n protesto m

protest^2 /prə'test/ vt/i protestar. ~**er** n (pol) manifestante mf

Protestant /'prɒtɪstənt/ a & n protestante (mf). ~**ism** /-ɪzəm/ n protestantismo m

protocol /'prəʊtəkɒl/ n protocolo m

prototype /'prəʊtətaɪp/ n protótipo m

protract /prə'trækt/ vt prolongar, arrastar

protrud|e /prə'tru:d/ vi sobressair, sair do alinhamento. ~**ing** a saliente

proud /praʊd/ a (er, -est) orgulhoso. ~**ly** adv orgulhosamente

prove /pru:v/ vt provar, demonstrar □ vi ~ **(to be) easy**/etc verificar-se ser fácil/etc. ~ **o.s.** dar provas de si. ~**n** /-n/ a provado

proverb /'prɒvɜ:b/ n provérbio m. ~**ial** /prə'vɜ:bɪəl/ a proverbial

provid|e /prə'vaɪd/ vt prover, munir (**sb with sth** alg de alguma coisa) □ vi ~ **for** providenciar para; (person) prover de, cuidar de; (allow for) levar em conta. ~**ed**, ~**ing (that)** conj desde que, contanto que

providence /'prɒvɪdəns/ n providência f

province /'prɒvɪns/ n província f; (fig) competência f

provincial /prə'vɪnʃl/ a provincial; (rustic) provinciano

provision /prə'vɪʒn/ n provisão f; (stipulation) disposição f. ~**s** (pl) (food) provisões fpl

provisional /prə'vɪʒənl/ a provisório. ~**ly** adv provisoriamente

proviso /prə'vaɪzəʊ/ n (pl -os) condição f

provo|ke /prə'vəʊk/ vt provocar. ~**cation** /prɒvə'keɪʃn/ n provocação f. ~**cative** /-'vɒkətɪv/ a provocante

prowess /'praʊɪs/ n proeza f, façanha f

prowl /praʊl/ vi rondar □ n **be on the** ~ andar à espreita. ~**er** n pessoa f que anda à espreita

proximity /prɒk'sɪmətɪ/ n proximidade f

proxy /'prɒksɪ/ n **by** ~ por procuração

prude /pru:d/ n puritano m, pudico m

pruden|t /'pru:dnt/ a prudente. ~**ce** n prudência f

prune^1 /pru:n/ n ameixa f seca

prune^2 /pru:n/ vt podar

pry /praɪ/ vi bisbilhotar. ~ **into** meter o nariz em, intrometer-se em

psalm /sɑ:m/ n salmo m

pseudo- /'sju:dəʊ/ pref pseudo-

pseudonym /'sju:dənɪm/ n pseudônimo m, (P) pseudónimo m

psychiatr|y /saɪ'kaɪətrɪ/ n psiquiatria f. ~**ic** /-ɪ'rætrɪk/ a psiquiátrico. ~**ist** n psiquiatra mf

psychic /'saɪkɪk/ a psíquico; (*person*) com capacidade de telepatia

psychoanalys|e /saɪkəʊ'ænəlaɪz/ vt psicanalisar. ~**t** /-ɪst/ n psicanalista mf

psychoanalysis /saɪkəʊə'næləsɪs/ n psicanálise f

psycholog|y /saɪ'kɒlədʒɪ/ n psicologia f. ~**ical** /-ə'lɒdʒɪkl/ a psicológico. ~**ist** n psicólogo m

psychopath /'saɪkəʊpæθ/ n psicopata mf

pub /pʌb/ n pub m

puberty /'pjuːbətɪ/ n puberdade f

public /'pʌblɪk/ a público; (*holiday*) feriado. **in** ~ em público. ~ **house** pub m. ~ **relations** relações fpl públicas. ~ **school** escola f particular; (*Amer*) escola f oficial. ~-**spirited** a de espírito cívico, patriótico. ~**ly** adv publicamente

publication /pʌblɪ'keɪʃn/ n publicação f

publicity /pʌ'blɪsətɪ/ n publicidade f

publicize /'pʌblɪsaɪz/ vt fazer publicidade de

publish /'pʌblɪʃ/ vt publicar. ~**er** n editor m. ~**ing** n publicação f. ~**ing house** editora f

pucker /'pʌkə(r)/ vt/i franzir

pudding /'pʊdɪŋ/ n pudim m; (*dessert*) doce m

puddle /'pʌdl/ n poça f de água, charco m

puerile /'pjʊəraɪl/ a pueril

puff /pʌf/ n baforada f □ vt/i lançar baforadas; (*breathe hard*) arquejar, ofegar. ~ **at** (*cigar etc*) dar baforadas em. ~ **out** (*swell*) inchar(-se). ~-**pastry** n massa f folhada

puffy /'pʌfɪ/ a inchado

pugnacious /pʌg'neɪʃəs/ a belicoso, combativo

pull /pʊl/ vt/i puxar; (*muscle*) distender □ n puxão m; (*fig: influence*) influência f, empenho m. **give a** ~ dar um puxão. ~ **a face** fazer uma careta. ~ **one's weight** (*fig*) fazer a sua quota-parte. ~ **sb's leg** brincar com alguém, meter-se com alguém. ~ **away** or **out** (*auto*) arrancar. ~ **down** puxar para baixo; (*building*) demolir. ~ **in** (*auto*) encostar-se. ~ **off** tirar; (*fig*) sair-se bem em, conseguir alcançar. ~ **out** partir; (*extract*) arrancar, tirar. ~ **through** sair-se bem. ~ **o.s. together** recompor-se, refazer-se. ~ **up** puxar para cima; (*uproot*) arrancar; (*auto*) parar

pulley /'pʊlɪ/ n roldana f

pullover /'pʊləʊvə(r)/ n pulôver m

pulp /pʌlp/ n polpa f; (*for paper*) pasta f de papel

pulpit /'pʊlpɪt/ n púlpito m

pulsat|e /pʌl'seɪt/ vi pulsar, bater, palpitar. ~**ion** /-'seɪʃn/ n pulsação f

pulse /pʌls/ n pulso m. **feel sb's** ~ tirar o pulso de alguém

pulverize /'pʌlvəraɪz/ vt (*grind, defeat*) pulverizar

pummel /'pʌml/ vt (*pt* **pummelled**) esmurrar

pump[1] /pʌmp/ n bomba f □ vt/i bombear; (*person*) arrancar or extrair informações de. ~ **up** encher com bomba

pump[2] /pʌmp/ n (*shoe*) sapato m

pumpkin /'pʌmpkɪn/ n abóbora f

pun /pʌn/ n trocadilho m, jogo m de palavras

punch[1] /pʌntʃ/ vt esmurrar, dar um murro or soco; (*perforate*) furar, perfurar; (*a hole*) fazer □ n murro m, soco m; (*device*) furador m. ~-**line** n remate m. ~-**up** n (*colloq*) pancadaria f

punch[2] /pʌntʃ/ n (*drink*) ponche m

punctual /'pʌŋktʃʊəl/ a pontual. ~**ity** /-'ælətɪ/ n pontualidade f

punctuat|e /'pʌŋktʃʊeɪt/ vt pontuar. ~**ion** /-'eɪʃn/ n pontuação f

puncture /'pʌŋktʃə(r)/ n (*in tyre*) furo m □ vt/i furar

pundit /'pʌndɪt/ n autoridade f, sumidade f

pungent /'pʌndʒənt/ a acre, pungente

punish /'pʌnɪʃ/ vt punir, castigar. ~**able** a punível. ~**ment** n punição f, castigo m

punitive /'pjuːnɪtɪv/ a (*expedition, measure etc*) punitivo; (*taxation etc*) penalizador

punt /pʌnt/ n (*boat*) chalana f

punter /'pʌntə(r)/ n (*gambler*) jogador m; (*colloq: customer*) freguês m

puny /'pjuːnɪ/ a (-ier, -iest) fraco, débil

pup(py) /'pʌp(ɪ)/ n cachorro m, cachorrinho m

pupil /'pjuːpl/ n aluno m; (*of eye*) pupila f

puppet /'pʌpɪt/ n (*lit & fig*) fantoche m, marionete f

purchase /'pɜːtʃəs/ vt comprar (**from sb** de alg) □ n compra f. ~**r** /-ə(r)/ n comprador m

pur|e /'pjʊə(r)/ a (-er, -est) puro. ~**ely** adv puramente. ~**ity** n pureza f

purgatory /'pɜːgətrɪ/ n purgatório m

purge /pɜːdʒ/ vt purgar; (*pol*) sanear □ n (*med*) purgante m; (*pol*) saneamento m

purif|y /'pjʊərɪfaɪ/ vt purificar. ~**ication** /-ɪ'keɪʃn/ n purificação f

puritan /'pjʊərɪtən/ n puritano m. ~**ical** /-'tænɪkl/ a puritano

purple /'pɜːpl/ a roxo, purpúreo □ n roxo m, púrpura f

purport /pə'pɔ:t/ *vt* dizer-se, (*P*) dar a entender. ~ **to be** pretender ser

purpose /'pɜ:pəs/ *n* propósito *m*; (*determination*) firmeza *f*. **on** ~ de propósito. **to no** ~ em vão. ~**-built** *a* construído especialmente.

purposely /'pɜ:pəslɪ/ *adv* de propósito, propositadamente

purr /pɜ:r/ *n* ronrom *m* □ *vi* ronronar

purse /pɜ:s/ *n* carteira *f*; (*Amer*) bolsa *f* □ *vt* franzir

pursue /pə'sju:/ *vt* perseguir; (*go on with*) prosseguir; (*engage in*) entregar-se a, dedicar-se a. ~**r** /-ə(r)/ *n* perseguidor *m*

pursuit /pə'sju:t/ *n* perseguição *f*; (*fig*) atividade *f*, (*P*) actividade *f*

pus /pʌs/ *n* pus *m*

push /pʊʃ/ *vt/i* empurrar; (*button*) apertar; (*thrust*) enfiar; (*colloq: recommend*) insistir □ *n* empurrão *m*; (*effort*) esforço *m*; (*drive*) energia *f*. **be** ~**ed for** (*time etc*) estar com pouco. **be** ~**ing thirty**/*etc* (*colloq*) estar beirando os trinta/*etc*. **give the** ~ **to** (*sl*) dar o fora em alguém. ~ **s.o. around** fazer alguém de bobo. ~ **back** repelir. ~**-chair** *n* carrinho *m* (de criança). ~**er** *n* fornecedor *m* (de droga). ~ **off** (*sl*) dar o fora. ~ **on** continuar. ~**-over** *n* canja *f*, coisa *f* fácil. ~ **up** (*lift*) levantar; (*prices*) forçar o aumento de. ~**-up** *n* (*Amer*) flexão *f*. ~**y** *a* (*colloq*) agressivo, furão

put /pʊt/ *vt/i* (*pt* put, *pres p* putting) colocar, pôr; (*question*) fazer. ~ **the damage at a million** estimar os danos em um milhão. **I'd** ~ **it at a thousand** eu diria mil. ~ **sth tactfully** dizer alg coisa com tato. ~ **across** comunicar. ~ **away** guardar. ~ **back** repor; (*delay*) retardar, atrasar. ~ **by** pôr de lado. ~ **down** pôr em lugar baixo; (*write*) anotar; (*pay*) pagar; (*suppress*) sufocar, reprimir. ~ **forward** (*plan*) submeter. ~ **in** (*insert*) introduzir; (*fix*) instalar; (*submit*) submeter. ~ **in for** fazer um pedido, candidatar-se. ~ **off** (*postpone*) adiar; (*disconcert*) desanimar; (*displease*) desagradar. ~ **s.o. off sth** tirar o gosto de alguém por alg coisa. ~ **on** (*clothes*) pôr; (*radio*) ligar; (*light*) acender; (*speed, weight*) ganhar; (*accent*) adotar. ~ **out** pôr para fora; (*stretch*) esticar; (*extinguish*) extinguir, apagar; (*disconcert*) desconcertar; (*inconvenience*) incomodar. ~ **up** levantar; (*building*) erguer, construir; (*notice*) colocar; (*price*) aumentar; (*guest*) hospedar; (*offer*) oferecer. ~**-up job** embuste *m*. ~ **up with** suportar

putrefy /'pju:trɪfaɪ/ *vi* putrefazer-se, apodrecer

putty /'pʌtɪ/ *n* massa de vidraceiro *f*, betume *m*

puzzl|e /'pʌzl/ *n* puzzle *m*, quebra-cabeça *m* □ *vt* deixar perplexo, intrigar □ *vi* quebrar a cabeça. ~**ing** *a* intrigante

pygmy /'pɪgmɪ/ *n* pigmeu *m*

pyjamas /pə'dʒɑ:məz/ *npl* pijama *m*

pylon /'paɪlən/ *n* poste *m*

pyramid /'pɪrəmɪd/ *n* pirâmide *f*

python /'paɪθn/ *n* píton *m*

Q

quack[1] /kwæk/ *n* (*of duck*) grasnido *m* □ *vi* grasnar

quack[2] /kwæk/ *n* charlatão *m*

quadrangle /'kwɒdræŋgl/ *n* quadrângulo *m*; (*of college*) pátio *m* quadrangular

quadruped /'kwɒdrʊped/ *n* quadrúpede *m*

quadruple /'kwɒdrʊpl/ *a* & *n* quádruplo (*m*) □ *vt/i* /kwɒ'drʊpl/ quadruplicar. ~**ts** /-plɪts/ *npl* quadrigêmeos *mpl*, (*P*) quadrigémeos *mpl*

quagmire /'kwægmaɪə(r)/ *n* pântano *m*, lamaçal *m*

quail /kweɪl/ *n* codorniz *f*

quaint /kweɪnt/ *a* (-er, -est) pitoresco; (*whimsical*) estranho, bizarro

quake /kweɪk/ *vi* tremer □ *n* (*colloq*) tremor *m* de terra

Quaker /'kweɪkə(r)/ *n* quaker *mf*, quacre *m*

qualification /kwɒlɪfɪ'keɪʃn/ *n* qualificação *f*; (*accomplishment*) habilitação *f*; (*diploma*) diploma *m*, título *m*; (*condition*) requisito *m*, condição *f*; (*fig*) restrição *f*, reserva *f*

qualif|y /'kwɒlɪfaɪ/ *vt* qualificar; (*fig: moderate*) atenuar, moderar; (*fig: limit*) pôr ressalvas *or* restrições a □ *vi* (*fig: be entitled to*) ter os requisitos (**for** para); (*sport*) classificar-se. **he** ~**ied as a vet** ele formou-se em veterinária. ~**ied** *a* formado; (*able*) qualificado, habilitado; (*moderated*) atenuado; (*limited*) limitado

quality /'kwɒlətɪ/ *n* qualidade *f*

qualm /kwɑ:m/ *n* escrúpulo *m*

quandary /'kwɒndərɪ/ *n* dilema *m*

quantity /'kwɒntətɪ/ *n* quantidade *f*

quarantine /'kwɒrənti:n/ *n* quarentena *f*

quarrel /'kwɒrəl/ *n* zanga *f*, questão *f*, discussão *f* □ *vi* (*pt* quarrelled) zangar-se, questionar, discutir. ~**some** *a* conflituoso, brigão

quarry[1] /'kwɒrɪ/ *n* (*prey*) presa *f*, caça *f*

quarry[2] /'kwɒrɪ/ *n* (*excavation*) pedreira *f*

quarter /'kwɔːtə(r)/ *n* quarto *m*; (*of year*) trimestre *m*; (*Amer: coin*) quarto *m* de dólar, 25 cêtimos *mpl*; (*district*) bairro *m*, quarteirão *m*. ~s (*lodgings*) alojamento *m*, residência *f*; (*mil*) quartel *m* □ *vt* dividir em quarto; (*mil*) aquartelar. **from all** ~s de todos os lados. ~ **of an hour** quarto *m* de hora. (a) ~ **past six** seis e quinze. (a) ~ **to seven** quinze para as sete. ~**final** *n* (*sport*) quarta *f* de final. ~**ly** *a* trimestral □ *adv* trimestralmente

quartet /kwɔː'tet/ *n* quarteto *m*

quartz /kwɔːts/ *n* quartzo *m* □ *a* (*watch etc*) de quartzo

quash /kwɒʃ/ *vt* reprimir; (*jur*) revogar

quaver /'kweɪvə(r)/ *vi* tremer, tremular □ *n* (*mus*) colcheia *f*

quay /kiː/ *n* cais *m*

queasy /'kwiːzɪ/ *a* delicado. **feel** ~ estar enjoado

queen /kwiːn/ *n* rainha *f*; (*cards*) dama *f*

queer /kwɪə(r)/ *a* (-er, -est) estranho; (*slightly ill*) indisposto; (*sl: homosexual*) bicha, maricas (*sl*); (*dubious*) suspeito □ *n* (*sl*) bicha *m*, maricas *m* (*sl*)

quell /kwel/ *vt* reprimir, abafar, sufocar

quench /kwentʃ/ *vt* (*fire, flame*) apagar; (*thirst*) matar, saciar

query /'kwɪərɪ/ *n* questão *f* □ *vt* pôr em dúvida

quest /kwest/ *n* busca *f*, procura *f*. **in** ~ **of** em demanda de

question /'kwestʃən/ *n* pergunta *f*, interrogação *f*; (*problem, affair*) questão *f* □ *vt* perguntar, interrogar; (*doubt*) pôr em dúvida *or* em causa. **in** ~ em questão *or* em causa. **out of the** ~ fora de toda a questão. **there's no** ~ **of** nem pensar em. **without** ~ sem dúvida. ~ **mark** ponto *m* de interrogação. ~**able** *a* discutível

questionnaire /kwestʃə'neə(r)/ *n* questionário *m*

queue /kjuː/ *n* fila *f*, (*P*) bicha *f* □ *vi* (*pres p* **queuing**) fazer fila, (*P*) fazer bicha

quibble /'kwɪbl/ *vi* tergiversar, usar de evasivas; (*raise petty objections*) discutir por coisas insignificantes

quick /kwɪk/ *a* (-er, -est) rápido □ *adv* depressa. **be** ~ despachar-se. **have a** ~ **temper** exaltar-se facilmente. ~**ly** *adv* rapidamente, depressa. ~**ness** *n* rapidez *f*

quicken /'kwɪkən/ *vt/i* apressar(-se)

quicksand /'kwɪksænd/ *n* areia *f* movediça

quid /kwɪd/ *n invar* (*sl*) libra *f*

quiet /'kwaɪət/ *a* (-er, -est) quieto, sossegado, tranquilo □ *n* quietude *f*, sossego *m*, tranqüilidade *f*. **keep** ~ calar-se. **on the** ~ às escondidas, na calada. ~**ly** *adv* sossegadamente, silenciosamente. ~**ness** *n* sossego *m*, tranqüilidade *f*, calma *f*

quieten /'kwaɪətn/ *vt/i* sossegar, acalmar(-se)

quilt /kwɪlt/ *n* coberta *f* acolchoada. **(continental)** ~ edredão *m* de penas □ *vt* acolchoar

quince /kwɪns/ *n* marmelo *m*

quintet /kwɪn'tet/ *n* quinteto *m*

quintuplets /kwɪn'tjuːplɪts/ *npl* quíntuplos *mpl*

quip /kwɪp/ *n* piada *f* □ *vt* contar piadas

quirk /kwɜːk/ *n* mania *f*, singularidade *f*

quit /kwɪt/ *vt* (*pt* **quitted**) deixar □ *vi* ir-se embora; (*resign*) demitir-se. ~ **doing** (*Amer*) parar de fazer

quite /kwaɪt/ *adv* completamente, absolutamente; (*rather*) bastante. ~ **(so)!** isso mesmo!, exatamente! ~ **a few** bastante, alguns/algumas. ~ **a lot** bastante

quiver /'kwɪvə(r)/ *vi* tremer, estremecer □ *n* tremor *m*, estremecimento *m*

quiz /kwɪz/ *n* (*pl* **quizzes**) teste *m*; (*game*) concurso *m* □ *vt* (*pt* **quizzed**) interrogar

quizzical /'kwɪzɪkl/ *a* zombeteiro

quorum /'kwɔːrəm/ *n* quorum *m*

quota /'kwəʊtə/ *n* cota *f*, quota *f*

quotation /kwəʊ'teɪʃn/ *n* citação *f*; (*estimate*) orçamento *m*. ~ **marks** aspas *fpl*

quote /kwəʊt/ *vt* citar; (*estimate*) fazer um orçamento □ *n* (*colloq: passage*) citação *f*; (*colloq: estimate*) orçamento *m*

R

rabbi /'ræbaɪ/ *n* rabino *m*

rabbit /'ræbɪt/ *n* coelho *m*

rabble /'ræbl/ *n* turba *f*. **the** ~ a ralé, a gentalha, o povinho

rabid /'ræbɪd/ *a* (*fig*) fanático, ferrenho; (*dog*) raivoso

rabies /'reɪbiːz/ *n* raiva *f*

race[1] /reɪs/ *n* corrida *f* □ *vt* (*horse*) fazer correr □ *vi* correr, dar uma corrida; (*rush*) ir em grande *or* a toda (a) velocidade. ~**track** *n* pista *f*

race[2] /reɪs/ *n* (*group*) raça *f* □ *a* racial

racecourse /'reɪskɔːs/ *n* hipódromo *m*

racehorse /'reɪshɔːs/ n cavalo m de corrida

racial /'reɪʃl/ a racial

racing /'reɪsɪŋ/ n corridas fpl. ~ car carro m de corridas

racis|t /'reɪsɪst/ a & n racista (mf). ~m /-zəm/ n racismo m

rack[1] /ræk/ n (for luggage) porta-bagagem m, bagageiro m; (for plates) escorredor m de prato □ vt ~ one's brains dar tratos à imaginação

rack[2] /ræk/ n go to ~ and ruin arruinar-se; (of buildings etc) cair em ruínas

racket[1] /'rækɪt/ n (sport) raquete f, (P) raqueta f

racket[2] /'rækɪt/ n (din) barulheira f; (swindle) roubalheira f; (sl: business) negociata f (colloq)

racy /'reɪsɪ/ a (-ier, -iest) vivo, vigoroso

radar /'reɪdɑː(r)/ n radar m □ a de radar

radian|t /'reɪdɪənt/ a radiante. ~ce n brilho m

radiator /'reɪdɪeɪtə(r)/ n radiador m

radical /'rædɪkl/ a & n radical (m)

radio /'reɪdɪəʊ/ n (pl -os) rádio f; (set) (aparelho de) rádio m □ vt transmitir pelo rádio. ~ station estação f de rádio, emissora f

radioactiv|e /reɪdɪəʊ'æktɪv/ a radioativo, (P) radioactivo. ~ity /'tɪvətɪ/ n radioatividade f, (P) radioactividade f

radiograph|er /reɪdɪ'ɒɡrəfə(r)/ n radiologista mf. ~y n radiografia f

radish /'rædɪʃ/ n rabanete m

radius /'reɪdɪəs/ n (pl -dii /-dɪaɪ/) raio m

raffle /'ræfl/ n rifa f □ vt rifar

raft /rɑːft/ n jangada f

rafter /'rɑːftə(r)/ n trave f, viga f

rag[1] /ræɡ/ n farrapo m; (for wiping) trapo m; (pej: newspaper) jornaleco m. ~s npl farrapos mpl, andrajos mpl. in ~s maltrapilho. ~ doll boneca f de trapos

rag[2] /ræɡ/ vt (pt ragged) zombar de

rage /reɪdʒ/ n raiva f, fúria f □ vi estar furioso; (of storm) rugir; (of battle) estar acesa. be all the ~ (colloq) fazer furor, estar na moda (colloq)

ragged /'ræɡɪd/ a (clothes, person) esfarrapado, roto; (edge) esfiapado, esgarçado

raid /reɪd/ n (mil) ataque m; (by police) batida f; (by criminals) assalto m □ vt fazer um ataque or uma batida or um assalto. ~er n atacante m, assaltante m

rail /reɪl/ n (of stairs) corrimão m; (of ship) amurada f; (on balcony) parapeito m; (for train) trilho m; (for cur-

tain) varão m. by ~ por estrada, (P) caminho de ferro

railings /'reɪlɪŋz/ npl grade f

railroad /'reɪlrəʊd/ n (Amer) = railway

railway /'reɪlweɪ/ n estrada f, (P) caminho m de ferro. ~ line linha f do trem. ~ station estação f ferroviária, (P) estação f de caminho de ferro

rain /reɪn/ n chuva f □ vi chover. ~ forest floresta f tropical. ~-storm n tempestade f com chuva. ~-water n água f da chuva

rainbow /'reɪnbəʊ/ n arco-íris m

raincoat /'reɪnkəʊt/ n impermeável m

raindrop /'reɪndrɒp/ n pingo m de chuva

rainfall /'reɪnfɔːl/ n precipitação f, pluviosidade f

rainy /'reɪnɪ/ a (-ier, -iest) chuvoso

raise /reɪz/ vt levantar, erguer; (breed) criar; (voice) levantar; (question) fazer; (price etc) aumentar, subir; (funds) angariar; (loan) obter □ n (Amer) aumento m

raisin /'reɪzn/ n passa f

rake /reɪk/ n ancinho m □ vt juntar, alisar com ancinho; (search) revolver, remexer. ~ in (money) ganhar a rodos. ~-off n (colloq) percentagem f (colloq). ~ up desenterrar, ressuscitar

rally /'rælɪ/ vt/i reunir(-se); (reassemble) reagrupar(-se), reorganizar(-se); (health) restabelecer(-se); (strength) recuperar as forças □ n (recovery) recuperação f; (meeting) comício m, assembléia f; (auto) rally m, rali m

ram /ræm/ n (sheep) carneiro m □ vt (pt rammed) (beat down) calcar; (push) meter à força; (crash into) bater contra

rambl|e /'ræmbl/ n caminhada f, perambulação f □ vi perambular, vaguear. ~e on divagar. ~er n caminhante mf; (plant) trepadeira f. ~ing a (speech) desconexo

ramp /ræmp/ n rampa f

rampage /ræm'peɪdʒ/ vi causar distúrbios violentos

rampant /'ræmpənt/ a be ~ vicejar, florescer; (diseases etc) grassar

rampart /'ræmpɑːt/ n baluarte m; (fig) defesa f

ramshackle /'ræmʃækl/ a (car) desconjuntado; (house) caindo aos pedaços

ran /ræn/ see run

ranch /rɑːntʃ/ n rancho m, estância f. ~er n rancheiro m

rancid /'rænsɪd/ a rançoso

rancour /'ræŋkə(r)/ n rancor m

random /'rændəm/ a feito, tirado etc ao acaso □ n at ~ ao acaso, a esmo, aleatoriamente

randy /'rændɪ/ a (-ier, -iest) lascivo, sensual

rang /ræŋ/ see **ring**

range /reɪndʒ/ n (distance) alcance m; (scope) âmbito m; (variety) gama f, variedade f; (stove) fogão m; (of voice) registro m, (P) registo m; (of temperature) variação f □ vt dispor, ordenar □ vi estender-se; (vary) variar. ~ of mountains cordilheira f, serra f. ~r n guarda m florestal

rank[1] /ræŋk/ n fila f, fileira f; (mil) posto m; (social position) classe f, categoria f □ vt/i ~ among contar(-se) entre. the ~ and file a massa

rank[2] /ræŋk/ a (-er, -est) (plants) luxuriante; (smell) fétido; (out-and-out) total

ransack /'rænsæk/ vt (search) espionar, revistar, remexer; (pillage) pilhar, saquear

ransom /'rænsəm/ n resgate m □ vt resgatar. **hold to** ~ prender como refém

rant /rænt/ vi usar linguagem bombástica

rap /ræp/ n pancadinha f seca □ vt/i (pt **rapped**) bater, dar uma pancada seca em

rape /reɪp/ vt violar, estuprar □ n violação f, estupro m

rapid /'ræpɪd/ a rápido. ~ity /rə-'pɪdətɪ/ n rapidez f

rapids /'ræpɪdz/ npl rápidos mpl

rapist /'reɪpɪst/ n violador m, estuprador m

rapport /ræ'pɔ:(r)/ n bom relacionamento m

rapt /ræpt/ a absorto. ~ **in** mergulhado em

raptur|e /'ræptʃə(r)/ n êxtase m. ~ous a extático; (welcome etc) entusiástico

rar|e[1] /reə(r)/ a (-er, -est) raro. ~ely adv raramente, raras vezes. ~ity n raridade f

rare[2] /reə(r)/ a (-er, -est) (culin) mal passado

rarefied /'reərɪfaɪd/ a rarefeito; (refined) requintado

raring /'reərɪŋ/ a ~ **to** (colloq) impaciente por, louco por (colloq)

rascal /'ra:skl/ n (dishonest) patife m; (mischievous) maroto m

rash[1] /ræʃ/ n erupção f cutânea, irritação f na pele (colloq)

rash[2] /ræʃ/ a (-er, -est) imprudente, precipitado. ~ly adv imprudentemente, precipitadamente

rasher /'ræʃə(r)/ n fatia f (de presunto or de bacon)

rasp /ra:sp/ n lixa f grossa, (P) lima f grossa

raspberry /'ra:zbrɪ/ n framboesa f

rasping /'ra:spɪŋ/ a áspero

rat /ræt/ n rato m, (P) ratazana f. ~ **race** (fig) luta renhida para vencer na vida, arrivismo m

rate /reɪt/ n (ratio) razão f; (speed) velocidade f; (price) tarifa f; (of exchange) (taxa m de) câmbio m; (of interest) taxa f. ~**s** (taxes) impostos mpl municipais, taxas fpl □ vt avaliar; (fig: consider) considerar. **at any** ~ de qualquer modo, pelo menos. **at the** ~ **of** à razão de. **at this** ~ desse jeito, desse modo

ratepayer /'reɪtpeɪə(r)/ n contribuinte mf

rather /'ra:ðə(r)/ adv (by preference) antes; (fairly) muito, bastante; (a little) um pouco. **I would** ~ **go** preferia ir

ratif|y /'rætɪfaɪ/ vt ratificar. ~ication /-ɪ'keɪʃn/ n ratificação f

rating /'reɪtɪŋ/ n (comm) rating m, (P) valor m; (sailor) praça f, marinheiro m; (radio, TV) índice m de audiência

ratio /'reɪʃɪəʊ/ n (pl **-os**) proporção f

ration /'ræʃn/ n ração f □ vt racionar

rational /'ræʃnəl/ a racional; (person) sensato, razoável. ~ize vt racionalizar

rattle /'rætl/ vt/i matraquear; (of door, window) bater; (of bottles) chocalhar; (colloq) agitar, mexer com os nervos de □ n (baby's toy) guizo m, chocalho m; (of football fan) matraca f; (sound) matraquear m, chocalhar m. ~ **off** despejar (colloq)

rattlesnake /'rætlsneɪk/ n cobra f cascavel

raucous /'rɔ:kəs/ a áspero, rouco

ravage /'rævɪdʒ/ vt devastar, causar estragos a. ~**s** npl devastação f, estragos mpl

rave /reɪv/ vi delirar; (in anger) urrar. ~ **about** delirar (de entusiasmo) com

raven /'reɪvn/ n corvo m

ravenous /'rævənəs/ a esfomeado; (greedy) voraz

ravine /rə'vi:n/ n ravina f, barranco m

raving /'reɪvɪŋ/ a ~ **lunatic** doido m varrido □ adv ~ **mad** loucamente

ravish /'rævɪʃ/ vt (rape) violar; (enrapture) arrebatar, encantar. ~ing a arrebatador, encantador

raw /rɔ:/ a (-er, -est) cru; (not processed) bruto; (wound) em carne viva; (weather) frio e úmido, (P) húmido; (immature) inexperiente, verde. ~ **deal** tratamento m injusto. ~ **material** matéria-prima f

ray /reɪ/ n raio m

raze /reɪz/ *vt* arrasar

razor /'reɪzə(r)/ *n* navalha *f* de barba. **~-blade** *n* lâmina *f* de barbear

re /riː/ *prep* a respeito de, em referência a, relativo a

re- /riː/ *pref* re-

reach /riːtʃ/ *vt* chegar a atingir; (*contact*) contatar; (*pass*) passar □ *vi* estender-se, chegar □ *n* alcance *m*. **out of** ~ fora de alcance. ~ **for** estender a mão para agarrar. **within** ~ **of** ao alcance de; (*close to*) próximo de

react /rɪ'ækt/ *vi* reagir

reaction /rɪ'ækʃn/ *n* reação *f*, (*P*) reacção *f*. **~ary** *a* & *n* reacionário (*m*), (*P*) reaccionário (*m*)

reactor /rɪ'æktə(r)/ *n* reator *m*, (*P*) reactor *m*

read /riːd/ *vt/i* (*pt* **read** /red/) ler; (*fig: interpret*) interpretar; (*study*) estudar; (*of instrument*) marcar, indicar □ *n* (*colloq*) leitura *f*. ~ **about** ler um artigo sobre. ~ **out** ler em voz alta. **~able** *a* agradável *or* fácil de ler; (*legible*) legível. **~er** *n* leitor *m*; (*book*) livro *m* de leitura. **~ing** *n* leitura *f*, (*of instrument*) registro *m*, (*P*) registo *m*

readily /'redɪlɪ/ *adv* de boa vontade, prontamente; (*easily*) facilmente

readiness /'redmɪs/ *n* prontidão *f*. **in** ~ pronto (**for** para)

readjust /riːə'dʒʌst/ *vt* reajustar □ *vi* readaptar-se

ready /'redɪ/ *a* (**-ier, -iest**) pronto □ *n* **at the** ~ pronto para disparar. **~-made** *a* pronto. ~ **money** dinheiro *m* vivo, (*P*) dinheiro *m* de contado, pagamento *m* à vista. **~-to-wear** *a* prêt-à-porter

real /rɪəl/ *a* real, verdadeiro; (*genuine*) autêntico □ *adv* (*Amer: colloq*) realmente. ~ **estate** bens *mpl* imobiliários

realis|t /'rɪəlɪst/ *n* realista *mf*. **~m** /-zəm/ *n* realismo *m*. **~tic** /'lɪstɪk/ *a* realista. **~tically** /'lɪstɪkəlɪ/ *adv* realisticamente

reality /rɪ'ælətɪ/ *n* realidade *f*

realiz|e /'rɪəlaɪz/ *vt* dar-se conta de, aperceber-se de, perceber; (*fulfil; turn into cash*) realizar. **~ation** /-'zeɪʃn/ *n* consciência *f*, noção *f*; (*fulfilment*) realização *f*

really /'rɪəlɪ/ *adv* realmente, na verdade

realm /relm/ *n* reino *m*; (*fig*) domínio *m*, esfera *f*

reap /riːp/ *vt* (*cut*) ceifar; (*gather; fig*) colher

reappear /riːə'pɪə(r)/ *vi* reaparecer. **~ance** *n* reaparição *f*

rear[1] /rɪə(r)/ *n* traseira *f*, retaguarda *f* □ *a* traseiro, de trás, posterior. **bring**

up the ~ ir na retaguarda, fechar a marcha. **~-view mirror** espelho *m* retrovisor

rear[2] /rɪə(r)/ *vt* levantar, erguer; (*children, cattle*) criar □ *vi* (*of horse etc*) empinar-se. ~ **one's head** levantar a cabeça

rearrange /riːə'remdʒ/ *vt* arranjar doutro modo, reorganizar

reason /'riːzn/ *n* razão *f* □ *vt/i* raciocinar, argumentar. ~ **with sb** procurar convencer alguém. **within** ~ razoável. **~ing** *n* raciocínio *m*

reasonable /'riːznəbl/ *a* razoável

reassur|e /riːə'ʃʊə(r)/ *vt* tranqüilizar, sossegar. **~ance** *n* garantia *f*. **~ing** *a* animador, reconfortante

rebate /'riːbeɪt/ *n* (*refund*) reembolso *m*; (*discount*) desconto *m*, abatimento *m*

rebel[1] /'rebl/ *n* rebelde *mf*

rebel[2] /rɪ'bel/ *vi* (*pt* **rebelled**) rebelar-se, revoltar-se, sublevar-se. **~lion** *n* rebelião *f*, revolta *f*. **~lious** *a* rebelde

rebound[1] /rɪ'baʊnd/ *vi* repercutir, ressoar; (*fig: backfire*) recair (**on** sobre)

rebound[2] /'riːbaʊnd/ *n* ricochete *m*

rebuff /rɪ'bʌf/ *vt* receber mal, repelir (*colloq*) □ *n* rejeição *f*

rebuild /riː'bɪld/ *vt* (*pt* **rebuilt**) reconstruir

rebuke /rɪ'bjuːk/ *vt* repreender □ *n* reprimenda *f*

recall /rɪ'kɔːl/ *vt* chamar, mandar regressar; (*remember*) lembrar-se de □ *n* (*summons*) ordem *f* de regresso

recant /rɪ'kænt/ *vi* retratar-se, (*P*) retractar-se

recap /'riːkæp/ *vt/i* (*pt* **recapped**) (*colloq*) recapitular □ *n* recapitulação *f*

recapitulat|e /riːkə'pɪtʃʊleɪt/ *vt/i* recapitular. **~ion** /-'leɪʃn/ *n* recapitulação *f*

reced|e /rɪ'siːd/ *vi* recuar, retroceder. **his hair is** ~**ing** ele está ficando com entradas. **~ing** *a* (*forehead, chin*) recuado, voltado para dentro

receipt /rɪ'siːt/ *n* recibo *m*; (*receiving*) recepção *f*. **~s** (*comm*) receitas *fpl*

receive /rɪ'siːv/ *vt* receber. **~r** /-ə(r)/ *n* (*of stolen goods*) receptador *m*; (*phone*) fone *m*, (*P*) auscultador *m*; (*radio/TV*) receptor *m*. (**official**) **~r** síndico *m* de massa falida

recent /'riːsnt/ *a* recente. **~ly** *adv* recentemente

receptacle /rɪ'septəkl/ *n* recipiente *m*, receptáculo *m*

reception /rɪ'sepʃn/ *n* recepção *f*; (*welcome*) acolhimento *m*. **~ist** *n* recepcionista *mf*

receptive /rɪ'septɪv/ *a* receptivo

recess /rɪ'ses/ *n* recesso *m*; (*of legisla-*

ture) recesso *m*; (*Amer: schol*) recreio *m*

recession /rɪ'seʃn/ *n* recessão *f*, depressão *f*

recharge /ri:'tʃɑ:dʒ/ *vt* tornar a carregar, recarregar

recipe /'resəpɪ/ *n* (*culin*) receita *f*

recipient /rɪ'sɪpɪənt/ *n* recipiente *m*; (*of letter*) destinatário *m*

reciprocal /rɪ'sɪprəkl/ *a* recíproco

reciprocate /rɪ'sɪprəkeɪt/ *vt/i* reciprocar(-se), retribuir, fazer o mesmo

recital /rɪ'saɪtl/ *n* (*music etc*) recital *m*

recite /rɪ'saɪt/ *vt* recitar; (*list*) enumerar

reckless /'reklɪs/ *a* inconsciente, imprudente, estouvado

reckon /'rekən/ *vt/i* calcular; (*judge*) considerar; (*think*) supor, pensar. ~ on contar com, depender de. ~ with contar com, levar em conta. ~ing *n* conta(s) *f* (*pl*)

reclaim /rɪ'kleɪm/ *vt* (*demand*) reclamar; (*land*) recuperar

reclin|e /rɪ'klam/ *vt/i* reclinar(-se). ~ing *a* (*person*) reclinado; (*chair*) reclinável

recluse /rɪ'klu:s/ *n* solitário *m*, recluso *m*

recognition /rekəg'nɪʃn/ *n* reconhecimento *m*. beyond ~ irreconhecível. gain ~ ganhar nome, ser reconhecido

recogniz|e /'rekəgnaɪz/ *vt* reconhecer. ~able /'rekəgnaɪzəbl/ *a* reconhecível

recoil /rɪ'kɔɪl/ *vi* recuar; (*gun*) dar coice □ *n* recuo *m*; (*gun*) coice *m*. ~ from doing recusar-se a fazer

recollect /rekə'lekt/ *vt* recordar-se de. ~ion /-ʃn/ *n* recordação *f*

recommend /rekə'mend/ *vt* recomendar. ~ation /-'deɪʃn/ *n* recomendação *f*

recompense /'rekəmpens/ *vt* recompensar □ *n* recompensa *f*

reconcil|e /'rekənsaɪl/ *vt* (*people*) reconciliar; (*facts*) conciliar. ~e o.s. to resignar-se a, conformar-se com. ~iation /-sɪlɪ'eɪʃn/ *n* reconciliação *f*

reconnaissance /rɪ'kɒnɪsns/ *n* reconhecimento *m*

reconnoitre /rekə'nɔɪtə(r)/ *vt/i* (*pres p* -tring) (*mil*) reconhecer, fazer um reconhecimento (de)

reconsider /ri:kən'sɪdə(r)/ *vt* reconsiderar

reconstruct /ri:kən'strʌkt/ *vt* reconstruir. ~ion /-ʃn/ *n* reconstrução *f*

record¹ /rɪ'kɔ:d/ *vt* registar; (*disc, tape etc*) gravar. ~ that referir/relatar que. ~ing *n* (*disc, tape etc*) gravação *f*

record² /'rekɔ:d/ *n* (*register*) registro *m*, (*P*) registo *m*; (*mention*) menção *f*, nota *f*; (*file*) arquivo *m*; (*mus*) disco

m; (*sport*) record(e) *m* □ *a* record(e) *invar*. have a (criminal) ~ ter cadastro. off the ~ (*unofficial*) oficioso; (*secret*) confidencial. ~-player *n* toca-discos *m invar*, (*P*) gira-discos *m invar*

recorder /rɪ'kɔ:də(r)/ *n* (*mus*) flauta *f* de ponta; (*techn*) instrumento *m* registrador

recount /rɪ'kaʊnt/ *vt* narrar em pormenor, relatar

re-count /'ri:kaʊnt/ *n* (*pol*) nova contagem *f*

recoup /rɪ'ku:p/ *vt* compensar; (*recover*) recuperar

recourse /rɪ'kɔ:s/ *n* recurso *m*. have ~ to recorrer a

recover /rɪ'kʌvə(r)/ *vt* recuperar □ *vi* restabelecer-se. ~y *n* recuperação *f*; (*health*) recuperação *f*, restabelecimento *m*

recreation /rekrɪ'eɪʃn/ *n* recreação *f*, recreio *m*; (*pastime*) passatempo *m*. ~al *a* recreativo

recrimination /rɪkrɪmɪ'neɪʃn/ *n* recriminação *f*

recruit /rɪ'kru:t/ *n* recruta *m* □ *vt* recrutar. ~ment *n* recrutamento *m*

rectang|le /'rektæŋgl/ *n* retângulo *m*, (*P*) rectângulo *m*. ~ular /-'tæŋgjʊlə(r)/ *a* retangular, (*P*) rectangular

rectify /'rektɪfaɪ/ *vt* retificar, (*P*) rectificar

recuperate /rɪ'kju:pəreɪt/ *vt/i* recuperar(-se)

recur /rɪ'kɜ:(r)/ *vi* (*pt* recurred) repetir-se; (*come back*) voltar (to a)

recurren|t /rɪ'kʌrənt/ *a* frequente, (*P*) frequente, repetido, periódico. ~ce *n* repetição *f*

recycle /ri:'saɪkl/ *vt* reciclar

red /red/ *a* (redder, reddest) encarnado, vermelho; (*hair*) ruivo □ *n* encarnado *m*, vermelho *m*. in the ~ em déficit. ~ carpet (*fig*) recepção *f* solene, tratamento *m* especial. R~ Cross Cruz *f* Vermelha. ~-handed *a* em flagrante (delito), com a boca na botija (*colloq*). ~ herring (*fig*) pista *f* falsa. ~-hot *a* escaldante, incandescente. ~ light luz *f* vermelha. ~ tape (*fig*) papelada *f*, burocracia *f*. ~ wine vinho *m* tinto

redden /'redn/ *vt/i* avermelhar(-se); (*blush*) corar, ruborizar-se

redecorate /ri:'dekəreɪt/ *vt* decorar/pintar de novo

red|eem /rɪ'di:m/ *vt* (*sins etc*) redimir; (*sth pawned*) tirar do prego (*colloq*); (*voucher etc*) resgatar. ~emption /rɪ'dempʃn/ *n* resgate *m*; (*of honour*) salvação *f*

redirect /ri:daɪ'rekt/ *vt* (*letter*) reendereçar

redness /'rednɪs/ n vermelhidão f, cor
f vermelha

redo /riː'duː/ vt (pt **-did**, pp **-done**)
refazer

redress /rɪ'dres/ vt reparar; (set right)
remediar, emendar. ~ **the balance**
restabelecer o equilíbrio □ n re-
paração f

reduc|e /rɪ'djuːs/ vt reduzir; (tempera-
ture etc) baixar. ~**tion** /rɪ'dʌkʃən/ n
redução f

redundan|t /rɪ'dʌndənt/ a redun-
dante, supérfluo; (worker) desempregado. **be made** ~**t** ficar desempregado. ~**cy** n demissão f por
excesso de pessoal

reed /riːd/ n cara f, junco m; (mus)
palheta f

reef /riːf/ n recife m

reek /riːk/ n mau cheiro m □ vi cheirar mal, tresandar. **he** ~**s of wine** ele
está com cheiro de vinho

reel /riːl/ n carretel m; (spool) bobina
f □ vi cambalear, vacilar □ vt ~ **off**
recitar (colloq)

refectory /rɪ'fektərɪ/ n refeitório m

refer /rɪ'fɜː(r)/ vt/i (pt **referred**) ~ **to**
referir-se a; (concern) aplicar-se a, dizer respeito a; (consult) consultar;
(direct) remeter a

referee /refə'riː/ n árbitro m; (for job)
pessoa f que dá referências □ vt (pt
refereed) arbitrar

reference /'refrəns/ n referência f;
(testimonial) referências fpl. **in** ~ **or**
with ~ **to** com referência a. ~ **book**
livro m de consulta

referendum /refə'rendəm/ n (pl
-dums or **-da**) referendo m, plebiscito m

refill¹ /riː'fɪl/ vt encher de novo; (pen
etc) pôr carga nova em

refill² /'riːfɪl/ n (pen etc) carga f nova,
(P) recarga f

refine /rɪ'faɪn/ vt refinar. ~**d** a refinado; (taste, manners etc) requintado.
~**ment** n (taste, manners etc) refina-
mento m, requinte m; (tech) refinação
f. ~**ry** /-ərɪ/ n refinaria f

reflect /rɪ'flekt/ vt/i refletir, (P) reflectir (**on/upon** em). ~**ion** /-ʃn/ n
reflexão f; (image) reflexo m. ~**or** n
refletor m, (P) reflector m

reflective /rɪ'flektɪv/ a refletor, (P) reflector; (thoughtful) refletido, (P) re-
flectido, ponderado

reflex /'riːfleks/ a & n reflexo (m)

reflexive /rɪ'fleksɪv/ a (gram) reflexivo, (P) reflexo

reform /rɪ'fɔːm/ vt/i reformar(-se) □ n
reforma f. ~**er** n reformador m

refract /rɪ'frækt/ vt refratar, (P) re-
fractar

refrain¹ /rɪ'freɪn/ n refrão m, estribilho m

refrain² /rɪ'freɪn/ vi abster-se (**from**
de)

refresh /rɪ'freʃ/ vt refrescar; (of rest
etc) restaurar. ~ **one's memory** avi-
var or refrescar a memória. ~**ing** a
refrescante; (of rest etc) reparador.
~**ments** npl refeição f leve; (drinks)
refrescos mpl

refresher /rɪ'freʃə(r)/ n ~ **course**
curso m de reciclagem

refrigerat|e /rɪ'frɪdʒəreɪt/ vt refri-
gerar. ~**or** n frigorífico m, refrige-
rador m, geladeira f

refuel /riː'fjuːəl/ vt/i (pt **refuelled**)
reabastecer(-se) (de combustível)

refuge /'refjuːdʒ/ n refúgio m, asilo m.
take ~ refugiar-se

refugee /refjuː'dʒiː/ n refugiado m

refund¹ /rɪ'fʌnd/ vt reembolsar

refund² /'riːfʌnd/ n reembolso m

refus|e¹ /rɪ'fjuːz/ vt/i recusar(-se).
~**al** n recusa f. **first** ~**al** preferência f, primeira opção f

refuse² /'refjuːs/ n refugo m, lixo m.
~**-collector** n lixeiro m, (P) homem
m do lixo

refute /rɪ'fjuːt/ vt refutar

regain /rɪ'geɪn/ vt recobrar, recuperar

regal /'riːɡl/ a real, régio

regalia /rɪ'ɡeɪlɪə/ npl insígnias fpl

regard /rɪ'ɡaːd/ vt considerar; (gaze)
olhar □ n consideração f, estima f;
(gaze) olhar m. ~**s** cumprimentos
mpl; (less formally) lembranças fpl,
saudades fpl. **as** ~**s**, ~**ing** prep no
que diz respeito a, quanto a. ~**less**
adv apesar de tudo. ~**less of** apesar
de

regatta /rɪ'ɡætə/ n regata f

regenerate /rɪ'dʒenəreɪt/ vt regenerar

regen|t /'riːdʒənt/ n regente mf. ~**cy**
n regência f

regime /reɪ'ʒiːm/ n regime m

regiment /'redʒɪmənt/ n regimento
m. ~**al** /-'mentl/ a de regimento,
regimental. ~**ation** /-en'teɪʃn/ n
arregimentação f, disciplina f excessiva

region /'riːdʒən/ n região f. **in the** ~
of por volta de. ~**al** a regional

regist|er /'redʒɪstə(r)/ n registro m,
(P) registo m □ vt (record) anotar;
(notice) fixar, registar, prestar atenção
a; (birth, letter) registar, (P) registar;
(vehicle) matricular; (emotions etc) exprimir □ vi inscrever-se. ~**er office**
registro m, (P) registo m. ~**ration**
/-'streɪʃn/ n registro m, (P) registo m;
(for course) inscrição f, matrícula f.
~**ration (number)** número m de
placa

registrar /redʒɪ'straː(r)/ n oficial m
do registro, (P) registo civil; (univ)
secretário m

regret /rɪ'gret/ *n* pena *f*, pesar *m*; (*repentance*) remorso *m*. **I have no ~s** não estou arrependido □ *vt* (*pt* regretted) lamentar, sentir (**to do** fazer); (*feel repentance*) arrepender-se de, lamentar. **~fully** *adv* com pena, pesarosamente. **~table** *a* lamentável. **~tably** *adv* infelizmente

regular /'regjʊlə(r)/ *a* regular; (*usual*) normal; (*colloq: thorough*) perfeito, verdadeiro, autêntico □ *n* (*colloq: client*) cliente *mf* habitual. **~ity** /-'lærətɪ/ *n* regularidade *f*. **~ly** *adv* regularmente

regulat|e /'regjʊleɪt/ *vt* regular. **~ion** /-'leɪʃn/ *n* regulação *f*; (*rule*) regulamento *m*, regra *f*

rehabilitat|e /ri:ə'bɪlɪteɪt/ *vt* reabilitar. **~ion** /-'teɪʃn/ *n* reabilitação *f*

rehash[1] /ri:'hæʃ/ *vt* apresentar sob nova forma, (P) cozinhar (*colloq*)

rehash[2] /'ri:hæʃ/ *n* (*fig*) apanhado *m*, (P) cozinhado *m* (*colloq*)

rehears|e /rɪ'hɜ:s/ *vt* ensaiar. **~al** *n* ensaio *m*. **dress ~al** ensaio *m* geral

reign /rem/ *n* reinado *m* □ *vi* reinar (**over** em)

reimburse /ri:ɪm'bɜ:s/ *vt* reembolsar. **~ment** *n* reembolso *m*

rein /rem/ *n* rédea *f*

reincarnation /ri:ɪnka:'neɪʃn/ *n* reencarnação *f*

reindeer /'remdɪə(r)/ *n invar* rena *f*

reinforce /ri:ɪn'fɔ:s/ *vt* reforçar. **~ment** *n* reforço *m*. **~ments** reforços *mpl*. **~d concrete** concreto *m* armado, (P) cimento *m* or betão *m* armado

reinstate /ri:ɪn'steɪt/ *vt* reintegrar

reiterate /ri:'ɪtəreɪt/ *vt* reiterar

reject[1] /rɪ'dʒekt/ *vt* rejeitar. **~ion** /-ʃn/ *n* rejeição *f*

reject[2] /'ri:dʒekt/ *n* (artigo de) refugo *m*

rejoic|e /rɪ'dʒɔɪs/ *vi* regozijar-se (**at/over** com). **~ing** *n* regozijo *m*

rejuvenate /ri:'dʒu:vəneɪt/ *vt* rejuvenescer

relapse /rɪ'læps/ *n* recaída *f* □ *vi* recair

relate /rɪ'leɪt/ *vt* relatar; (*associate*) relacionar □ *vi* **~ to** ter relação com, dizer respeito a; (*get on with*) entender-se com. **~d** *a* aparentado; (*ideas etc*) afim, relacionado

relation /rɪ'leɪʃn/ *n* relação *f*; (*person*) parente *mf*. **~ship** *n* parentesco *m*; (*link*) relação *f*; (*affair*) ligação *f*

relative /'relətɪv/ *n* parente *mf* □ *a* relativo. **~ly** *adv* relativamente

relax /rɪ'læks/ *vt/i* relaxar(-se), (*fig*) descontrair(-se). **~ation** /ri:læk'seɪʃn/ *n* relaxamento *m*; (*fig*) descontração *f*, (P) descontracção *f*;

(*recreation*) distração *f*, (P) distracção *f* **~ing** *a* relaxante

relay[1] /'ri:leɪ/ *n* turma *f*, (P) turno *m*. **~ race** corrida *f* de revezamento, (P) estafetas

relay[2] /rɪ'leɪ/ *vt* (*message*) retransmitir

release /rɪ'li:s/ *vt* libertar, soltar; (*mech*) desengatar, soltar; (*bomb, film, record*) lançar; (*news*) dar, publicar; (*gas, smoke*) soltar □ *n* libertação *f*; (*mech*) desengate *m*; (*bomb, film, record*) lançamento *m*; (*news*) publicação *f*; (*gas, smoke*) emissão *f*. **new ~** estréia *f*

relegate /'relɪgeɪt/ *vt* relegar

relent /rɪ'lent/ *vi* ceder. **~less** *a* implacável, inexorável, inflexível

relevan|t /'reləvənt/ *a* relevante, pertinente, a propósito. **be ~ to** ter a ver com. **~ce** *n* pertinência *f*, relevância *f*

reliab|le /rɪ'laɪəbl/ *a* de confiança, com que se pode contar; (*source etc*) fidedigno; (*machine etc*) seguro, confiável. **~ility** /-'bɪlətɪ/ *n* confiabilidade *f*

reliance /rɪ'laɪəns/ *n* (*dependence*) segurança *f*; (*trust*) confiança *f*, fé *f* (**on** em)

relic /'relɪk/ *n* relíquia *f*. **~s** vestígios *mpl*, ruínas *fpl*

relief /rɪ'li:f/ *n* alívio *m*; (*assistance*) auxílio *m*, assistência *f*; (*outline, design*) relevo *m*. **~ road** estrada *f* alternativa

relieve /rɪ'li:v/ *vt* aliviar; (*help*) socorrer; (*take over from*) revezar, substituir; (*mil*) render

religion /rɪ'lɪdʒən/ *n* religião *f*

religious /rɪ'lɪdʒəs/ *a* religioso

relinquish /rɪ'lɪŋkwɪʃ/ *vt* abandonar, renunciar a

relish /'relɪʃ/ *n* prazer *m*, gosto *m*; (*culin*) molho *m* condimentado □ *vt* saborear, apreciar, gostar de

relocate /ri:ləʊ'keɪt/ *vt/i* transferir (-se), mudar(-se)

reluctan|t /rɪ'lʌktənt/ *a* relutante (**to** em), pouco inclinado (**to** a). **~ce** *n* relutância *f*. **~tly** *adv* a contragosto, relutantemente

rely /rɪ'laɪ/ *vi* **~ on** contar com; (*depend*) depender de

remain /rɪ'mem/ *vi* ficar, permanecer. **~s** *npl* restos *mpl*; (*ruins*) ruínas *fpl*. **~ing** *a* restante

remainder /rɪ'memdə(r)/ *n* restante *m*, remanescente *m*

remand /rɪ'ma:nd/ *vt* reconduzir à prisão para detenção provisória □ *n* **on ~** sob prisão preventiva

remark /rɪ'ma:k/ *n* observação *f*, comentário *m* □ *vt* observar, comentar □ *vi* ~ **on** fazer observações *or* comentários sobre. ~**able** *a* notável

remarr|y /rɪ'mærɪ/ *vt/i* tornar a casar(-se) (com). ~**iage** *n* novo casamento *m*

remed|y /'remədɪ/ *n* remédio *m* □ *vt* remediar. ~**ial** /rɪ'miːdɪəl/ *a* (*med*) corretivo, (*P*) correctivo

rememb|er /rɪ'membə(r)/ *vt* lembrar-se de, recordar-se de. ~**rance** *n* lembrança *f*, recordação *f*

remind /rɪ'maɪnd/ *vt* (fazer) lembrar (**sb of sth** alg coisa a alguém). ~ **sb to do** lembrar a alguém que faça. ~**er** *n* o que serve para fazer lembrar; (*note*) lembrete *m*

reminisce /remɪ'nɪs/ *vi* (re)lembrar (coisas passadas). ~**nces** *npl* reminiscências *fpl*

reminiscent /remɪ'nɪsnt/ *a* ~ **of** que faz lembrar, evocativo de

remiss /rɪ'mɪs/ *a* negligente, descuidado

remission /rɪ'mɪʃn/ *n* remissão *f*, (*jur*) comutação *f* (de pena)

remit /rɪ'mɪt/ *vt* (*pt* **remitted**) (*money*) remeter. ~**tance** *n* remessa *f* (de dinheiro)

remnant /'remnənt/ *n* resto *m*; (*trace*) vestígio *m*; (*of cloth*) retalho *m*

remorse /rɪ'mɔːs/ *n* remorso *m*. ~**ful** *a* arrependido, com remorsos. ~**less** *a* implacável

remote /rɪ'məʊt/ *a* remoto, distante; (*person*) distante; (*slight*) vago, leve. ~ **control** comando *m* à distância, telecomando *m*. ~**ly** *adv* de longe, vagamente

remov|e /rɪ'muːv/ *vt* tirar, remover; (*lead away*) levar; (*dismiss*) demitir; (*get rid of*) eliminar. ~**al** *n* remoção *f*; (*dismissal*) demissão *f*; (*from house*) mudança *f*

remunerat|e /rɪ'mjuːnəreɪt/ *vt* remunerar. ~**ion** /-'reɪʃn/ *n* remuneração *f*

rename /riː'neɪm/ *vt* rebatizar, (*P*) rebaptizar

render /'rendə(r)/ *vt* retribuir; (*services*) prestar; (*mus*) interpretar; (*translate*) traduzir. ~**ing** *n* (*mus*) interpretação *f*; (*plaster*) reboco *m*

renegade /'renɪgeɪd/ *n* renegado *m*

renew /rɪ'njuː/ *vt* renovar; (*resume*) retomar. ~**able** *a* renovável. ~**al** *n* renovação *f*; (*resumption*) reatamento *m*

renounce /rɪ'naʊns/ *vt* renunciar a; (*disown*) renegar, repudiar

renovat|e /'renəveɪt/ *vt* renovar. ~**ion** /-'veɪʃn/ *n* renovação *f*

renown /rɪ'naʊn/ *n* renome *m*. ~**ed** *a* conceituado, célebre, de renome

rent /rent/ *n* aluguel *m*, (*P*) aluguer

m, renda *f* □ *vt* alugar, arrendar. ~**al** *n* (*charge*) aluguel *m*, (*P*) aluguer *m*, renda *f*; (*act of renting*) aluguel *m*, (*P*) aluguer *m*

renunciation /rɪnʌnsɪ'eɪʃn/ *n* renúncia *f*

reopen /riː'əʊpən/ *vt/i* reabrir(-se). ~**ing** *n* reabertura *f*

reorganize /riː'ɔːgənaɪz/ *vt/i* reorganizar(-se)

rep /rep/ *n* (*colloq*) vendedor *m*, caixeiro-viajante *m*

repair /rɪ'peə(r)/ *vt* reparar, consertar □ *n* reparo *m*, conserto *m*. **in good** ~ em bom estado (de conservação)

repartee /repa'tiː/ *n* resposta *f* pronta e espirituosa

repatriat|e /riː'pætrɪeɪt/ *vt* repatriar. ~**ion** /'eɪʃn/ *n* repatriamento *m*

repay /riː'peɪ/ *vt* (*pt* **repaid**) pagar, devolver, reembolsar; (*reward*) recompensar. ~**ment** *n* pagamento *m*, reembolso *m*

repeal /rɪ'piːl/ *vt* revogar □ *n* revogação *f*

repeat /rɪ'piːt/ *vt/i* repetir(-se) □ *n* repetição *f*; (*broadcast*) retransmissão *f*. ~**edly** *adv* repetidas vezes, repetidamente

repel /rɪ'pel/ *vt* (*pt* **repelled**) repelir. ~**lent** *a* & *n* repelente (*m*)

repent /rɪ'pent/ *vi* arrepender-se (**of** de). ~**ance** *n* arrependimento *m*. ~**ant** *a* arrependido

repercussion /riːpə'kʌʃn/ *n* repercussão *f*

repertoire /'repətwaː(r)/ *n* repertório *m*

repertory /'repətrɪ/ *n* repertório *m*

repetit|ion /repɪ'tɪʃn/ *n* repetição *f*. ~**ious** /-'tɪʃəs/, ~**ive** /rɪ'petətɪv/ *a* repetitivo

replace /rɪ'pleɪs/ *vt* colocar no mesmo lugar, repor; (*take the place of*) substituir. ~**ment** *n* reposição *f*; (*substitution*) substituição *f*; (*person*) substituto *m*

replenish /rɪ'plenɪʃ/ *vt* voltar a encher, reabastecer; (*renew*) renovar

replica /'replɪkə/ *n* réplica *f*, cópia *f*, reprodução *f*

reply /rɪ'plaɪ/ *vt/i* responder, replicar □ *n* resposta *f*, réplica *f*

report /rɪ'pɔːt/ *vt* relatar; (*notify*) informar; (*denounce*) denunciar, apresentar queixa de □ *vi* fazer um relatório. ~ (**on**) (*news item*) fazer uma reportagem (sobre). ~ **to** (*go*) apresentar-se a □ *n* (*in newspapers*) reportagem *f*; (*of company, doctor*) relatório *m*; (*schol*) boletim *m* escolar; (*sound*) detonação *f*; (*rumour*) rumores *mpl*. ~**edly** *adv* segundo consta. ~**er** *n* repórter *m*

repose /rɪ'pəʊz/ n repouso m

repossess /ri:pə'zes/ vt reapossar-se de, retomar de

represent /reprɪ'zent/ vt representar. ~ation /-'teɪʃn/ n representação f

representative /reprɪ'zentətɪv/ a representativo □ n representante mf

repress /rɪ'pres/ vt reprimir. ~ion /-ʃn/ n repressão f. ~ive a repressor, repressivo

reprieve /rɪ'pri:v/ n suspensão f temporária; (temporary relief) tréguas fpl □ vt suspender temporariamente; (fig) dar tréguas a

reprimand /'reprɪmɑ:nd/ vt repreender □ n repreensão f, reprimenda f

reprint /'ri:prɪnt/ n reimpressão f, reedição f □ vt /ri:'prɪnt/

reprisals /rɪ'praɪzlz/ npl represálias fpl

reproach /rɪ'prəʊtʃ/ vt censurar, repreender (sb for sth alguém por alg coisa, alg coisa a alguém) □ n censura f. above ~ irrepreensível. ~ful a repreensivo, reprovador. ~fully adv reprovadoramente

reproduc|e /ri:prə'dju:s/ vt/i reproduzir(-se). ~tion /-'dʌkʃn/ n reprodução f. ~tive /-'dʌktɪv/ a reprodutivo, reprodutor

reptile /'reptaɪl/ n réptil m

republic /rɪ'pʌblɪk/ n república f. ~an a & n republicano (m)

repudiate /rɪ'pju:dɪeɪt/ vt repudiar, rejeitar

repugnan|t /rɪ'pʌgnənt/ a repugnante. ~ce n repugnância f

repuls|e /rɪ'pʌls/ vt repelir, repulsar. ~ion /-ʃn/ n repulsa f. ~ive a repulsivo, repelente, repugnante

reputable /'repjʊtəbl/ a respeitado, honrado; (firm, make etc) de renome, conceituado

reputation /repjʊ'teɪʃn/ n reputação f

repute /rɪ'pju:t/ n reputação f. ~d /-ɪd/ a suposto, putativo. ~d to be tido como, tido na conta de. ~dly /-ɪdlɪ/ adv segundo consta, com fama de

request /rɪ'kwest/ n pedido m □ vt pedir, solicitar (of, from a)

requiem /'rekwɪəm/ n réquiem m; (mass) missa f de réquiem

require /rɪ'kwaɪə(r)/ vt requerer. ~d a requerido; (needed) necessário, preciso. ~ment n (fig) requisito m; (need) necessidade f, (demand) exigência f

requisite /'rekwɪzɪt/ a necessário □ n coisa necessária f, requisito m. ~s (for travel etc) artigos mpl

requisition /rekwɪ'zɪʃn/ n requisição f □ vt requisitar

resale /'ri:seɪl/ n revenda f

rescue /'reskju:/ vt salvar, socorrer (from de) □ n salvamento m; (help) socorro m, ajuda f. ~r /-ə(r)/ n salvador m

research /rɪ'sɜ:tʃ/ n pesquisa f, investigação f □ vt/i pesquisar, fazer investigação (into sobre). ~er n investigador m

resembl|e /rɪ'zembl/ vt assemelhar-se a, parecer-se com. ~ance n semelhança f, similaridade f (to com)

resent /rɪ'zent/ vt ressentir(-se de), ficar ressentido com. ~ful a ressentido. ~ment n ressentimento m

reservation /rezə'veɪʃn/ n (booking) reserva f; (Amer) reserva f (de índios)

reserve /rɪ'zɜ:v/ vt reservar □ n reserva f; (sport) suplente mf. in ~ de reserva. ~d a reservado

reservoir /'rezəvwɑ:(r)/ n (lake, supply etc) reservatório m; (container) depósito m

reshape /ri:'ʃeɪp/ vt remodelar

reshuffle /ri:'ʃʌfl/ vt (pol) remodelar □ n (pol) reforma f (do Ministério)

reside /rɪ'zaɪd/ vi residir

residen|t /'rezɪdənt/ a residente □ n morador m, habitante mf; (foreigner) residente mf; (in hotel) hóspede mf. ~ce n residência f; (of students) residência f, lar m. ~ce permit visto m de residência

residential /rezɪ'denʃl/ a residencial

residue /'rezɪdju:/ n resíduo m

resign /rɪ'zaɪm/ vt (post) demitir-se. ~ o.s. to resignar-se a □ vi demitir-se de. ~ation /rezɪg'neɪʃn/ n resignação f; (from job) demissão f. ~ed a resignado

resilien|t /rɪ'zɪlɪənt/ a (springy) elástico; (person) resistente. ~ce n elasticidade f; (of person) resistência f

resin /'rezɪn/ n resina f

resist /rɪ'zɪst/ vt/i resistir (a). ~ance n resistência f. ~ant a resistente

resolut|e /'rezəlu:t/ a resoluto. ~ion /-'lu:ʃn/ n resolução f

resolve /rɪ'zɒlv/ vt resolver. ~ to do resolver fazer □ n resolução f. ~d a (resolute) resoluto; (decided) resolvido (to a)

resonan|t /'rezənənt/ a ressonante. ~ce n ressonância f

resort /rɪ'zɔ:t/ vi ~ to recorrer a, valer-se de □ n recurso m; (place) estância f, local m turístico. as a last ~ em último recurso. seaside ~ praia f, balneário m, (P) estância f balnear

resound /rɪ'zaʊnd/ vi reboar, ressoar (with com). ~ing a ressoante; (fig) retumbante

resource /rɪ'sɔ:s/ n recurso m. ~s recursos mpl, riquezas fpl. ~ful a

expedito, engenhoso, desembaraçado.
~**fulness** *n* expediente *m*, engenho *m*
respect /rɪˈspekt/ *n* respeito *m* □ *vt*
respeitar. **with ~ to** a respeito de,
com respeito a, relativamente a.
~**ful** *a* respeitoso
respectab|le /rɪˈspektəbl/ *a* respeitá-
vel; (*passable*) passável, aceitável.
~**ility** /-ˈbɪlətɪ/ *n* res-peitabilidade *f*
respective /rɪˈspektɪv/ *a* respectivo.
~**ly** *adv* respectivamente
respiration /respəˈreɪʃn/ *n* respiração *f*
respite /ˈrespaɪt/ *n* pausa *f*, trégua *f*,
folga *f*
respond /rɪˈspɒnd/ *vi* responder (**to**
a); (*react*) reagir (**to** a)
response /rɪˈspɒns/ *n* resposta *f*; (*reaction*) reação *f*, (P) reacção *f*
responsib|le /rɪˈspɒnsəbl/ *a* respon-
sável; (*job*) de responsabilidade.
~**ility** /-ˈbɪlətɪ/ *n* responsabilidade
f
responsive /rɪˈspɒnsɪv/ *a* receptivo,
que reage bem. ~ **to** sensível a
rest[1] /rest/ *vt/i* descansar, repousar;
(*lean*) apoiar(-se) □ *n* descanso *m*, repouso *m*; (*support*) suporte *m*. ~-
room *n* (*Amer*) banheiro *m*, (P) toa-
letes *mpl*
rest[2] /rest/ *vi* (*remain*) ficar □ *n* (*remainder*) resto *m* (**of** de). **the ~ (of
the)** (*others*) os outros. **it ~s with
him** cabe a ele
restaurant /ˈrestrɒnt/ *n* restaurante
m
restful /ˈrestfl/ *a* sossegado, repou-
sante, tranqüilo, (P) tranquilo
restitution /restɪˈtjuːʃn/ *n* restituição
f; (*for injury*) indenização *f*, (P)
indemnização *f*
restless /ˈrestlɪs/ *a* agitado, desassos-
segado
restor|e /rɪˈstɔː(r)/ *vt* restaurar; (*give
back*) restituir, devolver. ~**ation**
/restəˈreɪʃn/ *n* restauração *f*
restrain /rɪˈstreɪn/ *vt* conter, reprimir. ~ **o.s.** controlar-se. ~ **sb
from** impedir alguém de. ~**ed** *a* comedido, reservado. ~**t** *n* controle *m*;
(*moderation*) moderação *f*, comedi-
mento *m*
restrict /rɪˈstrɪkt/ *vt* restringir,
limitar. ~**ion** /-ʃn/ *n* restrição *f*.
~**ive** *a* restritivo
result /rɪˈzʌlt/ *n* resultado *m* □ *vi* resultar (**from** de). ~ **in** resultar em
resum|e /rɪˈzjuːm/ *vt/i* reatar, reto-
mar; (*work, travel*) recomeçar.
~**ption** /rɪˈzʌmpʃn/ *n* reatamento *m*,
retomada *f*; (*of work*) recomeço *m*
résumé /ˈrezjuːmeɪ/ *n* resumo *m*
resurgence /rɪˈsɜːdʒəns/ *n* reapareci-
mento *m*, ressurgimento *m*

resurrect /rezəˈrekt/ *vt* ressuscitar.
~**ion** /-ʃn/ *n* ressureição *f*
resuscitat|e /rɪˈsʌsɪteɪt/ *vt* ressusci-
tar, reanimar. ~**ion** /-ˈteɪʃn/ *n*
reanimação *f*
retail /ˈriːteɪl/ *n* retalho *m* □ *a* & *adv* a
retalho □ *vt/i* vender(-se) a retalho.
~**er** *n* retalhista *mf*
retain /rɪˈteɪn/ *vt* reter; (*keep*) conservar, guardar
retaliat|e /rɪˈtælɪeɪt/ *vi* retaliar, exer-
cer represálias, desforrar-se. ~**ion**
/-ˈeɪʃn/ *n* retaliação *f*, represália *f*,
desforra *f*
retarded /rɪˈtaːdɪd/ *a* retardado, atrasado
retch /retʃ/ *vi* fazer esforço para vomitar, estar com ânsias de vômito
retention /rɪˈtenʃn/ *n* retenção *f*
retentive /rɪˈtentɪv/ *a* retentivo. ~
memory boa memória *f*
reticen|t /ˈretɪsnt/ *a* reticente. ~**ce** *n*
reticência *f*
retina /ˈretɪnə/ *n* retina *f*
retinue /ˈretɪnjuː/ *n* séquito *m*, comitiva *f*
retire /rɪˈtaɪə(r)/ *vi* reformar-se,
aposentar-se; (*withdraw*) retirar-se;
(*go to bed*) ir deitar-se □ *vt*
reformar, aposentar. ~**d** *a* reformado,
aposentado. ~**ment** *n* reforma *f*,
aposentadoria *f*, (P) aposentação *f*
retiring /rɪˈtaɪərɪŋ/ *a* reservado, retraído
retort /rɪˈtɔːt/ *vt/i* retrucar, retorquir
□ *n* réplica *f*
retrace /riːˈtreɪs/ *vt* ~ **one's steps**
refazer o mesmo caminho; (*fig*) recordar, recapitular
retract /rɪˈtrækt/ *vt/i* retratar(-se);
(*wheels*) recolher; (*claws*) encolher, recolher
retreat /rɪˈtriːt/ *vi* retirar-se; (*mil*) retirar, bater em retirada □ *n* retirada *f*;
(*seclusion*) retiro *m*
retrial /riːˈtraɪəl/ *n* novo julgamento
m
retribution /retrɪˈbjuːʃn/ *n* castigo
(merecido) *m*; (*vengeance*) vingança *f*
retriev|e /rɪˈtriːv/ *vt* ir buscar; (*res-
cue*) salvar; (*recover*) recuperar; (*put
right*) reparar. ~**al** *n* recuperação *f*.
information ~**al** (*comput*) acesso *m*
à informação. ~**er** *n* (*dog*) perdi-
gueiro *m*, (P) cobrador *m*
retrograde /ˈretrəɡreɪd/ *a* retrógrado
□ *vt* retroceder, recuar
retrospect /ˈretrəspekt/ *n* **in ~** em
retrospecto, (P) retrospectivamente.
~**ive** /-ˈspektɪv/ *a* retrospectivo; (*of
law, payment*) retroativo, (P) retroac-
tivo
return /rɪˈtɜːn/ *vi* voltar, regressar, re-
tornar (**to, a**) □ *vt* devolver; (*compli-*

ment, visit) retribuir; (*put back*) pôr de volta □ *n* volta *f*, regresso *m*, retorno *m*; (*profit*) lucro *m*, rendimento *m*; (*restitution*) devolução *f*. **in ~** for em troca de. **~ journey** viagem *f* de volta. **~ match** (*sport*) desafio *m* de desforra. **~ ticket** bilhete *m* de ida e volta. **many happy ~s (of the day)** muitos parabéns

reunion / riː'juːnɪən/ *n* reunião *f*

reunite /riːjuː'naɪt/ *vt* reunir

rev /rev/ *n* (*colloq: auto*) rotação *f* □ *vt/i* (*pt* **revved**) **~ (up)** (*colloq: auto*) acelerar (o motor)

reveal /rɪ'viːl/ *vt* revelar; (*display*) expor. **~ing** *a* revelador

revel /'revl/ *vi* (*pt* **revelled**) divertir-se. **~ in** deleitar-se com. **~ry** *n* festas *fpl*, festejos *mpl*

revelation /revə'leɪʃn/ *n* revelação *f*

revenge /rɪ'vendʒ/ *n* vingança *f*; (*sport*) desforra *f* □ *vt* vingar

revenue /'revənjuː/ *n* receita *f*, rendimento *m*. **Inland R~** Fisco *m*

reverberate /rɪ'vɜːbəreɪt/ *vi* ecoar, repercutir

revere /rɪ'vɪə(r)/ *vt* reverenciar, venerar

reverend /'revərənd/ *a* reverendo. **R~** Reverendo

reveren|t /'revərənt/ *a* reverente. **~ce** *n* reverência *f*, veneração *f*

revers|e /rɪ'vɜːs/ *a* contrário, inverso □ *n* contrário *m*; (*back*) reverso *m*; (*gear*) marcha *f* à ré, (P) atrás □ *vt* virar ao contrário; (*order*) inverter; (*turn inside out*) virar do avesso; (*decision*) anular □ *vi* (*auto*) fazer marcha à ré, (P) atrás. **~al** *n* inversão *f*, mudança *f* em sentido contrário; (*of view etc*) mudança *f*

revert /rɪ'vɜːt/ *vi* **~ to** reverter a

review /rɪ'vjuː/ *n* (*inspection; magazine*) revista *f*; (*of a situation*) revisão *f*; (*critique*) crítica *f* □ *vt* revistar, passar revista em; (*situation*) rever; (*book, film etc*) fazer a crítica de. **~er** *n* crítico *m*

revis|e /rɪ'vaɪz/ *vt/i* rever; (*amend*) corrigir. **~ion** /-ɪʒn/ *n* revisão *f*; (*amendment*) correção *f*

reviv|e /rɪ'vaɪv/ *vt/i* ressuscitar, reavivar; (*play*) reapresentar; (*person*) reanimar(-se). **~al** *n* reflorescimento *m*, renascimento *m*

revoke /rɪ'vəʊk/ *vt* revogar, anular, invalidar

revolt /rɪ'vəʊlt/ *vt/i* revoltar(-se) □ *n* revolta *f*

revolting /rɪ'vəʊltɪŋ/ *a* (*disgusting*) repugnante

revolution /revə'luːʃn/ *n* revolução *f*. **~ary** *a* & *n* revolucionário (*m*). **~ize** *vt* revolucionar

revolv|e /rɪ'vɒlv/ *vi* girar. **~ing door** porta *f* giratória

revolver /rɪ'vɒlvə(r)/ *n* revólver *m*

revulsion /rɪ'vʌlʃn/ *n* repugnância *f*, repulsa *f*

reward /rɪ'wɔːd/ *n* prêmio *m*, (P) prémio *m*; (*for criminal, for lost/stolen property*) recompensa *f* □ *vt* recompensar. **~ing** *a* compensador; (*task etc*) gratificante

rewind /riː'waɪnd/ *vt* (*pt* **rewound**) rebobinar

rewrite /riː'raɪt/ *vt* (*pt* **rewrote**, *pp* **rewritten**) reescrever

rhetoric /'retərɪk/ *n* retórica *f*. **~al** /rɪ'tɒrɪkl/ *a* retórico; (*question*) pro forma

rheumati|c /ruː'mætɪk/ *a* reumático. **~sm** /'ruːmətɪzm/ *n* reumatismo *m*

rhinoceros /raɪ'nɒsərəs/ *n* (*pl* **-oses**) rinoceronte *m*

rhubarb /'ruːbɑːb/ *n* ruibarbo *m*

rhyme /raɪm/ *n* rima *f*; (*poem*) versos *mpl* □ *vt/i* (fazer) rimar

rhythm /'rɪðəm/ *n* ritmo *m*. **~ic(al)** /'rɪðmɪk(l)/ *a* rítmico, compassado

rib /rɪb/ *n* costela *f*

ribbon /'rɪbən/ *n* fita *f*. **in ~s** em tiras

rice /raɪs/ *n* arroz *m*

rich /rɪtʃ/ *a* (**-er, -est**) rico; (*food*) rico em açúcar e gordura. **~es** *npl* riquezas *fpl*. **~ly** *adv* ricamente. **~ness** *n* riqueza *f*

rickety /'rɪkətɪ/ *a* (*shaky*) desconjuntado

ricochet /'rɪkəʃeɪ/ *n* ricochete *m* □ *vi* (*pt* **ricocheted** /-ʃeɪd/) fazer ricochete, ricochetear

rid /rɪd/ *vt* (*pt* **rid**, *pres p* **ridding**) desembaraçar (**of** de). **get ~ of** desembaraçar-se de, livrar-se de

riddance /'rɪdns/ *n* **good ~!** que alívio!, vai com Deus!

ridden /'rɪdn/ *see* **ride**

riddle¹ /'rɪdl/ *n* enigma *m*; (*puzzle*) charada *f*

riddle² /'rɪdl/ *vt* **~ with** crivar de

ride /raɪd/ *vi* (*pt* **rode**, *pp* **ridden**) andar (de bicicleta, a cavalo, de carro) □ *vt* (*horse*) montar; (*bicycle*) andar de; (*distance*) percorrer □ *n* passeio *m* or volta *f* (de carro, a cavalo etc); (*distance*) percurso *m*. **~r** /-ə(r)/ *n* cavaleiro *m*, amazona *f*; (*cyclist*) ciclista *mf*; (*in document*) aditamento *m*

ridge /rɪdʒ/ *n* aresta *f*; (*of hill*) cume *m*

ridicule /'rɪdɪkjuːl/ *n* ridículo *m* □ *vt* ridicularizar

ridiculous /rɪ'dɪkjʊləs/ *a* ridículo

riding /'raɪdɪŋ/ *n* equitação *f*

rife /raɪf/ *a* **be ~** estar espalhado; (*of illness*) grassar. **~ with** cheio de

riff-raff /'rɪfræf/ *n* gentinha *f*, povinho *m*, ralé *f*

rifle /'raɪfl/ *n* espingarda *f* □ *vt* revistar e roubar, saquear

rift /rɪft/ *n* fenda *f*, brecha *f*; (*fig: dissension*) desacordo *m*, desavença *f*, desentendimento *m*

rig[1] /rɪg/ *vt* (*pt* **rigged**) equipar □ *n* (*for oil*) plataforma *f* de poço de petróleo. ~ **out** enfarpelar (*colloq*). ~**-out** *n* (*colloq*) roupa *f*, farpela *f* (*colloq*). ~ **up** arranjar

rig[2] /rɪg/ *vt* (*pt* **rigged**) (*pej*) manipular. ~**ged** *a* (*election*) fraudulento

right /raɪt/ *a* (*correct, moral*) certo, correto, (*P*) correcto; (*fair*) justo; (*not left*) direito; (*suitable*) certo, próprio □ *n* (*entitlement*) direito *m*; (*not left*) direita *f*; (*not evil*) o bem □ *vt* (*a wrong*) reparar; (*sth fallen*) endireitar □ *adv* (*not left*) à direita; (*directly*) direito; (*exactly*) mesmo, bem; (*completely*) completamente. be ~ (*person*) ter razão (to em). be in the ~ ter razão. on the ~ à direita. put ~ acertar, corrigir. ~ of way (*auto*) prioridade *f*. ~ **angle** *n* ângulo reto *m*, (*P*) recto. ~ **away** logo, imediatamente. ~**-hand** *a* à *or* de direita. ~**-handed** *a* (*person*) destro. ~**-wing** *a* (*pol*) de direita

righteous /'raɪtʃəs/ *a* justo, virtuoso

rightful /'raɪtfl/ *a* legítimo. ~**ly** *adv* legitimamente, legalmente

rightly /'raɪtlɪ/ *adv* devidamente, corretamente, (*P*) correctamente; (*with reason*) justificadamente

rigid /'rɪdʒɪd/ *a* rígido. ~**ity** /rɪ-'dʒɪdətɪ/ *n* rigidez *f*

rigmarole /'rɪgmərəʊl/ *n* (*speech: procedure*) embrulhada *f*

rig|our /'rɪgə(r)/ *n* rigor *m*. ~**orous** *a* rigoroso

rile /raɪl/ *vt* (*colloq*) irritar, exasperar

rim /rɪm/ *n* borda *f*; (*of wheel*) aro *m*

rind /raɪnd/ *n* (*on cheese, fruit*) casca *f*; (*on bacon*) pele *f*

ring[1] /rɪŋ/ *n* (*on finger*) anel *m*; (*for napkin, key etc*) argola *f*; (*circle*) roda *f*, círculo *m*; (*boxing*) ringue *m*; (*arena*) arena *f*; (*of people*) quadrilha *f* □ *vt* rodear, cercar. ~ **road** *n* estrada *f* periférica *or* perimetral

ring[2] /rɪŋ/ *vt/i* (*pt* **rang**, *pp* **rung**) tocar; (*of words etc*) soar □ *n* toque *m*; (*colloq: phone call*) telefonadela *f* (*colloq*). ~ **the bell** tocar a campaínha. ~ **back** telefonar de volta. ~ **off** desligar. ~ **up** telefonar (a)

ringleader /'rɪŋliːdə(r)/ *n* cabeça *m*, cérebro *m*

rink /rɪŋk/ *n* rinque *m* de patinação

rinse /rɪns/ *vt* passar uma água, enxaguar □ *n* enxaguadura *f*, (*P*) enxaguadela *f*; (*hair tint*) rinsagem *f*

riot /'raɪət/ *n* distúrbio *m*, motim *m*; (*of colours*) festival *m* □ *vi* fazer distúrbios *or* motins. **run** ~ desenfrear-se, descontrolar-se; (*of plants*) crescer em matagal. ~**er** *n* desordeiro *m*

riotous /'raɪətəs/ *a* desenfreado, turbulento, desordeiro

rip /rɪp/ *vt/i* (*pt* **ripped**) rasgar(-se) □ *n* rasgão *m*. ~ **off** (*sl: defraud*) defraudar, enrolar (*sl*). ~**-off** *n* (*sl*) roubalheira *f* (*colloq*)

ripe /raɪp/ *a* (**-er, -est**) maduro. ~**ness** *n* madureza *f*, (*P*) amadurecimento *m*

ripen /'raɪpən/ *vt/i* amadurecer

ripple /'rɪpl/ *n* ondulação *f* leve; (*sound*) murmúrio *m* □ *vt/i* encrespar(-se), agitar(-se), ondular

rise /raɪz/ *vi* (*pt* **rose**, *pp* **risen**) subir, elevar-se; (*stand up*) erguer-se, levantar-se; (*rebel*) sublevar-se; (*sun*) nascer; (*curtain, prices*) subir □ *n* (*increase*) aumento *m*; (*slope*) subida *f*, ladeira *f*; (*origin*) origem *f*. **give** ~ **to** originar, causar, dar origem a. ~**r** /-ə(r)/ *n* **early** ~**r** madrugador *m*

rising /'raɪzɪŋ/ *n* (*revolt*) insurreição *f* □ *a* (*sun*) nascente

risk /rɪsk/ *n* risco *m* □ *vt* arriscar. **at** ~ em risco, em perigo. **at one's own** ~ por sua conta e risco. ~ **doing** (*venture*) arriscar-se a fazer. ~**y** *a* arriscado

risqué /'riːskeɪ/ *a* picante

rite /raɪt/ *n* rito *m*. **last** ~**s** últimos sacramentos *mpl*

ritual /'rɪtʃʊəl/ *a* & *n* ritual (*m*)

rival /'raɪvl/ *n* & *a* rival (*mf*); (*fig*) concorrente (*mf*), competidor (*m*) □ *vt* (*pt* **rivalled**) rivalizar com. ~**ry** *n* rivalidade *f*

river /'rɪvə(r)/ *n* rio *m* □ *a* fluvial

rivet /'rɪvɪt/ *n* rebite *m* □ *vt* (*pt* **riveted**) rebitar; (*fig*) prender, cravar. ~**ing** *a* fascinante

road /rəʊd/ *n* estrada *f*; (*in town*) rua *f*; (*small; fig*) caminho *m*. ~**-block** *n* barricada *f*. ~**-map** *n* mapa *m* das estradas. ~ **sign** *n* sinal *m*, placa *f* de sinalização. ~ **tax** imposto *m* de circulação. ~**-works** *npl* obras *fpl*

roadside /'rəʊdsaɪd/ *n* beira *f* da estrada

roadway /'rəʊdweɪ/ *n* pista *f* de rolamento, (*P*) rodagem *f*

roadworthy /'rəʊdwɜːðɪ/ *a* em condições de ser utilizado na rua/estrada

roam /rəʊm/ *vi* errar, andar sem destino □ *vt* percorrer

roar /rɔː(r)/ *n* berro *m*, rugido *m*; (*of thunder*) ribombo *m*, troar *m*; (*of sea,* *wind*) bramido *m* □ *vt/i* berrar, rugir; (*of lion*) rugir; (*of thunder*) ribombar, troar; (*of sea, wind*) bramir. ~ **with laughter** rir às gargalhadas

roaring /'rɔːrɪŋ/ *a* (*trade*) florescente; (*success*) enorme; (*fire*) com grandes chamas

roast /rəʊst/ *vt/i* assar □ *a* & *n* assado (*m*)

rob /rɒb/ *vt* (*pt robbed*) roubar (**sb of sth** alg coisa de alguém); (*bank*) assaltar; (*deprive*) privar (**of** de). ~**ber** *n* ladrão *m*. ~**bery** *n* roubo *m*; (*of bank*) assalto *m*

robe /rəʊb/ *n* veste *f* comprida e solta; (*dressing-gown*) robe *m*. ~**s** *npl* (*of judge etc*) toga *f*

robin /'rɒbɪn/ *n* papo-roxo *m*, (*P*) pintarroxo *m*

robot /'rəʊbɒt/ *n* robô *m*, (*P*) robot *m*, autômato *m*, (*P*) autómato *m*

robust /rəʊ'bʌst/ *a* robusto

rock[1] /rɒk/ *n* rocha *f*; (*boulder*) penhasco *m*, rochedo *m*; (*sweet*) pirulito *m*, (*P*) chupa-chupa *m* comprido. **on the ~s** (*colloq: of marriage*) em crise; (*colloq: of drinks*) com gelo. ~**bottom** *n* ponto *m* mais baixo □ *a* (*of prices*) baixíssimo (*colloq*)

rock[2] /rɒk/ *vt/i* balouçar(-se); (*shake*) abanar, sacudir; (*child*) embalar □ *n* (*mus*) rock *m*. ~**ing-chair** *n* cadeira *f* de balanço, (*P*) cadeira *f* de baloiço. ~**ing-horse** *n* cavalo *m* de balanço, (*P*) cavalo *m* de baloiço

rocket /'rɒkɪt/ *n* foguete *m*

rocky /'rɒkɪ/ *a* (**-ier, -iest**) (*ground*) pedregoso; (*hill*) rochoso; (*colloq: unsteady*) instável; (*colloq: shaky*) tremido (*colloq*)

rod /rɒd/ *n* vara *f*, vareta *f*; (*mech*) haste *f*; (*for curtains*) bastão *m*, (*P*) varão *m*; (*for fishing*) vara (de pescar) *f*

rode /rəʊd/ *see* **ride**

rodent /'rəʊdnt/ *n* roedor *m*

rodeo /rəʊ'deɪəʊ/ *n* (*pl* **-os**) rode(i)o *m*

roe /rəʊ/ *n* ova(s) *f* (*pl*) de peixe

rogue /rəʊg/ *n* (*dishonest*) patife *m*, velhaco *m*; (*mischievous*) brincalhão *m*

role /rəʊl/ *n* papel *m*

roll /rəʊl/ *vt/i* (fazer) rolar; (*into ball or cylinder*) enrolar(-se) □ *n* rolo *m*; (*list*) rol *m*, lista *f*; (*bread*) pãozinho *m*; (*of ship*) balanço *m*; (*of drum*) rufar *m*; (*of thunder*) ribombo *m*. **be ~ing in money** (*colloq*) nadar em dinheiro (*colloq*). ~ **over** (*turn over*) virar-se ao contrário. ~ **up** *vi* (*colloq*) aparecer □ *vt* (*sleeves*) arregaçar; (*umbrella*) fechar. ~**call** *n* chamada *f*. ~**ing-pin** *n* rolo *m* de pastel

roller /'rəʊlə(r)/ *n* cilindro *m*; (*wave*)

vagalhão *m*; (*for hair*) rolo *m*. ~**blind** *n* estore *m*. ~**coaster** *n* montanha *f* russa. ~**skate** *n* patim *m* de rodas

rolling /'rəʊlɪŋ/ *a* ondulante

Roman /'rəʊmən/ *a* & *n* romano (*m*). **R~ Catholic** *a* & *n* católico (*m*). ~ **numerals** algarismos *mpl* romanos

romance /rəʊ'mæns/ *n* (*love affair*) romance *m*; (*fig*) poesia *f*

Romania /ru'meɪnɪə/ *n* Romênia *f*, (*P*) Roménia *f*. ~**n** *a* & *n* romeno (*m*)

romantic /rəʊ'mæntɪk/ *a* romântico. ~**ally** *adv* românticamente. ~**ism** *n* romantismo *m*. ~**ize** *vi* fazer romance □ *vt* romantizar

romp /rɒmp/ *vi* brincar animadamente □ *n* brincadeira *f* animada. ~**ers** *npl* macacão *m* de bebê, (*P*) fato *m* de bebé

roof /ruːf/ *n* (*pl* **roofs**) telhado *m*; (*of car*) teto *m*, (*P*) capota *f*; (*of mouth*) palato *m*, céu *m* da boca □ *vt* cobrir com telhado. **hit the** ~ (*colloq*) ficar furioso. ~**ing** *n* material *m* para telhados. ~**rack** *n* porta-bagagem *m*. ~**top** *n* cimo *m* do telhado

rook[1] /rʊk/ *n* (*bird*) gralha *f*

rook[2] /rʊk/ *n* (*chess*) torre *f*

room /ruːm/ *n* quarto *m*, divisão *f*; (*bedroom*) quarto *m* de dormir; (*large hall*) sala *f*; (*space*) espaço *m*, lugar *m*. ~**s** (*lodgings*) apartamento *m*, cômodos *mpl*. ~**mate** *n* companheiro *m* de quarto. ~**y** *a* espaçoso; (*clothes*) amplo, largo

roost /ruːst/ *n* poleiro *m* □ *vi* empoleirar-se. ~**er** *n* (*Amer*) galo *m*

root[1] /ruːt/ *n* raiz *f*; (*fig*) origem *f* □ *vt/i* enraizar(-se), radicar(-se). ~ **out** extirpar, erradicar. **take** ~ criar raízes. ~**less** *a* sem raízes, desenraizado

root[2] /ruːt/ *vi* ~ **about** revolver, remexer. ~ **for** (*Amer sl*) torcer por

rope /rəʊp/ *n* corda *f* □ *vt* atar. **know the** ~**s** estar por dentro (do assunto). ~ **in** convencer a participar de

rosary /'rəʊzərɪ/ *n* rosário *m*

rose[1] /rəʊz/ *n* rosa *f*; (*nozzle*) ralo *m* (de regador). ~**bush** *n* roseira *f*

rose[2] /rəʊz/ *see* **rise**

rosé /'rəʊzeɪ/ *n* rosé *m*

rosette /rəʊ'zet/ *n* roseta *f*

rosewood /'rəʊzwʊd/ *n* pau-rosa *m*

roster /'rɒstə(r)/ *n* lista (de serviço) *f*, escala *f* de serviço

rostrum /'rɒstrəm/ *n* tribuna *f*; (*for conductor*) estrado *m*; (*sport*) podium *m*

rosy /'rəʊzɪ/ *a* (**-ier, -iest**) rosado; (*fig*) risonho

rot /rɒt/ *vt/i* (*pt rotted*) apodrecer □ *n*

putrefação f, podridão f; (sl: nonsense)
disparate m, asneiras fpl

rota /'rəʊtə/ n escala f de serviço

rotary /'rəʊtərɪ/ a rotativo, giratório

rotat|e /rəʊ'teɪt/ vt/i (fazer) girar,
(fazer) revolver; (change round)
alternar. ~ing a rotativo. ~ion /-ʃn/
n rotação f

rote /rəʊt/ n by ~ de cor, maquinal-
mente

rotten /'rɒtn/ a podre; (corrupt) corrupto; (colloq: bad) mau, ruim. ~
eggs ovos mpl podres. **feel** ~ (ill)
não se sentir nada bem

rotund /rəʊ'tʌnd/ a rotundo, redondo

rough /rʌf/ a (-er, -est) rude; (to
touch) áspero, rugoso; (of ground)
acidentado, irregular; (violent) violento; (of sea) agitado, encapelado; (of
weather) tempestuoso; (not perfect)
tosco, rudimentar; (of estimate etc)
aproximado □ n (ruffian) rufia m, desordeiro m □ adv (live) ao relento;
(play) bruto □ vt ~ **it** viver de modo
primitivo, não ter onde morar
(colloq). ~ **out** fazer um esboço
preliminar de. ~-and-ready a grosseiro mas eficiente. ~ **paper** rascunho m, borrão m. ~**ly** adv
asperamente, rudemente; (approximately) aproximadamente. ~**ness** n
rudeza f, aspereza f; (violence) brutalidade f

roughage /'rʌfɪdʒ/ n alimentos mpl
fibrosos

roulette /ru:'let/ n roleta f

round /raʊnd/ a (-er, -est) redondo □
n (circle) círculo m; (slice) fatia f,
(postman's) entrega f; (patrol) ronda
f; (of drinks) rodada f; (competition)
partida f, rodada f; (boxing) round
m; (of talks) ciclo m, série f □ prep &
adv em volta (de), em torno (de) □ vt
arredondar; (cape, corner) dobrar,
virar. **come** ~ (into consciousness)
voltar a si. **go** or **come** ~ **to** (a friend
etc) dar um pulo na casa de. ~ **about**
(nearby) por aí; (fig) mais ou menos.
~ **of applause** salva f de palmas. ~
off terminar. ~-**shouldered** a
curvado. ~ **the clock** noite e dia
sem parar. ~ **trip** viagem f de ida e
volta. ~ **up** (gather) juntar; (a figure)
arredondar. ~-**up** n (of cattle) rodeio
m; (of suspects) captura f

roundabout /'raʊndəbaʊt/ n carrossel m; (for traffic) rotatória f, (P) rotunda f □ a indireto, (P) indirecto

rous|e /raʊz/ vt acordar, despertar. **be**
~**ed** (angry) exaltar-se, inflamar-se,
ser provocado. ~**ing** a (speech) inflamado, exaltado; (music) vibrante;
(cheers) frenético

rout /raʊt/ n derrota f; (retreat) deban-

dada f □ vt derrotar; (cause to retreat)
pôr em debandada

route /ru:t/ n percurso m, itinerário
m; (naut, aviat) rota f

routine /ru:'ti:n/ n rotina f; (theat)
número m □ a de rotina, rotineiro.
daily ~ rotina f diária

rov|e /rəʊv/ vt/i errar (por), vaguear
(em/por). ~**ing** a (life) errante

row[1] /rəʊ/ n fila f, fileira f; (in knitting) carreira f. **in a** ~ (consecutive)
em fila

row[2] /rəʊ/ vt/i remar. ~**ing** n remo m.
~**ing-boat** n barco m a remo

row[3] /raʊ/ n (colloq: noise) barulho m,
bagunça f, banzé m (colloq); (colloq:
quarrel) discussão f, briga f. ~
(**with**) vi (colloq) brigar (com), discutir (com)

rowdy /'raʊdɪ/ a (-ier, -iest) desordeiro

royal /'rɔɪəl/ a real

royalty /'rɔɪəltɪ/ n família real f; (payment) direitos mpl (de autor, de patente, etc)

rub /rʌb/ vt/i (pt rubbed) esfregar;
(with ointment etc) esfregar, friccio-
nar □ n esfrega f; (with ointment etc)
fricção f. ~ **it in** repisar/insistir em.
~ **off on** comunicar-se a, transmitir-
se a. ~ **out** (with rubber) apagar

rubber /'rʌbə(r)/ n borracha f. ~
band elástico m. ~ **stamp** carimbo
m. ~-**stamp** vt aprovar sem
questionar. ~**y** a semelhante à borracha

rubbish /'rʌbɪʃ/ n (refuse) lixo m;
(nonsense) disparates mpl. ~ **dump**
n lixeira f. ~**y** a sem valor

rubble /'rʌbl/ n entulho m

ruby /'ru:bɪ/ n rubi m

rucksack /'rʌksæk/ n mochila f

rudder /'rʌdə(r)/ n leme m

ruddy /'rʌdɪ/ a (-ier, -iest) avermelhado; (of cheeks) corado, vermelho; (sl:
damned) maldito (colloq)

rude /ru:d/ a (-er, -est) mal-educado,
malcriado, grosseiro. ~**ly** adv grosseiramente, malcriadamente. ~**ness**
n má-educação f, má-criação f, grosseria f

rudiment /'ru:dɪmənt/ n rudimento
m. ~**ary** /-'mentrɪ/ a rudimentar

rueful /'ru:fl/ a contrito, pesaroso

ruffian /'rʌfɪən/ n desordeiro m

ruffle /'rʌfl/ vt (feathers) eriçar;
(hair) despentear; (clothes) amarrotar; (fig) perturbar □ n (frill) franzi-
do m, (P) folho m

rug /rʌg/ n tapete m; (covering) manta
f

rugged /'rʌgɪd/ a rude, irregular;
(coast, landscape) acidentado; (character) forte; (features) marcado

ruin /'ru:ın/ n ruína f □ vt arruinar; (fig) estragar. ~ous a desastroso

rule /ru:l/ n regra f; (regulation) regulamento m; (pol) governo m □ vt governar; (master) dominar; (jur) decretar; (decide) decidir □ vi governar. **as a ~** regra geral, por via de regra. **~ out** excluir. **~d paper** papel m pautado. ~r /-ə(r)/ n (sovereign) soberano m; (leader) governante m; (measure) régua f

ruling /'ru:lıŋ/ a (class) dirigente; (pol) no poder □ n decisão f

rum /rʌm/ n rum m

rumble /'rʌmbl/ vi ribombar, ressoar; (of stomach) roncar □ n ribombo m, estrondo m

rummage /'rʌmıdʒ/ vt revistar, remexer

rumour /'ru:mə(r)/ n boato m, rumor m □ vt **it is ~ed that** corre o boato de que, consta que

rump /rʌmp/ n (of horse etc) garupa f; (of fowl) mitra f. **~ steak** n bife m de alcatra

run /rʌn/ vi (pt ran, pp run, pres p running) correr; (flow) correr; (pass) passar; (function) andar, funcionar; (melt) derreter, pingar; (bus etc) circular; (play) estar em cartaz; (colour) desbotar; (in election) candidatar-se (for a) □ vt (manage) dirigir, gerir; (a risk) correr; (a race) participar em; (water) deixar correr; (a car) ter, manter □ n corrida f; (excursion) passeio m, ida f; (rush) corrida f, correria f; (in cricket) ponto m. **be on the ~** estar foragido. **have the ~** of ter à sua disposição. **in the long ~** a longo prazo. **~ across** encontrar por acaso, dar com. **~ away** fugir. **~ down** descer correndo; (of vehicle) atropelar; (belittle) dizer mal de, denegrir. **be ~ down** estar exausto. **~ in** (engine) ligar. **~ into** (meet) encontrar por acaso; (hit) bater em, ir de encontro a. **~ off** vt (copies) tirar; (water) deixar correr □ vi fugir. **~-of-the-mill** a vulgar. **~ out** esgotar-se; (lease) expirar. **I ran out of sugar** o açúcar acabou. **~ over** (of vehicle) atropelar. **~ up** deixar acumular. **the ~-up to** o período que precede

runaway /'rʌnəweı/ n fugitivo m □ a fugitivo; (horse) desembestado; (vehicle) desarvorado; (success) grande

rung¹ /rʌŋ/ n (of ladder) degrace m

rung² /rʌŋ/ see **ring**²

runner /'rʌnə(r)/ n (person) corredor m; (carpet) passadeira f. **~ bean** feijão m verde. **~-up** n segundo classificado m

running /'rʌnıŋ/ n corrida f; (functioning) funcionamento m □ a consecutivo, seguido; (water) corrente. **be in the ~** (competitor) ter probabilidades de êxito. **four days ~** quatro dias seguidos or a fio. **~ commentary** reportagem f, comentário m

runny /'rʌnı/ a derretido

runway /'rʌnweı/ n pista f de decolagem, (P) descolagem

rupture /'rʌptʃə(r)/ n ruptura f; (med) hérnia f □ vt/i romper(-se), rebentar

rural /'rʊərəl/ a rural

ruse /ru:z/ n ardil m, estratagema m, manha f

rush¹ /rʌʃ/ n (plant) junco m

rush² /rʌʃ/ vi (move) precipitar-se, (be in a hurry) apressar-se □ vt fazer, mandar etc a toda a pressa; (person) pressionar; (mil) tomar de assalto □ n tropel m; (haste) pressa f. **in a ~** as pressas. **~ hour** rush m, (P) hora f de ponta

rusk /rʌsk/ n bolacha f, biscoito m

russet /'rʌsıt/ a castanho avermelhado □ n maçã f reineta

Russia /'rʌʃə/ n Rússia f. ~n a & n russo (m)

rust /rʌst/ n (on iron, plants) ferrugem f □ vt/i enferrujar(-se). **~-proof** a inoxidável. **~y** a ferrugento, enferrujado; (fig) enferrujado

rustic /'rʌstık/ a rústico

rustle /'rʌsl/ vt/i restolhar, (fazer) farfalhar; (Amer: steal) roubar. **~ up** (colloq: food etc) arranjar

rut /rʌt/ n sulco m; (fig) rotina f. **in a ~** numa vida rotineira

ruthless /'ru:θlıs/ a implacável

rye /raı/ n centeio m

S

sabbath /'sæbəθ/ n (Jewish) sábado m; (Christian) domingo m

sabbatical /sə'bætıkl/ n (univ) período m de licença

sabot|age /'sæbəta:ʒ/ n sabotagem f □ vt sabotar. **~eur** /-'tɜ:(r)/ n sabotador m

sachet /'sæʃeı/ n saché m

sack /sæk/ n saco m, saca f □ vt (colloq) despedir. **get the ~** (colloq) ser despedido

sacrament /'sækrəmənt/ n sacramento m

sacred /'seıkrıd/ a sagrado

sacrifice /'sækrıfaıs/ n sacrifício m; (fig) sacrifício m □ vt sacrificar

sacrileg|e /'sækrılıdʒ/ n sacrilégio m. **~ious** /-'lıdʒəs/ a sacrílego

sad /sæd/ a (sadder, saddest) (person) triste; (story, news) triste. **~ly**

adv tristemente; (*unfortunately*) infelizmente. ~**ness** *n* tristeza *f*
sadden /'sædn/ *vt* entristecer
saddle /'sædl/ *n* sela *f* □ *vt* (*horse*) selar. ~ **sb with** sobrecarregar alguém com
sadis|m /'seɪdɪzəm/ *n* sadismo *m*. ~**t** /-ɪst/ *n* sádico *m*. ~**tic** /sə'dɪstɪk/ *a* sádico
safe /seɪf/ *a* (-er, -est) (*not dangerous*) seguro; (*out of danger*) fora de perigo; (*reliable*) confiável. ~ **from** salvo de risco de □ *n* cofre *m*, caixa-forte *f*. ~ **and sound** são e salvo. ~ **conduct** salvo-conduto *m*. ~ **keeping** custódia *f*, proteção *f*. **to be on the** ~ **side** por via das dúvidas. ~**ly** *adv* (*arrive etc*) em segurança; (*keep*) seguro
safeguard /'seɪfgaːd/ *n* salvaguarda *f* □ *vt* salvaguardar
safety /'seɪftɪ/ *n* segurança *f*. ~**-belt** *n* cinto *m* de segurança. ~**-pin** *n* alfinete *m* de fralda. ~**-valve** *n* válvula *f* de segurança
sag /sæg/ *vi* (*pt* **sagged**) afrouxar
saga /'saːgə/ *n* saga *f*
sage¹ /seɪdʒ/ *n* (*herb*) salva *f*
sage² /seɪdʒ/ *a* sensato, prudente □ *n* sábio *m*
Sagittarius /sædʒɪ'teərɪəs/ *n* (*astrol*) Sagitário *m*
said /sed/ *see* **say**
sail /seɪl/ *n* vela *f*; (*trip*) viagem *f* em barco à vela □ *vi* navegar; (*leave*) partir; (*sport*) velejar □ *vt* navegar. ~**ing** *n* navegação *f* à vela. ~**ing-boat** *n* barco *m* à vela
sailor /'seɪlə(r)/ *n* marinheiro *m*
saint /seɪnt/ *n* santo *m*. ~**ly** *a* santo, santificado
sake /seɪk/ *n* **for the** ~ **of** em consideração a. **for my/your/its own** ~ por mim/por isso
salad /'sæləd/ *n* salada *f*. ~ **dressing** *n* molho *m* para salada
salary /'sælərɪ/ *n* salário *m*
sale /seɪl/ *n* venda *f*; (*at reduced prices*) liquidação *f*. **for** ~ "vende-se". **on** ~ à venda. ~**s assistant**, (*Amer*) ~**s clerk** vendedor *m*. ~**s department** departamento *m* de vendas
sales|man /'seɪlzmən/ *n* (*pl* -**men**) (*in shop*) vendedor *m*; (*traveller*) caixeiro-viajante *m*. ~**woman** *n* (*pl* -**women**) (*in shop*) vendedora *f*; (*traveller*) caixeira-viajante *f*
saline /'seɪlaɪn/ *a* salino □ *n* salina *f*
saliva /sə'laɪvə/ *n* saliva *f*
sallow /'sæləʊ/ *a* (-er, -est) amarelado
salmon /'sæmən/ *n* (*pl invar*) salmão *m*
saloon /sə'luːn/ *n* (*on ship*) salão *m*; (*bar*) botequim *m*. ~ (**car**) sedã *m*

salt /sɔːlt/ *n* sal *m* □ *a* salgado □ *vt* (*season*) salgar; (*cure*) pôr em salmoura. ~**-cellar** *n* saleiro *m*. ~ **water** água *f* salgada, água *f* do mar. ~**y** *a* salgado
salutary /'sæljʊtrɪ/ *a* salutar
salute /sə'luːt/ *n* saudação *f* □ *vt/i* saudar
salvage /'sælvɪdʒ/ *n* (*naut*) salvamento *m*; (*of waste*) reciclagem *f* □ *vt* salvar
salvation /sæl'veɪʃn/ *n* salvação *f*
same /seɪm/ *a* & *n* mesmo (as que) □ *pron* **the** ~ o mesmo □ *adv* **the** ~ o mesmo. **all the** ~ (*nevertheless*) mesmo assim, apesar de tudo. **at the** ~ **time** (*at once*) ao mesmo tempo
sample /'saːmpl/ *n* amostra *f* □ *vt* experimentar, provar
sanatorium /sænə'tɔːrɪəm/ *n* (*pl* -**iums**) sanatório *m*
sanctify /'sæŋktɪfaɪ/ *vt* santificar
sanctimonious /sæŋktɪ'məʊnɪəs/ *a* santarrão, carola
sanction /'sæŋkʃn/ *n* (*approval*) aprovação *f*; (*penalty*) pena *f*, sanção *f* □ *vt* sancionar
sanctity /'sæŋktɪtɪ/ *n* santidade *f*
sanctuary /'sæŋktʃʊərɪ/ *n* (*relig*) santuário *m*; (*refuge*) refúgio *m*; (*for animals*) reserva *f*
sand /sænd/ *n* areia *f*; (*beach*) praia *f* □ *vt* (*with sandpaper*) lixar
sandal /'sændl/ *n* sandália *f*
sandbag /'sændbæg/ *n* saco *m* de areia
sandbank /'sændbæŋk/ *n* banco *m* de areia
sandcastle /'sændkaːsl/ *n* castelo *m* de areia
sandpaper /'sændpeɪpə(r)/ *n* lixa *f* □ *vt* lixar
sandpit /'sændpɪt/ *n* caixa *f* de areia
sandwich /'sænwɪdʒ/ *n* sanduíche *m*, (*P*) sandes *f invar* □ *vt* ~**ed between** encaixado entre. ~ **course** curso *m* profissionalizante envolvendo estudo teórico e estágio em local de trabalho
sandy /'sændɪ/ *a* (-ier, iest) arenoso; (*beach*) arenoso; (*hair*) ruivo
sane /seɪn/ *a* (-er, -est) (*not mad*) são *m*; (*sensible*) sensato, ajuizado
sang /sæŋ/ *see* **sing**
sanitary /'sænɪtrɪ/ *a* sanitário; (*system*) sanitário. ~ **towel**, (*Amer*) ~ **napkin** toalha *f* absorvente
sanitation /sænɪ'teɪʃn/ *n* condições *fpl* sanitárias, saneamento *m*
sanity /'sænɪtɪ/ *n* sanidade *f*
sank /sæŋk/ *see* **sink**
Santa Claus /'sæntəklɔːz/ *n* Papai Noel *m*
sap /sæp/ *n* seiva *f* □ *vt* (*pt* **sapped**) esgotar, minar

sapphire /'sæfaɪə(r)/ n safira f
sarcas|m /'saːrkæzəm/ n sarcasmo m.
~tic /saːr'kæstɪk/ a sarcástico
sardine /saː'diːn/ n sardinha f
sardonic /saː'dɒnɪk/ a sardônico
sash /sæʃ/ n (around waist) cinto m;
(over shoulder) faixa f. ~window n
janela f de guilhotina
sat /sæt/ see sit
satanic /sə'tænɪk/ a satânico
satchel /'sætʃl/ n sacola f
satellite /'sætəlaɪt/ n satélite m. ~
dish antena f de satélite. ~ television televisão f via satélite
satin /'sætɪn/ n cetim m
satir|e /'sætaɪə(r)/ n sátira f. ~ical
/sə'tɪrɪkl/ a satirical. ~ist /'sætərɪst/
n satirista mf. ~ize vt satirizar
satisfact|ion /sætɪs'fækʃn/ n satis-
fação f. ~ory /fæktərɪ/ a satisfatório
satisfy /'sætɪsfaɪ/ vt satisfazer; (convince) convencer; (fulfil) atender.
~ing a satisfatório
satura|te /'sætʃəreɪt/ vt saturar; (fig)
~ed a (wet) encharcado; (fat)
saturado. ~ion /'reɪʃn/ n saturação f
Saturday /'sætədɪ/ n sábado m
sauce /sɔːs/ n molho m; (colloq: cheek)
atrevimento m
saucepan /'sɔːspən/ n panela f, (P)
caçarola f
saucer /'sɔːsə(r)/ n pires m invar
saucy /'sɔːsɪ/ a (-ier, -iest) picante
Saudi Arabia /saʊdɪə'reɪbɪə/ n
Arábia f Saudita
sauna /'sɔːnə/ n sauna f
saunter /'sɔːntə(r)/ vi perambular
sausage /'sɒsɪdʒ/ n salsicha f,
linguiça f; (precooked) salsicha f
savage /'sævɪdʒ/ a (wild) selvagem;
(fierce) cruel; (brutal) brutal □ n selvagem mf □ vt atacar ferozmente.
~ry n selvageria f, ferocidade f
sav|e /seɪv/ vt (rescue) salvar; (keep)
guardar; (collect) colecionar; (money)
economizar; (time) ganhar; (prevent)
evitar, impedir (from de) □ n (sport)
salvamento m □ prep salvo, exceto.
~er n poupador m. ~ing n economia f, poupança f. ~ings npl econo-
mias fpl
saviour /'seɪvɪə(r)/ n salvador m
savour /'seɪvə(r)/ n sabor m □ vt
saborear. ~y a (tasty) saboroso; (not
sweet) salgado
saw¹ /sɔː/ see see¹
saw² /sɔː/ n serra f □ vt (pt sawed, pp
sawn or sawed) serrar
sawdust /'sɔːdʌst/ n serragem f
saxophone /'sæksəfəʊn/ n saxofone
m
say /seɪ/ vt/i (pt said /sed/) □ n have
a ~ (in) opinar sobre alg coisa. have

one's ~ exprimir sua opinião. I ~!
olhe! or escute! ~ing n ditado m,
provérbio m
scab /skæb/ n casca f, crosta f; (colloq:
blackleg) fura-greve mf invar
scaffold /'skæfəʊld/ n cadafalso m,
andaime m. ~ing /-əldɪŋ/ n andaime
m
scald /skɔːld/ vt escaldar, queimar □ n
escaldadura f
scale¹ /skeɪl/ n (of fish etc) escama f
scale² /skeɪl/ n (ratio, size) escala f;
(mus) escala f; (of salaries, charges)
tabela f. on a small/large/etc ~
numa pequena/grande/etc escala □
vt (climb) escalar. ~ down reduzir
scales /skeɪlz/ npl (for weighing)
balança f
scallop /'skɒləp/ n (culin) concha f de
vieira; (shape) concha f de vieira
scalp /skælp/ n couro m cabeludo □ vt
escalpar
scalpel /'skælpl/ n bisturi m
scamper /'skæmpə(r)/ vi sair correndo
scampi /'skæmpɪ/ npl camarões mpl
fritos
scan /skæn/ vt (pt scanned) (intently)
perscrutar, esquadrinhar; (quickly)
passar os olhos em; (med) examinar;
(radar) explorar □ n (med) exame m
scandal /'skændl/ n (disgrace)
escândalo m; (gossip) fofoca f. ~ous
a escandaloso
Scandinavia /skændɪ'neɪvɪə/ n
Escandinávia f. ~n a & n escandinavo (m)
scanty /'skæntɪ/ a (-ier, -iest) escasso;
(clothing) sumário
scapegoat /'skeɪpgəʊt/ n bode m expiatório
scar /skaː(r)/ n cicatriz f □ vt (pt
scarred) marcar; (fig) deixar marcas
scarc|e /skeəs/ a (-er, -est) escasso,
raro. make o.s. ~e (colloq) sumir,
dar o fora (colloq). ~ity n escassez
f. ~ely adv mal, apenas
scare /skeə(r)/ vt assustar, apavorar.
be ~d estar com medo (of de) □ n
pavor m, pânico m. bomb ~ pânico
m causado por suspeita de bomba
num local
scarecrow /'skeəkrəʊ/ n espantalho
m
scarf /skaːf/ n (pl scarves) (oblong)
cachecol m; (square) lenço m de cabelo
scarlet /'skaːlət/ a escarlate m
scary /'skeərɪ/ a (-ier, -iest) (colloq)
assustador, apavorante
scathing /'skeɪðɪŋ/ a mordaz
scatter /'skætə(r)/ vt (strew) espalhar;
(disperse) dispersar □ vi espalhar-se
scavenge /'skævɪndʒ/ vi procurar

comida *etc* no lixo. ~r /-ə(r)/ *n* (*person*) que procura comida *etc* no lixo; (*animal*) que se alimenta de carniça

scenario /sɪ'nɑːrɪəu/ *n* (*pl* -**os**) sinopse *f*, resumo *m* detalhado

scene /siːn/ *n* cena *f*; (*of event*) cenário *m*; (*sight*) vista *f*, panorama *m*. **behind the** ~**s** nos bastidores. **make a** ~ fazer um escândalo

scenery /'siːnərɪ/ *n* cenário *m*, paisagem *f*; (*theat*) cenário *m*

scenic /'siːnɪk/ *a* pitoresco, cênico

scent /sent/ *n* (*perfume*) perfume *m*, fragância *f*; (*trail*) rastro *m*, pista *f* □ *vt* (*discern*) sentir. ~**ed** *a* perfumado

sceptic /'skeptɪk/ *n* cético *m*. ~**al** *a* cético. ~**ism** /-sɪzəm/ *n* ceticismo *m*

schedule /'ʃedjuːl/ *n* programa *m*; (*timetable*) horário *m* □ *vt* marcar, programar. **according to** ~ conforme planejado. **behind** ~ atrasado. **on** ~ (*train*) na hora; (*work*) em dia. ~**d flight** *n* vôo *m* regular

scheme /skiːm/ *n* esquema *m*; (*plan of work*) plano *m*; (*plot*) conspiração *f*, maquinação *f* □ *vi* planejar, (*P*) planear; (*pej*) intrigar, maquinar, tramar

schism /'sɪzəm/ *n* cisma *m*

schizophreni|a /skɪtsəu'friːnɪə/ *n* esquizofrenia *f*. ~**c** /-'frenɪk/ *a* esquizofrênico, (*P*) esquizofrénico

scholar /'skɒlə(r)/ *n* erudito *m*, estudioso *m*, escolar *m*. ~**ly** *a* erudito. ~**ship** *n* erudição *f*, saber *m*; (*grant*) bolsa *f* de estudo

school /skuːl/ *n* escola *f*; (*of university*) escola *f*, faculdade *f* □ *a* (*age, year, holidays*) escolar □ *vt* ensinar; (*train*) treinar, adestrar. ~**ing** *n* instrução *f*; (*attendance*) escolaridade *f*

school|boy /'skuːlbɔɪ/ *n* aluno *m*. ~**girl** *n* aluna *f*

school|master /'skuːlmɑːstə(r)/, ~**mistress**, ~**teacher** *ns* professor *m*, professora *f*

schooner /'skuːnə(r)/ *n* escuna *f*; (*glass*) copo *m* alto

sciatica /saɪ'ætɪkə/ *n* ciática *f*

scien|ce /'saɪəns/ *n* ciência *f*. ~**ce fiction** ficção *f* científica. ~**tific** /-'tɪfɪk/ *a* científico

scientist /'saɪəntɪst/ *n* cientista *mf*

scintillate /'sɪntɪleɪt/ *vi* cintilar; (*fig: person*) brilhar

scissors /'sɪzəz/ *npl* (**pair of**) ~ tesoura *f*

scoff[1] /skɒf/ *vi* ~ **at** zombar de, (*P*) troçar de

scoff[2] /skɒf/ *vt* (*sl: eat*) devorar, tragar

scold /skəuld/ *vt* ralhar com. ~**ing** *n* repreensão *f*, (*P*) descompostura *f*

scone /skɒn/ *n* (*culin*) scone *m*, bolinho *m* para o chá

scoop /skuːp/ *n* (*for grain, sugar etc*) pá *f*, (*ladle*) concha *f*; (*news*) furo *m* □ *vt* ~ **out** (*hollow out*) escavar, tirar com concha *or* pá. ~ **up** (*lift*) apanhar

scoot /skuːt/ *vi* (*colloq*) fugir, mandar-se (*colloq*), (*P*) pôr-se a milhas (*colloq*)

scooter /'skuːtə(r)/ *n* (*child's*) patinete *f*, (*P*) trotinete *m*; (*motor cycle*) motoreta *f*, lambreta *f*

scope /skəup/ *n* âmbito *m*; (*fig: opportunity*) oportunidade *f*

scorch /skɔːtʃ/ *vt/i* chamuscar(-se), queimar de leve. ~**ing** *a* (*colloq*) escaldante, abrasador

score /skɔː(r)/ *n* (*sport*) contagem *f*, escore *m*; (*mus*) partitura *f* □ *vt* marcar com corte(s), riscar; (*a goal*) marcar; (*mus*) orquestrar □ *vi* marcar pontos; (*keep score*) fazer a contagem; (*football*) marcar um gol, (*P*) golo. **a** ~ (**of**) (*twenty*) uma vintena (de), vinte. ~**s** muitos, dezenas. **on that** ~ nesse respeito, quanto a isso. ~**board** *n* marcador *m*. ~**r** /-ə(r)/ *n* (*score-keeper*) marcador *m*; (*of goals*) autor *m*

scorn /skɔːn/ *n* desprezo *m* □ *vt* desprezar. ~**ful** *a* desdenhoso, escarninho. ~**fully** *adv* com desdém, desdenhosamente

Scorpio /'skɔːpɪəu/ *n* (*astr*) Escorpião *m*

scorpion /'skɔːpɪən/ *n* escorpião *m*

Scot /skɒt/ *n*, ~**tish** *a* escocês (*m*)

Scotch /skɒtʃ/ *a* escocês □ *n* uísque *m*

scotch /skɒtʃ/ *vt* pôr fim a, frustrar

scot-free /skɒt'friː/ *a* impune □ *adv* impunemente

Scotland /'skɒtlənd/ *n* Escócia *f*

Scots /skɒts/ *a* escocês. ~**man** *n* escocês *m*. ~**woman** *n* escocesa *f*

scoundrel /'skaundrəl/ *n* patife *m*, canalha *m*

scour[1] /'skauə(r)/ *vt* (*clean*) esfregar, arear. ~**er** *n* esfregão *m* de palha de aço *or* de nylon

scour[2] /'skauə(r)/ *vt* (*search*) percorrer, esquadrinhar

scourge /skɜːdʒ/ *n* açoite *m*; (*fig*) flagelo *m*

scout /skaut/ *n* (*mil*) explorador *m* □ *vi* ~ **about** (**for**) andar à procura de

Scout /skaut/ *n* escoteiro *m*, (*P*) escuteiro *m*. ~**ing** *n* escotismo *m*, (*P*) escutismo *m*

scowl /skaul/ *n* carranca *f*, ar *m* carrancudo □ *vi* fazer um ar carrancudo

scraggy /'skrægɪ/ *a* (-**ier**, -**iest**) descarnado, ossudo

scramble /'skræmbl/ *vi* trepar; (*crawl*) avançar de rastros, rastejar, arrastar-se □ *vt* (*eggs*) mexer □ *n* luta *f*, confusão *f*

scrap[1] /skræp/ *n* bocadinho *m*. ~**s**

npl restos *mpl* □ *vt* (*pt* **scrapped**) jogar fora, (*P*) deitar fora; (*plan etc*) abandonar, pôr de lado. **~-book** *n* álbum *m* de recortes. **~ heap** monte *m* de ferro-velho. **~-iron** *n* ferro *m* velho, sucata *f*. **~ merchant** sucateiro *m*. **~-paper** *n* papel *m* de rascunho. **~py** *a* fragmentário

scrap² /skræp/ *n* (*colloq: fight*) briga *f*, pancadaria *f* (*colloq*), rixa *f*

scrape /skreɪp/ *vt* raspar; (*graze*) esfolar, arranhar □ *vi* (*graze, rub*) roçar □ *n* (*act of scraping*) raspagem *f*; (*mark*) raspão *m*, esfoladura *f*; (*fig*) encrenca *f*, maus lençóis *mpl*. **~ through** escapar pela tangente, (*P*) à tangente; (*exam*) passar pela tangente, (*P*) à tangente. **~ together** conseguir juntar. **~r** /-ə(r)/ *n* raspadeira *f*

scratch /skrætʃ/ *vt/i* arranhar(-se); (*a line*) riscar; (*to relieve itching*) coçar(-se) □ *n* arranhão *m*; (*line*) risco *m*; (*wound with claw, nail*) unhada *f*. **start from ~** começar do princípio. **up to ~** à altura, ao nível requerido

scrawl /skrɔːl/ *n* rabisco *m*, garrancho *m*, garatuja *f* □ *vt/i* rabiscar, fazer garranchos, garatujar

scrawny /ˈskrɔːnɪ/ *a* (*-ier, -iest*) descarnado, ossudo, magricela

scream /skriːm/ *vt/i* gritar □ *n* grito *m* (agudo)

screech /skriːtʃ/ *vi* guinchar, gritar; (*of brakes*) chiar, guinchar □ *n* guincho *m*, grito *m* agudo

screen /skriːn/ *n* écran *m*, tela *f*; (*folding*) biombo *m*; (*fig: protection*) manto *m* (*fig*), capa *f* (*fig*) □ *vt* resguardar, tapar; (*film*) passar; (*candidates etc*) fazer a triagem de. **~ing** *n* (*med*) exame *m* médico

screw /skruː/ *n* parafuso *m* □ *vt* aparafusar, atarraxar. **~ up** (*eyes, face*) franzir; (*sl: ruin*) estragar. **~ up one's courage** cobrar coragem

screwdriver /ˈskruːdraɪvə(r)/ *n* chave *f* de parafusos *or* de fenda

scribble /ˈskrɪbl/ *vt/i* rabiscar, garatujar □ *n* rabisco *m*, garatuja *f*

script /skrɪpt/ *n* escrita *f*; (*of film*) roteiro *m*, (*P*) guião *m*. **~-writer** *n* (*film*) roteirista *m*, (*P*) autor *m* do guião

Scriptures /ˈskrɪptʃəz/ *npl* the **~** a Sagrada Escritura

scroll /skrəʊl/ *n* rolo *m* (de papel ou pergaminho); (*archit*) voluta *f* □ *vt/i* (*comput*) passar na tela

scrounge /skraʊndʒ/ *vt* (*colloq: cadge*) filar (*sl*), (*P*) cravar (*sl*) □ *vi* (*beg*) parasitar, viver às custas de alguém. **~r** /-ə(r)/ *n* parasita *mf*, filão *m* (*sl*), (*P*) crava *mf* (*sl*)

scrub¹ /skrʌb/ *n* (*land*) mato *m*

scrub² /skrʌb/ *vt/i* (*pt* **scrubbed**) esfregar, lavar com escova e sabão; (*colloq: cancel*) cancelar □ *n* esfrega *f*

scruff /skrʌf/ *n* **by the ~ of the neck** pelo cangote, (*P*) pelo cachaço

scruffy /ˈskrʌfɪ/ *a* (*-ier, -iest*) desmazelado, desleixado, mal ajambrado (*colloq*)

scrum /skrʌm/ *n* rixa *f*; (*Rugby*) placagem *f*

scruple /ˈskruːpl/ *n* escrúpulo *m*

scrupulous /ˈskruːpjʊləs/ *a* escrupuloso. **~ly** *adv* escrupulosamente. **~ly clean** impecavelmente limpo

scrutin|y /ˈskruːtɪnɪ/ *n* averiguação *f*, escrutínio *m*. **~ize** *vt* examinar em detalhes

scuff /skʌf/ *vt* (*scrape*) esfolar, safar □ *n* esfoladura *f*

scuffle /ˈskʌfl/ *n* tumulto *m*, briga *f*

sculpt /skʌlpt/ *vt/i* esculpir. **~or** *n* escultor *m*. **~ure** /-tʃə(r)/ *n* escultura *f* □ *vt/i* esculpir

scum /skʌm/ *n* (*on liquid*) espuma *f*; (*pej: people*) gentinha *f*, escumalha *f*, ralé *f*

scurf /skɜːf/ *n* películas *fpl*; (*dandruff*) caspa *f*

scurrilous /ˈskʌrɪləs/ *a* injurioso, insultuoso

scurry /ˈskʌrɪ/ *vi* dar corridinhas; (*hurry*) apressar-se. **~ off** escapulir-se

scurvy /ˈskɜːvɪ/ *n* escorbuto *m*

scuttle¹ /ˈskʌtl/ *n* (*bucket, box*) balde *m* para carvão

scuttle² /ˈskʌtl/ *vt* (*ship*) afundar abrindo rombos *or* as torneiras de fundo

scuttle³ /ˈskʌtl/ *vi* **~ away** *or* **off** fugir, escapulir-se

scythe /saɪð/ *n* gadanha *f*, foice *f* grande

sea /siː/ *n* mar *m* □ *a* do mar, marinho, marítimo. **at ~** no alto mar, ao largo. **all at ~** desnorteado. **by ~** por mar. **~bird** ave *f* marinha. **~-green** *a* verde-mar. **~ horse** cavalo-marinho *m*, hipocampo *m*. **~ level** nível *m* do mar. **~ lion** leão-marinho *m*. **~ shell** concha *f*. **~-shore** *n* litoral *m*; (*beach*) praia *f*. **~ water** água *f* do mar

seaboard /ˈsiːbɔːd/ *n* litoral *m*, costa *f*

seafarer /ˈsiːfeərə(r)/ *n* marinheiro *m*, navegante *m*

seafood /ˈsiːfuːd/ *n* marisco(s) *m* (*pl*)

seagull /ˈsiːɡʌl/ *n* gaivota *f*

seal¹ /siːl/ *n* (*animal*) foca *f*

seal² /siːl/ *n* selo *m*, sinete *m* □ *vt* selar; (*with wax*) lacrar. **~ing-wax** *n* lacre *m*. **~ off** (*area*) vedar

seam /siːm/ *n* (*in cloth etc*) costura *f*; (*of mineral*) veio *m*, filão *m*. **~less** *a* sem costura

seaman /'si:mən/ n (pl -men) marinheiro m, marítimo m

seamy /'si:mɪ/ a ~ **side** lado m (do) avesso; (fig) lado m sórdido

seance /'seɪɑ:ns/ n sessão f espírita

seaplane /'si:pleɪn/ n hidroavião m

seaport /'si:pɔ:t/ n porto m de mar

search /sɜ:tʃ/ vt/i revistar, dar busca (a); (one's heart, conscience etc) examinar □ n revista f, busca f; (quest) procura f, busca f; (official) inquérito m. **in** ~ **of** à procura de. ~ **for** procurar. **~-party** n equipe f de busca. **~-warrant** n mandado m de busca. **~ing** a (of look) penetrante; (of test etc) minucioso

searchlight /'sɜ:tʃlaɪt/ n holofote m

seasick /'si:sɪk/ a enjoado. **~ness** n enjôo m, P enjoo m

seaside /'si:saɪd/ n costa f, praia f, beira-mar f. ~ **resort** n balneário m, praia f

season /'si:zn/ n (of year) estação f, (proper time) época f; (cricket, football etc) temporada f □ vt temperar; (wood) secar. **in** ~ na época. **~able** a próprio da estação. **~al** a sazonal. **~ed** a (of people) experimentado. **~ing** n tempero m. **~-ticket** n (train etc) passe m; (theatre etc) assinatura f

seat /si:t/ n assento m; (place) lugar m; (of bicycle) selim m; (of chair) assento m; (of trousers) fundilho m □ vt sentar; (have seats for) ter lugares sentados para. **be ~ed, take a ~** sentar-se. ~ **of learning** centro m de cultura. **~-belt** n cinto m de segurança

seaweed /'si:wi:d/ n alga f marinha

seaworthy /'si:wɜ:ðɪ/ a navegável, em condições de navegabilidade

secateurs /'sekətɜ:z/ npl tesoura f de poda

seclu|de /sɪ'klu:d/ vt isolar. **~ded** a isolado, retirado. **~sion** /sɪ'klu:ʒn/ n isolamento m

second[1] /'sekənd/ a segundo □ n segundo m; (in duel) testemunha f. ~ **(gear)** (auto) segunda f (velocidade). **the ~ of April** dois de Abril. **~s** (goods) artigos mpl de segunda or de refugo □ adv (in race etc) em segundo lugar □ vt secundar. **~-best** a escolhido em segundo lugar. **~-class** a de segunda classe. **~-hand** a de segunda mão □ n (on clock) ponteiro m dos segundos. **~-rate** a medíocre, de segunda ordem. ~ **thoughts** dúvidas fpl. **on ~ thoughts** pensando melhor. **~ly** adv segundo, em segundo lugar

second[2] /sɪ'kɒnd/ vt (transfer) destacar (to para)

secondary /'sekəndrɪ/ a secundário. ~ **school** escola f secundária

secrecy /'si:krəsɪ/ n segredo m

secret /'si:krɪt/ a secreto □ n segredo m. **in** ~ em segredo. ~ **agent** n agente mf secreto. **~ly** adv em segredo, secretamente

secretar|y /'sekrətrɪ/ n secretário m, secretária f. **S~y of State** ministro m de Estado, (P) Secretário m de Estado; (Amer) ministro m dos Negócios Estrangeiros. **~ial** /-'teərɪəl/ a (work, course etc) de secretária

secret|e /sɪ'kri:t/ vt segregar; (hide) esconder. **~ion** /-ʃn/ n secreção f

secretive /'si:krətɪv/ a misterioso, reservado

sect /sekt/ n seita f. **~arian** /'teərɪən/ a sectário

section /'sekʃn/ n seção f, (P) secção f; (of country, community etc) setor m, (P) sector m; (district of town) zona f

sector /'sektə(r)/ n setor m, (P) sector m

secular /'sekjʊlə(r)/ a secular, leigo, P laico; (art, music etc) profano

secure /sɪ'kjʊə(r)/ a seguro, em segurança; (firm) seguro, sólido; (in mind) tranqüilo, P tranquilo □ vt prender bem or com segurança; (obtain) conseguir, arranjar; (ensure) assegurar; (windows, doors) fechar bem. **~ly** adv solidamente; (safely) em segurança

securit|y /sɪ'kjʊərətɪ/ n segurança f; (for loan) fiança f, caução f. **~ies** npl (finance) títulos mpl

sedate /sɪ'deɪt/ a sereno, comedido □ vt (med) tratar com sedativos

sedation /sɪ'deɪʃn/ n (med) sedação f. **under** ~ sob o efeito de sedativos

sedative /'sedətɪv/ n (med) sedativo m

sedentary /'sedntrɪ/ a sedentário

sediment /'sedɪmənt/ n sedimento m, depósito m

seduce /sɪ'dju:s/ vt seduzir

seduct|ion /sɪ'dʌkʃn/ n sedução f. **~ive** /-tɪv/ a sedutor, aliciante

see[1] /si:/ vt/i (pt **saw**, pp **seen**) ver; (escort) acompanhar. ~ **about** or **to** tratar de, encarregar-se de. ~ **off** vt (wave goodbye) ir despedir-se de; (chase) ~ **through** (task) levar a cabo; (not be deceived by) não se deixar enganar por. ~ **(to it) that** assegurar que, tratar de fazer com que. **~ing that** visto que, uma vez que. ~ **you later!** (colloq) até logo! (colloq)

see[2] /si:/ n sé f, bispado m

seed /si:d/ n semente f; (fig: origin) germe(n) m; (tennis) cabeça f de série; (pip) caroço m. **go to** ~ produzir sementes; (fig) desmazelar-se (colloq).

~**ling** *n* planta *f* brotada a partir da semente

seedy /'si:dɪ/ *a* (**-ier, -iest**) (com um ar) gasto, surrado; (*colloq: unwell*) abatido, deprimido, em baixo astral (*colloq*)

seek /si:k/ *vt* (*pt* **sought**) procurar; (*help etc*) pedir

seem /si:m/ *vi* parecer. ~**ingly** *adv* aparentemente, ao que parece

seemly /'si:mlɪ/ *adv* decente, conveniente, próprio

seen /si:n/ *see* **see**[1]

seep /si:p/ *vi* (*ooze*) filtrar-se; (*trickle*) pingar, escorrer, passar. ~**age** *n* infiltração *f*

see-saw /'si:sɔ:/ *n* gangorra *f*, (*P*) balanço *m*

seethe /si:ð/ *vi* ~ **with** (*anger*) ferver de; (*people*) fervilhar de

segment /'segmənt/ *n* segmento *m*; (*of orange*) gomo *m*

segregat|e /'segrɪgeɪt/ *vt* segregar, separar. ~**ion** /-'geɪʃn/ *n* segregação *f*

seize /si:z/ *vt* agarrar, (*P*) deitar a mão a, apanhar; (*take possession by force*) apoderar-se de; (*by law*) apreender, confiscar, (*P*) apresar □ *vi* ~ **on** (*opportunity*) aproveitar. ~ **up** (*engine etc*) grimpar, emperrar. **be** ~**d with** (*fear, illness*) ter um ataque de

seizure /'si:ʒə(r)/ *n* (*med*) ataque *m*, crise *f*; (*law*) apreensão *f*, captura *f*

seldom /'seldəm/ *adv* raras vezes, raramente, raro

select /sɪ'lekt/ *vt* escolher, selecionar, (*P*) seleccionar □ *a* seleto, (*P*) selecto. ~**ion** /-ʃn/ *n* seleção *f*, (*P*) selecção *f*; (*comm*) sortido *m*

selective /sɪ'lektɪv/ *a* seletivo, (*P*) selectivo

self /self/ *n* (*pl* **selves**) **the** ~ o eu, o ego

self- /self/ *pref* ~**-assurance** *n* segurança *f*. ~**-assured** *a* seguro de si. ~**-catering** *a* em que os hóspedes tem facilidades de cozinhar. ~**-centred** *a* egocêntrico. ~**-confidence** *n* autoconfiança *f*, confiança *f* em si mesmo. ~**-confident** *a* que tem confiança em si mesmo. ~**-conscious** *a* inibido, constrangido. ~**-contained** *a* independente. ~**-control** *n* autodomínio *m*. ~**-controlled** *a* senhor de si. ~**-defence** *n* legítima defesa *f*. ~**-denial** *n* abnegação *f*. ~**-employed** *a* autónomo. ~**-esteem** *n* amor *m* próprio. ~**-evident** *a* evidente. ~**-indulgent** *a* que não resiste a tentações; (*for ease*) comodista. ~**-interest** *n* interesse *m* pessoal. ~**-portrait** *n* auto-retrato *m*. ~**-possessed** *a* senhor de si. ~**-reliant** *a* independente, seguro de si.

~**-respect** *n* amor *m* próprio. ~**-righteous** *a* que se tem em boa conta. ~**-sacrifice** *n* abnegação *f*, sacrifício *m*. ~**-satisfied** *a* cheio de si, convencido (*colloq*). ~**-seeking** *a* egoísta. ~**-service** *a* auto-serviço, self-service. ~**-styled** *a* pretenso. ~**-sufficient** *a* auto-suficiente. ~**-willed** *a* voluntarioso

selfish /'selfɪʃ/ *a* egoísta; (*motive*) interesseiro. ~**ness** *n* egoísmo *m*

selfless /'selflɪs/ *a* desinteressado

sell /sel/ *vt/i* (*pt* **sold**) vender(-se). ~**by date** ~ **off** liquidar. **be sold out** estar esgotado. ~**-out** *n* (*show*) sucesso *m*; (*colloq: betrayal*) traição *f*. ~**er** *n* vendedor *m*

Sellotape /'seləʊteɪp/ *n* fita *f* adesiva, (*P*) fitacola *f*

semantic /sɪ'mæntɪk/ *a* semântico. ~**s** *n* semântica *f*

semblance /'sembləns/ *n* aparência *f*

semen /'si:mən/ *n* sêmen *m*, (*P*) sémen *m*, esperma *m*

semester /sɪ'mestə(r)/ *n* (*Amer: univ*) semestre *m*

semi- /'semɪ/ *pref* semi-, meio

semibreve /'semɪbri:v/ *n* (*mus*) semibreve *f*

semicirc|le /'semɪsɜ:kl/ *n* semicírculo *m*. ~**ular** /-sɜ:kjʊlə(r)/ *a* semicircular

semicolon /semɪ'kəʊlən/ *n* pontoe-vírgula *m*

semi-detached /semɪdɪ'tætʃt/ *a* ~ **house** casa *f* geminada

semifinal /semɪ'faɪnl/ *n* semifinal *f*, (*P*) meiafinal *f*

seminar /'semɪnɑ:(r)/ *n* seminário *m*

semiquaver /'semɪkweɪvə(r)/ *n* (*mus*) semicolcheia *f*

Semit|e /'si:maɪt/ *a* & *n* semita (*mf*). ~**ic** /sɪ'mɪtɪk/ *a* & *n* (*lang*) semítico (*m*)

semitone /'semɪtəʊn/ *n* (*mus*) semitom *m*

semolina /semə'li:nə/ *n* sêmola *f*, (*P*) sémola *f*, semolina *f*

senat|e /'senɪt/ *n* senado *m*. ~**or** /-ətə(r)/ *n* senador *m*

send /send/ *vt/i* (*pt* **sent**) enviar, mandar. ~ **back** devolver. ~ **for** (*person*) chamar, mandar vir; (*help*) pedir. ~ (**away** *or* **off**) **for** encomendar, mandar vir (por carta). ~**-off** *n* despedida *f*, bota-fora *m*. ~ **up** (*colloq*) parodiar. ~**er** *n* expedidor *m*, remetente *m*

senil|e /'si:naɪl/ *a* senil. ~**ity** /sɪ'nɪlətɪ/ *n* senilidade *f*

senior /'si:nɪə(r)/ *a* mais velho, mais idoso (**to** que); (*in rank*) superior; (*in service*) mais antigo; (*after surname*) sênior, (*P*) sénior □ *n* pessoa *f* mais velha; (*schol*) finalista *mf*. ~ **citizen**

pessoa *f* de idade *or* da terceira idade.
~**ity** /-'ɒreɪtɪ/ *n* (*in age*) idade *f*; (*in service*) antiguidade *f*
sensation /sen'seɪʃn/ *n* sensação *f*.
~**al** *a* sensacional. ~**alism** *n* sensacionalismo *m*
sense /sens/ *n* sentido *m*; (*wisdom*) bom senso *m*; (*sensation*) sensação *f*; (*mental impression*) sentimento *m*. ~**s** (*sanity*) razão *f* □ *vt* pressentir. **make** ~ fazer sentido. **make** ~ **of** compreender. ~**less** *a* disparatado, sem sentido; (*med*) sem sentidos, inconsciente
sensible /'sensəbl/ *a* sensato, razoável; (*clothes*) prático
sensitiv|e /'sensətɪv/ *a* sensível (**to** a); (*touchy*) susceptível. ~**ity** /-'tɪvətɪ/ *n* sensibilidade *f*
sensory /'sensərɪ/ *a* sensorial
sensual /'senʃʋəl/ *a* sensual. ~**ity** /-'ælətɪ/ *n* sensualidade *f*
sensuous /'senʃʋəs/ *a* sensual
sent /sent/ *see* send
sentence /'sentəns/ *n* frase *f*; (*jur: decision*) sentença *f*; (*punishment*) pena *f* □ *vt* ~ **to** condenar a
sentiment /'sentɪmənt/ *n* sentimento *m*; (*opinion*) modo *m* de ver
sentimental /sentɪ'mentl/ *a* sentimental. ~**ity** /-men'tæləti/ *n* sentimentalidade *f*, sentimentalismo *m*. ~ **value** valor *m* estimativo
sentry /'sentrɪ/ *n* sentinela *f*
separable /'sepərəbl/ *a* separável
separate[1] /-'seprət/ *a* separado, diferente. ~**s** *npl* (*clothes*) conjuntos *mpl*. ~**ly** *adv* separadamente, em separado
separat|e[2] /'sepəreɪt/ *vt/i* separar (-se). ~**ion** /-'reɪʃn/ *n* separação *f*
September /sep'tembə(r)/ *n* setembro *m*
septic /'septɪk/ *a* séptico, infectado
sequel /'si:kwəl/ *n* resultado *m*, sequela *f*, (*P*) sequela *f*; (*of novel, film*) continuação *f*
sequence /'si:kwəns/ *n* sequência *f*, (*P*) sequência *f*
sequin /'si:kwɪn/ *n* lantejoula *f*
serenade /serə'neɪd/ *n* serenata *f* □ *vt* fazer uma serenata para
seren|e /sɪ'ri:n/ *a* sereno. ~**ity** /-'enətɪ/ *n* serenidade *f*
sergeant /'sa:dʒənt/ *n* sargento *m*
serial /'sɪərɪəl/ *n* folhetim *m* □ *a* (*number*) de série. ~**ize** /-laɪz/ *vt* publicar em folhetim
series /'sɪərɪːz/ *n invar* série *f*
serious /'sɪərɪəs/ *a* sério; (*very bad, critical*) grave, sério. ~**ly** *adv* seriamente, gravemente, a sério. **take** ~**ly** levar a sério. ~**ness** *n* seriedade *f*, gravidade *f*

sermon /'sɜ:mən/ *n* sermão *m*
serpent /'sɜ:pənt/ *n* serpente *f*
serrated /sɪ'reɪtɪd/ *a* (*edge*) serr(e)ado, com serrilha
serum /'sɪərəm/ *n* (*pl* -**a**) soro *m*
servant /'sɜ:vənt/ *n* criado *m*, criada *f*, empregado *m*, empregada *f*
serv|e /sɜ:v/ *vt/i* servir; (*a sentence*) cumprir; (*jur: a writ*) entregar; (*mil*) servir, prestar serviço; (*apprenticeship*) fazer □ *n* (*tennis*) saque *m*, (*P*) serviço *m*. ~**e as/to** servir de/para. ~**e its purpose** servir para o que é (*colloq*), servir os seus fins. **it** ~**es you/him** *etc* **right** é bem feito. ~**ing** *n* (*portion*) dose *f*, porção *f*
service /'sɜ:vɪs/ *n* serviço *m*; (*relig*) culto *m*; (*tennis*) saque *m* (*P*) serviço *m*; (*maintenance*) revisão *f*. ~**s** (*mil*) forças *fpl* armadas □ *vt* (*car etc*) fazer a revisão de. **of** ~ **to** útil a, de utilidade a. ~ **area** área *f* de serviço. ~ **charge** serviço *m*. ~ **station** posto *m* de gasolina
serviceable /'sɜ:vɪsəbl/ *a* (*of use, usable*) útil, prático; (*durable*) resistente; (*of person*) prestável
serviceman /'sɜ:vɪsmən/ *n* (*pl* -**men**) militar *m*
serviette /sɜ:vɪ'et/ *n* guardanapo *m*
servile /'sɜ:vaɪl/ *a* servil
session /'seʃn/ *n* sessão *f*; (*univ*) ano *m* académico, (*P*) académico; (*Amer: univ*) semestre *m*. **in** ~ (*sitting*) em sessão, reunidos
set /set/ *vt* (*pt* set, *pres p* setting) pôr, colocar; (*put down*) pousar; (*limit etc*) fixar; (*watch, clock*) regular; (*example*) dar; (*exam, task*) marcar; (*in plaster*) engessar □ *vi* (*of sun*) pôr-se; (*of jelly*) endurecer, solidificar(-se) □ *n* (*of people*) círculo *m*, roda *f*; (*of books*) colecção *f*, (*P*) colecção *f*; (*of tools, chairs etc*) jogo *m*; (*TV, radio*) aparelho *m*; (*hair*) mise *f*, (*theat*) cenário *m*; (*tennis*) partida *f*, set *m* □ *a* fixo; (*habit*) inveterado; (*jelly*) duro, sólido; (*book*) do programa, (*P*) adoptado; (*meal*) a preço fixo. **be** ~ **on doing** estar decidido a fazer. ~ **about** *or* **to** começar a, pôr-se a. ~ **back** (*plans etc*) atrasar; (*sl: cost*) custar. ~-**back** *n* revés *m*, contratempo *m*, atraso *m* de vida (*colloq*). ~ **fire to** atear fogo a, (*P*) deitar fogo a. ~ **free** pôr em liberdade. ~ **in** (*rain etc*) pegar. ~ **off** *or* **out** partir, começar a viajar. ~ **off** (*mechanism*) pôr para funcionar, (*P*) pôr a funcionar; (*bomb*) explodir; (*by contrast*) realçar. ~ **out** (*state*) expor; (*arrange*) dispôr. ~ **sail** partir, içar as velas. ~ **square** esquadro *m*. ~ **the table** pôr a mesa. ~ **theory** teoria *f* de conjuntos. ~-**to** *n* briga *f*.

~ **up** (*establish*) fundar, estabelecer.
~**-up** *n* (*system*) sistema *m*, organização *f*; (*situation*) situação *f*

settee /se'ti:/ *n* sofá *m*

setting /'setɪŋ/ *n* (*framework*) quadro *m*; (*of jewel*) engaste *m*; (*typ*) composição *f*; (*mus*) arranjo *m* musical

settle /'setl/ *vt* (*arrange*) resolver; (*date*) marcar; (*nerves*) acalmar; (*doubts*) esclarecer; (*new country*) colonizar, povoar; (*bill*) pagar □ *vi* assentar; (*in country*) estabelecer-se; (*in house, chair etc*) instalar-se; (*weather*) estabilizar-se. ~ **down** acalmar-se; (*become orderly*) assentar; (*sit, rest*) instalar-se. ~ **for** aceitar. ~ **up** (**with**) fazer contas (com); (*fig*) ajustar contas (com). ~**r** /-ə(r)/ *n* colono *m*, colonizador *m*

settlement /'setlmənt/ *n* (*agreement*) acordo *m*; (*payment*) pagamento *m*; (*colony*) colônia *f*, (*P*) colónia *f*; (*colonization*) colonização *f*

seven /'sevn/ *a* & *n* sete (*m*). ~**th** *a* & *n* sétimo (*m*)

seventeen /sevn'ti:n/ *a* & *n* dezessete (*m*), (*P*) dezassete (*m*). ~**th** *a* & *n* décimo sétimo (*m*)

sevent|y /'sevntɪ/ *a* & *n* setenta (*m*). ~**ieth** *a* & *n* septuagésimo (*m*)

sever /'sevə(r)/ *vt* cortar. ~**ance** *n* corte *m*

several /'sevrəl/ *a* & *pron* vários, diversos

sever|e /sɪ'vɪə(r)/ *a* (-**er**, -**est**) severo; (*pain*) forte, violento; (*illness*) grave; (*winter*) rigoroso. ~**ely** *adv* severamente; (*seriously*) gravemente. ~**ity** /sɪ'verɪtɪ/ *n* severidade *f*; (*seriousness*) gravidade *f*

sew /səʊ/ *vt/i* (*pt* **sewed**, *pp* **sewn** *or* **sewed**) coser, costurar. ~**ing** *n* costura *f*. ~**ing-machine** *n* máquina *f* de costura

sewage /'sju:ɪdʒ/ *n* efluentes *mpl* dos esgotos, detritos *mpl*

sewer /'sju:ə(r)/ *n* cano *m* de esgoto

sewn /səʊn/ *see* **sew**

sex /seks/ *n* sexo *m* □ *a* sexual. **have** ~ ter relações. ~ **maniac** tarado *m* sexual. ~**y** *a* sexy *invar*, que tem sex-appeal

sexist /'seksɪst/ *a* & *n* sexista *mf*

sexual /'sekʃʊəl/ *a* sexual. ~ **harassment** assédio *m* sexual. ~ **intercourse** relações *fpl* sexuais. ~**ity** /'ælətɪ/ *n* sexualidade *f*

shabb|y /'ʃæbɪ/ *a* (-**ier**, -**iest**) (*clothes, object*) gasto, surrado; (*person*) maltrapilho, mal vestido; (*mean*) miserável. ~**ily** *adv* miseravelmente

shack /ʃæk/ *n* cabana *f*, barraca *f*

shackles /'ʃæklz/ *npl* grilhões *mpl*, algemas *fpl*

shade /ʃeɪd/ *n* sombra *f*; (*of colour*) tom *m*, matiz *m*; (*of opinion*) matiz *m*; (*for lamp*) abat-jour *m*, quebra-luz *m*; (*Amer: blind*) estore *m* □ *vt* resguardar da luz; (*darken*) sombrear. **a** ~ **bigger**/*etc* ligeiramente maior/*etc*. **in the** ~ à sombra

shadow /'ʃædəʊ/ *n* sombra *f* □ *vt* cobrir de sombra; (*follow*) seguir, vigiar. **S**~ **Cabinet** gabinete *m* formado pelo partido da oposição. ~**y** *a* ensombrado, sombreado; (*fig*) vago, indistinto

shady /'ʃeɪdɪ/ *a* (-**ier**, -**iest**) sombreiro, (*P*) que dá sombra; (*in shade*) à sombra; (*fig: dubious*) suspeito, duvidoso

shaft /ʃɑ:ft/ *n* (*of arrow, spear*) haste *f*; (*axle*) eixo *m*, veio *m*; (*of mine, lift*) poço *m*; (*of light*) raio *m*

shaggy /'ʃægɪ/ *a* (-**ier**, -**iest**) (*beard*) hirsuto; (*hair*) desgrenhado; (*animal*) peludo, felpudo

shake /ʃeɪk/ *vt* (*pt* **shook**, *pp* **shaken**) abanar, sacudir; (*bottle*) agitar; (*belief, house etc*) abalar □ *vi* estremecer, tremer □ *n* (*violent*) abanão *m*, safanão *m*; (*light*) sacudidela *f*. ~ **hands with** apertar a mão de. ~ **off** (*get rid of*) sacudir, livrar-se de. ~ **one's head** (*to say no*) fazer que não com a cabeça. ~ **up** agitar. ~**-up** *n* (*upheaval*) reviravolta *f*

shaky /'ʃeɪkɪ/ *a* (-**ier**, -**iest**) (*hand, voice*) trêmulo, (*P*) trémulo; (*unsteady, unsafe*) pouco firme, inseguro; (*weak*) fraco

shall /ʃæl/; *unstressed* /ʃəl/ *v aux* I/ **we** ~ **do** (*future*) farei/faremos. I/ **you/he** ~ **do** (*command*) eu hei de/ você há de/tu hás de/ele há de fazer

shallot /ʃə'lɒt/ *n* cebolinha *f*, (*P*) chalota *f*

shallow /'ʃæləʊ/ *a* (-**er**, -**est**) pouco fundo, raso; (*fig*) superficial

sham /ʃæm/ *n* fingimento *m*; (*jewel etc*) imitação *f*; (*person*) impostor *m*, fingido *m* □ *a* fingido; (*false*) falso □ *vt* (*pt* **shammed**) fingir

shambles /'ʃæmblz/ *npl* (*colloq: mess*) balbúrdia *f*, trapalhada *f*

shame /ʃeɪm/ *n* vergonha *f* □ *vt* (fazer) envergonhar. **it's a** ~ é uma pena. **what a** ~! que pena! ~**ful** *a* vergonhoso. ~**less** *a* sem vergonha, descarado; (*immodest*) despudorado, desavergonhado

shamefaced /'ʃeɪmfeɪst/ *a* envergonhado

shampoo /ʃæm'pu:/ *n* xampu *m*, (*P*) champô *m*, shampoo *m* □ *vt* lavar com xampu, (*P*) champô *or* shampoo

shan't /ʃɑ:nt/ = **shall not**

shanty /'ʃæntɪ/ *n* barraca *f*. ~ **town** favela *f*, (*P*) bairro(s) *m*(*pl*) da lata

shape /ʃeɪp/ *n* forma *f* □ *vt* moldar □ *vi* ~ **(up)** andar bem, fazer progressos. **take** ~ concretizar-se, avançar. ~**less** *a* informe, sem forma; (*of body*) deselegante, disforme

shapely /ˈʃeɪplɪ/ *a* (**-ier, -iest**) (*leg, person*) bem feito, elegante

share /ʃeə(r)/ *n* parte *f*, porção *f*; (*comm*) acção *f*, (P) acção *f* □ *vt/i* partilhar (**with** com, **in** de)

shareholder /ˈʃeəhəʊldə(r)/ *n* accionista *mf*, (P) accionista *mf*

shark /ʃɑːk/ *n* tubarão *m*

sharp /ʃɑːp/ *a* (**-er, -est**) (*knife, pencil etc*) afiado; (*pin, point etc*) pontiagudo, aguçado; (*words, reply*) áspero; (*of bend*) fechado; (*acute*) agudo; (*sudden*) brusco; (*dishonest*) pouco honesto; (*well-defined*) nítido; (*brisk*) rápido, vigoroso; (*clever*) vivo □ *adv* (*stop*) de repente □ *n* (*mus*) sustenido *m*. **six o'clock** ~ seis horas em ponto. ~**ly** *adv* (*harshly*) rispidamente; (*suddenly*) de repente

sharpen /ˈʃɑːpən/ *vt* aguçar; (*pencil*) fazer a ponta de, (P) afiar; (*knife etc*) afiar, amolar. ~**er** *n* afiadeira *f*; (*for pencil*) apontador *m*, (P) apára-lápis *m*, (P) afia-lápis *f*

shatter /ˈʃætə(r)/ *vt/i* despedaçar (-se), esmigalhar(-se); (*hopes*) destruir(-se); (*nerves*) abalar(-se). ~**ed** *a* (*upset*) passado; (*exhausted*) estourado (*colloq*)

shav|e /ʃeɪv/ *vt/i* barbear(-se), fazer a barba (de) □ *n* **have a** ~**e** barbear-se. **have a close** ~**e** (*fig*) escapar por um triz. ~**en** *a* raspado, barbeado. ~**er** *n* aparelho *m* de barbear, (P) máquina *f* de barbear. ~**ing-brush** *n* pincel *m* para a barba. ~**ing-cream** *n* creme *m* de barbear

shaving /ˈʃeɪvɪŋ/ *n* apara *f*

shawl /ʃɔːl/ *n* xale *m*, (P) xaile *m*

she /ʃiː/ *pron* ela □ *n* fêmea *f*

sheaf /ʃiːf/ *n* (*pl* **sheaves**) feixe *m*; (*of papers*) maço *m*, molho *m*

shear /ʃɪə(r)/ *vt* (*pp* **shorn** or **sheared**) (*sheep etc*) tosquiar

shears /ʃɪəz/ *npl* tesoura *f* para jardim

sheath /ʃiːθ/ *n* (*pl* ~**s** /ʃiːðz/) bainha *f*; (*condom*) preservativo *m*, camisa-de-Vénus *f*

sheathe /ʃiːð/ *vt* embainhar

shed[1] /ʃed/ *n* (*hut*) casinhola *f*; (*for cows*) estábulo *m*

shed[2] /ʃed/ (*pt* **shed**, *pres p* **shedding**) perder, deixar cair; (*spread*) espalhar; (*blood, tears*) deitar, derramar. ~ **light on** lançar luz sobre

sheen /ʃiːn/ *n* brilho *m*, lustre *m*

sheep /ʃiːp/ *n* (*pl invar*) carneiro *m*, ovelha *f*. ~**-dog** *n* cão *m* de pastor

sheepish /ˈʃiːpɪʃ/ *a* encabulado. ~**ly** *adv* com um ar encabulado

sheepskin /ˈʃiːpskɪn/ *n* pele *f* de carneiro; (*leather*) carneira *f*

sheer /ʃɪə(r)/ *a* mero, simples; (*steep*) íngreme, a pique; (*fabric*) diáfano, transparente □ *adv* a pique, verticalmente

sheet /ʃiːt/ *n* lençol *m*; (*of glass, metal*) chapa *f*, placa *f*; (*of paper*) folha *f*

sheikh /ʃeɪk/ *n* xeque *m*, sheik *m*

shelf /ʃelf/ *n* (*pl* **shelves**) prateleira *f*

shell /ʃel/ *n* (*of egg, nut etc*) casca *f*; (*of mollusc*) concha *f*; (*of ship, tortoise*) casco *m*; (*of building*) estrutura *f*, armação *f*; (*of explosive*) cartucho *m* □ *vt* descascar; (*mil*) bombardear

shellfish /ˈʃelfɪʃ/ *n* (*pl invar*) crustáceo *m*; (*as food*) marisco *m*

shelter /ˈʃeltə(r)/ *n* abrigo *m*, refúgio *m* □ *vt* abrigar; (*protect*) proteger; (*harbour*) dar asilo a □ *vi* abrigar-se, refugiar-se. ~**ed** *a* (*life etc*) protegido; (*spot*) abrigado

shelve /ʃelv/ *vt* pôr em prateleiras; (*fit with shelves*) pôr prateleiras em; (*fig*) engavetar, pôr de lado

shelving /ˈʃelvɪŋ/ *n* (**shelves**) prateleiras *fpl*

shepherd /ˈʃepəd/ *n* pastor *m* □ *vt* guiar. ~'**s pie** empadão *m* de batata e carne moída

sheriff /ˈʃerɪf/ *n* xerife *m*

sherry /ˈʃerɪ/ *n* Xerez *m*

shield /ʃiːld/ *n* (*armour, heraldry*) escudo *m*; (*screen*) anteparo *m* □ *vt* proteger (**from** contra, de)

shift /ʃɪft/ *vt/i* mudar de posição, deslocar(-se); (*exchange, alter*) mudar de □ *n* mudança *f*; (*workers; work*) turno *m*. **make** ~ arranjar-se

shiftless /ˈʃɪftlɪs/ *a* (*lazy*) molengão, preguiçoso

shifty /ˈʃɪftɪ/ *a* (**-ier, -iest**) velhaco, duvidoso

shimmer /ˈʃɪmə(r)/ *vi* luzir suavemente □ *n* luzir *m*

shin /ʃɪn/ *n* perna *f*. ~**-bone** *n* tíbia *f*, canela *f*. ~**-pad** *n* (*football*) caneleira *f*

shin|e /ʃaɪn/ *vt/i* (*pt* **shone**) (fazer) brilhar, (fazer) reluzir; (*shoes*) engraxar □ *n* lustro *m*. ~**e a torch (on)** iluminar com uma lanterna de mão. **the sun is** ~**ing** faz sol

shingle /ˈʃɪŋgl/ *n* (*pebbles*) seixos *mpl*

shingles /ˈʃɪŋglz/ *npl med* zona *f*, herpes-zóster *f*

shiny /ˈʃaɪnɪ/ *a* (**-ier, -iest**) brilhante; (*of coat, trousers*) lustroso

ship /ʃɪp/ *n* barco *m*, navio *m* □ *vt* (*pt* **shipped**) transportar; (*send*) mandar por via marítima; (*load*) embarcar. ~**ment** *n* (*goods*) carregamento *m*;

(*shipping*) embarque *m*. ~**per** *n* expedidor *m*. ~**ping** *n* navegação *f*; (*ships*) navios *mpl*

shipbuilding /'ʃɪpbɪldɪŋ/ *n* construção *f* naval

shipshape /'ʃɪpʃeɪp/ *adv* & *a* em (perfeita) ordem, impecável

shipwreck /'ʃɪprek/ *n* naufrágio *m*. ~**ed** *a* naufragado. be ~**ed** naufragar

shipyard /'ʃɪpjaːd/ *n* estaleiro *m*

shirk /ʃɜːk/ *vt* fugir a, furtar-se a, (*P*) baldar-se a (*sl*). ~**er** *n* parasita *mf*

shirt /ʃɜːt/ *n* camisa *f*; (*of woman*) blusa *f*. in ~**-sleeves** em mangas de camisa

shiver /'ʃɪvə(r)/ *vi* arrepiar-se, tiritar □ *n* arrepio *m*

shoal /ʃəʊl/ *n* (*of fish*) cardume *m*

shock /ʃɒk/ choque *m*, embate *m*; (*electr*) choque *m* elétrico, (*P*) eléctrico; (*med*) choque *m* □ *a* de choque □ *vt* chocar. ~ **absorber** (*mech*) amortecedor *m*. ~**ing** *a* chocante; (*colloq: very bad*) horrível

shod /ʃɒd/ *see* **shoe**

shoddy /'ʃɒdɪ/ *a* (-ier, -iest) mal feito, ordinário, de má qualidade. ~**ily** *adv* mal

shoe /ʃuː/ *n* sapato *m*; (*footwear*) calçado *m*; (*horse*) ferradura *f*; (*brake*) sapata *f*, (*P*) calço *m* (de travão) □ *vt* (*pt* **shod**, *pres p* **shoeing**) (*horse*) ferrar. ~ **polish** *n* pomada *f*, (*P*) graxa *f* para sapatos. ~**-shop** *n* sapataria *f*. on a ~**-string** (*colloq*) com/ por muito pouco dinheiro, na pindaíba (*colloq*)

shoehorn /'ʃuːhɔːn/ *n* calçadeira *f*

shoelace /'ʃuːleɪs/ *n* cordão *m* de sapato, (*P*) atacador *m*

shoemaker /'ʃuːmeɪkə(r)/ *n* sapateiro *m*

shone /ʃɒn/ *see* **shine**

shoo /ʃuː/ *vt* enxotar □ *int* xô

shook /ʃʊk/ *see* **shake**

shoot /ʃuːt/ *vt* (*pt* **shot**) (*gun*) disparar; (*glance, missile*) lançar; (*kill*) matar a tiro; (*wound*) ferir a tiro; (*execute*) executar, fuzilar; (*hunt*) caçar; (*film*) filmar, rodar □ *vi* disparar, atirar (at contra, sobre); (*bot*) rebentar; (*football*) rematar □ *n* (*bot*) rebento *m*. ~ **down** abater (a tiro). ~ **in/out** (*rush*) entrar/sair correndo *or* disparado. ~ **up** (*spurt*) jorrar; (*grow quickly*) crescer a olhos vistos, dar um pulo; (*prices*) subir em disparada. ~**ing** *n* (*shots*) tiroteio *m*. ~**ing-range** *n* carreira *f* de tiro. ~**ing star** estrela *f* cadente

shop /ʃɒp/ *n* loja *f*; (*workshop*) oficina *f* □ *vi* (*pt* **shopped**) fazer compras. ~ **around** procurar, ver o que há. ~

assistant empregado *m*, caixeiro *m*; vendedor *m*. ~**-floor** *n* (*workers*) trabalhadores *mpl*. ~**per** *n* comprador *m*. ~**-soiled**, (*Amer*) ~**-worn** *adjs* enxovalhado. ~ **steward** delegado *m* sindical. ~ **window** vitrina *f*, (*P*) montra *f*. **talk** ~ falar de coisas profissionais

shopkeeper /'ʃɒpkiːpə(r)/ *n* lojista *mf*, comerciante *mf*

shoplift|er /'ʃɒplɪftə(r)/ *n* gatuno *m* de lojas. ~**ing** *n* furto *m* em lojas

shopping /'ʃɒpɪŋ/ *n* (*goods*) compras *fpl*. **go** ~ ir às compras. ~ **bag** sacola *f* de compras. ~ **centre** centro *m* comercial

shore /ʃɔː(r)/ *n* (*of sea*) praia *f*, costa *f*; (*of lake*) margem *f*

shorn /ʃɔːn/ *see* **shear** □ *a* tosquiado. ~ **of** despojado de

short /ʃɔːt/ *a* (-er, -est) curto; (*person*) baixo; (*brief*) breve, curto; (*curt*) seco, brusco. be ~ **of** (*lack*) ter falta de □ *adv* (*abruptly*) bruscamente, de repente. **cut** ~ abreviar; (*interrupt*) interromper □ *n* (*electr*) curto-circuito *m*; (*film*) curta-metragem *f*, short *m*. ~**s** (*trousers*) calção *m*, (*P*) calções *mpl*, short *m*, (*P*) shorts *mpl*. **a** ~ **time** pouco tempo. **he is called Tom for** ~ o diminutivo dele é Tom. **in** ~ em suma. ~**-change** *vt* (*cheat*) enganar. ~ **circuit** (*electr*) curto-circuito *m* ~**-circuit** *vt/i* (*electr*) fazer *or* dar um curto-circuito (em). ~ **cut** atalho *m*. ~**-handed** *a* com falta de pessoal. ~ **list** pré-seleção *f*, (*P*) pré-selecção *f*. ~**-lived** *a* de pouca duração. ~**-sighted** *a* míope, (*P*) curto de vista. ~**-tempered** *a* irritadiço. ~ **story** conto *m*. ~ **wave** (*radio*) onda(s) *f*(*pl*) curta(s)

shortage /'ʃɔːtɪdʒ/ *n* falta *f*, escassez *f*

shortbread /'ʃɔːtbred/ *n* shortbread *m*, biscoito *m* de massa amanteigada

shortcoming /'ʃɔːtkʌmɪŋ/ *n* falha *f*, imperfeição *f*

shorten /'ʃɔːtn/ *vt/i* encurtar(-se), abreviar(-se), diminuir

shorthand /'ʃɔːthænd/ *n* estenografia *f*. ~ **typist** estenodactilógrafa *f*

shortly /'ʃɔːtlɪ/ *adv* (*soon*) em breve, dentro em pouco

shot /ʃɒt/ *see* **shoot** □ *n* (*firing, bullet*) tiro *m*; (*person*) atirador *m*; (*pellets*) chumbo *m*; (*photograph*) fotografia *f*; (*injection*) injeção *f*, (*P*) injecção *f*; (*in golf, billiards*) tacada *f*. **go like a** ~ ir disparado. **have a** ~ (at sth) experimentar (fazer alg coisa). ~**-gun** *n* espingarda *f*, caçadeira *f*

should /ʃʊd/; *unstressed* /ʃəd/ *v aux* **you** ~ **help me** você devia me ajudar. **I** ~ **have stayed** devia ter ficado. I ~ like to gostaria de *or* gostava de. if he ~ come se ele vier

shoulder /'ʃəʊldə(r)/ *n* ombro *m* □ *vt* (*responsibility*) tomar, assumir; (*burden*) carregar, arcar com. ~-**blade** *n* (*anat*) omoplata *f*. ~-**pad** *n* enchimento *m* de ombro, ombreira *f*

shout /ʃaʊt/ *n* grito *m*, brado *m*; (*very loud*) berro *m* □ *vt/i* gritar (**at** com); (*very loudly*) berrar (**at** com). ~ **down** fazer calar com gritos. ~**ing** *n* gritaria *f*, berraria *f*

shove /ʃʌv/ *n* empurrão *m* □ *vt/i* empurrar; (*colloq: put*) meter, enfiar. ~ **off** (*colloq: depart*) começar a andar (*colloq*), dar o fora (*colloq*), (*P*) cavar (*colloq*)

shovel /'ʃʌvl/ *n* pá *f*; (*machine*) escavadora *f* □ *vt* (*pt* **shovelled**) remover com pá

show /ʃəʊ/ *vt* (*pt* **showed**, *pp* **shown**) mostrar; (*of dial, needle*) marcar; (*put on display*) expor; (*film*) dar, passar □ *vi* ver-se, aparecer, estar à vista □ *n* mostra *f*, demonstração *f*, manifestação *f*; (*ostentation*) alarde *m*, espalhafato *m*; (*exhibition*) mostra *f*, exposição *f*; (*theatre, cinema*) espetáculo *m*, (*P*) espectáculo *m*, show *m*. **for** ~ para fazer vista. **on** ~ exposto, em exposição. ~-**down** *n* confrontação *f*. ~-**jumping** *n* concurso *m* hípico. ~ **in** mandar entrar. ~ **off** *vt* exibir, ostentar □ *vi* exibir-se, querer fazer figura. ~-**off** *n* exibicionista *mf*. ~ **out** acompanhar à porta. ~-**piece** *n* peça *f* digna de se expor. ~ **up** ser claramente visível, ver-se bem; (*colloq: arrive*) aparecer. ~**ing** *n* (*performance*) atuação *f*, performance *f*; (*cinema*) exibição *f*

shower /'ʃaʊə(r)/ *n* (*of rain*) aguaceiro *m*, chuvarada *f*; (*of blows etc*) saraivada *f*; (*in bathroom*) chuveiro *m*, ducha *f*, (*P*) duche *m* □ *vt* ~ **with** cumular de, encher de □ *vi* tomar um banho de chuveiro *or* uma ducha, (*P*) um duche. ~**y** *a* chuvoso

showerproof /'ʃaʊəpruːf/ *a* impermeável

shown /ʃəʊn/ *see* **show**

showroom /'ʃəʊrʊm/ *n* espaço *m* de exposição, show-room *m*; (*for cars*) stand *m*

showy /'ʃəʊɪ/ *a* (**-ier, -iest**) vistoso; (*too bright*) berrante; (*pej*) espalhafatoso

shrank /ʃræŋk/ *see* **shrink**

shred /ʃred/ *n* tira *f*, retalho *m*, farrapo *m*; (*fig*) mínimo *m*, sombra *f* □ *vt* (*pt* **shredded**) reduzir a tiras, estrançalhar; (*culin*) desfiar. ~**der** *n* trituradora *f*; (*for paper*) fragmentadora *f*

shrewd /ʃruːd/ *a* (**-er, -est**) astucioso,

fino, perspicaz. ~**ness** *n* astúcia *f*, perspicácia *f*

shriek /ʃriːk/ *n* grito *m* agudo, guincho *m* □ *vt/i* gritar, guinchar

shrift /ʃrɪft/ *n* **give sb short** ~ tratar alguém com brusquidão, despachar alguém sem mais cerimônias, (*P*) cerimónias

shrill /ʃrɪl/ *a* estridente, agudo

shrimp /ʃrɪmp/ *n* camarão *m*

shrine /ʃram/ *n* (*place*) santuário *m*; (*tomb*) túmulo *m*; (*casket*) relicário *m*

shrink /ʃrɪŋk/ *vt/i* (*pt* **shrank**, *pp* **shrunk**) encolher; (*recoil*) encolher-se. ~ **from** esquivar-se a, fugir a (+ *inf*)/de (+ *noun*), retrair-se de. ~**age** *n* encolhimento *m*; (*comm*) contração *f*

shrivel /'ʃrɪvl/ *vt/i* (*pt* **shrivelled**) encarquilhar(-se)

shroud /ʃraʊd/ *n* mortalha *f* □ *vt* (*veil*) encobrir, envolver

Shrove /ʃrəʊv/ *n* ~ **Tuesday** Terçafeira *f* gorda *or* de Carnaval

shrub /ʃrʌb/ *n* arbusto *m*. ~**bery** *n* arbustos *mpl*

shrug /ʃrʌɡ/ *vt* (*pt* **shrugged**) ~ **one's shoulders** encolher os ombros □ *n* encolher *m* de ombros. ~ **off** não dar importância a

shrunk /ʃrʌŋk/ *see* **shrink**. ~**en** *a* encolhido; (*person*) mirrado, chupado

shudder /'ʃʌdə(r)/ *vi* arrepiar-se, estremecer, tremer □ *n* arrepio *m*, tremor *m*, estremecimento *m*. **I** ~ **to think** tremo só de pensar

shuffle /'ʃʌfl/ *vt* (*feet*) arrastar; (*cards*) embaralhar □ *vi* arrastar os pés □ *n* marcha *f* arrastada

shun /ʃʌn/ *vt* (*pt* **shunned**) evitar, fugir de

shunt /ʃʌnt/ *vt/i* (*train*) mudar de linha, manobrar

shut /ʃʌt/ *vt* (*pt* **shut**, *pres p* **shutting**) fechar □ *vi* fechar-se; (*shop, bank etc*) encerrar, fechar. ~ **down** *or* **up** fechar. ~-**down** *n* encerramento *m*. ~ **in** *or* **up** trancar. ~ **up** *vi* (*colloq: stop talking*) calar-se □ *vt* (*colloq: silence*) mandar calar. ~ **up!** (*colloq*) cale-se!, cale a boca!

shutter /'ʃʌtə(r)/ *n* taipais *mpl*, (*P*) portada *f* de madeira; (*of laths*) persiana *f*; (*in shop*) taipais *mpl*; (*photo*) obturador *m*

shuttle /'ʃʌtl/ *n* (*of spaceship*) ônibus *m* espacial. ~ **service** (*plane*) ponte *f* aérea; (*bus*) navete *f*

shuttlecock /'ʃʌtlkɒk/ *n* volante *m*

shy /ʃaɪ/ *a* (**-er, -est**) tímido, acanhado, envergonhado □ *vi* (*horse*) assustar-se (**at** com); (*fig*) assustar-se (**at** *or* **away from** com). ~**ness** *n* timidez *f*, acanhamento *m*, vergonha *f*

Siamese /saɪə'miːz/ *a* & *n* siamês (*m*).
~ **cat** gato *m* siamês

Sicily /'sɪsɪlɪ/ *n* Sicília *f*

sick /sɪk/ *a* doente; (*humour*) negro. **be** ~ (*vomit*) vomitar. **be** ~ **of** estar farto de. **feel** ~ estar enjoado. ~**-bay** *n* enfermaria *f*. ~**-leave** *n* licença *f* por doença ~**-room** *n* quarto *m* de doente

sicken /'sɪkn/ *vt* (*distress*) desesperar; (*disgust*) repugnar □ *vi* **be** ~**ing for flu** *etc* começar a pegar uma gripe (*colloq*)

sickle /'sɪkl/ *n* foice *f*

sickly /'sɪklɪ/ *a* (-ier, -iest) (*person*) doentio, achacado; (*smell*) enjoativo; (*pale*) pálido

sickness /'sɪknɪs/ *n* doença *f*; (*vomiting*) náusea *f*, vômito *m*, (*P*) vómito *m*

side /saɪd/ *n* lado *m*; (*of road, river*) beira *f*, (*of hill*) encosta *f*; (*sport*) equipe *f*, (*P*) equipa *f* □ *a* lateral □ *vi* ~ **with** tomar o partido de. **on the** ~ (*extra*) nas horas vagas; (*secretly*) pela calada. ~ **by** ~ lado a lado. ~**-car** *n* sidecar *m*. ~**-effect** *n* efeito *m* secundário. ~**-show** *n* espetáculo *m*, (*P*) espectáculo *m* suplementar. ~**-step** *vt* (*pt* -**stepped**) evitar. ~**-track** *vt* (fazer) desviar dum propósito

sideboard /'saɪdbɔːd/ *n* aparador *m*

sideburns /'saɪdbɜːnz/ *npl* suíças *fpl*, costeletas *fpl*, (*P*) patilhas *fpl*

sidelight /'saɪdlaɪt/ *n* (*auto*) luz *f* lateral, (*P*) farolim *m*

sideline /'saɪdlaɪn/ *n* atividade *f*, (*P*) actividade *f* secundária; (*sport*) linha *f* lateral

sidelong /'saɪdlɒŋ/ *adv* & *a* de lado

sidewalk /'saɪdwɔːk/ *n* (*Amer*) passeio *m*

sideways /'saɪdweɪz/ *adv* & *a* de lado

siding /'saɪdɪŋ/ *n* desvio *m*, ramal *m*

sidle /'saɪdl/ *vi* ~ **up (to)** avançar furtivamente (para), chegar-se furtivamente (a)

siege /siːdʒ/ *n* cerco *m*

siesta /sɪ'estə/ *n* sesta *f*

sieve /sɪv/ *n* peneira *f*; (*for liquids*) coador *m* □ *vt* peneirar; (*liquids*) passar, coar

sift /sɪft/ *vt* peneirar; (*sprinkle*) polvilhar. ~ **through** examinar minuciosamente, esquadrinhar

sigh /saɪ/ *n* suspiro *m* □ *vt/i* suspirar

sight /saɪt/ *n* vista *f*; (*scene*) cena *f*; (*on gun*) mira *f* □ *vt* avistar, ver, divisar. **at** *or* **on** ~ à vista. **catch** ~ **of** avistar. **in** ~ à vista, visível. **lose** ~ **of** perder de vista. **out of** ~ longe dos olhos

sightsee|ing /'saɪtsiːɪŋ/ *n* visita *f*, turismo *m*. **go** ~**ing** visitar lugares turísticos. ~**r** /'saɪtsiːə(r)/ *n* turista *mf*

sign /sam/ *n* sinal *m*; (*symbol*) signo *m* □ *vt* (*in writing*) assinar □ *vi* (*make a sign*) fazer sinal. ~ **on** *or* **up** (*worker*) assinar contrato. ~**-board** *n* tabuleta *f*. ~ **language** *n* mímica *f*

signal /'sɪɡnəl/ *n* sinal *m* □ *vi* (*pt* **signalled**) fazer signal □ *vt* comunicar (por sinais); (*person*) fazer sinal para. ~**-box** *n* cabine *f* de sinalização

signature /'sɪɡnətʃə(r)/ *n* assinatura *f*. ~ **tune** indicativo *m* musical

signet-ring /'sɪɡnɪtrɪŋ/ *n* anel *m* de sinete

significan|t /sɪɡ'nɪfɪkənt/ *a* importante; (*meaningful*) significativo. ~**ce** *n* importância *f*; (*meaning*) significado *m*. ~**tly** *adv* (*much*) sensivelmente

signify /'sɪɡnɪfaɪ/ *vt* significar

signpost /'sampəʊst/ *n* poste *m* de sinalização □ *vt* sinalizar

silence /'saɪləns/ *n* silêncio *m* □ *vt* silenciar, calar. ~**r** /-ə(r)/ *n* (*on gun*) silenciador *m*; (*on car*) silencioso *m*

silent /'saɪlənt/ *a* silencioso; (*not speaking*) calado; (*film*) mudo. ~**ly** *adv* silenciosamente

silhouette /sɪlu'et/ *n* silhueta *f* □ *vt* **be** ~**d against** estar em silhueta contra

silicon /'sɪlɪkən/ *n* silicone *m*. ~ **chip** circuito *m* integrado

silk /sɪlk/ *n* seda *f*. ~**en**, ~**y** *adjs* sedoso

sill /sɪl/ *n* (*of window*) parapeito *m*; (*of door*) soleira *f*, limiar *m*

sill|y /'sɪlɪ/ *a* (-ier, -iest) tolo, idiota. ~**iness** *n* tolice *f*, idiotice *f*

silo /'saɪləʊ/ *n* (*pl* -os) silo *m*

silt /sɪlt/ *n* aluvião *m*, sedimento *m*

silver /'sɪlvə(r)/ *n* prata *f*; (*silverware*) prataria *f*, pratas *fpl* □ *a* de prata. ~ **paper** papel *m* prateado. ~ **wedding** bodas *fpl* de prata. ~**y** *a* prateado; (*sound*) argentino

silversmith /'sɪlvəsmɪθ/ *n* ourives *m*

silverware /'sɪlvəweə(r)/ *n* prataria *f*, pratas *fpl*

similar /'sɪmɪlə(r)/ *a* ~ (**to**) semelhante (a), parecido (com). ~**ity** /-ə'lærətɪ/ *n* semelhança *f*. ~**ly** *adv* de igual modo, analogamente

simile /'sɪmɪlɪ/ *n* símile *m*, comparação *f*

simmer /'sɪmə(r)/ *vt/i* cozinhar em fogo brando; (*fig: smoulder*) ferver, fremir; ~ **down** acalmar(-se)

simpl|e /'sɪmpl/ *a* (-er, -est) simples. ~**-minded** *a* simples; (*feeble-minded*) pobre de espírito, tolo. ~**icity** /-'plɪsətɪ/ *n* simplicidade *f*.

~y *adv* simplesmente; (*absolutely*) absolutamente, simplesmente

simpleton /'sɪmpltən/ *n* simplório *m*

simplif|y /'sɪmplɪfaɪ/ *vt* simplificar. ~**ication** /-ɪ'keɪʃn/ *n* simplificação *f*

simulat|e /'sɪmjʊleɪt/ *vt* simular, imitar. ~**ion** /-'leɪʃn/ *n* simulação *f*, imitação *f*

simultaneous /sɪml'teɪnɪəs/ *a* simultâneo, concomitante. ~**ly** *adv* simultaneamente

sin /sɪn/ *n* pecado *m* □ *vi* (*pt* **sinned**) pecar

since /sɪns/ *prep* desde □ *adv* desde então □ *conj* desde que; (*because*) uma vez que, visto que. ~ **then** desde então

sincer|e /sɪn'sɪə(r)/ *a* sincero. ~**ely** *adv* sinceramente. ~**ity** /-'serətɪ/ *n* sinceridade *f*

sinew /'sɪnjuː/ *n* (*anat*) tendão *m*. ~**s** músculos *mpl*. ~**y** *a* forte, musculoso

sinful /'sɪnfl/ *a* (*wicked*) pecaminoso; (*shocking*) escandaloso

sing /sɪŋ/ *vt/i* (*pt* **sang**, *pp* **sung**) cantar. ~**er** *n* cantor *m*

singe /sɪndʒ/ *vt* (*pres p* **singeing**) chamuscar

single /'sɪŋgl/ *a* único, só; (*unmarried*) solteiro; (*bed*) de solteiro; (*room*) individual; (*ticket*) de ida, simples □ *n* (*ticket*) bilhete *m* de ida *or* simples; (*record*) disco *m* de 45 r.p.m. ~**s** (*tennis*) singulares *mpl* □ *vt* ~ **out** escolher. **in** ~ **file** em fila indiana. ~**handed** *a* sem ajuda, sozinho. ~**minded** *a* decidido, aferrado à sua idéia, tenaz. ~ **parent** pai *m* solteiro, mãe *f* solteira. **singly** *adv* um a um, um por um

singsong /'sɪŋsɒŋ/ *n* **have a** ~ cantar em coro □ *a* (*voice*) monótono, monocórdico

singular /'sɪŋgjʊlə(r)/ *n* singular *m* □ *a* (*uncommon*; *gram*) singular; (*noun*) no singular. ~**ly** *adv* singularmente

sinister /'sɪnɪstə(r)/ *a* sinistro

sink /sɪŋk/ *vt* (*pt* **sank**, *pp* **sunk**) (*ship*) afundar, ir a pique; (*well*) abrir; (*invest money*) empatar; (*lose money*) enterrar □ *vi* afundar-se; (*of ground*) ceder; (*of voice*) baixar □ *n* pia *f*, (*P*) lava-louça *m*. ~ **in** □ (*fig*) ficar gravado, entrar (*colloq*). ~ **or swim** ou vai ou racha

sinner /'sɪnə(r)/ *n* pecador *m*

sinuous /'sɪnjʊəs/ *a* sinuoso

sinus /'saɪnəs/ *n* (*pl* **-es**) (*anat*) seio (nasal). ~**itis** /saɪnə'saɪtɪs/ *n* sinusite *f*

sip /sɪp/ *n* gole *m* □ *vt* (*pt* **sipped**) bebericar, beber aos golinhos

siphon /'saɪfn/ *n* sifão *m* □ *vt* ~ **off** extrair por meio de sifão

sir /sɜː(r)/ *n* senhor *m*. **S**~ (*title*) Sir *m*. **Dear S**~ Exmo Senhor. **excuse me**, ~ desculpe, senhor. **no**, ~ não, senhor

siren /'saɪərən/ *n* sereia *f*, sirene *f*

sirloin /'sɜːlɔɪn/ *n* lombo *m* de vaca

sissy /'sɪsɪ/ *n* maricas *m*

sister /'sɪstə(r)/ *n* irmã *f*; (*nun*) irmã *f*, freira *f*; (*nurse*) enfermeira-chefe *f*. ~**in-law** (*pl* ~**s-in-law**) cunhada *f*. ~**ly** *a* fraterno, fraternal

sit /sɪt/ *vt/i* (*pt* **sat**, *pres p* **sitting**) sentar(-se); (*of committee etc*) reunir-se. ~ **for an exam** fazer um exame, prestar uma prova. **be** ~**ting** estar sentado. ~ **around** não fazer nada. ~ **down** sentar-se. ~**in** *n* ocupação *f*. ~**ting** *n* reunião *f*, sessão *f*; (*in restaurant*) serviço *m*. ~**ting-room** *n* sala *f* de estar. ~ **up** endireitar-se na cadeira; (*not go to bed*) passar a noite acordado

site /saɪt/ *n* local *m*. (**building**) ~ terreno *m* para construção, lote *m* □ *vt* localizar, situar

situat|e /'sɪtʃʊeɪt/ *vt* situar. **be** ~**ed** estar situado. ~**ion** /-'eɪʃn/ *n* (*position, condition*) situação *f*; (*job*) emprego *m*, colocação *f*

six /sɪks/ *a* & *n* seis (*m*). ~**th** *a* & *n* sexto (*m*)

sixteen /sɪk'stiːn/ *a* & *n* dezesseis *m*, (*P*) dezasseis (*m*). ~**th** *a* & *n* décimo sexto (*m*)

sixt|y /'sɪkstɪ/ *a* & *n* sessenta (*m*). ~**ieth** *a* & *n* sexagésimo (*m*)

size /saɪz/ *n* tamanho *m*; (*of person, garment etc*) tamanho *m*, medida *f*; (*of shoes*) número *m*; (*extent*) grandeza *f* □ *vt* ~ **up** calcular o tamanho de; (*colloq: judge*) formar um juízo sobre, avaliar. ~**able** *a* bastante grande, considerável

sizzle /'sɪzl/ *vi* chiar, rechinar

skate[1] /skeɪt/ *n* (*pl* **invar**) (*fish*) (ar)raia *f*

skat|e[2] /skeɪt/ *n* patim *m* □ *vi* patinar. ~**er** *n* patinador *m*. ~**ing** *n* patinação *f*. ~**ing-rink** *n* rinque *m* de patinação

skateboard /'skeɪtbɔːd/ *n* skate *m*

skeleton /'skelɪtən/ *n* esqueleto *m*; (*framework*) armação *f*. ~**on crew** *or* **staff** pessoal *m* reduzido. ~**on key** chave *f* mestra. ~**al** *a* esquelético

sketch /sketʃ/ *n* esboço *m*, croqui(s) *m*; (*theat*) sketch *m*, peça *f* curta e humorística; (*outline*) idéia *f* geral, esboço *m* □ *vt* esboçar, delinear □ *vi* fazer esboços. ~**book** *n* caderno *m* de desenho

sketchy /'sketʃɪ/ *a* (**-ier**, **-iest**) incompleto, esboçado

skewer /'skjʊə(r)/ *n* espeto *m*

ski /ski:/ n (pl -s) esqui m □ vi (pt **ski'd** or **skied**, pres p **skiing**) esquiar; (go skiing) fazer esqui. **~er** n esquiador m. **~ing** n esqui m

skid /skɪd/ vi (pt **skidded**) derrapar, patinar □ n derrapagem f

skilful /ˈskɪlfl/ a hábil, habilidoso. **~ly** adv habilmente, com perícia

skill /skɪl/ n habilidade f, jeito m; (craft) arte f. **~s** aptidões fpl. **~ed** a hábil, habilidoso; (worker) especializado

skim /skɪm/ vt (pt **skimmed**) tirar a espuma de; (milk) desnatar, tirar a nata de; (pass or glide over) deslizar sobre, roçar □ vi **~ through** ler por alto, passar os olhos por. **~med milk** leite m desnatado

skimp /skɪmp/ vt (use too little) poupar em □ vi ser poupado

skimpy /ˈskɪmpɪ/ a (-ier, -iest) (clothes) sumário; (meal) escasso, racionado (fig)

skin /skɪn/ n (of person, animal) pele f; (of fruit) casca f □ vt (pt **skinned**) (animal) esfolar, tirar a pele de; (fruit) descascar. **~-diving** n mergulho m, caça f submarina

skinny /ˈskɪnɪ/ a (-ier, -iest) magricela, escanzelado

skint /skɪnt/ a (sl) sem dinheiro, na última lona (sl), (P) nas lonas

skip[1] /skɪp/ vi (pt **skipped**) saltar, pular; (jump about) saltitar; (with rope) pular corda □ vt (page) saltar; (class) faltar a □ n salto m. **~ping rope** n corda f de pular

skip[2] /skɪp/ n (container) container m grande para entulho

skipper /ˈskɪpə(r)/ n capitão m

skirmish /ˈskɜːmɪʃ/ n escaramuça f

skirt /skɜːt/ n saia f □ vt contornar, ladear. **~ing-board** n rodapé m

skit /skɪt/ n (theat) paródia f, sketch m satírico

skittle /ˈskɪtl/ n pino m. **~s** npl boliche m, (P) jogo m de laranjinha

skive /skaɪv/ vi (sl) eximir-se de um dever, evitar trabalhar (sl)

skulk /skʌlk/ vi (move) rondar furtivamente; (hide) esconder-se

skull /skʌl/ n caveira f, crânio m

skunk /skʌŋk/ n (animal) gambá m

sky /skaɪ/ n céu m. **~-blue** a & n azulceleste (m)

skylight /ˈskaɪlaɪt/ n clarabóia f

skyscraper /ˈskaɪskreɪpə(r)/ n arranha-céus m invar

slab /slæb/ n (of marble) placa f; (of paving-stone) laje f; (of metal) chapa f; (of cake) fatia f grossa

slack /slæk/ a (-er, -est) (rope) bambo, frouxo; (person) descuidado, negligente; (business) parado, fraco; (period, season) morto □ n the **~** (in rope) a parte bamba □ vt/i (be lazy) estar com preguiça, fazer cera (fig)

slacken /ˈslækən/ vt/i (speed, activity etc) afrouxar, abrandar

slacks /slæks/ npl calças fpl

slag /slæg/ n escória f

slain /sleɪn/ see **slay**

slam /slæm/ vt (pt **slammed**) bater violentamente com; (throw) atirar; (sl: criticize) criticar, malhar □ vi (door etc) bater violentamente □ n (noise) bater m, pancada f

slander /ˈslɑːndə(r)/ n calúnia f, difamação f □ vt caluniar, difamar. **~ous** a calunioso, difamatório

slang /slæŋ/ n calão m, gíria f. **~y** a de calão

slant /slɑːnt/ vt/i inclinar(-se); (news) apresentar de forma tendenciosa □ n inclinação f; (bias) tendência f; (point of view) ângulo m. **be ~ing** ser/estar inclinado or em declive

slap /slæp/ vt (pt **slapped**) (strike) bater, dar uma palmada em; (on face) esbofetear, dar uma bofetada em; (put forcefully) atirar com □ n palmada f, bofetada f □ adv em cheio. **~-up** a (sl: excellent) excelente

slapdash /ˈslæpdæʃ/ a descuidado; (impetuous) precipitado

slapstick /ˈslæpstɪk/ n farsa f com palhaçadas

slash /slæʃ/ vt (cut) retalhar, dar golpes em; (sever) cortar; (a garment) golpear; (fig: reduce) reduzir drasticamente, fazer um corte radical em □ n corte m, golpe m

slat /slæt/ n (in blind) ripa f, (P) lâmina f

slate /sleɪt/ n ardósia f □ vt (colloq: criticize) criticar severamente

slaughter /ˈslɔːtə(r)/ vt chacinar, massacrar; (animals) abater □ n chacina f, massacre m, mortandade f; (animals) abate m

slaughterhouse /ˈslɔːtəhaʊs/ n matadouro m

slave /sleɪv/ n escravo m □ vi mourejar, trabalhar como um escravo. **~driver** n (fig) o que obriga os outros a trabalharem como escravos, condutor m de escravos. **~ry** /-ərɪ/ n escravatura f

slavish /ˈsleɪvɪʃ/ a servil

slay /sleɪ/ vt (pt slew, pp slain) matar

sleazy /ˈsliːzɪ/ a (-ier, -iest) (colloq) esquálido, sórdido

sledge /sledʒ/ n trenó m. **~-hammer** n martelo m de forja, marreta f

sleek /sliːk/ a (-er, -est) liso, macio e lustroso

sleep /sliːp/ n sono m □ vi (pt slept) dormir □ vt ter lugar para, alojar. **go**

to ~ ir dormir, adormecer. **put to ~**
(*kill*) mandar matar. ~ **around** ser
promíscuo. **~er** *n* aquele que dorme;
(*rail: beam*) dormente *m*; (*berth*)
couchette *f*. **~ing-bag** *n* saco *m*
de dormir. **~ing-car** *n* carro-
dormitório *m*, carruagemcama *f*, (*P*)
vagon-lit *m*. **~less** *a* insone; (*night*)
em claro, insone. **~-walker** *n*
sonâmbulo *m*
sleep|y /'sli:pɪ/ *a* (**-ier, -iest**) sono-
lento. **be ~y** ter *or* estar com sono.
~ily *adv* meio dormindo
sleet /sli:t/ *n* geada *f* miúda □ *vi* cair
geada miúda
sleeve /sli:v/ *n* manga *f*; (*of record*)
capa *f*. **up one's ~** de reserva,
escondido. **~less** *a* sem mangas
sleigh /sleɪ/ *n* trenó *m*
sleight /slaɪt/ *n* **~ of hand** pres-
tidigitação *f*, passe *m* de mágica
slender /'slendə(r)/ *a* esguio, esbelto;
(*fig: scanty*) escasso. **~ness** *n* aspecto
m esguio, esbelteza *f*, elegância *f*;
(*scantiness*) escassez *f*
slept /slept/ *see* **sleep**
sleuth /slu:θ/ *n* (*colloq*) detective *m*
slew[1] /slu:/ *vi* (*turn*) virar-se
slew[2] /slu:/ *see* **slay**
slice /slaɪs/ *n* fatia *f* □ *vt* cortar em
fatias; (*golf, tennis*) cortar
slick /slɪk/ *a* (*slippery*) escorregadio;
(*cunning*) astuto, habilidoso; (*unctuous*) melífluo □ *n* (**oil**) **~** mancha *f*
de óleo
slid|e /slaɪd/ *vt/i* (*pt* **slid**) escorregar,
deslizar □ *n* escorregadela *f*, escorregão *m*; (*in playground*) escorrega *m*; (*for hair*) prendedor *m*, (*P*)
travessa *f*; (*photo*) diapositivo *m*, slide
m. **~e-rule** *n* régua *f* de cálculo.
~ing *a* (*door, panel*) corrediço, de
correr. **~ing scale** escala *f* móvel
slight /slaɪt/ *a* (**-er, -est**) (*slender,
frail*) delgado, franzino; (*inconsider-
able*) leve, ligeiro □ *vt* desconsiderar,
desfeitear □ *n* desconsideração *f*, desfeita *f*. **the ~est** a o/a menor. **not in
the ~est** em absoluto. **~ly** *adv* ligeiramente, um pouco
slim /slɪm/ *a* (**slimmer, slimmest**)
magro, esbelto; (*chance*) pequeno, remoto □ *vi* (*pt* **slimmed**) emagrecer.
~ness *n* magreza *f*, esbelteza *f*
slim|e /slaɪm/ *n* lodo *m*. **~y** *a* lodoso;
(*slippery*) escorregadio; (*fig: servile*)
servil, bajulador
sling /slɪŋ/ *n* (*weapon*) funda *f*; (*for
arm*) tipóia *f* □ *vt* (*pt* **slung**) atirar,
lançar
slip /slɪp/ *vt/i* (*pt* **slipped**) escorregar;
(*move quietly*) mover-se de mansinho
□ *n* escorregadela *f*, escorregão *m*;
(*mistake*) engano *m*, lapso *m*; (*petti-*

coat) combinação *f*; (*of paper*) tira *f*
de papel. **give the ~ to** livrar-se de,
escapar(-se) de. **~ away** esgueirar-se.
~ by passar sem se dar conta, passar
despercebido. **~-cover** *n* (*Amer*) capa
f para móveis. **~ into** (*go*) entrar de
mansinho, enfiar-se em; (*clothes*)
enfiar. **~ of the tongue** lapso *m*.
~ped disc disco *m* deslocado. **~-
road** *n* acesso *m* a autoestrada. **~
sb's mind** passar pela cabeça de
alguém. **~ up** (*colloq*) cometer uma
gafe. **~-up** *n* (*colloq*) gafe *f*
slipper /'slɪpə(r)/ *n* chinelo *m*
slippery /'slɪpərɪ/ *a* escorregadio;
(*fig: person*) que não é de confiança,
sem escrúpulos
slipshod /'slɪpʃɒd/ *a* (*person*) desleixado, desmazelado; (*work*) feito sem
cuidado, desleixado
slit /slɪt/ *n* fenda *f*; (*cut*) corte *m*; (*tear*)
rasgão *m* □ *vt* (*pt* **slit**, *pres p* **slitting**)
fender; (*cut*) fazer um corte em, cortar
slither /'slɪðə(r)/ *vi* escorregar, resvalar
sliver /'slɪvə(r)/ *n* (*of cheese etc*) fatia *f*;
(*splinter*) lasca *f*
slobber /'slɒbə(r)/ *vi* babar-se
slog /slɒg/ *vt* (*pt* **slogged**) (*hit*) bater
com força □ *vi* (*walk*) caminhar com
passos pesados e firmes; (*work*) trabalhar duro □ *n* (*work*) trabalheira *f*;
(*walk, effort*) estafa *f*
slogan /'sləʊgən/ *n* slogan *m*, lema *m*,
palavra *f* de ordem
slop /slɒp/ *vt/i* (*pt* **slopped**) transbordar, entornar. **~s** *npl* (*dirty water*)
água(s) *f*(*pl*) suja(s); (*liquid refuse*)
despejos *mpl*
slop|e /sləʊp/ *vt/i* inclinar(-se), for-
mar declive □ *n* (*of mountain*) encosta
f; (*of street*) rampa *f*, ladeira *f*. **~ing** *a*
inclinado, em declive
sloppy /'slɒpɪ/ *a* (**-ier, -iest**) (*ground*)
molhado, com poças de água; (*food*)
aguado; (*clothes*) desleixado; (*work*)
descuidado, feito de qualquer jeito *or*
maneira (*colloq*); (*person*) desmazelado; (*maudlin*) piegas
slosh /slɒʃ/ *vt* entornar; (*colloq:
splash*) esparrinhar; (*sl: hit*) bater
em, dar (uma) sova em □ *vi* chapinhar
slot /slɒt/ *n* ranhura *f*; (*in timetable*)
horário *m*; (*TV*) espaço *m*; (*aviat*) slot
m □ *vt/i* (*pt* **slotted**) enfiar(-se), me-
ter(-se), encaixar (-se). **~-machine** *n*
(*for stamps, tickets etc*) distribuidor
m automático; (*for gambling*) caça-
níqueis *m*, (*P*) slot machine *f*
sloth /sləʊθ/ *n* preguiça *f*, indolência
f; (*zool*) preguiça *f*
slouch /slaʊtʃ/ *vi* (*stand, move*) andar
com as costas curvadas; (*sit*) sentar
em má postura

slovenly /ˈslʌvnlɪ/ a desmazelado, desleixado

slow /sləʊ/ a (-er, -est) lento, vagaroso □ adv devagar, lentamente □ vt/i ~ (**up** or **down**) diminuir a velocidade, afrouxar; (auto) desacelerar. **be** ~ (clock etc) atrasar-se, estar atrasado. **in** ~ **motion** em câmara lenta. **~ly** adv devagar, lentamente, vagarosamente

slow|coach /ˈsləʊkəʊtʃ/, (Amer) **~poke** ns lesma m/f, pastelão m (fig)

sludge /slʌdʒ/ n lama f, lodo m

slug /slʌg/ n lesma f

sluggish /ˈslʌgɪʃ/ a (slow) lento, moroso; (lazy) indolente, preguiçoso

sluice /sluːs/ n (gate) comporta f; (channel) canal m □ vt lavar com jorros de água

slum /slʌm/ n favela f, (P) bairro m da lata; (building) cortiço m

slumber /ˈslʌmbə(r)/ n sono m □ vi dormir

slump /slʌmp/ n (in prices) baixa f, descida f; (in demand) quebra f na procura; (econ) depressão f □ vi (fall limply) cair, afundar-se; (of price) baixar bruscamente

slung /slʌŋ/ see **sling**

slur /slɜː(r)/ vt/i (pt slurred) (speech) pronunciar indistintamente, mastigar □ n (in speech) som m indistinto; (discredit) nódoa f, estigma m

slush /slʌʃ/ n (snow) neve f meio derretida. ~ **fund** (comm) fundo m para subornos. **~y** a (road) coberto de neve derretida, lamacento

slut /slʌt/ n (dirty woman) porca f, desmazelada f; (immoral woman) desavergonhada f

sly /slaɪ/ a (slyer, slyest) (crafty) manhoso; (secretive) sonso □ n **on the ~** na calada. **~ly** adv (craftily) astutamente; (secretively) sonsamente

smack[1] /smæk/ n palmada f; (on face) bofetada f □ vt dar uma palmada or tapa em; (on the face) esbofetear, dar uma bofetada em □ adv (colloq) em cheio, direto

smack[2] /smæk/ vi ~ **of sth** cheirar a alg coisa

small /smɔːl/ a (-er, -est) pequeno □ n ~ **of the back** zona f dos rins □ adv (cut etc) em pedaços pequenos, aos bocadinhos. ~ **change** trocado m, dinheiro m miúdo. ~ **talk** conversa f fiada, bate-papo m. **~ness** n pequenez f

smallholding /ˈsmɔːlhəʊldɪŋ/ n pequena propriedade f

smallpox /ˈsmɔːlpɒks/ n varíola f

smarmy /ˈsmaːmɪ/ a (-ier, -iest) (colloq) bajulador, puxa-saco (colloq)

smart /smaːt/ a (-er, -est) elegante;

(clever) esperto, vivo; (brisk) rápido □ vi (sting) arder, picar. **~ly** adv elegantemente, com elegância; (cleverly) com esperteza, vivamente; (briskly) rapidamente. **~ness** n elegância f

smarten /ˈsmaːtn/ vt/i ~ (**up**) arranjar, dar um ar mais cuidado a. ~ (**o.s.**) **up** embelezar-se, arrumar-se, (P) pôr-se elegante/bonito; (tidy) arranjar-se

smash /smæʃ/ vt/i (to pieces) despedaçar(-se), espatifar(-se) (colloq); (a record) quebrar; (opponent) esmagar; (ruin) (fazer) falir; (of vehicle) espatifar(-se) □ n (noise) estrondo m; (blow) pancada f forte, golpe m; (collision) colisão f; (tennis) smash m

smashing /ˈsmæʃɪŋ/ a (colloq) formidável, estupendo (colloq)

smattering /ˈsmætərɪŋ/ n leves noções fpl

smear /smɪə(r)/ vt (stain; discredit) manchar; (coat) untar, besuntar □ n mancha f, nódoa f; (med) esfregaço m

smell /smel/ n cheiro m, odor m; (sense) cheiro m, olfato m, (P) olfacto m □ vt/i (pt smelt or smelled) ~ (**of**) cheirar (a). **~y** a malcheiroso

smelt[1] /smelt/ see **smell**

smelt[2] /smelt/ vt (ore) fundir

smil|e /smaɪl/ n sorriso m □ vi sorrir. **~ing** a sorridente, risonho

smirk /smɜːk/ n sorriso m falso or afetado, (P) afectado

smithereens /smɪðəˈriːnz/ npl **to** or **in** ~ em pedaços mpl

smock /smɒk/ n guarda-pó m

smog /smɒg/ n mistura f de nevoeiro e fumaça, smog m

smoke /sməʊk/ n fumo m, fumaça f □ vt fumar; (bacon etc) fumar, defumar □ vi fumar, fumegar. **~-screen** n (lit & fig) cortina f de fumaça. **~less** a (fuel) sem fumo. **~r** /-ə(r)/ n (person) fumante mf, (P) fumador m. **smoky** a (air) enfumaçado, fumacento

smooth /smuːð/ a (-er, -est) liso; (soft) macio; (movement) regular, suave; (manners) lisonjeiro, conciliador, suave □ vt alisar. ~ **out** (fig) aplanar, remover. **~ly** adv suavemente, facilmente

smother /ˈsmʌðə(r)/ vt (stifle) abafar, sufocar; (cover, overwhelm) cobrir (**with** de); (suppress) abafar, reprimir

smoulder /ˈsməʊldə(r)/ vi (lit & fig) arder, abrasar-se

smudge /smʌdʒ/ n mancha f, borrão m □ vt/i sujar(-se), manchar(-se), borrar(-se)

smug /smʌg/ a (smugger, smuggest) presunçoso, convencido (colloq). **~ly** adv presunçosamente. **~ness** n presunção f

smuggl|e /'smʌgl/ *vt* contrabandear, fazer contrabando de. **~er** *n* contrabandista *mf*. **~ing** *n* contrabando *m*

smut /smʌt/ *n* fuligem *f*. **~ty** *a* cheio de fuligem; (*colloq: obscene*) indecente, sujo (*colloq*)

snack /snæk/ *n* refeição *f* ligeira. **~bar** *n* lanchonete *f*, (*P*) snack(-bar) *m*

snag /snæg/ *n* (*obstacle*) obstáculo *m*; (*drawback*) problema *m*, contra *m*; (*in cloth*) rasgão *m*; (*in stocking*) fio *m* puxado

snail /sneɪl/ *n* caracol *m*. **at a ~'s pace** em passo de tartaruga

snake /sneɪk/ *n* serpente *f*, cobra *f*

snap /snæp/ *vt/i* (*pt* **snapped**) (*whip, fingers*) (fazer) estalar; (*break*) estalar(-se), partir(-se) com um estalo, rebentar; (*say*) dizer irritadamente □ *n* estalo *m*; (*photo*) instantâneo *m*; (*Amer: fastener*) mola *f* □ *a* súbito, repentino. **~ at** (*bite*) abocanhar, tentar morder; (*speak angrily*) retrucar asperamente. **~ up** (*buy*) comprar rapidamente

snappish /'snæpɪʃ/ *a* irritadiço

snappy /'snæpɪ/ *a* (**-ier, -iest**) (*colloq*) vivo, animado. **make it ~** (*colloq*) vai rápido!, apresse-se! (*colloq*)

snapshot /'snæpʃɒt/ *n* instantâneo *m*

snare /sneə(r)/ *n* laço *m*, cilada *f*, armadilha *f*

snarl /snɑːl/ *vi* rosnar □ *n* rosnadela *f*

snatch /snætʃ/ *vt* (*grab*) agarrar, apanhar; (*steal*) roubar. **~ from sb** arrancar de alguém □ *n* (*theft*) roubo *m*; (*bit*) bocado *m*, pedaço *m*

sneak /sniːk/ *vi* (*slink*) esgueirar-se furtivamente; (*sl: tell tales*) fazer queixa, delatar □ *vt* (*sl: steal*) rapinar (*colloq*) □ *n* (*sl*) dedo-duro *m*, queixinhas *mf* (*sl*). **~ing** *a* secreto. **~y** *a* sonso

sneer /snɪə(r)/ *n* sorriso *m* de desdém □ *vi* sorrir desdenhosamente

sneeze /sniːz/ *n* espirro *m* □ *vi* espirrar

snide /snaɪd/ *a* (*colloq*) sarcástico

sniff /snɪf/ *vi* fungar □ *vt/i* **~ (at)** (*smell*) cheirar; (*dog*) farejar. **~ at** (*fig: in contempt*) desprezar □ *n* fungadela *f*

snigger /'snɪgə(r)/ *n* riso *m* abafado □ *vi* rir dissimuladamente

snip /snɪp/ *vt* (*pt* **snipped**) cortar com tesoura □ *n* pedaço *m*, retalho *m*; (*sl: bargain*) pechincha *f*

snipe /snaɪp/ *vi* dar tiros de emboscada. **~r** /-ə(r)/ *n* franco-atirador *m*

snivel /'snɪvl/ *vi* (*pt* **snivelled**) choramingar, lamuriar-se

snob /snɒb/ *n* esnobe *mf*, (*P*) snob *mf*. **~bery** *n* esnobismo *m*, (*P*) snobismo *m*. **~bish** *a* esnobe, (*P*) snob

snooker /'snuːkə(r)/ *n* snooker *m*, sinuca *f*

snoop /snuːp/ *vi* (*colloq*) bisbilhotar, meter o nariz em toda a parte. **~ on** espiar, espionar. **~er** *n* bisbilhoteiro *m*

snooty /'snuːtɪ/ *a* (**-ier, -iest**) (*colloq*) convencido, arrogante (*colloq*)

snooze /snuːz/ *n* (*colloq*) soneca *f* (*colloq*) □ *vi* (*colloq*) tirar uma soneca

snore /snɔː(r)/ *n* ronco *m* □ *vi* roncar

snorkel /'snɔːkl/ *n* tubo *m* de respiração, snorkel *m*

snort /snɔːt/ *n* resfôlego *m*, bufido *m* □ *vi* resfolegar, bufar

snout /snaʊt/ *n* focinho *m*

snow /snəʊ/ *n* neve *f* □ *vi* nevar. **be ~ed under** (*fig: be overwhelmed*) estar sobrecarregado (*fig*). **~-bound** *a* bloqueado pela neve. **~-drift** *n* banco *m* de neve. **~-plough** *n* limpa-neve *m*. **~y** *a* nevado, coberto de neve

snowball /'snəʊbɔːl/ *n* bola *f* de neve □ *vi* atirar bolas de neve (em); (*fig*) acumular-se, ir num crescendo, aumentar rapidamente

snowdrop /'snəʊdrɒp/ *n* (*bot*) fura-neve *m*

snowfall /'snəʊfɔːl/ *n* nevada *f*, (*P*) nevão *m*

snowflake /'snəʊfleɪk/ *n* floco *m* de neve

snowman /'snəʊmæn/ *n* (*pl* **-men**) boneco *m* de neve

snub /snʌb/ *vt* (*pt* **snubbed**) desdenhar, tratar com desdém □ *n* desdém *m*

snuff[1] /snʌf/ *n* rapé *m*

snuff[2] /snʌf/ *vt* **~ out** (*candles, hopes etc*) apagar, extinguir

snuffle /'snʌfl/ *vi* fungar

snug /snʌg/ *a* (**snugger, snuggest**) (*cosy*) aconchegado; (*close-fitting*) justo

snuggle /'snʌgl/ *vt/i* (*nestle*) aninhar-se, aconchegar-se; (*cuddle*) aconchegar

so /səʊ/ *adv* tão, de tal modo; (*thus*) assim, deste modo □ *conj* por isso, portanto, por conseguinte. **~ am I** eu também. **~ does he** ele também. **that is ~** é isso. **I think ~** acho que sim. **five or ~** uns cinco. **~ as to** de modo a. **~ far** até agora, até aqui. **~ long!** (*colloq*) até já! (*colloq*). **~ many** tantos. **~ much** tanto. **~ that** para que, de modo que. **~-and-** fulano *m*. **~-called** *a* pretenso, soidisant. **~-so** *a* & *adv* assim assim, mais ou menos

soak /səʊk/ *vt/i* molhar(-se), ensopar(-se), enchacar(-se). **leave to ~** pôr de molho. **~ in** *or* **up** *vt* absorver, embeber. **~ through** repassar. **~ing** *a* ensopado, encharcado

soap /səʊp/ *n* sabão *m*. **(toilet)** ~ sabonete *m* □ *vt* ensaboar. ~ **opera** (*radio*) novela *f* radiofônica, (*P*) radiofónica; (*TV*) telenovela *f*. ~ **flakes** flocos *mpl* de sabão. ~ **powder** sabão *m* em pó. ~**y** *a* ensaboado

soar /sɔ:(r)/ *vi* voar alto; (*go high*) elevar-se; (*hover*) pairar

sob /sɒb/ *n* soluço *m* □ *vi* (*pt* **sobbed**) soluçar

sober /ˈsəʊbə(r)/ *a* (*not drunk, calm, of colour*) sóbrio; (*serious*) sério, grave □ *vt/i* ~ **up** (fazer) ficar sóbrio, (fazer) curar a bebedeira (*colloq*)

soccer /ˈsɒkə(r)/ *n* (*colloq*) futebol *m*

sociable /ˈsəʊʃəbl/ *a* sociável

social /ˈsəʊʃl/ *a* social; (*sociable*) sociável; (*gathering, life*) de sociedade □ *n* reunião *f* social. ~**ly** *adv* socialmente; (*meet*) em sociedade. ~ **security** previdência *f* social; (*for old age*) pensão *f*. ~ **worker** assistente *mf* social

socialis|t /ˈsəʊʃəlɪst/ *n* socialista *mf*. ~**m** /-zəm/ *n* socialismo *m*

socialize /ˈsəʊʃəlaɪz/ *vi* socializar-se, reunir-se em sociedade. ~ **with** freqüentar, (*P*) frequentar, conviver com

society /səˈsaɪətɪ/ *n* sociedade *f*

sociolog|y /səʊsɪˈɒlədʒɪ/ *n* sociologia *f*. ~**ical** /-əˈlɒdʒɪkl/ *a* sociológico. ~**ist** *n* sociólogo *m*

sock¹ /sɒk/ *n* meia *f* curta; (*men's*) meia *f* (curta), (*P*) peúga *f*; (*women's*) soquete *f*

sock² /sɒk/ *vt* (*sl: hit*) esmurrar, dar um murro em (*colloq*)

socket /ˈsɒkɪt/ *n* cavidade *f*; (*for lamp*) suporte *m*; (*electr*) tomada *f*; (*of tooth*) alvéolo *m*

soda /ˈsəʊdə/ *n* soda *f*. **(baking)** ~ (*culin*) bicarbonato *m* de soda. ~ **(-water)** água *f* gasosa, soda *f* limonada, (*P*) água *f* gaseificada

sodden /ˈsɒdn/ *a* ensopado, empapado

sodium /ˈsəʊdɪəm/ *n* sódio *m*

sofa /ˈsəʊfə/ *n* sofá *m*

soft /sɒft/ *a* (-**er**, -**est**) (*not hard, feeble*) mole; (*not rough, not firm*) macio; (*gentle, not loud, not bright*) suave; (*tender-hearted*) sensível; (*fruit*) sem caroço; (*wood*) de coníferas; (*drink*) não alcoólico. ~**-boiled** *a* (*egg*) quente. ~ **spot** (*fig*) fraco *m*. ~**ly** *adv* docemente. ~**ness** *n* moleza *f*; (*to touch*) maciez *f*; (*gentleness*) suavidade *f*, brandura *f*

soften /ˈsɒfn/ *vt/i* amaciar, amolecer; (*tone down, lessen*) abrandar

software /ˈsɒftweə(r)/ *n* software *m*

soggy /ˈsɒgɪ/ *a* (-**ier**, -**iest**) ensopado, empapado

soil¹ /sɔɪl/ *n* solo *m*, terra *f*

soil² /sɔɪl/ *vt/i* sujar(-se). ~**ed** *a* sujo

solace /ˈsɒlɪs/ *n* consolo *m*; (*relief*) alívio *m*

solar /ˈsəʊlə(r)/ *a* solar

sold /səʊld/ *see* **sell** □ *a* ~ **out** esgotado

solder /ˈsəʊldə(r)/ *n* solda *f* □ *vt* soldar

soldier /ˈsəʊldʒə(r)/ *n* soldado *m* □ *vi* ~ **on** (*colloq*) perseverar com afinco, batalhar (*colloq*)

sole¹ /səʊl/ *n* (*of foot*) planta *f*, sola *f* do pé; (*of shoe*) sola *f*

sole² /səʊl/ *n* (*fish*) solha *f*

sole³ /səʊl/ *a* único. ~**ly** *adv* unicamente

solemn /ˈsɒləm/ *a* solene. ~**ity** /səˈlemnətɪ/ *n* solenidade *f*. ~**ly** *adv* solenemente

solicit /səˈlɪsɪt/ *vt* (*seek*) solicitar □ *vi* (*of prostitute*) aproximar-se de homens na rua

solicitor /səˈlɪsɪtə(r)/ *n* advogado *m*

solicitous /səˈlɪsɪtəs/ *a* solícito

solid /ˈsɒlɪd/ *a* sólido; (*not hollow*) maciço, cheio, compacto; (*gold etc*) maciço; (*meal*) substancial □ *n* sólido *m* ~**s** (*food*) alimentos *mpl* sólidos. ~**ity** /səˈlɪdətɪ/ *n* solidez *f*. ~**ly** *adv* solidamente

solidarity /sɒlɪˈdærətɪ/ *n* solidariedade *f*

solidify /səˈlɪdɪfaɪ/ *vt/i* solidificar(-se)

soliloquy /səˈlɪləkwɪ/ *n* monólogo *m*, solilóquio *m*

solitary /ˈsɒlɪtrɪ/ *a* solitário, só; (*only one*) um único. ~ **confinement** prisão *f* celular, solitária *f*

solitude /ˈsɒlɪtjuːd/ *n* solidão *f*

solo /ˈsəʊləʊ/ *n* (*pl* -**os**) solo *m* □ *a* solo. ~ **flight** vôo *m* solo. ~**ist** *n* solista *mf*

soluble /ˈsɒljʊbl/ *a* solúvel

solution /səˈluːʃn/ *n* solução *f*

solv|e /sɒlv/ *vt* resolver, solucionar. ~**able** *a* resolúvel, solúvel

solvent /ˈsɒlvənt/ *a* (dis)solvente; (*comm*) solvente □ *n* (dis)solvente *m*

sombre /ˈsɒmbə(r)/ *a* sombrio

some /sʌm/ *a* (*quantity*) algum(a); (*number*) alguns, algumas, uns, umas; (*unspecified, some or other*) um(a)... qualquer, uns... quaisquer, umas... quaisquer; (*a little*) um pouco de, algum; (*a certain*) um certo; (*contrasted with others*) uns, umas, alguns, algumas, certos, certas □ *pron* uns, umas, algum(a), alguns, algumas; (*a little*) um pouco, algum □ *adv* (*approximately*) uns, umas. **will you have** ~ **coffee**/*etc*? você quer café/*etc*? ~ **day** algum dia. ~ **of my friends** alguns dos meus amigos. ~ **people say**... algumas pessoas dizem... ~ **time ago** algum tempo atrás

somebody /'sʌmbədɪ/ *pron* alguém □ *n* be a ~ ser alguém

somehow /'sʌmhaʊ/ *adv* (*in some way*) de algum modo, de alguma maneira; (*for some reason*) por alguma razão

someone /'sʌmwʌn/ *pron* & *n* = **somebody**

somersault /'sʌməsɔːlt/ *n* cambalhota *f*; (*in the air*) salto *m* mortal □ *vi* dar uma cambalhota/um salto mortal

something /'sʌmθɪŋ/ *pron* & *n* uma/ alguma/qualquer coisa *f*, algo. ~ **good/etc** uma coisa boa/*etc*, qualquer coisa de bom/*etc*. ~ **like** um pouco como

sometime /'sʌmtaɪm/ *adv* a certa altura, um dia □ *a* (*former*) antigo. ~ **last summer** a certa altura no verão passado. **I'll go** ~ hei de ir um dia

sometimes /'sʌmtaɪmz/ *adv* às vezes, de vez em quando

somewhat /'sʌmwɒt/ *adv* um pouco, um tanto (ou quanto)

somewhere /'sʌmweə(r)/ *adv* (*position*) em algum lugar; (*direction*) para algum lugar

son /sʌn/ *n* filho *m*. ~**-in-law** *n* (*pl* ~**s-in-law**) genro *m*

sonar /'səʊnɑː(r)/ *n* sonar *m*

sonata /sə'nɑːtə/ *n* (*mus*) sonata *f*

song /sɒŋ/ *n* canção *f*. ~**-bird** *n* ave *f* canora

sonic /'sɒnɪk/ *a* ~ **boom** estrondo *m* sónico, (*P*) sónico

sonnet /'sɒnɪt/ *n* soneto *m*

soon /suːn/ *adv* (**-er**, **-est**) em breve, dentro em pouco, daqui a pouco; (*early*) cedo. **as** ~ **as possible** o mais rápido possível. **I would** ~**er stay** preferia ficar. ~ **after** pouco depois. ~**er or later** mais cedo ou mais tarde

soot /sʊt/ *n* fuligem *f*. ~**y** *a* coberto de fuligem

sooth|e /suːð/ *vt* acalmar, suavizar; (*pain*) aliviar. ~**ing** *a* (*remedy*) calmante, suavizante; (*words*) confortante

sophisticated /sə'fɪstɪkeɪtɪd/ *a* sofisticado, refinado, requintado; (*machine etc*) sofisticado

soporific /sɒpə'rɪfɪk/ *a* soporífico

sopping /'sɒpɪŋ/ *a* encharcado, ensopado

soppy /'sɒpɪ/ *a* (**-ier, -iest**) (*colloq: sentimental*) piegas; (*colloq: silly*) bobo

soprano /sə'prɑːnəʊ/ *n* (*pl* ~**s**) & *adj* soprano (*mf*)

sorbet /'sɔːbeɪ/ *n* (*water-ice*) sorvete *m* feito sem leite

sorcerer /'sɔːsərə(r)/ *n* feiticeiro *m*

sordid /'sɔːdɪd/ *a* sórdido

sore /sɔː(r)/ *a* (**-er, -est**) dolorido; (*vexed*) aborrecido (**at, with** com) □ *n* ferida *f*. **have a** ~ **throat** ter a garganta inflamada, ter dores de garganta

sorely /'sɔːlɪ/ *adv* fortemente, seriamente

sorrow /'sɒrəʊ/ *n* dor *f*, mágoa *f*, pesar *m*. ~**ful** *a* pesaroso, triste

sorry /'sɒrɪ/ *a* (**-ier, -iest**) (*state, sight etc*) triste. **be** ~ **to/that** (*regretful*) sentir muito/que, lamentar que; **be** ~ **about/for** (*repentant*) ter pena de, estar arrependido de. **feel** ~ **for** ter pena de. ~**!** desculpe!, perdão!

sort /sɔːt/ *n* gênero *m*, (*P*) género *m*, espécie *f*, qualidade *f*. **of** ~**s** (*colloq*) uma espécie de (*colloq, pej*). **out of** ~**s** indisposto □ *vt* separar por grupos; (*tidy*) arrumar. ~ **out** (*problem*) resolver; (*arrange, separate*) separar, distribuir

soufflé /'suːfleɪ/ *n* (*culin*) suflê *m*, (*P*) soufflé *m*

sought /sɔːt/ *see* **seek**

soul /səʊl/ *n* alma *f*. **the life and** ~ **of** (*fig*) a alma *f* de (*fig*)

soulful /'səʊlfl/ *a* emotivo, expressivo, cheio de sentimento

sound[1] /saʊnd/ *n* som *m*, barulho *m*, ruído *m* □ *vt/i* soar; (*seem*) dar a impressão de, parecer (**as if** que). ~ **a horn** tocar uma buzina, buzinar. ~ **barrier** barreira *f* de som. ~ **like** parecer ser, soar como. ~**-proof** *a* à prova de som □ *vt* fazer o isolamento sonoro de, isolar. ~**-track** *n* (*of film*) trilha *f* sonora, (*P*) banda *f* sonora

sound[2] /saʊnd/ *a* (**-er, -est**) (*healthy*) saudável, sadio; (*sensible*) sensato, acertado; (*secure*) firme, sólido. ~ **asleep** profundamente adormecido. ~**ly** *adv* solidamente

sound[3] /saʊnd/ *vt* (*test*) sondar; (*med; views*) auscultar

soup /suːp/ *n* sopa *f*

sour /'saʊə(r)/ *a* (**-er, -est**) azedo □ *vt/i* azedar, envinagrar

source /sɔːs/ *n* fonte *f*; (*of river*) nascente *f*

souse /saʊs/ *vt* (*throw water on*) atirar água em cima de; (*pickle*) pôr em vinagre; (*salt*) pôr em salmoura

south /saʊθ/ *n* sul *m* □ *a* sul, do sul; (*of country, people etc*) meridional □ *adv* a, ao/para o sul. **S~ Africa/ America** África *f*/América *f* do Sul. **S~ African/American** *a* & *n* sulafricano (*m*)/sul-americano (*m*). ~**east** *n* sudeste *m*. ~**erly** /'sʌðəlɪ/ *a* do sul, meridional. ~**ward** *a* ao sul. ~**ward(s)** *adv* para o sul. ~**-west** *n* sudoeste *m*

southern /'sʌðən/ *a* do sul, meridional, austral

souvenir /su:vəˈnɪə(r)/ n recordação f, lembrança f

sovereign /ˈsɒvrɪn/ n & a soberano (m). ~**ty** n soberania f

Soviet /ˈsəʊvɪət/ a soviético. **the S~ Union** a União Soviética

sow¹ /səʊ/ vt (pt sowed, pp sowed or sown) semear

sow² /saʊ/ n (zool) porca f

soy /ˈsɔɪ/ n ~ **sauce** molho m de soja

soya /ˈsɔɪə/ n soja f. ~**-bean** semente f de soja

spa /spa:/ n termas fpl

space /speɪs/ n espaço m; (room) lugar m; (period) espaço m, período m □ a (research etc) espacial □ vt ~ **out** espaçar

space|craft /ˈspeɪskra:ft/ n (pl invar), ~**ship** n nave espacial f

spacious /ˈspeɪʃəs/ a espaçoso

spade /speɪd/ n (gardener's) pá f de ferro; (child's) pá f. ~**s** (cards) espadas fpl

spadework /ˈspeɪdwɜ:k/ n (fig) trabalho m preliminar

spaghetti /spəˈgetɪ/ n espaguete m, (P) esparguete m

Spain /speɪn/ n Espanha f

span¹ /spæn/ n (of arch) vão m; (of wings) envergadura f; (of time) espaço m, duração f; (measure) palmo m □ vt (pt spanned) (extend across) transpor; (measure) medir em palmos; (in time) abarcar, abranger, estender-se por

span² /spæn/ see **spick**

Spaniard /ˈspænɪəd/ n espanhol m

Spanish /ˈspænɪʃ/ a espanhol □ n (lang) espanhol m

spaniel /ˈspænɪəl/ n spaniel m, epagneul m

spank /spæŋk/ vt dar palmadas or chineladas no. ~**ing** n (with hand) palmada f; (with slipper) chinelada f

spanner /ˈspænə(r)/ n (tool) chave f de porcas; (adjustable) chave f inglesa

spar /spa:(r)/ vi (pt sparred) jogar boxe, esp para treino; (fig: argue) discutir

spare /speə(r)/ vt (not hurt; use with restraint) poupar; (afford to give) dispensar, ceder □ a (in reserve) de reserva, de sobra; (tyre) sobressalente; (bed) extra; (room) de hóspedes □ n (part) sobressalente m. ~ **time** horas fpl vagas. **have an hour to** ~ dispôr de uma hora. **have no time to** ~ não ter tempo a perder

sparing /ˈspeərɪŋ/ a poupado. **be** ~ **of** poupar em, ser poupado com. ~**ly** adv frugalmente

spark /spa:k/ n centelha f, faísca f □ vt lançar faíscas. ~ **off** (initiate) desencadear, provocar. ~**(ing)-plug** n vela f de ignição

sparkle /ˈspa:kl/ vi cintilar, brilhar □ n brilho m, cintilação f

sparkling /ˈspa:klɪŋ/ a (wine) espumante

sparrow /ˈspærəʊ/ n pardal m

sparse /spa:s/ a esparso; (hair) ralo. ~**ly** adv (furnished etc) escassamente

spasm /ˈspæzəm/ n (of muscle) espasmo m; (of coughing, anger etc) ataque m, acesso m

spasmodic /spæzˈmɒdɪk/ a espasmódico; (at irregular intervals) intermitente

spastic /ˈspæstɪk/ n deficiente mf motor

spat /spæt/ see **spit**¹

spate /speɪt/ n (in river) enxurrada f, cheia f. **a** ~ **of** (letters etc) uma avalanche de

spatter /ˈspætə(r)/ vt salpicar (**with** de, **com**)

spawn /spɔ:n/ n ovas fpl □ vi desovar □ vt gerar em quantidade

speak /spi:k/ vt/i (pt spoke, pp spoken) falar (**to/with sb about sth** com alguém de/sobre alg coisa); (say) dizer. ~ **out/up** falar abertamente; (louder) falar mais alto. ~ **one's mind** dizer o que se pensa. **so to** ~ por assim dizer. **English/Portuguese spoken** fala-se português/inglês

speaker /ˈspi:kə(r)/ n (in public) orador m; (loudspeaker) alto-falante m; (of a language) pessoa f de língua nativa

spear /spɪə(r)/ n lança f

spearhead /ˈspɪəhed/ n ponta f de lança □ vt (lead) estar à frente de, encabeçar

special /ˈspeʃl/ a especial. ~**ity** /-ɪˈrælətɪ/ n especialidade f. ~**ly** adv especialmente. ~**ty** n especialidade f

specialist /ˈspeʃəlɪst/ n especialista mf

specialize /ˈspeʃəlaɪz/ vi especializar-se (**in** em). ~**d** a especializado

species /ˈspi:ʃɪz/ n (pl invar) espécie f

specific /spəˈsɪfɪk/ a específico. ~**ally** adv especificamente, explicitamente

specif|y /ˈspesɪfaɪ/ vt especificar. ~**ication** /-ɪˈkeɪʃn/ n especificação f. ~**ications** npl (of work etc) caderno m de encargos

specimen /ˈspesɪmɪn/ n espécime(n) m, amostra f

speck /spek/ n (stain) mancha f pequena; (dot) pontinho m, pinta f; (particle) grão m

speckled /ˈspekld/ a salpicado, manchado

specs /speks/ *npl* (*colloq*) óculos *mpl*

spectacle /'spektəkl/ *n* espetáculo *m*, (*P*) espectáculo *m*. (**pair of**) ~s (par *m* de) óculos *mpl*

spectacular /spek'tækjʊlə(r)/ *a* espetacular, (*P*) espectacular

spectator /spek'teɪtə(r)/ *n* espectador *m*

spectre /'spektə(r)/ *n* espectro *m*, fantasma *m*

spectrum /'spektrəm/ *n* (*pl* -tra) espectro *m*; (*of ideas etc*) faixa *f*, gama *f*, leque *m*

speculat|e /'spekjʊleɪt/ *vi* especular, fazer especulações *or* conjeturas, (*P*) conjecturas (**about** sobre); (*comm*) especular, fazer especulação (**in** em). ~**ion** /-'leɪʃn/ *n* especulação *f*, conjetura *f*, (*P*) conjectura *f*; (*comm*) especulação *f*. ~**or** *n* especulador *m*

speech /spi:tʃ/ *n* (*faculty*) fala *f*; (*diction*) elocução *f*; (*dialect*) falar *m*; (*address*) discurso *m*. ~**less** *a* mudo, sem fala (**with** com, **de**)

speed /spi:d/ *n* velocidade *f*, rapidez *f* □ *vt/i* (*pt* sped /sped/) (*move*) ir depressa *or* a grande velocidade; (*send*) despedir, mandar; (*pt* speeded) (*drive too fast*) ultrapassar o limite de velocidade. ~ **limit** limite *m* de velocidade. ~ **up** acelerar(-se). ~**ing** *n* excesso *m* de velocidade

speedometer /spi:'dɒmɪtə(r)/ *n* velocímetro *m*, (*P*) conta-quilómetros *m inv*

speed|y /'spi:dɪ/ *a* (-ier, -iest) rápido; (*prompt*) pronto. ~**ily** *adv* rapidamente; (*promptly*) prontamente

spell¹ /spel/ *n* (*magic*) sortilégio *m*

spell² /spel/ *vt/i* (*pt* spelled *or* spelt) escrever; (*fig: mean*) significar, ter como resultado. ~ **out** soletrar; (*fig: explain*) explicar claramente. ~**ing** *n* ortografia *f*

spell³ /spel/ *n* (*short period*) período *m* curto, breve espaço *m* de tempo; (*turn*) turno *m*

spend /spend/ *vt* (*pt* spent) (*money, energy*) gastar (**on** em); (*time, holiday*) passar. ~**er** *n* gastador *m*

spendthrift /'spendθrɪft/ *n* perdulário *m*, esbanjador *m*

spent /spent/ *see* spend □ *a* (*used*) gasto

sperm /spɜ:m/ *n* (*pl* sperms *or* sperm) (*semen*) esperma *m*, sêmen *m*, (*P*) sémen *m*; (*cell*) espermatozóide *m*

spew /spju:/ *vt/i* vomitar, lançar

sphere /sfɪə(r)/ *n* esfera *f*

spherical /'sferɪkl/ *a* esférico

spic|e /spaɪs/ *n* especiaria *f*, condimento *m*; (*fig*) picante *m* □ *vt* condimentar. ~**y** *a* condimentado; (*fig*) picante

spick /spɪk/ *a* ~ **and span** novo em folha, impecável

spider /'spaɪdə(r)/ *n* aranha *f*

spik|e /spaɪk/ *n* (*of metal etc*) bico *m*, espigão *m*, ponta *f*. ~**y** *a* guarnecido de bicos *or* pontas

spill /spɪl/ *vt/i* (*pt* spilled *or* spilt) derramar(-se), entornar(-se), espalhar(-se). ~ **over** transbordar, extravasar

spin /spɪn/ *vt/i* (*pt* spun, *pres p* spinning) (*wool, cotton*) fiar; (*web*) tecer; (*turn*) (fazer) girar, (fazer) rodopiar. ~ **out** (*money, story*) fazer durar; (*time*) (fazer) parar □ *n* volta *f*; (*aviat*) parafuso *m*. **go for a** ~ dar uma volta *or* um giro. ~-**drier** *n* centrifugadora *f* para a roupa, secadora *f*. ~**ning-wheel** *n* roda *f* de fiar. ~-**off** *n* bônus *m*, (*P*) bónus *m* inesperado; (*by-product*) derivado *m*

spinach /'spɪnɪdʒ/ *n* (*plant*) espinafre *m*; (*as food*) espinafres *mpl*

spinal /'spaɪnl/ *a* vertebral. ~ **cord** espina *f* dorsal

spindl|e /'spɪndl/ *n* roca *f*, fuso *m*; (*mech*) eixo *m*. ~**y** *a* alto e magro; (*of plant*) espigado

spine /spaɪn/ *n* espinha *f*, coluna *f* vertebral; (*prickle*) espinho *m*, pico *m*; (*of book*) lombada *f*

spineless /'spaɪnlɪs/ *a* (*fig: cowardly*) covarde, sem fibra (*fig*)

spinster /'spɪnstə(r)/ *n* solteira *f*; (*pej*) solteirona *f*

spiral /'spaɪərəl/ *a* (em) espiral; (*staircase*) em caracol □ *n* espiral *f* □ *vi* (*pt* spiralled) subir em espiral

spire /'spaɪə(r)/ *n* agulha *f*, flecha *f*

spirit /'spɪrɪt/ *n* espírito *m*; (*boldness*) coragem *f*, brio *m*. ~s (*morale*) moral *m*; (*drink*) bebidas *fpl* alcoólicas, (*P*) bebidas *fpl* espirituosas. **in high** ~s alegre □ *vt* ~ **away** dar sumiço em, arrebatar. ~-**level** *n* nível *m* de bolha de ar

spirited /'spɪrɪtɪd/ *a* fogoso; (*attack, defence*) vigoroso, enérgico

spiritual /'spɪrɪtʃʊəl/ *a* espiritual

spiritualism /'spɪrɪtʃʊəlɪzəm/ *n* espiritismo *m*

spit¹ /spɪt/ *vt/i* (*pt* spat *or* spit, *pres p* spitting) cuspir; (*of rain*) chuviscar; (*of cat*) bufar □ *n* cuspe *m*, (*P*) cuspo *m*. **the ~ting image of** o retrato vivo de, a cara chapada de (*colloq*)

spit² /spɪt/ *n* (*for meat*) espeto *m*; (*of land*) restinga *f*, (*P*) língua *f* de terra

spite /spaɪt/ *n* má vontade *f*, despeito *m*, rancor *m* □ *vt* aborrecer, mortificar. **in** ~ **of** a despeito de, apesar de. ~**ful** *a* rancoroso, maldoso. ~**fully** *adv* rancorosamente, maldosamente

spittle /'spɪtl/ *n* cuspe *m*, (*P*) cuspo *m*, saliva *f*

splash /splæʃ/ *vt* salpicar, respingar □ *vi* esparrinhar, esparramar-se. ~ **(about)** chapinhar □ *n* (*act, mark*) salpico *m*; (*sound*) chape *m*; (*of colour*) mancha *f*. **make a** ~ (*striking display*) fazer um vistão, causar furor

spleen /spliːn/ *n* (*anat*) baço *m*. **vent one's** ~ **on sb** descarregar a neura em alguém (*colloq*)

splendid /'splendɪd/ *a* esplêndido, magnífico; (*excellent*) estupendo (*colloq*), ótimo, (*P*) óptimo

splendour /'splendə(r)/ *n* esplendor *m*

splint /splɪnt/ *n* (*med*) tala *f*

splinter /'splɪntə(r)/ *n* lasca *f*, estilhaço *m*; (*under the skin*) farpa *f*, lasca *f* □ *vi* estilhaçar-se, lascar-se. ~ **group** grupo *m* dissidente

split /splɪt/ *vt*/*i* (*pt* split, *pres p* splitting) rachar, fender(-se); (*divide, share*) dividir; (*tear*) romper(-se) □ *n* racha *f*, fenda *f*; (*share*) quinhão *m*, parte *f*; (*pol*) cisão *f*. ~ **on** (*sl: inform on*) denunciar. ~ **one's sides** rebentar de risa. ~ **up** (*of couple*) separar-se. **a** ~ **second** uma fração de segundo. ~**ting headache** dor *f* de cabeça forte

splurge /splɜːdʒ/ *n* (*colloq*) espalhafato *m*, estardalhaço *m* □ *vi* (*colloq: spend*) gastar os tubos, (*P*) gastar à doida (*colloq*)

spool /spuːl/ *n* (*of sewing machine*) bobina *f*; (*for cotton thread*) carretel *m*, carrinho *m*; (*naut; fishing*) carretel *m*

splutter /'splʌtə(r)/ *vi* falar cuspindo; (*engine*) cuspir; (*fat*) crepitar

spoil /spɔɪl/ *vt* (*pt* spoilt *or* spoiled) estragar; (*pamper*) mimar □ *n* ~(**s**) (*plunder*) despojo(s) *m*(*pl*), espólios *mpl*. ~**-sport** *n* desmancha-prazeres *mf invar*. ~**t** *a* (*pampered*) mimado, estragado com mimos

spoke¹ /spəʊk/ *n* raio *m*

spoke², **spoken** /spəʊk, 'spəʊkən/ *see* speak

spokes|man /'spəʊksmən/ *n* (*pl* -men) ~**woman** *n* (*pl* -women) porta-voz *mf*

sponge /spʌndʒ/ *n* esponja *f* □ *vt* (*clean*) lavar com esponja; (*wipe*) limpar com esponja □ *vi* ~ **on** (*colloq: cadge*) viver à custa de. ~ **bag** bolsa *f* de toalete. ~ **cake** pão-de-ló *m*. ~**r** /-ə(r)/ *n* parasita *mf* (*colloq*) (*sl*). **spongy** *a* esponjoso

sponsor /'spɒnsə(r)/ *n* patrocinador *m*; (*for membership*) (sócio) proponente *m* □ *vt* patrocinar; (*for membership*) propor. ~**ship** *n* patrocínio *m*

spontaneous /spɒn'teɪnɪəs/ *a* espontâneo

spoof /spuːf/ *n* (*colloq*) paródia *f*

spooky /'spuːkɪ/ *a* (-ier, -iest) (*colloq*) fantasmagórico, que dá arrepios

spool /spuːl/ *n* (*of sewing machine*) bobina *f*; (*for thread, line*) carretel *m*, (*P*) carrinho *m*

spoon /spuːn/ *n* colher *f*. ~**-feed** *vt* (*pt* -fed) alimentar de colher; (*fig: help*) dar na bandeja para (*fig*). ~**ful** *n* (*pl* ~**fuls**) colherada *f*

sporadic /spə'rædɪk/ *a* esporádico, acidental

sport /spɔːt/ *n* esporte *m*, (*P*) desporto *m*. (**good**) ~ (*sl: person*) gente *f* fina, (*P*) bom tipo *m* (*colloq*), (*P*) tipo *m* bestial □ *vt* (*display*) exibir, ostentar. ~**s car/coat** carro *m*/casaco *m* esporte, (*P*) de desporto. ~**y** *a* (*colloq*) esportivo, (*P*) desportivo

sporting /'spɔːtɪŋ/ *a* esportivo, (*P*) desportivo. **a** ~ **chance** uma certa possibilidade de sucesso, uma boa chance

sports|man /'spɔːtsmən/ *n* (*pl* -men), ~**woman** (*pl* -women) desportista *mf*. ~**manship** *n* (*spirit*) espírito *m* esportivo, (*P*) desportivo; (*activity*) esportismo *m*, (*P*) desportismo *m*

spot /spɒt/ *n* (*mark, stain*) mancha *f*; (*in pattern*) pinta *f*, bola *f*; (*drop*) gota *f*; (*place*) lugar *m*, ponto *m*; (*pimple*) borbulha *f*, espinha *f*; (*TV*) spot *m* televisivo □ *vt* (*pt* spotted) manchar; (*colloq: detect*) descobrir, detectar (*colloq*). **a** ~ **of** (*colloq*) um pouco de. **be in a** ~ (*colloq*) estar numa encrenca (*colloq*), (*P*) estar metido numa alhada (*colloq*). **on the** ~ no local; (*there and then*) ali mesmo, logo ali. ~**-on** *a* (*colloq*) certo. ~ **check** inspeção *f*, (*P*) inspecção *f* de surpresa; (*of cars*) fiscalização *f* de surpresa. ~**ted** *a* manchado; (*with dots*) de pintas, de bolas; (*animal*) malhado. ~**ty** *a* (*with pimples*) com borbulhas

spotless /'spɒtlɪs/ *a* impecável, imaculado

spotlight /'spɒtlaɪt/ *n* foco *m*; (*cine, theat*) refletor *m*, holofote *m*

spouse /spaʊz/ *n* cônjuge *mf*, esposo *m*

spout /spaʊt/ *n* (*of vessel*) bico *m*; (*of liquid*) esguicho *m*, jorro *m*; (*pipe*) cano *m* □ *vi* jorrar, esguichar. **up the** ~ (*sl: ruined*) liquidado (*sl*)

sprain /spreɪn/ *n* entorse *f*, mau jeito *m* □ *vt* torcer, dar um mau jeito a

sprang /spræŋ/ *see* spring

sprawl /sprɔːl/ *vi* (*sit*) estirar-se, esparramar-se; (*fall*) estatelar-se; (*town*) estender-se, espraiar-se

spray¹ /spreɪ/ *n* (*of flowers*) raminho *m*, ramalhete *m*

spray² /spreɪ/ *n* (*water*) borrifo *m*, salpico *m*; (*from sea*) borrifo *m* de espuma; (*device*) bomba *f*, aerossol *m*; (*for perfume*) vaporizador *m*, atomizador *m* □ *vt* aspergir, borrifar, pulverizar; (*with insecticide*) pulverizar. **~-gun** *n* (*for paint*) pistola *f*

spread /spred/ *vt/i* (*pt* **spread**) (*extend, stretch*) estender(-se); (*news, fear, illness etc*) alastrar(-se), espalhar(-se), propagar(-se); (*butter etc*) passar; (*wings*) abrir □ *n* (*expanse*) expansão *f*, extensão *f*; (*spreading*) propagação *f*; (*paste*) pasta *f* para passar pão; (*colloq: meal*) banquete *m*. **~-eagled** *a* de braços e pernas abertos. **~-sheet** *n* (*comput*) folha *f* de cálculo

spree /spriː/ *n* **go on a ~** (*colloq*) cair na farra

sprig /sprɪg/ *n* raminho *m*

sprightly /ˈspraɪtlɪ/ *a* (-ier, -iest) vivo, animado

spring /sprɪŋ/ *vi* (*pt* **sprang**, *pp* **sprung**) (*arise*) nascer; (*jump*) saltar, pular □ *vt* (*produce suddenly*) sair-se com; (*a surprise*) fazer (**on sb** a alguém) □ *n* salto *m*, pulo *m*; (*device*) mola *f*; (*season*) primavera *f*; (*of water*) fonte *f*, nascente *f*. **~ from** vir de, originar, provir de. **~-clean** *vt* fazer limpeza geral. **~ onion** cebolinha *f*. **~ up** surgir

springboard /ˈsprɪŋbɔːd/ *n* trampolim *m*

springtime /ˈsprɪŋtaɪm/ *n* primavera *f*

springy /ˈsprɪŋɪ/ *a* (-ier, -iest) elástico

sprinkle /ˈsprɪŋkl/ *vt* (*with liquid*) borrifar, salpicar; (*with salt, flour*) polvilhar (**with** de). **~ sand/etc** espalhar areia/etc. **~r** /-ə(r)/ *n* (*in garden*) regador *m*; (*for fires*) sprinkler *m*

sprinkling /ˈsprɪŋklɪŋ/ *n* (*amount*) pequena quantidade *f*; (*number*) pequeno número *m*

sprint /sprɪnt/ *n* (*sport*) corrida *f* de pequena distância, sprint *m* □ *vi* correr em sprint *or* a toda a velocidade; (*sport*) correr

sprout /spraʊt/ *vt/i* brotar, germinar; (*put forth*) deitar □ *n* (*on plant etc*) broto *m*. (**Brussels**) **~s** couves *f* de Bruxelas

spruce /spruːs/ *a* bem arrumado □ *vt* **~ o.s. up** arrumar(-se)

sprung /sprʌŋ/ *see* **spring** □ *a* (*mattress etc*) de molas

spry /spraɪ/ *a* (**spryer**, **spryest**) vivo, ativo, (*P*) activo; (*nimble*) ágil

spud /spʌd/ *n* (*sl*) batata *f*

spun /spʌn/ *see* **spin**

spur /spɜː(r)/ *n* (*of rider*) espora *f*; (*fig: stimulus*) aguilhão *m*; (*fig*)

espora *f* (*fig*) □ *vt* (*pt* **spurred**) esporear, picar com esporas; (*fig: incite*) aguilhoar, esporear. **on the ~ of the moment** impulsivamente

spurious /ˈspjʊərɪəs/ *a* falso, espúrio

spurn /spɜːn/ *vt* desdenhar, desprezar, rejeitar

spurt /spɜːt/ *vi* jorrar, esguichar; (*fig: accelerate*) acelerar subitamente, dar um arranco súbito □ *n* jorro *m*, esguicho *m*; (*of energy, speed*) arranco *m*, surto *m*

spy /spaɪ/ *n* espião *m* □ *vt* (*make out*) avistar, descortinar □ *vi* **~ (on)** espiar, espionar. **~ out** descobrir. **~ing** *n* espionagem *f*

squabble /ˈskwɒbl/ *vi* discutir, brigar □ *n* briga *f*, disputa *f*

squad /skwɒd/ *n* (*mil*) pelotão *m*; (*team*) equipe *f*, (*P*) equipa *f*. **firing ~** pelotão *m* de fuzilamento. **flying ~** brigada *f* móvel

squadron /ˈskwɒdrən/ *n* (*mil*) esquadrão *m*; (*aviat*) esquadrilha *f*; (*naut*) esquadra *f*

squalid /ˈskwɒlɪd/ *a* esquálido, sórdido. **~or** *n* sordidez *f*

squall /skwɔːl/ *n* borrasca *f*

squander /ˈskwɒndə(r)/ *vt* desperdiçar

square /skweə(r)/ *n* quadrado *m*; (*in town*) largo *m*, pràça *f*; (*T-square*) régua-tê *f*; (*set-square*) esquadro *m* □ *a* (*of shape*) quadrado; (*metre, mile etc*) quadrado; (*honest*) direito, honesto; (*of meal*) abundante, substancial. (**all**) **~** (*quits*) quite(s) □ *vt* (*math*) elevar ao quadrado; (*settle*) acertar □ *vi* (*agree*) concordar. **go back to ~ one** recomeçar tudo do princípio, voltar à estaca zero. **~ brackets** parênteses *mpl* retos, (*P*) rectos. **~ up to** enfrentar. **~ly** *adv* diretamente, (*P*) directamente; (*fairly*) honestamente

squash /skwɒʃ/ *vt* (*crush*) esmagar; (*squeeze*) espremer; (*crowd*) comprimir, apertar □ *n* (*game*) squash *m*; (*Amer: marrow*) abóbora *f*. **lemon ~** limonada *f*. **orange ~** laranjada *f*. **~y** *a* mole

squat /skwɒt/ *vi* (*pt* **squatted**) acocorar-se, agachar-se; (*be a squatter*) ser ocupante ilegal □ *a* (*dumpy*) atarracado. **~ter** *n* ocupante *mf* ilegal de casa vazia, posseiro *m*

squawk /skwɔːk/ *n* grasnido *m*, crocito *m* □ *vi* grasnar, crocitar

squeak /skwiːk/ *n* guincho *m*, chio *m*; (*of door, shoes etc*) rangido *m* □ *vi* guinchar, chiar; (*of door, shoes etc*) ranger. **~y** *a* (*shoe etc*) que range; (*voice*) esganiçado

squeal /skwiːl/ *vi* dar gritos agudos,

guinchar □ n grito m agudo, guincho m. ~ (on) (sl: inform on) delatar, (P) denunciar

squeamish /'skwi:mɪʃ/ a (nauseated) que enjoa à toa

squeeze /skwi:z/ vt (lemon, sponge etc) espremer; (hand, arm) apertar; (extract) arrancar, extorquir (from de) □ vi (force one's way) passar à força, meter-se por □ n aperto m, apertão m; (hug) abraço m; (comm) restrições fpl de crédito

squelch /skwɛltʃ/ vi chapinhar or fazer chape-chape na lama

squid /skwɪd/ n lula f

squiggle /'skwɪgl/ n rabisco m, floreado m

squint /skwɪnt/ vi ser estrábico or vesgo; (with half-shut eyes) franzir os olhos □ n (med) estrabismo m

squirm /skwɜ:m/ vi (re)torcer-se, contorcer-se

squirrel /'skwɪrəl/ n esquilo m

squirt /skwɜ:t/ vt/i esguichar □ n esguicho m

stab /stæb/ vt (pt stabbed) apunhalar; (knife) esfaquear □ n punhalada f; (with knife) facada f; (of pain) pontada f; (colloq: attempt) tentativa f

stabilize /'steɪbəlaɪz/ vt estabilizar

stab|le[1] /'steɪbl/ a (-er, -est) estável. **~ility** /stə'bɪlətɪ/ n estabilidade f

stable[2] /'steɪbl/ n cavalariça f, estrebaria f. **~-boy** n moço m de estrebaria

stack /stæk/ n pilha f, montão m; (of hay etc) meda f □ vt ~ (up) empilhar, amontoar

stadium /'steɪdɪəm/ n estádio m

staff /sta:f/ n pessoal m; (in school) professores mpl; (mil) estado-maior m; (stick) bordão m, cajado m; (mus) (pl staves) pauta f □ vt prover de pessoal

stag /stæg/ n veado (macho) m, cervo m. **~-party** (colloq) reunião f masculina; (before wedding) despedida f de solteiro

stage /steɪdʒ/ n (theatre) palco m; (phase) fase f, ponto m; (platform in hall) estrado m □ vt encenar, pôr em cena; (fig: organize) organizar. **go on the ~** seguir a carreira teatral, ir para o teatro (colloq). **~ door** entrada f dos artistas. **~-fright** n nervosismo m

stagger /'stægə(r)/ vi vacilar, cambalear □ vt (shock) atordoar, chocar; (holidays etc) escalonar. **~ing** a atordoador, chocante

stagnant /'stægnənt/ a estagnado, parado

stagnat|e /stæg'neɪt/ vi estagnar. **~ion** /-ʃn/ n estagnação f

staid /steɪd/ a sério, sensato, estável

stain /steɪn/ vt manchar, pôr nódoa em; (colour) tingir, dar cor a □ n mancha f, nódoa f; (colouring) corante m. **~ed glass window** vitral m. **~less steel** aço m inoxidável

stair /steə(r)/ n degrau m. **~s** escada(s) f(pl)

stair|case /'steəkeɪs/, **~way** /-weɪ/ ns escada(s) f(pl), escadaria f

stake /steɪk/ n (post) estaca f, poste m; (wager) parada f, aposta f □ vt (area) demarcar, delimitar; (wager) jogar, apostar. **at ~** em jogo. **have a ~ in** ter interesse em. **~ a claim to** reivindicar

stale /steɪl/ a (-er, -est) estragado, velho; (bread) duro, mofado; (smell) rançoso; (air) viciado; (news) velho

stalemate /'steɪlmeɪt/ n (chess) empate m; (fig: deadlock) impasse m, beco-sem-saída m

stalk[1] /stɔ:k/ n (of plant) caule m

stalk[2] /stɔ:k/ vi andar com ar empertigado □ vt (prey) perseguir furtivamente, tocaiar

stall /stɔ:l/ n (in stable) baia f; (in market) tenda f, barraca f. **~s** (theat) poltronas fpl de orquestra; (cinema) platéia f, (P) plateia f □ vt/i (auto) enguiçar, (P) ir abaixo. **~ (for time)** ganhar tempo

stalwart /'stɔ:lwət/ a forte, rijo; (supporter) fiel

stamina /'stæmɪnə/ n resistência f

stammer /'stæmə(r)/ vt/i gaguejar □ n gagueira f, (P) gaguez f

stamp /stæmp/ vt/i ~ (one's foot) bater com o pé (no chão), pisar com força □ vt estampar; (letter) estampilhar, selar; (with rubber stamp) carimbar. **~ out** (fire, rebellion etc) esmagar; (disease) erradicar □ n estampa f; (for postage) selo m; (fig: mark) cunho m. (rubber) **~** carimbo m. **~-collecting** n filatelia f

stampede /stæm'pi:d/ n (scattering) debandada f; (of horses, cattle etc) tresma/hada f; debandada f; (fig: rush) corrida f □ vt/i (fazer) debandar; (horses, cattle etc) tresmalhar

stance /stæns/ n posição f, postura f

stand /stænd/ vi (pt stood) estar em pé; (keep upright position) ficar em pé; (rise) levantar-se; (be situated) encontrar-se, ficar, situar-se; (pol) candidatar-se (for por) □ vt pôr (de pé), colocar; (tolerate) suportar, agüentar, (P) aguentar □ n posição f; (support) apoio m; (mil) resistência f; (at fair) stand m, pavilhão m; (in street) quiosque m; (for spectators) arquibancada f, (P) bancada f; (Amer: witness-box) banco m das testemunhas. **~ a**

chance ter uma possibilidade. ~
back recuar. ~ **by** *or* **around** estar
parado sem fazer nada. ~ **by** (*be
ready*) estar a postos; (*promise, person*) manter-se fiel a. ~ **down** desistir, retirar-se. ~ **for** representar,
simbolizar; (*colloq: tolerate*) aturar.
~ **in for** substituir. ~ **out** (*be conspicuous*) sobressair. ~ **still** estar/fi-
car imóvel. ~ **still!** não se mexa!,
quieto! ~ **to reason** ser lógico. ~
up levantar-se, pôr-se em *or* de pé. ~
up for defender, apoiar. ~**s** (*morals*)
enfrentar. ~**-by** *a* (*for emergency*) de
reserva; (*ticket*) de stand-by □ *n* (*at
airport*) stand-by *m*. on ~**-by** (*mil*)
de prontidão; (*med*) de plantão. ~**-in**
n substituto *m*, suplente *mf*. ~**-offish**
a (*colloq: aloof*) reservado, distante
standard /'stændəd/ *n* norma *f*,
padrão *m*; (*level*) nível *m*; (*flag*) estandarte *m*, bandeira *f*. ~**s** (*morals*)
princípios *mpl* □ *a* regulamentar;
(*average*) standard, normal. ~ **lamp**
abajur *m* de pé. ~ **of living** padrão *m*
de vida, (*P*) nível *m* de vida
standardize /'stændədaɪz/ *vt* padronizar
standing /'stændɪŋ/ *a* em pé, de pé
invar; (*army, committee etc*) permanente □ *n* posição *f*; (*reputation*)
prestígio *m*; (*duration*) duração *f*. ~
order (*at bank*) ordem *f* permanente.
~**-room** *n* lugares *mpl* em pé
standpoint /'stændpɔɪnt/ *n* ponto *m*
de vista
standstill /'stændstɪl/ *n* paralisação *f*.
at a ~ parado, paralisado. **bring/
come to a** ~ (fazer) parar, parali-
sar(-se), imobilizar (-se)
stank /stæŋk/ *see* **stink**
staple¹ /'steɪpl/ *n* (*for paper*) grampo
m, (*P*) agrafo *m* □ *vt* (*paper*) gram-
pear, (*P*) agrafar. ~**r** /-ə(r)/ *n* gram-
peador *m*, (*P*) agrafador *m*
staple² /'steɪpl/ *a* principal, básico □ *n*
(*comm*) artigo *m* básico
star /sta:(r)/ *n* estrela *f*; (*cinema*) estrela *f*, vedete *f*; (*celebrity*) celebridade
f □ *vt* (*pt* **starred**) (*of film*) ter no
papel principal, (*P*) ter como actor
principal □ *vi* ~ **in** ser a vedete *or*
ter o papel principal em. ~**dom** *n*
celebridade *f*, estrelato *m*
starch /sta:tʃ/ *n* amido *m*, fécula *f*;
(*for clothes*) goma *f* □ *vt* pôr em goma,
engomar. ~**y** *a* (*of food*) farináceo,
feculento; (*fig: of person*) rígido, formal
stare /steə(r)/ *vi* ~ **at** olhar fixamente
□ *n* olhar *m* fixo
starfish /'sta:fɪʃ/ *n* (*pl invar*) estrela-
do-mar *f*
stark /sta:k/ *a* (-er, -est) (*desolate*) ári-

do, desolado; (*severe*) austero, severo;
(*utter*) completo, rematado; (*fact etc*)
brutal □ *adv* completamente. ~
naked nu em pêlo, (*P*) em pelota
(*colloq*)
starling /'sta:lɪŋ/ *n* estorninho *m*
starlit /'sta:lɪt/ *a* estrelado
starry /'sta:rɪ/ *a* estrelado. ~**-eyed** *a*
(*colloq*) sonhador, idealista
start /sta:t/ *vt/i* começar; (*machine*)
ligar, pôr em andamento; (*fashion
etc*) lançar; (*leave*) partir; (*cause*) causar, provocar; (*jump*) sobressaltar-se,
estremecer; (*of car*) arrancar, partir □
n começo *m*, início *m*; (*of race*) larga-
da *f*, partida *f*; (*lead*) avanço *m*;
(*jump*) sobressalto *m*, estremecimento *m*. **by fits and** ~**s** aosarrancos,
intermitentemente. **for a** ~ para
começar. **give sb a** sobressaltar alguém, pregar um susto a alguém. ~
to do começar a *or* pôr-se a fazer. ~**er**
n (*auto*) arranque *m*; (*competitor*) corredor *m*; (*culin*) entrada *f*. ~**ing-
point** *n* ponto *m* de partida
startl|e /'sta:tl/ *vt* (*make jump*) so-
bressaltar, pregar um susto a; (*shock*)
alarmar, chocar. ~**ing** *a* alarmante;
(*surprising*) surpreendente
starv|e /sta:v/ *vi* (*suffer*) passar fome;
(*die*) morrer de fome. **be** ~**ing** (*colloq:
very hungry*) ter muita fome, morrer
de fome (*colloq*) □ *vt* fazer passar fome
a; (*deprive*) privar. ~**ation** /-'veɪʃn/ *n*
fome *f*
stash /stæʃ/ *vt* (*sl*) guardar, esconder,
enfurnar (*colloq*)
state /steɪt/ *n* estado *m*, condição *f*;
(*pomp*) pompa *f*, gala *f*; (*pol*) Estado
m □ *a* de Estado, do Estado; (*school*)
público; (*visit etc*) oficial □ *vt* afirmar
(*that* que); (*views*) exprimir; (*fix*)
marcar, fixar. **in a** ~ muito abalado
stateless /'steɪtlɪs/ *a* apátrida
stately /'steɪtlɪ/ *a* (-ier, -iest)
majestoso. ~ **home** solar *m*, palácio
m
statement /'steɪtmənt/ *n* declaração *f*;
(*of account*) extrato *m*, (*P*) extracto *m*
de conta
statesman /'steɪtsmən/ *n* (*pl* -men)
homem *m* de estado, estadista *m*
static /'stætɪk/ *a* estático □ *n* (*radio,
TV*) estática *f*, interferência *f*
station /'steɪʃn/ *n* (*position*) posto *m*;
(*rail, bus, radio*) estação *f*; (*rank*)
condição *f*, posição *f* social □ *vt*
colocar. ~**-wagon** *n* perua *f*, (*P*) car-
rinha *f*. ~**ed at** *or* **in** (*mil*) estacionado em
stationary /'steɪʃnrɪ/ *a* estacionário,
parado, imóvel; (*vehicle*) estacionado,
parado
stationer /'steɪʃənə(r)/ *n* dono *m* de

papelaria. **~'s shop** papelaria *f*. **~y** *n* artigos *mpl* de papelaria; (*writing-paper*) papel *m* de carta

statistic /stə'tɪstɪk/ *n* dado *m* estatístico. **~s** *n* (*as a science*) estatística *f*. **~al** *a* estatístico

statue /'stætʃu:/ *n* estátua *f*

stature /'stætʃə(r)/ *n* estatura *f*

status /'steɪtəs/ *n* (*pl* **-uses**) situação *f*, posição *f*, categoria *f*; (*prestige*) prestígio *m*, importância *f*, status *m*. **~ quo** status quo *m*. **~ symbol** símbolo *m* de status

statut|e /'stætʃu:t/ *n* estatuto *m*, lei *f*. **~ory** /-ʊtrɪ/ *a* estatutário, regulamentar; (*holiday*) legal

staunch /stɔ:ntʃ/ *a* (**-er, -est**) (*friend*) fiel, leal

stave /steɪv/ *n* (*mus*) pauta *f* □ *vt* **~ off** (*keep off*) conjurar, evitar; (*delay*) adiar

stay /steɪ/ *vi* estar, ficar, permanecer; (*dwell temporarily*) ficar, alojar-se, hospedar-se; (*spend time*) demorar-se □ *vt* (*hunger*) enganar □ *n* estada *f*, visita *f*, permanência *f*. **~ behind** ficar para trás. **~ in** ficar em casa. **~ put** (*colloq*) não se mexer (*colloq*). **~ up** (*late*) deitar-se tarde. **~ing-power** *n* resistência *f*

stead /sted/ *n* **in my/your/***etc* **~** no meu/teu/*etc* lugar. **stand in good ~** ser muito útil

steadfast /'stedfa:st/ *a* firme, constante

stead|y /'stedɪ/ *a* (**-ier, -iest**) (*stable*) estável, firme, seguro; (*regular*) regular, constante; (*hand, voice*) firme □ *vt* firmar, fixar, estabilizar; (*calm*) acalmar. **go ~y with** (*colloq*) namorar. **~ily** *adv* firmemente; (*regularly*) regularmente, de modo constante

steak /steɪk/ *n* bife *m*

steal /sti:l/ *vt/i* (*pt* **stole**, *pp* **stolen**) roubar (**from sb** de alguém). **~ away/in/***etc* sair/entrar/*etc* furtivamente, esgueirar-se. **~ the show** pôr os outros na sombra

stealth /stelθ/ *n* **by ~** furtivamente, na calada, às escondidas. **~y** *a* furtivo

steam /sti:m/ *n* vapor *m* de água; (*on window*) condensação *f* □ *vt* (*cook*) cozinhar a vapor. **~ up** (*window*) embaciar. □ *vi* soltar vapor, fumegar; (*move*) avançar. **~-engine** *n* máquina *f* a vapor; (*locomotive*) locomotiva *f* a vapor. **~ iron** ferro *m* a vapor. **~y** *a* (*heat*) úmido, (*P*) húmido

steamer /'sti:mə(r)/ *n* (*ship*) barco a) vapor *m*; (*culin*) utensílio *m* para cozinhar a vapor

steamroller /'sti:mrəʊlə(r)/ *n* cilindro *m* a vapor, rolo *m* compressor

steel /sti:l/ *n* aço *m* □ *a* de aço □ *vpr* **o.s.** endurecer-se, fortalecer-se. **~ industry** siderurgia *f*

steep¹ /sti:p/ *vt* (*soak*) mergulhar, pôr de molho; (*permeate*) passar, impregnar. **~ed in** (*fig: vice, misery etc*) mergulhado em; (*fig: knowledge, wisdom etc*) impregnado de, repassado de

steep² /sti:p/ *a* (**-er, -est**) íngreme, escarpado; (*colloq*) exagerado, exorbitante. **rise ~ly** (*slope*) subir a pique; (*price*) disparar

steeple /'sti:pl/ *n* campanário *m*, torre *f*

steeplechase /'sti:pltʃeɪs/ *n* (*race*) corrida *f* de obstáculos

steer /stɪə(r)/ *vt/i* guiar, conduzir, dirigir; (*ship*) governar; (*fig*) guiar, orientar. **~ clear of** evitar passar perto de. **~ing** *n* (*auto*) direção *f*, (*P*) direcção *f*. **~ing-wheel** *n* (*auto*) volante *m*

stem¹ /stem/ *n* caule *m*, haste *f*; (*of glass*) pé *m*; (*of pipe*) boquilha *f*; (*of word*) radical *m* □ *vi* (*pt* **stemmed**) **~ from** provir de, vir de

stem² /stem/ *vt* (*pt* **stemmed**) (*check*) conter; (*stop*) estancar

stench /stentʃ/ *n* mau cheiro *m*, fedor *m*

stencil /'stensl/ *n* estêncil *m*, (*P*) stencil *m* □ *vt* (*pt* **stencilled**) (*document*) policopiar

step /step/ *vi* (*pt* **stepped**) ir andar □ *vt* **~ up** aumentar □ *n* passo *m*, passada *f*; (*of stair, train*) degrau *m*; (*action*) medida *f*, passo *m*. **~s** (*ladder*) escada *f*. **in ~** no mesmo passo, a passo certo; (*fig*) em conformidade (**with** com). **~ down** (*resign*) demitir-se. **~ in** (*intervene*) intervir. **~-ladder** *n* escada *f* portátil. **~ping-stone** *n* (*fig: means to an end*) ponte *f*, trampolim *m*

stepbrother /'stepbrʌðə(r)/ *n* meio-irmão *m*. **~daughter** *n* nora *f*, (*P*) enteada *f*. **~father** *n* padrasto *m*. **~mother** *n* madrasta *f*. **~sister** *n* meio-irmã *f*. **~son** *n* genro *m*, (*P*) enteado *m*

stereo /'sterɪəʊ/ *n* (*pl* **-os**) estéreo *m*; (*record-player etc*) equipamento *m* or sistema *m* estéreo □ *a* estéreo *invar*. **~phonic** /-ə'fɒnɪk/ *a* estereofônico, (*P*) estereofónico

stereotype /'sterɪətaɪp/ *n* estereótipo *m*. **~d** *a* estereotipado

steril|e /'steraɪl/ *a* estéril. **~ity** /stə'rɪlətɪ/ *n* esterilidade *f*

steriliz|e /'sterəlaɪz/ *vt* esterilizar. **~ation** /-'zeɪʃn/ *n* esterilização *f*

sterling /'stɜ:lɪŋ/ *n* libra *f* esterlina □ *a* esterlino; (*silver*) de lei; (*fig*) excelente, de (primeira) qualidade

stern¹ /stɜ:n/ a (**-er, -est**) severo

stern² /stɜ:n/ n (of ship) popa f, ré f

stethoscope /'steθəskəʊp/ n estetoscópio m

stew /stju:/ vt/i estufar, guisar; (fruit) cozer □ n ensopado m. ~**ed fruit** compota f

steward /'stjʊəd/ n (of club etc) ecônomo m, (P) ecónomo m, administrador m; (on ship etc) camareiro m (de bordo), (P) criado m (de bordo). ~**ess** /-'des/ n aeromoça f, (P) hospedeira f

stick¹ /stɪk/ n pau m; (for walking) bengala f; (of celery) talo m

stick² /stɪk/ vt (pt **stuck**) (glue) colar; (thrust) cravar, espetar; (colloq: put) enfiar, meter; (sl: endure) aguentar, (P) aguentar, aturar, suportar □ vi (adhere) colar, aderir; (remain) ficar enfiado or metido; (be jammed) emperrar, ficar engatado. ~ **in one's mind** ficar na memória. **be stuck with sb/sth** (colloq) não conseguir descartar-se de alguém/alg coisa (colloq). ~ **out** vt (head) esticar; (tongue etc) mostrar □ vi (protrude) sobressair. ~ **to** (promise) ser fiel a. ~**-up** n (sl) assalto m à mão armada. ~ **up for** (colloq) tomar o partido de, defender. ~**ing-plaster** n esparadrapo m, (P) adesivo m

sticker /'stɪkə(r)/ n adesivo m, etiqueta f (adesiva)

stickler /'stɪklə(r)/ n **be a ~ for** fazer grande questão de, insistir em

sticky /'stɪkɪ/ a (**-ier, -iest**) pegajoso; (label, tape) adesivo; (weather) abafado, mormacento

stiff /stɪf/ a (**-er, -est**) teso, hirto, rígido; (limb, joint; hard) duro; (unbending) inflexível; (price) elevado, puxado (colloq); (penalty) severo; (drink) forte; (manner) reservado, formal. **be bored/scared ~** (colloq) estar muito aborrecido/com muito medo (colloq). ~ **neck** torcicolo m. ~**ness** n rigidez f

stiffen /'stɪfn/ vt/i (harden) endurecer; (limb, joint) emperrar

stifl|e /'staɪfl/ vt/i abafar, sufocar. ~**ing** a sufocante

stigma /'stɪgmə/ n estigma m. ~**tize** vt estigmatizar

stile /staɪl/ n degrau m para passar por cima de cerca

stiletto /stɪ'letəʊ/ n (pl **-os**) estilete m. ~ **heel** n salto m alto fino

still¹ /stɪl/ a imóvel, quieto; (quiet) sossegado □ n silêncio m, sossego m □ adv ainda; (nevertheless) apesar disso, apesar de tudo. **keep ~!** fique quieto!, não se mexa! ~ **life** natureza f morta. ~**ness** n calma f

still² /stɪl/ n (apparatus) alambique m

stillborn /'stɪlbɔ:n/ a natimorto, (P) nado-morto

stilted /'stɪltɪd/ a afetado, (P) afectado

stilts /stɪlts/ npl pernas de pau fpl, (P) andas fpl

stimul|ate /'stɪmjʊleɪt/ vt estimular. ~**ant** n estimulante m. ~**ating** a estimulante. ~**ation** /-'leɪʃn/ n estimulação f

stimulus /'stɪmjʊləs/ n (pl **-li** /-laɪ/) (spur) estímulo m

sting /stɪŋ/ n picada f; (organ) ferrão m □ vt (pt **stung**) picar □ vi picar, arder. ~**ing nettle** urtiga f

stingy /'stɪndʒɪ/ a (**-ier, -iest**) pãoduro m, sovina (**with** com)

stink /stɪŋk/ n fedor m, catinga f, mau cheiro m □ vi (pt **stank** or **stunk**, pp **stunk**) ~ (**of**) cheirar (a), tresandar (a) □ vt ~ **out** (room etc) empestar. ~**ing** a malcheiroso. ~**ing rich** (sl) podre de rico (colloq)

stinker /'stɪŋkə(r)/ n (sl: person) cara m horroroso (colloq); (sl: sth difficult) osso m duro de moer

stint /stɪnt/ vi ~ **on** poupar em, apertar em □ n (work) tarefa f, parte f, quinhão m

stipulat|e /'stɪpjʊleɪt/ vt estipular. ~**ion** /-'leɪʃn/ n condição f, estipulação f

stir /stɜ:r/ vt/i (pt **stirred**) (move) mexer(-se), mover(-se); (excite) excitar; (a liquid) mexer □ n agitação f, rebuliço m. ~ **up** (trouble etc) provocar, fomentar. ~**ring** a excitante

stirrup /'stɪrəp/ n estribo m

stitch /stɪtʃ/ n (in sewing; med) ponto m; (in knitting) malha f, ponto m; (pain) pontada f □ vt coser. **in ~es** (colloq) às gargalhadas (colloq)

stoat /stəʊt/ n arminho m

stock /stɒk/ n (comm) estoque m, (P) stock m, provisão f; (finance) valores mpl, fundos mpl; (family) família f, estirpe f; (culin) caldo m; (flower) goivo m □ a (goods) corrente, comum; (hackneyed) estereotipado □ vt (shop etc) abastecer, fornecer; (sell) vender □ vi ~ **up with** abastecer-se de. **in ~** em estoque. **out of ~** esgotado. **take ~** (fig) fazer um balanço. ~**-car** n stock-car m. ~**-cube** n cubo m de caldo. ~ **market** Bolsa f (de Valores). ~**-still** a, adv imóvel. ~**-taking** n (comm) inventário m

stockbroker /'stɒkbrəʊkə(r)/ n corretor m da Bolsa

stocking /'stɒkɪŋ/ n meia f

stockist /'stɒkɪst/ n armazenista m

stockpile /'stɒkpaɪl/ n reservas fpl □ vt acumular reservas de, estocar

stocky /'stɒkɪ/ a (**-ier, -iest**) atarracado

stodg|e /stɒdʒ/ *n* (*colloq*) comida *f* pesada (*colloq*). ~**y** *a* (*of food, book*) pesado, maçudo

stoic /'stəʊɪk/ *n* estóico *m*. ~**al** *a* estoico. ~**ism** /-sɪzəm/ *n* estoicismo *m*

stoke /stəʊk/ *vt* (*boiler, fire*) alimentar, carregar

stole[1] /stəʊl/ *n* (*garment*) estola *m*

stole[2], **stolen** /stəʊl, 'stəʊlən/ *see* **steal**

stomach /'stʌmək/ *n* estômago *m*; (*abdomen*) barriga *f*, ventre *m* □ *vt* (*put up with*) aturar. ~**-ache** *n* dor *f* de estômago; (*abdomen*) dores *fpl* de barriga

ston|e /stəʊn/ *n* pedra *f*; (*pebble*) seixo *m*; (*in fruit*) caroço *m*; (*weight*) 6,348 kg; (*med*) cálculo *m*, pedra *f* □ *vt* apedrejar; (*fruit*) tirar o caroço de. **with-in a ~e's throw** (**of**) muito perto (de). ~**e-cold** gelado. ~**e-deaf** totalmente surdo. ~**ed** *a* (*colloq: drunk*) bebão *m* (*colloq*); (*colloq: drugged*) drogado. ~**y** *a* pedregoso. ~**y-broke** *a* (*sl*) duro, liso (*sl*)

stonemason /'stəʊnmeɪsn/ *n* pedreiro *m*

stood /stʊd/ *see* **stand**

stooge /stuːdʒ/ *n* (*colloq: actor*) ajudante *mf*; (*colloq: puppet*) antoche *m*, (*P*) comparsa *mf*, parceiro *m*

stool /stuːl/ *n* banco *m*, tamborete *m*

stoop /stuːp/ *vi* (*bend*) curvar-se, baixar-se; (*condescend*) condescender, dignar-se. ~ **to sth** rebaixar-se para (fazer) alg coisa □ *n* **walk with a ~** andar curvado

stop /stɒp/ *vt/i* (*pt* **stopped**) parar; (*prevent*) impedir (**from** de); (*hole, leak etc*) tapar, vedar; (*pain, noise etc*) parar; (*colloq: stay*) ficar □ *n* (*of bus*) parada *f*, (*P*) paragem *f*; (*full stop*) ponto *m* final. **put a ~ to** pôr fim a. ~ **it!** acabe logo com isso! ~**-over** *n* (*break in journey*) parada *f*, (*P*) paragem *f*; (*port of call*) escala *f*. ~**press** *n* notícia *f* de última hora. ~**-watch** *n* cronômetro *m*, (*P*) cronómetro *m*

stopgap /'stɒpgæp/ *n* substituto *m* provisório, tapa-buracos *mpl* (*colloq*) □ *a* temporário

stoppage /'stɒpɪdʒ/ *n* parada *f*, (*P*) paragem *f*; (*of work*) paralisação *f* de trabalho; (*of pay*) suspensão *f*

stopper /'stɒpə(r)/ *n* rolha *f*, tampa *f*

storage /'stɔːrɪdʒ/ *n* (*of goods, food etc*) armazenagem *f*, armazenamento *m*. **in cold ~** em frigorífico

store /stɔː(r)/ *n* reserva *f*, provisão *f*; (*warehouse*) armazém *m*, entreposto *m*; (*shop*) grande armazém *m*; (*Amer*) loja *f*; (*in computer*) memória *f* □ *vt* (*for future*) pôr de reserva, juntar, fazer provisão de; (*in warehouse*)

armazenar. **be in ~** estar guardado. **have in ~ for** reservar para. **set ~ by** dar valor a. ~**-room** *n* depósito *m*, almortarifado *m*, (*P*) armazém *m*

storey /'stɔːrɪ/ *n* (*pl* **-eys**) andar *m*

stork /stɔːk/ *n* cegonha *f*

storm /stɔːm/ *n* tempestade *f* □ *vt* tomar de assalto □ *vi* enfurecer-se. **a ~ in a teacup** uma tempestade num copo de água. ~**y** *a* tempestuoso

story /'stɔːrɪ/ *n* estória *f*, (*P*) história *f*; (*in press*) artigo *m*, matéria *f*; (*Amer: storey*) andar *m*; (*colloq: lie*) cascata *f*, (*P*) peta *f*. ~**-teller** *n* contador *m* de estórias, (*P*) histórias

stout /staʊt/ *a* (**-er, -est**) (*fat*) gordo, corpulento; (*strong, thick*) resistente, sólido, grosso; (*brave*) resoluto □ *n* cerveja *f* preta forte

stove /stəʊv/ *n* (*for cooking*) fogão *m* (de cozinha)

stow /stəʊ/ *vt* ~ (**away**) (*put away*) guardar, arrumar; (*hide*) esconder □ *vi* ~ **away** viajar clandestinamente

stowaway /'stəʊəweɪ/ *n* passageiro *m* clandestino

straddle /'strædl/ *vt* (*sit*) escarranchar-se em, montar; (*stand*) pôr-se de pernas abertas sobre

straggle /'strægl/ *vi* (*lag behind*) desgarrar-se, ficar para trás; (*spread*) estender-se desordenadamente. ~**r** /-ə(r)/ *n* retardatário *m*

straight /streɪt/ *a* (**-er, -est**) direito; (*tidy*) em ordem; (*frank*) franco, direto, (*P*) directo; (*of hair*) liso; (*of drink*) puro □ *adv* (*in straight line*) reto; (*directly*) direito, direto, (*P*) recto, directamente, (*P*) directamente □ *n* linha *f* reta, (*P*) recta. ~ **ahead** *or* **on** (*sempre*) em frente. ~ **away** logo, imediatamente. **go ~** viver honestamente. **keep a ~ face** não se desmanchar, manter um ar sério

straighten /'streɪtn/ *vt* endireitar; (*tidy*) arrumar, pôr em ordem

straightforward /streɪt'fɔːwəd/ *a* franco, sincero; (*easy*) simples

strain[1] /streɪn/ *n* (*breed*) raça *f*; (*streak*) tendência *f*, veia *f*

strain[2] /streɪn/ *vt* (*rope*) esticar, puxar; (*tire*) cansar; (*filter*) filtrar, passar; (*vegetables, tea etc*) coar; (*med*) distender, torcer; (*fig*) forçar, pôr à prova □ *vi* esforçar-se □ *n* tensão *f*; (*fig: effort*) esforço *m*; (*med*) distensão *f*. ~**s** (*music*) melodias *fpl*. ~ **one's ears** apurar o ouvido. ~**ed** *a* forçado; (*relations*) tenso. ~**er** *n* coador *m*, (*P*) passador *m*

strait /streɪt/ *n* estreito *m*. ~**s** estreito *m*; (*fig*) apuros *mpl*, dificuldades *fpl*. ~**-jacket** *n* camisa-de-força *f*. ~**-laced** *a* severo, puritano

strand /strænd/ n (*thread*) fio m; (*lock of hair*) mecha f, madeixa f

stranded /'strændɪd/ a (*person*) em dificuldades, deixado para trás, abandonado

strange /stremdʒ/ a (-er, -est) estranho. ~ly adv estranhamente. ~ness n estranheza f

stranger /'stremdʒə(r)/ n estranho m, desconhecido m

strangle /'stræŋgl/ vt estrangular, sufocar

stranglehold /'stræŋglhəʊld/ n **have a ~ on** ter domínio sobre

strangulation /stræŋgjʊ'leɪʃn/ n estrangulamento m

strap /stræp/ n (*of leather etc*) correia f; (*of dress*) alça f; (*of watch*) pulseira f com correia □ vt (pt strapped) prender com correia

strapping /'stræpɪŋ/ a robusto, grande

strata /'streɪtə/ see stratum

stratagem /'strætədʒəm/ n estratagema m

strategic /strə'tiːdʒɪk/ a estratégico; (*of weapons*) de longo alcance

strategy /'strætɪdʒɪ/ n estratégia f

stratum /'strɑːtəm/ n (pl strata) estrato m, camada f

straw /strɔː/ n palha f; (*for drinking*) canudo m, (P) palhinha f. **the last ~** a última gota f

strawberry /'strɔːbrɪ/ n (*fruit*) morango m; (*plant*) morangueiro m

stray /streɪ/ vi (*deviate from path etc*) extraviar-se, desencaminhar-se, afastar-se (**from** de); (*lose one's way*) perder-se; (*wander*) vagar, errar □ a perdido, extraviado; (*isolated*) isolado, raro, esporádico □ n animal m perdido or vadio

streak /striːk/ n risca f, lista f; (*strain*) veia f; (*period*) período m. ~ **of lightning** relâmpago m □ vt listrar, riscar □ vi ir como um raio. ~**er** n (*colloq*) pessoa f que corre nua em lugares públicos. ~y a listrado, riscado. ~y **bacon** toucinho m entremeado com gordura

stream /striːm/ n riacho m, córrego m, regato m; (*current*) corrente f; (*fig: flow*) jorro m, torrente f; (*schol*) nível m, grupo m □ vi correr; (*of banner, hair*) flutuar; (*sweat*) escorrer, pingar

streamer /'striːmə(r)/ n (*of paper*) serpentina f, (*flag*) flâmula f, bandeirola f

streamline /'striːmlam/ vt dar forma aerodinâmica a; (*fig*) racionalizar. ~**d** a (*shape*) aerodinâmico

street /striːt/ n rua f. **the man in the ~** (*fig*) o homem da rua. ~ **lamp** poste m de iluminação

streetcar /'striːtkɑː(r)/ n (*Amer*) bonde m, (P) carro m eléctrico

strength /streŋθ/ n força f; (*of wall*) solidez f; (*of fabric etc*) resistência f. **on the ~ of** à base de, em virtude de

strengthen /'streŋθn/ vt fortificar, fortalecer, reforçar

strenuous /'strenjʊəs/ a enérgico; (*arduous*) árduo, estrênuo, (P) estrénuo; (*tiring*) fatigante, esgotante. ~ly adv esforçadamente, energicamente

stress /stres/ n acento m; (*pressure*) pressão f, tensão f; (*med*) stress m □ vt acentuar, sublinhar; (*sound*) acentuar. ~**ful** a estressante

stretch /stretʃ/ vt (*pull taut*) esticar; (*arm, leg, neck*) estender, esticar; (*clothes*) alargar; (*truth*) forçar, torcer □ vi estender-se; (*after sleep etc*) espreguiçar-se; (*of clothes*) alargar-se □ n extensão f, trecho m; (*period*) período m; (*of road*) troço m □ a (*of fabric*) com elasticidade. **at a ~** sem parar. ~ **one's legs** esticar as pernas

stretcher /'stretʃə(r)/ n maca f, padiola f. ~**-bearer** n padioleiro m, (P) maqueiro m

strew /struː/ vt (pt strewed, pp strewed or strewn) (*scatter*) espalhar; (*cover*) juncar, cobrir

stricken /'strɪkən/ a ~ **with** atacado or acometido de

strict /strɪkt/ a (-er, -est) estrito, rigoroso. ~ly adv estritamente. ~ly **speaking** a rigor. ~**ness** n severidade f, rigor m

stride /straɪd/ vi (pt strode, pp stridden) caminhar a passos largos □ n passada f. **make great ~s** (*fig*) fazer grandes progressos. **take sth in one's ~** fazer alg coisa sem problemas

strident /'straɪdnt/ a estridente

strife /straɪf/ n conflito m , dissensão f, luta f

strike /straɪk/ vt (pt struck) bater (em); (*blow*) dar; (*match*) riscar, acender; (*gold etc*) descobrir; (*of clock*) soar, dar, bater (horas); (*of lightning*) atingir □ vi fazer greve; (*attack*) atacar □ n (*of workers*) greve f; (*mil*) ataque m; (*find*) descoberta f. **on ~** em greve. ~ **a bargain** fechar negócio. ~ **off** or **out** riscar. ~ **up** (*mus*) começar a tocar; (*friendship*) travar

striker /'straɪkə(r)/ n grevista mf

striking /'straɪkɪŋ/ a notável, impressionante; (*attractive*) atraente

string /strɪŋ/ n corda f, fio m; (*of violin, racket etc*) corda f; (*of pearls*) fio m; (*of onions, garlic*) réstia f; (*of lies etc*) série f; (*row*) fila f □ vt (pt strung) (*thread*) enfiar. **pull ~s** usar pistolão, (P) puxar os cordelinhos. ~ **out**

espaçar-se. **~ed** *a* (*instrument*) de cordas. **~y** *a* filamentoso, fibroso; (*meat*) com nervos

stringent /'strɪndʒənt/ *a* rigoroso, estrito

strip[1] /strɪp/ *vt/i* (*pt* **stripped**) (*undress*) despir(-se); (*machine*) desmontar; (*deprive*) despojar, privar. **~per** *n* artista *mf* de striptease; (*solvent*) removedor *m*

strip[2] /strɪp/ *n* tira *f*; (*of land*) faixa *f*. **comic ~** história *f* em quadrinhos, (*P*) banda *f* desenhada. **~ light** tubo *m* de luz fluorescente

stripe /straɪp/ *n* risca *f*, lista *f*, barra *f*. **~d** *a* listrado, com listras

strive /straɪv/ *vi* (*pt* **strove**, *pp* **striven**) esforçar-se (**to** por)

strode /strəʊd/ *see* **stride**

stroke[1] /strəʊk/ *n* golpe *m*; (*of pen*) penada *f*, (*P*) traço *m*; (*in swimming*) braçada *f*; (*in rowing*) remada *f*; (*med*) ataque *m*, congestão *f*. **~ of genius** rasgo *m* de genialidade. **~ of luck** golpe *m* de sorte

stroke[2] /strəʊk/ *vt* (*with hand*) acariciar, fazer festas em

stroll /strəʊl/ *vi* passear, dar uma volta □ *n* volta *f*, (*P*) giro *m*. **~ in/etc** entrar/*etc* tranquilamente

strong /strɒŋ/ *a* (**-er**, **-est**) forte; (*shoes, fabric etc*) resistente. **be a hundred**/*etc* **~** ser em número de cem/*etc*. **~-box** *n* cofre-forte *m*. **~ language** linguagem *f* grosseira, palavrões *mpl*. **~-minded** *a* resoluto, firme. **~-room** *n* casa-forte *f*. **~ly** *adv* (*greatly*) fortemente, grandemente; (*with energy*) com força; (*deeply*) profundamente

stronghold /'strɒŋhəʊld/ *n* fortaleza *f*; (*fig*) baluarte *m*, bastião *m*

strove /strəʊv/ *see* **strive**

struck /strʌk/ *see* **strike** □ *a* **~ on** (*sl*) apaixonado por

structur|e /'strʌktʃə(r)/ *n* estrutura *f*; (*of building etc*) edifício *m*, construção *f*. **~al** *a* estrutural, de estrutura, de construção

struggle /'strʌgl/ *vi* (*to get free*) debater-se; (*contend*) lutar; (*strive*) esforçar-se (**to, for** por) □ *n* luta *f*; (*effort*) esforço *m*. **have a ~ to** ter dificuldade em. **~ to one's feet** levantar-se a custo

strum /strʌm/ *vt* (*pt* **strummed**) (*banjo etc*) dedilhar

strung /strʌŋ/ *see* **string**

strut /strʌt/ *n* (*support*) suporte *m*, escora *f* □ *vi* (*pt* **strutted**) (*walk*) pavonear-se

stub /stʌb/ *n* (*of pencil, cigarette*) ponta *f*; (*of tree*) cepo *m*, toco *m*; (*counterfoil*) talão *m*, canhoto *m* □ *vt* (*pt* **stubbed**) **~ one's toe** dar uma topada. **~ out** esmagar

stubble /'stʌbl/ *n* (*on chin*) barba *f* por fazer; (*of crop*) restolho *m*

stubborn /'stʌbən/ *a* teimoso, obstinado. **~ly** *adv* obstinadamente, teimosamente. **~ness** *n* teimosia *f*, obstinação *f*

stubby /'stʌbɪ/ *a* (**-ier**, **-iest**) (*finger*) curto e grosso; (*person*) atarracado

stuck /stʌk/ *see* **stick**[2] □ *a* emperrado. **~-up** *a* (*colloq: snobbish*) convencido, esnobe

stud[1] /stʌd/ *n* tacha *f*; (*for collar*) botão *m* de colarinho □ *vt* (*pt* **studded**) enfeitar com tachas. **~ded with** salpicado de

stud[2] /stʌd/ *n* (*horses*) haras *m*. **~ (-farm)** *n* coudelaria *f*. **~(-horse)** *n* garanhão *m*

student /'stjuːdnt/ *n* (*univ*) estudante *mf*, aluno *m*; (*schol*) aluno *m* □ *a* (*life, residence*) universitário

studied /'stʌdɪd/ *a* estudado

studio /'stjuːdɪəʊ/ *n* (*pl* **-os**) estúdio *m*. **~ flat** estúdio *m*

studious /'stjuːdɪəs/ *a* (*person*) estudioso; (*deliberate*) estudado. **~ly** *adv* (*carefully*) cuidadosamente

study /'stʌdɪ/ *n* estudo *m*; (*office*) escritório *m* □ *vt/i* estudar

stuff /stʌf/ *n* substância *f*, matéria *f*; (*sl: things*) coisa(s) *f* (*pl*) □ *vt* encher; (*animal*) empalhar; (*cram*) apinhar, encher ao máximo; (*culin*) rechear; (*block up*) entupir; (*put*) enfiar, meter. **~ing** *n* enchimento *f*; (*culin*) recheio *m*

stuffy /'stʌfɪ/ *a* (**-ier**, **-iest**) abafado, mal arejado; (*dull*) enfadonho

stumbl|e /'stʌmbl/ *vi* tropeçar. **~e across** *or* **on** dar com, encontrar por acaso, topar com. **~ing-block** *n* obstáculo *m*

stump /stʌmp/ *n* (*of tree*) cepo *m*, toco *m*; (*of limb*) coto *m*; (*of pencil, cigar*) ponta *f*

stumped /stʌmpt/ *a* (*colloq: baffled*) atrapalhado, perplexo

stun /stʌn/ *vt* (*pt* **stunned**) aturdir, estontear

stung /stʌŋ/ *see* **sting**

stunk /stʌŋk/ *see* **stink**

stunning /'stʌnɪŋ/ *a* atordoador; (*colloq: delightful*) fantástico, sensacional

stunt[1] /stʌnt/ *vt* (*growth*) atrofiar. **~ed** *a* atrofiado

stunt[2] /stʌnt/ *n* (*feat*) façanha *f*, proeza *f*, (*trick*) truque *m*; (*aviat*) acrobacia *f* aérea. **~ man** *n* dublê *m*, (*P*) duplo *m*

stupefy /'stjuːpɪfaɪ/ *vt* estupefazer, (*P*) estupeficar

stupendous /stju:'pendəs/ *a* estupendo, assombroso, prodigioso

stupid /'stju:pɪd/ *a* estúpido, obtuso. **~ity** /-'pɪdətɪ/ *n* estupidez *f*. **~ly** *adv* estupidamente

stupor /'stju:pə(r)/ *n* estupor *m*, torpor *m*

sturdy /'stɜ:dɪ/ *a* (**-ier, -iest**) robusto, vigoroso, forte

stutter /'stʌtə(r)/ *vi* gaguejar □ *n* gagueira *f*, (*P*) gaguez *f*

sty /staɪ/ *n* (*pigsty*) pocilga *f*, chiqueiro *m*

stye /staɪ/ *n* (*on eye*) terçol *m*, terçolho *m*

styl|e /staɪl/ *n* estilo *m*; (*fashion*) moda *f*; (*kind*) gênero *m*, (*P*) género *m*, tipo *m*; (*pattern*) feitio *m*, modelo *m* □ *vt* (*design*) desenhar, criar. **in ~e** (*live*) em grande estilo; (*do things*) com classe. **~e sb's hair** fazer um penteado em alguém. **~ist** *n* (*of hair*) cabeleireiro *m*

stylish /'staɪlɪʃ/ *a* elegante, na moda

stylized /'staɪlaɪzd/ *a* estilizado

stylus /'staɪləs/ *n* (*pl* **-uses**) (*of record-player*) agulha *f*, safira *f*

suave /swa:v/ *a* polido, de fala mansa, (*P*) melífluo

sub- /sʌb/ *pref* sub-

subconscious /sʌb'kɒnʃəs/ *a* & *n* subconsciente (*m*)

subcontract /sʌbkən'trækt/ *vt* dar de subempreitada

subdivide /sʌbdɪ'vaɪd/ *vt* subdividir

subdue /səb'dju:/ *vt* (*enemy, feeling*) dominar, subjugar; (*sound, voice*) abrandar. **~d** *a* (*weak*) submisso; (*quiet*) recolhido; (*light*) velado

subject[1] /'sʌbdʒɪkt/ *a* (*state etc*) dominado □ *n* sujeito *m*; (*schol, univ*) disciplina *f*, matéria *f*; (*citizen*) súdito *m*. **~-matter** *n* conteúdo *m*, tema *m*, assunto *m*. **~ to** sujeito a

subject[2] /səb'dʒekt/ *vt* submeter. **~ion** /-kʃn/ *n* submissão *f*

subjective /sʌb'dʒektɪv/ *a* subjetivo, (*P*) subjectivo

subjunctive /səb'dʒʌŋktɪv/ *a* & *n* subjuntivo (*m*), (*P*) conjuntivo (*m*)

sublime /sə'blaɪm/ *a* sublime

submarine /sʌbmə'ri:n/ *n* submarino *m*

submerge /səb'mɜ:dʒ/ *vt* submergir □ *vi* submergir, mergulhar

submissive /səb'mɪsɪv/ *a* submisso

submi|t /səb'mɪt/ *vt/i* (*pt* **submitted**) submeter(-se) (**to** a); (*jur: argue*) alegar. **~ssion** /-'mɪʃn/ *n* submissão *f*

subnormal /sʌb'nɔ:ml/ *a* subnormal; (*temperature*) abaixo do normal

subordinate[1] /sə'bɔ:dmət/ *a* subordinado, subalterno; (*gram*) subordinado □ *n* subordinado *m*, subalterno *m*

subordinate[2] /sə'bɔ:dmeɪt/ *vt* subordinar (**to** a)

subpoena /səb'pi:nə/ *n* (*pl* **-as**) (*jur*) citação *f*, intimação *f*

subscribe /səb'skraɪb/ *vt/i* subscrever, contribuir (**to para**). **~ to** (*theory, opinion*) subscrever, aceitar; (*newspaper*) assinar. **~r** /-ə(r)/ *n* subscritor *m*, assinante *m*

subscription /səb'skrɪpʃn/ *n* subscrição *f*; (*to newspaper*) assinatura *f*

subsequent /'sʌbsɪkwənt/ *a* subseqüente, (*P*) subsequente, posterior. **~ly** *adv* subseqüentemente, a seguir, posteriormente

subservient /səb'sɜ:vɪənt/ *a* servil, subserviente

subside /səb'saɪd/ *vi* (*flood, noise etc*) baixar; (*land*) ceder, afundar; (*wind, storm, excitement*) abrandar. **~nce** /-əns/ *n* (*of land*) afundamento *m*

subsidiary /səb'sɪdɪərɪ/ *a* subsidiário □ *n* (*comm*) filial *f*, sucursal *f*

subsid|y /'sʌbsədɪ/ *n* subsídio *m*, subvenção *f*, (*P*) subsídio *m*. **~ize** /-ɪdaɪz/ *vt* subsidiar, subvencionar

subsist /səb'sɪst/ *vi* subsistir. **~ on** viver de. **~ence** *n* subsistência *f*. **~ence allowance** ajudas *fpl* de custo

substance /'sʌbstəns/ *n* substância *f*

substandard /sʌb'stændəd/ *a* de qualidade inferior

substantial /səb'stænʃl/ *a* substancial. **~ly** *adv* substancialmente

substantiate /səb'stænʃɪeɪt/ *vt* comprovar, fundamentar

substitut|e /'sʌbstɪtju:t/ *n* (*person*) substituto *m*, suplente *mf* (**for** de); (*thing*) substituto *m* (**for** de) □ *vt* substituir (**for** por). **~ion** /'tju:ʃn/ *n* substituição *f*

subterfuge /'sʌbtəfju:dʒ/ *n* subterfúgio *m*

subtitle /'sʌbtaɪtl/ *n* subtítulo *m*

subtle /'sʌtl/ *a* (**-er, -est**) sutil, (*P*) subtil. **~ty** *n* sutileza *f*, (*P*) subtileza *f*

subtotal /'sʌbtəʊtl/ *n* soma *f* parcial

subtract /səb'trækt/ *vt* subtrair, diminuir. **~ion** /-kʃn/ *n* subtração *f*, diminuição *f*

suburb /'sʌbɜ:b/ *n* subúrbio *m*, arredores *mpl*. **~an** /sə'bɜ:bən/ *a* dos subúrbios, suburbano. **~ia** /sə'bɜ:bɪə/ *n* (*pej*) os arredores

subver|t /səb'vɜ:t/ *vt* subverter. **~sion** /-ʃn/ *n* subverção *f*. **~sive** /-sɪv/ *a* subversivo

subway /'sʌbweɪ/ *n* passagem *f* subterrânea; (*Amer: underground*) metropolitano *m*

succeed /sək'si:d/ *vi* ser bem sucedido, ter êxito. **~ in doing sth** conseguir fazer alg coisa □ *vt* (*follow*) suceder a. **~ing** *a* seguinte, sucessivo

success /sək'ses/ *n* sucesso *m*, êxito *m*
succession /sək'seʃn/ *n* sucessão *f*; (*series*) série *f*. **in** ~ seguidos, consecutivos
successive /sək'sesɪv/ *a* sucessivo, consecutivo
successor /sək'sesə(r)/ *n* sucessor *m*
succinct /sək'sɪŋkt/ *a* sucinto
succulent /'sʌkjʊlənt/ *a* suculento
succumb /sə'kʌm/ *vi* sucumbir
such /sʌtʃ/ *a* & *pron* tal, semelhante, assim; (*so much*) tanto □ *adv* tanto. ~ **a book/etc** um tal livro/*etc* or um livro/*etc* assim. ~ **books/etc** tais livros/*etc* or livros/*etc* assim. ~ **courage/etc** tanta coragem/*etc*. ~ **a big house** uma casa tão grande. **as** ~ como tal. ~ **as** como, tal como. **there's no** ~ **thing** uma coisa dessa não existe. ~**-and-such** *a* & *pron* tal e tal
suck /sʌk/ *vt* chupar; (*breast*) mamar. ~ **in** or **up** (*absorb*) absorver, aspirar; (*engulf*) tragar. ~ **up to** puxar o saco a (*colloq*). ~ **one's thumb** chupar o dedo. ~**er** *n* (*sl: greenhorn*) trouxa *mf* (*colloq*); (*bot*) broto *m*
suckle /'sʌkl/ *vt* amamentar, dar de mamar a
suction /'sʌkʃn/ *n* sucção *f*
sudden /'sʌdn/ *a* súbito, repentino. **all of a** ~ de repente, de súbito. ~**ly** *adv* subitamente, repentinamente. ~**ness** *n* subitaneidade *f*, brusquidão *f*
suds /sʌdz/ *npl* espuma *f* de sabão; (*soapy water*) água *f* de sabão
sue /suː/ *vt* (*pres p* **suing**) processar
suede /sweɪd/ *n* camurça *f*
suet /'suːɪt/ *n* sebo *m*
suffer /'sʌfə(r)/ *vt/i* sofrer; (*tolerate*) tolerar, suportar. ~**er** *n* sofredor *m*, o que sofre; (*patient*) doente *mf*, vítima *f*. ~**ing** *n* sofrimento *m*
suffice /sə'faɪs/ *vi* bastar, chegar, ser suficiente
sufficien|t /sə'fɪʃnt/ *a* suficiente, bastante. ~**cy** *n* suficiência *f*, quantidade *f* suficiente. ~**tly** *adv* suficientemente
suffix /'sʌfɪx/ *n* sufixo *m*
suffocat|e /'sʌfəkeɪt/ *vt/i* sufocar. ~**ion** /'keɪʃn/ *n* sufocação *f*, asfixia *f*. ~**ing** *a* sufocante, asfixiante
sugar /'ʃʊgə(r)/ *n* açúcar *m* □ *vt* adoçar, pôr açúcar em. ~**-bowl** *n* açucareiro *m*. ~**-lump** *n* torrão *m* de açúcar, (*P*) quadradinho *m* de açúcar. **brown** ~ açúcar *m* preto, (*P*) açúcar *m* amarelo. ~**y** *a* açucarado; (*fig: too sweet*) delico-doce
suggest /sə'dʒest/ *vt* sugerir. ~**ion** /-tʃn/ *n* sugestão *f*. ~**ive** *a* sugestivo; (*improper*) brejeiro, picante. **be** ~**ive of** sugerir, fazer lembrar

suicid|e /'suːɪsaɪd/ *n* suicídio *m*. **commit** ~**e** suicidar-se. ~**al** /-'saɪdl/ *a* suicida
suit /suːt/ *n* terno *m*, (*P*) fato *m*; (*woman's*) costume *m*, (*P*) saia-casaco *m*; (*cards*) naipe *m* □ *vt* convir a; (*of garment, style*) ficar bem em; (*adapt*) adaptar. **follow** ~ (*fig*) seguir o exemplo. ~**ability** *n* (*of action*) conveniência *f*, oportunidade *f*; (*of candidate*) aptidão *f*. ~**able** *a* conveniente, apropriado (**for** para). ~**ably** *adv* convenientemente. ~**ed** *a* **be** ~**ed to** ser feito para, servir para. **be well** ~**ed** (*matched*) combinar-se bem; (*of people*) ser o ideal
suitcase /'suːtkeɪs/ *n* mala *f* (de viagem)
suite /swiːt/ *n* (*of rooms; mus*) suíte *f*, (*P*) suite *f*; (*of furniture*) mobília *f*
suitor /'suːtə(r)/ *n* pretendente *m*
sulk /sʌlk/ *vi* amuar, ficar emburrado. ~**y** *a* amuado, emburrado (*colloq*)
sullen /'sʌlən/ *a* carrancudo
sulphur /'sʌlfə(r)/ *n* enxofre *m*. ~**ic** /-'fjʊərɪk/ *a* ~**ic acid** ácido *m* sulfúrico
sultan /'sʌltən/ *n* sultão *m*
sultana /sʌl'taːnə/ *n* (*fruit*) passa *f* branca, (*P*) sultana *f*
sultry /'sʌltrɪ/ *a* (**-ier, -iest**) abafado, opressivo; (*fig*) sensual
sum /sʌm/ *n* soma *f*; (*amount of money*) soma *f*, quantia *f*, importância *f*; (*in arithmetic*) conta *f* □ *vt* (*pt* **summed**) somar. ~ **up** recapitular, resumir; (*assess*) avaliar, medir
summar|y /'sʌmərɪ/ *n* sumário *m*, resumo *m* □ *a* sumário. ~**ize** *vt* resumir
summer /'sʌmə(r)/ *n* verão *m*, estio *m* □ *a* de verão. ~**-time** *n* verão *m*, época *f* de verão. ~**y** *a* estival, próprio de verão
summit /'sʌmɪt/ *n* cume *m*, cimo *m*. ~ **conference** (*pol*) conferência *f* de cúpula, (*P*) reunião *f* de cimeira
summon /'sʌmən/ *vt* mandar chamar; (*to meeting*) convocar. ~ **up** (*strength, courage etc*) chamar a si, fazer apelo a
summons /'sʌmənz/ *n* (*jur*) citação *f*, intimação *f* □ *vt* citar, intimar
sump /sʌmp/ *n* (*auto*) cárter *m*
sumptuous /'sʌmptʃʊəs/ *a* suntuoso, (*P*) sumptuoso, luxuoso
sun /sʌn/ *n* sol *m* □ *vt* (*pt* **sunned**) ~ **o.s.** aquecer-se ao sol. ~**glasses** *npl* óculos *mpl* de sol. ~**-roof** *n* teto *m* solar. ~**-tan** *n* bronzeado *m*. ~**-tanned** *a* bronzeado. ~**-tan oil** *n* óleo *m* de bronzear
sunbathe /'sʌnbeɪð/ *vi* tomar um banho de sol

sunburn /'sʌnbɜ:n/ n queimadura f de sol. ~t a queimado pelo sol

Sunday /'sʌndɪ/ n domingo m. ~ **school** catecismo m

sundial /'sʌndaɪəl/ n relógio m de sol

sundown /'sʌndaʊn/ n = **sunset**

sundr|y /'sʌndrɪ/ a vários, diversos. ~**ies** npl artigos mpl diversos. **all and** ~**y** todo o mundo

sunflower /'sʌnflaʊə(r)/ n girassol m

sung /sʌŋ/ see **sing**

sunk /sʌŋk/ see **sink**

sunken /'sʌŋkən/ a (ship etc) afundado; (eyes) fundo

sunlight /'sʌnlaɪt/ n luz f do sol, sol m

sunny /'sʌnɪ/ a (-ier, -iest) (room, day etc) ensolarado

sunrise /'sʌnraɪz/ n nascer m do sol

sunset /'sʌnset/ n pôr m do sol

sunshade /'sʌnʃeɪd/ n (awning) toldo m; (parasol) pára-sol m, (P) guarda-sol m

sunshine /'sʌnʃaɪn/ n sol m, luz f do sol

sunstroke /'sʌnstrəʊk/ n (med) insolação f

super /'su:pə(r)/ a (colloq: excellent) formidável

superb /su:'pɜ:b/ a soberbo, esplêndido

supercilious /su:pə'sɪlɪəs/ a (haughty) altivo; (disdainful) desdenhoso

superficial /su:pə'fɪʃl/ a superficial. ~**ity** /-ɪ'ælətɪ/ n superficialidade f. ~**ly** adv superficialmente

superfluous /su:'pɜ:fluəs/ a supérfluo

superhuman /su:pə'hju:mən/ a sobre-humano

superimpose /su:pərɪm'pəʊz/ vt sobrepor (on a)

superintendent /su:pərɪn'tendənt/ n superintendente m; (of police) comissário m, chefe m de polícia

superior /su:'pɪərɪə(r)/ a & n superior (m). ~**ity** /-'ɒrətɪ/ n superioridade f

superlative /su:'pɜ:lətɪv/ a supremo, superlativo □ n (gram) superlativo m

supermarket /'su:pəma:kɪt/ n supermercado m

supernatural /su:pə'nætʃrəl/ a sobrenatural

superpower /'su:pəpaʊə(r)/ n superpotência f

supersede /su:pə'si:d/ vt suplantar, substituir

supersonic /su:pə'sɒnɪk/ a supersónico, (P) supersónico

superstiti|on /su:pə'stɪʃn/ n superstição f. ~**ous** a /-'stɪʃəs/ supersticioso

superstore /'su:pəstɔ:(r)/ n hipermercado m

supertanker /'su:pətæŋkə(r)/ n superpetroleiro m

supervis|e /'su:pəvaɪz/ vt supervisar, fiscalizar. ~**ion** /-'vɪʒn/ n supervisão f. ~**or** n supervisor m; (shop) chefe mf de seção; (firm) chefe mf de serviço. ~**ory** /'su:pəvaɪzərɪ/ a de supervisão

supper /'sʌpə(r)/ n jantar m; (late at night) ceia f

supple /'sʌpl/ a flexível, maleável

supplement¹ /'sʌplɪmənt/ n suplemento m. ~**ary** /-'mentrɪ/ a suplementar

supplement² /'sʌplɪment/ vt suplementar

supplier /sə'plaɪə(r)/ n fornecedor m

suppl|y /sə'plaɪ/ vt suprir, prover; (comm) fornecer, abastecer □ n provisão f; (of goods, gas etc) fornecimento m, abastecimento m □ a (teacher) substituto. ~**ies** (food) víveres mpl; (mil) suprimentos mpl. ~**y and demand** oferta e procura

support /sə'pɔ:t/ vt (hold up, endure) suportar; (provide for) sustentar, suster; (back) apoiar, patrocinar; (sport) torcer por □ n apoio m; (techn) suporte m. ~**er** n partidário m; (sport) torcedor m

suppos|e /sə'pəʊz/ vt/i supor. ~**e that** supondo que, na hipótese de que. ~**ed** a suposto. **he's** ~**ed to do** he deve fazer; (believed to) consta que ele faz. ~**edly** /-ɪdlɪ/ adv segundo dizem; (probably) supostamente, em princípio. ~**ing** conj se. ~**ition** /sʌpə'zɪʃn/ n suposição f

suppress /sə'pres/ vt (put an end to) suprimir; (restrain) conter, reprimir; (stifle) abafar, sufocar; (psych) recalcar. ~**ion** /-ʃn/ n supressão f; (restraint) repressão f; (psych) recalque m, (P) recalcamento m

suprem|e /su:'pri:m/ a supremo. ~**acy** /-eməsɪ/ n supremacia f

surcharge /'sɜ:tʃa:dʒ/ n sobretaxa f; (on stamp) sobrecarga f

sure /ʃʊə(r)/ a (-er, -est) seguro, certo □ adv (colloq: certainly) deveras, não há dúvida que, de certeza. **be** ~ **about** or **of** ter a certeza de. **be** ~ **to** (not fail) não deixar de. **he is** ~ **to find out** ele vai descobrir com certeza. **make** ~ assegurar. ~**ly** adv com certeza, certamente

surety /'ʃʊərətɪ/ n (person) fiador m; (thing) garantia f

surf /sɜ:f/ n (waves) ressaca f, rebentação f. ~**er** n surfista mf. ~**ing** n surfe m, (P) surf m, jacaré-na-praia m

surface /'sɜ:fɪs/ n superfície f □ a superficial □ vt/i revestir; (rise, become known) emergir. ~ **mail** via f marítima

surfboard /'sɜːfbɔːd/ n prancha f de surfe, (P) surf

surfeit /'sɜːfɪt/ n excesso m (of de)

surge /sɜːdʒ/ vi (waves) ondular, encapelar-se; (move forward) avançar □ n (wave) onda f, vaga f; (motion) arremetida f

surgeon /'sɜːdʒən/ n cirurgião m

surg|ery /'sɜːdʒərɪ/ n cirurgia f; (office) consultório m; (session) consulta f; (consulting hours) horas fpl de consulta. ~ical a cirúrgico

surly /'sɜːlɪ/ a (-ier, -iest) carrancudo, trombudo

surmise /sə'maɪz/ vt imaginar, supor, calcular □ n conjetura f, (P) conjectura f; hipótese f

surmount /sə'maʊnt/ vt sobrepujar, vencer, (P) superar

surname /'sɜːneɪm/ n sobrenome m, (P) apelido m

surpass /sə'pɑːs/ vt superar, ultrapassar, exceder

surplus /'sɜːpləs/ n excedente m, excesso m; (finance) saldo m positivo □ a excedente, em excesso

surpris|e /sə'praɪz/ n surpresa f □ vt surpreender. ~ed a surpreendido, admirado (at com). ~ing a surpreendente. ~ingly adv surpreendentemente

surrender /sə'rendə(r)/ vi render-se □ vt (hand over; mil) entregar □ n (mil) rendição f; (of rights) renúncia f

surreptitious /sʌrep'tɪʃəs/ a subreptício, furtivo

surrogate /'sʌrəgeɪt/ n delegado m. ~ mother mãe f de aluguel, (P) aluguer

surround /sə'raʊnd/ vt rodear, cercar; (mil etc) cercar. ~ing a circundante, vizinho. ~ings npl arredores mpl; (setting) meio m, ambiente m

surveillance /sɜː'veɪləns/ n vigilância f

survey¹ /sə'veɪ/ vt (landscape etc) observar; (review) passar em revista; (inquire about) pesquisar; (land) fazer o levantamento de; (building) vistoriar, inspecionar, (P) inspeccionar. ~or n (of buildings) fiscal m; (of land) agrimensor m

survey² /'sɜːveɪ/ n (inspection) vistoria f, inspeção f, (P) inspecção f; (general view) panorâmica f; (inquiry) pesquisa f

survival /sə'vaɪvl/ n sobrevivência f, (relic) relíquia f, vestígio m

surviv|e /sə'vaɪv/ vt/i sobreviver (a). ~or n sobrevivente mf

susceptib|le /sə'septəbl/ a (prone) suscetível (to a); (sensitive, impressionable) susceptível, sensível. ~ility /-'bɪlətɪ/ n susceptibilidade f

suspect¹ /sə'spekt/ vt suspeitar; (doubt, distrust) desconfiar de, suspeitar de

suspect² /'sʌspekt/ a & n suspeito (m)

suspen|d /sə'spend/ vt (hang, stop) suspender; (from duty etc) suspender. ~ded sentence suspensão f de pena. ~sion n suspensão f. ~sion bridge ponte f suspensa or pênsil

suspender /sə'spendə(r)/ n (presilha de) liga f. ~ belt n cintaliga f, (P) cinta f de ligas. ~s (Amer: braces) suspensórios mpl

suspense /sə'spens/ n ansiedade f, incerteza f; (in book etc) suspense m, tensão f

suspicion /sə'spɪʃn/ n suspeita f; (distrust) desconfiança f; (trace) vestígio m, (P) traço m

suspicious /səs'pɪʃəs/ a desconfiado; (causing suspicion) suspeito. be ~ of desconfiar de. ~ly adv de modo suspeito

sustain /sə'steɪn/ vt (support) suster, sustentar; (suffer) sofrer; (keep up) sustentar; (jur: uphold) sancionar; (interest, effort) manter. ~ed effort esforço m contínuo

sustenance /'sʌstməns/ n (food) alimento m, sustento m

swagger /'swægə(r)/ vi pavonear-se, andar com arrogância

swallow¹ /'swɒləʊ/ vt/i engolir. ~ up (absorb, engulf) devorar, tragar

swallow² /'swɒləʊ/ n (bird) andorinha f

swam /swæm/ see swim

swamp /swɒmp/ n pântano m, brejo m □ vt (flood, overwhelm) inundar, submergir. ~y a pantanoso

swan /swɒn/ n cisne m

swank /swæŋk/ vi (colloq: show off) gabar-se, mostrar-se (colloq)

swap /swɒp/ vt/i (pt swapped) (colloq) trocar (for por) □ n (colloq) troca f

swarm /swɔːm/ n (of insects, people) enxame m □ vi formigar. ~ into or round invadir

swarthy /'swɔːðɪ/ a (-ier, -iest) moreno, trigueiro

swat /swɒt/ vt (pt swatted) (fly etc) esmagar, esborrachar

sway /sweɪ/ vt/i oscilar, balançar(-se); (influence) mover, influenciar □ n oscilação f, balanceio m; (rule) domínio m, poder m

swear /sweə(r)/ vt/i (pt swore, pp sworn) jurar; (curse) praguejar, rogar pragas (at contra). ~ by jurar por; (colloq: recommend) ter grande fé em. ~-word n palavrão m

sweat /swet/ n suor m □ vi suar. ~y a suado

sweater /'swetə(r)/ *n* suéter *m*, (*P*) camisola *f*

sweatshirt /'swetʃɜ:t/ *n* suéter *m* de malha *or* algodão

swede /swi:d/ *n* couve-nabo *f*

Swed|e /swi:d/ *n* sueco *m*. ~**en** *n* Suécia *f*. ~**ish** *a* & *n* sueco (*m*)

sweep /swi:p/ *vt/i* (*pt* **swept**) varrer; (*go majestically*) avançar majestosamente; (*carry away*) arrastar; (*chimney*) limpar □ *n* (*with broom*) varredela *f*; (*curve*) curva *f*; (*movement*) gesto *m* largo. (**chimney-**)~ limpa-chaminés *m*. ~**ing** *a* (*action*) de grande alcance. ~**ing statement** generalização *f* fácil

sweet /swi:t/ *a* (**-er, -est**) doce; (*colloq: charming*) doce, gracinha; (*colloq: pleasant*) agradável □ *n* doce *m*. ~ **corn** milho *m*. ~ **pea** ervilha-de-cheiro *f*. ~ **shop** confeitaria *f*. **have a** ~ **tooth** gostar de doce. ~**ly** *adv* docemente. ~**ness** *n* doçura *f*

sweeten /'swi:tn/ *vt* adoçar; (*fig: mitigate*) suavizar. ~**er** *n* (*for tea, coffee*) adoçante *m* (artificial); (*colloq: bribe*) agrado *m*

sweetheart /'swi:tha:t/ *n* namorado *m*, namorada *f*; (*term of endearment*) querido *m*, querida *f*, amor *m*

swell /swel/ *vt/i* (*pt* **swelled**, *pp* **swollen** *or* **swelled**) (*expand*) inchar; (*increase*) aumentar □ *n* (*of sea*) ondulação *f* □ *a* (*colloq: excellent*) excelente; (*colloq : smart*) chique. ~**ing** *n* (*med*) inchação *f*, inchaço *m*

swelter /'sweltə(r)/ *vi* fazer um calor abrasador; (*person*) abafar (com calor)

swept /swept/ *see* **sweep**

swerve /swɜ:v/ *vi* desviar-se, dar uma guinada

swift /swɪft/ *a* (**-er, -est**) rápido, veloz. ~**ly** *adv* rapidamente. ~**ness** *n* rapidez *f*

swig /swɪg/ *vt* (*pt* **swigged**) (*colloq: drink*) emborcar, beber em longos tragos □ *n* (*colloq*) trago *m*, gole *m*

swill /swɪl/ *vt* passar por água □ *n* (*pig-food*) lavagem *f*, (*P*) lavadura *f*

swim /swɪm/ *vi* (*pt* **swam**, *pp* **swum**, *pres p* **swimming**) nadar; (*room, head*) rodar □ *vt* atravessar a nado; (*distance*) nadar □ *n* banho *m*. ~**mer** *n* nadador *m*. ~**ming** *n* natação *f*. ~**ming-bath**, ~**ming-pool** *ns* piscina *f*. ~**ming-cap** *n* touca *f* de banho. ~**ming-costume**, ~**suit** *ns* maiô *m*, (*P*) fato *m* de banho. ~**ming-trunks** *npl* calção *m* de banho

swindle /'swɪndl/ *vt* trapacear, fraudar, (*P*) vigarizar □ *n* vigarice *f*. ~**r** /-ə(r)/ *n* vigarista *mf*

swine /swaɪn/ *npl* (*pigs*) porcos *mpl* □

n (*pl invar*) (*colloq: person*) animal *m*, canalha *m* (*colloq*)

swing /swɪŋ/ *vt/i* (*pt* **swung**) balançar(-se); (*turn round*) girar □ *n* (*seat*) balanço *m*; (*of opinion*) reviravolta *f*; (*mus*) swing *m*; (*rhythm*) ritmo *m*. **in full** ~ no máximo, em plena actividade, (*P*) actividade. ~ **round** (*of person*) virar-se. ~-**bridge/door** *ns* ponte *f*/porta *f* giratória

swipe /swaɪp/ *vt* (*colloq: hit*) bater em, dar uma pancada em (*colloq*); (*colloq: steal*) afanar, roubar (*colloq*) □ *n* (*colloq: hit*) pancada *f* (*colloq*)

swirl /swɜ:l/ *vi* rodopiar, redemoinhar □ *n* turbilhão *m*, redemoinho *m*

swish /swɪʃ/ *vt/i* sibilar, zunir, (fazer) cortar o ar; (*with brushing sound*) roçar □ *a* (*colloq*) chique

Swiss /swɪs/ *a* & *n* suiço (*m*)

switch /swɪtʃ/ *n* interruptor *m*; (*change*) mudança *f* □ *vt* (*transfer*) transferir; (*exchange*) trocar □ *vi* desviar-se. ~ **off** desligar

switchboard /'swɪtʃbɔ:d/ *n* (*telephone*) PBX *m*, mesa *f* telefónica

Switzerland /'swɪtsələnd/ *n* Suíça *f*

swivel /'swɪvl/ *vt/i* (*pt* **swivelled**) (fazer) girar. ~ **chair** cadeira *f* giratória

swollen /'swəʊlən/ *see* **swell** □ *a* inchado

swoop /swu:p/ *vi* (*bird*) lançar-se, cair (**down on** sobre); (*police*) dar uma batida policial, (*P*) rusga

sword /sɔ:d/ *n* espada *f*

swore /swɔ:(r)/ *see* **swear**

sworn /swɔ:n/ *see* **swear** □ *a* (*enemy*) jurado, declarado; (*ally*) fiel

swot /swɒt/ *vt/i* (*pt* **swotted**) (*colloq: study*) estudar muito, (*P*) marrar (*sl*) □ *n* (*colloq*) estudante *m* muito aplicado, (*P*) marrão *m* (*sl*)

swum /swʌm/ *see* **swim**

swung /swʌŋ/ *see* **swing**

sycamore /'sɪkəmɔ:(r)/ *n* (*maple*) sicómoro *m*, (*P*) sicómoro *m*; (*Amer: plane*) plátano *m*

syllable /'sɪləbl/ *n* sílaba *f*

syllabus /'sɪləbəs/ *n* (*pl* **-uses**) programa *m*

symbol /'sɪmbl/ *n* símbolo *m*. ~**ic(al)** /-'bɒlɪk(l)/ *a* simbólico. ~**ism** *n* simbolismo *m*

symbolize /'sɪmbəlaɪz/ *vt* simbolizar

symmetr|y /'sɪmətrɪ/ *n* simetria *f*. ~**ical** /sɪ'metrɪkl/ *a* simétrico

sympathize /'sɪmpəθaɪz/ *vi* ~ **with** ter pena de, condoer-se de; (*fig*) compartilhar os sentimentos de. ~**r** *n* simpatizante *mf*

sympath|y /'sɪmpəθɪ/ *n* (*pity*) pena *f*, compaixão *f*; (*solidarity*) solidariedade *f*; (*condolences*) pêsames *mpl*, condolências *fpl*. **be in** ~**y with** estar de acordo com. ~etic /-'θetɪk/ a comprensivo, simpático; (*likeable*) simpático; (*showing pity*) compassivo. ~etically /-'θetɪklɪ/ adv compassivamente; (*fig*) compreensivamente

symphon|y /'sɪmfənɪ/ n sinfonia f □ a sinfônico, (P) sinfónico. ~ic /-'fɒnɪk/ a sinfônico, (P) sinfónico

symptom /'sɪmptəm/ n sintoma m. ~atic /-'mætɪk/ a sintomático (of de)

synagogue /'sɪnəgɒg/ n sinagoga f

synchronize /'sɪŋkrənaɪz/ vt sincronizar

syndicate /'sɪndɪkət/ n sindicato m

syndrome /'sɪndrəʊm/ n (*med*) síndrome m, (P) sindroma m

synonym /'sɪnənɪm/ n sinônimo m, (P) sinónimo m. ~ous /sɪ'nɒnɪməs/ a sinônimo, (P) sinónimo (with de)

synopsis /sɪ'nɒpsɪs/ n (pl -opses /-si:z/) sinopse f, resumo m

syntax /'sɪntæks/ n sintaxe f

synthesis /'sɪnθəsɪs/ n (pl -theses /-si:z/) síntese f

synthetic /sɪn'θetɪk/ a sintético

syphilis /'sɪfɪlɪs/ n sífilis f

Syria /'sɪrɪə/ n Síria f. ~n a & n sírio (m)

syringe /sɪ'rɪndʒ/ n seringa f □ vt seringar

syrup /'sɪrəp/ n (*liquid*) xarope m; (*treacle*) calda f de açúcar. ~y a (*fig*) melado, enjoativo

system /'sɪstəm/ n sistema m; (*body*) organismo m; (*order*) método m. ~atic /ˌsɪstə'mætɪk/ a sistemático

T

tab /tæb/ n (*flap*) lingueta f; (*for fastening, hanging*) aba f; (*label*) etiqueta f; (*loop*) argola f; (*Amer colloq: bill*) conta f. **keep** ~**s on** (*colloq*) vigiar

table /'teɪbl/ n mesa f; (*list*) tabela f, lista f □ vt (*submit*) apresentar; (*postpone*) adiar. **at** ~ à mesa. **lay** *or* **set the** ~ pôr a mesa. ~ **of contents** índice m (das matérias). **turn the** ~**s** inverter as posições. ~**-cloth** n toalha de mesa f. ~**-mat** n descanso m. ~ **tennis** pingue-pongue m

tablespoon /'teɪblspuːn/ n colher f grande de sopa. ~**ful** n (pl ~**fuls**) colher f de sopa cheia

tablet /'tæblɪt/ n (*of stone*) lápide f, placa f; (*drug*) comprimido m

tabloid /'tæblɔɪd/ n tablóide m. ~ **journalism** (*pej*) jornalismo m sensacionalista, imprensa f marron

taboo /tə'buː/ n & a tabu (m)

tacit /'tæsɪt/ a tácito

taciturn /'tæsɪtɜːn/ a taciturno

tack /tæk/ n (*nail*) tacha f; (*stitch*) ponto m de alinhavo; (*naut*) amura f; (*fig: course of action*) rumo m □ vt (*nail*) pregar com tachas; (*stitch*) alinhavar □ vi (*naut*) bordejar. ~ **on** (*add*) acrescentar, juntar

tackle /'tækl/ n equipamento m, apetrechos mpl; (*sport*) placagem f □ vt (*problem etc*) atacar; (*sport*) placar; (*a thief etc*) agarrar-se a

tacky /'tækɪ/ a (-ier, -iest) peganhento, pegajoso

tact /tækt/ n tato m, (P) tacto m. ~**ful** a cheio de tato, (P) tacto, diplomático. ~**fully** adv com tato, (P) tacto. ~**less** a sem tato, (P) tacto. ~**lessly** adv sem tato, (P) tacto

tactic /'tæktɪk/ n (*expedient*) tática f, (P) táctica f. ~**s** n(pl) (*procedure*) tática f, (P) táctica f. ~**al** a tático, (P) táctico

tadpole /'tædpəʊl/ n girino m

tag /tæg/ n (*label*) etiqueta f; (*on shoelace*) agulheta f; (*phrase*) chavão m, clichê m □ vi (pt **tagged**) etiquetar; (*add*) juntar □ vi ~ **along** (*colloq*) andar atrás, seguir

Tagus /'teɪgəs/ n Tejo m

tail /teɪl/ n cauda f, rabo m; (*of shirt*) fralda f. ~**s!** (*tossing coin*) coroa! □ vt (*follow*) seguir, vigiar □ vi ~ **away** *or* **off** diminuir, baixar. ~**-back** n (*traffic*) fila f, (P) bicha f. ~**-end** n parte f traseira, cauda f. ~**-light** n (*auto*) farolete m traseiro, (P) farolim m da rectaguarda

tailor /'teɪlə(r)/ n alfaiate m □ vt (*garment*) fazer; (*fig: adapt*) adaptar. ~**-made** a feito sob medida, (P) por medida. ~**-made for** (*fig*) feito para, talhado para

tainted /'teɪntɪd/ a (*infected*) contaminado; (*decayed*) estragado; (*fig*) manchado

take /teɪk/ vt/i (pt **took**, pp **taken**) (*get hold of*) agarrar em, pegar em; (*capture*) tomar; (*a seat, a drink; train, bus etc*) tomar; (*carry*) levar (to a, para); (*contain, escort*) levar; (*tolerate*) suportar, agüentar, (P) aguentar; (*choice, exam*) fazer; (*photo*) tirar; (*require*) exigir. **be** ~**n by** *or* **with** ficar encantado com. **be** ~**n ill** adoecer. **it** ~**s time to** leva tempo para. ~ **after** parecer-se a. ~**-away** n (*meal*) comida f para levar, takeaway m; (*shop*) loja f que só vende comida para ser consumida em outro lugar. ~ **away** levar. ~ **away from sb/sth** tirar de alguém/de alg coisa. ~ **back** aceitar de volta; (*return*) devolver; (*accompany*) acompanhar; (*statement*) retirar, retratar. ~ **down** (*object*) tirar para baixo; (*notes*) tirar, tomar. ~ **in** (*garment*) meter para dentro; (*include*) incluir; (*cheat*) enganar, levar (*colloq*); (*grasp*) compreender; (*receive*) receber. ~ **it that** supor que. ~ **off** *vt* (*remove*) tirar; (*mimic*) imitar, macaquear □ *vi* (*aviat*) decolar, levantar vôo. **~-off** *n* imitação *f*; (*aviat*) decolagem *f*, (P) descolagem *f*. ~ **on** (*task*) encarregar-se de; (*staff*) admitir, contratar. ~ **out** tirar; (*on an outing*) levar para sair. ~ **over** *vt* tomar conta de, assumir a direção, (P) direcção de □ *vi* tomar o poder. ~ **over from** (*relieve*) render, substituir; (*succeed*) suceder a. **~-over** *n* (*pol*) tomada *f* de poder; (*comm*) take-over *m*. ~ **part** participar *or* tomar parte (**in** em). ~ **place** ocorrer, suceder. ~ **sides** tomar partido. ~ **sides with** tomar o partido de. ~ **to** gostar de, simpatizar com; (*activity*) tomar gosto por, entregar-se a. ~ **up** (*object*) apanhar, pegar em; (*hobby*) dedicar-se a; (*occupy*) ocupar, tomar

takings /ˈteɪkɪŋz/ *npl* receita *f*

talcum /ˈtælkəm/ *n* talco *m*. ~ **powder** pó *m* talco

tale /teɪl/ *n* conto *m*, história *f*

talent /ˈtælənt/ *n* talento *m*. **~ed** *a* talentoso, bem dotado

talk /tɔːk/ *vt/i* falar; (*chat*) conversar □ *n* conversa *f*; (*mode of speech*) fala *f*; (*lecture*) palestra *f*. **small** ~ conversa *f* banal. ~ **into doing** convencer a fazer. ~ **nonsense** dizer disparates. ~ **over** discutir. ~ **shop** falar de assuntos profissionais. ~ **to o.s.** falar sozinho, falar com os seus botões. **there's** ~ **of** fala-se de. **~er** *n* conversador *m*. **~ing-to** *n* (*colloq*) descompostura *f*

talkative /ˈtɔːkətɪv/ *a* falador, conversador, tagarela

tall /tɔːl/ *a* (**-er, -est**) alto. ~ **story** (*colloq*) história *f* do arco-da-velha

tallboy /ˈtɔːlbɔɪ/ *n* cômoda *f*, (P) cómoda *f* alta

tally /ˈtælɪ/ *vi* corresponder (**with** a), conferir (**with** com)

tambourine /tæmbəˈriːn/ *n* tamborim *m*, pandeiro *m*

tame /teɪm/ *a* (**-er, -est**) manso; (*domesticated*) domesticado; (*dull*) insípido □ *vt* amansar, domesticar

tamper /ˈtæmpə(r)/ *vi* ~ **with** mexer indevidamente em; (*text*) alterar

tampon /ˈtæmpən/ *n* (*med*) tampão *m*; (*sanitary towel*) toalha *f* higiênica

tan /tæn/ *vt/i* (*pt* **tanned**) queimar, bronzear; (*hide*) curtir □ *n* bronzeado *m* □ *a* castanho amarelado

tandem /ˈtændəm/ *n* (*bicycle*) tandem *m*. **in** ~ em tandem, um atrás do outro

tang /tæŋ/ *n* (*taste*) sabor *m* or gosto

m característico; (*smell*) cheiro *m* característico

tangent /ˈtændʒənt/ *n* tangente *f*

tangerine /tændʒəˈriːn/ *n* tangerina *f*

tangible /ˈtændʒəbl/ *a* tangível

tangle /ˈtæŋgl/ *vt* emaranhar, enredar □ *n* emaranhado *m*. **become ~d** emaranhar-se, enredar-se

tank /tæŋk/ *n* tanque *m*, reservatório *m*; (*for petrol*) tanque *m*, (P) depósito *m*; (*for fish*) aquário *m*; (*mil*) tanque *m*

tankard /ˈtæŋkəd/ *n* caneca *f* grande

tanker /ˈtæŋkə(r)/ *n* carro-tanque *m*, camião-cisterna *m*; (*ship*) petroleiro *m*

tantaliz|e /ˈtæntəlaɪz/ *vt* atormentar, tantalizar. **~ing** *a* tentador

tantamount /ˈtæntəmaʊnt/ *a* **be ~ to** equivaler a

tantrum /ˈtæntrəm/ *n* chilique *m*, ataque *m* de mau gênio, (P) génio, birra *f*

tap¹ /tæp/ *n* (*for water etc*) torneira *f* □ *vt* (*pt* **tapped**) (*resources*) explorar; (*telephone*) gram-pear. **on** ~ (*colloq*: *available*) disponível

tap² /tæp/ *vt/i* (*pt* **tapped**) bater levemente. **~-dance** *n* sapateado *m*

tape /teɪp/ *n* (*for dressmaking*) fita *f*; (*sticky*) fita *f* adesiva. **(magnetic)** ~ fita *f* (magnética) □ *vt* (*tie*) atar, prender; (*stick*) colar; (*record*) gravar. **~-measure** *n* fita *f* métrica. **~ recorder** gravador *m*

taper /ˈteɪpə(r)/ *n* vela *f* comprida e fina □ *vt/i* ~ **(off)** estreitar(-se), afilar(-se). **~ed, ~ing** *adjs* (*fingers etc*) afilado; (*trousers*) afunilado

tapestry /ˈtæpɪstrɪ/ *n* tapeçaria *f*

tapioca /tæpɪˈəʊkə/ *n* tapioca *f*

tar /tɑː(r)/ *n* alcatrão *m* □ *vt* (*pt* **tarred**) alcatroar

target /ˈtɑːgɪt/ *n* alvo *m* □ *vt* ter como alvo

tariff /ˈtærɪf/ *n* tarifa *f*; (*on import*) direitos *mpl* aduaneiros

Tarmac /ˈtɑːmæk/ *n* macadame (alcatroado) *m*; (*runway*) pista *f*

tarnish /ˈtɑːnɪʃ/ *vt/i* (fazer) perder o brilho; (*stain*) manchar

tarpaulin /tɑːˈpɔːlɪn/ *n* lona *f* impermeável (alcatroada *or* encerada)

tart¹ /tɑːt/ *a* (**-er, -est**) ácido; (*fig: cutting*) mordaz, azedo

tart² /tɑːt/ *n* (*culin*) torta *f* de fruta, (P) tarte *f*; (*sl: prostitute*) prostituta *f*, mulher *f* da vida (*sl*) □ *vt* ~ **up** (*colloq*) embonecar(-se)

tartan /ˈtɑːtn/ *n* tecido *m* escocês □ *a* escocês

tartar /ˈtɑːtə(r)/ *n* (*on teeth*) tártaro *m*, (P) pedra *f*. ~ **sauce** molho *m* tártaro

task /tɑːsk/ *n* tarefa *f*, trabalho *m*.

take to ~ repreender, censurar. ~ **force** (*mil*) força-tarefa *f*

tassel /'tæsl/ *n* borla *f*

taste /teɪst/ *n* gosto *m*; (*fig: sample*) amostra *f* □ *vt* (*eat, enjoy*) saborear; (*try*) provar; (*perceive taste of*) sentir o gosto de □ *vi* ~ **of** or **like** ter o sabor de. **have a** ~ **of** (*experience*) provar. ~**ful** *a* de bom gosto. ~**fully** *adv* com bom gosto. ~**less** *a* insípido, insosso; (*fig: not in good taste*) sem gosto; (*fig: in bad taste*) de mau gosto

tasty /'teɪstɪ/ *a* (-**ier**, -**iest**) saboroso, gostoso

tat /tæt/ *see* **tit²**

tatter|s /'tætəz/ *npl* farrapos *mpl*. ~**ed** /-əd/ *a* esfarrapado

tattoo /tə'tuː/ *vt* tatuar □ *n* tatuagem *f*

tatty /'tætɪ/ *a* (-**ier**, -**iest**) (*colloq*) enxovalhado, em mau estado

taught /tɔːt/ *see* **teach**

taunt /tɔːnt/ *vt* escarnecer de, zombar de □ *n* escárnio *m*. ~**ing** *a* escarninho

Taurus /'tɔːrəs/ *n* (*astr*) Touro *m*, (*P*) Taurus *m*

taut /tɔːt/ *a* esticado, retesado; (*fig: of nerves*) tenso

tawdry /'tɔːdrɪ/ *a* (-**ier**, -**iest**) espalhafatoso e ordinário

tawny /'tɔːnɪ/ *a* fulvo

tax /tæks/ *n* taxa *f*, imposto *m*; (*on income*) imposto *m* de renda, (*P*) sobre o rendimento □ *vt* taxar, lançar impostos sobre, tributar; (*fig: put to test*) pôr à prova. ~-**collector** *n* cobrador *m* de impostos. ~-**free** *a* isento de imposto. ~ **relief** isenção *f* de imposto. ~ **return** declaração *f* do imposto de renda, (*P*) sobre o rendimento. ~ **year** ano *m* fiscal. ~**able** *a* tributável, passível de imposto. ~**ation** /-'seɪʃn/ *n* impostos *mpl*, tributação *f*. ~**ing** *a* penoso, difícil

taxi /'tæksɪ/ *n* (*pl* -**is**) táxi *m* □ *vi* (*pt* **taxied**, *pres p* **taxiing**) (*aviat*) rolar na pista, taxiar. ~-**cab** *n* táxi *m*. ~-**driver** *n* motorista *mf* de táxi. ~-**rank**, (*Amer*) ~ **stand** ponto *m* de táxis, (*P*) praça *f* de táxis

taxpayer /'tæksperə(r)/ *n* contribuinte *mf*

tea /tiː/ *n* chá *m*. **high** ~ refeição *f* leve à noite. ~-**bag** *n* saquinho *m* de chá. ~-**break** *n* intervalo *m* para o chá. ~-**cosy** *n* abafador *m*. ~-**leaf** *n* folha *f* de chá. ~-**set** *n* serviço *m* de chá. ~-**shop** *n* salão *m* or casa *f* de chá. ~-**time** *n* hora *f* do chá. ~-**towel** *n* pano *m* de prato

teach /tiːtʃ/ *vt* (*pt* **taught**) ensinar, lecionar, (*P*) leccionar (**sb sth** alg coisa a alguém) □ *vi* ensinar, ser

professor. ~**er** *n* professor *m*. ~**ing** *n* ensino *m*; (*doctrines*) ensinamento(s) *m* (*pl*) □ *a* pedagógico, de ensino; (*staff*) docente

teacup /'tiːkʌp/ *n* xícara *f* de chá, (*P*) chávena *f*

teak /tiːk/ *n* teca *f*

team /tiːm/ *n* equipe *f*, (*P*) equipa *f*; (*of oxen*) junta *f*; (*of horses*) parelha *f* □ *vi* ~ **up** juntar-se, associar-se (**with** a). ~-**work** *n* trabalho *m* de equipe, (*P*) equipa

teapot /'tiːpɒt/ *n* bule *m*

tear¹ /teə(r)/ *vt/i* (*pt* **tore**, *pp* **torn**) rasgar(-se); (*snatch*) arrancar, puxar; (*rush*) lançar-se, ir numa correria; (*fig*) dividir □ *n* rasgão *m*. ~ **o.s. away** arrancar-se (**from** de)

tear² /tɪə(r)/ *n* lágrima *f*. ~-**gas** *n* gases *mpl* lacrimogêneos, (*P*) lacrimogénios

tearful /'tɪəfl/ *a* lacrimoso, choroso. ~**ly** *adv* choroso, com (as) lágrimas nos olhos

tease /tiːz/ *vt* implicar; (*make fun of*) caçoar de

teaspoon /'tiːspuːn/ *n* colher *f* de chá. ~**ful** *n* (*pl* -**fuls**) colher *f* de chá cheia

teat /tiːt/ *n* (*of bottle*) bico *m*; (*of animal*) teta *f*

technical /'teknɪkl/ *a* técnico. ~**ity** /-'kælətɪ/ *n* questão *f* de ordem técnica. ~**ly** *adv* tecnicamente

technician /tek'nɪʃn/ *n* técnico *m*

technique /tek'niːk/ *n* técnica *f*

technolog|y /tek'nɒlədʒɪ/ *n* tecnologia *f*. ~**ical** /-ə'lɒdʒɪkl/ *a* tecnológico

teddy /'tedɪ/ *a* ~ (**bear**) ursinho *m* de pelúcia, (*P*) peluche

tedious /'tiːdɪəs/ *a* maçante

tedium /'tiːdɪəm/ *n* tédio *m*

tee /tiː/ *n* (*golf*) tee *m*

teem¹ /tiːm/ *vi* ~ (**with**) (*swarm*) pulular (de), fervilhar (de), abundar (em)

teem² /tiːm/ *vi* ~ (**with rain**) chover torrencialmente

teenage /'tiːneɪdʒ/ *a* juvenil, de/para adolescente. ~**r** /-ə(r)/ *n* jovem *mf*, adolescente *mf*

teens /tiːnz/ *npl* **in one's** ~ na adolescência, entre os 13 e os 19 anos

teeter /'tiːtə(r)/ *vi* cambalear, vacilar

teeth /tiːθ/ *see* **tooth**

teeth|e /tiːð/ *vi* começar a ter dentes. ~**ing troubles** (*fig*) problemas *mpl* iniciais

teetotaller /tiː'təʊtlə(r)/ *n* abstêmio *m*, (*P*) abstémio *m*

telecommunications /telɪkəmjuːnɪ-'keɪʃnz/ *npl* telecomunicações *fpl*

telegram /'telɪgræm/ *n* telegrama *m*

telegraph /'telɪgrɑːf/ *n* telégrafo *m* □

a telegráfico. ~ic /-'græfik/ *a* telegráfico

telepath|y /tɪ'lepəθɪ/ *n* telepatia *f*. ~ic /-ik/ *a* telepático

telephone /'telɪfəʊn/ *n* telefone *m* □ *vt* (*person*) telefonar a; (*message*) telefonar □ *vi* telefonar. ~ book lista *f* telefônica, (P) telefónica, guia *m* telefônico, (P) telefónico. ~ box, ~ booth cabine *f* telefônica, (P) telefónica. ~ call chamada *f*. ~ directory lista *f* telefônica, (P) telefónica, guia *m* telefônico, (P) telefónico. ~ number número *m* de telefone

telephonist /tɪ'lefənɪst/ *n* (*in exchange*) telefonista *mf*

telephoto /telɪ'fəʊtəʊ/ *n* ~ lens teleobjetiva *f*, (P) teleobjectiva *f*

telescop|e /'telɪskəʊp/ *n* telescópio *m* □ *vt/i* encaixar(-se). ~ic /-'skɒpɪk/ *a* telescópico

teletext /'telɪtekst/ *n* teletexto *m*

televise /'telɪvaɪz/ *vt* televisionar

television /'telɪvɪʒn/ *n* televisão *f*. ~ set aparelho *m* de televisão, televisor *m*

telex /'teleks/ *n* telex *m* □ *vt* transmitir por telex, telexar

tell /tel/ *vt* (*pt* told) dizer (sb sth alg coisa a alguém); (*story*) contar; (*distinguish*) distinguir, diferençar □ *vi* (*know*) ver-se, saber. I told you so bem lhe disse. ~ of falar de. ~ off (*colloq: scold*) ralhar, dar uma bronca em. ~ on (*have effect on*) afetar, (P) afectar; (*colloq: inform on*) fazer queixa de (*colloq*). ~-tale *n* mexeriqueiro *m*, fofoqueiro *m* □ *a* (*revealing*) revelador. tales mexericar, fofocar

telly /'telɪ/ *n* (*colloq*) TV *f* (*colloq*)

temp /temp/ *n* (*colloq*) empregado *m* temporário

temper /'tempə(r)/ *n* humor *m*, disposição *f*; (*anger*) mau humor *m* □ *vt* temperar. keep/lose one's ~ manter a calma/perder a calma *or* a cabeça, zangar-se

temperament /'temprəmənt/ *n* temperamento *m*. ~al /'mentl/ *a* caprichoso

temperance /'tempərəns/ *n* (*in drinking*) moderação *f*, sobriedade *f*

temperate /'tempərət/ *a* moderado, comedido; (*climate*) temperado

temperature /'temprətʃə(r)/ *n* temperatura *f*. have a ~ estar com *or* ter febre

tempest /'tempɪst/ *n* tempestade *f*, temporal *m*

tempestuous /tem'pestʃʊəs/ *a* tempestuoso

template /'templ(e)ɪt/ *n* molde *m*

temple¹ /'templ/ *n* templo *m*

temple² /'templ/ *n* (*anat*) têmpora *f*, fonte *f*

tempo /'tempəʊ/ *n* (*pl* -os) (*mus*) tempo *m*; (*pace*) ritmo *m*

temporar|y /'tempɪɪ/ *a* temporário, provisório. ~ily *adv* temporariamente, provisoriamente

tempt /tempt/ *vt* tentar. ~ sb to do dar a alguém vontade de fazer, tentar alguém a fazer. ~ation /-'teɪʃn/ *n* tentação *f*. ~ing *a* tentador

ten /ten/ *a* & *n* dez (*m*)

tenac|ious /tɪ'neɪʃəs/ *a* tenaz. ~ity /-'æsətɪ/ *n* tenacidade *f*

tenant /'tenənt/ *n* inquilino *m*, locatário *m*

tend¹ /tend/ *vt* tomar conta de, cuidar de

tend² /tend/ *vi* ~ to (*be apt to*) tender a, ter tendência para

tendency /'tendənsɪ/ *n* tendência *f*

tender¹ /'tendə(r)/ *a* (*soft, delicate*) terno; (*sore, painful*) sensível, dolorido; (*loving*) terno, meigo. ~-hearted *a* compassivo. ~ly *adv* (*lovingly*) ternamente, meigamente; (*delicately*) delicadamente. ~ness *n* (*love*) ternura *f*, meiguice *f*

tender² /'tendə(r)/ *vt* (*money*) oferecer; (*apologies, resignation*) apresentar □ *vi* ~ (for) apresentar orçamento (para) □ *n* (*comm*) orçamento *m*. legal ~ (*money*) moeda *f* corrente

tendon /'tendən/ *n* tendão *m*

tenement /'tenəmənt/ *n* prédio *m* de apartamentos de renda moderada; (*Amer: slum*) prédio *m* pobre

tenet /'tenɪt/ *n* princípio *m*, dogma *m*

tennis /'tenɪs/ *n* tênis *m*, (P) ténis *m*. ~ court quadra *f* de tênis, (P) court *m* de ténis

tenor /'tenə(r)/ *n* (*meaning*) teor *m*; (*mus*) tenor *m*

tense¹ /tens/ *n* (*gram*) tempo *m*

tense² /tens/ *a* (-er, -est) tenso □ *vt* (*muscles*) retesar

tension /'tenʃn/ *n* tensão *f*

tent /tent/ *n* tenda *f*, barraca *f*. ~-peg *n* estaca *f*

tentacle /'tentəkl/ *n* tentáculo *m*

tentative /'tentətɪv/ *a* provisório; (*hesitant*) hesitante. ~ly *adv* tentativamente, a título experimental; (*hesitantly*) hesitantemente

tenterhooks /'tentəhʊks/ *npl* on ~ em suspense

tenth /tenθ/ *a* & *n* décimo (*m*)

tenuous /'tenjʊəs/ *a* tênue, (P) ténue

tepid /'tepɪd/ *a* tépido, morno

term /tɜːm/ *n* (*word*) termo *m*; (*limit*) prazo *m*, termo *m*; (*schol etc*) período *m*, trimestre *m*; (*Amer*) semestre *m*; (*of imprisonment*) (duração de) pena *f*. ~s (*conditions*) condições *fpl* □ *vt* designar, denominar, chamar. on good/

bad ~s de boas/más relações. **not on speaking** ~s de relações cortadas. **come to** ~s **with** chegar a um acordo com; (*become resigned to*) resignar-se a. ~ **of office** (*pol*) mandato *m*

terminal /'tɜ:mml/ *a* terminal, final; (*illness*) fatal, mortal □ *n* (*oil, computer*) terminal *m*; (*rail*) estação *f* terminal; (*electr*) borne *m*. **(air)** ~ terminal *m* (de avião)

terminat|e /'tɜ:mmeɪt/ *vt* terminar, pôr termo a □ *vi* terminar. ~**ion** /-'neɪʃn/ *n* término *m*, (*P*) terminação *f*, termo *m*

terminology /tɜ:mɪ'nɒlədʒɪ/ *n* terminologia *f*

terminus /'tɜ:mməs/ *n* (*pl* -**ni** /-naɪ/) (*rail, coach*) estação *f* terminal

terrace /'terəs/ *n* terraço *m*; (*in cultivation*) socalco *m*; (*houses*) casas *fpl* em fileira contínua, lance *m* de casas. **the** ~**s** (*sport*) arquibancada *f*. ~**d house** casa *f* ladeada por outras casas

terrain /te'rem/ *n* terreno *m*

terribl|e /'terəbl/ *a* terrível. ~**y** *adv* terrivelmente; (*colloq: very*) extremamente, espantosamente

terrific /tə'rɪfɪk/ *a* terrífico, tremendo; (*colloq: excellent; great*) tremendo. ~**ally** *adv* (*colloq: very*) tremendamente (*colloq*); (*colloq: very well*) lindamente, maravilhosamente

terrif|y /'terɪfaɪ/ *vt* aterrar, aterrorizar. **be** ~**ied** of ter pavor de

territorial /terɪ'tɔ:rɪəl/ *a* territorial

territory /'terɪtrɪ/ *n* território *m*

terror /'terə(r)/ *n* terror *m*, pavor *m*

terroris|t /'terərɪst/ *n* terrorista *mf*. ~**m** /-zəm/ *n* terrorismo *m*

terrorize /'terəraɪz/ *vt* aterrorizar, aterrar

terse /tɜ:s/ *a* conciso, lapidar; (*curt*) lacônico, (*P*) lacónico

test /test/ *n* teste *m*, exame *m*, prova *f*; (*schol*) prova *f*, teste *m*; (*of goods*) controle *m*; (*of machine etc*) ensaio *m*; (*of strength*) prova *f* □ *vt* examinar; (*check*) controlar; (*try*) ensaiar; (*pupil*) interrogar. **put to the** ~ pôr à prova. ~ **match** jogo *m* internacional. ~**-tube** *n* proveta *f*. ~**-tube baby** bebê *m* de proveta

testament /'testəmənt/ *n* testamento *m*. **Old/New T**~ Antigo/Novo Testamento *m*

testicle /'testɪkl/ *n* testículo *m*

testify /'testɪfaɪ/ *vt/i* testificar, testemunhar, depôr

testimonial /testɪ'məʊnɪəl/ *n* carta *f* de recomendação

testimony /'testɪmənɪ/ *n* testemunho *m*

tetanus /'tetənəs/ *n* tétano *m*

tether /'teðə(r)/ *vt* prender com corda □ *n* **be at the end of one's** ~ não poder mais, estar nas últimas

text /tekst/ *n* texto *m*

textbook /'tekstbʊk/ *n* compêndio *m*, manual *m*, livro *m* de texto

textile /'tekstaɪl/ *n* & *a* têxtil (*m*)

texture /'tekstʃə(r)/ *n* (*of fabric*) textura *f*; (*of paper*) grão *m*

Thai /taɪ/ *a* & *n* tailandês (*m*). ~**land** *n* Tailândia *f*

Thames /temz/ *n* Tâmisa *m*

than /ðæn/; *unstressed* /ðən/ *conj* que, do que; (*with numbers*) de. **more/less** ~ **ten** mais/menos de dez

thank /θæŋk/ *vt* agradecer. ~ **you!** obrigado! ~**s!** (*colloq*) (*P*) obrigadinho! (*colloq*). ~**s** *npl* agradecimentos *mpl*. ~**s to** graças a. **T**~**sgiving (Day)** (*Amer*) Dia *m* de Ação, (*P*) Acção de Graças

thankful /'θæŋkfl/ *a* grato, agradecido, reconhecido (**for** por). ~**ly** *adv* com gratidão; (*happily*) felizmente

thankless /'θæŋklɪs/ *a* ingrato, mal agradecido

that /ðæt/; *unstressed* /ðət/ *a* & *pron* (*pl* those) esse/essa, esses/essas; (*more distant*) aquele/aquela, aqueles /aquelas; (*neuter*) isso *invar*; (*more distant*) aquilo *invar* □ *adv* tão, tanto, de tal modo □ *rel pron* que □ *conj* que. ~ **boy** esse/aquele rapaz. **what is** ~? o que é isso? **who is** ~? quem é? **is** ~ **you?** é você? **give me** ~ **(one)** dá-me esse. ~ **is (to say)** isto é, quer dizer. **after** ~ depois disso. **the day** ~ o dia em que. ~ **much** tanto assim, tanto como isto

thatch /θætʃ/ *n* colmo *m*. ~**ed** *a* de colmo. ~**ed cottage** casa *f* com telhado de colmo

thaw /θɔ:/ *vt/i* derreter(-se), degelar; (*food*) descongelar □ *n* degelo *m*, derretimento *m*

the /*before vowel* ðɪ/, *before consonant* ðə/, *stressed* ði:/ *a* o, a (*pl* os, as). **of** ~, **from** ~ do, da (*pl* dos, das). **at** ~, **to** ~ ao, à (*pl* aos, às), para o/a/os/ as. **in** ~ no, na (*pl* nos, nas). **by** ~ **hour** a cada hora □ *adv* **all** ~ **better** tanto melhor. ~ **more...** ~ **more...** quanto mais... tanto mais...

theatre /'θɪətə(r)/ *n* teatro *m*

theatrical /θɪ'ætrɪkl/ *a* teatral

theft /θeft/ *n* roubo *m*

their /ðeə(r)/ *a* deles, delas, seu

theirs /ðeəz/ *poss pron* o(s) seu(s), a(s) sua(s), o(s) deles, a(s) delas. **it is** ~ é (o) deles/delas *or* o seu

them /ðem/; *unstressed* /ðəm/ *pron* os, as; (*after prep*) eles, elas. **(to)** ~ lhes

theme /θi:m/ *n* tema *m*

themselves /ðəm'selvz/ *pron* eles

mesmos/próprios, elas mesmas/ próprias; (*reflexive*) se; (*after prep*) si (mesmos, próprios). **by ~** sozinhos. **with ~** consigo

then /ðen/ *adv* (*at that time*) então, nessa altura; (*next*) depois, em seguida; (*in that case*) então, nesse caso; (*therefore*) então, portanto, por conseguinte □ *a* (de) então. **from ~ on** desde então

theolog|y /θɪˈɒlədʒɪ/ *n* teologia *f*. **~ian** /θɪəˈlɒʊdʒən/ *n* teólogo *m*

theorem /ˈθɪərəm/ *n* teorema *m*

theor|y /ˈθɪərɪ/ *n* teoria *f*. **~etical** /ˈretɪkl/ *a* teórico

therapeutic /θerəˈpjuːtɪk/ *a* terapêutico

therap|y /ˈθerəpɪ/ *n* terapia *f*. **~ist** *n* terapeuta *mf*

there /ðeə(r)/ *adv* aí, ali, lá; (*over there*) lá, acolá □ *int* (*triumphant*) pronto, aí está; (*consoling*) então, vamos lá. **he goes ~** ele vai aí *or* lá. **~ he goes** aí vai ele. **~ is, ~ are** há. **~ you are** (*giving*) toma. **~ and then** logo ali. **~abouts** *adv* por aí. **~after** *adv* daí em diante, depois disso. **~by** *adv* desse modo

therefore /ˈðeəfɔː(r)/ *adv* por isso, portanto, por conseguinte

thermal /ˈθɜːml/ *a* térmico

thermometer /θəˈmɒmɪtə(r)/ *n* termômetro *m*, (*P*) termómetro *m*

Thermos /ˈθɜːməs/ *n* garrafa *f* térmica, (*P*) termo *m*

thermostat /ˈθɜːməstæt/ *n* termostato *m*

thesaurus /θɪˈsɔːrəs/ *n* (*pl* **-ri** /-raɪ/) dicionário *m* de sinônimos, (*P*) sinónimos

these /ðiːz/ *see* **this**

thesis /ˈθiːsɪs/ *n* (*pl* **theses** /-siːz/) tese *f*

they /ðeɪ/ *pron* eles, elas. **~ say** (**that**)... diz-se *or* dizem que...

thick /θɪk/ *a* (**-er, -est**) espesso, grosso; (*colloq: stupid*) estúpido □ *adv* = **thickly** □ *n* **in the ~ of** no meio de. **~-skinned** *a* insensível. **~ly** *adv* espessamente; (*spread*) em camada espessa. **~ness** *n* espessura *f*, grossura *f*

thicken /ˈθɪkən/ *vt/i* engrossar, espessar(-se). **the plot ~s** o enredo complica-se

thickset /θɪkˈset/ *a* (*person*) atarracado

thief /θiːf/ *n* (*pl* **thieves** /θiːvz/) ladrão *m*, gatuno *m*

thigh /θaɪ/ *n* coxa *f*

thimble /ˈθɪmbl/ *n* dedal *m*

thin /θɪn/ *a* (**thinner, thinnest**) (*slender*) estreito, fino, delgado; (*lean, not plump*) magro; (*sparse*) ralo, escasso;

(*flimsy*) leve, fino; (*soup*) aguado; (*hair*) ralo □ *adv* = **thinly** □ *vt/i* (*pt* **thinned**) (*of liquid*) diluir(-se); (*of fog etc*) dissipar(-se); (*of hair*) rarear. **~ out** (*in quantity*) diminuir, reduzir; (*seedlings etc*) desbastar. **~ly** *adv* (*sparsely*) esparsamente. **~ness** *n* (*of board, wire etc*) finura *f*; (*of person*) magreza *f*

thing /θɪŋ/ *n* coisa *f*. **~s** (*belongings*) pertences *mpl*. **the best ~ is to** o melhor é. **for one ~** em primeiro lugar. **just the ~** exatamente o que era preciso. **poor ~** coitado

think /θɪŋk/ *vt/i* (*pt* **thought**) pensar (**about, of** em); (*carefully*) reflectir, (*P*) reflectir (**about, of** em). **I ~ so** eu acho que sim. **~ better of it** (*change one's mind*) pensar melhor. **~ nothing of** achar natural. **~ of** (*hold opinion of*) pensar de, achar de. **~ over** pensar bem em. **~-tank** *n* comissão *f* de peritos. **~ up** inventar. **~er** *n* pensador *m*

third /θɜːd/ *a* terceiro □ *n* terceiro *m*; (*fraction*) terço *m*. **~-party insurance** seguro *m* contra terceiros. **~-rate** *a* inferior, medíocre. **T~ World** Terceiro Mundo *m*. **~ly** *adv* em terceiro lugar

thirst /θɜːst/ *n* sede *f*. **~y** *a* sequioso, sedento. **be ~y** estar com *or* ter sede. **~ily** *adv* sofregamente

thirteen /θɜːˈtiːn/ *a & n* treze (*m*). **~th** *a & n* décimo terceiro (*m*)

thirt|y /ˈθɜːtɪ/ *a & n* trinta (*m*). **~ieth** *a & n* trigésimo (*m*)

this /ðɪs/ *a & pron* (*pl* **these**) este, esta □ *pron* isto *invar*. **~ one** este, esta. **these ones** estes, estas. **~ boy** este rapaz. **~ is** isto é. **after ~** depois disto. **like ~** assim. **~ is the man** este é o homem. **~ far** até aqui. **~ morning** esta manhã. **~ Wednesday** esta quarta-feira

thistle /ˈθɪsl/ *n* cardo *m*

thorn /θɔːn/ *n* espinho *m*, pico *m*. **~y** *a* espinhoso; (*fig*) bicudo, espinhoso

thorough /ˈθʌrə/ *a* consciencioso; (*deep*) completo, profundo; (*cleaning, washing*) a fundo. **~ly** *adv* (*clean, study etc*) completo, a fundo; (*very*) perfeitamente, muito bem

thoroughbred /ˈθʌrəbred/ *n* (*horse etc*) puro-sangue *m invar*

thoroughfare /ˈθʌrəfeə(r)/ *n* artéria *f*. **no ~** passagem *f* proibida

those /ðəʊz/ *see* **that**

though /ðəʊ/ *conj* se bem que, embora, conquanto □ *adv* (*colloq*) contudo, no entanto

thought /θɔːt/ *see* **think** □ *n* pensamento *m*; idéia *f*. **on second ~s** pensando bem

thoughtful /'θɔːtfl/ a pensativo; (*considerate*) atencioso, solícito. ~ly *adv* pensativamente; (*considerately*) com consideração, atenciosamente

thoughtless /'θɔːtlɪs/ a irrefletido, (P) irreflectido; (*inconsiderate*) pouco atencioso. ~ly *adv* sem pensar; (*inconsiderately*) sem consideração

thousand /'θaʊznd/ a & n mil (*m*). ~s of milhares de. ~th a & n milésimo (*m*)

thrash /θræʃ/ *vt* surrar, espancar; (*defeat*) dar uma surra *or* sova em. ~ **about** debater-se. ~ **out** debater a fundo, discutir bem

thread /θred/ *n* fio *m*; (*for sewing*) linha *f* de coser; (*of screw*) rosca *f* □ *vt* enfiar. ~ **one's way** abrir caminho, furar

threadbare /'θredbeə(r)/ a puído, surrado

threat /θret/ *n* ameaça *f*

threaten /'θretn/ *vt/i* ameaçar. ~ingly *adv* com ar ameaçador, ameaçadoramente

three /θriː/ a & n três (*m*)

thresh /θreʃ/ *vt* (*corn etc*) malhar, debulhar

threshold /'θreʃəʊld/ *n* limiar *m*, soleira *f*; (*fig*) limiar *m*

threw /θruː/ *see* throw

thrift /θrɪft/ *n* economia *f*, poupança *f*. ~y a económico, (P) económico, poupado

thrill /θrɪl/ *n* arrepio *m* de emoção, frêmito *m*, (P) frémito *m* □ *vt* excitar(-se), emocionar(-se), (fazer) vibrar. be ~ed estar/ficar encantado. ~ing a excitante, emocionante

thriller /'θrɪlə(r)/ *n* livro *m or* filme *m* de suspense

thriv|e /θraɪv/ *vi* (*pt* **thrived** *or* **throve**, *pp* **thrived** *or* **thriven**) prosperar, florescer; (*grow strong*) crescer, dar-se bem (**on** com). ~ing a próspero

throat /θrəʊt/ *n* garganta *f*. have a sore ~ ter dores de garganta

throb /θrɒb/ *vi* (*pt* **throbbed**) (*wound, head*) latejar; (*heart*) palpitar, bater; (*engine; fig*) vibrar, trepidar □ *n* (*of pain*) latejo *m*, espasmo *m*; (*of heart*) palpitação *f*, batida *f*; (*of engine*) vibração *f*, trepidação *f*. ~bing a (*pain*) latejante

throes /θrəʊz/ *npl* in the ~ of (*fig*) às voltas com, no meio de

thrombosis /θrɒm'bəʊsɪs/ *n* trombose *f*

throne /θrəʊn/ *n* trono *m*

throng /θrɒŋ/ *n* multidão *f* □ *vt/i* apinhar(-se); (*arrive*) afluir

throttle /'θrɒtl/ *n* (*auto*) válvula-borboleta *f*, estrangulador *m*, acelerador *m* de mão □ *vt* estrangular

through /θruː/ *prep* através de, por; (*during*) durante; (*by means or way of, out of*) por; (*by reason of*) por, por causa de □ *adv* através; (*entirely*) completamente, até o fim □ a (*train, traffic etc*) direto, (P) directo. be ~ ter acabado (**with** com); (*telephone*) estar ligado. **come** *or* **go** ~ (*cross, pierce*) atravessar. **get** ~ (*exam*) passar. be **wet** ~ estar ensopado *or* encharcado

throughout /θruː'aʊt/ *prep* durante, por todo. ~ **the country** por todo o país afora. ~ **the day** durante toda a dia, pelo dia afora □ *adv* completamente; (*place*) por toda a parte; (*time*) durante todo o tempo

throw /θrəʊ/ *vt* (*pt* **threw**, *pp* **thrown**) atirar, jogar, lançar; (*colloq: baffle*) desconcertar □ *n* lançamento *m*; (*of dice*) lance *m*. ~ **a party** (*colloq*) dar uma festa. ~ **away** jogar fora, (P) deitar fora. ~ **off** (*get rid of*) livrar-se de. ~ **out** (*person*) expulsar; (*reject*) rejeitar. ~ **over** (*desert*) abandonar, deixar. ~ **up** (*one's arms*) levantar; (*resign from*) abandonar; (*colloq: vomit*) vomitar

thrush /θrʌʃ/ *n* (*bird*) tordo *m*

thrust /θrʌst/ *vt* (*pt* **thrust**) arremeter, empurrar, impelir □ *n* empurrão *m*, arremetida *f*. ~ **into** (*put*) enfiar em, mergulhar em. ~ **upon** (*force on*) impôr a

thud /θʌd/ *n* som *m* surdo, baque *m*

thug /θʌɡ/ *n* bandido *m*, facínora *m*, malfeitor *m*

thumb /θʌm/ *n* polegar *m* □ *vt* (*book*) manusear. ~ **a lift** pedir carona, (P) boleia. **under sb's** ~ completamente dominado por alguém. ~-**index** *n* índice *m* de dedo

thumbtack /'θʌmtæk/ *n* (*Amer*) percevejo *m*

thump /θʌmp/ *vt/i* bater (em), dar pancadas (em); (*with fists*) dar murros (em); (*piano*) martelar (em); (*of heart*) bater com força □ *n* pancada *f*; (*thud*) baque *m*. ~ing a (*colloq*) enorme

thunder /'θʌndə(r)/ *n* trovão *m*, trovoada *f*; (*loud noise*) estrondo *m* □ *vi* (*weather, person*) trovejar. ~ **past** passar como um raio. ~y a (*weather*) tempestuoso

thunderbolt /'θʌndəbəʊlt/ *n* raio *m* e ribombo *m* de trovão; (*fig*) raio *m* fulminante (*fig*)

thunderstorm /'θʌndəstɔːm/ *n* tempestade *f* com trovoadas, temporal *m*

Thursday /'θɜːzdɪ/ *n* quinta-feira *f*

thus /ðʌs/ *adv* assim, desta maneira. ~ **far** até agora

thwart /θwɔːt/ *vt* frustrar, contrariar

thyme /taɪm/ *n* tomilho *m*

tiara /tɪ'ɑːrə/ *n* tiara *f*, diadema *m*

tic /tɪk/ n tique m

tick¹ /tɪk/ n (sound) tique-taque m; (mark) sinal (V) m; (colloq: moment) instantinho m □ vi fazer tique-taque □ vt ~ (off) marcar com sinal (V). ~ off (colloq: scold) dar uma bronca em (colloq). ~ over (engine, factory) funcionar em marcha lenta, (P) no "ralenti"

tick² /tɪk/ n (insect) carrapato m

ticket /'tɪkɪt/ n bilhete m; (label) etiqueta f; (for traffic offence) aviso m de multa. ~-collector n (railway) guarda m. ~-office n bilheteira f

tickle /'tɪkl/ vt fazer cócegas; (fig: amuse) divertir □ n cócegas fpl, comichão m

ticklish /'tɪklɪʃ/ a coceguento, sensível a cócegas; (fig) delicado, melindroso

tidal /'taɪdl/ a de marés, que tem marés. ~ wave onda f gigantesca; (fig) onda f de sentimento popular

tiddly-winks /'tɪdlɪwɪŋks/ n (game) jogo m da pulga

tide /taɪd/ n maré f; (of events) marcha f, curso m. high ~ maré f cheia, preia-mar f. low ~ maré f baixa, baixa-mar f □ vt ~ over (help temporarily) agüentar, (P) aguentar

tid|y /'taɪdɪ/ a (-ier, -iest) (room) arrumado; (appearance, work) asseado, cuidado; (methodical) bem ordenado; (colloq: amount) belo (colloq) □ vt arrumar, arranjar. ~ily adv com cuidado. ~iness n arrumação f, ordem f

tie /taɪ/ vt (pres p tying) atar, amarrar, prender; (link) ligar, vincular; (a knot) dar, fazer □ vi (sport) empatar □ n fio m, cordel m; (necktie) gravata f; (link) laço m, vínculo m; (sport) empate m. ~ in with estar ligado com, relacionar-se com. ~ up amarrar, atar; (animal) prender; (money) imobilizar; (occupy) ocupar

tier /tɪə(r)/ n cada fila f, camada f, prateleira f etc colocada em cima de outra; (in stadium) bancada f; (of cake) andar m; (of society) camada f

tiff /tɪf/ n arrufo m

tiger /'taɪɡə(r)/ n tigre m

tight /taɪt/ a (-er, -est) (clothes) apertado, justo; (rope) esticado, tenso; (control) rigoroso; (knot, schedule, lid) apertado; (colloq: drunk) embriagado (colloq) □ adv = tightly. be in a ~ corner (fig) estar em apuros or num aperto, (P) estar entalado (colloq). ~-fisted a sovina, pão-duro, (P) agarrado (colloq). ~ly adv bem; (squeeze) com força

tighten /'taɪtn/ vt/i (rope) esticar; (bolt, control) apertar. ~ up on apertar o cinto

tightrope /'taɪtrəʊp/ n corda f (de acrobacias). ~ walker funâmbulo m

tights /taɪts/ npl collants mpl, meias-colant fpl

tile /taɪl/ n (on wall, floor) ladrilho m, azulejo m; (on roof) telha f □ vt ladrilhar, pôr azulejos em; (roof) telhar, cobrir com telhas

till¹ /tɪl/ vt (land) cultivar

till² /tɪl/ prep & conj = until

till³ /tɪl/ n caixa (registadora) f

tilt /tɪlt/ vt/i inclinar(-se), pender □ n (slope) inclinação f. (at) full ~ a toda a velocidade

timber /'tɪmbə(r)/ n madeira f (de construção); (trees) árvores fpl

time /taɪm/ n tempo m; (moment) momento m; (epoch) época f, tempo m; (by clock) horas fpl; (occasion) vez f, (rhythm) compasso m. ~s (multiplying) vezes □ vt escolher a hora para; (measure) marcar o tempo; (sport) cronometrar; (regulate) acertar. at ~s às vezes. for the ~ being por agora, por enquanto. from ~ to ~ de vez em quando. have a good ~ divertir-se. have no ~ for não ter paciência para. in no ~ num instante. in ~ a tempo; (eventually) com o tempo. in two days ~ daqui a dois dias. on ~ na hora, (P) a horas. take your ~ não se apresse. what's the ~? que horas são? ~ bomb bomba-relógio f. ~-limit n prazo m. ~ off tempo m livre. ~-sharing n time-sharing m. ~ zone fuso m horário

timeless /'taɪmlɪs/ a intemporal; (unending) eterno

timely /'taɪmlɪ/ a oportuno

timer /'taɪmə(r)/ n (techn) relógio m; (with sand) ampulheta f

timetable /'taɪmteɪbl/ n horário m

timid /'tɪmɪd/ a tímido; (fearful) assustadiço, medroso. ~ly adv timidamente

timing /'taɪmɪŋ/ n (measuring) cronometragem f; (of artist) ritmo m; (moment) cálculo m do tempo, timing m. good/bad ~ (moment) momento m bem/mal escolhido

tin /tɪn/ n estanho m; (container) lata f □ vt (pt tinned) estanhar; (food) enlatar. ~ foil papel m de alumínio. ~-opener n abridor m de latas, (P) abre-latas m. ~ plate lata f, folha(-de-Flandes) f. ~ned foods conservas fpl. ~ny a (sound) metálico

tinge /tɪndʒ/ vt ~ (with) tingir (de); (fig) dar um toque (de) □ n tom m, matiz m; (fig) toque m

tingle /'tɪŋgl/ vi (sting) arder; (prickle) picar □ n ardor m; (prickle) picadela f

tinker /'tɪŋkə(r)/ n latoeiro m ambulante □ vi ~ **(with)** mexer (em), tentar consertar

tinkle /'tɪŋkl/ n tinido m, tilintar m □ vt/i tilintar

tinsel /'tɪnsl/ n fio m prateado/dourado, enfeites mpl metálicos de Natal; (fig) falso brilho m, ouropel m

tint /tɪnt/ n tom m, matiz m; (for hair) tintura f, tinta f □ vt tingir, colorir

tiny /'taɪnɪ/ a (-ier, -iest) minúsculo, pequenino

tip[1] /tɪp/ n ponta f. **(have sth) on the ~ of one's tongue** ter alg coisa na ponta de língua

tip[2] /tɪp/ vt/i (pt **tipped**) (tilt) inclinar(-se); (overturn) virar(-se); (pour) colocar, (P) deitar; (empty) despejar(-se) □ n (money) gorjeta f; (advice) sugestão f, dica f (colloq); (for rubbish) lixeira f. **~ off** avisar, prevenir. **~-off** n (warning) aviso m; (information) informação f

tipsy /'tɪpsɪ/ a ligeiramente embriagado, alegre, tocado

tiptoe /'tɪptəʊ/ n **on ~** na ponta dos pés

tir|**e**[1] /'taɪə(r)/ vt/i cansar(-se) (of de). **~eless** a incansável, infatigável. **~ing** a fatigante, cansativo

tire[2] /'taɪə(r)/ n (Amer) pneu m

tired /taɪəd/ a cansado, fatigado. **~ of** (sick of) farto de. **~ out** morto de cansaço

tiresome /'taɪəsəm/ a maçador, aborrecido, chato (sl)

tissue /'tɪʃuː/ n tecido m; (handkerchief) lenço m de papel. **~-paper** n papel m de seda

tit[1] /tɪt/ n (bird) chapim m, canário-da-terra m

tit[2] /tɪt/ n **give ~ for tat** pagar na mesma moeda

titbit /'tɪtbɪt/ n petisco m

titillate /'tɪtɪleɪt/ vt excitar, titilar, (P) dar gozo a

title /'taɪtl/ n título m. **~-deed** n título m de propriedade. **~-page** n página f de rosto, (P) frontispício m. **~-role** n papel m principal

titter /'tɪtə(r)/ vi rir com riso abafado

to /tuː/; unstressed /tə/ prep a, para; (as far as) até; (towards) para; (of attitude) para (com) □ adv **push** or **pull ~** (close) fechar. **~ Portugal** (for a short time) a Portugal; (to stay) para Portugal. **~ the baker's** para o padeiro, (P) ao padeiro. **~ do/sit/etc** (infinitive) fazer/sentar-se/etc; (expressing purpose) para fazer/para se sentar/etc. **it's ten ~ six** são dez para as seis, faltam dez para as seis. **go ~ and fro** andar de um lado para outro. **husband/etc-~-be** n futuro marido

m/etc. **~-do** n (fuss) agitação f, alvoroço m

toad /təʊd/ n sapo m

toadstool /'təʊdstuːl/ n cogumelo m venenoso

toady /'təʊdɪ/ n lambe-botas mf, puxa-saco m □ vi puxar saco

toast /təʊst/ n fatia f de pão torrado, torrada f; (drink) brinde m, saúde f □ vt (bread) torrar; (drink to) brindar, beber à saúde de. **~er** n torradeira f

tobacco /tə'bækəʊ/ n tabaco m

tobacconist /tə'bækənɪst/ n vendedor m de tabaco, homem m da tabacaria (colloq). **~'s shop** tabacaria f

toboggan /tə'bɒgən/ n tobogã m, (P) toboggan m

today /tə'deɪ/ n & adv hoje (m)

toddler /'tɒdlə(r)/ n criança f que está aprendendo a andar

toe /təʊ/ n dedo m do pé; (of shoe, stocking) biqueira f □ vt **~ the line** andar na linha. **on one's ~s** alerta, vigilante. **~-hold** n apoio (precário) m. **~-nail** n unha f do dedo do pé

toffee /'tɒfɪ/ n puxa-puxa m, (P) caramelo m. **~-apple** n maçã f caramelizada

together /tə'geðə(r)/ adv junto, juntamente, juntos; (at the same time) ao mesmo tempo. **~ with** juntamente com. **~ness** n camaradagem f, companheirismo m

toil /tɔɪl/ vi labutar □ n labuta f, labor m

toilet /'tɔɪlɪt/ n banheiro m, (P) casa f de banho; (grooming) toalete f. **~-paper** n papel m higiênico, (P) higiénico. **~-roll** n rolo m de papel higiênico, (P) higiénico. **~ water** água-de-colônia f

toiletries /'tɔɪlɪtrɪz/ npl artigos mpl de toalete

token /'təʊkən/ n sinal m, prova f; (voucher) cheque m; (coin) ficha f □ a simbólico

told /təʊld/ see **tell** □ a **all ~** (all in all) ao todo

tolerabl|**e** /'tɒlərəbl/ a tolerável; (not bad) sofrível, razoável. **~y** adv (work, play) razoavelmente

toleran|**t** /'tɒlərənt/ a tolerante (of para com). **~ce** n tolerância f. **~tly** adv com tolerância

tolerate /'tɒləreɪt/ vt tolerar

toll[1] /təʊl/ n pedágio m, (P) portagem f. **death ~** número m de mortos. **take its ~** (of age) fazer sentir o seu peso

toll[2] /təʊl/ vt/i (of bell) dobrar

tomato /tə'maːtəʊ/ n (pl -oes) tomate m

tomb /tuːm/ n túmulo m, sepultura f

tomboy /'tɒmbɔɪ/ n menina f levada (E masculinizada), (P) maria-rapaz f

tombstone /'tu:mstəʊn/ n lápide f, pedra f tumular

tome /təʊm/ n tomo m, volume m

tomfoolery /tɒm'fu:lərɪ/ n disparates mpl, imbecilidades fpl

tomorrow /tə'mɒrəʊ/ n & adv amanhã (m). ~ **morning/night** amanhã de manhã/à noite

ton /tʌn/ n tonelada f (= 1016 kg). **(metric)** ~ tonelada f (= 1000 kg). ~**s of** (colloq) montes de (colloq), (P) carradas de (colloq)

tone /təʊn/ n tom m; (of radio, telephone etc) sinal m; (colour) tom m, tonalidade f; (med) tonicidade f □ vt ~ **down** atenuar □ vi ~ **in** combinarse, harmonizar-se (**with** com). ~ **up** (muscles) tonificar. ~-**deaf** a sem ouvido musical

tongs /tɒŋz/ n tenaz f; (for sugar) pinça f; (for hair) pinça f

tongue /tʌŋ/ n língua f. ~-**in-cheek** a & adv sem ser a sério, com ironia. ~-**tied** a calado. ~-**twister** n trava-língua m

tonic /'tɒnɪk/ n (med) tônico m, (P) tónico m; (mus) tônica f, (P) tónica f □ a tônico, (P) tónico

tonight /tə'naɪt/ adv & n hoje à noite, logo à noite, esta noite (f)

tonne /tʌn/ n (metric) tonelada f

tonsil /'tɒnsl/ n amígdala f

tonsillitis /tɒnsɪ'laɪtɪs/ n amigdalite f

too /tu:/ adv demasiado, demais; (also) também, igualmente; (colloq: very) muito. ~ **many** a demais, demasiados. ~ **much** a & adv demais, demasiado

took /tʊk/ see take

tool /tu:l/ n (carpenter's, plumber's etc) ferramenta f; (gardener's) utensílio m; (fig: person) joguete m. ~-**bag** n saco m de ferramenta

toot /tu:t/ n toque m de buzina □ vt/i ~ **(the horn)** buzinar, tocar a buzina

tooth /tu:θ/ n (pl teeth) dente m. ~**less** a desdentado

toothache /'tu:θeɪk/ n dor f de dentes

toothbrush /'tu:θbrʌʃ/ n escova f de dentes

toothpaste /'tu:θpeɪst/ n pasta f de dentes, dentifrício m

toothpick /'tu:θpɪk/ n palito m

top[1] /tɒp/ n (highest point; upper part) alto m, cimo m, topo m; (of hill; fig) cume m; (upper surface) cimo m, topo m; (surface of table) tampo m; (lid) tampa f; (of bottle) rolha f; (of list) cabeça f □ a (shelf etc) de cima, superior; (in rank) primeiro; (best) melhor; (distinguished) eminente; (maximum) máximo □ vt (pt topped) (exceed) ultrapassar, ir acima de. **from** ~ **to bottom** de alto a baixo. **on** ~ **of** em

cima de; (fig) além de. **on** ~ **of that** ainda por cima. ~ **gear** (auto) a velocidade mais alta. ~ **hat** chapéu m alto. ~-**heavy** a mais pesado na parte de cima. ~ **secret** ultra-secreto. ~ **up** encher. ~**ped with** coberto de

top[2] /tɒp/ n (toy) pião m. **sleep like a** ~ dormir como uma pedra

topic /'tɒpɪk/ n tópico m, assunto m

topical /'tɒpɪkl/ a da atualidade, (P) actualidade, corrente

topless /'tɒplɪs/ a com o peito nu, topless

topple /'tɒpl/ vt/i (fazer) desabar, (fazer) tombar, (fazer) cair

torch /tɔ:tʃ/ n (electric) lanterna f elétrica, (P) eléctrica; (flaming) archote m, facho m

tore /tɔ:(r)/ see tear[1]

torment[1] /'tɔ:mənt/ n tormento m

torment[2] /tɔ:'ment/ vt atormentar, torturar; (annoy) aborrecer, chatear

torn /tɔ:n/ see tear[1]

tornado /tɔ:'neɪdəʊ/ n (pl -oes) tornado m

torpedo /tɔ:'pi:dəʊ/ n (pl -oes) torpedo m □ vt torpedear

torrent /'tɒrənt/ n torrente f. ~**ial** /tə'renʃl/ a torrencial

torrid /'tɒrɪd/ a (climate etc) tórrido; (fig) intenso, ardente

torso /'tɔ:səʊ/ n (pl -os) torso m

tortoise /'tɔ:təs/ n tartaruga f

tortoiseshell /'tɔ:təsʃel/ n (for ornaments etc) tartaruga f

tortuous /'tɔ:tʃʊəs/ a (of path etc) que dá muitas voltas, sinuoso; (fig) tortuoso, retorcido

torture /'tɔ:tʃə(r)/ n tortura f, suplício m □ vt torturar. ~**r** /-ə(r)/ n carrasco m, algoz m, torturador m

Tory /'tɔ:rɪ/ a & n (colloq) conservador (m), (P) tóri (m)

toss /tɒs/ vt atirar, jogar, (P) deitar; (shake) agitar, sacudir □ vi agitar-se, debater-se. ~ **a coin**, ~ **up** tirar cara ou coroa

tot[1] /tɒt/ n criancinha f, (colloq: glass) copinho m

tot[2] /tɒt/ vt/i (pt totted) ~ **up** (colloq) somar

total /'təʊtl/ a & n total (m) □ vt (pt totalled) (find total of) totalizar; (amount to) elevar-se a, montar a. ~**ity** /-'tælətɪ/ n totalidade f. ~**ly** adv totalmente

totalitarian /təʊtælɪ'teərɪən/ a totalitário

totter /'tɒtə(r)/ vi cambalear, andar aos tombos; (of tower etc) oscilar

touch /tʌtʃ/ vt/i tocar; (of ends, gardens etc) tocar-se; (tamper with) mexer em; (affect) comover □ n (sense) ta-to m, (P) tacto m; (contact) toque m; (of *colour*) toque *m*, retoque *m*. **a ~ of** (*small amount*) um pouco de. **get in ~ with** entrar em contato, (*P*) contacto com. **lose ~** perder contato, (*P*) contacto. **~ down** (*aviat*) aterrissar, (*P*) aterrar. **~ off** disparar; (*cause*) dar início a, desencadear. **~ on** (*mention*) tocar em. **~ up** retocar. **~-and-go** *a* (*risky*) arriscado; (*uncertain*) duvidoso, incerto. **~-line** *n* linha *f* lateral

touching /'tʌtʃɪŋ/ *a* comovente, comovedor

touchy /'tʌtʃɪ/ *a* melindroso, suscetível, (*P*) susceptível, que se ofende facilmente

tough /tʌf/ *a* (**-er, -est**) (*hard, difficult*) duro; (*strong*) forte, resistente □ *n* ~ (**guy**) valentão *m*, durão *m* (*colloq*). **~ luck!** (*colloq*) pouca sorte! **~ness** *n* dureza *f*; (*strength*) força *f*, resistência *f*

toughen /'tʌfn/ *vt/i* (*person*) endurecer; (*strengthen*) reforçar

tour /tʊə(r)/ *n* viagem *f*; (*visit*) visita *f*; (*by team etc*) tournée *f* □ *vt* visitar. **on ~** em tournée

tourism /'tʊərɪzəm/ *n* turismo *m*

tourist /'tʊərɪst/ *n* turista *mf* □ *a* turístico. **~ office** agência *f* de turismo

tournament /'tʊənəmənt/ *n* torneio *m*

tousle /'taʊzl/ *vt* despentear, esguedelhar

tout /taʊt/ *vi* angariar clientes (**for** para) □ *vt* (*try to sell*) tentar revender □ *n* (*hotel etc*) angariador *m*; (*ticket*) cambista *m*, (*P*) revendedor *m*

tow /təʊ/ *vt* rebocar □ *n* reboque *m*. **on ~** a reboque. **~ away** (*vehicle*) rebocar. **~-path** *n* caminho *m* de sirga. **~-rope** *n* cabo *m* de reboque

toward(s) /tə'wɔːd(z)/ *prep* para, em direção, (*P*) direcção a, na direção, (*P*) direcção de; (*of attitude*) para com; (*time*) por volta de

towel /'taʊəl/ *n* toalha *f*; (*tea towel*) pano *m* de prato □ *vt* (*pt* **towelled**) esfregar com a toalha. **~-rail** *n* toalheiro *m*. **~ling** *n* atoalhado *m*, (*P*) pano *m* turco

tower /'taʊə(r)/ *n* torre *f* □ *vi* **~ above** dominar. **~ block** prédio *m* alto. **~ing** *a* muito alto; (*fig: of rage etc*) violento

town /taʊn/ *n* cidade *f*. **go to ~** (*colloq*) perder a cabeça (*colloq*). **~ council** município *m*. **~ hall** câmara *f* municipal. **~ planning** urbanização *f*

toxic /'tɒksɪk/ *a* tóxico

toy /tɔɪ/ *n* brinquedo *m* □ *vi* **~ with** (*object*) brincar com; (*idea*) considerar, cogitar

trace /treɪs/ *n* traço *m*, rastro *m*, sinal *m*; (*small quantity*) traço *m*, vestígio *m* □ *vt* seguir *or* encontrar a pista de; (*draw*) traçar; (*with tracing-paper*) decalcar

tracing /'treɪsɪŋ/ *n* decalque *m*, desenho *m*. **~-paper** *n* papel *m* vegetal

track /træk/ *n* (*of person etc*) rastro *m*, pista *f*; (*race-track, of tape*) pista *f*; (*record*) faixa *f*; (*path*) trilho *m*, carreiro *m*; (*rail*) via *f* □ *vt* seguir a pista *or* a trajetória, (*P*) trajectória de. **keep ~ of** manter-se em contato com; (*keep oneself informed*) seguir. **~ down** (*find*) encontrar, descobrir; (*hunt*) seguir a pista de. **~ suit** conjunto *m* de jogging, (*P*) fato *m* de treino

tract /trækt/ *n* (*land*) extensão *f*; (*anat*) aparelho *m*

tractor /'træktə(r)/ *n* trator *m*, (*P*) tractor *m*

trade /treɪd/ *n* comércio *m*; (*job*) ofício *m*, profissão *f*; (*swap*) troca *f* □ *vt/i* comerciar (em), negociar (em) □ *vt* (*swap*) trocar. **~ in** (*used article*) trocar. **~-in** *n* troca *f*. **~ mark** marca *f* de fábrica. **~ on** (*exploit*) tirar partido de, abusar de. **~ union** sindicato *m*. **~r** /-ə(r)/ *n* negociante *mf*, comerciante *mf*

tradesman /'treɪdzmən/ *n* (*pl* **-men**) comerciante *m*

trading /'treɪdɪŋ/ *n* comércio *m*. **~ estate** zona *f* industrial

tradition /trə'dɪʃn/ *n* tradição *f*. **~al** *a* tradicional

traffic /'træfɪk/ *n* (*trade*) tráfego *m*, tráfico *m*; (*on road*) trânsito *m*, tráfego *m*; (*aviat*) tráfego *m* □ *vi* (*pt* **trafficked**) traficar (**in em**). **~ circle** (*Amer*) giratória *f*, (*P*) rotunda *f*. **~ island** ilha *f* de pedestres, (*P*) refúgio *m* para peões. **~ jam** engarrafamento *m*. **~-lights** *npl* sinal *m* luminoso, (*P*) semáforo *m*. **~ warden** guarda *mf* de trânsito. **~ker** *n* traficante *mf*

tragedy /'trædʒədɪ/ *n* tragédia *f*

tragic /'trædʒɪk/ *a* trágico

trail /treɪl/ *vt/i* arrastar(-se), rastejar; (*of plant, on ground*) rastejar; (*of plant, over wall*) trepar; (*track*) seguir □ *n* (*of powder, smoke etc*) esteira *f*, rastro *m*, (*P*) rasto *m*; (*track*) pista *f*; (*beaten path*) trilho *m*

trailer /'treɪlə(r)/ *n* reboque *m*; (*Amer: caravan*) reboque *m*, caravana *f*, trailer *m*; (*film*) trailer *m*, apresentação *f* de filme

train /treɪn/ *n* (*rail*) trem *m*, (*P*) comboio *m*; (*procession*) fila *f*; (*of dress*) cauda *f*; (*retinue*) comitiva *f* □ *vt* (*instruct, develop*) educar, formar, treinar; (*plant*) guiar; (*sportsman, animal*) treinar; (*aim*) assestar, apontar □ *vi* estudar, treinar-se. **~ed** *a* (*skilled*) qualificado; (*doctor etc*) diplomado. **~er** *n* (*sport*) treinador *m*; (*shoe*) tênis *m*. **~ing** *n* treino *m*

trainee /treɪ'niː/ *n* estagiário *m*

trait /treɪ(t)/ *n* traço *m*, característica *f*

traitor /'treɪtə(r)/ *n* traidor *m*

tram /træm/ *n* bonde *m*, (P) (carro) eléctrico *m*

tramp /træmp/ *vi* marchar (com passo pesado) □ *vt* percorrer, palmilhar □ *n* som *m* de passos pesados; (*vagrant*) vagabundo *m*, andarilho *m*; (*hike*) longa caminhada *f*

trample /'træmpl/ *vt/i* **~ (on)** pisar com força; (*fig*) menosprezar

trampoline /'træmpəliːn/ *n* (lona *f* usada como) trampolim *m*

trance /trɑːns/ *n* (*hypnotic*) transe *m*; (*ecstasy*) êxtase *m*, arrebatamento *m*; (*med*) estupor *m*

tranquil /'træŋkwɪl/ *a* tranqüilo, (P) tranqüilo, sossegado. **~lity** /-'kwɪlətɪ/ *n* tranqüilidade *f*, (P) tranquilidade *f*, sossego *m*

tranquillizer /'træŋkwɪlaɪzə(r)/ *n* (*drug*) tranqüilizante *m*, (P) tranquilizante *m*, calmante *m*

transact /træn'zækt/ *vt* (*business*) fazer, efetuar, (P) efectuar. **~ion** /-kʃn/ *n* transação *f*, (P) transacção *f*

transcend /træn'send/ *vt* transcender. **~ent** *a* transcendente

transcri|be /træn'skraɪb/ *vt* transcrever. **~pt**, **~ption** /-ɪpʃn/ *ns* transcrição *f*

transfer¹ /træns'fɜː(r)/ *vt* (*pt* **transferred**) transferir; (*power, property*) transmitir □ *vi* mudar, ser transferido; (*change planes etc*) fazer transferência. **~ the charges** (*telephone*) ligar a cobrar

transfer² /'trænsfɜː(r)/ *n* transferência *f*; (*of power, property*) transmissão *f*; (*image*) decalcomania *f*

transfigure /træns'fɪgə(r)/ *vt* transfigurar

transform /træns'fɔːm/ *vt* transformar. **~ation** /-ə'meɪʃn/ *n* transformação *f*. **~er** *n* (*electr*) transformador *m*

transfusion /træns'fjuːʒn/ *n* (*of blood*) transfusão *f*

transient /'trænzɪənt/ *a* transitório, transiente, efêmero, (P) efémero, passageiro

transistor /træn'zɪstə(r)/ *n* (*device, radio*) transistor *m*

transit /'trænsɪt/ *n* trânsito *m*. **in ~** em trânsito

transition /træn'zɪʃn/ *n* transição *f*. **~al** *a* transitório

transitive /'trænsətɪv/ *a* transitivo

transitory /'trænsɪtərɪ/ *a* transitório

translat|e /trænz'leɪt/ *vt* traduzir. **~ion** /-ʃn/ *n* tradução *f*. **~or** *n* tradutor *m*

translucent /trænz'luːsnt/ *a* translúcido

transmi|t /trænz'mɪt/ *vt* (*pt* **transmitted**) transmitir. **~ssion** *n* transmissão *f*. **~tter** *n* transmissor *m*

transparen|t /træns'pærənt/ *a* transparente. **~cy** *n* transparência *f*, (*photo*) diapositivo *m*

transpire /træn'spaɪə(r)/ *vi* (*secret etc*) transpirar; (*happen*) suceder, acontecer

transplant¹ /træns'plɑːnt/ *vt* transplantar

transplant² /'trænsplɑːnt/ *n* (*med*) transplantação *f*, transplante *m*

transport¹ /træn'spɔːt/ *vt* (*carry, delight*) transportar. **~ation** /'teɪʃn/ *n* transporte *m*

transport² /'trænspɔːt/ *n* (*of goods, delight etc*) transporte *m*

transpose /træn'spəʊz/ *vt* transpor

transverse /'trænzvɜːs/ *a* transversal

transvestite /trænz'vestaɪt/ *n* travesti *mf*

trap /træp/ *n* armadilha *f*, ratoeira *f*, cilada *f* □ *vt* (*pt* **trapped**) apanhar na armadilha; (*cut off*) prender, bloquear. **~per** *n* caçador *m* de armadilha (esp de peles)

trapdoor /træp'dɔː(r)/ *n* alçapão *m*

trapeze /trə'piːz/ *n* trapézio *m*

trash /træʃ/ *n* (*worthless stuff*) porcaria *f*; (*refuse*) lixo *m*; (*nonsense*) disparates *mpl*. **~ can** *n* (*Amer*) lata *f* do lixo, (P) caixote *m* do lixo. **~y** *a* que não vale nada, porcaria

trauma /'trɔːmə/ *n* trauma *m*, traumatismo *m*. **~tic** /-'mætɪk/ *a* traumático

travel /'trævl/ *vi* (*pt* **travelled**) viajar; (*of vehicle, bullet, sound*) ir □ *vt* percorrer □ *n* viagem *f*. **~ agent** agente *mf* de viagem. **~ler** *n* viajante *mf*. **~ler's cheque** cheque *m* de viagem. **~ling** *n* viagem *f*, viagens *fpl*, viajar *m*

travesty /'trævəstɪ/ *n* paródia *f*, caricatura *f*

trawler /'trɔːlə(r)/ *n* traineira *f*, (P) arrastão *m*

tray /treɪ/ *n* tabuleiro *m*, bandeja *f*

treacherous /'tretʃərəs/ *a* traiçoeiro

treachery /'tretʃərɪ/ *n* traição *f*, perfídia *f*, deslealdade *f*

treacle /'triːkl/ *n* melaço *m*

tread /tred/ *vt/i* (*pt* **trod**, *pp* **trodden**) (*step*) pisar; (*walk*) andar, caminhar; (*walk along*) seguir □ *n* passo *m*, maneira *f* de andar; (*of tyre*) trilho *m*. **~ sth into** (*carpet*) esmigalhar alg coisa sobre/em

treason /'tri:zn/ n traição f
treasure /'treʒə(r)/ n tesouro m □ vt ter o maior apreço por; (store) guardar bem guardado. ~r n tesoureiro m
treasury /'treʒərɪ/ n (building) tesouraria f; (department) Ministério m das Finanças or da Fazenda; (fig) tesouro m
treat /tri:t/ vt/i tratar □ n (pleasure) prazer m, regalo m; (present) mimo m, gentileza f. ~ sb to sth convidar alguém para alg coisa
treatise /'tri:tɪz/ n tratado m
treatment /'tri:tmənt/ n tratamento m
treaty /'tri:tɪ/ n (pact) tratado m
treble /'trebl/ a triplo □ vt/i triplicar □ n (mus: voice) soprano m. ~y adv triplamente
tree /tri:/ n árvore f
trek /trek/ n viagem f penosa; (walk) caminhada f □ vi (pt trekked) viajar penosamente; (walk) caminhar
trellis /'trelɪs/ n grade f para trepadeiras, treliça f
tremble /'trembl/ vi tremer
tremendous /trɪ'mendəs/ a (fearful, huge) tremendo; (colloq: excellent) fantástico, formidável
tremor /'tremə(r)/ n tremor m, estremecimento m. (earth) ~ abalo (sísmico) m, tremor m de terra
trench /trentʃ/ n fossa f, vala f; (mil) trincheira f
trend /trend/ n tendência f; (fashion) moda f. ~y a (colloq) na última moda, (P) na berra (colloq)
trepidation /trepɪ'deɪʃn/ n (fear) receio m, apreensão f
trespass /'trespəs/ vi entrar ilegalmente (on em). no ~ing entrada f proibida. ~er n intruso m
trestle /'tresl/ n cavalete m, armação f de mesa. ~-table n mesa f de cavaletes
trial /'traɪəl/ n (jur) julgamento m, processo m; (test) ensaio m, experiência f, prova f; (ordeal) provação f. on ~ em julgamento. ~ and error tentativas fpl
triangle /'traɪæŋgl/ n triângulo m. ~ular /-'æŋgjʊlə(r)/ a triangular
tribe /traɪb/ n tribo f. ~al a tribal
tribulation /trɪbjʊ'leɪʃn/ n tribulação f
tribunal /traɪ'bju:nl/ n tribunal m
tributary /'trɪbjʊtərɪ/ n afluente m, tributário m
tribute /'trɪbju:t/ n tributo m. pay ~ to prestar homenagem a, render tributo a
trick /trɪk/ n truque m; (prank) partida f; (habit) jeito m □ vt enganar. do the ~ (colloq: work) dar resultado

trickery /'trɪkərɪ/ n trapaça f
trickle /'trɪkl/ vi pingar, gotejar, escorrer □ n fio m de água etc; (fig: small number) punhado m
tricky /'trɪkɪ/ a (crafty) manhoso; (problem) delicado, complicado
tricycle /'traɪsɪkl/ n triciclo m
trifle /'traɪfl/ n ninharia f, bagatela f; (sweet) sobremesa f feita de pão-de-ló e frutas e creme □ vi ~ with brincar com. a ~ um pouquinho, (P) um poucochinho
trifling /'traɪflɪŋ/ a insignificante
trigger /'trɪgə(r)/ n (of gun) gatilho m □ vt ~ (off) (initiate) desencadear, despoletar
trill /trɪl/ n trinado m, gorjeio m
trilogy /'trɪlədʒɪ/ n trilogia f
trim /trɪm/ a (trimmer, trimmest) bem arranjado, bem cuidado; (figure) elegante, esbelto □ vt (pt trimmed) (cut) aparar; (sails) orientar, marear; (ornament) enfeitar, guarnecer (with com) □ n (cut) aparadela f, corte m leve; (decoration) enfeite m; (on car) acabamento(s) m(pl), estofado m. in ~ em ordem; (fit) em boa forma. ~ming(s) n(pl) (dress) enfeite m; (culin) guarnição f, acompanhamento m
Trinity /'trɪnətɪ/ n the (Holy) ~ a Santíssima Trindade
trinket /'trɪŋkɪt/ n bugiganga f; (jewel) bijuteria f, berloque m
trio /'tri:əʊ/ n (pl -os) trio m
trip /trɪp/ vi (pt tripped) (stumble) tropeçar, dar um passo em falso; (go or dance lightly) andar/dançar com passos leves □ vt ~ (up) fazer tropeçar, passar uma rasteira a □ n (journey) viagem f, (outing) passeio m, excursão f; (stumble) tropeção m, passo m em falso
tripe /traɪp/ n (food) dobrada f, tripas fpl; (colloq: nonsense) disparates mpl
triple /'trɪpl/ a triplo, tríplice □ vt/i triplicar. ~ts /-plɪts/ npl trigêmeos mpl, (P) trigêmeos mpl
triplicate /'trɪplɪkət/ n in ~ em triplicata
tripod /'traɪpɒd/ n tripé m
trite /traɪt/ a banal, corriqueiro
triumph /'traɪəmf/ n triunfo m □ vi triunfar (over sobre); (exult) exultar, rejubilar-se. ~al /-'ʌmfl/ a triunfal. ~ant /-'ʌmfənt/ a triunfante. ~antly /-'ʌmfəntlɪ/ adv em triunfo, triunfantemente
trivial /'trɪvɪəl/ a insignificante
trod, trodden /trɒd, 'trɒdn/ see tread
trolley /'trɒlɪ/ n carrinho m. (tea-)~ carrinho m de chá
trombone /trɒm'bəʊn/ n (mus) trombone m
troop /tru:p/ n bando m, grupo m. ~s

(*mil*) tropas *fpl* □ *vi* ~ **in/out** entrar/
sair em bando *or* grupo. ~**ing the
colour** a saudação da bandeira. ~**er**
n soldado *m* de cavalaria

trophy /'trəʊfɪ/ *n* troféu *m*

tropic /'trɒpɪk/ *n* trópico *m.* ~**s**
trópicos *mpl.* ~**al** *a* tropical

trot /trɒt/ *n* trote *m* □ *vi* (*pt* **trotted**)
trotar; (*of person*) correr em passos
curtos, ir num *or* a trote (*colloq*). **on
the** ~ (*colloq*) a seguir, a fio. ~ **out**
(*colloq: produce*) exibir; (*colloq: state*)
desfiar

trouble /'trʌbl/ *n* (*difficulty*) dificul-
dade(s) *f*(*pl*), problema(s) *m*(*pl*);
(*distress*) desgosto(s) *m*(*pl*), aborreci-
mento(s) *m*(*pl*); (*pains, effort*) cuidado *m*, trabalho *m*, maçada *f*;
(*inconvenience*) transtorno *m*, incómodo *m*, (*P*) incómodo *m*; (*med*)
doença *f*. ~**(s)** (*unrest*) agitação *f*,
conflito(s) *m*(*pl*) □ *vt/i* (*bother*) inco-
modar(-se), (*P*) maçar(-se); (*worry*)
preocupar(-se); (*agitate*) perturbar.
be in ~ estar em apuros, estar em
dificuldades. **get into** ~ meter-se em
encrenca/apuros. **it is not worth the**
~ não vale a pena. ~**-maker** *n* desordeiro *m*, provocador *m*. ~**-shooter**
n mediador *m*, negociador *m*. ~**d** *a*
agitado, perturbado; (*of sleep*) agitado; (*of water*) turvo

troublesome /'trʌblsəm/ *a* problemático, importuno, (*P*) maçador

trough /trɒf/ *n* (*drinking*) bebedouro
m; (*feeding*) comedouro *m*. ~ (**of low
pressure**) depressão *f*, linha *f* de
baixa pressão

trounce /traʊns/ *vt* (*defeat*) esmagar;
(*thrash*) espancar

troupe /truːp/ *n* (*theat*) companhia *f*,
troupe *f*

trousers /'traʊzəz/ *npl* calça *f*, (*P*)
calças *fpl*. **short** ~ calções *mpl*

trousseau /'truːsəʊ/ *n* (*pl* -**s** /-əʊz/) (*of
bride*) enxoval *m* de noiva

trout /traʊt/ *n* (*pl invar*) truta *f*

trowel /'traʊəl/ *n* (*garden*) colher *f* de
jardineiro; (*for mortar*) trolha *f*

truan|t /'truːənt/ *n* absenteísta *mf*, (*P*)
absentista *mf*; (*schol*) gazeteiro *m*.
play ~**t** fazer gazeta. ~**cy** *n* absenteísmo *m*, (*P*) absentismo *m*

truce /truːs/ *n* trégua(s) *f*(*pl*),
armistício *m*

truck /trʌk/ *n* (*lorry*) camião *m*; (*barrow*) carro *m* de bagageiro; (*wagon*)
vagão *m* aberto. ~**-driver** *n* motorista *mf* de camião, (*P*) camionista *mf*

truculent /'trʌkjʊlənt/ *a* agressivo,
brigão

trudge /trʌdʒ/ *vi* caminhar com dificuldade, caminhar a custo, arrastar-
se

true /truː/ *a* (**-er, -est**) verdadeiro; (*accurate*) exato, (*P*) exacto; (*faithful*)
fiel. **come** ~ (*happen*) realizar-se,
concretizar-se. **it is** ~ é verdade

truffle /'trʌfl/ *n* trufa *f*

truism /'truːɪzəm/ *n* truísmo *m*, verdade *f* evidente, (*P*) verdade *f* do Amigo Banana (*colloq*)

truly /'truːlɪ/ *adv* verdadeiramente;
(*faithfully*) fielmente; (*truthfully*) sinceramente

trump /trʌmp/ *n* trunfo *m* □ *vt* jogar
trunfo, trunfar. ~ **up** forjar, inventar.
~ **card** carta *f* de trunfo; (*colloq:
valuable resource*) trunfo *m*

trumpet /'trʌmpɪt/ *n* trombeta *f*

truncheon /'trʌntʃən/ *n* cassetete *m*,
(*P*) cassetête *m*

trundle /'trʌndl/ *vt/i* (*fazer*) rolar rui-
dosamente/pesadamente

trunk /trʌŋk/ *n* (*of tree, body*) tronco
m; (*of elephant*) tromba *f*; (*box*) mala *f*
grande; (*Amer, auto*) mala *f*. ~**s** (*for
swimming*) calção *m* de banho. ~ **call**
n chamada *f* interurbana. ~ **road** *n*
estrada *f* nacional

truss /trʌs/ *n* (*med*) funda *f* □ *vt* atar,
amarrar

trust /trʌst/ *n* confiança *f*; (*association*) truste *m*, (*P*) trust *m*, consórcio
m; (*foundation*) fundação *f*; (*responsibility*) responsabilidade *f*; (*jur*) fideicomisso *m* □ *vt* (*rely on*) ter confiança
em, confiar em; (*hope*) esperar □ *vi* ~
in *or* **to** confiar em. **in** ~ em
fideicomisso. **on** ~ (*without proof*)
sem verificação prévia; (*on credit*) a
crédito. ~ **sb with** confiar em
alguém. ~**ed** *a* (*friend etc*) de confiança, seguro. ~**ful**, ~**ing** *adjs*
confiante. ~**y** *a* fiel

trustee /trʌs'tiː/ *n* administrador *m*;
(*jur*) fideicomissário *m*

trustworthy /'trʌstwɜːðɪ/ *a* (digno)
de confiança

truth /truːθ/ *n* (*pl* -**s** /truːðz/) verdade
f. ~**ful** *a* (*account etc*) verídico; (*person*) verdadeiro, que fala verdade.
~**fully** *adv* sinceramente

try /traɪ/ *vt/i* (*pt* **tried**) tentar, experimentar; (*be a strain on*) cansar, pôr à
prova; (*jur*) julgar □ *n* (*attempt*) tentativa *f*, experiência *f*; (*Rugby*) ensaio
m. ~ **for** (*post, scholarship*) candidatar-se a; (*record*) tentar alcançar. ~
on (*clothes*) provar. ~ **out**
experimentar. ~ **to do** tentar fazer.
~**ing** *a* difícil

tsar /zɑː(r)/ *n* czar *m*

T-shirt /'tiːʃɜːt/ *n* T-shirt *f*, camiseta *f*
de algodão de mangas curtas

tub /tʌb/ *n* selha *f*; (*colloq: bath*) tina *f*,
banheira *f*

tuba /'tjuːbə/ *n* (*mus*) tuba *f*

tubby /'tʌbɪ/ *a* (**-ier, -iest**) baixote e gorducho

tub|e /tjuːb/ *n* tubo *m*; (*colloq: railway*) metrô *m*. **inner ~e** câmara *f* de ar. **~ing** *n* tubos *mpl*, tubagem *f*

tuber /'tjuːbə(r)/ *n* tubérculo *m*

tuberculosis /tjuːbɜːkjʊ'ləʊsɪs/ *n* tuberculose *f*

tubular /'tjuːbjʊlə(r)/ *a* tubular

tuck /tʌk/ *n* (*fold*) prega *f* cosida; (*for shortening or ornament*) refego *m* □ *vt/i* fazer pregas; (*put*) guardar, meter, enfiar; (*hide*) esconder. **~ in** *or* **into** (*colloq: eat*) atacar. **~ in** (*shirt*) meter as fraldas para dentro; (*blanket*) prender em; (*person*) cobrir bem, aconchegar. **~-shop** *n* (*schol*) loja *f* de balas, (*P*) pastelaria *f* (junto à escola)

Tuesday /'tjuːzdɪ/ *n* terça-feira *f*

tuft /tʌft/ *n* tufo *m*

tug /tʌg/ *vt/i* (*pt* **tugged**) puxar com força; (*vessel*) rebocar □ *n* (*boat*) rebocador *m*; (*pull*) puxão *m*. **~ of war** cabo-de-guerra *m*, (*P*) jogo *m* da guerra

tuition /tjuː'ɪʃn/ *n* ensino *m*

tulip /'tjuːlɪp/ *n* tulipa *f*

tumble /'tʌmbl/ *vi* tombar, baquear, dar um trambolhão □ *n* tombo *m*, trambolhão *m*. **~-drier** *n* máquina *f* de secar (roupa)

tumbledown /'tʌmbldaʊn/ *a* em ruínas

tumbler /'tʌmblə(r)/ *n* copo *m*

tummy /'tʌmɪ/ *n* (*colloq: stomach*) estômago *m*; (*colloq: abdomen*) barriga *f*. **~-ache** *n* (*colloq*) dor *f* de barriga/de estômago

tumour /'tjuːmə(r)/ *n* tumor *m*

tumult /'tjuːmʌlt/ *n* tumulto *m*. **~uous** /'mʌltʃʊəs/ *a* tumultuado, barulhento, agitado

tuna /'tjuːnə/ *n* (*pl invar*) atum *m*

tune /tjuːn/ *n* melodia *f* □ *vt* (*engine*) regular; (*piano etc*) afinar □ *vi* **~ in** (**to**) (*radio, TV*) ligar (em), (*P*) sintonizar. **~ up** afinar. **be in ~/out of ~** (*instrument*) estar afinado/desafinado; (*singer*) cantar afinado/desafinado. **~ful** *a* melodioso, harmonioso. **~r** *n* afinador *m*; (*radio*) sintonizador *m*

tunic /'tjuːnɪk/ *n* túnica *f*

Tunisia /tjuː'nɪzɪə/ *n* Tunísia *f*. **~n** *a* & *n* tunisiano (*m*), (*P*) tunisino (*m*)

tunnel /'tʌnl/ *n* túnel *m* □ *vi* (*pt* **tunnelled**) abrir um túnel (**into** em)

turban /'tɜːbən/ *n* turbante *m*

turbine /'tɜːbaɪn/ *n* turbina *f*

turbo- /'tɜːbəʊ/ *pref* turbo-

turbot /'tɜːbət/ *n* rodovalho *m*

turbulen|t /'tɜːbjʊlənt/ *a* turbulento. **~ce** *n* turbulência *f*

tureen /tə'riːn/ *n* terrina *f*

turf /tɜːf/ *n* (*pl* **turfs** *or* **turves**) gramado *m*, (*P*) relva *f*, relvado *m* □ *vt* **~ out** (*colloq*) jogar fora, (*P*) deitar fora. **the ~** (*racing*) turfe *m*, hipismo *m*. **~ accountant** corretor *m* de apostas

turgid /'tɜːdʒɪd/ *a* (*speech, style*) pomposo, empolado

Turk /tɜːk/ *n* turco *m*. **~ey** *n* Turquia *f*. **~ish** *a* turco *m* □ *n* (*lang*) turco *m*

turkey /'tɜːkɪ/ *n* peru *m*

turmoil /'tɜːmɔɪl/ *n* agitação *f*, confusão *f*, desordem *f*. **in ~** em ebulição

turn /tɜːn/ *vt/i* virar(-se), voltar(-se), girar; (*change*) transformar(-se) (**into** em); (*become*) ficar, tornar-se; (*corner*) virar, dobrar; (*page*) virar, voltar □ *n* volta *f*; (*in road*) curva *f*, (*of mind, events*) mudança *f*; (*occasion, opportunity*) vez *f*; (*colloq*) ataque *m*, crise *f*; (*colloq: shock*) susto *m*. **do a good ~** prestar (um) serviço. **in ~** por sua vez, sucessivamente. **speak out of ~** dizer o que não se deve, cometer uma indiscrição. **take ~s** revezar-se. **~ of the century** virada *f* do século. **~ against** virar-se *or* voltar-se contra. **~ away** *vi* virar-se *or* voltar-se para o outro lado □ *vt* (*avert*) desviar; (*reject*) recusar; (*send back*) mandar embora. **~ back** *vi* (*return*) devolver; (*vehicle*) dar meia volta, voltar para trás □ *vt* (*fold*) dobrar para trás. **~ down** recusar; (*fold*) dobrar para baixo; (*reduce*) baixar. **~ in** (*hand in*) entregar; (*colloq: go to bed*) deitar-se. **~ off** (*light etc*) apagar; (*tap*) fechar; (*road*) virar (para rua transversal). **~ on** (*light etc*) acender, ligar; (*tap*) abrir. **~ out** *vt* (*light*) apagar; (*empty*) esvaziar, despejar; (*pocket*) virar do avesso; (*produce*) produzir □ *vi* (*transpire*) vir a saber-se, descobrir-se; (*colloq: come*) aparecer. **~ round** virar-se, voltar-se. **~ up** *vi* aparecer, chegar; (*be found*) aparecer □ *vt* (*find*) desenterrar; (*increase*) aumentar; (*collar*) levantar. **~-out** *n* assistência *f*. **~-up** *n* (*of trousers*) dobra *f*

turning /'tɜːnɪŋ/ *n* rua *f* transversal; (*corner*) esquina *f*. **~-point** *n* momento *m* decisivo

turnip /'tɜːnɪp/ *n* nabo *m*

turnover /'tɜːnəʊvə(r)/ *n* (*pie, tart*) pastel *m*, empada *f*; (*money*) faturamento *m*, (*P*) facturação *f*; (*of staff*) rotatividade *f*

turnpike /'tɜːnpaɪk/ *n* (*Amer*) autoestrada *f* com pedágio, (*P*) portagem

turnstile /'tɜːnstaɪl/ *n* (*gate*) torniquete *m*, borboleta *f*

turntable /'tɜ:nteɪbl/ n (for record) prato m do toca-disco, (P) giradiscos; (record-player) toca-disco m, (P) gira-discos m

turpentine /'tɜ:pəntam/ n terebentina f, aguarrás m

turquoise /'tɜ:kwɔɪz/ a turquesa invar

turret /'tʌrɪt/ n torreão m, torrinha f

turtle /'tɜ:tl/ n tartaruga-do-mar f. ~-neck a de gola alta

tusk /tʌsk/ n (tooth) presa f; (elephant's) defesa f, dente m

tussle /'tʌsl/ n luta f, briga f

tutor /'tju:tə(r)/ n professor m particular; (univ) professor m universitário

tutorial /tju:'tɔ:rɪəl/ n (univ) seminário m

TV /ti:'vi:/ n tevê f

twaddle /'twɒdl/ n disparates mpl

twang /twæŋ/ n (mus) som m duma corda esticada; (in voice) nasalação f □ vt/i (mus) (fazer) vibrar, dedilhar

tweet /twi:t/ n pio m, pipilo m □ vi pipilar

tweezers /'twi:zəz/ npl pinça f

twel|ve /twelv/ a & n doze (m). ~ (o'clock) doze horas. ~fth a & n décimo segundo (m). T~fth Night véspera f de Reis

twent|y /'twentɪ/ a & n vinte (m). ~ieth a & n vigésimo (m)

twice /twaɪs/ adv duas vezes

twiddle /'twɪdl/ vt/i ~ (with) (fiddle with) torcer, brincar (com). ~ one's thumbs girar os polegares

twig /twɪg/ n galho m, graveto m

twilight /'twaɪlaɪt/ n crepúsculo m □ a crepuscular

twin /twɪn/ n & a gêmeo (m), (P) gémeo (m) □ vt (pt twinned) (pair) emparelhar, emparceirar. ~ beds par m de camas de solteiro. ~ning n emparelhamento m

twine /twaɪn/ n guita f, cordel m □ vt/i (weave together) entrançar; (wind) enroscar(-se)

twinge /twɪndʒ/ n dor f aguda e súbita, pontada f; (fig) pontada f, (P) ferroada f

twinkle /'twɪŋkl/ vi cintilar, brilhar □ n cintilação f, brilho m

twirl /twɜ:l/ vt/i (fazer) girar; (moustache) torcer

twist /twɪst/ vt torcer; (weave together) entrançar; (roll) enrolar; (distort) torcer, deturpar □ vi (rope etc) torcer-se, enrolar-se; (road) dar voltas or curvas, serpentear □ n (act of twisting) torcedura f, (P) torcedela f; (of rope) nó m; (of events) reviravolta f. ~ sb's arm (fig) forçar alguém

twit /twɪt/ n (colloq) idiota mf

twitch /twɪtʃ/ vt/i contrair(-se) □ n (tic) tique m; (jerk) puxão m

two /tu:/ a & n dois (m). in or of ~ minds indeciso. put ~ and ~ together tirar conclusões. ~-faced a de duas caras, hipócrita. ~-piece n (garment) duas-peças m invar. ~-seater n (car) carro m de dois lugares. ~-way a (of road) mão dupla

twosome /'tu:səm/ n par m

tycoon /taɪ'ku:n/ n magnata m

tying /'taɪŋ/ see **tie**

type /taɪp/ n (example, print) tipo m; (kind) tipo m, gênero m, (P) género m; (colloq: person) cara m, (P) tipo m (colloq) □ vt/i (write) bater à máquina, datilografar, (P) dactilografar

typescript /'taɪpskrɪpt/ n texto m datilografado, (P) dactilografado

typewrit|er /'taɪpraɪtə(r)/ n máquina f de escrever. ~ten /-ɪtn/ a batido à máquina, datilografado, (P) dactilografado

typhoid /'taɪfɔɪd/ n ~ (fever) febre f tifóide

typhoon /taɪ'fu:n/ n tufão m

typical /'tɪpɪkl/ a típico. ~ly adv tipicamente

typify /'tɪpɪfaɪ/ vt ser o (protó)tipo de, tipificar

typing /'taɪpɪŋ/ n datilografia f, (P) dactilografia f

typist /'taɪpɪst/ n datilógrafa f, (P) dactilógrafa f

tyrann|y /'tɪrənɪ/ n tirania f. ~ical /tɪ'rænɪkl/ a tirânico

tyrant /'taɪərənt/ n tirano m

tyre /'taɪə(r)/ n pneu m

U

ubiquitous /ju:'bɪkwɪtəs/ a ubíquo, onnipresente

udder /'ʌdə(r)/ n úbere m

UFO /'ju:fəʊ/ n OVNI m

ugl|y /'ʌglɪ/ a (-ier, -iest) feio. ~iness n feiúra f, (P) fealdade f

UK abbr see **United Kingdom**

ulcer /'ʌlsə(r)/ n úlcera f

ulterior /ʌl'tɪərɪə(r)/ a ulterior. ~ motive razão f inconfessada, segundas intenções fpl

ultimate /'ʌltɪmət/ a último, derradeiro; (definitive) definitivo; (maximum) supremo; (basic) fundamental. ~ly adv finalmente

ultimatum /ʌltɪ'meɪtəm/ n (pl -ums) ultimato m

ultra- /'ʌltrə/ pref ultra-, super-

ultraviolet /ʌltrə'vaɪələt/ a ultravioleta

umbilical /ʌm'bɪlɪkl/ a ~ cord cordão m umbilical

umbrage /'ʌmbrɪdʒ/ n take ~ (at sth) ofender-se or melindrar-se (com alg coisa)

umbrella /ʌmˈbrelə/ n guardachuva m

umpire /'ʌmpaɪə(r)/ n (sport) árbitro m □ vt arbitrar

umpteen /'ʌmptiːn/ a (sl) sem conta, montes de (colloq). for the ~th time (sl) pela centésima or enésima vez

UN abbr (United Nations) ONU f

un- /ʌn/ pref não, pouco

unable /ʌnˈeɪbl/ a be ~ to do ser incapaz de/não poder fazer

unabridged /ʌnəˈbrɪdʒd/ a (text) integral

unacceptable /ʌnəkˈseptəbl/ a inaceitável, inadmissível

unaccompanied /ʌnəˈkʌmpənɪd/ a só, desacompanhado

unaccountable /ʌnəˈkaʊntəbl/ a (strange) inexplicável; (not responsible) que não tem que dar contas

unaccustomed /ʌnəˈkʌstəmd/ a desacostumado. ~ to não acostumado or não habituado a

unadulterated /ʌnəˈdʌltəreɪtɪd/ a (pure, sheer) puro

unaided /ʌnˈeɪdɪd/ a sem ajuda, sozinho, por si só

unanim|ous /juːˈnænɪməs/ a unânime. ~ity /-əˈnɪmətɪ/ n unanimidade f. ~ously adv unânimemente, por unanimidade

unarmed /ʌnˈaːmd/ a desarmado, indefeso

unashamed /ʌnəˈʃeɪmd/ a desavergonhado, sem vergonha. ~ly /-ɪdlɪ/ adv sem vergonha

unassuming /ʌnəˈsjuːmɪŋ/ a modesto, despretencioso

unattached /ʌnəˈtætʃt/ a (person) livre

unattainable /ʌnəˈteɪnəbl/ a inacessível

unattended /ʌnəˈtendɪd/ a (person) desacompanhado; (car, luggage) abandonado

unattractive /ʌnəˈtræktɪv/ a sem atrativos, (P) atractivos; (offer) de pouco interesse

unauthorized /ʌnˈɔːθəraɪzd/ a não-autorizado, sem autorização

unavoidabl|e /ʌnəˈvɔɪdəbl/ a inevitável. ~y adv inevitavelmente

unaware /ʌnəˈweə(r)/ a be ~ of desconhecer, ignorar, não ter consciência de. ~s /-eəz/ adv (unexpectedly) inesperadamente. catch sb ~s apanhar alguém desprevenido

unbalanced /ʌnˈbælənst/ a (mind, person) desequilibrado

unbearable /ʌnˈbeərəbl/ a insuportável

unbeat|able /ʌnˈbiːtəbl/ a imbatível. ~en a não vencido, invicto; (unsurpassed) insuperado

unbeknown(st) /ʌnbɪˈnəʊn(st)/ a ~ to (colloq) sem o conhecimento de

unbelievable /ʌnbɪˈliːvəbl/ a inacreditável, incrível

unbend /ʌnˈbend/ vi (pt unbent) (relax) descontrair. ~ing a inflexível

unbiased /ʌnˈbaɪəst/ a imparcial

unblock /ʌnˈblɒk/ vt desbloquear, desobstruir; (pipe) desentupir

unborn /'ʌnbɔːn/ a por nascer; (future) vindouro, futuro

unbounded /ʌnˈbaʊndɪd/ a ilimitado

unbreakable /ʌnˈbreɪkəbl/ a inquebrável

unbridled /ʌnˈbraɪdld/ a desequilibrado, (P) desenfreado

unbroken /ʌnˈbrəʊkən/ a (intact) intato, (P) intacto, inteiro; (continuous) ininterrupto

unburden /ʌnˈbɜːdn/ vpr ~ o.s. (open one's heart) desabafar (to com)

unbutton /ʌnˈbʌtn/ vt desabotoar

uncalled-for /ʌnˈkɔːldfɔː(r)/ a injustificável, gratuito

uncanny /ʌnˈkænɪ/ a (-ier, -iest) estranho, misterioso

unceasing /ʌnˈsiːsɪŋ/ a incessante

unceremonious /ʌnserɪˈməʊnɪəs/ a sem cerimônia, (P) cerimónia, brusco

uncertain /ʌnˈsɜːtn/ a incerto. be ~ whether não saber ao certo se, estar indeciso quanto a. ~ty n incerteza f

unchang|ed /ʌnˈtʃeɪndʒd/ a inalterado, sem modificação. ~ing a inalterável, imutável

uncivilized /ʌnˈsɪvɪlaɪzd/ a não civilizado, bárbaro

uncle /'ʌŋkl/ n tio m

uncomfortable /ʌnˈkʌmfətəbl/ a (thing) desconfortável, incômodo, (P) incómodo; (unpleasant) desagradável. feel or be ~ (uneasy) sentir-se or estar pouco à vontade

uncommon /ʌnˈkɒmən/ a pouco vulgar, invulgar, fora do comum. ~ly adv invulgarmente, excepcionalmente

uncompromising /ʌnˈkɒmprəmaɪzɪŋ/ a intransigente

unconcerned /ʌnkənˈsɜːnd/ a (indifferent) indiferente (by a)

unconditional /ʌnkənˈdɪʃənl/ a incondicional

unconscious /ʌnˈkɒnʃəs/ a inconsciente (of de). ~ly adv inconscientemente. ~ness n inconsciência f

unconventional /ʌnkənˈvenʃənl/ a não convencional, fora do comum

uncooperative /ʌnkəʊˈɒpərətɪv/ a

(*person*) pouco cooperativo, do contra (*colloq*)

uncork /ʌn'kɔ:k/ *vt* desarolhar, tirar a rolha de

uncouth /ʌn'ku:θ/ *a* rude, grosseiro

uncover /ʌn'kʌvə(r)/ *vt* descobrir, revelar

unctuous /'ʌŋktʃʊəs/ *a* untuoso, gorduroso; (*fig*) melífluo

undecided /ʌndɪ'saɪdɪd/ *a* (*irresolute*) indeciso; (*not settled*) por decidir, pendente

undeniable /ʌndɪ'naɪəbl/ *a* inegável, incontestável

under /'ʌndə(r)/ *prep* debaixo de, sob; (*less than*) com menos de; (*according to*) conforme, segundo □ *adv* por baixo, debaixo. ~ **age** menor de idade. ~ **way** em preparo

under- /'ʌndə(r)/ *pref* sub-

undercarriage /'ʌndəkærɪdʒ/ *n* (*aviat*) trem *m* de aterrissagem, (*P*) trem *m* de aterragem

underclothes /'ʌndəkləʊðz/ *npl see* **underwear**

undercoat /'ʌndəkəʊt/ *n* (*of paint*) primeira mão *f*, (*P*) primeira demão *f*

undercover /ʌndə'kʌvə(r)/ *a* (*agent, operation*) secreto

undercurrent /'ʌndəkʌrənt/ *n* corrente *f* subterrânea; (*fig*) filão *m* (*fig*), tendência *f* oculta

undercut /ʌndə'kʌt/ *vt* (*pt* **undercut**, *pres p* **undercutting**) (*comm*) vender a preços mais baixos que

underdeveloped /ʌndədɪ'veləpt/ *a* atrofiado; (*country*) subdesenvolvido

underdog /ʌndə'dɒg/ *n* desprotegido *m*, o mais fraco (*colloq*)

underdone /'ʌndədʌn/ *a* (*of meat*) mal passado

underestimate /ʌndə'restɪmeɪt/ *vt* subestimar, não dar o devido valor a

underfed /ʌndə'fed/ *a* subalimentado, subnutrido

underfoot /ʌndə'fʊt/ *adv* debaixo dos pés; (*on the ground*) no chão

undergo /ʌndə'gəʊ/ *vt* (*pt* **-went**, *pp* **-gone**) (*be subjected to*) sofrer; (*treatment*) ser submetido a

undergraduate /ʌndə'grædʒʊət/ *n* estudante *mf* universitário

underground¹ /ʌndə'graʊnd/ *adv* debaixo da terra; (*fig: secretly*) clandestinamente

underground² /'ʌndəgraʊnd/ *a* subterrâneo; (*fig: secret*) clandestino □ *n* (*rail*) metro(politano) *m*

undergrowth /'ʌndəgrəʊθ/ *n* mato *m*

underhand /'ʌndəhænd/ *a* (*deceitful*) sonso, dissimulado

under|lie /ʌndə'laɪ/ *vt* (*pt* **-lay**, *pp* **-lain**, *pres p* **-lying**) estar por baixo de. ~**lying** *a* subjacente

underline /ʌndə'laɪn/ *vt* sublinhar

undermine /ʌndə'maɪn/ *vt* minar, solapar

underneath /ʌndə'ni:θ/ *prep* sob, debaixo de, por baixo de □ *adv* abaixo, em baixo, por baixo

underpaid /ʌndə'peɪd/ *a* mal pago

underpants /'ʌndəpænts/ *npl* (*man's*) cuecas *fpl*

underpass /'ʌndəpa:s/ *n* (*for cars, people*) passagem *f* inferior

underprivileged /ʌndə'prɪvɪlɪdʒd/ *a* desfavorecido

underrate /ʌndə'reɪt/ *vt* subestimar, depreciar

underside /'ʌndəsaɪd/ *n* lado *m* inferior, base *f*

underskirt /'ʌndəskɜ:t/ *n* anágua *f*

understand /ʌndə'stænd/ *vt/i* (*pt* **-stood**) compreender, entender. ~**able** *a* compreensível. ~**ing** *a* compreensivo □ *n* compreensão *f*; (*agreement*) acordo *m*, entendimento *m*

understatement /'ʌndəsteɪtmənt/ *n* versão *f* atenuada da verdade, litotes *f*

understudy /'ʌndəstʌdɪ/ *n* substituto *m*

undertak|e /ʌndə'teɪk/ *vt* (*pt* **-took**, *pp* **-taken**) empreender; (*responsibility*) assumir. ~**e to** encarregar-se de. ~**ing** *n* (*task*) empreendimento *m*; (*promise*) compromisso *m*

undertaker /'ʌndəteɪkə(r)/ *n* agente *m* funerário, papa-defuntos *m* (*colloq*)

undertone /'ʌndətəʊn/ *n* **in an ~** a meia voz

undervalue /ʌndə'vælju:/ *vt* avaliar por baixo, subestimar

underwater /ʌndə'wɔ:tə(r)/ *a* submarino □ *adv* debaixo de água

underwear /'ʌndəweə(r)/ *n* roupa *f* interior *or* de baixo

underweight /'ʌndəweɪt/ *a* **be ~** estar com o peso abaixo do normal, ter peso a menos

underwent /ʌndə'went/ *see* **undergo**

underworld /'ʌndəwɜ:ld/ *n* (*of crime*) submundo *m*, bas-fonds *mpl*

underwriter /'ʌndəraɪtə(r)/ *n* segurador *m*; (*marine*) underwriter *m*

undeserved /ʌndɪ'zɜ:vd/ *a* imerecido, injusto

undesirable /ʌndɪ'zaɪərəbl/ *a* indesejável, inconveniente

undies /'ʌndɪz/ *npl* (*colloq*) roupa *f* de baixo *or* interior

undignified /ʌn'dɪgnɪfaɪd/ *a* pouco digno, sem dignidade

undisputed /ʌndɪ'spju:tɪd/ *a* incontestado

undo /ʌn'du:/ *vt* (*pt* **-did**, *pp* **-done** /dʌn/) desfazer; (*knot*) desfazer, desatar; (*coat, button*) abrir. **leave ~ne**

não fazer, deixar por fazer. **~ing** n desgraça f, ruína f

undoubted /ʌn'daʊtɪd/ a indubitável. **~ly** adv indubitavelmente

undress /ʌn'dres/ vt/i despir(-se). get **~ed** despir-se

undu|e /ʌn'dju:/ a excessivo, indevido. **~ly** adv excessivamente, indevidamente

undulate /'ʌndjʊleɪt/ vi ondular

undying /ʌn'daɪɪŋ/ a eterno, perene

unearth /ʌn'ɜ:θ/ vt desenterrar; (fig) descobrir

unearthly /ʌn'ɜ:θlɪ/ a sobrenatural, misterioso. **~ hour** (colloq) hora f absurda or inconveniente

uneasy /ʌn'i:zɪ/ a (ill at ease) pouco à vontade; (worried) preocupado

uneconomic /ʌni:kə'nɒmɪk/ a antieconômico. **~al** a antieconômico

uneducated /ʌn'edʒʊkeɪtɪd/ a (person) inculto, sem instrução

unemploy|ed /ʌnɪm'plɔɪd/ a desempregado. **~ment** n desemprego m. **~ment benefit** auxílio-desemprego m

unending /ʌn'endɪŋ/ a interminável, sem fim

unequal /ʌn'i:kwəl/ a desigual. **~led** a sem igual, inigualável

unequivocal /ʌnɪ'kwɪvəkl/ a inequívoco, claro

uneven /ʌn'i:vn/ a desigual, irregular

unexpected /ʌnɪk'spektɪd/ a inesperado. **~ly** a inesperadamente

unfair /ʌn'feə(r)/ a injusto (to com). **~ness** n injustiça f

unfaithful /ʌn'feɪθfl/ a infiel

unfamiliar /ʌnfə'mɪlɪə(r)/ a estranho, desconhecido. be **~ with** desconhecer, não conhecer, não estar familiarizado com

unfashionable /ʌn'fæʃənəbl/ a fora de moda

unfasten /ʌn'fa:sn/ vt (knot) desatar, soltar; (button) abrir

unfavourable /ʌn'feɪvərəbl/ a desfavorável

unfeeling /ʌn'fi:lɪŋ/ a insensível

unfinished /ʌn'fɪnɪʃt/ a incompleto, inacabado

unfit /ʌn'fɪt/ a sem preparo físico, fora de forma; (unsuitable) impróprio (for para)

unfold /ʌn'fəʊld/ vt desdobrar; (expose) expor, revelar □ vi desenrolar-se

unforeseen /ʌnfɔ:'si:n/ a imprevisto, inesperado

unforgettable /ʌnfə'getəbl/ a inesquecível

unforgivable /ʌnfə'gɪvəbl/ a imperdoável, indesculpável

unfortunate /ʌn'fɔ:tʃənət/ a (unlucky) infeliz; (regrettable) lamen-

tável. it was very **~ that** foi uma pena que **~ly** adv infelizmente

unfounded /ʌn'faʊndɪd/ a (rumour etc) infundado, sem fundamento

unfriendly /ʌn'frendlɪ/ a pouco amável, antipático, frio

unfurnished /ʌn'fɜ:nɪʃt/ a sem mobília

ungainly /ʌn'geɪnlɪ/ a desajeitado, desgracioso

ungodly /ʌn'gɒdlɪ/ a ímpio. **~ hour** (colloq) hora f absurda, às altas horas (colloq)

ungrateful /ʌn'greɪtfl/ a ingrato

unhapp|y /ʌn'hæpɪ/ a (-ier, -iest) infeliz, triste; (not pleased) descontente, pouco contente (with com). **~ily** adv infelizmente. **~iness** n infelicidade f, tristeza f

unharmed /ʌn'ha:md/ a incólume, são e salvo, ileso

unhealthy /ʌn'helθɪ/ a (-ier, -iest) (climate etc) doentio, insalubre; (person) adoentado, com pouca saúde

unheard-of /ʌn'hɜ:dɒv/ a inaudito, sem precedentes

unhinge /ʌn'hɪndʒ/ vt (person, mind) desequilibrar

unholy /ʌn'həʊlɪ/ a (-ier, -iest) (person, act etc) ímpio; (colloq: great) incrível, espantoso

unhook /ʌn'hʊk/ vt desenganchar; (dress) desapertar

unhoped /ʌn'həʊpt/ a **~ for** inesperado

unhurt /ʌn'hɜ:t/ a ileso, incólume

unicorn /'ju:nɪkɔ:n/ n unicórnio m

uniform /'ju:nɪfɔ:m/ n uniforme m □ a uniforme, sempre igual. **~ity** /'fɔ:mətɪ/ n uniformidade f. **~ly** adv uniformemente

unif|y /'ju:nɪfaɪ/ vt unificar. **~ication** /-ɪ'keɪʃn/ n unificação f

unilateral /ju:nɪ'lætrəl/ a unilateral

unimaginable /ʌnɪ'mædʒɪnəbl/ a inimaginável

unimportant /ʌnɪm'pɔ:tnt/ a sem importância, insignificante

uninhabited /ʌnɪn'hæbɪtɪd/ a desabitado

unintentional /ʌnɪn'tenʃənl/ a involuntário, não propositado

uninterest|ed /ʌn'ɪntrəstɪd/ a desinteressado (in em), indiferente (in a). **~ing** a desinteressante, sem interesse

union /'ju:nɪən/ n união f; (trade union) sindicato m. **~ist** n sindicalista mf; (pol) unionista mf. **U~ Jack** bandeira f britânica

unique /ju:'ni:k/ a único, sem igual

unisex /'ju:nɪseks/ a unisexo

unison /'ju:nɪsn/ n **in ~** em uníssono

unit /'ju:nɪt/ *n* unidade *f*; (*of furniture*) peça *f*, unidade *f*, (*P*) módulo *m*

unite /ju:'naɪt/ *vt/i* unir(-se). **U~d Kingdom** *n* Reino *m* Unido. **U~d Nations (Organization)** *n* Organização *f* das Nações Unidas. **U~ States (of America)** Estados *mpl* Unidos (da América)

unity /'ju:nətɪ/ *n* unidade *f*; (*fig: harmony*) união *f*

universal /ju:nɪ'vɜ:sl/ *a* universal

universe /'ju:nɪvɜ:s/ *n* universo *m*

university /ju:nɪ'vɜ:sətɪ/ *n* universidade *f* □ *a* universitário; (*student, teacher*) universitário, da universidade

unjust /ʌn'dʒʌst/ *a* injusto

unkempt /ʌn'kempt/ *a* desmazelado, desleixado; (*of hair*) despenteado, desgrenhado

unkind /ʌn'kaɪnd/ *a* desagradável, duro. **~ly** *adv* mal

unknowingly /ʌn'nəʊɪŋlɪ/ *adv* sem saber, inconscientemente

unknown /ʌn'nəʊn/ *a* desconhecido □ *n* the ~ o desconhecido

unleaded /ʌn'ledɪd/ *a* sem chumbo

unless /ʌn'les/ *conj* a não ser que, a menos que, salvo se, se não

unlike /ʌn'laɪk/ *a* diferente □ *prep* ao contrário de

unlikely /ʌn'laɪklɪ/ *a* improvável

unlimited /ʌn'lɪmɪtɪd/ *a* ilimitado

unload /ʌn'ləʊd/ *vt* descarregar

unlock /ʌn'lɒk/ *vt* abrir (com chave)

unluck|y /ʌn'lʌkɪ/ *a* (**-ier, -iest**) infeliz, sem sorte; (*number*) que dá azar. **be ~y** ter pouca sorte. **~ily** *adv* infelizmente

unmarried /ʌn'mærɪd/ *a* solteiro, celibatário

unmask /ʌn'ma:sk/ *vt* desmascarar

unmistakable /ʌnmɪs'teɪkəbl/ *a* (*voice etc*) inconfundível; (*clear*) claro, inequívoco

unmitigated /ʌn'mɪtɪɡeɪtɪd/ *a* (*absolute*) completo, absoluto

unmoved /ʌn'mu:vd/ *a* impassível; (*indifferent*) indiferente (**by** a), insensível (**by** a)

unnatural /ʌn'nætʃrəl/ *a* que não é natural; (*wicked*) desnaturado

unnecessary /ʌn'nesəserɪ/ *a* desnecessário; (*superfluous*) supérfluo, dispensável

unnerve /ʌn'nɜ:v/ *vt* desencorajar, desmoralizar, intimidar

unnoticed /ʌn'nəʊtɪst/ *a* **go ~** passar despercebido

unobtrusive /ʌnəb'tru:sɪv/ *a* discreto

unofficial /ʌnə'fɪʃl/ *a* oficioso, que não é oficial; (*strike*) ilegal, inautorizado

unorthodox /ʌn'ɔ:θədɒks/ *a* pouco ortodoxo, não ortodoxo

unpack /ʌn'pæk/ *vt* (*suitcase etc*) desfazer; (*contents*) desembalar, desempacotar □ *vi* desfazer a mala

unpaid /ʌn'peɪd/ *a* não remunerado; (*bill*) a pagar

unpalatable /ʌn'pælətəbl/ *a* (*food, fact etc*) desagradável, intragável

unparalleled /ʌn'pærəleld/ *a* sem paralelo, incomparável

unpleasant /ʌn'pleznt/ *a* desagradável (**to** com); (*person*) antipático

unplug /ʌn'plʌg/ *vt* (*pt* **-plugged**) (*electr*) desligar a tomada, (*P*) tirar a ficha da tomada

unpopular /ʌn'pɒpjʊlə(r)/ *a* impopular

unprecedented /ʌn'presɪdentɪd/ *a* sem precedentes, inaudito, nunca visto

unpredictable /ʌnprə'dɪktəbl/ *a* imprevisível

unprepared /ʌnprɪ'peəd/ *a* sem preparação, improvisado; (*person*) desprevenido

unpretentious /ʌnprɪ'tenʃəs/ *a* despretencioso, sem pretensões

unprincipled /ʌn'prɪnsəpld/ *a* sem princípios, sem escrúpulos

unprofessional /ʌnprə'feʃənl/ *a* (*work*) de amador; (*conduct*) sem consciência profissional

unprofitable /ʌn'prɒfɪtəbl/ *a* não lucrativo

unqualified /ʌn'kwɒlɪfaɪd/ *a* sem habilitações; (*success etc*) total, absoluto. **be ~ to** não estar habilitado para

unquestionable /ʌn'kwestʃənəbl/ *a* incontestável, indiscutível

unreal /ʌn'rɪəl/ *a* irreal

unreasonable /ʌn'ri:znəbl/ *a* pouco razoável, disparatado; (*excessive*) excessivo

unrecognizable /ʌn'rekəɡnaɪzəbl/ *a* irreconhecível

unrelated /ʌnrɪ'leɪtɪd/ *a* (*facts*) desconexo, sem relação (**to** com); (*people*) não aparentado (**to** com)

unreliable /ʌnrɪ'laɪəbl/ *a* que não é de confiança

unremitting /ʌnrɪ'mɪtɪŋ/ *a* incessante, infatigável

unreservedly /ʌnrɪ'zɜ:vɪdlɪ/ *adv* sem reservas

unrest /ʌn'rest/ *n* agitação *f*, distúrbios *mpl*

unrivalled /ʌn'raɪvld/ *a* sem igual, incomparável

unroll /ʌn'rəʊl/ *vt* desenrolar

unruffled /ʌn'rʌfld/ *a* calmo, tranqüilo, imperturbável

unruly /ʌn'ru:lɪ/ *a* indisciplinado, turbulento

unsafe /ʌnˈseɪf/ a (*dangerous*) que não é seguro, perigoso; (*person*) em perigo

unsaid /ʌnˈsed/ a leave ~ não mencionar, não dizer, deixar algo por dizer

unsatisfactory /ʌnsætɪsˈfæktərɪ/ a insatisfatório, pouco satisfatório

unsavoury /ʌnˈseɪvərɪ/ a desagradável, repugnante

unscathed /ʌnˈskeɪðd/ a ileso, incólume

unscrew /ʌnˈskru:/ vt desenroscar, desparafusar

unscrupulous /ʌnˈskru:pjʊləs/ a sem escrúpulos, pouco escrupuloso, sem consciência

unseemly /ʌnˈsi:mlɪ/ a inconveniente, indecoroso, impróprio

unsettle /ʌnˈsetl/ vt perturbar, agitar. ~d a perturbado; (*weather*) instável, variável; (*bill*) não saldado

unshakeable /ʌnˈʃeɪkəbl/ a (*person, belief etc*) inabalável

unshaven /ʌnˈʃeɪvn/ a com a barba por fazer, por barbear

unsightly /ʌnˈsaɪtlɪ/ a feio

unskilled /ʌnˈskɪld/ a inexperiente; (*work, worker*) não especializado; (*labour*) mão-de-obra f não especializada

unsociable /ʌnˈsəʊʃəbl/ a insociável, misantropo

unsophisticated /ʌnsəˈfɪstɪkeɪtɪd/ a insofisticado, simples

unsound /ʌnˈsaʊnd/ a pouco sólido. of ~ mind (*jur*) não estar em plena posse das suas faculdades mentais (*jur*)

unspeakable /ʌnˈspi:kəbl/ a indescritível; (*bad*) inqualificável

unspecified /ʌnˈspesɪfaɪd/ a não especificado, indeterminado

unstable /ʌnˈsteɪbl/ a instável

unsteady /ʌnˈstedɪ/ a (*step*) vacilante, incerto; (*ladder*) instável; (*hand*) pouco firme

unstuck /ʌnˈstʌk/ a (*not stuck*) descolado. come ~ (*colloq: fail*) falhar

unsuccessful /ʌnsəkˈsesfl/ a (*candidate*) mal sucedido; (*attempt*) malogrado, fracassado. be ~ não ter êxito. ~ly adv em vão

unsuit|able /ʌnˈs(j)u:təbl/ a impróprio, pouco apropriado, inadequado (for para). ~ed a inadequado (to para)

unsure /ʌnˈʃʊə(r)/ a incerto

unsuspecting /ʌnsəˈspektɪŋ/ a sem desconfiar de nada, insuspeitado

untangle /ʌnˈtæŋgl/ vt desemaranhar, desenredar

unthinkable /ʌnˈθɪŋkəbl/ a impensável, inconcebível

untid|y /ʌnˈtaɪdɪ/ a (-ier, -iest) (*room, desk etc*) desarrumado; (*appearance*) desleixado, desmazelado; (*hair*) despenteado. ~ily adv sem cuidado. ~iness n desordem f; (*of appearance*) desmazelo m

untie /ʌnˈtaɪ/ vt (*knot, parcel*) desatar, desfazer; (*person*) desamarrar

until /ənˈtɪl/ prep até. not ~ não antes de □ conj até que

untimely /ʌnˈtaɪmlɪ/ a inoportuno, intempestivo; (*death*) prematuro

untold /ʌnˈtəʊld/ a incalculável

untoward /ʌntəˈwɔ:d/ a inconveniente, desagradável

untrue /ʌnˈtru:/ a falso

unused[1] /ʌnˈju:zd/ a (*new*) novo, por usar; (*not in use*) não utilizado

unused[2] /ʌnˈju:st/ a ~ to não habituado a, não acostumado a

unusual /ʌnˈju:ʒʊəl/ a insólito, fora do comum. ~ly adv excepcionalmente

unveil /ʌnˈveɪl/ vt descobrir; (*statue, portrait etc*) desvelar

unwanted /ʌnˈwɒntɪd/ a (*useless*) que já não serve; (*child*) indesejado

unwarranted /ʌnˈwɒrəntɪd/ a injustificado

unwelcome /ʌnˈwelkəm/ a desagradável; (*guest*) indesejável

unwell /ʌnˈwel/ a indisposto

unwieldy /ʌnˈwi:ldɪ/ a difícil de manejar, pouco jeitoso

unwilling /ʌnˈwɪlɪŋ/ a relutante (to em), pouco disposto (to a)

unwind /ʌnˈwaɪnd/ vt/i (*pt* unwound /ʌnˈwaʊnd/) desenrolar(-se); (*colloq: relax*) descontrair(-se)

unwise /ʌnˈwaɪz/ a imprudente, insensato

unwittingly /ʌnˈwɪtɪŋlɪ/ adv sem querer

unworthy /ʌnˈwɜ:ðɪ/ a indigno

unwrap /ʌnˈræp/ vt (*pt* unwrapped) desembrulhar, abrir, desfazer

unwritten /ʌnˈrɪtn/ a (*agreement*) verbal, tácito

up /ʌp/ adv (to higher place) cima, para cima, para o alto; (*in higher place*) em cima, no alto; (*out of bed*) acordado, de pé; (*up and dressed*) pronto; (*finished*) acabado; (*sun*) alto □ prep no cimo de, em cima de, no alto de. ~ the street/river/etc pela rua/pelo rio/etc acima □ vt (*pt* upped) (*increase*) aumentar. be ~ against defrontar, enfrentar. be ~ in (*colloq*) saber. be ~ to (*do*) estar fazendo; (*plot*) estar tramando; (*task*) estar à altura de. feel ~ to doing (*able*) sentir-se capaz de fazer. it is ~ to you depende de você. come or go ~ subir. have ~s and downs (*fig*) ter (os seus) altos e baixos. **walk ~ and down** andar dum lado para o outro *or* para a frente e para trás. **~-and-coming** *a* prometedor. **~-market** *a* requintado, fino

upbringing /'ʌpbrɪŋɪŋ/ *n* educação *f*

update /ʌp'deɪt/ *vt* atualizar, (*P*) actualizar

upheaval /ʌp'hi:vl/ *n* pandemônio *m*, (*P*) pandemónio *m*, revolução *f* (*fig*); (*social*, *political*) convulsão *f*

uphill /'ʌphɪl/ *a* ladeira acima, ascendente; (*fig*: *difficult*) árduo □ *adv* /ʌp'hɪl/ **go ~** subir

uphold /ʌp'həʊld/ *vt* (*pt* upheld) sustentar, manter, apoiar

upholster /ʌp'həʊlstə(r)/ *vt* estofar. **~y** *n* estofados *mpl*, (*P*) estofo(s) *m* (*pl*)

upkeep /'ʌpki:p/ *n* manutenção *f*

upon /ə'pɒn/ *prep* sobre

upper /'ʌpə(r)/ *a* superior □ *n* (*of shoe*) gáspea *f*. **have the ~ hand** estar por cima, estar em posição de superioridade. **~ class** aristocracia *f*. **~most** *a* (*highest*) o mais alto, superior

upright /'ʌpraɪt/ *a* vertical; (*honourable*) honesto, honrado, (*P*) recto

uprising /'ʌpraɪzɪŋ/ *n* insurreição *f*, sublevação *f*, levantamento *m*

uproar /'ʌprɔ:(r)/ *n* tumulto *m*, alvoroço *m*

uproot /ʌp'ru:t/ *vt* desenraizar; (*fig*) erradicar, desarraigar

upset¹ /ʌp'set/ *vt* (*pt* upset, *pres p* upsetting) (*overturn*) entornar, virar; (*plan*) contrariar, transtornar; (*stomach*) desarranjar; (*person*) contrariar, transtornar, incomodar □ *a* aborrecido

upset² /'ʌpset/ *n* transtorno *m*; (*of stomach*) indisposição *f*; (*distress*) choque *m*

upshot /'ʌpʃɒt/ *n* resultado *m*

upside-down /ʌpsaɪd'daʊn/ *adv* (*lit* & *fig*) ao contrário, de pernas para o ar

upstairs /ʌp'steəz/ *adv* (*at/to*) em/para cima, no/para o andar de cima □ *a* /'ʌpsteəz/ (*flat etc*) de cima, do andar de cima

upstart /'ʌpstɑ:t/ *n* arrivista *mf*

upstream /ʌp'stri:m/ *adv* rio acima, contra a corrente

upsurge /'ʌpsɜ:dʒ/ *n* recrudescência *f*, recrudescimento *m*; (*of anger*) acesso *m*, ataque *m*

uptake /'ʌpteɪk/ *n* **be quick on the ~** pegar rapidamente as coisas; (*fig*) ser de compreensão rápida, ser vivo

up-to-date /'ʌptədeɪt/ *a* moderno, atualizado, (*P*) actualizado

upturn /'ʌptɜ:n/ *n* melhoria *f*

upward /'ʌpwəd/ *a* ascendente, voltado para cima. **~s** *adv* para cima

uranium /jʊ'reɪnɪəm/ *n* urânio *m*

urban /'ɜ:bən/ *a* urbano

urbane /ɜ:'beɪn/ *a* delicado, cortês, urbano

urge /ɜ:dʒ/ *vt* aconselhar vivamente (**to a**) □ *n* (*strong desire*) grande vontade *f*. **~ on** (*impel*) incitar

urgen|t /'ɜ:dʒənt/ *a* urgente. **be ~t** urgir. **~cy** *n* urgência *f*

urinal /jʊə'raɪnl/ *n* urinol *m*

urin|e /'jʊərɪn/ *n* urina *f*. **~ate** *vi* urinar

urn /ɜ:n/ *n* urna *f*; (*for tea*, *coffee*) espécie *f* de samovar

us /ʌs/; *unstressed* /əs/ *pron* nos; (*after preps*) nós. **with ~** conosco. **he knows ~** ele nos conhece

US *abbr* United States

USA *abbr* United States of America

usable /'ju:zəbl/ *a* utilizável

usage /'ju:zɪdʒ/ *n* uso *m*

use¹ /ju:z/ *vt* usar, utilizar, servir-se de; (*exploit*) servir-se de; (*consume*) gastar, usar, consumir. **~ up** esgotar, consumir. **~r** /-ə(r)/ *n* usuário *m*, (*P*) utente *mf*. **~r-friendly** *a* fácil de usar

use² /ju:s/ *n* uso *m*, emprego *m*. **in ~** em uso. **it is no ~ shouting**/*etc* não serve de nada *or* não adianta gritar/*etc*. **make ~ of** servir-se de. **of ~** útil

used¹ /ju:zd/ *a* (*second-hand*) usado

used² /ju:st/ *pt* **he ~ to** ele costumava, ele tinha por costume *or* hábito □ *a* **~ to** acostumado a, habituado a

use|ful /'ju:sfl/ *a* útil. **~less** *a* inútil; (*person*) incompetente

usher /'ʌʃə(r)/ *n* vagalume *m*, (*P*) arrumador *m* □ *vt* **~ in** mandar entrar. **~ette** *n* vagalume *m*, (*P*) arrumadora *f*

usual /'ju:ʒəl/ *a* usual, habitual, normal. **as ~** como de costume, como habitualmente. **at the ~ time** na hora de costume, (*P*) à(s) hora(s) de costume. **~ly** *adv* habitualmente, normalmente

USSR *abbr* URSS

usurp /ju:'zɜ:p/ *vt* usurpar

utensil /ju:'tensl/ *n* utensílio *m*

uterus /'ju:tərəs/ *n* útero *m*

utilitarian /ju:tɪlɪ'teərɪən/ *a* utilitário

utility /ju:'tɪlətɪ/ *n* utilidade *f*. **(public) ~** serviço *m* público. **~ room** área *f* de serviço (para as máquinas de lavar a roupa e a louça)

utilize /'ju:tɪlaɪz/ *vt* utilizar

utmost /'ʌtməʊst/ *a* (*furthest, most intense*) extremo. **the ~ care**/*etc* (*greatest*) o maior cuidado/*etc* □ *n* **do one's ~** fazer todo o possível

utter[1] /'ʌtə(r)/ a completo, absoluto. ~**ly** adv completamente

utter[2] /'ʌtə(r)/ vt proferir; (sigh, shout) dar. ~**ance** n expressão f

U-turn /'juːtɜːn/ n retorno m

V

vacan|t /'veɪkənt/ a (post, room, look) vago; (mind) vazio; (seat, space, time) desocupado, livre. ~**cy** n (post) vaga f; (room in hotel) vago m

vacate /və'keɪt/ vt vagar, deixar vago

vacation /və'keɪʃn/ n férias fpl

vaccinat|e /'væksmeɪt/ vt vacinar. ~**ion** /-'neɪʃn/ n vacinação f

vaccine /'væksiːn/ n vacina f

vacuum /'vækjʊəm/ n (pl -**cuums** or -**cua**) vácuo m, vazio m. ~ **flask** garrafa f térmica, (P) termo(s) m. ~ **cleaner** aspirador m de pó

vagina /və'dʒaɪnə/ n vagina f

vagrant /'veɪgrənt/ n vadio m, vagabundo m

vague /veɪg/ a (-er, -est) vago; (outline) impreciso. **be** ~ **about** ser vago acerca de, não precisar. ~**ly** adv vagamente

vain /veɪn/ a (-er, -est) (conceited) vaidoso; (useless) vão, inútil; (fruitless) infrutífero. **in** ~ em vão. ~**ly** adv em vão

valentine /'væləntaɪn/ n (card) cartão m do dia de São Valentin

valet /'vælɪt, 'væleɪ/ n (manservant) criado m de quarto; (of hotel) camareiro m □ vt (car) lavar e limpar o interior

valiant /'væliənt/ a corajoso, valente

valid /'vælɪd/ a válido. ~**ity** /və'lɪdətɪ/ n validade f

validate /'vælɪdeɪt/ vt validar, confirmar, ratificar

valley /'vælɪ/ n vale m

valuable /'væljʊəbl/ a (object) valioso, de valor; (help, time etc) precioso. ~**s** npl objetos mpl, (P) objectos mpl de valor

valuation /væljʊ'eɪʃn/ n avaliação f

value /'væljuː/ n valor m □ vt avaliar; (cherish) dar valor a. ~ **added tax** imposto m de valor adicional, (P) acrescentado. ~**r** /-ə(r)/ n avaliador m

valve /vælv/ n (anat, techn, of car tyre) válvula f; (of bicycle tyre) pipo m; (of radio) lâmpada f, válvula f

vampire /'væmpaɪə(r)/ n vampiro m

van /væn/ n (large) camião m; (small) camionete f, comercial m; (milkman's, baker's etc) camionete f; (rail) bagageiro m, (P) furgão m

vandal /'vændl/ n vândalo m. ~**ism** /-əlɪzəm/ n vandalismo m

vandalize /'vændəlaɪz/ vt destruir, estragar

vanguard /'vængaːd/ n vanguarda f

vanilla /və'nɪlə/ n baunilha f

vanish /'vænɪʃ/ vi desaparecer, sumir-se, desvanecer-se

vanity /'vænətɪ/ n vaidade f. ~ **case** bolsa f de maquilagem

vantage-point /'vaːntɪdʒpɔɪnt/ n (bom) ponto m de observação

vapour /'veɪpə(r)/ n vapor m; (mist) bruma f

vari|able /'veərɪəbl/ a variável. ~**ation** /-'eɪʃn/ n variação f. ~**ed** /-ɪd/ a variado

variance /'veərɪəns/ n **at** ~ em desacordo (**with** com)

variant /'veərɪənt/ a diverso, diferente □ n variante f

varicose /'værɪkəʊs/ a ~ **veins** varizes fpl

variety /və'raɪətɪ/ n variedade f; (entertainment) variedades fpl

various /'veərɪəs/ a vários, diversos, variados

varnish /'vaːnɪʃ/ n verniz m □ vt envernizar; (nails) pintar

vary /'veərɪ/ vt/i variar. ~**ing** a variado

vase /vaːz/ n vaso m, jarra f

vast /vaːst/ a vasto, imenso. ~**ly** adv imensamente, infinitamente. ~**ness** n vastidão f, imensidão f, imensidade f

vat /væt/ n tonel m, dorna f, cuba f

VAT /viːˈɜːtiː, væt/ abbr ICM m, (P) IVA m

vault[1] /vɔːlt/ n (roof) abóbada f; (in bank) casa-forte f; (tomb) cripta f; (cellar) adega f

vault[2] /vɔːlt/ vt/i saltar □ n salto m

vaunt /vɔːnt/ vt/i gabar(-se), ufanar (-se) (de), vangloriar(-se)

VD abbr see **venereal disease**

VDU abbr see **visual display unit**

veal /viːl/ n (meat) vitela f

veer /vɪə(r)/ vi virar, mudar de direção, (P) direcção

vegan /'viːgən/ a & n vegetariano (m) estrito

vegetable /'vedʒɪtəbl/ n hortaliça f, legume m □ a vegetal

vegetarian /vedʒɪ'teərɪən/ a & n vegetariano (m)

vegetate /'vedʒɪteɪt/ vi vegetar

vegetation /vedʒɪ'teɪʃn/ n vegetação f

vehement /'viːəmənt/ a veemente. ~**ly** adv veementemente

vehicle /'viːɪkl/ n veículo m

veil /veɪl/ n véu m □ vt velar, cobrir com véu; (fig) esconder, disfarçar

vein /veɪn/ n (in body; mood) veia f; (in rock) veio m, filão m; (of leaf) nervura f

velocity /vɪ'lɒsətɪ/ n velocidade f

velvet /'velvɪt/ n veludo m. ~y a aveludado

vendetta /ven'detə/ n vendeta f

vending-machine /'vendɪŋməʃi:n/ n vendedora f automática, (P) máquina f de distribuição

vendor /'vendə(r)/ n vendedor m. street ~ vendedor m ambulante

veneer /və'nɪə(r)/ n folheado m; (fig) fachada f, máscara f

venerable /'venərəbl/ a venerável

venereal /və'nɪərɪəl/ a venéreo. ~ disease doença f venérea

venetian /və'ni:ʃn/ a ~ blinds persiana f

Venezuela /venɪz'weɪlə/ n Venezuela f. ~n a & n venezuelano (m)

vengeance /'vendʒəns/ n vingança. with a ~ furiosamente, em excesso, com mais força do que se pretende

venison /'venɪzn/ n carne f de veado

venom /'venəm/ n veneno m. ~ous /'venəməs/ a venenoso

vent[1] /vent/ n (in coat) abertura f

vent[2] /vent/ n (hole) orifício m, abertura f, (for air) respiradouro m □ vt (anger) descarregar (on para cima de). give ~ to (fig) desabafar, dar vazão a

ventilat|e /'ventɪleɪt/ vt ventilar. ~ion /-'leɪʃn/ n ventilação f. ~or n ventilador m

ventriloquist /ven'trɪləkwɪst/ n ventríloquo m

venture /'ventʃə(r)/ n empreendimento m arriscado, aventura f □ vt/i arriscar(-se)

venue /'venju:/ n porto m de encontro

veranda /və'rændə/ n varanda f

verb /vɜ:b/ n verbo m

verbal /'vɜ:bl/ a verbal; (literal) literal

verbatim /vɜ:'beɪtɪm/ adv literalmente, palavra por palavra

verbose /vɜ:'bəʊs/ a palavroso, prolixo

verdict /'vɜ:dɪkt/ n veredicto m; (opinion) opinião f

verge /vɜ:dʒ/ n beira f, borda f □ vi ~ on estar à beira de. on the ~ of doing prestes a fazer

verify /'verɪfaɪ/ vt verificar

veritable /'verɪtəbl/ a autêntico, verdadeiro

vermicelli /vɜ:mɪ'selɪ/ n aletria f

vermin /'vɜ:mɪn/ n animais mpl nocivos; (lice, fleas etc) parasitas mpl

vermouth /'vɜ:məθ/ n vermute m

vernacular /və'nækjʊlə(r)/ n vernáculo m; (dialect) dialeto m, (P) dialecto m

versatil|e /'vɜ:sətaɪl/ a versátil; (tool) que serve para vários fins. ~ity /-'tɪlətɪ/ n versatilidade f

verse /vɜ:s/ n (poetry) verso m, poesia f; (stanza) estrofe f, (of Bible) versículo m

versed /vɜ:st/ a ~ in versado em, conhecedor de

version /'vɜ:ʃn/ n versão f

versus /'vɜ:səs/ prep contra

vertebra /'vɜ:tɪbrə/ n (pl -brae /-bri:/) vértebra f

vertical /'vɜ:tɪkl/ a vertical. ~ly adv verticalmente

vertigo /'vɜ:tɪgəʊ/ n vertigem f

verve /vɜ:v/ n verve f, vivacidade f

very /'verɪ/ adv muito □ a (actual) mesmo, próprio; (exact) preciso, exato, (P) exacto. the ~ day/etc o próprio or o mesmo dia/etc. at the ~ end mesmo or precisamente no fim. the ~ first/best/etc (emph) o primeiro/melhor/etc de todos. ~ much muito. ~ well muito bem

vessel /'vesl/ n vaso m

vest[1] /vest/ n corpete m, (P) camisola f interior; (Amer: waistcoat) colete m

vest[2] /vest/ vt conferir (in a). ~ed interests interesses mpl

vestige /'vestɪdʒ/ n vestígio m

vestry /'vestrɪ/ n sacristia f

vet /vet/ n (colloq) veterinário m □ vt (pt vetted) (candidate etc) examinar atentamente, estudar

veteran /'vetərən/ n veterano m. (war) ~ veterano m de guerra

veterinary /'vetərɪnərɪ/ a veterinário. ~ surgeon veterinário m

veto /'vi:təʊ/ n (pl -oes) veto m; (right) direito m de veto □ vt vetar, opor o veto a

vex /veks/ vt aborrecer, irritar, contrariar. ~ed question questão f muito debatida, assunto m controverso

via /'vaɪə/ prep por, via

viab|le /'vaɪəbl/ a viável. ~ility /-'bɪlətɪ/ n viabilidade f

viaduct /'vaɪədʌkt/ n viaduto m

vibrant /'vaɪbrənt/ a vibrante

vibrat|e /vaɪ'breɪt/ vt/i (fazer) vibrar. ~ion /-ʃn/ n vibração f

vicar /'vɪkə(r)/ n (Anglican) pastor m; (Catholic) vigário m, pároco m. ~age n presbitério m

vicarious /vɪ'keərɪəs/ a vivido indiretamente, (P) indirectamente

vice[1] /vaɪs/ n (depravity) vício m

vice[2] /vaɪs/ n (techn) torno m

vice- /vaɪs/ pref vice-. ~-chairman vice-presidente m. ~-chancellor n vice-chanceler m; (univ) reitor m. ~-consul n vice-cônsul m. ~-president n vice-presidente mf

vice versa /'vaɪsɪ'vɜ:sə/ adv vice-versa

vicinity /vɪ'sɪnətɪ/ n vizinhança f,

cercania(s) *fpl*, arredores *mpl*. **in the ~ of** nos arredores de

vicious /ˈvɪʃəs/ *a* (*spiteful*) mau, maldoso; (*violent*) brutal, feroz. **~ circle** círculo *m* vicioso. **~ly** *adv* maldosamente; (*violently*) brutalmente, ferozmente

victim /ˈvɪktɪm/ *n* vítima *f*

victimiz|e /ˈvɪktɪmaɪz/ *vt* perseguir. **~ation** /-ˈzeɪʃn/ *n* perseguição *f*

victor /ˈvɪktə(r)/ *n* vencedor *m*

victor|y /ˈvɪktərɪ/ *n* vitória *f*. **~ious** /-ˈtɔːrɪəs/ *a* vitorioso

video /ˈvɪdɪəʊ/ *a* vídeo □ *n* (*pl* -os) (*colloq*) vídeo □ *vt* (*record*) gravar em vídeo. **~ cassette** video-cassete *f*. **~ recorder** videocassete *m*

vie /vaɪ/ *vi* (*pres p* **vying**) rivalizar, competir (**with** com)

view /vjuː/ *n* vista *f* □ *vt* ver; (*examine*) examinar; (*consider*) considerar, ver; (*a house*) visitar, ver. **in my ~** a meu ver, na minha opinião. **in ~ of** em vista de. **on ~** em exposição, à mostra; (*open to the public*) aberto ao público. **with a ~ to** com a intenção de, com o fim de. **~er** *n* (*TV*) telespectador *m*; (*for slides*) visor *m*

viewfinder /ˈvjuːfaɪndə(r)/ *n* visor *m*

viewpoint /ˈvjuːpɔɪnt/ *n* ponto *m* de vista

vigil /ˈvɪdʒɪl/ *n* vigília *f*; (*over corpse*) velório *m*; (*relig*) vigília *f*

vigilan|t /ˈvɪdʒɪlənt/ *a* vigilante. **~ce** *n* vigilância *f*. **~te** /vɪdʒɪˈlæntɪ/ *n* vigilante *m*

vig|our /ˈvɪgə(r)/ *n* vigor *m*. **~orous** /ˈvɪgərəs/ *a* vigoroso

vile /vaɪl/ *a* (*base*) infame, vil; (*colloq: bad*) horroroso, péssimo

vilify /ˈvɪlɪfaɪ/ *vt* difamar

villa /ˈvɪlə/ *n* vivenda *f*, vila *f*; (*country residence*) casa *f* de campo

village /ˈvɪlɪdʒ/ *n* aldeia *f*, povoado *m*. **~r** *n* aldeão *m*, aldeã *f*

villain /ˈvɪlən/ *n* patife *m*, mau-caráter *m*. **~y** *n* infâmia *f*, vilania *f*

vindicat|e /ˈvɪndɪkeɪt/ *vt* vindicar, justificar. **~ion** /-ˈkeɪʃn/ *n* justificação *f*

vindictive /vɪnˈdɪktɪv/ *a* vingativo

vine /vaɪn/ *n* (*plant*) vinha *f*

vinegar /ˈvɪnɪgə(r)/ *n* vinagre *m*

vineyard /ˈvɪnjəd/ *n* vinha *f*, vinhedo *m*

vintage /ˈvɪntɪdʒ/ *n* (*year*) ano *m* de colheita de qualidade excepcional □ *a* (*wine*) de colheita excepcional e de um determinado ano; (*car*) de museu (*colloq*), fabricado entre 1917 e 1930

vinyl /ˈvaɪnɪl/ *n* vinil *m*

viola /vɪˈəʊlə/ *n* (*mus*) viola *f*, violeta *f*

violat|e /ˈvaɪəleɪt/ *vt* violar. **~ion** /-ˈleɪʃn/ *n* violação *f*

violen|t /ˈvaɪələnt/ *a* violento. **~ce** *n* violência *f*. **~tly** *adv* violentamente, com violência

violet /ˈvaɪələt/ *n* (*bot*) violeta *f*; (*colour*) violeta *m* □ *a* violeta

violin /vaɪəˈlɪn/ *n* violino *m*. **~ist** *n* violinista *mf*

VIP /viːaɪˈpiː/ *abbr* (*very important person*) VIP *m*, personalidade *f* importante

viper /ˈvaɪpə(r)/ *n* víbora *f*

virgin /ˈvɜːdʒɪn/ *a & n* virgem (*f*); **~ity** /vəˈdʒɪnətɪ/ *n* virgindade *f*

Virgo /ˈvɜːgəʊ/ *n* (*astr*) Virgem *f*, (*P*) virgo *m*

viril|e /ˈvɪraɪl/ *a* viril, varonil. **~ity** /vɪˈrɪlətɪ/ *n* virilidade *f*

virtual /ˈvɜːtʃʊəl/ *a* que é na prática embora não em teoria, verdadeiro. **a ~ failure**/*etc* praticamente um fracasso/*etc*. **~ly** *adv* praticamente

virtue /ˈvɜːtʃuː/ *n* (*goodness, chastity*) virtude *f*; (*merit*) mérito *m*. **by** *or* **in ~ of** por *or* em virtude de

virtuos|o /vɜːtʃʊˈəʊsəʊ/ *n* (*pl* -si /-siː/) virtuoso *m*, virtuose *mf*. **~ity** /-ˈɒsətɪ/ *n* virtuosidade *f*, virtuosismo *m*

virtuous /ˈvɜːtʃʊəs/ *a* virtuoso

virulen|t /ˈvɪrʊlənt/ *a* virulento. **~ce** /-ləns/ *n* virulência *f*

virus /ˈvaɪərəs/ *n* (*pl* -es) vírus *m*; (*colloq: disease*) virose *f*

visa /ˈviːzə/ *n* visto *m*

viscount /ˈvaɪkaʊnt/ *n* visconde *m*. **~ess** /-ɪs/ *n* viscondessa *f*

viscous /ˈvɪskəs/ *a* viscoso

vise /vaɪs/ *n* (*Amer: vice*) torno *m*

visib|le /ˈvɪzəbl/ *a* visível. **~ility** /-ˈbɪlətɪ/ *n* visibilidade *f*. **~ly** *adv* visivelmente

vision /ˈvɪʒn/ *n* (*dream, insight*) visão *f*; (*seeing, sight*) vista *f*, visão *f*

visionary /ˈvɪʒənərɪ/ *a* visionário; (*plan, scheme etc*) fantasista, quimérico □ *n* visionário *m*

visit /ˈvɪzɪt/ *vt* (*pt* **visited**) (*person*) visitar, fazer uma visita a; (*place*) visitar □ *vi* estar de visita □ *n* (*tour, call*) visita *f*; (*stay*) estada *f*, visita *f*. **~or** *n* visitante *mf*; (*guest*) visita *f*

visor /ˈvaɪzə(r)/ *n* viseira *f*; (*in vehicle*) visor *m*

vista /ˈvɪstə/ *n* vista *f*, panorama *m*

visual /ˈvɪʒʊəl/ *a* visual. **~ display unit** terminal *m* de vídeo. **~ly** *adv* visualmente

visualize /ˈvɪʒʊəlaɪz/ *vt* visualizar; (*foresee*) imaginar, prever

vital /ˈvaɪtl/ *a* vital. **~ statistics** estatísticas *fpl* demográficas; (*colloq: woman*) medidas *fpl*

vitality /vaɪˈtælətɪ/ *n* vitalidade *f*

vitamin /ˈvɪtəmɪn/ *n* vitamina *f*

vivac|ious /vɪˈveɪʃəs/ *a* cheio de vida,

vivo, animado. ~ity /-'væsətɪ/ n vivacidade f, animação f

vivid /'vɪvɪd/ a vívido; (*imagination*) vivo. ~ly adv vividamente

vivisection /vɪvɪ'sekʃn/ n vivissecção f

vixen /'vɪksn/ n raposa f fêmea

vocabulary /və'kæbjʊlərɪ/ n vocabulário m

vocal /'vəʊkl/ a vocal; (*fig: person*) eloqüente, (P) eloquente. ~ cords cordas fpl vocais. ~ist n vocalista mf

vocation /və'keɪʃn/ n vocação f; (*trade*) profissão f. ~al a vocacional, profissional

vociferous /və'sɪfərəs/ a vociferante

vodka /'vɒdkə/ n vodka m

vogue /vəʊg/ n voga f, moda f, popularidade f. in ~ em voga, na moda

voice /vɔɪs/ n voz f □ vt (*express*) exprimir

void /vɔɪd/ a vazio; (*jur*) nulo, sem validade □ n vácuo m, vazio m. make ~ anular, invalidar. ~ of sem, destituído de

volatile /'vɒlətaɪl/ a (*substance*) volátil; (*fig: changeable*) instável

volcano /vɒl'keɪnəʊ/ n (pl -oes) vulcão m. ~ic /-ænɪk/ a vulcânico

volition /və'lɪʃn/ n of one's own ~ de sua própria vontade

volley /'vɒlɪ/ n (*of blows etc*) saraivada f; (*of gunfire*) salva f; (*tennis*) voleio m. ~ball n voleibol m, vôlei m

volt /vəʊlt/ n volt m. ~age n voltagem f

voluble /'vɒljʊbl/ a falante, loquaz

volume /'vɒljuːm/ n (*book, sound*) volume m; (*capacity*) capacidade f

voluntary /'vɒləntərɪ/ a voluntário; (*unpaid*) não-remunerado. ~ily /-trəlɪ/ adv voluntariamente

volunteer /vɒlən'tɪə(r)/ n voluntário m □ vi oferecer-se (to do para fazer); (*mil*) alistar-se como voluntário □ vt oferecer espontaneamente

voluptuous /və'lʌptʃʊəs/ a voluptuoso, sensual

vomit /'vɒmɪt/ vt/i (pt vomited) vomitar □ n vômito m, (P) vómito m

voodoo /'vuːduː/ n vodu m

voracious /və'reɪʃəs/ a voraz. ~ously adv vorazmente. ~ty /və'ræsətɪ/ n voracidade f

vote /vəʊt/ n voto m; (*right*) direito m de voto □ vt/i votar. ~er n eleitor m. ~ing n votação f; (*poll*) escrutínio m

vouch /vaʊtʃ/ vi ~ for responder por, garantir

voucher /'vaʊtʃə(r)/ n (*for meal, transport*) vale m; (*receipt*) comprovante m

vow /vaʊ/ n voto m □ vt (*loyalty etc*) jurar (to a). ~ to do jurar fazer

vowel /'vaʊəl/ n vogal f

voyage /'vɔɪɪdʒ/ n viagem (por mar) f. ~r /-ə(r)/ n viajante m

vulgar /'vʌlgə(r)/ a ordinário, grosseiro; (*in common use*) vulgar. ~ity /-'gærətɪ/ n (*behaviour*) grosseria f, vulgaridade f

vulnerable /'vʌlnərəbl/ a vulnerável. ~ility /-'bɪlətɪ/ n vulnerabilidade f

vulture /'vʌltʃə(r)/ n abutre m, urubu m

vying /'vaɪɪŋ/ see vie

W

wad /wɒd/ n bucha f, tampão m; (*bundle*) maço m, rolo m

wadding /'wɒdɪŋ/ n enchimento m

waddle /'wɒdl/ vi bambolear-se, rebolar-se, gingar

wade /weɪd/ vi ~ through (*fig*) avançar a custo por; (*mud, water*) patinhar em

wafer /'weɪfə(r)/ n (*biscuit*) bolacha f de baunilha; (*relig*) hóstia f

waffle[1] /'wɒfl/ n (*colloq: talk*) lenga-lenga f, papo m, conversa f; (*colloq: writing*) □ vi (*colloq*) escrever muito sem dizer nada de importante

waffle[2] /'wɒfl/ n (*culin*) waffle m

waft /wɒft/ vi flutuar □ vt espalhar, levar suavemente

wag /wæg/ vt/i (pt wagged) abanar, agitar, sacudir

wage[1] /weɪdʒ/ vt (*campaign, war*) fazer

wage[2] /weɪdʒ/ n ~(s) (*weekly, daily*) salário m, ordenado m. ~claim n pedido m de aumento de salário. ~earner n trabalhador m assalariado. ~freeze n congelamento m de salários

wager /'weɪdʒə(r)/ n (*bet*) aposta f □ vt apostar (that que)

waggle /'wægl/ vt/i abanar, agitar, sacudir

wagon /'wægən/ n (*horse-drawn*) carroça f; (*rail*) vagão m de mercadorias

waif /weɪf/ n criança f abandonada

wail /weɪl/ vi lamentar-se, gemer lamentosamente □ n lamentação f, gemido m lamentoso

waist /weɪst/ n cintura f. ~line n cintura f

waistcoat /'weɪskəʊt/ n colete m

wait /weɪt/ vt/i esperar □ n espera f. ~ for esperar. ~ on servir. lie in ~ (for) estar escondido à espera (de), armar uma emboscada (para). keep sb ~ing fazer alguém esperar. ~ing-list n lista *f* de espera. **~ing-room** *n* sala *f* de espera

wait|er /'weɪtə(r)/ *n* garçon *m*, (P) criado *m* (de mesa). **~ress** *n* garçonete *f*, (P) criada *f* (de mesa)

waive /weɪv/ *vt* renunciar a, desistir de

wake¹ /weɪk/ *vt/i* (*pt* woke, *pp* woken) **~ (up)** acordar, despertar □ *n* (*before burial*) velório *m*

wake² /weɪk/ *n* (*ship*) esteira (de espuma) *f*. **in the ~ of** (*following*) atrás de, em seguida a

waken /'weɪkən/ *vt/i* acordar, despertar

Wales /weɪlz/ *n* País *m* de Gales

walk /wɔːk/ *vi* andar, caminhar; (*not ride*) ir a pé; (*stroll*) passear □ *vt* (*streets*) andar por, percorrer; (*distance*) andar, fazer a pé, percorrer; (*dog*) (levar para) passear □ *n* (*stroll*) passeio *m*, volta *f*; (*excursion*) caminhada *f*; (*gait*) passo *m*, maneira *f* de andar; (*pace*) passo *m*; (*path*) caminho *m*. **it's a 5-minute ~** são 5 minutos a pé. **~ of life** meio *m*, condição *f* social. **~ out** (*go away*) sair; (*go on strike*) fazer greve. **~ out on** abandonar. **~-over** *n* vitória *f* fácil

walker /'wɔːkə(r)/ *n* caminhante *mf*

walkie-talkie /wɔːkɪ'tɔːkɪ/ *n* walkie-talkie *m*

walking /'wɔːkɪŋ/ *n* andar (a pé) *m*, marcha (a pé) *f* □ *a* (*colloq: dictionary*) vivo. **~-stick** *n* bengala *f*

Walkman /'wɔːkmæn/ *n* walkman *m*

wall /wɔːl/ *n* parede *f*; (*around land*) muro *m*; (*of castle, town, fig*) muralha *f*; (*of stomach etc*) parede(s) *f* (*pl*) □ *vt* (*city*) fortificar; (*property*) murar. **go to the ~** sucumbir, falir; (*firm*) ir à falência. **up the ~** (*colloq*) fora de si

wallet /'wɒlɪt/ *n* carteira *f*

wallflower /'wɔːlflaʊə(r)/ *n* (*bot*) goivo *m*. **be a ~** (*fig*) tomar chá de cadeira, (P) levar banho de cadeira

wallop /'wɒləp/ *vt* (*pt* walloped) (*sl*) espancar (*colloq*) □ *n* (*sl*) pancada *f* forte

wallow /'wɒləʊ/ *vi* (*in mud*) chafurdar, atolar-se; (*fig*) regozijar-se

wallpaper /'wɔːlpeɪpə(r)/ *n* papel *m* de parede □ *vt* forrar com papel de parede

walnut /'wɔːlnʌt/ *n* (*nut*) noz *f*; (*tree*) nogueira *f*

walrus /'wɔːlrəs/ *n* morsa *f*

waltz /wɔːls/ *n* valsa *f* □ *vi* valsar

wan /wɒn/ *a* pálido

wand /wɒnd/ *n* (*magic*) varinha *f* mágica *or* de condão

wander /'wɒndə(r)/ *vi* andar ao acaso, vagar, errar; (*river*) serpentear; (*mind, speech*) divagar; (*stray*) extra-

viar-se. **~er** *n* vagabundo *m*, andarilho *m*. **~ing** *a* errante

wane /weɪn/ *vi* diminuir, minguar; (*decline*) declinar □ *n* **on the ~** em declínio; (*moon*) no quarto minguante

wangle /'wæŋgl/ *vt* (*colloq*) conseguir algo através de pistolão

want /wɒnt/ *vt* querer (**to do** fazer); (*need*) precisar (de); (*ask for*) exigir, requerer □ *vi* **~ for** ter falta de □ *n* (*need*) necessidade *f*, precisão *f*; (*desire*) desejo *m*; (*lack*) falta *f*, carência *f*. **for ~ of** por falta de. **I ~ you to** go eu quero que você vá. **~ed** *a* (*criminal*) procurado pela polícia; (*in ad*) precisa(m)-se

wanting /'wɒntɪŋ/ *a* falho, falto (**in** de). **be found ~** não estar à altura

wanton /'wɒntən/ *a* (*playful*) travesso, brincalhão; (*cruelty, destruction etc*) gratuito; (*woman*) despudorado

war /wɔː(r)/ *n* guerra *f*. **at ~** em guerra. **on the ~-path** em pé de guerra

warble /'wɔːbl/ *vt/i* gorjear

ward /wɔːd/ *n* (*in hospital*) enfermaria *f*; (*jur: minor*) pupilo *m*; (*pol*) círculo *m* eleitoral □ *vt* **~ off** (*a blow*) aparar; (*anger*) desviar; (*danger*) prevenir, evitar

warden /'wɔːdn/ *n* (*of institution*) diretor *m*, (P) director *m*; (*of park*) guarda *m*

warder /'wɔːdə(r)/ *n* guarda (de prisão) *m*, carcereiro *m*

wardrobe /'wɔːdrəʊb/ *n* (*place*) armário *m*, guarda-roupa *m*, (P) guarda-fato *m*, (P) roupeiro *m*; (*clothes*) guarda-roupa *m*

warehouse /'weəhaʊs/ *n* (*pl* -s /-haʊzɪz/) armazém *m*, depósito *m* de mercadorias

wares /weəz/ *npl* (*goods*) mercadorias *fpl*, artigos *mpl*

warfare /'wɔːfeə(r)/ *n* guerra *f*

warhead /'wɔːhed/ *n* ogiva (de combate) *f*

warlike /'wɔːlaɪk/ *a* marcial, guerreiro; (*bellicose*) belicoso

warm /wɔːm/ *a* (-er, -est) quente; (*hearty*) caloroso, cordial. **be** *or* **feel ~** estar com *or* ter *or* sentir calor □ *vt/i* **~ (up)** aquecer(-se). **~-hearted** *a* afetuoso, (P) afectuoso, com calor humano. **~ly** *adv* (*heartily*) calorosamente. **wrap up ~ly** agasalhar-se bem. **~th** *n* calor *m*

warn /wɔːn/ *vt* avisar, prevenir. **~ sb off sth** (*advise against*) pôr alguém de prevenção *or* de pé atrás com alg coisa; (*forbid*) proibir alg coisa a alguém. **~ing** *n* aviso *m*. **~ing light** lâmpada *f* de advertência. **without ~ing** sem aviso, sem prevenir

warp /wɔːp/ vt/i (wood etc) empenar; (fig: pervert) torcer, deformar, desvirtuar. ~ed a (fig) deturpado, pervertido

warrant /'wɒrənt/ n autorização f; (for arrest) mandato (de captura) m; (comm) título m de crédito, warrant m □ vt justificar; (guarantee) garantir

warranty /'wɒrəntɪ/ n garantia f

warring /'wɔːrɪŋ/ a em guerra; (rival) contrário, antagônico, (P) antagónico

warrior /'wɒrɪə(r)/ n guerreiro m

warship /'wɔːʃɪp/ n navio m de guerra

wart /wɔːt/ n verruga f

wartime /'wɔːtaɪm/ n in ~ em tempo de guerra

wary /'weərɪ/ a (-ier, -iest) cauteloso, prudente

was /wɒz/; unstressed /wəz/ see be

wash /wɒʃ/ vt/i lavar(-se); (flow over) molhar, inundar □ n lavagem f; (dirty clothes) roupa f para lavar; (of ship) esteira f; (of paint) fina camada f de tinta. **have a** ~ lavar-se. ~**-basin** n pia f, (P) lavatório m. ~**-cloth** n (Amer: face-cloth) toalha f de rosto. ~ **one's hands of** lavar as mãos de. ~ **out** (cup etc) lavar; (stain) tirar lavando. ~**-out** n (sl) fiasco m. ~**-room** n (Amer) banheiro m, (P) casa f de banho. ~ **up** lavar a louça; (Amer: wash oneself) lavar-se. ~**able** a lavável. ~**ing** n (dirty) roupa f suja; (clean) roupa f lavada. ~**ing-machine** n máquina f de lavar roupa. ~**ing-powder** n detergente m em pó. ~**ing-up** n lavagem f da louça

washed-out /wɒʃt'aʊt/ a (faded) desbotado; (exhausted) exausto

washer /'wɒʃə(r)/ n (machine) máquina f de lavar roupa, louça f, (P) loiça f; (ring) anilha f

wasp /wɒsp/ n vespa f

wastage /'weɪstɪdʒ/ n desperdício m, perda f. **natural** ~ desgaste m natural

waste /weɪst/ vt desperdiçar, esbanjar; (time) perder □ vi ~ **away** consumir-se □ a (useless) inútil; (material) de refugo □ n desperdício m, perda f; (of time) perda f; (rubbish) lixo m. **lay** ~ assolar, devastar. ~ **(land)** (desolate) região f desolada, ermo m; (unused) (terreno) baldio m. ~**-disposal unit** triturador m de lixo. ~ **paper** papéis mpl velhos. ~**-paper basket** cesto m de papéis

wasteful /'weɪstfl/ a dispendioso; (person) esbanjador, gastador, perdulário

watch /wɒtʃ/ vt/i ver bem, olhar com atenção, observar; (game, TV) ver; (guard, spy on) vigiar; (be careful about) tomar cuidado com □ n vigia f, vigilância f; (naut) quarto m; (for telling time) relógio m. ~**-dog** n cão m de guarda. ~ **out** (look out) estar à espreita (for de); (take care) acautelar-se. ~**-strap** n correia f, pulseira f do relógio. ~**-tower** n torre f de observação. ~**ful** a atento, vigilante

watchmaker /'wɒtʃmeɪkə(r)/ n relojoeiro m

watchman /'wɒtʃmən/ n (pl -men) (of building) guarda m. **(night-)**~ guarda-noturno m

watchword /'wɒtʃwɜːd/ n lema m, divisa f

water /'wɔːtə(r)/ n água f □ vt regar □ vi (of eyes) lacrimejar, chorar. ~ **down** juntar água a, diluir; (milk, wine) aguar, batizar, (P) baptizar (colloq); (fig: tone down) suavizar. ~**-closet** n WC m, banheiro m, (P) lavabos mpl. ~**-colour** n aquarela f. ~**-ice** n sorvete m. ~**-lily** n nenúfar m. ~**-main** n cano m principal da rede. ~**-melon** n melancia f. ~**-pistol** n pistola f de água. ~ **polo** pólo m aquático. ~**-skiing** n esqui m aquático. ~**-wheel** n roda f hidráulica

watercress /'wɔːtəkres/ n agrião m

waterfall /'wɔːtəfɔːl/ n queda f de água, cascata f

watering-can /'wɔːtərɪŋkæn/ n regador m

waterlogged /'wɔːtəlɒɡd/ a saturado de água; (land) empapado, alagado; (vessel) inundado, alagado

watermark /'wɔːtəmɑːk/ n (in paper) marca-d'água f, filigrana f

waterproof /'wɔːtəpruːf/ a impermeável; (watch) à prova d'água

watershed /'wɔːtəʃed/ n (fig) momento m decisivo; (in affairs) ponto m crítico

watertight /'wɔːtətaɪt/ a à prova d'água, hermético; (fig: argument etc) inequívoco, irrefutável

waterway /'wɔːtəweɪ/ n via f navegável

waterworks /'wɔːtəwɜːks/ n (place) estação f hidráulica

watery /'wɔːtərɪ/ a (colour) pálido; (eyes) lacrimoso; (soup) aguado; (tea) fraco

watt /wɒt/ n watt m

wav|e /weɪv/ n onda f; (in hair; radio) onda f; (sign) aceno m □ vt acenar com; (sword) brandir; (hair) ondular □ vi acenar (com a mão); (hair etc) ondular; (flag) tremular. ~**eband** n faixa f de onda. ~**e goodbye** dizer adeus. ~**elength** n comprimento m de onda. ~**y** a ondulado

waver /'weɪvə(r)/ vi vacilar; (hesitate) hesitar

wax[1] /wæks/ n cera f □ vt encerar; (car) polir. **~en**, **~y** adjs de cera

wax[2] /wæks/ vi (of moon) aumentar, crescer

waxwork /'wækswɜːk/ n (dummy) figura f de cera. **~s** npl (exhibition) museu m de figuras de cera

way /weɪ/ n (road, path) caminho m, estrada f, rua f (to para); (distance) percurso m; (direction) (P) direção f; (manner) modo m, maneira f; (means) meios mpl; (respect) respeito m. **~s** (habits) costumes mpl □ adv (colloq) consideravelmente, de longe. **be in the ~** atrapalhar. **be on one's** or **the ~** estar a caminho. **by the ~** a propósito. **by ~ of** por, via, através. **get one's own ~** conseguir o que quer. **give ~** (yield) ceder; (collapse) desabar; (auto) dar a preferência. **in a ~** de certo modo. **make one's ~** ir. **that ~** dessa maneira. **this ~** desta maneira. **~ in** entrada f. **~ out** saída f. **~-out** a (colloq) excêntrico

waylay /weɪ'leɪ/ vt (pt -laid) (assail) armar uma cilada para; (stop) interceptar

wayward /'weɪwəd/ a (wilful) teimoso; (perverse) caprichoso, difícil

WC /dʌb(ə)ljuː'siː/ n WC m, banheiro m, (P) casa f de banho

we /wiː/ pron nós

weak /wiːk/ a (-er, -est) fraco; (delicate) frágil. **~en** vt/i enfraquecer; (give way) fraquejar. **~ly** adv fracamente. **~ness** n fraqueza f; (fault) ponto m fraco. **a ~ness for** (liking) um fraco por

weakling /'wiːklɪŋ/ n fraco m

wealth /welθ/ n riqueza f; (riches, resources) riquezas fpl; (quantity) abundância f

wealthy /'welθɪ/ a (-ier, -iest) rico

wean /wiːn/ vt (baby) desmamar; (from habit etc) desabituar

weapon /'wepən/ n arma f

wear /weə(r)/ vt (pt wore, pp worn) (have on) usar, trazer; (put on) pôr; (expression) ter; (damage) gastar. **~ black/red/etc** vestir-se de preto/vermelho/etc □ vi (last) durar; (become old, damaged etc) gastar-se □ n (use) uso m; (deterioration) gasto m, uso m; (endurance) resistência f; (clothing) roupa f. **~ and tear** desgaste m. **~ down** gastar; (person) extenuar. **~ off** passar. **~ on** (time) passar lentamente. **~ out** gastar; (tire) cansar, esgotar

wear|y /'wɪərɪ/ a (-ier, -iest) fatigado, cansado; (tiring) fatigante, cansativo □ vi **~y of** cansar-se de. **~ily** adv com

lassidão, cansadamente. **~iness** n fadiga f, cansaço m

weasel /'wiːzl/ n doninha f

weather /'weðə(r)/ n tempo m □ a meteorológico □ vt (survive) agüentar, (P) aguentar, resistir a. **under the ~** (colloq: ill) indisposto, achacado. **~-beaten** a curtido pelo tempo. **~-forecast** n boletim m meteorológico. **~-vane** n cata-vento m

weathercock /'weðəkɒk/ n (lit & fig) cata-vento m

weav|e[1] /wiːv/ vt (pt wove, pp woven) (cloth etc) tecer; (plot) urdir, criar □ n (style) tipo m de tecido. **~er** /-ə(r)/ n tecelão m, tecelã f. **~ing** n tecelagem f

weave[2] /wiːv/ vi (move) serpear; (through traffic, obstacles) ziguezaguear

web /web/ n (of spider) teia f; (fabric) tecido m; (on foot) membrana f interdigital. **~bed** a (foot) palmado. **~bing** n (in chair) tira f de tecido forte. **~-footed** a palmípede

wed /wed/ vt/i (pt wedded) casar(-se)

wedding /'wedɪŋ/ n casamento m. **~-cake** n bolo m de noiva. **~-ring** n aliança (de casamento) f

wedge /wedʒ/ n calço m, cunha f; (cake) fatia f; (of lemon) quarto m; (under wheel etc) calço m, cunha f □ vt calçar; (push) meter or enfiar à força; (pack in) entalar

Wednesday /'wenzdɪ/ n quarta-feira f

weed /wiːd/ n erva f daninha □ vt/i arrancar as ervas, capinar. **~-killer** n herbicida m. **~ out** suprimir, arrancar. **~y** a (fig: person) fraco

week /wiːk/ n semana f. a **~ today/tomorrow** de hoje/de amanhã a oito dias. **~ly** a semanal □ a & n (periodical) (jornal) semanário (m) □ adv semanalmente, todas as semanas

weekday /'wiːkdeɪ/ n dia m de semana

weekend /'wiːkend/ n fim-de-semana m

weep /wiːp/ vt/i (pt wept) chorar (for sb por alguém). **~ing willow** (salgueiro-)chorão m

weigh /weɪ/ vt/i pesar. **~ anchor** levantar âncora or ferro, zarpar. **~ down** (weight) sobrecarregar; (bend) envergar; (fig) acabrunhar. **~ up** (colloq: examine) pesar

weight /weɪt/ n peso m. **lose ~** emagrecer. **put on ~** engordar. **~less** a imponderável. **~-lifter** n halterofilista m. **~-lifting** n halterofilia f. **~y** a pesado; (subject etc) de peso; (influential) influente

weighting /'weɪtɪŋ/ n suplemento m salarial

weir /wɪə(r)/ n represa f, açude m

weird /wɪəd/ a (-er, -est) misterioso; (strange) estranho, bizarro

welcom|e /'welkəm/ a agradável; (timely) oportuno □ int (seja) benvindo! □ n acolhimento m □ vt acolher, receber; (as greeting) dar as boas vindas a. **be ~e** ser bem-vindo. **you're ~e!** (after thank you) não tem de quê!, de nada! **~e to do** livre para fazer. **~ing** a acolhedor

weld /weld/ vt soldar □ n solda f. **~er** n soldador m. **~ing** n soldagem f, soldadura f

welfare /'welfeə(r)/ n bem-estar m; (aid) assistência f, previdência f social. **W~ State** Estado-Providência m

well[1] /wel/ n (for water, oil) poço m; (of stairs) vão m; (of lift) poço m

well[2] /wel/ adv (better, best) bem □ a bem (invar) □ int bem! **as ~** também. **we may as ~ go** é melhor irnos andando. **as ~ as** tão bem como; (in addition) assim como. **be ~** (healthy) ir or passar bem. **do ~** (succeed) sairse bem, ser bem sucedido. **very ~** muito bem. **~ done!** bravo!, muito bem! **~-behaved** a bem comportado, educado. **~-being** n bem-estar m. **~-bred** a (bem) educado. **~-done** a (of meat) bem passado. **~-dressed** a bem vestido. **~-heeled** a (colloq: wealthy) rico. **~-informed** a versado, bem informado. **~-known** a (bem-)conhecido. **~-meaning** a bem intencionado. **~-off** a rico, próspero. **~-read** a instruído. **~-spoken** a bem-falante. **~-timed** a oportuno. **~-to-do** a rico. **~-wisher** n admirador m, simpatizante mf

wellington /'welɪŋtən/ n (boot) bota f alta de borracha

Welsh /welʃ/ a galês □ n (lang) galês m. **~man** n galês m. **~woman** n galesa f

wend /wend/ vt **~ one's way** dirigirse, seguir o seu caminho

went /went/ see **go**

wept /wept/ see **weep**

were /wɜ:(r)/; unstressed /wə(r)/ see **be**

west /west/ n oeste m. **the W~** (pol) o Oeste, o Ocidente □ a ocidental, do oeste □ adv ao oeste, para o oeste. **W~ Indian** a & n antilhano (m). **the W~ Indies** as Antilhas. **~erly** a ocidental, oeste. **~ward** a para a oeste. **~ward(s)** adv para o oeste

western /'westən/ a ocidental, do oeste; (pol) ocidental □ n (film) filme m de cowboys, bangue-bangue m

westernize /'westənaɪz/ vt ocidentalizar

wet /wet/ a (wetter, wettest) molhado; (of weather) chuvoso, de chuva; (colloq: person) fraco. **get ~** molharse □ vt (pt wetted) molhar. **~ blanket** (colloq) desmancha-prazeres mf invar (colloq). **~ paint** pintado de fresco. **~ suit** roupa f de mergulho

whack /wæk/ vt (colloq) bater em □ n (colloq) pancada f. **~ed** a (colloq) morto de cansaço, rebentado (colloq). **~ing** a (sl) enorme, de todo o tamanho

whale /weɪl/ n baleia f

wharf /wɔ:f/ n (pl wharfs) cais m

what /wɒt/ a (interr, excl) que. **~ time is it?** que horas são? **~ an idea!** que idéia! □ pron (interr) (o) quê, como, o que, qual, quais; (object) o que; (after prep) que; (that which) o que, aquilo que. **~?** (o) quê?, como? **~ is it?** o que é? **~ is your address?** qual é o seu endereço? **~ is your name?** como se chama? **~ can you see?** o que é que você pode ver? **this is ~ I write with** é com isto que escrevo. **that's ~ I need** é disso que eu preciso. **do ~ you want** faça o que or aquilo que quiser. **~ about me/ him/**etc? e eu/ele/etc? **~ about doing sth?** e se fizéssemos alg coisa? **~ for?** para quê?

whatever /wɒt'evə(r)/ a **~ book/**etc qualquer livro/etc que seja □ pron (no matter what) qualquer que seja; (anything that) o que quer que, tudo o que. **nothing ~** absolutamente nada. **~ happens** aconteça o que acontecer. **do ~ you like** faça o que quiser

whatsoever /wɒtsəʊ'evə(r)/ a & pron = **whatever**

wheat /wi:t/ n trigo m

wheedle /'wi:dl/ vt convencer, persuadir, levar a

wheel /wi:l/ n roda f □ vt empurrar □ vi rodar, rolar. **at the ~** (of vehicle) ao volante; (helm) ao leme

wheelbarrow /'wi:lbærəʊ/ n carrinho m de mão

wheelchair /'wi:ltʃeə(r)/ n cadeira f de rodas

wheeze /wi:z/ vi respirar ruidosamente □ n respiração f difícil

when /wen/ adv, conj & pron quando. **the day/moment ~** o dia/momento em que

whenever /wen'evə(r)/ conj & adv (at whatever time) quando quer que, quando; (every time that) (de) cada vez que, sempre que

where /weə(r)/ adv, conj & pron onde, aonde; (in which place) em que, onde; (whereas) enquanto que, ao passo que. **~ is he going?** aonde é que ele vai? **~abouts** adv onde □ n paradeiro m.

~by *adv* pelo que. **~upon** *adv* após o que, depois do que

whereas /weər'æz/ *conj* enquanto que, ao passo que

wherever /weər'evə(r)/ *conj* & *adv* onde quer que. **~ can it be?** onde pode estar?

whet /wet/ *vt* (*pt* **whetted**) (*appetite, desire*) aguçar, despertar

whether /'weðə(r)/ *conj* se. **not know ~** não saber se. **~ I go or not** caso eu vá ou não

which /wɪtʃ/ *interr a* & *pron* qual, que **~ bag is yours?** qual das malas é a sua? **~ is your coat?** qual é o seu casaco? **do you know ~ he's taken?** sabe qual/quais é que ele levou? □ *rel pron* que, o qual; (*referring to whole sentence*) o que; (*after prep*) que, o qual, cujo. **at ~** em qual/que. **from ~** do qual/que. **of ~** do qual/de que. **to ~** para o qual/o que

whichever /wɪtʃ'evə(r)/ *a* **~ book/etc** qualquer livro/etc que seja, seja que livro/etc for. **take ~ book you wish** leve o livro que quiser □ *pron* qualquer, quaisquer

whiff /wɪf/ *n* (*of fresh air*) sopro *m*, lufada *f*; (*smell*) baforada *f*

while /waɪl/ *n* (espaço de) tempo *m*, momento *m*. **once in a ~** de vez em quando □ *conj* (*when*) enquanto; (*although*) embora; (*whereas*) enquanto que □ *vt* **~ away** (*time*) passar

whim /wɪm/ *n* capricho *m*

whimper /'wɪmpə(r)/ *vi* gemer; (*baby*) choramingar □ *n* gemido *m*; (*baby*) choro *m*

whimsical /'wɪmzɪkl/ *a* (*person*) caprichoso; (*odd*) bizarro

whine /waɪn/ *vi* lamuriar-se, queixar-se; (*dog*) ganir □ *n* lamúria *f*, queixume *m*; (*dog*) ganido *m*

whip /wɪp/ *n* chicote *m* □ *vt* (*pt* **whipped**) chicotear; (*culin*) bater □ *vi* (*move*) ir a toda a pressa. **~-round** *n* (*colloq*) coleta *f*, vaquinha *f*. **~ up** excitar; (*cause*) provocar; (*colloq: meal*) preparar rapidamente. **~ped cream** creme *m* chantilly

whirl /wɜːl/ *vt/i* (fazer) rodopiar, girar □ *n* rodopio *m*

whirlpool /'wɜːlpuːl/ *n* redemoinho *m*

whirlwind /'wɜːlwɪnd/ *n* redemoinho *m* de vento, turbilhão *m*

whirr /wɜː(r)/ *vi* zunir, zumbir

whisk /wɪsk/ *vt/i* (*snatch*) levar/tirar bruscamente; (*culin*) bater; (*flies*) sacudir □ *n* (*culin*) batedeira *f*. **~ away** (*brush away*) sacudir

whisker /'wɪskə(r)/ *n* fio *m* de barba. **~s** *npl* (*of animal*) bigode *m*; (*beard*) barba *f*; (*sideboards*) suíças *fpl*

whisky /'wɪskɪ/ *n* uísque *m*

whisper /'wɪspə(r)/ *vt/i* sussurrar, murmurar; (*of stream, leaves*) sussurrar □ *n* sussurro *m*, murmúrio *m*. **in a ~** baixinho, em voz baixa

whist /wɪst/ *n* uíste *m*, (*P*) whist *m*

whistle /'wɪsl/ *n* assobio *m*; (*instrument*) apito *m* □ *vt/i* assobiar; (*with instrument*) apitar

Whit /wɪt/ *a* **~ Sunday** domingo *m* de Pentecostes

white /waɪt/ *a* (-er, -est) branco, alvo; (*pale*) pálido □ *n* (*colour; of eyes; person*) branco *m*; (*of egg*) clara (de ovo) *f*. **go ~** (*turn pale*) empalidecer; (*of hair*) branquear, embranquecer. **~ coffee** café *m* com leite. **~-collar worker** empregado *m* de escritório. **~ elephant** (*fig*) trambolho *m*, elefante *m* branco. **~ lie** mentirinha *f*. **~ness** *n* brancura *f*, alvura *f*

whiten /'waɪtn/ *vt/i* branquear

whitewash /'waɪtwɒʃ/ *n* cal *f*; (*fig*) encobrimento *m* □ *vt* caiar; (*fig*) encobrir

Whitsun /'wɪtsn/ *n* Pentecostes *m*

whittle /'wɪtl/ *vt* **~ down** aparar, cortar aparas; (*fig*) reduzir gradualmente

whiz /wɪz/ *vi* (*pt* **whizzed**) (*through air*) zunir, sibilar; (*rush*) passar a toda a velocidade. **~-kid** *n* (*colloq*) prodígio *m*

who /huː/ *interr pron* quem □ *rel pron* que, o(a) qual, os(as) quais

whoever /huː'evə(r)/ *pron* (*no matter who*) quem quer que, seja quem for; (*the one who*) aquele que

whole /həʊl/ *a* inteiro, todo; (*not broken*) intacto. **the ~ house/etc** toda a casa/etc □ *n* totalidade *f*; (*unit*) todo *m*. **as a ~** no conjunto, como um todo. **on the ~** de um modo geral. **~-hearted** *a* de todo o coração; (*person*) dedicado. **~-heartedly** *adv* sem reservas, sinceramente

wholefood /'həʊlfuːd/ *n* comida *f* integral

wholemeal /'həʊlmiːl/ *a* **~ bread** pão *m* integral

wholesale /'həʊlseɪl/ *n* venda *f* por grosso *or* por atacado □ *a* (*firm*) por grosso, por atacado; (*fig*) sistemático, em massa □ *adv* (*in large quantities*) por atacado; (*fig*) em massa, em grande escala. **~r** /-ə(r)/ *n* grossista *mf*, atacadista *mf*

wholesome /'həʊlsəm/ *a* sadio, saudável

wholewheat /'həʊlwiːt/ *a* = **wholemeal**

wholly /'həʊlɪ/ *adv* inteiramente, completamente

whom /huːm/ *interr pron* quem □ *rel*

pron (that) que; *(after prep)* quem, que, o qual

whooping cough /'huːpɪŋkɒf/ *n* coqueluche *f*

whore /hɔː(r)/ *n* prostituta *f*

whose /huːz/ *rel pron & a* cujo, de quem □ *interr pron* de quem. ~ **hat is this?**, ~ **is this hat?** de quem é este chapéu? ~ **son are you?** de quem é que o senhor é filho?

why /waɪ/ *adv* porque, por que motivo, por que razão, porquê. **she doesn't know** ~ **he's here** ela não sabe porque *or* por que motivo ele estáaqui. **she doesn't know** ~ ela não sabe porquê. **do you know** ~? você sabe porquê? □ *int (protest)* ora, ora essa; *(discovery)* oh. ~ **yes/ etc**

wick /wɪk/ *n* torcida *f*, mecha *f*, pavio *m*

wicked /'wɪkɪd/ *a* mau, malvado; *(mischievous, spiteful)* maldoso. ~**ly** *adv* maldosamente. ~**ness** *n* maldade *f*, malvadeza *f*

wicker /'wɪkə(r)/ *n* verga *f*, vime *m*. ~-**work** *n* trabalho *m* de verga *or* de vime

wicket /'wɪkɪt/ *n (cricket)* arco *m*

wide /waɪd/ *a* (-er, -est) largo; *(extensive)* vasto, grande, extenso. **two metres** ~ com dois metros de largura □ *adv* longe; *(fully)* completamente. **open** ~ *(door, window)* abrir(-se) de par em par, escancarar(-se); *(mouth)* abrir bem. ~ **awake** desperto, acordado. **far and** ~ por toda a parte. ~**ly** *adv* largamente; *(travel, spread)* muito; *(generally)* geralmente; *(extremely)* extremamente

widen /'waɪdn/ *vt/i* alargar(-se)

widespread /'waɪdspred/ *a* muito espalhado, difundido

widow /'wɪdəʊ/ *n* viúva *f*. ~**ed** *a (man)* viúvo; *(woman)* viúva. **be** ~**ed** enviuvar, ficar viúvo *or* viúva. ~**er** *n* viúvo *m*. ~**hood** *n* viuvez *f*

width /wɪdθ/ *n* largura *f*

wield /wiːld/ *vt (axe etc)* manejar; *(fig: power)* exercer

wife /waɪf/ *n (pl* **wives**) mulher *f*, esposa *f*

wig /wɪg/ *n* cabeleira (postiça) *f*, *(judge's etc)* peruca *f*

wiggle /'wɪgl/ *vt/i* remexer(-se), retorcer(-se), mexer(-se) dum lado para outro

wild /waɪld/ *a* (-er, -est) selvagem; *(of plant)* silvestre; *(mad)* louco; *(enraged)* furioso, violento □ *adv* a esmo; *(without control)* à solta. ~**s** *npl* regiões *fpl* selvagens. ~-**goose chase** falsa pista *f*, tentativa *f* inútil. ~**ly**

adv violentamente; *(madly)* loucamente

wildcat /'waɪldkæt/ *a* ~ **strike** greve *f* ilegal

wilderness /'wɪldənɪs/ *n* deserto *m*

wildlife /'waɪldlaɪf/ *n* animais *mpl* selvagens

wile /waɪl/ *n* artimanha *f*; *(cunning)* astúcia *f*, manha *f*

wilful /'wɪlfl/ *a (person)* voluntarioso; *(act)* intencional, propositado

will¹ /wɪl/ *v aux* **you** ~ **sing/he** ~ **do/etc** tu cantarás/ele fará/*etc*. *(1st person: future expressing will or intention)* **I** ~ **sing/we** ~ **do**/*etc* eu cantarei/nós faremos/*etc*. ~ **you have a cup of coffee?** quer tomar um cafézinho? ~ **you shut the door?** quer fazer o favor de fechar a porta?

will² /wɪl/ *n* vontade *f*; *(document)* testamento *m*. **at** ~ à vontade, quando *or* como se quiser □ *vt (wish)* querer; *(bequeath)* deixar em testamento. ~-**power** *n* força *f* de vontade

willing /'wɪlɪŋ/ *a* pronto, de boa vontade. ~ **to** disposto a. ~**ly** *adv (with pleasure)* de boa vontade, de bom grado; *(not forced)* voluntariamente. ~**ness** *n* boa vontade *f*, disposição *f* (**to do** em fazer)

willow /'wɪləʊ/ *n* salgueiro *m*

willy-nilly /wɪlɪ'nɪlɪ/ *adv* de bom ou de mau grado, quer queira ou não

wilt /wɪlt/ *vi* murchar, definhar

wily /'waɪlɪ/ *a* (-ier, -iest) manhoso, matreiro

win /wɪn/ *vt/i (pt* **won**, *pres p* **winning**) ganhar □ *n* vitória *f*. ~ **over** *vt* convencer, conquistar

wince /wɪns/ *vi* estremecer, contrair-se. **without** ~**ing** sem pestanejar

winch /wɪntʃ/ *n* guincho *m* □ *vt* içar com guincho

wind¹ /wɪnd/ *n* vento *m*; *(breath)* fôlego *m*; *(flatulence)* gases *mpl*. **get** ~ **of** *(fig)* ouvir rumor de. **put the** ~ **up** *(sl)* assustar. **in the** ~ no ar. ~ **instrument** *(mus)* instrumento *m* de sopro. ~-**swept** *a* varrido pelo vento

wind² /waɪnd/ *vt/i (pt* **wound**) enrolar(-se); *(wrap)* envolver, pôr em volta; *(of path, river)* serpentear. ~ **(up)** *(clock etc)* dar corda em. ~ **up** *(end)* terminar, acabar; *(fig: speech etc)* concluir; *(firm)* liquidar. **he'll** ~ **up in jail** *(colloq)* ele vai acabar na cadeia. ~**ing** *a (path)* sinuoso; *(staircase)* em caracol

windfall /'wɪndfɔːl/ *n* fruta *f* caída; *(fig: money)* sorte *f* grande

windmill /'wɪndmɪl/ *n* moinho *m* de vento

window /'wɪndəʊ/ *n* janela *f*; *(of shop)* vitrine *f*, *(P)* montra *f*; *(counter)* guichê *m*, (*P*) guichet *m*. ~-box *n* jardineira *f*, (*P*) floreira *f*. ~-cleaner *n* limpador *m* de janelas. ~-dressing *n* decoração *f* de vitrines; (*fig*) apresentação *f* cuidadosa. ~-ledge *n* peitoril *m*. ~-pane *n* vidro *m*, vidraça *f*. go ~-shopping ir ver vitrines. ~-sill *n* peitoril *m*

windpipe /'wɪndpaɪp/ *n* traquéia *f*, (*P*) traqueia *f*

windscreen /'wɪndskri:n/ *n* pára-brisa *m*, (*P*) pára-brisas *m invar*. ~-wiper /-waɪpə(r)/ *n* limpador *m* de pára-brisa

windshield /'wɪndʃi:ld/ *n* (*Amer*) = windscreen

windsurf|er /'wɪndsɜ:fə(r)/ *n* surfista *mf*. ~ing *n* surfe *m*

windy /'wɪndɪ/ *a* (-ier, -iest) ventoso. it is very ~ está ventando muito

wine /waɪn/ *n* vinho *m*. ~ bar bar *m* para degustação de vinhos. ~-cellar *n* adega *f*, cave *f*. ~-grower *n* vinicultor *m*. ~-growing *n* vinicultura *f*. ~-list *n* lista *f* de vinhos. ~-tasting *n* prova *f* or degustação *f* de vinhos. ~ waiter garçon *m*

wineglass /'waɪnglɑ:s/ *n* copo *m* de vinho; (*with stem*) cálice *m*

wing /wɪŋ/ *n* asa *f*; (*mil*) flanco *m*; (*archit*) ala *f*; (*auto*) pára-lamas *m invar*, (*P*) guarda-lamas *m invar*. ~s (*theat*) bastidores *mpl*. under sb's ~ debaixo das asas de alguém. ~ed *a* alado

wink /wɪŋk/ *vi* piscar o olho; (*light, star*) cintilar, piscar □ *n* piscadela *f*. not sleep a ~ não pregar olho

winner /'wɪnə(r)/ *n* vencedor *m*

winning /'wɪnɪŋ/ *see* win □ *a* vencedor, vitorioso; (*number*) premiado; (*smile*) encantador, atraente. ~-post *n* meta *f*, poste de chegada *f*. ~s *npl* ganhos *mpl*

wint|er /'wɪntə(r)/ *n* inverno *m* □ *vi* hibernar. ~ry *a* de inverno, invernoso; (*smile*) glacial

wipe /waɪp/ *vt* limpar; (*dry*) enxugar, limpar □ *n* limpadela *f*. ~ off limpar. ~ out (*destroy*) aniquilar, limpar (*colloq*); (*cancel*) cancelar. ~ up enxugar

wir|e /'waɪə(r)/ *n* arame *m*; (*colloq: telegram*) telegrama *m*. (electric) ~e fio elétrico *m*, (*P*) eléctrico □ *vt* (*a house*) montar a instalação elétrica em; (*colloq: telegraph*) telegrafar. ~e netting rede *f* de arame. ~ing *n* (*electr*) instalação *f* elétrica, (*P*) eléctrica

wireless /'waɪəlɪs/ *n* rádio *f*; (*set*) rádio *m*

wiry /'waɪərɪ/ *a* (-ier, -iest) magro e rijo

wisdom /'wɪzdəm/ *n* sagacidade *f*, sabedoria *f*; (*common sense*) bom senso

m, sensatez *f*. ~ tooth dente *m* (do) sizo

wise /waɪz/ *a* (-er, -est) (*person*) sábio, avisado, sensato; (*look*) entendedor. ~ guy (*colloq*) sabichão *m* (*colloq*), sabetudo *m* (*colloq*). none the ~r sem entender nada. ~ly *adv* sensatamente

wisecrack /'waɪzkræk/ *n* (*colloq*) (boa) piada *f*

wish /wɪʃ/ *n* (*desire, aspiration*) desejo *m*, vontade *f*; (*request*) pedido *m*; (*greeting*) desejo *m*, voto *m*. I have no ~ to go não tenho nenhum desejo *or* nenhuma vontade de ir □ *vt* (*desire, bid*) desejar; (*want*) apetecer, ter vontade de, desejar (to do fazer) □ *vi* ~ for desejar. ~ sb well desejar felicidades a alguém. I don't ~ to go não me apetece ir, não tenho vontade de ir, não desejo ir. I ~ he'd leave eu gostaria que ele partisse. with best ~es (*formal: in letter*) com os melhores cumprimentos, com saudações cordiais; (*on greeting card*) com desejos *or* votos (for de)

wishful /'wɪʃfl/ *a* ~ thinking sonhar acordado

wishy-washy /'wɪʃɪwɒʃɪ/ *a* sem expressão, fraco, inexpressivo

wisp /wɪsp/ *n* (*of hair*) pequena mecha *f*; (*of smoke*) fio *m*

wistful /'wɪstfl/ *a* melancólico, saudoso

wit /wɪt/ *n* inteligência *f*; (*humour*) presença *f* de espírito, humor *m*; (*person*) senso *m* de humor. be at one's ~'s *or* ~s' end não saber o que fazer. keep one's ~s about one estar alerta. live by one's ~s ganhar a vida de maneira suspeita. scared out of one's ~s apavorado

witch /wɪtʃ/ *n* feiticeira *f*, bruxa *f*. ~craft *n* feitiçaria *f*, bruxaria *f*, magia *f*

with /wɪð/ *prep* com; (*having*) de; (*because of*) de; (*at the house of*) em casa de. the man ~ the beard o homem de barbas. fill/*etc* ~ encher/*etc* de. laughing/shaking/*etc* ~ a rir/a tremer/*etc* de. I'm not ~ you (*colloq*) não estou compreendendo-o

withdraw /wɪð'drɔ:/ *vt/i* (*pt* withdrew, *pp* withdrawn) retirar (-se); (*money*) tirar. ~al *n* retirada *f*; (*med*) estado *m* de privação. ~n *a* (*person*) retraído, fechado

wither /'wɪðə(r)/ *vt/i* murchar, secar. ~ed *a* (*person*) mirrado. ~ing *a* (*fig: scornful*) desdenhoso

withhold /wɪð'həʊld/ *vt* (*pt* withheld) negar, recusar; (*retain*) reter; (*conceal, not tell*) esconder (from de)

within /wɪ'ðɪn/ *prep* & *adv* dentro (de), por dentro (de); (*in distances*) a menos de. ~ **a month** (*before*) dentro de um mês. ~ **sight** à vista

without /wɪ'ðaʊt/ *prep* sem. ~ **fail** sem falta. **go** ~ **saying** não ser preciso dizer

withstand /wɪð'stænd/ *vt* (*pt* **withstood**) resistir a, opor-se a

witness /'wɪtnɪs/ *n* testemunha *f*; (*evidence*) testemunho *m* □ *vt* testemunhar, presenciar; (*document*) assinar como testemunha. **bear** ~ **to** testemunhar, dar testemunho de. ~-**box** *n* banco *m* das testemunhas

witticism /'wɪtɪsɪzəm/ *n* dito *m* espirituoso

witty /'wɪtɪ/ *a* (-**ier**, -**iest**) espirituoso

wives /waɪvz/ *see* **wife**

wizard /'wɪzəd/ *n* feiticeiro *m*; (*fig: genius*) gênio *m*, (*P*) génio *m*

wizened /'wɪznd/ *a* encarquilhado

wobbl|e /'wɒbl/ *vi* (*of jelly, voice, hand*) tremer; (*stagger*) cambalear, vacilar; (*of table, chair*) balançar. ~**y** *a* (*trembling*) trêmulo; (*staggering*) cambaleante, vacilante; (*table, chair*) pouco firme

woe /wəʊ/ *n* dor *f*, infortúnio *m*

woke, woken /wəʊk, 'wəʊkən/ *see* **wake**[1]

wolf /wʊlf/ *n* (*pl* **wolves** /wʊlvz/) lobo *m* □ *vt* (*food*) devorar. **cry** ~ dar alarme falso. ~-**whistle** *n* assobio *m* de admiração

woman /'wʊmən/ *n* (*pl* **women**) mulher *f*. ~**hood** *n* as mulheres, o sexo feminino; (*maturity*) maturidade *f*. ~**ly** *a* feminino

womb /wuːm/ *n* seio *m*, ventre *m*; (*med*) útero *m*; (*fig*) seio *m*

women /'wɪmn/ *see* **woman**. ~'s **movement** movimento *m* feminista

won /wʌn/ *see* **win**

wonder /'wʌndə(r)/ *n* admiração *f*; (*thing*) maravilha *f* □ *vt* perguntar-se a si mesmo (**if** se) □ *vi* admirar-se (**at** de, com), ficar admirado, espantar-se (**at** com); (*reflect*) pensar (**about** em). **it is no** ~ não admira (**that** que)

wonderful /'wʌndəfl/ *a* maravilhoso. ~**ly** *adv* maravilhosamente. **it works** ~**ly** funciona às mil maravilhas

won't /wəʊnt/ = **will not**

wood /wʊd/ *n* madeira *f*, pau *m*; (*for burning*) lenha *f*. ~(**s**) *n* (*pl*) (*area*) bosque *m*, mata *f*, floresta *f*. ~**ed** *a* arborizado. ~**en** *a* de *or* em madeira, de pau; (*fig: stiff*) rígido; (*fig: inexpressive*) inexpressivo, de pau

woodcut /'wʊdkʌt/ *n* gravura *f* em madeira

woodland /'wʊdlənd/ *n* região *f* arborizada, bosque *m*, mata *f*

woodlouse /'wʊdlaʊs/ *n* (*pl* -**lice** /laɪs/) baratinha *f*, tatuzinho *m*

woodpecker /'wʊdpekə(r)/ *n* (*bird*) pica-pau *m*

woodwind /'wʊdwɪnd/ *n* (*mus*) instrumentos *mpl* de sopro de madeira

woodwork /'wʊdwɜːk/ *n* (*of building*) madeiramento *m*; (*carpentry*) carpintaria *f*

woodworm /'wʊdwɜːm/ *n* caruncho *m*

woody /'wʊdɪ/ *a* (*wooded*) arborizado; (*like wood*) lenhoso

wool /wʊl/ *n* lã *f*. ~**len** *a* de lã. ~**lens** *npl* roupas *fpl* de lã. ~**ly** *a* de lã; (*vague*) confuso □ *n* (*colloq: garment*) roupa *f* de lã

word /wɜːd/ *n* palavra *f*; (*news*) notícia(s) *f*(*pl*); (*promise*) palavra *f* □ *vt* exprimir, formular. **by** ~ **of mouth** de viva voz. **have a** ~ **with** dizer duas palavras a. **in other** ~**s** em outras palavras. ~-**perfect** *a* que sabe de cor seu papel, a lição etc. ~ **processor** processador *m* de textos. ~**ing** *n* termos *mpl*, redação *f*, (*P*) redacção *f*. ~**y** *a* prolixo

wore /wɔː(r)/ *see* **wear**

work /wɜːk/ *n* trabalho *m*; (*product, book etc*) obra *f*; (*building etc*) obras *fpl*. **at** ~ no trabalho. **out of** ~ desempregado. ~**s** *npl* (*techn*) mecanismo *m*; (*factory*) fábrica *f* □ *vt/i* (*of person*) trabalhar; (*techn*) fazer funcionar, (*fazer*) andar; (*of drug etc*) agir, fazer efeito; (*farm, mine*) explorar; (*land*) lavrar. ~ **sb** (*make work*) fazer alguém trabalhar. ~ **in** introduzir, inserir. ~ **loose** soltar-se. ~ **off** (*get rid of*) descarregar. ~ **out** *vt* (*solve*) resolver; (*calculate*) calcular; (*devise*) planejar □ *vi* (*succeed*) resultar; (*sport*) treinar-se. ~-**station** *n* estação *f* de trabalho. ~-**to-rule** *n* greve *f* de zelo. ~ **up** *vt* criar □ *vi* (*to climax*) ir num crescendo. ~**ed up** (*person*) enervado, transtornado, agitado

workable /'wɜːkəbl/ *a* viável, praticável

workaholic /wɜːkə'hɒlɪk/ *n* **be a** ~ (*colloq*) trabalhar como um possesso (*colloq*)

worker /'wɜːkə(r)/ *n* trabalhador *m*, trabalhadora *f*; (*factory*) operário *m*

working /'wɜːkɪŋ/ *a* (*day, clothes, hypothesis, lunch etc*) de trabalho. **the** ~ **class(es)** a classe operária, a(s) classe(s) trabalhadora(s), o proletariado. ~-**class** *a* operário, trabalhador. ~ **mother** mãe *f* que trabalha. ~ **party** comissão *f* consultiva, de estudo etc. ~**s** *npl* mecanismo *m*. **in** ~ **order** em condições de funcionamento

workman /'wɜːkmən/ *n* (*pl* -**men**)

trabalhador *m*; (*factory*) operário *m*.
~**ship** *n* trabalho *m*, execução *f*, mão-
de-obra *f*; (*skill*) arte *f*, habilidade *f*
workshop /'wɜːkʃop/ *n* oficina *f*
world /wɜːld/ *n* mundo *m* □ *a*
mundial. **a** ~ **of** muito(s), grande
quantidade de, um mundo de. ~-
wide *a* mundial, universal
worldly /'wɜːldlɪ/ *a* terreno; (*devoted
to the affairs of life*) mundano. ~
goods bens *mpl* materiais. ~-**wise** *a*
com experiência do mundo
worm /wɜːm/ *n* verme *m*; (*earth-
worm*) minhoca *f* □ *vt* ~ **one's way
into** insinuar-se, introduzir-se, enfiar-se. ~-**eaten** *a* (*wood*) caruncho-
so; (*fruit*) bichado, bichoso
worn /wɔːn/ *see* **wear** □ *a* usado. ~-
out *a* (*thing*) completamente gasto;
(*person*) esgotado
worr|y /'wʌrɪ/ *vt/i* preocupar(-se) □ *n*
preocupação *f*. **don't** ~**y** fique des-
cansado, não se preocupe. ~**ied** *a*
preocupado. ~**ying** *a* preocupante,
inquietante
worse /wɜːs/ *a & adv* pior □ *n* pior *m*.
get ~ piorar. **from bad to** ~ de mal a
pior. ~ **luck** pouca sorte, pena
worsen /'wɜːsn/ *vt/i* piorar
worship /'wɜːʃɪp/ *n* (*reverence*)
reverência *f*, veneração *f*; (*religious*)
culto *m* □ *vt* (*pt* **worshipped**) adorar,
venerar □ *vi* fazer as suas devoções,
praticar o culto. ~**per** *n* (*in church*)
fiel *m*. **Your/His W**~ Vossa/Sua
Excelência *f*
worst /wɜːst/ *a & n* (**the**) ~ (o/a) pior
(*mf*) □ *adv* pior. **if the** ~ **comes to
the** ~ se o pior acontecer, na pior
das hipóteses. **do one's** ~ fazer todo
o mal que se quiser. **get the** ~ **of it**
ficar a perder. **the** ~ (**thing**) **that** o
pior que
worth /wɜːθ/ *a* **be** ~ valer; (*deser-
ving*) merecer □ *n* valor *m*, mérito *m*.
ten pounds ~ of dez libras de. **it's** ~
it, **it's** ~ **while** vale a pena. **it's not**
~ **my while** não vale a pena. **it's** ~
waiting/*etc* vale a pena esperar/*etc*.
for all one's ~ (*colloq*) dando tudo
por tudo. ~**less** *a* sem valor
worthwhile /'wɜːθ'waɪl/ *a* que vale a
pena; (*cause*) louvável, meritório
worthy /'wɜːðɪ/ *a* (-**ier**, -**iest**) (*deser-
ving*) digno, merecedor (**of** de); (*laudable*) meritório, louvável □ *n* (*person*)
pessoa *f* ilustre
would /wʊd/; *unstressed* /wəd/ *v aux*
he ~ **do/you** ~ **sing**/*etc* (*conditional
tense*) ele faria/você cantaria/*etc*. **he**
~ **have done** ele teria feito. **she** ~
come every day (*used to*) ela vinha *or*
costumava vir aqui todos os dias. ~
you please come here? chegue aqui

por favor. ~ **you like some tea?** você
quer um chazinho? **he** ~**n't go** (*re-
fused to*) ele não queria ir. ~-**be
author/doctor**/*etc* aspirante a
autor/médico/*etc*
wound[1] /wuːnd/ *n* ferida *f* □ *vt* ferir.
the ~**ed** os feridos *mpl*
wound[2] /waʊnd/ *see* **wind**[2]
wove, woven /wəʊv, 'wəʊvn/ *see*
weave
wrangle /'ræŋgl/ *vi* disputar, discutir,
brigar □ *n* disputa *f*, discussão *f*, briga
f
wrap /ræp/ *vt* (*pt* **wrapped**) ~ (**up**)
embrulhar (**in** em); (*in cotton wool,
mystery etc*) envolver (**in** em) □ *vi* ~
up (*dress warmly*) abrigar-se bem,
agasalhar-se bem □ *n* xale *m*. ~**ped
up in** (*engrossed*) absorto em, mergulhado em. ~**per** *n* (*of sweet*) papel
m; (*of book*) capa *f* de papel. ~**ing** *n*
embalagem *f*
wrath /rɒθ/ *n* ira *f*. ~**ful** *a* irado
wreak /riːk/ *vt* ~ **havoc** (*of storm etc*)
fazer estragos
wreath /riːθ/ *n* (*pl* -**s** /-ðz/) (*of flowers,
leaves*) coroa *f*, grinalda *f*
wreck /rek/ *n* (*sinking*) naufrágio *m*;
(*ship*) navio *m* naufragado; restos *mpl*
de navio; (*remains*) destroços *mpl*;
(*vehicle*) veículo *m* destroçado □ *vt*
destruir; (*ship*) fazer naufragar, afundar; (*fig: hope*) acabar. **be a nervous**
~ estar com os nervos arrasados.
~**age** *n* (*pieces*) destroços *mpl*
wren /ren/ *n* (*bird*) carriça *f*
wrench /rentʃ/ *vt* (*pull*) puxar;
(*twist*) torcer; (*snatch*) arrancar
(**from** a) □ *n* (*pull*) puxão *m*; (*of
ankle, wrist*) torcedura *f*; (*tool*) chave
f inglesa; (*fig*) dor *f* de separação
wrest /rest/ *vt* arrancar (**from** a)
wrestl|e /'resl/ *vi* lutar, debater-se
(**with com** *or* contra). ~**er** *n* lutador
m. ~**ing** *n* luta *f*
wretch /retʃ/ *n* desgraçado *m*,
miserável *mf*; (*rascal*) miserável *mf*
wretched; /'retʃɪd/ *a* (*pitiful, poor*)
miserável; (*bad*) horrível, desgraçado
wriggle /'rɪgl/ *vt/i* remexer(-se), contorcer-se
wring /rɪŋ/ *vt* (*pt* **wrung**) (*twist;
clothes*) torcer. ~ **out of** (*obtain from*)
arrancar a. ~**ing wet** encharcado; (*of
person*) encharcado até os ossos
wrinkle /'rɪŋkl/ *n* (*on skin*) ruga *f*;
(*crease*) prega *f* □ *vt/i* enrugar(-se)
wrist /rɪst/ *n* pulso *m*. ~-**watch** *n*
relógio *m* de pulso
writ /rɪt/ *n* (*jur*) mandado *m* judicial
write /raɪt/ *vt/i* (*pt* **wrote**, *pp* **written**) escrever. ~ **back** responder. ~
down escrever, tomar nota de. ~ **off**
(*debt*) dar por liquidado; (*vehicle*) des-

tinar à sucata. ~-**off** n perda f total.
~ **out** (*in full*) escrever por extenso.
~ **up** (*from notes*) redigir. ~-**up** n
relato m; (*review*) crítica f
writer /'raɪtə(r)/ n escritor m, autor
m
writhe /raɪð/ vi contorcer(-se)
writing /'raɪtɪŋ/ n escrita f. ~(**s**)
(*works*) escritos mpl, obras fpl. **in** ~
por escrito. ~-**paper** n papel m de
carta
written /'rɪtn/ see **write**
wrong /rɒŋ/ a (*incorrect, mistaken*)
mal, errado; (*unfair*) injusto; (*wicked*)
mau; (*amiss*) que não está bem; (*mus:
note*) falso; (*clock*) que não está certo
□ adv mal □ n mal m; (*injustice*)
injustiça f □ vt (*be unfair to*) ser injusto com; (*do a wrong to*) fazer mal a.
what's ~? qual é o problema? **what's**
~ **with it?** (*amiss*) o que é que não
vai bem?; (*morally*) que mal há nisso?, que mal tem? **he's in the** ~ (*his
fault*) ele não tem razão. **go** ~ (*err*)
desencaminhar-se; (*fail*) ir mal;
(*vehicle*) quebrar. ~**ly** adv mal;
(*blame etc*) sem razão, injustamente
wrongful /'rɒŋfl/ a injusto, ilegal
wrote /rəʊt/ see **write**
wrought /rɔːt/ a ~ **iron** ferro m
forjado. ~-**up** a excitado
wrung /rʌŋ/ see **wring**
wry /raɪ/ a (**wryer, wryest**) torto;
(*smile*) forçado. ~ **face** careta f

X

Xerox /'zɪərɒks/ n fotocópia f, xerox
m □ vt fotocopiar, xerocar, tirar um
xerox de
Xmas /'krɪsməs/ n Christmas
X-ray /'eksreɪ/ n raio X m; (*photograph*) radiografia f □ vt radiografar.
have an ~ tirar uma radiografia
xylophone /'zaɪləfəʊn/ n xilofone m

Y

yacht /jɒt/ n iate m. ~**ing** n iatismo
m, andar m de iate; (*racing*) regata f
de iate
yank /jæŋk/ vt (*colloq*) puxar bruscamente □ n (*colloq*) puxão m
Yank /jæŋk/ n (*colloq*) ianque mf
yap /jæp/ vi (*pt* yapped) latir
yard[1] /jaːd/ n (*measure*) jarda f (=
0,9144 m). ~**age** n medida f em jardas
yard[2] /jaːd/ n (*of house*) pátio m;
(*Amer: garden*) jardim m; (*for storage*) depósito m
yardstick /'jaːdstɪk/ n jarda f; (*fig*)
bitola f, craveira f

yarn /jaːn/ n (*thread*) fio m; (*colloq:
tale*) longa história f
yawn /jɔːn/ vi bocejar; (*be wide open*)
abrir-se, escancarar-se □ n bocejo m.
~**ing** a escancarado
year /jɪə(r)/ n ano m. **school/tax** ~
ano m escolar/fiscal. **be ten/** etc ~**s
old** ter dez/etc anos de idade. ~-**book**
n anuário m. ~**ly** a anual □ adv
anualmente
yearn /jaːn/ vi ~ **for, to** desejar, ansiar por, suspirar por. ~**ing** n desejo
m, anseio m (**for** de)
yeast /jiːst/ n levedura f
yell /jel/ vt/i gritar, berrar □ n grito
m, berro m
yellow /'jeləʊ/ a amarelo; (*colloq: cowardly*) covarde, poltrão □ n amarelo m
yelp /jelp/ n (*of dog etc*) ganido m □ vi
ganir
yen /jen/ n (*colloq: yearning*) grande
vontade f (**for** de)
yes /jes/ n & adv sim (m). ~-**man** n
(*colloq*) lambe-botas m invar, puxa-
saco m
yesterday /'jestədɪ/ n & adv ontem
(m). ~ **morning/afternoon/even-
ing** ontem de manhã/à tarde/à
noite. **the day before** ~ anteontem.
~ **week** há oito dias, há uma semana
yet /jet/ adv ainda; (*already*) já □ conj
contudo, no entanto. **as** ~ até agora,
por enquanto. **his best book** ~ o seu
melhor livro até agora
yew /juː/ n teixo m
Yiddish /'jɪdɪʃ/ n ídiche m
yield /jiːld/ vt (*produce*) produzir, dar;
(*profit*) render; (*surrender*) entregar □
vi (*give way*) ceder □ n produção f;
(*comm*) rendimento m
yoga /'jəʊgə/ n ioga f
yoghurt /'jɒgət/ n iogurte m
yoke /jəʊk/ n jugo m, canga f; (*of garment*) pala f □ vt jungir; (*unite*) unir,
ligar
yokel /'jəʊkl/ n caipira m, labrego m
yolk /jəʊk/ n gema (de ovo) f
yonder /'jɒndə(r)/ adv acolá, além
you /juː/ pron (*familiar*) tu, você (*pl*
vocês); (*polite*) vós, o(s) senhor(es),
a(s) senhora(s); (*object: familiar*) te,
lhe (*pl* vocês); (*polite*) o(s), a(s), lhes,
vós, o(s) senhor(es), a(s) senhora(s);
(*after prep*) ti, si, você (*pl* vocês); (*polite*) vós, o senhor, a senhora (*pl* os
senhores, as senhoras); (*indefinite*)
se; (*after prep*) si, você. **with** ~ (*familiar*) contigo, consigo, com você (*pl*
com vocês); (*polite*) com o senhor/a
senhora (*pl* convosco, com os senho-
res/as senhoras). **I know** ~ (*familiar*) eu te conheço, eu o/a
conheço (*pl* eu os/as conheço); (*polite*) eu vos conheço, conheço o

senhor/a senhora (*pl* conheço os senhores/as senhoras). **~ can see the sea** você pode ver o mar

young /jʌŋ/ *a* (**-er, -est**) jovem, novo, moço □ *n* (*people*) jovens *mpl*, a juventude *f*, a mocidade *f*; (*of animals*) crias *fpl*, filhotes *mpl*

youngster /'jʌŋstə(r)/ *n* jovem *mf*, moço *m*, rapaz *m*

your /jɔː(r)/ *a* (*familiar*) teu, tua, seu, sua (*pl* teus, tuas, seus, suas); (*polite*) vosso, vossa, do senhor, da senhora (*pl* vossos, vossas, dos senhores, das senhoras)

yours /jɔːz/ *poss pron* (*familiar*) o teu, a tua, o seu, a sua (*pl* os teus, as tuas, os seus, as suas); (*polite*) o vosso, a vossa, o/a do senhor, o/a da senhora (*pl* os vossos, as vossas; os/as do(s) senhor(es), os/as da(s) senhora(s)). **a book of ~** um livro seu. **~ sincerely/faithfully** atenciosamente, com os cumprimentos de

yourself /jɔː'self/ (*pl* **-selves** /-'selvz/) *pron* (*familiar*) tu mesmo/a, você mesmo/a (*pl* vocês mesmos/as); (*polite*) vós mesmo/a, o senhor mesmo, a senhora mesma (*pl* vós mesmos/as, os senhores mesmos, as senhoras mesmas); (*reflexive: familiar*) te, a ti mesmo/a, se, a si mesmo/a (*pl* a vocês mesmos/as); (*polite*) ao senhor mesmo, à senhora mesma (*pl* aos senhores mesmos, às senhoras mesmas); (*after prep: familiar*) ti mesmo/a, si mesmo/a, você mesmo/a (*pl* vocês mesmos/as); (*after prep: polite*) vós mesmo/a, o senhor mesmo, a senhora mesma (*pl* vós mesmos/as, os senhores mesmos, as senhoras mesmas). **with ~** (*familiar*) contigo mesmo/a, consigo mesmo/a, com você (*pl* com vocês); (*polite*) convosco, com o senhor, com a senhora (*pl* com os senhores, com as senhoras). **by ~** sozinho

youth /juːθ/ *n* (*pl* **-s** /-ðz/) mocidade *f*, juventude *f*; (*young man*) jovem *m*, moço *m*. **~ club** centro *m* de jovens.

~ hostel albergue *m* da juventude. **~ful** *a* juvenil, jovem

yo-yo /'jəʊjəʊ/ *n* (*pl* **-os**) ioiô *m*

Yugoslav /'juːgəslaːv/ *a & n* iogoslavo (*m*), (*P*) jugoslavo (*m*). **~ia** /-'slaːvɪə/ *n* Iogoslávia *f*, (*P*) Jugoslávia *f*

Z

zany /'zeɪnɪ/ *a* (**-ier, -iest**) tolo, bobo

zeal /ziːl/ *n* zelo *m*

zealous /'zeləs/ *a* zeloso. **~ly** *adv* zelosamente

zebra /'zebrə, 'ziːbrə/ *n* zebra *f*. **~ crossing** faixa *f* para pedestres, (*P*) passagem *f* para peões

zenith /'zenɪθ/ *n* zênite *m*, (*P*) zénite *m*, auge *m*

zero /'zɪərəʊ/ *n* (*pl* **-os**) zero *m*. **~ hour** a hora H. **below ~** abaixo de zero

zest /zest/ *n* (*gusto*) entusiasmo *m*; (*fig: spice*) sabor *m* especial; (*lemon or orange peel*) casca *f* de limão/laranja ralada

zigzag /'zɪgzæg/ *n* ziguezague *m* □ *a & adv* em ziguezague □ *vi* (*pt* **zigzagged**) ziguezaguear

zinc /zɪŋk/ *n* zinco *m*

zip /zɪp/ *n* (*vigour*) energia *f*, alma *f*. **~(-fastener)** fecho *m* ecler □ *vt* (*pt* **zipped**) fechar o fecho eclerde □ *vi* ir a toda a velocidade. **Z~ code** (*Amer*) CEP de endereçamento postal *m*, (*P*) código *m* postal

zipper /'zɪpə(r)/ *n* = **zip(-fastener)**

zodiac /'zəʊdɪæk/ *n* zodíaco *m*

zombie /'zɒmbɪ/ *n* zumbi *m*; (*colloq*) zumbi *m*, (*P*) autómato *m*

zone /zəʊn/ *n* zona *f*

zoo /zuː/ *n* jardim *m* zoológico

zoolog|y /zəʊˈʊlədʒɪ/ *n* zoologia *f*. **~ical** /-əˈlɒdʒɪkl/ *a* zoológico. **~ist** *n* zoólogo *m*

zoom /zuːm/ *vi* (*rush*) sair roando **~ lens** zum *m*, zoom *m*. **~ off** *or* **past** passar zunindo

zucchini /zuːˈkiːnɪ/ *n* (*pl invar*) (*Amer*) courgette *f*

Portuguese Verbs · Verbos portugueses

Introduction
Portuguese verbs can be divided into three categories: regular verbs, those with spelling peculiarities determined by their sound and irregular verbs.

Regular verbs
in -ar (*e.g.* **comprar**)
Present: compr|o, ~as, ~a, ~amos, ~ais, ~am
Future: comprar|ei, ~ás, ~á, ~emos, ~eis, ~ão
Imperfect: compr|ava, ~avas, ~ava, ~ávamos, ~áveis, ~avam
Preterite: compr|ei, ~aste, ~ou, ~amos (*P*:~ámos), ~astes, ~aram
Pluperfect: compr|ara, ~aras, ~ara, ~áramos, ~áreis, ~aram
Present subjunctive: compr|e, ~es, ~e, ~emos, ~eis, ~em
Imperfect subjunctive: compr|asse, ~asses, ~asse, ~ássemos, ~ásseis, ~assem
Future subjunctive: compr|ar, ~ares, ~ar, ~armos, ~ardes, ~arem
Conditional: comprar|ia, ~ias, ~ia, ~íamos, ~íeis, ~iam
Personal infinitive: comprar, ~es, ~, ~mos, ~des, ~em
Present participle: comprando
Past participle: comprado
Imperative: compra, comprai

in ~er (*e.g.* **bater**)
Present: bat|o, ~es, ~e, ~emos, ~eis, ~em
Future: bater|ei, ~ás, ~á, ~emos, ~eis, ~ão
Imperfect: bat|ia, ~ias, ~ia, ~íamos, ~íeis, ~iam
Preterite: bat|i, ~este, ~eu, ~emos, ~estes, ~eram
Pluperfect: bat|era, ~eras, ~era, ~êramos, ~êreis, ~eram
Present subjunctive: bat|a, ~as, ~a, ~amos ~ais, ~am
Imperfect subjunctive: bat|esse, ~esses, ~esse, ~êssemos, ~êsseis, ~essem
Future subjunctive: bat|er, ~eres, ~er, ~ermos, ~erdes, ~erem
Conditional: bater|ia, ~ias, ~ia, ~íamos, ~íeis, ~iam
Personal infinitive: bater, ~es, ~, ~mos, ~des, ~em
Present participle: batendo
Past participle: batido
Imperative: bate, batei

in ~ir (*e.g.* **admitir**)
Present: admit|o, ~es, ~e, ~imos, ~is, ~em

Future: admitir|ei, ~ás, ~á, ~emos, ~eis, ~ão
Imperfect: admit|ia, ~ias, ~ia, ~íamos, ~íeis, ~iam
Preterite: admit|i, ~iste, ~iu, ~imos, ~istes, ~iram
Pluperfect: admit|ira, ~iras, ~ira, ~íramos, ~íreis, ~iram
Present subjunctive: admit|a, ~as, ~a, ~amos, ~ais, ~am
Imperfect subjunctive: admit|isse, ~isses, ~isse, ~íssemos, ~ísseis, ~issem
Future subjunctive: admit|ir, ~ires, ~ir, ~irmos, ~irdes, ~irem
Conditional: admitir|ia, ~ias, ~ia, ~íamos, ~íeis, ~iam
Personal infinitive: admitir, ~es, ~, ~mos, ~des, ~em
Present participle: admitindo
Past participle: admitido
Imperative: admite, admiti

Regular verbs with spelling changes:

-ar verbs:
in -car (*e.g.* **ficar**)
Preterite: fiquei, ficaste, ficou, ficamos (*P*: ficámos), ficais, ficam
Present subjunctive: fique, fiques, fique, fiquemos, fiqueis, fiquem

in -çar (*e.g.* **abraçar**)
Preterite: abracei, abraçaste, abraçou, abraçamos (*P*: abraçámos), abraçastes, abraçaram
Present subjunctive: abrace, abraces, abrace, abracemos, abraceis, abracem

in -ear (*e.g.* **passear**)
Present: passeio, passeias, passeia, passeamos, passeais, passeiam
Present subjunctive: passeie, passeies, passeie, passeemos, passeeis, passeiem
Imperative: passeia, passeai

in -gar (*e.g.* **apagar**)
Preterite: apaguei, apagaste, apagou, apagamos (*P*: apagámos), apagastes, apagaram
Present subjunctive: apague, apagues, apague, apaguemos, apagueis, apaguem

in -oar (*e.g.* **voar**)
Present: vôo (*P*: voo), voas, voa, voamos, voais, voam

averiguar
Preterite: averigüei (*P*: averiguei), averiguaste, averiguou, averiguamos (*P*: averiguámos), averiguastes, averiguaram
Present subjunctive: averigúe, averigúes, averigúe, averigüemos (*P*: averiguemos), averigüeis (*P*: averigueis), averigúem

enxaguar
Present: enxáguo, enxáguas, enxágua, enxaguamos, enxaguais, enxáguam
Preterite: enxagüei (*P*: enxaguei), enxaguaste, enxaguou, enxaguamos (*P*: enxaguámos), enxaguastes, enxaguaram
Present subjunctive: enxágüe, enxágües, enxágüe, enxagüemos, enxagüeis, enxágüem (*P*: enxágue, enxágues, enxágue, enxaguemos, enxagueis, enxáguem)
Similarly: aguar, desaguar

saudar
Present: saúdo, saúdas, saúda, saudamos, saudais, saúdam
Present subjunctive: saúde, saúdes, saúde, saudemos, saudeis, saúdem
Imperative: saúda, saudai

-er verbs:
in -cer (*e.g.* **tecer**)
Present: teço, teces, tece, tecemos, teceis, tecem
Present subjunctive: teça, teças, teça, teçamos, teçais, teçam

in -ger (*e.g.* **proteger**)
Present: protejo, proteges, protege, protegemos, protegeis, protegem
Present subjunctive: proteja, protejas, proteja, protejamos, protejais, protejam

in -guer (*e.g.* **erguer**)
Present: ergo, ergues, ergue, erguemos, ergueis, erguem
Present subjunctive: erga, ergas, erga, ergamos, ergais, ergam

in -oer (*e.g.* **roer**)
Present: rôo (*P*: roo), róis, rói, roemos, roeis, roem
Imperfect: roía, roías, roía, roíamos, roíeis, roíam
Preterite: roí, roeste, roeu, roemos, roestes, roeram
Past participle: roído
Imperative: rói, roei

-ir verbs:
in -ir with -e- in stem (*e.g.* **vestir**)
Present: visto, vestes, veste, vestimos, vestis, vestem

Present subjunctive: vista, vistas, vista, vistamos, vistais, vistam
Similarly: mentir, preferir, refletir, repetir, seguir, sentir, servir

in -ir with -o- in stem (*e.g.* **dormir**)
Present: durmo, dormes, dorme, dormimos, dormis, dormem
Present subjunctive: durma, durmas, durma, durmamos, durmais, durmam
Similarly: cobrir, descobrir, tossir

in -ir with -u- in the stem (*e.g.* **subir**)
Present: subo, sobes, sobe, subimos, subis, sobem
Similarly: consumir, cuspir, fugir, sacudir, sumir

in -air (*e.g.* **sair**)
Present: saio, sais, sai, saímos, saís, saem
Imperfect: saía, saías, saía, saíamos, saíeis, saíam
Preterite: saí, saíste, saiu, saímos, saístes, saíram
Pluperfect: saíra, saíras, saíra, saíramos, saíreis, saíram
Present subjunctive: saia, saias, saia, saiamos, saiais, saiam
Imperfect subjunctive: saísse, saísses, saísse, saíssemos, saísseis, saíssem
Future subjunctive: sair, saíres, sair, sairmos, sairdes, saírem
Personal infinitive: sair, saíres, sair, sairmos, sairdes, saírem
Present participle: saindo
Past participle: saído
Imperative: sai, saí

in -gir (*e.g.* **dirigir**)
Present: dirijo, diriges, dirige, dirigimos, dirigis, dirigem
Present subjunctive: dirija, dirijas, dirija, dirijamos, dirijais, dirijam

in -guir (*e.g.* **distinguir**)
Present: distingo, distingues, distingue, distinguimos, distinguis, distinguem
Present subjunctive: distinga, distingas, distinga, distingamos, distingais, distingam

in -uir (*e.g.* **atribuir**)
Present: atribuo, atribuis, atribui, atribuímos, atribuís, atribuem
Imperfect: atribuía, atribuías, atribuía, atribuíamos, atribuíeis, atribuíam
Preterite: atribuí, atribuíste, atribuiu, atribuímos, atribuístes, atribuíram
Pluperfect: atribuíra, atribuíras, atribuíra, atribuíramos, atribuíreis, atribuíram

Present subjunctive: atribua, atribuas, atribua, atribuamos, atribuais, atribuam
Imperfect subjunctive: atribuísse, atribuísses, atribuísse, atribuíssemos, atribuísseis, atribuíssem
Future subjunctive: atribuir, atribuíres, atribuir, atribuirmos, atribuirdes, atribuírem
Personal infinitive: atribuir, atribuíres, atribuir, atribuirmos, atribuirdes, atribuírem
Present participle: atribuindo
Past participle: atribuído
Imperative: atribui, atribuí

proibir
Present: proíbo, proíbes, proíbe, proibimos, proibis, proíbem
Present subjunctive: proíba, proíbas, proíba, proibamos, proibais, proíbam
Imperative: proíbe, proibi
Similarly: coibir

reunir
Present: reúno, reúnes, reúne, reunimos, reunis, reúnem
Present subjunctive: reúna, reúnas, reúna, reunamos, reunais, reúnam
Imperative: reúne, reuni

in -struir (*e.g.* **construir**) - like atribuir except:
Present: construo, constróis/construis, constrói/construi, construímos, construís, constroem/construem
Imperative: constrói/construi, construí

in -duzir (*e.g.* **produzir**)
Present: produzo, produzes, produz, produzimos, produzis, produzem
Imperative: produz(e), produzi
Similarly: luzir, reluzir

Irregular verbs

caber
Present: caibo, cabes, cabe, cabemos, cabeis, cabem
Preterite: coube, coubeste, coube, coubemos, coubestes, couberam
Pluperfect: coubera, couberas, coubera, coubéramos, coubéreis, couberam
Present subjunctive: caiba, caibas, caiba, caibamos, caibais, caibam
Imperfect subjunctive: coubesse, coubesses, coubesse, coubéssemos, coubésseis, coubessem
Future subjunctive: couber, couberes, couber, coubermos, couberdes, couberem

dar
Present: dou, dás, dá, damos, dais, dão
Preterite: dei, deste, deu, demos, destes, deram
Pluperfect: dera, deras, dera, déramos, déreis, deram
Present subjunctive: dê, dês, dê, demos, deis, dêem
Imperfect subjunctive: desse, desses, desse, déssemos, désseis, dessem
Future subjunctive: der, deres, der, dermos, derdes, derem
Imperative: dá, dai

dizer
Present: digo, dizes, diz, dizemos, dizeis, dizem
Future: direi, dirás, dirá, diremos, direis, dirão
Preterite: disse, disseste, disse, dissemos, dissestes, disseram
Pluperfect: dissera, disseras, dissera, disséramos, disséreis, disseram
Present subjunctive: diga, digas, diga, digamos, digais, digam
Imperfect subjunctive: dissesse, dissesses, dissesse, disséssemos, dissésseis, dissessem
Future subjunctive: disser, disseres, disser, dissermos, disserdes, disserem
Conditional: diria, dirias, diria, diríamos, diríeis, diriam
Present participle: dizendo
Past participle: dito
Imperative: diz, dizei

estar
Present: estou, estás, está, estamos, estais, estão
Preterite: estive, estiveste, esteve, estivemos, estivestes, estiveram
Pluperfect: estivera, estiveras, estivera, estivéramos, estivéreis, estiveram
Present subjunctive: esteja, estejas, esteja, estejamos, estejais, estejam
Imperfect subjunctive: estivesse, estivesses, estivesse, estivéssemos, estivésseis, estivessem
Future subjunctive: estiver, estiveres, estiver, estivermos, estiverdes, estiverem
Imperative: está, estai

fazer
Present: faço, fazes, faz, fazemos, fazeis, fazem
Future: farei, farás, fará, faremos, fareis, farão
Preterite: fiz, fizeste, fez, fizemos, fizestes, fizeram
Pluperfect: fizera, fizeras, fizera, fizéramos, fizéreis, fizeram

Present subjunctive: faça, faças, faça, façamos, façais, façam
Imperfect subjunctive: fizesse, fizesses, fizesse, fizéssemos, fizésseis, fizessem
Future subjunctive: fizer, fizeres, fizer, fizermos, fizerdes, fizerem
Conditional: faria, farias, faria, faríamos, faríeis, fariam
Present participle: fazendo
Past participle: feito
Imperative: faz(e), fazei

frigir
Present: frijo, freges, frege, frigimos, frigis, fregem
Present subjunctive: frija, frijas, frija, frijamos, frijais, frijam
Imperative: frege, frigi

ir
Present: vou, vais, vai, vamos, ides, vão
Imperfect: ia, ias, ia, íamos, íeis, iam
Preterite: fui, foste, foi, fomos, fostes, foram
Pluperfect: fora, foras, fora, fôramos, fôreis, foram
Present subjunctive: vá, vás, vá, vamos, vades, vão
Imperfect subjunctive: fosse, fosses, fosse, fôssemos, fôsseis, fossem
Future subjunctive: for, fores, for, formos, fordes, forem
Present participle: indo
Past participle: ido
Imperative: vai, ide

haver
Present: hei, hás, há, hemos/havemos, haveis/heis, hão
Preterite: houve, houveste, houve, houvemos, houvestes, houveram
Pluperfect: houvera, houveras, houvera, houvéramos, houvéreis, houveram
Present subjunctive: haja, hajas, haja, hajamos, hajais, hajam
Imperfect subjunctive: houvesse, houvesses, houvesse, houvéssemos, houvésseis, houvessem
Future subjunctive: houver, houveres, houver, houvermos, houverdes, houverem
Imperative: há, havei

ler
Present: leio, lês, lê, lemos, ledes, lêem
Imperfect: lia, lias, lia, líamos, líeis, liam
Preterite: li, leste, leu, lemos, lestes, leram
Pluperfect: lera, leras, lera, lêramos, lêreis, leram

Present subjunctive: leia, leias, leia, leiamos, leiais, leiam
Imperfect subjunctive: lesse, lesses, lesse, lêssemos, lêsseis, lessem
Future subjunctive: ler, leres, ler, lermos, lerdes, lerem
Present participle: lendo
Past participle: lido
Imperative: lê, lede
Similarly: crer

odiar
Present: odeio, odeias, odeia, odiamos, odiais, odeiam
Present subjunctive: odeie, odeies, odeie, odiemos, odieis, odeiem
Imperative: odeia, odiai
Similarly: incendiar

ouvir
Present: ouço (*P also*: oiça), ouves, ouve, ouvimos, ouvis, ouvem
Present subjunctive: ouça, ouças, ouça, ouçamos, ouçais, ouçam (*P also*: oiça, oiças, oiça, oiçamos, oiçais, oiçam)

pedir
Present: peço, pedes, pede, pedimos, pedis, pedem
Present subjunctive: peça, peças, peça, peçamos, peçais, peçam
Similarly: despedir, impedir, medir

perder
Present: perco, perdes, perde, perdemos, perdeis, perdem
Present subjunctive: perca, percas, perca, percamos, percais, percam

poder
Present: posso, podes, pode, podemos, podeis, podem
Preterite: pude, pudeste, pôde, pudemos, pudestes, puderam
Pluperfect: pudera, puderas, pudera, pudéramos, pudéreis, puderam
Present subjunctive: possa, possas, possa, possamos, possais, possam
Imperfect subjunctive: pudesse, pudesses, pudesse, pudéssemos, pudésseis, pudessem
Future subjunctive: puder, puderes, puder, pudermos, puderdes, puderem

polir
Present: pulo, pules, pule, polimos, polis, pulem
Present subjunctive: pula, pulas, pula, pulamos, pulais, pulam
Imperative: pule, poli

pôr
Present: ponho, pões, põe, pomos, pondes, põem

Future: porei, porás, porá, poremos, poreis, porão
Imperfect: punha, punhas, punha, púnhamos, púnheis, punham
Preterite: pus, puseste, pôs, pusemos, pusestes, puseram
Pluperfect: pusera, puseras, pusera, puséramos, puséreis, puseram
Present subjunctive: ponha, ponhas, ponha, ponhamos, ponhais, ponham
Imperfect subjunctive: pusesse, pusesses, pusesse, puséssemos, pusésseis, pusessem
Future subjunctive: puser, puseres, puser, pusermos, puserdes, puserem
Conditional: poria, porias, poria, poríamos, poríeis, poriam
Present participle: pondo
Past participle: posto
Imperative: põe, ponde
Similarly: compor, depor, dispor, opor, supor etc

prover
Present: provejo, provês, provê, provemos, provedes, provêem
Present subjunctive: proveja, provejas, proveja, provejamos, provejais, provejam
Imperative: provê, provede

querer
Present: quero, queres, quer, queremos, quereis, querem
Preterite: quis, quiseste, quis, quisemos, quisestes, quiseram
Pluperfect: quisera, quiseras, quisera, quiséramos, quiséreis, quiseram
Present subjunctive: queira, queiras, queira, queiramos, queirais, queiram
Imperfect subjunctive: quisesse, quisesses, quisesse, quiséssemos, quisésseis, quisessem
Future subjunctive: quiser, quiseres, quiser, quisermos, quiserdes, quiserem
Imperative: quer, querei

requerer
Present: requeiro, requeres, requer, requeremos, requereis, requerem
Present subjunctive: requeira, requeiras, requeira, requeiramos, requeirais, requeiram
Imperative: requer, requerei

rir
Present: rio, ris, ri, rimos, rides, riem
Present subjunctive: ria, rias, ria, riamos, riais, riam
Imperative: ri, ride
Similarly: sorrir

saber
Present: sei, sabes, sabe, sabemos, sabeis, sabem
Preterite: soube, soubeste, soube, soubemos, soubestes, souberam
Pluperfect: soubera, souberas, soubera, soubéramos, soubéreis, souberam
Present subjunctive: saiba, saibas, saiba, saibamos, saibais, saibam
Imperfect subjunctive: soubesse, soubesses, soubesse, soubéssemos, soubésseis, soubessem
Future subjunctive: souber, souberes, souber, soubermos, souberdes, souberem
Imperative: sabe, sabei

ser
Present: sou, és, é, somos, sois, são
Imperfect: era, eras, era, éramos, éreis, eram
Preterite: fui, foste, foi, fomos, fostes, foram
Pluperfect: fora, foras, fora, fôramos, fôreis, foram
Present subjunctive: seja, sejas, seja, sejamos, sejais, sejam
Imperfect subjunctive: fosse, fosses, fosse, fôssemos, fôsseis, fossem
Future subjunctive: for, fores, for, formos, fordes, forem
Present participle: sendo
Past participle: sido
Imperative: sê, sede

ter
Present: tenho, tens, tem, temos, tendes, têm
Imperfect: tinha, tinhas, tinha, tínhamos, tínheis, tinham
Preterite: tive, tiveste, teve, tivemos, tivestes, tiveram
Pluperfect: tivera, tiveras, tivera, tivéramos, tivéreis, tiveram
Present subjunctive: tenha, tenhas, tenha, tenhamos, tenhais, tenham
Imperfect subjunctive: tivesse, tivesses, tivesse, tivéssemos, tivésseis, tivessem
Future subjunctive: tiver, tiveres, tiver, tivermos, tiverdes, tiverem
Present participle: tendo
Past participle: tido
Imperative: tem, tende

trazer
Present: trago, trazes, traz, trazemos, trazeis, trazem
Future: trarei, trarás, trará, traremos, trareis, trarão
Preterite: trouxe, trouxeste, trouxe, trouxemos, trouxestes, trouxeram

Pluperfect: trouxera, trouxeras, trou-xera, trouxéramos, trouxéreis, trou-xeram

Present subjunctive: traga, tragas, tra-ga, tragamos, tragais, tragam

Imperfect subjunctive: trouxesse, trouxesses, trouxesse, trouxéssemos, trouxésseis, trouxessem

Future subjunctive: trouxer, trouxeres, trouxer, trouxermos, trouxerdes, trouxerem

Conditional: traria, trarias, traria, traríamos, traríeis, trariam

Imperative: traze, trazei

valer
Present: valho, vales, vale, valemos, valeis, valem

Present subjunctive: valha, valhas, va-lha, valhamos, valhais, valham

ver
Present: vejo, vês, vê, vemos, vedes, vêem

Imperfect: via, vias, via, víamos, víeis, viam

Preterite: vi, viste, viu, vimos, vistes, viram

Pluperfect: vira, viras, vira, víramos, víreis, viram

Present subjunctive: veja, vejas, veja, vejamos, vejais, vejam

Imperfect subjunctive: visse, visses, visse, víssemos, vísseis, vissem

Future subjunctive: vir, vires, vir, vir-mos, virdes, virem

Present participle: vendo

Past participle: visto

Imperative: vê, vede

vir
Present: venho, vens, vem, vimos, vindes, vêm

Imperfect: vinha, vinhas, vinha, vínha-mos, vínheis, vinham

Preterite: vim, vieste, veio, viemos, viestes, vieram

Pluperfect: viera, vieras, viera, viéra-mos, viéreis, vieram

Present subjunctive: venha, venhas, venha, venhamos, venhais, venham

Imperfect subjunctive: viesse, viesses, viesse, viéssemos, viésseis, viessem

Future subjunctive: vier, vieres, vier, viermos, vierdes, vierem

Present participle: vindo

Past participle: vindo

Imperative: vem, vinde